MENTAL HEALTH AND PSYCHIATRIC NURSING
A CARING APPROACH

JANET L. DAVIES, R.N., PH.D.

Director of Nursing
St. John's Home
Rochester, New York

Adjunct Assistant Professor
University of Rochester
Rochester, New York

ELLEN H. JANOSIK, R.N., M.S.

Associate Professor Emeritus
Alfred University
Alfred, New York

Adjunct Professor
Roberts Wesleyan College
Rochester, New York

JONES AND BARTLETT PUBLISHERS
BOSTON

To our parents,

who taught us the meaning of caring

Editorial, Sales, and Customer Service Offices

Jones and Bartlett Publishers
20 Park Plaza
Boston, MA 02116

Portions of this book first appeared in *Psychiatric Mental Health Nursing* by Ellen H. Janosik and Janet L. Davies, copyright © 1989 by Jones and Bartlett Publishers, Inc.

Library of Congress Cataloging-in-Publication Data

Davies, Janet L.
    Mental health and psychiatric nursing : a caring approach / Janet L. Davies, Ellen H. Janosik.
        p.   cm.
    Includes bibliographical references and index.
    ISBN 0-86720-442-7
    1. Psychiatric nursing. I. Janosik, Ellen Hastings. II. Title. [DNLM: 1. Psychiatric Nursing. WY 160 D256m]
    RC440.D38   1991
    610.73'68—dc20
    DNLM/DLC
    for Library of Congress   90–15624
                                                                      CIP

ISBN: 0-86720-442-7

Printed in the United States of America
10 9 8 7 6 5 4 3 2 1

Cover illustration: *Imaginary Landscape* by the Spanish painter Antonio Povedano
Cover design: Hannus Design Associates

The selection and dosage of drugs presented in this book are in accord with standards accepted at the time of publication. The authors and publisher have made every effort to provide accurate information. However, research, clinical practice, and government regulations often change the accepted standard in this field. Before administering any drug, the reader is advised to check the manufacturer's product information sheet for the most up-to-date recommendations on dosage, precautions, and contraindications. This is especially important in the case of drugs that are new or seldom used.

When preparing this textbook, we were mindful of Emerson's warning: "He teaches who gives and he learns who receives. There is no learning until the pupil is brought into the same state and principle in which you are." Conscientious teachers are concerned with attitudes as well as information. Because we believe that nurses must respect the uniqueness of each client, we have tried to lead students into sharing our principles and state of mind. In persuading nurses to respect the individuality of clients, we endorse the value of caring *about* clients as well as caring *for* them.

The theoretical structure on which this text is based is a *continuum of caring* that requires the rational involvement of nurses in the total well-being of their clients. The continuum of caring is described theoretically in the first chapter and applied clinically in subsequent chapters. Many nurses already subscribe to holistic approaches in their practice. This is important, but holism without rational caring may be empty and ineffectual. We identify rational caring as a prime requisite in all nursing practice. We believe that rational caring is especially significant in psychiatric mental health nursing, where clients are very vulnerable and tend to be greatly affected by uncaring interpersonal transactions. Like holism, caring in itself may not be enough. Rationality must be superimposed on caring so that the emotional involvement of nurses is under control and cognitive processes guide all nursing activities. In professional practice, caring is not merely an emotional response but is also an intellectual one. Rational caring consists of concern for clients that is best expressed through knowledge and reasoning.

As practitioners and educators, we are also aware of Emerson's admonition: "No man can learn what he has no preparation for learning, however near to his eyes is the object . . . we cannot see things that stare us in the face until the hour arrives when the mind is ripened." In order to prepare and ripen the mind of the student, we have tried to present in clear, coherent language the essential knowledge on which psychiatric mental health nursing depends. Some of this knowledge may seem confus-

ing and contradictory at first glance, but we have tried to clarify and simplify without sacrificing accuracy.

No single volume can possibly include all pertinent knowledge, and we have had to be somewhat selective. We have chosen concepts and theories that have proven their relevance and worth in clinical and classroom settings. We believe that the presentation of psychiatric mental health content in this text is comprehensive and holistic, but condensed to fit the time constraints operating in nursing programs. Because we have been selective in organizing content, we have chosen to call the clinical chapters "guidelines" for nursing practice. However, we are confident that this textbook contains all the material necessary for a rigorous, intensive course in psychiatric mental health nursing. In addition to presenting the essence of the subject, these guidelines reflect contemporary issues and directions in nursing. In combining caring with rationality, we have tried to integrate affective learning with cognitive learning, so that students and clients have the best of both worlds.

We have entitled the book *Mental Health and Psychiatric Nursing* because we did not want to limit its scope to psychiatric diagnoses and disorders, and we strongly endorse the application of mental health principles to every clinical encounter, regardless of setting. Therefore, we have adopted a broad viewpoint that applies mental health concepts to many varieties of human experience. Disruptions and variations that result in psychiatric syndromes are presented in depth, but parameters of this text extend to human reactions that may not be psychiatric disorders but nevertheless call for an understanding of mental health and psychiatric theory.

New developments in the field of psychiatric mental health nursing are included in the text, especially those in areas of nursing research and theory building.

Mental Health and Psychiatric Nursing is organized into six sections, each dealing with an important aspect of psychiatric nursing. Part One, "Foundations of Mental Health Nursing," introduces the

Caring Continuum, which is the theoretical structure of the book. This organizing structure serves as a reminder of what nursing is all about; it is broad enough and strong enough to support the essential theories and practice of mental health nursing. The historical background and contributing theories of mental health nursing appear in this section. A chapter is devoted to nursing practice and process in mental health care. Again, an effort has been made to combine philosophical abstract thought with clinical relevance so that students may grasp the usefulness of nursing process applied to mental health nursing. The section concludes with a discussion of assessment and testing mechanisms as these pertain to nursing practice.

Part Two presents variations and disruptions in mental health, using holistic approaches that emphasize biological, psychological, and social perspectives. We have tried to avoid stressing the medical aspects of mental health, believing that holism demands appropriate attention to all viewpoints. In using a caring approach with clients, nurses must forego a competitive or adversarial relationship with any approach designed to meet the client's needs. For example, a nurse may not accept behaviorism in its pure Skinnerian version, but at the same time employ behavioral principles in clinical practice. We do not champion any particular modality. We present various perspectives as clearly and accurately as possible, discuss their applicability to nursing practice, and endorse the holistic use of various modalities, all of which are based on the rational caring actions of the nurse.

Part Three discusses critical tasks and transitions, maturational and situational problems. Guidelines for crisis intervention are included in this section. Part Four presents five approaches to mental health and psychiatric nursing: behavior, family, group, community, and combined or eclectic. The chapters give students a solid understanding of the underlying principles of these approaches, as well as their uses and limitations. Part Five includes many contemporary issues and trends in psychiatric and mental health nursing. This section encourages nurses to think beyond the scope of their own practice and look at the contemporary forces that affect the profession. Nurses are also reminded of their potential as political forces and as planning agents. The concluding chapters remind nurses that rational caring may take many forms and that understanding current political, economic, and legal issues is a basic part of rational caring.

Features of this book that should prove useful and attractive to teachers and students include:

- Consistent use of *Continuum of Rational Caring* as a supporting framework
- Comprehensive theoretical content, clearly explained and clinically applied
- Integration of Nursing Diagnoses with DSM-III-R
- Adherence to Nursing Process sequence throughout
- Multiple case studies and clinical examples in every chapter
- Nursing care plans for expanded case studies
- Sample generic care plans
- Content outline for every chapter
- Objectives for every chapter
- Summaries and review questions for every chapter
- Suggested annotated readings for every chapter
- Multiple research summaries
- Comprehensive glossary and index
- Appendices: Nursing diagnoses
  DSM-III-R
  List of psychological tests
  Review of psychotropic drugs

Clinical examples apply various nursing diagnoses in ways that show their compatibility with multi-axial psychiatric diagnoses in current use. We believe that nursing diagnoses and psychiatric diagnoses do not conflict with one another, but are compatible and complementary when understood and used properly. Every chapter contains case studies and nursing care plans that integrate nursing and psychiatric diagnoses in a meaningful fashion. Throughout the textbook, summaries of relevant research studies appear. The summaries illustrate some features of what is being done to enrich the knowledge of nurses practicing in clinical and academic settings. We have endeavored to present nursing as a vital, expanding profession that utilizes the contributions of theorists representing many disciplines, but applies them in a caring way that is unique to nursing. Moreover, nursing does more than draw upon the work done in other disciplines. Many nursing models developed within nursing by nurses have gained wide acceptance. A number of these models are described and contrasted. The formulation and application of nursing models, like the profession itself, effectively utilize abstract thinking in order to enrich clinical practice.

Every chapter concludes with a brief list of suggested annotated readings. The readings are representational rather than comprehensive. Each was selected because it highlights some aspect dealt with in the previous chapter. Often the readings were chosen to capture the interest of students and motivate further reading. Many of the books and articles in the annotated list contain references or bibliographies that may help students explore a particular subject in greater depth. The annotated lists are simply a learning tool; many teachers will wish to add to the list or substitute selections of their own choice.

We wish to acknowledge our indebtedness to the significant people in our lives who taught us the meaning of caring. We are also indebted to the colleagues and nurses in hospital, home, community, and academic settings who demonstrate a commitment to rational caring every day of their lives. Perhaps in a small way this book acknowledges, but cannot repay, these debts. Every teacher was once a student. Good teachers, in fact, remain students forever. We hope that our efforts will make the tasks of teaching and of learning less arduous and more pleasurable. If we succeed, we will have advanced the concept of rational caring upon which our profession was established.

We would also like to acknowledge our production editor, Anne Benaquist, who combined thoroughness with tactfulness. Her meticulous work and her genuine interest in the book heightened our respect for the editorial process. We extend thanks for her generosity and enthusiasm.

The statements made in this book represent the opinions of the authors and do not represent the views of any institutions with which they are affiliated. We are sensitive to the use of sexist pronouns and have used plural nouns and pronouns wherever possible. Where plural expressions would be awkward, gender pronouns have been alternately used.

Janet L. Davies
Ellen H. Janosik

C O N T E N T S

FOUNDATIONS OF MENTAL HEALTH NURSING

1

The Caring Approach in Mental Health Nursing

Learning Objectives

After reading this chapter the student should be able to:

1. Define the concept of holism and describe its implications for nurses as they provide care to individuals, families, and groups.

2. Explain the importance for nurses of introspection while interacting with individuals, families, and groups.

3. Identify the polarities of the *Caring Continuum of Nursing Process*. Outline the characteristics of each polarity.

4. Compare vertical and horizontal communication patterns, and their effect on nurse-client interactions.

5. Describe sequence of confirming behavior by caregivers, and the probable effect on clients. Contrast this with the sequence of negating behaviors.

Overview

The unifying concept of this book is *caring* as it influences and relates to mental health and psychiatric nursing. The unifying framework of the book is the *Caring Continuum of Nursing Process*, which is presented as a nursing model. The Caring Continuum is a reference point for nurses as they study and apply the principles of mental health and psychiatric nursing to clinical practice. The major purpose of the Caring Continuum is to help nurses analyze their attitudes toward clients in general, and toward psychiatric clients in particular. Through introspection and self-analysis nurses can better understand their own strengths and weaknesses, and monitor their interactions with clients.

The Caring Continuum of Nursing Process illustrates two diverse and opposite ways of providing health care to clients. Between these diverse polarities, points exist on the continuum that are close to one extreme or the other. One polarity of the continuum represents therapeutic or benign ways of interacting with clients. The other polarity represents untherapeutic, or malignant, ways of interacting with clients. Two separate lists of adjectives further differentiate the extreme points on the continuum; each of these adjectives is explained at some length.

Health and health care are described in holistic terms. Health and illness are not presented as opposite states. Instead, health is presented as the optimal functioning of which people are capable. Less than optimal functioning is discussed as a variation or disruption of function rather than a disease entity. The role enactment of nurses in the field of mental health was the center of controversy a few decades ago and is briefly reviewed, along with the contributions of several pioneer nurse theorists. Among the nurse theorists are Peplau, Orlando, and Mellow, all of whom expanded the range of nursing process. The chapter concludes by discussing the questions "What is mental health?" and "What is nursing?"

INTRODUCTION TO THE CARING APPROACH

In its commitment to comprehensive, multidimensional health care, the nursing profession has embraced the concept of holism. A holistic view of human existence must be broad enough to include the physical, psychological, and social experiences of individuals, families, and communities. Thus, holistic nursing is biopsychosocial in scope. Holism not only includes biopsychosocial aspects of life, but is also concerned with the unity and wholeness of experience throughout the life cycle. Holistic health care sees function, variations of function, and disruptions of function not as isolated events but as on-going processes within individuals, or between individuals and their external environment. This basic text utilizes a holistic approach in presenting principles of psychiatric and mental health nursing as these apply to clinical practice. A holistic approach is essential to the understanding of clients' attitudes and behaviors. It is equally essential to the understanding of nurses' attitudes and behaviors in their professional practice.

The commitment to holistic care may seem overwhelming to nurses at the start of their professional careers. This is especially true of nursing students trying to master the large body of theory on which psychiatric mental health nursing principles are based, and to apply that theory appropriately and effectively. A sensible beginning is to think about the personal qualities that nurses bring to all aspects of their work. In psychiatric mental health nursing, the tasks that nurses perform are often less crucial than the manner in which activities are carried out. The challenge of providing holistic care, therefore, begins by analyzing the attitudes, behaviors, and interactional style that the nurse brings to clinical practice. To promote self-awareness and monitor their professional actions, students must begin to engage in introspection and self-analysis while interacting with clients in psychiatric and other clinical settings.

The term *introspection* simply means looking within oneself in order to understand the reasons and motives for one's own actions and reactions. Introspection encourages self-awareness that, in turn, aids in maintaining self-control and professionalism. Since internal feelings greatly affect external behaviors, awareness by nurses of their inner feelings increases their ability to develop nurse-client relationships that are beneficial to all concerned. Increasing one's self-awareness is an important first step toward providing holistic care. Like the concept of holism, self-awareness may seem difficult to accept. To reduce the concept of holism to manageable proportions and to foster self-awareness on the part of nurses, it is helpful to turn to a scheme or model called the Caring Continuum of Nursing Process.

Nursing models, like models used in other disciplines, are diagrammatic forms of shorthand. In nursing, models are widely used by practitioners, teachers, and researchers to explain ideas, show directions, and clarify variables found in a variety of clinical, community, and laboratory settings. The Caring Continuum of Nursing Process focuses attention on the interpersonal style and professional behavior of persons engaged in nursing process activities.

CARING CONTINUUM OF NURSING PROCESS

The nursing model used to unify this text is a continuum with two opposite extremes or poles, one of which is benign in its effects and the other malignant. The continuum represents nursing process activities that can be accomplished in different ways, ranging from the most to the least therapeutic. When nursing actions are performed in a caring, careful manner they belong at a point on the continuum close to the benign pole. When nursing actions are performed in an uncaring, careless manner, they belong at a point on the continuum near the untherapeutic or malignant pole. As Figure 1–1 shows, each polarity has contrasting characteristics that shape the role performance of the nurse. The Caring Continuum is a reference point for students to keep in mind as they grasp and apply the principles of psychiatric-mental health nursing.

Nursing process consists of certain on-going, essential activities: assessment, planning, implementation and evaluation. All are crucial to meeting clients' needs. Equally important is the way these

Figure 1–1. Caring continuum of nursing process

Benign Polarity	Malignant Polarity
←	→
Caring/Careful	Uncaring/Careless
Thoughtful	Thoughtless
Rational	Irrational
Consistent	Inconsistent
Horizontal	Vertical
Confirming	Negating
Inclusive	Exclusive
Humanistic	Mechanistic
Holistic	Simplistic

activities are undertaken, especially those in which nurses and clients interact directly. It is possible to be thorough in carrying out nursing process activities and still perform them in ways that are untherapeutic. Technical proficiency is admirable, but psychiatric nursing is an area where technical skills are less consequential than interpersonal and intrapersonal awareness. In addition, psychiatric nursing requires cognitive knowledge. To meet this requirement, a number of theoretical frameworks are discussed in this text and placed in the context of nursing process activities. The unifying concept of this text is caring, and the unifying framework is the Caring Continuum of Nursing Process.

CHARACTERISTICS OF CARING

The Caring Continuum is process-oriented, not product-oriented. It is nonspecific in that it does not outline specific services nurses should offer clients. It is specific, however, in stating *how* nurses should offer services to clients. If the model were product-oriented, cures and curing might be included. Although cures and curing are worthwhile, they are not basic to nursing process. Cures and curing tend to be responses to symptoms of disease or distress at a particular moment, and may overlook what has gone before and what may come after. Additionally, cures and curing convey an impression of actions performed on rather than shared with the client. An interesting comparison may be drawn between the terms "caretakers" and "caregivers." The first conveys a sense of authority and superiority; the second suggests benevolence and equality. Caring is essential to caregiving, for it humanizes the knowledge and techniques that nurses possess. Yet caring is not the same as overinvolvement with clients or ignoring one's own needs. Such behavior often starts dedicated nurses on the path to burnout, and burnout usually signifies the absence of caring, and preoccupation only with one's own inadequacies and the overwhelming demands being made. Recovery from burnout requires respite, relaxation, and realism, with the last probably the most important. Realistic recognition of one's own resources and those of clients leads to self-awareness and realization that caring nurses do make a difference, even if they cannot always predict with certainty the results of their efforts.

Students entering a psychiatric mental health setting for clinical practice are likely to be very anxious. To begin with, psychiatric mental health settings are seldom task-oriented, and usually they are relatively unstructured. Technical proficiency may be less highly regarded than interpersonal

skills. This means that psychiatric mental health facilities rarely allow nurses to distance themselves from clients by becoming extremely busy. Most students have absorbed some misconceptions from the media about the nature and behaviors of persons with psychiatric or mental disorders. Their first reaction, then, is to regard psychiatric clients as different from other people in almost every respect. This initial reaction fades within a short time, as students learn that clients in a psychiatric facility or mental health center are individuals not so very different from anyone else, despite their limitations. Throughout the whole clinical experience in a psychiatric or any other facility, nursing process actions can be powerful tools to increase the comfort level of both students and clients, especially if the activities focus on the unique needs of the client who is probably even more anxious than the student about a new encounter. Building and maintaining a therapeutic relationship with the client is the essence of psychiatric mental health nursing, and it is objective, concerned caring that creates an atmosphere of trust so that the interventions of the nurse are accepted by the client (Benner and Wrubel 1989).

Caring: Thoughtful and Rational

One consequence of utilizing a Caring Continuum is that it reminds nurses to monitor their interactions with clients so that they are neither overly involved nor overly detached. Controlled caring links the term "carefulness" to the entire nursing plan formulated for the client. The caring nurse is careful and deliberate in all client-nurse transactions. He is able to adopt a dual perspective, seeing himself as subject or caregiver and at the same time seeing himself as the object of the client's interpretations and reactions. It is not enough for the nurse to analyze only the client's behavior; the nurse must also be willing to consider what he brought to the transaction that affected the client's actions. What works well with one client may not work well with another, and there is no interactional style that can be learned by rote and used with all clients. This means that qualities of inflexibility, superficiality, and thoughtlessness must give place to nursing actions that are carefully thought through, planned, scrutinized and evaluated by the nurse.

This is not to say that a nurse practicing in a psychiatric mental health setting is barred from ever being spontaneous. It does mean, however, that a rationale should support whatever a nurse says or does in any encounter with clients. A rationale is a supporting reason or justification for the nurse's interventions. The rationale may be based on a theoretical construct, on assessment of the client, on the formulated care plan, on the policy of the facility or agency, or on the nurse's clinical judgment at that particular point in time. The important requirement for rationales is that they must be rational, which means that they are based on data that is sound and valid.

Consistent, Horizontal, and Confirming

A client's need for help and degree of acceptance will vary from time to time, and this may be disconcerting to the nurse trying to offer continuous health care. Even though the client's needs and behaviors fluctuate, the caring nurse remains consistent in her willingness to accommodate the client wherever possible, provided that the interests of the client are not at risk. Consistency is not another word for automation or inflexibility. It simply means that the nurse is consistently responsive to messages transmitted by the client, is alert to the underlying needs that are being expressed verbally or nonverbally. Of course it is not always possible to gratify every request a client makes. Sometimes for consistency or for therapeutic reasons a client's expressed desire may have to be delayed or refused. This is especially true if the client's desires are contrary to the care plan that has been developed. For example, a hospitalized client whose home situation is unsuitable or even dangerous and whose self-control is questionable might ask for a pass for an overnight visit home. If it has been determined that the client is currently unable to handle the home visit or that progress might be undermined, the criteria of consistency and therapeutic adherence to the agreed-upon care plan support refusing the request. The client is entitled to know the reason for the refusal, but may find it hard to understand why goals of the health care plan take priority over immediate gratification of any and all requests. Consistency in meeting clients' needs does not always mean giving permission or granting privileges. It sometimes means that these must be deferred or withheld. Consistency is easier for nurses to uphold if they rely on clinical judgment and on the health care plan as the basis for their decisions.

Social actions between two friends or peer colleagues are almost always horizontal in nature. When persons involved in an interaction are equal in status, they are on the same footing, with neither occupying a higher or lower level. This means that lines of communication between them are direct and parallel, or horizontal. Messages sent and received are transmitted directly and easily so that there is relatively little chance of ambiguity or misunderstanding. In nurse-client interactions, the participants may not see themselves as having equal status. Clients receiving care often perceive caregivers as very powerful and themselves as powerless. This perception is reinforced by nurses who are not comfortable with horizontal communication patterns between themselves and clients, and resort to vertical patterns that place the nurse in a position above and at a distance from the client. This pattern may reduce the anxiety of the nurse, but it further impairs the client's feelings of personal competence and self-worth. Since raising a client's self-esteem is a major nursing objective, the nurse who maintains horizontal communication patterns usually operates near the benign pole of the Caring Continuum. Nurses guide, support, reassure, and set limits, as the occasion demands, but it is possible to do all this and still maintain horizontal communication that confirms rather than demeans the client, and thus strengthens the ability to participate in the health care regimen.

If the activities of the nurse are consistently directed toward positive goals, and if communication patterns are horizontal, not vertical, the client is likely to believe that his or her unique worth has been confirmed rather than negated. When communication patterns are vertical, messages may easily travel downward from nurse to client, but upward communication from client to nurse may be less easily transmitted. An unfortunate effect of vertical communication is to minimize clients' feeling of importance because the authenticity and merit of their perceptions and feelings are not understood or confirmed, but are negated or dismissed by caregivers. Figure 1–2 shows horizontal and vertical communication patterns.

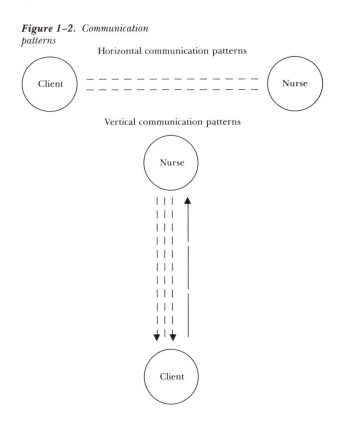

Figure 1–2. *Communication patterns*

Horizontal communication patterns

Client — — — — — — — — — — Nurse

Vertical communication patterns

Nurse

Client

All clients, even those who seem confident and in charge of circumstances, are somewhat dependent on the knowledge and authority of the caregiver. Whenever the power of one person overshadows that of another, the person with lesser power becomes extremely sensitive to the emotional tone of interactions between them. This means that caregivers must meet the deepened sensitivity of clients with objective professional sensitivity. It is necessary to assess clients' reactions to events, to identify the psychological state of the client, and to accept the client as a thinking, feeling, social being. Confirmation has been defined as the clients' realization that caregivers understand their feelings and accept these feelings as real and valid for the clients (Engel 1980). Along similar lines, Kestenbaum (1982) wrote that no person's subjective, inner experience should be disconfirmed or negated, because for all individuals their inner experience *is* reality.

In every encounter, the nurse has the ability to confirm or negate the truth of the client's experience. Negation and confirmation are processes that originate during interactions between clients and caregivers, and grow out of clients' reactions to the behavior of caregivers. Drew (1986) found that clients who experienced confirmation of their worth described the energy, attention, and enthusiasm expended on their behalf by caregivers. Almost any nursing action was interpreted as positive and confirming if the caregiver seemed relaxed and unhurried. Tone of voice, calmness, clarity, and audibility were noted by clients and interpreted as positive messages from caregivers.

The emotional response to positive messages from caregivers was one of hopefulness and reassurance. The cognitive response of clients experiencing confirmation was the maintenance of heightened self-image, with renewed confidence in their own powers of decision and strength (Drew 1986). The study concluded that confirmation by caregivers supplied additional energy to clients, while negating messages from caregivers depleted clients' energy.

Inclusive, Humanistic, and Holistic

An exclusive club is one that makes rules to limit membership and participation; i.e., to keep people out. The caring nurse is a person who does not formulate or enforce exclusionary rules. The agenda of a caring nurse is to include in the health care plan not only other professionals but also the client and any support systems that might be productive. At times it is hard to understand why some clients comply with a health care regimen while others who seem equally motivated do not. Every client, no matter how docile or eager to please, goes through a period of deciding whether there are

---

BEHAVIOR OF NEGATING CAREGIVERS

■ Used indifferent, uninvolved, flat manner
■ Conveyed sense of being hurried
■ Indicated dislike or distaste for the task at hand
■ Avoided eye contact with the client
■ Maintained great spatial distance from the client
■ Employed abrupt, brusque manner of speaking
■ Displayed little animation or interest in the client
■ Used terminology unsuited to client's level of understanding

BEHAVIOR OF CONFIRMING CAREGIVERS

■ Displayed an appropriate range of feeling and affect
■ Conveyed an impression of being unhurried yet energetic
■ Dealt with setbacks and mishaps in a calm, accepting manner
■ Maintained eye contact with the client
■ Preserved appropriate spatial proximity to the client
■ Used a range of voice tones, inflections, and modulations
■ Employed terminology suited to the client's level of understanding

---

advantages to following a recommended course of action. Changes that seem obvious to the nurse may be less obvious to the client for whom the changes may represent sacrifices and shifts in priorities. If the client is included in the planning process, and if the care plan reflects the client's views and preferences as much as possible, the chance of goal achievement increases. Careful assessment enables nurses to consider client attitudes and prejudices when planning care (Fielo and Rizzolo 1988).

Inclusive health care is collaborative and participatory. The first person to include is the client, since without client participation, progress toward goals is unlikely. Inclusionary steps lead to the involvement of significant family members, of available community resources and networks, and (in some instances) of social institutions, such as church, school, or government. Inclusion causes nurses to

SEQUENCE OF NEGATING BEHAVIOR BY CAREGIVERS

- Nurse's actions are performed in ways that threaten client's importance
- Nurse's actions are performed in ways that ignore client's individuality
- Client interprets nurse's actions as hostile and negative
- Client reacts by feeling angry, ashamed, and afraid
- Client's sense of self-esteem and self-worth is lowered
- Client's energy levels are reduced or wasted
- Client has less energy to invest in reaching the goals of the health care plan

SEQUENCE OF CONFIRMING BEHAVIOR BY CAREGIVERS

- Nurse's actions are performed in ways that acknowledge the client's importance
- Nurse's actions are performed in ways that consider the client's individuality
- Client interprets nurse's action as beneficial and positive
- Client reacts by feeling reassured, comfortable, and safe
- Client's sense of self-esteem and self-worth is raised
- Client's energy levels are maintained or heightened
- Client has more energy to invest in meeting the goals of the health care plan

give up control in favor of shared responsibility and expanded resources.

There are few caregivers who are capable of total commitment, sensitivity, and self-awareness every hour of every day. By following an inclusive approach nurses can avoid fostering the dependency of the client on any one person. Sharing responsibility with other health professionals lessens the burden of the nurse without jeopardizing client care. Inclusive care encourages the entry of family members and of health care team members who have something to contribute. When inclusive care is offered, the efforts of health team members are directed toward common goals, even though each member may have special expertise. No single approach or treatment modality can be assumed to be the best choice for every client. Instead of clinging to one or two formula-like approaches, the nurse who is committed to inclusionary methods will examine various possibilities, excluding no individual or avenue that seems promising in meeting the unique needs of the client.

A mechanistic viewpoint promotes the belief that most processes can be explained by laws governing physical forces. Chemistry, physics, and the biological sciences help us explain and predict the consequences of certain forces or events. A humanistic viewpoint, on the other hand, is more concerned with modes of thought or action that involve humankind in one way or another. The humanist believes that the nature of humankind has no parallel in the world, and to understand it one must apply more than laws governing physical forces. For some people humanism means the denial of divine authority. In this textbook the term *humanistic* is used in a broader sense. On the Nursing Caring Continuum, being humanistic merely means believing in the potential and uniqueness of every human being.

WHAT IS HEALTH?

In its 1980 policy statement, the American Nurses Association defined *health* as "a dynamic state of being in which the development and behavioral potential of an individual is realized to the fullest extent possible (Hall and Allen 1986). This definition is compatible with the ideas of Florence Nightingale, who believed in mobilizing people's healing potential by providing relief from external stresses and environmental pollutants (Reverby 1987).

Although the unifying framework of this book is a continuum, there is danger in discussing health and illness as if they were opposite poles of human existence, and distinct, separate entities. Engel (1960) noted that disease is failure or disturbance in the growth, development, functions, or adjustments of the organism as a whole or any of its systems. This description of disease as an interaction within the organism or between the organism and the environment is compatible with Martha Roger's idea that the individual and the environment inhabited by the individual are one and the same (1970). Another theorist who did not see health and illness as opposite poles was Abraham Maslow (1970). He identified a hierarchy of needs that must be satisfied in order to retain or regain health (see Figure 1–3).

Maslow's hierarchy of needs may be explained simply. At the bottom of the hierarchy are basic survival needs. Satisfaction of these basic needs

Figure 1-3. *Maslow's Hierarchy of Needs.*
SOURCE: Based on Maslow (1970).

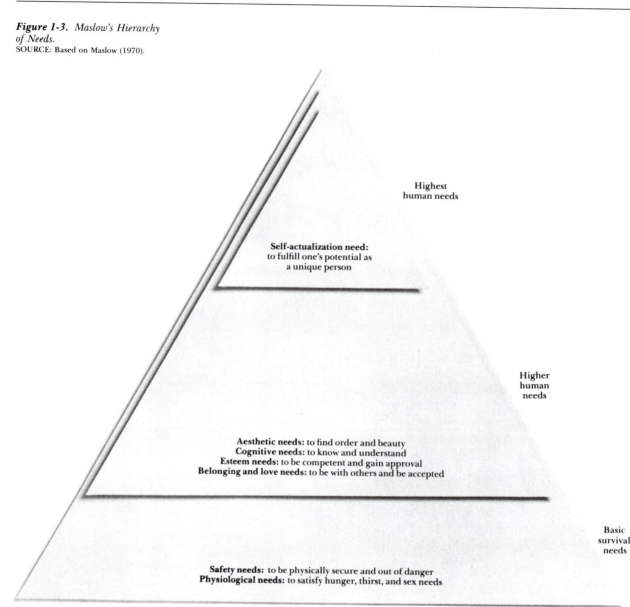

Highest
human needs

Self-actualization need:
to fulfill one's potential as
a unique person

Higher
human
needs

Aesthetic needs: to find order and beauty
Cognitive needs: to know and understand
Esteem needs: to be competent and gain approval
Belonging and love needs: to be with others and be accepted

Basic
survival
needs

Safety needs: to be physically secure and out of danger
Physiological needs: to satisfy hunger, thirst, and sex needs

leads to desire for gratification of higher needs. As the lower needs are met, the next higher level of needs becomes dominant. According to Maslow, the desire for higher levels of need fulfillment is a powerful motivator and shaper of behavior. When the entire list of needs is considered, Maslow's hierarchy depicts a holistic view of health, although this is implied rather than stated.

In addition to Martha Rogers, a number of nurse theorists approach health as a holistic concept. Margaret Newman (1979) linked health and holism, interpreting illness as a manifestation of life patterns that existed before the onset of illness and will persist after the illness subsides. Like Rogers, Newman explained illness as an indication of an ongoing process in a person's life rather than a separate, isolated event.

Whenever health and illness are seen as extreme opposites, the result is the application of a mechanistic model that is likely to be more suited to medicine than to nursing. In the medical model, diseases and symptoms are classified, labeled, and treated. Because the medical model is not central to nursing theory and practice, caring nurses avoid approaches that define health as merely the absence of illness. Instead of emphasizing health versus illness or normality versus abnormality, nurses are concerned with variations and disruptions of function that appear as people try to meet the demands of everyday life. From the perspective of nursing, health is described, not as the opposite of illness, but as the optimal functioning level of individuals, families, and groups. This perspective allows apparently adverse variations and disruptions of function that threaten the well-being of individuals, families, and groups to be interpreted as their attempts to cope with the conditions in which they live.

Among nurse theorists, King (1971) proposed a holistic definition of health as a dynamic process in which people must continuously adapt to their internal and external environment. Existence is not static, but is rather an ongoing process, with optimal functioning a goal that is sometimes but not always reached. Because everyone experiences growth and change over the life span, variations and disruptions of function are frequent and inevitable.

Successful functioning depends on the resources available to individuals and on their ability and willingness to use those resources. Available resources consist not only of the physiological and psychological characteristics of individuals but also their coping skills, and life experiences. Coping skills and problem-solving ability may be weakened or strengthened by responses to life experiences. When individuals function successfully in one situation, they acquire confidence and skills that are transferable to other situations. When individuals fail to function successfully in one situation, functioning patterns are changed or disrupted in ways that fail to gratify the individual and society.

WHAT IS NURSING?

The 1980 policy statement of the American Nurses' Association defined *nursing* as "the diagnosis and treatment of human responses to actual or potential health problems." The definition is broad and health-oriented, but it has been criticized in some quarters for using words like *diagnosis* and *treatment*. However, subsequent sections of this text show how nursing has conferred special meaning on such terminology (Hall and Allen 1986). Many principles advocated by Florence Nightingale (1820–1910) remain part of current nursing practice. Among the Nightingale principles are informed observation, concern for the client as a person, maintenance of a wholesome environment, and implementation of preventive health measures. The founder of modern nursing considered the duties of an administrator, nutritionist, spiritual counselor, and social worker all to be within the sphere of nursing (Woodham-Smith 1951).

The uniqueness of nursing is valued by members of the profession, some of whom have opposed nursing role expansion in order to protect this unique quality. Many early nurse leaders urged nurses to leave psychotherapeutic work to members of other disciplines, but this advice was opposed by other leaders. A prominent advocate of

nursing role expansion in the care of the mentally ill was Euphemia Taylor at Johns Hopkins Hospital in Baltimore. Taylor advocated comprehensive care for all clients, not just those with mental disorders. Her statement is a clear description of holistic nursing care (Taylor 1926).

It is imperative that all nurses have an understanding of the patient as a whole and there is no such thing as mental nursing apart from general nursing or general nursing apart from mental nursing. They form a oneness and make up the whole. From our knowledge of how the whole organism acts, it is obvious that what affects one part affects the other, and a sense of well-being in either mind or body brings about reactions which are not confined to one part alone but affect the whole body.

One of the most influential figures in the expansion of roles in psychiatric-mental health nursing was Hildegarde Peplau (1962), who described the scope of psychiatric nursing and asserted that nurses should be counselors, not mothers or managers. In her book *Interpersonal Relations in Nursing* (1952), Peplau wrote that "counseling in nursing has to do with helping the client to remember and to understand fully what is happening to him in the present situation so that the experience can be integrated with, rather than dissociated from, other experiences in life" (p. 64). In other words, Peplau envisioned mental health nurses actively performing psychotherapeutic activities with clients. She went on to differentiate surface from in-depth psychotherapeutic work, insisting that both types of intervention are within the capacity of well-prepared nurses. Peplau (1962) believed that nursing interventions should aid clients in recognizing their dysfunctional behavior, help them describe the behavior verbally, connect the causes and consequences of their behavior, search for more functional behavior, and transfer the improved behavior to other situations. She stated that nursing is an educational instrument and a force for promoting progress toward constructive and productive living.

In the same article, in which Peplau (1962) wrote that the primary role of the psychiatric nurse was that of counselor, she distinguished between generalist staff nurses working in psychiatric facilities and specialist nurses with graduate education working in psychiatric facilities. (See Table 1–1) Her insistence on clinical competence and on graduate education for psychiatric nurse specialists had two consequences. One was to keep psychiatric nursing within the aegis of the nursing profession. The second was to encourage the National Institute of Mental Health to recognize psychiatric mental health nursing as one of the four major mental

Table 1–1. Psychiatric Nursing Certification Requirements (Generalist and Clinical Specialist)

Certifying organization	Specialty	Initials conferred	Education required	Experience required
American Nurses' Association 2420 Pershing Road Kansas City, MO 64108	Psychiatric and Mental Health Nursing	RN, C	RN	Spends at least four hours a week in direct patient care, and worked in specialty for two of the last four years
	Clinical Specialist in Adult Psychiatric-Mental Health Nursing	RN, CS	MSN or master's degree in related field	Worked in specialty for two years, with eight hours a week in direct patient care, or for four years, with four hours a week in direct patient care; has spent 100 hours working under the clinical supervision of a member of the mental health disciplines
	Clinical Specialist in Child/Adolescent Psychiatric-Mental Health Nursing	RN, CS		

Key to Abbreviations   C: Certified   CS: Certified Specialist   RN: Registered Nurse

health professions, the others being psychiatry, psychology, and social work.

Another nurse concerned with psychotherapeutic work with clients was June Mellow (1968), who worked with schizophrenic clients and advocated an intense, close relationship between nurse and client. Although Mellow based her work on psychoanalytic principles, she did not maintain the detachment and aloofness of a psychoanalyst. Rather, she urged nurses to establish a warm emotional relationship through routines of helping the client bathe, dress, and engage in planned activities. Mellow thought that by building trust and nurturing the client, the nurse would become a positive identification figure and lead the client to a corrective emotional experience.

Ida Orlando's (1961) conceptualization of the dynamic nurse-client relationship is applicable to all nurse-client interactions, regardless of setting. The nurse helps clients explore their behavioral patterns in order to identify underlying causes and motives. Within the dynamic relationship, the nurse assesses the meaning of the client's behavior and shares the assessment with the client. For example, a client who has quarreled with her parents during visiting hours might later become involved in an argument with a staff member. The nurse might then suggest to the client that there was perhaps a connection between the dispute with parents and the argument with the staff member. The nurse's reactions to the client's actions could be disclosed in order to facilitate the client's awareness of the meaning beneath these actions.

Nursing intervention follows observation of behavior and assessment of needs expressed by the behavior. A client with a gastrointestinal disorder being cared for on a medical facility might be seen as making excessive demands of staff while at the same time criticizing the care received. On observing this behavior, the nurse might conclude that the client's underlying need is for reassurance that the staff is concerned and that he will be allowed to control most aspects of the care being given. Improvement after an intervention indicates that the client's real needs have been understood and gratified. If improvement does not follow an intervention, the nurse must continue to observe behaviors, validate observations with the client, try to assess the needs expressed through the behavior, and respond to the needs rather than to the behavior only.

In the 1950s and 1960s, controversy over nurses functioning as counselors and psychotherapists abated somewhat, partly because the need for qualified care providers was so great. By the mid 1960s psychotherapeutic intervention by nurses was an integral part of the health care delivery system. The work of psychiatric-mental health nurses was often presented as a therapeutic one-to-one relationship, and relationship therapy was widely accepted as the basis of psychiatric nursing.

In extending a caring approach to clients experiencing psychological distress, regardless of whether they have a psychiatric label, nurses can operate on any or all of three levels. Nurses can work directly with the client on a one-to-one basis. They can work with significant groups of which the client is a member. The group may be the family of the client, an in-patient population, or an out-patient group meeting at a community facility. Nurses can also work with professional and community groups of which the client is not a member; such groups have as their purpose the allocation of health care resources and the management of health care delivery. The health care team is a prime example of nurses working at this level. In psychiatric mental health nursing the setting where care is provided may not be a hospital and the health care team may include persons who do not belong to the four major health care professions (medicine, nursing, social work, and psychology). This means that much is expected of psychiatric nurses in terms of flexibility and the ability to practice effectively in hospitals, clinics, homes, and community agencies.

TYPES OF PSYCHIATRIC NURSES

THE GENERALIST NURSE The generalist nurse is most often a staff member of a hospital or facility in which the clients are treated for acute or chronic psychiatric disabilities. Most nurses who work with psychiatric clients are generalists, even though they may be called psychiatric nurses or mental health nurses. As generalists, they have received undergraduate education in nursing in a two-year associate degree program, a three-year diploma program, or a four-year baccalaureate program. They have passed a state board examination and are licensed in the state in which they practice as professional nurses. Whether graduates of a two-, three-, or four-year program, they have completed an introductory course in mental health nursing that combines classroom instruction with supervised clinical practice. In addition to this basic course in mental health nursing, most programs integrate mental health concepts throughout the curriculum, particularly in schools that emphasize biopsychosocial nursing.

At the generalist level, registered nurses participate in the activities of a therapeutic community that may be a day treatment program or an inpatient unit. Community mental health nurses and community health nurses are generalist nurses who make frequent home visits to monitor the progress of clients. Most regions require community health nurses to have a minimum of a baccalaureate degree. Generalist nurses may function as formal or informal leaders of short-term groups, may engage in some forms of family guidance or teaching, and may evaluate the effects of prescribed medication. Often, the generalist is concerned with communication issues, problems of daily living, and health teaching.

The generalist nurse in a mental health setting is usually a member of a health care team. Although a member from another discipline, such as medicine or psychology, may head the team, the generalist nurse is usually also accountable to a supervisory nurse with graduate education in psychiatric mental health nursing.

THE CLINICAL SPECIALIST The clinical specialist in mental health nursing usually has a master's degree that represents two years of education beyond the baccalaureate level. Nurses with such advanced training provide direct care to clients and families in addition to overseeing the clinical performance of generalist nurses. The American Nurses' Association, recognizing the differing levels of expertise among nurses working in mental health settings, has offered certificates to both generalists and clinical specialists who meet certain standards. Certification at the generalist level means that the nurse has a minimum of two years' experience as a registered nurse working in a mental health facility, is currently engaged in practice, and has given evidence of theoretical knowledge and clinical skills. Certification as a clinical specialist means that the nurse has at least a master's degree in psychiatric mental health nursing, has a minimum of two years of postgraduate clinical experience, and has demonstrated by examination and peer review a superior level of theoretical knowledge and clinical skills.

WHAT IS MENTAL HEALTH?

If definitions of health and illness are subtle, definitions of mental health and mental illness are even more so. Definitions of mental disorders as disease entities have been inadequate, but definitions of mental disorders as either behavioral, psychological, or social deficiencies have proved equally unsatisfactory. As with definitions of health, holistic definitions of mental health are the most meaningful for nurses. During the period between World Wars I and II, William A. White (1921) an eminent American psychiatrist, emphasized the relationships between physiological and psychological factors in

(text continues on page 15)

C L I N I C A L E X A M P L E

UTILIZING THE CARING CONTINUUM OF NURSING PROCESS

When 19-year-old Gloria sought help from the welfare department she was raising her two children in a single-parent household. Flossie was an active, energetic three-year-old; her sister Ruthie was a responsive but placid six-month-old baby. The two children had different fathers. Ruthie was the child of a legal marriage between Gloria and Joe, a part-time member of the household. Many of Joe's activities were illegal. Periodically he had to drop from sight to avoid arrest, and he had already served two prison terms for burglary. Although Joe was violent at times and unreliable in contributing financially to the household, Gloria regarded him highly because he had married her. Ruthie received adequate care from her mother, due partly to the baby's pleasant disposition and partly to the fact that Ruthie's father was Gloria's legal husband. In Gloria's social circles there was some status in being a legal wife.

Flossie, on the other hand, had characteristics that caused Gloria to have negative feelings about her older child. Alert and energetic in temperament, Flossie was restless and inquisitive. As a baby, she had been a poor sleeper. Once she started to walk, she tested the limits of her environment and her mother's patience. Her behavior and the nature of her father's relationship with Gloria caused recurring incidents in which Flossie was the target of her mother's anger and frustration.

The relationship between Gloria and Gus, Flossie's father, had been stormy. Gloria remembered Gus as a hard, uncaring man who seduced her when she was fifteen years old. Their life together was marked by drug and alcohol abuse, and bitter fights followed by brief reconciliations. When Gus needed money, he insisted that Gloria walk the streets looking for sexual partners who would pay for her services. When Gloria became pregnant with Flossie, Gus left, saying he wasn't going to support a kid that might not be his. Gloria was sure Gus had fathered her child, and she saw in Flossie many physical resemblances to Gus.

Gloria's behavior toward her children reflected her attitude toward their respective fathers. Ruthie was fed fairly regularly, hugged and rocked to sleep occasionally. With Flossie, Gloria acted more like another child than like a mother. She often yelled at Flossie and slapped her. When Flossie cried, Gloria would pinch her arms or legs to make her stop. Gloria bought toys for both children, but she placed Flossie's on a high shelf where the child could only gaze longingly at them. Gloria's explanation was that she couldn't afford two sets of toys, that Flossie was such a roughneck that she would break everything and there would be no toys left for Ruthie when she was ready for them.

Sometimes Gloria tried to hug Flossie, but the child pulled away. When Gloria felt sad or lonely she would turn to Flossie and ask, "You do love your mommy, don't you, honey?" Flossie would giggle nervously or stare round-eyed and silent at her mother. Usually this made Gloria lose her temper. She would tell the puzzled three-year-old, "Well, if you don't love me, I damn sure don't love you." When Gloria completely lost control, she might drag Flossie across the room and lock her in a closet. Flossie's frightened crying enraged Gloria even more. She would scream at Flossie not to wake the baby and threaten to throw Flossie off the fire escape if her sister awakened. Eventually Flossie would cry herself to sleep. In the morning a contrite Gloria would unlock the closet, cook Flossie a big breakfast, and then put the bewildered child in bed to make up for spending the night in the closet. Even though Flossie was not especially sleepy, she learned quickly that it was a good idea to stay in bed rather than risk another isolation period in the closet.

ASSESSMENT

As a child, Gloria had been abused by an alcoholic father and ignored by an indifferent mother. She left school in the tenth grade to live with Gus and soon became pregnant. She had never experienced tenderness from her parents and had no knowledge of how to mother her own children. Her knowledge of child development was equally inadequate and distorted. Because Ruthie was a calm, cuddly baby, Gloria loved her and felt that the child loved her in return. In contrast, her feelings about Flossie were in conflict. Flossie was a typical target child for many reasons. Brighter and more active than Ruthie, she made more demands on her mother's patience. Moreover, the resentment Gloria felt toward Gus was displaced on Flossie.

The behavior that Gloria expected from Flossie was unsuited to the child's age and temperament. Gloria had deep-seated needs for affection that had never been met, so she turned to her children to meet these needs. From Flossie she also demanded obedience and a level of maturity that were impossible for any three-year-old. Gloria was so ignorant about child development that she interpreted Flossie's behavior as a sign of "badness" and punished the child wildly and irrationally. Because Flossie had a vitality that was not easily subdued, she constantly reminded Gloria of the man who had mistreated her. Since he was beyond her reach, she made his child the target of her pent-up rage.

PLANNING

Except for a few girlfriends with small children of their own, Gloria led an isolated existence. She and her daughters received public assistance, and it was a visitor from the welfare department who first noticed bruises on Flossie's small face and body. After Flossie pointed out the closet as her bedroom, the welfare visitor began a systematic inquiry into Gloria's child-rearing practices. As a result, the family was referred to the local Children's Protective Association, to a community health nurse for ongoing supervision, and to the neighborhood mental health center for an evaluation of Gloria.

After Gloria was evaluated at the mental health center and no serious psychiatric disorder was found, she was assigned to a psychiatric nurse practitioner for help with problems of immaturity, impulse control, and poor self-esteem. The worker from the Children's Protective Association considered the family to be at risk, especially Flossie. Ongoing supervision was advised, and a protective worker began to visit the household regularly.

Regular meetings of the three caregivers were scheduled. At the first meeting discussion centered on the possibility of removing Flossie and perhaps Ruthie from the home. Because there was agreement that Gloria was always guilty and remorseful after mistreating Flossie, the caregivers considered how to make the home a safe place for both children. It was obvious that there were multiple problems in the home that should be addressed differently by each professional. The community health nurse would visit to oversee the physical well-being of the children, to assist Gloria in obtaining routine health care, and to teach her about growth and development so that Gloria's expectations of her children would be more realistic. The psychiatric nurse practitioner would not deal directly with the children, but would concentrate on helping Gloria work through some of her feelings about her parents and about the victimization she had experienced in relationships with men. The protective worker, who represented an agency with legal enforcement powers, functioned as case coordinator.

IMPLEMENTATION

The caregivers functioned as a single team. They identified relevant problems and met regularly to formulate and revise goals as needed and to report progress.

Focus of the Community Health Nurse

Since Gloria had no understanding of the developmental stages and capacities of preschool children, an essential goal was to give her this information in a way that she would accept. Gloria also needed to understand the differences in the temperaments of her two children. The community health nurse also tried to prepare Gloria for the changes that would occur in Ruthie as she moved from infancy into toddlerhood.

Although the children had different fathers, both of them belonged to Gloria, and she needed to accept Flossie as a child who needed love and attention as much as Ruthie did. The community health nurse began to relabel Flossie's behavior so that Gloria would appreciate the liveliness and intelligence in Flossie that now provoked her anger. The nurse saw some similarities between Gloria and Flossie, and pointed these out to Gloria to encourage closeness between mother and daughter.

Focus of the Psychiatric Nurse Practitioner

Gloria was hampered by her ignorance of child development and by her own experience with a mother figure. In meetings with the psychiatric nurse practitioner, she described her mother as cold and neglectful but not abusive. Gloria remembered her mother as never praising or punishing, but always letting her children fend for themselves. Gloria's father had been abusive, and he abandoned the family when Gloria was still in grade school. After he left, a succession of men lived with Gloria's mother. Some of them were violent toward Gloria and her three brothers. Flossie's father had been living with Gloria's mother when his sexual relationship with Gloria began.

Gloria had suffered nurturing deficiencies that prevented her from being a good mother. She needed to learn how to be tender and caring with her children, but first she had to experience acceptance and tenderness. The psychiatric nurse practitioner, with the concurrence of the other caregivers, proposed that Gloria be permitted a period of dependency on the psychiatric nurse. Having won the trust and confidence of Gloria, the psychiatric nurse would direct her interventions toward raising Gloria's self-esteem and increasing her self-control.

In helping Gloria control her impulsive reactions, the psychiatric nurse practitioner used behavior modification. When Flossie made Gloria angry, the mother was told to walk away immediately without responding to Flossie's behavior. She was to call one of the caregivers on the phone and discuss what happened. If none was available, Gloria was to leave a message and call the 24-hour crisis line to talk about what happened and plan her response to Flossie. Only then would she deal with the child and the behavior that made her so angry.

A referral was made for Gloria to Parents Anonymous, a self-help group formed to prevent child abuse, and arrangements were made for group members to visit Gloria and accompany her to the first meetings.

Nursing Diagnosis	Goal	Nursing Action	Outcome Criteria	Outcome Evaluation
Knowledge deficit	Client will learn about age-appropriate behavior of children.	Weekly visits by community nurse focus on child development.	Client will have realistic standards of child behavior.	Client told community nurse the children are "just kids" after all.
Altered role performance	Client will talk about her feelings about her own mother with encouragement from the psychiatric nurse.	Biweekly visits by psychiatric nurse offer support to client.	Client will exhibit more appropriate parenting behavior.	Client expressed appreciation for having help for her own problems, not just the children's.
Self-esteem disturbance	Phone connection will be arranged by nurses for client to use when angry.	Suggest substitute actions instead of punishing children.	Client will not deal with children while angry.	Client has not hit toddler or put her in closet for three weeks. Reports child is easier to handle.
	Client will feel better about herself and her life as a result of various efforts to raise her self-esteem.	Reinforce client's efforts to be more patient and confident.	Client will feel less inadequate compared to her friends who are mothers.	Client reported to psychiatric nurse that friend called her for advice in dealing with a troublesome two-year-old.
	With help of nurses, client will develop a social network to reduce isolation.	Obtain home phone. Establish phone links with health team members. Arrange respite child care.	Client will maintain phone contact with friends and health team.	Client using phone. Calls nurses 3–4 times weekly, escorts toddler to and from day care.

Focus of the Child Protective Worker

Because Gloria had a very limited income, she had never managed to save enough money to install a telephone. This meant that she was isolated, especially in the winter when her girlfriends could not visit with their children. The protective worker decided that a telephone was essential if Gloria was to carry out the behavior modification plan devised by the psychiatric nurse practitioner. The protective worker also thought that having a communication line to her friends would make Gloria feel less stressed and alone. With help from the protective agency, a phone was installed.

At first the protection worker was dubious about leaving Flossie in the home but ultimately agreed that the child could remain if close supervision was maintained. Arrangements were made for Flossie to attend day care at the nearby home of an agency-approved mother. Since other preschoolers would be present, the socialization would provide structure and outlets for Flossie's energy. The day care mother would also be able to observe any signs of abuse and note Flossie's day-to-day progress.

EVALUATION

The plan for the family was comprehensive in that the needs of all three family members were included in the health care plan. The plan was individualized and required collaboration by caregivers from several agencies. The caregivers did not present themselves as critics or faultfinders. Although their agenda emphasized the safety of the children, they realized that the most useful course of action would be to strengthen the skills and resources of the mother. All the caregivers saw some potential for change in Gloria, provided

they could win her trust. Their goal was not to blame Gloria for her deficiencies but to help her overcome them. When Gloria learned what to expect from her children as they moved through normal growth stages, she was less inclined to believe that Flossie was "bad" or that Ruthie would remain an adorable baby forever. All the caregivers intervened to alter Gloria's attitude toward herself and to alter her behaviors toward both her children. In effect, Gloria's home was under close supervision, but the coordinated care plan and the caring interventions employed by the health care team allowed the family to stay together and interact in ways that were more beneficial for all concerned.

Nursing Diagnoses

Knowledge deficit
(related to ignorance of normal child development)

Altered role performance
(related to harsh life experiences, inadequate mothering, deficient impulse control)

Self-esteem disturbance
(related to social isolation and single mother status)

Multiaxial Psychiatric Diagnoses

Axis I   799.90   Diagnosis deferred
Axis II   301.84   Passive-aggressive personality disorder
Axis III   No diagnosis
Axis IV   Code 3   Moderate psychosocial stressors
Axis V   Global assessment of functioning (GAF scale) Code 40 Moderate impairment

health and illness. His writings and those of Dunbar (1935) in the area of psychosomatic investigation supported multifaceted explanations for illness and led to recognition that psychiatric and mental disorders that vary or disrupt function may be physiological or behavioral responses to psychological stress confronted by the individual. Connections noted between physiological and psychological factors led to an awareness that people are social beings whose problems can be understood only if their social relationships are taken into account.

Definitions of mental health and mental illness can have far-reaching cultural and political implications. Labeling people as mentally ill has been criticized by Thomas Szasz (1961, 1970, 1987), who claims that mental illness is actually a myth perpetuated by society, and that individuals presumed to be mentally ill merely have problems in living that make them unacceptable to society. Although some of Szasz's allegations are questionable, there is historical evidence that prevailing beliefs and norms do indeed determine what many believe constitutes mental health and illness. Historically such beliefs have affected the treatment given those considered mentally ill, as will become evident in the next chapter.

The report of the Joint Commission on Mental Illness and Health (1971) stated that persons who experienced mental disorders often faced social rejection and disapproval. Because mental illness rarely follows a simple cause-and-effect course, there is an element of uncertainty and unpredictability that adds to the problems of mentally ill clients and their families. One encouraging sign is the rising popular recognition that mental illness may originate in physiological as well as psychological factors, and that mental illness expresses itself in behaviors that influence what others think of the client and what the client thinks of himself. If the client's problems in living are to be modified in positive ways, blaming must be avoided, and nonconforming behaviors must be interpreted as dysfunctional variations and disruptions that are aspects of the disorder. Although the client must be willing to change and to participate in the recovery program, caregivers must demonstrate attitudes and behaviors that permit the client to engage in interactions and establish relationships that do not threaten but rather enhance his feelings of being accepted and valued. This is done by developing a problem-solving collaboration between nurse and client that supports the health potential of the client, regardless of the behavioral responses that he is currently using.

SUMMARY

Caring is a concept that may be applied to all nursing process activities performed on behalf of a client. At the same time, caring is a concept that must be adapted and differentiated to meet the assessed needs of each specific client. Approaches that were indicated in one clinical situation may be contraindicated in another. All nursing interventions should be characterized by carefulness and deliberation. Caring activities offered by nurses are planned and implemented in response to client behaviors and the underlying needs expressed through the behaviors. In this textbook client needs and behaviors are assessed and interpreted according to prevailing biopsychosocial theories as presented in succeeding chapters.

Review Questions

1. Define the term *introspection*. Explain why introspection is important in professional nursing.
2. List several benign characteristics of the Caring Continuum of Nursing Process.
3. What is meant by *horizontal communication*?
4. Describe the behaviors of a nurse who strives to "confirm" the status of a client. How is this different from the behaviors of a nurse who uses exclusionary tactics?
5. In your own words define the following terms: *health, nursing, mental health, holism, certification, expanded roles.*

Research Report

The purpose of this study was to examine the role perceptions and role models identified by new graduate nurses. Twenty-five senior nursing students in a generic baccalaureate program answered questionnaires one month before their graduation and three months after working in a clinical facility. The subjects were asked to identify their professional role models and to answer items that indicated whether their orientation to the nursing role was professional or bureaucratic in nature. Results showed that before graduation the role models identified by students were more likely to be faculty members with professional orientations. After the students worked three months in a clinical facility, the number of faculty members chosen as role models declined, while the number of role models in the clinical area increased. In addition, the role perceptions of the recent graduates were more oriented toward technical proficiency and clinical competence than toward professionalism.

After exposure to the realities of the clinical setting, the new graduates became more bureaucratic, reflecting the attitudes of more experienced nurses with whom they worked. Not only the technical proficiency of more experienced nurses was emulated, but also their values and beliefs. One conclusion permitted by the study was that professionally oriented nurses who enter the work force have relatively little impact on bureaucratically oriented systems or coworkers. Instead the professional orientation of new graduates diminishes as they are socialized into a bureaucratic, performance-oriented system. The findings are not altogether surprising, since nurses new to any clinical setting are unlikely to wield immediate influence. Further studies are needed to isolate the specific factors that perpetuate a bureaucratic working environment at the expense of professionalism.

Relationships between Role Models and Role Perceptions of New Graduates Gloria J. Green, *Nursing Research* 37, no. 4 (July/August 1988): 238–244.

Suggested Annotated Readings

Backer, B. A., P. M. Dubbert, and E. J. P. Eisenman. *Psychiatric Mental Health Nursing: Contemporary Readings, Part One*. 2d. ed. Monterey, California: Wadsworth, 1985.

Part One of this book of readings is a collection of articles by six notable nurse leaders. Subject matter includes the nature of psychiatric nursing and the role enactment of psychiatric nurses. The concept of caring is extended to health care providers themselves, who need to develop support systems and stress management techniques in order to remain responsive to the full gamut of client needs.

Benner, P., and J. Wrubel. "Caring Comes First." *American Journal of Nursing* 88, no. 8 (1988): 1072–1075.

Caring is essential to nursing and must be present if nursing is to be truly effective. Caring enables nurses to notice which interventions are helpful and which are not. It causes nurses to notice signs of improvement or deterioration, and facilitates nurse-client collaboration. Caring for oneself cannot be ignored, for neglect of self leads to burnout. Burnout denotes an absence of caring either for clients or for oneself. Recovery from burnout means a return to caring, both for the client and for oneself.

Eucker, B. "Walk a Shift in My Shoes." *American Journal of Nursing* 88, no. 5 (May 1988): 672–673.

A medical-surgical nurse describes one day of trying to meet the unceasing demands of clients. Exhausted at the end of the day, she renews her commitment by imagining how she would feel if the clients she cares for were her loved ones. Going further, she imagines what it would feel like to need such care herself, and concludes by urging nurses to take a closer look at the people for whom they provide care.

Glazer, G. "The *Good* Patient." *Nursing and Health Care* 2 (1981): 144–147.

The author questions whether the so-called good patient, who makes few demands of the health care system or on providers, is really acting in his own best interests and suggests that caregivers change their definition of what constitutes a good patient.

Leininger, M. *Caring: the Essence and Central Focus of Nursing*. American Nursing Foundation Research Report 12, no. 1 (February 1977).

No concept is more central to nursing than caring. Because it is so crucial, caring should be a rich area for teaching, research, and practice in nursing. Nurses need to direct attention to the caring behaviors they exhibit or fail to exhibit. Attention to the way care is provided and to caring attitudes, values, and outcomes ensures that nursing will remain professional rather than technological. This report by the nurse who developed the subspeciality of transcultural nursing contains insights into the concept of caring.

Lundh, Soder, M., and K. Waerness. "Nursing Theories: A Critical View." *Image* 20, no. 1 (Spring 1988): 36–40.

Nursing theories to date consist of descriptions of what nursing is (process) and of the environments where nursing takes place (systems). During the 1970s various nursing theories were developed, among them Orem's "self-care" theory. Orem divided the nursing process into an intellectual phase and a practical phase. The first phase is concerned with assessment and planning, the second with implementation and evaluation. The authors of the article question emphasis by nurses on cognitive and pragmatic aspects, and our lack of emphasis on the intuitive, caring aspects. The concept of self-care obscures our view of people as interdependent, social beings. Unlike self-care, caring is a relationship concept and includes such considerations as nearness, empathy, and understanding. As a guideline for nursing practice and research, self-care seeks advances and results that may ignore the urgent needs of persons who cannot achieve self-care, no matter how well-intentioned or knowledgeable their caregivers are. The article is a call to substitute rational caring for excessive intellectualization of our clients' problems. It also issues a warning about the abstract nature of nursing research at this time.

References

Benner, P., and E. Wrubel. *The Primacy of Caring.* Menlo Park, California: Addison-Wesley, 1989.

Drew, N. "Exclusion and Confirmation: A Phenomenology of Patients' Experiences with Caregivers." *Image* 18, no. 2 (Summer 1986):39–47.

Dunbar, H. *Emotions and Bodily Changes: A Survey of Literature on Psychosomatic Co-Relationships 1910–1933.* New York: Columbia University Press, 1935.

Engel, G. L. "A Unified Concept of Health and Disease." *Perspectives on Biology and Medicine.* Chicago: University of Chicago Press, 1960.

Engel, N. "Confirmation and Validation: The Caring that Is Professional Nursing." *Image* 12, no. 2 (Summer 1980):55–56.

Fielo, S. B., and M. A. Rizzolo. "Handle with Caring." *Nursing and Health Care* 9, no. 4 (April 1988):192–195.

Hall, B. A., and J. D. Allen. "Focus on Health." *Nursing and Health Care* 7, no. 6 (June 1986):314–320.

Joint Commission on Mental Illness and Health. Action for Mental Health: Final Report. New York: Basic Books, 1971.

Kestenbaum, V. *The Humanity of the Ill.* Knoxville: University of Tennessee, 1982.

King, I. M. *Toward a Theory of Nursing.* New York: John Wiley & Sons, 1971.

Maslow, A. *Toward a Psychology of Being*, 2d. ed. New York: Van Nostrand Reinhold, 1970.

Mellow, J. "Nursing Therapy." *American Journal of Nursing* 11 (1968):2365–2369.

Newman, M. *Theory Development in Nursing.* Philadelphia: F. A. Davis, 1979.

Orlando, I. *The Dynamic Nurse-Patient Relationship.* New York: Putnam, 1961.

Peplau, H. *Interpersonal Relationships in Nursing.* New York: Putnam, 1952.

——— . "Interpersonal Techniques: The Crux of Psychiatric Nursing." *American Journal of Nursing* 6 (June 1962):53–54.

Reverby, S. "A Caring Dilemma: Womanhood and Nursing in Historical Perspective." *Nursing Research* 36, no. 1 (January/February 1987):5–11.

Rogers, M. *An Introduction to the Theoretical Basis of Nursing.* Philadelphia: F. A. Davis, 1970.

Szasz, T. *The Myth of Mental Illness.* New York: Dell Press, 1961.

——— . *Ideology and Insanity.* New York: Doubleday, 1970.

——— . *Insanity: The Idea and Its Consequences.* New York: John Wiley & Sons, 1987.

Taylor, E. S. "Psychiatry and the Nurse." *American Journal of Nursing* 26 (August 1926):133–134.

White, W. A. *Foundations of Psychiatry.* New York: Nervous and Mental Disease Publishing, 1921.

Woodham-Smith, C. *Florence Nightingale: 1820–1910.* New York: McGraw-Hill, 1951.

2

Historical Developments in Mental Health Care

Learning Objectives

After reading this chapter, the student should be able to:

1. Identify major historical developments in psychiatric care and psychiatric mental health nursing.

2. Evaluate the impact of the community mental health movement on psychiatric mental health nursing.

3. Describe the concepts of primary, secondary, and tertiary levels of prevention as they relate to psychiatric mental health nursing.

4. Trace the various developments that influenced the roles and functions of psychiatric mental health nurses.

5. Compare the educational preparation and clinical responsibilities of generalists and clinical specialists in psychiatric mental health nursing.

Overview

This chapter traces social attitudes toward mental disturbance through the ages and describes the influence of prevalent attitudes on the treatment of mentally disturbed persons. At various times in history mental disturbances were regarded as supernatural visitations, as shameful stigma, as afflictions, as illnesses, and as psychodynamic disruptions. As societies relinquished the idea that mental disturbance was supernatural or disgraceful, measures were taken to meet the needs of mentally disturbed persons. Gradually mental institutional systems were established by well-intentioned reformers who believed in humane care. Unfortunately, their efforts contributed to promoting institutional care that was less than humane at times.

Government involvement in mental health care expanded with public awareness that mental health needs were not being met. The community mental health movement was a new approach to the delivery of mental health services. It stemmed from dissatisfaction with institutional care that promoted long periods of expensive hospitalization, and from the development of medication that permitted new therapeutic methods to be adopted for persons once considered beyond help. Despite the advances in mental health care delivery and the goals of the community mental health movement, release of large numbers of mental health clients from state institutions into the community often created problems for the clients, their families, and the communities they reentered. Many persons discharged after years of institutional care found the adjustment difficult. In addition, some communities were deficient in providing follow-up care. The outcomes of deinstitutionalization depended largely on adequate planning and community resources. When community programs were not overwhelmed by a great influx of deinstitutionalized clients, when clients were carefully prepared for their reentry, and when health care delivery systems were flexible and individualized, the deinstitutionalization process was relatively successful.

The problem of homelessness is a community issue that has been linked to deinstitutionalization. A disproportionate number of homeless persons seem to have mental health problems for which they are not receiving treatment, partly because many of them refuse treatment and partly because programs are not available that truly meet their needs. One response to the problems of the homeless has been to return to the institutionalization of persons not in treatment who are judged to be mentally ill. However, the movement toward reinstitutionalization is unlikely to be a fully adequate or acceptable solution either for the problems of the homeless or for the care of the mentally ill.

The concluding section of the chapter deals with members of the four core health disciplines (nursing, psychiatry, psychology, and social work) that comprise the mental health team. Standards of psychiatric/mental health nursing practice are reviewed. Psychiatric diagnoses of the Diagnostic Standard Manual III-Revised are presented and the coding method is explained. The origin and significance of nursing diagnoses are described in a manner that demonstrates how nursing diagnoses and psychiatric diagnoses augment and reinforce one another. Used appropriately, the two diagnostic systems facilitate communication among health professionals and permit a holistic assessment of clients and their families.

MENTAL DISTURBANCE AS SUPERNATURAL

In early times mental disturbance was thought to be sent from the gods and therefore to be beyond the control of ordinary mortals. Feelings of powerlessness led to the belief that mentally disturbed people could be helped only if and when the gods were willing. As a result, little care was provided except in the form of physical restraint for those whose actions were considered violent or dangerous. Acceptance of the idea that mental disturbance was supernatural in origin caused the ancient Greeks to decide that disturbed persons should not be considered legally responsible for their behavior. This decision led citizens to delegate responsibility for mentally disturbed persons to legal authorities. The idea that mental disturbance was caused by the gods meant that priests and other religious figures also played an important part in the care of the mentally ill.

The Greek physician Hippocrates attempted to explain mental illness rationally. In doing this he opposed the popular beliefs of the day and tried to contradict the popular idea that mental illness came from the gods. He wrote that epilepsy, which was generally thought to be divinely caused, was much like any other illness, with its own identifiable symptoms. In addition, Hippocrates described the interaction of four body fluids, or *humors*—blood, black bile, yellow bile, and phlegm—and suggested that each humor was associated with a particular temperament or disposition: sanguine, choleric,

---

THE FIRST AMERICAN PSYCHIATRIC TEXTBOOK

A year before his death in 1813, Dr. Benjamin Rush published a compilation of his observations and conclusions regarding mental illness based on his work at Pennsylvania Hospital and as medical professor at the University of Pennsylvania. Rush regarded insanity as a disease of the brain, noting that the cause of madness was seated primarily in the blood vessels of the brain and was a chronic illness attacking that part of the brain containing the mind. This volume was published in Philadelphia, was well regarded in most quarters, and for seventy years was the only available American textbook on the subject of mental illness.

---

melancholic, or phlegmatic. In current terminology, the sanguine temperament might be characterized by hopefulness, the choleric by anger, the melancholic by sadness, and the phlegmatic by passivity. Conflict between the body humors was thought to create a state of imbalance called *dyscrasia*, the treatment for which was purging with strong cathartic drugs.

Like members of most other early societies, the Romans allowed fear and superstition to dominate their attitudes toward persons thought to be mentally disturbed. It was in the area of legal or forensic psychiatry that the Romans made an original contribution. Not only were the mentally disturbed neglected or mistreated, but they were also deprived of freedom and often deemed incompetent to manage their own affairs. Relatives or court-appointed guardians were made custodians of persons judged incompetent or irresponsible. At the same time, however, the Romans were tolerant of excess alcohol consumption, and drunkenness was considered an acceptable reason for overlooking otherwise reprehensible behavior.

During the Middle Ages, belief persisted that mental illness had a supernatural cause, although by this time devotion to many gods had been replaced by devotion to one god.

From 500 to 1500, there was widespread interest in demonology and witchcraft. The medieval church recognized human beings as having a body (soma) and a soul (psyche). Individuals were often seen as arenas in which evil forces contended for control of the soul. When evil forces seemed to possess a human being, various tactics were used to exorcise or drive them out. Sometimes the methods of exorcism were benign, but more often they were brutal. It was considered advisable to deal forcefully with any person inhabited by a demon in order to punish the malignant spirit dwelling within. Beatings, starvation, exposure, and similar procedures were used.

Exorcism was based on the assumption that the person possessed was an unwilling victim. No such assumption was made for persons accused of witchcraft. These unfortunates were generally accused of willingly making a pact with the devil and were treated accordingly. Preoccupation with witchcraft continued through the eighteenth century and traveled from Europe to colonies in the New World. Witch hunting ultimately abated, but belief that mental illness represented an association with demons aggravated the inhuman treatment endured by those afflicted (Coleman, Butcher and Carson 1984).

Mental Disturbance as Stigma

For many years ostracism or segregation of the mentally disturbed was customary. Occasionally mentally disturbed persons were placed on sailing vessels and sent forth in search of their lost reason, thus giving rise to the expression "ship of fools." Confinement became the usual treatment, effectively isolating the mentally disturbed from the rest of the community. Also included within the ranks of the mentally disturbed were the poor; the physically handicapped; the developmentally impaired; and the impoverished, unproductive elderly (Mora 1980).

To a great extent, facilities for the mentally disturbed were considered correctional as much as custodial institutions. Because idleness was thought to be a source of rebelliousness and upheaval, hard work was offered as a remedy for madness. The madhouse was a place "where the morality of the majority in a society could be imposed on the minority" (Church 1987, p. 48).

For decades the mentally disturbed were seen with a mixture of horror and fascination. Often they were subjected to taunts and public display; at the same time the curious were warned that the sight of deranged patients might through suggestibility and imagination provoke similar disturbances in onlookers (Kraepelin 1962).

Mental Disturbance as Affliction

During the seventeenth and eighteenth centuries, society gradually relinquished exclusive belief in supernatural and religious forces for an interest in scientific investigation. In England, Thomas Sydenham (1624–1689) introduced to medicine the systematic clinical observation of patients, and Robert Burton (1577–1640), in *The Anatomy of Melancholy*, identified the causative factors of such mental disturbances as jealousy, solitude, unrewarded affection, and religiosity. Some years later the Society of Friends opened a facility in York, England, for about thirty mentally disturbed persons, who were treated kindly and were not subjected to physical restraint or purely medical procedures. Across the English Channel, Philippe Pinel (1745–1826), a superintendent of French institutions that housed criminals, the mentally retarded, and the mentally disturbed, introduced humane treatment, classified the symptoms of his charges, and arranged for the participation of inmates in structured activities (Freedman, Kaplan, and Sadock 1972).

About the same time, Benjamin Franklin encouraged the Pennsylvania Hospital in Philadelphia to become the first public institution in the United States to admit mentally disturbed persons. Benjamin Rush (1745–1813), a physician at the hospital (and a signer of the Declaration of Independence), is considered the father of American psychiatry. Although he adopted some moderate practices in his work at Pennsylvania Hospital, he also used harsh methods, such as the use of a specially designed chair in which agitated patients were tied and suspended.

A treatment modality known as "moral management" was an outgrowth of Pinel's humane methods of caring for the mentally disturbed. This new approach to care was a stark contrast to treatment previously accorded the mentally ill. Moral management resembled what is now called milieu therapy in that it included not only physical but also social, psychological, spiritual, and aesthetic dimensions of care. Even with the arrival of moral therapy, however, traditional medical measures continued to be used. Difficult patients were subjected to bloodletting, extremes of temperature, drugs, and physical restraint so as to make them more tractable and amenable to moral management.

Mental Disturbance as Illness

MENTAL INSTITUTIONAL SYSTEMS The nineteenth century saw the establishment of a number of small mental hospitals and larger state institutions. Among them was McLean Asylum in Massachusetts, which was founded in 1818 and which opened the first school for psychiatric nurses in 1882. The school offered a two-year program that stressed training rather than education, and it established the precedent of preparing psychiatric nurses in psychiatric institutions. The woman acknowledged to be the first American psychiatric nurse was Linda Richards, an 1873 graduate of the nursing program of the New England Hospital for Women and Children in Boston. She was noted for her work in improving nursing care in state mental hospitals in the United States.

Much of the impetus for placing the mentally disturbed in large state institutions came from Dorothea Lynde Dix (1802–1887), a teacher and social reformer. Her efforts were well intended but ultimately fostered a system of impersonal, segregated care in specialized facilities. A New England school teacher, Dix first encountered the plight of the mentally disturbed when she volunteered to teach inmates of a Massachusetts prison. She found to her lifelong horror that the treatment of the mentally disturbed population housed there was far worse than that of the prisoners. Dix was an activist who traveled widely in her own country and abroad on behalf of her cause. Tirelessly she lobbied on behalf of the mentally ill before various legislative bodies and claimed "It is cheaper to take charge of the insane in a curative institution than to support them elsewhere for life. Well organized hospitals are the only fit residences for the insane of all classes; ill conducted institutions are worse than none at all." (Cullen 1978, p. 16).

Dorothea Dix was enormously effective in persuading legislatures to allocate funds for the construction and maintenance of specialized facilities for the mentally disturbed. Her effectiveness was due to her adherence to dominant medical thinking, her emphasis on the curability of mental illness, and her linking of curability with specialization and institutionalization.

THE MENTAL HYGIENE MOVEMENT The first decade of the twentieth century saw the development of the National Mental Hygiene Movement. Adolf Meyer (1866–1950), a physician, broadened the range of psychiatric thinking by proposing to emphasize the idea of mental hygiene rather than mental illness. Meyer claimed that institutional care was restrictive in that it overlooked community conditions in which mental illness arose. He said that communities should learn what they contribute in the form of mental problems and wasted human opportunities. This knowledge could then be used to make mental health care balanced and more preventive (Meyer 1922).

In 1908 Clifford Beers published an account of his personal experiences as a psychiatric patient. *A Mind That Found Itself*, which described the importance of social factors in the author's illness, was widely read and was instrumental in advancing the mental hygiene movement. The mere fact that a former mental patient was taken seriously was previously unheard of; even though he did not succeed in eradicating custodial care, Beers forcefully brought to public attention the need for improved, personalized standards of care. In 1909 the National Mental Hygiene Movement was established as the National Society for Mental Hygiene (Dain 1964).

Mental Disturbance as Psychodynamic

Around the turn of the century, Sigmund Freud (1856–1939) introduced the school of psychodynamic psychiatry, which greatly altered treatment of the mentally disturbed and brought new optimism to clinical practice. In contrast to the belief that mental disorders are affliction or illness. Freud believed that individuals possess drives and instincts that are gradually modified by childhood experiences. Unresolved conflict between instinctual forces and the expectations of family and society can lead to maladaptive behavior in adulthood: the person behaves in ways that perpetuate childhood patterns even when these behaviors do not produce the desired results. Freud devised the therapeutic technique of *psychoanalysis* to explore, analyze, and eventually correct such maladaptive patterns.

Freud's insistence on the absolute importance of the relationship between psychoanalyst and cli-

ent had the effect of reducing the importance of other therapeutic relationships. In addition, psychoanalysis could only be afforded by persons of means. Moreover, many individuals undergoing psychoanalysis remained unhospitalized or received care in private facilities. Thus, the number of nurses using a psychodynamic approach with clients was limited. The influence of psychoanalysis as therapy has diminished in recent years, although it continues to be important theoretically (Adams 1979).

Government Involvement in Health Care

One of the lasting effects of the Depression was to bring the federal government into greater involvement with the American health care system. The first milestone of this involvement was the passage of the Social Security Act in 1935, which increased the revenues of the federal government as it assumed new responsibilities for aid to the blind, dependent children, and the elderly.

The Mental Health Systems Act, passed in 1980 during the administration of President Carter, restated the responsibility of the federal government for mental health care. It expressed concern for the young, the elderly, minorities, and the chronically mentally ill. In the early 1980s most of the provisions of the act were repealed as part of the budgetary constraints of President Reagan's administration.

Inherent in the early community mental health movement was commitment to comprehensive, continuous care and the use of indigenous paraprofessionals as community coordinators and liaison workers. The 1960s were a time of great enthusiasm for deinstitutionalization; the 1970s were a time of reassessment and evaluation, particularly for great urban centers like New York City, where difficulties in caring for the mentally disturbed in the community were compounded by their nomadic homelessness.

The success of deinstitutionalization varied greatly from one locality to another. When clients were carefully prepared for returning to the community and when adequate follow-up care was available, outcomes were relatively successful. In other instances, large numbers of clients were denied much-needed support and became victims of a "revolving door" policy, in which discharge to community care was followed by repeated hospitalization, release, and rehospitalization.

THE IMPACT OF DEINSTITUTIONALIZATION

When state asylums or mental institutions were originally founded, they were perceived by society as humane refuges for persons who could not manage on their own. More recently, society has become disenchanted with such institutions. Early in this century it was apparent that the state mental hospital network, once a proud tribute to an era of reform, had largely turned into a rigid bureaucracy where inmates were housed but often neglected, exploited, and even abused.

Disenchantment with the system of state mental institutions coincided with the emergence of the community mental health movement. The result was *deinstitutionalization*, or the discharge of large numbers of hospitalized psychiatric clients into the community.

Deinstitutionalization is a dramatic example of the impact that one health care trend can have on communities. When the community mental health movement undertook the task of returning large numbers of psychiatric clients to the community, the results were mixed. Many persons who had supported deinstitutionalization in principle became opposed to it in fact when it became evident that discharged psychiatric clients might become their neighbors. Deinstitutionalization aroused fears among established residents, particularly when they were not informed or reassured about the presence of discharged psychiatric clients in their midst. Some people interpreted deinstitutionalization as a legitimate wish by society to free individuals from confinement and restraint; others saw it as neglect and abandonment of chronic psychiatric clients (Coleman, Butcher, and Carson 1984).

In theory, deinstitutionalization seemed workable. It was believed that the staffs of the newly organized community mental health centers would be equal to the task of providing adequate followup care and that government costs would be less than were needed to support state mental institutions. But despite the best efforts of many well-intentioned professionals and lay persons, unexpected problems arose. According to one source, "The needs of chronic patients had no place in the original federal mandate for the community mental health center" (Pepper and Ryglewiecz 1982, p. 389).

Lamb (1986) observed that problems arose because there were so many different kinds of chronic mental health patients and they varied so greatly in the extent to which they could be rehabilitated. Many persons discharged to the community found it difficult, if not impossible, to adjust to community living. Apparently, community mental health centers were better equipped to help clients during acute episodes of psychological impairment than to deal with chronic impairment.

One critic of deinstitutionalization used the example of a young male client who had been admitted to psychiatric hospitals or wards thirty-one times in eleven years (Smith 1981). Between hospital admissions, the client was arrested more than a dozen times. He was assaulted, beaten, and raped. He made numerous suicide attempts by jumping off bridges, slashing his wrists, and taking drug overdoses. The revolving door through which this client and others move is a consequence of current methods of dealing with the mentally ill. These methods include limited hospitalization and permissive forms of confinement in which clients are relatively free to wander about in the community. According to Smith (1981), the policy of trying to care for mental patients in the community has not meant better or more humane care but only recurrent worry and frustration for clients, their families, and the community. Others have pointed out that perhaps deinstitutionalization and return to the community were oversold and that benefits were lost because of the inability of the mental health care system to adjust to sudden changes in the delivery of mental health services (Lamb 1986, 1988).

Pepper and Ryglewiecz (1982) expressed concern regarding another population, referred to as the "uninstitutionalized." They describe them as persons who in the past might have been institutionalized for lengthy periods but who now spend just enough time in an institution to be stabilized and are then returned to the same stressful community conditions that they left.

During the decades of the sixties and seventies, deinstitutionalization was a highly regarded process. More recently questions have been raised as to its ethical and practical value. The driving force for deinstitutionalization came from two very different groups. One group was composed of moralists who were concerned about abuses and practices in public mental facilities that infringed on the civil rights of clients. The second group was composed of pragmatists who were concerned with the high costs of maintaining public mental facilities even at minimal standards. Thus the two groups were united in a common goal but for very different reasons. Since deinstitutionalization was introduced more than two decades ago, the inpatient population of publicly supported mental hospitals has been greatly reduced, but a number of shortcomings have become evident. Mental patients have returned to the community with only the most acute symptoms under control. Such people need a slow, gradual introduction to the activities of independent living. They need ongoing attention and help in obtaining food, clothing, and medication, but this help is often unavailable or given in ways that are unacceptable to them (Appleby and Desai 1987).

The eighties and nineties are, in effect, a postinstitutional era during which questions have been and will continue to be raised about the whole deinstitutionalization process. The plight of the homeless, many of whom are mentally disturbed, is a community problem for which no easy remedy is at hand. Homeless people make comfortable citizens less comfortable. The sight of bag ladies and of other ragged people sleeping on steam grates or bathing in public lavatories has raised a cry for reinstitutionalization.

Lamb (1988) called the condition of the homeless a symptom of a general lack of comprehensive health care in modern life, noting that "though the homeless have become an everyday part of today's society, they are nameless; the great majority are not on the case load of any mental health professional or mental health agency. Hardly anyone is looking out for them, for they are not officially missing. By and large the system does not know who they are or where they came from" (p. 941). Some researchers prefer the term *residential instability* to *homelessness*, believing that frequent mobility is the real problem, rather than homelessness. Goldfinger and Chavetz (1984) found that only 10 percent of high mental health service users were homeless on every admission. This finding, however, does not refute the fact that many homeless people who need care do not receive it because they are suspicious of established services and do not seek aftercare. They fail to keep appointments, are unwilling to conform to schedules, or comply with treatment regimens.

In evaluating deinstitutionalization, it must be kept in mind that some aspects have gone well. It is true that the homeless mentally ill are very visible and their condition tends to persuade the public that deinstitutionalization was a mistake. Yet the chronically mentally ill population has more freedom than before and many have adapted relatively well to community living. Perhaps *where* people live is less important than how well their clinical needs are met. Most of us would agree that poor mental health care can be found in inpatient and in community settings. The chronic mentally disturbed population is not homogeneous, and what are appropriate services for some persons may not be appropriate for others. There are wide differences in the ability of chronic mentally disturbed people to tolerate stress in the form of social relationships, vocational training, and independent living arrangements. For persons who can live only in a very structured environment, inpatient care may be advisable, even for considerable periods of time. Maintaining this group at their current functioning levels may be more therapeutic than discharging them to more demanding living arrangements where a cycle of stress-noncompliance and decompensation occurs. Genuine independence is difficult for chronic clients to maintain. Without sup-

portive care that realistically appraises their capabilities, clients take their medications erratically, neglect personal habits, and eat poorly. When their lives become disorganized and chaotic, they often become street people or rehospitalized mental patients (Lamb 1988).

The policy of deinstitutionalization placed great demand on clients, families, and on the health care system, partly because the benefits were oversold and the need for support services underestimated. Current demands for a sweeping return to the former system are another form of overreaction. A number of individualized mental health care programs must be developed to ease the hazards of deinstitutionalization, not only for the homeless, but for all mental health clients who prefer freedom and mobility to conformity and stability (Bachrach 1984).

The Mental Health Care Team

Responsibility for providing care to persons suffering psychiatric disorders is usually assumed by a mental health care team comprised of members of various disciplines. Nurses, whether generalists or specialists, are usually members.

The four core mental health disciplines—nursing, psychiatry, psychology, and social work—are usually represented on the team. Depending on the resources and program of the agency involved, the team may include occupational and/or recreational therapists. Considerable overlapping of knowledge and function occurs, since team members share a similar body of knowledge, augmented by the special expertise of their respective disciplines. However, even on interdisciplinary teams there is agreement that some specialization is necessary. Perhaps the most prominent characteristic of the interdisciplinary team is its collegiality. The designated team leader may be a member of any discipline concerned with program implementation. Often a nurse heads the team, partly because of nursing's commitment to comprehensive holistic care.

Interdisciplinary teams require clear communication channels between members, mutual respect, efficient coordination, and agreed-upon expectations and goals. Depending on their experience and preparation, all team members perform psychotherapeutic tasks compatible with the policies and programs of the agency involved.

THE PSYCHIATRIST AS MENTAL HEALTH TEAM MEMBER Psychiatrists have a medical degree followed by a two- or three-year residency in clinical psychiatry. As a rule, psychiatrists on mental health teams are responsible for the medical aspect of clients' care and with prescribing somatic regimens, such as chemotherapy or electric shock therapy. With other team members, psychiatrists participate in assessment, diagnosis, planning, implementation, and evaluation of care. They may or may not be certified by the American Board of Medical Specialists. Board certification is a lengthy process involving written, oral, clinical practice testing administered only to qualified candidates.

THE CLINICAL PSYCHOLOGIST AS MENTAL HEALTH TEAM MEMBER The preparation of a clinical psychologist requires graduate work at the doctor's level. Clinical fieldwork and a postdoctoral residency of one, two, or three years have usually been completed. Many functions of the clinical psychologist as team member coincide with those of other members; the special task of the clinical psychologist is the administration and interpretation of various psychological tests used to assist the team in formulating diagnoses and in assessing the strengths and weaknesses affecting a client's health potential. Clinical psychologists may not prescribe medication but can maintain an independent practice if they wish. They are adequately prepared to offer individual, group, and family psych' therapy.

THE PSYCHIATRIC SOCIAL WORKER AS MENTAL HEALTH TEAM MEMBER The special expertise of the social worker is the identification and assessment of significant family and social facets of the client's life. The social worker is cognizant of social services available in the community and acts as a resource person for clients and for team members. Occasionally the social worker may be prepared at the baccalaureate level. More often a graduate program at the master's level has been completed; such programs are usually two years in length and include supervised field experience. Only social workers with a master's degree may be admitted to the National Association of Social Workers (NASW). Social work has a dual focus: (1) direct service to clients and (2) social action and community organization. Members of NASW are qualified to engage in independent practice as well as work for hospitals, schools, and family agencies. Clinical doctoral programs in social work are available for practitioners who wish to engage in advanced administration, policy making, research, and practice.

THE OCCUPATIONAL THERAPIST AS MENTAL HEALTH TEAM MEMBER Established as a legitimate profession in 1917, occupational therapy usually requires preparation at the master's level (Freedman, Kaplan, and Sadock 1972). The purpose of occupational therapy is to help clients participate in mean-

ingful activities, either to reduce dysfunctional responses to health problems or to expand the clients' range of functional behaviors. Clients who need assistance in managing activities of daily living are encouraged to participate in self-care through activities that foster self-esteem and competence. The occupational therapist may introduce new interests and activities or encourage clients to regain lost skills and abilities. Often occupational therapists collaborate with nurses to plan for clients and encourage sustained participation in planned programs. They are instrumental in helping clients in their return to community living by guiding them through job placement and vocational programs. Sheltered workshops and rehabilitation and training centers are often staffed by occupational therapists (Kaplan and Sadock 1985).

THE ACTIVITIES THERAPIST AS MENTAL HEALTH TEAM MEMBER Alternatively, an activities therapist may be called a recreational therapist or a leisure therapist. Whatever the name, the purpose is the effective use or structuring of leisure time. Preferably, preparation for an activities therapist is at the master's level, although some baccalaureate programs offer a major in this field. Clients are encouraged to cultivate pastimes and hobbies that will enable them to lead richer, more rewarding lives. It is essential to assess a client's strengths and limitations before introducing any activities. Inducing a physically fragile client to engage in strenuous sports is counterproductive, as is teaching flower arranging to a macho wrestling fan. There is some confusion regarding distinctions between occupational therapists and recreational therapists. One difference may be the greater formalization of occupational therapy as a profession, with stated qualifications and requirements. Where actual functions are concerned, the distinctions may be blurred. As shown in Table 2–1, many forms of therapy are available for clients under the umbrella of recreational therapy.

Standards of Psychiatric and Mental Health Nursing Practice

The Standards of Psychiatric and Mental Health Nursing Practice were developed in 1973 and revised in 1982 by the Division on Psychiatric and Mental Health Nursing Practice of the American Nurses' Association. Only the basic standards are reprinted here; in their entirety, the standards are accompanied by specific rationales and measurement criteria. The rationales explain the basic premise on which each standard is based. The criteria suggest various mechanisms that may be

Table 2–1. Forms of Recreational Therapy

Form	Purpose
Dance therapy	Rhythmic body movements help clients express thoughts and feelings in nonverbal, nonthreatening ways.
Music therapy	Sound and rhythm soothe or stimulate clients who may listen quietly, sing, or keep time. Feelings evoked by the music may be explored verbally after listening.
Art therapy	Art forms created by clients help to control or release feelings. The art may be used as a vehicle for assessment. This therapy form requires sensitivity and experience from therapists, who can help clients deal with the emotional content of the art they created.
Pet therapy	Animals are used to reach lonely, withdrawn clients who fear human relationships but can respond to an animal's need for love and attention.
Plant therapy	Nurturing seedlings and plants promotes responsibility and competence. Horticulture makes minimal social demands and is a good first step for anxious, asocial clients.

employed to judge adherence to or attainment of a particular standard.

The Standards of Psychiatric and Mental Health Nursing are written in broad terms and are intended to guide practitioners regardless of the setting or the population being served. Standards distinguish between generalist nurses and specialist nurses. All standards apply to generalists and specialists alike, except for Standard V-F and Standard X. The first of these deals with psychotherapy and the second with community health systems; both of these standards are addressed to clinical specialists in psychiatric and mental health nursing.

The Standards of Psychiatric and Mental Health Nursing are organized according to the dimensions of nursing process and include data collection (assessment), diagnosis, planning, implementation, and evaluation. The first standard deals with theory and makes a strong case for scholarly and knowledgeable utilization of theoretical concepts as the foundation of all professional nursing practice, whether the practitioner is a generalist or a specialist in psychiatric and mental health nursing.

Most of the eleven standards are concerned with professional practice, but an important few are concerned with aspects of professional performance beyond offering clinical care. The performance standards focus on peer review as an evaluation tool, acceptance of lifelong learning as a professional obligation, and collaboration with other health care disciplines. The importance of nursing research is addressed in the final standard of professional performance. In effect, the Standards of Psychiatric and Mental Health Nursing Practice support and guide the enactment of expanded roles for nurses within the framework of professional accountability, lifelong growth, and commitment to excellence in client care.

Professional Practice Standards

Standard I: Theory
The nurse applies appropriate theory that is scientifically sound as a basis for decisions regarding nursing practice.

Standard II: Data Collection
The nurse continuously collects data that are comprehensive, accurate, and systematic.

Standard III: Diagnosis
The nurse utilizes nursing diagnoses and standard classification of mental disorders to express conclusions supported by recorded assessment data and current scientific premises.

Standard IV: Planning
The nurse develops a nursing care plan with specific goals and interventions delineating nursing actions unique to each client's needs.

Standard V: Intervention
The nurse intervenes, as guided by the nursing care plan to implement nursing actions that promote, maintain, or restore physical and mental health, prevent illness, and effect rehabilitation.

Standard V-A: Psychotherapeutic Interventions
The nurse (generalist) uses psychotherapeutic interventions to assist clients to regain or improve their previous coping abilities and to prevent further disability.

Standard V-B: Health Teaching
The nurse assists clients, families, and groups to achieve satisfying and productive patterns of living through health teaching.

Standard V-C: Self-care Activities
The nurse uses activities of daily living in a goal-directed way to foster adequate self-care and physical and mental well-being of clients.

Standard V-D: Somatic Therapies

The nurse uses knowledge of somatic therapies and applies related clinical skills in working with clients.

Standard V-E: Therapeutic Environment

The nurse provides, structures, and maintains a therapeutic environment in collaboration with the client and other health care providers.

Standard V-F: Psychotherapy

The nurse (specialist) utilizes advanced clinical expertise in individual, group, and family psychotherapy, child psychotherapy, and other treatment modalities to function as a psychotherapist and recognizes professional accountability for nursing practice.

Standard VI: Evaluation

The nurse evaluates client responses to nursing actions in order to revise the data base, nursing diagnoses, and nursing care plan.

Professional Performance Standards

Standard VII: Peer Review

The nurse participates in peer review and other means of evaluation to assure quality of nursing care provided for clients.

Standard VIII: Continuing Education

The nurse assumes responsibility for continuing education and professional development and contributes to the professional growth of others.

Standard IX: Interdisciplinary Collaboration

The nurse collaborates with interdisciplinary teams in assessing, planning, implementing, and evaluating programs and other mental health activities.

Standard X: Utilization of Community Health Systems

The nurse (specialist) participates with other members of the community in assessing, planning, implementing, and evaluating mental health services and community systems that include the promotion of the broad continuum of primary, secondary, and tertiary prevention of mental illness.

Standard XI: Research

The nurse contributes to nursing and the mental health field through innovations in theory and practice and participation in research.

Revisions in psychiatric classification systems and a growing list of nursing diagnoses represent converging trends that enhance the effectiveness of mental health care teams. The psychiatric classification systems and the nursing diagnostic system represent not final but on-going processes that are subject to scrutiny, validation, and refinement over time.

Psychiatric Diagnoses

The current official guide to psychiatric classification is the *Diagnostic and Statistical Manual of Mental Disorders-III-Revised* (DSM-III-R), which was approved in December 1986 by its sponsor, the American Psychiatric Association (APA). This version of the DSM is the fourth to appear. Like its predecessors, the DSM-III-R is fairly faithful to the medical model but moves toward a descriptive, behavioral, and social understanding of the manifestations of the clinical entities called *mental disorders*. Because the DSM-III-R is often used by interdisciplinary and multidisciplinary health care teams, nurses should have a general understanding of the system. It is also helpful to trace the evolution of various versions of the DSM.

DSM-I The first official version was prepared by the APA and published in 1952. It included a descriptive glossary of the diagnostic categories, and the term *reaction* was commonly applied to various disorders. This reflected the beliefs of Adolf Meyer that mental disorders were reactions of the personality to social, psychological, and biological influences.

DSM-II In developing the second version, the APA based its classification system on the relevant sections of the *International Classification of Diseases*, eighth edition (ICD-8). Work on the DSM-II and on the ICD-8 (the latter sponsored by the World Health Organization) occurred concurrently, and both appeared in 1968. The chief characteristic of the DSM-II was the elimination of the term *reaction* and the avoidance of any theoretical bias, except for using the psychoanalytic term *neurosis*.

DSM-III The third version of the DSM stemmed from the APA's desire to produce a classification system acceptable in the United States yet compatible with ICD-9, which was then in preparation. Therefore, the DSM-III adopted diagnostic terms used in the ICD-9, which in January 1979 became the official system used in the United States and abroad for recording all diseases, injuries, impairment, symptoms, and causes of death.

The preparation of DSM-III, which took five years, was an effort to resolve a number of problematic issues that had plagued the first two versions:

1. Tendencies among psychiatric clinicians, researchers, and educators to classify *people* rather than disorders. Instead of discussing clients as having various symptoms, they used labels such as *schizophrenic* or *alcoholic*.

2. The inaccurate but widespread belief that all

persons with the same disorder are similar, tend to behave alike, and tend to respond in the same way to similar interventions.

3. Lack of concordance or agreement regarding diagnosis, even among experienced professionals.

4. Inadequate criteria in DSM-I and DSM-II on which to base a reliable diagnosis.

5. Discrepancies in treatments offered persons with the same psychiatric diagnosis, and inconsistent outcomes even when similar treatment was offered to clients with the same diagnosis.

6. Attempts of DSM-I and DSM-II to explain the *causes* of symptoms. In other words, theoretical explanations were offered even though they were untested and unproven.

In response to these problems, the task force appointed to revise the DSM took upon itself the following objectives:

1. Formulation of reliable diagnostic categories acceptable to professionals with different orientations.

2. Clinical testing of new diagnostic categories before final approval.

3. Development of mechanisms for data collection and for describing degrees of psychiatric disturbance, biopsychosocial influences, and complicating factors.

The result of this effort was a descriptive multiaxial framework. DSM-III requires each client to be assessed on five *axes*, each of which provides specific information. The first three axes constitute the physical and psychiatric diagnosis; the last two permit rating of psychosocial stressors and levels of adaptive function. Every client is assessed on each axis.

DSM-III-R The current classification manual was published in 1987; many features of the DSM-III were unchanged. With minor changes the same multiaxial system remained. There was more emphasis on clinical criteria and more reliance on research data, but the same goals and descriptive atheoretical approach were retained. When proposals were made to add or delete diagnostic categories, the following two basic questions were asked: (1) Does the new category meet the DSM-III definition of mental disorder? and (2) How compelling is the clinical or research need for this category?

Some of the changes introduced in the DSM-III-R were controversial. In particular, three diagnostic categories proposed for inclusion generated objections from professionals and the public: late

---

MULTIAXIAL CLASSIFICATION SYSTEMS

DSM-III Axes

Axis I	Clinical syndromes or disorders Conditions not attributable to a mental disorder that are a focus of attention or treatment Additional codes
Axis II	Personality disorders Specific developmental disorders
Axis III	Physical disorders or conditions
Axis IV	Severity of psychosocial stressors
Axis V	Highest level of adaptive functioning in the past year

DSM-III-R Axes

Axis I	Clinical syndromes V codes*
Axis II	Developmental disorders Personality disorders
Axis III	Physical disorders and conditions
Axis IV	Severity of psychosocial stressors
Axis V	Global assessment of functioning

* V Codes are used for conditions not attributable to a mental disorder that are a focus of treatment or deferred or unspecified diagnoses. See Appendix B.

---

luteal phase dysphoric disorder, self-defeating personality disorder, and sadistic personality disorder. Critics of these categories claimed that supporting research data were lacking and that the categories had a propensity for misuse and stigma for women. Therefore, these diagnostic categories are listed only in an appendix under the heading "Proposed Diagnostic Categories Needing Further Study." The DSM-III-R warns clinicians to be sensitive to ethnic and cultural effects so as to avoid labeling "pathological" those behaviors and experiences that are culturally normal. Another warning included in the DSM-III-R is that the diagnoses are to be used for clinical purposes only and not to fulfill legal definitions of mental illness, disability, or competence. This is compatible with the stated purpose of the DSM-III-R: to deal primarily with reliable clinical observations and valid research data in order to promote consistency among various practitioners.

Axes I and II include all the clinical entities known as mental disorders. Sometimes multiple diagnoses are necessary, as when substance abuse is superimposed on another psychiatric disorder. Personality disorders are recorded on Axis II; notation of a code number on Axis II indicates that a specific personality *disorder* is present, not merely a trait. Any current physical disability that has a bearing on treatment management is recorded on Axis III.

Axis IV enables clinicians to report the severity of psychosocial stressors on a scale of 1 to 6 (from no acute or enduring psychosocial stressors to catastrophic psychosocial stressors). A rating of 0 is given if information is inadequate for assessment purposes. Axis V indicates the clinician's assessment of global functioning (GAF). Using a rating scale of 90 to 1, the clinician indicates good functioning with a rating of 90. A rating of 10 or less indicates persistent inability to function or persistent danger of hurting the self or others or serious suicidal act.

The DSM-III-R, like its immediate predecessor, helps clinicians to assess the biopsychosocial status of the client, to determine the most appropriate diagnostic category, and to report the data in an organized fashion. Data collection along the five axes provides an informed basis for making clinical decisions about target symptoms and treatment goals. Because the collected data are descriptive rather than theoretical, they tend to be readily accepted by clinicians regardless of their particular preferences and orientation.

Axes IV and V, psychosocial stressors and global functioning levels, are most relevant for nurses. It has been proposed that psychiatric nurses add a sixth axis based on clients' responses to psychiatric problems. This could then be used by all members of a mental health team to design the treatment plan (Williams and Wilson, 1982). While this direction is not presently pursued by nurses, the development of nursing diagnoses may be an avenue to broaden the contributions of nurses to comprehensive assessment and intervention. The classification system of the DSM-III-R may be found in Appendix B.

Nursing Diagnosis

Nursing diagnosis has been defined as "a statement that describes the human response of an individual or group that the nurse can legally identify and for which the nurse can offer definitive interventions to maintain the health state or to reduce, eliminate, or prevent alterations" (Carpenito 1987, p. x). In simpler terms, nursing theorist Johnson (1974) described nursing diagnosis as identifying and defining real or potential health problems. The development of approved or official nursing diagnoses is an ongoing process under the direction of the North American Nursing Diagnosis Association (NANDA). In formulating nursing diagnostic categories, NANDA continues to review and amend the approved diagnoses. Some of the early diagnoses were awkward and cumbersome for nurses to use, but NANDA has made progress in simplifying the categories. (See Table 2–2.) Some nurses believe that data obtained by assessing the client requires nursing diagnoses not on the approved list and permit themselves freedom to add to or revise the list as needed, while adhering as much as possible to terminology approved by NANDA. If nurses find there is a sustained need for new or revised nursing diagnoses, they should submit suggestions to NANDA for study.

Making a nursing diagnosis begins with a comprehensive assessment of the client's total health status. In developing nursing diagnoses for clients, the following steps should be taken.

Table 2–2. Simplified Nursing Diagnostic Labels Approved by NANDA

Previous Terminology	Simplified Terminology
Bowel elimination, altered: constipation	Constipation
Bowel elimination, altered: diarrhea	Diarrhea
Bowel elimination, altered: incontinence	Bowel incontinence
Cardiac output, altered: decreased	Decreased cardiac output
Comfort, altered: pain	Pain
Role performance, altered	Altered role performance
Self-care deficit: feeding	Feeding self-care deficit
Self-care deficit: bathing/hygiene	Bathing/hygiene self-care deficit
Self-care deficit: dressing/grooming	Dressing/grooming self-care deficit
Self-care deficit: toileting	Toileting self-care deficit
Self-concept, disturbance in: body image	Body image disturbance
Self-concept, disturbance in: personal identity	Personal identity disturbance
Self-concept, disturbance in: self-esteem	Self-esteem disturbance

SOURCE: Adapted from Tribulski (1988).

1. Gather data regarding the health status of the client.

2. Analyze the data and identify patterns of insufficiency, discrepancy, dominance, and incompatibility.

3. Formulate a specific statement, noting actual or potential health problems. (This is the nursing diagnosis.)

4. Organize the nursing care plan around the nursing diagnosis or diagnoses.

This nursing care plan may be adapted according to the policies of the sponsoring agency or facility, but the focus is the nursing diagnosis as stated.

The nurse involved in the care of clients suffering a mental disorder follows the same procedures used by a nurse caring for clients whose major problems are medical. The first step in reaching a diagnosis is to make a comprehensive (holistic) assessment of the client's needs. Client strengths as well as client weaknesses should be included. If the client's needs require any nursing intervention, a nursing diagnosis can be made. Because nursing diagnoses give direction to nursing intervention, the diagnosis often has two parts. The first part is a statement of the client's needs. This part is a description of the client's responses (physiological, psychological, or social) to the conditions she is experiencing. The second part of the nursing diagnosis is an explanation of the cause, or *etiology*, of the client's response. The two parts are usually connected by the phrase *related to*, although the space limitations of some nursing care plans may cause the causal (etiological) explanation to be abbreviated or even omitted. For example, a nursing diagnosis of self-care deficit might be attributable to either drug abuse, malnutrition, cerebral hemorrhage, or severe depression. Depending on the nursing care plans used by specific agencies or facilities, the statement of the client's needs and the

statement of the probable cause lead to the formulation of client goals. The goals lead in turn to nursing interventions, and to reasonable outcome criteria by which to evaluate progress toward the goals. Table 2–3 shows the significance of the nursing diagnosis statement and the etiological statement. Table 2–4 illustrates diagnostic and etiological connections in a nursing care plan format.

NANDA continues to review and refine the approved list of diagnoses. Recently the diagnostic categories were expanded to nine. Each category is identified by number. Under the category or pattern number, approved diagnoses are listed. Each diagnosis bears the number of the pattern or category in which it belongs. The diagnosis is further identified with its own number. For example, the diagnosis *Impaired Verbal Communication* is placed in pattern 2, *Communicating*. It is the first diagnosis listed in this pattern and is numbered 2.1.1.1. The names of the nine patterns are listed below. A complete list of nursing diagnoses may be found in Appendix A of the text.

Pattern 1: Exchanging

Pattern 2: Communicating

Pattern 3: Relating

Pattern 4: Valuing

Pattern 5: Spiritual distress (distress of the human spirit)

Pattern 6: Moving

Pattern 7: Perceiving

Pattern 8: Knowing

Pattern 9: Feeling

An important advantage of the numerical coding system is that it allows computer processing.

Nursing diagnosis is a systematic effort to establish a better knowledge base for informed practice. Although less extensive than the DSM categories,

Table 2–3. Significance of Nursing Diagnosis and Etiological Statement

Nursing Diagnosis (description of the client's actual or potential responses)	Related to	Etiology (probable causes of the client's responses)
Self-care deficit	related to	Severe depression

Goals	Nursing Interventions
Client will bathe daily	Assist client with bathing and grooming
Client will change clothing daily	Help client decide how and when to proceed with self-care
Client will make his bed with assistance and encouragement	Negotiate with client to set acceptable minimal self-care standards

Table 2–4. Nursing Care Plan Format Showing Diagnostic and Etiological Connections

Nursing Diagnosis	Goal	Nursing Action	Outcome Criteria
Noncompliance related to refusal to take prescribed Rx.	Increased client willingness to take prescribed medication.	Explore causes of refusal to take prescribed medication.	Client will follow prescribed medication regimen.
Noncompliance related to alcohol abuse.	Reduced client ingestion of and reliance on alcohol.	Discuss client's preferences regarding medication.	Client will no longer ingest alcohol.
		Refer client to AA.	Client will attend AA meetings.

official nursing diagnoses are part of the scientific, autonomous direction nursing is pursuing. All diagnoses tentatively approved by the North American Nursing Diagnosis Association undergo clinical testing and validation. Further work is required to refine terminology, to delineate criteria, and to test the diagnoses in clinical and laboratory situations. The formulation of nursing diagnoses is a sign of progress in expanding and applying nursing theory.

There are many areas of agreement between psychiatric and nursing diagnostic classifications, especially in regard to Axes IV and V. Like the DSM categories, nursing diagnoses make client assessment and care planning more specific and consistent.

Work on expanding and refining nursing diagnoses continues, but controversy has arisen between two groups. One is concerned with the lack of health-oriented statements in the current listing of accepted diagnoses. Nurses supporting this premise want to include coping abilities, actual and potential; support systems functioning effectively; maintenance of independent self-care, and other references to positive aspects of the client's resources. At present the North American Nursing Diagnostic Association is utilizing a problem-etiology format that identifies areas where nursing intervention is largely involved at secondary and tertiary prevention levels. The group that proposes to continue the present approach to developing nursing diagnoses believes the present method helps nurses communicate with clients and with care providers from other disciplines. Each faction makes a strong case for its position. Supporters of the present format contend that the approach now being used is adequate. Nursing process begins with assessment, and assessment includes observation and consideration of client strengths as well as client problems. Since client strengths are noted in assessing the client, there seems to be little justification for expanding the problem-oriented method, according to those who advocate no change. At the same time that this major controversy is occurring, there is a move toward having specialty subgroups in nursing formulate nursing diagnoses applicable to a specific specialty area. A committee comprised of psychiatric mental health nurses has already undertaken this task. It is quite clear that the expansion and refinement of nursing diagnoses is an evolving process in which many nurses are participating. It is also clear that compromises and modifications will be made by NANDA as the work proceeds (Baretich and Anderson 1987, Popkiss-Vawter and Pinnell 1987).

In the early years of the community mental health movement, nurses were in the vanguard, and they often made the difference between happy and unhappy outcomes of deinstitutionalization. Working as health team members, they organized and coordinated the activities related to discharge into community care. They led predischarge groups in psychiatric hospitals and postdischarge groups in halfway houses and other community settings. Such groups were a means of resocializing clients and reactivating long-forgotten skills. Clients were taught to practice such ordinary activities as shopping and handling money, using a laundromat, and riding a bus, and nurses reassured clients made anxious by impending change. For many nurses and clients the community mental health movement continues to bring challenges and opportunities for growth.

LEVELS OF PREVENTION The prevention concepts formulated by Gerald Caplan (1964) have been important in the community mental health movement. According to Caplan, a major goal in community mental health work is *primary prevention*, which is designed to reduce the incidence of new cases of mental disturbance. Another goal is *secondary prevention*, which is accomplished through case findings, diagnosis, and treatment. *Tertiary prevention* is concerned with reducing residual disabling effects of mental disturbance by promoting physical, psychological, vocational, and social rehabilitation. These three levels of prevention are no longer limited to community mental health work and have become fundamental principles used extensively by nurses in clinical and community settings.

(*Text continues on page 35.*)

CLINICAL EXAMPLE

CONVERGENCE OF PSYCHIATRIC AND NURSING DIAGNOSES

The client is a 60-year-old woman who suffered a cardiovascular accident. She has residual paralysis of the left side that is severe enough to require the use of a walker. Prior to the cardiovascular accident Mrs. Evans had lived alone in a small apartment, but afterward she had to be admitted to a skilled nursing facility, following a month's stay in a general hospital.

While in the nursing facility, Mrs. Evans became seriously depressed and was then transferred to an inpatient psychiatric unit where she could be observed more closely. Because she was so depressed, suicide precautions were instituted. Mrs. Evans was distrustful and suspicious of everyone with whom she came in contact. She was afraid that staff members and other clients would disturb her possessions and steal her belongings if she left her room even to attend physical therapy. At the same time, she refused to allow staff members to lock the door of her room.

Mrs. Evans had few friends and no visitors except for her landlady. Her husband was dead and her only son lived many miles away. In general, her behavior was withdrawn and seclusive. She spent most of her time in her room, lying in bed staring into space. Her daytime inactivity contributed to nighttime insomnia. She was indifferent to her appearance, often objecting to taking a bath or combing her hair even with assistance. Mrs. Evans never initiated conversations and responded with monosyllables when others spoke to her. At times she was abrupt and rude toward the staff and fellow clients. She never attended activities or programs organized for clients in the facility. Her extreme resistance to involvement of any kind impeded her physical and social rehabilitation.

Psychiatric and nursing assessments of the client led to the formulation of the following nursing and psychiatric diagnoses:

Nursing Diagnoses

Altered role performance
(related to social isolation and loss of independence)

Personal identity disturbance
(related to psychiatric hospitalization and loss of mobility)

Self-care deficit: bathing/hygiene dressing/grooming
(related to depression and low self-esteem)

Diversional activity deficit
(related to feelings of hopelessness and altered feelings of self-worth and confidence)

Knowledge deficit
(related to uncertainty about the future)

Multiaxial Psychiatric Diagnoses

Axis I	Clinical syndromes
	296.23 Major depression, single episode, with melancholia
	V15.81 Noncompliance with medical regimen
	V62.89 Life circumstance problem
Axis II	Personality and developmental disorders
	Atypical paranoid disorder
	(Code number is not used in Axis II except to indicate personality disorder rather than a trait)
Axis III	Physical disorders or conditions
	Cardiovascular accident
Axis IV	Severe psychosocial stressors
	Psychological factors affecting physical condition
	Psychiatric hospitalization
	Lack of support networks
	Loss of autonomy
Axis V	GAF 50: Current
	GAF 60: Highest in past year

Nursing Diagnosis	Goal	Nursing Action	Outcome Criteria	Outcome Evaluation
Altered role performance	Client will demonstrate increased independence and social interaction.	Assist with personal and room care: collaborate with client on setting up a daily schedule.	Client will gradually take more responsibility for self and room care.	Schedule revised at request of client to allow for one hour alone in a.m.
Personal identity disturbance	Client will demonstrate increased comfort and trust.	Permit client to bring her handbag and radio to nurses' station when she is out of her room.	Client will be comfortable with community living situation on the unit.	Client is now giving more assistance to primary nurse; little interaction with other clients.
	Client will cooperate in rehabilitation regimen.	Refer to physiotherapist; accompany client to physiotherapy. Help client practice prescribed exercise daily on her own.	Client will understand and follow exercise schedule.	Client asked about possibility of "graduating" from a walker.
Self-care deficit	Client will reduce sense of hopelessness and low self-esteem.	Give honest praise for signs of progress. Help client fix hair becomingly. Permit client to decide how and when self-care will proceed within reasonable limits. Assure client of her own worth and staff's interest.	Client will show more interest in her appearance. Client will begin to make decisions about self-care.	Client is often angry during a.m. care; protests but follows schedule regarding self-care.
Diversional activity deficit	Client will participate in activities of her choosing.	Refer to activities therapist. Explore client's interests.	Client will engage in two activities daily.	Client needs persuasion to attend activities periods; has begun to seek help of another client when doing needlework.
Knowledge deficit	Client will understand prospects for recovery of function.	Discuss client's prospects realistically with her. Emphasize client's role in restoration of function.	Client will accept her situation and begin to participate in her own recovery.	Client has begun to ask questions about her "stroke."

LEVELS OF PREVENTION

Primary: Activities and programs to reduce the incidence of new health problems. Example: Alateen groups for the children of alcoholics, since these children are at risk of developing alcoholism or other problems.
Secondary: Activities and programs to find persons with health problems, to diagnose problems, and to offer remedial intervention. Example: Home health care for a diabetic amputee and his wife, providing personal care, education, and family support.
Tertiary: Activities and programs to reduce the disabling effects of health problems. Example: Resocialization group experiences for elderly, withdrawn residents of a nursing home.

SUMMARY

A review of the history of psychiatric care and psychiatric nursing reveals certain trends. Over the ages mental disturbance has been seen in turn as supernatural in origin, as a stigma, an affliction, as illness, as a product of psychodynamic factors, and finally as a social and community responsibility. For many years psychiatry and psychiatric nursing were separate and divisible, with the scope of psychiatric nursing limited by whatever treatment approaches were fashionable and available. In the United States, governmental involvement in health and health care delivery led to the community mental health movement. Out of the community mental health movement came innovations and influences that expanded the roles and responsibilities of psychiatric nurses. When long-term, chronic psychiatric clients left institutions and reentered the community, it was often the psychiatric nurse and the community health nurse who prepared clients to return to community living and coordinated their aftercare. Without the discovery of somatic treatment in the form of chemotherapy, the deinstitutionalization of psychiatric clients would have been virtually impossible.

Deinstitutionalization has increased the problem of homelessness because many persons discharged to the community are not receiving the care they need. In some cases this is because adequate resources are not available or are offered in forms that are unacceptable to persons in need.

Some health care professionals are hesitant about becoming professionally involved with clients identified as having mental disorders. This attitude is generated by the belief that mental disorders are intractable conditions with an unknown etiology and a hopeless future. What is often overlooked is that diagnostic categories or labels have little relevance in psychiatric nursing. It is much more useful for nurses to think of mental disorders as reactions to overwhelming conditions in everyday life. The person with a psychiatric problem is less mysterious and more approachable if nurses rely on their powers of observation and on systematic assessment. Observation and assessment are assisted by the use of nursing diagnoses.

As in other fields of nursing, application of a nursing diagnosis is not dependent upon a medical or psychiatric label, but evolves from ongoing assessment of a client's social, psychological, and physical responses.

Research Report

Analysis of a Decade of Nursing Practice Research 1977–1986

The study analyzed nursing research over a ten-year period. Seven hundred and twenty articles were reviewed and analyzed according to specific criteria for inclusion. In addition to looking at research design and methodology, the study also assessed nursing research articles within the taxonomy (classification groups) of NANDA. Two thirds of the articles chosen for review were assessment-oriented; one third was intervention-oriented. Over the ten-year period use of nursing conceptual models increased, but models borrowed from psychology, physiology, or sociology were used more frequently. The decade also saw improvement in nursing research methodology, and in reported reliability and validity.

Classification of research articles according to NANDA categories showed that nurse researchers dealt mostly with knowledge deficit, coping, health maintenance, parenting, and noncompliance. For various reasons some of the research articles were difficult to classify. Thirty-two percent of the sample (229 articles) were classified under the catchall category of "other." Within this miscellaneous category, possible new NANDA categories were evident: breastfeeding, childbirth, health promotion, labor, nausea, parental bonding, menstruation, and menopause.

Authors of the review concluded that nurse researchers should give more attention to theory-based research, adequate sample selection and sample size. Improvement in these areas would allow nurse researchers to explain and analyze their data more appropriately, and to make predictions about future events based on their analyzed findings.

Linda E. Moody, Margaret E. Wilson, Kathleen Smyth, Rosanne Schwartz, Mart Tittle, Mary Lou Van Cott. *Nursing Research* 37, no. 6 (November/December 1988):374–379.

Review Questions

1. Describe the effect on mental health care of the popular belief that mental illness was supernatural.

2. Explain the role of Dorothea Dix in the care and treatment of the mentally ill. Do you consider her accomplishment to be positive or negative? Give supporting evidence for your answer.

3. Describe the origin and primary aspects of the community mental health movement.

4. Explain how the DSM-III-R and the nursing diagnoses approved by NANDA augment and reinforce each other.

5. Using a clinical example, explain how assessment leads to nursing diagnoses that in turn lead to goals, intervention, and evaluation of outcomes.

6. Based on your experience and your reading, what clinical issues in psychiatric nursing deserve investigation by nurse researchers?

Suggested Annotated Readings

Anderson, Joan E., and Lynn L. Briggs, "Nursing Diagnosis: A Study of Quality and Supportive Evidence." *Image* 20, no. 3 (Fall 1988):141–144.

This article deals with the number and quality of nursing diagnoses made by practicing nurses and with the evidence supporting the diagnoses. Forty-four percent of the diagnoses studied (12 out of 34) were not supported by assessment data. Nurses had difficulty writing etiological statements based on assessment data and in identifying problems for which independent nursing actions were appropriate. The authors suggest that nurses are uncertain as to what independent nursing actions really are, and have difficulty transferring assessment data into the descriptive and etiological components of nursing diagnoses. Although the article is fairly sophisticated in style and in data analysis, it should encourage students to use assessment data as a basis for nursing diagnosis and for verifying the diagnosis.

Culpepper, Marilyn Mayer, and Pauline Gordon Adams. "Nursing in the Civil War" *American Journal of Nursing* 88, no. 7 (July 1988):981–984.

In an unpretentious way this article describes some of the sacrifices and achievements of nineteenth century nurses exploring the dimensions of new roles in a new profession. Often their efforts met with suspicion, condescension, and even contempt. Within their own ranks they encountered stern discipline and stringent rules. Yet they continued to function as bedside nurses, hygienists, physical therapists, mental health counselors, spiritual advisers, and staunch friends and advocates for their patients. This is an interesting and inspiring account.

Derdiarian, Anayis. "A Valid Profession Needs Valid Diagnoses." *Nursing and Health Care* 9, no. 3 (March 1988):137–140.

The author deplores the lack of research studies dealing with the validity of nursing diagnoses and urges nurse clinicians and nurse researchers to join forces to remedy this deficiency. Various validation methods applicable to nursing diagnoses are presented in understandable language. According to the author, valid nursing diagnoses are the key to verifying client outcomes and ultimately to justifying nursing as a cost-effective professional service.

Donahue, M. Patricia. *Nursing: the Finest Art*. Mosby: St. Louis, Missouri, 1985.

This beautifully illustrated and well-organized book presents a selective history of nursing from early times to the present. The book is not encyclopedic in nature, for space considerations prevented the inclusion of some significant persons and events. Instead, it is more like a documentary in which significant individuals and developments are used to highlight the struggles and changes that characterize what Florence Nightingale described as "the finest of fine arts."

Drew, Barbara J. "Devaluation of Biological Knowledge." *Image* 20, no. 1 (Spring 1988):25–27.

The author of this article calls for a biopsychosocial model for nursing, with renewed emphasis on biological frameworks. She rejects the biomedical model as unacceptable because it is solely medical, being limited to cause/effect and cure. Yet nursing must not neglect biological knowledge, since this is virtually the only area that nursing does not share with the social and behavioral sciences. Knowledge of physiological disorders and their manifestations is essential to modern professional nursing. Nurses can demonstrate their value to clients and to society, not by overlooking biology, psychology, or sociology, but by maintaining a balance among the three.

Gilberg, Lillian, and Lawrence S. Linn. "Social and Physical Health of Homeless Adults Previously Treated for Mental Health Problems." *Hospital and Community Psychiatry* 39, no. 5 (May 1988):510–516.

The sample described in this article consisted of 529 homeless adults with a history of mental health problems. The purpose was to determine relationships between previous use of mental health services and medical services, as well as personal habits affecting the clients' health. Significant differences were found between subjects who had been hospitalized for psychiatric reasons and those who had been treated only on an outpatient basis. The previously hospitalized subjects had more serious physical problems, expressed more reasons for not obtaining necessary medical care, were more likely to obtain their food from garbage cans, and had poorer personal hygiene habits. In short, the homeless adults previously hospitalized for psychiatric reasons had far worse physical health than the other subjects. Researchers found companionship to be the need most often named by the homeless. Therefore companionship and accessibility were advocated as important aspects of health programs designed for the homeless. Programs are likely to be more effective if physical and psychiatric services are combined at a single site, and if they are provided in community outreach facilities rather than in traditional health care facilities.

References

Adams, V. A. "Freud's Work Thrives as Theory Not Therapy." *The New York Times* (August 14):1979.

American Psychiatric Association. *Diagnostic and Statistical Manual of Mental Disorders*. 3d. ed., rev. Washington, D.C.: American Psychiatric Association, 1987.

Appleby, L., and P. Desai. "Residential Instability: A Prospective on System Imbalance." *American Journal of Orthopsychiatry* 4, no. 57 (October 1987):515–524.

Bachrach, L. *Deinstitutionalization*. San Francisco, California:1984.

Baretich, D. M., and L. B. Anderson. "Stick to the Problems." *American Journal of Nursing* 87, no. 9 (September 1987):1211–1212.

Caplan, G. *Principles of Preventive Psychiatry*. New York: Basic Books, 1964.

Carpenito, L. *Handbook of Nursing Diagnoses*. Philadelphia: Lippincott, 1987.

Church, O. M. "From Custody to Community in Psychiatric Nursing." *Nursing Research* 36, no. 1 (January/February 1987):48–55.

Coleman, J. C., J. N. Butcher, and R. C. Carson. *Abnormal Psychology in Modern Life*. Baltimore: Williams & Wilkins, 1984.

Cullen, J. "Dorothea Dix: Forgotten Crusader." *American History Illustrated* (April 1978):13–14.

Dain, N. *Concepts of Insanity in the United States*. New Brunswick, New Jersey: Rutgers University, 1964.

Freedman, A. M., H. I. Kaplan, and B. J. Sadock. *Modern Synopsis of Psychiatry*. Baltimore: Williams & Wilkins, 1972.

Goldfinger, S. M., and L. Chavetz. "Developing a Better Service Delivery System for the Homeless Mentally Ill." In *The Homeless Mentally Ill*, Lamb, H. R. ed., Washington, D.C.: American Psychiatric Association, 1984.

Hollingshead, A., and F. C. Redlich. *Social Class and Mental Illness*. New York: John Wiley & Sons, 1958.

Johnson, D. E. "Development of Theory: Prerequisite of Nursing as a Primary Profession." *Nursing Research* 23, no. 5 (September/October 1974):372–377.

Kaplan, H. I., and B. J. Sadock. *Comprehensive Textbook of Psychiatry*. 4th ed. Baltimore: Williams & Wilkins, 1985.

Kraepelin, E. *One Hundred Years of Psychiatry*. New York: Philosophical Library, 1962.

Lamb, H. R. *The Homeless Mentally Ill: Task Force Report*. Washington, D.C.: American Psychiatric Association, 1986.

———. "Deinstitutionalization at the Crossroads." *Hospital and Community Psychiatry* 39, no. 9 (September 1988):941–945.

Meyer, A. "Historical Sketch and Outlook of Psychiatry and Social Work." *Hospital Social Services* (May 1922):13–14.

Mora, G. "Historical and Theoretical Trends in Psychiatry." In *Comprehensive Textbook of Psychiatry*. 3d ed. H. I. Kaplan, A. M. Freedman, and B. J. Sadock, eds. Baltimore: Williams & Wilkins, 1980.

Pepper, B., and H. Ryglewiecz. *Advances in Treating the Young Adult Chronic Patient*. San Francisco: Jossey Bass, 1984.

Popkiss-Vawter, S., and N. Pinnell. "Accentuate the Positive." *American Journal of Nursing* 87, no. 9 (September 1987):1216–1217.

Smith, J. A. *The Idea of Health: Implications for the Nursing Profession*. New York: Columbia Teachers College, 1981.

Tribulski, J. A. "Nursing Diagnosis: Waste of Time or Valued Tool?" *RN* (December 1988):30–34.

Williams, J. B. W., and H. S. Wilson. "A Psychiatric Nursing Perspective on DSM-III" *Journal of Psychosocial Nursing and Mental Health Services* 20, no. 4 (April 1982):14–20.

Communication and Interaction in Mental Health Nursing

Learning Objectives

After reading this chapter the student should be able to:

1. Describe the purpose and major components of therapeutic communication.

2. Outline the characteristics of the therapeutic relations and explain their purpose.

3. Apply principles of therapeutic communication to the nursing process.

4. Utilize documents in recording the care given to clients.

5. Explain what is meant by nurse-client collaboration and its importance to the delivery of health care.

Overview

Communication is a process that takes place among all human beings, regardless of their age, objective, or context. Whenever there is an encounter or transaction between two or more persons, some form of communication occurs, for it is impossible not to communicate. Verbal communication is important, but is by no means the entire process. When one chooses not to answer a letter or return a phone call, a powerful kind of communication is occurring. Indeed, it is through behavior rather than language that most feelings are expressed in everyday life. There are major differences between social communication and therapeutic communication; these differences are emphasized in the chapter. Social communication is a dynamic interpersonal process or exchange between two or more persons that may or may not be goal-directed or equally important to those involved. Therapeutic communication is a mutual interpersonal process that is goal-directed, facilitative, and significant for all persons involved. The first section of this chapter underlines the importance of collaboration and explains the therapeutic relationship as the basic step toward maintaining collaboration, formulating a therapeutic contract, and setting goals. The final sections describe techniques and methods of communicating effectively with clients and identify hazards to avoid. Standard methods of documenting care and communicating information to colleagues are suggested. Examples of typical forms of documentation based on their purpose are included; these examples are representational and illustrative only. All forms of documentation vary in format from one clinical agency to another, even though underlying principles remain consistent and intact.

INTRODUCTION TO THERAPEUTIC COMMUNICATION

In mental health settings, communication takes many forms and is transmitted in many ways. Sometimes communication is only the flicker of an eyelash or the slight movement of an outstretched hand. Sometimes it is a quiet, repeated muttering: "Oh no, no, no, no . . ." At other times it is a loud and angry shout: "Get away from me! Get away!" Sometimes the words come haltingly, hesitantly, painfully slow, after what has seemed to be interminable periods of silence. Sometimes the flow of words does not even seem to be in any known language: "Ya, pa, dee, may, may." At other times the words seem quite ordinary: "I'm hungry" or "I'm so tired." And sometimes the words seem to carry many messages: "I don't like what's going on around here" or "I don't understand what's happening."

Thus, an infinite variety of messages reach out to psychiatric nurses, sometimes eluding them, sometimes threatening them, sometimes discouraging them. But in all their infinite forms and varieties, the messages are the expressions of the clients' deep-seated needs.

Just as varied are the responses made by the nurse. When nurses respond to clients, they choose their words carefully, selecting them to achieve specific purposes. Often the nursing response is nonverbal—reaching for a trembling hand, lightly touching a shoulder, leaning toward a client, or smiling quietly (Burnside 1973). All these responses used by the psychiatric nurse are a part of *therapeutic communication.*

Therapeutic communication between client and nurse, regardless of the nature of the health care needs, is far more than the transmission of a message from sender to receiver. It is the reaching out of one human being for another. When a psychiatric nurse uses a simple phrase such as "I'll walk with you to breakfast now," she is offering her presence, support, guidance, strength, judgment, and protection to a client who may be feeling so overwhelmed, so weighed down by sadness, that motion seems impossible, or so anxious that the very appearance of the nurse arouses suspicion and fear. The communication that is developed and nurtured between nurse and client should be carefully planned and implemented so that the client feels protected, recognizes acceptance, and dares to attempt further communication, which in turn becomes the vehicle of progress and recovery.

ESTABLISHING A THERAPEUTIC RELATIONSHIP

Establishing a therapeutic relationship is a process that takes time. It must be carefully guided by the nurse and it must be predicated on *trust.* Trust between client and nurse occurs when the client is able to rely on the nurse's integrity, ability, character, and commitment to the client's well-being.

Creating a climate of trust begins with the *offering of self*, the reaching out of one person to another. A nurse reaches out to the client by offering his help: "I am Jim Williams. While you are here, I'll be your nurse. Please let me know if there is anything I can do to help you." Sometimes the nurse uses words that are less explicit but that are a clear statement of caring: "You seem upset; would you like me to stay with you for a while?" The nurse may also demonstrate caring without words, as by touching a hand or just staying with a client who is silent and withdrawn or anxious. Regardless of the specific way in which the nurse reaches out, the message conveyed is the same: "I'm interested in you and I care about you." When a client entrusts herself to a nurse, she demonstrates confidence that she will be accepted, respected, and helped.

Another important step in establishing a therapeutic relationship is clarifying identities, roles, and expectations: "I am Beth Thomas, the nurse in charge on this unit. I will be helping the other nurses to help you. I'll be stopping by to see how you are at least once a day. If there's anything that concerns you about your care or your stay here on the floor, please let me know."

It is important to make clear not only what the client can expect of the nurse but also what the nurse expects of the client: "We eat together in a dining room at the end of the hall. I will expect to see you there each mealtime" or "We meet once a week for community meetings. We expect all residents to join us."

Making clear the expectations in relationships helps decrease anxiety and prevent misunderstandings. Clear expectations also create an atmosphere that feels safe because expectations that are clear can more easily be met. And feeling safe in the hospital environment may enable the client to adapt in more healthful and effective ways.

Above all else, trust in the nurse-client relationship depends on consistent behavior on the part of the nurse. This is particularly important because many persons seeking mental health care have not experienced positive, trusting relationships before.

The nurse must ensure that his words and actions are congruent and that he keeps commitments to the client. A nurse who says he will return at a specified time or will pursue a particular question demonstrates consistency and reliability when he does what he has promised to do. The nurse must also display congruence between verbal and nonverbal communication. The nurse who says that a behavior is acceptable but who nevertheless appears angry is giving the client an inconsistent and therefore confusing message.

A therapeutic relationship must be based on respect as well as trust. Respect means acknowledging the value of the client, accepting and valuing her individuality and recognizing her rights and needs. The nurse demonstrates respect for the client by listening to her viewpoint, respecting her preferences, giving her choices, and treating her with dignity.

Honesty is another prerequisite for trust. It is important that the client be able to believe what the nurse says. If a nurse says, "You can have your medicine in 30 minutes," it is essential that the client indeed receive the medicine on time. Even in setting limits the nurse must be honest, because honesty, like consistency, helps clients develop a sense of security.

ELEMENTS IN THE THERAPEUTIC COMMUNICATION PROCESS

Therapeutic communication is not a simple, unidirectional, one-dimensional transmission of a message but rather a multidimensional, complex interaction between two human beings. Each person must be viewed holistically and understood as a living system if communication is to be therapeutically effective. Both the nurse and the client bring to the interaction their memories, feelings, fears, expectations, values, strengths, weaknesses, skills, and limitations. The overt message is only a clue to the full meaning of the interaction.

Berlo (1960) developed a classic model of communication with five components: sender, receiver, message, feedback, and context. Berlo also included a communication component called the referent, which is defined as the cause or precipitating factor of communication. (See Figure 3–1.)

The nurse wishing to analyze any interaction should first ask, "What is the referent?" That is, what originally precipitated the interaction? Was it the return of the voices the client had been hearing, a sudden unexpected sound outside the client's door, the slow awakening into consciousness of a client who had been heavily medicated, the anticipation and anxiety that arise as visiting hours approach? What need prompted the client to initiate communication? Or, did the nurse initiate communication herself because she is trying to stimulate the client to greater activity and independence? Is the nurse perhaps trying to reassure a client who seems visibly distressed?

Once the nurse has identified what began the communication process, she should consider the perspectives of both the sender/encoder and the receiver/decoder. Sometimes the client is the sender and the nurse is the receiver who must

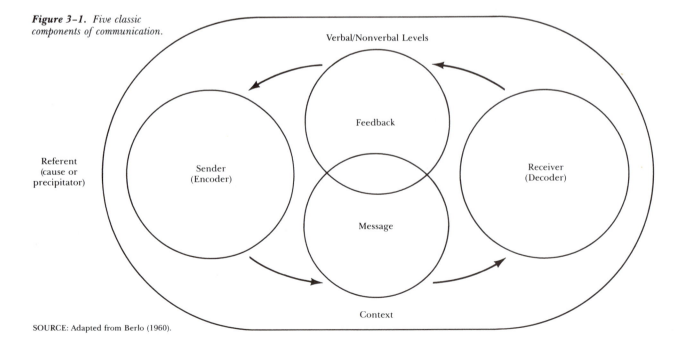

Figure 3–1. Five classic components of communication.

Verbal/Nonverbal Levels

Feedback

Referent (cause or precipitator)

Sender (Encoder)

Message

Receiver (Decoder)

Context

SOURCE: Adapted from Berlo (1960).

decode and interpret the message. At other times the roles are reversed. In either case, certain questions can be asked: What past experiences, perceptual difficulties, beliefs, hopes, and fears have influenced the way in which the message has been sent and received?

Sometimes the level or channel selected for the message gives a clue about the meaning the message has for either sender or receiver. The client who always whispers or who refuses to speak and insists on writing things is indicating something about the personal meaning that the communication process holds for him. So, too, is the client whose feelings are so overwhelming that her only form of communication is to glance and quickly turn away. There are many different meanings for such silence. For example, a silent client may be trying to avoid anxiety or to control hostile impulses that are not acceptable to the client's value system. In either case the silence has a meaning that requires attention and interpretation by the nurse.

Sometimes the medium by which the message is sent seems to conflict with other messages being sent at the same time. One of the most important things to look for in analyzing communication is congruence between the verbal and nonverbal expressions of an individual. The nurse will often see clients whose nonverbal behavior seems not to correspond to their verbal behavior or whose nonverbal behavior seems somehow inappropriate for the message being sent. The client who says, "I really feel much better today; I feel much less nervous" but who continually paces and fidgets is displaying a lack of congruence that reveals her conflicting inner feelings.

The body language of both the client and the nurse also communicates a great deal of meaning. Messages of acceptance or rejection can be transmitted by posture, stance, and body movements. The amount of space maintained between two persons is also believed to convey much meaning about the amount of closeness desired in the interaction. Clients vary in the amount of personal space they need. Some indicate a preference for maintaining physical distance while others show an acceptance of physical closeness. It is important that nurses not violate a client's personal space by standing or sitting too close. Such a violation could cause extreme resentment and anger and could even precipitate panic in a severely anxious client. The nurse should be guided by the messages conveyed by the client, permitting the client to maintain whatever physical distance is comfortable. Sometimes a client will endeavor to reduce physical distance by moving close to the nurse. In such cases the nurse should react in a way that is role-appropriate and professional. Nurses can use physical closeness to indicate caring, acceptance, and respect for the client, and they can gain clues about a client's desire for or fear of closeness by observing his use of space.

Another aspect to consider is the client's demands on the nurse's time. The client who attempts to monopolize all the nurse's time is indicating an urgent need for the nurse's attention. It is important to analyze why this is so important to the client. The nurse can control excessive demands in ways that communicate an important message to the client. Her willingness to commit certain amounts of time to the client reaffirms her valuing of and interest in him. But she must also set limits on time spent together to indicate to the client that she will help impose external controls when he is unable to set appropriate limits on his own behavior. Such limits also force the client to accept realities such as being alone at times.

COGNITIVE AND AFFECTIVE CHARACTERISTICS OF THERAPEUTIC COMMUNICATION

The characteristics of therapeutic communication should not be entirely new to nurses studying psychiatric mental health nursing, for therapeutic communication is part of nursing practice in all settings. It is the central process in the nurse-client interaction system in any health care setting, regardless of the nature of the client's needs. However, certain characteristics of therapeutic communication are so essential to the psychiatric mental health setting that it is important to review them here. These characteristics include client-centeredness, goal-directedness, authenticity, self-disclosure, confidentiality, and acceptance.

Client-Centeredness

The purpose of a therapeutic relationship is to promote a client's health and well-being. It is therefore a *client-centered* relationship. All that the nurse says and does is designed to meet the client's health care needs. This is in sharp contrast to ordinary social communication, in which both parties expect to have their needs attended to and gratified. It is particularly important that nurses who are beginning to develop expertise in therapeutic communication keep this purpose in mind and avoid unknowingly using interactions with clients to meet their own needs. A nurse's needs for reassurance, self-esteem, affection, and belonging are, of course, quite legitimate and very important, but the skillful nurse will seek appropriate ways to meet personal needs, such as through interactions with instructors, peers, friends, and family members. Once personal needs are met, nurses can use their energy creatively to meet clients' needs.

Even a need as deceptively innocent as intellectual curiosity is an inappropriate intrusion into the therapeutic relationship. The nurse should seek information from the client only when it is needed to plan for and evaluate the client's care. Similarly, there should be little if any personal talk about the nurse, except perhaps as a way to establish trust or to achieve some specific goal in the client's plan of care.

The client-centered nature of the therapeutic interaction is important because it affirms the client's importance and value. Clients with mental health alterations suffer from poor self-esteem; therapeutic interaction serves to enhance that self-esteem.

At first therapeutic communication may seem awkward to the nurse, since she may become absorbed in techniques to the neglect of the client's needs. For example, when student nurses first learn the technique of reflection (discussed later in this chapter), they may find themselves so eager to try this technique in their interactions with others that they become oblivious to the effect it may have on the other parties. True therapeutic communication focuses not on technique but rather on the sensitivities, needs, comfort, and individuality of the client (Scheideman 1979).

Goal-Directedness

The second critical characteristic of therapeutic communication is that it always be directed toward a goal. Each interaction between the client and the nurse should have a specific purpose related to the client's health needs. Early in the relationship, the purpose may be as fundamental as establishment of trust or assessment of the client's needs. Later interactions may focus on developing a therapeutic contract or on clarifying goals and expectations. In the working phase, therapeutic communication becomes the instrument by which the nursing care plan is implemented. At each stage, an awareness of the goal helps the nurse maintain client-centered therapeutic communication. (See Figure 3–2.) Therapeutic communication must also be guided by the logical thought processes of the nurse; it cannot be intuitive and spontaneous, as social interactions often are.

Empathy

One way to demonstrate to clients that you have accepted them at their unique level of need is through *empathy*, or the extension of support and understanding to the client. Brammer and Shostrom (1982) called empathic responses attempts to think with rather than for or about another person. Empathy is different from sympathy, which may cause the nurse to be overwhelmed by her own feelings of concern. There is a cognitive base as well as a feeling base to empathy. The empathic nurse is not flooded with feeling, but comprehends what the client is feeling and uses that comprehension to help. Cormier, Cormier, and Weisser (1984) listed some guidelines for empathic communication:

- Actively concentrate on the client's messages, verbal and nonverbal.

- Give yourself time to think and reflect instead of answering immediately.

- Formulate an answer that accurately responds to the intensity of the client's message, but

Figure 3–2. Tasks and phases of nurse-client therapeutic collaboration.

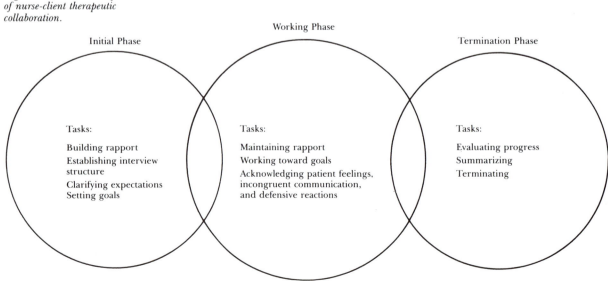

Initial Phase

Working Phase

Termination Phase

Tasks:

Building rapport
Establishing interview structure
Clarifying expectations
Setting goals

Tasks:

Maintaining rapport
Working toward goals
Acknowledging patient feelings, incongruent communication, and defensive reactions

Tasks:

Evaluating progress
Summarizing
Terminating

neither magnifies nor diminishes what the client has communicated.

- Offer a concise response that is clear and straightforward.
- Employ language similar to that used by the client.
- Use language, verbal and nonverbal, that is congruent and consistent with the feeling level shown by the client.

Respect

Like empathy, *respect* is an internal attitude the nurse holds and conveys to clients in innumerable small ways. Respect is akin to acceptance but is more positive in nature. Acceptance is acknowledgement of a client's uniqueness; respect is acknowledgement of a client's inalienable right to be different. Respect is rarely communicated in words, but is exhibited by nurses who integrate confirming gestures into whatever they do. Four guidelines that convey respect to clients should prove constructive.

- Try to understand the client's situation and viewpoint.
- Avoid negative or overly-critical judgments.
- Show commitment and concern for the client.
- Avoid actions that seem hasty, cold, or uncaring.

Inevitably, there are times when nurses must care for persons whose values and lifestyle seem different and even deviant. Nurses can express respect for clients verbally through the use of neutral and inoffensive terminology. When caring for an angry or defensive client, nonjudgmental phrasing and a matter-of-fact demeanor may diminish a client's angry reactions. Even when they fail to do this, they won't add fuel to the client's negativism. When nurses and clients inhabit different worlds or disagree about issues, respect can take the form of recognizing differences. A nurse who recognizes differences without imposing his views on the client might say, "I don't quite agree, but I can see how you arrived at that opinion" or "I'm not sure your method will work, but you have the right to try it out." Recognizing differences gives the nurse and the client freedom to have different opinions. The nurse does not express disapproval but voices uncertainty, and she does not infringe on the client's position in the matter.

Another important characteristic of therapeutic communication is *authenticity*, or acting in accord

with one's attitudes, beliefs, and values. When schools of nursing first began to emphasize the importance of the communication process in the late 1950s and early 1960s, nursing school curricula often revealed a preoccupation with techniques such as clarification, reflection, restatement, and the use of open-ended and closed questions. Nurses have since learned that they must not allow technique to take precedence over therapy and thus lose the human dimension in interactions with clients (Ramaekers 1979).

Nurses who can remain true to their individual beliefs and values while taking advantage of proven communication techniques are likely to be effective in their work. Authentic nurses let their warmth and concern for the client show. They communicate all the more skillfully because they are willing to learn specific communication techniques appropriate for certain situations, but they never let the techniques obscure the caring and shared humanity.

Authentic nurses do not use approaches that are personally uncomfortable. For example, if touching does not come naturally to a nurse, she does not touch a client just because she has read that touch can be therapeutic. Touch offered without authenticity may well be perceived as impersonal and awkward. Authentic nurses are acutely aware of their inner feelings regarding interaction with the client. They constantly seek to develop insight into the meanings behind their responses and to incorporate their personal responses into ever more authentic, and therefore more therapeutic, interactions.

Self-Disclosure

Another characteristic that distinguishes therapeutic communication from social communication is the amount and type of *self-disclosure* made by each participant in the interaction. In social communication, self-disclosure is generally done by both persons, although not necessarily to the same degree. In therapeutic communication, there is a concerted effort to facilitate self-disclosure by the client in order to promote the client's insight into his problems, feelings, and behaviors (Almore 1979). Self-disclosure by the nurse, on the other hand, is not appropriate. It can put additional stress on the client, who may become concerned with the nurse's needs. Keeping in mind the client-centered and goal-directed nature of the therapeutic communication process will enable the nurse to avoid inappropriate self-disclosure.

Confidentiality

All nurse-client interactions are understood to be confidential, except when there is a need to share certain kinds of information with other health care providers for the client's benefit. The nurse may wish to explain this important exception to the client. In social interactions, confidentiality is not assumed unless it is specifically requested.

Acceptance

Another characteristic of therapeutic communication is the obligation to accept the client at his or her present level of functioning. The nurse may work with clients whose communication and social interaction skills are limited and whose behavior seems offensive, unpleasant, or even bizarre. The nurse must remain nonjudgmental while assisting the client toward more healthy adaptation and more effective communication.

Perhaps the most important factor influencing the emotional climate of therapeutic communication is the nurse's *acceptance* of the client as she is, including whatever strengths, weaknesses, needs, and problems she possesses. Acceptance of the client often presents formidable challenges, for clients may display behavior considered unacceptable or at least unappealing in social situations, such as whining, crying, moaning, drooling, pacing, showing bluntness, anger, hostility, or excessive touching or avoidance of touching. The nurse's ability to accept these behaviors in a nonjudgmental way is critical to promoting therapeutic communication.

Introspection refers to the inner examination of one's own behavior, thoughts, and feelings. Helping a client practice introspection and develop insight into his problems is often the key to successful outcomes in psychiatric mental health nursing. The nurse may help clients develop the capacity for introspection by suggesting meaning for expressed feelings. To the client who talks of feeling "lost" after the death of a friend, the nurse might suggest, "Sometimes people feel that way when they have lost something they care about a great deal." Another method of encouraging introspection is to ask the client to consider the thoughts and feelings that accompany certain behaviors: "What do you usually think about when you follow people in the halls? What are you feeling when you do that?" Or the nurse may make specific requests for the purpose of encouraging introspection: "Will you write down just how you feel at the times you ask for your medication?"

Introspection must in turn be based on *self-awareness*, or the recognition of one's own memories, ideas, feelings, fears, and wishes. The nurse can be instrumental in helping the client become more self-aware by pointing out significant behaviors: "I have noticed that you leave the room every time other patients come in" or "I see that you talk very little in group meetings, yet the rest of the time you talk a great deal." Sometimes the nurse can help the client become increasingly self-aware by asking questions that require him to consider his own behavior, feelings, and self-image: "How do you feel when people address you like that?" "How would you describe yourself?" "What do you usually do when you are angry?"

Techniques in Therapeutic Communication

Communication processes that encourage clients to express their needs and feelings include active listening, questioning, the use of general leads, and the use of silence. Strategies used to refine and pinpoint meanings include clarification, validation, restatement, and reflection. Additional strategies, such as focusing, interpreting, confronting, and summarizing, may also be used to help the client increase self-awareness and acquire insights into her thoughts and feelings. Communication techniques that help clients control certain behaviors or shape behaviors into more socially acceptable ones include limit setting and positive reinforcement. Many of these strategies are summarized in the accompanying box.

The nurse working with psychiatric clients needs to learn how to use these techniques to facilitate therapeutic communication. Because these strategies are useful in various settings, many nurses are already familiar with some of them and need only to learn how to use them effectively with psychiatric mental health clients.

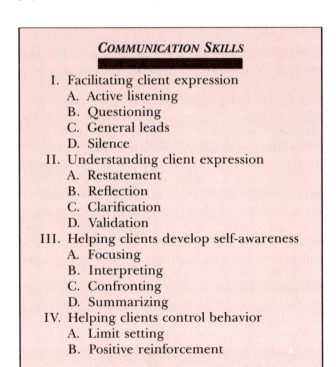

COMMUNICATION SKILLS

I. Facilitating client expression
   A. Active listening
   B. Questioning
   C. General leads
   D. Silence
II. Understanding client expression
   A. Restatement
   B. Reflection
   C. Clarification
   D. Validation
III. Helping clients develop self-awareness
   A. Focusing
   B. Interpreting
   C. Confronting
   D. Summarizing
IV. Helping clients control behavior
   A. Limit setting
   B. Positive reinforcement

Two major goals of therapeutic communication are facilitating and understanding client expression. Another important goal is to foster the client's self-awareness in order to promote self-control.

FACILITATING CLIENT EXPRESSION Facilitating the client's verbal expression is one of the nurse's primary aims. Hearing the client express what he or she is perceiving, feeling, and thinking provides the nurse with essential information that can be used to assess the client's needs and to develop a plan of care.

Active Listening One of the most effective ways of facilitating client expression is *active listening*. Active listening means attending closely to all that the client is communicating through verbal and nonverbal channels. The nurse should actively attend to what the client is saying, identifying themes in the client's communication. He should also observe the client's behavior, posture, facial expressions, gestures, mannerisms, use of space, and use of and reactions to touch. He should listen to the client's tone of voice, rate of speech, and choice of words to discern underlying feelings.

Such active listening is useful in two ways. First, it gives the nurse the maximum amount of data with which to make assessments of the client's needs. Second, it indicates to the client that full attention is being paid to her, thereby indicating acceptance of and concern for her.

Questioning A second way in which the nurse may facilitate client expression is through *questioning*. By asking the client carefully formulated questions, the nurse elicits information about what the client feels, thinks, and perceives. Generally, the nurse should ask open-ended questions that encourage the client to respond with more than a few words and that allow the client to retain some control over the interaction. Such questions as "How are you feeling right now?" and "What brought you to the hospital?" invite the client to share as much information as he chooses.

Closed questions, in contrast, are those that can be answered by yes, no, or other limited responses. Examples of closed-ended questions include: "How many pills do you take each evening?" "Do you ever feel dizzy when you stand up?" and "Have you ever been in the hospital before?" Such questions can be useful for obtaining specific information and are particularly useful in crisis situations in which immediate intervention is imperative and specific information is required. They should be used sparingly, however, because they do limit client responses. Examples of closed questions that might be useful in a crisis include: "How many pills have

you taken?" "Have you ever had chest pain before?" and "Do you know where you are?"

General Leads *General leads* are neutral expressions that encourage the client to continue talking, such as "I see," "Go on," and "Mmm hmm . . ." General leads let the client know that the nurse is actively listening, that she is interested in what the client is saying, and that she wishes to hear more.

General leads are used when the nurse wishes the client to continue, but they should not be used when the client is rambling in a way that does not contribute to assessment of needs or the achievement of goals. General leads should not be used when the client is using nonsense syllables or other forms of vocal behavior that the nurse cannot understand.

Silence The thoughtful and appropriate use of silence is another helpful communication strategy. This refers to the conscious and purposeful choice of letting silence occur or continue in order to achieve some specific purpose in an interaction. Silence can offer both the nurse and the client an opportunity to collect their thoughts, review what has been said, and determine the direction they would like the next part of the interaction to take. Silence can provide them with the opportunity to consider the meaning of what has been said. If the interaction has aroused strong emotional responses in the client, silence offers him the opportunity to express these emotions, by crying for example, or to regain his composure. Silence also conveys the nurse's full acceptance, since the nurse is staying with the client regardless of whether he speaks or is silent.

Many people, including nurses, are intensely uncomfortable during periods of silence. Therefore, nurses need to develop the ability to tolerate silence comfortably. They need to learn how to sit quietly with a client without speaking, in spite of any discomfort they may feel, for gradually extended periods of time. To a novice, the period of silence may seem to last much longer than it actually does. It may therefore be helpful to time the silence, if this can be done unobtrusively. Periods of silence may initially be no longer than 15 to 30 seconds, but as the nurse becomes more comfortable, she will be able to remain silent for a full minute or even longer. It is also essential to assess the client's reaction to silence and to judge whether the client is benefiting from the technique or is feeling acutely uncomfortable.

UNDERSTANDING CLIENT EXPRESSION In addition to facilitating client expression, techniques of therapeutic communication can be used to gain an understanding of the meaning of the client's communications—that is, the client's perceptions, thoughts, and feelings. Strategies used to determine the meaning of the client's communication include restatement, reflection, clarification, and validation.

Restating and Reflecting   *Restatement* and *reflection* are two of the most commonly used techniques of therapeutic communication, and most nurses become familiar with them in classroom and clinical settings. Both have the same purpose: to encourage the client to say more in order to clarify his intended meaning.

Restatement is a technique in which the nurse repeats to the client exactly what he just said, using the client's own words. This is usually done with the intonation of a question. Restatement has the dual effect of increasing the client's awareness of what he has said and of encouraging further explanation. Following is a dialogue that illustrates the use of restatement:

NURSE: Tell me what brought you to the hospital today.

CLIENT: I was so nervous I couldn't stand it. I felt like I was going to jump out of my skin. I was afraid I was going to do something terrible.

NURSE: You were afraid you were going to do something terrible?

CLIENT: Yes, like hit the baby or something. I felt like if she cried one more time I'd smash her into a million pieces.

In contrast to restatement, reflection is a technique in which the nurse repeats what she understands to be the essence of the client's message but rephrases it in her own words. For example, the nurse in the preceding example might have used reflection to continue the interaction: "You were afraid you were going to hurt the baby?"

Clarifying   It is not uncommon for the full meaning of a client's message to be somewhat obscure to the listener. In such cases the nurse may use *clarification* in order to reach a more precise understanding of what the client is trying to say. There are several ways in which the nurse can seek clarification, including questioning, use of examples, and contrast and comparison. For example, in the situation just cited, the nurse might ask, "What did you mean when you said you were afraid you might do something terrible?" In a different situation, the nurse might ask the client to provide examples to illustrate his meaning. For example:

CLIENT: I really feel uptight when people treat me like that.

NURSE: Can you give me an example of what you mean?

Sometimes clarification can best be achieved by the use of comparisons with other topics on which mutual understanding has already been reached. For example, a nurse might ask a client who is complaining of "feeling funny" to compare this feeling with feelings experienced at another time: "How do your feelings right now compare with the way you felt when you came into the hospital?" At other times clarification is best achieved by eliciting contrasting examples: "Do I understand you to be saying that your feelings now are much different from your feelings last night when Susan got angry?"

Once the nurse understands the client's meaning, he should verify the accuracy of his understanding through the technique called *validation*. A nurse using validation states his interpretation to the client and asks the client to verify whether it is correct. After an admission interview, for example, the nurse might validate his initial assessments with a statement such as "So the thing that bothers you the most is being alone?" or "So the thing that you feared the most about coming to the hospital is what other people would think?"

HELPING CLIENTS DEVELOP SELF-AWARENESS   A third major purpose of therapeutic interaction is to help clients develop greater self-awareness. Several specific communication strategies are used to accomplish this, including focusing, interpreting, confronting, and summarizing.

Focusing   In *focusing*, the nurse selects portions of what the client has expressed and directs the client's attention to those areas in order to explore them more fully. The nurse makes her selection based on her judgment of what part of the message is most relevant to the client's health care needs. The nurse focuses the client's attention by a direct request:

"Let's talk more about what happened at breakfast today."

"I'd like to hear more about how you feel when your wife visits."

"It sounds like the relationship with your stepdaughter is very stressful to you. Try to tell me more about what that is like."

Interpreting   A second way in which the nurse can help the client develop self-awareness is through *interpretation* of his communication and behavior.

The nurse can be helpful in this regard by first describing what seems to be happening: "I see that it is very hard for you to talk about this." Then the nurse suggests an interpretation for the behavior: "I wonder if it is hard to talk about the incident because you found it so frightening." At times the nurse may interpret the client's nonverbal behavior: "I notice that you become very restless when we discuss your marriage. You seem anxious and uncomfortable."

Confronting One of the most difficult yet important strategies available to the psychiatric mental health nurse is *confrontation*. To confront means to come face to face with, or to bring close together for comparison or examination. When the nurse confronts the client with something, she is making a demand that the client take note of a behavior and examine it. The nurse may elect to confront the client with a description of the particular behavior:

> "You ask for your medicine an hour or more before it is scheduled each day."
>
> "You say you want to lose weight, but I often see you eating candy and donuts."
>
> "You rarely come to meals unless a staff member asks you to."

In this manner the nurse requires the client to acknowledge certain behaviors and respond.

Sometimes the client who is confronted in this way reacts in a defensive or angry manner. It is important that the nurse accept this type of response without becoming defensive in turn about why confrontation was used. The nurse must not deviate at this point but must repeat, if necessary, her confrontational statement. As long as the client feels that the nurse's acceptance has not been withdrawn, he will usually be able to deal with the facts the nurse has presented.

Summarizing Another way in which the nurse can help the client gain self-awareness is through periodically *summarizing* what has been discussed. In summarizing, the nurse identifies and reiterates the main points of the total interaction. This helps the client review the interaction and hear how his communication has been perceived by others.

HELPING CLIENTS CONTROL BEHAVIOR The nurse can use two main techniques in helping clients control their behavior in appropriate ways: limit setting and positive reinforcement.

Limit Setting *Limit setting* is required when clients are not able to adapt in positive, constructive, appropriate ways to the stressors they are experiencing and therefore behave in ways considered socially unacceptable or potentially injurious to themselves or others. Limits must be set on such behaviors for the well-being of clients and of those around them.

In deciding whether limits should be set, the nurse should first assess the undesirable behavior, noting its nature and extent, the frequency with which it is used, and its actual and potential effects. For example, a client who frequently spits on the floor is creating a health hazard and is offending the aesthetic sensibilities of others. Another client who obsessively spits into tissues and throws them into a wastebasket may be behaving in a manner that is irritating, but he is not posing a threat to others' well-being. Thus, setting limits is more urgent in the former case than in the latter. Whenever possible, the nurse should also assess the meaning the behavior has for the client and what actions might be appropriately instituted. For example, the client who spits on the floor may be responding to distorted thought processes that require psychotherapeutic intervention involving medical as well as nursing measures. The client using tissues may be trying to get rid of an irritation caused by certain medications and may respond to reassurance and the use of throat lozenges. In both instances, the meaning of the behavior must be investigated in order to set appropriate limits.

Limits should be set in a specific and direct manner, stating explicitly what aspect of the behavior is unacceptable: "Spitting on the floor is not acceptable, Mr. Smith. Tell me what makes you unwilling to use a tissue." Consequences of violating the limits should also be clearly stated: "Here are tissues to use when you spit. If you continue spitting on the floor, you may not remain in the TV room."

The type of communication that is most effective for setting limits consists of short declarative sentences delivered in a calm, quiet, courteous manner. It should always be clear to the client that the limits that are being set represent the nurse's unwillingness to accept certain behaviors but do not constitute a rejection of the client. Clients often test limits by repeatedly trying to break them. The nurse may have to communicate the same message repeatedly: "You may not spit on the floor, Mr. Smith. If you do, you must leave the TV room."

Occasionally it is necessary to use medications, seclusion, or physical restraints to assist clients in controlling their behavior when they have shown the inability to respond to limits communicated verbally. The careful use of medications and restraint with severely disturbed clients has value, but nurses should remember that medication, seclusion, and physical restraint are forms of communication that must be used carefully and without punitive intent in order to be therapeutic for clients with poor impulse control.

Positive Reinforcement *Positive reinforcement* involves rewarding clients for engaging in desirable behaviors. Such reinforcement may take the form of acknowledgment, recognition, or some other sign of approval of the behavior. Reinforcement should express an opinion or comment rather than a value judgment. It is not particularly useful to label behaviors as "good" or "bad." Instead of making such value judgments, it is often preferable to indicate a neutral reaction to the desirable behavior:

"I see that you are up and dressed before breakfast time, Mary."

"This is the first day I've found you waiting your turn for medication, Sam."

Sometimes positive reinforcement is used to convey actual rewards that have been agreed upon as the consequence of specific behaviors: "We agreed that if you ate your entire meal you could have a pass to the canteen. You ate all your lunch. Here is your pass."

When using positive reinforcement, the nurse should clearly indicate to the client which behavior is being rewarded, praised, or reinforced so that the client knows which behavior to repeat.

COLLABORATION

Traditionally, the mental health client has been placed in a dependent, passive position, while the nurse has assumed a directive role. In contrast, therapeutic communication is based on a *collaborative* effort between the client and nurse, who hold equally important positions, although their unique needs and characteristics are acknowledged and respected. The client is actively involved in the interactive process and works together with the nurse to identify problems, establish goals, formulate plans of action, work toward goals, and evaluate progress.

When a nurse and client collaborate together, they must have a mutual respect, each recognizing that the other brings unique qualities, needs, and resources to the situation. Until the nurse is able to engage the client in active collaboration, it will not

be possible for the client to make progress toward improved health status. Clients must ultimately take responsibility for their own mental health, and willingness to become active participants in the nurse-client interaction is an important indicator of readiness to assume that responsibility. (See Figure 3–3.)

The Collaborative Continuum

Sometimes the amount and type of collaboration of which a client is capable are limited. For example, the profoundly depressed individual who has not spoken for days may be capable of no more than nonverbal assent to certain aspects of the daily routine. By agreeing to stand up, walk to the door, and accompany the nurse to the dining room for meals, the client may be collaborating, albeit in a limited way. It is essential to recognize the extent to which the client is capable of collaborating at any time and it is equally essential to continue to assess a client's ability to take a more active role in the therapeutic process.

Some clients actively resist any kind of collaborative effort, refusing to participate in activities suggested by the nurse or to discuss their problems, goals, and plan of care. In such cases, the nurse must initially take a strong leadership role, setting limits on certain client behaviors and identifying consequences of particular kinds of behaviors. Strategies such as limit setting and positive reinforcement are ways of promoting a collaborative relationship. Each member of the relationship has a special role, and in some instances the role of the client may be to adhere to reasonable limits, while

Figure 3–3. *The changing balance of responsibility in nurse/client collaboration.*

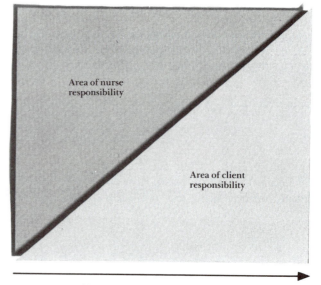

Area of nurse responsibility

Area of client responsibility

Movement toward increasing wellness

COMMUNICATION TECHNIQUES

Type of Question	Definition	Example
Open-ended question	A question beginning with "what," "how," "when," "where," or "who" that asks for information without specifying the content and requires more elaboration than a one-word response	What did you think of the discharge meeting?
Closed question	A question beginning with words like "are," "do," "did," "is," or "can," which asks for a specific fact or piece of information and can be answered with one word or a short phrase	Did you keep your appointment at the mental health clinic?
Focused question	A question often beginning with "have you," "can you," "do you," which narrows or defines the topic by asking for a specific response	Have you told anyone how upset you were?
Clarifying question	A question asking the patient to rephrase or restate a previous message	I don't understand. Will you tell me again?
Restatement of facts	A statement rephrasing the cognitive part of a patient message	So you still intend to leave tomorrow as planned.
Reflection of feelings	A statement rephrasing the affective part or emotional tone of a patient message	You sound both happy and sad about going home.
Summarizing statement	A collection of several paraphrased or reflected responses that condenses patient messages or an interview or series of interviews	You seem to be saying you have mixed feelings about leaving. You were upset today, but you told the clinic nurse and you intend to keep your appointments at the mental health clinic.

the role of the nurse may be to set such limits. As the client moves in the direction of mental and emotional wellness, both client and nurse will work toward the time when the client will be able to set his or her own limits. Thus, collaboration can be seen as occurring along a continuum in which the balance between the amount of leadership taken by the nurse and the amount of initiative and responsibility taken by the client changes over time. (See Figure 3–3.)

The Therapeutic Contract

Establishing a *therapeutic contract* is a crucial step in building an effective nurse-client relationship. The therapeutic contract is the process by which the nurse and client identify the client's problems and establish mutually acceptable goals for both the short term and the long term.

Sometimes a considerable amount of time may be required to reach agreement about the client's needs, since clients often have difficulty identifying their own problems and setting priorities. Therefore, early goals may relate to identification and exploration of urgent problems.

Once agreement has been reached about which problems should be addressed, specific short-term and long-term goals should be explored and defined. For example, a nurse with a highly anxious client may agree that attention should be given to the client's feelings of apprehension about leaving her hospital room. Exploration of the client's feelings will help the nurse understand the client's perception of the problem. This understanding can then guide formulation of goals for the client. Short-term goals for this particular client might include the following:

1. The client will leave the room accompanied by the nurse for meals and for medications.

2. Within three days, the client will go to meals unaccompanied, meeting the nurse in the dining room.

3. By the end of the week, the client will also leave the room once in the morning and once in the afternoon for a walk around the unit, accompanied by the nurse.

Long-term goals might include:

4. The client will move about the unit freely, unaccompanied by the nurse, and will stay out of her room at least once during half of her waking hours.

A contract with this client might also include an agreement that, after each excursion outside the room, the nurse and client will spend a few minutes discussing the experience and the client's feelings about it. As progress is made toward achievement of the goals, the contract can be reviewed and revisions may be made.

Another example of a therapeutic contract might be one made with a severely depressed person who has not been taking responsibility for hygiene and self-care. The nurse and client might discuss appropriate behavior in different areas of hygiene, such as mouth care, bathing, and grooming, and develop a plan whereby the client assumes increasing responsibility for these areas, with gradually decreasing amounts of assistance from the nurse. The nurse will want to verbally reinforce the client's progress while providing the amount of support and assistance that has been agreed upon. Sometimes a contract of this sort needs to be tied to certain requirements. For example, the contract may state that the client must brush his teeth and

dress before breakfast or that she must finish showering before watching television.

The types of agreements that may be made part of the therapeutic contract vary with client needs and with the ways in which clients express their needs. The nurse who devotes time and effort to developing a highly individualized contract with a client will find that considerable progress can be made within the terms of the contract.

Mutual agreement about contract terms is essential. For the contract to succeed, there must be mutual accountability and a sense of shared ownership. This makes both participants more committed to the designated goals and more aware of progress that is made. Once goals have been achieved, the contract should be revised so that the client assumes greater responsibility for his or her own well-being.

Therapeutic Communication and the Nursing Process

The concepts, principles, and techniques of therapeutic communication are inextricably interwoven with the nursing process at each stage of its application. The effectiveness with which the nurse uses the nursing process is highly dependent on his or her skill with therapeutic communication.

ASSESSMENT AND DIAGNOSIS The same factors that contribute to the development of therapeutic communication also contribute to effective data gathering during the assessment phase of the nursing process. The more comfortable the client feels in his relationship with the nurse, the more readily he will answer questions and share information.

The nurse may use a variety of communication strategies to collect data needed to develop a health assessment and plan of care. Open-ended questions and broad leads may encourage the client to share information; closed questions may elicit specific information. Through a client-centered, goal-directed approach, the nurse can collect data quickly and efficiently, conserving the client's emotional energy without sacrificing completeness or accuracy.

The nurse may also need to gather data from secondary sources, such as the client's family, other health care providers, and past records. Because secondary data may be subject to inaccuracies, the nurse should be particularly careful to clarify and validate such information.

After collecting data about the client, the nurse should review and analyze the information in order to draw conclusions about its meaning. The process of data analysis leads to the formulation of nursing diagnoses that will serve as the basis for the client's plan of care. Validation of diagnoses is helpful with clients in all settings, but it is particularly critical in the mental health setting, for two reasons. First, nursing diagnoses of mental and emotional alterations may be more difficult to make than those of physical alterations and therefore may be more subject to error. Validation of the diagnoses with the client reduces or eliminates the likelihood of such error. Second, collaboration with the mental health client is crucial to the success of his therapy. Collaboration is in turn dependent on a mutual agreement about which problems are to be addressed.

The nurse can validate diagnoses with the client by sharing the assessments that have been made and by asking for feedback. Assessments may be worded a bit differently in discussions with the client than in documentation on the client's record. For example, a diagnosis recorded as "alteration in body image related to perceptual distortions" may be described to the client as "troubled feelings about your body because of the way things seem to you." Similarly, "anxiety regarding interactions with other people related to poor self-esteem" might be described to the client as "nervousness about talking with other people because you think they will not find you interesting." In each case, the nurse would ask the client to validate the assessment: "Would you agree that this seems to be the problem?" or "Would you agree that this is one of the problems troubling you now?"

PLANNING Planning nursing care is highly dependent on collaboration among the nurse and client, the client's family, and various members of the health care team. Collaboration is in turn based on effective communication and on clear statements about roles and expectations. Whether collaboration is with the client, a family member, or other members of the health care team, clear, direct communication is essential. It enables both parties to agree on the problems to be addressed, to identify and consider possible interventions, and to select those interventions that will form the plan of care. During the planning phase, the nurse and client should reach agreement about priorities so that those areas considered most urgent will be dealt with first.

Once a plan of care has been developed, it should be available in writing to all members of the health care team. Nursing diagnoses should be stated clearly and concisely; short-term and long-term goals should be identified; and interventions should be stated as lucid, precise nursing orders. A portion of a care plan might be stated as in Table 3–1.

IMPLEMENTATION The actual implementation of the nursing care plan is highly dependent on effective communication. In the case of the client referred to in Table 3–1, the establishment of a trusting, effective nurse-client relationship is a prerequisite to the implementation of the plan. Specific aspects of the plan will succeed only to the extent that communication is used effectively. The nurse accompanying the client to the dining room should indicate acceptance and empathy but also convey the clear expectation that the client will comply. "It is time to go to the dining room for lunch," the nurse might say. "I know it is hard for you to do that, but we have agreed that you will eat meals with the other residents. I am going to walk with you to the dining room and stay with you until you feel more comfortable."

EVALUATION As the nursing care plan is implemented, ongoing evaluation occurs. In the evaluation phase of the nursing process, the nurse should note the client's reactions to the care plan. For example, the nurse may invite the client to share her reactions and feelings about eating meals with others: "You seem less tense than you did at breakfast. Tell me how you feel now." The nurse may also help the client interpret her nonverbal messages: "You seem to be upset right now. Tell me what you are feeling."

Regardless of the nature of the client's problems or the interventions included in the individual care plan, exploration of the client's thoughts and feelings is central to care. There may, for example, be a goal for the client to verbalize feelings instead of expressing them behaviorally. Because the verbal expression of feelings is difficult to quantify and does not involve psychomotor skills such as those the nurse uses in other settings, its importance may

Table 3–1. Portion of a Nursing Care Plan

Nursing Diagnosis	Short-Term Goals	Long-Term Goals	Nursing Orders
Social isolation secondary to depression	The client will eat all meals in dining room beginning 11/21	The client will interact with others at mealtime by 11/25	1. Accompany client to dining room for all meals. 2. Seat client with others who are likely to interact with him. 3. Document interactions at meals.

sometimes be underestimated. Encouraging clients to verbalize their feelings is often the most critical intervention of all and can only be achieved through effective communication. The nurse caring for mental health clients must therefore develop genuine skill in the area of therapeutic communication, which will enable her to provide high-quality, meaningful nursing care.

DOCUMENTATION OF CARE

There are four ways to document the nursing process in the mental health setting (the nurse will probably be familiar with them from other settings): the health status profile, the problem list, progress notes, and the discharge plan and summary.

The Health Status Profile

The *health status profile* contains the data gathered when the client enters or reenters the health care system. A designated nurse usually conducts a thorough, systematic interview, called an *intake interview* or an *initial nursing assessment*. Typically, this interview deals with the client's present health status, the nature of the problems that brought the client to the health care system, the client's past health history, and the client's support systems, resources, and constraints.

It is helpful to note first the client's perception of what brought him to the health care setting and his description of the onset and characteristics of the current problem. The nurse might record a summary that indicates both the client's own words, referred to as the *subjective data*, and the nurse's observations of the client, or *objective data*, as follows:

Subjective:
"My husband brought me in. He said I had to come here because I wouldn't eat any more. He said I had to find out what is wrong."

Objective:
This thin, pale young woman was brought to the Emergency Department by her husband, who states client has not eaten for four days. Client speaks only when spoken to but responds to questions in a cooperative manner. Avoids eye contact. Affect is flat. Lies motionless in bed, seeming to stare at the wall.

During the initial assessment, the nurse should explore with the client the dimensions of the present problem, including its onset and duration, the ways in which it is manifested, and anything that aggravates or relieves the problem.

The nurse should then take a complete health history, unless the client's condition precludes it. In addition to the client's own health history, the nurse should investigate the client's family history and social history, including the present living situation, major roles and responsibilities, and potential or actual support systems. The health history interview is usually accompanied by a physical health assessment of the client. The format for a comprehensive health assessment is the same for mental health clients as for all other clients. Particular attention should be paid to the mental status examination and assessment.

Once the initial assessment has been conducted by the nurse and by the other appropriate members of the health care team, all the data should be documented in an orderly fashion in the client's record, where it serves as the health status profile. The health status profile then provides the basis for diagnosing the client's health care problems and planning appropriate care.

The Problem List

The nursing diagnoses, as well as those made by other health care professionals, are listed on the client's *problem list* in the record. The problem list serves as a guide for all those participating in the client's care and also is used as the basis for organizing a record of the client's progress.

Progress Notes

The *progress notes* comprise the body of the client's record and describe the changing condition of the client. The frequency with which progress notes are written will depend on the rate at which the client's condition changes and the policies of the particular institution. All progress notes should be directed at a specific problem from the client's problem list and should contain subjective and objective data related to the problem, the nurse's assessment and evaluation of the meaning of the data, and the care plan revisions required by the assessment and evaluation. The progress notes make it possible for all those providing care to review quickly the client's progress and to use that knowledge as the basis for further work with the client. Accurate, concise progress notes are essential to comprehensive and continuous nursing care and also serve as the legal record of the nursing care provided to the client.

Discharge Plans and Summary

When the client is ready to be discharged from the health care facility, the record should indicate the plans for discharge and for any follow-up care. Each of the client's identified problems should be addressed, and the plans for continued treatment

SAMPLE PROGRESS NOTES

PROBLEM: Anxiety related to marital difficulties

Subjective: "I dread hearing his car in the driveway. I just know he'll start yelling about something as soon as he comes in the door. I feel so scared I just pretend I am not there. I hope he won't even see me."

Objective: Client talks in quiet, hesitant manner, staring down at her hands, which she twists nervously. Makes no eye contact with nurse. Occasionally eyes well with tears, which she brushes away. Client appears pale and poorly groomed; smokes absentmindedly at intervals.

Assessment: Expressing feelings more readily today, but still visibly upset when discussing marriage. Smoking less than yesterday.

Plan: Continue daily periods of exploration of feelings about husband. Assist client in focusing on herself as a person and on her grooming and physical care. Develop contract regarding personal hygiene.

PROBLEM: Grief and suicidal ideation related to loss of pregnancy

Subjective: "If I can't have a baby there is nothing to live for." "Just leave me alone."

Objective: Client is crying hysterically, sitting in corner of room with arms drawn around flexed legs, rocking back and forth. Client was originally quite agitated when nurse entered room but quieted somewhat after a few minutes.

Assessment: Client continues to express feelings of hopelessness. Suicide risk still a possibility.

Plan: Continue suicide precautions. Discuss response to medications with physician. Continue supportive interactions with encouragement to express feelings about loss of pregnancy.

of any unresolved problems should be indicated in the discharge summary. Specifically, the names of persons and agencies who have responsibility for the client's ongoing care should be noted.

In addition to the specific discharge plan, a brief summary should be written indicating the client's condition at discharge and summarizing the care provided. Examples of discharge plans and discharge summaries are provided in the accompanying boxes.

Process Recording

In addition to the written documentation that forms the client's record of care, the nurse may wish to use other forms of written communication to enhance understanding of the client or for the use of the interdisciplinary health care team. In psychiatric mental health settings, one form of written communication that is a commonly used and highly effective learning tool is the *process recording*. A process recording is merely a verbatim recording of what was said by each participant in the interaction, using alternating columns so that the

communication of each person is clearly identified. A third column is then used to identify the meanings assigned to the interaction.

The purposes of a process note are:

1. To provide a mechanism for studying and analyzing the interaction by helping the nurse identify and understand the meaning of behavior, thoughts, and feelings exhibited by both the nurse and the client.

2. To provide a method of systematically observing and noting nonverbal and verbal communication.

3. To assist the nurse in examining and evaluating nursing interventions.

4. To offer a means by which the nurse can validate perceptions and interpretations.

5. To help the nurse collect, organize, interpret, analyze, and synthesize raw data gathered in the course of a nurse-client interaction.

SAMPLE DISCHARGE PLAN

Problem	Status at Discharge	Plans for Follow-up
1. Anxiety	Client has good awareness of her own anxiety level; is using imaging and relaxation techniques with some benefit. Adequately controlled on Valium 5 mg p.o. every 4 hr. p.r.n.	Dr. R. Jones to follow. First appointment Nov. 30. Client will continue to attend relaxation group on weekly basis.
2. Anorexia	Client has stabilized weight at 110 pounds. Goal now is maintenance. Was instructed to continue calorie count to maintain intake at 1500 calories per day.	Client to be weighed weekly after group meeting. Dietitian available p.r.n. Clinic nurses to evaluate weight and diet history weekly.
3. Concern regarding ability to carry pregnancy to term	Initial meeting with gynecologist consult went well; client is receptive to further workup.	Has appointment with Dr. B. Gunther on Dec. 1.
4. Lack of social supports	Client has acknowledged need for structured activities outside home; has made commitment to join weekly discussion group and to seek part-time employment.	Client has obtained information about discussion group meeting on 11/28. Plans to attend. To be referred to Bureau of Vocational Rehabilitation for intake interview and vocational testing if she expresses interest in this.

6. To facilitate the application of theoretical concepts to clinical practice.

7. To promote ongoing assessment, planning, and evaluation of nursing intervention with a specific client.

There are times when nurses must obtain critical information as quickly as possible, for example, when a drug overdose is suspected. More often, however, nurses prefer a communication style that is a "joint exploration of the patient's experience, involving negotiation and consensus more than interrogation, inquisition, and prescription" (Kasch 1986, p. 44). Many clients who are dealing with strong emotions or hard decisions are unwilling or unable to reveal their deepest needs unless they are given time and permission to do so. A number of researchers have studied ways of encouraging clients to be less reticent. One early researcher (Feinstein 1967) suggested that caregivers ask clients why they were seeking help at that particular time. When the effects of this question were systematically tested in an outpatient psychiatric clinic, it was found that clients interpreted the question as an accusation. Later investigators found that clients were more comfortable if the question were phrased as, "How do you think I might be able to help you today?" (Eisenthal and Lazare 1976).

The nondirective nature of nurses' interaction and communication with clients makes the process recording extremely important. A detailed process note contains objective and subjective material; it includes implicit as well as explicit information. In a sense, the process note is a historical record of an encounter and is used to help nurses search for the underlying meaning of the encounter.

SAMPLE DISCHARGE SUMMARY

Mrs. Anderson is a 24-year-old married woman who was admitted on 10/4/90 following an attempted suicide with a Librium overdose. The attempt was apparently precipitated by the loss of a pregnancy by spontaneous abortion on 9/29/90, following which she had grown profoundly depressed, refused meals, suffered marked weight loss, withdrawn from all social contact, and stayed secluded in her room. This is her third spontaneous abortion; she has no living children.

Mrs. Anderson has responded well to the plan of care, making rapid progress in acknowledging and dealing with her own problems. She has responded well to medication (Imipramine 100 mg q.d. at h.s.; Valium 5 mg p.o. every 4 hours p.r.n.), daily therapy with Dr. R. Jones, and supportive therapy from the nursing and activities staffs.

She has participated in the relaxation group and community meetings. Her weight has stabilized at 110 pounds, and she has assumed responsibility for keeping her own calorie counts and planning her intake to meet a goal of 1500 calories per day. She has a realistic perception of her gynecologic difficulties and is aware of the options remaining to her for having a child. She has consented to further gynecologic workup.

Mrs. Anderson now recognizes the relationship between her anxiety and depression and her lack of social supports and is taking steps to make commitments outside her home, including a search for a part-time job and a commitment to join a discussion group.

She will be followed by Dr. Jones and by the outpatient staff of the mental health and gynecologic clinic.

FORMAT OF A PROCESS NOTE

Place where interaction occurred: _____ Name of nurse: _____

Time and date of interaction: _____ Client initials: _____

Purpose or goal of interaction: _____ Presenting problem(s): _____

Client Communication (verbal and nonverbal)	Nurse Communication (verbal and nonverbal, including thoughts, feelings, opinions)	Interpretation, Rationale, and Evaluation
What does the client say? How does the client act? How does the client seem to the nurse? Tense? Anxious? Angry? Sad? Changeable or labile?	What is the emotional, cognitive, verbal, and nonverbal response of the nurse to the client, the environment, and the communication exchanged?	What is the client really communicating? Is verbal communication congruent with nonverbal communication? On what level does the client usually communicate? Behavioral? Cognitive? Emotional? Is the nurse communicating on the same level as the client? Does the client understand and accept what the nurse is trying to communicate? Was the communication of the nurse effective? If not, what alternative responses might have been made? Why might the alternatives have been more effective?

C L I N I C A L   E X A M P L E

STAFF-CLIENT COMMUNICATION IMPASSE

Mrs. Mason is a middle-aged alcoholic who has liver damage and neurological impairment due to long years of excessive drinking. She is being cared for in a 30-day residential program for alcoholics, and her stay is almost over. She is a widow and a "loner." Before entering the program, she lived alone and had difficulty managing her daily activities. She has difficulty walking, and staff members doubt her ability to care for herself at home. She has some funds and they have suggested that she consider living in a modest proprietary residence where she will have access to nursing supervision and minimal responsibility for cooking, housekeeping, or grocery shopping. Mrs. Mason has cooperated with staff recommendations until now, but she insists that she is able to take care of herself at home. She becomes very angry when staff members urge her to be more realistic about her future. Staff members are feeling pressure from administrators who want Mrs. Mason discharged as soon as possible. Most of them are truly concerned about her, believe that she needs residential care immediately, and consider her a stubborn, unreasonable old woman. The situation has deteriorated to the point that Mrs. Mason and staff members have almost stopped speaking to one another. Mrs. Mason talks with other residents about her plans to go home, but she doesn't share information with the staff. If she did tell them her plans to return home, she is sure they would prevent her from doing what she wants. The problem has not been resolved, even though Mrs. Mason is scheduled for discharge at the end of the week.

Nursing Diagnoses

Altered role performance
(related to self-care deficits)

Impaired home maintenance management
(related to problems with activities of daily living)

Impaired physical mobility
(related to ataxia and neurological problems)

Social isolation
(related to lack of family and friends)

Multiaxial Psychiatric Diagnoses

Axis I   303.9x Alcohol dependence
Axis II   None
Axis III   Alcohol liver disease, peripheral neuropathy
Axis IV   Code 2 Mild psychosocial stressor
Axis V   G.A.F. 50: current
              G.A.F. 55: highest in past year

PROCESS NOTE

Place: Client's room
Time and date: 2 P.M. July 23
Goal of the interview: To further explore the issues of discharge and aftercare.

Nurse: K. Winslow
Client initials: L.M.
Presenting problems: Impaired mobility, self-care deficits, social isolation

CLIENT	NURSE	INTERPRETATION AND RATIONALE
	Hello, Mrs. M. When we talked last week, you told me that you hoped to return to your home. I'd like to talk with you about this during our time together today. (Looks inquiringly at client. Nurse really wants to explore this issue and doesn't want client to say no.)	Stating purpose of interview. Seeking collaboration and permission.

CLIENT	NURSE	INTERPRETATION AND RATIONALE
Are you going to help me get home? The social worker says I can't go home.		Asking nurse to define her role. What can the nurse do for the client?
	No, I probably won't be able to help you get home. (Wishes she knew how to get client home.) I didn't know you had talked to the social worker. It must have been very discouraging to hear her say that!	Attempting to ascertain client's underlying feelings.
I don't believe I won't be able to go home. I've had that home for 25 years. (Gestures angrily around room) I'm waiting.		Client is angry but not discouraged because she doesn't believe she's not able to return home.
	You're waiting? (Nurse wonders if client is waiting for something to happen. Is she using denial to cope with being here? Nurse wouldn't especially like living here, either. Doesn't know what to say.)	Reflection—nurse needs more information.
(Leans closer to nurse and drops her voice.) I keep myself busy, you know. I work my puzzles in the morning; then I have lunch; then I read a little in the afternoon, and sometimes I work on my knitting. I've done a lot of that. I know that I'll be able to take care of myself at home.		Communicating on behavioral level. Client has changed subject and is trying to show nurse how capable she is. Client derives satisfaction from handiwork skills.
	You knit well. You certainly do a nice job! Have you sold some of your things? (Somewhat relieved that subject has changed to a safer topic.)	Nurse goes along with changed subject. [No evidence noted that client was getting anxious in talking about house, except for change of subject. Nurse could have said, "What are you thinking about while you keep yourself so busy?" If client answered, "I don't know," it might indicate she didn't want to talk about it. On the other hand, she had introduced the topic.]
I sold a lot of things at the sidewalk sale.		
	That's good. (Looks brightly at client.)	
(Looks brightly back.)		
	(Realizing that client really doesn't want to talk about knitting or the sidewalk sale, nurse starts feeling a little anxious.)	

CLIENT	NURSE	INTERPRETATION AND RATIONALE
(Leans back in chair, looks away from nurse and starts to work on the puzzle.)		Nonverbal. Client is not interested in this topic, either.
	Well, I'll talk to you next week. Good-bye.	Responding to nonverbal communication from client. [Nurse does not achieve solution regarding the client's feelings about going home. Nurse is relieved when client talks about topics other than going home and allows the client to digress. The goal of the interaction has not been met fully.]
Good-bye Honey.	(Nurse leaves, wondering if there is any meaning to the client's use of the word "honey." She has an uneasy sense of being ineffective with the client.)	

Nursing Diagnosis	Goal	Nursing Action	Outcome Criteria	Outcome Evaluation
Ineffectual individual coping	Client will collaborate in formulating discharge plan for follow-up care.	Inform client of available services for home care and residential care. Accompany client on site visit to residential facility.	Client will make informed decision regarding coping and self-care.	Client accepted discharge plan. Client now uses support services as needed.
Impaired home management	Client will help formulate activities of daily living schedule. Client will use homemaker services.	Nurse and client will make predischarge home visit. Refer client to community nursing service. Initiate homemaker visits through community nursing service. Initiate contact with Meals on Wheels program.	Client will consider alternatives to self-care at home if necessary. Client will accept assistance and supervision in home management. Community nurse and homemaker will visit regularly.	Client performs appropriate home management activities. Homemaker visits 3 times a week to help with shopping/cooking. Client refused meals on wheels. Prefers own cooking.
Impaired physical mobility	Client will remain ambulatory as long as possible. Client will live in her home as long as possible.	Arrange for wheelchair and walker before and after discharge. Teach client to use equipment. Allow client as much autonomy as possible.	Client will move about more easily and safely.	Client is now more mobile at home. Client is now able to leave her home with assistance.
Social isolation	Client will join AA or support group for alcoholics.	Refer client to alcoholism program of her choice. Arrange transportation through community support services. Coordinate discharge plans with community nurse.	Client will attend group meetings. Client will use transportation as arranged.	Client now participates in group sessions and activities. Client allows some group members to visit or phone her at home: they provide transportation to meetings.

SUMMARY

Therapeutic communication is the process that unites the nurse and the client in their collaborative search for improvement in the client's health status. The nurse-client interaction system is dependent on the therapeutic communication skills of the nurse through every phase of the nursing process.

By establishing trust, offering empathy, and communicating her acceptance of and respect for the client, the nurse begins the therapeutic relationship. Verbal and nonverbal messages are exchanged as the nurse guides the client-centered, goal-directed process that leads to growth and improved functioning.

Through a combination of authenticity and specific communication techniques, the nurse facilitates collaboration with the client and guides the establishment of a therapeutic contract. The nurse and client then use the communication process to pursue specific goals on the client's behalf. The nurse's ability to convey empathy and to facilitate increasing self-awareness and introspection on the part of the client helps the client move toward achieving the goals mutually set by client and nurse. A variety of communication strategies enable the nurse to deal effectively with the individual needs of different clients.

The nurse also uses the communication process to collaborate with other members of the health team and to document the assessment, planning, and implementation of nursing care and to evaluate the client's response to that care.

Review Questions

1. Describe four ingredients essential for establishing therapeutic relationships.

2. Use the Berlo model of communication to analyze the elements of an interaction you recently experienced with a client.

3. Explain the role of each of these five essential qualities in the process of therapeutic communication: client-centeredness, goal-directedness, authenticity, self-disclosure, and confidentiality.

4. Define and describe the collaboration process.

5. Explain what is meant by a therapeutic contract.

6. Give one example of each of the following specific communication strategies:
   a. Open-ended questioning
   b. General leads
   c. Clarification
   d. Validation
   e. Restatement
   f. Reflection
   g. Focusing
   h. Interpreting
   i. Confronting

7. Explain how each of the following helps the client who has difficulty with emotional adaptation:
   a. Active listening
   b. Use of silence
   c. Summarizing

8. List and illustrate two ways in which communication can be used therapeutically to control behavior.

Research Report

The community mental health movement which fostered a change from a medical to a psychological model of care encouraged nurses to change from traditional uniforms to street clothes. This study was done on an inpatient unit in response to contentions from visiting physicians that psychiatric patients were confused by receiving care from non-uniformed nurses. The purpose was to ascertain whether uniforms facilitated the identification of caregiver as nurses. Testing was done by having patients examine full-length photographs of staff nurses caring for them; photographs of actual caregivers were interspersed with photographs of persons working elsewhere in the hospital. Half of the persons in the photographs wore uniforms and half wore street clothes. Ratio of actual caregivers to noncaregivers in the photographs was 1 to 4. Testing consisted of showing the subjects the collection of photographs at weekly intervals up to a period of three weeks and asking them to identify the nurses actually providing their care. Researchers found no differences in the subjects' ability to recognize their caregivers, regardless of whether persons in the photographs were or were not in uniform. What separated recognized from unrecognized nursing staff members was a combination of the nurses' personal characteristics and the shifts they worked. Evening nursing staff were more often recognized than day shift staff, perhaps because fewer staff members worked evening hours and because the overall activity level was less. The researchers concluded that even persons with deficits in recent memory recognize their nurses on the basis of who they are and what they do, rather than what they wear.

A Study of Whether Uniforms Help Recognize Nurses. Henry Pinsker and William Vingiano. *Hospital and Community Psychiatry* 39, no. 1 (January 1988):78–79.

Suggested Annotated Readings

Bennett, H. "Why Patients Don't Follow Instructions" *RN* (March 1986):45–47.

Sharpening communication and negotiation skills can help nurses encourage client understanding and compliance. Getting to know the client and the family is essential before teaching begins. Setting small, reachable goals with the client is usually more successful than attempting to impose sweeping changes in lifestyle. Search for ways of doing things that are acceptable to the client, since some progress is better than none at all. The article concludes by stating that a caring, trusting relationship is basic to client compliance.

Bergerson, S. P. "Charting With a Jury in Mind." *Nursing 88* 18, no. 4 (April 1988):51–58.

In litigation where the defendant is a health care professional or agency, the chart is the best indicator of what happened. It is impossible for nurses to be too careful. Even good charting may sometimes be manipulated and discredited by a plaintiff's attorneys. Primary prevention is necessary in charting so as to forestall legal consequences. Subjective terminology should be avoided. Ambiguous phrases like "Client was restless" or "Client was anxious" should be replaced by descriptions of what the client did or said to denote restlessness or anxiety. Nurses are warned not to chart for a colleague and not to wait a long time before recording data. If time elapses before an incident is recorded, the nurse should note the time of the entry. Besides being complete, litigation-proof records must be meticulous and honest.

DeBaca, V. "So Many Patients, So Little Time" *RN* (April 1987):33–34.

The author acknowledges the frustration nurses often feel when excessive demands are made on them, especially in times of understaffing and short hospitalization stays. Orienting new patients to inpatient routines and telling them what to expect can reduce later questioning. Clients feel more secure with nurses who listen actively, anticipate needs, set goals, and re-evaluate priorities.

Eggland, E. T. "Charting: How and Why to Document Care Daily and Fully." *Nursing 88* 18, no. 11 (November 1988):76–84.

This extensive article reviews the basic rules of charting, from narrative nursing notes through SOAPE notes to computer processing. The holistic charting that uses DAR (Data, Action, and Response) is described as a form of focus charting. The need to supplement nursing care plans with additional relevant information is emphasized. A checklist is provided to organize relevant data, and common charting errors are noted. The author states that for nurses no day is mechanical or routine; therefore, no charting should be. In summary, routine, mechanical charting equals no charting at all.

Manglass, L. "Psychiatric Interventions You Can Use in an Emergency." *RN* (November 1986):38–39.

Psychiatric emergencies occur when people feel they cannot cope with their psychological or emotional distress. At such times in-depth counseling is not appropriate; nursing interventions should be aimed at assisting the client through the immediate situation that is so threatening. Preventing the distressed client from harming himself or others is a primary goal, and seeking aid from other caregivers is advisable. Regardless of the cause, only the current circumstances require attention until the client regains control.

McElroy, D., and K. Herbelin. "Writing a Better Care Plan." *Nursing 88* 18, no. 2 (January 1988):50–51.

A set of guidelines for writing nursing care plans is presented in an interesting, concise format. The purpose of care plans is to ensure quality care by providing a core of information regarding client needs, goals, nursing actions, and documentation of progress. A sample care plan is included as well as an analysis of why nursing care plans are sometimes inadequate. The authors say that care plans are important for numerous reasons: to maintain high standards of care; to provide legal protection, and to safeguard reimbursement procedures. In any clinical situation, comprehensive care plans protect nurses from the allegation "If it wasn't documented, it wasn't done."

References

Berlo, D. K. *The Process of Communication.* San Francisco: Rinehart Press, 1960.

Brammer, L. M., and E. I. Shostrom. *Therapeutic Psychology: Fundamentals of Counseling and Psychotherapy.* 4th ed. Englewood Cliffs, New Jersey: Prentice Hall, 1982.

Burnside, I. M. "Touching Is Talking." *American Journal of Nursing* 73 (1973):2060–2063.

Cormier, L. S., W. H. Cormier, and R. J. Weisser. *Interviewing and Helping Skills for Health Professionals.* Boston: Jones and Bartlett Publishers, 1986.

Eisenthal, S., and A. Lazare. "Evaluation of the Initial Interview in a Walk-In Clinic: The Patient's Perspective." *Journal of Nervous and Mental Diseases*, 162 (1976):169–176.

Feinstein, A. R. *Clinical Judgment*. Baltimore: Williams & Wilkins, 1967.

Kasch, C. R. "Establishing a Collaborative Nurse-Patient Relationship." *Image*, 18, no. 2 (Summer 1986):44–47.

Ramaekers, M. J. "Communication Blocks Revisited." *American Journal of Nursing* 79 (1979):1079–1081.

Scheideman, M. "Problem Patients Do Not Exist." *American Journal of Nursing* 79 (1979):1082–1084.

4

Contributing Theories in Mental Health Nursing

FORMAL AND INFORMAL PERSPECTIVES

THEORIES AND THEORETICAL FRAMEWORKS
Psychogenic
Interpersonal
Sociological
Existential
Cognitive
Biogenic

Learning Objectives

After reading this chapter the student should be able to:

1. Contrast the strengths and limitations of various theories used in mental health nursing.
2. Trace the major contributions of Erikson to our understanding of personality development and compare his contribution to that of Freud.
3. Describe the development of the self system as outlined by Sullivan and explain its importance in social interactions.
4. Discuss the relevance of sociological theory to mental health nursing.
5. Compare the relevance of cognitive theory and of existentialist theory to mental health nursing.
6. Discuss the relevance of biogenic theory to mental health nursing.

Overview

Every individual possesses a certain viewpoint, or perspective, that helps him or her to focus observations and enhances understanding of internal and external experience. For scientists and scholars, perspectives guide the formulation of theories and of theoretical frameworks. In mental health nursing, the perspectives of a number of major theorists help us to maintain a biopsychosocial approach to clients. The theoretical frameworks presented in this chapter are the psychogenic, the interpersonal, the sociological, the existential, the cognitive, and the biogenic. Systems theory is a perspective often used by nurses to understand the interactions of individuals and groups. Learning and behavior theory are other perspectives that also help nurses to understand human behavior. These theories for organizational reasons are discussed separately in later chapters of this text. Nursing theory is a rapidly growing field that is being enriched by abstract and philosophical formulations of nurse theorists, and by the clinical investigations of nurse scholars and researchers. Nursing theory and process are discussed in Chapter 5.

FORMAL AND INFORMAL PERSPECTIVES

A perspective is simply a way of directing one's attention; and every human being, whether expert or amateur, has a perspective that is unique and original, derived from the sum total of his or her experience. Thus, a perspective is a set of beliefs used to focus observations and organize data collection. Perspectives help us to determine what to look for and why. They also suggest questions to ask and answers to pursue.

Perspectives guide us, but they also limit us to some degree. By sharpening our powers of observation, they influence what and how we see; but they also tend to exclude from our vision other insights that might prove enlightening. Moreover, the perspective of many individuals is characterized by inconsistency, perhaps because the informal perspectives we use are amalgams of sensation, cognition, emotion, physiology, and social context. In effect, a perspective is a form of bias that enables us to see some things clearly and others not at all. Since it is impossible for even the most observant, fair-minded person to note everything that is going on, all of us rely on a perspective to help us determine relevant aspects of the observations we make (Ruch 1984).

THEORIES AND THEORETICAL FRAMEWORKS

A theory is a formalized perspective or statement of something a theorist believes to be true or untrue. Theories begin with observable facts or data; laws or rules generalize facts. The generalization of facts or data in an understandable manner is a basic step of theory building. Another step of theory building is to make predictions based on facts or data, and the soundest theories are those in which predictions are demonstrated to be factual. Theories, then, are bridges between hypothetical facts not yet proven and facts already tested and proven. Hypothetical data must be retested, modified, or discarded according to the extent of their provability. This is the research strategy now underway in the development of nursing theory. The perspectives of nursing research are expansive, but the scientific, humanistic, and statistical strategies now being used are subjected to increasingly rigorous testing and replication.

Factual knowledge is the basis of psychiatric nursing, but isolated facts tend to seem irrelevant and to be easily forgotten. Knowledge must therefore be organized systematically into a coherent pattern, using theoretical frameworks. A *theory* may be defined as a set of related principles that can be used to explain, predict, or analyze certain phenomena. Theories permit inferences or generalizations to be made on the basis of principles that are applicable to more than one situation. *Theoretical frameworks* are organizing structures that reveal relationships and connections and that therefore increase our understanding of phenomena. No theoretical framework is all inclusive. Rather, each offers a particular perspective that helps illuminate a part of the whole.

Theoretical frameworks are composed of selected concepts and constructs. *Concepts* are general abstract ideas. They are not "objects" that can be perceived or witnessed, because they exist only in the mind. Most concepts have a collective meaning that is shared by the people who use them. *Constructs* are collections or syntheses of concepts, but the terms are sometimes used interchangeably. (See Table 4–1 for theory definitions and terminology.)

Theoretical frameworks promote the analysis and synthesis of knowledge in a way that mere facts do not. For these reasons, many nurse educators rely on theoretical frameworks to transmit the knowledge on which professional expertise depends.

Theoretical frameworks are also important in the research conducted by nurses working in clinical and laboratory settings. Although there is a growing body of nursing theory based on research, many theoretical formulations in nursing remain "a synthesis of principles, concepts, laws, and theories drawn from the natural and social sciences" (King 1971, p. 3). However, nurse researchers continue to be involved in building a theory base that is unique to nursing.

Table 4–1. Theory Definitions and Terminology

Theory	Set of related principles that can be used to explain, predict, or analyze events or phenomena
Theoretical Frameworks	Organizing structures that show relationships and connections between concepts and constructs
Concepts	Abstract ideas existing primarily in the mind
Constructs	Collections or combinations of concepts

Every theoretical framework has a particular viewpoint that reveals some phenomena but excludes others. The same concepts may appear in more than one framework, but they are interpreted differently in each. Because psychiatric nursing is a complex field in which there are few definitive answers, no single framework is fully satisfactory. It is important, therefore, for nurses to be familiar with those theories of biopsychosocial functioning that are the most influential.

The essence of knowledge is *generalization*. That fire can be produced by rubbing wood in a certain way is a knowledge derived by generalization from individual experiences; the statement means that rubbing wood in this way will *always* produce fire. The art of discovery is therefore the art of correct generalization. What is irrelevant, such as the particular shape or size of the piece of wood used, is to be excluded from the generalization; what is relevant, for example, the dryness of the wood, is to be included in it. The meaning of the term "relevant" can thus be defined: that which is relevant must be mentioned for the generalization to be valid. The separation of the relevant from the irrelevant factors is the beginning of knowledge (Reichenback 1968, p. 5).

PSYCHOGENIC FRAMEWORK

The psychogenic framework is primarily represented in this text by Freud's psychosexual theory and Erikson's psychosocial theory.

Psychosexual Theory

Psychosexual theory is a term applied to the developmental aspects of the psychoanalytic approach of Sigmund Freud (1856–1939). Freud believed that civilization depends on the control of sexual impulses. Energy that is diverted from sexual gratification becomes available for cultural and social improvement. He thought that society is repressive because it frustrates human sexual desires and that there is always danger that primitive sexual impulses will be released and threaten social stability. His idea that sexuality begins in infancy created a great deal of hostility, which he attributed to fear on the part of society (Freud 1961).

Freud asserted that human beings, like lower animals, possess instinctual drives that influence behavior patterns. Drives are the source of psychic energy; they operate from birth and promote personality development. Two opposing drives, erotic and aggressive, are part of the *id*, which is the primitive or instinctual part of the personality. Every individual possesses erotic (libidinous) and ag-

gressive drives that operate simultaneously, so that many human acts have both loving and destructive components. Freud's description of the duality of drives helps explain the ambivalence that individuals feel in many situations. A good example is the mother who is devoted to the welfare of her family but sometimes resents their demands and wishes to be free of responsibility in order to pursue her own career goals.

Freud explained that psychic energy, like physical energy, is limited in quantity. When one individual bestows affection on someone else, this results in a loss of psychic energy unless the affection is returned. Love that is returned restores psychic energy, but unreturned love depletes the lover. The fact that psychic energy can be exhausted helps explain the fatigue that follows excessive psychologic demands on an individual.

In his theory, Freud distinguished two ways of thinking and relating: primary and secondary. *Primary process thinking* is not rooted in reality but is controlled by impulsive id forces that seek instant gratification. This way of thinking sometimes enhances the creative processes that produce art, literature, and music. Primary process may also include psychotic thinking and can be discerned in the thought patterns of persons who are in acute states of mental disturbance. *Secondary process thinking* originates in the ego and is rooted in reality. It utilizes conscious reasoning, comprehension, logic, and judgment.

PERSONALITY STRUCTURES According to Freud, in the first months of life the infant is motivated entirely by id or instinctual forces. Contact with the environment modifies the id; maturation is achieved through both frustration and gratification of the id, provided always that frustration is not excessive. The *ego* begins to develop when the infant is about six months old. The primary purpose of the ego is to maintain a sense of reality, to negotiate with reality, and to adapt to reality. Development of the ego is assisted by the increasing perceptual, cognitive, and language ability of the child (Brenner 1955).

Besides dealing with reality, additional ego functions include the following (Bellak, Hurvick, and Gediman 1973):

1. Reality testing, or the ability to differentiate internal stimuli from external stimuli. Hallucinations and delusions indicate failure of reality testing.

2. Judgment, or the ability to control impulses and predict the consequences of one's behavior.

Inability to tolerate delayed gratification is a sign of poor judgment.

3. Subjective awareness of what reality is and where selfhood begins and ends. When this awareness is impaired, individuals feel isolated from reality or merged with reality.

4. Regulation of moods and drives without acting them out behaviorally.

5. Establishment of object relatedness, or the ability to form and maintain relationships.

6. Maintenance of thought processes such as memory, concept formation, and language skills.

7. Regression in the service of the ego, or the ability to reduce functioning temporarily in order to rest, feel pleasure, or engage in creative work. Sleep, vacations, and orgasm are examples of regression in the service of the ego.

8. Maintenance of a stimulus barrier to permit concentration or prevent being overwhelmed by stimuli. Inadequacies in the stimulus barrier lead to confusion and feelings of disorientation.

9. Performance of complex mental functions related to learning, perception, logical thinking, and complex skills.

10. Integration and synthesis of contradictory values and attitudes in order to establish meaningful relationships and attain appropriate goals.

11. Maintenance of mastery and competence related to self-control and control of one's environment.

The third personality structure to develop is the *superego* (see Figure 4–1). The superego represents the internalized attitudes of the parents and of society. It includes the *ego ideal*, which is the self as one would like to be. Because much of the superego is controlled by unconscious attitudes, it is not a reliable means of dealing with reality. It is the emergence of the superego at about age six that leads to the feeling of guilt. *Shame* is an earlier experience that results from one's failure to live up to the ego ideal. Shame is rarely felt unless one's unacceptable behavior is discovered by others. *Guilt* is an internal experience caused by failure to conform to the standards of the superego, and it is felt even when one's inner thoughts and desires are unknown to others.

Freud also described three levels of mental activity: the *unconscious*, the *preconscious*, and the *conscious* (see Figure 4–2). Of the three, the unconscious is by far the largest. Memories and feelings that are unacceptable to the individual are pushed out of awareness into the unconscious by means of a mental process called *repression*. Unacceptable memories and feelings are *ego-alien*, or *ego-dystonic*, and produce anxiety unless they are repressed. Acceptable memories and feelings are *ego-syntonic* and do not produce anxiety. The preconscious level contains material not immediately available but

Figure 4–1. Psychoanalytic personality structure and function.

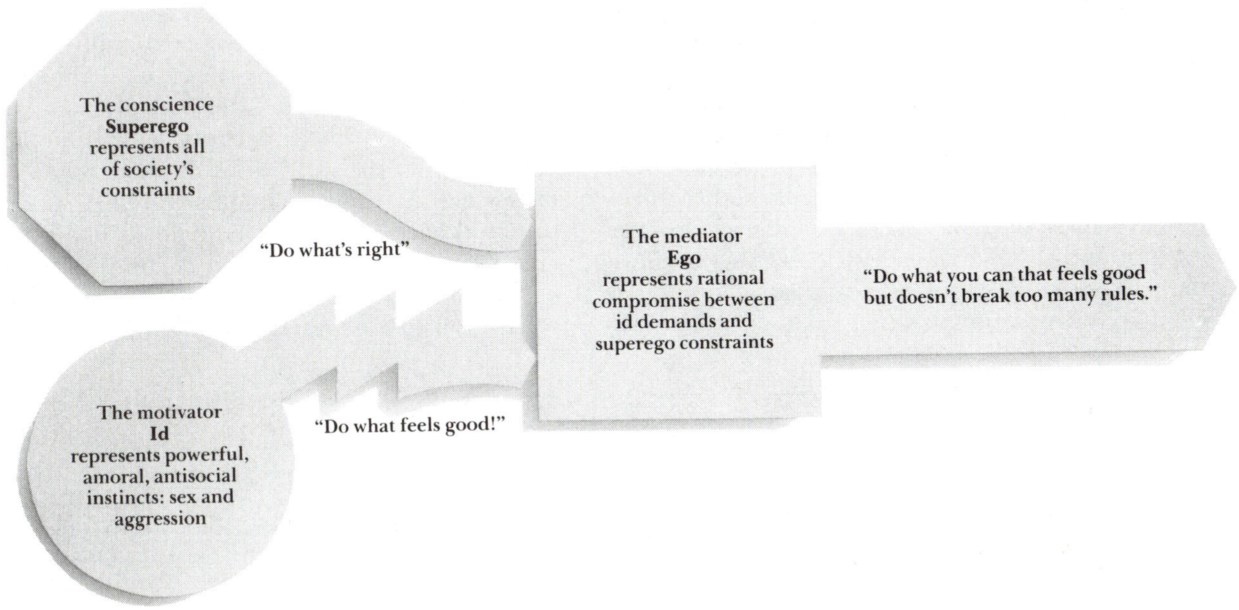

The conscience
Superego
represents all of society's constraints

"Do what's right"

The mediator
Ego
represents rational compromise between id demands and superego constraints

"Do what you can that feels good but doesn't break too many rules."

The motivator
Id
represents powerful, amoral, antisocial instincts: sex and aggression

"Do what feels good!"

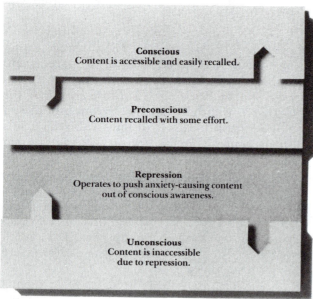

Figure 4-2. Levels of mental awareness.

subject to recall if one tries. The conscious level is the smallest and contains material that is accessible and easily remembered. Table 4–2 outlines the relationship between personality structures and levels of consciousness.

PSYCHOSEXUAL STAGES Freud suggested that each person, beginning at birth, undergoes a uniform, predetermined sequence of *psychosexual stages* and that each developmental stage is related to a particular psychosexual conflict. In psychoanalytic theory, a conflict is explained as a wish for something and a simultaneous fear of the consequences if that wish is fulfilled. For example, a person who is in conflict about dependency might want to depend on others but fear the loss of freedom that dependency often brings. Individuals can progress from one psychosexual phase to another, can be *fixated* in one phase without advancing further, or can progress and later *regress* to an earlier developmental phase. Within each phase, specific body orifices (mouth, anus, or genitals) are the objects of erotic interest and instinctual energy. Table 4–3 outlines the psychosexual stages, chronologic ages, and related conflicts formulated by Freud.

In Greek mythology, Oedipus was a ruler who unknowingly killed his father, wed his mother, and suffered for his misdeeds. According to Freud, the Oedipal romance is enacted in every family during the phallic phase of childhood. For all infants the mother is the first love object. As the child matures, the parent of the opposite sex becomes a love object and the parent of the same sex becomes a rival in the mind of the child. The task of the boy is considered to be less complicated because for him the mother can remain the primary love object, but girls must cope with the transformation of mother from love object into rival.

Sexual feelings for one parent and resentment for the other create a fear of punishment in the child. Freud called this fear of impending punishment *castration anxiety*, and out of this fear emerges the *superego*, the conscience or censor of the personality. Freud believed that because girls have no penis, they suffer less castration anxiety. The effect is to prolong the Oedipal conflict in girls and to make the female's superego less strict and punitive than the male's, according to Freud..

Freud saw the Oedipal conflict as an explanation for the adult fantasies of childhood seduction that he encountered in his practice. He hypothesized that such fantasies of rape and seduction by a parent arose out of sexual interest in the parent of the opposite sex. Many clinicians working in the field of child abuse today feel that the Freudian viewpoint has seriously damaged the credibility of children who have been victims of actual sexual abuse.

ANXIETY Freud described several causes and manifestations of anxiety. He attributed castration anxiety, which surfaces during the Oedipal conflict, to unacceptable erotic wishes and saw superego anxiety is as arising from internalized guilt. *Separation anxiety* is triggered first by the trauma of birth and later by separation from beloved persons, places, and possessions. The concept of separation anxiety helps explain the difficulties many people experience when they must relinquish familiar surroundings and friendships. Extreme forms of separation anxiety are felt by persons dealing with death, either their own or that of loved ones. *Anaclitic* separation anxiety is caused by early loss of the

Table 4-2. Personality Structures and Level of Consciousness

Structure	Basis	Level of Consciousness	Principle Followed	Process Used
Id	Instincts for sex and aggression	Unconscious	Pleasure principle	Primary process thinking
Ego	Learned behaviors in response to reality	Mostly conscious	Reality principle	Secondary process thinking
Superego	Learned social inhibitions	Partly conscious	—	—

Table 4–3. Psychosexual Stages

Psychosexual Stage	Age	Related Conflict
Oral	Birth to 1 year	Dependency
Anal	1 to 3 years	Control
Phallic (Oedipal)	3 to 5 or 6 years	Competition
Latency	5 or 6 years to puberty	Mastery
Genital	Puberty and onward	Intimacy

mothering figure. When this happens in the first year of life, the child may react by withdrawing and by failing to thrive, behaviors considered by some theorists to be a form of depression (Engel 1964). *Signal* or *anticipatory anxiety* is based on the memory of early experiences that had produced anxiety. Repetitions or recollection of the early experiences reactivate feelings of anxiety. Freud believed that anxiety is generally useful because it calls into play defenses that help control irrational impulses and reactions (Brenner 1955).

DEFENSE MECHANISMS Freud considered the ego to be a defensive structure that mediates between the excessive demands of the id and the excessive restrictions of the superego. It was Freud's daughter, Anna (1953), who formulated a comprehensive list of *defense mechanisms* employed by the ego. Anna Freud contended that everyone uses a variety of defenses, some of which are more functional than others. The major defense mechanisms she identified are as follows:

1. *Repression*, the central defense mechanism, is the inability to remember material that is unacceptable to the individual. By means of repression, ideas, impulses, and emotions pass out of conscious awareness. For example, the individual who cannot acknowledge hostile feelings toward an old friend may "forget" the friend's name.

2. *Displacement* is the transferral of emotion from one target to another. The man who is angry with his employer but does not want to lose his job may displace his anger by yelling at family members.

3. *Reaction formation* is the transformation of unacceptable impulses into opposite behavior. For example, hostile feelings toward someone may be expressed by behaviors that are excessively kind and loving.

4. *Isolation* is the separation of an idea from the emotion surrounding it. The idea itself may or may not be forgotten, but the accompanying emotion always is. Thus, a college freshman may ignore feelings of homesickness even though she often has thoughts of returning home.

5. *Undoing* is an effort to cancel out certain actions, real or imaginery. Undoing may be accomplished through apologies, atonement, or ceremonies and rituals. An adolescent who engages in masturbation may try to undo the behavior by repeated, ritualistic handwashing, for example.

6. *Rationalization* is the formation of reasonable explanations, which may or may not be valid, for certain events or behaviors. Rationalization is used to conceal one's real motives or shortcomings from oneself or from others. An example is the alcoholic who says that he needs to drink in order to "wind down" from daily pressures.

7. *Intellectualization* is similar to rationalization and involves the use of intellectual processes to avoid emotional expression. An incompatible couple may use intellectualization to avoid discussing their actual feelings about each other.

8. *Denial* is a partial or complete rejection of something. That is, one may deny a total experience or only the emotion that accompanies the experience. Denial is quite common and may be adaptive or maladaptive, depending on the circumstances. Dealing with loss often begins by denying the reality of the loss.

9. *Projection* is a mechanism by which individuals attribute their own feelings and desires to others. Thus, a student with hostile feelings toward a certain instructor may assume that the instructor is in fact hostile toward her.

10. *Regression* enables people to return to an earlier stage of functioning in order to avoid the tension and demands of a later stage. The five-year-old whose world is invaded by a new sibling may, for example, return to the oral or anal stage, where gratification was assured.

11. *Introjection* is the eradication of distinctions between the individual and an early love object. When all the characteristics of a love object are internalized, the sense of being a separate entity is lost. Thus, a child who adopts all the characteristics of a parent may lose his sense of being separate or different from the parent.

12. *Identification* is the imitation or acquisition of certain attributes of a significant person. The son of a famous baseball player who tries to emulate his father is using the mechanism of identification.

13. *Sublimation* is the expression of psychic energy in socially acceptable ways by controlling or delaying instinctual drives. Sublimation of the erotic drive may be seen in the behavior of a childless woman who expresses her mothering capacities by teaching preschool children. Sublimation of the aggressive drive may be seen in the behavior of an adolescent who becomes a competitive and successful athlete.

PSYCHOANALYSIS Freud's theory is the basis of *psychoanalysis*, a treatment of which the ambitious goal is the restructuring of personality. Classical psychoanalysis assumes that a great deal of mental activity is outside our conscious awareness, that human beings experience psychological conflicts, and that people tend to continue behaving in familiar ways even if the results produce unhappiness. In psychoanalytic treatment, conflicts of early life are explored so that the client can understand and resolve them. Because of the time and expense required, relatively few people undergo complete psychoanalysis. However, psychoanalytic concepts continue to be important, not only within the health professions, but in literature, history, social sciences, and the arts (Adams 1979).

During this early part of his career Freud introduced the concept of *psychic determinism*, which states that all behavior is meaningful even when it seems accidental. (See Table 4–4 for definitions of common Freudian terms.) At this time, Freud was using hypnosis to eradicate the symptoms of his clients. Inconsistent results obtained with hypnosis caused him to substitute the technique of *free association*, in which clients reconstruct disturbing events they have "forgotten." In free association the psychoanalyst remains silent so as not to interfere with the clients' flow of associated thoughts.

The detachment of the psychoanalyst promotes powerful transferences on the part of the client. *Transference* is a distortion in which the client acts as if the therapist were a significant person from the client's own life. For example, a client might react as if the therapist were a parent or other authority figure from the past. Exploring the transference helps clients bring irrational feelings and conflicts into conscious awareness so that a corrective emotional experience can occur. *Countertransference* occurs when transference is felt by the psychoanalyst toward the client. Countertransference can be dealt with by introspection on the part of the psychoanalyst and by a personal training analysis.

Freud admitted the absence of objective data in his work. He was an astute observer, but his clinical experience was limited to persons exhibiting hysterical, obsessive-compulsive, and phobic behavior. Much of his data are intuitive in the sense of not being tested or validated systematically. It would be foolish to reject all Freud's insights but equally foolish to accept them without question. There is no doubt that he was a man of his times and that his view of behavior and of personality development was colored by the values and customs of the society in which he lived.

NURSING IMPLICATIONS OF PSYCHOSEXUAL THEORY Although nurses do not engage in classical psychoanalytic work, many of Freud's concepts are useful to nurses working with clients. The idea that human behavior has purpose and meaning is extremely important in psychiatric nursing. The theories of the conscious, preconscious, and unconscious levels of awareness help explain the underlying dynamics of some behaviors. Freud's descriptions of various forms of anxiety have proved durable, particularly the concepts of separation anxiety and of anaclitic depression generated when the infant is separated from his or her mother in the first year of life. The idea that psychological energy is limited can be validated by clinical observation and personal experience. Depletion of psychological energy as a factor in the onset and course of physical illness has been documented in many clinical and experimental situations. In some respects psychoanalytic theory is narrow and restrictive, but its emphasis on the importance of early childhood experiences cannot be entirely discounted.

Table 4–4. Freudian Terms in Common Use	
Psychic determinism	The concept that all behavior has meaning and purpose
Free association	A technique of psychoanalysis in which the client tries to bring forgotten material into conscious awareness
Transference	A thought distortion in which the client acts as if another person were a significant figure from the past
Countertransference	A thought distortion in which the analyst (or caregiver) acts as if the client were a significant figure from the past

Psychosocial Theory

Erik Erikson (1963) devised a psychosocial theory of personality development that retained a core of Freudian theory but broadened its scope. He suggested that a triad of forces shapes personality development; this triad includes constitutional, psychological, and social factors. As these three types of factors converge on an individual, a period of ascendency or urgency occurs, during which essential life tasks must be accomplished.

Erikson not only broadened Freudian theory but diverged from it in certain respects. Whereas Freud believed that personality is formed by the age of five or six years, Erikson asserted that personality continues to develop throughout the whole life cycle, moving sequentially through eight critical developmental stages. The second change Erikson made was to emphasize the importance of the ego. According to Erikson, the ego is an independent structure of the personality and is neither dependent upon nor subservient to the id. Ego development is influenced by one's parents, but is also influenced by a host of social, environmental, and biological impulses. The third divergence from Freudian theory was the importance Erikson attributed to cultural and historical forces on personality development. Between 1938 and 1943, Erikson studied child rearing methods of two dissimilar Indian tribes, the Sioux Indians of South Dakota and the Yurok Indians of Northern California. His observations made him acutely aware of the role of custom and tradition in forming personality and shaping identity. Out of his anthropological studies and his work with emotionally disturbed veterans of World War II, Erikson formulated the concept of identity (role) confusion. He attributed the absence of a sense of identity to cultural uprootedness and, in the case of the veterans, to traumatic experiences (Schultz 1981).

Freud believed that each developmental stage has its own relevant task to achieve. Erikson accepted this to some extent, but he divided the life cycle into eight successive stages, each of which with its own critical task. Each of the eight stages contains two opposing poles representing success or failure in accomplishing the critical task (see Table 4–5). If tasks are not completed at the appointed time, they may never be fully resolved. Furthermore, faulty resolution of early tasks endangers the resolution of later ones. The bipolar aspect of Erikson's framework helps explain the progressive (positive) and regressive (negative) trends in the recurrent behaviors of many individuals.

In Erikson's view, society alternately grants and withholds, thus giving children messages from which they must build *ego strength*. The ego is seen as an

Table 4–5. Stages and Critical Tasks of Erikson's Psychosocial Framework

Stage	Task
Oral-sensory (birth to 1 year)	Trust versus mistrust
Muscular-anal (1 to 3 years)	Autonomy versus shame and doubt
Locomotor-genital (3 to 6 years)	Initiative versus guilt
Latency (6 to 11 years)	Industry versus inferiority
Puberty and adolescence (11 to 19 years)	Ego identity versus role confusion
Young adulthood	Intimacy versus isolation
Adulthood	Generativity versus stagnation
Old age	Ego integrity versus despair

integrator of multiple factors operating throughout the life cycle. Figure 4–3 compares the ego functions presented by Freud with those described by Erikson.

ERIKSON'S DEVELOPMENTAL STAGES Erikson's stages extend through the complete life cycle, from birth to old age.

Trust versus Mistrust In the first months of life, the interaction between infant and mother is crucial. From this interaction the infant develops a sense of trust that basic needs will be gratified. If needs are frustrated more often than gratified, the infant will be disappointed, and basic trust will not be established. During the second six months of life, the infant adds biting to its initial sucking activities. In psychoanalytic terms, dual drives are operating: erotic (sucking) and aggressive (biting) (Abraham 1953). Gradually the infant realizes this separateness from his mother, and if early experiences have been positive, he has developed a reservoir of trust and hopefulness from which to draw.

Autonomy versus Shame and Doubt As children learn to walk, talk, and control excretory processes, they are given a choice between holding on and letting go. According to Erikson, the period of toilet training is one of madness and mystery for the child, and he warns against excessive parental expectations. If toilet training is not accompanied by shaming tactics, and if parenting is consistent and moderate, the child gains confidence and takes pleasure in autonomous actions. Children subjected to excessive control, on the other hand, become prone to self-doubt.

Initiative versus Guilt The child's growing initiative may produce conflict between her desires and

Figure 4–3. Comparison of Freud's and Erikson's theories of personality structure.

Defensive Ego Functioning (Freud)

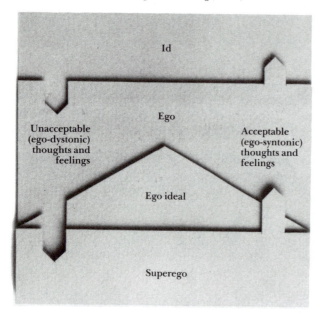

The ego mediates instinctual drives of the id and the imposed restrictions of the superego

Integrative Ego Functioning (Erikson)

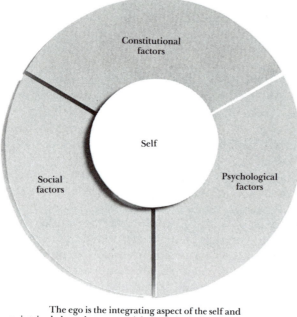

The ego is the integrating aspect of the self and maintains balance between social, psychological, and constitutional influences on the self

permitted experimentation and innovation. Otherwise, her capacity for initiative is impaired and she may experience guilt. The accompanying box contrasts the shame of the previous period with the guilt that can occur at this stage.

Industry versus Inferiority At this point the child can become confident of the ability to work productively, or, losing confidence, can sacrifice industriousness. The child who feels inferior becomes afraid of tasks and enterprises and is reluctant to try them. In addition, as the child's world expands, it becomes necessary to reconcile parental values with those of the outside world.

Ego Identity versus Role Confusion During the teen years, the child is less inclined to accept the guidance of parents and is greatly influenced by peers. Confusion and indecision may be concealed by a facade of rebelliousness. Erikson was sympathetic toward the dilemma of adolescence and called these years a "moratorium" between parental values that were once accepted by the child and a new adult code of ethics not yet determined.

Intimacy versus Isolation A meaningful relationship with another person is needed in order to avoid the egocentricity, or self-centeredness, that is fostered by social isolation. In genuine intimacy there is giving as well as taking. Ideally, love and sexuality are not isolated from each other but rather are fundamental to establishing reciprocal adult relationships.

Generativity versus Stagnation Generativity refers not to procreation but to constructive activities performed for the betterment of society. Stagnation results when middle-aged adults become self-engrossed, living only for their own pleasure and comfort. In Erikson's view, preoccupation with self is detrimental to society and to the individual.

Ego Integrity versus Despair As people grow old, they must come to terms with their own mortality. The idea of death—their own and that of loved ones—brings despair unless they can achieve a sense of purpose and acceptance of their own place in the progression of generations. A backward look at one's own life and accomplishments can promote ego integrity if the retrospective view is positive. However, if retrospection focuses on failures and disappointments in life, the result is despair.

NURSING IMPLICATIONS OF PSYCHOSOCIAL Erikson's work has been extremely influential in nursing education, practice, and research. The comprehensive life cycle approach, the focus on converging

her parents' restrictions. Gradually, she accepts parental values, identifies with them, and eventually internalizes them. However, a compromise is necessary so that child is protected from risk but is social factors. Freud attributed differences in the psychosexual development of males and females to such biological influences as the absence of a penis in girls and the possession of a penis by boys, which lead to greater castration anxiety for boys. Erikson also noted differences between the sexes in the ways they dealt with spatial relationships, but he placed less emphasis on purely biological considerations because he believed that culture and tradition were also important and he interpreted differences as the result of the interaction of biology, psychology, and culture.

INTERPERSONAL FRAMEWORK

Harry Stack Sullivan (1892–1949) disagreed with the psychoanalytic view that mental disturbance lies within the individual. He believed instead that interpersonal and environmental conditions are the source of emotional difficulties. Sullivan called his work a theory of *interpersonal relationships* because of the vast influence of such relationships on personality development. He admitted that individual differences exist among people but insisted that everyone shares attributes and experiences that are uniquely human. According to Sullivan, all human beings pursue two goals: satisfaction and security. The goal of satisfaction is biological, whereas the goal of security is social and cultural.

The notion that we are all uniquely human, called the *one genus postulate*, is central to interpersonal theory. Because of this common humanity, Sullivan objected to professionals who consider themselves superior to or even different from clients. He claimed that many professionals do things *to* clients and do not try to be in touch *with* clients. In his opinion, the restoration of self-respect and self-esteem should be the objective of all health care (Sullivan 1953).

Self System

According to Sullivan, the sense of self, or *self system*, begins to evolve during the first year of life as a consequence of interpersonal experiences between child and mother. Everyone is born with the need for a self system. Personality evolves from the interaction between interpersonal relationships and defensive operations that the individual uses to reduce anxiety and maintain self-esteem.

As a result of early interaction, the self system acquires three main components: the "good me," the "bad me," and the "non-me" (see Table 4–6). Sullivan used the word "mother" in describing the early interactions of infants, but the mothering person might not be the biological parent or even female. It is the primary nurturer of the child. A

constitutional, social, and psychological forces in development, and the idea of a period of ascendance or urgency for accomplishing critical tasks all provide a holistic view of humankind. Application of psychosocial formulations is appropriate in primary, secondary, and tertiary prevention and helps promote a biopsychosocial approach to health care.

Freud and Erikson differed in their explanation of gender differences in the behaviors of males and females. Freud attributed differences to biological factors and Erikson attributed differences to mother who is warm and nurturing gives her child a feeling of acceptance so that he experiences the self as the "good me." A tense, rejecting mother gives her child a feeling of being a "bad me." When there are few affectionate gestures from the mother, the child perceives the self as more bad than good; good self-appraisals are lost and bad self-appraisals dominate. When the mother uses forbidding or disapproving gestures against certain activities of the child, such as thumbsucking or genital exploration, the effect is to separate or dissociate the genital and oral regions from the child's sense of what is good and acceptable. Sometimes a child will isolate or separate these forbidden regions and behaviors, disown them, and make them part of the "non-me" aspect of the self system.

Sullivan described an undesirable process called *malevolent transformation* in which a child who feels "bad" sees badness in everyone else. Because the child is so aware of being bad, the only way for him to feel human like everyone else is to search for the worst in others. In this, the child is rarely disappointed; the result is that he believes the world is full of enemies. This line of reasoning helps explain suspiciousness and paranoid thinking as outcomes of low self-esteem. Another implication of this theory is that self-love and self-respect are necessary if one is to be able to love and respect others.

Communication between mother and child occurs through a process called *empathy*, which allows one person to understand and identify with the feelings of another. When the mother feels anxiety, it is transmitted by empathy to the child. Thus, for Sullivan, feelings of anxiety arise out of dependency on others for security. Generated first in the interaction between mother and child, anxiety becomes part of every subsequent interpersonal transaction and is the primary cause of problematic relationships and difficulties in living.

Table 4–6. Components of Sullivan's Self System

Component	Description
Good me	Self-personification of experiences in which the child received nurture and tenderness
Bad me	Self-personification of experiences in which the child failed to receive nurture and tenderness
Non-me	Self-personification of experiences in which the child experienced excessive anxiety due to disapproving emotions transmitted by the nurturer

Modes of Experience

Sullivan's conceptualization of *experience* included the inner meaning of everything people live through or undergo. He described three distinct modes of experience: prototaxic, parataxic, and syntaxic.

The *prototaxic* mode of experience is that known to the very young infant. It is a continuous flow with no differentiation; there are no connections, no causes or effects, and there is no awareness of self as distinct from others. The separate world does not exist; the infant is the entire world.

The *parataxic* mode of experience is broken, but the fragments are unconnected and unrelated. Parataxic experience belongs only to the person involved in it, and its uniqueness cannot be shared with others. Older infants, many children, and some creative people engage in parataxic experience. At times of acute mental disturbance the subjective experience of a client may become a parataxic distortion. The transference that can develop in psychoanalysis and in everyday life is one example of parataxic distortion.

Syntaxic experience can be validated consensually by means of language and symbols. In syntaxic experience, meanings and principles can be shared with others and can be accepted by others as true or untrue based on common understanding. In general, syntaxic experience is accepted as valid by a group (Sullivan 1953).

Elaboration of the three modes of experience led Sullivan to describe several strategies people use to handle interpersonal transactions. *Consensual validation* is an efficient strategy that involves measuring one's perceptions against the perceptions of others in order to reduce any distortions. *Selective inattention* is the screening out of an anxiety-provoking content so that it can be overlooked or forgotten. Thus, selective inattention actually operates to *prevent* consensual validation of perceptions and interpretations. Persons denying the significance of a serious illness often resort to the anxiety-reducing technique of selective inattention. *Focal awareness* is a means by which people see and hear what they want to and emphasize content that is reassuring. The parents of developmentally impaired children will often use focal awareness and direct all their attention to small signs of progress, thereby fostering unrealistic hopes (Griffin 1980).

Like Freud and Erikson, Sullivan described a developmental progression of stages (see Table 4–7). The first period, *infancy*, lasts from birth to one and a half years and is characterized by the dominant influence of the mother. During this period, experience is prototaxic. The infant can rarely be "spoiled," as mothers sometimes fear, since the idea of cause and effect has not yet

Table 4–7. Stages and Tasks of Sullivan's Interpersonal Framework

Period	Age	Characteristics
Infancy	Birth to 1½ years	Dominant maternal influence
Childhood	1½ to 6 years	Increasing peer influence
Juvenile	6 to 9 years	Gradual movement into the world
Preadolescent	9 years to puberty	Decreasing egocentricity; increasing socialization
Early adolescence	12 to 14 years	Increasing independence, interest in opposite sex
Late adolescence	15 to 21 years	Increasing sexuality, intimacy

SOURCE: Adapted from Sullivan (1953).

evolved. *Childhood* lasts from the end of infancy until the time when the child begins to cooperate with peers. This period, from age one and a half to six, is marked by clashes between the wishes of the child and those of the parents. Consistent limit setting is necessary if the child is to have a realistic perception of the world. During the *juvenile* period, which lasts from age six to nine, the child moves further from the home into the world. *Preadolescence*, which lasts from age nine to puberty, introduces movement from what is termed egocentricity toward a more socialized orientation. In the preadolescent period, peer influence is important, and having a best friend reinforces the effect of interpersonal experiences on personality development.

Adolescence is divided into early and later stages. *Early adolescence* lasts from age twelve to fourteen and is usually characterized by growing independence and interest in the opposite sex. *Late adolescence* lasts from fifteen to twenty-one years of age and is a time in which sexuality is enriched by establishing a lasting, satisfying intimacy. In discussing sexuality Sullivan expressed concern that the biological sexuality of young people was inhibited by social factors that discourage sexual expression—a concern that may be less true now than it was in his day.

Nursing Implications of Sullivan's Theory

Sullivan devoted much attention to specific therapeutic techniques, for he considered himself primarily a clinician. He objected to remote, authoritarian attitudes on the part of professionals and preferred the role of participant-observer. Moreover, he thought that clients should be helped to understand just how their problems developed. He extended kindness and acceptance to clients, allowing them to sit, stand, or walk as they chose during therapeutic sessions. When anxious clients were distracted from the topic at hand, Sullivan was not reluctant to reintroduce pertinent issues. He termed these digressions by anxious clients "substitute systems of thought" and considered them to be security operations (Thompson 1950). The purpose of security operations such as digressions is to reduce anxiety.

Unlike Freud, who believed that only neurotic clients could be helped by techniques of psychoanalysis, Sullivan was willing to work with clients who were psychotic or out of touch with reality. He defined "cure" as the gradual realization by clients of the nature of their problems in interpersonal relationships.

Sullivan's interpersonal framework has been used as a basis for building nursing theory. Peplau (1952) described nursing as an interpersonal process that has as its chief purpose promoting the health of individuals and communities. In her view, conflict and anxiety cause tension that results either in actions to confront and solve the problem or actions to avoid the problem. Along with Sullivan, Peplau believed that anxiety is nonspecific and that security represents freedom from anxiety. Because one of the most compelling human desires is to be anxiety-free, a great deal of human behavior is directed toward reaching this goal. In addition to defining anxiety operationally, Peplau expanded and refined this concept. She developed a paradigm showing the effects and manifestations of anxiety and suggested appropriate nursing responses (see Table 4–8). Her work in this area constitutes a major contribution to nursing theory.

SOCIOLOGICAL FRAMEWORK

The sociological framework deals with the relationships of individuals and families to social institutions and to society at large. A number of theorists from the health professions and the social sciences agree that the self emerges through social interaction taking place within the individual's social milieu. Sociological theory acknowledges the contradictory norms and values that exist in society and the confusion that these contradictions sometimes create.

Table 4–8. Effect of Anxiety on Perception and Behavior

Levels of Anxiety	Perception	Behaviors	Nursing Interventions
Mild anxiety	Sounds seem louder; irritability, restlessness, and energy increase.	Alertness and vigilance increase.	1. Observe what is occurring. 2. Describe occurrences. 3. Compare what was expected with what actually occurred. 4. Validate impressions with others. 5. Determine whether the situation or expectations can be changed.
Moderate anxiety	Concentration, communication, and perception decrease; tension increases; somatic discomforts (sweating, rapid pulse, etc.) occur.	Visual and auditory attention to details decreases; selective inattention occurs.	1. Recognize that attention is decreased. 2. Recognize that meanings and connections may be lost. 3. Try to identify precipitators or causes. 4. Try to reduce anxiety to mild levels.
Severe anxiety	Feelings of dread, awe, loathing arise; emotional discomfort increases; physical discomfort increases.	Details and occurrences are incomprehensible; focal awareness increases distortion.	1. Encourage severely anxious people to talk to a willing listener. 2. Encourage severely anxious people to work at a simple task. 3. Provide opportunity for motor activities such as walking and games. 4. Permit emotional outlet of tears.
Panic	Details and occurrences are distorted by being exaggerated or overlooked.	Rational communication and behavior are lost; fight/flight actions occur; herd instincts prevail.	1. Provide structure and firm direction—people in panic obey a stronger leader. 2. Increase safety and comfort by taking charge of the situation.

SOURCE: Adapted from Sullivan (1953) and Peplau (1952).

Social Institutions

A major focus of sociological theories is social institutions. Such institutions exhibit both manifest and latent functions that often exist side by side. *Manifest functions* include all the acknowledged and obvious reasons for the existence of an institution; *latent functions* include the unacknowledged and hidden reasons for its existence. For example, state mental hospitals have the manifest function of providing care for persons suffering a mental disorder. However, their latent function may be to isolate clients and permit society at large to ignore their existence as much as possible (Clausen 1980). The express purpose of psychiatric facilities—to care for clients—is often incompatible with its unacknowledged purpose, which is to label and segregate clients. This chasm between expressed purpose and unacknowledged purpose has been widened by the subordinate positions in which psychiatric clients are placed. Sociologists have been highly critical of this situation, with many citing the degrading practices sometimes imposed on psychiatric clients by care providers (Goffman 1961).

Social Epidemiology

The sociological approach to any issue, including mental health, is a collective one that examines social groups, processes, and institutions in order to identify the effects of variables such as social class, gender differences, and place of residence. A landmark sociological study was published in 1958 by Hollingshead (a sociologist) and Redlich (a psychiatrist). The researchers compared public and private mental patients, inpatients and outpatients, to a sample from the general, nonpatient population. Race, ethnicity, lifestyle, occupation, education, and place of residence were used to classify the subjects' socioeconomic status. In their investigation Hollingshead and Redlich developed a classification of social class that became a widely used measure of social stratification, and the widely read study added to the impetus for the community mental health center program.

Another important sociological study was the Midtown Manhattan study of the 1950s. The purpose of this study was to determine the genuine prevalence of mental disorders in a large urban community. Like Hollingshead and Redlich, the Midtown Manhattan investigators found a significant relationship between sociodemographic variables, psychiatric treatment, diagnosis, and outcome (Langner and Michael 1963).

The findings of these investigations are summarized in accompanying boxes.

A 1986 study of the effect of sociodemographic variables and care given clients at a mental health center produced less clear-cut results. Mollica and

Milic (1986) found that social class was not the major predictor of treatment assigned to clients. Three interactive factors were more influential: gender, diagnosis, and work history. Although lower-class clients were less likely to receive psychotherapy than other forms of treatment, they had access to the community mental health center serving their neighborhood and tended to remain in treatment until termination was a mutual decision. An interesting discovery was the fact that female clients were more likely to be given psychotherapy, while blacks of either gender were less likely. One implication of this study is that the establishment of community mental health centers has alleviated the neglect and inaccessability that lower-class clients so often confronted in earlier decades.

Upward and downward social mobility were also found to be related to the prevalence of psychiatric symptoms. That is, individuals whose education and achievements exceeded those of their parents and individuals whose education and achievements did not reach those of their parents were more likely to suffer mental disorders than persons who had attained but not surpassed the status of their parents.

Symbolic Interactionism

An important sociological perspective from which to explain the behavior of individuals in a society is *symbolic interactionism* (Mead 1933, Blumer 1969). The focus of this perspective is *socialization*, which is considered a process of interpreting and responding to social meanings (the intentions underlying the acts of others). Social organization and social meanings are culturally determined. Every individual analyzes others' intentions and responds on the basis of these analyses. It is therefore important to understand the behavior of others in order to guide one's own responses. Social stability depends on accurate analysis of the behavior of other people and on the capacity to regulate one's own behavior.

The enactment of social roles always requires the participation of more than one person. One can only be a mother if one has children; one can only be a teacher if one has students. Small children see themselves as different people depending on what

---

CLASSIC SOCIOLOGICAL STUDY
INDEX AND FINDINGS

Index of Social Position

Class I Upper	Included business and professional leaders in the community; contained two segments: (1) core group with inherited wealth and tradition, (2) upwardly mobile group with acquired education and wealth
Class II Upper middle	Included persons with post-high school education, usually functioning as managers or as members of less high status professions
Class III Lower middle	Included high school graduates, usually working as salaried employees and enjoying some degree of economic security
Class IV Working class	Included semi-skilled workers, usually with a grade school education, demonstrating little generational or educational upward mobility
Class V Lower class	Included persons who had not completed elementary school, usually functioning as unskilled workers and demonstrating little interest or participation in community organizations

Findings

Class I was relatively free of psychotic or anxiety problems.
Class II had the highest proportion of anxiety problems.
Class IV and V had more mental disorder and more disabling forms than other groups.
Class V had eleven times more persons diagnosed as having schizophrenia than did Class I.

The lower the social class of a client, the greater the use of organic treatment, the less use of psychotherapy, the fewer the number of visits, the greater likelihood of assignment to a lesser-prepared care provider, and the briefer the therapeutic contact visit.

Hollingshead and Redlich, 1958

role they are enacting. The same child may well be the oldest child at home but the smallest child in the classroom, and behave accordingly. Group attitudes greatly determine what role the child enacts, and role enactment helps children integrate all the diverse aspects of selfhood.

Integration of self results from the way others appraise and evaluate us. The term *reference group* is applied to groups whose standards are used to evaluate some aspects of ourselves (Mead 1933). Our school, profession, or religious denomination may function as a reference group. The term *generalized other* has been used to describe group attitudes; our internalized social attitudes are derived from generalized others. It is our internalized attitudes regarding the meaning of events that establish our social environment and influence how we behave.

Social Roles

Role theory is indebted to Talcott Parsons (1951) for describing attributes and expectations attached to the *sick role*. Enactment of the sick role entails privileges and obligations. When persons assume the sick role, they are exempted from certain duties and allowed certain rights. They have the right to receive care, but they also have an obligation to accept help, to cooperate, and to try to recover.

MIDTOWN MANHATTAN PROJECT FINDINGS

Mental disorders were more prevalent among the lower class than among other groups.

Those clients rated as most impaired were of lower-class strata, were between 50 and 59 years of age, and had grown up in conditions of poverty.

Large numbers of mentally disturbed persons were living in the community without professional help or social supports.

Stress was found to be an important factor in mental disorders. This was explained in two ways.

1. Members of the lower social class had to cope with more adverse conditions but had fewer resources at their disposal.
2. More mental illness in lower-class families is partly attributable to the tendency of persons with mental problems to drift downward rather than continue in the same or a higher social class.

Clients with some types of disorders, such as substance abuse, may be rejected by care providers because they do not fully accept sick role obligations. Many persons with mental disorders seem to defy customary enactment of the sick role. As a result, their motivation to seek help, to follow a treatment regimen, and to try to recover is questioned by relatives, friends, and health professionals. This is discussed in more detail in Chapter 19.

Social Stratification

Social class differences can have a significant impact on childrearing practices and therefore on individual personality development. For example, many working-class parents emphasize external standards and encourage conformity, whereas middle-class parents are more likely to stress internal standards and to encourage individuality (Scheinfeld 1983). In middle-class families, praise and encouragement are more generously bestowed, fathers are more involved in childrearing, and less authoritarian measures are used (Miller and Janosik 1980). Lower-class children may suffer culture shock early in life as they move from disadvantaged homes into schools and communities, whereas middle-class children are less likely to find a great discrepancy between standards inside and outside the home, so for them adjustment is usually less difficult.

Deviant behavior and society's reaction to it are also influenced by social class. Lower-class status increases the likelihood of being sent to prison for legal infractions, of being hospitalized for mental disorders, and of being hospitalized for longer periods (Hollingshead and Redlich 1958).

Social deviance is a concept that has interested sociologists since Durkheim (1951) demonstrated that suicide rates correlated inversely with people's sense of being integrated with and belonging to a meaningful group. Acceptance by and integration into a group requires some acceptance of group values. Actions that disrupt the rules and norms of the group are perceived as deviant, and the members who engage in deviant behavior often become targets of negative or punitive reactions.

Human behavior is directed through meanings that are communicated, interpreted, and modified by social interaction. For all of us, the reality we inhabit is a social climate constructed in part by ourselves and in part by those around us. Social control is preserved by adhering to the rules, norms, and values of the majority, either because we have accepted these standards or because we respect the powerful institutions (family, school, church, and law) that have the means to punish infractions. It is the majority of participants in the structure of social reality who decide what behavior is acceptable and what is not. Social deviancy is also complicated by the fact that norms and values are different for different groups and that most of us are subject to the standards of the various groups and subgroups to which we belong and in which we are expected to play different roles.

Whenever behavior is considered deviant enough to disrupt the stability of a family, group, or community, the persons who display deviant behavior are stigmatized, sometimes to the extent of being labeled bizarre or mentally disturbed. To be labeled as delinquent, alcoholic, or criminal is to be regarded as incompetent to some extent. However, in certain segments of society, some forms of delinquency, substance abuse, or criminality are not considered deviant but are examples of behavior conforming to peer or group pressure. In such situations a conventional form of social competence has been replaced by a far more destructive one. Thus deviancy in one culture may be conformity in another.

In examining deviance one must deal in relative, not absolute terms. The labeling process usually entails the following steps, regardless of the group conferring the label.

Labeling Deviance

- Prevailing social groups create the potential for deviance by establishing standards of behavior.

- Failure of group members to follow established standards results in behavior considered disruptive to the group.

- Questionable behavior is described as a threat to group standards and is therefore labeled deviant.

- Deviance is not a quality inherent in the behavior itself but is a judgment made by the group.

- Deviance in one group may be equivalent to conformity in another group, because deviance is a comparative definition of behavior, not an absolute one.

The persuasiveness of psychiatric labeling was shown in one study (Rosenhan 1973) in which normal, functioning persons posed as schizophrenic clients and were admitted to a number of different mental hospitals across the country. Once admitted, the subjects resumed their normal behavior but their label as mental patients was sufficient to keep them hospitalized for an average of nineteen days. A precondition for their release was that their caregivers accept the idea that the supposed clients were stabilized and in remission. The range of their hospital stays was from seven to fifty-two days. In this study psychiatric labeling proved more powerful, at least for a time, than observable data on whether their behavior was appropriate (normal) or inappropriate (abnormal).

Sociologists working in the field of mental health study the channels by which clients enter treatment and the choice of treatment modalities available to them. In general, lower-class and minority group members are referred by police, courts, and social agencies, while middle- and upper-class persons are family-, physician-, or self-referred. Community mental health centers have accepted considerable responsibility for serving neighborhood populations more equitably, and the centers have been receptive to sociological methods of assessing needs, surveying populations, studying outcomes, and analyzing cultural variables.

Nursing Implications of Sociological Approaches

The viewpoint of sociologists is that mental disorders result from the interplay of many factors on individuals and families. Therefore, they tend to be distrustful of purely medical approaches. As members of a discipline that concentrates on social issues, they often examine public policies and public programs related to mental health.

A number of nurse scientists trained at the doctoral level are currently engaged in health-related research that uses sociological and anthropological approaches. Even though social and cultural factors do not fully explain the occurrence and course of mental disturbance, they are essential to a holistic perspective. Nurses who are sensitive to cultural variations, who are interested in community organization, and who hope to influence public health policy will incorporate sociological concepts into their enactment of their professional role.

EXISTENTIAL FRAMEWORK

Existential theory is relatively unstructured. Its basic premise is that individuals do not exist separately in the world; rather, the world exists only because there are people to experience it. Behavior is not merely the result of external forces acting on the individual but is a complicated response to the individual's interpretation of external events. Individual existence is not predetermined, nor is it instinctual or biologic; instead, it depends entirely on the daily choices the person makes. Self-determination lies within the grasp of everyone.

Marram (1978) outlined the following existential beliefs:

1. Every individual has the freedom to reach maximum potential.

2. Recognition of immediate reality increases and enhances the potential for change.

3. For an individual to resolve problems it is necessary only to know what they are and not why they exist.

The fundamental problem facing individuals is to determine whether their existence is authentic (based on truth) or inauthentic (based on deception). According to existential theory, few people reach their full potential, but anyone who chooses to try can achieve a more authentic existence. The search for an authentic existence requires courage, and few people are courageous all the time. Most individuals vacillate between progressing and regressing. For an existentialist, however, regression may not always be detrimental; in fact, it may become a new beginning. For example, an alcoholic who loses his job, his family, and his self-respect may be inspired by desperation to begin again.

Children in particular have great potential unless they are damaged by adverse conditions early in life. Whenever a child is greatly burdened with guilt or anxiety, he or she is likely to become an adult who avoids responsibility and whose life lacks truth or authenticity. But even persons damaged in childhood can be aided by receiving love and acceptance from other people—provided that they accept responsibility and self-determination.

A basic premise of existentialism is that human beings and their lives are more important than any theory or therapy. The question of who or what one is can only be settled by one's own choices and actions. Nothing and no one is predetermined by social or biological forces, since each of us shapes our own behavior. Although existentialists are humanists, they do not accept the idea of universal human nature, since they believe that everyone forms his own nature and his own being.

Existentialists differentiate responsibility from obligation. People are responsible for their actions, but there is no obligation to make choices merely to please others or to live on terms that others dictate. When choices are motivated by obligation, the result is self-deception and self-violation.

Existentialism is a humanistic philosophy that respects people's potential to solve their problems in a manner that enhances their own lives and contributes to society. In reinforcing responsibility and self-determination, humanists oppose rigid beliefs about psychic determinism, asserting that most people have the capacity to grow, to progress, and to break away from the chains of the past, if they so choose.

Existential theory has had an impact on a number of therapeutic modalities, including rational-emotive therapy (Ellis and Harper 1961), logo therapy (Frankl 1959), and reality therapy (Glasser 1965). These treatment approaches differ in detail, but all emphasize personal responsibility and self-determination.

COGNITIVE FRAMEWORK

The cognitive framework is based primarily on principles formulated by the Swiss psychologist Jean Piaget (1974). Piaget identified four variables that influence the development of cognitive processes: (1) biological development, (2) interaction with the physical world, (3) interaction with the social world, and (4) integration of new and past experiences as the child matures.

Piaget traced the cognitive progress of children from the primitive concrete thought of infancy to the mature abstract thinking of adolescence. He saw biological, social, and environmental influences as all playing roles in the emergence of selfhood in children. A more extensive treatment of Piaget's theory is provided in Chapter 15, which deals with the critical tasks of maturation and development.

Moving beyond a theoretical model of cognitive development in children, Aaron T. Beck, a psychiatrist, formulated a framework of cognitive principles and clinical interventions (1976, 1985). Interventions for dysfunctional cognitive variations have been proposed by a number of theorists and therapists, including Sigmund Freud (1953), Albert Bandura (1977), B. F. Skinner (1972), and Carl Rogers (1980, 1985). Thus, cognitive theory has

Table 4–9. Cognition and Behavior			
Cognitive Interpretation	Emotional State	Mood Response	Behavior Response
Perceived loss	Sadness	Depression	Contract/conserve
Perceived reward	Joyousness	Hypomania	Expand/expend
Perceived threat	Fearfulness	Anxiety	Retreat/withdraw
Perceived punishment	Anger	Suspiciousness	Defend/attack

SOURCE: Adapted from Beck (1985).

been broadened by contributions from psychoanalytic theory, learning theory, behaviorism, and existentialism.

Cognition may be described generally as the visual and verbal images derived from our perceptions, attitudes, and beliefs. People whose cognitive patterns habitually distort reality and misjudge meanings cannot deal effectively with everyday life. Cognitive errors cause them to misinterpret events, respond incorrectly, and engage in self-defeating behavior. The cognitive framework links perception, thinking, and behavior. As a result, cognitive therapy is a blend of psychological, cognitive, and behavioral correction.

According to Beck, the cognitive framework utilizes the following principles:

- The way participants cognitively structure a situation determines their reaction to it. For example, people who believe they are in danger will behave defensively or offensively to protect themselves from the danger they perceive.

- Depending on the nature of the cognitive structure and the perceived situation, people experience an emotional reaction and behave accordingly. Individuals who react with resentment or anger tend to adopt a fight posture. Those who react with anxiety or fear tend to adopt a flight posture. People who react with affection or helplessness tend to adopt an approach posture. Individuals who react with hopelessness or sadness tend to adopt an avoidance posture (Table 4–9).

The care provider using a cognitive approach is active and guides the client to refocus on problems, to alter erroneous thought patterns, and to rehearse new behavior patterns. The rigid beliefs and attitudes of the client are questioned, directly and indirectly, and the ultimate goal is the transformation of error and misperception into open-mindedness and accurate cognitive patterns.

Implications for Nursing

Cognitive principles are compatible with the nursing process and may be adapted to a variety of situations. Some techniques of behavior therapy are used but not in a simplistic, mechanical way. The behavior modification methods of Skinner and others differ greatly from the supportive, client-centered interventions of Carl Rogers, yet both methods are used to correct dysfunctional ways of thinking and acting.

Chapter 8, which deals with mood variations and disruptions, describes the application of cognitive principles in the clinical setting.

BIOGENIC FRAMEWORK

Biogenic approaches are those that emphasize the role of biological factors in mental disorders. They look to constitutional, genetic, and chemical factors for the causes of psychological difficulties.

Constitutional Factors

In the late nineteenth century, the prevailing view was that mental disorders could be explained on the basis of physiological imbalance. As a result, physicians and others with a medical orientation dominated psychiatric treatment and research. The work of Emil Kraepelin (1856–1926) in describing and classifying mental disorders did much to reinforce biological explanations of mental disturbance. In a classic textbook published in 1883 and revised many times thereafter, Kraepelin classified mental disorders according to symptomatology.

About this time attempts were made to correlate physical endowment with personality traits and with predisposition to mental disorders. William Sheldon developed a constitutional typology that classified people according to three main body types: ectomorphs, endomorphs, and mesomorphs (see Figure 4–4). Each body type was not only associated with particular personality traits, but with susceptibility to mental disorders. Ectomorphs were assumed to be more prone to schizophrenic disorders, and endomorphs were assumed to be more vulnerable to manic-depressive episodes (Freedman, Kaplan, and Sadock 1973). Mesomorphs were seen as the least susceptible to mental disorders of all types.

Genetic Factors

Another biogenic approach has been to focus on the role of genetic factors in mental disorders. Kallmann (1953, 1962) found the concordance rate (a measure of correlation) for schizophrenia to be 14.7 percent for nonidentical twins, 14.3 percent for full siblings, 7.1 percent for half-siblings, and more than 85.8 percent for identical twins. When identical twins were reared apart, the schizophrenia concordance rates remained significantly high. Other studies of schizophrenia have produced similar results (Cohen et al. 1972, Gottesman and Shields 1972).

The possibility of genetic influence on affective disorders such as depression and mania has been documented using twin and family studies. Connors (1979) attributed the mood vulnerability of the children of depressed parents to a highly anxious, overreactive nervous system. Wierzbicki (1987) found that monozygotic (identical) twins resembled each other more closely than dizygotic

Figure 4–4. *Typology according to Sheldon's body types.*

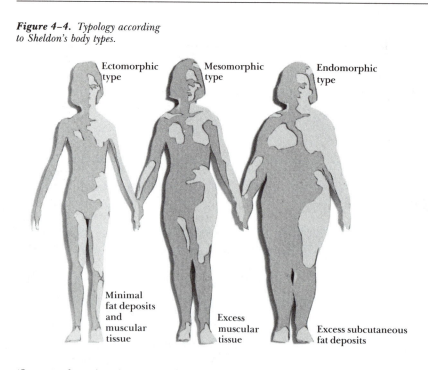

Ectomorphic type

Mesomorphic type

Endomorphic type

Minimal fat deposits and muscular tissue

Excess muscular tissue

Excess subcutaneous fat deposits

(fraternal) twins in mood level and mood lability. However, the data from this and similar studies may be biased by the interference of uncontrolled behavioral, cognitive, and social factors. Specific research is needed on the genetic basis of mood disorders before generalization is possible. As Chess, Thomas, and Hassibi (1983) noted, temperament may be a partially inherited state, but it is undoubtedly modified by a host of nongenetic, nonbiological influences. While it is true that there are some indications of genetic factors as mood disorder forces, precise models focusing on genetic inheritability must be developed to clarify available findings.

These findings indicate that some mental disorders are familial, even though data pointing specifically to heredity are inconclusive. Heredity and environment are influences that moderate or intensify each other. Genetic predisposition can be altered by life experiences, and inherited tendencies can modify environmental factors. The nature versus nurture controversy has yet to be resolved to everyone's satisfaction. At best one can state that heredity and environment are interactive influences on physical and mental well-being.

Chemical Imbalance

Neurochemical imbalance is suspected as a factor in some mental disorders. Kety (1959), for example, showed that schizophrenia may result from defective transmethylation, the molecular transformation of one catecholamine to another. There are three major catecholamines that serve as neuro-

transmitters in the body: dopamine, serotonin, and norepinephrine. In persons with schizophrenia, transmethylation of catecholamines produces a hallucinogenic, mescalinelike substance that is detectible in the urine. Furthermore, the antipsychotic (neuroleptic) drugs used to treat schizophrenia block central nervous system dopamine receptors—an action that helps explain the Parkinsonian symptoms that are frequent side effects of these drugs. Research on neurochemical imbalance as a factor in schizophrenia is promising, but the results are not yet definitive.

Research on neurochemical imbalance as a causative factor in affective, or mood, disorders has been more conclusive. Depressive states have been correlated with deficits of neurotransmitters, especially norepinephrine, while manic or elated states have been correlated with excesses of norepinephrine. It is possible that alterations in catecholamine metabolism may be partly responsible for some of the drastic mood swings of adolescents, of women experiencing menopause, and of elderly people, but this has not been substantiated as yet. In these stressful periods of the life cycle, many individuals experience strong feelings of depression or elation that could be related to natural chemical changes occurring in the body. It must be acknowledged that this is a rather simplistic explanation, considering the complex processes involved, and much additional research on neurochemical imbalance remains to be done.

Every process and system in the body, including blood cell levels, blood pressure, hormone levels, body temperature, heartbeat, renal function, and sleep, has its own rhythm that fluctuates regularly within intervals of a second, minute, day, week, month, or year. An excellent example is the monthly menstrual cycle of women that begins at menarche and ends at menopause. Cycles that occur more often, on a daily, or *circadian*, rhythm are shown in Figure 4–5.

Reputable studies indicate that biological rhythms can profoundly affect physical and psychological well-being (Brody 1981).

Figure 4–5. Biological rhythms. Many aspects of human physiology show clear-cut circadian cycles, changing regularly over each 24-hour period. Some of the more important ones are shown here.

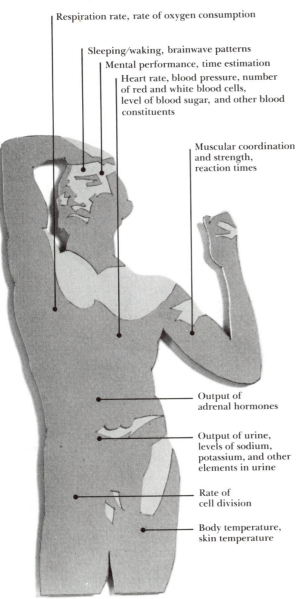

Respiration rate, rate of oxygen consumption

Sleeping/waking, brainwave patterns

Mental performance, time estimation

Heart rate, blood pressure, number of red and white blood cells, level of blood sugar, and other blood constituents

Muscular coordination and strength, reaction times

Output of adrenal hormones

Output of urine, levels of sodium, potassium, and other elements in urine

Rate of cell division

Body temperature, skin temperature

A number of economical procedures have been devised for recording an individual's many biological rhythms. One is autorhythmometry, a technique in which individuals are taught to record their own blood pressure, temperature, pulse, grip strength, and mood by means of ratings that can then be computerized. Another technique is the psychophysiological diary, which enables individuals to record quantitative information about physiological processes and about subjective experiences such as mood, hunger, and satiation. When such information is computerized, it becomes possible to detect individual changes in patterns of living and functioning and to make comparisons within and between groups. Because every individual pattern is unique, deviations may provide guidance in preventing, detecting, or alleviating maladaptive internal conditions.

Nursing Implications of Biogenic Approaches

As might be expected, proponents of the biogenic framework favor somatic forms of treatment, which include chemotherapy, psychosurgery, and shock therapy induced by insulin or electrical current. Some clients have been helped, while others have been hurt, by somatic treatments that are popular for a time and later discarded. Treatments that alter moods, thoughts, and behaviors continue to be used despite the fact that the underlying reasons for their effects are largely unknown. The biological causes of mental disorders remain a matter for conjecture and study, and understanding of how and why somatic treatments work awaits further investigation. Because somatic intervention demands the skills of knowledgeable, competent nurses, this approach in some respects enhances the role of the psychiatric nurse. In other respects, however, a reliance on somatic measures restricts the scope of nursing intervention.

A significant effect of the biogenic framework is its tendency to reduce the stigmatization that many psychiatric clients endure. If mental disorders are considered the result of physiological dysfunction, the client is less likely to be blamed for her symptoms. The other side of the coin, however, is that biogenic explanations also tend to reduce the client's responsibility for changing maladaptive behavior. Furthermore, adherence to such a medical model changes the focus of care, making clients passive recipients of treatment rather than active participants in their own recovery. Another drawback to the biogenic approach is that it increases distances between clients and care providers. Interventions take the form of procedures done *to* the

(Text continues on page 89.)

C L I N I C A L   E X A M P L E

THEORETICAL FRAMEWORKS IN NURSING ASSESSMENT

Edith Bailey was brought to a mental health facility by her husband at the suggestion of a community health nurse who had visited their home. Three months earlier Mrs. Bailey had given birth to a baby boy after a long and difficult labor. She was 32 years old and was the mother of another son, Jimmy, age 4. Because Mrs. Bailey was uncommunicative, her husband, Bob, gave most of the information to the intake nurse. He reported that after the birth of their first child, Edith had seemed tired and upset but gradually recovered without hospitalization or specific treatment. She seemed to improve steadily as her first child progressed through the toddler years.

The second child had been planned, but Mrs. Bailey had hoped for a daughter and was disappointed when it turned out to be a boy. Upon returning home after the birth, she had seemed silent and withdrawn. She was indifferent about her appearance and seldom bothered to dress or comb her hair. She ate little but slept for long periods of time. When awake, she smoked constantly and ignored the crying of the baby. The older boy was being cared for by his maternal grandmother. Mr. Bailey took time off from work to help his wife and arranged for a community health nurse to visit daily and a housekeeper to come in for a few hours a day. Mr. Bailey cared for the baby and did the cooking when he was not at work. In his free moments he visited Jimmy.

During the initial assessment interview, the nurse observed that Mrs. Bailey was oriented as to time, place, and person. However, she appeared apathetic and indifferent to her surroundings. She did not look at her husband or at the nurse but fixed her eyes on the floor. Often she did not seem to hear what was being said to her. When she did respond, her words were hard to understand. Several times she mumbled that she felt bad because she deserved to feel bad.

Mr. Bailey explained that his wife had experienced an unhappy childhood because her father drank too much. The family was poor and Edith had to take care of her younger brothers while her mother worked. Mr. Bailey added that his own childhood had not been a bed of roses. He had married in the hope of enjoying a happy family life, and he felt that he had always been a good provider. Prior to Jimmy's birth, he believed that he and his wife enjoyed a good relationship. Although

Edith was distant and aloof after Jimmy's birth, he tried to be understanding. He said that after his wife had "pulled herself together" their relationship was again harmonious. Although concerned about his wife and children, Mr. Bailey was beginning to feel angry about the heavy burden he was assuming. He was particularly worried about the new baby, in whom no one but himself seemed interested.

Based on Mrs. Bailey's behavior and level of functioning, a decision was made to admit her for observation. Since Edith's mother was willing, plans were made for her to care for the new baby as well as for Jimmy, who seemed delighted to welcome his new brother. The health care team considered it important for Mr. Bailey to stay in close touch with the children and for Mrs. Bailey to see them as soon as her condition permitted.

Members of the health team used a number of theoretical frameworks in assessing Mrs. Bailey and in trying to understand her behavior. Although the frameworks differed in focus, they yielded few genuine contradictions. In many respects the various frameworks supported and supplemented one another, as can been seen in the following applications.

PSYCHOGENIC FRAMEWORK

Assessment of Mrs. Bailey: (1) regression to early developmental levels, (2) conflict related to dependency needs, (3) repressed aggression, (4) failure to achieve basic trust, and (5) failure to achieve autonomy.

As a child Edith Bailey had taken on many adult responsibilities. Her mother was not unkind, but she had to work hard to support her daughter and three sons. The irresponsibility of Edith's father had left a residue of distrust in her that a successful marriage had failed to overcome. She had enjoyed the childless years of her marriage, and after a period of adjustment she was able to respond warmly to her first little boy. However, the arrival of a second son reactivated her sense of resentment for her lost childhood.

Edith was a woman with strong dependency needs that had never been fully met. As a result she was torn between her wish to be cared for and the current demands being made on her. Consequently, she

regressed to an immature level of functioning where her helplessness was apparent to all.

INTERPERSONAL FRAMEWORK

Assessment of Mrs. Bailey: (1) feelings of low self-esteem, (2) excessive interpersonal insecurity, and (3) poorly integrated self system.

Mrs. Bailey's self-esteem depended on her being considered loving and good. In childhood she had performed the tasks her mother expected of her and was rewarded by her mother's approval. As a married woman, she had continued to seek approval by doing whatever was asked of her, even when it meant sacrificing her own wishes. At the age of ten she had been expected to cook, clean, and care for her little brothers. After marrying and becoming a parent, she had doubts about having a second child but could not oppose her husband. When her pregnancy advanced, she began to hope for a baby girl. The birth of a second son disappointed her—looking at the new baby and thinking of her other boy, she was reminded of the constant care that her little brothers had required. Her mood did not improve after she returned home from the hospital. She was irritated by her husband's attentions, and his pride in the new baby annoyed her even more. Unable to break the habits of a lifetime, she did not disclose her feelings to anyone but retreated into a world where no one could intrude.

For years Mrs. Bailey had concealed inner anxiety and insecurity. The self system she had constructed was neither integrated nor realistic. When she asked for something she wanted, she felt like the "bad me." She disclaimed negative emotions and considered herself "good" only when she sacrificed herself for others.

SOCIOLOGICAL FRAMEWORK

Mrs. Bailey, like her husband, had grown up in a working-class family where the struggle to earn a living left family members with little time or energy to meet the emotional needs of all the members. Both partners had married in the hope of finding in family life the affection and nurture that had been absent in their formative years. Mrs. Bailey, in particular, had been pushed prematurely into assuming an adult role. With the arrival of her second child she felt she had returned to the role enactment of her childhood. In her resentment she overlooked the resources now available to her that were absent in her childhood. She failed to recognize the contributions of a devoted husband and a cooperative mother. Rejecting her responsibilities as a wife and mother, she moved into enactment of the sick role. This exempted her from her responsibilities but isolated her from her husband and children. She was then able to ignore the legitimate needs of her family and avoid seeing that her husband's physical and emotional reserves were nearly exhausted. All her life Mrs. Bailey had tried to enact roles that conformed to the expectations of others, but she was no longer able or willing to do this. Because role expectation was overwhelming and inappropriate in her family of origin, Mrs. Bailey saw her present situation as similar. She did not express her reactions directly, but for the first time in her life she chose to be deviant rather than a conformist. Her enactment of the sick role freed her from family interactions in which she believed that too much was expected from her.

EXISTENTIAL FRAMEWORK

Edith Bailey had spent her life trying to please everyone else and ignoring her own feelings. Trying first to be the perfect daughter and later the perfect wife, she had lost the ability to speak up for herself and state what she truly wanted. She had no confidence in herself and none in anyone else. Her disappointment in her father had caused her to turn inward and to expect little for herself. Although outwardly well-adjusted, she based her life on self-sacrifice and self-deception, always concealing her inner resentment. Her relationships with her husband and her mother were essentially dishonest. She pretended to herself and others that she was happy until she eventually became incapable of continuing the pretense. When that point was reached, Edith engaged in extreme withdrawal, abandoning her family just as surely as her father had abandoned her so many years before.

COGNITIVE FRAMEWORK

Mrs. Bailey could not meet the demands of daily life because she was not thinking of herself as a competent wife and mother who meant a great deal to her husband and children. She saw herself as a woman who

Nursing Diagnosis	Goal	Nursing Action	Outcome Criteria	Outcome Evaluation
Self concept disturbance	Client will attend unit activities of her choice, with staff input.	Negotiate with client for client to attend aerobics group in exchange for being allowed to join music appreciation group.	Client will attend group meetings with reminders from staff, if needed.	Client needs fewer reminders to attend group. Asked to change from aerobic to cooking group.
Self-care deficit	Client will take more interest in self-care and grooming.	Help client set up schedule for bathing, dressing, etc.; acknowledge efforts of client in this area.	Client will take more responsibility for self-care; client will permit husband and mother to bring clothing and personal articles from home.	Client adheres to schedule. Client has 2 clothing changes, wears each on alternate days.
Altered role performance	Client will begin to ask husband and mother about affairs at home.	Encourage family to ask client's opinion about what she wants done at home. Permit client to express feelings of being overwhelmed by her responsibilities.	Client will initiate discussion about how things are going at home.	Client shows little interest in home management. Client asked for pictures of her children to be brought to her.
	Client will permit visit from older son.	Express interest in pictures of the children. Discuss impending visit of older son; explore client's feelings about the visit.	Client will tolerate visit from older son; client will interact appropriately during visit.	Client permitted older boy to visit three times; says she is not ready to have the baby visit.
	Client will attend evening support group for young mothers while in hospital and after discharge.	Arrange for client to meet group leader; group goals and contract explained.	Client will agree to join group and live up to agreement.	Client attends meetings but has not yet agreed to continue after leaving the hospital.

had been exploited all her life and who now was expected to sacrifice her own welfare on behalf of her thoughtless husband and self-centered children. She interpreted her situation as hopeless, using cognitive misperceptions that magnified the problems in her life and minimized her proven record of competence and regeneration. The anxiety that pervaded so much of her social interaction caused her to give up. As a result of her feelings of hopelessness, she withdrew from her family. Her flight behavior and avoidance tactics permitted her to ignore the unhappiness and deprivation her husband and children were feeling. This withdrawal reduced the chances of correcting her distorted perceptions but gave her the opportunity to express her negativism in an extreme, nonverbal manner.

BIOGENIC FRAMEWORK
Assessment of Mrs. Bailey: (1) physical exhaustion, (2) hormonal changes, and (3) possible biochemical imbalance.

the birth of her second child. A difficult labor and delivery drained her physically and made her dread the demands of running a household and caring for two small children. After the birth of her first child she had experienced similar feelings but had rallied and managed to function fairly well. Because of the two recurrent episodes, it was apparent that the stress of parturition made Mrs. Bailey susceptible to depression. The biological explanation for her depression was physical exhaustion aggravated by postpartal hormonal and biochemical changes and by the stresses of her life situation.

PSYCHIATRIC AND NURSING DIAGNOSES
The following nursing and psychiatric diagnoses were made for Mrs. Bailey:

Nursing Diagnoses

Self concept disturbance
(related to client's apathy and regressed behavior)
Self-esteem disturbance
Personal identity disturbance

Self-care deficit
(related to client's neglect of her person)
Bathing/hygiene
Dressing/grooming

Altered role performance
(related to client's neglect of children and home)
Parenting
Home maintenance

Multiaxial Psychiatric Diagnoses

Axis I	Clinical syndrome
	296.33 Recurrent major depression, with melancholia
Axis II	Personality disorders
	301.60 Dependent personality
Axis III	Physical disorders and conditions
	Postpartum maladjustment
Axis IV	Code 4—Severe psychosocial stressors
Axis V	GAF 45: Current
	GAF 70: Highest in past year

client rather than *with* the client and reinforce the medical model.

The medical model also helps perpetuate the position of the physician as director of the therapeutic program, making health care teams hierarchical rather than egalitarian and multi-disciplinary rather than interdisciplinary. A physician is usually in charge of the health team, with members working according to the traditional scope of their respective disciplines. As a consequence, the dependent functions of psychiatric nurses are likely to be emphasized, while their independent nursing functions are given less opportunity for expression. Psychotherapeutic interactions between clients and nurses may then become secondary to administrative and managerial responsibilities. In a study of four health care teams, each composed of a physician, two nurses, and a dietitian, investigators found that although the physicians enjoyed dominant status in all cases, the team that produced the most successful outcomes for clients scored highest on "collegiality" between members. Interactions on the most successful team were characterized by mutual sharing of information and opinions (Schmitt 1982).

In general, the medical model tends to use a specific problem-solving rather than a holistic approach to care. However, the model has provided some benefits to nursing in that many somatic measures that are part of the medical model require careful monitoring by professional nurses who must observe, explain, teach, and reassure clients undergoing such treatment.

SUMMARY

Theoretical frameworks organize knowledge systematically by means of related concepts and con-structs. No one framework is all inclusive; each offers a distinct but limited perspective. A number of major frameworks provide insights into biopsychosocial development, adaptation, and maladaptation.

The theories of Freud and Erikson are representative of the psychogenic framework. Freud emphasized psychic determinism, the belief that all behavior is meaningful and purposeful. He described personality as composed of id, ego, and superego and identified three levels of mental awareness: conscious, unconscious, and preconscious. A major ego function is reality testing, or the ability to differentiate internal stimuli from external stimuli. Hallucinations and delusions are internal stimuli that are mistakenly thought to be external; they are indicative of failure in reality testing. Freud considered the ego to be a defensive structure that mediates between the demands of the id and the restrictions of the superego. Freud outlined five psychosexual stages of development, each characterized by a conflict to be resolved if development is to progress. His initial work on defense mechanisms was elaborated by his daughter, Anna, who developed a comprehensive list of adaptive and maladaptive defense mechanisms utilized by the ego.

Erikson accepted some of Freud's ideas but modified others. He believed that the ego has an integrative rather than a defensive purpose. He explained that constitutional, psychological, and social factors create a compelling period of urgency during which critical life tasks should be accomplished. Erikson's framework encompasses the entire life cycle, which he divided into eight stages, each of which has its own maturational task.

Sullivan developed the interpersonal framework for explaining personality. He described a self system that evolves as a consequence of interpersonal experiences between mother and child.

Everyone engages in interpersonal security operations designed to reduce anxiety. These security operations include selective inattention and focal awareness, both of which allow individuals to overlook information that threatens security. Peplau refined and expanded interpersonal definitions of anxiety and applied them to the nursing process.

Sociologists are interested in the relationships of individuals and families to society. They focus on the effects of such social factors as institutions, socialization, social roles, and stratification. Social institutions may have both manifest and latent functions that justify their existence. Symbolic interactionism explains how our interpretation of underlying social meanings enables us to regulate our behaviors. Roles and attitudes are acquired from interaction with others. Social class influences have a deep effect on childrearing practices and on how mental disorders are diagnosed and treated. It is the opinion of many sociologists that mental disorders result from the interplay of diverse variables. Although social and cultural factors do not fully explain the occurrence or course of mental disorders, they cannot be discounted.

Proponents of the biogenic framework favor somatic treatments, such as psychosurgery, insulin shock therapy, electroconvulsive therapy, and chemotherapy. Many of the currently used somatic treatments are effective, even though the rationale for their use is not clearly understood. Among biogenic sources of mental disorders currently being explored are genetic factors and chemical imbalance. Chronobiology (the study of biological rhythms) is used to monitor a range of human functions and to record characteristic patterns. Because every individual pattern of biological rhythms is unique, deviations may provide guidelines in preventing, detecting, or alleviating internal maladaptations.

The quality and quantity of human sleep can be viewed as a regular, recurrent cycle. There is great variation in the amount of sleep different people need; requirements change with age and vary with the physical and psychological status of the individual. Attention to the sleeping problems of clients is a responsibility often delegated to nurses. Effectiveness of nursing measures is enhanced by an understanding of the complex nature of the human sleep cycle.

Additional frameworks for explaining biopsychosocial development include the existential approach, which emphasizes self-determination and striving for authentic existence, and the cognitive approach, which emphasizes cognitive factors in emergence of the self.

Review Questions

1. Define the following terms and explain their relevance to psychiatric mental health nursing: *theories, theoretical frameworks, concepts*.

2. What do the terms *ego-alien* (dystonic) and *ego-syntonic* mean? What is their relationship to repression?

3. Describe the ego function known as *reality testing*. What manifestations frequently indicate failure of reality testing?

4. What role does the unconscious play in mental life, according to Freud?

5. How did Peplau adapt Sullivan's interpersonal framework to nursing theory and practice?

6. What are the major differences among the formulations of Freud, Erikson, and Sullivan?

7. What advantages are derived from viewing mental disorders as physiological in origin? What are the disadvantages of this viewpoint?

Research Report

Nurse Performance: Strengths and Weaknesses

Little research has attempted to measure nurse performance, particularly nurses' strengths and weaknesses. This report compares head nurses' ratings of staff nurses' performance on 52 specific nursing skills with the staff nurses' self-evaluations. Two sets of head nurses and two sets of staff nurses comprised the sample. Results indicated that nurses, regardless of educational level, experience, or type of clinical unit shared many of the same strengths and weaknesses. Although head nurses generally gave lower ratings, their rankings of skills performed best and worst agreed with staff nurses' self-evaluations. Staff nurses and head nurses alike identified professional development skill at the top and teaching/collaboration skills at the bottom in terms of performance. The data suggest that nurse educators, academic and in-service, should emphasize teaching/collaboration, planning/evaluation, and leadership skills of students and practicing nurses. The performance of technical skills such as suctioning and intravenous procedures was rated highly by the staff nurses and by the head nurses. Although technological changes may demand continuous academic and inservice education in these areas the study indicated that hospitals and nursing schools are endeavoring to meet the technological demands that nurses confront. Higher level skills such as teaching/collaboration and planning/evaluation perhaps need more attention than they are currently receiving. Another possibility is that these skills are more complex, harder to master and therefore require graduate level education. The researchers also suggested the possibility that these higher level skills received lower performance ratings because they are considered by the practice facility to be less important. Future research might well include study of excellence as well as competence by examining the performance of experienced nurses and of nurses with graduate education within specific settings and across various settings.

Joanne Comi McCloskey and Bruce McCain. *Nursing Research* 37, no. 5 (September/October 1988):308–313.

Suggested Annotated Readings

Antai-Otong, D. "Dealing with Demanding Patients." *Nursing 88* 19, no. 1 (January 1989):94–95.

This interesting article uses a casebook method to induce nurses to think of ways to deal with demanding clients when pressures at work seem overwhelming. The key to coping with very demanding clients is to try to understand what is motivating the objectionable behavior, and to learn to work with the clients instead of engaging in battle against them. Included are a helpful list of rules for coping effectively with demanding clients and a rationale for using certain strategies.

Collins, H. L. "The Patients Your Colleagues Hate to Nurse." *RN* (December 1987):46–53.

Nurses across the United States were surveyed to discover which kinds of patients they most disliked treating. A factor in the replies of nurses was their apparent inability to help a particular person. The three categories that nurses most disliked caring for were psychiatric clients, persons with AIDS, and seriously ill children. One respondent stated that it was impossible to eradicate the pain of psychiatric clients. Another said that she hated to see psychiatric clients waste their lives on emotional problems. Some respondents admitted that lack of knowledge made them feel inadequate in caring for psychiatric clients; others were impatient with the endless needs this group of clients often manifests. Alcoholics, in particular, seemed to arouse strong feelings of anger in respondents, many of whom believed that these clients create their own difficulties. Persons with AIDS were high on the most disliked list, because the disease is contagious and incurable. Homophobia also plays a part in making

nurses dislike AIDS clients. The emotional distress of caring for very sick children causes many nurses to try to avoid this task, especially if they have children of their own. The article contains a list of techniques to help nurses handle their feelings as they care for clients who arouse emotional turmoil.

Fitzpatrick, J. J. "How Can We Enhance Nursing Knowledge and Practice?" *Nursing and Health Care* 9, no. 9 (November/December 1988):516–521.

Academic programs in nursing have tended to emphasize interdisciplinary involvement, sometimes at the expense of disciplinary content. The author goes on to state that nursing's weakest claim to professionalism lies in its limited body of unique knowledge. She attributes this limitation in part to the long domination of nursing by medicine, yet she believes that nursing is strengthened by a synthesis of knowledge from a range of disciplines. She believes that the systematic efforts to identify, validate, and use nursing diagnoses amounts to a revolution in the management of information by nurses. The arrival of computerization within the health care system has added to the necessity of codifying nursing assessments and actions. There is enormous potential for the utilization of computer technology in nursing. At the same time there is an ongoing need for what the author calls conceptual clarity within the profession regarding what nurses do. Information management and new technology may well speed the professionalization of nursing as we move into the twenty-first century.

Kidd, P., and E. F. Morrison. "The Progression of Knowledge in Nursing: A Search for Meaning." *Image* 20, no. 4 (Winter 1988):222–224.

In this nonexperimental article the authors call for the use of multiple theories in the scholarly work of nurses. They also advocate the use of theories by clinical nurses with different levels of expertise. A comparison is made between the stages of growth of "women's knowledge" and the stages of theory development in nursing, and interesting similarities are shown. Stages of nursing research and of the clinical use of theory are also traced. Various forms of knowledge are relevant to nursing, and current nursing research tends to be somewhat narrow and reductionistic. Drawing upon all types of knowledge in nursing practice, education, and research will help move the profession toward a vision of human beings as integrated, unified persons.

Expert nurses do not rely only upon explicit rules or guidelines, but allow their practices to become extensions of knowledge, intuition, and their clients' experiences. Expert nurses have a clear understanding of theory and apply this understanding to clinical assessment. They also understand that theories that work well in one clinical situation may not work well in another. As a result, expert nurses use theory in a flexible way. They do not hesitate to disregard or modify theory when the theory is not working, when professional intuition contradicts theory, or when moral or ethical obligations refute or supercede theory. The article relies on a literature search and the author's reflections to support the viewpoints presented.

Watson, J. "Human Caring as a Moral Context for Nursing Education." *Nursing and Health Care* 9, no. 8 (October 1988):422–425.

This thoughtful article criticizes the emphasis in contemporary nursing education on science and technology. According to the author, nurses may be technically and scientifically correct and still make moral errors. What is needed is a shift to a new moral standard that guides the nurse through all caregiving activities. This shift is especially important because of the trend in nursing toward specialization. In order to uphold a moral context for nursing, schools must change a number of their traditions, notably the custom of treating students as objects and fostering power/dependency relationships between teachers and students. The author accuses schools of nursing of creating "competency without compassion," and urges a liberalization of nursing education that includes art, literature, music, and movement as ways of extending nurses' understanding of subjective and objective responses to health and illness.

References

Abraham, K. *Selected Papers in Psychoanalysis*. New York: Basic Books, 1953.

Adams, V. A. "Freud's Work Thrives as Theory, Not Therapy." *The New York Times* (August 14, 1979).

Bandura, A. *Social Learning Theory*. Englewood Cliffs, New Jersey: Prentice-Hall, 1977.

Beck, A. T. *Cognitive Therapy and the Emotional Disorders*. New York: International Universities Press, 1976.

——. "Cognitive Therapy." In *Comprehensive Textbook of Psychiatry*, 4th ed. H. I. Kaplan and B. J. Sadock, eds., 1432–1438. Baltimore: Williams & Wilkins, 1985.

Bellak, L., and M. Hurvick, and H. K. Gediman. *Ego Functions in Schizophrenics, Neurotics, and Normals*. New York: John Wiley & Sons, 1973.

Blumer, H. *Symbolic Interaction: Perspective and Method*. Englewood Cliffs, New Jersey: Prentice-Hall, 1969.

Brenner, C. *An Elementary Textbook of Psychoanalysis*. New York: International Universities Press, 1955.

Brody, J. E. "Body's Many Rhythms Send Messages on When to Work and Play." *The New York Times* (August 11, 1981).

Chess, S., A. Thomas, and M. Hassibi. "Depression in Childhood and Adolescence." *Journal of Nervous and Mental Disorders* 171 (1983):411–420.

Clausen, J. A. "Sociology and Psychiatry." In *Comprehensive Textbook of Psychiatry*, 3d. ed. H. I. Kaplan, A. M. Freedman, and B. J. Sadock, eds. Baltimore: Williams & Wilkins, 1980.

Cohen, S. M., M. G. Allen, W. Pollin, and Z. Hrubec. "Relationships of Schizo-Affective Psychosis to Manic-Depressive Psychosis and Schizophrenia." *Teaching of General Psychiatry* 26 (1972):539–546.

Connors, C. K., et al. "Children of Parents with Affective Illness." *American Academy of Child Psychology* 18:600–607.

Durkheim, E. *Suicide*. Glencoe, New York: Free Press, 1951.

Ellis, A., and R. A. Harper. *A Guide to Rationale Living*. Englewood Cliffs, New Jersey: Prentice-Hall, 1961.

Engel, G. L. "Grief and Grieving." *American Journal of Nursing* 64 (1964):93–98.

Erikson, E. H. *Childhood and Society*, 2d ed. New York: W. W. Norton, 1963.

Frankl, V. *Man's Search for Meaning*. New York: Beacon Press, 1959.

Freedman, A. M., H. I. Kaplan, and B. J. Sadock. *Modern Synopsis of Psychiatry*. Baltimore: Williams & Wilkins, 1973.

Freud, A. *The Ego and Mechanisms of Defense*. New York: International Universities Press, 1953.

Freud, S. *A General Introduction to Psychoanalysis*. New York: Simon & Schuster, 1953.

——. "Civilization and Its Discontents." In *Standard Edition of Psychological Works of Sigmund Freud*, Vol. 21. London: Hogarth Press, 1961.

Gendlin, E. T. "The Experiential Response." In *Use of Interpretation in Treatment*, E. J. Hammer, ed. New York: Grune & Stratton, 1968.

Glasser, W. *Reality Therapy: A New Approach to Psychiatry*. New York: Harper & Row, 1965.

Goffman, E. *Asylums*. New York: Doubleday, 1961.

Gottesman, I. I., and J. Shields. *Schizophrenia and Genetics*. New York: Academic Press, 1972.

Griffin, J. Q. "Physical Illness in the Family." In *Family—Focus of Care*, J. R. Miller and E. H. Janosik, eds. New York: McGraw-Hill, 1980.

Hollingshead, A., and F. C. Redlich. *Social Class and Mental Illness*. New York: John Wiley & Sons, 1958.

Kallmann, F. J. *Heredity in Health and Mental Disorder*. New York: W. W. Norton, 1953.

——. *Expanding Goals of Genetics in Psychiatry*. New York: Grune & Stratton, 1962.

Kety, S. S. "Biochemical Theories of Schizophrenia." *Science* 129 (1959):1528, 1590.

King, I. M. *Toward a Theory of Nursing*. New York: John Wiley & Sons, 1971.

Langner, T. S., and S. T. Michael. *Life Stress and Mental Health: Midtown Manhattan Study*. Glencoe, New York: Free Press, 1963.

Marram, G. *The Group Approach in Nursing Practice*, 2d ed. St. Louis: C. V. Mosby, 1978.

Mead, G. H. *Mind, Self, and Society*. Chicago: University of Chicago Press, 1933.

Miller, J. R., and E. H. Janosik, eds. *Family-Focused Care*. New York: McGraw-Hill, 1980.

Mollica, R. F., and M. Milic. "Social Class and Psychiatric Practice." *American Journal of Psychiatry* 143, no. 1 (1986):12–17.

Morgan, A. J., and M. D. Morgan. *Manual of Primary Mental Health Care*. Philadelphia: J. B. Lippincott, 1980.

Parsons, T. *The Social System*. New York: Free Press, 1951.

Peplau, H. E. *Interpersonal Relations in Nursing*. New York: Putnam, 1952.

Piaget, J. *The Origins of Intelligence in Children*. New York: International Universities Press, 1974.

Reichenback, H. *The Rise of Scientific Philosophy*. Berkeley: University of California Press, 1968.

Rogers, C. R. *A Way of Being*. Boston: Houghton Mifflin, 1980.

Rogers, C. R., and R. Stanford. "Client-Centered Psychotherapy." In *Comprehensive Textbook of Psychiatry*, 4th ed. H. I. Kaplan and B. J. Sadock, eds. Baltimore: Williams & Wilkins, 1985.

Rosenhan, D. I. "On Being Sane in Insane Places." *Science* 179 (1973):250–258.

Ruch, S. C. *Psychology: The Personal Science*. Belmont, California: Wadsworth, 1984.

Scheinfeld, D. R. "Family Relationships and School Achievement among Boys of Lower Income Urban Black Families." *American Journal of Orthopsychiatry* 53, no. 1 (1983):127–143.

Schmitt, M. "Working Together in Health Teams." In *Life Cycle Group Work in Nursing*. E. H. Janosik and L. B. Phipps, eds. Monterey, California: Wadsworth Health Sciences, 1982.

Schultz, D. *Theories of Personality*, 2d ed. Monterey, California: Wadsworth Health Sciences, 1981.

Skinner, B. F. *Science and Human Behavior*. New York: Macmillan, 1953.

——. *Beyond Freedom and Dignity*. New York: Macmillan, 1972.

Sullivan, H. S. *The Interpersonal Theory of Psychiatry*. New York: W. W. Norton, 1953.

Thompson, C. *Psychoanalyses: Evolution and Development*. New York: Grune & Stratton, 1950.

Wierzbicki, M. "Similarity of Monozygotic and Dizygotic Twins in Level and Lability of Sub-clinically Depressed Mood." *American Journal of Orthopsychiatry* 57, no. 1 (1987):33–40.

5

Nursing Process and Practice in Mental Health Care

Learning Objectives

After reading this chapter, the student should be able to:

1. Apply the nursing process to the care of clients with a variety of problem behaviors.

2. Use nursing care plan guidelines to develop plans that have a wide application in clinical practice.

3. Determine which nursing interventions are appropriate for various problematic client behaviors.

Overview

The therapeutic techniques used by psychiatric mental health nurses have evolved from several sources, including psychiatry, psychology, sociology, and, most recently, the work of nurses themselves. This chapter describes components of the nursing process, a systematic method of identifying problems, planning and providing holistic care, and evaluating the effectiveness of the care provided. Generic care plans for common problem behaviors are presented as guidelines that can be used but must be individualized to fit each client and family. The second section of this chapter describes some problem behaviors and delineates the use of the nursing process in therapeutic relationships with clients who demonstrate these behaviors. Therapeutic and nontherapeutic methods of interaction with clients are emphasized, as well as the need for continual self-assessment on the part of the nurse.

Regardless of a client's psychiatric diagnosis, inappropriate coping patterns are often present.

The primary problems that follow are usually ineffective problem-solving ability, faulty reality testing and difficulty with interpersonal relationships. Psychiatric nursing consists of interventions by which nurses help clients to use new or healthy coping patterns in ways that are consistent and continuous. The nurse and the client must collaborate in a problem solving process to determine the strengths of the client in order to modify inappropriate variations and disruptions that are present.

Nurses who work with psychiatric clients are challenged not only to assist the clients to resolve difficulties and alter problem behaviors but to continually monitor their own actions and reactions during a therapeutic interchange. The nursing process is the most effective means of problem solving and of incorporating ongoing introspection into coordinating and delivering care to the client.

THE NURSING PROCESS

Because of the wide range of problems presented by clients, nurses must be adept at problem-solving techniques. To manage and care for clients effectively, nurses must overcome four barriers to efficient problem solving, according to Sorensen and Luckmann (1979):

1. Failing to specify goals and purposes.

2. Jumping to conclusions about the cause of a problem and then proceeding on a course of action that may or may not solve the problem.

3. Plunging into action before considering all relevant alternatives.

4. Failing to consider the probable consequences of a course of action.

The use of systematic problem solving can help nurses overcome the barriers to effective solutions and make logical decisions concerning client care. The systematic process that facilitates problem solving is termed the nursing process, and the impetus guiding the nursing process is caring, regardless of the clinical setting in which it takes place.

The nursing process involves four sequential, interrelated, interdependent steps: (1) identifying the client's health problems (making nursing diagnoses), (2) formulating plans to solve the problem, (3) implementing the plans or delegating implementation to others, and (4) evaluating the effectiveness of the plans in resolving the problems that have been identified. Implicit in the nursing process are the need to involve the client and the family and the need to individualize the approach for each client's particular needs (Kozier and Erb 1983).

The purpose of the nursing process is to provide direction and structure for the delivery of nursing care to meet the health needs of the individual, family, and community. The four steps of the process provide the organizational structure necessary to accomplish its purpose.

Utilizing the nursing process model has several benefits. Its flexibility and versatility make it applicable to a wide variety of health care recipients. By being client-centered, the nursing process model addresses the individual needs of each client. It also creates a health data base, identifies actual or potential health problems, establishes priorities for nursing action, and defines specific nursing responsibilities. Because care is planned and organized, the process encourages innovative nursing care and provides alternatives for nursing action. In addition, it develops nursing autonomy and

accountability (Carlson et al. 1982). Because of the steps involved in this system, the nurse can utilize the process to monitor the progress of the client as well as her own reactions to the relationship.

The Components of the Nursing Process

The four steps of the nursing process can be identified as assessment, planning, implementation, and evaluation. These components are diagrammed in Figure 5–1.

ASSESSMENT An assessment is a deliberate, systematic, and logical collection of data. Data collection regarding the health status of the client begins with the initial contact. In addition to observing and interviewing the client, the nurse should acquire supplementary information from family members, from previous charts and records, and from participating members of the health team. The adequacy of an assessment is largely dependent on the data base collected. It is often necessary to accept the fact that early data collection may be less than complete. The compilation of information about any client must always be ongoing and continuous. The following categories of information are helpful to bear in mind when gathering data:

Physical, psychological, and mental status of the client

Client's perception of the current situation

Impact of social, familial, and environmental variables on the clients

Present habits, activities, and lifestyle of the client

Previous habits, activities, and lifestyle of the client

Figure 5–1. *The nursing process is client-centered.*

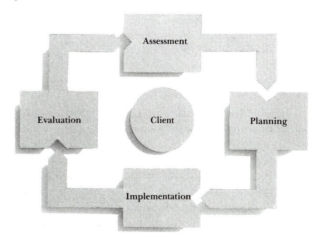

After the initial assessment is completed, the nurse assigns meaning to the data by writing a statement about the client's problems—that is, the client's specific disruption or potential disruption in health status which is called a *nursing diagnosis.* Nursing diagnoses are concise terms that accurately and effectively describe client needs, problems, and objectives. According to Neal et al. (1980), making a nursing diagnosis requires interpreting various data that concerns the client. Information about the client is clarified, validated, and categorized so that connecting relationships can be recognized.

Nursing diagnosis is concerned with identifying the client's presenting problems. The diagnosis may be descriptive, as in "limited response to auditory and tactile stimulation"; it may be etiologic, as in "lessened intestinal sounds"; it may be primarily physiological, as in "inability to void"; or it may be psychological, as in "feelings of powerlessness."

PLANNING The purpose of planning client care is to develop guidelines for helping the client attain or maintain the state of optimal wellness. The plan is based on the nursing diagnosis and is designed to build in the client's strengths that have been identified in the assessment phase.

Planning includes consideration of various goals, objectives, and expected outcomes, which may be long-term, short-term, or a combination of both. Goals are statements of the desired, achievable outcomes to be attained within a predicted time span, given the presenting situation and available resources. Goals give direction and purpose for nursing action. Short-term goals are those whose focus is immediate achievement; they are probably the most concrete and tangible since they deal with expectations for the here and now. Long-term goals spell out the final desired outcome; they give the overall direction for care.

It is important to include the client in the process of establishing goals. Goals and objectives should be behaviorally stated in terms of what the client will be doing or of what the expected outcome will be for the client rather than for the nurse. The most usual ways of expressing client-centered goals, objectives, or outcomes is to state simply that "The client will . . . ." It is important for nurses to realize that the terminology does not denote any degree of coercion but merely outlines identifiable, objective goals. As much as possible, the goals, objectives, and outcomes expected for the client should be specific. Whenever possible, a predetermined standard of measurement should be stated. For example, it might be noted that a socially isolated client will arrange to visit a friend once a week

or attend a club meeting. At least one goal, objective, or expected outcome should accompany nearly every nursing diagnosis. These may be of a long- or short-term nature and should be so described. If a client has multiple problems, it may be necessary to prioritize goals and begin work on the most troublesome or on goals that will give the most chance for success to initiate the relationship.

IMPLEMENTATION Implementation involves putting into action the nursing interventions that have been planned. To intervene means to "come between." Nursing intervention, sometimes called nursing care, consists of actions taken by the nurse to assist the client. The nurse "comes between" a problem and its resolution by carrying out actions directed toward solving the problem.

Nursing interventions include all the nursing measures used to achieve the goals, objectives, and outcomes developed from the nursing diagnoses that emerged from the data collection and assessment. Some nursing interventions help clients achieve short-term goals. In turn, the achievement of short-term goals eventually facilitates the attainment of long-term objectives and outcomes.

Nursing interventions should be described simply and concisely in the care plan. A statement such as "encourage socialization" is less useful for other staff members than specific interventions such as "accompany client on daily walks." General instructions such as "reward," "discourage," and "reinforce" are more apt to be clearly understood and consistently followed if they are accompanied by specific directions.

Involving the client to the greatest extent possible is an important part of nursing care. It is well-documented in nursing literature that expressions of client satisfaction are directly proportional to clients' involvement in their care. Client involvement may entail more of the nurse's time, but in the long run the extra time expenditure is worthwhile and generally helps the client to become more independent.

To be helpful in assisting the client to meet mutually established goals, nursing interventions should be (Sorensen and Luckmann 1979):

1. Consistent with the nursing care plan and the medical plan of care.
2. Designed to solve problems.
3. Therapeutically safe.
4. Specific to the nursing diagnosis.
5. Individualized to the client's needs, resources, and abilities.

6. Developed to use appropriate health facility resources.

7. Scheduled to coincide with the client's need for rest, exercise, food, sleep, recreation, and other activities.

8. Organized to allow both the client and family to participate.

9. Used to teach the client self-care and avoidance of complications and setbacks.

10. Modified in accordance with changes in the client's condition and situation.

EVALUATION Evaluation is the process of determining to what extent the goals of nursing care have been attained. Sometimes it is possible to evaluate a client's response to a nursing measure after 24 hours. At other times longer periods may be needed. Evaluation of the client's response is essential for reassessment, reordering of priorities, and ongoing revision of the care plan.

If the client's problems and goals have been identified in precise terms, evaluation is relatively simple: either the client has responded as expected, short-term goals have been achieved but long-term goals have not yet been met, no goals have been achieved, or new problems have arisen.

If apparent progress toward desired goals has been made, no major changes of the nursing care plan may be indicated. If little or no progress is evident, there are certain questions to be asked. A basic question is whether major revision or merely a difference in emphasis is needed. Appropriate issues to be considered include the following:

1. Was the problem correctly identified?

2. Are the goals/objectives realistic for the client at this time?

3. What factors affected the attainment of the goals?

4. Is a reordering of the priorities necessary?

5. Are there alternative measures that might be adopted to reach goals or objectives?

6. Have the nursing measures emerged naturally and coherently, based on nursing assessment, diagnosis, and planning?

7. Based on evaluation of client responses, what aspects of the nursing care need reassessment and revision? What aspects do not?

The evaluation is carried out in a purposeful and organized way. It is an intellectual activity in which the client is assessed in terms of previously identified goals. Both the client and the nurse should participate whenever possible.

During the evaluation, the nurse may consider a number of questions: What factors affected the attainment of the goals? Was the problem correctly identified? If the problem was not resolved, why not? Was the nursing intervention directed toward the stated goals? What other nursing interventions would be more likely to assist the client to attain the stated goals? In addition, the nurse must ask how the outcomes were affected by her own actions and reactions to the client during her contacts with the client. Was she aware of the meaning of the verbal and non-verbal communication of the client? Did she attend to her own feelings in response to the client's progress and behaviors? What interventions were effective and therapeutic? Why? Which ones were not and why?

The nursing process may seem complicated, and in some ways perhaps it is, since human behavior is complex. On the other hand, following the nursing process is less difficult than describing it and using the process elevates problem solving to professional levels. Once the fundamental skills that comprise nursing process actions are mastered, they can be carried out easily and confidently throughout each step in the process.

THE NURSING CARE PLAN

The nursing care plan is a written statement that documents the evidence of the nursing process. It indicates the objectives of nursing intervention and provides a guide to client-centered care, a means of communication, a guide for supervision, and a basis for evaluating the care.

The following questions can be used as a guide for evaluating the nursing care plan:

1. Do the diagnoses reflect actual or potential disruptions in the health status of the client?

2. Are the diagnoses logically derived from the data available?

3. Are the diagnoses stated in nursing terms, or are they medical diagnoses?

4. Are the diagnoses merely stating subjective and objective data, or do they reflect the client's basic needs?

5. Do the goals relate to the identified problems?

6. Is the short-term goal a required step in reaching a long-term goal?

7. Are the goal statements client-centered rather than nurse-centered?

8. Are the goals relevant, understandable, measurable, behaviorally stated, and attainable?

9. Are the interventions specific and related to the identified goals?

10. Are the interventions clearly stated and written in nursing terms?

11. Is the plan of care individualized, and does it provide for continuity of care?

12. Is the plan clear and concise, providing direction for those caring for the client?

13. Is the plan realistic, and does it allow for evaluation of nursing interventions?

Generic nursing care plans that can be used as a basis for planning are provided next. These plans are designed to be used as guidelines only and must be individualized for each client.

Generic Nursing Care Plans

With the development of officially recognized nursing diagnoses, it has become possible to adopt a standard format for care plans. The format of generic care plans may vary from one facility to another, but most plans use the four stages of the nursing process.

The trend toward the use of generic plans is part of an attempt to provide clear, concise information that will facilitate the therapeutic nursing regimen. Generic plans are not all-purpose guides, but when adopted by an agency or facility, they can bring a high degree of consistency and professionalism to record keeping. Four examples of generic plans are provided here. They suggest some common nursing diagnoses and appropriate nursing interventions for four types of behavioral manifestations displayed by clients. It should be remembered that any generic plan must be tailored to the needs of the specific client and must adhere to the format approved by the facility providing care.

THE PRACTICE OF PSYCHIATRIC NURSING

The application of the nursing process to actual nursing care situations is the focus of the rest of this chapter. As each type of problem behavior is discussed, guidelines are provided for assessment, planning, implementation, and evaluation.

The Anxious Client

Anxiety is a subjective phenomenon that everyone experiences to a lesser or greater degree when confronted with situations that they perceive as threatening. It is an internal response to danger of an unknown specific nature, and it can occur when people face circumstances that previously provoked anxiety or confront certain new situations or new roles. Anxiety may vary from mild feelings of uneasiness and nervousness to acute feelings of dread and apprehension. The degree of anxiety depends on the individual's evaluation of the severity of the threat. Intervention is indicated if the anxiety impairs the functioning of the individual. If not dealt with adequately in its early stages, anxiety tends to increase.

Normal anxiety is a reaction that is proportionate to the actual threat and does not require dysfunctional behavior for its management. It can be dealt with on the level of conscious awareness or can be relieved if the situation is altered. Extreme dysfunctional anxiety is a reaction that is out of proportion to the threat or danger.

ASSESSMENT A variety of behaviors are indicative of the anxious state. Clients may appear to be vague, uneasy, tense, nervous, or apprehensive. These emotions are shown by body language (sweating, pacing, jaw clenching) or by verbal mannerisms (slow, rapid, or evasive speech). Anxious clients may complain of feeling helpless, alone, insecure, and rejected. At times they may act sarcastic, angry, irritable, or tearful; or they may use derogatory or belittling remarks. Incessant talking, excessive demands on others' time and attention, and repeated questioning of the dependability and sincerity of others are also frequently seen in anxious clients.

Somatic symptoms of anxiety may include restlessness, increased muscular tension, breathlessness, chest pain, heart palpitations, tightness in the throat, sweating, headache, fatigue, and insomnia. Anxiety frequently affects the gastrointestinal tract, producing nausea, vomiting, diarrhea, and loss of appetite.

PLANNING Appropriate nursing goals for the anxious client should include the following:

1. To intervene when the client is unable to handle her anxiety.

2. To reduce anxiety in order to increase the client's comfort.

3. To help the client recognize that his behaviors are related to anxiety.

4. To assist the client in gaining insight into the reasons for the anxiety.

5. To help the client accept anxiety as an inevitable part of life and learn to tolerate and benefit from mild degrees of anxiety.

Generic Nursing Care Plan: The Client Who Exhibits Delusional Thinking

Date	Assessment: Nursing Diagnosis	Planning: Goals/Outcomes	Implementation: Nursing Orders/ Interventions	Evaluation
	Altered thought processes Sensory-perceptual alteration Impaired home maintenance management Anxiety	Client will maintain control and avoid behavior upsetting to others. Client will begin to verbalize feelings instead of enacting them. Client will establish a trusting relationship with a care provider. Client will manifest improved orientation to reality. Client will manifest lower levels of anxiety.	Employ suicide precautions. Monitor eating and activity patterns. Assess *general nature* of delusions. Note events preceding manifestations of delusional thinking. Note and record behaviors indicative of delusional thinking. Note manifestations of sensory misperceptions. Do not explore delusions in depth. Offer empathy but reinforce reality. Provide limits for inappropriate actions and discussions. Interpret delusions as reactions to stress and anxiety. Encourage family involvement to promote understanding and support for the client. Explain medication regimen (rationale, therapeutic effects, precautions, side effects).	

Revised ___ Discontinued ___ Continued ___ Reviewed ___

Generic Nursing Care Plan: The Client Who Exhibits Hypervigilance and Suspiciousness

Date	Assessment: Nursing Diagnosis	Planning: Goals/Outcomes	Implementation: Nursing Orders/ Interventions	Evaluation
	Altered thought processes Social isolation due to egocentricity and extreme distrust Anxiety	Client will be able to distinguish objective (external) from subjective (internal) reasons for suspiciousness. Client will manifest less hypervigilance and will show improved ability to interact with others. Client will establish a trusting relationship with one or more care providers.	Assess potential for aggressive or violent behavior. Avoid excessive friendliness or extreme aloofness. Avoid behavior such as whispering that suggests secrecy or concealment. Discourage competitive activities. Communicate clearly and simply; avoid confrontation or argument. Provide brief frequent contacts. Avoid physical contact with the client. Maintain a consistent, predictable schedule. Do not mix medication with food.	

Revised ___ Discontinued ___ Continued ___ Reviewed ___

IMPLEMENTATION Clients' anxiety will only increase if they are urged to apply more insight to a situation than they can deal with at a given time. To facilitate understanding, it is first necessary to reduce anxiety to manageable levels. After anxiety lessens, nurses can help clients make necessary connections between anxiety-producing situations, the feelings engendered by those situations, and the behaviors prompted by the underlying feelings. Anxiety that is not recognized by nurses may result in inappropriate interventions that only increase the discomfort of the clients. Knowledge of the various ways that anxiety is expressed will guide nurses in helping clients cope with their feelings,

Generic Nursing Care Plan: The Client Who Exhibits Hyperactivity

Date	Assessment: Nursing Diagnosis	Planning: Goals/Outcomes	Implementation: Nursing Orders/ Interventions	Evaluation
	Altered health maintenance	Client will maintain adequate physical health.	Set limits on intrusive or disruptive behavior.	
	Altered nutrition: less than body requirements	Client will maintain reality orientation.	Present limit setting as protective for the client.	
	Potential fluid volume deficit	Client will express recognition of the need for a protected environment.	Observe and monitor activity level.	
	Bathing, dressing, feeding, self-care deficit	Client will express understanding of need for medication, side effects, and necessary precautions.	Observe nutritional habits. Monitor intake and output. Weigh daily; note signs of dehydration and weight loss.	
	Sleep pattern disturbance		Decrease external stimuli. Negotiate and set regular bedtime.	
	Impaired home maintenance management		Offer moderate, noncompetitive physical activity. Make "finger foods" available. Encourage adequate fluid intake. Give simple, brief, clear messages. Seclude if necessary to reduce overstimulation and protect client from exhaustion. Involve the spouse in health teaching and anticipatory guidance.	

Revised ___ Discontinued ___ Continued ___ Reviewed ___

Generic Nursing Care Plan: The Client Who Exhibits Self-destructive Behavior

Date	Assessment: Nursing Diagnosis	Planning: Goals/Outcomes	Implementation: Nursing Orders/ Interventions	Evaluation
	Potential for injury	Client's health and safety will be maintained.	Assess suicide potential, present and past; assess lethality of plan.	
	Dysfunctional grieving	Client will not engage in self-destructive acts or gestures.	Initiate suicide precautions: Check every 15 minutes, place on 1:1 supervision p.r.n., seclude or restrain to ensure safety.	
	Sleep pattern disturbance	Client will engage in active grieving.	Explore underlying sadness and client's perception of loss.	
	Ineffective individual coping	Client will begin to develop alternative coping behaviors.	Encourage verbalization of feeling.	
		Client will recognize and utilize available support networks.	Help client realize that self-destructive actions only intensify feelings of frustration and depression.	
			Help client realize the danger of impulsive behavior.	
			Negotiate an agreement to seek help from specific sources of support whenever self-destructive impulses are activated.	
			Assess response of significant others to client's self-destructive behavior.	
			Observe for signs of physical injury: lacerations, burns, etc.	
			Encourage problem solving and alternative means of coping.	

Revised ___ Discontinued ___ Continued ___ Reviewed ___

find relief, and avoid deterioration. During the implementation phase, it may also be necessary to seek the advice of other health professionals or to refer clients for more specialized help. Various anxiety-associated problems and suggested nursing interventions are described in Table 5–1.

Table 5–1. Problems Associated with Anxiety and Suggested Nursing Interventions	
Identified Problems	**Nursing Interventions**
Insecurity	1. Accept the client's anxiety without being provoked into sharing it. 2. Be willing to listen. Just talking may help the client alleviate his anxiety. 3. Recognize and acknowledge the client's distress and discomfort. 4. Provide control by a matter-of-fact attitude that combines structure with empathy. 5. Assess the situation from the client's point of view; avoid evaluating stress levels from personal standards.
Confusion	1. Identify behaviors that betray the anxiety the client is experiencing. 2. Help the client identify and describe her feelings and locate the source of distress. 3. Endeavor to help the client realize what she was thinking or doing before the anxious behaviors became apparent. 4. Explore what actually happened to the client and what she expected to happen. Discuss differences between expectations and reality. 5. List the sequence of other experiences that produced anxiety. 6. List the sequence of behaviors that have brought relief before.
Agitation	1. Provide outlets for expending energy by arranging activity or diversion. Suggest motor behaviors, such as walking and pacing. 2. Administer appropriate medication when needed, as prescribed. 3. Help the client talk when he is ready, but do not force or probe. 4. Validate feelings the client has about his immediate situations.
Cognitive distortion	1. Offer feedback to correct thought distortions. 2. Relate new experiences to familiar ones to increase client's insight. 3. Help client discover relationships between feelings, thoughts, and actions. 4. Help client learn from experiences with difficult situations. Help client learn to tolerate some anxiety. Replace the concepts of self that cause anxiety with concepts of self that are realistic and functional. 5. Use anticipatory planning to prepare client for similar situation in the future.

EVALUATION A number of factors may be considered if an anxious client does not respond to nursing intervention. Perhaps a nurse's own anxiety interfered with the ability to reduce the client's anxiety. A certain amount of anxiety and emotional insecurity is present in everyone, including nurses. Anxiety can be contagious; an anxious client may heighten a nurse's anxiety. It is important for nurses to be aware of their own responses in order to remain effective in such a situation.

Timing is also important in dealing with anxious clients. The failure to recognize anxiety in a client or the failure to intervene promptly and appropriately before anxiety escalates to panic may explain why a client does not respond to nursing interventions.

The Delusional Client

Delusional individuals hold false, fixed beliefs that they maintain despite evidence to the contrary. Their delusions are attempts to deal with conflicts, problems, and stresses, and may also be used as a symbolic means of communication or as a means of escaping reality. Confusion, misinterpretation, and distortion of reality help preserve delusions.

Delusions are thought to result from the displacement of unacceptable feelings from the objects or individuals that caused them toward other, less frightening objects or individuals. They are sometimes used to increase a person's self-esteem or to minimize the power the client thinks others possess.

Two layers of expression and belief characterize a delusion: the material or content that is verbalized and the material or content that the client actually believes. A delusion may be based on actual childhood experiences. Many delusions reflect the client's cultural orientation. For example, religious delusions are less common today than they were in times when religious beliefs were more strongly held. Many delusions common today have a pseudoscientific flavor borrowed from notions of the space age. The delusion may also be an attempt to symbolically communicate ideas.

Regardless of the question of truth, a belief that has its foundation in experience and expresses elements of the personality carries a strong sense of reality for the client. Such beliefs cannot be changed without first changing the client's external experience and making reality more acceptable.

ASSESSMENT Delusional clients often have difficulty in admitting their own misperceptions, and they take pride in intellectualizing and in being considered correct. They are often adept at manipulating people and facts, and tend to think in literal terms. They often resent being dominated, yet they themselves are often dominating and provocative, patronizing toward others, and inclined to misinterpret others' speech and actions. They are sensitive to minor injustices and are often resentful and hypercritical of health care personnel. Testing to determine others' trustworthiness may also occur within the context of a delusion.

PLANNING Appropriate nursing goals for assisting the delusional client should include the following:

1. To assist the client in recognizing the distortions of reality and gaining a realistic perception of self.

2. To help the client find more satisfactory ways of relating to others.

3. To accept the reality of the client's belief in the delusional ideation but to reject the reality of the ideation itself.

4. To create an atmosphere in which the client may safely examine reality.

5. To provide opportunities for corrective experiences in emotional relationships.

IMPLEMENTATION Problems associated with delusional thinking and suggested nursing interventions are provided in Table 5–2.

EVALUATION Failure to help a client who is experiencing delusions is sometimes caused by inconsistency in approach by staff. Once a care plan is formulated and agreed upon, it is necessary for all staff members to follow it. Lack of success in dealing with a delusional client may also be due to misunderstanding of the client's behavior or to feelings of inadequacy on the part of staff members. If nurses reinforce delusional beliefs or become incorporated in the client's delusions, the delusions will strengthen and expand, and corrective measures will have to be taken.

The Demanding Client

When nurses label clients as "demanding," they may mean that the staff simply cannot give clients what they ask for. A large number of clients, inadequate staffing, and the pressures of other duties may contribute to the perception that the clients are demanding. If nurses allow their feelings, reactions, and perceptions to influence their responses to clients, then clients may indeed become demanding. Annoyance and anger toward clients frequently exaggerate demands, because the more frustrated and unfulfilled clients feel, the more demanding their behavior will become. On the

Table 5–2. Problems Associated with Delusional Thinking and Suggested Nursing Interventions

Identified Problems	Nursing Interventions
Insecurity	1. Demonstrate acceptance of the client as a worthwhile individual, without judgment. 2. Avoid demands for drastic change as long as behavior is not harmful or overtly destructive. 3. Respond to feelings indicated by the tone of the client's comments. 4. Allow expression of negative emotions without fear of punishment or rejection. 5. Contribute to security by being consistent. Let the client know what behavior is acceptable or unacceptable. 6. Make your identity and professional position clear. Describe your role to avoid becoming part of the delusional system. 7. Satisfy the client's need for control by allowing as many choices as possible among routines and activities.
Autistic communication	1. Ask the client to explain the meaning of his communication in order to understand what he is saying or experiencing. 2. Describe clearly and distinctly the reasons for hospitalization or treatment. 3. Reinforce the appropriate and nonthreatening nature of reality. 4. Avoid debate or argument of any kind. Accept, without necessarily approving, the client's right to feel as he does. 5. Avoid exploring delusional content or displaying great interest in it. 6. Set an example of reality-based thinking with clear, and consistent communication. 7. Divert focus from delusions to discussion of reality. 8. Identify themes of client's delusions (e.g., persecution, grandiosity, religiosity). 9. Do not leave openings that permit encouragement of the delusion. 10. Search for underlying needs expressed by delusional thinking.
Inclusion of the nurse in delusional thinking	1. Take no action without the client's knowledge. 2. Contact no one about the client without her permission. 3. Do not make decisions about care without including the client. 4. If client believes substances are poisoned, permit her to watch others as they ingest or serve food or medicines. 5. Avoid tasting the client's food or medicines to convince her that substances are harmless. This does not reassure, but merely takes away the client's defense mechanism and may cause her to include the nurse in the delusional pattern.

other hand, if clients develop the conviction that staff members want to help them and are interested in meeting their requests, they may become less demanding.

There may be several reasons for excessively demanding behavior. Many clients are demanding because of conflicting feelings about dependency. Some resent being dependent and react by giving orders in a bold, urgent way. Others seem to enjoy being dependent and regress to immature, cajoling behavior. Yet others act insecure and helpless and dread being abandoned. Whatever the outward behavior, it may mask feelings of anxiety, helplessness, inadequacy, hostility, fear of being deprived, or a need for attention. Demanding individuals wish to control others and direct attention to themselves.

ASSESSMENT Demanding clients usually make requests in an authoritative way, believing they have the right to have their demands met. These clients ask many questions, want a great deal of staff time, and seek constant attention. Others may be just as demanding but choose to adopt a whining, "poor me" attitude. Still others act helpless and insecure.

PLANNING In dealing with the excessively demanding client, appropriate nursing goals should include the following:

1. To convey an attitude of concern for the client's needs and to meet realistic demands and requests.

2. To help the client derive satisfaction from relationships with others who are not staff members.

3. To assist the client in developing feelings of security and self-esteem that come from within, rather than from outside sources.

4. To encourage the client to look at interaction as a two-way process of giving and taking rather than as a one-way process of taking.

5. To help the client use more acceptable methods of getting needs met than demanding or whining.

6. To help the client understand and deal with underlying fears of being neglected or abandoned.

IMPLEMENTATION Reassurance and acceptance help demanding clients maintain contact with others and remain in touch with reality. Types of excessively demanding behaviors and suggested interventions are discussed in Table 5–3.

EVALUATION The usual reason for continued demanding behavior is an inconsistent approach in implementing the care plan. Staff members are often caught in a vicious cycle of overreacting to the client's demands with impatience and anger.

Table 5–3. Problems Associated with Demanding Behavior and Suggested Nursing Interventions

Identified Problems	Nursing Interventions
Insecurity	1. Recognize your own reactions of anger at the client's incessant demands so that you can control it. 2. Show consideration for and sincere interest in trying to meet requests in a reasonable way. 3. Provide consistency when responding to requests. 4. Allow the client to verbalize irritation at necessary restrictions. 5. Avoid punishing or withdrawing from the client. 6. Reassure the client that essential needs are and will continue to be met.
Authoritative, hostile behavior	1. Clarify expectations for the client. 2. Determine what needs underlie the demanding, hostile behavior. 3. Set limits and keep within these limits without rejecting the client. 4. Let the client know what will be offered in terms of time and attention. Be sure to live up to this part of the contract. 5. Spend time with the client when she is not demanding, to reinforce appropriate behavior.
Regressive, placating behavior	1. Create an accepting climate in which it is safe to express needs openly. 2. Accept the client's right to think and feel as he does. 3. Provide a consistent relationship in order to build trust. 4. Identify any of the client's interests and talents, and reinforce abilities and skills to reduce regression. 5. Devise ways to redirect the client's energy; reinforce and reward what is good, constructive, and useful in client's behavior.

Such reactions only increase the client's insecurity and demanding behavior. The nurse may not recognize her own feelings of anger and may fail to realize that the client's behavior is a protective mechanism for covering true feelings. When nurses react by physically and psychologically withdrawing from clients or by becoming punitive, retaliatory, or rejecting, they only aggravate the problem behavior.

The Hallucinating Client
Hallucinations are false or distorted perceptions of objects or events. They often carry a compelling sense of reality. Hallucinations tend to originate during periods of extreme emotional stress in which the individual is unable to cope successfully with the situation. The flight from reality represented

by hallucinations is usually a way of expressing some phase of a troublesome problem in the inner life of the individual.

ASSESSMENT Clients with hallucinations are often introspective individuals who have not had satisfactory interpersonal relationships. These clients tend to withdraw from others and to discourage interpersonal approaches and communication. Their hallucinations often substitute for human relationships. Hallucinating clients appear unaware of what is going on around them and have a low frustration tolerance to changes in their routine. Many assume a listening, watchful attitude and appear apprehensive without cause. They may follow "commands" or "voices," talk to themselves, or talk out of context while a conversation is going on around them. If a hallucination is threatening, the client may be terrified of the experience.

PLANNING Appropriate nursing goals in caring for clients experiencing hallucinations should include the following:

1. To interrupt the pattern of hallucination by helping the client interact with other people and establish satisfying relationships.

2. To involve the client in activities that reduce time for introspection.

3. To find alternative methods of working through or releasing anxiety so that clients can relinquish hallucinations.

IMPLEMENTATION Correction of sensory distortion occurs not through arguing or confrontation but through concrete experience. A sincere interest in and honest response to clients often results in the disappearance of the hallucination. Problems associated with hallucinations and suggested interventions are provided in Table 5–4.

EVALUATION Failure to help clients who are hallucinating may be due to the staff's lack of knowledge about how to interrupt the hallucinations and replace them with more socially acceptable behaviors. Sometimes staff members are intimidated by clients who are hallucinating. At times, staff may behave inappropriately around clients, not realizing that the hallucinating client remains acutely aware of her surroundings. It is not therapeutic to react with annoyance to the client's incomprehensible behavior or to instruct her to stop hallucinating. Exhibiting surprise at her fantastic perceptions or imposing unnecessary security measures retards the establishment of a trusting relationship. The staff's

Table 5–4. Problems Associated with Hallucinations and Suggested Nursing Interventions

Identified Problems	Nursing Interventions
Insecurity	1. Provide a structured environment with a routine that has few changes. 2. Explain any changes shortly before they occur, so the client knows what to expect. 3. Provide supervision to prevent the client from injuring himself or others. 4. Reassure client whose hallucinations are fearful or threatening.
Break with reality	1. Initiate interactions with the client for short periods of time, increasing time as the client's toleration increases. 2. Respond to any comments based in reality. 3. Avoid nonverbal approaches such as shaking your head or motioning with your hands; they may add to the hallucinations. 4. Ask client to let you know when hallucinations intrude into conversations and to tell you his reactions. 5. Validate the nature of the situation before making the assumption that the client is hallucinating. 6. Avoid conveying in any way that the hallucination is real. Let the client know that the "voices" are real for her but not for other people. Do not reinforce hallucinations by deep exploration. Be clear and specific in communication. 7. Help the client identify impersonal pronouns. If possible, use proper names in conversation.
Social withdrawal	1. Explore ways the client can relieve his anxiety in a more acceptable manner. 2. Help the client recognize his strengths and accomplishments. Reinforce healthy aspects of his personality. 3. Gradually increase the client's interaction with others, widening the circle of people he trusts. 4. Help the client develop relationships with others so that interactions cause less fear. 5. Recognize that even though clients may appear remote and detached, consistent accepting approaches are probably having some beneficial influence.

anxiety may cause them to ignore the hallucinating client in an effort to increase their own comfort.

The Angry Client

Anger is a response to something that is perceived as a frustration or a threat, such as an illness, a change in body image, a sense of inadequacy, a fear of loss, or an actual loss. It is an emotion that can range from mild irritation to uncontrollable rage. Every person feels anger on occasion. It can be healthy in some situations and pathological in others. A person will often become less angry when helped to identify the threat and when given alternative ways of dealing with the threat.

Anger is a derivative of anxiety, which in turn is usually the result of a feeling of powerlessness that may be rational or irrational. When anxiety is converted to anger, the underlying powerlessness and the irrationality are hidden. But suppression and repression do not eliminate anger; suppression forbids the expression of anger, while repression hides it from awareness.

ASSESSMENT Angry clients are inclined to harm themselves or others. The feelings surrounding anger include hate, rage, and aggression. Angry behaviors may take the form of gossiping, swearing, scapegoating, arguing, demanding, attacking, threatening, or abusing (physically or verbally). Less obvious expressions of anger include joking at the expense of others, deceptive sweetness, sarcasm or derision, suspiciousness, and lack of cooperation.

PLANNING Appropriate nursing goals in caring for angry clients should include the following:

1. To protect the client from harming himself or others until he can resume this responsibility himself.

2. To help the client express feelings of anger verbally, specifically, and in a safe, acceptable manner.

3. To facilitate the appropriate exploration and ventilation of anger without fear of judgment or retaliation.

4. To guide the client to recognize problems created by angry behavior.

5. To help the client cope with angry feelings in a way that will eliminate trauma to herself and others.

6. To facilitate the client's understanding of the cause of her anger.

IMPLEMENTATION Anger generally provokes anger in others. The first step in helping a client deal with anger is to be aware of one's own reactions to the client's anger so that they do not prevent therapeutic interactions. Working with angry clients requires a great deal of stamina and self-control. One should remember that anger protects the client from emotional states that are too powerful to face. Suggested nursing interventions for the angry client are listed in Table 5–5.

EVALUATION If the nursing intervention does not succeed with the angry client, it may be that the

Table 5–5. Problems Associated with Anger and Suggested Nursing Interventions	
Identified Problems	**Nursing Interventions**
Insecurity	1. Recognize the client's feelings of anger. 2. Refrain from joking, laughing at, or teasing a client who is angry. 3. Use a matter-of-fact response when the client displays unacceptable, angry behavior. 4. Accept the client's anger without making value judgments. 5. Let the client know it is all right to feel angry. 6. Accept anger as legitimate but help client monitor the way she expresses anger. 7. Avoid close personal contact with the angry client except when protection of the client or others is needed.
Hostile behavior	1. Help the client become aware of the angry feelings causing his behavior. 2. Identify early clues or conditions that triggered feelings of anger. 3. Confront the client's unacceptable behavior and discuss alternative ways of reacting. 4. Find out what happened to cause the anger and what the client thinks about it. Reconstruct the events as the client experienced them. 5. Avoid coercing the client if she is not ready to face or deal with the problem of anger. 6. Withdraw attention when the client is acting in an unacceptable manner. 7. Do not intervene unless the anger is reaching dangerous proportions. 8. Encourage the client to assume responsibility for his own behavior and to exercise self-control.
Inappropriate outlets for anger	1. Help the client find constructive ways of expending physical energy and releasing anger, such as motor activities. 2. Help the client find healthy, competitive outlets for anger.

staff members are not aware of the factors likely to cause anger in him. If staff members tried to ignore the anger in the hope that it would fade away, the client learned nothing about handling his anger. Similarly, if the affective component of a statement was ignored and only the content heeded, there may have been no opportunity to explore the causes of an angry remark. If the staff became defensive or angry in response to the client's expression of anger, the client may only have become more angry. Avoiding the angry client or probing too deeply or prematurely into causes of his anger may have made him confused or so antagonistic that a therapeutic relationship may have been impossible to establish or maintain.

The Hypochondriacal Client

Hypochondriasis is the persistent conviction that one is or is likely to become ill when illness is neither present nor likely. The hypochondriac client is not a malingerer; her suffering and symptoms are very real. A physical disability, real or imagined, can serve as a method of escape from life's pressures or as an excuse for personal failure. Being physically ill provides a method of controlling others and monopolizing their attention.

The psychodynamics of hypochondriasis are extremely complex. Often a hypochondriacal client has been raised in an environment that focused on physical complaints and illness. Oversolicitous parents may have reinforced concerns about health. Perhaps a prolonged childhood illness caused excessive preoccupation with the workings of the body.

ASSESSMENT Hypochondriacal clients exhibit a marked anxiety about health, an overconcern regarding body processes, and an exaggeration of any organic problems. Symptoms may relate to any body system, may range from mild to severe, and may be chronic or intermittent.

PLANNING Appropriate nursing goals in caring for the hypochondriacal client should include the following:

1. To assist the client in tolerating average discomfort without becoming an emotional cripple.

2. To assist the client in finding other means of satisfaction and in developing healthy relationships with others.

3. To decrease the client's need for somatic symptoms as a means of controlling others.

IMPLEMENTATION Reassurance is of only temporary value in the treatment of hypochondriacal clients because they often do not wish to be relieved of their symptoms. Legitimate medical issues should be addressed, but treatment should focus primarily on understanding the underlying conflict and assisting the client to find better ways of dealing with conflicts and meeting needs. Hypochondriacal clients who have some legitimate concerns can learn to live with their weaknesses and deficiencies and to mobilize available strengths. Suggested nursing interventions for the care of the hypochondriacal clients are provided in Table 5–6.

EVALUATION If a client has used somatic symptoms as a way of relating to others for a long time, it may be extremely difficult to induce change. Frustration and an unaccepting attitude on the part of the staff

Table 5–6. Problems Associated with Hypochondriasis and Suggested Nursing Interventions	
Identified Problems	Nursing Interventions
Insecurity	1. Accept the client as a person who is suffering and in need of help. 2. Show interest rather than impatience even though the symptoms are repeated frequently. 3. Refer all physical complaints to the attention of appropriate personnel. Some symptoms may indicate actual somatic disorders. 4. Recognize the negative feelings aroused in caregivers and others when dealing with hypochondriacal clients. 5. Reduce the client's interactions with those who reinforce his symptoms.
Preoccupation with physical symptoms	1. Listen attentively, but do not make symptoms the focus of the interaction. 2. Indicate awareness of physical complaints but guide conversation to other topics. 3. Help the client recognize how he uses symptoms to avoid dealing with life's problems. 4. Discourage the client from remaining unoccupied or inactive for long periods of time. 5. Plan activities in which the client can feel successful to enhance his self-esteem. 6. Help the client develop new interests and skills to reduce his preoccupation with somatic complaints.

members may have been transmitted to the client and aggravated his behavior. Implying that the client should be able to control her symptoms may have made a therapeutic relationship difficult to establish. If symptoms were ignored or belittled, the hypochondriacal client may have developed more severe complaints in order to retain the attention of staff members and others.

The Manipulative Client

Manipulation is an interpersonal process that occurs consciously and unconsciously in virtually all interpersonal behavior. If manipulation is used constructively, the individual's interpersonal capabilities and strengths are applied to promoting successful relations with others. Destructive manipulation, by contrast, is the exploitation of other people or the extraction of favors or behaviors from others for egotistical purposes that create difficulties in relationships and inhibit personal growth. Destructive manipulation entails a series of interpersonal operations: one individual's needs are not met by another; therefore, anxiety levels rise. The needs of the other person are then disregarded, and manipulative adaptive maneuvers are tried. If these maneuvers are successful, the person's initial needs are met, anxiety decreases, and the pattern of manipulation become entrenched.

Manipulation is usually learned in childhood. A common tactic is to induce sympathy or guilt in another person in order to make him unable to refuse a request. Often the client does not trust others to fulfill her needs if she approaches them directly.

ASSESSMENT The manipulative client may bargain with, threaten, demand, flatter, or intimidate others. He is adept at finding other's weaknesses and using them to his own advantage. He may act as a helper, tale carrier, gift giver, or flatterer. Setting up one staff member or client against another through comparisons is common. The manipulative client can be charming and subservient when it serves his purpose. He may use tears and feign helplessness while making multiple demands and pressing unpleasant issues. The manipulator is attracted to staff members who unknowingly foster his behavior. Frequently he exploits caregivers' generosity and desire to be liked. He is indifferent to distinctions between truth and falsehood, feels little guilt, and has little capacity for insight.

PLANNING Appropriate nursing goals for the manipulative client should include the following:

1. To help the client become aware of her behavior in relation to others and find more appropriate ways to obtain what she needs.
2. To foster her ability to trust others to meet her needs without having to resort to manipulation and exploitation.
3. To mutually agree on consistent expectations and limits.
4. To teach the client the advantages of cooperation, compromise, and collaboration over manipulation.

IMPLEMENTATION If the manipulative client can learn to trust nurses in a therapeutic relationship and to employ direct methods of having his needs met, he may be able to generalize this experience to others and learn to interact in a more constructive manner. Setting reasonable limits allows a manipulative client to experiment with new behaviors, achieve self-control, and replace manipulative tactics with more constructive interactions. The purpose of limit setting is not to control clients but to give them consistent expectations and guidance toward self-control. Suggested nursing interven-

tions for care of the manipulative client are presented in Table 5–7.

EVALUATION The most common reason for failure to improve the behavior of manipulative clients is an inconsistent approach by staff members. These clients are adept at discovering those staff members who will be likely to respond to their efforts at manipulation. Often these clients are able to take advantage of staff members' own anxiety and need for approval. Hostility toward these clients is easily aroused, especially when staff members discover they have been manipulated. This hostility may cause staff to avoid manipulative clients or to respond in a punitive manner. Although this may protect staff members from further manipulation, it is not therapeutic for clients and may intensify their manipulative tendencies.

The Regressed Client

Regression is a defense mechanism that involves reversion to cognitive and behavioral patterns that were appropriate and brought pleasure at an earlier stage of development. Some regression is a normal and necessary part of life. Most people enjoy an occasional nap, shouting at football games, or going to costume parties. Society also endorses

Table 5–7. Problems Associated with Manipulative Behavior and Suggested Nursing Interventions

Identified Problems	Nursing Interventions
Insecurity	1. Provide consistent limits and reasonable expectations. 2. Allow reasonable freedom within the limits. 3. Communicate expectations and limits to all staff to prevent the manipulation of any one member. 4. Recognize the feelings, positive and negative, that the client arouses in the nurse and other caregivers.
Attempt to control others	1. Identify the client's attempts to manipulate staff and others. 2. Recognize the client's behavioral patterns and prevent her from using these patterns in an exploitive way. 3. Inform the client that you understand what she is trying to accomplish. 4. Help the client analyze what she is doing and why she needs to do it. 5. Refuse promises, gifts, and compliments from the client in return for favors or concessions. 6. Provide verbal reinforcement when the client functions within the established limits. 7. Encourage open and direct forms of communication.

regression in other circumstances, particularly during illness when persons are usually expected to relinquish responsibilities. However, regression may become a fixed pattern that interferes with an individual's potential for growth.

By regressing, a person may retreat from responsibility for interpersonal conflicts, settle for lowered aspirations, and seek immediate gratification of his desires. Often regression is related to unmet dependency needs. Changes in relationships can result in regressive behaviors that lead to chronic dependency.

ASSESSMENT Regressed clients appear helpless and may be unable to take care of basic needs such as washing, feeding, or eliminating. They often lack confidence in making decisions and show clinging behavior. Severely regressed clients are preoccupied with themselves, have low aspirations, rebel against authority, and search for nurturing persons. Often they exhibit impaired reality testing and altered human relationships. Infantile behavior such as bedwetting, thumbsucking, and temper tantrums may be seen in extreme cases. In even more severe cases, the client may become autistic or mute and may even assume a fetal position.

PLANNING Appropriate nursing goals in caring for the regressed client should include the following:

1. To avoid fostering dependency and reinforcing childlike attitudes.
2. To expect the client to accept a partnership in the treatment.
3. To help the client tolerate unavoidable stress and anxiety without regressing further.
4. To help the client find gratification in the environment and in his accomplishments instead of dwelling on failures and inadequacies.

IMPLEMENTATION Problems associated with regression and suggested nursing interventions are listed in Table 5–8.

EVALUATION Failure to achieve stated goals with regressed clients is frequently due to staff actions that foster dependency rather than encourage the acceptance of responsibilities. Hospitalization is a situation that requires some regressive behavior in any circumstances, but tolerance of consistently regressed behavior only promotes the possibility of the behavior becoming a continual disruption. Family attitudes may contribute to clients' regression by isolating the clients or by not permitting them to resume their previous roles after hospitalization.

Table 5–8. Problems Associated with Regressed Behavior and Suggested Nursing Interventions

Identified Problems	Nursing Interventions
Insecurity	1. Be direct, clear, and simple in all verbal communications. 2. Avoid punishment following periods of regression. 3. Explore the meaning of the regression if the client can tolerate it.
Dependency on others	1. Avoid taking over any tasks the client is able to perform herself. 2. Convey a partnership attitude by soliciting the client's contributions to planning and decision making. 3. Accept the client's present level; do not assign tasks that he is unable to accomplish. 4. Treat the client as an adult; do not use nicknames that detract from his dignity. 5. Avoid establishing a custodial environment. Permit maximum possible freedom. 6. Do not pretend to understand what the client is talking about unless you really do. 7. Indicate that the regressed behavior is unacceptable but only temporary. 8. Throughout hospitalization, discuss plans for eventual discharge. 9. Do not reinforce or encourage regressed behavior. 10. Avoid acting like a disapproving parent.
Preoccupation with self	1. Involve clients in motor activities and verbal interactions. 2. Encourage group activities. 3. Emphasize talking and acting on a reality-oriented level. 4. Acknowledge clients' efforts when they assume greater responsibility.
Regression due to a psychotic episode	1. Tolerate regression during acute stages. 2. Use minimal pressure to limit regression during acute psychosis or periods of extreme distress. 3. Emphasize contact, trust, and reality orientation, even when clients seem to be unresponsive. 4. Convey the expectation that regression is only temporary and that the client's coping ability will improve. 5. Provide for rest, food and fluid intake, exercise, and elimination.

The Ritualistic Client

Compulsive behavior is an irresistible impulse to perform a procedure repeatedly and in exactly the same way. Compulsive rituals are usually related to superstitious concepts and magical thinking. Fears and tensions are often discharged through ritualistic behavior, but the relief is only temporary. Ritualism also helps the person avoid making decisions yet maintain control over himself and others. The total body may be involved in the ritualistic behaviors, which may be physically exhausting or damaging to the individual.

ASSESSMENT The ritualistic client's behavior patterns may involve repeating an act in exactly the same manner each time or performing various seemingly meaningless acts. Examples of common ritualistic behaviors are continual handwashing, hoarding of unneeded items, and bizarre mannerisms. Ordinary precautions, such as checking to see whether the lights are turned off or whether windows are locked, may become ritualistic if the client must continually repeat the process.

PLANNING Ritualistic clients seldom ask for help because they have found their own methods of relieving anxiety and because they have a strong need for self-control. Appropriate nursing measures for the ritualistic client should include the following:

1. To intervene early in the anxiety-building process and try to reduce the need for ritualism.
2. To help the client gain some insight into why the ritual is necessary.
3. To find alternative methods for dealing with anxiety.
4. To allow the client sufficient time to complete the anxiety-reducing ritual.
5. To encourage social interactions immediately after the ritual has been completed, when anxiety is at its lowest level.

IMPLEMENTATION Trying to prevent the ritualistic act may cause panic and terror in the clients. Although it is sometimes possible to substitute a less harmful ritual, it is not advisable to prohibit the ritualistic behavior entirely. Suggested nursing interventions for dealing with ritualistic clients are provided in Table 5–9.

EVALUATION The ritualistic client's failure to respond to nursing interventions may be the result of the staff members' failure to recognize the underlying cause of the ritualistic behavior. Critical reactions from nurses and others may have caused increased feelings of guilt and reinforced the need for the ritual. The hospital environment itself often seems confusing and inconsistent to ritualistic clients, who value order and uniformity. It requires a concerted effort on the part of the staff to provide a safe haven for these anxiety-prone clients so that they may improve.

Table 5–9. Problems Associated with Ritualistic Behavior and Suggested Nursing Interventions

Identified Problems	Nursing Interventions
Insecurity	1. Accept ritualism without scolding or ridicule. 2. Set consistent limits to prevent actual harm to the client or others. 3. Allow episodes of ritualism when the client finds this the only way to reduce anxiety. 4. Allow the client as much autonomy as possible.
Need for control	1. Establish routines for daily living and avoid anxiety-producing changes. 2. Provide activities that can lead to a sense of accomplishment and self-worth. 3. Provide assignments that the client can complete successfully. 4. Assign a living area that is as private as possible. 5. Encourage verbalization of feelings. 6. Substitute less harmful rituals, such as using an antiseptic hand lotion for excessive handwashing. 7. Allow the client sufficient time to complete rituals. 8. Arrange activities just after ritual is completed and anxiety is relatively low. 9. Observe client for signs of mounting anxiety. 10. Observe the client's physical needs. Self-neglect is possible because of preoccupation with ritualism.

The Suspicious Client

Trust and confidence in others are acquired throughout life as a result of experiences that do not result in harm. Suspicious clients have not learned to trust themselves, to trust others, nor to test reality. They have not experienced feelings of adequacy and approval and thus tend to resort to the defense mechanism of projection. Projection is the attribution of one's own feelings, attitudes, or desires to others. Suspicious clients who feel inadequate and unworthy themselves project their feelings of inadequacy and unworthiness onto others.

ASSESSMENT Suspicious clients may appear aloof, mistrustful, irritable, quarrelsome, and extremely sensitive, with a tendency toward impulsive, destructive behavior. These clients are frequently hospitalized against their wishes and therefore see their environment as hostile and threatening. They blame others for their own discomfort and set unrealistic goals for themselves and others. Frequently, suspicious clients attempt to set one person against another. They often search for evidence of error to prove their suspicions are correct.

PLANNING Appropriate nursing goals for the suspicious client should include the following:

1. To assist the suspicious client in feeling secure and developing trust.
2. To divert excess energy into satisfying activities.
3. To provide an atmosphere that fosters feelings of acceptance and belonging and provides opportunities for success.

IMPLEMENTATION Demonstrations of genuine concern and interest may build trust and confidence in suspicious clients. Nurses working with suspicious clients must also realize the necessity of providing outlets for anger. Suspicious clients often have a limited capacity for coping with anger, and unexpressed or indirectly expressed anger inhibits their ability to relate to others. Behind the angry facade of the suspicious person is a lonely individual who is terrorized by the thought of being exposed as inadequate. Verbalization of anger should be permitted without adverse consequences, but the client should also be encouraged to direct the anger at specific incidents and should be discouraged from expressing anger that is generalized to every situation and person that is encountered. Suggested nursing interventions for the suspicious client are provided in Table 5–10.

EVALUATION Staff members may be ineffectual with suspicious clients because they fear working with a hostile person and are unwilling to become targets of the hostility. Often nurses will avoid a suspicious person because they are uncomfortable with the client's mistrust. On the other hand, nurses may expect too much too soon from a suspicious client and attempt to establish a reciprocal trust prematurely. It is important to differentiate between the client who is merely suspicious and the client who is actively delusional because the treatment approach for each is different. The merely suspicious client may slowly develop trust based on reality. The delusional client avoids the need to trust by creating a new reality that exists only for himself.

The Withdrawn Client

An individual's relationships are influenced by the self-concept and ability to cope with life situations. Repeated failures in relationships decrease self-esteem and cause a person to avoid others because of fear of failure. Withdrawn clients deny themselves the opportunity to share experiences and develop relationships. To replace the threatening world of reality, they may create a fantasy world that is free of stress, or they may remain in touch with reality and observe interactions around them carefully, even though they choose not to participate.

ASSESSMENT Clients who become withdrawn may be lonely, isolated, frightened, suspicious, and helpless. These clients often daydream, seem indifferent to others, sit alone, and stare into space. They seem to have a diminished capacity to tolerate the feelings that accompany interaction, and they cannot or will not invest in emotional attachments. They show a marked indifference to pursuing normal interests, a blunting of emotions, and a resistance to outside influences.

Table 5–10. Problems Associated with Suspicious Behavior and Suggested Nursing Interventions

Identified Problems	Nursing Interventions
Insecurity	1. Keep contact with diverse staff at minimum; assign the same staff members if possible. 2. Watch for signs that the client is becoming more angry or vigilant. 3. Accept rebuffs and abusive language as symptoms and not as personal attacks. 4. Be scrupulously honest. Keep promises and maintain a consistent approach. 5. Be aware of negative feelings the client's behavior arouses in staff members. 6. Be aware of the client's distrust of others and dissatisfaction with herself. 7. Allow verbalization of feelings without becoming defensive, angry, or punitive.
Distrustful behavior	1. Do not whisper or act secretively in the presence of the client. 2. Limit physical contact to that which is absolutely necessary. 3. Taste food only if requested to do so by the client. 4. Do not mix medication with food. 5. Allow the client to set extent of closeness and distance. 6. Start with solitary or one-on-one activities, then gradually advance to group activities. 7. Inform the client about schedules and what can be expected. 8. Avoid laughing or talking with others when the client can observe but not hear what is being said.
Sense of inadequacy	1. Assign meaningful tasks to encourage feelings of adequacy. 2. Avoid competitive activities. 3. Provide appropriate outlets for anger and aggression. Verbalization and motor activities may be helpful. 4. Make opportunities for demonstrating skills. 5. Confer recognition for work well done. 6. Give the client the right to complain. Deal with the issues in a calm, rational manner.

PLANNING Appropriate nursing goals for the withdrawn client should include the following:

1. Help the client modify her perception of her relationships to others.
2. Reduce the client's autistic and regressive tendencies.
3. Provide relationships that will foster the willingness to interact with others.
4. Help clients feel safe in a one-to-one relationship.

IMPLEMENTATION Problems associated with withdrawal and suggested nursing interventions are listed in Table 5–11.

EVALUATION Lack of success with withdrawn clients may be due to the staff's misunderstanding of their bizarre and seemingly illogical behavior. Frequently nurses become impatient because of the

large investment of time and energy required by these clients and the slow progress made. Withdrawn clients tend to arouse anxiety in the staff, so the staff in turn may label them as "wanting to be alone" to justify paying less attention to them. With self-awareness and practice, nurses can learn to become comfortable even with clients who remain silent or who continually rebuff efforts to interact or communicate. Another common problem is the tendency of staff members to become accustomed to the behavior of withdrawn clients and to not see the behavior as a problem. Since these clients make few demands on the staff, it is important not to overlook their needs in the course of caring for more troublesome clients.

SUMMARY

An overview of the nursing process and its application to several problem behaviors have been presented in this chapter. The systematic use of assessment, planning, implementation, and evaluation was emphasized as the process was individualized to meet client and family needs.

One of the most important elements in working with clients with problem behaviors is providing a therapeutic atmosphere in which clients can find the security they need to begin to solve their problems and change behaviors. There is no substitute for genuineness in relationships with clients, and it is imperative that nurses become aware of the feelings that certain clients can generate in them. Lack of success with clients can often be attributed to a lack of acceptance or understanding of their difficulties on the part of the nurse.

Table 5–11. Problems Associated with Withdrawal and Suggested Nursing Interventions

Identified Problems	Nursing Interventions
Insecurity	1. Provide a choice of activities that are neither monotonous nor excessively stimulating. 2. Avoid making demands that cannot be met by the client. 3. Avoid mutual withdrawal. 4. Observe for signs of physical consequences of apathy and inactivity. 5. Protect withdrawn client from being exploited by aggressive clients. 6. Avoid placing the client in situations where failure is inevitable.
Interpersonal and environmental withdrawal	1. Keep the client as active as possible in the hospital routine. 2. Recognize that the client is isolating himself as a protective maneuver. 3. Recognize the patten of actions through which the client withdraws. 4. Seek out the client regularly without being intrusive. 5. Stay with the client, sitting in silence if necessary. 6. Initiate nonthreatening conversations in which the client can give brief responses. 7. Use simple language and nonthreatening words. 8. Focus on everyday experiences. Comment on routine events. 9. Relieve client of decision making until he is able to make decisions. 10. Make consistent attempts to elicit a response but without demanding a response. 11. Indicate to the client that he may be less withdrawn at some later time and that you will continue to be available.

Review Questions

1. Define *anxiety* and describe its implications for the therapeutic relationship between nurse and client.
2. Explain the importance of remaining outside the client's delusional system, and describe ways that this can be accomplished.
3. Discuss the importance of self-assessment for the psychiatric nurse and its role in the nursing process.
4. Describe the most important differences between caring for a client who has delusions and caring for a client who is suspicious.
5. Discuss healthy and pathological means of manipulation and ways that nurses can recognize

(text continues on page 117)

C L I N I C A L   E X A M P L E

AN ANXIOUS CLIENT

Julie Morgan is a 44-year-old married mother of four children, who range in age from 14 to 24 years of age. Their family life has been one of continual stress and disagreements. When the children were young and Julie was home with them, she was able to maintain authority over them, but as the oldest child approached adolescence, Julie went to work and was less able to exert any influence on them. As the children grew older, Julie experienced periods of discouragement and frustration when her word was no longer accepted without question and she began to feel guilty about not remaining home with the children. She was unable to tolerate some of their behaviors, such as refusing to help around the house and smoking marijuana, which led to arguments with her husband, who seemed undisturbed by the children's behavior. When the children failed to become more obedient, Julie withdrew from the family and blamed herself for not being able to influence them.

Although Julie is devoted to her husband and dependent on him for comfort and security, her relationship with him is less than happy. He is sexually demanding yet mechanical in his approach to lovemaking, and she often feels used and unappreciated by him because of his perceived coldness.

Julie has worked as an accountant for a large company for the past ten years, and despite her delayed entry into the business world, she has had several promotions and is in charge of the marketing department. In this capacity, it is frequently necessary for her to make formal presentations before large groups of people. Although she performs very well during these lectures, she approaches them with severe apprehension and is constantly afraid of being embarrassed by forgetting her speech or being unable to answer questions from the group.

Julie has suffered from acute attacks of anxiety for several years. In some instances, such as during a presentation, she is able to identify the cause of the anxiety, but at other times she cannot find a cause for her panic. She says these occasions cause her heart to beat "so fast I can feel it," and make her feel dizzy, afraid of suffocating, and unable to control or stop the panicky feeling. These episodes frequently occur shortly after she goes to bed at night when she would like to reach out for her husband but is reluctant to do so because her gesture would indicate to him that she wants sexual intercourse. Occasionally she has felt an attack coming on at work, but she has been able to control the feelings long enough to leave the area and go for a walk to pull herself together. The panic attacks leave her exhausted and barely able to function the next day, although she does force herself back to work. Her exhaustion leads to a variety of minor physical complaints, which she tries to explain to her husband, who responds only with impatience.

Julie has been in and out of outpatient treatment for several years but has had little success in curbing her anxiety. On the latest occasion, she presented for treatment because she was about to undergo surgery for gall bladder removal and felt she would be unable to face hospitalization because of fear of "dying on the table" and didn't think she could stand to spend the nights away from her husband.

ASSESSMENT

In the first interview, Julie presented as a stylishly dressed woman, who looked younger than her age and sat rigidly in the chair, making very little eye contact with the nurse. She spoke rapidly in a monotone and frequently asked the nurse if she was "crazy" or if other people had similar problems. She was fully oriented to time, place, and person, and the nurse estimated that she was of above average intelligence. Based on the history and clinical picture, the following diagnoses were made:

Nursing Diagnoses

Anxiety
(related to attacks ranging from mild to panic)

Ineffective individual coping
(related to the inability to maintain the influence she deserved in the family)

Fear
(related to job performance and feelings of abandonment)

Disturbance in self-esteem
(related to dependence on husband and lack of confidence in her job)

Knowledge deficit
(related to surgical procedure)

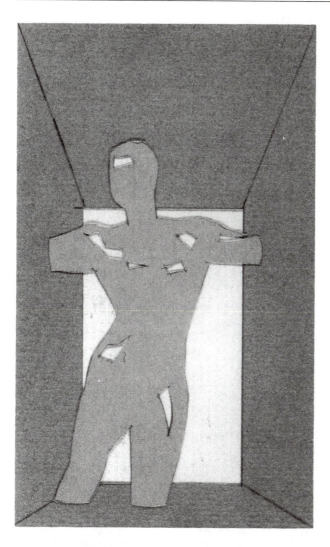

Multiaxial Psychiatric Diagnoses

Axis I   300.01 Panic disorder
Axis II   301.60 Dependent personality
Axis III   Cholecystitis
Axis IV Impending surgery, marital discord, job
           dissatisfaction
           Severity: 3 moderate
Axis V   Current GAF: 51
           Highest GAF past year: 60

PLANNING

Because of the complexity of Julie's problems, the nurse used a number of approaches in planning her care. It was important to engage Julie in a one-to-one relationship in which she would be able to freely express her fears and explore the causes of her anxiety. The focus of the interaction would deal with her insecurity and fear of dying. Interest and concern had to be demonstrated so that Julie would feel that her problems were recognized as very real and worth

listening to. An unjudgmental, interested attitude was important to let her know that the nurse cared, was willing to work with her and would not reject her because her complaints were repetitious. Values that Julie held regarding her role as wife and mother needed to be explored and compared to ways in which she had been able to function. Julie needed to develop ways of nurturing and caring for herself in periods of stress. Support through surgery was indicated and the hospital experience could be used as a period of learning and development. The skills that she already possessed needed reinforcement to increase her self-esteem. Her achievements as wife, mother, and career woman needed recognition to persuade her to take pleasure in these accomplishments. Relaxation techniques were indicated to help her cope when she felt panic approaching, and couple therapy was planned to help her husband realize her need to be close to him without sexual contact.

IMPLEMENTATION

The first task of the outpatient nurse was to establish a contract with Julie for individual sessions of which the initial focus was on preparation for surgery. Because there were only four weeks until the operation was scheduled, it was necessary to provide some external structure for Julie. A decision was made, which Julie approved, for the nurse to explain Julie's near-panic state to her surgeon because she was unable to talk with the surgeon herself. Plans were also made for a preoperative visit to the hospital and a "walking tour" through the procedure. During the period prior to hospitalization, Julie was given the opportunity to transfer some of her dependency needs to the nurse. Subsequent sessions focused on helping Julie to develop a sense of autonomy and self-confidence. The nurse began relaxation training sessions and referred Julie to a consulting psychologist for training in self-hypnosis to begin after the surgery.

As Julie became comfortable in her therapeutic relationship with the nurse and was able to talk about her fears freely, she acknowledged that she felt safe in the sessions. Although an effective nurse-client relationship had been built, it became apparent that Julie's husband should also be involved in the plan.

Before Julie's hospitalization, a session that included her husband was arranged. In this session only Julie's fears of separation from her husband and home were discussed. Her feelings were interpreted to her husband not as deficiencies on his part but as her strong commitment to her home and family. During this session, her husband indicated some appreciation and recognition of Julie's strengths and feelings. In this context, the nurse was able to help the husband realize that there were many areas in which Julie depended on him and needed his support, such as during the impending hospitalization. With the help of the nurse and the increased participation of the husband, Julie underwent surgery with only minor feelings of anxiety. Having seen the couple together, the nurse realized that future sessions should involve the husband so that he would have a better understanding of what Julie's nonverbal behavior was actually communicating. Julie's husband seemed to be a somewhat insensitive but not malevolent individual. Postoperative sessions had the general goal of helping the couple to understand the unstated, behaviorally expressed needs each had for the other. Plans were made for a regular structured exercise schedule that Julie could undertake whenever she felt her anxiety level begin to rise.

EVALUATION

With the help of the nurse, Julie underwent surgery without an anxiety attack. As he became involved in counseling, Julie's husband became aware of Julie's dependency needs. He acknowledged her contributions to the well-being of the family, and Julie's self-esteem began to flourish. Her husband's agreement to attend future sessions was an indication that the prehospital meetings were of value to him as well as to Julie.

Nursing diagnoses	Goal	Nursing actions	Outcome criteria	Outcome evaluation
Anxiety	Client will decrease anxiety to mild level, eliminate panic attacks.	Engage in one-to-one relationship to discuss insecurity and fear of dying. Teach relaxation techniques. Refer for self-hypnosis training. Teach new skills, such as exercise for coping with anxiety.	Client will be able to express fears and explore causes of anxiety. She will learn new ways of managing anxiety attacks.	Client became comfortable with the nurse, was able to talk about her fears and feel safe in the relationship. She was amenable to plans for learning a structured exercise program and relaxation.
Fear	Client will reduce fear of failure in job performance and family role.	Convey interest and concern with nonjudgmental, caring attitude. Explore values about role of wife, mother, career woman, and determine incongruence between expectations and performance.	Client will realize that her problems are recognized as being real and she is worth listening to.	Repetitive complaints decreased during sessions. Client was able to recognize fears and expectations. Job performance increased with fewer episodes of panic.
Ineffective individual coping	Client will increase comfort level in family role.	Engage client and husband in couple sessions. Interpret her feelings as a strong commitment to family, not as deficiencies on his part. Assist both in identifying needs and expressing the meaning of their behaviors.	Client's husband will realize her need to be close to him and to help her decrease her dependency on him. Both will have an understanding of each other's unstated behaviorally communicated expressed needs.	Client's husband indicated some recognition of her strengths, weaknesses. He was able to see other areas where she needed support (hospitalization). Future sessions should involve him to increase understanding of the nonverbal behaviors.
Knowledge deficit	Client will get information *re* surgery to relieve anxiety.	Arrange a preoperative visit to hospital and a walking tour through the procedure.	Client's new knowledge of surgical procedure will promote self-confidence through anticipatory guidance.	Walking tour enabled client to transfer some dependency needs to nurse. She was still unable to talk to the physician. The nurse must intervene.
Self-esteem disturbance	With assistance, client will develop ways of nurturing and caring for herself during stress.	Support through surgery, provide meaningful presence, use hospital experience as period of learning and development.	Client will undergo surgery with only minor feelings of anxiety. Ability to handle anxiety will be transferred to other areas of her life.	Client underwent surgery without an anxiety attack. Her husband was able to realize dependency needs and acknowledge her contributions to the family. She became comfortable with her need for his approval.

manipulation and avoid being manipulated by clients.

Suggested Annotated Readings

Doenges, M. E., M. F. Jefferies, and M. F. Moorhouse. *Nursing Care Plans: Nursing Diagnosis in Planning Patient Care.* Philadelphia: F. A. Davis Co., 1984.

This book gives directions for the development and use of individualized nursing care and is a reference for clinical practice. The authors explain why interventions are important and give related pathophysiology when applicable. The importance of care plans for the practitioner as well as the student is emphasized in all areas of nursing practice. The use of the nursing process is reviewed to formulate plans and the nurse's role in the delivery of care.

Dunlap, L. C. *Mental Health Concepts Applied to Nursing.* New York: John Wiley & Sons, 1978.

Mental health concepts are applied in both traditional and nontraditional settings. The themes of the book encompass the reality of working with the emotional aspect of the individual and the existential awareness of one's own humanness. The uniqueness of each individual is stressed and mental health concepts are applied to the hospital setting, the community, and to speciality areas.

Longo, D. C., and R. A. Williams. *Clinical Practice in Psychosocial Nursing.* Norwalk, Connecticut: Appleton-Century-Crofts, 1986.

The assessment process is presented so that the reader can see more clearly the relationship between theory and practice. Physical health and psychological variables are integrated for a holistic approach to patient care. All ages are included so that generalists can benefit from specialist experience and gain an understanding of patients in all stages of development.

Paterson, Josephine, and Loretta Zderad. *Humanistic Nursing.* New York: John Wiley & Sons, 1976.

Two nursing theorists postulate that nursing is "a lived experience" and the mandate of nursing is to share. Humanistic nursing is "a being and a doing," which is experienced and developed. The focus of the philosophy is on the meaning of human caring. In the process of caring and sharing, nurses help themselves and others to become more human.

References

Carlson, J., C. Craft., and A. McGuire. *Nursing Diagnosis.* Philadelphia: W. B. Saunders, 1982.

Kozier, B., and G. Erb. *Fundamentals of Nursing: Concepts and Procedures.* Menlo Park, California: Addison-Wesley, 1983.

Neal, M. C., P. F. Cohen, P. G. Cooper, and J. Reighley. *Nursing Care Planning Guides for Psychiatric and Mental Health Care.* Boston: Jones and Bartlett Publishers, 1980.

Sorensen, K., and J. Luckmann. *Basic Nursing: A Psychological Approach.* Philadelphia: W. B. Saunders, 1979.

6

Assessment and Testing in Mental Health Nursing

Learning Objectives

After reading this chapter, the student should be able to:

1. Describe the nature of holistic interaction and recognize its relevance to psychiatric mental health nursing.

2. Discuss adaptation as a general behavioral concept and the implications of adaptation as a nursing theory.

3. Recognize the usefulness of assessment guidelines that adopt a holistic perspective.

4. Identify major tests and measures developed to facilitate data collection and comprehensive assessment of clients' needs.

5. Define and differentiate defense mechanisms and evaluate the effectiveness of various defense mechanisms as adaptive or maladaptive behavioral responses.

Overview

In this chapter holistic interaction is presented as a unifying framework for psychiatric mental health nursing. Attention to holism requires nurses to reach beyond the mind-body paradigm and consider all the ramifications of human interaction: physical, psychological, social, political, cognitive, and spiritual. The concept of adaptation may be understood in a broad sense as a characteristic of every living organism, beginning at the cellular level. Like other living organisms, human beings engage in operations to preserve their internal balance or equilibrium. The equilibrium of human beings may be threatened by excessive stimuli and by deficient stimuli. Each of these conditions demands adaptational responses from the affected persons.

The chapter differentiates functional and dysfunctional behavior patterns and emphasizes the holistic nature of human interaction.

A number of well-known tests and measures have been developed by members of other disciplines to facilitate clinical data collection for purposes of assessment. Since many of these procedures are widely used and provide useful information, they are described briefly in this chapter.

HOLISTIC CARING

Concern for the biopsychosocial needs of clients is readily accepted by nurses committed to meeting the total needs of clients. Holistic caring is not a responsibility imposed on nurses but a natural response to client needs. Moreover, it is a response made by no other profession. Nursing is a practice profession. The practice professions differ from purely scientific endeavors, which are preoccupied with abstractions, explanations, and causation. Like other practice professions, nursing relies on theory-based application, but the scope of nursing is broader than that of other practice professions. Medicine, for example, concentrates on treating disease and illness; education focuses on teaching and learning. Nursing, however, seeks to maintain, restore, and strengthen the wholesome functioning of clients to the fullest extent possible. Lynaugh and Fagin (1988) wrote that historically, when home and family care are insufficient, the task of caring is transferred from family to nursing. The range of nursing is educational, assistive, empathic, sustaining, and managerial. When our early leaders conceptualized nursing, they included all actions needed to ensure a safe environment, share knowledge, and care for the whole person. What is noteworthy about this conceptualization is its sweeping scope. It is not specific, looks to no single theory, and excludes no aspect of life. A hierarchy of needs must be established in assessing clients and planning care, but for nurses committed to holistic caring, no factor may be discarded as irrelevant. Even in the decades when illness and treatment formed the organizing structure for health care delivery, nurses organized their care around people and families rather than diseases. Interventionist, treatment-oriented models of care are often questioned by health planners interested in promoting holism. At the same time, nurses live and work in a climate where technical proficiency and interpersonal skills share importance. Nurses are committed to humanistic and holistic care, but they often practice in situations where laboratory (hard) data must be integrated with client-oriented (soft) information. In this chapter, as in nursing practice, the objective is to strike a proper balance.

HOLISTIC INTERACTION

People do not exist as solitary beings in the world but as acting, reacting, and interacting organisms that must respond to changing conditions at all levels of existence: physical, psychological, and social. From this holistic viewpoint, the individual and the environment are a single but changing configuration shaped by the individual's efforts to bring order and meaning into life experiences.

According to Maslow (1968), individual response to internal and external events requires not merely the acquisition of new habits but a shifting of the whole organism as it continues to interact with its inner and outer worlds. Thus, a holistic approach to biopsychosocial development focuses on the individual's ability to *adapt* in his or her ongoing interactions.

Interactions may be functional or dysfunctional. *Functional interaction* has been defined as the "constant, positive alterations which individuals make in their pattern of interaction to stimuli within the environment. These alterations perpetuate the survival of the individual and increase the individual's utility, performance, and pleasure within the chosen environment" (Goosen and Bush 1979, p. 66). In contrast, *dysfunctional interaction* consists of responses to environmental stimuli that result in conditions of disruption, disorganization, and displeasure. Functional interaction is achieved when responses to internal and external conditions preserve the integrity and well-being of the individual, family, or community. Dysfunctional interaction results from responses that threaten or destroy this integrity and well-being.

Functional and dysfunctional interaction patterns can be found at every level of human existence. A physiological example is the fight-or-flight response. When people face conditions that require high expenditures of energy, adrenocorticotropic hormone (ACTH) is released from the hypothalamus. The sympathetic nervous system is then activated, causing large amounts of epinephrine and norepinephrine to be produced. Increased amounts of these hormones help prepare the individual for fight or flight. Mobilization for fight-or-flight behavior was functional for primitive humans, but this form of physiological response is less adaptive and less functional in the modern world, where more selective responses are needed. For example, the employee who reacts by venting anger or by leaving whenever things go wrong on the job is not likely to be highly regarded by her employer or her coworkers.

Reciprocal interaction is the capacity of organisms to adjust to external change by altering internal conditions and, conversely, to cause external change by means of internal modifications. Changes within a system may also be reciprocal in that such changes inevitably have an effect on other systems coexisting in the environment.

Human beings engage in holistic interactions that are reciprocal and extremely complex. On a physiological level, the human fetus is accustomed to the uterine environment, but with its first breath it interacts in response to extrauterine conditions. Psychologically, reciprocal interaction can be seen in adjustment to separation or loss, in which grieving is followed by a willingness to establish new relationships. An example of reciprocal sociocultural interaction is the immigrant who begins to master English as a second language. The immigrant's respone to conditions within the dominant culture is to master a new language; her way of experiencing and acting upon the culture will alter as her mastery of the English language grows.

For most individuals, internal conditions may be altered in response to existing, remembered, or anticipated environmental changes. A ballplayer warming up before a big game is displaying reciprocal interaction designed to meet the demands being made, or about to be made, upon him. If the athlete proves unequal to the demands of the situation, this failure will affect the conditions surrounding his next game. And the memory of a satisfactory or unsatisfactory experience will affect future interactions in positive or negative ways.

FUNCTIONAL AND DYSFUNCTIONAL ADAPTATION

Because human existence is dynamic, not static, people must accept the inevitability of change in themselves, in their environment, and between themselves and their environment. This means that *adaptation* takes place continuously, despite great variability in the adaptive capacities of individuals. Adaptive ability depends on a number of factors, including personality traits, life experiences, and learned behaviors. Some basic characteristics of adaptation are listed in the accompanying box.

As a rule, successful adaptation depends on congruence between the adaptive capacities of individuals and the nature of the demands made on them (Mechanic 1976). For example, an elderly person who must give up an independent lifestyle for supervised residential placement may react adaptively or maladaptively. An angry or bitter reaction is likely to evoke resentment in others and prevent an easy adjustment to the new situation, whereas a reaction of acceptance will probably elicit positive gestures from staff and fellow residents, thereby promoting adjustment.

Some individuals are capable of displaying adaptive behaviors as long as the demand is not prolonged. For example, a divorced father or mother may be willing to take care of the children

---

CHARACTERISTICS OF ADAPTATION

Adaptation is an essential process in the life cycle, involving conscious and unconscious responses.

The same conditions will elicit different adaptive responses from different individuals.

The same conditions will elicit different adaptive responses from the same individual at different times.

The same conditions will be perceived and interpreted differently by different individuals.

The same conditions will be perceived and interpreted differently by the same individual at different times.

---

on occasional weekends but may be unwilling to accept sustained parental responsibility. The presence or absence of rewards for certain behaviors may determine whether adaptive or maladaptive behaviors occur. A child whose efforts to succeed are acknowledged only by greater parental demands may become discouraged and fearful of ultimate failure and may stop trying. When demands exceed the capacities of the individual, or when adaptive behaviors are unrewarded, maladaptive responses usually follow. In other words, every individual, family, and group has a certain point at which they become overwhelmed by the conditions in which they must try to function. Whenever this breaking point is reached, responsive behavior is likely to be maladaptive.

Adaptation to Life Changes

Every life change creates a new demand for adaptation, and each adaptational demand exacts a price that alters efficiency, consumes energy, and jeopardizes equilibrium to some extent. Ability to adapt to life change varies, but there is general agreement that frequent changes within a brief period of time predispose people to physical and psychological distress. It does not matter whether the change is positive, such as marriage or career advancement, or negative, such as divorce or unemployment. The crucial factor seems to be that any life change for which new responses are needed places people at risk.

Holmes and Rahe (1967) devised a way to assess the effects of life change by developing what they called the Social Readjustment Rating Scale. They assigned quantitative values, using "life change units," to various life changes, ranging from 100 units for the most stressful event, death of a spouse, to 19 units for such lesser events as vacations and minor legal infractions (see Table 6–1). The assumption made by Holmes and Rahe was that the higher a person's life change score, the greater the likelihood that physical or psychological illness would follow within a year or two. Among subjects whose life change index exceeded 300 units in a year, 86 percent suffered adverse health effects in the following two years. Among subjects who scored from 150 to 300, 48 percent suffered adverse health effects in the same time frame.

The Social Readjustment Rating Scale is a useful assessment tool because it ranks specific life changes according to the amount of adaptation needed to cope and it permits accumulated life changes to be identified and quantified. Because some life changes can be anticipated and regulated in advance, it is possible to help clients control the rate of change in their lives so that their adaptive capacities are not depleted. Helping clients monitor their rate of change is a form of primary prevention that helps clients avoid adverse reactions to a number of drastic changes occurring in rapid succession.

Table 6–1. Social Readjustment Rating Scale

Rank	Life Event	Mean Value
1	Death of a spouse	100
2	Divorce	73
3	Marital separation	65
4	Jail term	63
5	Death of close family member	63
6	Personal injury or illness	53
7	Marriage	50
8	Fired from job	47
9	Marital reconciliation	45
10	Retirement	45
11	Change in health of family member	44
12	Pregnancy	40
13	Sexual problems	39
14	Addition of new family member	39
15	Business readjustments	39
16	Change in financial status	38
17	Death of a close friend	37
18	Change to a new line of work	36
19	Increased dissension with spouse	35
20	Mortgage disproportionate to income	31
21	Foreclosure of loan or mortgage	30
22	Change in responsibilities at work	29
23	Son or daughter leaving home	29
24	Trouble with in-laws	29
25	Outstanding personal achievement	28
26	Spouse begins or quits job	26
27	Beginning or ending school	26
28	Change in living conditions	25
29	Change in personal habits	24
30	Trouble with boss at work	23
31	Change in residence	20
32	Change of schools	20
33	Change in working hours or conditions	20
34	Change in recreation habits	19
35	Change in church activities	19
36	Change in social activities	19
37	Mortgage or loan over $10,000	19
38	Change in sleeping habits or eating habits	19
39	Change in number of family visits	19
40	Vacation	19
41	Christmas	19
42	Minor legal infractions	19

SOURCE: Holmes and Rahe (1967).

PATTERNS OF BEHAVIOR

Human response to the demands of everyday life ranges from adaptive to maladaptive behaviors. Adaptive behaviors are reality-based, task-oriented, problem-solving actions that enable people to cope and interact in a functional manner. Among the functional coping behaviors are reasoning, concentration, learning, advance preparation, and accurate perception of meaning. Many motor activities, such as walking and running, are also functional in that they reduce anxiety, discharge anger, or release tension without hurting the self or others. Emotional expression in the form of tears, laughter, or verbalization, can also help individuals deal with difficult situations. Postponing immediate gratification, working toward a goal, and establishing rewarding social relationships are other methods of coping successfully.

The essential characteristic of adaptive coping behaviors is that they are not restricted to one or two rigid patterns. Adaptive coping involves the use of many coping methods chosen for their usefulness in a particular situation. Many persons when under stress resort to habitual behaviors without trying to modify their responses according to circumstances. In the realm of interpersonal relationships, Horney (1937, 1950) described three dysfunctional patterns of social interaction: (1) moving toward other people (dependency), (2) moving away from other people (detachment), and (3) moving against other people (domination). Moving away from others is a form of flight behavior; moving against others is a form of fight behavior. Moving against others can be seen in persons who show hostility toward others, either directly or indirectly. The pattern of moving toward others is not a true aspect of flight-fight behavior, but is a variation that provides a third psychosocial option. All three response patterns are disruptive when used exclusively or in exaggerated forms, because a fragile sense of interpersonal safety is obtained at the expense of healthy personality development.

Dependency Pattern The individual who has a dependency pattern adopts a submissive, compliant attitude in order to obtain acceptance and approval. Since this openly dependent individual engages in an endless search for nurture and emotional support from others, the dependency needs are never fully met and must constantly be replenished. Therefore, there is movement in the direction of social interaction, since that is the source of psychological nourishment.

Domination Pattern Like the individual who is openly dependent, the individual who shows a domination pattern may have an underlying wish to be accepted and protected. However, the prospect of being dependent on others is so frightening that the individual denies or represses such ideas, concealing them by adopting authoritarian, controlling, demanding, or angry behaviors.

Detachment Pattern The individual who has a detachment pattern seeks neither to dominate nor to be accepted, for these behaviors require some closeness. It is interpersonal closeness that threatens the detached person. Detachment is achieved by rationalization and intellectualization, and through social and psychological distancing from other people.

Behavior Variations and Disruptions

Defense mechanisms are sometimes adaptive and sometimes maladaptive in dealing with life situations. When used adaptively, defense mechanisms effectively regulate instinctual drives and impulses that are not acceptable to the individual, the family, or society (Freud 1948). However, many defense mechanisms are dysfunctional because they prevent rather than promote adequate coping. Vaillant (1977) developed four levels of defense mechanisms, ranging from psychotic, to immature, to neurotic, and finally to mature mechanisms. The classifications are subjective and somewhat arbitrary, but they indicate that most of us use a variety of mental processes, mature and immature, to deal with life experiences. Even psychotic thinking is within the reach of most of us in certain circumstances.

LEVELS OF DEFENSE MECHANISMS

Level 1 *Psychotic mechanisms*, such as distortion, delusions, and extreme denial, are common in children up to five years of age and in the dreams and fantasies of adults. If the mechanisms intrude beyond these limits, they are inappropriate and dysfunctional.

Level 2 *Immature mechanisms*, such as fantasy, projection, passive-aggressive behaviors, and hypochondria, are evident in children, in adolescents, and among adults experiencing depression, physical illness, or substance abuse disorders.

Level 3 *Neurotic mechanisms*, such as intellectualization, repression, reaction formation, displacement, and dissociation, are responses that often can be modified through counseling, introspection, and analysis of behavior.

Level 4 *Mature mechanisms*, such as altruism, humor, suppression, and sublimation, expedite adaptation during the life cycle.

SYSTEMS THEORY APPROACHES

Holism implies interrelatedness among a host of variables operating at different levels. *Systems theory* is based on the idea of interrelatedness among components that are separated from the environment and from one another by boundaries. Thus, systems theory shares with holism the idea of interrelatedness but negates the notion of holism by introducing boundaries and substituting the less expansive concept of interdependent interaction.

Basic Concepts of Systems Theory

Adaptation to changes in the environment requires individuals, families, and groups to function as *systems* that can exchange material, information, and energy across system boundaries. There is usually a higher rate of transaction and interaction *within* the boundaries of a system than *across* the boundaries. Because the components and elements within a system are interrelated and interdependent, alteration in one part of the system produces alteration in other parts. Regardless of the extent of internal alterations, the dual purpose of any system is to maintain a steady, balanced state and to continue functioning. When the system can no longer maintain this dual purpose, the result is malfunction of the whole system or some of its parts.

Open systems have boundaries that are easily penetrated, while *closed systems* permit only limited amounts of exchange across boundaries. This means that closed systems can operate with considerable predictability because their rate of transaction and change is relatively slow. The operations of open systems may be less predictable, since they permit the entry of large amounts of energy and information. Closed systems are less tolerant of change than open systems, are less accessible to input from outside, and are more susceptible to rising internal tension because of difficulty in discharging output across their boundaries.

One example of a relatively closed system is the traditional family that tries to preserve its values by isolating itself from mainstream society. This isolation is usually imposed by older members and may be resented by younger members who are eager to adapt to the dominant culture. The result may be conflict within the family system and tension among members that is dysfunctional and generates maladaptive behaviors. Conversely, a family system that is too open often lacks stability and is overly responsive to changes in the surrounding environment.

In order to discuss systems theory in a meaningful fashion, it is important to define some of the terms commonly used. Systems possess patterns of *structure* and *function*; specific terms used to describe these patterns and related phenomena are defined in the accompanying box.

Systems Variations and Disruptions

In all living systems, operations and interactions constantly occur in order to maintain a state of balance or equilibrium. An example of this is the behavior of a person who perspires on a hot day, feels thirsty, and promptly replaces lost fluids so that thirst signals subside. Virtually all living systems maintain equilibrium by means of negative feedback that causes the system to correct dysfunction. However, any adjustment or adaptation is achieved at the cost of lost energy or reduced efficiency, at least for a time. When demands for adaptation are excessive or prolonged, the resources of the organism are apt to be depleted or exhausted. With the energy of the organism impaired, future adaptation is more difficult, and the stability of the organism is threatened. Karl Menninger wrote that equilibrium is the basic element of physical and psychological well-being (1963). He described some variations and disruptions used by persons unable to engage in more adaptive behavior. The following variations and disruptions are listed in order of their decreasing effectiveness.

- Nervousness: tension, slight impairment of customary resilient behavior
- Dysfunctional behaviors of hysterical, obsessional, or anxiety-laden nature
- Violent, aggressive actions, characterized by repetitiveness and loss of control
- Denial or distortion of reality, loss of contact with reality, disorientation, severe disorganization
- Malignant disorganization, intolerable anxiety, depression, psychotic thinking, and self-destructive behavior

The social climate in which most people work and live contains many contradictory expectations for themselves and others. Contemporary society pays lip service to altruism and social commitment, for example, but often rewards aggressive, competitive behavior. Individual freedom and choices are highly valued, but repetition and monotony flourish in many educational and occupational settings (McLean 1980).

PRINCIPLES OF SYSTEMS THEORY

- Systems theory differentiates functional and dysfunctional patterns, thereby facilitating identification of individual and family interactions for which corrective feedback is indicated.
- Systems theory interprets human behavior as adjustment between social demands and personal needs.

Developmental changes and situational stressors require ongoing adjustment within a system or between several systems.

- Systems theory includes external factors (input) and internal responses (output) that affect social, psychological, and biological expressions of human behavior.

SOURCE: Anderson and Carter (1978).

SYSTEMS TERMINOLOGY

System: An arrangement of units or components in which relationships exist among the components or units. The state of each component is affected by the state of other components.

Structure: The organization or arrangement of various components within a system. Even in a relatively stable system, structure can be described only at a given moment.

Function: The enactment of certain behaviors that permit the operations of the system to continue.

Process: An exchange of energy, information, or transactions within a system, between systems, or between a system and the surrounding environment.

Level: A hierarchy of systems which exist in the universe, each more complex than any lower level systems.

■ Cells are the lowest level of living systems and are composed of atoms, molecules, and molecular clusters.

■ Organs are composed of collective cells organized to form tissues.

■ Organisms are composed of collective organs whose structure and function are organized to form an example of a species.

■ Groups are composed of collective organisms that for human beings are organized to form families, tribes, teams, communities, nations, etc.

Species: Any living system related genetically at cellular and organism levels so that interbreeding is possible. Human beings represent one species.

Type: Any group of living systems having in common a number of similar, shared characteristics. Blood type is an example of such grouping.

Subsystem: A component or unit within a system that carries out a particular function. In families mothers and fathers make up the parental subsystem; children make up the sibling subsystem.

Suprasystem: A larger system to which smaller systems relate or of which they form a part. A community is a suprasystem to which families relate.

Boundaries: The limits or periphery of a system that holds the components together, protects them from environmental stressors by excluding some input from outside system boundaries and by permitting entry of other input. Boundaries also permit output from the system to enter the environment; thus boundaries are more or less permeable.

External Variables: Conditions, factors, or influences outside the boundaries of a system.

Internal Variables: Structural patterns and functional processes inside the boundaries of a system.

Feedback: A process that includes both input and output. Output discharged by a system is returned by external sources in the form of input to the system.

Negative Feedback: Feedback that produces change in order to correct error.

Positive Feedback: Feedback that maintains the status quo by validating or reinforcing current operations of a system.

Deficient Stimulation

Under ordinary conditions most individuals are able to adjust the rate and flow of stimuli reaching them by adjusting the environment and altering the social field. Adjusting the rate and flow of stimuli is perhaps more difficult to accomplish when available stimuli are deficient or entirely absent. Sensory deprivation in the form of stimuli deficits has been studied extensively (Miller 1980) and it has been found that for individuals to function adequately a certain amount of stimulation must be present in the environment. Miller found that reactions to sensory deprivation were often predictable and tended to follow a sequential pattern.

Phase 1: Subjects are preoccupied with their own thoughts and ideas.

Phase 2: Subjects become drowsy and tend to fall asleep.

Phase 3: Subjects cannot think clearly or direct their thoughts when awake.

Phase 4: Subjects become restless, irritable, hostile.

Phase 5: Subjects fantasize and display child-like, emotional behaviors.

Phase 6: Subjects experience visual, auditory, or kinesthetic hallucinations.

Phase 7: Subjects experience feelings of depersonalization and nonbeing, of merging with the environment or with others.

Excessive Stimulation

Excessive stimulation, sometimes called information overload, can also produce maladaptive responses. When individuals are bombarded with large amounts of sensory stimuli, they have difficulty screening or separating irrelevant material from that which is worthy of attention. People who are subjected to stimuli overload use processes such as filtering out and ignoring some stimuli, selectively concentrating on other stimuli, and searching for alternative behaviors that require less expenditure of time and energy. Some individuals experiencing stimuli overload simply use flight tactics in which all incoming stimuli are ignored or unanswered. Others may resort to fight tactics that cause them to react aggressively. In general, a range of behaviors is employed by people enduring excessive stimulation. Many individuals try to respond appropriately, but if demands on them are prolonged, they may respond less adaptively as follows (Miller 1980).

- Errors in responsive behaviors and performances
- Incoherence in speech: lapses, slips of the tongue, forgetfulness
- Poverty of speech patterns: omissions, retardation, repetitiveness
- Social and interpersonal withdrawal: silence, apathy, catatonic reactions
- Reduced attention span, narrowed attention range

Intensive care units are places where deficient interpersonal stimulation may cause clients to retreat from reality into a delusional or depersonalized world. The disrupted thinking that intensive care clients experience is aggravated by physiological problems; thus physiological measures must be instituted promptly. Physiological measures can be greatly enhanced by nursing measures that orient clients to their surroundings and give them a sense of interpersonal safety. The client in an intensive care unit "knows that something bad has happened to him. He finds himself in unfamiliar surroundings at the mercy of strangers and hemmed in by

machines with disturbing noises and blinking lights. To make matters worse, hospital rules often keep his family away, and he may feel abandoned" (Ramsey 1986, p. 44).

To counteract the feelings of isolation and abandonment, nurses need to introduce and reintroduce themselves by name, and to tell clients just what they are doing. Touching can be a convincing way of expressing solicitude, as can speaking slowly and calmly. Adequate lighting in an intensive care unit helps enlarge a client's visual field, and makes menacing shadows disappear. In constantly orienting a client to the reality of the intensive care unit, it is futile to try to reason with his irrational feelings. At the same time, careful explanation and reassurance through interpersonal communication reduce a client's confusion and disorganization.

Altering conditions of sensory deprivation by introducing interpersonal contact does not produce immediate relief. Return to reality-based thinking may require a period of several days. Sensory deprivation is a frightening experience and adds to the problem of providing holistic care. Therefore, primary prevention measures should be undertaken to avoid the consequences. For nurses the necessity of offering frequent interpersonal contact to persons being treated in intensive care units or secluded in solitary units cannot be overstated. In psychiatric facilities there is sometimes a need to protect clients from excessive stimulation, but even in these instances a degree of stimulation is necessary, if they are to think clearly and react appropriately. There are individual differences in the amount of stimulation that is optimal, but there is consensus that deficient stimulation impairs the adaptive functioning of the human organism.

CLINICAL TESTING AND ASSESSMENT

Nursing assessment is concerned with obtaining all available data pertaining to the client. By collecting as much information as possible, the nurse is better able to collaborate with the client and the health team. Many clients cannot explain themselves, and their behaviors, although meaningful to the clients, may be puzzling to the nurse. Although there is no substitute for attentiveness and careful observation, a number of testing and assessment methods have been designed to supplement the observations of nurses and other professionals in an effort to better understand client behaviors.

The terms *assessment*, *examination*, and *testing* are sometimes used interchangeably, but they are not synonymous. *Testing* is a rather limited activity that is usually carried out by a technician, whereas *assessment* requires the skills of a professional who relates to the client in a special way. A technician may perform blood tests or electrocardiograms, but only a professional can derive meaning from the data and safely use it. *Examination* is a broad term applied to testing or assessment, depending on the methods employed and the results obtained (Kaplan and Sadock 1980). Although nurses are more concerned with assessing than with testing and examining, as professionals they should understand the relevance of information obtained from tests and examinations. It is therefore highly appropriate to describe the implications of several widely used testing and examining procedures. Here we shall focus on three main types of measures: intelligence testing, mental status assessment, and personality assessment.

Intelligence Testing

Intelligence is defined as the ability to solve new problems through reasoning and cognitive processes (Matarazzo 1980). In the hands of competent professionals, measures of intelligence yield valuable information. However, when intelligence scores are considered in isolation or are used to label people, they have destructive potential. With this warning in mind, health care professionals will find that measures of intelligence may be helpful adjuncts to comprehensive assessment.

Intelligence tests are *standardized* by administering them to large representative groups of people. Those who achieve the median score on the test are assigned an IQ of 100 (see Figure 6–1). Because their test scores exceeds that of 50 percent of other people, they are said to rank at the 50th percentile of the general population. The higher the percentile rank, the higher the individual stands in the group. Thus, a person at the 90th percentile surpasses 90 percent of the group and is

surpassed by 10 percent. Percentile rankings on IQ tests provide an indication of how the test taker performed in comparison to other test takers and, unlike IQ scores, do not stigmatize the individual.

Reliability and validity are important concepts in testing of any kind. A test is *reliable* when repeated administration under similar conditions yields consistent results; a test is *valid* when the test measures what it is intended to measure. Intelligence scores indicate only what a person may be capable of achieving, and many persons do not perform up to their intellectual capacity. Persons of limited intelligence cannot achieve beyond their capacity, but their progress may be influenced by learning activities geared to their abilities.

Tests that measure intelligence are more reliable when administered individually, but for economic reasons they are often given to groups of subjects. The most commonly used individual tests are the Weschler Adult Intelligence Scales and the Weschler Intelligence Scales for Children. Individual testing allows the examiner to monitor the attitudes and behaviors of the subjects as they are tested. Most group tests are paper-and-pencil measures that reflect the reading skills of the subjects. Such tests rely on choices and short answers, making speed another intruding factor. In situations where subjects are emotionally unstable or unmotivated, group testing is not recommended. For subjects who are under stress, whatever the cause, individual testing, even when abbreviated, is always more valid and more reliable than group testing.

Critics of intelligence testing claim that there are many different kinds of intelligence, and that available tests measure language and mathematic abilities, while ignoring others. Gardner (1988) identified a number of abilities that have received scant attention from testers. A list of these more elusive abilities follows.

Figure 6–1. *Normal curve for IQ test scores.*

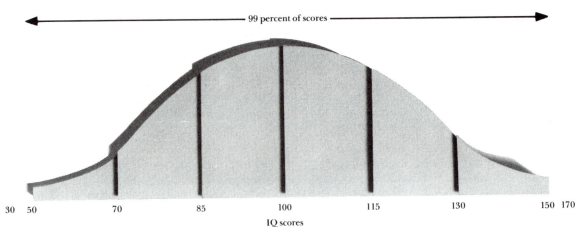

Spatial Intelligence The ability to form a spatial image of size and distance, and operate according to that image

Musical Intelligence The ability to recall, reproduce, and identify tones through sound and sight

Kinesthetic Intelligence The ability to utilize the musculo-skeletal system with strength, vigor, and deftness

Interpersonal Intelligence The ability to understand others and to work cooperatively with them

Intrapersonal Intelligence The ability to form an accurate self-image and operate realistically according to that image

There is no inherent danger in measuring intelligence, but there is danger in believing that what is measured is the whole picture of individual accomplishment or potential (Ogbu 1988). White (1988) listed a number of warnings on the subject of intelligence testing.

- IQ scores are of limited value in predicting occupational success.

- IQ scores are of limited value in measuring nonacademic intellectual skills.

- IQ scores do not measure innate (genetic) intelligence, actual or potential.

- IQ scores and scoring methods penalize nonconventional answers, and thus reflect a bias against minority groups.

- IQ scores restrict rather than broaden our understanding of intelligence and mental capacity.

Mental Status Assessment

The mental status examination is an assessment tool used to obtain information with or without the client's active participation and cooperation. Because active client participation is not mandatory, nurses can readily make an informal mental status assessment of every client with whom they come in contact. A more formal mental status examination with active client participation is desirable at the beginning of a relationship with a client or whenever changes in the client's mental status are suspected. In many respects, mental status assessment is impressionistic rather than definitive. Even so, such assessment is important enough to be made a routine part of nursing practice.

There are many variations in the form of the mental status examination, but its purpose is uniform: (1) to note significant features in the appearance, manner, and behavior of the client, (2) to for-mulate impressions regarding problematic areas, and (3) to develop hypotheses concerning the client's strengths and weaknesses that will assist in setting realistic mutual goals. The reason for recording mental status data is to give a precise description of the client's emotional and intellectual functioning at a specific point in time.

ASSESSMENT GUIDELINES Most forms of the mental status examination contain categories that provide organizational guidelines (MacKinnon 1980). A typical mental status examination is likely to follow the format provided in the accompanying box. A narrative style is generally used in reporting mental status information, although some facilities or health care professionals may prefer a comparable checklist.

Appearance and General Behavior The mental status examination begins with a detailed description of the client's appearance and general behavior according to the categories listed in the box. In providing such descriptions, it is important to select words that are exact and that do not convey value judgments. For example, the phrase "careless grooming" should be used only if it is followed by a precise description of the client's apparel and personal hygiene to support this evaluation. If general behavior is described as "withdrawn" or "hostile," examples of such behaviors should be provided. Motor activities are important, especially manifestations of restlessness, tremors, tics, or ataxia. Again, these characteristics should be described and not just labeled.

Affect and Mood *Mood* is the inner emotional state of the client; *affect* is the outward expression of the internal mood. A client's mood can be assessed by the content of verbal communication, by voice tone, by facial expression, by posture, and by gestures. Affect is considered appropriate only if it is congruent with the subject matter being discussed. Thus, a client speaking of loss or deprivation in a laughing or jocular fashion would be described as showing inappropriate affect. Affect that is narrow or constricted in range may be described as *flat* or *blunted*. Affect that changes from moment to moment is usually termed *labile*.

When possible, affect and mood should be reported in the client's own words. If a client is not verbally responsive, the nurse should note signs and indications of subjective emotional reactions. Tearfulness, sweating, blushing, and rapid respirations are signs of emotional distress that deserve mention.

is a subjective, internal experience, the perceptions of clients are difficult to comprehend fully. Verbal exploration and observation of behavior are two ways of investigating what the client perceives. Behavior, both verbal and nonverbal, is the client's outward response to what he perceives and is shaped by his perception of events (Jess 1988).

Distortions of perception include illusions, hallucinations, and delusions. *Illusions* are misperceptions attached to external sensory stimuli in the environment. *Hallucinations* are sensory misperceptions that occur without external stimuli. *Delusions* are false, entrenched beliefs that do not respond to reason or reassurance. Popular perceptual distortions are described in the box below.

Cognitive Functions   A client who is oriented as to time, place, and person is functioning on at least minimal levels of awareness. Disorientation as to time, place, and person can result from functional or organic problems, social isolation, or sensory deprivation. Whatever the cause, disorientation is a significant factor in assessing the mental status of the client.

Other cognitive functions to assess include memory, concentration, judgment, and insight. The quality of recent memory can be ascertained simply by asking about events that occurred the day before, such as what the client had for dinner. A general estimate of concentration and recall ability may be made by asking questions that require a decision, such as how to dress on a wintry day. Even without asking direct questions, the nurse can collect information about the client's judgment merely by observing the safety and suitability of the client's behavior in ordinary situations. Insight is presumed to be present to some extent when the client is aware of not functioning well and is able to

Thought Processes   Information about the client's thought processes can be obtained by asking questions or by allowing the client to talk at will. Ideas, vocabulary, and subject matter make up the content of the client's thought. Logic and clarity determine the client's coherence, regardless of the content (Cohen 1981). Dissociated thinking is characterized by fragmentation and a lack of logical connections.

Perceptions   Perception refers to the client's awareness of events by means of the senses: tactile, olfactory, auditory, visual, and gustatory. Since perception acknowledge this lack. Greater insight is evident when the client is aware of not functioning well, can recognize some reasons for it, and begins moving toward altering maladaptive patterns (Freedman, Sadock, and Kaplan 1973).

To test clients' ability to engage in abstract thinking, it is customary to ask them to compare different objects, such as a pencil and typewriter, or apples, oranges, and pears. An acceptable answer is that the first two are used to write, or that the latter three are fruits. If clients describe differences instead of similarities among the groups, then abstract thinking is impaired. Common quotations are also used to assess abstract powers. The client who responds to the adage, "Rolling stones gather no moss" with "Moss won't grow in stony places," is demonstrating concrete rather than abstract thinking.

RELIABILITY OF MENTAL STATUS ASSESSMENT When assessing the mental status of a client, observations must be distinguished from inferences. An *observation* is made up of behaviors or events witnessed through the senses. An *inference*, on the other hand, is an interpretation of the observed behavior or event. The same observation may be interpreted differently by different observers because inferences are subjective. One way to determine the reliability of inferences is to compare those made by various observers. Because mental status assessment has few objective standards, observations and inferences made about clients should be discussed and validated with colleagues. The more staff members who share observations and agree on inferences, the more accurate the assessment of the client is likely to be (Cohen 1981).

Personality Assessment

Personality assessment is concerned with conscious and unconscious attitudes, behaviors, impulses, conflicts, and traits. Tests of personality include the MMPI and a variety of projective tests.

THE MINNESOTA MULTIPHASIC PERSONALITY INVENTORY (MMPI). The most extensively used personality test is the Minnesota Multiphasic Personality Inventory (MMPI). It is a paper-and-pencil test consisting of 399 to 550 statements, depending on the preference of the examiner. Subjects respond to questions pertaining to general health, neurological and physiological factors, personal habits, family dynamics, sexual attitudes, religious beliefs, and political opinions. The subject is asked to label each statement as true, false, or don't know; when the subject cannot decide, that item is not counted.

The MMPI test items are classified into nine clinical scales, each of which has been validated empirically by administering the test to various populations. These MMPI scales are listed in the accompanying box.

There are a number of disadvantages to using the MMPI. The test asks intimate questions that may seem threatening, and many of the items provoke anxiety, especially because they are written in the first person. Another problem with the test is that it tends to make subjects who can censor their responses appear better adjusted than they actually may be. It is possible for some subjects, for example, to anticipate what inferences may be drawn from certain questions and as a result to answer in a way they think will put them in the best light. The test does, however, discriminate well between depressed and nondepressed psychotic subjects and can therefore help identify suicidal behaviors (Freedman, Sadock, and Kaplan 1973). The MMPI, like most tests, is an adjunct to but not a substitute for informed, ongoing observation.

PROJECTIVE TESTS Several tests of personality are called *projective tests* because subjects *project* aspects of their internal selves into their responses to ambiguous images or words. Subjects' patterns of reacting to projective tests vary not only from person to person but may vary for the same person on successive tests. The most commonly used projective tests are the Rorschach, the TAT, and word association and completion tests.

The Rorschach Test The purpose of the Rorschach inkblot test is to identify personality attributes by analyzing a subject's responses to a series of ambiguous shapes. The subject is shown ten symmetrical inkblots printed on cards (see Figure 6–2). Five of the inkblots are black, gray, and white; two are red and gray; and three are multicolored. The subject is asked to hold the cards and describe the images formed by the inkblots. The examiner may then question the subject about descriptions for purposes of clarification. Subjects are free to elaborate on their descriptions, but the examiner makes no direct suggestions. Scores on the Rorschach test are divided into four groups:

1. *Area scores.* These indicate what portions of the image were described—the whole inkblot, a detail, or the white part of the card.
2. *Form scores.* These indicate what movements, colors, shadings, and shapes were described.
3. *Content scores.* These indicate what animate, inanimate, human, or animal figures were described.
4. *Accuracy scores.* These indicate the accuracy of descriptions applied to respective inkblots: the description is labeled good, poor, or indeterminate.

MINNESOTA MULTIPHASIC PERSONALITY INVENTORY (MMPI)

The MMPI consists of 399 to 550 items dealing with multiple areas of functioning, both physical and psychological. Scores are obtained for nine different clinical scales, differentiated for males and females. Scoring is complex and requires each scale to be related to other scales in order to obtain an accurate profile. Computerized scoring is available but should be augmented with clinical judgment. It is important that examiners be proficient in administering, scoring, and interpreting this complex test. Social class, education, religion, and race are considered factors that may influence MMPI responses. Subjects answer test items with True, False, and Don't Know responses. The nine clinical scales are:

Hs Hypochondriasis Scale: 30 items dealing with bodily function.

D Depression Scale: 60 items dealing with discouragement, self-esteem, and worry.

Hy Hysteria Scale: 60 items dealing with specific somatic complaints and with the use of denial and repression.

Pd Psychopathic Deviate Scale: 50 items dealing with social maladjustment and deficient interpersonal bonds.

Mf Masculinity-Femininity Scale: 60 items dealing with aesthetic and vocational interests and with passive as opposed to active role preferences.

Pa Paranoia Scale: 40 items dealing with sensitivity, suspiciousness, and rejection.

Pt Psychasthenia Scale: 40 items dealing with narcissism, magical thinking, sado-masochism, anxiety, and self-doubt.

Sc Schizophrenia Scale: 78 items dealing with social alienation, family dysfunction, delusional thinking, bizarre emotions, unusual somatic complaints, and external influences.

Ma Hypomania Scale: 40 items dealing with expansiveness, excessive activity, flightiness, distractibilty, and irritability.

SOURCE: After Carr (1980).

In addition to analyzing the responses themselves, the examiner records the manner in which responses are made. Failures to respond, delays in responding, and recurring themes are noted and interpreted by the examiner, who is usually a psychologist.

When properly administered, the test is considered valid and reliable. It can be used to identify and differentiate depressive and schizophrenic response patterns and can assist in making differential diagnoses of other psychiatric disorders (Carr 1980).

Thematic Apperception Test (TAT) The Thematic Apperception Test (TAT) is a series of pictures showing men and women of various ages either alone or in groups. The subject is shown one picture card at a time and is asked to make up a story describing the experiences of the persons in the picture, their emotions, and the probable outcome of events. A similar test for children (the CAT) uses animals in the picture cards instead of people.

The TAT requires more than one session, and the number of pictures shown at a session is usually ten. Among the set of pictures is a blank card for which a story must be told. The blank card normally evokes wishes or fantasies about affection, affiliation, and security. If it provokes stories of fear, violence, or failure, this is considered an indicator of mood disturbances.

In interpreting the TAT, both the *content narrative* (the story that is told) and the *process narrative* (nonverbal behavior and gestures) are considered. Depressed subjects take a long time to react and are pessimistic in their content narrative. Obsessive subjects show indecision and inability to form definite opinions about the figures depicted on the cards. The TAT is less able to differentiate psychotic responses than is the Rorschach test (Carr 1980).

Word Association and Completion Tests Information obtained from word association and sentence completion tests is apt to be questionable because norms for such tests are deficient. Interpretation is therefore dependent on the expertise of the examiner. Experienced clinicians are often able to correlate symptomatology with the responses of the client. For some word association tests, norms are available that consist of lists of words most often associated. Several sentence completion tests also offer norms for certain age and gender groups.

NEUROLOGICAL ASSESSMENT AND TESTING

Neurological assessment is a form of screening that should be part of a nurse's observation of any

Figure 6–2. Inkblots similar to those used in the Rorschach test.

client. The screening process may be formal or informal but in all cases should yield relevant information concerning the client's status. The mental status examination is part of neurological screening. Other aspects are assessment of the client's muscle strength and movements, and pupillary reaction in terms of time and uniformity. In addition to muscle strength, coordination and balance need to be observed. When there is any doubt about a client's balance and coordination, precautions should be taken to prevent a fall. Sensory abilities may be tested by placing a small object such as a coin, key, or safety pin in the client's hands, asking her to identify it. Using one's powers of observation to assess a client's appearance, speech, gait, memory, orientation, and judgment can be of enormous help to the health care team responsible for planning care. Needless to say, all information obtained by preliminary and ongoing assessment should be carefully documented, and if significant, reported verbally as well.

In addition to assessment procedures and various psychological tests that are available, there are some common neurological tests with which nurses should be generally familiar. Knowing the significance of neurological diagnostic tests enables nurses to offer explanations and reassurance. Specific techniques are not outlined, since the emphasis here is on the reason for testing and what happens during the procedure. To a great extent, caring for clients undergoing neurological testing and assisting with procedures are interdependent responsibilities in which nurses and physicians collaborate.

Lumbar and Cisternal Punctures

Both these procedures are done by the physician at the client's bedside, and involve inserting a needle into the spinal canal to measure cerebral spinal fluid pressure and obtain spinal fluid samples. Cisternal puncture is used when problems in the lumbar area necessitate needle insertion at the base of the neck just above the spine. Both forms of puncture are done to detect blockage or central nervous system infection such as meningitis, syphilis, or multiple sclerosis. After the procedure the client is asked to lie flat in bed for 24 hours. The most common complaint afterwards is headache, but there may be nausea, malaise leg pain, or local irritation at the injection site. The most dangerous complication is brain herniation caused by sudden cerebral pressure changes. This complication is likely to occur during the procedure; the signs include increased intercranial pressure, pupillary changes, and loss of consciousness. The client should be monitored closely for the first 24 hours and observed frequently thereafter, especially if headache or other discomfort persists (Fisher 1987).

Myelography

A myelogram is an x-ray of the spinal subarachnoid space. The test is used to diagnose a tumor, herniated disc, or other cause of nerve or spinal cord compression. The test is administered in a radiology department where a lumbar puncture is done and opaque dye injected into the subarachnoid space. Postprocedural care is like that of clients who have undergone lumbar or cisternal

THE THEMATIC APPERCEPTION TEST (TAT)

The purpose of the TAT is to explore the dimensions of normal personality by means of a series of pictures. The subject is asked to make up a story about each picture that is shown, describing what led up to the event in the picture, the event itself, and the probable outcome. The test is thought to reveal feelings that subjects have about themselves and other people and to reveal interactional patterns that exist between subjects and significant persons in their life. Out of the available cards the examiner usually selects twenty or so pictures that seem likely to shed light on a subject's needs and conflicts. The following pictures are among those frequently selected:

Young boy looking at a violin.

Country scene showing a young woman carrying books, a man working, and an older woman watching.

Young boy with a downcast, bowed head.

Young woman covering her face with her right hand.

Elderly woman with her back turned toward a young man with a puzzled expression on his face.

Woman grasping the shoulders of a man who looks angry.

Gray-haired man looking at a younger man.

Older woman sitting on a sofa next to a young girl holding a doll.

Elderly man leaning over a young man on a sofa.

Young man standing and looking down at a partially undressed woman lying in bed.

Blank card.

SOURCE: After Carr (1980).

puncture. Clients must be closely watched for headache, neck stiffness, low grade fever, and elevated white cell count. These symptoms indicate that the client was probably sensitive to the dye, but discomfort should subside in a few days as the substance leaves the client's body. Before the procedure is done, nurses should inquire whether an oil-based dye (such as Pantopaque) or a water-based dye (such as Amique) has been used. If a water-based dye was used, the head of the bed should be ele-

vated for 8 to 16 hours after the test. This keeps the dye from moving to the client's head and reduces the risk of headache, vomiting, and seizures. If an oil-based dye has been used, clients should lie flat in bed for 24 hours.

Brain Scans and CT Scans

Brain scans and computed tomography (CT) scans are done to obtain x-rays of intracranial soft tissues and ventricles. The tests are done to discover causes of difficulties thought to be of cerebral origin. The tests are performed in a radiology department, where the client is usually given an intravenous injection of a radioisotope. The client is placed next to a scanner resembling a geiger counter that transmits signals from the isotope to a TV monitor. If stroke or transient ischemic attacks are suspected, scanning is done immediately after injecting the isotope. If the client's problem is less specific, an hour or two should elapse before the scanning so that the isotope has time to penetrate the brain tissue. After a brain or CT scan, no special follow-up is required. Clients often seek assurance that they will not become radioactive as a result of the procedure.

Angiography

Cerebral angiograms are x-rays of the flow of blood in cerebral and extracranial arteries, in order to determine the cause of motor weakness, stroke, seizure, or intractable headache. Again the test is done in a radiology department where a major artery (usually the femoral or brachial artery) is entered and a flexible catheter inserted. A baseline x-ray is taken after insertion of the catheter; contrast dye is then injected, and x-rays or computer images are taken of the cerebral vessels. When the needle and catheter are removed, pressure is applied on the area and a pressure dressing is applied. Three minutes of applied pressure are sufficient for a venous puncture area; 10 to 15 minutes of pressure are needed for an arterial puncture area.

Electroencephalography

An electroencephalogram detects and records electrical impulses from the brain. The patterns of electrical impulse help to diagnose brain tumors, infections, or dementias. The EEG also yields information concerning the cause and type of seizure disorders. Since low blood sugar can alter EEG readings, the client is permitted to eat normally. As a rule, the EEG is done in an insulated room, where 16 to 22 electrodes are placed on the client's scalp. The client sits or lies down during the procedure. Sometimes clients are asked to blink their eyes

INFORMAL COGNITIVE ASSESSMENT

In the initial assessment of a client's gross level of mental function, a questionnaire composed of the following items is often used. If possible, the purpose of the questions should be explained in an empathic, nonthreatening way (Kermis 1986).

1. Where are you now?
2. What is this place?
3. What day is this?
4. What month is it?
5. What year is it?
6. How old are you?
7. When is your birthday?
8. What year (or where) were you born?
9. Who is president of the United States?
10. Who was the president before this one?

Scores of zero to 2 errors mean *mild* or *no impairment*. Scores of 3 to 8 errors mean *moderate impairment*, and 9 to 10 errors mean *severe impairment*. This test does not make fine distinctions. Anyone who scores in the moderate range or more should receive additional testing by a qualified health professional. The questionnaire deals only with cognitive function, and does not deal with mood, affect, or any other psychological dimensions.

several times, to watch a flashing light, or to hyperventilate for a few minutes. These behaviors may activate abnormal electrical impulses. Occasionally, a sleep EEG will be done and the client may require medication in order to fall asleep under these relatively stressful conditions. No special aftercare is needed unless the procedure has been done on an outpatient basis and a sedative given, in which case the client should rest until the effects of sedation have disappeared.

Electromyography

An electromyelogram traces muscle activity and is conducted to determine whether a client's problems originate in the muscles or in the nerves supplying them. The test assists in diagnosing muscular dystrophy, myesthenia gravis, or polyneuropathy due to diabetes or alcoholism, among other conditions. Electrodes are applied to the client's skin surface. Mild electric shocks are administered as the apparatus records the rate of electrical conduction. In addition muscle punctures are done. An electrode is inserted directly into a muscle and the client is asked to move the muscle carefully. As this is done, electrodes pick up impulses from the muscle, transmit and record them. The number and location of the muscle punctures depend on the client's condition. Although not terribly painful, the procedure does cause some discomfort, especially if the client is already tense or anxious.

The procedure requires no extraordinary nursing measure except for careful explanation and constant reassurance before and during the procedure.

Nursing Implications of Neurological Testing

Neurological procedures are mysterious and frightening ordeals for clients and their families. A degree of discomfort accompanies some of the tests, but beyond that, clients are terrified because they don't know what to expect. The basic features are summarized here, but nurses whose clients are scheduled for a neurological procedure should obtain additional information. Only nurses with accurate knowledge of neurological procedures can reduce their clients' fears by explaining in simple language the purpose of the test and what they can expect. It's better to be truthful than to tell a client that there will be no discomfort. Explanations should be tailored to a client's ability to understand. In some facilities a client's primary nurse is encouraged to accompany the client to the area where testing will take place. Even if this is not possible, it alleviates misgivings when clients know that they will be cared for after the procedure by nurses they already know and trust. Sophisticated technology helps identify and localize the source of a client's discomfort, and nurses can contribute to the smooth administration of neurological tests.

(Text continues on page 138.)

CLINICAL EXAMPLE

ASSESSMENT OF HOLISTIC INTERACTION IN AN AMBULATORY CLIENT

Robert Bates is a 60-year-old man who attends a community day treatment center three days each week. He has a long history of problem drinking but has been sober for the last three years. Mr. Bates lives in a modest home with his wife of 40 years; his children are grown and have established families of their own. Before retiring on disability income, he had worked as a machinist. Some years ago Mr. Bates suffered several frightening episodes of delirium tremens that helped convince him to control his drinking.

The client's wife acts like a mother toward him. She takes care of his clothing, cooks for him, and supervises the routine activities of his life. His attendance at the day treatment center is partly due to his wife's need for relief from his presence. At the center he attends alcoholism and nutrition groups and engages in occupational activities. He is proud of the handcrafted articles that he makes and usually gives them to his wife or other family members.

At present Mr. Bates is in good physical health, but his years of excessive drinking have caused mental and emotional deficits that are thought to be organic in origin. Except for the episodes of delirium tremens, the organic brain damage has not produced psychotic reactions (loss of contact with reality). There are days when he seems confused and has trouble fully comprehending the interactions going on around him. When this happens, he turns to his friends in the day treatment center or to the staff for guidance. At home his wife is available to direct him and to clarify matters that are confusing.

Mrs. Bates realizes that her husband is very dependent on her but she accepts this situation. She says her husband has always looked to her for advice and assistance. She refers to herself as the "family manager" and has told her husband that she will no longer tolerate his drinking. Unless he maintains sobriety, either he or she will move out of the house. She is a religious woman and a regular churchgoer; her husband accompanies her to church irregularly.

Mr. Bates is frequently assessed by the staff of the day treatment center, all of whom are aware of the usual signs of organic brain damage. Staff members use the acronym *JOCAM* in observing and assessing his behavior, since organic brain deficits are often indicated by disturbances in judgment, orientation, comprehension, affect, and memory. The extent of functional impairment can sometimes be correlated with the extent of organic damage, but function is greatly influenced by environmental conditions.

New situations and demands tend to increase the client's confusion, whereas familiar surroundings and social support decrease his functional impairment.

The staff consider Mr. Bates to be in a stable condition. For the present he is controlling his drinking, and the circumstances in which he lives are acceptable to him and his wife. Considering the adverse effects of years of excessive drinking, Mr. Bates is handling his disability well. Ongoing assessment is needed, however, to help the client and his wife maintain their current level of adaptation.

It is an agency policy that all clients attending the day treatment center be assessed by designated staff members, who try to recognize changes in their clients' physical, social, and emotional status. For clients like Mr. Bates, who have chronic disorders, a weekly progress note is written. This is in addition to a monthly summary that includes a formal mental status assessment. Daily notes are recorded for clients who are unstable or in acute distress.

MENTAL STATUS EXAMINATION OF MR. BATES

Appearance

The client is a 60-year-old white male who looks his stated age. He is smooth shaven and his hair is thin; skin, hair, and fingernails appear clean. His clothing is somewhat worn but adequate. He dresses appropriately for the weather but says, "My wife always tells me what to wear." When sitting or standing the client seems relaxed. His posture does not show tension or rigidity. Usually the client presents himself as affable and smiling. He rarely initiates conversation but responds pleasantly to conversational overtures by other people. His voice is of normal volume, and there is no discernible speech impairment.

Weight is within normal range at present. Client joined a nutrition group at the day treatment center and has lost a substantial amount of weight in the last three months. As a result, his clothing looks too large for him. Despite this, the client says he is pleased with the weight loss and so is his wife.

He moves about rather easily. There is no sign of ataxia, tremor, or restricted movement. However, he tends to move slowly. The same slowness is evident in his speech patterns and reaction time. It is the consensus of the staff that this retardation is due to the client's efforts to concentrate to avoid making mistakes.

General Behavior

The client is congenial and cooperative in most interactions. He seems to fear giving offense, and expresses himself in a self-effacing manner. When group decisions must be made, he is reluctant to vote or express an opinion. If projects are suggested, he is slow to join in. With encouragement he does participate and gives signs of enjoying himself. He has not been observed acting in a hostile or suspicious manner.

Affect and Mood

Mr. Bates's affect is somewhat flat; he seems neither euphoric nor depressed, and there are no extreme mood swings. The client seems responsive and eager to please, but he is more comfortable when discussing superficial topics. When interacting with some of the other members, he expresses anger indirectly through sarcasm. He does not show anger toward staff or toward day treatment members whom he considers to be his friends.

Thought Processes

There is no evidence of dissociated thinking, but the conversation of the client is sometimes tangential or circumstantial. Occasionally he can't find the word he wants and calls himself "stupid." Recent memory is somewhat impaired and he often must be reminded of the day treatment center schedule. He carries a small notebook and asks other people to write down reminders for him.

Perception

Mr. Bates shows no signs of perceptual disorders. Hallucinations and delusional thoughts are not apparent. His reality testing seems intact except for intervals of slight confusion.

Cognitive Functions

The client is oriented as to time, place, and person. Remote memory is good but recent recall is unreliable. Concentration is sufficient to permit him to work on crafts and to play cards. Judgment is sufficient to enable him to follow a schedule with help, attend group meetings, and assume minor responsibilities. His inability or unwillingness to deal with abstract thought makes it difficult to assess his capacity for insight, but he acknowledges that his past drinking has affected his memory.

PSYCHIATRIC AND NURSING DIAGNOSES

The following nursing and psychiatric diagnoses were made for Mr. Bates.

Nursing Diagnoses

Altered role performance
(related to forced retirement and dependence on others)

Altered thought processes
(related to confusion and difficulties in comprehending)

Multiaxial Psychiatric Diagnosis

Axis I	303.93 Alcohol dependence in remission
	310.10 Organic personality syndrome
Axis II	Dependent personality
Axis III	None
Axis IV	Code 2—Minimal severity
Axis V	Level 4—Moderate impairment in social and occupational functioning

Nursing Diagnosis	Goal	Nursing Action	Outcome Criteria	Outcome Evaluation
Altered role performance	Client will develop more positive self-image.	Reinforce self-esteem by recognizing client's efforts and achievements.	Client and wife will attend group meetings regularly.	Client and wife attend group meetings and participate.
	Client will maintain sobriety.	Refer client to support group for alcoholics and spouses. Meet with client and wife to discuss group.	Client will take responsibility for writing reminders instead of depending on others.	Client is writing reminders for himself.
		Reinforce value of client's written reminders.	Client will not call himself stupid when he is confused or forgetful.	No angry outbursts with staff in last week. Client remains sober.
Altered thought processes	Client will engage in relevant conversation.	Help client to stay on a topic by discouraging digressions.	Client will be able to stay on a topic without digressing.	Client is less confused and is able to stay on one topic.
	Client will stay on one topic for 3–5 minutes.	Validate client's right to hold and express his opinions.	Client will refer to his written schedule and reminders to orient himself.	Client adheres to written schedule.
	Client will be able to express his opinions and preferences.	Help client formulate a consistent schedule for activities of daily living.		Client expressed an opinion rationally and appropriately in community meeting.
	Client will follow a consistent daily schedule.	Help client write out his daily schedule, based on activities he prefers.		

Moreover, careful nursing assessment and attention to the quality, intensity, and duration of a client's distress is of great value. This is especially true of clients with psychiatric diagnoses whose complaints may be overlooked or discounted. For all clients, the constant assessment by nurses may lead in some instances to avoiding unnecessary procedures and in other instances to recommending beneficial procedures to the health care team.

SUMMARY

Holistic interaction is an approach to health that enables nurses to view human actions in their entirety and to consider both functional and dysfunctional implications of human behavior. A holistic approach requires the use of guidelines developed by nurse theorists and by members of other disciplines, many of whom have developed methods that facilitate data collection and assessment of client needs.

Adaptability, a quality possessed by all living systems, is related to the physiological, psychological, and social competence of individuals, families, and groups. Levels of adaptation range from dysfunctional defense mechanisms to functional coping mechanisms. Adaptive capacity is finite and limited. Therefore, prolonged or excessive demands for adaptive responses may deplete the resources of individuals, families, and communities.

Clinical assessment requires nurses to understand the relevance of data obtained through assessment, examination, and testing. The mental status examination that nurses use formally and informally provides general information about clients. Personality tests include the Minnesota Multiphasic Personality Inventory (MMPI), the Rorschach Test, and the Thematic Apperception Test (TAT). Although personality tests are commonly administered by psychologists, data provided by these tests make a valuable contribution to client assessment, and the nature of these tests should be understood by nurses and other members of the health team.

The administration of neurological testing is an interdependent function shared by nurses and physicians, but preparatory and follow-up measures are primarily done by nurses. Since many of these procedures are frightening for clients, nurses should know about them to guide and reassure clients about the nature and purpose of neurological tests.

Review Questions

1. What is holistic interaction? How does holistic interaction influence the practice of psychiatric mental health nursing?

2. What mechanisms do *you* employ in making adaptive responses to changing situations?

3. From your own experience or observation, give examples of successful adaptation to life demands.

4. From your own experience or observation, give examples of unsuccessful or questionable adaptation to life demands.

5. Describe the concepts of functional and dysfunctional patterns of adaptation.

6. What is the major purpose of a mental status examination? What are the strengths and limitations of this assessment tool?

7. What are the purposes and implications of projective tests of personality?

8. What are the implications of stimuli excesses and deficits in nursing care?

Research Report

Congruence between Intershift Reports and Patients' Actual Conditions

This study examines the congruence, incongruence, and omissions between the stated condition of hospitalized patients and their actual condition. The cause of the discrepancies is not explored, only the occurrence. In conducting the study, a convenience sample was used, and consent was obtained from clients and nurses involved. The investigator listened to each shift report and then visited the patients involved, with or without the presence of the incoming nurse, in accord with the unit's preference. Fifty-seven shift reports and 19 units were used. The overall congruence was 70 percent; for the day shift, congruence was 70 percent; for the evening shift, congruence was 72 percent; for the night shift, 68 percent. Most incongruence was about intake and output records, and IV sites or status. Congruence of 100 percent was not found in any intershift reports; and important, relevant information was omitted or reported incorrectly. It was suggested that quantitative and qualitative overload may explain the shortcomings to some extent. The investigator emphasized the need for a standard verifying procedure in the form of "walking rounds" before the outgoing shift is relieved and the incoming shift assumes responsibility. Guidelines for verifying intershift reports should be established by inservice instructors, supervisors, and nurse executive officers. To support the warning that nurses who do not check patients before accepting responsibility for their care may risk litigation, the author cites two eminent jurists: Justice Holmes, who noted in 1903, "What usually is done may be evidence of what ought to be done, but what ought to be done is fixed by a standard of reasonable prudence, whether it is usually complied with or not," and Justice Hand, who wrote three decades later, "There are precautions so imperative that even their universal disregard will not excuse their omission."

Judith A. Richard. *Image* 20, no. 1 (Spring 1988):4–6.

Suggested Annotated Readings

Coburn, K. L., C. H. Sullivan, and J. Hundley, "High-Tech Maps of the Brain." *American Journal of Nursing* 88, no. 11 (November 1988):1500–1501.

Using colorful illustrations and clear terms, the authors explain how computers use EEG readings to map the electrical activity of the brain. The mapping shows subtle changes that cannot be distinguished in traditional EEG readings. Tips are given for easing clients through the brain mapping process. Special caution is needed in giving drugs, since some EEG procedures require alertness in the subject, while others require relaxation. The goal of the article is to enhance nurses' knowledge of EEG computerized technology so they can prepare clients for EEG procedures by imparting accurate, understandable information.

Halloran, E. J. "Computerized Nurse Assessments." *Nursing and Health Care* 9, no. 9 (November/December 1988):496–499.

Need of clients for nursing care constitutes a rationale for hospital admission, and degree of nurse dependency affects clients' length of stay. Degree of nurse dependency affects amount of time nurses spend with clients. This, in turn affects cost of nursing services. Even though every client is unique, this study of many clients over time reveals consistent patterns of need that are comparable within client groups, between clinical units, and among hospitals. Information from such broad-scale study can be used to construct data-based information about nurse dependency and cost effectiveness. Client assessment is the most crucial step of the whole process because all nursing care stems from assessed client need. The language of nursing diagnoses summarizes nursing assessment by defining client problems in terms meaningful to all nurses. Until now, failure to develop retrievable information systems concerning clients' functional levels and nurses' clinical judgments has caused clinical and analytic deficiencies. One new system is an automated client classification scheme that utilizes nurses' judgments. The content of the system was developed by NANDA, and elements of it have been used to refine a nursing minimum data set applicable to all settings where nurses practice. Health care planners are looking more closely at methods of recording, computerizing, and retrieving information from nurses about their clients.

Jess, L. W. "Investigating Impaired Mental Status." *Nursing 88* 18, no. 6 (June 1988):42–50.

This illuminating article uses a case study to demonstrate the specific steps comprising mental status assessment. Key indicators of mental function, such as level of consciousness, attention, memory, and judgment are outlined. The mental status of a client with a neurological problem is compared with that of a client with a psychiatric problem. A sample mental status protocol is provided and a self-test is offered for nurses wishing to earn continuing education credits for mastering the material in the article.

Marchette, L., and F. Hollman. "A First-Hand Report on the New Body Scanners." *RN* (November 1985):28–31.

This article reports the reactions of a nurse who volunteered for an MRI (Magnetic Resonance Image) scan so physicians could perfect their technique in this form of diagnostic radiology. In addition to explaining how and why an MRI is done, the article describes the subject's sensations and perceptions in the procedure, particularly the feelings of claustrophobia and the difficulty in remaining perfectly still when she was entirely encased in a cylindrical tunnel. The same volunteer also reported her reactions to a PET scan, describing this as more tedious but less traumatic than the MRI.

Moore, P. C. "When You Have to Think Small for a Neurological Exam." *RN* (June 1988):38–44.

The author assures nurses that doing a baseline neurological assessment only requires observant eyes, ears, hands, and some general knowledge. Special measures are suggested when the client is a child. Specific guidance is outlined for dealing with infants, toddlers, preschoolers, gradeschoolers, and adolescents. In performing neurological assessments, nurses are advised not to be intimidated by terminology but to record exactly what the child's responses

are without trying to condense the assessment into language that may or may not be clear and precise.

"Reliability and Validity of Mental Status Questionnaires in Elderly Hospitalized Patients." *Nursing Research* 36, no. 4 (July/August 1987):216–220.

Three different mental status questionnaires were used to assess 66 persons over the age of 65 years. Of the three forms, the Cognitive Capacity Screening Examination (CCSE) was found to be the most valid and reliable for this hospitalized population. The two other questionnaires were less accurate clinically. All three were comparable in regard to internal consistency. Although the CCSE was superior from a psychometric viewpoint, it was longer than the other questionnaires used. For persons with moderate to severe cognitive impairment, the length of the CCSE might produce unreliable or invalid results. In these cases the Mini Mental State Examination (MMSE) or the Short Portable Mental Status Examination (SPMSE) might be preferable. These mental status questionnaires are approximately one third the length of the CCSE.

Werley, H. H., E. C. Devine, and C. R. Zorn. "Nursing Needs Its Own Minimum Data." *American Journal of Nursing* 88, no. 12 (December 1988): 1651–1653.

The deficiency of freestyle documentation in this age of computerization is addressed here. The Nursing Minimum Data Set (NMDS) is proposed as a system that draws data from nursing records and presents the retrieved data in a uniform way. Through the NMDS it is possible to compare nursing data across clinical populations, clinical settings, geographical areas, nursing diagnoses, and nursing resources. Pilot testing of the NMDS showed a satisfactory rate of 91 percent intercoder agreement when used to review client records from four different clinical agencies. Existing nursing records seemed to provide sufficient information to implement the proposed system.

References

Anderson, R. E., and I. Carter. *Human Behavior in the Social Environment: A Social Systems Approach.* Chicago: Aldine, 1978.

Carr, A. C. "Psychological Testing of Personality." In *Comprehensive Textbook of Psychiatry,* 3d ed. H. I. Kaplan, A. M. Freedman, and B. J. Sadock, eds. Baltimore: Williams & Wilkins, 1980.

Cohen, S. "Mental Status Assessment." *American Journal of Nursing* 81, no. 8 (1981):1493–1518.

Fisher, J. "What You Need to Know about Neurological Testing." *RN* (January 1987):47–53.

Freedman, A. M., B. J. Sadock, and H. I. Kaplan. *Comprehensive Textbook of Psychiatry*. Baltimore: Williams & Wilkins, 1973.

Freud, S. *The Ego and Mechanisms of Defense*. London: Hogarth, 1953.

Gardner, H. "Beyond the I.Q.: Education and Human Development." *National Forum* 68, no. 2 (Spring 1988):4–7.

Goosen, G. M., and H. A. Bush. "Adaptation: A Feedback Process." *Advances in Nursing Science* 1, no. 4 (1979): 51–65.

Holmes, T., and R. Rahe. "The Social Readjustment Rating Scale." *Journal of Psychosomatic Research* 11 (1967):213–218.

Horney, K. *The Neurotic Personality of Our Time*. New York: W. W. Norton, 1937.

Jess, L. W. "Investigating Impaired Mental Status: An Assessment Guide You Can Use." *Nursing 88* 18, no. 6 (June 1988):42–50.

Kaplan, H. I., and B. J. Sadock. "Psychiatric Report" and "Typical Signs and Symptoms of Psychiatric Illness." In *Comprehensive Textbook of Psychiatry*, 3d ed. H. I. Kaplan, A. M. Freedman, and B. J. Sadock, eds. Baltimore: Williams & Wilkins, 1980.

Kermis, M. D. *Mental Health in Late Life: The Adaptive Process*. Boston: Jones and Bartlett Publishers, 1986.

Lynaugh, J. E., and C. M. Fagin. "Nursing Comes of Age." *Image* 20, no. 4 (Winter 1988):184–190.

MacKinnon, R. A. "Psychiatric History and Mental Status Examination." In *Comprehensive Textbook of Psychiatry*, 3d ed. H. I. Kaplan, A. M. Freedman, and B. J. Sadock, eds. Baltimore: Williams & Wilkins, 1980.

Maslow, A. H. *Toward a Psychology of Being*, 2d ed. New York: Van Nostrand Reinhold, 1968.

Matarazzo, J. D. "Psychological Assessment of Intelligence." In *Comprehensive Textbook of Psychiatry*, 3d ed. H. I. Kaplan, A. M. Freedman, and B. J. Sadock, eds. Baltimore: Williams & Wilkins, 1980.

McLean, A. A. "Occupational Psychiatry." In *Comprehensive Textbook of Psychiatry*, 3d ed. H. I. Kaplan, A. M. Freedman, and B. J. Sadock, eds. Baltimore, Maryland: Williams & Wilkins, 1980.

Mechanic, D. "Stress, Illness, and Illness Behavior." *Journal of Human Stress* 2, no. 2 (1976):2–7.

Menninger, K. A. *The Vital Balance*. New York: Viking Press, 1965.

Miller, J. G. "General Living Systems Theory." In *Comprehensive Textbook of Psychiatry*, vol. I, 3d ed. H. I. Kaplan, A. M. Freedman, and B. J. Sadock, eds. Baltimore: Williams & Wilkins, 1980.

Ogbu, J. U. "Human Intelligence Testing: A Cultural Ecological Perspective." *National Forum* 68, no. 2 (Spring 1988):22–29.

Ramsey, P. W. "Bringing a Patient through ICU Psychosis." *RN* (September 1986):43–45.

Vaillant, G. *Adaptations to Life*. Boston: Little, Brown, 1977.

White, S. W. "Opportunity and Intelligence." *National Forum* 68, no. 2 (Spring 1988):2–3.

PART TWO

VARIATIONS AND DISRUPTIONS IN MENTAL HEALTH

7

Thought Variations and Disruptions

Learning Objectives

After reading this chapter, the student should be able to:

1. Describe biochemical, genetic, psychodynamic, and developmental theories explaining the etiology of schizophrenia.

2. Explain the concept of expressed emotion and its link to psychoeducation therapy.

3. In terms of the nursing process, formulate appropriate nursing interventions with clients whose altered thoughts and perceptions are expressed behaviorally.

4. Describe the functions and responsibilities of the nurse in the administration of antipsychotic medication.

5. Explain the principles of relationship therapy in caring for clients with alterations of thought and perception.

6. Describe the major components of milieu therapy as they relate to the nursing process.

Overview

Disruptions and variations of thinking and perceiving are the subject of this chapter, with special emphasis on persons considered to be schizophrenic. A wide range of life stresses, organic problems, and personality traits can lead to disrupted, dysfunctional thinking. Schizophrenia, however, is a broad term applied to a serious group of disorders characterized by withdrawal of interest from other people and from reality, and preoccupation with an inner world shaped by the nature of the disrupted thinking.

In the first part of this chapter genetic, biochemical, developmental, and psychodynamic theories about the etiology of schizophrenia are discussed. Next, the forms of thought variation and disruption characteristic of schizophrenia are described behaviorally. The last section deals with therapeutic methods of caring for the schizophrenic client.

Schizophrenia is not a single, homogeneous disorder, but is a number of disorders whose manifestations and outcomes have great variability. The etiology of this group of disorders is assumed to be multifaceted. Therapeutic approaches are also multifaceted, and include psychotropic drug therapy, relationship therapy, milieu therapy, family therapy, and psychoeducational therapy. Nursing functions and responsibilities in implementing and coordinating these approaches are presented. Finally, factors influencing the outcomes of therapy are described in comparative terms.

THEORETICAL AND HISTORICAL PERSPECTIVES

Schizophrenia is a diagnosis that has alarming connotations and carries a degree of stigma. Thoughtful clinicians admit that the condition may well be overdiagnosed, and that the diagnosis itself may accelerate the downward course of some clients. Psychiatrists and other health care personnel often think that diagnosis should come first and come quickly, so that a treatment plan can be instituted. In responding to these concerns, the DSM III-R clarified the criteria for schizophrenia, but the diagnostic problem remains. The multiaxial system does, however, encourage clinicians to examine other factors, such as substance abuse, personality attributes, and life stressors that may simulate schizophrenia. Pepper and Ryglewicz (1988) urge clinicians to move beyond psychiatric categories and instead examine the lives of clients and families in a comprehensive, ongoing fashion. Nurses have already adopted a biopsychosocial perspective; nursing assessment and nursing diagnoses are primarily directed to observing and responding to thought variations and disruptions that are indicators of a disorganized inner life, whatever the psychiatric diagnosis.

There are two very different ways of viewing the deviant behaviors that are generally described as schizophrenic. At one extreme are those who do not acknowledge that schizophrenic manifestations represent illness but choose to see certain clusters of behaviors as nonconforming but rational adjustments to the demands of an irrational world. At the opposite extreme are those who prefer the traditional medical model and are preoccupied with investigating biological structures and processes to explain the existence of illness and symptoms. Between these extremes are large numbers of researchers and clinicians from various disciplines who are willing to include and consider any biopsychosocial factors that appear to influence the onset, course, and outcome of this altered pattern of thought and perception.

The clinical picture presented by persons thought to be schizophrenic is variable, heterogeneous, and often puzzling. Most of the victims of schizophrenia endure a multitude of fears and doubts—about themselves, about the people around them, and about the confusing, terrifying world in which they must live. One young schizophrenic woman described her condition not as an illness but as a way of life that consigned her to overwhelming pain and darkness as she struggled to escape from the embrace of shapes and ghosts, and from the threats of disembodied voices. Many

PSYCHIATRIC DIAGNOSTIC PUZZLES

A 19-year-old girl with a poorly repaired cleft palate has a child born as the result of a casual encounter. Her sex life is promiscuous; she flies into wild rages during which she slashes her clothing and breaks her furniture. Her explanation is that she does this to keep from hitting her child. She drinks alcohol excessively and smokes marijuana when she can get it. She is excitable; her speech is rapid to the point of incoherence. As a child, she was sexually molested by her father and brothers. She has been diagnosed as schizophrenic, and a major tranquilizer has been prescribed. Lately she has been using cocaine with male friends. Schizophrenia, substance abuse, or personality disorder?

A 35-year-old-man lives with his mother. He has no friends or social outlets except for her. His mother permits him to drink in his room because he is quiet and easy to manage when intoxicated. When he does not drink, he is hostile and surly toward her. The psychiatric diagnosis is schizophrenia. Schizophrenia or alcoholism?

A 20-year-old college freshman has stopped attending class. He is enrolled in the demanding college from which his father graduated, but he was not asked to join his father's fraternity. Unshaven and unwashed, he spends his time alone listening to music. After a few attempts to break through the apathy, his roommate moved out. The student health service labeled the freshman schizophrenic and moved for his dismissal, after he expressed thoughts of suicide. Schizophrenia or depression?

schizophrenic persons have tried to express in words and art the loneliness and desperation they feel. It is essential that nurses realize that grotesque and bizarre behaviors are indicators of deep human needs that clients cannot express in any other way. Even when a nurse cannot comprehend the precise need being communicated, he must see schizophrenic behaviors as a client's struggle to deal with a confused, distorted perception of the inner self in relation to the outside world.

In general, mental illness is a public health problem of overwhelming proportions, affecting adversely as many as 41 million persons in the

Can I ever forget that I am schizophrenic? I am isolated and I am alone. I am never real. I play-act my life, touching and feeling only shadows . . . What good is physical freedom if the human feelings are trapped inside, unable to escape? I am in my own prison . . . The totally frustrating part of this illness is that it is always growing, always changing. There are always new symptoms, new fears to conquer . . . I am so ambivalent that my mind can divide on a subject, and those two parts subdivide over and over until my mind feels like it is in pieces . . . I feel like I am trapped inside my head, banging against its walls, trying desperately to escape while my lips can utter only nonsense.

Anonymous, 1986

United States. The severe disabilities stemming from mental illness cripple human relationships and human productivity. In 1984 mental illness cost the nation 65 billion dollars in health care costs and lost productivity. In 1987 the cost was reported as 106 billion dollars, or 10 percent of the whole federal budget (Wyden 1987).

Within the United States alone 2 million Americans can be expected to experience serious disruption of thought and perception during their lifetime. Compounding the problem is the fact that initial episodes usually affect young adults, and a sizable number of those affected follow a pattern of gradual deterioration and chronic disability. The peak years of onset are between the end of the second decade and the beginning of the third decade—years that should be useful and rewarding (Cancro 1985).

The relatively high prevalence of schizophrenic disorders and the lack of agreement regarding diagnosis, etiology, and treatment contribute to the challenges of dealing with the altered patterns of thought and perception known as schizophrenia. Because of differences in methodology and diagnostic criteria, statistics on the incidence and prevalence of schizophrenia vary considerably. Worldwide incidence rates have been estimated at between 1 and 2 percent, but it is impossible to make reliable comparisons from one culture to another. (*Prevalence* refers to the number of persons suffering from a disorder at the time of a survey; *incidence* refers to the number of new cases within a given period.)

For clinicians concerned with psychiatric classification, there are no unique identifying signs for schizophrenia, nor are there conclusive laboratory indicators. When there is lack of agreement regarding the psychiatric classification to which the client has been assigned, there are some general guidelines to consider. Most clients presumed to be experiencing schizophrenic alterations of thought and perception develop idiosyncratic interpretations of events that are revealed by inconsistent, confused, illogical statements or bizarre behaviors. Thoughts and ideas are randomly and incoherently comprehended and expressed, and learning abilities may be impaired. The person may withdraw from interaction with the external world and become preoccupied with subjective internal stimuli.

ETIOLOGIC THEORIES

Etiologic explanations for the cluster of disorders classified as schizophrenia remain inconclusive, despite some progress in this regard. Current explanations are based on interactions among genetic, biochemical, psychological, and interpersonal factors that as yet are incompletely understood. These multifactorial interactive explanations suggest that a number of variables may be present, some of which remain unidentified. The most plausible theories to date suggest that the clinical manifestations of schizophrenia are mediated by neurotransmitters in the brain and central nervous system. Although considerable laboratory research points in the direction of biochemical causes, other etiologic explanations should be noted as well. Careful investigation of family and social factors is essential to understanding not only the etiology but also the nature of schizophrenia. Faulty communication patterns and inappropriate role enactment in families are considered significant in the development and prognosis of schizophrenic behaviors manifested by a family member. In this section genetic and developmental theories are presented in some detail because of the relevance of these theories to the nursing process. Biochemical theories merit attention because of their primacy in research studies and because biochemical theories support and explain many aspects of pharmacologic treatment of schizophrenia.

Genetic Theories

Investigative studies indicate that genetic factors may influence the onset of schizophrenic disorders. It has been noted that the closer the biological relationship between an individual and a person considered to be schizophrenic, the greater the risk of that individual developing the disorder. Vulnerability seems to decrease as biological relationships become more distant. When one parent is identified as being schizophrenic, the probability of offspring becoming schizophrenic is 12 to 15 percent (Heston 1977, Rosen 1978). If both parents are diagnosed as schizophrenic, the probability of offspring developing the disorder increases to 35 percent.

Research on the etiology of schizophrenia involves the study of concordance rates for schizophrenia in monozygotic (identical) and dizygotic (fraternal) twins. Concordance rates in twins may be measured in several ways, so that it is possible for the same data to yield different statistics. Another problem with twin studies is that the subjects identified as schizophrenic may not have been held to consistent diagnostic standards. Even so, 10 out of 11 twin studies done before 1970 reported markedly higher concordance rates in monozygotic twins (Cancro 1985). Studies done in the late 1970s and early 1980s that employed sounder methods also upheld the genetic hypothesis to a significant extent (Weiner 1985).

Biochemical Theories

Biochemical explanations of the etiology of schizophrenia propose that the disorder is caused by physiological dysfunction. Biochemical investigations have not established the existence of a dominant causative factor, but in general, the evidence of biochemical research points to *bioamine* transmission as a likely factor, since bioamines act as neurotransmitters in the limbic system of the brain and mediate such functions as awareness, sleep, emotion, and sensations of pain and pleasure.

There are two broad categories of bioamines: the *catecholamines* (norepinephrine and dopamine) and the *indolamines* (serotonin and tryptamine). These bioamines are converted into metabolites that can be detected and measured in the urine. Studies of bioamine production and metabolism tend to confirm the idea that a relationship exists between the bioamines and schizophrenia. For example, urinalyses of schizophrenic persons have revealed abnormally high levels of indolamine metabolites. Researchers studying persons with schizophrenia found that one to five days before the onset of behavioral signs, levels of tryptamine increased in the urine. Levels remained high until the day before behavioral manifestations appeared, at which time the levels of tryptamine suddenly dropped. Additionally, when behavioral manifestations developed, urinary levels of catecholamine metabolites increased. Catecholamine levels in the urine began to rise prior to the appearance of behavioral signs and continued to increase as psy-

chotic behavior became more pronounced. When the behavioral manifestations of schizophrenia escalated, urinary levels of indolamines and catecholamines both rose; when an individual showed signs of tension without behavioral manifestations of schizophrenia, only the catecholamine levels rose.

When the specific role of *serotonin* in the etiology of schizophrenia has been studied, it has been shown that administration of a monoamine oxidase (MAO) inhibitor is followed by increased levels of serotonin in the brain and the appearance of schizophrenic behaviors. Conversely, the phenothiazine group of drugs has been shown to block the action of dopamine and to reduce the behavioral signs of schizophrenia. Some investigators have therefore postulated that the schizophrenic process may be initiated and perpetuated by excesses of serotonin and dopamine.

Biochemical research is at present the main focus in the study of schizophrenia. Computer images of the brain have made it possible to study both the structure and functioning of the brain. The cerebral cortex in some victims shows abnormalities in terms of size and activity. It is not yet known whether such biological changes are the consequence or the cause of the schizophrenic process. Some researchers believe two distinct groups of symptoms may be connected to biological processes in the brain. The hallucinations, rages, and feelings of being controlled by external forces are termed the "positive" signs of the disorder. It is this type of symptom that is most responsive to antipsychotic medication and is most closely related to biochemical changes in the brain. The "negative" signs of the disorder consist of withdrawal, indifference, apathy, and regression. Even when antipsychotic medication is administered, these negative behaviors persist. Often it is the negative features of the disorder that create street people who carry all their possessions with them as they try to survive but remain apart from the rest of society (Schmeck 1986, Harding, Zubin, and Strauss 1987).

In addition to statistical evidence that biological relatives of persons with schizophrenia are at greater risk, the following data support theories of genetic transmission (Gottesman 1978):

- The incidence of schizophrenia in identical twins is three times greater than the incidence in fraternal twins and at least thirty times greater than in the general population.
- The incidence of schizophrenia in identical twins reared apart is about the same as that in identical twins reared together.

■ The incidence of the disorder in children of schizophrenic parents placed early in life with other families is higher than that in the general population; data from some studies show incidence rates as high as if the children had been reared by their biological parents.

■ The incidence of schizophrenia is not greater in children adopted into homes where an adoptive parent develops schizophrenia.

■ In a study of monozygotic (identical) twin pairs where only one twin became schizophrenic, the incidence of schizophrenia in offspring of the unaffected twin equaled that in offspring of the affected twin.

From a genetic perspective, schizophrenia may be explained either by a *monogenic* or a *polygenic* theory. The monogenic theory holds that the disorder classified as schizophrenia is influenced by the transmission of a single gene that produces susceptibility to the disorder. The extent to which the gene is expressed behaviorally depends on environmental influences to which the susceptible person is exposed. Under stress, a genetically vulnerable person is likely to become schizophrenic, but under benign conditions this is less likely to occur. According to the polygenic theory, schizophrenia is caused by the inheritance of more than one gene. A person might inherit all the genes involved in schizophrenia and therefore be at high risk, or she might inherit only some of the genes involved and therefore be at less risk.

Whether of polygenic or monogenic etiology, precipitating factors in the appearance of schizophrenic behaviors seem to be related to social or environmental stresses. The high incidence of schizophrenia among relatives of persons with the disorder supports the possibility of inherited vulnerability. The extent to which inherited vulnerability leads to clinical manifestations of the disorder seems to depend on (1) the extent of inherited susceptibility, and (2) the amount of life stress encountered by the vulnerable individual (Goleman 1984). What is less certain is the nature of the processes and structures involved in a genetic predisposition to schizophrenia (Barham 1984).

Developmental Theories

It is generally accepted by theorists and clinicians that all behavior has meaning and purpose, even if neither can immediately be discerned. It is also accepted that childhood experiences influence adult behaviors. Thus, developmental theories are considered a useful frame of reference for explaining the etiology of schizophrenia. Knowledge and understanding of developmental stages enable nurses to assess behaviors in the context of the client's past experience. Two developmental theorists whose work has contributed to the conceptualization of interpersonal and psychosocial issues

The Cerebral Cortex at Work

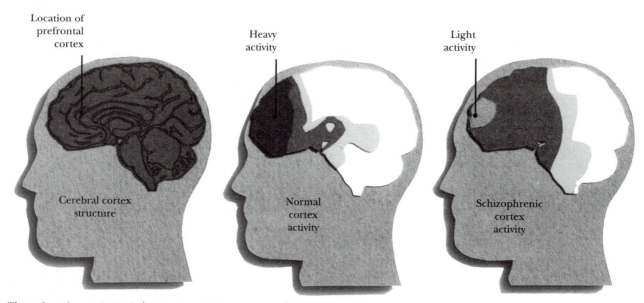

The prefrontal cortex is involved in such mental processes as analytic thinking. Computerized images are now available to compare mental activity in normal and in schizophrenic persons. In normal subjects analytic thinking causes the cortex image to be clearly shown, reflecting the activity. By comparison, the cortex image is dim in schizophrenic persons engaged in the same tasks. Such findings cause researchers to suspect that structural and chemical variations in the brain may be associated with schizophrenia.
SOURCE: Adapted from National Institute of Mental Health (1986).

are Harry Stack Sullivan (1953) and Erik Erikson (1968). Their theories (introduced in Chapter 4) are summarized in Tables 7–1 and 7–2.

According to Erikson, the process of thought disturbance may start early in life when the relationship between the child and the primary caregiver is impaired or inadequate. As a result of deficient nurturing in infancy, the child has difficulty learning to interact with others. Erikson (1968) believes that if trust does not develop between the child and the caregiver during the first year of life, the child's ability to trust himself and others will be permanently impaired. According to Sullivan (1953), the person who has never experienced a secure, comforting relationship with another human being is at risk for developing mental disturbances. Such an individual is deprived of the kind of interpersonal relationships that promote self-esteem and establish a firm identity. The capacity to establish anxiety-free associations with other people fails to develop. As a consequence, such an individual feels like a failure. Interpersonal rela-

tionships, regardless of their surface appearance, are menacing and potentially painful. Therefore, the individual feels that they must be avoided.

Both Erikson and Sullivan contend that maladjustment is more likely to occur when an individual has been neglected, rejected, and deprived of consistent nurture and affection in early life. Children who experience ridicule, abuse, or unpredictable actions at the hands of parents or other significant persons react by becoming insecure and anxious. The person or persons caring for the child may give mechanical attention or open rejection. Sometimes the child is treated as an inconvenience or nuisance by the parents and consequently feels inferior and devalued. An outside observer might not recognize the emotional trauma that is concealed by a semblance of appropriate family behavior. Disguised rejection is extremely detrimental to the child since it is often easier to deal with open rejection than with antagonism masked by apparent attention and concern. In this sort of situation, the

Table 7–1. Erikson's Psychosocial Theory

Developmental Stage	Time Frame	Developmental Task	Implication
Sensory	0–18 months	Trust vs. mistrust	Consistent loving care fosters trust; inconsistent harsh care fosters mistrust; some mistrust remains in every adult.
Muscular	1–3 years	Autonomy vs. shame and doubt	Desire arises to control own thoughts and actions; success leads to sense of control over body and environment.
Locomotor	3–6 years	Initiative vs. guilt	Child needs to explore world via senses, actions, imagination; conscience begins to develop, guiding initiative; negative relationships with parents promote a sense of guilt.
Latency	6–12 years	Industry vs. inferiority	Child understands and accepts rules, engages in productive work, starts and completes tasks; excessive parental expectations induce feelings of inferiority.
Adolescence	12–20 years	Identity vs. role diffusion	Adolescent attempts to rework problems of earlier stages; usually demonstrates interest in members of opposite sex; tries to integrate past and present experiences; copes with changing body image; searches for identity and a place in society.
Young adulthood	18–25 years	Intimacy vs. isolation	Adult achieves sufficient identity to establish intimacy, accepts personal commitments, tries to understand others and to be understood by others; isolation results when intimacy is not attained.

SOURCE: Adapted from Erikson (1968).

Table 7–2. Sullivan's Interpersonal Theory

Stage of Development	Self System	Cognitive Experiences	Developmental Tasks	Relationships
Infancy: Birth to emergence of speech, about 1½ years	Barely emerging	Largely prototaxic	Learning to count on others to gratify needs and to satisfy wishes	During this period, an infant cannot be spoiled. Meeting an infant's needs lays a firm foundation for the development of trust.
Childhood: 1½ years to the emergence of the need to associate with peers, about 6 years	Sex-role recognition	Largely parataxic emerging to syntaxic	Learning to accept interference with wishes in relative comfort, to delay gratification	The child must have realistic limits set. The limits must be consistent if the child is to develop a sense of reality about the environment.
Juvenile period: 6 years to the beginning of capacity to love, about 9 years	Integrating needs—internal controls	Syntaxic most of the time; fascination with symbols	Learning to form satisfactory relationships with peers	The child learns to attend to peers' wishes in order to have needs met. Family rules may be ignored in deference to friends' ideas.
Preadolescense: 9 years to the first evidence of puberty, about 12 years	Somewhat stabilized	Syntaxic	Learning to relate to a friend of the same sex	More allegiance to friends than to family. The opposite sex is shunned and best friend shares secrets, dreams, and fantasies.
Early adolescence: 12 years to the completion of primary and secondary changes, about 14 years	Confused, but continuingly stabilized	Syntaxic (highly sexually oriented)	Learning to master independence and to establish satisfactory relationships with members of the opposite sex	Rebellion and dependence mark this era. Sexual relationships and peer values are more influential than family allegiance.
Late adolescence: 14 years to establishment of durable situations of intimacy, about 21 years	Integrated and stabilized	Fully syntaxic	Developing an enduring intimate relationship with a member of the opposite sex	During this period, a love relationship is established and marriage usually follows.

SOURCE: Adapted from Sullivan (1953).

child passes through the formative years constantly expecting pain and failure from interpersonal relationships, as significant persons have taught him to expect nothing else. Such a person perceives all aspects of the social world as intimidating and tends to attribute these feelings of dread to deficiencies in himself.

Sullivan believed that the frightening non-me experiences of early life (the sum of experiences that create such intense feelings of fear or dread that they have to be disowned—see Chapter 4) dominate some people's awareness and initiate schizophrenic episodes. According to Sullivan, the schizophrenic process is a withdrawal from interpersonal relationships into a timeless, spaceless world in which normal cause and effect cease to exist. The negative feelings about the world and the self originate in the bad me (the sum of experiences

in which the infant's need for tenderness is not met) and non-me components of the self system and contribute to schizophrenic withdrawal from reality.

Sullivan believed that along with interpersonal withdrawal, the schizophrenic person discards the commonly understood or consensually validated words and meanings by which most people make themselves comprehensible to others. Language no longer is a means of reaching out and communicating with others but becomes a way of encapsulating and concealing the self. Shared meanings that can be consensually validated and understood by others become distorted as the schizophrenic person withdraws from reality and regresses to earlier developmental levels. Without language, the schizophrenic person loses the ability to preserve ways of thinking, acting, and feeling that make

RISK FACTORS FOR SCHIZOPHRENIA

Identification of high-risk groups currently points to inherited susceptibility to schizophrenia as an essential etiologic factor that is greatly intensified when combined with the following additional risk factors (Goleman 1984):

- Childbirth problems, including low birth weight and unusual birth position.
- Poor maternal bonding in the first three years of life.
- Poor motor coordination in infancy.
- Separation from parents or multiple placements in early childhood.
- Intellectual deficits, especially in verbal skills.
- Cognitive deficits, especially in concentration and attention.
- Social incompetence, especially contentiousness with peers and others.
- Confusion in family communication patterns.
- Hostility of parents toward the child.

sense to other people. Consequently, the person with schizophrenia loses the ability to communicate and comprehend ordinary ideas, perceptions, and symbols. All these things are interpreted in a private, special way by the schizophrenic person. The consequence of interpersonal withdrawal, followed by loss of shared language and meanings, sets the stage for the appearance of internal experiences that take the form of hallucinations and delusions.

Schizophrenic persons often use thought patterns that are uncommon in everyday life and are therefore subject to misinterpretation by others. In expressing thoughts, the person with schizophrenia does not link subjects together, as most people do, but links predicates instead. Since coherent thinking and comprehensible communication are oriented to subjects or topics, the language of the schizophrenic client becomes individualistic, or *parataxic*, to use the terminology coined by Sullivan. An example of this incoherence is the following sentence: "Tall ships sail (sale) of people weep me a river flowing blood to the sea." In this sentence, the associations are not between the nouns but between the verbs or predicates. The rapid change of subject matter makes the meaning obscure until the mes-

sage is seen as a form of communication based on predicate thinking. Only then can the association be understood by the listener. The time and energy needed to decipher such thought processes are enormous. In the meantime the person with schizophrenia manages to remain a riddle misunderstood by others and relatively inaccessible.

Certain interactional patterns have been noted in the families of children who develop schizophrenia. Although both parents are important to the psychological development of the child, the maternal relationship is considered crucial, especially in the early years. The mother whose attitudes and behaviors have been labeled schizophrenogenic has been described as overinvolved with the child yet anxious, ungiving, and unpredictable (Fromm-Reichmann 1948, Lidz 1958, Rosen 1962). The schizophrenogenic father, on the other hand, has been described as a weak, ineffectual role model (Lidz, Fleck, and Cornelius 1965), or as self-engrossed and seductive (Lidz 1958, Wolman 1976).

Additional theorists have studied the entire family system and explored dysfunctional interaction among all family members (Sullivan 1929, Arieti 1974, Wolman 1976). In the schizophrenogenic family the relationships among all members are intricate and confusing. Longitudinal research undertaken in Europe and the United States validates some earlier work that attributed schizophrenia to flawed family interactional patterns. Researchers have discovered significant differences in the families of young people who become schizophrenic and those who do not. Among the habitual communication and interactional patterns noted in the families of schizophrenic persons are (Goleman 1984):

1. Parents of schizophrenic children engaged in attacks on the characters of their children. Instead of criticizing a behavior, they assaulted the whole child, labeling him as deficient or inferior.

2. Parents of schizophrenic children were very intrusive in the life of their children. Instead of acknowledging how their child thought or felt, the parents told her what to think or feel. For example, a child who wanted something was told that she did not really want it. As a result, the child became unsure of what she actually wanted, thought, or felt.

3. Parents of schizophrenic children employed an erratic communication style in which words were used inappropriately or ambiguously. Denial, distortion, and circumstantiality were employed in ways that caused the child to distrust his own perception of reality. From this communication distortion, the child learned chaotic,

bizarre patterns of thinking and reasoning. As a result the child's cognitive and language abilities became deficient, unstable, and more likely to deteriorate during periods of stress.

Regressive thought processes cause the person with schizophrenia to engage in language patterns whose meaning cannot be understood easily by others. Three main patterns of cognitive and language distortion can be discerned: concretization, desymbolization, and desocialization.

CONCRETIZATION In the process of *concretization* there is a loss of consensually validated words, symbols, and meanings. As a result of this loss, knowledge is not easily transferred from one experience to another, and each situation encountered by the schizophrenic person seems new and unique. The person resorts to a vigilant, watchful, listening attitude. As she tries to organize life experiences into meaningful patterns, abstract feelings are transformed into concrete ideas and sensations. Thus, an inner sense of being weak and vulnerable becomes a concrete idea that "someone is out to get me"; this concretization of an inner feeling of helplessness has been projected to the outside world. The next step is for the individual to reinforce the image of external enemies by means of visual and auditory experiences that take the form of hallucinations or false sensory experiences. When this happens, the essential ego function of *reality testing* is lost. Reality testing is the ability to differentiate between internal and external stimuli. What the individual sees, hears, feels, tastes, or smells in the form of a hallucination supports what she already believes—namely, that she is weak, helpless, and at the mercy of powerful forces.

CONCEPTS FROM HARRY STACK SULLIVAN

- The *one genus postulate*: No matter how much individuals differ from one another, differences between humans are far less than differences between humans and other species.

- *Personality* is the result of the evolution of the self from recurrent patterns of interpersonal experience.

- *Foresight* is the ability to choose actions appropriate to an experience; it helps maintain the integrity of the self.

- *Instincts* are not predetermined but labile and are continuously modified by experience, maturation, and individual differences.

- *Self-concept* is related to self-esteem. It evolves from the reflected appraisals of others. Evolution of the self-concept is gradual, but the need for self-esteem is present from birth.

- The *good me* is the personification of experience in which the infant is rewarded by tenderness.

- The *bad me* is the personification of experience in which satisfaction is withheld because the mother's tension and anxiety are transferred to the infant.

- The *non-me* is the personification of the emotions of dread, fear, awe, loathing, and horror that are dissociated or disowned as components of the self system.

- *Anxiety* is related to the need for security. It is rooted in infantile dependency on the mother for survival and for the gratification of biological needs.

- *Consensual validation* is the measuring of personal perceptions against the perceptions of others in order to correct distortion or validate accurate perceptions.

- The *prototaxic mode* is the first experiential state of the infant. Experience at this time has a wholeness; before and after concepts are unknown. There is no connection between cause and consequences, no awareness of the self as separate from the rest of the world. Experience is undifferentiated, without limits, cosmic. The infant *is* the world.

- In the *parataxic mode* the undifferentiated wholeness of experience is broken, but parts are not connected. Experiences are unrelated, illogical, fragmented.

- In the *syntaxic mode*, experience is consensually validated; meaning is acquired from group, interpersonal, and social involvement.

- *Selective inattention* operates to prevent consensual validation and preserve distortion by ignoring information that is unwanted or unacceptable.

DESYMBOLIZATION AND DESOCIALIZATION Symbols are a form of condensed language in which the symbol has meaning and implications far beyond its linguistic parameters. For example, a red cross has international significance recognized by millions. Gold medals and blue ribbons are other symbols, both of which convey recognition of excellence and achievement. Figure 7–1 shows various symbols encountered in everyday life that have commonly understood meanings. When an individual suffers a psychotic episode, the meanings commonly attached to symbols are replaced by more primitive connotations understood only by that individual. Since the acquisition of shared meaning occurs through socialization and communication, *desymbolization*—the loss of consensually understood symbolic meanings—results in *desocialization* and isolation (Arieti 1974).

Psychodynamic Theories

Psychodynamic theories suggest that schizophrenic thought processes are largely the result of the formation of a fragile ego, which cannot withstand the demands of external reality. The individual with impaired ego development cannot cope with the stress of internal and external pressures that produce conflict. Conflict arises when there is a disparity between the psychological needs of an individual and sociocultural expectations. This disparity produces subjective discomfort, which is relieved by social withdrawal and other regressive behaviors.

According to traditional psychoanalytic theory, mothers often feel both love and hate toward their child. The regressed behavior of the schizophrenic child represents a renunciation of normal separation and individuation; the child sacrifices emotional maturation for the sake of the mother. Frequently, the mother herself has inner feelings of emptiness and worthlessness that make her unable to tolerate the child's self-sacrificing love. As a result the mother acts in a way that makes it extremely difficult for the child to separate but then resents the child's inability to do so. Since any attempts on the part of the child to separate from his mother generate guilt and anxiety, the recourse of the child is to continue to exist in a state of psychological entrapment, anxiety, and conflict.

One unfortunate result of explaining the etiology of schizophrenia by means of psychodynamic theory is the tendency to blame the family, especially the mother, for the breakdown of the child. Present-day investigators question the value of any generalizations that give simple answers to complicated questions and also add guilt to the distress already present in the family. Blaming the mother for a child's problems remains a common practice (Chess 1982) even though theorists have stressed the importance of a child's attachment to both mother and father in the early stages of life (Lamb 1984). The widespread scapegoating of mothers is due to some theorists' efforts to fit all families into the psychoanalytic model. It is irresponsible, however, and certainly not holistic to make assessments based on a rather narrow ideology. Early etiological studies of schizophrenia were based on psychoanalytic concepts that tended to blame the mother without taking into account additional relevant variables.

To counteract the assigning of blame that may occur when psychoanalytic guidelines are being used, Caplan and Hall-McCorquodale have made the following recommendations (1985):

Figure 7–1. *Symbol substitutes for verbal messages. (a) Road sign for "falling rocks." (b) Shipping symbol for "keep frozen." (c) Hobo cat symbol for "kind lady lives here." (d) Navy signal flag for "I need assistance."*

(a)

(b)

(c)

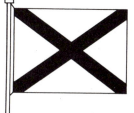

(d)

■ Attention to parent/child interaction should replace focus on mother/child interaction.

■ Contributions and influences of all family members should be considered.

■ Characteristics of a child's innate temperament and developing personality must be considered.

■ Etiological factors of schizophrenia are too complex to assign sole responsibility for it to any single person or event.

THE PROCESS OF THOUGHT DISTURBANCE

Schizophrenia is sometimes depicted not as a single disorder but as a group of disorders, each of which exhibits both similarities with and differences from the others (American Psychiatric Association 1987). A common denominator among the schizophrenic disorders is thought and language distortion, which is manifested in various ways.

Another common denominator is the regressive sequence followed by persons in the grip of the schizophrenic process.

The sequential manifestations of schizophrenia may be described in a general way. Table 7–3 identifies sequential steps of the schizophrenic process, the underlying emotions, and their behavioral consequences.

Types of Thought Disruption

Emil Kraepelin was the first to differentiate this disorder, to classify it according to observable behaviors, and to label it *dementia praecox*, which means "madness of the young" (Lehmann 1980). The disorder was renamed "schizophrenia" by Eugene Bleuler in 1911, based on what Bleuler saw as a splitting of psychological functions. The person suffering from schizophrenia does not have a "split personality" but rather suffers a split, or departure, from reality. Another splitting aspect of schizophrenia is the separation between thought and affect that frequently develops. For instance, persons with this disorder may feel gratified but give no outward sign, or react to their grief by singing or laughing boisterously. In some instances, schizophrenic persons may weep and smile simultaneously without apparent cause.

When Kraepelin identified and differentiated schizophrenia on the basis of systematic observation, his approach was descriptive, not etiologic. Interestingly, this early descriptive approach has been revived in DSM-III-R. One rationale for reviving descriptive classifications was the lack of agreement among researchers and clinicians on the issue of etiologic or causative factors.

Table 7–4 presents the typology of schizophrenic disorders found in the DSM-III-R, along with the behaviors that often accompany them. Because this typology is based on behaviors that can be identified and described, there is some overlap. The same person might demonstrate catatonic behavior in one acute episode but not in another; another individual may return to the same behavioral pattern during every psychotic episode. A wide range of diversity prevails in the clinical manifestations of schizophrenia. However, the use of a typology provides researchers and clinicians with a common language so that the manifestations can be identified and described.

Primary Manifestations

Bleuler (1950) described four primary indicators that are pervasive and identifiable in all persons with schizophrenia, regardless of typology. Each of the four primary indicators begins with the letter *A*,

---

Table 7–3. Sequential Steps of the Schizophrenic Process		
Experiential State	**Emotional Response**	**Behavioral Consequences**
Inability to trust	Fearfulness, insecurity, ambivalence	Avoidance behaviors to decrease fear and insecurity and to handle ambivalence
Dissociation	Loneliness, isolation, unhappiness	Withdrawal from the social and physical environment
Depersonalization	Preoccupation with the self, narcissism, alienation	Replacement of attachments to others by self-attachment
Delusions	Retreat from reality into a self-created world; excessive self-absorption and autism	Loss of contact with reality—the real world no longer exists, and only the fantasized world is real; behavior is shaped by events within the self-created world
Projection	Attribution of inner thoughts and feelings to people or objects in the external environment; thoughts and feelings are generated by conditions within the fantasized world	Denial of inner feelings; projection of inner feelings to others in order to avoid responsibility and self-determination

Table 7-4. Typology of Schizophrenia Based on Behaviors

Type	Predominant Behaviors
Catatonic	Psychomotor disturbances, such as stupor, rigidity, posturing, negativism, excitement, alternating excitement and stupor, mutism, and waxy flexibility (retaining a position until the previous posture is gradually resumed)
Disorganized	Incoherence and/or flat, incongruous, inappropriate or silly affect; fragmented delusions and/or hallucinations; social eccentricity in the form of grimaces, mannerisms; hypochondriacal complaints; social withdrawal
Paranoid	Delusions and/or hallucinations that are persecutory or grandiose; demonstrations of anger, anxiety, argumentativeness, aggressiveness; doubts regarding gender identity
Residual	At least one previous episode of schizophrenia but no psychotic signs currently present; residual features persist in the form of illogical thinking, bizarre behavior, loose associations, blunt or unresponsive affect, social withdrawal
Undifferentiated	Obvious and prominent psychotic features that do not fit into other categories or that meet the criteria for more than one category

POSSIBLE NURSING DIAGNOSES RELATED TO THOUGHT VARIATIONS AND DISRUPTIONS

Impaired social interaction
Social isolation
Altered role performance
Altered family processes
Altered sexuality patterns
Ineffective individual coping
Impaired adjustment
Defensive coping
Noncompliance (specify)
Sleep pattern disturbance
Altered health maintenance
Self-esteem disturbance
Personal identity disturbance
Sensory/perceptual alterations (specify type: visual, auditory, kinesthetic, gustatory, tactile, olfactory)
Hopelessness
Powerlessness
Altered thought processes
Potential for violence: directed at self or others
Anxiety
Fear

The above are nursing diagnoses likely to be observed in clients with thought variations and disruptions, but possible nursing diagnoses are not limited to the list shown above. Manifestations of thought variations and disruptions are individualistic and fluctuating. In some instances the manifestations are persistent and consistent, but often they are not.

which can serve as a mnemonic device: (1) associative looseness, (2) autism, (3) ambivalence, and (4) alterations of affect.

ASSOCIATIVE LOOSENESS The schizophrenic client exhibits alteration in normal modes of thinking. Instead of the logical thought patterns characteristic of adult thinking, the individual reverts to early, primitive modes of thinking. Unable to think or reason logically, the schizophrenic person cannot act in a rational manner. His irrational thinking is maintained because his thoughts and actions are based on personalized interpretations of reality that cannot be validated or understood by others.

Loose associations are thought and communication patterns characterized by unclear connections between one idea and the next. The individual has great difficulty in organizing thoughts, and her ideas are not followed to a logical conclusion. Consequently, her language is confusing and difficult to understand. An example of loose association is the statement of one schizophrenic client, "I like Tarzan, but the car doesn't eat bananas."

Magical thinking is another form of associative thought alteration. The person who engages in magical thinking believes that thoughts have the power to change events. As a result, the person is convinced that thoughts can bring about good or bad outcomes. If the client thinks negatively about someone and that person suffers misfortune, the client attributes this to the power of his thoughts. This also means that the individual believes that the thoughts of other people can be harmful and dangerous.

AUTISM Regression is a common phenomenon in schizophrenia that results in the individual's energies being directed toward the self. This defense mechanism enables the individual to return to an earlier stage of development regarding thoughts, feelings, and behaviors. As regression continues, she may return to infantile ways of relating to others. This causes deterioration in social relationships that depend on mutuality. The social environment is ignored, and a new environment is invented where customary ways of interacting can be abandoned and the client can become totally self-engrossed.

AMBIVALENCE The person with schizophrenia tends to have mixed feelings of love, hate, and fear toward persons he is expected to love. There are similar feelings of ambivalence toward the self and toward objects, situations, events, and relationships. Ambivalence may be so great that the person is immobilized and can only cling to inactivity and apathy. Most people have ambivalent feelings about events and individuals in their lives. The difference between the normal ambivalence with which everyone must deal and the excessive ambivalence of schizophrenia is the degree to which ambivalence affects behavior. An example is the response of a client hospitalized on an inpatient unit who was given the privilege of leaving the unit unescorted for one hour. The client had been looking forward to this privilege but, when the time came to leave the unit, he decided not to go and expressed a desire to remain on the unit and play cards with a staff member instead.

Another way that ambivalence can be expressed is through negativism. The negativistic client refuses to participate in appropriate activities or to cooperate voluntarily. Repeated refusals indicate that she may be trying to handle ambivalent feelings that intensify anxiety. Such clients are equally likely either to refuse to begin doing something or to refuse to stop doing it. For example, a client may refuse to follow the routine of a treatment facility, resisting suggestions to get out of bed in the morning, to dress, to eat, or to participate in activities. Yet once the client becomes involved in an activity

it may be equally difficult for staff members to persuade him to do anything else.

Some clients express ambivalence through repeated, ceaseless activity that appears to have no meaning. An example is the client who sits in a chair for a few minutes, gets up, looks out the window, returns to the chair, and repeats these maneuvers for hours if permitted to do so.

Other clients express their ambivalence by complying with everything that is asked of them but refusing to do anything unless asked specifically and told how to do it. Such clients must be told when to go to bed, when to get up, and what to wear, and they need detailed instructions about how these actions should be performed (Haber et al. 1982).

ALTERATIONS OF AFFECT When judged by ordinary standards, the emotions and outward affect of the individual with schizophrenia seem extraordinary. The terms "affect" and "emotion" are often used interchangeably, but it should be emphasized that *emotion* refers to the inner, somatic expression of feeling whereas *affect* refers to the outward behavior engendered by emotion (Kolb and Brodie 1982). Affective reactions permeate the psychic life of individuals, influencing their acceptance and rejection of events and experiences. The affective alterations noted in schizophrenic clients stem from their need to cope with intense feelings that might evoke unbearable anxiety if confronted directly. These affective alterations are distancing or protective actions

---

DSM III-R CLASSIFICATION OF DISORDERS OF THOUGHT AND PERCEPTION

Schizophrenia

295.2x	Catatonic
295.1x	Disorganized
295.3x	Paranoid (specify if stable type)
295.9x	Undifferentiated
295.6x	Residual (specify if late onset)

Delusional (Paranoid) Disorder

297.10	Delusional (paranoid) disorder (specify type: erotomanic, grandiose, jealous, persecutory, somatic, unspecified)

Psychotic Disorders Not Elsewhere Classified

298.80	Brief reactive psychosis
295.40	Schizophreniform disorder (specify with good prognostic features or without good prognostic features)
295.70	Schizoaffective disorder (specify bipolar type or depressive type)
297.30	Induced psychotic disorder
298.90	Psychotic disorder NOS (not otherwise specified) (atypical psychosis)

taken to isolate or overcome painful emotions. Alterations of affect take the form of inappropriate affect, blunted affect, and apathy.

Inappropriate affect is an outward display of emotion that is not in harmony with reality. The client demonstrates a mood that is unsuited to the situation. An example is the client who breaks into boisterous laughter on being told that a faithful pet dog has been killed by a speeding car.

Blunted affect is an extreme decrease in the intensity of the client's response to any person, idea, or experience. For example, the loss of a month's stipend would be expected to arouse a strong negative response, but a schizophrenic individual might appear quite indifferent to the loss. People whose affect is blunted usually present themselves as unresponsive to events around them, whether pleasant or unpleasant. Their reactions are unemotional, flat, and dull, regardless of the nature of their experiences.

Apathy is a behaviorally demonstrated indifference to one's social and physical environment, characterized by a lack of commitment and involvement. For instance, a client's family might enter the dayroom of a psychiatric facility, carrying brightly wrapped packages and a cake aglow with candles, singing "Happy Birthday" to the client. Instead of responding with pleasure, the client might remain seated in a chair, ignoring the song, the cake, and the gifts, giving no outward sign or response to the celebration. In contrast, a person showing blunted affect would respond minimally to such an event but would be capable of acknowledging its occurrence. Often apathy and blunted affect appear in combination.

The client who is apathetic tends to be consistent in showing this affective state. Nursing records of such clients indicate little change in affect regardless of the client's situation. A graphic record of the affect of an apathetic client would consist simply of a straight line. The term *flatness of affect* is often used to describe the absence of emotional responsiveness characteristic of schizophrenic clients who display apathy and blunted affect.

Secondary Manifestations

In addition to the primary features of schizophrenia identified by Bleuler, there are a number of secondary characteristics, which include alterations in language, perception, self-image, and thought.

ALTERATIONS IN LANGUAGE Verbal interaction depends on the ability to exchange thoughts and ideas, to express feeling, and to share perceptions. Schizophrenic alterations in language and communication reduce the ability of the individual to form relationships. Serious alterations or disruptions in thought patterns are reflected in the way that language is used. An alteration of language comes about for two reasons: (1) the individual cannot usually utilize language effectively and has thus developed a private language that no one else can understand (Beck, Rawlings, and Williams 1984); (2) the person is unable to synthesize segments of thought into a whole and his language often identifies only fragments or part of an idea. As a result schizophrenic alterations in language frequently take the forms of echolalia, clang associations, neologisms, and word salad.

Echolalia is the purposeless repetition of a word or phrase that someone else has just spoken. For example, the nurse might say to the client, "In the next step blue yarn is used." The client would respond, "Yarn is used, yarn is used, yarn is used."

A *clang association* is a repetition of words or phrases having a similar sound but no other relationship. For example, when the client is asked, "What would you like to drink?" she responds by saying, "Drink, think, stink, blink."

A *neologism* is a private word or phrase that has special meaning for the client but that cannot be understood by others. For example, when a client is asked a question about a favorite television show, the response might be "Fodda sodda kor."

Word salad is a linking of words and phrases in a meaningless, disconnected way. As an example, a client seated at a dining table might say, "Coffee is innocent, and when the dog runs, the chair melts."

ALTERATIONS IN PERCEPTION *Perception* is the process of recognizing and interpreting stimuli. Perception is influenced by both cognitive and emotional processes. All people sometimes perceive stimuli accurately and sometimes distort or misinterpret them. An example of perceptual distortion with schizophrenia is provided in Figure 7–2. When distortion or misinterpretation of perceptions becomes habitual, the result may be the development of hallucinations.

Hallucinations are false sensory perceptions that have no basis in reality and that are generated by internal rather than external stimuli. They most often are auditory or visual misperceptions, although olfactory, gustatory, and tactile hallucinations are also experienced. Tactile hallucinations are usually the result of an organic condition or drug or alcohol toxicity. There are five types of hallucinations:

1. *Auditory hallucinations* are sounds or voices heard only by the client. Often the voices berate and accuse the client; they are considered

Figure 7–2. *Progressive perceptual distortions in altered patterns of thought and perception. These drawings were made by an artist with schizophrenia (Louis Wain, 1860–1939) over the course of his disorder.*
SOURCE: © 1985 Aspect: Derek Bayes, CLICK/Chicago.

(a)

(b)

to be projections of the client's anxiety-producing thoughts and feelings, which must be disclaimed and attributed to external sources. An example of a person with an auditory hallucination is the client who hears voices telling her that her parents must not visit in the hospital. These messages may originate because the client fears parental disapproval of the hospitalization.

2. *Gustatory hallucinations* are sensations of tastes and flavors that reflect the internal experience of the client and have no basis in reality. An example of a gustatory hallucination is the experience of a client who learns of the death of her husband while drinking a particular soft drink and later experiences a bitter taste whenever she tries to drink this beverage.

3. *Olfactory hallucinations* are odors and aromas smelled only by the client that seem to emanate from specific or unknown sources. An example

of an olfactory hallucination is the experience of a client who smells sulfurous fumes whenever a clergyman is present.

4. *Tactile hallucinations* are unusual somatic sensations that cannot be explained factually. An example of this type of hallucination is the experience of the client who believes that insects are crawling under his skin or that worms infest his vital organs.

5. *Visual hallucinations* are visual images that appear to the client in the absence of valid external stimuli. An example of a visual hallucination is the experience of the client who sees deceased friends, historical figures, or threatening spectres. Another form of visual hallucination involves distortions in how things are perceived. For most people four perceptual constancies act to promote accurate visual perception: constancy of size, color, shape, and location. In some visual hallucinations one or more perceptual constancies may be lost and objects seem to change unpredictably. Table 7–5 describes and gives examples of major perceptual constancies that may be lost during a visual hallucinatory experience.

(c)

(d)

ALTERATIONS IN SELF-IMAGE Often the client with schizophrenia experiences distortions in how he perceives himself. These distortions may affect body image, or they may affect ego boundaries. For many schizophrenic persons, body image is not a stable concept. Parts of the body are subject to imagined change, and the client may become preoccupied with changes not apparent to anyone else. When looking into a mirror, the client may believe that the reflected image really belongs to someone else or that her nose is becoming an eagle's beak.

Body image and ego boundaries are closely associated for the person with schizophrenia. The somatic and psychological boundaries that define the individual as a separate entity are sometimes so indistinct that the client is not able to maintain a sense of himself as an entity, distinct and separate from the environment. *Depersonalization* is the term used to define feelings of unreality and instability about the self. The result of depersonalization is a sense of living in a dream, an inability to discriminate between the inner and outer parts of one's body, and feelings of not being in control. When ego boundaries are indistinct, clients may believe that they have merged with the environment and are lost. For example, a client walking in the grass may feel that she has become part of Mother Nature. Feelings of depersonalization may render clients unable to reconcile body image with their assigned gender. Thus, a female client may believe that her body is masculine or a male client may feel that his mind is feminine.

ALTERATIONS IN THOUGHT The schizophrenic person may reveal gross or subtle alterations in normal modes of thought. Instead of the mature thought patterns characteristic of adult thinking, the schizophrenic person may return to the thought modes of childhood. When unable to think clearly or reason logically, the individual finds it difficult to act like other people. Thus, the altered thought modes produce individualistic interpretations that lead to puzzling, incomprehensible behaviors. Alterations that affect thinking and cognition may take various forms, including autistic thinking, concrete thinking, and delusions.

Autistic thinking is a form of thinking that endeavors to gratify unfulfilled desires and needs. Thoughts manifest themselves as daydreams, fantasies, and delusions. The unconscious level of mental awareness is the most active in autistic thinking.

Table 7–5. Definitions and Examples of Major Perceptual Constancies

Perceptual Constancy	Definition	Example
Size constancy	Objects are perceived as remaining the same size even though their visual images change at different distances.	Approaching objects such as automobiles seem to get closer, while distant objects are perceived as distant.
Color constancy	Objects are perceived as being of a stable color regardless of the amount of light in the environment.	A white object appears white even in a dim light and a black object appears black even in a bright light.
Shape constancy	Objects are perceived as having a stable shape even though their visual images change when they are seen at different angles.	Round objects such as wheels are seen as circles even when the visual image is an ellipse; rectangular objects such as doors are seen as rectangular shapes even when their visual image is trapezoid.
Location constancy	Objects are correctly perceived as stationary or moving, despite movement of their visual images.	Persons riding in an automobile see immobile objects being passed as stationary even though the images change with the car's movement.

Most people utilize stimuli and impressions gathered from the outside world to organize their experience in a meaningful way. The excessive anxiety of the schizophrenic person causes the self rather than the outside world to be used as a frame of reference in organizing experience. The outside world does not provide gratification, so the client looks inward for validation and satisfaction. Consequently, the client attaches personal and private meanings to experience to which no one else has access. Habitual autistic thought patterns in turn can lead to concrete thinking, delusions, loose associations, and magical thinking.

Concrete thinking is a primitive form of thinking in which thoughts are organized and coherent but generalizations and abstractions are deficient or absent. When engaging in concrete thinking, individuals can sort and classify cognitive material but cannot generalize from specific examples. Inductive reasoning powers are absent, as is the ability to understand logical implications surrounding events and experiences. For example, when a schizophrenic client is told by a laboratory technician, "I'm here to draw your blood," the client might reply, "You forgot your crayons and paper. How can you draw without them?"

Delusions are distorted thought processes in which the client's ability to evaluate and test reality is seriously impaired. A delusion is a false, fixed idea generated within the client in the absence of external stimuli. Delusions tend to repeat certain themes even though details may change over time. The forms that delusions often take and their content themes are presented in Table 7–6.

THERAPEUTIC APPROACHES

For nurses and other health professionals caring for clients with schizophrenia, there is no precise set of

Table 7–6. Forms of Delusion and Content Themes

Form of Delusion	Content Themes
Delusions of persecution	False beliefs that one is being singled out for punishment or harassment. *Example:* A client may feel that coworkers are noisy because they want to interfere with her work.
Delusions of grandeur	False beliefs about one's power or authority. *Example:* A client may believe that he is a reigning monarch and should be treated like royalty.
Delusions of control or undue influence	False beliefs that one is being controlled by others. *Example:* A client believes that beings from another plant control all the appliances in the kitchen.
Delusions of infidelity	False beliefs that a spouse or lover is unfaithful. *Example:* A husband is convinced that his wife is having an affair with the postman and that their letters are written in a secret code.
Somatic delusions	False beliefs about the body or a part of the body. *Example:* A client believes that her heart or kidneys are failing despite medical reassurance to the contrary.
Ideas of reference	False beliefs that certain statements or events have a special meaning for the client. *Example:* A panel of experts is discussing immorality on a television program and the client believes that she is being discussed.

rules or techniques that are uniformly applicable. Nurses need to respond to the behavioral signs of each client's internal experience and to avoid dealing with clients as psychiatric entities rather than as troubled human beings. Nursing process requires an encompassing perspective that considers all dimensions of a client's experience and formulates appropriate nursing interventions based on the client's individualized needs as they are manifested in his behaviors.

Psychotropic Drug Therapy

The discovery of antipsychotic medications has made it possible to control many extreme behavioral manifestations that accompany schizophrenic disorders. By means of appropriate medication, clients who might otherwise be unapproachable are now able to engage in human interactions that make rehabilitation possible.

ANTIPSYCHOTIC MEDICATIONS The first and most widely used antipsychotic drug, chlorpromazine (Thorazine), was discovered by chance. It was considered an antihistamine and was not used for antipsychotic purposes until 1952, when it was noted that the drug had profound effects on the thinking, perception, affect, and behavior of schizophrenics. Antipsychotic medications, among which chlorpromazine is a prime example, cause the schizophrenic person to be less out of touch with reality, less withdrawn, less delusional, and less anxious.

Nurses usually do not prescribe medication, but they do administer medication and supervise clients who take medication on their own, and they frequently make recommendations based on their assessments of clients. The nurse is responsible for instructing clients, for noting the effects of the medication, and for monitoring and dealing with side effects. Most clients receiving an antipsychotic drug or any other psychotropic medication will be taking the drug for considerable periods of time and should know as much as possible about the action of the drug and any necessary precautions. Because nurses are closely involved in the aftercare of clients taking psychotropic medication, they should have accurate, up-to-date information regarding range of dosage, therapeutic action, and possible side effects.

The specific action of major tranquilizers administered to control manifestations of schizophrenia is not fully understood. One hypothesis is that in certain areas of the central nervous system there is excessive activity of the neurotransmitter dopamine, which is thought to precipitate the psychotic reaction. Antipsychotic drugs block dopamine receptors in the brain and central nervous system, thus reducing the severity of the psychotic reaction. The antipsychotic drugs used for schizophrenia differ only in their potency and side effects; the therapeutic effectiveness of most of the antipsychotic drugs is similar, although their range of dosages is not equivalent.

PRIMARY SYMPTOMS OF ALTERED PATTERNS OF THOUGHT AND PERCEPTION (4 A's)

- *Ambivalence*. Mixed, conflicted feelings about self, others, events, or relationships.
- *Autism*. Self-engrossment accompanied by regressed behaviors.
- *Altered affect*. Inappropriate, blunted, inconsistent emotional responses.
- *Loose associations*. Unclear connections between one thought and the next.

Table 7–7 lists the generic and trade names of the most often used antipsychotic drugs, their dosage range, and the forms in which the drugs are available.

Antipsychotic medications are relatively safe for most clients, but there are a number of troublesome side effects. Truly dangerous side effects, such as cardiac arrhythmias, are rare, but there are more frequent side effects that prove uncomfortable and sometimes frightening for clients. Before antipsychotic medication is prescribed, the general health of the individual should be evaluated. Electrocardiograms should be done initially and at regular intervals thereafter. When side effects do occur, they should be identified promptly and measures should be instituted to restore the client's comfort. The common side effects of antipsychotic medications can be classified according to the physiological structures that are involved.

Allergic Reactions Blood dyscrasias are among the hypersensitive reactions that may develop. These include agranulocytosis, which often begins as a sore throat and fever, and eosinophilia, which is usually benign. Blood tests should be done regularly to monitor any blood changes. If a client has a history of blood dyscrasia, these side effects are more likely to appear, and when they do occur it is usually early in treatment.

Contact dermatitis is another reaction that is distressing to clients. Sometimes a skin reaction takes the form of urticaria, and the itching can be very uncomfortable. Pigment deposits in the skin cause darkened areas, especially if the client is taking chlorpromazine. Heightened sensitivity to sunlight is also a common side effect.

Autonomic Nervous System Reactions In some clients antipsychotic drugs cause dry mouth, constipation, and blurred vision. Persons with cerebrovascular insufficiency, renal insufficiency, or cardiac

Table 7–7. Antipsychotic Medications

Drugs by Category	Trade Name	Oral Dosage (mg/day)	Available Forms
Phenothiazines			
Chlorpromazine	Thorazine	50–1200	Tablet, liquid, injection, suppository
Promazine	Sparine	100–2400	Tablet, liquid, injection
Triflupromazine	Vesprin	30–150	Tablet, liquid, injection
Piperazines			
Acetophenazine	Tindal	40–120	Tablet
Butaperazine	Repoise	50–1000	Tablet
Carphenazine	Proketazine	25–40	Tablet, liquid
Fluphenazine	Prolixin	2–25	Tablet, liquid, injection
Perphenazine	Trilafon	12–64	Tablet, liquid, injection
Trifluoperazine	Stelazine	5–40	Tablet, liquid, injection
Piperidines			
Mesoridazine	Serentil	150–400	Tablet, liquid, injection
Piperacetazine	Quide	40–160	Tablet, injection
Thioridazine	Mellaril	50–800	Tablet, liquid
Butyrophenones			
Droperidol	Inapsine	None	Injection
Haloperidol	Haldol	2–100	Tablet, liquid, injection
Dibenzoxazepines			
Loxapine	Loxitane	15–100	Tablet
Oxoiodoles			
Molindone	Moban	15–225	Tablet
Thioxanthenes			
Chlorprothizene	Taractin	75–600	Tablet, liquid, injection
Thiothixene	Navane	5–60	Tablet, injection

reserve insufficiency may be susceptible to hypotensive episodes and should be observed closely.

Choleostatic jaundice may appear during the first months of drug therapy; it is accompanied by yellowing of the sclera and skin and discoloration of urine and stools. Usually jaundice is preceded by flulike symptoms appearing in the first month of treatment. The medication should be discontinued if these conditions occur. Clients with a history of liver damage are at risk when taking antipsychotic medication, for they may not be able to detoxify the drugs.

The anticholinergic properties of the antipsychotic drugs may cause urinary retention or hesitancy. Men who have prostatic hypertrophy are at greater risk for these problems when taking an antipsychotic drug. Male clients may report inability to sustain an erection or to ejaculate. Occasionally males develop priapism.

Priapism is persistent, abnormal erection of the penis, accompanied by considerable pain and tenderness. The name is derived from Priaps, a king of ancient Greece who seduced a daughter of the gods. His punishment, according to legend, was to remain forever in a state of erection without ejaculation.

Priapism is sometimes a side effect of psychotropic medication, but it also occurs in spinal cord injuries or diseases. It may also result from vesical calculus or trauma to the penis itself.

Compliance in taking appropriate medication helps clients avoid periodic relapses that sometimes occur. Many clients resist taking medication regularly for a variety of reasons. It may be difficult for young male schizophrenics to introduce their concerns about erection and ejaculation. A nurse trying to discover the reasons for a client's noncompliance is fully justified in asking the client if he is experiencing such problems. The information that similar side effects have occurred in others is reassuring to the client. Often it is necessary to change a dosage or substitute another medication that the client can tolerate better.

Endocrine Reactions Side effects that involve the endocrine system can be particularly embarrassing for clients. Breast enlargement or lactation may occur in males and females and is especially upsetting to the male client. Female clients may suffer menstrual irregularities, such as amenorrhea, which can cause fears of pregnancy. Weight gain may be a source of concern for both male and female clients, especially if they are already troubled by body image changes.

NEUROLOGIC REACTIONS One third of those taking an antipsychotic medication will experience extrapyramidal side effects. When extrapyramidal effects go unnoticed or untreated, the client may become frightened enough to refuse further medication. There are four general types of extrapyramidal symptoms: (1) parkinsonism, (2) akathisia, (3) dystonia, and (4) tardive dyskinesia.

Drug-induced parkinsonism is similar to Parkinson's disease and can appear after the first week of taking an antipsychotic drug. If it is to occur, it usually appears before eight weeks of drug administration. Akinesia (changes in posture, shuffling gait, muscular rigidity, and drooling) are manifestations of this drug reaction. Clients with akinesia also exhibit a lack of ambition and interest, fatigue, and slowed movements.

Akathisia is an uneasy feeling of restlessness and agitation. The client has great difficulty sitting still; when urged to do so the client will squirm, fidget, stand up, walk around, and sit down for only short periods. Akathisia appears after approximately two weeks of drug therapy and peaks at six to ten weeks. It is more common in women than men.

Dystonias are bizarre, uncoordinated movements of the neck, face, eyes, tongue, body, and arm and leg muscles. There may be a backward rolling of the eyes in their sockets (ocular gyration), sideways twisting of the neck (torticollis), spasms of the back muscles (opisthotonos), and protrusion of the tongue. The onset is sudden and dramatic, and as a result the client is usually very frightened. The spasms can be so severe that the client may suffer respiratory distress or be unable to swallow or talk. Dystonias may occur any time after the first dose of

an antipsychotic drug, and each episode may last from a few minutes to two hours. Reassurance is often enough to calm the client as the reaction subsides. Diphenhydramine (Benadryl) injected intramuscularly is often administered to counteract this type of reaction.

Tardive dyskinesia is a disorder characterized by rhythmic, involuntary chewing, sucking, licking movements of the mouth, tongue, and lower jaw. Frowning, blinking, and tongue protrusion are often present. Two of the earliest indications of tardive dyskinesia are fine vermiform movements of the tongue and excessive blinking. Tardive dyskinesia is irreversible, and its manifestations tend to increase when the causative drug is discontinued. Because the condition is persistent once it develops, it is important to be alert to early signs. Occasional "drug holidays" are advisable if the client can manage to forgo medication for a short while. Another preventive measure is to change the antipsychotic drug the client is taking. Some clients can be maintained on a minor tranquilizer such as Librium, which has some antipsychotic properties.

The medications used to control parkinsonism and other extrapyramidal effects of antipsychotic drugs are referred to as *anticholinergic agents*. Sometimes these medications are given as soon as an antipsychotic medication is prescribed. At other times these medications are only administered when side effects become apparent. The most frequently used antiparkinsonian agents are outlined in Table 7–8.

The possible side effects of antipsychotic medications vary in severity as well as in form. The well-informed nurse can help clients deal with troublesome side effects and intervene if side effects are contributing to the client's distress. When teaching clients about the action and complicating factors of psychotropic medications, nurses should explore clients' emotional reactions to taking medication in

Table 7–8. Antiparkinsonian Medications

Drug	Trade Name	Dose (mg/day) PO	IM	Available Forms
Diphenhydramine hydrochloride	Benadryl	25–50 T.i.d.	10–100 T.i.d./Q.i.d.	Capsule, elixir, ampule
Biperiden hydrochloride	Akineton	1–2 T.i.d.	1–15 Q.i.d.	Tablet, ampule
Procyclidine hydrochloride	Kemadrin	2–5 T.i.d.		Tablet
Trihexyphenidyl hydrochloride	Artane	1–5 T.i.d.		Tablet
Benztropine mesylate	Cogentin	1–4 T.i.d.	1–2 Q.i.d.	Tablet, ampule

addition to their physiologic reactions. Table 7–9 summarizes the side effects of antipsychotic medications and outlines specific nursing interventions.

Neuroleptic Malignant Syndrome A neuroleptic drug is a pharmacological agent that produces an antipsychotic effect. Not all psychotropic drugs are neuroleptics, but most of the medications taken by schizophrenic clients can be classified as neuroleptics. The serious side effect known as neuroleptic malignant syndrome was not identified until the late 1960s, when Dutch researchers presented it as a rare phenomenon. Later statistics indicate that NMS is far less rare than was once believed. Caroff (1980) wrote that NMS is a life-threatening problem of major proportions, considering the large numbers of persons who take antipsychotic medications for many years. Estimates of mortality range from 20 to 30 percent (Sternberg 1986). Death occurs within 3 to 30 days of onset; cause of death is respiratory failure, cardiovascular collapse, and acute renal failure (Pope, Keck, and McElroy 1986).

All persons taking antipsychotic medication are at risk for NMS. It does not seem to be dose related, and some persons who have tolerated a medication for years may suddenly develop the syndrome. It is believed that NMS is caused by neuroleptic-induced blockage of dopamine receptors. It is more common in the young, particularly males who are less than 40 years old. The onset is sudden and explosive. Only a few hours may elapse between the suggestive first symptoms and the debilitating ones that follow.

As soon as the imminence or onset of NMS is suspected, supportive nursing measures should be initiated, along with medical and psychiatric consultation.

Relationship Therapy

The role of the primary therapist is usually enacted by a professional care provider with graduate

---

INDICATORS OF NEUROLEPTIC MALIGNANT SYNDROME ONSET

- Incontinence
- Dysphagia
- Mutism
- Tachypnea
- Cogwheeling
- Opisthotonus
- Retrocolis
- Delirium
- Stupor/Coma
- Recovery/Death

LEVELS OF NURSING INTERVENTION FOR NEUROLEPTIC MALIGNANT SYNDROME

Primary

- Regularly monitor blood pressure and vital signs of all clients taking antipsychotic medication
- Carefully observe muscle tone and rigidity in clients taking antipsychotic medication
- Carefully assess objective or subjective signs of hyperpyrexia, diaphoresis, confusion, or disorientation

Secondary

- Discontinue antipsychotic medication upon appearance of symptoms
- Continue administering antiparkinsonian medication. Notify physician and clinical nurse specialist
- Initiate supportive measures to reduce fever
- Monitor blood pressure and vital signs
- Monitor electrolyte balance
- Monitor intake and output flow

Tertiary

- Review psychiatric status of client as soon as vital signs are stable
- Consider alternative psychotropic medications
- Monitor neuroleptic serum level while client is taking antipsychotic medication
- Initiate and maintain ongoing client and family teaching regarding NMS

INDICATORS OF IMMINENT OR POSSIBLE NEUROLEPTIC MALIGNANT SYNDROME

- Elevated temperature (hyperpyrexia)
- Severe extrapyramidal rigidity
- Elevated blood pressure, especially the diastolic
- Autonomic instability (diaphoresis, tachycardia)
- Altered levels of consciousness (confusion, disorientation)

Table 7–9. Side Effects of Antipsychotic Medications and Nursing Interventions

Side Effects	Nursing Interventions
Allergic reactions Blood dyscrasias	1. Assess the client and note increased temperature, itching of the skin, sore throat, bruises, nosebleeds. 2. Withhold medication until the client can be evaluated further.
Contact dermatitis	1. Treat the symptoms and reassure the client. 2. Obtain a medical order for appropriate topical and oral medications. 3. Withhold antipsychotic medication until the client can be evaluated further.
Sunlight sensitivity	1. Advise client to wear sunglasses if necessary. 2. Advise client to use sunburn preventives when outdoors. 3. Advise client to avoid direct sunlight and to cover exposed skin with clothing when outdoors. 4. Remind clients with dark complexions that they may be sensitive to sunlight and are also at risk.
Autonomic nervous system reactions Arrythmias and T-wave abnormalities	1. Monitor pulse for irregularities. 2. Arrange for routine electrocardiogram. 3. Notify nursing and medical staff members.
Blurred vision	1. Arrange for periodic examination of client to determine whether retinitis pigmentosa is present. 2. Reassure client that visual disturbance is usually temporary and will probably subside in 2–6 weeks.
Constipation	1. Encourage client to maintain adequate fluid intake. Encourage greater intake of fresh fruits, prunes, and bran. 2. Offer stool softeners and mild laxatives if necessary. 3. Encourage more activity and physical exercise. 4. If condition is severe, withhold medication and notify physician so as to prevent paralytic ileus.
Dry mouth	1. Offer glycerine mouth swabs. 2. Encourage frequent sips of water. 3. Suggest sugarless gum or lozenges. 4. Examine for fungal infections.
Ejaculatory inhibition	1. Reassure client and explain probable cause. 2. Inform client that medication can be changed or dosage altered with approval of physician. 3. Be sensitive to covert indications from client that this may be a problem. 4. Provide an open, permissive attitude to enable the client to discuss the problem freely. 5. Include information regarding the possibility of this problem when teaching the client about medication.
Jaundice	1. Observe client for yellowing of skin and sclera. 2. Assess for discoloration of urine and stools. 3. Withhold medication until client is evaluated further.
Hypotension or hypertensive crisis	1. Instruct the client to arise slowly from a supine to a sitting position, dangling the legs before standing. 2. Help client stand after rising if dizziness or disorientation occurs. 3. When antipsychotic medication is initiated, record sitting and standing blood pressure. If systolic reading drops more than 20 mm, withhold medication temporarily. Take blood pressure reading in 30 minutes. If unchanged, consult physician before administering medication.
Tachycardia	1. Monitor pulse rate. 2. Withhold medication and consult physician if resting pulse is 120 or more.
Urinary hesitancy or retention	1. Record intake and output to establish urinary baseline. 2. Observe client for signs of obstruction or infection. 3. Withhold medication if client continues to be unable to void and notify physician.
Endocrine system reactions Breast enlargement, lactation, amenorrhea, weight gain	1. Offer explanations of how the medication works, adapted to client's level of understanding. 2. Reassure client concerning the seriousness of side effects. 3. Inform female clients that amenorrhea does not indicate the absence of ovulation. 4. Encourage weight control through exercise and proper diet.
Neurological reaction Akathisia and akinesia	1. Reassure client that the condition is reversible. 2. Differentiate side effects from other features of client's condition, such as recurrence of psychosis. 3. Administer an antiparkinsonian agent as prescribed.
Dystonia	1. Obtain a p.r.n. order for an antiparkinsonian agent when an antipsychotic drug is prescribed, especially if client has a history of such side effects. 2. Teach the client to recognize the onset of side effects. 3. Remain with the client for the duration of an episode, offering reassurance. 4. Obtain help from other staff members in order to administer p.r.n. antiparkinsonian agent by IM or IV routes, since oral medication may be contraindicated during dystonic episode.
Tardive dyskinesia	1. Use antiparkinsonian agents concurrently with antipsychotic medication. 2. When necessary, use parenteral antiparkinsonian medication. 3. Use preventive measures such as "drug holidays." 4. Suggest reduced dosages or change of medication at first indications of tardive dyskinesia. 5. Assess all clients regularly who are receiving antipsychotic drugs. Report early signs of this complication immediately.

preparation, but generalist nurses function as caregivers in many psychiatric settings in the hospital and the community. The care offered by the generalist nurse to clients with schizophrenic disorders is often based on principles of relationship therapy, which may be augmented by medication, group therapy, or individual therapy. Relationship therapy is the establishment of a one-to-one therapeutic relationship between nurse and client in which the nursing process is used to meet the client's needs.

The client's current level of functioning reflects the setting in which the nurse encounters the client. If, for example, the client is experiencing an acute psychotic episode, in all likelihood care will be provided in a hospital setting. If the client is living in the community, his behavioral symptoms are probably being controlled reasonably well by medication and supportive care.

Interpersonal communication and therapeutic relationships are areas in which schizophrenic clients are likely to experience problems and in which nurses can be extremely helpful. Initially, the nurse must try to understand how the client is experiencing the world. In beginning to establish a therapeutic relationship the nurse must convey a sincere wish to understand and to communicate, even if this is likely to be a slow process. Relationship therapy is effective only when trust is established and when the client experiences the feeling of being understood and accepted. Arnold (1976) proposed four principles of therapeutic interaction for these clients: acceptance, acknowledgement, authenticity, and awareness.

Acceptance The nurse must accept the client at the developmental and behavioral level at which he is functioning. Moreover, the nurse must recognize and accept the existence of her personal and private reactions to the client in order to foster self-awareness and preserve therapeutic objectivity.

Acknowledgment Whenever the client is not accepted as a unique human being and her communication efforts are not acknowledged in a caring and honest manner, she will feel that her legitimate needs have not been sufficiently acknowledged or fulfilled. The schizophrenic client needs to know that the nurse and other caregivers are attempting to understand the obscure messages that she is verbally and behaviorally conveying. It is important for the nurse to indicate to the client whether a message has been understood. For a nurse to pretend that he comprehends a message when in fact he has not is a way of negating the client's self-worth and dignity.

Authenticity The nurse who works with schizophrenic clients should try not to engage in deception of any kind. Schizophrenic clients are highly sensitive to the emotional overtones of other people. Indeed, their extreme sensitivity probably contributed to the onset of their disorder. Every interaction between the nurse and the client should be honest and oriented to reality.

Awareness In order for the nurse and client to communicate effectively, the nurse must acknowledge and analyze the reactive feelings, thoughts, and actions that the client arouses in the nurse. Self-understanding on the part of the nurse, augmented by knowledge of verbal and nonverbal levels of communication, is essential to the establishment and continuation of a trusting relationship with the client.

Schizophrenia is a disturbance that includes cognitive and affective changes but eventually is expressed behaviorally. The nursing care plan must be tailored to the particular behaviors exhibited. Understanding the theoretical explanations for the client's behavior helps the nurse to realize that dysfunctional behaviors are part of the disorder rather than deliberate challenges. Table 7–10 enumerates some of the behavioral manifestations of schizophrenia and outlines some appropriate nursing interventions that can be adapted to individual client needs.

Schizophrenic clients who have been successfully treated with relationship therapy tend to see their caregivers as protective, friendly, and strong (Arieti 1974) and to recognize that efforts are being made to help but that excessive demands are not being imposed on them (Wolman 1976).

Milieu Therapy
Relationship therapy is an approach fully compatible with the nursing process and role. Milieu therapy is a variation of relationship therapy offered on a larger scale.

The basic principle of milieu therapy is that all of the client's surroundings, physical and interpersonal, constitute part of the therapeutic environment. The facility, whether an inpatient unit, a day treatment center, or a halfway house, should not be just a place where care is given but an actual component of the total treatment program. The concept of milieu therapy incorporates the idea of a therapeutic community devoted to holistic health care. The old-fashioned term *asylum* once implied a place of refuge, a safe retreat from the threats and dangers of the outside world. It is true that some emotionally disturbed people may indeed benefit from spending time in a safe, tranquil environment

Table 7–10. Behavioral Manifestations of Schizophrenic Clients	
Behavioral Manifestations	**Nursing Interventions**
Withdrawal	Promote client's participation in grooming and personal hygiene by giving positive reinforcement for self-care activities. Protect the client's self-esteem by avoiding derogatory comments. Praise any efforts directed toward self-care or greater involvement. Encourage remotivation and resocialization group activities. Encourage and support the client as participation in structured activities is renewed.
Mutism	Recognize that mutism is a form of withdrawal. Exercise patience and communicate an attitude of hopefulness. Comment on nonverbal messages transmitted by the client. Communicate in a clear, simple fashion that does not require a verbal answer.
Immobility	Utilize nursing measures to prevent circulatory deficits, spasticity, or loss of muscle tone. Be attentive to general health needs. Offer exercise, diet, and adequate rest to clients whose coping skills consist of social isolation and self-neglect.
Excessive activity	Recognize that frenzied activity may be used to block out reality. Offer interventions directed to preserving physical well-being. Encourage activities and games that are not physically or mentally demanding.
Suspicion of others	Maintain a matter-of-fact attitude. Avoid close physical contact. Maintain eye contact judiciously. Maintain physical distance that is neither very close nor very distant. Do not put medication into food or liquids without the client's knowledge. Avoid power struggles with the client.
Communication deficits	Permit the client to make decisions when possible. Speak clearly and concisely. Avoid emotionally charged words. Speak in tones that are neither very loud nor very soft. Ask for clarification when the client's message is unclear. Let the client know when it is hard to understand autistic communication.
Inappropriate behavior	Protect the client from embarrassment. Protect others from anxiety-producing situations.
Delusions and hallucinations	Let the client know that you do not consider the delusions and hallucinations to be real. Encourage the client not to discuss these issues with others. Do not argue with the client about the reality of delusions or hallucinations. Accept the fact that they are real for the client. Distract the client by encouraging a return to reality through activities or interpersonal involvement. For example, say to a client who is responding to internal stimuli, "You don't seem to be listening to what I am saying . . . Try to concentrate on what is going on in this room."

where they are not bombarded with excessive stimuli or subjected to stress. For people like this an asylum that lived up to its name might be quite helpful. However, the majority of clients with psychological problems already tend to withdraw from others and to avoid responsibility and involvement. Therefore, they need an atmosphere where they feel relatively secure but are encouraged to keep busy and to engage in positive social interactions. For schizophrenic clients, the inclination to regress and to become self-engrossed should be balanced by therapeutic programs that encourage outward rather than inward interests. Milieu therapy is a comprehensive approach that attempts to accomplish this goal.

The purpose of milieu therapy is to oppose regression and to foster in clients a sense of personal worth, to enhance their ability to interact with others, and to increase their social competence so that a return to a more rewarding lifestyle is possible. Milieu therapy is flexible enough to provide security and safety for some clients, limit setting for others, and provide remotivation and resocialization activities for all. Perhaps the most important function of milieu therapy is the restoration or

maintenance of self-confidence and autonomy. This is done by providing an environment in which the individuality of each client is respected, where participation of staff and clients is cooperative rather than coercive, and where democratic policies guide the daily activities that compose the program.

Milieu therapy may be adapted for use in various types of facilities and modified according to the functioning level of the clients who are being served. Although milieu therapy may be offered in an acute care facility, the regressive behavior of clients will necessitate modifications in the way milieu therapy is implemented. In most instances, group activities in the form of community meetings and various collective enterprises are prominent in milieu therapy. As much as possible, clients are given freedom to make decisions for themselves, to discharge responsibilities, and to carry out commitments they have made. The clients and staff members of the facility share in developing and enforcing policies and rules. Clients and staff contribute to decision making and problem solving. If milieu therapy is to be successful, everyone involved must have a positive attitude. This means clients and

---

SUGGESTIONS FOR THERAPEUTIC INTERACTIONS

1. *Unconditional acceptance and support.* The nurse accepts the client as an individual by treating the client with respect and dignity.
2. *Flexibility of interaction.* Interactions depend on circumstances and the situation. For example, a client with catatonic behaviors might be permitted to sit in a lotus position when alone but would be expected to sit in a chair like other clients when a community meeting is in session.
3. *Individualization of treatment.* Rules should not be enforced arbitrarily but rather adapted to the needs of each client. For some clients limit setting is necessary, while for others reassurance and support are more effective.
4. *Reinforcement of reality testing.* The client who appears to be listening to internal voices should be distracted or invited to participate in interactions in the real environment.
5. *Parsimony of interpretation.* The nurse may engage in an internal interpretation of the meaning of a client's behavior; however, interpretation need not always be shared immediately with the client.

Often an interpretation should be validated further before being shared; premature or inaccurate interpretations are counterproductive.

6. *Management of transference.* Schizophrenics often regress to infantile levels and become quite dependent on the caregiver. For this reason, nurses should maintain a professional attitude that protects the client but also promotes his eventual maturity to a point where protection and guidance are less necessary.
7. *Management of countertransference.* Self-awareness and introspection help the caregiver avoid inappropriate intimacy, which creates confusion and inhibits the emotional growth of the client.
8. *Control of hostility.* The schizophrenic client sometimes acts out hostile impulses. Physical expressions of violence are not acceptable. Not only are such expressions threatening to others, they are also damaging to the client's self-esteem. Clients should be reassured that hostile feelings are normal but that expressions of hostility must be limited to the verbalization of feelings.

---

personnel at all levels, including professional, administrative, and housekeeping staff. Inservice education for staff members is essential so that new employees can become familiar with and accept the philosophy that underlies milieu therapy. Every individual with whom clients come in contact must have a constructive attitude and be a willing participant in establishing and preserving therapeutic interpersonal relationships.

The physical environment of the care facility is important to milieu therapy. Provision should be made for meeting the physical needs of the clients. Safety measures, cleanliness, harmonious colors, and comfortable furnishings all positively influence the behaviors of staff and clients. There should be rooms of different sizes so that large and small groups can meet. Provision should be made for occasional privacy and for the client who is upset or overwhelmed and needs to be alone or with one staff member for a while. Most clients with psychiatric disorders, especially schizophrenia, have difficulty trusting and relating to others. In a facility devoted to milieu therapy the staff members model appropriate communication and behaviors. Self-

control is encouraged, but some limit setting is inevitable. Ideally, limits are not imposed by the staff but are generated by the clients themselves. Limit setting may seem inconsistent with the democratic policies advocated in milieu therapy, but structure and respect for others reinforce the realities of living in a social world.

Group interaction is considered an effective way of modifying maladaptive behaviors. In group meetings clients learn to communicate with others, to become aware of how they appear to others, and to improve their communication skills. The emphasis is not on the past but on the present, as clients begin to understand the impact of their own and others' behavioral patterns. Clients are encouraged to learn as much as possible about what is going on in the facility. They have a voice in decisions, and their full participation is an important element of the program. Because staff and clients are actively involved in so many aspects of day-to-day activities, clients can be expected to begin to relinquish the passive behaviors that ensure safety but inhibit their progress.

The collaboration and role sharing in a therapeutic community can be intimidating for staff and clients alike. Professionals may be uncomfortable over their loss of authority over clients, while clients may search for staff members who will think and decide for them. When the search for a controlling, directive staff member is fruitless, clients may become angry for a time. Any nurse who chooses to practice milieu therapy must be willing to work in an egalitarian environment where staff and clients are engaged in a mutual process of shared responsibility and self-awareness.

One milieu that is appropriate for recovering schizophrenics is a halfway house. A halfway house is a community facility dedicated to tertiary prevention, or the prevention of further decompensation or impairment after an acute episode has been resolved. For clients with schizophrenia, tertiary prevention consists of a collaborative rehabilitative effort that involves client and family members in addition to health care providers. After the acute episode of schizophrenia has been dealt with, it is important to add structure and organization to the client's everyday existence. A halfway house that offers some freedom and some supervision can be a temporary home for the client whose family is less than wholehearted in its support.

A halfway house does not remove a client from society but instead places the client in a protected society. Clients recovering from an acute schizophrenic episode need follow-up care and a hiatus before returning to the everyday world. The halfway house may expose clients to the same pressures that are found elsewhere but more slowly and with better timing, so that the recovering client has an opportunity to modify behavior on the basis of insight into the nature of his problems.

Family Therapy

Family therapy is recommended and used by many caregivers in the treatment of clients with schizophrenia. The principles and use of family therapy are discussed in Chapter 19. Generalist nurses who cannot engage in family therapy *per se* can perform family assessments and use a family approach in caring for schizophrenic clients.

Psychodynamic theories about the family's role in the etiology of mental illness, especially schizophrenia, sometimes alienated the family and caused them to sabotage or at least not support treatment. One consequence of the alienation of the family was that guilt and blaming were added to the family's distress. At present families are asked to be involved in the care plan, and support is extended to these worried relatives as they come to grips with chronic mental illness. Family involvement is monitored so that it does not become too intense. Efforts are made to educate the family about schizophrenia and to help members formulate specific measures in dealing with the client. The family's guilt and frustration are alleviated as much as possible, and they are encouraged to be satisfied with small signs of progress instead of hoping for major immediate changes (Hatfield et al. 1986, McFarlane 1983).

Basic Guidelines for Long-term Care of Schizophrenic Clients

- Maintain and enhance the client's self-esteem
- Offer support combined with clear expectations
- Set modest, reachable goals
- Avoid extremes of overstimulation or understimulation
- Involve the family at cognitive rather than emotional levels
- Foster a sense of mastery in the client through specific problem solving
- Coordinate work of inpatient staff, family, and community staff
- Promote the participation of the client as an agent in his or her care
- Attend to the client as a whole person rather than as a cluster of irritating symptoms

The section on relationship therapy made the point that persons with schizophrenia are extremely sensitive to excessive stimulation. The precise reason for this sensitivity is not yet known, but its effects have been documented (Yalom 1983, Bernheim and Lehmann 1985). It may be that these clients suffer a defect in processing that demands privacy, distance, and isolation from others. A fragile sense of self may cause them to feel controlled and overwhelmed by any intensity of feeling. Therefore, the involvement of the family with the client requires a delicate balance so that the family is not alienated by therapeutic actions aimed at curtailing their overinvolvement. A description of the concept of *expressed emotion* in families should clarify this point.

Expressed Emotion in Families The emotional climate in the families of schizophrenic persons continues to be of interest to researchers and clinicians trying to understand relationships between the disorder and family life. Out of the family studies has emerged the concept called *Expressed Emotion*. Expressed emotion deals with three aspects of family interaction: (1) criticism of the client, (2) hostility toward the client, and (3) overinvolvement with the client. The concept of expressed emotion assumed importance when it was noted that chronic schizophrenic males who returned to live with spouses or parents after hospitalization were more prone to relapse than their counterparts who returned to community facilities or lived with more distant relatives (Koenigsberg and Handley 1986). In differentiating families with high levels of emotional intensity from families with low levels, four characteristics were noted (Leff and Vaugn 1985, Leff, Kuipers, and Berkowitz 1983).

Family Characteristics of Low Emotional Intensity

- Controlled, concerned but not acutely anxious about the client
- Respectful of the client's need for social distance
- Accepting of the client as one who is ill rather than a malingerer
- Tolerant rather than critical and impatient with the client's behavior

Family Characteristics of High Emotional Intensity

- Very concerned, acutely anxious, and involved with the client
- Resentful of the client's need for social distance
- Describing the client as malingering or choosing to be ill
- Intolerant, critical, and impatient with the client's behavior

A scale or index of expressed emotion in families has been developed and is considered a reliable indicator of relapse if a client lives with the family. The index is not an indicator of long-term outcomes, only of rehospitalization. Other studies are needed to determine whether reductions in family emotional intensity have long-term benefits. Most studies thus far have not controlled for intervening variables, such as compliance with medication schedules. Even so, the fact that expressed family emotion correlates with relapse and rehospitalization offers direction for family assessment and intervention. Some clients living with critical or intrusive close relatives need to be protected. Merely reducing the weekly hours of contact between the client and the family may prove helpful. This may be accomplished by encouraging the client to make other living arrangements, or suggesting a daytime program that gets the client out of the house for most of the day. It is better to recommend activities for the client than to recommend that more time should be spent in his or her own room. If for some reason the only way to reduce family tension is for the client to withdraw, time spent alone should be regulated in order to forestall the client's inclination to regress.

Family intervention may be indicated in some instances. The assessment process should include family meetings during which caregivers can observe the ways in which family members interact with the client. Educating the family about the disorder helps them to understand that the client has not chosen to behave strangely but may not be able to act otherwise. Very often close relatives may blame themselves for the disorder. In a sense, this is an example of overinvolvement and intrusiveness. Reassuring parents or spouses that they alone could not cause schizophrenic behaviors not only helps increase emotional distance between the client and the family but mitigates the anger and guilt that add to the emotional intensity of the family. Supportive or educational groups for relatives are often valuable (Francis et al. 1987).

The concept of expressed emotion need not be limited to families of schizophrenic clients. It goes without saying that criticism, hostility, and overinvolvement are impediments to recovery in almost any disorder. At present it is widely accepted that high emotional intensity in families may be detrimental for schizophrenic clients. What is not yet known is the point at which low-intensity families may become detrimental. Additional studies are needed to differentiate family tolerance of the client's behavior from indifference to the client's welfare. Therapeutic actions require assessment of prevailing family attitudes of overinvolvement versus underinvolvement, and of hostility versus indifference. Following the assessment of the emotional climate of the family, attention should be directed toward modifying extremes that are counterproductive (Kanter, Lamb, and Loeper 1987).

Psychoeducational Therapy

The concept of expressed emotion in families has led to growing interest in psychoeducational therapy as a means of helping schizophrenic clients and their families. Psychoeducation was introduced as a useful way to help families and clients deal with residual symptoms of schizophrenia. Researchers have pointed out the lack of emphasis on education for psychiatric clients as compared to persons with physiological problems. This may be due to belief that clients with mental disorders cannot understand the concepts being taught, that they are unwilling to accept responsibility for their own care, and that they will be disheartened by learning more about their specific diagnosis (Goldman and Quinn 1988). Yet some investigators using psychoeducation report greater compliance, reduced defensiveness, and greater self-esteem among clients who received formal instruction about the nature

Generic Nursing Care Plan for Client with Thought and Perceptual Alterations

Identified Problem	Goal or Need	Specific Interventions	Rationale
Alterations in psychological comfort level resulting in increasing anxiety	Client will identify cause of anxiety; client will verbalize feelings of anxiety.	1. Help client look at possible cause for anxiety and allow him to see if reasons are valid. 2. Explore ways to alleviate causes of anxiety. 3. Encourage client to talk out feelings of anxiety. 4. Explore actions that could be taken to alleviate anxiety. 5. Accept client's anxiety without being provoked into reciprocal anxiety. 6. Avoid pushing client ahead by probing into areas that he is not ready to explore. 7. Offer client unconditional acceptance. 8. Encourage interest in activities outside of himself. 9. Provide reassurance and support.	To help client recognize and label anxiety. To allow client to consider alternatives to master situation, learn new techniques for handling situation, and explore realm of anxiety. To help client describe feelings related to source of distress, allowing client to set pace.
Decreased capacity for interpersonal contact resulting in emotional withdrawal	Client will take part in one group activity every day.	1. Encourage socialization. 2. Encourage verbal expression of hurt and anger. 3. Help client recognize when he is isolating himself. 4. Respect client's body space. 5. Help client realize destructiveness of withdrawal to him as person. 6. Avoid making demands on him that he cannot meet. 7. Make consistent steady attempts to draw client into responding, but do not demand any response. 8. Use a warm, nonpressure approach.	To promote client's interaction with other people.
Alteration in level of cognitive functioning resulting in unrealistically based thinking	Client will verbally validate experiences with staff members.	1. Identify client's habitual mode of responding, and maneuvers he uses to avoid closeness. 2. Help client to learn trust. 3. Be honest and consistent in interactions with client. 4. Be neutral, neither agreeing nor disagreeing with contents of client's delusion. 5. Listen carefully to client's account and question any obscurities.	To understand general nature of client's delusional system. To establish trust. To encourage development of therapeutic relationship.

of their disability (Brown, Wright, and Christiansen 1987). In addition to providing cognitive information to families, psychoeducational methods focus on self-care and self-management. They purposely reduce high levels of emotion by offering support, collaboration, and practice in skills needed to manage everyday life. When problems arise or seem imminent, specific solutions are sought by the client and the clinician in the hope that acquired skills may ultimately be transferred from one situation to another. Psychoeducational programs do seem to rely to some extent on a medical model, but their aim is to promote independence and self-control. The psychoeducator may be a member of any health care profession but monitors the expression of strong emotion, avoids confrontation, and uses structured exercises to teach and to maintain an atmosphere of understanding and faith in clients' ability to move forward (Bernheim and Lehmann 1985).

Many schizophrenic clients either live with families or with other clients in group homes or community residences. Family psychoeducation may be used with family members or in nonfamilial group settings. Regardless of the setting, family psychoeducation provides a forum and a moderator so that questions can be answered and grievances discussed in a neutralized environment. Bernheim and Switalski (1988) found that the families of persons suffering mental illness complained of not receiving information about the illness, of not being helped with management problems or informed of available resources. Families reported that interactions with health professionals made them feel guilty, frustrated, and helpless. In short, they placed mental health professionals at the bottom of their list of helpful, supportive people. Psychoeducation offers hope for more family involvement, on a nonrandom basis. Nurses working as case managers or taking primary responsibility for a client's care can add psychoeducational considerations to the care plan.

- Explain hospital or agency procedures and their rationale to families.
- Explain what a treatment plan is, and what the major goals are.
- Involve family members as well as the client in discharge planning.
- Act as resource persons or consultants when families have questions.
- Advise families on how to avoid tensions and expressions of hostility.
- Instruct families regarding the nature of the client's illness and the monitoring of medications.
- Help families recognize their own (and the client's) areas of strength and resilience.
- Encourage the client and the family to devise a living situation that allows all members a degree of comfort and autonomy.

PREDICTIVE FACTORS

The prognosis for the client with schizophrenia is mixed. Favorable predictive factors are abrupt onset, short duration of the psychotic episode, and a stable and supportive social background. If there is an identifiable precipitating event, such as a loss or disappointment, the prognosis also seems to be enhanced. Other predictive factors that influence prognosis:

- Prognosis seems to be best for those suffering catatonic schizophrenic episodes.

- Prognosis seems to be poorest for those suffering from chronic and undifferentiated forms of schizophrenia. Prognosis is also poor for persons with paranoid delusions.
- Prognosis seems to be related to age; the younger the person at time of onset, the poorer the prognosis.

The label "chronic schizophrenic" is widely applied and accentuates the pessimism that surrounds the care of many persons with schizophrenia. One group of researchers suggested that the term "prolonged schizophrenia" is more accurate and more hopeful. In addition, the term "brief or short-term schizophrenia" might well be substituted for "acute schizophrenia." It is true that many persons with schizophrenia seem to be permanently impaired and capable of functioning only marginally. It is also true that many of the practices of the past, such as institutionalization and psychosurgery, probably contributed to the prevalence of chronicity. At present, even the most experienced clinicians are unable to predict who will lapse into chronicity and who will recover. Therefore nurses and other health professionals must care for clients in ways that maximize the potential for improvement, even when progress is slow and faltering.

Current treatment systems are available for clients in acute episodes of schizophrenia and for clients who have been labeled chronic, but there are few programs devoted to persons whose disturbance is prolonged but who have the potential to improve. The course of a schizophrenic disorder frequently lasts several years or more. It is unfortunate that sometimes when clients just begin to change direction toward improvement, caregivers, families, and the clients themselves have become resigned to never getting better. Permanent commitment from caregivers and from significant persons in clients' lives is needed to avoid premature giving in and giving up (Harding, Zubin, and Strauss 1987).

SUMMARY

Statistics on the incidence and prevalence of schizophrenia are unreliable because of disagreement about diagnosis and other factors, but the disorder is acknowledged to be a major public health problem. A comparatively large percentage of young people are affected, and a sizable number of affected persons follow a pattern of gradual deterioration. There are no laboratory tests to indicate the

(Text continues on page 177.)

CLINICAL VIGNETTE

SUCCESSFUL PSYCHOEDUCATION STRATEGIES FOR A LONG-TERM SCHIZOPHRENIC CLIENT

Anna York is a middle-aged woman with a history of psychiatric hospitalizations for paranoid schizophrenia. Since her late twenties she has periodically shown delusions of persecution, sleeplessness, and alternate periods of withdrawal and unrestrained hostile outbursts. She is unreliable about taking medication, stops periodically, and within a short period of time becomes disorganized and difficult to manage. She lives at home with her father, a retired postal worker, and a widowed sister who does the cooking and housekeeping. During her most recent hospitalization Anna was agitated and had delusions that through her breathing she could control the people around her. She insisted that unseen forces wanted to rob her of her powers. After a few weeks of hospitalization, during which Anna resumed medication, her symptoms subsided to a great extent.

When the time came to plan for Anna's discharge a number of problems arose. Her sister and her father wanted Anna to be placed in a state hospital instead of returning home. Both relatives felt that caring for Anna was too great a burden, and described occasions when she became very violent and had to be restrained by police. Anna's sister was an active church woman and was embarrassed by Anna's language and behavior. Objections to Anna's returning home made her become delusional again, especially when state hospital placement was mentioned. Family meetings were scheduled to deal with the relatives' reluctance to let Anna return home and to explain why state hospital placement was not a useful option.

FAMILY PSYCHOEDUCATION MEASURES

Because Anna had already shown herself to be unreliable about taking oral management, she was given a long-term injectable drug. Anna agreed to this as a condition for returning home and the new medication lowered family conflict over her management. Because the family was so apprehensive, Anna was admitted to a hospital day treatment center where staff members could observe her daily. The day treatment program offered respite for Anna's father and sister, and countered their feelings of abandonment. In the family sessions the day treatment program was explained as a place where there would be structured activities of Anna's choosing as well as social and recreational activities supervised by staff.

The day treatment program included a weekly multifamily group attended by clients and family members. This was a support group in which schizophrenia was discussed in a calm, cognitive manner that defused its mystery and reduced fears. Medications, significant behaviors, stress reduction, and community resources were among the topics discussed. Families and clients shared experiences and coping methods. For the clients, the multifamily group was a forum where they felt at ease and could practice social behavior.

As part of the psychoeducation component of the day care center, families learned facts that helped them understand their relatives better. They learned of the negative impact that extreme emotions have on schizophrenic persons and on the entire household. Families were reminded repeatedly that they were not the cause of the schizophrenic illness, but that they could learn to communicate in uncritical language without pressuring or nagging. Home visits were made by nurses to increase family members' sense of participation. Instruction was informal and friendly, with nurses acting as role models for family members in their interactions with clients.

Anna went home to an overall plan that was better than the one she left. In the day care center she practiced everyday routines, such as greeting people, keeping appointments, and managing small sums of money. There was a primary nurse with whom she could bring up problems and who knew her family. With her nurse, Anna set up target goals to achieve, and decided how to reach them. Teaching methods consisted of meetings, discussions, homework, and role play.

Through psychoeducation Anna's family was stabilized and her prospects were brightened. Neither she nor her family were interested in psychodynamic explanations or in acquiring insight. Psychodynamic explanations often help caregivers to understand clients, but families experiencing the rigors of a recent psychiatric hospitalization derive more benefit from psychoeducation aimed at allaying their misgivings and renewing their efforts to assist their schizophrenic relative.

IMPLICATIONS FOR NURSING

Schizophrenia is neither simple nor homogeneous in its course or outcomes. Because the course of the disorder is chronic, caregivers and families become frustrated unless they accept the fact that maintenance and rehabilitation of the client will require long-range care and planning. Unfortunately the work of caregivers, including nurses, has largely centered on responding to acute episodes rather than constructing a longitudinal approach (Mechanic 1986). Hospitalization of the schizophrenic client may be needed in agitated, psychotic episodes, but with the availability of medication, the current trend is to hospitalize the client for relatively brief periods. Among the risks of lengthy hospitalization are loss of self-esteem, loss of community and family supports, and lowered competence in self-care and role performance. During hospitalization, goals should be specific and time-limited. Nursing care should be supportive and promote trust. Regressive tendencies on the part of the client should be discouraged without adopting threatening tactics.

Extremes of environmental stimulation in the form of sensory overload or sensory deprivation are harmful to the schizophrenic client. The neglect and lack of stimulation that were features of large state institutions contributed to the deterioration of institutionalized clients, who reacted to environmental conditions by becoming apathetic, withdrawn, dependent, and even mute. At one time this clinical picture was called institutionalization, but it is now known that the same regressed behaviors can appear when clients are discharged to the community without adequate follow-up care. At the other end of the spectrum is overstimulation, which may occur in some short-term inpatient facilities and in some families where the emotional climate is intense and where clients are pushed beyond their ability to cope. One of the least therapeutic strategies for schizophrenic clients is direct confrontation, which attacks the clients' defenses. These clients benefit from interactions with caregivers who provide support, structure, limits, practical advice, and opportunity for shared problem solving. Clearexpectations and directions help reduce the ambivalence and confusion that are part of the clinical picture. Emphasis should be on the realities of everyday life, and on the establishment of trust between the client and the primary caregivers. Caregivers who strive for quick cures rather than slow healing only foster regression and prolong the psychotic defenses (Drake and Sederer 1986).

The population of people with schizophrenia is not one group but many subgroups with different levels of disability. Because of changes in treatment methods over the last 50 years, some segments of the schizophrenic population have avoided the deterioration once thought to be almost inevitable. Although the etiology is blurred, there is continuing interest in research of all kinds, using social, developmental, and biological factors. Progress has been made in eradicating extreme psychotic behavior by means of drugs. Less progress has been made in controlling the undesirable side effects of many psychotropic drugs. Future pharmacological devel- opments and neurological discoveries may offer hope.

A challenge relevant for the nursing profession is devising and staffing wide-ranging services in home, hospital, and community that can alleviate incapacitating thought disturbance, reduce secondary deterioration, and help clients and families function as well as possible. Besides acting a therapeutic role with clients, nurses have the potential to act as case managers. Case management requires coordination between the client and community services, and between the psychiatric care system and the generalized care system. Prepared and caring nurses can bring to case management not only psychosocial knowledge but background in biological sciences, permitting the comprehensiveness that the care of schizophrenic persons demands (Shepherd 1984, Grob 1983).

CLINICAL EXAMPLE

ONSET OF AN ACUTE EPISODE OF THOUGHT AND PERCEPTUAL DISRUPTION

Lance Walters is the oldest of three brothers. Shortly after the birth of his youngest brother, Lance's mother became indifferent to the needs of the children. Lance's father was an affable individual who had little sense of responsibility and worked only when he felt like it. He did not assume much responsibility for his wife and children. As a result, the children were marginally nourished and inadequately clothed. The family moved frequently and often lived in unsuitable places. Once they lived in a condemned building that had no heat or hot water and was infested with rats. When Lance was about six years old, the family lived over a tavern where noise and violence occurred frequently. His father was out of the home for days at a time, and the children were so neglected that neighbors reported the situation to the local health department. An official investigation resulted in Lance's mother's being committed to a community psychiatric hospital with the diagnosis of undifferentiated schizophrenia. The children became wards of the state.

Lance and his two younger brothers, who were four and two years old, went to live with a foster family. The two younger boys adjusted fairly well and responded to the care and attention they received from their foster parents. The foster parents stated later that Lance was different from his brothers even when he first came to them. He was timid and turned often to his four-year-old brother for direction. He was afraid of the dark, and had trouble sleeping at night. He argued with his new foster mother and had temper tantrums whenever he was frustrated or even gently reprimanded.

As time passed Lance seemed to adjust to his new situation. He rarely asked questions about his mother but sometimes wondered aloud why his father never visited. He became very fond of his foster mother, helping her around the house so much that his brothers sometimes teased him about it. As Lance grew older it became apparent that he was gifted intellectually. He was conscientious and hard-working and therefore attracted favorable attention from his teachers. He preferred to keep to himself but often complained that children in the neighborhood disliked him. In high school he was a member of the school choir and the orchestra but was not interested in sports.

When he was a junior in high school, Lance began to neglect his schoolwork and to lose interest in the choir and orchestra. His habits changed gradually. Instead of attending practice sessions after school, he began to go home to his room as soon as classes were over. He interacted less and less with his brothers and foster parents, spending most of his free time alone in his room listening to his records. At first his foster parents attributed the changed behavior to the fact that Lance was growing up. They became more concerned when Lance began to go out late at night and to not return until early morning. When his foster mother questioned him, he became defiant although they had always had a close relationship.

Lance had worked after school but was fired when he stopped showing up. When this happened, his worried foster mother arranged for him to be seen by the family physician. The physician had known Lance for years and was concerned about his behavioral changes. The physician informed the foster parents that Lance was on the verge of a "nervous breakdown" and in need of help. He referred Lance to a community mental health clinic, but it was three weeks before Lance could be seen. By this time Lance was hearing voices. He thought that his clothes were being worn by invisible people who watched him and called him filthy names.

Although it had never been discussed, Lance knew that his mother was in a mental institution. He told his foster mother, "I know what's wrong with me. I'm going crazy like my mother." Sometimes Lance talked sensibly, but often he seemed confused and unaware of his surroundings. When his brothers asked why he acted as he did, Lance said, "When these thoughts come to me, I don't understand anything or anybody." His brothers began to be afraid of Lance because he was so unpredictable. One night, during one of his nocturnal journeys, Lance was picked up by the police. He was confused, incoherent, and wandering aimlessly. His foster parents were notified, and Lance was hospitalized for a psychiatric evaluation.

ASSESSMENT

Lance was admitted to an inpatient facility for assessment. An interdisciplinary team observed him in a number of different situations, administered psychological tests, compiled a history, and most important, tried to get to know Lance and win his trust. The interdisciplinary team identified the following factors in their assessment:

A history of abuse and neglect before the age of six years.

An unstable mother figure with whom the client identified.

A distant, uncaring father figure with whom Lance could not identify.

Two younger brothers for whom Lance felt responsible.

Superior intellectual abilities that contributed to difficulties with peers.

Resurgence of early anxiety with the onset of adolescence.

It was the opinion of the persons assessing Lance that the factors that made him vulnerable—his superior mental ability, his affection for his foster mother, and his concern for his younger brothers—could become his sources of strength.

Nursing Diagnoses

5.1.1.1	Ineffective individual coping
7.2	Sensory/perceptual alterations
8.3	Altered thought processes
3.1.2	Social isolation

Multiaxial Psychiatric Diagnoses

Axis I   295.31 Schizophrenia, paranoid
Axis II V71.09 No diagnosis
Axis III No diagnosis
Axis IV Code 5—Severe psychosocial stressors
Axis V GAF 25: Current
            GAF 40: Highest in past year

PLANNING AND INTERVENTION

Lance was hospitalized for a period of about one month. During that time he was given antipsychotic medication to reduce the thought and perceptual distortions that were adversely influencing his behavior. Because Lance had never had the opportunity to relate to a strong, caring male figure, he was cared for by male nurses during hospitalization and by a male therapist after discharge. The consensus of persons on the interdisciplinary health team was that the prognosis for Lance was quite good. Despite the deprivation of his early years, he remained a person who was able to show concern for others as well as for himself. His

devotion to his foster mother and his affection for his younger brothers opposed his autistic tendencies and were sources of strength for him.

One strength that the health team hoped to mobilize on Lance's behalf was his impressive intellectual ability, which was a source of both anxiety and self-esteem for him.

The difficulties that caused Lance to be hospitalized originated many years before, in his family of origin. His problems seemed to stem from a resurgence of anxiety, often a characteristic of adolescence. Lance had maintained good adjustment for about ten years. After a brief hospitalization augmented by good aftercare, Lance would probably return to his previous level of adjustment and perhaps be strengthened by his regressive psychotic behaviors, which drew attention to his inner turmoil. Although the prognosis for Lance was favorable, intervention would be of long duration. In addition, Lance's problem was closely tied to the inadequacies of his biological parents and the needs of his younger brothers. A holistic approach would include Lance and his brothers as integral components of a family-focused approach and the foster parents as secondary influences.

EVALUATION

After a three-month hospitalization Lance was discharged to a community halfway house. He went to this facility because he and his foster parents had decided that this was better for all concerned than returning home. Lance was discharged with an adequate supply of antipsychotic medication, about which he had been fully informed.

In the halfway house Lance was finally able to feel that he belonged. His natural parents had made him feel guilty for having been born, and his foster home was a place where he felt he had to adjust. In the halfway house Lance encountered people who were as lonely and as lost as he was. For the first time he was truly able to appreciate his intellectual gifts as he embarked on programs to improve his deficient interpersonal skills. In the halfway house a formal vocational assessment was done on Lance. This assessment, combined with a review of Lance's skills, interests, strengths, education, and intelligence, was enough to make his counselors optimistic about his future, and their enthusiasm was transmitted to Lance.

One of the rules of the halfway house was that residents must be involved in a daytime program. This rule gave Lance the impetus to return to high school, even though he found the prospect frightening. On Sundays he frequently visited his former foster home; as his own problems became manageable he became better able to relate to his younger brothers, who continued to look up to and admire him.

The prognosis for Lance was favorable in spite of the deprivation that characterized so much of his early life. His adjustment after being placed in a foster home had been good, due primarily to his superior intellectual gifts and the positive attitudes of his teachers. His concern for his younger brothers was an obligation but also a source of strength. Lance was wise enough to know that his success or failure would have a profound impact on his brothers. It would be too soon to predict outcomes with any degree of certainty, but there were a number of factors to indicate that Lance would be one of those fortunate persons who suffer a single schizophrenic episode, are rehabilitated, and experience no further relapses.

Nursing Diagnosis	Goal	Nursing Action	Outcome Criteria	Outcome Evaluation
Ineffective individual coping	Client will receive educational and vocational assessment and testing. Client will participate in discharge planning.	Reinforce client's self-esteem and autonomy. Refer to psychologist for testing.	Client will learn of his ability and potential. Client will return to school.	Client has followed through on post-discharge plans. Client is progressing satisfactorily in school.
Sensory/perceptual alterations	Client will take antipsychotic medication as prescribed. Client's reality testing will improve.	Reinforce reality testing. Orient client to reality. Teach client rationale, safeguards, and possible side effects of medication.	Client will continue in treatment as community mental health center outpatient.	Internally generated stimuli (hallucinations, ideas of reference, delusions of persecution) have decreased. Self-esteem and self-confidence improved.
Altered thought processes (Ideas of reference/delusions of persecution)	Client's hallucinations will be controlled. Ideas of reference and of persecution will diminish.	Refer client to community mental health center for psychotherapy and follow-up care.	Client will comply with medication regimen.	Reality testing and reality orientation now prevail; no signs of altered thought patterns.
Social isolation	Client will be discharged to halfway house.	Primary nurse will accompany client on predischarge visit to halfway house. Arrange admission to halfway house for client. Coordinate care of client with halfway house staff. Recommend that client join group activities at halfway house.	Client will accept living arrangement at halfway house. Client will join support group at halfway house.	Client has adjusted to new residence. Client now accepts assigned responsibilities at residence. Client now interacts with staff and peers in a positive way.
	Client will see his brothers and foster parents regularly.	Meet with client and family to discuss visits and value of ongoing relationship with all concerned.	Family support will be available.	Relationship with siblings continues positive. Social isolation and withdrawal have lessened.

presence of schizophrenia, and the disorder is often confused with organic brain syndrome, manic-depressive illness, or drug toxicity.

Etiologic explanations regarding the cause of the disorder remain inconclusive. Research indicates that genetic factors may play a role in the onset of schizophrenia. The closer the biological relationship between an individual and an identified person with schizophrenia, the greater is the risk of developing the disorder. Biochemical investigations suggest that the clinical signs of schizophrenia are associated with bioamines that act as neurotransmitters and mediate such functions as awareness, sleep, emotion, and sensations of pain and pleasure.

Developmental theories are a useful frame of reference for understanding the etiology of schizophrenia. Erikson and Sullivan believed that adverse experiences in early life cause a child to perceive the social world as frightening and to attribute these anxieties and fears to deficiencies in the self. Family relationships may play a role in the vulnerability of certain individuals. In the families of persons with schizophrenia, relationships among members are intricate and enmeshed, and relationships between the child and the primary caregiver (usually the mother) seem particularly crucial to the development of the child's identity. Psychodynamic explanations of schizophrenia also emphasize the influence of the mother's inhibition of the child's progress toward individuation and separation.

Schizophrenia is sometimes considered not one disorder but a group of disorders with some common characteristics. All are characterized by thought and language distortion that can be expressed behaviorally in a number of ways. The following are types of schizophrenia: catatonic, disorganized, paranoid, residual, and undifferentiated. An individual may demonstrate the same behaviors in every acute schizophrenic episode or may demonstrate one kind of behavior in one episode and a different kind in another episode.

Although schizophrenia is a thought disorder, its behavioral manifestations are used as the bases for assessing the client and developing a comprehensive care plan.

The altered thought patterns of the schizophrenic client are accompanied by alterations in perception, which in turn may result in the development of hallucinations, or false sensory perceptions that have no basis in reality. Hallucinations may be auditory, visual, olfactory, gustatory, or tactile.

The schizophrenic client may also develop delusions, or false, fixed beliefs that have no basis in reality. The content of delusions varies, but usually a dominant theme can be identified, such as persecution, grandeur, control by others, or somatic distortions. Delusions are defenses used to avoid awareness of distressing thoughts or feelings. Therefore, they are persistent, and the client is reluctant to relinquish or modify them.

The discovery of antipsychotic medication has made it possible for clients with schizophrenia to engage in the human interactions that make rehabilitation possible. Most clients taking antipsychotic medication need to take the drugs for long periods and should know as much as possible about their action and possible side effects. Some side effects to antipsychotic medication are merely uncomfortable; others can be disfiguring or life-threatening. Nurses need to have accurate, current information regarding dosage, action, side effects, and precau-

tions relating to these drugs. Teaching and ongoing assessment of clients taking antipsychotic medication are important nursing responsibilities.

The therapeutic approach most suitable for generalist nurses working with schizophrenic clients is relationship therapy. The nurse must try to understand the way the client is experiencing the world and convey to the client a sincere wish to help. Relationship therapy is effective only after trust is established and the client experiences the feeling of being understood and accepted. Successfully treated schizophrenic clients tend to see the caregiver as protective, friendly, and strong. It seems to be important to them that caregivers make efforts on their behalf without imposing excessive demands.

Milieu therapy is an approach compatible with the nursing process and role. It is a variation of relationship therapy on a larger scale. The purpose of milieu therapy is to oppose regression and to foster a sense of personal worth, social competence, and autonomy. In milieu therapy, as in most therapeutic approaches appropriate for clients with schizophrenia, the client's behavior is used to assess needs and offer care. Some clients require support and reassurance, while others respond to more structured intervention. Individualized nursing care is based on what the client's behavior expresses about his distortion of thought and perception.

Review Questions

1. Describe three theories concerning the etiology of schizophrenia.

2. List the various types of schizophrenic disorders and describe their identifying characteristics.

3. Describe three alterations in affect manifested by clients with schizophrenia.

4. Identify the basic premise of relationship therapy, and explain why it is compatible with the nursing role and process.

5. Describe the major principles of milieu therapy.

6. Describe therapeutic approaches appropriate for generalist nurses to offer in caring for clients with schizophrenia.

7. Describe three levels of nursing interventions useful in dealing with neuroleptic malignant syndrome.

8. Explain the concept of expressed emotion in families and its effects on the client with schizophrenia.

Research Report

Training Chronic Mental Patients to Independently Practice Personal Grooming Skills.

The article reports on a practical and inexpensive program used at a state mental hospital in California for teaching personal grooming skills to hospitalized chronic clients. Schizophrenic clients, particularly those who are institutionalized, have-little interest in their appearance. Their indifference to good grooming and personal care impairs their social relationships and inhibits their chances for successful adjustment to community living. Often their outward appearance stigmatizes persons with schizophrenia and may endanger physical well-being. Although programs to enhance social and living skills of psychiatrically disabled persons are in use, there are few controlled studies of the impact of a complete personal grooming program on a psychiatric population. An 11-category checklist was used to evaluate the progress of subjects. In addition to obtaining positive results in clients' grooming, investigators found that a brief two-week training period for staff nurses enabled the nurses to implement the training program within an entire hospital unit. Training of the staff nurses in social and material reinforcements of behavior therapy was carried out by a registered nurse and a master's prepared psychologist, both of whom had had considerable experience in behavior therapy.

Stephen E. Wong, Stephen G. Flanagan, Timothy G. Kuehnel, Robert P. Liberman, Ron Hunnicutt and Jean Adams-Badgett. *Hospital and Community Psychiatry* 39, no. 8 (August 1988):874–879.

Suggested Annotated Readings

Blair, J. P., and B. K. Greenspan. "Teams: Teamwork Training for Interns, Residents, and Nurses." *Hospital and Community Psychiatry* 36, no. 6 (June 1986):633–635.

Nurses and physicians work together but are seldom brought together in an educational setting to work on shared problems. The program *Training Effectiveness through Assertiveness in a Medical Setting* (TEAMS) was developed in response to stress, communication failure, and role conflict between nurses and physicians working in a hospital setting. Participation in the nine-week program was voluntary. Group sessions dealt with work-related issues, not exploration of feelings. The program received high marks from participants, all of whom scored better on a post-group questionnaire than on a pre-group questionnaire. The tests were an inventory of psychological health and self-actualization scores.

Program sponsors thought the project successful but thought the sessions would have been more rewarding if members had had the same amount of experience. It was considered preferable to conduct separate sessions for interns and less experienced nurses, and for residents and more experienced nurses.

Dennis, K. E. "Dimensions of Client Control." *Nursing Research* 36, no. 3 (May/June 1987):151–156.

This study was done to identify actions that give clients a feeling of control during hospitalization. Knowing and understanding what was being done during the experiment was important to all 70 subjects. Although all wanted cognitive knowledge, some wanted decision-making power and some did not. Behavioral independence was also reported as important to a sense of control. Data suggest that dimensions and definitions of control vary among clients and that individualization is needed in administering nursing care. Since cognitive knowledge was valued by all subjects, findings indicated that nurses should translate information into language that clients can understand. Interestingly, persons with cancer were predominant in wanting to be involved in making decisions.

Detzer, E., and L. Huston. "When Schizophrenia Complicates Med/Surg Care." *RN* (January 1986):51–53.

People who are mentally ill often need hospitalization on a medical or surgical unit, where nurses are relatively inexperienced in caring for persons with severe psychiatric problems. Such clients find it hard to adjust to the hospital environment because their disorganized thinking makes the hospital experience very frightening. Often hospitalization intensifies their psychotic thought processes. Two psychiatric specialists offer good advice on direct interventions to use with these clients and suggest how and when to call upon psychiatric clinical specialists for help.

Fulop, G., J. J. Strain, M. C. Fans, J. S. Hammer, and J. S. Lyons. "Medical Disorders Associated with Psychiatric Comorbidity and Prolonged Hospital Stay." *Hospital and Community Psychiatry* 4, no. 1 (January 1989):80–82.

Lengthier stays are associated with psychiatric disorders in persons hospitalized for medical reasons. Findings suggest that psychiatric care should be instituted and evaluated for cost effectiveness when medical illnesses are complicated by psychiatric disorder. Collaboration between caregivers and researchers with expertise in psychiatry and their counterparts in medical and surgical practice can help contain hospital costs and contribute to speedier recovery rates.

Schwartz, H. I., W. Vingiano, and C. B. Perez. "Autonomy and the Right to Refuse Treatment: Patients' Attitudes after Involuntary Medication." *Hospital and Community Psychiatry* 19, no. 10 (October 1988):49–54.

The legal system tends to assume that refusal of treatment by clients is based on autonomous, voluntary refusal. This assumption was tested by exploring the reactions of 24 psychiatric clients medicated against their will. At discharge from the hospital, a majority (17) said that refusing medication was a manifestation of their illness and not the result of a wish for autonomy or disbelief in the treatment being given. They stated that their refusal of treatment was correctly overruled and that they wanted to be treated against their will in the future if necessary. Findings suggest that refusal of treatment is a clinical issue and should not be subject to judicial review.

References

American Psychiatric Association. *Diagnostic and Statistical Manual of Mental Disorders*, 3d ed. Washington, D.C.: The Association, 1987.

Arieti, S. *Interpretation of Schizophrenia*, 2d ed. New York: Basic Books, 1974.

Arnold, H. M. "Working with Schizophrenic Patients." *American Journal of Nursing* 78 (1976):941–947.

Barham, P. *Schizophrenia and Human Value*. London: Blackwell Press, 1984.

Beck, C., R. P. Rawlings, and S. Williams. *Mental Health Psychiatric Nursing*. St. Louis: C. V. Mosby, 1984.

Bernheim, K. F., and A. F. Lehmann. *Working with Families of the Mentally Ill*. New York: W. W. Norton, 1985.

Bernheim, K. F., and T. Switalski. "Mental Health Staff and Patients' Relatives: How They View Each Other." *Hospital and Community Psychiatry* 39, no. 1 (January 1988):63–67.

Bleuler, E. *Dementia Praecox on the Group of Schizophrenias*, tr. J. Zinki. New York: International Press, 1950.

Brown, C. S., R. G. Wright, and D. B. Christiansen. "Association between Type of Medication Instruction and Patients' Knowledge: Side Effects and Compliance." *Hospital and Community Psychiatry* 38, no. 1 (January 1987):55–60.

Cancro, R. "History and Overview of Schizophrenia." In *Comprehensive Textbook of Psychiatry*, 4th ed., H. I. Kaplan and B. J. Sadock, eds. Baltimore: Williams & Wilkins, 1985.

Caplan, P. J., and I. Hall-McCorquodale. "The Scapegoating of Mothers: A Call for Change." *American Journal of Orthopsychiatry* 55, no. 4 (October 1985):610–613.

Caroff, S. N. "Neuroleptic Malignant Syndrome." *Journal of Clinical Psychology* 41, no. 1 (January 1980):79–83.

Chess, S. "Blame the Mother Ideology." *International Journal of Mental Health* 11, no. 1 (January 1982):95–107.

Drake, R. E., and L. I. Sederer. "Inpatient Psychosocial Treatment of Chronic Schizophrenia: Negative Effects and Current Guidelines." *Hospital and Community Psychiatry* 37, no. 9 (September 1986):897–901.

Erikson, E. *Childhood and Society*. New York: W. W. Norton, 1968.

Francis, A., B. Hoffman, T. Pass, and S. Andrews. "A Schizophrenic Woman in a High Expressed Emotion Family." *Hospital and Community Psychiatry* 38, no. 7 (July 1987):707–708, 717.

Fromm-Reichmann, F. "Notes on the Development of Treatment of Schizophrenia by Psychoanalytic Psychotherapy." *Psychiatry* 11 (1948):263–273.

Goldman, C. R., and F. L. Quinn. "Effects of a Patient Education Program in the Treatment of Schizophrenia." *Hospital and Community Psychiatry* 39, no. 3 (March 1988):282–286.

Goleman, D. "Schizophrenia: Early Signs Found." *The New York Times* (December 11, 1984).

Gottesman, I. I. "Schizophrenia and Genetics: Where Are We? Are You Sure?" In *The Nature of Schizophrenia*, L. C. Wynne, R. D. Cromwell, and S. Matheses, eds. New York: John Wiley & Sons, 1978.

Grob, G. N. *Mental Illness and American Society: 1875–1940*. Princeton, New Jersey: Princeton University Press, 1983.

Haber, J., A. M. Leach, S. M. Shudy, and B. F. Sideleau. *Comprehensive Psychiatric Nursing*, 2d ed. New York: McGraw-Hill, 1982.

Harding, C. M., J. Zubin, and J. Strauss. "Chronicity in Schizophrenia: Fact, Partial Fact, or Artifact." *Hospital and Community Psychiatry* 38, no. 5 (May 1987):477–486.

Hatfield, A. D., and H. P. Lefley. *Families of the Mentally Ill: Coping and Adaptation*. New York: Guilford, 1986.

Heston, L. L. "Genetic Factors." *Hospital Practice* 12 (June 1977):43–49.

Kanter, J., R. H. Lamb, and C. Loeper. "Expressed Emotion in Families: A Critical Review." *Hospital and Community Psychiatry* 38, no. 4 (April 1987):374–380.

Koenigsberg, H. W., and R. Handley. "Expressed Emotion: From Predictive Index to Clinical Construct." *American Journal of Psychiatry* 143, no. 11 (November 1986):1361–1373.

Kolb, L., and K. Brodie. *Modern Clinical Psychiatry*, 10th ed. Philadelphia: W. B. Saunders, 1982.

Kyes, J., and C. Hofling. *Basic Psychiatric Concepts in Nursing*. Philadelphia: J. B. Lippincott, 1980.

Lamb, H. R. *The Homeless Mentally Ill*. Washington, D.C.: American Psychiatric Association, 1984.

Leff, J. P., L. Kuipers, and R. Berkowitz. "Controlled Study of Social Intervention in Families of Schizophrenic Patients." *British Journal of Psychiatry* 141, no. 1 (January 1983):121–141.

Leff, J. P., and C. E. Vaugn. *Expressed Emotion in Families*. New York: Guilford, 1985.

Lehmann, H. "History of Schizophrenia." In *Comprehensive Textbook of Psychiatry*, 3d ed., H. I. Kaplan, A. M. Freedman, and B. J. Sadock, eds. Baltimore: Williams & Wilkins, 1980.

Lidz, T. "Intrafamilial Environment of Schizophrenic Patients: Marital Schism and Marital Skew." *American Journal of Psychiatry* 114 (1958):241–248.

Lidz, T., S. Fleck, and A. Cornelius. *Schizophrenia and the Family*. New York: International Universities Press, 1965.

McFarlane, W. R. *Family Therapy in Schizophrenia*. New York: Guilford, 1983.

Mechanic, D. "Nursing and Mental Health Care." In *Nursing in the 80s*, L. Aiken, ed. Philadelphia: Lippincott, 1986.

Pepper, B., and H. Ryglewicz. "What's in a Diagnosis and What Isn't." *Hospital and Community Psychiatry* 39, no. 1 (January 1988):7.

Pope, H. G., P. E. Keck, and S. L. McElroy. "Frequency and Presentation of Neuroleptic Malignant Syndrome in a Large Psychiatric Hospital." *American Journal of Psychiatry* 143, no. 10 (October 1986):1227–1232.

Rosen, H. *A Guide to Clinical Psychiatry*. Coral Gables, Florida: Mnemosyne, 1978.

Rosen, J. N. *Direct Psychoanalytic Psychiatry*. New York: Grune & Stratton, 1962.

Schmeck, H. M. "Schizophrenia Focus Shifts to Dramatic Changes in Brain." *The New York Times* (March 18, 1986).

Shepard, G. *Institutional Care and Rehabilitation*. New York: Longman, 1984.

Sternberg, D. E. "Neuroleptic Malignant Syndrome: The Pendulum Swings." *American Journal of Psychiatry* 143, no. 10 (October 1986):1273–1275.

Sullivan, H. S. *The Interpersonal Theory of Psychiatry*. New York: W. W. Norton, 1953.

——. "Research in Schizophrenia." *American Journal of Psychiatry* 9 (1929):533–567.

Weiner, H. "Schizophrenia: Etiology." In *Comprehensive Textbook of Psychiatry*, 4th ed., H. I. Kaplan and B. J. Sadock, eds. Baltimore: Williams & Wilkins, 1985.

Wolman, B. B. *Manual of Child Psychopathology*. New York: McGraw-Hill, 1976.

Wyden, R. "Mental Illness Awareness Week." *Hospital and Community Psychiatry* 38, no. 10 (October 1987):1037.

Yalom, I. D. *Inpatient Group Psychotherapy*. New York: Basic Books, 1983.

8

Mood Variations and Disruptions

Learning Objectives

After reading this chapter, the student should be able to:

1. Discuss psychodynamic, biochemical, genetic, and existential factors contributing to altered patterns of mood and affect.

2. Compare various therapeutic approaches to working with depressed clients.

3. Compare various therapeutic approaches to working with elated clients.

4. Describe somatic interventions used with clients experiencing dysfunctional alterations of mood and affect.

5. Recognize the responsibilities and contributions of the nurse in the administration of somatic interventions.

6. Identify nursing functions in preventing and alleviating dysfunctional alterations of mood and affect.

7. Differentiate functional grief from dysfunctional responses to loss.

Overview

Variations and disruptions of mood and affect are universal responses to loss, change, and life transitions. Variations and disruptions may range from temporary states of joy or sorrow to extreme, prolonged states of elation or depression where the quality of life deteriorates and awareness of reality is impaired. This chapter discusses the nature of mood variations and disruptions, etiological theories, risk factors, therapeutic approaches, and nursing responsibilities in caring for depressed or elated clients. The last part of the chapter describes grief and mourning as adaptive responses that help people resolve their feelings and resume normal living. Nursing strategies are suggested that help clients deal with grief and mourning. Anticipatory grief is a form of primary prevention that may alleviate the distress of persons facing loss. In some circumstances anticipatory grieving is not acceptable to clients or their families. In this, as in other nursing interventions, it is necessary to assess clients carefully and to offer care that they are ready to accept.

INTRODUCTION TO MOOD VARIATIONS AND DISRUPTIONS

Emotions of joy and sadness are part of the pattern of life and should be differentiated from sustained disruptions of mood. Loss is an unavoidable experience which all of us must face at various times. Loss may be caused by the death of a loved one, by the occurrence of trauma or illness, or by episodes of defeat or disappointment over the course of the life span. Although difficult to endure, loss is an experience to which most people eventually adjust after a painful time of grief and mourning. Such periods of grief and mourning are adaptive behaviors that help integrate the experience of loss. Prolonged depression, on the other hand, is a disruption of mood that is maladaptive. Transient feelings of depression are universal, and for most people the sense of helplessness and hopelessness that are characteristic of depression disappear within a relatively short time. A basic question, then, is why depression appears in some people as a recurring or long-standing disruption, often without any identifiable loss or precipitating factor. A number of explanations are supported by research and clinical observation. Among these are psychodynamic, biogenic, and existential theories.

Depression is the most common disruption of mood, but often the disruption takes the form of mania. Mania is a state of hyperactivity, excitement, grandiosity, and euphoria. Clinically, the manic state seems to be a reversed image of the depressed state, but it is more accurately described as a compensatory mechanism that allows the client to deny underlying feelings of depression. The term "affective disorder" is generally used in the United States and other countries where English is the primary language, although the term "mood disorder" is preferred internationally.

INCIDENCE AND PREVALENCE OF DEPRESSION

Depression is a complex reaction generated by the convergence of many influences: past, present, and future. Causes of depression exist at biological and psychological levels, and the depressed state is expressed through biological and psychological pathways. People function as systems whose operations are influenced by input from many sources. Some input is derived from biological structures and processes; other input comes from life experiences that are stressful, and from the psychological impact of stressful experiences, both pleasant and unpleasant. Figure 8–1 depicts some of the input sources. Over a lifetime almost one out of four persons experiences some form of severe mood disruption. Overall rates of occurrence are about 18 percent; ranging from 15 percent in men to 20 percent in women. Gender rates in manic disorders are about equal.

Depression is the most prevalent psychiatric disorder and is thought to be 10 times more prevalent than disruptions of thought and perception known as schizophrenia. About 25 percent of clients in state mental hospitals carry the diagnosis of depression; 40 percent, in outpatient psychiatric clinics; and 50 percent of clients treated in private mental facilities. Up to 70 percent of psychiatric diagnoses in nonpsychiatric settings are for depression (Cancro 1985).

For some persons, depression is a chronic condition that lasts a lifetime. These persons are a burden to society, to their families, and to themselves. They are unlikely to be very productive citizens, and tend to be constant users of health care services in their search for relief. Many depressed persons attribute their distress to physical causes, and in searching for diagnostic clues caregivers may overlook the possibility of depression. Conversely, depression may be prematurely diagnosed

Figure 8–1. Determining factors in depression.

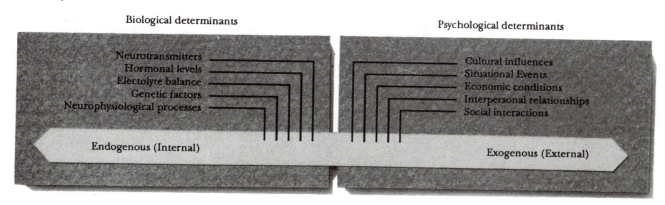

Biological determinants

Neurotransmitters
Hormonal levels
Electrolyte balance
Genetic factors
Neurophysiological processes

Endogenous (Internal)

Psychological determinants

Cultural influences
Situational Events
Economic conditions
Interpersonal relationships
Social interactions

Exogenous (External)

when the underlying cause is physiological rather than psychological.

Culture, social class, and race have not been correlated with overall rates of mood disorders. However, sociocultural factors do seem to influence the clinical signs of the disorder. Somatic complaints, worry, tension, and irritability are more evident in lower socioeconomic groups. Interesting differences have been noted in the form depression takes from one country to another, especially in industrial and nonindustrial nations. Differences have also been found in manifestations of depression in Western cultures with Judeo-Christian traditions and in non-Western cultures that uphold other religious beliefs. In nonindustrial countries, depressed persons' complaints take somatic forms that are culturally acceptable. Their complaints center on physical dysfunction, such as indigestion, constipation, loss of sexual function, and fatigue. These depressed persons may have paranoid delusions of being mistreated or persecuted, but seldom express feelings of guilt or worthlessness, and rarely commit suicide. In industrial societies where Judeo-Christian traditions prevail, guilt feelings are often expressed, but even in these societies there has been a sharp decline in the frequency and severity of feelings of guilt reported by depressed persons. It is estimated that guilt was once characteristic of 75 percent of clinically depressed clients but now is characteristic of 30 to 40 percent. Instead of reporting feelings of guilt, depressed clients are more likely to express a sense of personal inadequacy and concern for their own fulfillment. Despite cultural differences, there are enough commonalities in the way depression is expressed for nurses making a careful assessment to recognize the condition (Robert, Hirschfeld, and Shea 1985).

DETERMINING FACTORS IN DEPRESSION

As a clinical entity, depression is hard to define clearly. The problem of differentiating depression from natural reactions of grief or sadness is greatly influenced by the orientation of the caregiver. There are two extremely different views of depression, with many caregivers taking positions between the two extremes. One view is that depression is biologically determined even though situational factors may contribute. At the other extreme is the view that depression is psychologically determined, with situational factors being primary causes (see Figure 8–1). In recent years research has made much progress in connecting chemical imbalance with depression, but these imbalances have not yet been proved to cause depression, only to be associated with its occurrence (Robert, Hirschfeld, and Shea 1985).

DEPRESSION AS A DYSFUNCTIONAL RESPONSE

Statistics on rates of depression probably underestimate its prevalence because clinical signs vary so much. This is especially true of people who mask their feelings and seem cheerful, or who develop somatic complaints that explain their apathy and lack of pleasure (anhedonia). Although depression has been described as a universal phenomenon, certain people are more likely than others to become depressed: the elderly, young people, alcoholics, and those who have suffered a meaningful loss of some kind.

Increased longevity has contributed to the incidence of depression among elderly persons who

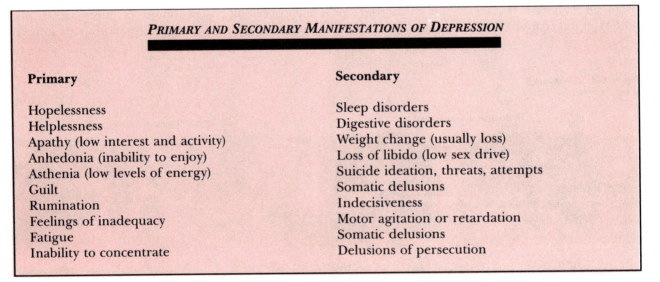

PRIMARY AND SECONDARY MANIFESTATIONS OF DEPRESSION

Primary	Secondary
Hopelessness	Sleep disorders
Helplessness	Digestive disorders
Apathy (low interest and activity)	Weight change (usually loss)
Anhedonia (inability to enjoy)	Loss of libido (low sex drive)
Asthenia (low levels of energy)	Suicide ideation, threats, attempts
Guilt	Somatic delusions
Rumination	Indecisiveness
Feelings of inadequacy	Motor agitation or retardation
Fatigue	Somatic delusions
Inability to concentrate	Delusions of persecution

no longer feel useful or productive. Many elderly people must deal with *transition overload*, and adaptive responses become more difficult for them with each additional life change. Among other transitions, the elderly encounter restricted relationships as loved ones die or move away, and role reduction or reversal as their vigor declines. Their resulting depressed moods are often attributed to the inevitable effects of aging and therefore receive little attention. To complicate matters, many elderly persons use drugs, either by prescription or by choice, that cause depressive reactions that are apt to go unrecognized.

Among children and adolescents, underlying depression may be expressed in rebellious or in withdrawn behavior. The aggressive child who is hyperactive, the passive-aggressive teenager who resists schooling, and the worried overachiever may each be exhibiting depression in his or her own way. Authority figures such as teachers, parents, or police officers who deal with these young people often interpret their behavior as delinquent rather than as depressed.

In very young children who can neither verbalize nor act out their feelings, depressed reactions are usually expressed physiologically. Spitz (1946) noted that infants deprived of mothering withdraw from their environment, and similar infantile responses were observed by Engel (1962). Somewhat older children may develop skin disorders, gastrointestinal disturbances, headaches, or anorexia. In meeting the needs of such children, nurses should recommend medical investigation and treatment for the focal symptoms, followed by family meetings to examine the context in which the dysfunctional responses developed (Hochman 1986).

Alcoholism is a condition that can cause significant alterations of mood and affect. Despite its popularity as a relaxer and social lubricant, alcohol is a central nervous system depressant that acts to aggravate physical and mental depression. Alcoholics who suffer loss of control, family discord, and occupational difficulties tend to increase their consumption of alcohol, thereby adding to their problems.

Most people who develop depression have experienced a loss of some kind. The loss may be recent, in the past, or a combination of the two. Furthermore, the loss may be actual, anticipated, or symbolic. Whatever its characteristics, the loss is always perceived by the depressed persons as meaningful and excessive. Significant losses that are likely to provoke depressive reactions in vulnerable individuals are listed in Table 8–1. Demographic risk factors are described in Tables 8–2 and 8–3.

Table 8–1. Significant Factors in Depressive Reactions

Type of Loss or Change	Examples of Loss or Change
Loss of meaningful relationships	Alienation or estrangement from a loved one: death, divorce, separation from a loved one
Change in body image or self-image	Physical or functional change in self-concept due to disease, trauma, or aging
Loss of status or prestige	Career demotion or disappointment; social or interpersonal inadequacy
Loss of confidence and self-assurance	Lowered sense of competence, autonomy, and independence
Loss of security and safety	Economic or social reverses; loss of control; unpredictable future outcomes
Loss of dreams, fantasies, and goals	Unfulfilled hopes; unrealized and unreachable ambitions

CLASSIFICATION OF MOOD VARIATIONS AND DISRUPTIONS

Although human beings are capable of a wide range of emotions—fear, anger, anxiety, joy, amazement, and so on—the clinical manifestations of affective disorders take the form of depression and its opposite extreme, mania.

Major depression is characterized by a history of one or more episodes of depression. Whenever a period of mania (elation and heightened activity) has occurred, with or without a history of depression, the category of *bipolar disorder* is used. *Cyclothymic disturbances* resemble bipolar disorders but are less severe. *Dysthymic disorders* resemble major depression but are shorter in duration and less severe, and they are not preceded or followed by manic episodes.

At one time depression was classified as *neurotic* (mild in form and reactive to external events) or *psychotic* (severe in form and reactive to internal conditions). A similar typology classified depressive states as *endogenous* (arising from biological or physiological causes) or *exogenous* (arising from situational or environmental causes). Depressions that were considered endogenous were usually treated with such somatic interventions as electroconvulsive therapy and drugs. Depressions classified as exogenous were thought to be more responsive to psychotherapeutic intervention or environmental modification than endogenous depressions.

Table 8-2. Demographic Risk Factors in Variations and Disruptions of Mood: Depression

Risk Factor	Epidemiological Data
Gender	In almost all industrialized countries more women than men are found to be clinically depressed. Data may be biased because help-seeking behavior is more acceptable for women. Furthermore, alcohol use and aggressive behavior may mask depression in men. Other factors accounting for greater prevalence in women are more precarious thyroid function, use of steroidal contraceptives, premenstrual and postpartum endocrine changes.
Age	Early studies indicated that incidence of depression in women was greatest between 35 and 45 years of age; in men incidence was greatest between 45 and 55 years of age. More recent studies show that the median age of onset is the mid-twenties for both. High rates of depression are now reported in children and adolescents, due to recognition that depression is not confined to adults.
Race	Black Americans receive less treatment for depression than whites. As health care systems were integrated, diagnosis and treatment of depression in black Americans rose significantly. Community-based studies now indicate that race is not a significant risk factor.
Social class	No association has been reported been social class and clinical evidence of depression. This is a contrast to bipolar disorders (mania) where social class is a significant factor.
Religion	No association between religion and depression has been proved, partly because genetic and cultural factors intrude.
Family influence	Family history of depression doubles or triples the risk. Depression concordance rates for identical twins are less than bipolar concordance rates. Evidence for genetic mission of depression is less convincing than for bipolar alterations. Family studies are complicated by symmetrical mating (likelihood of depressed persons to have a depressed spouse). It is unclear whether depressed persons choose mates with similar problems or whether depression in one partner is contagious for the other. Children of two depressed parents are twice as likely to be clinically depressed as the children in families where only one parent is depressed.

SOURCE: Adapted from Weissman and Boyd (1985), Kerr, Hoier, and Versi (1985), and Wierzbicki (1987).

Table 8-3. Demographic Risk Factors in Variations and Disruptions of Mood: Mania (Bipolar)

Risk Factor	Epidemiological Data
Gender	Most of the incidence and prevalence studies now show equal rates for men and women. Earlier studies showed higher overall rates for women.
Age	Recent studies show onset occurring most often in late teens or early twenties. Earlier studies showed incidence to rise until age 35, followed by decline. With advancing age, time between manic episodes may shorten and duration lengthen. NIMH (National Institute of Mental Health) studies consistently show earlier onset (late 20s) for mania, and later onset (late 30s) for major depression.
Social class	Bipolar disorder is more common in upper socioeconomic groups. Persons with bipolar disorders usually reach higher educational and occupational status than comparable control groups comprised of normal subjects.
Race	No relationship has been found between race and bipolar disorders.
Religion	Because intermarriage within religious groups may introduce genetic and cultural influences, no association between religion and bipolar disorders has been proved.
Personality	Most studies of this factor are inconclusive. An NIMH study compared recovered bipolar persons with a normal sample and found the only significant difference to be greater obsessive-compulsive tendencies in the bipolar group.
Family influences	Abundant evidence shows that bipolar disorders are familial and probably genetic. In a study of paired twins, there was three times as much concordance between identical as between fraternal twins. Adopted persons with biological family histories of bipolar disorders were three times more likely to develop the disorder than adoptive parents or siblings with no family history of bipolar disorders.

SOURCE: Adapted from Weissman and Boyd (1985), and Wierzbicki (1987).

At present, the differences between endogenous and exogenous depression are indistinct. Indeed, it is now believed that both internal and external changes accompany *all* alterations of mood and affect. External problems such as marital conflict or occupational discontent may follow depression or precede it. Thus, rather than trying to separate cause from effect, it is more useful to examine interrelated factors in the etiology of mood and affective disturbances.

ETIOLOGY OF MOOD VARIATIONS AND DISRUPTIONS

Psychodynamic Factors

According to psychoanalytic theory, depressive tendencies can begin early (see Table 8–4). In the first year of life the dependency needs of the child are

---

NURSING DIAGNOSES RELATED TO MOOD VARIATIONS AND DISRUPTIONS

Perceived constipation
Impaired verbal communication
Impaired social interaction
Altered parenting
Sexual dysfunction
Altered family processes
Altered sexuality patterns

Ineffective individual coping
Impaired adjustment
Ineffective denial
Ineffective family coping: disabling
Ineffective family coping: compromised
Decisional conflict
Fatigue
Sleep pattern disturbance
Diversional activity deficit
Impaired home maintenance management
Altered health maintenance
Bathing/hygiene self-care deficit
Dressing/grooming self-care deficit

Body image disturbance
Self-esteem disturbance
Chronic low self-esteem
Situational low self-esteem
Personal identity disturbance
Sensory/perceptual alterations (specify)
Hopelessness
Powerlessness

Altered thought processes
Dysfunctional grieving
Anticipatory grieving
Potential for violence: self-directed or
    directed at others
Anxiety
Fear

The above are the more likely diagnoses related to mood variations and disruptions. Applicable nursing diagnoses are not limited to the list shown here. Manifestations of these disorders are individualistic even though certain patterns prevail.

Table 8–4. Crucial Assessment Areas in Childhood Depression

Area	Warning Signs
Eating patterns	Child has lost weight or failed to gain weight. Child has lost interest in food . . . OR Child has gained an unusual amount of weight.
Sleeping patterns	Child is tired all the time and can hardly get up in the morning . . . OR Child is agitated and sleepless at night.
Energy level	Child is listless, lethargic, and uninterested in activities previously enjoyed . . . OR Child is agitated, hyperactive, unmanageable . . . OR Child develops mannerisms such as stuttering, twisting his hair, yelling/whispering inappropriately.
Mental function	Child has trouble concentrating; thinking is slowed; decision making is difficult . . . OR Child is fearful, anxious; is excessively worried about his health.
Self-esteem	Child expresses doubts about his abilities and value. Child performs far below his ability at school and at home, and doesn't seem to care. Child is seldom spontaneous or enthusiastic. Child feels that family and schoolmates dislike him.
Age-related patterns	School-aged child is reluctant to separate from parent to attend school. School-aged child may develop temper outbursts. Adolescents engage in antisocial actions. Adolescents become aggressive, violent. Adolescents engage in substance abuse. Adolescents run away from home. Any prolonged or sudden change in attitude or behavior may stem from depression.

DSM III-R CLASSIFICATION OF AFFECTIVE DISORDERS

Major Depression

296.2x	Single
296.3x	Recurrent
	(Specify: chronic, seasonal, melancholic type)

Bipolar Disorder

296.6x	Mixed
296.4x	Manic
296.5x	Depressed

Other Specific Affective Disorders

301.13	Cyclothymia
300.40	Dysthymia (depressive neurosis) Specify: Primary or secondary, early or late onset, seasonal pattern

met by the mother or mother figure. Oral needs predominate, and if these needs are not sufficiently satisfied, the child develops a longing for love and security.

Eventually, the child comes to see the world as disorderly and unpredictable, and he feels confused and guilty because his surrounding world lacks meaning. Unable to rely on external sources of love or to establish order in the world, the child blames himself and feels angry and inferior. The result is a fragile sense of self-esteem and competence (Freud 1957).

When nurturing is insufficient or inconsistent, children develop a wish or craving for affection and approval that lasts a lifetime. Two modes of behavior are apt to result. The individual may try to obtain what she needs from others by becoming openly dependent, or she may deny dependency needs by adopting high, unrealistic standards of performance. Thus, the psychoanalytic explanation connects depressive tendencies with unmet dependency needs in early life. The findings of Bowlby (1973, 1980) that early experiences of loss threaten abilities of individuals to cope with later losses support this explanation.

During the 1940s René Spitz, a European psychiatrist, studied the behavior of 123 young children being raised in a South American nursery. He found that a significant number of the children habitually avoided social interaction with others, ate poorly, lost weight, and had difficulty sleeping. Further investigation showed Spitz that the children who behaved in this way had been separated from their mothers between their sixth and eighth month of life, and that the separation was of three months duration or more. In the nursery surroundings no surrogate mother was supplied. Spitz also found that when separation from mother lasted less than six months, the children soon recovered after reunion. However, when mothers did not return, the condition of the children worsened, and 24 out of 91 children who were not reunited with their mothers died. The work of Spitz is the basis for the widespread belief that the origin of childhood depression is loss of some kind. It may be loss of a parent or sibling through death. It may be the loss of security that children experience when parents are divorced, or it may even be the loss of a familiar home and friends when a family moves (Spitz 1946).

Childhood loss of a parent does not lead inevitably to mood disorder, but a history of loss in childhood may prevent the acquisition of mature coping skills, and lead to lack of confidence and low self-esteem which in turn encourage feelings of depression. Two aspects of modern life are blamed for a rising incidence of depression in children. The dissolution of families by divorce and geographic separation means that many children are deprived of needed family supports. Children are more aware of what is going on in the family than parents realize. Without being told, they recognize conflict between parents, whether the cause is money worries or extramarital affairs. More often than not, children blame themselves for the family's problems. They may become troubleshooters and try to

ANACLITIC DEPRESSION

René Spitz (1946) and John Bowlby (1969, 1982) were among the first to note that physical separation from the mother during infancy can cause apathy, withdrawal, and failure to thrive in the child. This condition, known as *anaclitic* separation or depression, is marked by conservation of energy and withdrawal from the social environment (Engel 1962). In fact, many behaviors observed clinically in depressed children resemble the listlessness and inertia of some depressed adults who make no demands on the environment but wish only to be left alone.

solve the family's problems. Since they rarely have the power to do this, they become increasingly anxious and depressed. Some children endure much emotional deprivation and physical abuse without giving any sign of being depressed. In such cases there may be subtle safety precautions that protect the child. Some children are lucky enough to find a surrogate in the form of a teacher, an older sibling, or a scout leader who gives them stability and a feeling of value. And many single parents, in spite of all their responsibilities, give their children reassurance and confidence.

Although traumatic experiences during the oral phase of life may generate excessive needs for affection and approval in later life, such vulnerability is not limited to the oral period. Bibring (1953) suggested that fixation or regression at any stage of psychosexual development may contribute to depressive personality traits. In his view, depression is associated with the lowering of self-esteem that occurs when the mastery of developmental tasks is impaired. Trauma in the toilet-training phase, for example, may incite lifelong feelings of failure around issues of control. Similarly, difficulties during the phallic period may result in extreme competitiveness or in an exaggerated fear of competing. Problems arising either in the stage of autonomy versus shame and doubt or in the stage of initiative versus guilt pose threats to the person's sense of competence and self-worth (Erikson 1963).

Existential Factors

Existential factors in affective disturbances include accumulated or multiple life events that seem to predispose individuals to such problems. It is difficult, if not impossible, to separate life experiences from psychodynamic influences because personality traits, life experiences, and reactive behaviors are intertwined. Rejection by parents in childhood, poor marital adjustment, economic problems, and frustrated ambitions are only a few of the existential conditions that can influence mood and affect. In addition, some individuals spend their formative years in homes where there is a sustained atmosphere of hopelessness and a chronic expectation of failure. Such family depression can be contagious, and it is hard for any person living under such conditions to remain optimistic.

Individuals suffering bipolar disorder often come from families that are upwardly mobile, socially and economically, but somewhat isolated from the community (Gardner 1982). The mother may have considerable authority in the family but is apt to be distant and unloving. The father is likely to be kinder but less powerful than the mother. The family member who develops bipolar disorder

may have been the child expected to achieve high social and academic success, with parental approval conditional on the performance of the child.

During periods of depression, persons with bipolar disorder have feelings of failure and inferiority. During episodes of mania, their basic feelings are the same but are kept from conscious awareness by activity and energy that compensate for the underlying sense of inferiority. In periods of mania, as in depression, low self-esteem and fear of rejection persist but are disguised by grandiosity. Some theorists believe that manic behaviors are used to avoid reality, that sociability is compulsive rather than spontaneous, and that hyperactivity enables the individual to escape underlying fears and frustrations.

Few people get through life without encountering stress, loss, or disappointment. Any persistent life problem or recurring adversity may eventually lead to a state of depression characterized by feelings of worthlessness, hopelessness, guilt, and apathy. Negative feelings about one's self and the world arise when life events threaten one's self-esteem. If self-esteem is linked to achievement and recognition, status and prestige are very important. If external reminders of status and prestige are lost, a vulnerable person will react by becoming depressed. Individuals less interested in status may rely more on their internal feelings of competence and confidence. Such persons suffer a loss of confidence and self-assurance when their feelings of competence are threatened. Another kind of person may be concerned with security rather than status and will become depressed when security is endangered. Loss of dreams and fantasies are abstractions that may cause depression when individuals realize that their lifelong ambitions will probably not be realized. Loss of meaningful roles and relationships are other circumstances that may engender depression.

The term *Involutional Melancholia* is no longer included in the DSM III-R but midlife depression remains prevalent. Depression in midlife usually occurs in women about the time of menopause during their fourth decade, and in men about ten years later. The disorder is more prevalent in men than in women, but studies linking midlife depression to hormonal changes related to menopause have been inconclusive (Klerman 1980, Wolpert 1980). In midlife people have finished raising their families. Children, for the most part, have been launched, and the nest is empty except for the parents, who are no longer young. They have achieved some goals but not others. Unachieved goals no longer seem close at hand, but rather seem out of reach. Retirement nears, and with it comes the prospect of lowered income and additional role losses (Roy 1981). The increased life span of very elderly people has added to the burden of the middle-aged, particularly women who must assume the major responsibility for incapacitated parents.

Many people who develop midlife depression have been conforming, conscientious, and hardworking all their lives but feel they have not been sufficiently rewarded or appreciated. Loss of youth and negative attitudes toward aging may contribute to their distress. Some are disappointed in themselves but project their feelings of worthlessness on to others, becoming bitter and complaining. In general, midlife depression is marked by feelings of guilt, anger, and anxiety. Some persons begin by thinking they have committed unpardonable sins but gradually project these sins to others, becoming convinced that the sins have been committed against them. Delusions of persecution are common, as are somatic delusions that they are ill and diseased (Minot 1986).

The risk of suicide is quite high, and the sufferings of clients and families can be extensive. Although it is no longer differentiated from other forms of depression, midlife depression merits particular attention from nurses because of its prevalence and distressing manifestations. In both men and women midlife depression often takes the form of an agitated depressed mood. The clients' agitation and the nature of their delusions can be very difficult for family members, who need support and reassurance when dealing with a relative who has changed so much. The client and family members can truthfully be told that the condition is self-limiting and that the eventual outcome is hopeful, particularly when relief is provided in the form of psychotherapy and suitable somatic measures, such as antidepressant medication or electroconvulsive treatment.

Many elderly people adjust well to the changes in their lives and maintain the ego integrity that Erikson described so eloquently. Nevertheless, old age and depression occur together with some frequency. Unfortunately, depression in the elderly is often mistaken for the dysfunction popularly known as senility. The indications of depression and of organic brain damage (impaired memory, disorientation, confusion, agitation or apathy) resemble one another to the extent that the underlying depression of many elderly persons is overlooked (Shapira, Schlesinger, and Cummings 1986).

BIOLOGICAL DETERMINING FACTORS

Biochemical Factors

Alterations of mood and affect undoubtedly involve complex biochemical changes in the body. Among the identified changes are electrolyte imbalance of sodium and potassium and altered functioning of the thyroid, adrenocortex, gonads, and autonomic nervous system. In the last few decades the belief has grown that affective disorders are related to the transmission of nerve impulses across the synaptic cleft (see Figure 8–2) by neurotransmitters, especially the biogenic amines. Both groups of biogenic amines seem to be involved: the catecholamines (dopamine and norepinephrine) and the indolamines (serotonin). Two altered neurotransmission patterns have been identified: norepinephrine deficiency in depression and serotonin deficiency in periodic mania and depression (bipolar disorder) (Wolpert 1980). Although the results of biochemical investigation point to deficient amounts of norepinephrine as a major factor in depression, mania seems to be related to dopamine and serotonin function as well as to excess norepinephrine levels. Biochemical theories explaining mania and depression appear to be valid, but extensive investigation continues (Usdin 1977, Wolpert 1980).

The possibility that biochemical changes might contribute to mania and depression first came to light when it was observed that certain drugs can have major effects on mood and affect. It was noted,

Figure 8–2. *Diagram showing action of neurotransmitters within a neural synapse.*

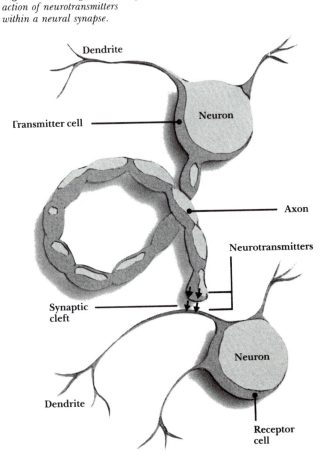

for example, that when certain drugs were prescribed to reduce hypertension, the incidence of depression and suicide increased among persons taking these drugs. Subsequent research showed that the drugs used to alleviate hypertension depleted levels of norepinephrine, serotonin, and dopamine in the brain and neural synapses. About the same time it was noted that patients given monamine oxidase (MAO) inhibitors for treatment of tuberculosis experienced a state of elation or euphoria. When administered as antidepressants, these drugs proved to have the ability to elevate the mood of depressed persons. It was also discovered that these drugs *increased* the levels of norepinephrine, serotonin, and dopamine in the central nervous system. Currently it is thought that MAO inhibitors and another group of drugs called tricyclics produce their antidepressant effects by interfering with deamination of norepinephrine, thus increasing the availability of this biogenic neurotransmitter.

The possibility that hormonal levels might be linked to depression arose from clinical observation of the mood changes of clients with hypothyroidism and other endocrine disorders such as Cushing's and Addison's syndromes. The many sophisticated studies that have been done have conflicted data, but one conclusion has emerged. Various hormonal changes are associated with altered patterns of mood and affect. The best documented changes concern the hypothalamic-pituitary-adrenal axis (HPA), the hypothalamic-pituitary-thyroid axis (HPT), and the hypothalamic-pituitary-growth hormone (HPGH) (Schildkraut, Green, and Mooney 1985). Table 8–5 shows hormonal changes in alterations of mood and affect. Table 8–6 describes somatic conditions associated with depression.

At present it is uncertain whether biochemical changes cause alterations of mood and affect, whether they are the results of alterations of mood and affect, or whether both factors interact in reciprocal ways (Hanin and Usdin 1982). The fact that biochemical changes are associated with affective disturbances does not rule out psychological or situational influences in mania and depression. Human beings adapt both physiologically and psychologically to internal and external conditions. For example, the fight or flight behaviors induced by anxiety are related to autonomic nervous system activity that influences the whole organism. In short, life experiences, past and present, can promote generalized and localized reactions that are both psychogenic and biogenic (Selye 1956).

Genetic Factors

Some researchers are convinced that genetic factors play a significant role in mood and affective

Table 8–5. Hormonal Changes in Alterations of Mood and Affect	
HPA (Hypothalamic-pituitary-adrenal axis)	Hyperactive secretion in depressed persons Disruption of normal circadian (24-hour) rhythm Alteration of minimal activity period (early morning)
HPT (Hypothalamic-pituitary-thyroid axis)	Reduction of thyroid-stimulating hormone (TSH) in depressed persons Reduction of thyroid releasing hormone (TRH) in depressed persons
HPGH (Hypothalamic-pituitary-growth hormone)	No clear evidence of HPGH change in depressed persons Increase in growth hormone (GH) in 50 percent of persons classified as having unipolar or bipolar depression

SOURCE: Data compiled from Schildkraut, Green, and Mooney (1985).

disorders, especially the bipolar types. Kallman (1953) considered manic-depressive disorders to be caused by a dominant gene with incomplete penetration and variable manifestation. That is, the gene is probably dominant, but its behavior is unpredictable. It has indeed been found that close relatives of persons with bipolar disorder seem to be more susceptible than the general population, to developing the disorder, and susceptibility increases with the closeness of the relationship: The monozygotic twin of a person with a bipolar disorder is more susceptible than a dizygotic twin, and a dizygotic twin is more susceptible than a regular sibling. Although current research supports the theory of a genetic factor in explaining the prevalence of bipolar disorder in some families, social factors in these families cannot be discounted (Juel-Nielson 1980, Lumsden and Wilson 1981, Gershon, Nurnberger, Berrettini, and Goldin 1985).

WORKING WITH DEPRESSED CLIENTS

The clinical manifestations of depressed individuals offer a challenge to the nurse who recognizes that all behavior has meaning and purpose even when it seems self-defeating. In assessing a depressed client, it is important to go beyond outward behavior and consider every possible aspect. For example, many physical conditions manifest themselves as alterations of mood and affect, including carcinoma, cerebrovascular accidents (stroke), malnutrition, anemia, hypothyroidism, and multiple sclerosis. It is therefore unwise to assume that alterations of mood, whether depressive or manic,

Table 8–6. Somatic Conditions Associated with Depression	
Cardiovascular	Over 50% of cardiac clients in treatment are depressed; 30% develop depression within 18 months of a myocardial infarction.
Neurological	Huntington's chorea, multiple sclerosis, and dementias are often associated with depression.
Endocrine	Depression is shown in low-energy levels and apathy: thyroid dysfunctions, Addison's syndrome, Cushing's syndrome.
Rheumatic	About 50% of clients with rheumatoid arthritis exhibit depressive features.
Malignant (Cancer)	Depression is often the earliest indication. Clients receiving chemotherapy are extremely prone to depression.
Nutritional	Protein and Vitamin B deficiencies result in depression. Poor eating habits and inefficient absorption of nutrients lead to depression, especially among elderly clients.

SOURCE: Adapted from Lehmann (1985).

are primarily psychogenic until a full investigation of all factors has been made.

Assessment

Comprehensive assessment should include psychological, physiological, cognitive, and related factors.

PSYCHOLOGICAL MANIFESTATIONS Depressed people who are able to verbalize their feelings may describe themselves as helpless, worthless, hopeless, and despairing. They may feel guilty about deeds they imagine they have committed or resentful of misdeeds they believe have been committed against them.

Psychoanalytic theory considers depressed people to be carriers of anger. This anger is obvious in the behavior of complaining, demanding clients who try to punish everyone in the vicinity because they do not believe their needs are being met, but it is less identifiable in depressed persons who mask their anger in some way and prefer to make their demands silently or indirectly. The nurse should remember that the behavior of a passive, withdrawn client may be just as directed toward winning attention as the behavior of the demanding client. Both behavioral expressions—aggressive and passive—tend to increase the power of the client over others.

In moderate to severe forms of depression, many individuals become indecisive and indifferent to their appearance or their surroundings. Others may engage obsessively in routine tasks and become preoccupied with unimportant details. Ru-

THE COGNITIVE TRIAD OF DEPRESSION

Negative View of the Self

The depressed person generally perceives the self as deficient and inferior. Failure and frustration are attributed to physical, mental, or moral defects in the self. Therefore, the self is unlovable and unacceptable.

Negative View of the World

The depressed person believes that the world makes excessive demands and at the same time causes constant frustration. Actions meet with defeat; life is full of burdens, impediments, and disappointments.

Negative View of the Future

The depressed person assumes that the dismal conditions of the present will continue in the future. No relief can be seen; only a life of failure and hardship looms ahead.

mination (prolonged thinking about the same issue) is typical and is a factor in self-deprecation and indecisiveness. Attention span is often reduced to the extent that ordinary tasks require enormous amounts of energy and effort. Failure to accomplish or complete tasks then adds to feelings of guilt or worthlessness. Many depressed clients have distorted viewpoints and interpretations of reality that come to dominate their behavior. For example, some severely depressed individuals may develop somatic delusions, believing that their vital organs are diseased or decaying.

During depressive episodes, the whole quality of life seems to deteriorate. The person suffers from a poverty of ideas, restricted interests, loss of energy and spontaneity, and the belief that life is grim and unrewarding. Anhedonia (lack of pleasure) interferes with the individual's participation in activities that he or she once enjoyed. Anhedonia is accompanied by reduced sexual interest and desire, and by inhibited sexual excitement and orgasm in men and in women. Such sexual dysfunction may then jeopardize the individual's sexual relationships.

Some depressed persons lose weight as a result of anorexia, but others overeat as they try to relieve feelings of emptiness. Depressed clients express many somatic complaints, sometimes to the point of hypochondria. Because some complaints may have a realistic basis, it is essential to investigate and respond appropriately to any somatic problems, whether real or imaginary.

Psychomotor retardation may cause the client to move, think, and speak slowly. Constipation may become a problem, although it may be the expression of an emotional state rather than a direct result of physiological retardation. Not every depressed person exhibits psychomotor retardation; in fact, many engage in aimless, unproductive activity. When depression takes the form of agitation rather than psychomotor retardation, the individual becomes restless and fidgety, but the activity is often purposeless and undirected. Tasks are begun but rarely finished, further contributing to feelings of inadequacy.

COGNITIVE MANIFESTATIONS The psychoanalytic explanation that depressed persons carry anger that has been internalized and turned against the self was questioned by Beck (1969, 1972), who formulated a different explanation for depression. Beck began by analyzing the dreams of several hundred depressed and nondepressed subjects. He found that the dreams of depressed persons could be characterized by these common themes: (1) the dreamer tried to do or obtain something but was frustrated, (2) the dreamer lost an object or person of value, or (3) the dreamer was deficient in health, appearance, or ability. Beck followed these dream studies with investigations of the thought content revealed by depressed clients. He found that depressed persons hold a number of negative attitudes toward themselves, their world, and their future. Beck labeled this group of negative attitudes the *cognitive triad of depression*; it is presented in the accompanying box and illustrated in Figure 8–3.

Having noted the distortions in the cognitive patterns of depressed persons, Beck tried to identify the mechanisms used to interpret situations negatively. He found that depressed persons overgeneralize by drawing global conclusions from a single, isolated event. A selective focus causes them to take details out of context, exaggerating negative features and ignoring positive ones. In addition, they reject pieces of evidence that contradict their negative interpretations. Errors in judgment are ignored or exaggerated, depending on which distortion is needed to support negative viewpoints.

When Beck's findings were applied clinically, it was apparent that depressed persons responded favorably to positive feedback given upon the successful completion of graded tasks. Rewards, in the form of praise and attention, had to be immediate to be effective, however. Exposure to consistent rewards and the experience of successful achievement contradicted the depressed client's conviction that success was impossible. Interventions that suggested that failure was not inevitable also seemed to reduce feelings of pessimism and ineffectiveness.

Planning

Nurses planning care for depressed clients should identify major problems, including the possibility of

Figure 8–3. *Cognitive Triad of Depression.*

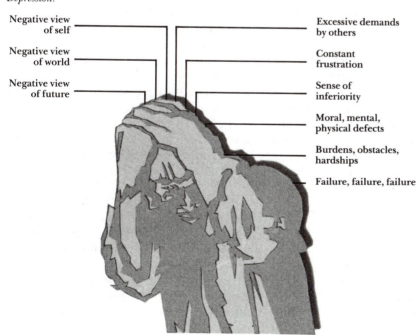

Negative view of self

Negative view of world

Negative view of future

Excessive demands by others

Constant frustration

Sense of inferiority

Moral, mental, physical defects

Burdens, obstacles, hardships

Failure, failure, failure

Table 8–7. Planning Care for Depressed Clients

Client's Problem	Goal	Nursing Intervention
Feelings of inadequacy and helplessness	Client will experience a sense of acceptance.	Listen actively and give honest reassurance.
Rumination and indecision	Client will ruminate less and decide issues more easily.	Clarify issues so decision making and problem solving are simplified.
Apathy and regression	Client will participate in appropriate activity and interaction.	Encourage verbalization and social interaction.
Direct and indirect expressions of anger	Client will be less afraid to express negative feelings.	Accept expressions of anger without retaliating.
Psychomotor retardation	Client will feel less inferior and incapable.	Allow time for activities to be completed; encourage motor activities that client can tolerate.
Somatic complaints	Client will realize that staff will respond realistically to somatic complaints.	Work with health team to investigate and treat.
Sleep disturbance: hypersomnia	Client will sleep an appropriate number of hours.	Design schedule of activities with the help of the client.
Sleep disturbance: insomnia	Client will sleep or rest an adequate number of hours.	Promote relaxing bedtime routines: warm milk, bathing, quiet conversation.

a suicide attempt. Every depressed client is a suicide risk. When deeply depressed, a client may lack the energy or motivation to put a suicide plan into action. Thus, the danger of suicide is actually greatest just as the depression begins to lift. Not only does the client now have the energy to act on a suicide plan, but inexperienced staff members may be relaxing their vigilance.

In cases of potential suicide, hospitalization may be indicated unless social supports are reliable and available for the client. Suicide precautions are a routine procedure for depressed clients in psychiatric inpatient facilities and require staff members to know the exact whereabouts of the suicidal client at every moment. A discussion of the assessment of suicide risk, types of suicide, and nursing responsibility for suicidal clients is provided in Chapter 16, which deals with situational crises.

Many depressed clients suffer from sleep disturbances. Clients may be unable to fall asleep or may fall asleep readily but waken early. Some individuals sleep fitfully while others regress by sleeping day and night. When clients are wakeful, sedatives may promote sleep for a time, but they fail to solve the fundamental problems. Alert nurses have observed that administration of sedation to inpatients rises or falls depending on the staff assigned to evening or night rotations. Thus, at times sedation seems to be administered on the basis of staff needs rather than client needs.

Before deciding to administer sedation, the nurse should explore the possible causes of sleep disturbance. Many depressed clients behave in ways that encourage insomnia. They may sleep during the day or engage in activities such as watching television that are neither constructive nor rewarding. When bedtime arrives, these clients cannot sleep because they are not tired or because the day has seemed wasted. Occasionally, family visits have been upsetting, making the client agitated and unable to sleep.

To address these causes, the nurse can plan activities for daytime hours so that tendencies to sleep all day and stay awake all night are discouraged. The nurse might also talk quietly with the client about unresolved incidents of the day or may attend to specific complaints that prevent the client from sleeping. Giving nonstimulating beverages or assisting with relaxing baths may be more effective in the long run than medication. Moreover, these measures assure the client that the nurse is concerned and wants to help. Table 8–7 discusses ways to plan care for depressed clients.

Implementation

Many depressed clients are reluctant to engage in social interaction because of apathy and poor motivation. Their lack of confidence and feelings of worthlessness lead them to doubt their ability to converse or to inspire positive responses in anyone. Depressed clients may inadvertently cause staff members to withdraw and avoid them unless deliberate efforts are made by staff to prevent mutual withdrawal. Staff members should spend some portion of each day with hospitalized depressed clients, talking or listening in an accepting way or perhaps just sitting with them in order to communicate interest and a wish to help. Extreme cheerfulness on the part of caregivers is not helpful, as it conveys to the client that feelings of sadness are unacceptable.

Depressed clients seem to become resigned to their situation and want to give up. These feelings can be counteracted by using Beck's cognitive approach to correct distortions. When depressed clients express feelings of helplessness, it is appropriate to ask, "Are you really so helpless, or do you have some strengths you're not using?" If clients express feelings of hopelessness, suggest that "there are people available who want to help you begin to help yourself."

Feelings of worthlessness can be reduced by providing opportunities to succeed. Because the client's concentration and energy are limited, activities should be noncompetitive, undemanding, and of short duration. Indecisiveness in depressed clients is troublesome and intensifies their feelings of inadequacy. Therefore, a schedule or routine that eliminates some decisions can be helpful. When decisions must be made, the nurse can help the client reduce the number of alternatives so that confusion is lessened.

Consistency is needed from the nurse, as is the ability to tolerate anger without becoming angry in turn. When the client is angry, the nurse should be matter-of-fact rather than defensive. Motor activities such as walking and exercising can help to discharge anger and aggression without provoking additional guilt on the part of the client.

Because the clinical picture presented by depressed clients is not uniform, individual signs and behaviors must be considered in developing a care plan. Collaboration with the client is always an objective, but sometimes active collaboration must wait until the client becomes capable of participation.

Clients who become troubled by a sleep problem may be told truthfully that this is not a permanent condition but rather a part of being depressed. In dealing with the problem the nurse and client should work together rather than at cross purposes. It is far easier to dispense medication than to establish routines that promote sleep, but only the latter is an independent nursing function. A number of interventions appropriate for sleep disturbance and other problems are listed in Table 8–8.

Table 8–8. Classic Manifestations of Depression and Nursing Interventions

Altered Pattern	Manifestation	Nursing Intervention
Low self-esteem	"I'm not worth anything to any one" (self-care deficits)	Seek out client and give recognition for any accomplishments, however minor.
Anger: hidden or open	"No one is concerned with my comfort" (sarcasm, ridicule, or silent resistance to social overtures)	Accept client's anger without retaliating. Teach client to recognize presence and cause of anger. Encourage physical activity as outlet for anger. Suggest client keep daily "complaint list" and review this with client.
Powerlessness	"Everybody tells me what to do and how to do it" (active or passive resistance to therapeutic regimen)	Explain reason for various aspects of care. Permit client to have some control over daily routine. Offer alternative actions when possible.
Helplessness	"I can't manage alone—I need someone to look after me" (indifference, passivity, regression)	Encourage client to take increasing responsibility but indicate that help is available if needed.
Hopelessness	"There is nothing anyone can do to help me" (withdrawal, apathy, despair)	Reassure client that others will help if client permits them. Help client deal with fears of abandonment.
Guilt	"I deserve to feel bad—I brought this on myself" (self-blame, rumination, and wish to atone for past sins)	Hear and accept emotional state of client. Oppose idea that feeling bad is punishment.
Indecisiveness	"I feel so confused; I can't seem to make up my mind about anything. Tell me what I should do." (inability to decide; ambivalence)	Don't offer solutions, but help client look at various options. Discuss advantages and disadvantages of options. Help client reduce range of options to a few desirable choices.
Self-destructiveness	"I can't go on. I have nothing to live for" (suicide ideation, threats, or attempts)	Assure client of your belief in and commitment to his/her survival. Arrange for strong social support system where possible. If client is hospitalized, institute suicide precautions. In absence of social supports, be available to unhospitalized clients in person or by phone.

SOURCE: Adapted from Kline and Chernecky (1987).

Evaluation

Making a nursing assessment, reaching a nursing diagnosis, identifying problems, and establishing priorities make clinical evaluation possible. One way to evaluate the progress of a depressed client is to note the client's increased involvement in self-care and decision making. Observations of the client's psychological, physiological, and cognitive responses in therapeutic interaction, accurate recording of observations, progress toward identified goals, and the abatement of subjective discomfort are used by the nurse to evaluate the effectiveness of the care plan and to modify specific treatment goals as needed.

WORKING WITH ELATED CLIENTS

Depression and mania represent two poles of the same continuum. Although the outward manifestations of the two affective states are diametrically opposed, their dynamics are similar.

Whereas depression involves a devaluation of self in response to a loss, mania represents a denial of loss and a temporary restoration of self-esteem. Manic states may or may not be triggered by a precipitating event, and episodes of mania may be followed by periods of normalcy or of depression. Mania occurs more commonly before age thirty-five, while depression occurs more commonly after that age. In any form of bipolar disorder, little deterioration occurs between the maladaptive episodes, which may be separated by intervals of weeks, months, or years.

Assessment

Comprehensive assessment should include psychological, physiological, and cognitive factors.

PSYCHOLOGICAL MANIFESTATIONS Clients in a manic state are attempting to remove their doubts and conflicts by behaving in ways that free them from the restraints of logic and rationality. In *hypomania*, which is a less severe state than mania, hyperactive behavior may remain purposeful, goal-directed, and productive. When full blown mania erupts, however, the client becomes elated, euphoric, and grandiose. To maintain the illusion of omnipotence, she may engage in reckless spending or may embark on impractical schemes to impress others. The defense mechanisms of denial and reaction formation are used to disguise feelings of dependence and insecurity. The manic client is demanding, exploitive, manipulative, and self-centered, but

underneath she is uncertain and needs approval. The client may be easily angered because of her low tolerance for frustration.

Although the client seems eager for social interaction, she does not tolerate intimacy well and is quite sensitive to rejection. Because the client is sensitive to and fears rejection, she constantly tests and manipulates others in an effort to achieve reassurance. The client expects much from others, is insensitive to their needs, and tries to control the social environment.

PHYSIOLOGICAL MANIFESTATIONS The client in a manic state engages in frenzied, unceasing activity that makes it possible for him to ignore reality-based messages from others. During the manic state, external stimuli are not screened adequately, and the client is easily distracted. His speech, thoughts, and actions are speeded to the point of incoherence. Singing, rhyming, dancing, dressing, and undressing proceed in rapid order until onlookers (but not the client) feel exhausted. The client's limitless energy and responsiveness to all stimuli make it difficult for him to maintain adequate nutrition or rest. Unless prompt measures are taken, he will suffer from total exhaustion and depletion of energy. The stages of a typical manic episode are illustrated in Figure 8–4.

COGNITIVE MANIFESTATIONS Mania not only blocks out input from others but also enables the client to feel powerful. He has flights of ideas in which the content is somewhat related but is so fragmented that listeners find it hard to understand what he means.

The manic client has little awareness of experiencing impaired reality testing and is convinced of being superior to others. He adopts a cheerful, boisterous conviviality to disperse anxiety and self-doubt. However, this facade is fragile and easily threatened. Whenever the manic client has cause to distrust his effectiveness, he may become angry, accusatory, or hostile.

Nursing assessment of the manic client consists of analyzing the connections between the client's behavior and the contradictory feelings beneath. As with depressed clients, assessment proceeds more easily if specific problems are identified and ranked in order of priority and if responsive interventions are formulated for the problems. Some of the typical problems resulting from the psychological, physiological, and cognitive manifestations of the manic client are described in Table 8–9.

Planning

A client in a manic state may be difficult to manage initially; usually medication in the form of a major

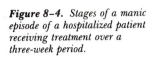

Figure 8–4. *Stages of a manic episode of a hospitalized patient receiving treatment over a three-week period.*

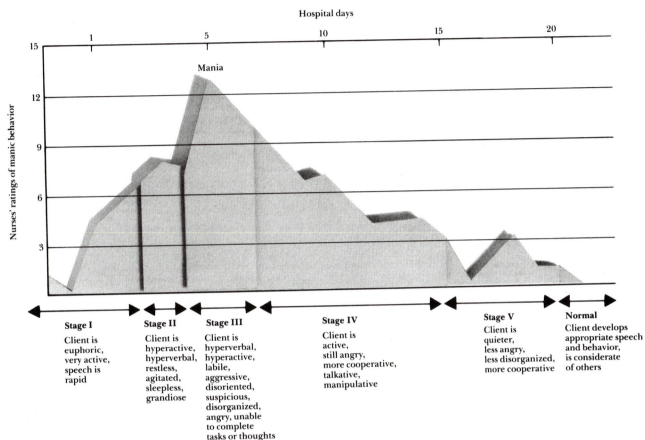

tranquilizer or lithium carbonate is administered, but it may be several days before the medication takes effect. Two major considerations must be taken into account in planning the care of a manic client. One consideration is the maintenance of adequate food and rest until the manic behaviors are brought under control. The second consideration is the elimination of unnecessary sources of stimulation and distraction. Manic clients should be cared for by the same nurse or health care team during hospitalization. Even with this arrangement, the potential for manipulation of staff members remains. One way to avoid such manipulation is to include all staff members in explanations of the approaches to be used. As with any client, staff members who participate in planning are less likely to deviate from the agreed upon approach.

Implementation

The client who is in a manic state needs to know that staff members will help control unacceptable behaviors. Although the client may engage in grandiose schemes and manipulative tactics, she has

underlying fears of losing control. She may interpret a permissive attitude on the part of staff members as a sign of indifference.

In setting limits, the staff should address specific behaviors and whenever possible suggest substitute behaviors so that the client cannot complain that "nothing" is allowed by the staff. For example, walking is a motor activity that is not too strenuous. Sketching and painting are other activities that help a manic client satisfy the need for action.

The grandiose behaviors of manic clients may annoy some people and their outbreaks of anger may frighten others. It is thus important for everyone concerned that staff members clearly indicate the range of acceptable behaviors and institute procedures to modify unacceptable actions (Klerman 1980). Establishing a regular schedule that alternates periods of rest and activity can help if all staff members are consistent in adhering to the regimen.

Therapeutic interventions should have a moderating effect on the client's disruptive, self-destructive behaviors. Suggested nursing interventions are provided in Table 8–9.

Table 8–9. Planning Care for Manic Clients

Client's Problem	Goal	Nursing Intervention
Inadequate nutrition	Client will maintain adequate food intake.	Offer "finger foods" that may be eaten without sitting still.
Inadequate sleep	Client will avoid total exhaustion.	Encourage short rest periods if client cannot sleep longer.
Poor personal hygiene	Client will comply with relaxed standards of dress and hygiene.	Enforce minimal standards of dress and grooming.
High energy expenditure	Client will accept a regimen that does not deplete energy.	Suggest sedentary but interesting activities, such as drawing or painting; offer motor activities in moderation to relieve tension; avoid competitive games or activities.
Excessive responsiveness to stimuli	Client will avoid unnecessary external stimuli.	Remove client from situations that are highly stimulating; remove unnecessary objects from immediate environment; arrange for the same staff members to deal with client.
Belief in personal omnipotence	Client will be protected from opportunity to test powers recklessly.	Safeguard client from physical risks.
Unrealistic attitudes toward financial and legal matters	Client will refrain from making purchases that prove detrimental to self or family; client will avoid adverse legal entanglements.	Cooperate with family to discourage the client from making large expenditures or legal commitments.
Demanding, manipulative behaviors	Client will understand what behaviors are acceptable; client will be treated consistently by staff; client will be diverted from unacceptable actions.	Define and explain acceptable behaviors; negotiate limits with client; offer alternative activities; avoid frustrating the client unnecessarily; use diversion as a therapeutic tool.

Anger, expressed or hidden, is considered a component of mood disturbance regardless of whether depression or mania is evident. For some depressed persons anger is a way of avoiding more painful feelings. Even though the manic person appears elated and euphoric, she does not tolerate limit setting or frustration easily and is apt to become very angry with caregivers. Nurses must remember that anger may stem from feelings of powerlessness and lack of internal control. Since nurses are rarely powerless in their interactions with clients, and since internal control is part of professionalism, the nurse must never meet anger by becoming angry in turn. By controlling their own emotions, nurses can help clients control theirs. In some situations nurses must enlist the help of other staff members, but in most instances nurses can remain in command, and discover that calmness can be contagious. A number of specific suggestions are shown in Table 8–10 to help nurses deal therapeutically with angry clients (Antai-Otong 1988).

If frustrated, the manic client may become physically or verbally abusive toward staff members and others. When the client is in the grip of mania, primary prevention measures must be used constantly to keep the client from losing control. Firmness and consistency by caregivers, vigilance, limit setting, and control of social space are essential.

Maier et al. (1987) reported that aggressive behaviors arise when there is overcrowding in inpatient settings, when activities are unstructured, and when the staff demand participation from reluctant clients. It is essential to let the manic client understand what behaviors are acceptable and what the consequences of unacceptable behavior will be. Within this framework the client should be permitted to engage in safe, nonthreatening activities of her choice for stated periods of time.

Clients' aggressive acts may arouse anger in caregivers. Opportunities should be made available to staff members to discuss their feelings about this issue so that their role performance remains therapeutic. Verbal aggression is difficult for caregivers to endure, but it is physical aggression that makes them fearful, defensive, and even punitive. When aggression takes the form of physical assault, staff members usually react as to an emergency. If the assault is clearly not dangerous, they try to respond by providing structure and reassurance simultaneously. If the assault has taken or is about to take place in a public, populated area it is wise to persuade the client to move, in the company of staff members, to a more private place where there are fewer witnesses. This indicates to other clients that the staff is in control of the situation, helps calm the assaultive client, and reduces the client's need to

Table 8–10. Therapeutic Nursing Responses to Angry Clients

Nursing Actions	Rationale
Keep your own emotions under control.	Emotional control of yourself promotes rational thinking.
Speak in a calm, reassuring manner.	Calmness reduces the client's fears of being helpless or threatened.
Observe the client's body language.	Body language reveals the extent of the anger and the possibility of physical violence. For example, are his fists clenched? Have objects been thrown or broken?
Let the client verbalize his anger.	Verbalization lessens tension and anger. Listening to the client enhances his self-esteem and reduces his fearfulness.
Involve the client by suggesting alternative behaviors.	Activity or diversion can lower levels of anger. Escorting a client to an area where there are fewer spectators is often beneficial.
Don't touch the angry client or invade his personal space.	Moving too close may threaten the client and cause him to react violently.
Don't scold or reprimand the client. Accept his right to be angry.	Patronizing the client or treating him like a child encourages childish behavior.
Provide external controls and limits as needed.	Protect yourself by having other staff members nearby. Take a position near the door. Avoid having the client stand between you and the door. Familiarize yourself with restraint and seclusion policies and procedures.

SOURCE: Adapted from Antai-Otong (1988).

save face by continuing belligerent behavior. If these measures seem unsafe, the client may have to be restrained or secluded temporarily.

In caring for a client during a manic episode it is advisable to develop a nursing care plan that considers all contingencies that might arise during hospitalization (Brenners, Harris, and Weston 1987). Because the manic client is distractible and forgetful, a written contract is helpful in providing direction and limits. The contract is signed by the client and the nurse responsible for care; a copy of the contract is left with the client and a second copy is available in the nurses' station. The contract should be written in clear, explicit language and should deal wtih the following issues.

■ Activities of daily living for which the client is responsible, with assistance from staff members if necessary. Activities include attention to personal hygiene, selection of suitable clothing, eating, toileting, and access to the telephone at designated times. If permitted, the manic client may wear wildly unsuitable outfits, change clothing twenty or thirty times a day, and monopolize the telephone by calling friends and strangers all over the world. The contract helps promote appropriate activities and control inappropriate behavior.

■ Explicit schedules that outline where the client is to be at specified times of the day. During the acute manic phase the client may be asked to spend 45 minutes of every hour in her room and 15 minutes out of it. As the manic phase subsides the time spent out of the room is gradually increased. Because the manic client is rarely aware of hunger or fatigue, scheduling should allow time for frequent, brief meals and for periods when expenditure of great physical energy is discouraged.

■ Behaviors and conditions (loss of control, outbreaks of physical and verbal assault) that will cause the client to be placed in a quiet room or seclusion room until sufficiently controlled to return to her own room.

In bipolar disorders where there are recurrent periods of mania and depression, the client and the family need to understand certain dynamics. Assurance may be given that the condition is controllable if the client complies with the therapeutic regimen. Those concerned for the client's well-being must learn to recognize early signs of mood shifts. When the manic phase gives place to depression, the client's needs change drastically. Limiting stimulation and asking them to stay alone in a room cause depressed people to withdraw further and foster their tendencies to engage in self-blame, guilt, and obsessive rumination. Lithium is effective in the long-term care of many clients with bipolar disorders but must be used with caution. Whether clients are receiving lithium or not, they and their families need to know as much as possible about early signs of mood changes and their possible consequences. Between episodes these clients suffer little deterioration and are often creative, achieving people. It is tragic for an individual to recover from a manic episode only to confront the economic and social consequences of reckless, extravagant acts.

Evaluation

A problem-oriented care plan with specific interventions allows both nurse and client to determine whether expected outcomes have been reached.

During periods of mania, the client has little awareness of maladaptive behavior; thus, until symptoms subside the treatment plan should be largely supportive. After the acute phase of the manic episode has abated, it may be advisable to help the client explore feelings experienced before, during, and after the episode. The client with a bipolar disorder who learns to identify early symptoms is in a better position to seek help and to learn methods of coping.

SOMATIC TREATMENT MEASURES

Clients with severe alterations of mood and affect often require somatic intervention in the form of electroconvulsant therapy (ECT) or drug therapy. Drug therapy is important in treating clients experiencing mania or depression, and ECT, although controversial, has a place in the treatment of persons with moderate to severe depression who may be suicidal or for whom medication has proved ineffective. Nurses have an important part to play in the administration of such treatments and in preparing, supporting, and teaching clients. They should therefore understand the rationale and implications of such measures.

Electroconvulsive Therapy

Electroconvulsive therapy was introduced in the 1930s when it was noticed that psychiatric clients who had suffered spontaneous convulsions or seizures became less disturbed and that epileptic convulsions and schizophrenia were rarely present in the same individual. Two Italian psychiatrists, Cerletti and Bini, were the first to apply electrodes to the temporal region of psychiatric clients for the purpose of inducing therapeutic convulsions. The electrodes sent an alternating electric current through the head strong enough to cause the client to lose consciousness and to have a seizure of grande mal proportions (Lerer, Weiner, and Belmaker 1986).

A number of theories have attempted to explain the ability of ECT to alleviate depression. The behavioral explanation is that depression is a learned way of behaving and that the electrical charge interrupts neural pathways that may be maintaining the depressed responses. Interrupting these neural pathways is thought to permit a return to more adaptive responses. Another theory is that guilt, a major component of depression, is reduced by a treatment so unpleasant that it seems like a punishment. This punishment theory is indirectly supported by the reports of some clients who say that they fear ECT but "deserve" to undergo it.

Since its introduction, ECT has been called barbarous by its critics, and with some justification. At first it was used indiscriminately for many types of psychiatric disorders and on people of all ages. It was also administered repeatedly without due regard for the possible consequences to the client. The convulsions induced were sufficiently severe to cause fractures and dislocations in some clients. Today the basic apparatus remains the same, but the techniques of administration have been greatly modified. Among the modifications is the use of atropine to reduce secretions and vagal stimulation. A muscle relaxant such as succinylcholine chloride (Anectine) is used to block the transmission of impulses to the skeletal muscles, thereby preventing muscle spasms. Because of precautions now taken, the convulsions are not severe and may be evident only in the involuntary movements of the client's toes as the current is applied.

A preliminary medical workup is necessary for every client receiving ECT, including a complete blood count, electrocardiograph, chest x-ray, urinalysis, and x-ray of the lateral aspects of the spine. Cardiac arrhythmias may develop during the seizures, and the potential for problems should be known in advance. As ECT is usually given in the morning, the client takes nothing by mouth after midnight. Dentures, metal hairpins, and shoes or slippers should be removed before treatment.

When ECT is administered, an anesthesiologist injects a short-acting anesthetic such as thiopental (Pentothal) or methohexital intravenously. Before the electrical charge is administered, the client is oxygenated. An airway is inserted into the mouth, and the arms are restrained at the sides of the body. Electrodes are placed on the temples at a point midway between the eyes and the top of the ears. Application of the electric current induces a tonic seizure lasting 5 to 15 seconds, followed by clonic seizures lasting 10 to 60 seconds. A single course of ECT consists of three treatments a week on alternate days over a period of three weeks, followed by a recess. Additional treatments may be given if indicated.

After several ECT treatments the client becomes confused and forgetful. As the treatments continue, the confusion and amnesia increase. These effects usually disappear in time, although some clients say that the forgetfulness never fully disappears. Immediately after a treatment the client is apt to be disoriented and must be reoriented to time, place, and person as he regains consciousness. Vital signs are taken every 15 minutes as he recovers. When he becomes aware of his surroundings and can walk, a nurse accompanies him to his room, where he then sleeps for several hours.

Every state has its own laws regulating the administration of ECT, and there are legal and ethical dilemmas surrounding this treatment that nurses should understand. Before ECT is given a nurse may be asked to obtain written permission from the client or next of kin. Informed consent is the right of every client, but a severely depressed person may not be capable of making a rational choice. Families may then have to give written consent instead of the client. The procedure should be fully explained to families, including the limited information about how or why the procedure works. Providing information about the confusion and memory loss that follow ECT not only fulfills legal requirements but also reduces the concern of family members as they deal with the aftermath of the treatments (Kermis 1986).

Attitudes of nurses can greatly affect clients receiving ECT. If the nurse has ambivalent feelings about the treatment, he should keep these feelings under control to avoid giving negative messages to the client. Clients may be frightened by the confusion and amnesia that increase with each treatment and will want explanations. Support and reassurance should be based on the facts that the gross aftereffects do disappear and that depressed people who have not responded to other forms of treatment almost always improve as a result of ECT.

Antidepressant Medication

Drug therapy is often indicated for depressed persons, and clinicians may select from two groups of antidepressant drugs, the monamine oxidase inhibitors and the tricyclic antidepressants. A third group of drugs, the tetracyclates, are also available but are less common. When using drug therapy it should be remembered that it constitutes but one aspect of the plan of care. Although biological and psychosocial approaches are concerned with different aspects of the client and employ different interventions, the approaches should be seen as complementary, not competitive or mutually exclusive (Wolpert 1980).

MONAMINE OXIDASE INHIBITORS The therapeutic effect of *monamine oxidase* (MAO) *inhibitors* is to relieve depression and to act as psychic energizers. Because the MAO inhibitors are stimulants, some clients may experience euphoric, hypomanic, or manic reactions to them. Such reactions may occur at any time during the course of drug treatment. Furthermore, this group of drugs may intensify schizophrenic tendencies, making susceptible clients agitated or actively delusional.

MAO inhibitors act by blocking the metabolism of certain neurotransmitters, thereby increasing the amounts available. The drugs are long-lasting and are thought to remain in the body for as long as two weeks after the last dose. Because their effects are cumulative, the antidepressant action of the MAO inhibitors are not apparent for one to two weeks after treatment is begun. Dosages of the MAO inhibitors must be regulated and clients carefully observed for undesirable side effects. The most widely used MAO inhibitors and their recommended dosages are shown in Table 8–11.

MAO inhibitors reduce the body's ability to metabolize epinephrine and thus should not be given with certain medications containing ephedrine. Because ephedrine is an ingredient of many nonprescription cold remedies, decongestants, and allergy preparations, clients taking an MAO inhibitor must be explicitly warned of the danger. In addition, the MAO inhibitors potentiate a number of other drugs such as morphine, meperidine, barbiturates, atropine derivatives, antihistamines, and some diuretics. Among the potential side effects of MAO inhibitors resulting from anticholinergic effects are blurred vision, constipation, dry mouth, and delayed micturition.

In addition to avoiding compounds containing ephedrine, persons taking an MAO inhibitor should avoid foods containing tryamine. When combined with an MAO inhibitor tryamine releases norepinephrine, and a hypertensive crisis results. Clients must be warned not to eat foods containing tryamine for several days prior to drug therapy, during drug therapy, and for two weeks after the drug is discontinued. If a client does eat foods on the restricted list while taking an MAO inhibitor, an emetic is usually given to induce vomiting. The accompanying box shows the major food substances to be avoided by persons taking an MAO inhibitor.

Table 8–11. Monamine Oxidase Inhibitors and Dosages		
Generic Name	**Trade Name**	**Range of Dosages**
Isocarboxazid	Marplan	10–30 mg/day
Phenelzine	Nardil	15–30 or more mg/day
Tranylcypromine	Parnate	20–30 mg/day

SOURCE: Appleton and Davis (1980).

DIETARY REGULATIONS FOR USERS OF MAO INHIBITORS

Forbidden Substances

Aged cheeses, such as cheddar or Swiss
Sour cream
Yogurt
Brewer's yeast
Beer, sherry, ale, or wine
Raisins, canned figs
Bananas
Lima beans, kidney beans, bean pods, split peas
Pizza
Liver
Pickled herring

Permitted Substances

Cottage cheese, creamed cheese
Sanka (liberal amounts)
Coffee (small amounts)
Tea (small amounts)
Cola drinks (small amounts)
Chocolate (small amounts)
Licorice (small amounts)
Bread (liberal amounts)

Table 8–12. Tricyclic Antidepressants and Dosages

Generic Name	Trade Name	Range of Dosages
Amitriptyline	Elavil	50–300 mg/day
Imipramine	Tofranil	50–300 mg/day
Nortriptyline	Aventyl	20–200 mg/day
Dioxepin	Sinequan	25–300 mg/day
Protriptyline	Vivactyl	15–60 mg/day

As with MAO inhibitors, it takes two to three weeks for therapeutic effects to become noticeable. Although the drugs promote alertness in clients, they rarely cause excessive excitability or agitation. This is particularly true of Elavil and Sinequan, which have sedating and antianxiety properties that counteract stimulating effects. Tofranil, another drug in this group, does not have significant sedating or antianxiety properties and is often accompanied by antianxiety medications to avoid causing agitated behaviors. The tricyclic antidepressants are not cumulative in effect and seldom potentiate the action of other medications.

It is customary to give tricyclic antidepressants, particularly dioxepin (Sinequan) and amitriptyline (Elavil), in a single nighttime dose to reduce insomnia. This procedure reduces the need for additional sleep medication, which is often dangerous in the hands of a depressed client.

Like the MAO inhibitors, the tricyclic antidepressants are anticholinergic, so clients with cardiovascular problems should be carefully monitored by means of electrocardiograph. Tricyclics are contraindicated for clients with a history of glaucoma, urinary retention, benign prostatic hypertrophy, seizure disorder, or renal deficiency.

Most clinicians do not recommend the concurrent use of MAO inhibitors and tricyclic antidepressants. In fact, a washout period of at least a week is usually arranged before changing from an MAO inhibitor to a tricyclic antidepressant because of the danger of hypertension or hyperpyrexia if the drugs are both used within a brief time frame.

OTHER ANTIDEPRESSANTS Other antidepressants are available that are structurally unrelated to the MAO inhibitors and the tricyclic antidepressants (see Table 8–13). These include amoxapine (Asendin) and maprotiline (Ludiomil), which offer the advantage of more rapid improvement and less frequent occurrence of cardiovascular reactions. Little is known about their specified therapeutic action or their effect on neurotransmitters.

When a client is unresponsive to other antidepressant medications, a psychomotor stimulant is sometimes used to alleviate depression. These

Contraindications for the use of MAO inhibitors are glaucoma, liver disease, renal impairment, hyperthyroidism, hypertension, and cardiovascular disease. Because of the hazards in taking MAO inhibitors, they are usually prescribed only when tricyclic preparations prove ineffective. However, MAO inhibitors seem more effective for clients suffering fluctuating, atypical depression. For clients suffering severe depression with psychomotor retardation, the tricyclic drugs seem to produce greater improvement (Mansky 1981, Gerald and O'Bannon 1981).

TRICYCLIC ANTIDEPRESSANTS About 70 percent of individuals with depressive disorders of clinical proportions are relieved by antidepressants belonging to the *tricyclic* group.

These antidepressants do not block neurotransmitter metabolism but rather prevent the reuptake of neurotransmitters into the presynaptic cleft, thus increasing the amounts of neurotransmitters available. Table 8–12 shows the generic and trade names of commonly used tricyclic antidepressants and their range of dosages.

Table 8–13. Other Drugs Used as Antidepressants and Usual Dosages

Generic Name	Trade Name	Range of Dosages
Amoxapine	Asendin	150–400 mg/day
Maprotiline	Ludiomil	75–300 mg/day
Trazodone	Desyrel	150–500 mg/day
Trimipramine maleate*	Surmontil	75–300 mg/day
Dextroamphetamine*	Dexedrine	5–15 mg/day
Methamphetamine*	Methedrine	5–15 mg/day
Methylphenidate*	Ritalin	10–30 mg/day
Phenmetrazine*	Preludin	25–75 mg/day
Amphetamine sulfate*	Benzedrine	5–15 mg/day
Fluoxetine hydrochloride	Prozac	20 mg/day

*Psychomotor stimulants—used with caution for selected clients.

Table 8–14. Side Effects of Antidepressant Drugs

Effects	Nursing Interventions
Anxiety, agitation, excitement	Continue drug, but inform physician. Antidepressant with sedating action or antianxiety medication may be needed.
Disorientation, delusions, mania	Withhold drug and inform physician immediately. As depression lifts, a psychotic or bipolar episode may be revealed.
Fine tremor, ataxia	If severe, withhold medication and inform physician.
Convulsions	Withhold medication and inform physician immediately. Institute seizure precautions.
Tachycardia	Monitor vital signs, especially pulse. Withhold medication if pulse exceeds 120 beats. Notify physician.
Orthostatic hypotension	Record sitting and standing blood pressure. Withhold medication and inform physician if systolic pressure drops significantly.
Arrhythmias and T-wave abnormalities	Monitor pulse. Withhold medication and notify physician immediately. Suggest electrocardiograph if client has a history of conduction problems.
Drowsiness, slowed responses	Advise client not to drive or operate power tools. Administer most of medication at bedtime. Inform physician if symptoms persist.
Decreased or increased sexual desire; ejaculatory disturbance (premature or inhibited); failure to achieve or maintain erection	Reassure client that problem may be temporary. Inform physician, since sexual dysfunction may cause client to stop taking medication. Explore with physician possibility of altering dosage or using alternative medication.
Dry mouth	Offer water frequently. Suggest sugarless hard candy or lubricating mouth swabs.
Constipation	Encourage fluid intake. Increase amounts of whole-grain cereals, fruits, and vegetables in diet. Observe client for signs of impaction or paralytic ileus.
Urinary retention or delayed micturition	Monitor intake and output. Note signs of abdominal distention. Notify physician if client cannot void. Suggest catheterization if client is uncomfortable.
Diaphoresis	Offer fluids to replace lost amounts. Monitor electrolyte balance.

drugs stimulate the central nervous system, thereby increasing mental alertness and elevating the client's mood. However, the psychomotor stimulants are rarely effective when the client is severely depressed, so they are generally used only with mild to moderate states of depression, when increased activity is desired. There are risks to the use of psychomotor stimulants for depressed clients because the energizing effects are short-lived. When the effects of the drugs wear off, the client experiences a return of the depressed state or even a worsening of the symptoms. In addition, use of psychomotor stimulants may result in drug dependency and drug abuse. However, there are instances where psychomotor stimulants are used for relatively short periods and for selected clients.

Nursing Measures Nurses can do a great deal to prevent or relieve the troublesome side effects of antidepressant medications. Serious side effects such as cardiac arrhythmias can be avoided by teaching clients to note and report reactions promptly. Regular electrocardiogram evaluation should be part of the care plan for clients with a history of cardiac conduction problems. Dietary restriction and its rationale must be explained to persons using MAO inhibitors. Any client on antidepressant medications should avoid central nervous system depressants. Specific side effects of antidepressants and suggested nursing interventions are shown in Table 8–14.

Nurses working with depressed clients receiving antidepressant medication need to monitor compliance. It is possible, for instance, to commit suicide by taking an overdose of a prescribed antidepressant. Some deaths have been attributed to antidepressants at dosages as low as 700 mg, especially when alcohol has been ingested at the same time. For this reason, it is important to question clients about how and when the antidepressant is being taken, to check on the remaining quantity of the medication, and to make available only enough for a week to ten days.

Antidepressant drugs are often continued for several months after symptoms subside. When the medication is discontinued, clients and family members should be taught to recognize incipient indications of depression. Usually the same manifestations occur as in previous episodes.

Lithium Therapy

Until the early 1970s, people with bipolar disorders faced long years of disruptive mood changes for which no satisfactory treatment was available. This situation changed with the discovery that *lithium carbonate* could be used to control episodes of mania and that, when offered on a long-term basis, it could prevent recurrences of both mania and depression.

Lithium carbonate is a salt that is readily absorbed in the gastrointestinal tract. It easily crosses cellular membranes and is therefore readily distributed throughout the body. The drug is not metabolized, is excreted by the kidneys, and has a serum half-life of 24 hours; that is, within 24 hours 50 percent of lithium in the body is eliminated. In acute manic episodes, symptom control requires 7 to 10 days. Because there is a delay in reaching therapeutic levels of lithium, antipsychotic medication in the form of a phenothiazine may be given concurrently for a time.

LITHIUM TOXICITY The range between therapeutic and toxic levels of lithium is narrow. Therefore, it is essential to regulate lithium levels frequently, particularly when the client is being stabilized on the drug. Initially, serum lithium levels may be taken twice weekly, then weekly, and later at monthly intervals. Once a client is stabilized on a maintenance dose, serum lithium levels should be taken every two to three months. Lithium levels between 0.8 and 1.5 mEq/l are considered within therapeutic range. Many clients show early signs of toxicity when serum lithium levels reach 1.5 mEq/l, and virtually all clients show severe signs of toxicity when serum lithium levels exceed 2.0 mEq/l (Fieve 1980).

During the first few days of taking the drug, clients may complain of nausea and mild tremors, but these early reactions usually subside. Nausea developing after the first few days may be an indication of toxicity. The onset of lithium toxicity is indicated by increased drowsiness, tremors that progress from fine to gross movements, nausea, vomiting, diarrhea, neurologic impairment leading to ataxia, visual difficulties, loss of consciousness, and coma (see Table 8–15). As a rule, mild to moderate lithium toxicity can be relieved by discontinuing or reducing the dosage of the drug.

LITHIUM MAINTENANCE When the client has regained a normal mood, lithium maintenance may be considered. This decision is made only after

Table 8–15. Indications of Lithium Toxicity

Serum Lithium Levels	Early Signs	Later Signs
Therapeutic: 0.8 to 1.5 mEq/l	Thirst Nausea Dizziness Fine tremor Increased urine	Polyuria Polydipsia Edema Weight gain Goiter Hypothyroidism
Imminent toxicity: 1.5 to 2.0 mEq/l	Vomiting Diarrhea Vertigo Sluggishness Dysarthia	Slurred speech Tinnitus Twitching Increased tremor Increased muscle tone
Actual toxicity: 2.0 to 7.0 mEq/l	Hyperreflexia Nystagmus Seizures Oliguria Confusion Dyskinesia	Visual hallucinations Tactile hallucinations Anuria Coma Death

clients have undergone more than one cyclical episode of mania with or without depression. Once the symptoms of mania have subsided, tolerance for lithium subsides and toxicity may develop. Thus, the maintenance dosages of lithium are apt to be less than the amounts needed to control acute mania. Most clients who take lithium for long periods of time respond well; even those who continue to have mood swings will experience less severe episodes. A maintenance lithium regimen seems to be most effective with clients diagnosed as having bipolar disorders. When clients experience recurrent episodes of depression without intervening periods of mania or hypomania, they may not respond well to the prophylactic use of lithium. For such clients either antidepressant or electroconvulsant therapy may be more effective.

NURSING MEASURES Lithium carbonate, whether used for remedial or preventive purposes, is a drug that requires considerable precautions (see Table 8–16). Before lithium therapy is begun, a complete medical examination is necessary, with special emphasis on cardiovascular, renal, and thyroid function. Lithium is rapidly absorbed and reaches its peak effect in two to three hours. Therefore, clients are usually instructed to take the drug in two or three divided doses daily.

Because lithium is a gastrointestinal irritant, the client should be instructed to take the drug with meals or just after eating. If a dose is forgotten, clients should be warned not to compensate by taking a double amount the next time, since this may cause a temporary reaction. Clients must be taught to maintain adequate sodium intake, because reduced sodium increases the possibility of a toxic reaction. Any unusual physical conditions, such as fever or lowered food or fluid intake, may predispose the client to dangerous lithium levels and should be reported to the person responsible for monitoring the drug regimen. Blood for monitoring of lithium levels should be drawn in the morning, 10 to 14 hours after the last dose. If the level is measured at any other time, particularly when the client has taken lithium a few hours before, the reading will not be accurate.

Women in the childbearing years who are taking lithium should be advised to practice contraception. If pregnancy is being considered or is a possibility, nurses should recommend preliminary consultation with a physician. Because lithium will cross the placental barrier, there may be some risk to the fetus, so the value of continuing lithium therapy must be weighed carefully. Nursing mothers who receive lithium should be warned that there may be traces in their milk. Again, there is a need for consultation that includes both psychiatric and physiological considerations (Harris 1988, 1989).

Maintenance on lithium means that clients will be taking the drug for a number of years. The signs of lithium toxicity and the importance of regular testing should be emphasized to clients and their families. Whenever a client is being maintained on lithium, all of the care providers involved with the client should be informed. Because of the prolonged nature of lithium therapy, need for various other medications may arise. Lithium is compatible with most antidepressants and major tranquilizers, but there are a number of drugs that are unsafe for persons taking lithium. The accompanying box lists a number of drugs that may be used concurrently with lithium and some that may not.

Somatic remedies in the form of electroconvulsive therapy and drug therapy enable psychiatric

---

Table 8–16. Important Information about Lithium Carbonate

- Clinical relief occurs after a period of 5 to 14 days (average 7 days).
- After initial improvement, regulation of lithium maintenance may take one year.
- Persons on lithium maintenance need serum levels checked from 1 to 3 months; thyroid and renal function should be checked annually or semiannually.
- Lithium toxicity may occur at any time. Doubling up to compensate for missing a dose, crash dieting, or extreme sweating may cause toxicity. Reduced fluid intake, diarrhea, or vomiting will increase serum lithium levels.
- The half-life of lithium is 24 hours; therefore mild toxicity may be treated by omitting the next two or three doses.
- In cases of severe toxicity ipecac may be given by mouth if the person is conscious and by gastric lavage if the person is unconscious. Immediate hospitalization is indicated. Occasionally hemodyalysis or peritoneal dialysis may be necessary.
- Persons on lithium maintenance need careful teaching and supervision, especially in the first weeks or months. Severe lithium toxicity may cause permanent neurological or renal damage.
- Candidates for long-term lithium maintenance are persons who have had two severe mood swings in the previous year. If mood swings are not severe or are several years apart, lithium therapy may be necessary only until the current episode subsides.

Side Effect	Intervention
Thirst	Encourage client to drink enough fluids to quench thirst.
Nausea, abdominal distress, diarrhea	Remind client to take lithium with meals, especially with milk. A different form of lithium may be needed.
Muscle weakness, fatigue	Consider giving smaller, more frequent doses. Discuss with physician possibility of using a slow-release form of lithium. Reassure client these signs may be temporary.
Polyuria	Assure client that this is usual. Polyuria may be controlled through dose reduction, a slow-release preparation, or a single dose of lithium. Have client measure 24 hour urine output. More than 3 liter output calls for renal workup.
Tremors	Advise client to avoid caffeine substances. Dose reduction, slow-release form, or frequent doses may be indicated.
Edema	Advise client that it may be necessary to restrict salt intake and balance this with reduction of lithium dosage.
Weight gain	Assure client that this is usual. Advise that moderate calorie reduction and more exercise will help. Warn against extreme fluid or salt restriction, or crash dieting.
Hypothyroidism	Assure client that this is not unusual. Advise client that condition can be treated by thyroid hormone replacement.
Hair loss	Investigate thyroid function.

SOURCE: Adapted from Harris (1988).

clients to escape the disruptive effects of maladaptive mood alterations. For the vast majority of people, however, altered mood and affect do not result in a psychiatric diagnosis. Such milder alterations of mood and affect, particularly in the form of depression, are extremely prevalent in modern life. In fact, no matter what setting nurses choose for clinical practice, they will encounter depression and its disguised counterpart, mania or hypomania.

For clients who become depressed as a result of life stress, loss, or change, the intervention of a concerned nurse may reduce the suffering and disruption that mood alterations sometimes bring. Similarly, for the grief and sadness that are an inevitable part of the human experience, the intervention of another person who exhibits informed interest and empathy may be more appropriate than somatic treatments.

An educational program for clients and their families who are dealing with disruptions of mood and affect should enable them to do the following:

■ Recognize the name of the condition; know its manifestations

■ Understand the usual course of the condition

■ Recognize early signs of depressive and manic states

■ Know the names of medications being given and their purpose

■ Understand or have access to the following information:
  Dosage, schedule, and side effects of medications
  Signs of lithium toxicity, if prescribed
  Need for periodic checkups, including laboratory testing
  Additive effects of alcohol and prescribed medications
  Dietary restrictions of prescribed medications

■ Recognize the importance of ongoing health care and supervision. Understand the nature and importance of primary, secondary, and tertiary health care in mood and affective alterations

■ Acknowledge the prospect of a rewarding, productive life if the client controls mood shifts instead of being controlled by them

GRIEF AND MOURNING

Grief and mourning are normal responses to loss or separation from meaningful persons or objects. *Mourning* is the word generally applied to behav-

ioral responses to loss, while *grief* is the inner subjective feeling. Although grief and mourning are often associated with the death of a loved one, there are many other causes, including the loss of important relationships or the loss of certain possessions or surroundings. Homesickness is an example of this specific and common grief reaction. People who have lost something that was highly valued must allow themselves to feel grief and to mourn their loss before trying to resume normal life. In many respects active mourning, or *grief work* is a painful but necessary response to loss (Engel 1962, Jacoby 1983).

Freud (1957) described the mourning process as a gradual withdrawal of attachment from whatever or whoever was lost, ultimately followed by readiness to make new attachments in the form of relationships and commitments. This means that people who feel grief are those who have learned to form attachments. Freud distinguished mourning from melancholia or depression, and Bibring (1953) pointed out that lowered self-esteem is a significant feature of depression that is not present in mourning.

Although it is necessary to withdraw attachment from a lost loved one in order to resolve grief, this withdrawal is not easy to accomplish. According to Schoenberg (1980), the activity of mourning is "carried out tediously and painfully, and at great expense in order to prolong the existence of the deceased" (p. 1349). Because many mourners feel that they cannot survive without the lost relationship, they seek to continue it, and the mourner may even adopt mannerisms once belonging to the deceased (Parks and Stevenson-Hinde 1982). Such behaviors may indicate that attachment to or identification with the deceased has reached unhealthy proportions and that the mourner has refused to accept the reality of the loss. An effective intervention in such circumstances is to encourage the mourner to weep, to verbalize negative as well as positive emotions toward the deceased, and to engage in a life review by reminiscing about experiences in which the deceased person was a participant. This permits emotional and cognitive expression that emphasizes the loss of the relationship as well as its importance.

Functional and Dysfunctional Adaptation to Grief

Normal grief may be distinguished from pathologic grief by the functioning level of the bereaved and by the length of time that elapses before grief is overcome. Rubin (1981) noted that acute grief lasts from three to twelve weeks, after which less extreme mourning may continue for a year or two.

The circumstances surrounding a death influence the mourning process. When death is untimely or unexpected, or when the mourner feels responsible in some way, the grief reaction may be more intense (Kirkley-Best and Kellner 1982). The age of the mourner also influences how grief is expressed and its extent. Older people whose personal worlds have narrowed to a few cherished persons or objects may feel especially desolate. Adolescents mourn much as adults do, but younger children whose cognitive and language development are incomplete have difficulty comprehending or expressing feelings of grief.

The younger a child, the more difficult the grieving process is. Since grieving is a form of primary prevention against later depression, children need help from family members. When children want to talk about a relative who has died they should be permitted to do so without being diverted. Adults who listen ease the child's pain and may even find their own grief lightened. Denial of loss and avoidance of grieving are defenses that are not helpful.

In studying the behaviors of survivors of a nightclub fire that claimed many lives, Lindemann (1944) found that acute grief reactions could appear immediately after the loss, could be delayed, could take exaggerated forms, or could fail to appear. He inferred that losses are difficult for everyone to endure but that reaction to loss is less adaptive when the bereaved person is unwilling or unable to mourn. Severe or prolonged depression is more likely to develop in the absence of grief work and may even be a defense against the pain that active mourning brings.

Holistic Grief Model

Many health professionals believe that grief is time limited and progresses in stages (Caplan 1964, Bowlby 1973, 1982). The value of sequential models is that observed behaviors can be readily identified and understood, but sequential models have limitations. A well-known sequential model is that of Elisabeth Kübler-Ross (1969), who described five stages terminally ill persons undergo: denial, anger, bargaining, despair, and acceptance. Griffin (1980) warned that these stages vary and that for some persons the sequence may never be completed. For example, an individual who has reached the stage of acceptance may revert to anger or bargaining, while another may never progress beyond denial.

More important than fixed sequences is awareness that different behaviors may arise at different

Sequential Phases of Grief Work	
Phase	**Characteristics**
Protest	Mourners are preoccupied with and attached to the deceased. All resources of the bereaved are used to prolong attachment and to protest loss. At this time mourners resent advice to accept the loss. Anger, tears, reproaches, and recriminations characterize the protest phase.
Despair	Efforts to continue the attachment give way to gradual acceptance of permanent loss. As the reality of loss is recognized, despair mounts. Behavior formerly devoted to preserving or regaining the lost relationship now becomes disorganized. Restlessness, anxiety, and sadness become apparent.
Detachment	This is the phase of reorganization, as the bereaved become resigned to the loss. As the permanency of loss is realized, acute grief begins to subside. When longing for the deceased does not lessen and hope of restoration is not discarded, the grief reaction may become pathologic, and depression follows.

SOURCE: Adapted from Bowlby (1969).

times. According to one viewpoint, genuine grief is never fully resolved but is carried for a lifetime. This view may be valid, as evidenced by the phenomenon in which anniversaries of loss reactivate old grief.

Designating specific stages of grief according to the Kübler-Ross concepts is not a holistic perspective that enables nurses to recognize the many masks that grief may wear (Archer and Smith 1988). A holistic perspective on grief recognizes that grief reactions are individual and originate out of a person's total experience. Not everyone goes through different stages, but everyone does react in various dimensions of life: physical, emotional, mental, social, family, and spiritual. When a holistic perspective is applied to grief, any number of different behaviors may be observed in bereaved persons.

Giacquinta (1977) formulated a guide for caregivers working with terminal cancer patients and their families.

- *1: Living with terminal illness.* At this point families learn the diagnosis and must deal with the immediate consequences of the illness. Nursing planning and interventions should be directed toward solving problems of daily living for the client and the family.

- *2: Restructuring in the living-dying period.* As the condition of the ill member worsens, the family reassigns roles and responsibilities. Families

DRUGS INTERACTIONS WITH LITHIUM

Safe Drug Combinations

- *Antipsychotic drugs:* May be used during the time lag between initial administration of lithium and therapeutic effect. Chlorpromazine (Thorazine) and haldoperidol (Haldol) are commonly used in this way.

- *Antidepressants:* May be used to oppose the depressive reactions that occur at times even with lithium maintenance therapy. Both the MAO inhibitors and the tricyclics may be used with lithium.

- *Disulfiram* (Antabuse—used for adversive treatment of alcoholics): May be taken by lithium users.

Unsafe Drug Combinations

- *Diuretics:* May decrease lithium excretion and increase danger of toxicity.

- *Nephrotoxins:* The tetracyclines and spectinomycine may promote lithium toxicity.

- *Anti-inflammatory agents:* May cause lithium retention and possible toxicity; reported with indomethacin (Indocin) and phenylbutazone (Butazolidin).

- *Antihypertensives:* May cause temporary lithium retention.

- *Digoxin:* Decreased intracellular potassium resulting from lithium may lead to digoxin toxicity, nodal bradycardia, and atrial fibrillation. Combining lithium, digoxin, and a diuretic is especially hazardous.

- *Alcohol:* Intoxication in clients taking lithium produces more extreme confusion, uncoordination, and ataxia.

- *Narcotics:* May increase effects of morphine.

- *Muscle relaxants and anesthetics:* Effects are prolonged in clients taking lithium. Lithium should be withheld for 48 to 72 hours before surgery.

LOSS AND BODY IMAGE

Body image is one's mental picture of one's own body. Body image is determined in part by the appraisals of others and in part by the appraisal of the individual. Most people are dissatisfied with their body image, or at least parts of it. For example, a man may be proud of his physique but embarrassed by his thinning hair. A woman may take satisfaction in having a pretty face but dislike her size 10 feet. Such minor discontents with body image are shared by vast numbers of people.

Of greater consequence is the loss of any body part or function, for even the best-adjusted person will have difficulty dealing with such losses. Changing from a perception of oneself as whole to a perception of oneself as defective is comparable to grief felt at the death of a loved one. When a limb or breast is lost by surgery or trauma, phantom pain in the removed part lingers and is a bitter reminder of what was lost. Nurses and other care providers must permit expressions of protest and despair as the individual mourns for the intact person who no longer exists. Severe grief reactions also follow sensory losses, heart attacks, miscarriages, or any discovery of inadequacy or dysfunction in the body. Active mourning for what was lost is essential to eventual reorganization. Therefore, an extreme reaction to changed body image should be considered as being more adaptive than a failure to react at all.

"framing memories," helps the dying person remain a living presence even as his strength fades.

- *3: Bereavement.* This is the stage of actual separation and loss. Only through active mourning can the death be accepted. Denial of loss or avoidance of grief is dysfunctional, for mourning is the only way to proceed to the next stage.

- *4: Reestablishment.* This is the period when the family begins to return to earlier routines and patterns of living and to reestablish activities given up during the time of impending loss.

As death approaches the family needs to understand as much as they can about their loved one's condition. They need reassurance that the caregivers are truly concerned about the loved one

should now be encouraged to engage in retrospection that retains the dying person in the collective history of the family. This activity, called and are trying to make him or her as comfortable as possible. When death does come, family members should have time alone with their dead if they wish this. In all instances they need a quiet place and privacy as they begin the long process of mourning and adjusting. If nurses have given evidence of caring and solicitude before the death, the family will be ready to accept their help after the death has occurred. Some families turn to friends or relatives for help and may ask nurses to make phone calls for them. They may ask that a rabbi, minister, or priest be notified. Hospital policies should guide nurses in responding to these requests. Unless a family is wholly demoralized by the death, it is advisable for the members to begin to be involved in making arrangements. More often than not, one or two family members emerge as more competent than the others. From a therapeutic standpoint, family members need to feel that they are in control of the situation and somehow will get through the ordeal.

As the finality of death is realized, families are often comforted just by the presence of a nurse who has cared for their loved one. Usually they are helped by a nurse who simply sits with them, answers their questions, and demonstrates understanding of their feelings by being gentle, unhurried, and soft-spoken. A great deal has been said of the value of touch during times of bereavement, but nurses are sometimes uncertain about holding the hand of or putting an arm around a person who has been recently bereaved. In this, as in all situations, the nurse should be guided by the behavior of the family members. Some families are uncomfortable with touching, even among themselves. Other families find physical contact extremely comforting. While sharing the waiting period with the family, nurses can observe how members behaved under stress and whether they move toward or away from physical contact. Because nurses, like the relatives, are participants in the waiting period, they can note family preferences and extend help accordingly.

Rituals can be used to ease grief reactions. Funerals, wakes, and memorial services help resolve grief by offering acceptable outlets for its expression. Informal rituals such as family reminiscing or examining family albums are also productive. The bereaved and bystanders should realize that grief is not something to avoid but to experience, however difficult at the time.

Persons dealing with loss should be allowed to proceed at their own pace as much as possible while receiving assurances that any feelings, even negative ones, will be understood. If the mourner's feelings toward the deceased were ambivalent or inconsistent, grief is more difficult to overcome

Response Dimensions	Behaviors
Physical	Tears, fatigue, insomnia, headache, palpitations, appetite loss, dizziness, nausea, vomiting, diarrhea, constipation Subjective complaints of a lump in the throat, heaviness in the chest, weakness, lassitude, apathy, and a sense of emptiness
Emotional (Note range of emotions)	Irritability, anger, rage; anxiety, fearfulness, panic; sadness, sorrow, despair, suicidal intention; doubt, misgivings, regret, guilt
Mental	Denial, forgetfulness, absentmindedness; loss of concentration, disorganization; intellectualization, rationalization; premature optimism and reorganization
Social	Preoccupation with one's own loss and needs; detachment and indifference toward others; contempt and disregard toward mourning rituals; immersion and deep regard for mourning rituals
Family	Adaptive: all family members accept grief responses of other members and give support Maladaptive: Some members grieve too much while others do not grieve at all; family members turn away from each other and look elsewhere for comfort; each family member mourns alone without a shared sense of loss; family members assign responsibility and blame on each other
Spiritual	Some persons turn toward religious sources for help and answers with renewed spiritual faith; some persons bitterly reject help from religious sources or look for new sources of spiritual guidance

SOURCE: Adapted from Archer and Smith (1988).

because guilt becomes a prominent component. Even with losses where the relationship with the deceased was a devoted one, the mourner may be angry at the deceased for having abandoned him or her. Expressions of anger toward nurses and other professionals who did not perform life-saving miracles are also to be expected, and this anger should be interpreted as displacement used to defend against pain.

Some well-intentioned remarks disturb the person they are meant to comfort. The statement "I know how you feel" may be interpreted by the grief stricken as an implication that their feelings are neither unique nor painful. Saying that the bereaved should not be so upset and should "look at the bright side of things" may be heard as a criticism of a mourner's behavior. Giving advice

CONDOLENCES THAT HURT

Comforter's Statement	Griever's Reaction
"What happened was all for the best."	Best for whom? Who knows what is for the best?
"It might have been worse."	How could it be any worse?
"Try not to think about what happened."	I need to think about it. I want to think it through.
"Don't talk about him (or her) so much."	Talking about it comforts me a little.
"Snap out of it. Nothing lasts forever."	I don't want things to change so soon.
"Don't be so sad. Life goes on."	How can life go on when I feel like this?
"I never understood what you saw in him (or her)."	You are glad he (or she) is gone.
"You should be glad his (or her) suffering is over."	His (or her) suffering may be over but mine goes on and on.

that has not been asked for may arouse resentment. Effective advice may be given by persons who have been in the same situation, but only if the bereaved indicates that the advice is welcome. Even then advice should be given in a manner that permits the bereaved to reject it without offending the adviser.

SUMMARY

Alterations of mood and affect are prevalent in modern life, but the symptoms are variable and are sometimes misinterpreted or unrecognized. Among psychiatric categories of affective disturbances are major depression and bipolar disorder. The notable feature of bipolar disorder is mania, with or without episodes of depression.

The etiology of depression involves the interaction of psychodynamic, biochemical, genetic, and existential factors. In dealing with depressed persons, nurses are advised to use an approach in which problems are identified and specific interventions planned. Problem identification and solving facilitates evaluation procedures, as outcomes can be measured against specific goals.

Mania appears to be the opposite of depression but in actuality shares many dynamics. Like the depressed individual, the manic client engages in psychological, physiological, and cognitive distortions. Nurses working with clients who display manic behaviors are guided by two major considerations: the protection of the clients from physical risk or exhaustion, and the protection of the client from excessive environmental stimulation.

A number of somatic measures are available for clients who experience drastic alterations of mood and affect. One somatic measure is electroconvulsive therapy, which is controversial but still has a place in the treatment of severely depressed individuals who are unresponsive to drug therapy. Among antidepressants available for depressed clients are the MAO inhibitors and the tricyclic antidepressants. Lithium carbonate is used to control symptoms of mania and to prevent recurrence of cyclical mood changes. Clients taking antidepressants or lithium need to be made aware of possible side effects in order to improve the likelihood of compliance.

Nursing responsibilities in administering somatic treatment to persons with affective and mood disorders are considerable. Careful observation is important, as is education of clients and families. Because clients may be unaware of the recurrence of a mood swing, families need to be included in educational sessions. Somatic treatment is beneficial in the care of persons experiencing severe mood alterations, but the availability of these measures does not reduce the need for a psychotherapeutic approach.

The experience of loss is unavoidable for persons who have learned to form attachments and make commitments. Grief and mourning are normal, adaptive responses to loss, and depression is often experienced by those who are unable or unwilling to engage in the pain of grief work.

Review Questions

1. Depression is sometimes described as a compensatory mechanism used to avoid the pain of grieving. Explain this statement.

2. Mania is sometimes described as a compensatory mechanism used to avoid depression. Explain this statement.

3. What precautions are essential in caring for a client in an acute manic state?

(Text continues on page 217.)

CLINICAL EXAMPLE

RATIONAL CARING IN MEETING THE NEEDS OF A DEPRESSED WOMAN

Greta is a heavy-set, slow-moving woman who seems much older than her 40 years. Her voice is low-pitched, and her manner is timid and self-effacing. She is dressed in a brown dress that resembles a tent. Her dark hair is pulled tightly back from her round face. She wears no jewelry and no makeup. Blue, myopic eyes look out of old-fashioned, granny-type glasses. She avoids eye contact with the nurse who interviews her on her first visit to the community mental health center. Several times during the interview Greta's eyes fill with tears and her voice breaks so that it is difficult to understand what she is saying.

Greta says that she feels ashamed for coming to the mental health center because only crazy people come to such places. In order to lower Greta's anxiety, the nurse tells her that a mental health center is just a place to visit when you need a safe person to talk to. The nurse adds that coming to the center is a sign of strength, not weakness. When Greta becomes more composed, she is able to talk about why she has come.

Greta is employed by a company that manufactures photographic equipment. For the past five years she has worked as a packer of film. This means that she sits all day in a darkened room in front of an assembly belt sealing rolls of film into little boxes. Other people work nearby on similar assembly lines, but in the darkened room they don't talk very much to each other. Even during break time or after work, Greta has very little communication with her coworkers. She thinks that they don't like her very much because her English is poor and because she is a speedy worker. She also thinks they play tricks on her, such as going into her locker and moving her belongings around, disturbing her neat arrangement of her locker. She acknowledges that nothing has ever been taken from her. When talking about the people she works with, Greta seems more angry than sad.

Greta tells the nurse that she came to the United States with her parents many years ago and that English is not her native language. She has two teenage sons who are in school and doing fairly well academically. However, they do little to help Greta around the house and pay attention to her only when they want money. She thinks that they ask for too much money but she never refuses their requests. Greta is a single parent who is separated but not divorced from her sons' father. She has not heard from him in many years but knows that he left her and the boys for another woman. She has a male friend, a man from the "old country" whom she has known for a few years. He is a bachelor who has dinner with Greta and her sons almost every week night. On weekends he takes Greta to dinner and to see a movie. She has no complaints about the arrangement except that her boys complain because the man visits so much. They look down on the man, who is employed as a janitor.

Greta states that her life is very dull and that everyone she knows seems to take her for granted. She believes herself to be a good mother and a good worker, but she feels that she is fat and unattractive. She has repeatedly tried to lose weight but has never succeeded. During the day she eats little, but after work she eats from the time she gets home until she goes to bed. Her boys tease her about her appetite, telling her they don't need a garbage can when Mom is around. She tries to smile when she tells this to the nurse but her expression is forlorn.

Because Greta is obviously despondent, the nurse asks her if she has ever thought about committing suicide. She strongly denies this, adding that she is a devout Roman Catholic, that she wants to finish raising her boys and give them a good start in life. When the nurse comments that Greta seems to take good care of other people and asks what Greta does to take care of herself, the client looks surprised and does not answer. The nurse then suggests that perhaps coming to the center is a good way to begin taking care of Greta.

ASSESSMENT

Nursing Diagnoses

Chronic low self-esteem
(related to client's low sense of personal value)

Ineffective individual coping
(related to difficulties at work and at home)

Ineffective family coping: compromised
(related to inability to deal with and set limits for sons)

Social isolation
(related to fear and distrust of others)

Powerlessness
(related to feelings that she could not manage her life)

Altered nutrition: More than body requirements (related to binge eating)

Multiaxial Psychiatric Diagnoses

Axis I   311.00 Depressive disorder, seasonal pattern

Axis II   301.82 Personality disorder, avoidant type

Axis III   307.50 Eating disorder

Axis IV   Code 3—Moderate Psychosocial stressors

Axis V   Level 55—Current GAF

           Level 60—Highest GAF in past year

In the initial interview Greta presented herself as a passive, depressed woman with low self-esteem. The nurse elicited from Greta information that she suffered from seasonal bouts of despondency, beginning in December and lasting until spring. At other times of the year she said she felt better, but the nurse suspected that Greta was always somewhat depressed.

Because of her low self-image, she made no effort to improve her appearance, either by dieting or dressing more attractively. Even though she complained about the financial demands her sons made, these expenditures gave her another excuse for not buying anything for herself. She had a vague sense that she was being exploited by her male friend, but defended him to her sons and to herself. Shortly before coming to the clinic, Greta had agreed to do his laundry in addition to providing most of his meals. She was afraid that if she refused his request, then she would lose her one friend.

Greta's suspiciousness of her coworkers also stemmed from low self-esteem. Her self-image was that of being a chronic victim. In order to preserve her identity as a victim, she convinced herself that other people were out to take advantage of her. She had no idea of how she came across to other people, nor that her fearfulness might be interpreted as hostility. Knowing that it was hard for her to assert herself and believing that new friends would only take advantage of her, Greta misconstrued and rejected any friendly overtures that were made toward her.

The nurse formulated the preceding nursing and psychiatric diagnoses, based on information obtained from the client and clinical observations made by the nurse in conjunction with the mental health care team.

PLANNING

After consulting with colleagues on the mental health team, the nurse determined that the basis of Greta's problems was her poor opinion of herself. Even though she was a productive member of society, Greta still thought of herself as weak and powerless. In her own mind, she was still the bewildered immigrant girl who had immigrated so long ago. Despite Greta's long-standing problems, the team members thought that

Greta had many strengths that could be mobilized on her own behalf. A combined cognitive/behavioral approach was adopted.

The first objective in the therapeutic sessions was to improve Greta's opinion of herself so that she could learn to give to herself as well as to other people. Along with assuring Greta that she was entitled to treat herself better, the nurse provided consistent feedback regarding Greta's genuine competence as family provider and single parent. Rather than attack the weight problem immediately and directly, the nurse suggested that other forms of self-indulgence could replace the nightly food binges. If losing weight became the focus of the nurse's work, the result might be to weaken rather than strengthen Greta's self-esteem.

To improve Greta's sense of power and autonomy, the nurse asked Greta what issues she wanted to work on first. As an illustration, Greta was asked whether she wanted first to make friends with her coworkers or to practice saying no to her sons and her male friend when she felt they were asking too much from her. She chose first to work on learning to say no, perhaps because she found her coworkers more intimidating. A hierarchy of objectives was drawn up, based on what Greta thought she could accomplish. The objectives were formulated and ranked as follows:

1. Practice saying no to someone at least twice a week.
2. Spend at least one hour a day on personal grooming.
3. Substitute some enjoyable activity for the nightly binging.
4. Invite her two sons to join her in one or two counseling sessions.
5. Exchange greetings with coworkers at the beginning and end of the day.

IMPLEMENTATION

Three facets to the nursing care plan were developed for Greta: behavioral, cognitive, and affective. As part of the behavioral facet, schedules were prepared so that Greta could record things she had accomplished, such as saying no to an unreasonable request, or failing to say no. She was also asked to record the amount of time she spent on self-care and what grooming activities she performed. Shampooing her hair, giving herself a manicure, and going to a hairdresser were among the activities Greta reported. At first she complained about the time she was wasting, but she was pleased when her sons and her male friend noticed her improved appearance.

Using a cognitive approach, the nurse explained that Greta's nightly eating was a futile effort to make herself feel less empty inside. The nurse reminded Greta of how much energy she used up at work and at home. The result of expending so much energy was a feeling of fatigue and depletion at the end of the day.

Instead of gorging on junk food, Greta was encouraged to reward herself in other ways. Buying makeup, perfume, or inexpensive accessories was suggested as a substitute for binging. For a while Greta resisted these suggestions for change. When the cause of resistance was explored, it became evident that according to Greta's old world standards, wives and mothers should not devote themselves to becoming more attractive. Far from discounting Greta's resistance in this area, the nurse listened respectfully and negotiated compromises that were acceptable to Greta, such as choosing brighter colors and taking care of her skin and hair.

With Greta's consent, her sons were invited to attend two therapeutic sessions. By this time the sessions had become very meaningful to Greta and she was unwilling to share more than two sessions. The meetings at which the boys were present were used to help them understand what their mother was working toward and enlisting their cooperation. An affective note was introduced when the nurse asked Greta to tell her sons some of her experiences as a young immigrant and of the adjustments she had to make. Until then Greta had told her sons very little about her native country and she was surprised at the interest they showed.

EVALUATION

In working toward the objectives the nurse permitted Greta to set her own priorities and proceed at her own pace. Many of the new tasks were difficult for Greta and there were numerous setbacks. This was particularly true of the nightly food binges that Greta found

hard to change. Greta found the setbacks discouraging and engaged in self-blame that the nurse did not encourage. When the client dwelled on her lack of progress, the nurse used the written record to convince Greta of what had been accomplished. An unexpected consequence of Greta's improved appearance, even though she had not lost much weight, was the changed attitude of her coworkers. They began of their own accord to greet her and try to engage her in short conversations. With encouragement from the nurse, Greta tried to be responsive in turn.

Antidepressant medication was not prescribed for Greta because she was able to function even in winter, which was her worst time. When her depression was deepest, she managed to take herself to a mental health center, partly because she was afraid she was going "crazy." Her fears were relieved by the caring, common sense tactics of the nurse, who worked with Greta to establish reasonable goals. Even the cognitive explanation that winter time increased Greta's sadness was reassuring. When explanations are given in language that clients can understand, fears are more easily handled. No treatment was given except for the sessions with the mental health nurse. The trusting relationship formed between nurse and client meant that Greta could be observed over time to determine if she had a tendency toward manic as well as depressive episodes. The seasonal nature of Greta's depression indicated that she might be the victim of a cyclical mood disorder. If this proved true, Greta had already established strong ties to the mental health care delivery system that would facilitate long-term care if this proved necessary.

Nursing Diagnosis	Goals	Nursing Action	Outcome Criteria	Outcome Evaluation
Chronic low self-esteem	Client will improve self-image. Client will increase self-esteem.	Give positive feedback on competence as a parent and wage earner.	Client will acknowledge her achievements and derive satisfaction from them.	After 6 therapy sessions client verbalized pride in sons' school records. Client reported that she was given a 5-year pin by employer for reliable service.
Ineffective individual coping	Client will take more interest in appearance and grooming.	Use behavior modification to encourage interest in personal appearance. Discuss American values about female grooming.	Client will improve self-care beyond basic hygienic routines. Client will accept some American grooming standards.	Client resisted change for several weeks but gradually exhibited some pride in her appearance. She responded to sons' approval of her new "American look" with pleasure.
Social isolation	Client will reduce mistrust of other people.	Explore reasons for mistrust. Help client separate rational from irrational mistrust. Introduce the idea that what is unfamiliar is more fearful than what is familiar. Encourage client to discuss adjustment to different culture.	Client will alter her withdrawal and avoidance tactics.	Client is not spontaneous or open but is getting along better with coworkers. Refused suggestion to join single parents' support group.
Powerlessness	Client will develop self-assertiveness.	Use behavior modification and role play to encourage and rehearse assertiveness.	Client will refuse to let others exploit her by learning to say no to unreasonable requests.	Client still finds it hard to say no but reported that after she had said no a few times, unreasonable requests from others lessened.
Ineffective family coping	Client will set limits for teenage sons.	Involve sons in family meetings.	Client will be able to refuse sons' unreasonable requests.	Client has negotiated amounts for sons' regular allowance.
Altered nutrition: more than body requirements	Client will reduce amount and frequency of food binges.	Avoid focusing attention on obesity so as to protect self-esteem. Suggest positive forms of self-indulgence to replace destructive binging. Use behavior modification: ask client to record binging and/or substitute activities.	Client will engage in harmless forms of self-indulgence (shopping for herself, reading, playing scrabble, etc.) to replace eating.	Binge eating recurred periodically, especially if client was tired or upset. Binge eating became less excessive and less frequent as client began to fill her evenings with other activities. She reports that she is less preoccupied with food.

4. Under what circumstances is electroconvulsive therapy considered an appropriate treatment? What nursing responsibilities accompany the administration of electroconvulsive therapy before and after the procedure?

5. A depressed client is taking an MAO inhibitor. What information should be included in teaching the client about this group of antidepressants?

6. A client with a bipolar affective disorder is receiving lithium. What information should be included in teaching this client about lithium maintenance?

7. What types of loss are likely to produce grief reactions? Give an example of each type.

8. What principles should be kept in mind by nurses as they attempt to comfort grieving individuals and families?

Suggested Annotated Readings

Ferstz, G. G., and P. B. Taylor. "When Your Patient Needs Spiritual Comfort" *Nursing 88* 18, no. 4 (April 1988):48–49.

Spiritual distress is a nursing diagnosis that may be expressed through anger, fear, or grief. The authors reinforce the value of listening and not offering glib expressions of sympathy. Nurses are warned not to impose their own beliefs, prayers, or rituals on grieving families. Suggestions are given about how to help families who have no religious faith of their own. The authors are also concerned with nurses' search for meaning as they try to find answers to their own existential questions.

Larson, D. B., A. A. Hohmann, L. G. Kessler, K. G. Meador, J. H. Boyd, and E. McSherry. "The Couch and the Cloth: the Need for Linkage" *Hospital and Community Psychiatry* 31, no. 10 (October 1988): 1064–1069.

Persons providing mental health services were classified into four groups: clergy only, mental health specialists only, both clergy and mental health specialists, and neither source. Clients receiving care from both clergy and mental health specialists were more likely to have affective or panic disorders than persons who obtained care from clergy or mental health specialists only, or those who sought care from neither group. Those in the exclusive care of mental health specialists were more likely to have substance abuse disorders. Persons in the care of clergy only were just as likely to have serious mental disorders as those seeing mental health specialists only. The findings show a genuine need for formal linkage between clergy and mental health specialists and for clergy to refer clients to mental health professionals in certain instances. The study also indicated that substance abusers may prefer help from mental health counselors rather than clergy.

Lion, J. R. "Training for Battle: Thoughts on Managing Aggressive Patients" *Hospital and Community Psychiatry* 38, no. 8 (August 1987):882–884.

This article openly admits the large number of assaultive incidents that take place in psychiatric facilities and deplores the lack of attention given to the problem. Psychiatrists, in particular, are held accountable for denying the problem and for not participating in staff education programs designed to help. The article describes a management training program instituted in Maryland where nursing staff receive instruction in "talk down" techniques and in "take down" techniques for clients who are physically threatening others. The author states that procedures to deal with aggressive clients should be taught and mastered with the same seriousness as cardiopulmonary resuscitation. Only trainees who are certified in the designated procedures are permitted to teach them to other nurses.

Raphael, B., and W. Middleton. "Mental Health Responses in a Decade of Disasters: Australia 1974–1983" *Hospital and Community Psychiatry* 38, no. 12 (December 1987):1331–1337.

After a series of major disasters in Australia, mental health systems tried to develop adequate responses. Gradually, they were able to coordinate techniques that led to greater community acceptance and program effectiveness. Lessons learned from one disaster were used in responding to the next. Research and review revealed considerable psychological trauma as a result of disasters, especially among children and relief workers. Data showed that relief workers provided practical aid but usually overlooked the mental health consequences of disasters. Disaster research is growing and is being incorporated into relief work.

Richardson, B. K. "Psychiatric Inpatient's Perceptions of the Seclusion Room Experience" *Nursing Research* 36, no. 4 (July/August 1987):234–238.

The purpose of this study was to explore the client's perception of the seclusion room experience, the controversial practice in some inpatient facilities of locking a client alone in a room.

The investigators found differences in the reasons given by staff and by clients for seclusion. In no instance was reduction of sensory stimulation given as a reason. Subjects described *events* leading up to seclusion, while staff members described aggressive *behavior* by the client. The clients and staff members gave reasons that acknowledged out-of-control impulses or social relationship problems existing at the time seclusion was instituted. Attacking a staff member was the reason most commonly cited by the staff.

Half the subjects said seclusion protected them and 44 percent said it protected others. One third said they felt better, calmer, relieved when secluded. However, almost half said that a different approach by the staff would have made seclusion unnecessary. Half the subjects regarded seclusion as punishment but some of these thought their preseclusion actions deserved to be punished. A majority could recall the visits of staff members while they were secluded. Those clients who reported feeling out of control or experiencing intense social relationships felt that their attitudes toward staff and fellow clients were more positive after seclusion.

Tisdale, S. "On the Other Side of Midnight" *Hippocrates* 2, no. 2 (March/April 1988):40–50.

This article describes sleep stages and analyzes sleep problems. It gives an excellent explanation of REM sleep and its importance to the sleeper. Physiological and psychological aspects of sleeping are contrasted. The language of the author is clear and interesting, and the article is far-reaching in scope.

References

Antai-Otong, D. "What You Should and Shouldn't Do When Your Patient Is Angry." *Nursing 88* 18, no. 2 (February 1988):44–45.

Archer, D. N., and A. C. Smith. "Sorrow Has Many Faces: Helping Families Cope with Grief." *Nursing 88* 18, no. 5 (May 1988):43–45.

Beck, A. T. *Cognition and Psychopathology in Depression: Clinical, Experimental, and Theoretical Aspects.* New York: Harper & Row, 1969.

——. *Depression: Causes and Treatment.* Philadelphia: University of Pennsylvania, 1972.

Bibring, E. "The Mechanisms of Depression." In *Affective Disorders*, P. Greenacre, ed. New York: International Universities Press, 1953.

Bowlby, J. *Attachment and Loss: Attachment.* New York: Basic Books, 1969.

——. *Attachment and Loss: Separation.* New York: Basic Books, 1973.

——. *Attachment and Loss: Loss.* New York: Basic Books, 1980.

——. "Attachment and Loss: Retrospect and Prospect." *American Journal of Orthopsychiatry* 52 (1982):644–678.

Brenners, D. K., B. Harris, and P. S. Weston. "Managing Manic Behaviors." *American Journal of Nursing* 87, no. 5 (May 1987):620–623.

Cancro, R. "Overview of Affective Disorders." In *Comprehensive Textbook of Psychiatry*, 4th ed., H. I. Kaplan and B. J. Sadock, eds. Baltimore: Williams & Wilkins, 1985.

Caplan, G. *Principles of Preventative Psychiatry.* New York: Basic Books, 1964.

Collison, C., and S. Miller. "Using Images of the Future in Grief Work." *Image* 19, no. 1 (Spring 1987):9–11.

Engel, G. *Psychological Development in Health and Disease.* Philadelphia: W. B. Saunders, 1962.

Erikson, E. H. *Childhood and Society.* New York: W. W. Norton, 1963.

Fieve, R. R. "Lithium Therapy." In *Comprehensive Textbook of Psychiatry*, 3d ed., H. I. Kaplan, A. M. Freedman, and B. J. Sadock, eds. Baltimore: Williams & Wilkins, 1980.

Freud, S. "Mourning and Melancholia." In *Standard Edition of the Works of Sigmund Freud*, Vol. 14. London: Hogarth, 1957.

Gardner, R. "Mechanisms in Manic Depressive Disorder: An Evolutionary Model." *Archives of General Psychiatry* 39 (1982):1436–1444.

Gerald, M. C., and F. V. O'Bannon. *Nursing Pharmacology and Therapeutics.* Englewood Cliffs, New Jersey: Prentice-Hall, 1981.

Gershon, E. S., J. I. Nurnberger, W. H. Berrettini, and L. R. Goldin. "Affective Disorders: Biochemical Aspects." In *Comprehensive Textbook of Psychiatry*, 4th ed., H. I. Kaplan and B. J. Sadock, eds. Baltimore: Williams & Wilkins, 1985.

Giacquinta, B. "Helping Families Face the Crisis of Cancer." *American Journal of Nursing* 77 (1977):1585–1588.

Griffin, J. Q. "Physical Illness in the Family." In *Family-Focused Care*, J. R. Miller and E. H. Janosik, eds. New York: McGraw-Hill, 1980.

Hanin, I., and E. Usdin. *Markers in Psychiatry and Psychology.* New York: Pergamon Press, 1982.

Harris, E. "Psych Drugs." *American Journal of Nursing* 88, no. 11 (November 1988):1507–1516.

——. "Lithium—in a Class by Itself." *American Journal of Nursing* 89, no. 2 (February 1989):190–195.

Hochman, G. "Childhood Depression." *New York Times Magazine* (June 15, 1986):12–28.

Jacoby, S. "Grief Should Be Allowed to Run Its Natural Course." *New York Times* (April 21, 1983).

Juel-Nielson, J. *Individual and Environment: Monozygotic Twins Reared Apart.* New York: International Universities Press, 1980.

Kermis, M. D. *Mental Health in Late Life*. Boston: Jones and Bartlett, 1986.

Kerr, M. M., T. S. Hoier, and M. Versi. "Methodological Issues in Childhood Depression: Review of the Literature." *American Journal of Orthopsychiatry* 57, no. 2 (1985):193–198.

Kirkley-Best, E., and K. R. Kellner. "The Forgotten Grief: A Review of the Psychology of Stillbirth." *American Journal of Orthopsychiatry* 52 (1982):420–429.

Klerman, G. L. "Overview of Affective Disorders." In *Comprehensive Textbook of Psychiatry*, 3d ed., H. I. Kaplan, A. M. Freedman, and B. J. Sadock, eds. Baltimore: Williams & Wilkins, 1980.

Kline, P. M., and C. C. Chernecky. "Heading Off Depression in the Chronically Ill." *RN* (October 1987):44–49.

Kübler-Ross, E. *On Death and Dying*. New York: Macmillan, 1969.

Lehmann, H. E. "Affective Disorders: Clinical Features." In *Comprehensive Textbook of Psychiatry*, 4th ed., H. I. Kaplan and B. J. Sadock, eds. Baltimore: Williams & Wilkins, 1985.

Lerer, B., R. D. Weiner, and R. H. Belmaker. *ECT: Basic Mechanisms*. Washington, D. C.: American Psychiatric Press, 1986.

Lewis, J. M. "Dying with Friends." *American Journal of Psychiatry* 139 (1982):261–266.

Lindemann, E. "Symptomatology and Management of Acute Grief." In *American Journal of Psychiatry* 101 (1944):141–148.

Lumsden, C. J., and E. D. Wilson. *Genes, Mind, and Culture: The Coevolutionary Process*. Cambridge, Massachusetts: Harvard University Press, 1981.

Maier, G. J., L. J. Stava, B. R. Morrow, G. J. Van Rybroek, and K. G. Bauman. "A Model for Understanding and Managing Cycles of Aggression among Psychiatric Inpatients." *Hospital and Community Psychiatry* 38, no. 5 (May 1987):520–527.

Mansky, P. A. "Treatment of Depression." In *Psychiatric Medicine Update*, T. C. Manschreck, ed. New York: Elsevier, 1981.

Minot, R. S. "Depression: What Does It Mean?" *American Journal of Nursing* 96, no. 3 (1986):284–288.

Naylor, A. "Premature Mourning and Failure to Mourn: The Relationship to Conflict between Mothers and Intellectually Normal Children." *American Journal of Orthopsychiatry* 52 (1982):679–687.

Parker, G. B., and L. B. Brown. "Coping Behaviors That Mediate Life Events and Depression." *Archives of General Psychiatry* 39 (1982):1386–1392.

Parkes, R. *Bereavement: Studies of Grief in Adult Life*. London: Tavistock, 1972.

Parks, C. M., and J. Stevenson-Hinde. *The Place of Attachment in Human Behavior*. New York: Basic Books, 1982.

Robert, M., A. Hirschfeld, and T. Shea. "Affective Disorders: Psychosocial Treatment." In *Comprehensive Textbook of Psychiatry*, 4th ed., H. I. Kaplan and B. J. Sadock, eds. Baltimore: Williams & Wilkins, 1985.

Roy, E. "Specificity of Risk Factors for Depression." *American Journal of Psychiatry* 138 (1981):959–964.

Rubin, S. "A Two-Track Model of Bereavement." *American Journal of Orthopsychiatry* 51 (1981):101–109.

Schildkraut, J. J., A. I. Green, and J. J. Mooney. "Affective Disorders: Biochemical Aspects." In *Comprehensive Textbook of Psychiatry*, 4th ed., H. I. Kaplan and B. J. Sadock, eds. Baltimore: Williams & Wilkins, 1985.

Schoenberg, B. "Grief, Mourning, and Simple Bereavement." In *Comprehensive Textbook of Psychiatry*, 3d ed., H. I. Kaplan, A. M. Freedman, and B. J. Sadock, eds. Baltimore: Williams & Wilkins, 1980.

Seyle, H. *The Stress of Life*. New York: McGraw-Hill, 1956.

Shapira, J., R. Schlesinger, and J. L. Cummings. "Distinguishing Dementias." *American Journal of Nursing* 86, no. 6 (June 1985):698–702.

Spitz, R. A. "Anaclitic Depression." In *Psychoanalytic Study of the Child*, Vol. 2., P. Greenacre, ed. New York: International Universities Press, 1946.

Stockdale, L., and T. Hutzenbiler. "How You Can Comfort a Grieving Family." *Nursing Life* 6, no. 3 (May/June 1986):22–26.

Usdin, G. *Depression: Clinical, Biological and Psychological Perspectives*. New York: Brunner/Mazel, 1977.

Weissman, M. M., and J. H. Boyd. "Affective Disorders: Epidemiology." In *Comprehensive Textbook of Psychiatry*, 4th ed., H. I. Kaplan and B. J. Sadock, eds. Baltimore: Williams & Wilkins, 1985.

Wierzbicki, M. "Similarity of Monozygotic and Dyzygotic Child Twins in Level and Lability of Subclinically Depressed Mood." *American Journal of Orthopsychiatry* 57, no. 1 (January 1987):33–40.

Wolpert, E. A. "Major Affective Disorders." In *Comprehensive Textbook of Psychiatry*, 3d ed., H. I. Kaplan, A. M. Freedman, and B. J. Sadock, eds. Baltimore: Williams & Wilkins, 1980.

9

Relationship Variations and Disruptions

Learning Objectives

After reading this chapter, the student should be able to:

1. Discuss the influence of anxiety on the development of variations and disruptions in relationships.

2. Describe the clinical manifestations and underlying dynamics of the various relationship variations and disruptions.

3. Discuss therapeutic modalities and nursing activities appropriate for clients manifesting relationship variations and disruptions.

Overview

Variations and disruptions in relationships are functional disturbances of the personality that arise when inner conflicts manifest themselves in altered behavior patterns. These functional disturbances include neurotic disorders and personality disorders as well as borderline conditions.

Neurotic disorders are psychological or behavioral disruptions characterized primarily by anxiety. Maladaptive behaviors are adapted by neurotic individuals in order to cope with the anxiety. The neurotic disorders include generalized anxiety states, phobias, obsessive-compulsive states, dissociative states, conversion disorders, posttraumatic stress syndrome and hypochondriasis. Personality disorders are syndromes in which the individual's inner difficulties are revealed by patterns of living that seek immediate gratification of impulses and instinctual needs without regard for society's laws, mores, or customs and without censorship of personal conscience. The personality disorders include the following types: schizoid, compulsive, histrionic, antisocial, passive-aggressive/passive-dependent, and paranoid.

Clients with borderline personalities have not developed the capacity to love and to work. They are individuals with almost no sense of who they really are or what they are feeling.

The purpose of this chapter is to familiarize the student with the variations and disruptions of relationships and with the nursing process as it is utilized to help clients manifesting these conditions.

In order to achieve and maintain successful interpersonal relationships, people must be able to perceive themselves and the manner in which they are perceived by others in an accurate way. When people relate to each other, they need to have a sense of who they are, who the other people are, and how they are seen by others. The ability to see both points of view is necessary for give-and-take relationships. People who have variations and disruptions in relatedness cannot maintain relationships that are reciprocal because they do not have the ability to see themselves as they are seen by others.

It has been stated that all people are "neurotic" to some extent, but this is not entirely true. Although everyone is likely to experience neurotic conflicts at times, most people have an extensive collection of defenses and coping mechanisms on which they can rely. On the other hand, a person suffering from a dysfunctional variation in relatedness clings to a few rigid, maladaptive behaviors that tend to be repetitive. Even when these patterned behaviors do not produce the desired results, the individual's limited coping style causes him to use these maladaptive behaviors repeatedly.

People who have relationship variations and disruptions show difficulty in certain areas of living but may be entirely competent in other areas. Despite their difficulties in coping with everyday life, they remain in touch with reality. Although they suffer a great deal, they are less disabled than individuals with psychotic alterations of thought or affect, who exhibit gross distortions of reality. Persons with neurotic disorders may have an intellectual grasp of their problems, but they remain trapped in conflict and are not comfortable with these patterns. Persons with personality disorders may also have an understanding of how their dysfunctional behavior has caused difficulties in relationships, but they have become comfortable with the pattern.

Both neurotic and personality disorders are functional rather than organic problems, but organic workups are always necessary to rule out any organic problems. An organic disorder is one in which there is a change in the structure of the body, for example, an infection, traumatic injury, or malformation of an anatomic structure. In a functional illness, there is no demonstrable change in structure; the symptoms are based on the unhealthy psychological responses of the individual. An example is conversion disorder, in which there is no physiological reason for a disability such as blindness or paralysis. Many clients assumed to have a neurotic or personality disorder have been found on later examination to have definite organic pathology. The psychological trauma to an individual who is aware of physical problems only to have them dismissed as "neurotic" can be considerable. Delay in receiving appropriate treatment can also result in more extensive debility and complications.

The prevalence of neurotic dysfunction is so great that nurses will inevitably encounter clients who display signs of disturbed relatedness. Greenberg (1977) believes that approximately 80 percent of Americans are, to some extent, impaired by neurotic disorders, many of which go undiagnosed and untreated.

COMPARISON OF HEALTHY AND ALTERED SENSE OF SELF

In order to understand the manifestations of neurotic and personality disorders, it is necessary to be aware of the differences between the person who has developed a healthy sense of self and the person who has an altered sense of self.

The Healthy Self

A healthy sense of self is possessed by people who have more or less fully developed their mental and physical faculties (Greenberg 1977). Healthy people are basically courageous. Because they are not afraid, they are open and curious and can look calmly at the world around them. They are not afraid of new situations and can tolerate risks and uncertainty. They are not afraid to try new things, and they can learn from experiences that enable them to do better the next time.

Healthy people are realists who see things accurately and do not confuse what *is* with what *should be*. These people do not expect something for nothing and respect the limitations of time, energy, and money. Because they realize that they cannot do everything, they concentrate on what is most important to them. They do not seek the impossible; their best is good enough. They accept their own limitations and are not too uncomfortable with their shortcomings.

Healthy people are mature and disciplined. In the course of their development, they have worked out a set of values that are appropriate for them. They do not have to satisfy all their impulses and needs immediately; they are oriented toward growth and do not allow themselves to be diverted from their real goals by needs that clamor for immediate gratification. Healthy people are in control of their own lives; they listen to others but make up their own minds and take responsibility for their own actions.

Good judgment is another quality of healthy people. They can simplify problems and get down to essentials. They do not get lost in unimportant details and trivial issues. They do not look for perfect solutions but for the best available means of solving problems.

Healthy people have self-respect and self-esteem. They appreciate themselves and do not constantly seek approval from others. Healthy people are productive and creative; they take advantage of their abilities to experience the joys of living.

People who are healthy have good contact with their own feelings and can express them. They are also sensitive to the feelings of others. They are good observers of themselves and their circumstances. These people know who they are, what they want, and in what direction they are going.

Finally, healthy people have good relations with other people. They can be generous and helpful to others because they are not always preoccupied with their own problems. Healthy people are capable of experiencing both love and work to the fullest extent.

The Altered Self

People who have not developed a solid sense of self feel vulnerable, insecure, and inferior. They are too frightened to look at themselves realistically and are afraid to see their limitations and shortcomings. Instead, by distorting or ignoring reality, they create a picture of themselves that they believe will impress others and of which they can be proud. The creation of an idealized self-image has far-reaching consequences for every aspect of their lives: it becomes more important to live up to the image than to appreciate and recognize their real needs.

People with an altered sense of self cannot function without their idealized image; it is needed to help them feel unique, superior, secure, and confident. This image furnishes a direction and shapes their interactions with others.

Frequently, the idealized self-image dictates standards that are so high that these people become engaged in a hopeless and never-ending struggle to mold themselves into their idea of a perfect being. Whereas healthy people live in reality and respect it, people with an altered sense of self live in an illusory world where nothing is impossible. Whatever enhances and glorifies the idealized image becomes desirable and important. Conversely, those qualities and tendencies that diminish or detract from this image are undesirable and must be avoided. This type of thinking leads to a set of standards in which all qualities and tendencies are considered either good or bad, to be proud of or ashamed of. People with an altered sense of self do not do things that are in their own interests but rather things that maintain their self-image. They have lost control over their own lives and sacrificed their genuine needs in the pursuit of self-esteem according to the idealized image.

A comparison of the healthy person and the person with an altered sense of self is provided in Table 9–1.

The Role of Anxiety and Fear

The central process in disruptions in relatedness is anxiety and defense against anxiety. People suffering from these disorders do not consciously know what they are anxious about and are too frightened to look at their anxiety accurately and realistically.

Horney (1945) postulated that the basis of anxiety is the feeling of being isolated and helpless in a hostile world. It is the terror of being abandoned, of feeling impotent, inadequate, unlovable, and worthless. Anxiety is the prevailing experiential state of neurotic persons.

The common elements of anxiety are fear of exposure and of loss of control. Exposure of one's inner conflict and turmoil can lead to feelings of inferiority, embarrassment, shame, and of being ridiculed. Many people harbor feelings that are unacceptable to them, and the fear that these feelings will become known to others creates intense anxiety. Feelings of anxiety usually mean that a person's methods of coping with stress are no longer functional—that an uncomfortable conflict is surfacing.

Both fear and anxiety are emotional reactions to danger. With fear the cause is obvious, but with anxiety it is not. Most people are afraid of fire and war, for example; they are real dangers. Because the threat is known, it is possible to be frightened yet deal with the problem. The individual who experiences anxiety, however, does not know the origin of her fear. The source is diffuse and nonspecific, arising from within the person rather than from external dangers.

A variety of events can trigger anxiety. If the anxiety is general, not associated with one particular thing, it is called a *free-floating* anxiety. Anxiety may also be triggered by specific objects or classes of objects, such as dogs, heights, or enclosed spaces. These objects are substitutes for the real cause of the anxiety. Since the real cause is not consciously recognized by the individual, anxiety creates feelings of helplessness, shame, and inferiority. The anxious person feels as though she has lost control over her life.

Table 9–1. Comparison of the Healthy Self and the Altered Self

Healthy Self	Altered Self
Courageous	Fearful
Realistic	Given to wishful thinking
Disciplined	Impulsive
Fair	Given to extremes
Open-minded	Closed-minded
Spontaneous	Driven, compulsive
Flexible	Rigid
Assertive	Hostile, vindictive
Loving	Clinging, dependent
Has zest for living	Apathetic, impoverished
Sincere	Self-deceiving
Shows deep feelings	Numb
Relates well	Exploits or is exploited
Productive, creative	Wasteful
Oriented toward growth	Oriented toward fame, prestige
Has sense of identity	Alienated, stranger to self

SOURCE: Adapted from Greenberg (1977).

THEORETICAL FRAMEWORKS

Several conceptual frameworks are widely used in understanding the dynamics of neurotic and personality disorders. For additional information regarding these frameworks, see Chapter 3.

Psychosexual or Psychodynamic Model

According to psychodynamic theory, the neurotic conflict represents a struggle between the ego (the part of the psyche that experiences the external world through the senses, organizes thought processes rationally and governs action) and the id (the part of the psyche that is the reservoir of instinctual drives and is dominated by the pleasure principle and irrational wishing). Freud believed that the ego mediates between the id and the superego—the part of the psyche that is critical of the self and enforces moral standards.

A conflict usually represents the wish to behave in a certain way and a fear of the consequences of doing so. For example, a student might wish to excel in class and win the instructor's approval but fears that outstanding achievement might lead to being resented by classmates. Anxiety is the end product of these opposing urges.

Repression is one way of dealing with a conflict. Freud described the defense mechanism of repression as resulting from a traumatic experience, usually of a sexual nature, during childhood (Freedman, Kaplan, and Sadock 1976). Because the experience was painful, it was forgotten and repressed. But the excitement elicited by the sexual stimulation was not extinguished and stayed in the unconscious as a repressed memory. Later, in response to another uncomfortable experience, the memory is revived, and the repressive mechanism fails. When repression fails, anxiety increases. Because the memories are unacceptable to the person, the original sexual excitement is expressed by a new means—the neurotic symptom. The neurotic symptoms or behaviors are invoked to control the anxiety and protect the ego against forbidden impulses and memories.

Freud believed that neurotic conflict occurs because of traumatic childhood experiences before the age of five or six. He described three early stages of psychosexual development, each characterized by a specific conflict (Table 9–2). Failure to resolve that conflict results in the person's becoming fixated at that level of psychosexual development. This view is no longer widely accepted. Other psychodynamic theorists have suggested that a person may develop neurotic patterns later in life when he experiences sufficient stress. The stress causes regression or fixation at immature levels, producing neurotic symptoms.

Identification of the basic conflict makes it possible to locate the psychosexual stage when the conflict originated, and gives direction to nursing process activities designed to facilitate conflict res-olution. The use of the psychoanalytic framework dictates that treatment be long-term and be aimed at the client's ultimate recognition of the nature of the conflict.

Psychosocial Model

Erik Erikson (1963), like Freud, proposed a developmental model, but his model used three influences to explain the modification of experiences: biological, psychological, and cultural. In this framework, the appearance or nonappearance of neurotic symptoms is determined by inborn sensitivity and temperament, parenting, ethnic and cultural factors as well as psychological strengths and weaknesses. Neurotic disorders may develop from critical tasks that are incompletely resolved. If critical tasks are resolved prematurely or belatedly, they may not be dealt with adequately, and incomplete resolution of early critical tasks has a detrimental effect on resolution of later tasks.

Interpersonal Model

Harry Stack Sullivan (1953), like Freud, looked for developmental fixation or regression to explain mental illness. But, unlike Freud, Sullivan believed that such developmental arrests are caused by inadequacies in personal relations in the home, school, and community. In addition, he thought that the personality structure of a person takes more than 20 years to develop rather than just the first 5 years of life. At any stage of development, favorable or unfavorable events can be influential.

According to Sullivan, anxiety always pertains to interpersonal relations. This anxiety causes the person to focus on experiences that will meet with social approval. The person thus develops in relation to social norms and behavior patterns.

As a result of unpleasant past experiences, individuals can develop views and attitudes about themselves that are not validated by others (Freedman, Kaplan, and Sadock 1976). These distorted views propel them into inappropriate situations

Table 9–2. Psychosexual Etiology of Neurotic Disorders		
Developmental Stage	**Objective**	**Pathologic Manifestation**
Oral (birth to age one)	Establish trusting dependence, gratification of oral needs without conflict	Dependency, counter-dependency; dependence on others for maintenance of self-esteem; biting, sucking *Example:* depression, alcoholism
Anal (ages one to three)	Achieve autonomy and independence without shame or self-doubt from loss of control	Orderliness, abstinence, parsimony, defense against anal eroticism *Example:* obsessive-compulsive disorder
Phallic (ages three to five)	Focus erotic interest on genital area, lay foundation for gender identity	Unresolved Oedipal complex; lack of feelings of achievement, power *Example:* phobias

and cause anxiety, which in turn leads to unclear thoughts, inaccurate perceptions, and inappropriate behaviors.

Social Learning Model

Learning theorists see anxiety and fear as unconditioned responses to a dangerous external stimuli capable of providing a powerful motivating force for shaping learned behavioral patterns (Kaplan, Freedman, and Sadock 1980). Children learn anxiety responses, neurotic behavior patterns, and repression through interactions with their parents. During the growth process, the future neurotic adult learns to associate interpersonal needs with an internal response of danger or anxiety. The threatening signals are perceived by children as originating from the disapproving reactions of parental figures.

Conflict between wishes and fears, which is a predominant aspect of neurotic disorders, manifests itself when clients attempt to meet interpersonal needs but avoid situations with issues that create anxiety. When clients banish thoughts from their mind that they have learned to associate with internal danger, there is weakened cognitive functioning and they are unable to plan and solve problems (Dollard and Miller 1950).

By intervening in the process, health care providers can alter the system so that the social environment begins to respond in a positive manner. Modeling can be used to increase functional behavior and enhance the acquisition of new behaviors such as social skills (Goodpastor et al. 1983).

Cognitive Model

Advocates of this framework maintain that neurotic disorders are caused by distortions in thinking and perceiving. Past experiences impact on a person to determine her perception of future experiences and dictate the patterns of relationships. For the individual with neurotic disorders, there are areas of unawareness or "not knowing," which prevent logical thinking and restrict opportunities for growth. Treatment is aimed at correction of the distortions and integration of an event with the experience (Barnett 1980).

COMPARISON OF VARIATIONS AND DISRUPTIONS IN FUNCTIONING

As mentioned earlier, psychosis, neurosis, and personality disorder are different forms of altered patterns of functioning. In clinical practice, it is sometimes difficult to distinguish among these patterns with absolute accuracy. Tables 9–3 and 9–4 are presented as guides to help nurses differentiate between neurotic and psychotic patterns of functioning and between neurotic and personality disorders.

The most distinguishing features of psychotic alterations are failure of reality testing and inability to differentiate between internal and external stimuli. Persons with neurotic disorders do not experience such a gross loss of contact with reality. The major differentiating factor of personality disorders is an acceptance of and comfort with the variations and disruptions in relatedness. Persons with neurotic styles of relating, on the other hand, are not comfortable with their conflict and repeatedly try to resolve it.

RELATIONSHIP VARIATIONS AND DISRUPTIONS: NEUROTIC PATTERNS

Although each neurotic disorder has its own manifestations, several characteristics are commonly displayed by all (Greenberg 1977). For example, all neurotic persons develop some type of symptom to relieve their anxiety. According to psychoanalytic theory, the symptom is the result of a compromise between unacceptable impulses and the forces that operate to repress those impulses. The symptom contains elements of both; a compromise is more tolerable for the individual than the conflict and reduces anxiety. In addition, symptoms have another advantage: Whenever an individual suffers from an ailment, other people are sympathetic and not only offer assistance but excuse the person from customary responsibilities. These are secondary gains that may be of considerable benefit to the neurotic person. But since neurotic symptoms impair functioning and cause suffering, the benefit is only temporary.

Neurotic persons are frightened of the demands of everyday living. They would like to guarantee that unpleasant things will not happen to them. As a result, they construct a plan of defense that will protect them from dangers, assuming that if they do certain things in certain ways, they will always be

Table 9–3. Comparison of Neurotic and Personality Alterations

Factor	Neurotic Disorder	Personality Disorder
Conflict	Continual, needs to be dealt with repeatedly	Resolved
Anxiety	Continually present	Not present
Feelings, thoughts, behaviors	Undesirable, distressing, irritating; are ego-dystonic	Felt as part of the self; are ego-syntonic

Table 9–4. Comparison of Neurotic Alterations and Psychotic Alterations

Factor	Neurotic Alteration	Psychotic Alteration
General behavior	Mild degree of personality decompensation; reality contact impaired, but client not incapacitated in social functioning	Severe degree of personality decompensation; reality contact markedly impaired; client incapacitated in social functioning
Nature of symptoms	Wide range of complaints but no hallucinations or other markedly deviant behavior	Wide range of complaints, with delusions, hallucinations, and other severely deviant behavior
Orientation	Client rarely loses orientation to environment	Client frequently loses orientation to environment
Insight	Client often has some insight into nature of the behavior; feels suffering keenly, wishes to get well on a conscious level	Client rarely has insight into nature of the behavior; usually doesn't recognize that illness is present
Social aspects	Behavior usually not injurious or dangerous to client or society; social adjustment impaired but not prevented	Behavior frequently injurious or dangerous to client or society
Treatment	Client rarely needs institutional care; psychotherapy usually only treatment necessary	Client usually needs institutional care; shock and other somatic therapies in addition to psychotherapy frequently necessary
Thoughts	Delusions never present; thoughts, feelings, actions maintain normal relationships	Delusions common; thoughts, feelings, actions lose relationship to each other
Repression	Repression is maintained, but repressed matter finds expression in distorted form that is relatively acceptable to the ego	Repression may be destroyed; ego is overwhelmed with unacceptable impulses

safe from harm and get what they want. Such beliefs tend to be unrealistic and magical, with little regard for others. The defensive strategy is fixed and rigid. Consequently, the neurotic person is not prepared to meet difficult or novel situations when they present themselves. Neurotic individuals also expect too much from themselves. By setting up impossible standards, they give themselves a continued stream of orders to perform in a certain way without regard for conditions that exist at the time. Horney (1950) called this the "tyranny of the shoulds."

Despite their problems, individuals with neurotic styles of functioning can manage fairly well for long periods of time. However, as the neurotic pattern increases in severity, it becomes more difficult to carry out the necessary functions of life. Because of the energy expended in maintaining a neurotic way of life, these individuals tend to be underachievers, repeaters of mistakes, and subject to extremes of behavior and poor judgment. The most common reaction in neuroses is depression. Neurotic persons often feel alienated from themselves, which can lead to extreme self-hatred and self-destruction.

In the rest of this section we shall examine the specific types of neurotic patterns. In general, neurotic reactions show a progression from primitive behavior, in which anxiety is discharged through direct somatic channels as a generalized *anxiety disor-*der, to more sophisticated manifestations. *Obsessive-compulsive disorders* use both mental and behavioral channels for dealing with anxiety. *Phobias*, which are the highest level of neurotic behavior, use external methods by displacing or projecting the anxiety to specific external objects. *Conversion disorders* utilize sensory motor channels; *dissociative disorders* involve mental processes. Following the discussion of each of these disorders, appropriate nursing assessments and approaches are presented.

Anxiety Reactions

Anxiety is the number one psychiatric disorder in the United States, with an estimated 13.1 million Americans suffering from this condition. People under 45 years of age have higher rates of a diagnosis of anxiety disorder, and this rate is about double that for people over 45 (Smith 1986).

Anxiety is part of normal development; the spectrum of developmental anxiety reactions runs from mild to severe. Absence of anxiety in development is considered pathological. Separation-stranger anxiety is universal in infants from 8 to about 18 months of age and is a part of learning to trust and develop primary relationships with others. The child at this stage clings to the mother and cries when approached by a stranger. These demands for continued closeness decrease as the child becomes involved in toddler explorations. Separation anxiety becomes evident again as the child begins school. Normal anxieties include fear of strange people, places, animals, and the dark. Coping strategies learned at this stage set the style for those used in later life. In the absence of support, the child may be prone to developing other manifestations of anxiety later in life.

Panic attacks are common in adolescence and may be brought on by a first date or a difficult examination. Because of the psychological growth and turmoil experienced in this stage of development, some episodes of severe anxiety can be expected.

Developmental anxieties are not considered serious unless they continue past the appropriate age and increase to the point of interfering with growth. Normal anxieties about social situations are part of the process that paces psychosexual development to enable persons to monitor their own behaviors (Saucier 1984).

In generalized anxiety reactions, the threat to the consciousness of the individual arises from repressed emotions such as hostility and resentment (Mereness and Karnash 1966). External events, such as loss of a job, divorce, or threats to personal security can be important causative factors. Since there are no elaborate symptoms, an anxiety reaction is considered to be the most primitive mechanism for handling conflict. The anxiety is neither focused nor displaced but rather involves the whole organism. It is usually experienced in the form of physical symptoms that center around the vital organs of the body (heart palpitations, upset stomach, constriction of the throat) but can involve other areas as well (numbness in extremities). These symptoms are frightening, and the person frequently becomes depressed, has difficulty concentrating and working, and dwells on fears about dying or becoming insane. Severe anxiety attacks may cause a person to fear being left alone, which results in clinging to familiar situations and being unable to work because of the fear of impending doom.

Occasionally, anxiety attacks can reach panic proportions. Panic is a sudden upsurge of terror and can last for minutes or hours. The client may complain of tremulousness, sweating, inability to breathe, and palpitations. Panic attacks typically begin between the ages of 15 and 35. Some clients improve spontaneously but if attacks occur for over a year, they are likely to continue. The cause of these frightening and disturbing events may or may not be known to the individual. For some persons, anxiety attacks may be mild enough to be noticeable only to themselves. For example, talking too much or not talking at all in stressful situations may indicate a mild form of anxiety attack.

The importance of a thorough physical workup cannot be overemphasized, as certain somatic conditions may simulate anxiety attacks. The most common organic causes are thyrotoxicosis, hypoglycemia, amphetamine usage, and synergistic or idiosyncratic drug reactions.

Proponents of psychodynamic theory advocate insight-oriented psychotherapy if the client has sufficient ego strength and demonstrates motivation and capacity for introspection. Supportive psychotherapy with reassurance and encouragement to face anxiety-producing situations may be helpful even if not curative. Relaxation techniques taught by hypnotists and behavioral therapists may also prove effective for some clients (Kaplan, Freedman, and Sadock 1980).

Advocates of cognitive therapy believe that alteration of danger-laden cognitions associated with anxiety will relieve the anxiety itself. This can be approached intellectually by identifying misconceptions, testing validity and substituting more appropriate concepts, and experientially by exposing clients to experiences that are powerful enough to change misconceptions.

NURSING ASSESSMENT AND APPROACH The absence of systematic, repetitive defensive behaviors indicates a favorable prognosis. Spontaneous remission may occur without intervention, or chronic anxiety attacks may result. These attacks may be precursors of other forms of neuroses, such as phobias and obsessive-compulsive disorders. As with all neuroses, interventions should deal less with the real circumstances surrounding the attack and more with the client's perception of her inner experience. It is important to examine the context in which the symptoms occur but also to remember that extraneous factors may be crucial. Reassurance that the attack is not life-threatening or permanent are caring approaches. Supportive measures should be offered at first, but long-term treatment consists of helping the client to develop insight into the nature of the conflict causing the symptoms. For further nursing interventions, see Chapter 5.

Obsessive-Compulsive Reactions

An obsessive-compulsive disorder is an emotional dysfunction in which certain ideas and behaviors occupy the client to such a degree that they interfere with normal work and social activity. In the obsessive-compulsive individual, conflicts are expressed in repetitious thoughts, words, and acts.

An *obsession* is a thought that occurs persistently despite the person's wish to avoid or ignore it. A *compulsion* is an act that is carried out, in some degree against the client's wishes, to avoid or control anxiety. The obsessive person may also be occupied with rumination, which involves not just single thoughts but large topics around which repetitive thoughts revolve without resolution or decision.

According to psychodynamic theory, obsessive-compulsive individuals are fixated or regressed to the anal stage of development. The underlying conflicts are related to cleanliness, authority, and control. Individuals may be very clean or very dirty. Behaviors are usually symbolic of holding on or letting go, for example, hoarding items or giving everything away. Ritualistic behaviors may be sadomasochistic. The abnormal fears of the obsessive-compulsive person usually develop out of disagreeable and socially unacceptable ideas. These ideas, with associated intense emotions, are repressed into the unconscious. The repressed energy attaches itself to an activity or idea that seemingly has no relationship to the original problem. A sense of relief from tension and anxiety is obtained when the ritual is performed, but the relief is only temporary, so the person is compelled to repeat the act.

The defense mechanisms used by obsessive-compulsive individuals include regression, isolation, reaction formation, and undoing (see Chapter 3). A well-structured obsessive-compulsive ritual protects against psychosis. Usually the obsessive-compulsive person who fears hurting others is in no danger of doing so—the idea of violence is frightening. An example of the interplay of defense mechanisms is illustrated by a woman who had ambivalent feelings about bearing a child and becoming a mother. When caring for her child, she developed a ritualistic behavior about keeping the baby clean, sterilizing all food or objects that the child came in contact with, and washing her hands continually. In this manner, she dealt with her hostile (and unacceptable) feelings toward her child through ritualized behavior. She repressed her hostility and unconscious wish to harm the child and instead devoted all her energy to keeping the child and the environment impeccably clean (a reaction formation). Furthermore, the continual handwashing (undoing) alleviated her guilt by making demands and causing discomfort (sadomasochism).

Erikson (1963) proposed that obsessive-compulsive character traits are generated during the developmental stage of autonomy versus shame and doubt. During the maturation of the anal musculature, the child discovers that self-control, tidiness, and cleanliness gain parental approval, whereas carelessness prompts punishment and rejection. Throughout childhood, controlling oneself and the environment continues to be a major issue. Meticulous and detailed behavior becomes integrated into the character structure and this developmental stage is not successfully resolved.

Shapiro (1965) defined obsessive-compulsive behavior as a style of functioning and a way of thinking and perceiving. During intellectual development, the person comes to view the world with rigidity and indecisiveness. The behavior is dependent on the perceptual mode of the environment in which the child was raised.

Gelfman (1970) described obsessive-compulsive neuroses as a faulty practice in living and a value system evolved over a lifetime in which the individual abdicates a responsible role to others yet chooses to maintain control over them by giving the illusion of superiority. This illusion is perpetuated by the obsessional traits that present the person as being perfect, uniquely ideal and above question. The process creates conflict because the client attempts to maintain the image of competence and is not willing to assume the related responsibilities. Decompensation usually is evident when the posture of superiority is realistically challenged.

Another approach is presented by learning theorists, who believe that obsession represents a conditioned stimulus to anxiety. Because of an association with an anxiety-producing stimulus, the obsessional thought gains the capacity to arouse anxiety. A compulsion is established when a person learns that certain actions reduce anxiety; these actions become fixed into a learned pattern.

Within the last decade, the treatment of obsessive-compulsive disorders has improved with the introduction of response prevention and deliberate exposure to feared situations either in fantasy or in real situations. Actual exposure to the feared situation is a technique that has been used most extensively with phobic clients but is proving to be useful with obsessive-compulsive behavior.

Response prevention, the blocking of the ritualistic behavior that relieves anxiety, is helpful in reinforcing the exposure technique. In cases where actual experience is not feasible, for example, where anxiety is generated by fears of possible disasters (death, disease, fire), the presentation of these situations in fantasy has been effective (Sketetee, Foa, and Grayson 1982).

NURSING ASSESSMENT AND APPROACH Obsessive-compulsive individuals rarely become suicidal, because their defenses protect them from acting out their impulses. They frequently engage in magical thinking, believing that thinking equals acting. It is important to negate this belief and reassure them that there are differences between thoughts and acts. Symptoms must be assessed in the context of the client's lifestyle and social supports. These clients usually have a chronic condition and show few prospects for growth. It is unrealistic to try to modify their behavior or personality radically. Often the symptoms increase as the client ages. It is usually more realistic to modify the external situation and to help the client cope with the demands of her ritualistic behaviors by reducing them or substituting less demanding behaviors, if possible. If long-term therapy is contemplated, the original source of the anxiety should be investigated, a task for the primary therapist.

The outlook for a client displaying an obsessive-compulsive reaction is related to the severity of his symptoms, including the rigidity in thinking and behaving, the quality of relationships with others, the tolerance for anxiety, the ability to tolerate introspection, and the capacity for insight. For specific nursing interventions, see Chapter 5.

Posttraumatic Stress Syndrome

Posttraumatic stress syndrome is a pattern of psychological symptoms brought about by the experience of a highly traumatic event (Ziarnowski 1984). The syndrome involves such a severe stressor that almost anyone experiencing it could be subject to psychological distress. Victims of rape or assault, veterans of military combat, and survivors of natural or human-made disasters are all vulnerable to posttraumatic stress reactions and have the potential to manifest serious psychological impairment. Posttraumatic stress disorder was first identified in Viet Nam combat veterans, but it can be seen in the survivors of other traumatic situations as well.

The indications of posttraumatic stress reactions are dramatic and compelling. First, there is a tendency to relive the event in some way; through nightmares, intrusive thoughts, or other obsessive ruminations. Flashbacks—the feeling of "being there again" set off by some seemingly neutral stimulus in the environment—are common. A second major indicator is the tendency to insulate oneself from one's emotions and feelings, known as "psychic numbing." Trauma involves a range of experiences and feelings that include fear, panic, guilt, anger, and physical and emotional pain. When one is traumatized, the normal inclination is to withdraw or escape both physically and emotionally. People with posttraumatic stress disorder have been psychologically scarred and try to isolate themselves from the event and its emotional overlay. However, the experience is so complex that they cannot dissociate themselves from the event and its emotional overlay without shutting down a good part of their emotional lives. By not feeling deeply, they can avoid being hurt again. Interpersonal relations can be profoundly affected. Things that were once enjoyable no longer hold any pleasure, and the client appears blunted, perhaps even schizophrenic in some cases.

Because of the isolation, these clients seem unable to relate to others or to express emotions. They remain involved with the stressful experience, which has resulted in unresolved conflict. Since they are unable to deal with the conflict, they develop an overwhelming sense of apathy toward the present environment. This inability to cope alienates family and friends, and the defenses that are utilized produce a cycle of isolation and rejection that leaves the clients feeling depressed and helpless.

Preoccupation with the distressing event may impair memory and ability to concentrate on other things. The unresolved conflict consumes energy and does not leave many resources to cope with present situations. When the coping mechanisms of avoidance and withdrawal are not successful, the client may attempt to increase these mechanisms by using drugs and alcohol. Alcohol abuse is more common because of its availability, social acceptance and lower cost. Alcohol is used to avoid memories and to further isolate oneself from exposure to events that trigger reenactment of the traumatic event. However, the use of alcohol can frequently lead to situations in which the client completely loses control of rage and violent impulses. The combination of alcohol and suppressed hostility often results in violent acting out behavior.

In addition to reliving and psychic numbing, these clients may manifest hyperalertness, disturbances of sleep, survivor guilt, memory impairment, trouble concentrating, and avoidance of activities that are reminiscent of the trauma, or intensification of symptoms if such activities cannot be avoided. Anxiety and depression (often with suicidal ideation) are common, along with lowered stress tolerance and explosiveness. The most dramatic illustration of PTSD in recent years has been the occurrence of this disorder in the men and women who served in the Vietnam War.

NURSING ASSESSMENT AND APPROACHES The primary symptoms of PTSD can range from anxiety to drug and alcohol abuse to marital problems. Anxiety and depression are the most common symptoms. A nursing assessment should include the determination of the traumatic event. For veterans, information about the combat experience should be obtained. Information on the psychosocial history is needed to establish the presence of delayed stress. Questions concerning interpersonal relationships and feelings toward others help to determine if emotional numbing has occurred. If the family is available for interview, members can provide information concerning the differences in the client before and after the traumatic event.

It should be determined whether or not the client has been able to talk with anyone about the experience. He may have an unsteady employment record because of difficulty in dealing with authority figures or other job stressors. There may be legal problems related to the rage and frustration associated with the feelings of betrayal. Information related to alcohol and drug abuse as well as homocidal and suicidal thoughts should be elicited.

The main goal of treatment is to help clients recognize that the stressful event has produced a psychological arrest in their lives. They must come to know the traumatic event and resolve the conflicts to be able to deal with the present. The most popular form of treatment is participation in group therapy, or "rap" sessions, where stressful events can be reviewed in detail in a supportive group situation. The focus should be on the reality of past events as well as the reality of the present. A num-

ber of other treatment approaches can complement group therapy. Hypnotherapy has proved to be useful to cope with intrusive thoughts, sleep disturbances, and anxious feelings. Individual therapy can be helpful as a means of learning to trust in the therapeutic relationship. Whatever the modality, the client must eventually resume responsibility for his own behavior. He cannot remain a victim of the situation and dwell on that aspect of his life. He must be able to resolve that period and proceed with life in the present. Therapy for PTSD should be directed toward that syndrome alone. Treatment for other problems should be given separately but concurrently. For example, anxiety can be treated with medication, alcohol and drug abuse attended to in separate programs (Casper 1984).

Nurses can play a key role in assisting the client to work through the traumatic experience. Crisis management can be combined with other forms of therapy.

Phobic Reactions

A *phobia* is dread of an object that realistically is not dangerous but has come to represent a danger and is specific enough to transform anxiety into fear. Phobias are sometimes called the normal neuroses of childhood because they may result from inadequate parental protection or from fearfulness conveyed by a parent. Some common phobias are listed in Table 9–5.

According to psychoanalytic theory, a phobia may begin when a real threat causes fear and anxiety; the phobia then develops as a means of decreasing the anxiety. The particular phobic object symbolizes the conflict that is causing the anxiety. By replacing the anxiety with fear of the specific object, the person can reduce psychic discomfort by avoiding the feared object. For example, if one is afraid of heights, one avoids high places.

Some phobias involve the use of the defense mechanism of *displacement*. For example, a woman may wish to hurt her mother, but since these feelings are unacceptable to her, she displaces her feelings of hostility onto kitchen knives and becomes afraid of them because they represent her true feelings. Other phobias involve the use of both displacement and *projection*. In the story of Little Hans (Freud 1955), the child had a wish to hurt his father, but because this wish was unacceptable to him, he projected his feelings onto his father, believing that his father wished to hurt him. Since this, too, was unacceptable, he displaced the fear of his father onto horses, developing a phobia about them.

Persons with phobic disorders have relatively mature ego structures. Since their fear is placed outside themselves, the mechanism is less punitive than in an anxiety or hysterical disorder. However,

Table 9–5. Common Phobias

Phobia	Fear of
Acrophobia	High places
Agoraphobia	Open places
Algophobia	Pain
Astraphobia	Thunder and lightning
Claustrophobia	Closed places
Coprophobia	Excreta
Hematophobia	Blood
Hydrophobia	Water
Lalophobia	Speaking
Mysophobia	Dirt, contamination
Necrophobia	Dead bodies
Nyctophobia	Night, darkness
Pathophobia	Disease
Peccatophobia	Sinning
Photophobia	Strong light
Sitophobia	Eating
Taphophobia	Being buried alive
Thanatophobia	Death
Toxophobia	Being poisoned
Xenophobia	Strangers
Zoophobia	Animals

SOURCE: Adapted from Freedman, Kaplan, and Sadock (1976).

phobias can become generalized, causing discomfort and interfering with daily functioning. For example, a man may experience an accident or near-accident in an airplane, causing him to become afraid of flying; subsequently, his fear may become generalized to all moving vehicles and progress until he is afraid to leave his home for any reason.

A different explanation of phobias is offered by learning theorists, who use the traditional Pavlovian stimulus-response model of the conditioned reflex to account for the initial creation of a phobia. They suggest that fear becomes attached to an inappropriate object when anxiety is aroused by a frightening stimulus in the presence of that neutral object. Because of this association, the object acquires the ability to arouse anxiety on its own.

Cognitive therapists use an approach that begins with the presumption that people suffering from phobic attacks are responding to the unchallenged thought that something terrible is going to happen. Clients tend to see and overestimate danger in a situation where none exists. They also underestimate their ability to cope with situations. When this happens, there is a distressing physical response which increases the fear. This fear then increases the physical symptoms. In cognitive therapy, clients learn to challenge automatic thoughts and to think realistically about the threats they

perceive. They then learn strategies for coping rationally with the anxious moments or situations that occur. Clients also learn to induce the symptoms of panic in themselves thereby learning that if they can induce them, they can control them (Corr 1986).

NURSING ASSESSMENT AND APPROACHES The prognosis for the client who is phobic is uncertain. Some phobic persons are stable and do not experience a major disruption in their lives because the object of their fear can easily be avoided. However, for others, fear may broaden to the point of incapacitation. The degree of impairment created by the phobia needs careful assessment because, in many cases, there is no need for treatment. If the phobia is incapacitating or if the client expresses a need to be rid of it, several techniques may be successful. In *desensitization*, the client is repeatedly exposed to situations that cause progressively greater levels of anxiety until the client no longer feels great anxiety in the presence of the feared object. In *reciprocal inhibition*, an anxiety-producing stimulus is paired with an anxiety-suppressing stimulus until the anxiety is no longer uncomfortable. Reciprocal-inhibition techniques include meditation, yoga, and biofeedback. At times insight work is helpful. All these methods require special training and are to be used only after careful evaluation of the client's particular circumstances.

Since recent research (Brody 1983) has indicated that the cause of phobias and panic attacks may be biologic, some new approaches to treatment involve the use of antidepressant medication combined with behavior modification. The drugs most frequently used are imipramine (Tofranil) and MAO inhibitors. Many clients repond to the three-phase approach of support, medication, and behavior modification. One advantage of this approach is that the client is helped to realize that the feared object is not the cause of the problem.

Conversion Reactions

In a *conversion reaction*, functioning of sensory systems or voluntary muscles are altered to control anxiety (Hofling and Leininger 1960). These alterations are never peripheral and are unrelated to the distribution of nerve pathways. Psychodynamically, conversions can be explained in terms of the ego's ability to control the sensory and motor apparatus by refusing to acknowledge incoming stimuli (as by blindness) or to carry out a particular motor function (as by paralysis of one hand). This control is always below the level of conscious awareness. In a conversion reaction, the conflict is not expressed in diffuse symptoms as it is in generalized anxiety. In fact, the symptoms have a specific meaning to the client. Neither is the anxiety displaced to an external object, as in a phobic reaction. Instead, it is expressed symbolically by altered functioning.

When considering the etiology of conversion reactions, the student should be aware of the sociological view that illnesses often reflect the expectations of valued persons and health care providers (see Chapter 2). According to Parsons (1951), the sick role is characterized by passivity—others are permitted to make all the decisions for the client. This enforced dependency diminishes the client's sense of autonomy and supports a state of helplessness.

People suffering from conversion reactions are sometimes misdiagnosed as malingerers. However, malingering is a conscious endeavor, whereas a conversion disorder is unconscious. The client with a conversion reaction has real symptoms and experiences discomfort from them; the malingerer does not. The person with a conversion disorder may be inconsistent in exhibiting symptoms because he or she does not fear detection; there is no feigning involved. The malingerer, on the other hand, will show considerable consistency; his symptoms and complaints are well thought through because he fears being exposed. People with conversion reactions cannot modify their disabilities of their own volition; malingerers can.

Repression is the fundamental defense mechanism in conversion reactions. The production of the symptom depends on keeping unacceptable thoughts and feelings in the unconscious. Since the symptom actually serves unconscious purposes, clients have a relative lack of distress toward their symptoms. The symptom binds the anxiety, thereby relieving distress. This has led to the use of the term *la belle indifference* to describe the casual attitude of the client.

Alleviation of anxiety is the primary gain of behaviors in all neurotic disorders—"primary" in the sense that the client receives advantages from the behaviors that are independent of the response of the environment. However, secondary gains may also be accrued from the environment. For example, a woman who has developed conversion blindness because she does not wish to "see" the evidence that her husband is having an affair with another woman also receives the secondary gain of increased attention from her family because of her disability. Secondary gain comes from the attention one receives; it is not part of the conversion reaction but is instead a complication. Removal of the secondary gain does not decrease the conversion reaction.

As in all instances where a functional disorder is suspected, it is important first to rule out the possibility of physiological pathology. For example, multiple sclerosis sometimes causes bizarre symptoms that are unrelated to nerve distribution.

NURSING ASSESSMENT AND APPROACHES Clients with a conversion reaction are usually suggestible and are fond of attention. Guilt is rarely a prominent feature. Conversion disorders are often associated with sexual repression and disapproval of sexual feelings in early life. Fewer cases are diagnosed than formerly, probably because of changing attitudes about sex and sexuality.

In the treatment of clients with a conversion reaction, therapists should not try to remove the symptom too quickly. If the symptom is suddenly removed but the conflict remains, emergency defenses such as depression or suicide may follow. Expressive exploratory therapy that brings the conflict into conscious awareness can increase insight and decrease the need for repression. The symptom should never be the target; rather, the client should be allowed to retain the symptom while insight, self-understanding, and change take place. Because clients cannot make the cognitive connection between the way they feel and the cause of their symptoms, therapy should aim at achieving this cognitive connection.

Effective care of clients with conversion reactions is largely dependent on the attitudes and acceptance of health care professionals. It is at times difficult for caretakers to respond to the demands of these clients when their symptoms lack demonstrable physical cause. Treatment planning must be based on an acceptance of the symptoms as being real and on a search for the meaning of the symptoms.

Dissociative Reactions

In dissociative reactions, denial and ego splitting are used to decrease anxiety. The alteration is in mental functions rather than in sensory or motor functions. Portions of the ego are separated from the total personality and forced into the unconscious. The client still, however, possesses the majority of mental material, such as knowledge and skills related to work performance. Examples of dissociative reactions include amnesia and multiple personality. Modern literature has helped to create public interest in these conditions through such works as *The Three Faces of Eve* and *Sybil*. In these examples of brief amnesias with the emergence of new personalities and the alteration of two or more personalities, a portion of the person's psychic material was separated (dissociated) from other portions.

According to the psychoanalytic model, all hysterical neurotic reactions are related to the oral and

DSMm-III-R Axis I Diagnostic Classifications

Anxiety Disorders

300.21	Panic disorder with agoraphobia
300.01	Panic disorder without agoraphobia
300.22	Agoraphobia without panic disorder
300.23	Social phobia
300.29	Simple phobia
300.30	Obsessive-compulsive disorder
309.89	Posttraumatic stress disorder
300.02	Generalized anxiety disorder
300.00	Anxiety disorder not otherwise specified

Somatoforms Disorders

300.70	Body dysmorphic disorder
300.11	Conversion disorder
300.70	Hypochondriasis
300.81	Somatization disorder
307.80	Somatoform pain disorder
300.70	Undifferentiated somatoform disorder
300.70	Somatoform disorder NOS

Dissociative Disorders

300.14	Multiple personality disorder
300.13	Psychogenic fugue
300.12	Psychogenic amnesia
300.60	Depersonalization disorder
300.15	Dissociative disorder

Personality Disorders (coded on Axis II)

301.00	Paranoid
301.20	Schizoid
301.22	Schizotypal
301.70	Antisocial
301.83	Borderline
301.50	Histrionic
301.81	Narcissistic
301.82	Avoidant
301.60	Dependent
301.40	Obsessive-compulsive
301.84	Passive-aggressive
301.90	Personality disorder NOS

Most researchers in the field believe that this condition is the result of severe sexual, physical, or emotional abuse in childhood. Because of the severe trauma, clients are forced to create their own, more harmonious worlds. A mental structure arises that seems to take on a life of its own. Multiple personality disorder is a coping mechanism that allows the child to compartmentalize the trauma and no longer live continuously with the memory of the abuse. While being forced to live in the abusing environment, the different personalities allow the child to live without being in constant fear. The problems arise when the child grows up and leaves the context of the abuse and has to function with a continuous sense of identity and continuity.

The disorder is characterized by the existence within the client of more than two distinct personalities, each with little or no awareness of the others and each with its own behavioral patterns. Blackouts or amnesia are common among these clients because, while the information has been recorded in memory, it cannot be recaptured.

Clients with multiple personalities usually have a typical set of classic characters: the "child," who is frightened and guards the memories of childhood trauma; the "internal persecutor," who attempts to harm the other personalities; the "host," who provides the social facade to the outside world; the "memory trace," who keeps a chronological memory of life; the "self helper," who aids the therapist in treatment; the "moderator," who comments on the dynamics of the family within; the "protector," who defends against injury or harm; the "anesthetic," who feels no pain; and a person who handles sexuality (Talan 1985).

Although abuse may be the primary cause of the disorder, recent research has yielded the possibility that the ability to split may have a genetic link. It has been shown that the changes in personality are accompanied by changes in brain activity. Therapy is directed toward helping the personalities to fuse and become whole. Frightening memories must be recalled and relived to be released (Scotta 1988).

NURSING ASSESSMENT AND APPROACHES In the past, dissociative ("hysterical") reactions were thought to occur only in women. However, recent research has shown that these reactions are at least as common, and perhaps more so, in men (Luisada, Peele, and Pillard 1974). Both men and women initially seek treatment in their late teens or early twenties and both usually have a history of suicidal gestures. They are often scholastic underachievers and rarely express having had sexual satisfaction. Misuse of alcohol and drugs is common, as are unreliability and misrepresentation.

phallic phases of development. The sexual seductiveness often displayed by the hysterical person indicates an Oedipal conflict, with a wish to regress to oral levels where love and security can be found.

Previously, the existence of clients with multiple personality disorder were thought to be relatively rare. Current estimates now indicate that MPD occurs in one in every 10,000 Americans.

Treatment should focus on the client rather than on the symptoms. Therapy should not become a long, self-rewarding process that reinforces the manipulative and dependent behavior commonly seen in these clients.

Hypochondriacal Reactions

Clients suffering from hypochondriacal reactions have an unrealistic interpretation of physical signs or symptoms as being abnormal, which leads to a preoccupation with the fear or belief that they have a serious disease. Physical evaluations do not uncover any physical disorders that can account for the sensations. In this disorder, the unrealistic fear persists despite medical reassurance and impairs the person's social or occupational functioning (Strain 1985).

The condition differs from a hysterical disorder in that there are no actual losses or distortions in function. Symptoms of the condition may appear in childhood but usually peak in the fourth decade for men and the fifth decade for women. The symptoms are diffuse and can involve many areas of the body.

Psychoanalytical approaches suggest that hypochondriacal behavior reflects the physical effects of a narcissistic withdrawal of love from objects to organs; the complaints are the result of increased tension on the organs, caused by the blocked libido. Others have postulated a psychophysiological explanation that allows for an elevated basal level of physiological arousal and heightened perceptual sensitivity leading to a tendency to perceive more bodily sensations.

A third framework argues that somatic complaints and behavior may serve as strategies for reducing negative implications of poor performance, thereby maintaining the person's self-esteem. These clients may be responding to a threat to self-esteem by offering an excuse for poor performance based on illness and physical symptoms. Self-handicapping strategies give clients a ready excuse for possible failure (Smith et al. 1983).

Development of hypochondriasis may be founded in the earliest human relationships and develop as an adaptive style based on the relationship with one's parents. Illness and suffering may be the vehicle to maintain social interaction and receive attention.

A hypochondriacal reaction can be a primary, temporary, or secondary disorder. As a primary disorder, the condition is not the product of another psychiatric reaction. It is a functional disorder that is a lifelong style of behavior that may worsen with stress. Hypochondriacal symptoms may be secondary to another psychiatric problem, such as depression. Temporary hypochondriasis is manifested by persons under extreme stress who temporarily experience a conviction of illness and transient somatic symptoms.

Hypochondriasis should be distinguished from pseudohypochondriasis, which is seen most often in the aged. With the biological changes inherent in the aging process, it is not surprising that the elderly frequently express vague somatic complaints. An excessive concern with bodily functions might be expected as normal in the aged. Both hypochondriasis and pseudohypochondriasis clients attempt, on the basis of their illness, to establish a relationship with health care providers which they view as a social contact. Clients in both groups have few social relations but the social isolation of the elderly is age-related, whereas the true hypochondriacal client lacks relationships as a consequence of lifelong behavior. The hypochondriacal client may respond to reassurance with anger and increased complaints, whereas the pseudohypochondriacal is relieved by a favorable diagnosis. Clients in the latter group derive little comfort from undergoing complex, costly diagnostic procedures and do not characteristically level accusations of neglect, rejection, or incompetence against health care personnel.

Clients with hypochondriacal reactions should not be confused with malingerers, who do not actively experience physical symptoms. Both have primary gains but hypochondriacal clients express unacceptable dependency needs through their suffering and do not consciously try to deceive anyone (Strain 1985).

NURSING ASSESSMENT AND APPROACHES A client with hypochondriasis will present his or her symptoms at length and in great detail. The content of the client's thoughts is entirely centered on bodily complaints and on unsuccessful attempts to achieve relief. In contrast to the indifference shown by clients with conversion reactions, these clients are frequently worried and anxious. They usually have a long history of repeated physician visits and multiple surgeries. Many show obsessive-compulsive traits such as defiance, obstinancy, miserliness, and egocentricity to the extent that they exclude any concern for others.

The hypochondriacal client should be encouraged to verbalize her feelings to decrease her need to demonstrate them with body language. The client's physical symptoms should be accepted by the nurse but should not become the *focus* of the interaction. Honest and simple explanations for symptoms should be given without showing overconcern. Physical complaints should be discreetly brought to the attention of appropriate staff, as some may be legitimate and in need of further evaluation. The best therapy for a hypochondriacal client is an understanding and supportive relationship with sympathetic listening. The family should be included in the plan of care to assist them to understand the nature of the client's complaints.

PSYCHOPHARMACOLOGICAL APPROACHES

The most common drugs used in therapy for neurotic disorders are the antianxiety agents, sometimes known as minor tranquilizers. They are used to control moderate to severe daytime anxiety and tension without causing excessive sedation or drowsiness. The most commonly used agents are listed in Table 9–6.

The therapeutic actions of these drugs are thought to result from actions at subcortical sites, particularly depression of the limbic system (Eisenhauer and Gerald 1984). High doses can also depress the cerebral cortex, producing sedation. Many antianxiety agents also possess anticonvulsant and skeletal muscle relaxant properties.

Antianxiety drugs are contraindicated with hypersensitive clients or those with a history of drug dependence. The most common side effects are drowsiness, lethargy, fainting, nausea, vomiting, and general gastrointestinal distress. At times, transient hypotension can be a problem. Blood pressure should be monitored before and after administration of the medication. Because these drugs may impair physical and mental performance, clients should be warned not to operate a car or potentially dangerous machinery until the intensity of the drug response has been assessed. Clients should also be advised not to consume alcoholic beverages while receiving these drugs because of the combined depressant effects. Elderly clients should receive reduced doses of these drugs because they are more susceptible to drug-induced drowsiness, dizziness, and hypotension than younger clients.

Sudden withdrawal of a drug after long periods of administration may worsen the neurotic state and precipitate withdrawal effects. Long-term administration may lead to the development of psychological dependence, tolerance, and possibly physical dependence.

RELATIONSHIP VARIATIONS AND DISRUPTIONS: PERSONALITY DISORDERS

Personality disorders are lifelong behavior patterns that are acceptable to the individual but that create conflict with others. Although the behaviors may resemble the patterns of some neurotic disorders, they are usually acceptable to the individual (egosyntonic) and do not create anxiety because of their acceptability to the ego. Unlike neurotic persons, who must deal with their conflicts repeatedly, persons with a character disorder seem to have resolved their libidinous and aggressive conflicts once and for all. Latent anxiety may exist, but it does not usually surface unless the coping style is challenged or is no longer effective.

Personality traits are patterns of thinking, feeling, acting, and relating that are not confined to one aspect of the person or to a specific time period. When these traits are inflexible and maladaptive, and cause significant impairment in functioning, they are considered personality disorders. The defining characteristics of the disorders are chronicity, pervasiveness, and maladaptivity. If one of these symptoms is not manifested, the condition is considered a trait rather than a disorder. Clients with personality disorders constitute a large percentage of outpatient clinical practice (Widiger and Frances 1985).

Usually, people with personality disorders do not see the problem as theirs but as that of others. They express discontent only if their behavior pattern fails to obtain fulfillment of their needs. Their common complaint is that they are treated unfairly by others or by life in general. The ego structure of such persons causes them to react poorly to anxiety and depression. The behavior pattern is frequently a prolonged maladaptive way of interacting with others and usually becomes worse when a situation is stressful.

Little is known about the causes of specific personality disorders (Kaplan, Freedman, and Sadock 1980). Genetic factors have been considered, since research has shown that monozygotic twins have a higher concordance of personality disorders

Table 9–6. Commonly Used Antianxiety Agents

Generic Name	Trade Name	Usual Dose Range
Alprazolam	Xanax	0.25–0.5 mg tid
Chlordiazepoxide	Librium	5–10 mg tid
Chlorazepate	Tranxene	15–60 mg qd
Diazepam	Valium	2–10 mg tid
Flurazepam	Dalmane	15–30 mg qd hs
Halazepam	Paxipam	20–40 mg tid
Lorazepam	Ativan	2–6 mg qd
Oxazepam	Serax	15–30 mg tid
Prazepam	Centrax	20–60 mg qd
Temazepam	Restoril	30 mg qd
Trizaolam	Halcion	0.25–0.5 mg qd

than dizygotic twins (Pollin et al. 1969) and studies have indicated that children of parents with borderline schizophrenia raised by adoptive parents had a higher than average rate of schizotypal personalities (Wender 1976).

Constitutional factors have been thought to play a role in personality disorders because some clients with emotionally unstable character disorders have shown an increase in neurologic deficits (Quitkin, Rifkin, and Klein 1976). Other researchers have suggested that children with minimal brain dysfunction are predisposed to later development of personality disorders (Satterfield and Centwell 1972). These factors have been useful in the explanation of personality disorders, but firm evidence has not been established.

Sociocultural aspects may also contribute to the etiology. Learning theorists suggest that persistent maladaptive social behavior is reinforced and maintained by rewards—usually social—that are present in the environment (Feldman 1977).

Treatment Approaches

Most of the personality disorders are not responsive to drug therapy. Medication may be useful when focused on a particular target symptom. Treatment is then limited to one particular aspect of the disorder but it is also possible that success in one area may generalize to others. Change in affects may result in change in cognition, behavior or interpersonal relationships if the target symptom, such as anxiety, is a core characteristic of the client.

Behavior therapy is a symptom-focused treatment that may have a limited or generalized effect on the personality. However, these techniques require motivation for change and cooperation that may not be present in these clients, since most are comfortable with their disorders.

Cognitive-behavioral techniques focus on the irrational assumptions that underlie the clients' beliefs and behaviors. The clients with personality disorders often have debilitating cognitive styles; e.g., compulsive clients who govern their actions by severe moralistic standards may respond to rational-emotive therapy.

Family therapy may be helpful when a disordered personality is considered as a disordering system of relationships. Using an interpersonal model, the personality entails a pattern of relating to others. These disorders can be considered to be interpersonal patterns in which one person's debilitating behavior elicits complementary behavior that reinforces the original behavior. Even if an interpersonal or systems perspective is not utilized, the quality of the clients' relationships must be considered, since these interactions are often an integral part of the disorder, and relationships will be affected by and will affect any individual therapy.

Psychodynamic psychotherapies focus treatment techniques explicitly on the personality structure. The concepts of transference and countertransference are particularly relevant in the treatment of these clients. Since a therapist may develop a complementary response to the client's pathology, the task of treatment is to identify the basis of the client's relationship style, manage it within the therapeutic relationship, and break the pattern through insight and corrective interpersonal experiences. The choice of this treatment modality depends in part on the client's psychological-mindedness and motivation for insight and change. Some of the clients are more appropriate than others for insight-oriented therapy. At some times, it is necessary to support the client's personality style to help her cope with difficult stressors such as medical problems (Widiger and Frances 1985).

The main types of dysfunctional personality patterns are termed schizoid, compulsive, histrionic, antisocial, passive-aggressive/passive-dependent, and paranoid.

Schizoid Type

People with schizoid personality disorders have problems with relationships, tend to withdraw from others, and are frequently seen as loners. Despite this behavior pattern, such persons may be very aware of their intense need for others and may fear that if their needs are expressed they will overwhelm and hurt other people. They maintain a distance to protect themselves and others from being hurt. This style is often thought to be a way of avoiding homosexual impulses, as relations with the opposite sex are frightening. These clients often have a childhood history of poor relations with distant or cruel parents; they have essentially given up hope of love and caring.

Because of their hunger for a satisfactory relationship, these clients may be quick to form relationships with helping persons. They are frequently hypersensitive to rejection and have fragile defenses. The nurse must be aware of both their need for human contact and their need for distance from others. These clients should not be allowed to develop a dependency on one practitioner but should be exposed to a variety of clinicians. In some cases, group therapy may be most helpful.

Compulsive Type

Compulsive individuals are usually meticulous, conscientious, disciplined, and reliable. Because of the many pressures generated within, they tend to be relatively inflexible. If they are fortunate enough to have an appropriate job, they may function quite well, but adaptation to change is difficult. The conflict for these clients centers on control and aggression, which are dispelled by obsessive-compulsive activity. Often there are underlying fears of aggression, which the client is afraid of expressing. The childhood history may show authoritarian and rigid parents. Treatment should focus on helping clients to deal with their fears of closeness and aggression as well as to reduce some of the self-induced stresses. In addition, clients should be assisted in regaining some control over their environment by appropriate verbal interaction.

Histrionic Type

Histrionic persons tend to be emotional and flamboyant with an appearance of seductiveness, which is actually competition with the opposite sex. In women, the origin may be a wish to have the power that men possess, and in men, there may be a wish to be cared for. These persons frequently have difficulty in mixed groups because they become competitive with persons of the same sex and seductive to persons of the opposite sex. The sexual behavior is usually deceptive, since it is actually a way of asking to be cared for.

Treatment should aim at reducing the self-destructive nature of the behavior and encouraging the development of the person's potential. Clients should be assisted to reduce the affective and emotional intensity of their behavior. Female nurses can help by providing nurturing responses in competitive situations, whereas male nurses can help by providing caring, nonsexual responses.

Antisocial Type

The person with an antisocial personality often manifests abnormal behavior that is in violation of laws, mores, and customs. Lacking a conscience, the antisocial person seeks immediate gratification of his needs, is unable to tolerate delays or frustration, and is unable to postpone pleasure. Many of these people may appear quite charming in order to get their needs met. A comprehensive history often reveals ambivalent or inconsistent parenting in childhood.

Such people usually lack a sense of loyalty or concern for others and have little ability to maintain close and lasting relationships. Because they lack anxiety or guilt feelings and do not learn from experience, punishment is rarely effective. The criminal who returns to prison repeatedly is an example of this personality style.

These persons frequently have poor school and work records because of their inability to conform to standards and relate to authority figures. Promiscuous sexual behavior with a variety of partners (who mean little to them), as well as socially unacceptable activities are frequently seen. In many instances, the problems are compounded by abuse of alcohol and drugs.

Treatment focuses on helping clients to take more responsibility for their own behavior and to realize that their problems come from within themselves.

Passive-Aggressive/Passive-Dependent Type

For individuals with passive-aggressive or passive-dependent personality disorders, the prominent trait may be either aggression or dependency that is expressed indirectly. Passive persons of either type are subject to depression if their needs are not met. The cause of these disorders may be inadequate mothering, as in schizoid disorders, but whereas the schizoid has given up hope of love, the

---

DIAGNOSTIC SEXUAL BIAS CONTROVERSY

Since both dependent and histrionic disorders are diagnosed more frequently in women than in men, it has been argued that this occurs because of a sex bias in the diagnostic criteria. "Symptoms" of each disorder are commonly seen in normal women, but they may be deemed symptomatic of a personality disorder because of the masculine bias about what is healthy. Women who conform to their sex role stereotype may be inappropriately labeled as disordered. It can be argued that men express dependency in equally pathological ways, such as overreliance on others to maintain home and children.

Opponents of this view respond that there are some personality disorders more commonly seen in men—antisocial and compulsive. Because personality disorders are exaggerations of common personality traits, it is not surprising that women exaggerate stereotypic feminine traits and men exaggerate stereotypic masculine traits.

Clinicians should be cognizant of a possible sex bias in diagnosis and treatment because it is not clear when a behavior conforms too much or too little to a sex role and when it should be considered pathological. Feminist therapy and feminist consciousness-raising groups should be considered for dependent women struggling not only with personal conflicts but with a sex role stereotype as well.

SOURCE: Widiger and Frances (1985).

passive-aggressive/passive-dependent person has not. He tends to search for the person who will meet all his needs, but since his needs are insatiable, the search is doomed to failure.

Masochism is often a factor in this personality structure. Masochists derive pleasure from being the victim and behave in ways that will increase the chances of their own exploitation. Many times they will hurt themselves in order to hurt others.

Treatment should be aimed at identifying underlying dependency needs and uncovering underlying aggression. Passive-dependent clients are unaware of their underlying anger and see themselves as good and kind. Therapy should focus on self-responsibility. Group therapy is often the treatment of choice. Passive-aggressive individuals often have conflicts with authority. They need to be encouraged to express their needs directly to obtain what they want.

Paranoid Type

Persons with paranoid personality disorders are usually hypersensitive, rigid, suspicious, jealous, envious, and excessively self-important. They tend to project their inadequacies onto others and to blame them for their own difficulties. The interpersonal relationships of these individuals are extremely disturbed, and they are in constant conflict with friends, spouses, and people in positions of authority. The paranoid personality disorder may be a residual or latent schizophrenic process. People with paranoid personalities may be shy and reclusive or aggressive and outwardly hostile. They expend a great deal of energy in searching for clues to confirm their suspicions. They are extremely sensitive to slight rejections and inadvertent oversights.

Treatment should be aimed at strengthening self-confidence, improving reality testing, and increasing a sense of security. The client's sense of autonomy should be fostered whenever possible and freedom of choice given when feasible.

General Nursing Approaches

Treatment of clients with personality disorders is difficult since they experience relatively little discomfort. Confrontation is necessary, but since interpersonal skills are poor, the confrontation must be carefully timed. It is difficult to get these clients to accept treatment, and they frequently drop out before any progress can be made. Group treatment is often effective.

Many clients instinctively resolve their own difficulties by choosing a mate who is complementary to them. For example, the passive-aggressive individual may choose a masochistic partner, or the obsessive-compulsive individual may find a hysterical partner.

It is often helpful to these clients to trace the course of their interpersonal difficulties rather than merely identifying the dysfunctional patterns.

RELATIONSHIP VARIATIONS AND DISRUPTIONS: BORDERLINE CONDITIONS

The concept of the borderline personality has been described and labeled in a variety of ways since the early 1900s. At the turn of the century, the term *borderline* was used to refer to a group of individuals considered to be enemies of society and criminal personalities whose pathology was secondary to a degenerative hereditary process. Today the term refers to clients who are psychiatrically ill but who are not suffering from psychotic or neurotic disturbances.

One framework for understanding the borderline client is based on object relations theory (Kernberg 1967). A normal infant passes through four stages to develop an integrated mental representation of self and others: (1) the infant and mother (self and object) are undifferentiated in the child's mind (this occurs during the first month of life); (2) the infant imagines two dyads to be coexistent, the good self and the good mother, and the bad self and the bad mother (there is no differentiation between self and mother—only between good and bad); (3) the emerging differentiation of infant from mother when the infant begins to imagine her self as separate from her mother and (4) the integration of the good and bad self into the beginnings of a self concept. Objects and self are no longer all good or all bad but are an integration of both.

The borderline client was thought to be arrested in the third stage, which resulted in a relatively sound ability to differentiate inner from outer reality but a failure to integrate good and bad mental representations of self and others.

The primitive defense mechanisms noted in the borderline client all function to preserve the all-good and all-bad view of the world. Splitting is the primary characteristic of the personality organization. The world is seen in a series of all or none, black or white encounters. Significant individuals are either overvalued or undervalued. If the manifestations of the splitting operation are not recognized by a treatment team, internal strife and nontherapeutic interactions can result. This concept is discussed further under Nursing Approaches.

Projective identification is also used, in which the client sees others as being aggressive when in fact he is only projecting his own aggressive feelings onto others.

A biogenic framework (Davis and Akiskal 1986) suggests that endorphins play a major role in separation-attachment behaviors; early object loss may lead to a disturbance in endorphin function that results in long-term behavior disorders.

Behaviorally, according to the DSM-III-R, the individual with a borderline personality disorder displays unstable and intense interpersonal relationships, impulsivity and unpredictability, inappropriate anger, identity disturbance, affective instability, intolerance of being alone, chronic feelings of emptiness, and self-destructive threats/behaviors.

Assessment

Borderline clients are often bright, verbal people who present a variety of physical and emotional symptoms. These are individuals with almost no sense of who they really are or what they are feeling; there is no sense of personal consistency or cohesiveness. The self is experienced as a series of loose collections of parts rather than an integrated whole.

Persons with borderline personalities do not become psychotic as schizophrenic clients do and do not develop a fixed delusional system. They rarely withdraw from interpersonal contact because they cannot bear to be alone for long. Psychotic episodes are usually precipitated by interpersonal stress or drug use.

These clients often pretend to have an identity and feelings and are continually drawn into intense interpersonal relationships that are unstable and unsatisfying. Because they are so uncertain of others, clients' relationships tend to be either highly dependent and clinging or very distant and cold. Clients may have long-standing relationships but demonstrate almost no understanding of the partners' feelings or motivations. A striking characteristic of these clients is their way of perceiving other people as either all good or all bad; this perception can also be suddenly reversed without warning and can be disconcerting to health care providers.

Borderline clients sometimes present with what appears to be a variety of neurotic symptoms, such as anxiety, phobias, hysteria, or obsessive-compulsive phenomenon, but while the neurotic client usually has one predominant symptom, borderline clients present with multiple symptoms as well as a history of brief psychotic episodes. Several physical complaints without an organic basis that may be quite disabling may also be present.

Depression is quite common. In addition to the guilt and sense of wrongdoing that are present in neurotic and psychotic depression, these clients feel empty and isolated. They are also subject to a particularly intense anxiety that is pervasive, omnipresent, and overwhelming—a symptom called pananxiety.

Anger is about the only emotion that these clients can feel without pretending. They have a great deal of rage in reaction to real or perceived emotional deprivation in childhood. These clients are often irritable and critical, demanding special treatment. In reality, their emotional needs are almost insatiable, and they cannot adequately define them. They often act in self-defeating ways as a result of their insecurity, immaturity, and hopelessness.

Because of their depression and anxiety, the act which draws clients into treatment may be a suicidal gesture or attempt. In some cases, the gesture may have nothing to do with dying but is a deliberately inflicted painful injury in a desperate attempt to feel something, to prove that they exist (Charry 1983).

Self-mutilation is an extremely self-destructive act that is not uncommon among certain populations in the psychiatric setting. Two major manifestations have been identified. The first is severe, bizarre, and grotesque, such as self-enucleation or autocastration that is seen in clients suffering from schizophreniform disorders. This type is usually associated with psychotic symptoms such as delusional thinking and hallucinations. The other type, which is more common, consists of superficial slashing of the body, usually the extremities. The client who does this type of mutilation tends to have symptoms which fit the category of borderline personality disorder. Self-destructive acts are an important criteria for the disorder in DSM-III-R (Schaffer et al. 1982).

Treatment Approaches

Because the term *borderline* encompasses a wide and diverse group of clients, many of whom have additional diagnoses, the types of treatments vary as well.

PSYCHOTHERAPY Individual psychotherapy with the borderline client aims at increasing the capacity of the ego to resist regression, to tolerate frustration, delay gratification, control impulses, and to bear painful affective states. Efforts are made to assist the client in conflict resolution and to deal with ambivalence.

A frequent aspect of therapy with these clients is the swift and sudden emergence of intense transference reactions, both positive and negative. It is important to insist on a consistent and thorough interpretation of the negative transference and the clients' tendencies to act out. Some clients form a negative therapeutic reaction; for these clients, pleasure in defeating the treatment efforts by not getting well is so rewarding that it overcomes the pleasure of getting better.

Another problem encountered in therapy is the development of intense countertransference situations. At times the clients find ways of provoking what is really a sadomasochistic struggle in which they induce the therapist to assault them through confrontation as they persistently deny understanding what is happening. The clients' constant projection of distorted internal objects and their insistance that the therapist conform to these projections produces considerable stress for the therapist (Egan 1986).

PHARMOTHERAPY For borderline personality disorder clients, there is no single drug treatment, but some medications may be useful to treat certain symptoms. When the main feature is emotional lability, neuroleptics may be used. When dysphoria is evident, monamine oxidase has been used, and some clients respond to tricyclic antidepressants. Minor tranquilizers are given if the primary symptom is anxiety. Lithium has been tried to treat emotional instability, with inconsistent results (Davis and Akiskal 1986).

BEHAVIOR THERAPY Several common behavioral patterns are associated with the borderline conditions (Linehan 1987). Borderline clients are emotionally vulnerable, extremely sensitive, and unable to regulate their emotional responses. They tend to oversimplify problem solving and invalidate their affective experiences. Many have learned that extreme emotional displays are necessary to get the help and attention they need. These clients approach problems with a learned helplessness pattern which results in emotional clinging and demanding behaviors, going from problem to problem in a state of "unrelenting crises." Repeated stressful events, along with the inability to fully recover from one event, lead to such emergency behaviors as suicide. Since they cannot control their emotional experiences, clients resort to inhibiting feelings, and are unable to grieve in a healthy manner when necessary. The task of therapy is to help these clients understand their reaction patterns and learn grieving skills and coping strategies needed to accept and recognize their current lives without lost objects. The client's emotional experiences and difficulties must be validated.

Implications for Nursing

Clients with borderline personality disorders have unique characteristics that make inpatient treatment extremely difficult. Since they have an insatiable need for special attention and communicate a sense of entitlement, they often evoke angry reactions from clients and staff alike. They are often negativistic, demanding, self-destructive, and prone to a multitude of acting out behaviors. With their decreased capacity for anxiety, frustration, delay and impulse control, they present with suspicion,

distrust, and a sensitivity to rejection that borders on a true paranoia. The interaction in the therapeutic milieu is often complicated by the complex splitting process between the clients and the hospital social structure, which causes tension and conflict among staff. The interplay among the milieu, individual, family, group, and occupational therapies is essential to foster basic personality change.

The various functions of milieu therapy can be integrated with psychotherapy to restore and enhance socially adaptive skills. The milieu can help the borderline clients counteract the regressive pull and provide experiences in which they can gain behavioral insight. The clients will rapidly get a sense from other clients of what level of acting out will and will not be tolerated. Responsible behavior should be an expectation; both other clients and staff should be actively involved in limit setting. Milieu work is most effective if it focuses on the reality of expectations, the process of decision making and the interactional behaviors and dynamics of the here and now.

Since most borderline clients are enmeshed in a family system that impedes development and makes change difficult, it is important to understand ways in which the family creates and maintains a structure into which the clients must fit.

Family theory attributes borderline development to the structure of roles assigned within a family unit. Family group defenses of splitting and projective identification ascribe good and bad roles to family members. The unspoken ground rule is that independence and separation from the family will dangerously reject family values. Parents enact their own developmental conflicts through their children. Dysfunctional features of these families include restrictiveness from the rest of the world, absense of authority, confusion of parental executive and nurturing roles, blurred boundaries, and irrational forms of thinking and relating. Treatment of clients with borderline personality disorders is much more effective if family therapy is a part of the plan.

Group therapy can provide these clients with a corrective experience and aids in diluting the transference response. Expressions of anger and criticism are facilitated in the group setting and the group can provide an "unfreezing" experience for passive clients by enabling them to identify with both the aggressor and the victim in emotional interchanges in the life of a group.

Because these clients frequently have an insatiable need for special attention, the feedback from the group can help them understand the inappropriateness of their expectations and help them modulate their rage from frustration. Many of these clients have very vulnerable self-esteem and can find the group experience supportive and gratifying if they are able to become significant figures in the life of another person.

The vocational histories of these clients usually reveal severe functional deficits because the work environment becomes fused with the clients' struggle to maintain a self identity that is separate from those with whom they interact. Work patterns are characterized by inconsistency, intense involvement followed by precipitous termination, troubled relationships, and lack of satisfaction with work. They feel hopeless about their abilities and are frightened about their futures. Occupational therapy groups can offer the borderline personality client a milieu that encourages the redirection of behaviors toward functional adaptation (Kaplan 1986).

Because these clients often exhibit regressed behavior and a need to control their course of treatment, the nursing staff must develop consistent plans of care to meet the needs of these clients. Behavioral contracting has been suggested as a process to assist the nurse and the clients to meet the specific goals (McEnany and Tescher 1985, O'Brien et al. 1985). With a treatment contract, both the nurse and the clients are engaged in a mutual task. Roles change from all-good or all-bad mother and child to that of equal adults. Clear, written expectations about the clients' responsibilities establish a concrete reality against which the magical fantasy wish for the all-good mothering can be tested. The goals and responsibilities must be within the scope of the clients' abilities or the resulting frustration will be another stress for the clients. However, if the goals do not present a challenge, there will not be any pressure for change and adaptation.

Structure and close nursing supervision are necessary in behavioral management, as the challenge relating to control is often viewed as threatening to these clients and an opportunity for testing. Contracting with these clients is not a simple, easy approach to care. The nurses using this modality should be well versed in an understanding of the personality disorder and its behavioral manifestations. It is essential that the nurses discriminate in deciding which clients are selected for behavioral contracting. The clients must have the intellectual ability to follow a negotiating process and the motivation to work toward specific goals.

A therapeutic approach to borderline clients must be aimed at minimizing the potential for destructive interplay between the clients' personality structure and the hospital social system. Therapeutic change can occur only when the clients no longer receive the same detrimental messages. The problems that occur in the management of these clients are manifestations of the defense mechanisms of splitting and projective identification. Treatment teams can be torn apart by this structure. In projective identification, the clients project various parts of the self onto the staff. Staff members are accosted outside their level of awareness and they may act like projected parts, reacting in a punishing manner or in an overprotective indulgent way. When the aspects of the clients' feelings are projected on to staff members, some are seen as good and helpful, others as bad and destructive. This is liable to split the treatment team into two groups—those that feel the clients are manipulative and mean and need more structure or punishment and those who feel the clients are in pain and need more attention and understanding. In this situation, team members become distrustful of each other and begin to mimic the patterns of relating that brought the clients to the hospital in the first place.

The extent to which the organizational structure of the treatment team promotes effective functioning is an essential factor in the treatment of borderline clients. Staff members must have a strong sense of connectedness to the team. The team must have a clearly defined philosophy of treatment that is shared by all members and avoids a one-dimensional view of clients. Team members need to meet frequently to discuss planning, evaluate progress and encourage each member to share experiences and attitudes.

Borderline clients are provocative, manipulative, and have an uncanny ability to exaggerate staff members' idiosyncrasies. Unless staff members understand what the clients are doing and how it affects their own emotions, they will not be able to deal with the clients in a therapeutic way. Countertransference should be assumed when staff members have strong emotional reactions that are unlike their usual way of responding (Kaplan 1986). Caring with the borderline client necessitates limit setting and constant awareness by the nurse of her emotional response to the client.

SUMMARY

Conditions that cause relationship variations and disruptions include neurotic and personality disorders as well as borderline conditions. These problems are usually the result of an altered sense of self, in which the individual feels vulnerable, insecure, and inferior.

Clients suffering from neurotic patterns of relatedness have lost control of some aspect of their lives; they are frightened and prone to increasing

(Text continues on page 245.)

C L I N I C A L   E X A M P L E

Stress Disorder

Maria is a 30-year-old ex-army nurse who served two tours of duty in Viet Nam. She is engaged to marry Greg, a 34-year-old respiratory therapist.

Maria grew up in a large metropolitan area, the oldest of four daughters. Because of her position in the family, Maria always assumed a great deal of the responsibility of mothering the younger sisters while her widowed mother worked long hours on a factory assembly line to support the family. Maria did well in school but had few friends because her time was filled with her studies and her home duties.

Because the family consisted of five women essentially on their own, Maria's mother continually worried that some danger would befall the girls and was especially afraid that they would be molested or attacked in their city environment. Consequently, she often spoke to the girls, particularly Maria, about the "evils of men" and the need for caution when they were out of the house. She was also very resistent to dating and male friends for the girls.

Maria did not date in high school and only went on a few group outings in mixed company during her three years in nursing school. After she completed her education, she enlisted in the army and volunteered to serve in Viet Nam. Although the first tour of duty was very difficult for her, she felt compelled to sign on for a second tour because she gained some feelings of satisfaction from helping as she could. She was assigned to the operating room and was exposed to death on a massive scale as well as extensive injuries and mutilation.

During her second tour, when she was on leave in Japan, she was raped by three men who forced her into an alley next to her hotel. Her immediate reaction to the rape was that she had done something wrong and failed her mother by not being careful enough. She told no one of the experience because of her shame.

After completing her service time, Maria returned to the city where her family lived and took a position at one of the metropolitan hospitals. There she met Greg, and despite the protests from her mother, began dating him regularly. Maria and Greg dated throughout the summer and decided to get married after the new year. One night in Greg's apartment, he attempted sexual relations with her. Although she consented at first, she experienced pain when he attempted penetration. After the futile attempt, she

tearfully explained that her reaction was due to her previous experience. Greg was understanding and sympathetic, and he assured her that he would be patient and kind in their sexual relationship.

After their marriage, Maria started having nightmares about events that happened in Viet Nam. She would awaken during the night extremely frightened and look to Greg for comfort. Having little understanding of the situation, Greg began to withdraw and wonder if Maria was losing her mind. Maria, in turn, became more isolated emotionally and was unable to communicate with Greg.

Despite Greg's vow to be patient and understanding in their sexual relations, difficulties continued. Maria was able to tolerate penetration only about 20 percent of the time intercourse was attempted, and there was no enjoyment for her and little for Greg, other than physical release. Greg was becoming irritable, and Maria was expressing feelings of depression. Finally, at Greg's insistence, Maria went to her local mental health center to seek assistance with her sexual problem and her nightmares.

Assessment

The nurse who interviewed Maria saw a slender, attractive young woman who was stylishly dressed and appeared to be quite uncomfortable. She spoke in a quiet voice, almost a monotone, but she maintained good eye contact with the nurse. Although she verbalized feelings of depression, she laughed and smiled frequently when discussing sensitive events. She stated she would like to be able to have sexual intercourse on a regular basis to please her husband. When she talked of her experiences in Viet Nam, she only spoke superficially and appeared emotionally blunted with this content.

Based on the history and assessment interview, the following nursing and psychiatric diagnoses were made:

Nursing Diagnoses

Rape trauma syndrome
(related to being sexually molested)

Sexual dysfunction
(related to her difficulty in responding to sexual intercourse)

Ineffective individual coping
(related to her nightmares and difficulty communicating

Ineffective family coping
(related to the inability of the couple to share feelings and understand each other's problems)

Multiaxial Psychiatric Diagnoses

Axis I	306.01 Functional vaginismus
	309.89 Posttraumatic stress disorder
Axis II	None
Axis III	None
Axis IV	Marital discord, primarily enduring circumstances
	Severity: 3
Axis V	Current GAF: 75
	Highest GAF past year: 80

PLANNING

The treatment team agreed that the plan for Maria should include several modalities. It was generally thought that her difficulties with sexual intercourse were related to the rape she had experienced and had never discussed or worked through, probably compounded by her experiences in Viet Nam. It was felt that Maria might benefit from a women's support rape group to facilitate the expression of feelings surrounding the incident. Relaxation techniques would also be of help. Plans were made for separate and conjoint interviews with Greg to evaluate progress in the relationship. A gynecologic workup was arranged to rule out any organic problems.

IMPLEMENTATION

Maria was assigned to a nurse clinician for a weekly supportive session, relaxation training, and coordination of referrals to appropriate disciplines. The gynecologic examination was negative. Maria proved to be an avid student of relaxation techniques. However, in the group sessions, she was unable to do more than relate the facts of the rape as she remembered them. When speaking in the groups, her affect was quite flat, and she never showed any emotion or dealt with the feelings surrounding the incident in other than an intellectual way. Maria and Greg reported that their sexual relationship was improving as Maria seemed able to relax more and penetration became easier.

After a few months, Maria's nightmares were not decreasing and she began to experience flashbacks at work. She became fearful that her job would be in jeapordy and appealed to her nurse clinician to help her obtain some different treatment, perhaps medication, to deal with the fears. Greg began to distance himself emotionally again and became angry at Maria whenever she would try to discuss the problem.

The treatment team met again to reconsider the plan and decided that a rap group for women veterans might provide more support than the rape group because the experience in Viet Nam could be dealt with in its entirety in the former. The need for couple therapy on a more intensive basis was also apparent.

the rape experience was superimposed on the grotesque encounters in the Viet Nam War. It was necessary to find the appropriate treatment modality that would best meet her needs. The rap group facilitated her ability to talk in a meaningful way about the experiences in Nam, including the rape. Since Greg had little understanding of the problem, he and Maria needed couple therapy to help Maria share her needs and give Greg some insight into her experiences.

EVALUATION

The case of Maria highlights the difficulties in treating a client who has experienced multiple traumatic events without the opportunity to successfully resolve the emotional content surrounding each one. For Maria,

Nursing Diagnoses	Goal	Nursing Actions	Outcome Criteria	Outcome Evaluation
Rape trauma syndrome	Client will resolve feelings and fears related to rape.	Enroll client in women's support rape group.	Client will be able to participate in group, share feelings, and decrease intellectualization.	Client enrolled in group but participation was on a superficial level. Rap group was recommended to free up emotional response.
Sexual dysfunction	Client will be able to participate in sexual intercourse without pain.	Schedule GYN workup to rule out organic problems. Teach relaxation techniques in supportive sessions.	Client will be able to perform intercourse by relaxing and learning to enjoy closeness.	Sexual relationship improved but occurrence of flashbacks caused more distancing.
Ineffective individual coping	Client will cease to have nightmares and flashbacks.	Enroll in rap group.	Client will resolve emotional experiences from Viet Nam.	Client participated more fully in this group. She was able to communicate with the members and deal with her trauma.
Ineffective family coping	Couple will be able to discuss experiences and needs. Husband will understand the Viet Nam experience.	Conjoint session with educational component for husband.	Husband will know the problems with client's experiences. Communication will improve.	Husband gained an understanding of client's trauma and needs. Emotional distancing decreased and he was able to support her when she indicated her distress.

anxiety. The anxiety is usually controlled by the development of behaviors that differ according to the type of neurotic reaction. This anxiety formation can be understood from a variety of theories including psychosexual, psychosocial, and interpersonal models as well as social learning and cognitive theories. Neurotic conditions are classified as anxiety reactions, obsessive-compulsive reactions, posttraumatic stress reactions, phobic reactions, conversions, dissociative, and hypochondriacal reactions.

Personality disorders are life-long behavior patterns that may be schizoid, compulsive, histrionic,

antisocial, passive-aggressive/passive-dependent, or paranoid. Clients who suffer from altered personality patterns are comfortable with their altered relatedness and do not have increased anxiety unless their particular style is threatened. Treatment for these conditions is difficult because clients rarely experience discomfort or a need for change.

Borderline clients have severe deficits in their capacities to love and to work. They are generally dissatisfied with life. Well-defined goals and limit setting are important aspects of treatment.

Review Questions

1. Contrast the clinical picture of a client with a healthy sense of self with that of a client with an altered sense of self.

2. What are the major nursing principles in caring for clients with anxiety disorders?

3. What are the major nursing principles in caring for clients with personality disorders?

4. Describe the differences between neurotic disorders and personality disorders.

5. Discuss the personality deficits that are present in borderline clients.

Research Report

Effects of Relaxation on Anxiety in Children: Implications for Coping with Stress.

Relaxation techniques have been shown to be effective in the adult population for reducing anxiety but little research has been conducted to assess the effect of this technique on children. This study was an attempt to provide information about relaxation as a strategy that may be useful to children for managing stress. Forty-six children were administered a tool that measured anxiety before and after a relaxation training program consisting of ten stories that led the children in muscle relaxation and guided imagery. Anxiety levels decreased after treatment, which indicated that relaxation training has a potential for reducing anxiety in children.

L. L. Lamontagne, K. R. Mason, and J. T. Hepworth. *Nursing Research* 34 (September/October 1985):289–292.

Suggested Annotated Readings

Giovacchini, P. *Psychoanalysis of Character Disorders.* New York: Jason Aronson, 1975.

This volume represents a wide spectrum of clinical interest in the study of psychopathology, in the exploration of developmental and psychological problems and investigation of a variety of object relations. Written from a psychoanalytic framework, the book discusses clinical issues in psychotherapy as applied to cases not usually deemed appropriate for psychoanalytic technique.

Greenberg, S. I. *Neurosis is a Painful Style of Living.* New York: The New American Library, 1971.

This practical book, written simply with a minimum of theoretical and technical terms, explains the process of neurosis and its consequences. The author describes the typical kinds of feelings, reactions, and consequent behaviors that tend to be neurotic. Methods for defusing those forces and for practicing other and more effective modes of response are presented.

Masterson, J. F. *Psychotherapy of the Borderline Adult: A Developmental Approach.* New York: Brunner/Mazel, 1976.

This book presents an object relations theory which becomes the developmental origin of the borderline syndrome and makes effective therapy possible. Supportive therapy as well as reconstructive psychotherapy are presented.

Shapiro, D. *Neurotic Styles.* New York: Basic Books, Inc., 1965.

Four major neurotic styles are outlined as a form or mode of functioning identifiable in an individual by his behavior: obsessive-compulsive, paranoid, hysterical, and impulsive. Ways of thinking, perceiving, experiencing emotion, and modes of subjective experience are applied to the various pathologies.

Wishnie, H. *The Impulsive Personality.* New York: Plenum Press, 1977.

The goal of this book is to present clinical information to support the belief that many of society's allegedly untreatable people can be helped to change their destructive patterns of living. It presents a clear conceptualization of the problem for professionals in health care as well as those in the correction field. The chapters discuss the author's beliefs, experiences, and theoretical understandings. Practical approaches and concepts are presented.

References

Barnett, J. "Cognitive Repair in the Treatment of Neuroses." *Journal of the American Academy of Psychoanalysis* 8 (1980):39–55.

Brody, J. E. "Panic Attacks: The Terror Is Treatable." *The New York Times* (October 19, 1983).

Charry, D. "The Borderline Personality." *Association of Family Practitioners* 3 (1983):195–202.

Casper, E. "Helping Veterans to Get on with Their Lives." *Consultant* 24 (1984):191–203.

Corr, J. "Therapy That Strikes the Panic from the Panic Stricken." *The Philadelphia Enquirer* (November 2, 1986).

Davis, G. C., and H. S. Akiskal. "Descriptive, Biological and Theoretical Aspects of Borderline Personality Disorder." *Hospital and Community Psychiatry* 37 (1986): 685–691.

Dollard, J., and N. Miller. *Personality and Psychiatry*. New York: McGraw-Hill, 1950.

Egan, J. "Etiology and Treatment of Borderline Personality Disorders in Adolescents." *Hospital Community Psychiatry* 37 (1986):613–618.

Eisenhauer, L. A., and M. D. Gerald. *The Nurses' 1984–1985 Guide to Drug Therapy*. Englewood Cliffs, New Jersey: Prentice-Hall, 1984.

Erikson, E. H. *Childhood and Society*. New York: W. W. Norton, 1963.

Feldman, M. P. *Criminal Behavior*. New York: John Wiley & Sons, 1977.

Freedman, A. M., H. E. Kaplan, and B. J. Sadock. *Modern Synopsis of Psychiatry II*. Baltimore: Williams & Wilkins, 1976.

Freud, S. "Analysis of a Phobia in a Five-Year-Old Boy." In *Standard Edition of the Complete Psychological Works of Sigmund Freud*, Vol. 10, London: Hogarth Press, 1955.

Gelfman, M. "The Role of Irresponsibility in Obsessive-Compulsive Neuroses." *Contemporary Psychoanalysis* 7 (1970):36–47.

Goodpastor, W. A., W. M. Pitts, S. Snyder, C. Sajadi, and Q. L. Gustin. "A Social Learning Approach to Group Psychotherapy for Hospitalized DSM-III Borderline Patients." *Journal of Psychiatric Treatment and Evaluation* 5 (1983):331–335.

Greenberg, S. I. *Neurosis is a Painful Style of Living*. New York: Signet Books, 1977.

Hofling, C. K., and M. D. Leininger. *Basic Psychiatric Concepts in Nursing*. Philadelphia: J. B. Lippincott, 1960.

Horney, K. *Neuroses and Human Growth*. New York: W. W. Norton, 1945.

Kaplan, C. A. "The Challenge of Working with Patients Diagnosed as Having Borderline Personality Disorders." *Nursing Clinics of North America* 21 (1986): 429–438.

Kaplan, H. I., A. M. Freedman, and B. J. Sadock. *Comprehensive Textbook of Psychiatry III*, 3d ed. Baltimore: Williams & Wilkins, 1980.

Kernberg, O. "Borderline Personality Organization." *Journal of American Psychoanalytical Association* 15 (1967): 641–685.

Linehan, M. "Dialectical Behavior Therapy for Borderline Personality Disorders." *Bulletin of Menninger Clinic* 51 (1987):261–276.

Luisada, P. V., R. Peele, and E. A. Pillard. "The Hysterical Personality in Men." *American Journal of Psychiatry* 131 (1974):518–522.

McEnany, G. W., and B. E. Tescher. "Contracting for Care." *Journal of Psychosocial Nursing* 23 (1985):11–18.

Mereness, D., and L. J. Karnash. *Essentials of Psychiatric Nursing*. St. Louis: C. V. Mosby, 1966.

O'Brien, P., C. Caldwell, and C. Transeau. "Destroyers: Written Treatment Contracts Can Help Cure Self-Destructive Behaviors of the Borderline Patient." *Journal of Psychosocial Nursing* 23 (1985):19–23.

Parsons, T. *The Social System*. New York: Free Press, 1951.

Pollin, W. G., G. Marlin, A. Hoffer, J. R. Stabeneau, and Z. Hrubee. "Psychopathology in 15,901 Pairs of Veteran Twins." *American Journal of Psychiatry* 126 (1969):597.

Quitkin, F., A. Rifkin, and D. Klein. "Neurologic Soft Signs in Schizophrenia and Character Disorders." *Archives of General Psychiatry* 33 (1976):845.

Saucier, R. P. "Panic Attacks and Generalized Anxiety States." *Nurse Practitioner* 9 (1984):35–37.

Satterfield, J. H., and Centwell, D. P. "Psychopharmacology in the Prevention of Antisocial and Delinquent Behaviors." *International Journal of Mental Health* 1 (1972):227.

Schaffer, C. B., J. Carroll, and S. I. Abramowitz. "Self-Mutilation and the Borderline Personality." *Journal of Nervous and Mental Disease* 170 (1982):468–473.

Scotta, K. J. "Learning to Live as One." *Democrat and Chronicle*. Rochester, New York (March 5, 1988).

Shapiro, D. *Neurotic Styles*. New York: Basic Books, 1965.

Sketetee, G., E. Foa, and J. Grayson. "Recent Advances in the Behavioral Treatment of Obsessive-Compulsives." *Archives of General Psychiatry* 39 (1982):1365–1371.

Smith, T. W., C. R. Ryder, S. C. Perkins. "Anxiety Disorders: America's Leading Mental Health Problem." *AAOHN Journal* 34:42–43.

——. "The Self-Serving Function of Hypochondriacal Complaints." *Journal of Personality and Social Psychology* 44:787–797.

Strain, J. "Hypochondriasis: Keep the Patient and Yourself from Becoming Its Victims." *Consultant* 25 (1985):67–73.

Sullivan, H. S. *The Interpersonal Theory of Psychiatry*. New York: W. W. Norton, 1953.

Talan, J. "Too Many Voices." *Times-Union*, Rochester, New York (September 30, 1985).

Wender, P. H., D. Rosenthal, J. D. Rainer, L. Greenhill, and M. B. Sarlin. "Schizophrenics' Adoptive Parents." *Archives of General Psychiatry* 33 (1976):845.

Widiger, T. A., and A. Frances. "Axis II Personality Disorders: Diagnostic and Treatment Issues." *Hospital and Community Psychiatry* 36 (1985):619–627.

Ziarnowski, A. P. "A Typical Crisis: Delayed Stress Reaction." In *Crisis Counseling*, E. Janosik, ed. Boston: Jones and Bartlett, 1984.

C H A P T E R

10

Adjustment Variations and Disruptions

Learning Objectives

After reading this chapter, the student should be able to:

1. Trace the psychological, physiological, and social variables affecting substance abuse.

2. Discuss the psychological, physiological, and social consequences of alcoholism and drug abuse.

3. Discuss approaches used in the acute toxic phases of alcoholism and drug abuse.

4. Discuss approaches used in long-term rehabilitation for alcohol- and drug-abusing clients.

5. Analyze the role of the nurse during various aspects of care for clients who abuse substances, stressing the importance of objectivity and consistency.

Overview

Throughout history, members of virtually every society have used drugs to change their moods, thoughts, and feelings. Within societies, there have always been individuals who digressed from accepted social customs for use of these potent drugs, employing them as a means of coping with the stresses and problems of existence and rendering them at odds with society's norms and values. As a result, such individuals have developed variations and disruptions of societal adjustment.

Any drug, whether obtained legally or illegally, is subject to misuse. The term "substance abuse" is usually used in connection with drugs that drastically alter levels of consciousness. This chapter describes various factors relating to substance abuse and discusses its causes, treatment, and complications, as well as the application of nursing measures that alleviate substance abuse problems. Because of its widespread use and acceptability in society, alcohol is treated separately from other commonly abused drugs. However, it is important to remember that alcohol is indeed a drug that changes mood, thoughts, and feelings, despite the assertion of some alcoholic clients that they have never used "drugs" in their lives.

DRUG TERMINOLOGY

The term *drug abuse* refers to the use of any drug in a manner that is different from the approved medical or social pattern in a given culture (Jaffee 1983). Because this definition is largely a social one, it is not surprising that there are varying opinions of what constitutes abuse. For example, using a barbiturate to produce sleep is socially acceptable, but using the same drug to produce a feeling of tranquility in a social situation is considered a form of abuse. Similarly, using opiates to relieve pain is acceptable but using them to produce euphoria is not.

Nonmedical drug use is a term that, although nonjudgmental, is so general that it includes everything from occasional drug use to compulsive drug use. Nonmedical use encompasses experimental drug use motivated by curiosity or by conformity to peer pressure, the casual or recreational use of a drug for its pleasurable effects, the circumstantial use of drugs (such as of amphetamines to stay awake while studying), and the intensive use of drugs to an extent commonly thought of as drug abuse.

Compulsive drug use usually results when individuals develop a dependence (psychological or physical) on a drug. Such individuals have less flexibility in their behavior toward a particular drug. Therefore, they continue to take the drug despite adverse medical and social consequences, and they behave as if they need the drug in order to continue to function. If their drug of choice is difficult to obtain, these users become preoccupied with ways to ensure their supply of the drug.

Compulsive drug use is commonly, but not necessarily, associated with the development of tolerance and physical dependence. *Tolerance* occurs when increasingly large doses must be taken to obtain the same effects experienced with original, smaller doses. *Physical dependence* refers to an altered physiological state produced by repeated use of the drug, necessitating continued use to prevent withdrawal effects. *Withdrawal symptoms* are physical disturbances that result when the person stops taking the drug. Withdrawal symptoms are characterized by rebound effects in the same physiological systems initially depressed by the drug. For example, amphetamines act to alleviate fatigue, suppress appetite, and elevate mood; thus, amphetamine withdrawal brings a reactive lack of energy, hyperphagia, and depression.

Psychological dependence can occur with all drugs of abuse. With psychological dependence, the user feels he needs the drug in order to reach a maximum level of functioning or well-being, regardless of whether he is physically dependent on the drug.

"Addiction" was previously associated almost exclusively with drug use but is now commonly applied to a variety of behaviors, from playing tennis to reading *The New York Times*. In this chapter, *addiction* refers to a behavioral pattern of drug use characterized by an overwhelming preoccupation with the compulsive use of a drug, the securing of a supply, and a tendency to readdiction after withdrawal. "Addiction" cannot be used interchangeably with "physical dependence" because it is possible to be physically dependent on a drug without being addicted. For example, it is possible to experience withdrawal symptoms after therapeutic doses of morphine given four times a day for as short a period as two to three days. Yet people in this situation are not addicted to the drug and have no psychological craving once the physical condition that dictated the use of morphine is alleviated. Similarly, a large number of men who served in Viet Nam used heroin regularly, but only about half became addicted; the rest simply stopped using heroin without any special treatment.

Cross-addiction refers to the ability of one drug to suppress the manifestations of physical dependence produced by another drug and to maintain the physically dependent state. For example, alcohol can suppress the symptoms of barbiturate withdrawal and barbiturates can suppress the effects of alcohol withdrawal. Many alcoholics attempt to maintain sobriety by using marijuana, Librium, or Valium as a substitute for alcohol.

NURSING ATTITUDES

Nurses working with clients who are alcohol and drug abusers need to be aware of their own attitudes toward addiction and addicts. As the roles and functions of nurses expand, they will have increased exposure to such clients. Stereotyped pictures of the addict have influenced public attitudes for many years. Nurses, although they have chosen a helping profession, are not immune to the influence of such negative stereotypes. Clients are able to intuitively sense negative attitudes and an air of moral superiority on the part of nurses. A therapeutic atmosphere can be established only if nurses are nonjudgmental and accepting of clients. This accepting attitude is not possible unless nurses examine their own attitudes and values regarding drug abuse and drug abusers.

Alcohol and drug abusers are extremely difficult clients to work with. Several factors contribute to this difficulty. Drug abusers tend to be skilled at manipulation, and they use flattery and ingenuity to get their needs met. The highly seductive tactics of the drug addict can be ego-enhancing for the nurse, who then becomes discouraged when seductiveness is withdrawn or demands become insatiable. Intermittent relapse may be a frustration for nurses working with a "revolving door" client who seems unable to change or to utilize treatment. Such behavior often causes nurses to become disappointed and angry. Although most nurses profess to believe that addiction is a disease, many still carry an underlying attitude that drug-abusing clients could stop their behavior if only they persevered. However, this attitude is as unrealistic as expecting clients to stop having diabetes or cancer if only they choose to do so.

Dealing with addictive clients can be a challenging and rewarding experience for caregivers who are able to monitor their own feelings and accept their clients as people in need of help. Frustration can be kept to a minimum by maintaining realistic expectations and by goal setting. The nurse must realize that the client may have been an abuser for years; expecting to reverse the process within a short time would not only be frustrating for the nurse but would also lead to inadequate treatment planning for the client.

PREVALENCE OF ALCOHOL USE AND ABUSE

Alcoholism is a problem of enormous proportion. More than two thirds of Americans drink more than just occasionally. The peak years of alcohol consumption are between the ages of 16 and 25, gradually decreasing thereafter. At any stage of life, the chances of becoming a person who consumes alcohol (not necessarily an alcoholic client) are highest for people with greater education and higher socioeconomic status. The average American consumes 2.7 gallons of absolute alcohol per year, spending billions of dollars that represent almost 3 percent of total personal expenditures (Schuckit 1979).

Recent statistics indicate that alcohol addiction alters the lives of 70 million Americans. An estimated 14 million are victims of alcoholism and 56 million people are directly affected by them. Alcohol-related disease accounts for 30 to 50% of all hospital admissions (Frank 1985).

USE AND ABUSE OF ALCOHOL

Alcohol has been around for a long time—evidence of wine and beer drinking has been found in archeologic records of the oldest civilizations. Early on, humans learned that fruits and grains could be fermented to become beverages with mood-changing effects. Alcohol soon became an integral part of religious rituals and offerings. It replaced fluids such as water or milk and honey because it was more suitable for evoking the moods of release, mystification, and ecstasy that were essential for communicating with invisible powers. The role of alcohol in religious ceremonies tended to give an aura of sanctity and solemnity to its use, and it became mandatory in worship, magic, and festivals.

The attitudes of Americans toward alcohol abuse have been ambiguous (Smithers Foundation 1968). The alcoholic person has often been an object of scorn and derision. In religious thinking, the drinker has been considered a sinner; in social and economic thinking, the problem drinker has been considered useless and hopeless.

Even in the early days of the nation, widespread use of alcohol caused civic leaders concern. In particular, Benjamin Rush, a signer of the Declaration of Independence and surgeon general of the Continental Army, was the first American to call the intemperate use of spirits a "disease." Worries about the effects of alcohol abuse laid the foundation for the temperance movement, which began around 1850 and was led by the Antisaloon League and the Women's Christian Temperance Union (WCTU). Their campaign resulted in the eighteenth Amendment to the Constitution, adopted in 1919, which imposed nationwide Prohibition.

Paradoxically, the era of Prohibition made drinking fashionable. Speakeasies were open to men and women, and for the first time women could drink hard spirits in public places. After thirteen years of a national trial, Prohibition was repealed. One reason for the success of the repeal movement may have been a growing feeling among Americans that they had the right to choose their own behavior. In the years since Prohibition, the proportion of drinkers has steadily increased, but attitudes toward alcoholic individuals have been slow to change.

During the 1940s, a small group of persons who openly admitted to their problem joined together in an effort to remain sober and to help others to do so. This program, which centered around the concept that alcoholism is a disease, became known as Alcoholics Anonymous (AA). Since then, AA has grown to include several thousand groups functioning in 90 countries.

Also during the 1940s, medical and scientific articles dealing with the idea of alcoholism as a disease began to appear with regularity in newspapers and magazines. Local committees composed of private citizens and professional people were formed to discuss the problems of alcoholism. These committees later became the National Council on Alcoholism. By the 1960s the concept of alcoholism as an illness had been accepted by many professionals. E.M. Jellinek, coordinator of the Yale Center of Alcohol Studies, conducted extensive research on alcoholism and published his book *The Disease Concept of Alcoholism* (1960), which has become a classic reference in the field. His classification system for alcoholism is discussed in the following section.

Classification and Diagnosis of Alcoholism

Opinions of what constitutes the disease alcoholism are diverse. One of the most widely accepted definitions is that given by the National Institute of Mental Health (1968):

Alcoholism is a chronic disease, a disorder of behavior characterized by the repeated drinking of alcoholic beverages to an extent that exceeds customary dietary use or ordinary compliance with the social drinking customs of the community, and which interferes with the drinker's health, interpersonal relations, or economic functioning.

Jellinek (1960) divided people suffering from alcoholism into five major categories: (1) alpha alcoholism—a purely psychological continual dependence or reliance on the effect of alcohol to relieve bodily or emotional pain, (2) beta alcoholism—a type in which complications may occur without physical or psychological dependence, (3) gamma alcoholism—a type which involves tissue tolerance to alcohol, adaptive cell metabolism, withdrawal, and craving, (4) delta alcoholism—a type like gamma but involving inability to abstain rather than loss of control, and (5) epsilon—a periodic type, also known as binge drinking.

In another type of classification, Freedman, Kaplan, and Sadock (1976) described alcoholic clients as either reactive or addictive. The reactive alcoholic client becomes preoccupied with alcohol whenever she feels overwhelmed by external stress. In contrast, the addictive alcoholic client is often preoccupied with alcohol from the first experience and drinks without apparent reason.

Other typologies have also been used, but those that we have described here are adequate to show the diversity involved in definition and classification of alcoholism. In this chapter, the term *alcoholic client* is used to describe those persons who have variations and disruptions of adjustment to society as a result of alcohol abuse. It should be kept in mind, however, that the label "alcoholic client" should not be used pejoratively or as a means of stereotyping.

Abuse is defined as a pattern of pathological use for at least one month and impairment in social or occupational functioning. Dependence indicates the presence of tolerance or withdrawal symptoms. Both nursing diagnoses and the multiaxial psychiatric diagnoses are important in the nursing approach to the alcoholic client. Alcoholism causes clinical symptoms that are not attributable to any other psychiatric diagnoses. Personality disorders frequently accompany alcoholism. Axis V can be particularly useful in defining variations in functioning: for example, the client may currently be drinking heavily but may have had long periods of sobriety during which functioning was adequate.

CAUSES OF ALCOHOLISM

Physiological Theories

Alcoholism has long been known to be prevalent in certain families. The Greek philosopher Aristotle declared that drunken women brought forth children like themselves. During the so-called gin epidemic in eighteenth century England, the notion that alcoholism was not only familial but hereditary enjoyed a sizable acceptance, causing many people to denounce the consumption of spirits on the grounds that it engendered alcoholism in the offspring (Warner and Rosett 1975). Later explanations favored the idea of genetic mutation—that exposure of the sperm or ovum to alcohol caused changes leading to the development of alcoholism in the offspring. Eventually, the heredity and mutation theories were discarded in favor of the idea that alcoholism was the result of poor upbringing and crowded living conditions. In the past few years, however, the possibility of heredity as a factor in alcoholism has received renewed attention.

Family studies have consistently found a high prevalence of alcoholism among relatives of alcoholic clients, and twin studies have demonstrated that identical twins share a similar incidence of alcoholism more often than fraternal twins (Goodwin 1979, 1982). Although studies continue to indicate a familial relationship in alcoholism, more research is needed to isolate the biological from the environmental factors before addressing the question of how alcoholism is transmitted.

Research efforts are providing increased evidence that the disease of alcoholism is biologically determined rather than caused by psychological problems. In 1979, Mendelson and Mello reported that biological factors were thought to protect some individuals against the development of alcoholism. Many persons of the oriental races, for example, have an enhanced sensitivity to the effects of alcohol; that is, they experience flushing, abdominal discomfort, muscle weakness, tachycardia, and decreased blood pressure even with small doses of alcohol. Such sensitivity may guard the individual from progressing to alcoholism because the uncomfortable effects are felt sooner, before physiological damage can be done.

These researchers also determined that alcoholism is more prevalent in certain racial and ethnic groups than in the general population; it has therefore been suggested that people in these groups metabolize alcohol differently. Results from various studies have been conflicting; varying rates of alcoholism have been found in all races and ethnic groups.

Currently it is believed that people with alcoholism do not metabolize alcohol properly and some people may be born with a faulty liver enzyme system that can lead to addiction. Preliminary tests have indicated that this malfunctioning enzyme system precedes the development of alcoholism and might be used to predict a predisposition to the disease (Frank 1985). The new knowledge of biochemistry of alcoholism is being applied through use of nutrition therapy to repair the liver and amino acid supplements to correct enzyme imbalances. Many experts now agree that the deep psychological problems often characteristic of the alcoholic client are a consequence rather than a cause of the disease.

DSM-III-R AXIS I
DIAGNOSTIC CLASSIFICATION

DSM-III-R classifies alcohol problems under Psychoactive Substance Use Disorders and Psychoactive Substance-Induced Organic Mental Disorders

303.90	Alcohol dependence
305.00	Alcohol abuse
303.00	Alcohol intoxification
291.40	Alcohol idiosyncratic intoxication
291.80	Uncomplicated alcohol withdrawal
291.00	Alcohol withdrawal delerium
291.30	Alcohol hallucinosis
291.10	Alcohol amnestic disorder
291.20	Dementia associated with alcoholism

Sociocultural Theories

The consumption of alcohol is a common occurrence in almost every culture and society. However, the amount used is determined by the norms and regulations for the use of alcohol. Most cultural norms are based on the ideas that (1) alcohol is a drug that causes loss of control, (2) people are permitted to relax social and personal control under the influence of alcohol, and (3) alcohol abuse is associated with undesirable behavior (Jessor, et al. 1968). Through society's reactions to their drinking behavior, alcoholic clients become publicly labeled as deviants and are forced by that society to live a deviant lifestyle. Merton (1957) proposed that alcoholic clients' deviant behavior was affected by the discrepancy between the prevalent goals in a society and the means of achieving these goals; for example, the American Dream of success and happiness is, in reality, far out of reach for many people. Failure to achieve this dream is a reality harsh enough to cause some individuals to escape by drinking to excess.

Psychological Theories

Psychological approaches to alcoholism generally assume that it is a symptom of an underlying personality or emotional disorder.

PSYCHOANALYTIC THEORY Freud thought that alcohol allowed the expression of repressed urges because of its ability to release inhibition. He hypothesized that these repressed tendencies—including oral dependency and latent homosexuality—developed in childhood because of problems in the parent-child relationship (McCord and McCord 1960). Otto Fenichel (1945) maintained that alcoholic clients were passive, dependent, narcissistic people who used their mouths as a primary means of achieving gratification. Karl Menninger (1938) placed greater emphasis on the self-destructive tendencies of alcohol abuse, asserting that people abused alcohol for oral gratification and self-punishment because of anger against their parents, thereby accomplishing a symbolic revenge. Others have postulated that alcoholism is a striving for power to compensate for feelings of inferiority and to bolster feelings of self-esteem (McCord and McCord 1960). Psychoanalytic theories are difficult to test and are therefore inconclusive, but these ideas have continued to be used in the treatment of alcoholic clients, often with limited success.

PERSONALITY TRAIT THEORIES The search for an "alcoholic personality" has been the object of much research but has failed to find a single personality structure that can be described as *the* alcoholic personality. What have been identified instead are a variety of personality patterns or traits that have been associated with alcohol abuse. The most significant of these are (Burkhalter 1975):

1. *Dependency-independency.* A predominant personality characteristic of the alcoholic is a conflict between the need to be dependent and the need to be independent, with dependency being most apparent. Because the alcoholic is unable to confront the conflict, he represses either his independent or his dependent needs to avoid the conflict. The desire to assert the repressed needs serves only to increase the desire for relief, which alcohol can provide. Since the conflict remains unresolved, a pattern becomes established and the need for alcohol is maintained.

2. *Anger and frustration.* Anger and frustration are often the result of strong dependency needs. Anger often arises from the inability to express feelings of worthlessness, failure, and inadequacy; alcohol allows the expression of this anger and serves as an excuse for the angry behavior. Also characteristic of many alcoholics is a low tolerance for frustration. The frustration caused by the inability to cope with daily stress is often the stimulus that leads to continued drinking.

3. *Feelings of omnipotence.* The desire to feel powerful and in control of one's destiny is expressed through the alcoholic's search for omnipotence. The feelings of power that can be stimulated by alcohol help to momentarily ease feelings of frustration, guilt, and self-denigration. The basic need to feel important, valued, and respected is in conflict with the alcoholic's behavior; when she begins to sober up and realize this inconsistency, she experiences greater feelings of failure, which act as a motivator to resume drinking.

4. *Depression.* The depression experienced by many alcoholics can be viewed as an initial stimulus to drink (to self-medicate the depression), as the result of excessive drinking when the alcoholic realizes that his relationships with others are changing, or as a reason to continue drinking to decrease and mask the depression. Unfortunately, using alcohol for the relief of depression is self-reinforcing; it fosters the need for relief that alcohol brings, but drinking only increases the depression.

5. *Defense mechanisms.* Denial (and the rationalizations and projections associated with it) is a major defense mechanism used by alcoholics. Most deny that they have a problem controlling their alcohol intake, and many claim that they are not drinking at all. When they begin to suspect that their behavior is changing, they will invent reasons for the behavior and will project blame for their actions onto others who, in their minds, have driven them to drink. These mechanisms allow the alcoholic to continue to drink and to justify the drinking.

Various psychological tests used in an attempt to isolate alcoholic personality traits have met with mixed results. The major difficulty with personality trait theories is that it is still unknown whether the personality traits predate the onset of alcoholism or are a consequence of the alcoholism.

Learning Theories

From the social learning point of view, psychological functioning can be best understood in terms of a continuous, reciprocal interaction between behavior and the conditions of the environment. In this perspective, the behaviors of alcohol use and misuse are considered to be socially acquired through a variety of methods, including vicarious learning, peer and parental modeling, social reinforcement, and the anticipated effects of alcohol as a tension-reducing agent (Donovan and Marlatt 1980). Learning theorists see alcohol ingestion as a reflex response aimed at reducing fear or anxiety. Drinking alcohol reduces tension and replaces this unpleasant feeling with sensations of well-being. Although the pain and discomfort experienced as the result of long-term drinking should appear to serve as punishment and as a deterrent to drinking, the immediate effect of drinking is pleasurable. The alcoholic client goes for the short-term relief, not thinking of the long-term consequences.

Because finding a single cause for alcoholism appears to be unrealistic, most current practitioners use a multifaceted approach to this problem. More research is needed to gain a better understanding of the causes of alcoholism, so that better and more specific treatment interventions can be developed.

ALCOHOLISM IN SUBGROUPS OF THE POPULATION

Although alcoholism is not a disease found predominantly in one particular group, research efforts and descriptive literature have, in the past, focused almost exclusively on the male adult population. Recently there has been increased recognition of the presence of this disease in other groups. Women, children, and older adults are receiving more professional attention and there has been a significant realization of the implication of alcoholism among health care providers. This next section discusses some of the concepts related to these groups.

Women

The incidence of alcoholism among women has been on the rise during most of the twentieth century. Morbidity and mortality associated with alcoholism, such as suicide, death from accidents and cirrhosis, is significantly greater for them than for men (Nathan 1983). The suggestion that the causes of alcohol misuse are different in men from those in women has received some attention in the literature. Drinking in response to stressful events such as death, divorce, and role changes has been emphasized (Beckman 1975, Plant 1980).

One of the greatest concerns about women consuming alcoholic drinks is that they will incur Fetal Alcohol Syndrome (FAS). A safe level of alcohol consumption during pregnancy or a safe time to consume alcohol during pregnancy has not been established. The first trimester is the most vulnerable time for the fetus. Alcohol use during the second trimester is associated with spontaneous abortions and during the third trimester with interference with growth and weight gain (Anderson, Anderson, and Smith 1986).

In addition to the prevalence of FAS, studies of social drinking during pregnancy have shown that alcohol consumption is related to increased incidence of still births, congenital malformations, growth deficiencies, and low activity levels. FAS is preventable and dictates the necessity for professionals to take an active role in influencing the drinking behaviors of their clients. Public education and awareness are essential in an effort to alleviate these occurrences.

Children

The increased use of alcohol by children and teenagers has received much attention in the media as well as in the professional literature. Programs for adolescents that are available include alcohol education in schools, counseling of youths in legal difficulties, and attention to adolescent drunk drivers.

Along with the growth in concern for children who drink, there is an increasing interest in children of alcoholic parents, who need recognition and understanding. In alcoholic families, the trust, affection, and emotional support needed for growing children are limited if not nonexistent. The denial process affects the whole family and can impede the development of reality testing. If the secret of alcoholism is disclosed within the family but not to others, the family sets up rigid and impermeable boundaries to guard the family integrity.

Latency-age children comprise a particularly vulnerable group because they must cope with direct effects of alcohol use on their family as well as deal with an inconsistent environment. They frequently have to learn to discount their own needs in order to fulfill roles that have been abandoned by adults. These children experience significant gaps in growth and development that result from unpredictable and inconsistent parenting which leaves problems in issues of control, trust, dependency, and expression of feelings. They are at high risk for problems and have a difficult time disengaging from the family system and developing constructive peer interactions (Bingham and Bargar 1985).

The Elderly

Alcoholism is as serious a condition in older adults as it is in younger populations, but for a variety of reasons is not recognized as readily. Many complaints that the elderly present are assumed to be secondary to the aging process and are missed as symptoms of alcoholism. Depression, paranoia, and symptoms of organic mental syndrome may be manifestations of heavy alcohol use but are not recognized or treated as such. Many elderly persons also live alone, are retired, and do not come to the attention of health care workers and/or families who might be of assistance in obtaining treatment for them.

The older person who turns to alcohol to find a release from the distresses of aging has only recently drawn public attention. Alcohol use is associated with loneliness and social isolation, which frequently accompany old age. Alcoholic clients who begin drinking later in life should be distinguished from older adults who have been drinking all their lives. Problems for these individuals are more likely to be related to external, situational factors and are therefore easier to confront. The clients who abuse alcohol in response to loneliness need help to develop new relationships and adaptive coping skills.

Caution must be used in treating the elderly alcoholic client with drugs because of the metabolic and circulatory changes associated with aging. Antabuse is not recommended for the elderly because of its possible adverse cardiovascular effects. The aged can be helped by appropriate care, but negative attitudes should be altered toward the elderly person who drinks.

Chemical Dependency among Nurses

Nurses with chemical dependency, along with other professional groups, are becoming the focus of research, treatment, and rehabilitation efforts. Two factors in chemical dependency are identified as attitude and accessibility. Nurses sometimes feel immunized against disease by their profession. Most have difficulty assuming the "sick role" and like to view themselves as being in control of their own problems. Easy accessibility, loosely enforced controlled substance protocols in some facilities give nurses more opportunity to divert drugs. Addiction to drugs and alcohol should be regarded as an occupational hazard in nursing.

Impaired nurses present a dilemma to their colleagues. Nurses bear a moral and legal responsibility for quality care. The nurse who is chemically impaired and is diverting medications from clients for personal use is not only committing theft but is guilty of ethical misconduct. The nurse who is chemically dependent will also have impaired judgment and there exists a real possibility of negligence and gross incompetence. The nurse's behavior becomes suspect by showing slurred speech, chronic tardiness, erratic mood swings. Clients may complain of not receiving pain medication and prescription blanks may be missing. Events, behaviors, and professional performance should be documented. Discovering that a nurse has a drug or alcohol problem isn't difficult but confronting her is. It is important for nurses to help others in facing the illness, seeking treatment, and returning to productive lives. Nursing should "take care of its own" by lobbying for legislation to set up and fund state-wide model programs for addicted nurses and encourage hospitals to start such programs (Lachman 1986).

PHYSIOLOGICAL CONSEQUENCES OF ALCOHOL ABUSE

Heavy alcohol use has been implicated, either directly or indirectly, in a variety of illnesses. Alcoholics are subject to an exceptionally high rate of illness and death; their life span is reduced by as much as ten to twelve years, compared with the general population. Not only do alcohol abuse and alcoholism contribute to many pathologic conditions, but they complicate other illnesses that alcoholics may incur. Many of these alcohol-related conditions can be alleviated or reversed with appropriate treatment.

Alcohol and the Brain

Alcohol produces several syndromes that are the result of damage to brain cells or of the release of longstanding personality disturbances.

Blackouts occur frequently with excessive alcohol use and are an early sign of alcoholism. A person who experiences a blackout cannot remember his activities during a period of time, yet to those around him he appeared outwardly normal during the blackout period. Most frequently, the person cannot remember an evening of drinking by the next day; however, blackouts can extend for longer periods of time. Some alcoholic clients have traveled across the country in a blackout state, unable to recall any of the journey, and finding themselves in a different place several weeks later. The mechanism of blackouts is unclear; explanations range from drug-induced amnesia, to a dissociative reaction, to a means of sustaining a psychological defense.

Pathologic intoxication is a state of agitation and altered consciousness that has a dramatic and sudden onset. Increasing anxiety, aggressiveness, and rage may be accompanied by confusion, disorientation, delusions, and hallucinations. Suicide attempts are common. This state may last from a few moments to a day or more and ends with a long period of sleep. Persons who experience such states may have a high level of anxiety and tension; alcohol provides loss of control and release of aggression.

Delirium tremens (DTs) is an acute psychotic state that follows cessation of drinking. The onset is usually 24 to 72 hours following the last drink. The delirium is usually preceded by restlessness, irritability, tremulousness, and disturbed sleep. Confusion and disorientation as to time and place are common. Other characteristics include visual hallucinations of spiders and snakes, severe agitation, fever, sweating, tachycardia, tachypnea, and seizure activity.

Acute alcoholic hallucinosis usually follows a long drinking bout. In contrast to the visual hallucinations of delirium tremens, this syndrome is characterized by auditory hallucinations, usually of a threatening nature. The alcoholic client is still oriented to time and place and fits the hallucinations into her real environment, creating an elaborate delusional system. After recovery, the person can recall the events and feelings.

Wernicke's syndrome is characterized by clouding of consciousness and paralysis of eye nerves. It is associated with severe deficiency of Vitamin B_1, which occurs because the alcoholic is malnourished. Delirium, memory loss, confabulation, apathy, and ataxia result from neuronal and capillary lesions in the gray matter of the brain stem and in structures in the third and fourth ventricles

Korsakoff's syndrome is characterized by amnesia, falsification of memory, disorientation to time and place, and peripheral neuropathy. It is mainly the result of a deficiency of thiamine and niacin. Memory loss is progressive. A superficial mood of light-heartedness is common.

Alcoholic paranoia is characterized by delusions of jealousy, suspicion, and distrust. Projection is intense. Because alcohol use weakens repression, forbidden impulses may arise that are defended against by an elaborate delusional system. Prognosis is guarded, as symptoms frequently reoccur after treatment.

Alcohol and the Liver

Since the liver is the organ involved with processing alcohol in the body, it is often the most seriously affected by heavy alcohol use. Alcohol does not require digestion but passes directly into the bloodstream through the stomach or intestinal walls. As the alcohol travels through the liver, it is acted upon by enzymes that begin the process of changing alcohol into acetaldehyde. The acetaldehyde then breaks down into acetate (which can be used for energy), carbon dioxide, and water. A small part of the alcohol (10 percent) is eliminated by the kidneys, lungs, and sweat glands. Because the majority of alcohol is processed by the liver and there is no mechanism to adjust the rate of metabolism, the liver can be severely damaged by alcohol. Blood lactic acid is increased, which slows the excretion of uric acid by the kidneys and may give rise to symptoms of gout (Leiber et al. 1962). In addition, red blood cells in the capillaries tend to clump, which may result in inefficient oxygen transport to body cells (Moskow, Pennington, and Knisely 1968).

Alcohol metabolism releases excess hydrogen in the liver, which inhibits certain metabolic functions important to producing energy. Energy is produced by burning hydrogen rather than fatty acids, and the unburned fats become deposited in the liver. This accumulation of fat ("fatty liver") is the first liver dysfunction caused by alcohol. It has few consequences and is usually reversible if alcohol intake stops.

Alcohol hepatitis is an inflammatory liver disorder that usually follows years of heavy alcohol abuse. It is characterized by fever, increased white blood cell count, pain in the upper abdomen, and jaundice. While it may recede if drinking stops, it often progresses to cirrhosis despite decreased intake.

Alcoholic cirrhosis, which occurs in about 10 percent of alcoholics, is a scarring of the liver. The scarring of the small veins in the liver causes narrowing and distortion of liver tissue by impairing circulation, which in turn leads to hypertension in the veins feeding the liver, often seen as esophageal varicies. If drinking continues, the person may die from hepatic failure or as the result of hemorrhage from portal hypertension. In some cases cancer of the liver may develop.

Alcohol and the Gastrointestinal Tract

The effects of alcohol on parts of the gastrointestinal system other than the liver have not been studied as extensively, but it is known that alcohol stimulates acid production in the stomach, which damages the stomach lining and causes gastritis and gastric ulcers. Malabsorption of vitamins such as thiamine, folic acid, and vitamin B_{12} may occur in the small intestine. Alcoholism is also associated with pancreatitis and pancreatic insufficiency.

Malnutrition is a common disorder in alcoholics because the alcohol itself represents a source of calories, reducing the appetite for food to fulfill caloric needs. Because alcoholic beverages provide "empty calories," the drinker has a deficient intake of protein, vitamins, minerals, and other nutrients. In addition, heavy alcohol intake can interfere with the process of food digestion and absorption.

Alcohol and the Heart

Long-term alcohol abuse can lead to *alcoholic cardiomyopathy*, with slow or sudden onset of left- and right-sided congestive failure. Manifestations include an enlarged heart, distended neck veins, narrow pulse pressure, elevated diastolic pressure, and peripheral edema. Significant EKG changes occur, tachycardia is common, and there may be episodes of atrial fibrillation.

Alcohol and the Muscles

Alcohol use affects the muscle system in three forms: subclinical myopathy, acute alcoholic myopathy, and clinical alcoholic myopathy. In the subclinical variety, there is an increase in the enzyme creatine phosphokinase (CPK) in the blood serum and a diminished rise of lactic acid in the blood after ischemic exercise. Acute myopathy is characterized by episodes of sudden muscle cramps in the extremities. The most severe form brings myoglobinuria, a concentration of muscle pigment in the urine; it is manifested by severe, painful swelling of involved muscles and by pronounced weakness. If alcohol use is discontinued, recovery usually follows, but the myoglobinuria may precipitate renal failure. With a history of prolonged alcoholism, chronic myopathy may develop, bringing weakness and atrophy, particularly to the muscles of the legs.

Alcohol and the Endocrine System

When alcohol is ingested repeatedly, the sensitive endocrine system is forced to adapt to maintain the body's internal balance. Although experimental data have been inconclusive, alcohol appears to affect the hypothalamic-pituitary-adrenal axis, causing adrenocortical insufficiency. It may also affect aldosterone, which induces retention of sodium, potassium, and chloride and increases the excretion of catecholamines. Alcohol affects urinary excretion by inhibiting the antidiuretic hormone of the pituitary gland.

Researchers have noted similarities between the symptoms of alcoholic clients and clients with endocrine disorders. It has therefore been suggested that failure of the endocrines may be a cause of alcoholism. However, cause and effect can be confused when studying people who already have alcoholism, and conflicting research results leave this theory open to question (U.S. Department of Health, Education and Welfare).

Alcohol and the Reproductive System

The male alcoholic client may experience erection problems that can become permanent if alcohol intake is excessive. Sexual functioning will usually return with abstinence. However, both sexes may have decreased sexual desire with continued alcohol use.

ALCOHOLISM AND THE NURSING PROCESS

Application of the nursing process in dealing with alcoholic clients occurs in two stages: the acute phase and the rehabilitation phase.

Acute Stage

ASSESSMENT When clients are admitted for treatment in an intoxicated state, the nurse must make an assessment in several areas. At this point, the client's physical well-being is of paramount importance, as acute intoxication can be a medical emergency.

A thorough assessment must include several aspects. The presence and severity of withdrawal symptoms must be determined by noting tremulousness, shaking, difficulties with coordination, short attention span, insomnia, hyperactivity, anorexia, and tachycardia. If the client is hallucinating, severe anxiety, disorientation, and DTs can be expected. Nutritional status must be determined by checking for loss of muscle tissue, underweight, and signs of vitamin deficiencies such as gum disease. The fluid balance of the body is assessed by checking skin turgor and moisture, mucous membranes, and the specific gravity of the urine. Circulatory status can be checked by noting edema, pulse arrhythmias, respiratory status, the presence of congestion and purulent sputum, and the warmth and color of the extremities.

Since many people injure themselves easily under the influence of alcohol, the client should be checked for the presence of trauma, including scars, burns, and head injuries. The reaction of the pupils and the strength of the hand grasp should be noted. Mental status is determined by noting the client's orientation to person, place, and time and the stability of this orientation.

Table 10–1. Interventions in the Acute Stage of Alcoholism

Client's Problems	Nursing Interventions
Withdrawal from alcohol	Monitor vital signs; observe closely for signs of convulsions and impending delirium tremens.
Inadequate food and fluid intake	Provide high-protein diet, vitamin and mineral supplements. Record intake and output. Test urine for specific gravity and stool for blood. Encourage fluid intake. If client is not dehydrated, supply according to thirst.
Risk of self-injury	Provide adequate supervision while client is confused and disoriented. Remove potentially harmful items. Allow client to smoke (but not unattended) if this relieves anxiety.
Lack of self-care	Administer personal physical care if client is unable. Explain that this is a temporary measure. Delay unnecessary procedures.
Need for rest and relaxation	Use measures to induce sleep and rest, such as warm showers and darkened rooms. Avoid sudden approaches to client to prevent frightening him or contributing to his hyperactivity.
Increased anxiety	Administer antianxiety drugs as ordered. Do not undersedate, as client has been accustomed to large amounts of alcohol. Explain reasons for all tests and procedures. Provide opportunities for ventilating fear and anger. Continually orient client to reality if confusion, delusions, or hallucinations are present.

PLANNING AND IMPLEMENTATION Potential problems and nursing interventions for these problems are listed in Table 10–1. If the client is experiencing delirium tremens, visitors should be banned, as they may add to the client's confusion and irritation. Siderails and restraints may be necessary to prevent injury. A light should be left on in the room to prevent distortions in perception. Unnecessary stimulation, such as a radio or TV, should be avoided.

It is of primary importance for the nurse to accept the alcoholic client as being worthy of his best possible efforts and to convey a kind, caring, accepting attitude while still maintaining objectivity.

EVALUATION When the client has been successfully detoxified, she will have regained her optimum physical health and will be free of all mood-altering drugs. Once this stage has been reached, the detoxification period has been completed and rehabilitation begins.

Rehabilitation Stage

ASSESSMENT After the client has been successfully detoxified, he needs to be assessed for the appropriateness of entering a rehabilitation program that will facilitate his return to the community. The client must be evaluated as to the degree of insight he has into his problem, his understanding of the disease, and his stage of denial. If the client is not yet recognizing that he has a problem, support will be needed to facilitate this process.

Clients enter rehabilitation programs for a variety of reasons. The amount of motivation for change is a crucial component in the client's recovery. Clients who participate because of external pressure (such as a wife's insistence or a lawyer's encouragement in hopes of reducing a sentence) are usually less motivated to change their behavior.

A thorough drinking history should include any experiences with blackouts, DTs or seizures; previous attempts at treatment and the client's understanding of reasons for failure; degree of depression and any suicidal ideation or suicide attempts; other acting out or violent behavior. Significant events in the past that the client has not yet resolved, such as divorce or death of a loved one, should be explored.

The nurse should assess the presence of support systems in the environment, the attitudes of significant others toward the drinking, the presence of a co-alcoholic or an enabler, and any problems with the law or the employer. It is important for the nurse to determine the role of alcohol in helping the alcoholic client cope. If alcohol abuse serves as an adaptive mechanism, it is easier to understand why the client drinks.

PLANNING AND IMPLEMENTATION Potential problems and suggested nursing interventions for these problems are listed in Table 10–2.

Intervention for rehabilitation of the alcoholic can take place on several levels and from a variety of approaches. Nurses need to be aware of different kinds of treatment not only to participate but to refer clients appropriately.

Intrapsychic Approaches Many professionals treating alcoholics believe that the problem is a result of conscious or unconscious emotional factors. While this assumption is controversial, many experts agree that an important part of any treatment program is fostering trust. Individual therapy is the method of choice for some clients, but there are hazards in this approach. Because the therapeutic relationship tends to be prolonged and intense, the caregiver has to be wary of the client's developing an overwhelming dependency on the therapist. Group therapy is thus often the treatment of choice

Table 10–2. Interventions in the Rehabilitation Stage of Alcoholism

Client's Problems	Nursing Interventions
Denial of illness	Guide client toward acceptance of fact that at least some of the difficulties in her life are due to drinking. Help her realize she must manage her life without alcohol. Confront the use of denial and manipulation to satisfy needs to avoid responsibility for her own behavior.
Lack of understanding of the disease	Educate the client about the disease of alcoholism and its influence, including the psychological, social, and economic effects of alcohol abuse.
Lack of self-esteem	Help the client regain self-respect and confidence by providing tasks that lead to success. Explore areas of competence and ways to broaden interests and complete projects. Verbalize the hope of arresting the alcoholism.
Loneliness	Provide experiences showing that satisfaction and support can be obtained from relating to others. Assist the client to directly verbalize needs and fear of change. Identify ways of preventing or alleviating feelings of loneliness.
Low frustration tolerance	Help the client find alternative methods of relieving tension and anxiety and develop constructive coping skills.
Possibility of relapse	Make appropriate discharge plans to facilitate return to the community. Determine feasibility of plans for the particular client. Inform client of available support systems.

because it dilutes dependency and provides opportunities for confrontation of the alcoholic by his peers. In many instances, alcoholic clients will more readily accept the exposure of denial and game playing from another alcoholic than from a nonalcoholic therapist.

Aversion Therapy Aversion therapy, based on learning theory, is designed to associate a painful experience with alcohol use. The most commonly used technique is administration of the drug disulfiram (Antabuse), which interferes with the metabolism of alcohol and increases the amount of acetaldehyde (a toxic substance) in the blood. Drinking alcohol while taking Antabuse creates a physiological reaction that mimics severe shock, with deep flushing, a rise in blood pressure, difficulty in breathing, and violent vomiting. While the drug has few side effects when taken by abstainers, it can be lethal for clients with certain medical problems who drink while taking the drug. For this reason, Antabuse is not given to individuals with cardiac or kidney problems.

Interpersonal Approaches Interpersonal approaches focus on marital and family dysfunction and their influences on the alcoholic client. In some marriages, the nonalcoholic spouse unconsciously resists the attempts of the alcoholic client to recover because the family dynamics have come to be based on the illness. The spouse has been forced to assume most of the responsibility for the family, and it may be difficult for the spouse to give up some of these responsibilities as his or her partner gains sobriety.

Attention should be given to the life pattern of the alcoholic and to the role that the spouse plays in this pattern. Many partners find themselves contributing to the continuation of problem drinking by inadvertently rescuing the alcoholic and assuming responsibility for the alcoholic's actions. That is, they become "enablers." Others perpetuate the problem because they are more comfortable when the alcoholic is actively drinking—they are in control when the alcoholic is drunk.

Al-Anon and Ala-Teen are organizations available in most communities to help the spouse and children understand the problem and help themselves and the alcoholic person.

Ells (1986) presented a framework for dealing with the alcoholic family based on Bowen's family system theory. Alcoholism creates a destructive pattern of family dynamics that is harmful both to the alcoholic client and family members. The child in the family sees severe conflict between the parents, and witnesses severe dysfunction in one or both of them. As the alcoholism progresses, the nonalcoholic parent is alternatively emotionally out of control or smothers the child with overcloseness. High levels of anxiety and tension are present. The child cannot be a child in a normal sense and cannot negotiate age-appropriate developmental tasks; nor, because of the families closed system, can develop a supportive outside network. The child initially sees himself as a victim or rescuer. This image is fortified by acting out behaviors, withdrawal, underachievement or overachievement, as this coping mechanism becomes inadequate. At times the child abuses alcohol as the teen years pass. Despite the presence of the child's symptom, the spouse of the alcoholic client needs attention.

Therapeutic work is most successful with a family member who is willing to work in therapy. This is usually the spouse, often called the co-alcoholic. The spouse enters treatment after unsuccessfully trying to control the drinking and reaching a point of frustration. To intervene effectively with the spouse, it is necessary to deal with the fusion or undifferentiation of the spouse that is experienced. The spouse should be coached to define a self by using "I" positions in stating beliefs and convictions. The spouse has often begun the process of differentiating of self when seeking treatment, going to Al-Anon and joining support groups. The resulting distancing from the alcoholic client lessen the emotionally fused nature of the relationship and brings some emotional relief. When the spouse begins to distance, the alcoholic client frequently hits bottom and enters treatment.

The spouse often assumes the role of overfunctioner, which helps the alcoholic client to continue to be irresponsible. The spouse needs to be confronted on the issue to relinquish the inappropriate taking on of the alcoholic client's responsibilities.

When working with spouses of alcoholic clients, it frequently becomes apparent that they have cut themselves off emotionally and/or geographically from their families of origin, thus adding to the intensity of emotion and fusion in the alcoholic family. As the spouse learns to recognize patterns of cutoff and the mechanisms used when anxiety rises in the system, relationships and contact with families of origin can be re-established and bring symptomatic relief.

A child is frequently "triangled in" when tension arises, and this child becomes the most dysfunctional child in the family. As the couple experiences disappointment in the relationship, they hope that the child will achieve and provide satisfaction they haven't found through marriage. The first step is to teach the co-alcoholic about triangles and help him or her de-triangle and stay in touch with both other persons in the triangle. Attempts to differentiate a self and define a self while in a triangle are an effective way to reduce marital conflict. Triangulation as a maladaptive family pattern is presented in more detail later in this book in the section "Family Guidelines in Nursing Practice."

Family intervention is a necessary condition for complete recovery of the alcoholic client and the family. The family system is a more powerful force than the addiction itself and can overcome or sustain the alcoholism.

Social Approaches The best example of social and small-group treatment for alcoholic clients is Alcoholics Anonymous. The aim of this organization is to help members maintain their sobriety. Their program is based on twelve steps designed to help the alcoholic client recover. The organization is self-supporting and consists solely of lay people, not members of the helping professions (unless they, too, are alcoholic).

Another form of social therapy for the alcoholic client is community halfway houses designed to fill

THE ROLE OF THE SPOUSE

Spouses who wish to be helpful to their alcoholic partners should be aware of certain factors:

■ Alcoholism is a family disease, and each family member must be involved in treatment to facilitate change.

■ Family members should be educated about the disease of alcoholism.

■ The spouse should stop protecting the alcoholic and allow him to take responsibility for his own behavior.

■ Nagging and pouring out the alcohol will not stop the drinking.

■ Developing a feeling of detachment and independence from the problem will help resolve the spouse's guilt and increase the spouse's sense of self-worth.

■ It may be necessary to create a crisis to get the alcoholic to accept treatment.

the gap between hospitalization and independent living. These houses provide group therapy, a healthy environment with regular meals, and structure and peer support while residents job hunt or undertake vocational rehabilitation programs.

Alcoholism is a complex disorder, but it can be treated successfully. When the unique needs of each client are considered, the outlook is considerably optimistic. The nurse's role in the rehabilitation of the alcoholic extends from inpatient programs to outpatient care to involvement in community services. Whatever the modality, a kind, firm approach, based on knowledge and understanding, and a spirit of hopefulness will facilitate the client's progress and promote success.

EVALUATION Several factors should be considered in determining whether treatment has been successful. If the client has returned to drinking, his perception of events that may have precipitated this relapse should be taken into account in planning future treatment. If the client has remained sober, there has been a measure of success.

Goals should be re-evaluated for their appropriateness to the individual client. While complete abstinence is the ideal goal for most treatment, relapses seem to be a necessary part of the process. It is unrealistic to expect that all alcoholic clients who enter treatment will remain sober forever.

Change takes time, and each attempt adds more insight and education. By keeping goals manageable, staff and clients are less subject to discouragement and feelings of failure.

When a client returns for additional treatment, the staff should re-evaluate their attitudes regarding the client. Alcoholic clients can make the professional staff feel guilty if they don't get well or respond to treatment. Many times such clients are not "good" clients, which can lead to nontherapeutic responses from the staff—condescension, impatience, unwillingness to take time to listen, annoyance, resentment, and so on.

An additional area for evaluation is the role of support systems in a client's return to drinking. The previous treatment plan should be scrutinized to determine what areas should receive more consideration this time, such as greater family involvement, different housing arrangements, or more reliance on AA.

USE AND ABUSE OF DRUGS

Throughout recorded history, human beings have used drugs to alter their state of consciousness and to relieve the tension or monotony of existence. Over time, various mind-altering drugs have gained and lost popularity from culture to culture. Our contemporary society is highly drug-oriented. We take pills to calm us or to excite us, to wake us up or to put us to sleep, to help us gain or lose weight.

The dividing line between use and abuse of drugs is often determined by social sanctions. For example, the teenage use of marijuana or stimulants to achieve a "high" is frequently considered abuse by the adult population, but youngsters claim their drug habits are no different from those of parents who use alcohol or tobacco.

Often the legal system decides what constitutes use and abuse (Burkhalter 1975). The Harrison Narcotics Act of 1914 was the first national attempt to control the flow of narcotics and opiates in particular. This act was aimed at regulating the supply available for persons dependent on these drugs. Although considered beneficial, this act led to the beginning of illegal drug traffic. Physicians could no longer legally prescribe accustomed doses of narcotics to addicts to keep them comfortable, forcing them to turn to illegal sources. The Harrison Act was challenged in 1925 when the guilty verdict for a physician who had prescribed a narcotic for a known addict was overturned by the Supreme Court. For the first time, narcotic abuse was described as an illness that could be legally treated.

PREVALENCE OF DRUG ABUSE

It is estimated that there are about 300,000 heroin addicts nationwide, but the actual number may be two to three times that amount. About 1950, the typical heroin addict was a member of a minority group, lived in a large city, and was about 30 years old. Since that time, there has been a shift toward younger and younger addicts. New York City Addiction Services recently found that 42 percent of participants in drug abuse programs were black, 21 percent were Puerto Rican, and the rest were Caucasian. According to the Bureau of Narcotics and Dangerous Drugs, 51 percent of the addicts in the United States are white, with the average age being twenty-three (Freedman, Kaplan, and Sadock 1976).

The prevalence of other widely used drugs has been reported by Schuckit (1979) as follows:

- Marijuana has been tried by some 36 million Americans, with over 50 percent of people ages eighteen to twenty-five reporting some use, 20 percent using it two or more times per week, and 8 percent using it daily. One in five adults report having used marijuana at some time.
- Hallucinogens are used on an occasional basis by 20 percent of the youth population.
- Solvents are usually taken intermittently by adolescents. About 20 percent of girls and 33 percent of boys have used solvents at least once.
- Depressants are prescribed in approximately 90 percent of hospitalized cases. More than 15 percent of American adults use these drugs during any one year. Psychological dependence is between 10 percent and 30 percent for individuals who have received these drugs for medical purposes, and physical dependence is between 5 percent and 10 percent.

In 1937, the Uniform Narcotics Law created a consistent method for record keeping at federal and state levels, but it left penalties for use, possession, and sale of narcotics up to the individual states. In 1956 the Federal Narcotics Control Act increased the penalties for narcotics and marijuana violations, imposing sentences that ranged from 10 to 40 years.

Society's perception of drug abuse has followed much the same course as that of alcohol abuse. In recent years, an effort has been made to treat drug abuse problems as illnesses rather than as criminal or immoral acts. In 1962, a court case in California established that a person could not be punished as a criminal on the sole grounds of being a drug abuser. This decision helped emphasize the idea of drug dependence as an illness. In 1966, Congress established a policy for the treatment of narcotics abusers. Abusers found guilty of violating federal criminal law might be sentenced to prison or sent to a drug treatment center for detoxification and rehabilitation. But before confinement, it had to be determined whether the person could benefit from and respond to treatment efforts, which had the effect of screening out abusers judged to be potential failures.

The most recent legislation was the 1970 Compulsive Drug Abuse Control and Prevention Act. Penalties for violations were brought into greater accord with the danger and intended uses of the drugs. Under this law, a judge is free to arrive at alternative penalties, such as volunteer work for youthful offenders, rather than imprisonment.

COMMONLY ABUSED DRUGS

Drugs that are commonly abused fall into six major categories: (1) stimulants, (2) opiates, (3) depressants, (4) cannabinols, (5) hallucinogens, and (6) inhalants.

Stimulants

The *stimulants* comprise a variety of drugs that have the ability to stimulate the central nervous system at a number of levels. They include amphetamines, cocaine, and caffeine. As a group, they work by causing the release of neurotransmitters such as norepinephrine. Common stimulants are listed in Table 10–3. These drugs act on the central and peripheral nervous systems and on the cardiovascular system, causing euphoria, a decrease in fatigue, a decrease in appetite, and an increase in energy. They may increase feelings of sexuality and may interfere with normal sleep patterns. In some cases they produce tremor of the hands, restlessness, and tachycardia.

Tolerance to stimulants develops within hours or days. Whether physical dependence occurs is still being debated by researchers and clinicians,

Table 10–3. Common Stimulants

Generic Name	Trade Name	Street Names
Amphetamine	Benzedrine	Bennies, greenies, footballs
Methamphetamine	Desoxyn	Speed, crystal, meth
Dextroamphetamine	Dexedrine	Dexies, hearts, oranges, Christmas trees
Cocaine		Snow, dust, "C," gold dust
Caffeine		

but many feel that a physical syndrome does exist. There is no doubt, however, that psychological dependence can occur.

In the emergency room, any individual presenting with dilated pupils, increased heart rate, dry mouth, increased reflexes and temperature, sweating, and behavioral abnormalities should be considered a possible stimulant abuser. Panic reaction (fear of losing control or of going crazy) and amphetamine psychosis (high level of suspiciousness and paranoid delusions) may develop. Because of the short action and rapid metabolism of these drugs, flashbacks rarely occur.

Opiates and Related Analgesics

The major *opiates* include natural substances such as opium, morphine, and codeine; semisynthetic drugs such as heroin, Percodan, and Dilaudid; and synthetic analgesics such as Darvon and Demerol (see Table 10–4). These drugs all produce analgesia, drowsiness, changes in mood, and, at high doses, clouding of mental functioning through depression of the central nervous system and of cardiac activity.

Table 10–4. Common Opiates and Related Analgesics

Generic (Trade) Name	Street Name
Heroin	Horse, smack, H, junk
Morphine	Morf, monkey, white stuff
Codeine	Schoolboy
Hydromorphine (Dilaudid)	Lords, little D
Oxycodone (Percodan)	Perkies
Methadone (Dolophine)	Dollies
Meperidine (Demerol)	Demies
Diphenoxylate (Lomotil)	
Pentazocine (Talwin)	T's
Combination of heroin and cocaine taken intravenously	Hot shot

Opiate substances are highly addicting, and physical dependence develops with short-term use. Tolerance develops rapidly. Even therapeutic doses of morphine given four times a day for three days can result in mild withdrawal symptoms; clients returning home after surgery often experience a runny nose, tearing, and yawning that they attribute to a cold contracted in the hospital.

Physical signs and symptoms of opiate use include increased pigmentation over the veins, thrombosed veins, skin lesions and abscesses, constricted pupils, swollen nasal mucosa (if drug has been snorted), enlarged liver, and swollen lymph glands. Panic reactions and flashbacks are rare.

An opiate overdose is a medical emergency; usual signs include decreased respiration, pale or cyanotic skin and lips, pinpoint pupils, pulmonary edema, shock, cardiac arrhythmias, and convulsions. Death may occur from the respiratory depression and pulmonary edema.

The withdrawal syndrome usually begins at the time of the next scheduled dose. The pattern of this syndrome is outlined in the accompanying box.

Depressants

Central nervous system *depressants* include a variety of medications such as hypnotics and antianxiety drugs (see Table 10–5). All have clinical usefulness and potential for abuse. The main effects are lethargy and sleepiness. Overdose can lead to death from respiratory and circulatory depression. Some depressant drugs can produce a paradoxical reaction, that of extreme excitement, when given to children and the elderly.

OPIATE WITHDRAWAL

Opiate withdrawal occurs in the following pattern:

1. Within 12 hours—physical discomfort, tearing of the eyes, runny nose, sweating, and yawning.

2. 12 to 14 hours—restless sleep.

3. 2 to 3 days—dilated pupils, loss of appetite, gooseflesh ("cold turkey"), back pain, and tremor.

4. 3 to 4 days—insomnia, incessant yawning, flulike symptoms, gastrointestinal upsets, chills, muscle spasms, and abdominal pain.

5. 5 days—symptoms decrease, usually disappearing in a week to 10 days.

Table 10–5. Common Depressants

Generic Name	Trade Name	Street Name
Hypnotics		
Thiopental	Pentothal	Barbs, sleepies
Methohexital	Brevital	
Pentobarbital	Nembutal	Yellow jackets
Secobarbital	Seconal	Red devils, red birds
Amobarbital	Amytal	Blues
Phenobarbital	Luminal	Phennies, pink lady
Methaqualone	Quaalude	Sopers, ludes, love drug
Ethchlorvynol	Placidyl	Dyls
Chloral hydrate	Noctec	
Antianxiety drugs		
Chlordiazepoxide	Librium	Libs
Diazepam	Valium	Blues (10 mg), yellows (5 mg)
Oxazepam	Serax	
Chlorazepate	Tranxene	
Meprobamate	Miltown, Equanil	

Tolerance occurs both metabolically and through adaptation of the CNS. If two depressant drugs, such as alcohol and barbiturates, are taken at the same time, they will compete for metabolism in the liver. Since the liver can handle only a certain amount at one time, neither drug will be metabolized properly, and the effects of one drug will enhance the effects of the other, because drugs remain in the blood longer.

All CNS depressants produce a withdrawal state when drug taking stops abruptly. Physical signs and symptoms of withdrawal include tremor, gastrointestinal upsets, muscle aches, increased pulse and respiration, fever, and grand mal seizures. These symptoms may last three to seven days for short-acting drugs but longer for drugs like Valium.

Panic reactions and flashbacks are rarely seen. A toxic reaction can develop in a matter of hours, occurring either unintentionally or as the result of suicidal overdose. Depressants can also produce a temporary psychosis, manifested by acute onset of auditory hallucinations and paranoid delusions.

Cannabinols (Marijuana)

Marijuana is the second most widely used mood-altering drug in America, after alcohol. Marijuana comes from the dried leaves of the marijuana plant, *Cannabis sativa*; hashish is made from the resins of the plant flowers. The active ingredient, tetrahy-drocannabinol (THC), can cause panic reactions, toxic reactions, and generalized anxiety. Marijuana can be smoked, eaten, or injected intravenously.

Marijuana is primarily a hallucinogen, but at usual doses the dominant effects are euphoria and change in level of consciousness without hallucinations. Marijuana use increases the cardiac workload and causes fine tremors, decreased muscle strength, decreased coordination, and breathing problems with prolonged use. It may also precipitate seizures. High doses can produce short-term memory loss, paranoia, and, with toxic doses, confusion, disorientation, and panic. Tolerance and physical dependence do not appear to be a problem, but there is some debate as to whether withdrawal symptoms occur. Flashbacks—the recurrence of feelings and perceptions experienced in the intoxicated state—are commonly seen in marijuana users.

Of concern to nurses are recent findings associating marijuana use with a decrease in the body's responses, impairment of sperm production, and destruction of lung tissue (Weiten 1983).

Hallucinogens

Hallucinogens (also called psychedelics) increase awareness of sensory input, provide a feeling of enhanced mental activity and altered body image, and decrease the ability to distinguish between oneself and one's surroundings. Common hallucinogens are listed in Table 10–6. Physical signs of use include dilated pupils, flushing, tremors, increased blood pressure, elevated blood sugar levels, and increased temperature. Tolerance develops rapidly but decreases in about a week if drug use is discontinued. There do not appear to be any withdrawal symptoms with these drugs. Flashbacks can occur, lasting from several minutes to a few hours.

Some users experience "bad trips"—states of high anxiety and fear. The individual is highly stimulated, frightened, hallucinating, and fearful of losing his mind. Hallucinogen-induced psychosis

Table 10–6. Common Hallucinogens

Generic Name	Street Names
Lysergic acid diethylamide (LSD)	Acid, hawk, royal blue, sugar cubes, pearly gates, instant zen
Psilocybin	Magic mushrooms
Dimethyltryptamine	DMT
Mescaline (peyote)	Big chief, cactus, half moon
Phencyclidine	PCP, angel dust, hog, peace pill
Dimethoxymethyl amphetamine	DOM, STP ("serenity, tranquility, peace")

can occur but usually clears within hours to days. In cases where psychosis does not clear, a preexisting psychotic problem, such as schizophrenia, is likely to have been present.

Inhalants

Inhalants include glues, solvents, and aerosols (see Table 10–7). These substances can produce generalized CNS depression. They are popular because they readily produce euphoria and are available, cheap, and legal. Usually the high begins within minutes and lasts about a half hour, with the person feeling giddy and lightheaded. The person may experience a decrease in inhibitions, misperceptions or illusions, clouding of thoughts, and drowsiness. Acute intoxication causes irritation of the eyes, double vision, ringing in the ears, and irritation of the mucous membranes of the nose and mouth.

Tolerance develops quickly, but withdrawal symptoms do not develop. Overdose causes a life-threatening syndrome, characterized by respiratory depression, cardiac arrhythmias, loss of consciousness, and possibly death.

CAUSES OF DRUG ABUSE

In discussing the etiology of drug abuse and drug dependence, it should be emphasized that there may be a difference between the factors that initially lead to abuse and those that tend to maintain the state of dependence once it has been established. The fear of symptoms caused by abstinence is, for the abuser, an important reason for staying on a drug. Many addicted persons resist hospitalization out of fear they will be asked to go "cold turkey." Others return to drugs after trying to withdraw themselves and suffering for several days.

While the exact causes of drug dependence are not known, it is possible to discuss the possible factors in three categories: the "host" (mental or personality makeup of the user), the environment, and the agent (the pharmacologic nature of the drug) (Glatt 1974).

Role of the Host

As with the alcoholic client, a great deal of research has focused on trying to establish a personality

---

DSM-III-R AXIS I
DIAGNOSTIC CLASSIFICATION

Drug abuse is classified under Psychoactive Substance Use Disorders. Additional codes for organic related disorders are found under Psychoactive Substance-Induced Organic Mental Disorders

Amphetamine
304.40 Dependence
305.70 Abuse

Cannabis
304.30 Dependence
305.20 Abuse

Cocaine
304.20 Dependence
305.60 Abuse

Hallucinogen
304.50 Dependence
305.30 Abuse

Inhalant
304.60 Dependence
305.90 Abuse

Nicotine
305.10 Withdrawal

Opioid
304.00 Dependence
305.50 Abuse

PCP
304.50 Dependence
305.90 Abuse

Sedatives, hypnotics, anxiolytics
304.10 Dependence
305.40 Abuse

Polysubstance dependence
304.90

Psychoactive substance dependence not otherwise specified
304.90

Psychoactive substance abuse not otherwise specified
305.90

Table 10–7. Commonly Abused Inhalants

Substance	Active Ingredients
Glues	Toluene, naphtha, benzene, chloroform
Cleaning solutions	Carbon tetrachloride
Nail polish remover	Acetone
Aerosols	Fluorinated hydrocarbons, nitrous oxide
Petroleum products	Gasoline, ether
Paint thinners	Toluene, methanol

makeup for the drug abusing client. Some similarities have been found among abusing individuals, particularly (1) emotional immaturity, (2) a wish to ignore reality, (3) low tolerance for frustration, (4) an unwillingness to cope with tension, and (5) inability to persist at a task (Glatt 1974). Certain emotionally vulnerable people tend to look for ways to obtain relief from discomfort or to achieve a higher degree of satisfaction than previously experienced. For them, drugs are a means to these ends. Some drugs, such as alcohol, release aggressive impulses; others, such as heroin, weaken them. Therefore, the choice of drug may be somewhat determined by the individual's values and his ego ideal (the type of person he wishes to be and to portray to his peers).

As with alcohol abuse, genetic and environmental factors are difficult to separate. It is presently believed that genetic factors play less of a role in predisposition to drug dependence than to alcoholism. However, inherited factors may play a role in drug abuse in clients who also suffer from schizophrenia or manic-depressive conditions (Glatt 1974).

In Western culture, alcohol is widely accepted socially, but most other mind-altering drugs aren't. It is therefore likely that the proportion of immature and insecure personalities is much higher among abusers of other drugs than among alcohol abusers. Drugs are frequently taken as a rebellious act against authority. Since alcohol use is more accepted, it is not an acting-out method as much as other drug use is. Young people generally find drugs attractive for different reasons than alcohol. Curiosity, glamour, excitement, risk taking, a feeling of bravery, and the lure of the unknown may be factors in drug experimentation. It has been said that young people take drugs to rebel against their parents but take alcohol to emulate them (Glatt 1974). In contrast, middle-aged drug abusing clients seem to have begun their abuse by a different route: self-medication. For example, a middle-aged woman who abuses amphetamines may have originally begun using them as a means of weight control.

Role of the Environment

Drug-dependent individuals will often revert to drug taking long after the physical dependence has disappeared. This relapse mainly occurs when they resume contact with their former friends and subculture. They commonly return to their old neighborhoods because they have no place else to go, but in many cases, abusing clients return because of the need to belong; they feel more comfortable in their old environments.

Environmental factors also play a role in the increasing use of drugs within the teenage population. Youngsters who engage in activities that are frowned on by authority figures become alienated from society's values, such as having a steady job, maintaining family ties, getting an education, and so on. Many sociologists suggest that the blame for drug abuse rests on our "sick" society rather than on the "weak personality" of the addict. Old social standards have largely disappeared without new guidelines to replace them. As a result, many young people feel insecure and bewildered. In this state of anxiety and insecurity, many reject society and look for new ways to gain satisfaction, including drugs (Glatt 1974).

Another environmental factor that affects drug abuse is membership in a particular ethnic group or subculture. The low incidence of alcoholism among Jews, for example, is believed to exist because in Jewish culture drunkenness is frowned upon and holding one's liquor is not a status symbol. However, abuse of other drugs is more common among Jews, possibly because they have no clear-cut established attitudes against drug taking.

Easy access to certain drugs also appears to influence drug patterns. Thus, military personnel and businessmen, whose main access is to alcohol, may be more likely to abuse this drug, whereas doctors, pharmacists, and nurses have a greater access to opiates and other prescription drugs and are thus more likely to abuse these drugs.

Role of the Agent

The pharmacologic properties of a drug may play a role in the process of addiction. Most people become physically dependent on opiates after using even small amounts, in a matter of a week or two. Barbiturate users, on the other hand, usually do not become addicted even after two to three months of administration slightly over therapeutic dose range. And it takes a long period of consuming large amounts for people using alcohol to develop a physical dependence. In general, drugs that can be injected produce dependence sooner than those taken by mouth.

Another factor in drug abuse is the drug's ability to serve as a reinforcer. The drug of choice gives a reward, whether the relief of tension or feelings of euphoria. With each use, the reward continues and drug usage is reinforced. Many times the pattern of drug use is begun with social reinforcement; then the desired effects take over as the reinforcement. Addicted persons also find that withdrawal symptoms provide *negative* reinforcement for continued drug use. Formerly clients addicted to heroin have been known to experience withdrawal symptoms upon seeing drug equipment (syringe, needles) despite having been physically detoxified from the drug.

Drug abuse is a complex health problem, the causes of which are not completely understood. Research in this area is especially difficult because the main source of information is current users, who are highly defensive about their behavior. In addition, the reasons one person chooses a certain drug may be entirely different from the reasons another person chooses the same drug. Furthermore, people may abuse different drugs at different times in their lives. Nurses therefore need to be aware of the variety of factors that can contribute to beginning and maintaining drug abuse patterns.

CAUSAL INTERACTION IN THE ADOLESCENT AND YOUNG ADULT CHRONIC USERS Substance abuse is a growing problem for the adolescent and young adult population.

The reasons for drug use among adolescents are many and complex. The adolescents' perception of drug use by parents, peers, and others may be one of the most important factors. Frequently these teenagers learn that drugs allow temporary escape from dysphoric moods and unpleasant life circumstances.

In assessing the drug use problems of this age group, it is critical to determine parental psychoactive drug usage and the overall functioning of the family. Parents should be asked about direct evidence of drug use in their child and information should be obtained about their reactions to their findings and the child's reaction to the confrontation. Indirect evidence of drug use may be a personality change, declining academic and behavioral performance, increased absenteeism, rebelliousness, and changes in peer relationships.

When working with adolescents, the attitude of the health care team is of primary importance. Care must be taken not to relate to the teenager as a "bad person" because of the drug use. The concept of "tough love" should be used sparingly. This is often described as a willingness by the parents to do whatever is necessary to facilitate recovery, including allowing the child to suffer the consequences of drug use and his or her behaviors. However, they should not be allowed to suffer dangerous or fatal consequences. To simply watch an adolescent engage in overtly dangerous activity usually reflects a passive-aggressive acting out of the parents' own hostility and does not help the child.

Honesty and accuracy are important in the long-term management. Neither the risks involved nor any other aspects of the problem should be exaggerated or distorted (Niven 1986).

PHYSIOLOGICAL CONSEQUENCES OF DRUG ABUSE

Long-term drug abuse is associated with a variety of complications.

Circulatory and Respiratory Complications

Bacterial endocarditis is a common complication of intravenous drug use. The infecting organism is usually *Staphylococcus aureus*. The left side of the heart and the aortic, mitral, and tricuspid valves are usually involved. Heroin addicts with bacterial endocarditis have a mortality rate of 28 to 75 percent.

Gangrene, caused by injection of drugs into an artery instead of a vein, can occur in the extremity distal to the arterial injection site. The damage is believed to be caused by chemical action on the intimal lining of the artery.

Vascular disorders such as acute and chronic thrombophlebitis and sclerosing of the veins are common. If contaminated drugs are injected, the result may be severe extremity lymphedema because of obstruction of veins and lymphatics. Intracranial hemorrhage has been reported with amphetamine use because of its hypertensive effect.

Pulmonary embolism occurs when foreign particles such as talc, cornstarch, and cotton are injected into the circulatory system. When emboli reach the lungs, granulomas or pulmonary fibrosis can result.

Respiratory infections occur with a high frequency in drug addicts because of general lack of health care, poor diet, and poor living conditions. Heroin addicts frequently develop pneumonia, tuberculosis, and pulmonary abscesses.

Hepatic Dysfunction

Acute and chronic hepatitis are common problems resulting from use of contaminated needles. Hepatitis is one of the most frequent medical complications of drug abuse, with 10 to 15 percent of heroin addicts showing signs of the acute process and another 60 to 75 percent showing signs of chronic hepatitis and liver disease.

Gastrointestinal Disturbances

Severe and rapid weight loss is common with amphetamine abuse. Long-term heroin users are troubled with vitamin deficiencies, severe constipation, and hemorrhoids.

Skin Complications

Skin problems develop at the site of drug injections and include scarring, abscesses, cellulitis, and ulcerations. When drugs are injected into surrounding tissue rather than the vein, necrotic ulcerating lesions appear. Such subcutaneous "skin popping" increases the potential for systemic infections.

Muscular Disorders

Long-term subcutaneous injection can cause a fibrosing myopathy, in which the veins become blocked, resulting in edema, and possibly leading to cellulitis and myositis, with chronic muscle damage.

Miscellaneous Complications

There is a high incidence of tetanus in the heroin-abusing population, as skin popping provides an excellent avenue of entry for infection. The mortality rate for tetanus among addicts is extremely high.

Eye emboli are caused by foreign substances, producing retinal hemorrhages with edema. In most cases, this problem is temporary.

Traumatic injury occurs because of decreased mental alertness, producing burns, fractures, lacerations, and contusions.

PRESCRIPTION DRUG MISUSE

While most efforts at studying and treating drug abuse are aimed at illicit drugs, there is a substantial problem in this country with misuse of prescription drugs. Two groups appear to be especially vulnerable to this difficulty: women and the elderly.

Prescription psychotropic drug dependence affects women twice as often as men. As men use alcohol at least twice as much as women, substance abuse appears to be manifested in men by socially-sanctioned alcohol use and in women by the "illness of prescription pill taking." Women report more symptoms to physicians than men do; disproportionate prescribing to women (women receive 70 percent of psychoactive prescriptions) is seen as a treatment for emotional problems.

The reasons for this are complex. Women may experience a greater responsibility for the well-being of others than men do and are subject to distinct socioeconomic stressors that are chronic and lack ready solutions. Emotional ventilation may be an appropriate coping mechanism. In addition, women are socialized to be more emotionally expressive than men. Women's conversations deal freely with emotions and interpersonal interactions.

It may be that this form of communication is misinterpreted by male physicians as an emotional state needing drug therapy. Issues of stereotyping, socially-reinforced self-negation, and other forces which impact on the interaction between practitioner and client must be considered when assessing this problem (Ogur 1986).

Another segment of the population that is a risk for drug misuse is the elderly, who consume 25 percent of all prescription drugs sold in the United States. Older persons experience more adverse drug reactions and the occurrence of side effects is three times greater. Most elderly Americans are not in institutions and are unsupervised in their use of drugs; these factors increase the risk of drug use substantially.

Underuse of drugs is the most common type of drug misuse: a large proportion of misusers make errors in the dosage of their medications or fail to take the medication at all. Others are self-medicators and take drugs that were not intended to be used over long periods of time.

Several factors have been identified as contributing to drug misuse in the older population. The tendency of older persons to develop multiple chronic pathologies may prompt the elderly to make greater use of both prescription and over-the-counter drugs, which leads to an increased risk of toxicity.

For some clients, old age is a time of social isolation and withdrawal that can result in a reliance on drugs in response to psychosomatic illness or in the misuse of antidepressants and sleeping medication. The media directly influences this consumer group by providing continuous information and sales campaigns aimed at the elderly for a variety of conditions. Many elderly persons also have financial constraints. Living on a fixed income may result in an attempt to save money by not filling a prescription or using a medication from a previous illness (Raffoul 1986).

The elderly who are institutionalized are also at risk for drug misuse. There is a widespread use of psychotropic medications with the elderly clients in nursing homes. Surveys reveal that between 43 and 75 percent of nursing home residents have a prescription for a major or minor tranquilizer.

There are many pressures inherent in many nursing homes today. Short and inadequate staff, high turnover rates, absenteeism. Waxman, Klein, and Carter (1985) postulate that the overuse of psychotropic medications is a symptom of these pressures since the medications are effective in reducing the burden on the staff. Personnel are uncomfortable with clients who are behaviorally disruptive. The misuse of psychotropic medications by institutions serves the same stress-reducing function as drug abuse by individuals.

The potential for drug misuse in the elderly is a problem that demands a coordinated multidisciplinary focus. Nursing must play a crucial role in the detection, treatment, referral, and follow-up of these clients, in the hospital, outpatient, and community settings.

DRUG ABUSE AND THE NURSING PROCESS

Application of the nursing process in dealing with drug abusing clients occurs in two stages: the acute phase and the rehabilitation phase.

Acute Stage

ASSESSMENT The client with an acute drug reaction can present a medical emergency, especially if he has received an overdose. If the client is unable to respond, detective work is necessary to determine which drug was used. Comprehensive knowledge of the signs and symptoms of the various drugs will assist the nurse in this process. At times, verification can be made by someone accompanying the client.

A thorough physical assessment should include an inspection for scars, needle points, and abscesses. The possibility of overdose should be determined by assessing pupil size and reaction, reflex responses, vital signs, respiratory status, tremors, convulsions, and breath odor. Clothing should be inspected for signs of drugs and drug implements. Nutritional and hygiene status can be assessed by looking for signs of nutritional deficiencies and personal neglect. The assessment should also include determining the level of consciousness and looking for the presence of hallucinations or delusions, confusion, signs of complications, and physical injuries.

PLANNING AND IMPLEMENTATION As with alcohol treatment, the primary concern during the acute stage of drug detoxification is the physical well-being of the client, with attention to providing comfort and alleviating fear. Common problems and appropriate nursing interventions are presented in Table 10–8.

EVALUATION When the client is medically stable, referral for continued care can be made.

Rehabilitation Stage

ASSESSMENT Many of the assessments discussed for the alcoholic client also apply to the rehabilitating drug abuser. Attention must be given to the motivation for treatment and the reasons for requesting treatment. Available support systems, including those that may encourage a return to drug abuse, need evaluation. Current living conditions may need to be included in the plan for change. It is especially important to assess the client's past treatment history, including types of programs attempted (such as abstinence and methadone maintenance), to determine the reasons for past failures and what might work better in the future.

Table 10–8. Interventions for Acute Drug Problems

Client's Problem	Nursing Interventions
Decreased circulatory and respiratory function	Monitor vital signs and neurologic reflex responses. Be prepared for emergencies, including CPR, keeping an airway open. Suction as necessary.
Impending withdrawal	Determine the stage of withdrawal. Medicate as ordered to alleviate discomfort. Approach the client calmly; avoid touching her without explanation. Limit visitors.
Potential for self-injury	Use restraints as necessary; remove all harmful objects. Monitor suicidal behavior.
Panic and flashback reactions	Have staff attend as much as possible. Provide a caring presence and opportunity to ventilate feelings. Try to talk client down. Reassure him through this difficult period. Orient him to person, time, and place. Do not support delusions and hallucinations. Let client know that these are very real for him but that you do not experience the same things.
Poor nutritional status, personal hygiene	Give conscientious skin care, being aware of the likelihood of skin breakdown. Record nutritional and fluid intake and output. Administer and monitor IV solutions until oral intake can be established. Provide small, frequent feedings when indicated.
Fear of "cold turkey," unavailability of treatment	Give honest reassurance about the client's condition. Begin education about drug abuse. Make plans for continued treatment. Discuss available treatment modalities. Have a recovered addict visit client.

PLANNING AND IMPLEMENTATION Whatever the chosen modality for continued treatment, certain problems will arise that need attention by nursing personnel. Such problems and suggested interventions are examined in Table 10–9.

The past decade has seen the development of a multitude of treatment possibilities for substance abuse, including maintenance, detoxification, use of antagonists, and drug-free communities. These types of treatment offer different approaches to drug abuse and may be most effectively used in combination at various points in rehabilitation. However, all too often proponents of one type of therapy have attempted to pit it against other types of therapy, thereby ignoring the potential benefits of each type and reducing the overall effectiveness of treatment by forcing an inappropriate approach on the client (O'Brien, Woody, and McLellan 1983).

Maintenance The assumption that basic addiction is a metabolic disease is the basis for methadone maintenance. The basic idea of this treatment is that if

POSSIBLE NURSING DIAGNOSES RELATED TO CLIENTS WITH ALCOHOL AND DRUG PROBLEMS

Anxiety
Chronic pain
Ineffective individual coping
Ineffective family coping
Altered family processes
Diversional activity deficit
Impaired home maintenance management
Altered health maintenance
Hopelessness
Potential for injury
Knowledge deficit
Noncompliance
Altered nutrition
Altered parenting
Feeding/bathing/toileting/dressing self-care deficit
Self-esteem disturbance
Sensory-perceptual alterations
Impaired skin integrity
Social isolation
Potential for violence

*The above are the more likely diagnoses related to clients with alcohol and drug problems. Nursing diagnoses are not limited to the list shown above. Manifestations of these disorders are individualistic even though certain prevailing patterns are identifiable.

Table 10–9. Interventions in Drug Rehabilitation

Client's Problem	Nursing Interventions
Denial of illness	Confront the client regarding his problem behavior. Help him recognize his avoidance of responsibility. Identify projection of blame or defensiveness that prevents honesty.
Isolation	Encourage group participation, physical exercise, and new interests and activities. Help the client seek support from others.
Avoidance of responsibility	Encourage decision making and verbal expression of anger and depression. Provide a structured environment and planned routine. Prepare the client for a change in lifestyle after discharge.
Lack of knowledge about consequences of drug abuse	Provide education to help the client understand drug abuse as an illness.
Return to drug abuse	Encourage compliance with the planned treatment program. Explore goals for appropriateness and client resistance.

addicted clients are supplied with adequate quantities of opiate in the form of methadone, they will no longer have to engage in criminal activity to maintain their supply. Oral doses of methadone do not produce euphoria but do satisfy the physiological desire for the drug and prevent onset of withdrawal symptoms. Although methadone maintenance programs have met with some success, they have also created medical, social, and legal problems, including sale on the illegal market and death from overdose. These difficulties have usually evolved when appropriate support services have been neglected (O'Brien, Woody, and McLellan 1983).

An alternative approach, *heroin maintenance*, is highly controversial. Proponents believe that because heroin is the drug of choice for most addicted clients, providing a controlled supply of heroin keeps more addicts in treatment. Opponents of this program believe that it creates more problems than it solves because it makes addiction less costly and more socially acceptable, gives a free supply of heroin to potential addicts, and discourages other, more effective treatment plans.

Antagonists Narcotic antagonists block or antagonize the opiates, preventing them from acting. They do not provide the psychological effects of narcotics and are not addictive. Nalorphine (Nalline) has been used in the treatment of opiate overdose. Antagonists used for treatment include cyclazocine, naloxone, and naltrexane. A problem with this approach is the lack of any mechanism to compel the addicted person to continue taking the antagonist. If he decides to eliminate the dose on one day, the effects of heroin can be experienced on the next day.

Drug-Free Communities Another treatment approach is drug-free therapeutic communities, usually within a residential treatment facility. Formerly addicted clients live together and participate in group therapy sessions. Synanon, one of the first groups of this type, has stressed harsh group confrontation, re-education, and hard work. The basic idea underlying such communities is that drug abuse is symptomatic of an underlying antisocial personality problem or behavior pattern.

Many treatment types can be combined effectively for subgroups of client populations. A client may begin on maintenance, progress to detoxification, then spend several months on an antagonist and eventually become drug-free. A variety of psychologic therapies have been found to add to the overall effectiveness of treatment by addressing the particular group of problems often associated with

THE ROLE OF THE NURSE IN DRUG ABUSE TREATMENT

The following nursing approaches are applicable to inpatient programs, day hospital treatment, and less intensive outpatient care.

■ Establish and maintain the therapeutic milieu by explaining policies and routines.

■ Assess the client's ability to handle stress and to participate in multidisciplinary team planning.

■ Be alert for drug use, realizing that clients may try to smuggle in drugs or, if outpatients, continue to use drugs. Continuous assessment of physical and behavioral characteristics helps monitor abstinence.

■ Teach new forms of interpersonal behavior by role modeling and confronting inappropriate behavior.

■ Participate in group therapy and encourage client participation, being alert to client's expressed feelings and assisting her to become aware of them.

■ Provide a full schedule of activities, encouraging new interests and development of potential abilities.

■ Give medications as prescribed, being aware that clients may hoard medication to get a "high" later, may feign physical pain to obtain drugs, or may "cheek" medications to avoid effects.

■ Evaluate the appropriateness of follow-up care and refer as indicated.

drug involvement. Individual psychotherapy has been found to be effective with clients on methadone maintenance. A variety of behavior modification techniques, often used in conjunction with naltrexone, have been reported to have benefits in extinguishing drug-conditioned responses that may lead to relapse. Family therapy, vocational guidance, and legal counseling have also proved to be beneficial.

Psychotropic medication, particularly antidepressants, adds another dimension. When schizophrenia or affective disorders are present, neuroleptics or lithium may be combined with maintenance, drug-free, or antagonist programs. Even benzodiazepines, which themselves have a potential for abuse, may be used with naltrexone to reduce protracted withdrawal symptoms and to improve program compliance (O'Brien, Woody, and McLellan 1983).

EVALUATION There are three major reasons why treatment fails to initiate change for a drug abusing client. First, the original goals may have been unrealistic. Success for the drug abusing client is often defined as being drug-free, being legally employed, and not engaging in crime. These are excellent goals, but for a drug program to adopt them as standards may be unfair to the client. It is unreasonable to expect that freedom from drugs will make other areas immediately improve. Employment, for example, is partly a function of skills and habits developed before drug involvement and is also related to economic conditions.

A second reason for failure is not taking into account the heterogeneity and complexity of problems found among drug-abusing clients. Unless the client's unique problems are assessed and incorporated into the plan, failure is likely.

The third main reason for failure is inappropriate choice of treatment program. The proper utilization of available modalities is a necessary component of treatment for the abuser. Only a few places presently provide all the available treatment approaches. The nurse can make a valuable contribution to the health care of the abusing client by making accurate diagnoses and helping to match the client with the most appropriate program.

SUMMARY

Substance abuse has been a problem for centuries. Social perception of individuals who abuse drugs has varied over time; in recent years, knowledgeable members of the helping professions have come to see substance abusers as people suffering from an illness that is amenable to treatment. These clinicians are beginning to take an active role in research, case finding, and planning of treatment designed to assist clients who are unable to monitor or control their use of various substances. Abuse of alcohol has resulted in problem drinking to the point of alcoholism for approximately 14 million Americans and it affects the lives of 56 million others.

The etiology of alcoholism has been explained by a variety of theories ranging from physiological (Text continues on page 275.)

C L I N I C A L   E X A M P L E

*MULTIPLE SUBSTANCE ABUSE
IN AN ADULT FEMALE*

Sally Mason is a 34-year-old white female, divorced for five years. She is currently unemployed and receives welfare benefits from the county in which she lives. Sally attended college for two years but dropped out when she became pregnant and married. The marriage lasted only a short time; her husband deserted her and she still has no idea as to his whereabouts. Because Sally had few job skills, she was unable to find any employment and joined the street scene, supplementing her income with prostitution. In addition to her alcohol intake of one or two six-packs of beer and a pint or more of whiskey per day, Sally smokes marijuana and has used heroin. As a result of her heroin usage, she contacted hepatitis and now has a chronic liver condition.

Currently Sally lives in a run-down apartment with two other women who also use drugs and engage in prostitution. She has no other support people in her life; her parents died several years ago and she was an only child. Sally has attempted treatment at several facilities but has been unable to remain sober or abstain from marijuana use for any length of time. She no longer uses heroin. She has developed cirrhosis of the liver and was recently hospitalized for emergency surgery because of ruptured esophageal varicies. She was told at that time that it was unlikely that she could survive another serious drinking binge. She has been referred for outpatient follow-up care.

ASSESSMENT

The nurse who interviewed Sally saw a woman who was casually dressed, poorly groomed, and wearing very heavy makeup. She was fully oriented, alert to her surroundings, and engaged easily in conversation. She tended to ramble at length when recounting her past life. She was otherwise articulate, using words effectively to communicate ideas. The nurse estimated Sally's verbal IQ to be within the bright average to superior range, although the client did appear to have some cognitive deficits that showed up in abstract reasoning and some memory distortion. Her affect was inappropriate. As she verbalized concern over her behavioral and drinking problems, she was cheerful and laughed frequently. Throughout the interview, the nurse commented on these discrepancies, and Sally was able to say that this was her way of handling her nervousness and that she was quite frightened about her poor physical condition but knew that fear alone would not keep her abstinent. She said she had no reason to believe that this attempt at treatment would be any more successful than previous ones.

Based on Sally's history and clinical picture, the following nursing and psychiatric diagnoses were formulated:

Nursing Diagnoses

Anxiety
(related to feelings of inadequacy, conflicts over past life)

Ineffective individual coping
(related to drug-related lifestyle, lack of support systems)

Diversional activity deficit
(related to reliance on drug and prostitution activities to fill the day)

Noncompliance with treatment

Self-esteem disturbance
(related to fear of failure)

Multiaxial Psychiatric Diagnoses

Axis I	303.90 Alcohol dependence
	305.50 Opioid abuse
	304.30 Cannabis dependence
Axis II	Schizoid personality
Axis III	Poststatus esophageal repair
	Chronic hepatitis
	Cirrhosis of liver
Axis IV	Psychosocial stressors—serious chronic illness
	Acute and chronic enduring circumstances
	Severity 5: extreme
Axis V	Current GAF: 35
	Highest GAF past year: 41

PLANNING

The health team agreed that Sally could achieve sobriety only with drastic changes in her lifestyle. Because of past failures at treatment, she needed a highly structured milieu and close contact with a counselor for support and guidance. Sally's lack of constructive activity and continued contact with peers who abused drugs and practiced prostitution was contributing to her return to drinking and marijuana use. Because of her lack of job skills, she had been content to exist on welfare payments without making an effort to obtain some stability in and direction to, her life. Sally's avoidance of work may have been caused by fear of failure or of being recognized by "clients"; thus the health team emphasized the need to set small attainable goals. Sally needed some experience with success.

The team also noted the necessity of designing challenging and rewarding tasks for Sally that would help her redefine herself as a person and as a functioning individual in society. In addition, it was necessary to plan individual counseling sessions to enable her to work through her feelings about being abandoned by her parents and her husband. Because of her liver condition and poor physical health, Antabuse was not considered an option. Contacts with a volunteer group that provides companions for substance abusers were initiated to determine their ability to provide some healthy support and company for Sally.

IMPLEMENTATION

In order to maintain contact and establish the therapeutic relationship, Sally's psychiatric nurse initiated a short-term contract with her for keeping appointments and beginning planned activities to structure her day. Since she had previously attended AA meetings in her neighborhood but had only participated superficially, it was arranged for her to take part in the care of the AA meeting place and to be responsible for the coffee hour. Although she was not stable enough to become a sponsor for others, her responsibilities at the center were designed to increase her involvement in a businesslike, nonthreatening manner.

To give Sally some sense of accomplishment and a feeling that she could become a contributing member of society, she was placed in a community vocational evaluation program to assess her potential for either vocational training or constructive volunteer work. The program had the added benefit of providing a schedule and a task for each day. Sally also accepted placement at a community halfway house to get a new environment and a new, nonsubstance-abusing peer group.

EVALUATION

The goal of social rehabilitation for Sally required the participation of caregivers representing a variety of disciplines and agencies. Medical follow-up was provided by physicians, placement and vocational rehabilitation was organized by the social worker, and the psychiatric nurse was responsible for the individual counseling, coordination with AA and the companion organization, and the comprehensive planning. A primary responsibility of the psychiatric nurse was to coordinate these diverse efforts so that consistent goals were maintained and manipulation on Sally's part was kept to a minimum.

Coordination was a not only essential but difficult activity that required preservation of the territoriality of the caregivers. In addition, it was necessary to ensure that the client did not receive any mixed messages from the personnel involved.

As with all alcoholic clients, continuity of care was essential, and the presence of a primary stabilizing caregiver who maintained interest in the overall progress was paramount to beginning successful treatment. Most relationships had been transient and fleeting in Sally's life. The progress she made would have been impossible without the ongoing presence of one individual who made the rehabilitation program consistent with realistic goals that were acceptable to the client.

Nursing Diagnoses	Goal	Nursing Actions	Outcome Criteria	Outcome Evaluation
Anxiety	Clients anxiety will be reduced to mild level to facilitate functioning.	Focus on fears, feelings of inadequacy in individual sessions. Explore conflict of feelings over abandonment by parents and husband.	Client will be able to talk about her concerns without resorting to joking and changing the subject, will be able to identify her coping strategies in the session, and will come to some realization about her fears of abandonment.	After 12 sessions, client was able to discuss many of her past experiences and realize their effect on her lifestyle now. When anxiety reached a certain level, she would again resort to joking but was able to identify this before the nurse pointed it out. She needed more time to work through feelings about parents.
Ineffective individual coping	Client will change lifestyle.	Provide close contact with nurse for support and guidance. Contact volunteer agency to determine its capability.	Companion will help to structure client's day and place limits on her behavior.	Companion established a working relationship with nurse and agreed to continue with client as long as necessary.
Diversional activity deficit	Client will become involved in activities that will reinforce new lifestyle.	Explore possibilities for constructive tasks to replace style of living.	Client will devise a schedule for daily activities and keep to it.	Client accepted placement in halfway house to give her a new peer group and facilitate her planned schedule.
Noncompliance with treatment	Client will increase compliance with short-term goals.	Initiate short-term contract for keeping appointments. Provide close contact, enroll in group therapy and AA.	Client will attend group therapy and AA for 3 months.	Client attended all meetings but at the end of 3 months was feeling that she no longer needed this support. A new contract was made for 3 more months.
Self-esteem disturbance	Client will set small goals to allow for success.	Contact social worker to arrange meaningful tasks in connection with AA.	Client will be responsible for the coffee hour at AA to increase her involvement in a nonthreatening manner.	Client was still somewhat uncomfortable with the AA group. Plans were made to continue tasks until she could be a fully participating member.

to psychological, sociocultural, and learning theories. Recently there have been new discoveries in the biochemical arena which are adding new dimensions to the study of alcoholism. Women, children, and the elderly evidence special problems when alcohol is used.

Other drugs commonly abused fall into six major categories: (1) stimulants, (2) opiates, (3) depressants, (4) cannabinols, (5) hallucinogens, and (6) inhalants. Each of these drugs has particular presenting symptoms of misuse and varies in its ability to induce tolerance, withdrawal, and dependence. Physical complications can be severe and often life-threatening.

Prescription drug misuse is becoming an increasing problem, especially for women and older adults.

Nurses who have contact with substance abusing clients can find the work challenging and rewarding if they are able to examine their own attitudes toward substance abuse and the client, accept the clients for themselves, provide a caring and nonjudgmental relationship, and set realistic goals for themselves and their clients.

Review Questions

1. Describe your understanding of alcoholism and how this understanding will affect your plan of care for the alcoholic client.

2. Describe alcohol's effect on the liver and the conditions that may result.

3. What are the important psychological factors that need to be taken into account when assessing a client's motivations for a rehabilitation program?

4. Describe the various treatment modalities available for the substance abusing client and give your ideas about the timing and appropriateness of each.

5. Nursing attitudes toward the substance abusing client can affect progress of treatment either favorably or unfavorably. Discuss this statement.

Research Report

The Role of Alcohol in Family Violence.

Alcohol use and family violence are problems affecting substantial proportions of all segments of the population. Since both conditions cause difficulties within families, the link between the two was studied to obtain a better understanding of the relationships that exist. A sample of men who had been identified as being violent toward their partners were administered three instruments to assess drinking habits and tactics used during conflicts. Contrary to most studies that identify the father's alcohol use as being significant, the alcohol use by the mother of the batterer was associated with his alcohol use. Attention should be given to the influence of mothers on the drinking patterns of their sons.

J.L. Davies, Paper presented at the University of Rochester School of Nursing, May 1984.

Suggested Annotated Readings

Beauchamp, D. *Beyond Alcoholism.* Philadelphia: Temple University Press, 1980.

The book traces a set of ideas that have evolved as the concept of alcoholism. While the alcoholic client is no longer defined as being morally deficient, he is still considered basically different or ill, which assumes that everyone will realize that the problem resides with the deviant. The author presents these theories for debate and discussion.

Corrigan, E. *Problem Drinkers Seeking Treatment.* New Brunswick, New Jersey: Rutgers Center of Alcohol Studies, 1974.

This monograph describes a study to understand what happens to a person who seeks help for a difficult and misunderstood problem. It explores characteristics of problem drinkers that prevent them from continuing their quest and why institutions fail when help is needed.

Perez, J. *Counseling the Alcoholic Group.* New York: Gardner Press Inc., 1986.

Guidelines are presented for counselors to function effectively as leaders of alcoholism groups. Practical and theoretical aspects of the group process, group leadership, techniques, therapeutic activities, and dynamics of group members are presented.

Steiner, C. *Games Alcoholics Play.* New York: Ballantine Books, 1971.

This book describes a transactional analysis approach to the problem of the drinking client. Ways to break up the games and scripts that are frequently played by these clients are presented. The aim is to provide lay and professional readers with information leading to the understanding and more effective treatment of alcoholism and other addictions.

Sullivan, E., L. Bissell, and E. Williams. *Chemical Dependency in Nursing: the Deadly Diversion.* Menlo Park, CA: Addison Wesley Publishing Co., 1988.

The authors attempt to end the "throwaway nurse syndrome." This comprehensive guide tells how to deal effectively and humanely with the problem, from identification of the chemically dependent nurse through intervention, treatment, and re-entry into the job market. The aim is to bring the problem into the open and provide practical methods to work with.

References

Anderson, R. C., K. E. Anderson, and A. Smith. "The Effects of Alcohol Consumption during Pregnancy." *American Association of Occupational Health Nurses* 34 (1986):88–91.

Beckman, L. J. "Women Alcoholics: A Review of Social and Psychological Studies." *Journal of Studies on Alcohol* 36 (1975):797–824.

Bingham, A., and J. Bargar. "Children of Alcoholic Families." *Journal of Psychosocial Nursing* 23 (1985):13–15.

Burkhalter, P. *Nursing Care of the Alcoholic and Drug Abuser.* New York: McGraw-Hill, 1975.

Donovan, D., and C. Marlatt. "Assessment of Expectancies and Behavior Associated with Alcohol Consumption." *Journal of Studies on Alcohol* 41 (1980):1153–1185.

Eells, M. A. "Interventions with Alcoholics and Their Families." *Nursing Clinics of North America* 21 (1986):493–503.

Fenichel, O. *The Psychoanalytic Theory of Neuroses.* New York: W. W. Norton, 1945.

Frank, L. "A New Attack on Alcoholism." *The New York Times Magazine* (October 20, 1985):47–50, 61–69.

Freedman, P. M., H. I. Kaplan, and B. Sadock. *Modern Synopsis of Psychiatry II.* Baltimore: Williams & Wilkins, 1976.

Glatt, M. N. *A Guide to Addiction and Its Treatment.* New York: John Wiley & Sons, 1974.

Goodwin, D. "Alcoholism and Heredity: A Review and Hypothesis. *Archives of General Psychiatry* 36 (1979):57–61.

——. "Genetic Aspects of Alcoholism." *Drug Therapy* 6 (1982):57–66.

Jaffee, J. "Drug Addiction and Drug Abuse." Paper presented at Northeast Regional Medical Education Center, Northport, New York, 1983.

Jellinek, E. M. *The Disease Concept of Alcoholism.* New Haven: Hillhouse Press, 1960.

Jessor, R., T. Graves, R. Hanson, and S. Jessor. *Society, Personality and Deviant Behavior.* New York: Holt, Rinehart and Winston, 1968.

Lachman, V. D. "Why We Must Take Care of Our Own." *Nursing* 86 (April 1986):41.

Leiber, C. S., D. P. Jones, M. Lasowsky, and C. Davidson. "Interrelations of Uric Acid and Ethanol Metabolism in Man." *Journal of Clinical Investigation* 41 (1962): 1863–1870.

McCord, W., and J. McCord. *Origins of Alcoholism.* Stanford: Stanford University Press, 1960.

Mendelson, J., and N. Mello. "Biologic Concommitants of Alcoholism." *New England Journal of Medicine* 30 (1979):912–921.

Menninger, K. *Man Against Himself.* New York: Harcourt, Brace and Co., 1938.

Merton, R. *Social Theory and Social Structure.* New York: Free Press, 1957.

Moskow, H., R. Pennington, and M. Knisely. "Alcohol, Sludge, and Hypoxic Areas of the Nervous System, Liver and Heart." *Microvascular Research* 1 (1968):174–185.

Nathan, P. E. "Failure of Prevention: Why We Can't Prevent the Devastating Effect of Alcoholism and Drug Abuse." *American Psychologist* 38 (1983):459–467.

National Institute of Mental Health. *Alcohol and Alcoholism.* Washington, D. C.: U.S. Public Health Service, 1968.

Niven, R. G. "Adolescent Drug Abuse." *Hospital and Community Psychiatry* 37 (1986):596–607.

O'Brien, C. P., G. E. Woody, and A. McLellan. "Modern Treatment of Substance Abuse." Paper presented at Northeast Regional Medical Education Center, Northport, New York, 1983.

Ogur, B. "Long Day's Journey into Night: Women and Prescription Drug Abuse." *Women and Health* 11 (1986): 99–115.

Plant, O. "Women with Drinking Problems." *British Journal of Psychiatry* 137 (1980):280–290.

Raffoul, P. R. "Drug Misuse among Older People: Focus for Interdisciplinary Efforts." *Health and Social Work* 11 (1986):197–203.

Schuckit, M. D. *Drug and Alcohol Abuse.* New York: Plenum Press, 1979.

Smithers Foundation. *Understanding Alcoholism.* New York: Charles Scribner's Sons, 1968.

Warner, R., and H. Rosett. "The Effects of Drinking on Offspring: A Historical Survey of the American and British Literature." *Journal of Studies on Alcohol* 36 (1975):1395–1420.

Waxman, H. M., M. Klein, and E. A. Carner. "Drug Misuse in Nursing Homes: An Institutional Addiction?" *Hospital and Community Psychiatry* 36 (1985): 886–887.

Weiten, W. *Psychology Applied to Modern Life.* Monterey: Brooks/Cole, 1983.

Congenital Variations and Disruptions

Learning Objectives

After reading this chapter, the student should be able to:

1. Discuss the influence of heredity on the etiology of variations and disruptions of congenital origin.

2. Contrast the effects of biological, social, and environmental factors on variations and disruptions of congenital origin.

3. Emphasize the importance of multidimensional data collection in formulating nursing approaches for clients and families confronting variations and disruptions of congenital origin.

4. Utilize primary, secondary, and tertiary levels of prevention in nursing approaches to clients experiencing or at risk for variations and disruptions of congenital origin.

Overview

Years ago, the trend was to segregate persons with physical and mental disabilities from the mainstream of society and to limit their rights as individuals. Over time, however, many positive changes have occurred in the treatment of the disabled. Trends such as normalization and mainstreaming have brought the disabled out of institutions and into their communities. As a result, more health care providers are interfacing with these people, and nurses in all areas of specialization are being challenged in the care of this population.

It is essential for psychiatric nurses in particular to understand the various types of variations and disruptions of congenital origin, including their etiology, impact on health and development, and complications as well as current treatments and prevention. With this knowledge, the psychiatric nurse can appropriately assess client needs and plan nursing interventions, independently or in collaboration with others. The purpose of this chapter is to address these issues and guide the psychiatric nurse in a caring approach to increase the coping skills of the disabled and chronically ill populations.

Growing up with a physical or mental disability is a profound challenge for any child and his family. As the individual with a variation or disruption of congenital origin enters adulthood, his physical and mental impairments can impede his ability to meet the expectations of society, putting him at risk for psychosocial maladjustment. Often it is the psychological impact of a chronic illness

or disability rather than the physical complications that interferes with the person's ability to maintain health status and to function at the highest level of potential (Hamburg 1983). For these reasons, psychiatric nurses can play a major role in the care of individuals with variations and disruptions of congenital origin.

For purposes of the chapter, "variations and disruptions of congenital origin" is used as a generic term to describe birth defects and disabilities. In caring for individuals with such problems, the psychiatric nurse should be familiar with the following definitions:

Variations and disruptions of congenital origins are abnormalities in growth, physical structure, and genetic makeup that result in cognitive and physical impairments.

Developmental disability is any severe, chronic disability attributable to a mental or physical impairment that is manifested before age 22, that is likely to continue, and that will result in substantial functional limitations in self-care, language, mobility, self-direction and motivation, or the capacity for independent living (American Academy of Pediatrics 1979).

Chronic illness is any illness with a protracted course that can be progressive and fatal or that is associated with a relatively normal life span despite impaired mental or physical functioning (Mattsson 1972). It has also been defined as any illness that lasts for more than three months in any given year or that requires one month or more of continued hospitalization.

ETIOLOGY OF VARIATIONS AND DISRUPTIONS OF CONGENITAL ORIGIN

Altered patterns of congenital origin vary greatly in their presentation and in their visibility, extent of involvement, potential for cure, and rate of occurrence. A wide range of factors are known to be involved in the etiology of these disorders. Genetic and environmental factors interact to produce the physical, mental, and biochemical characteristics of the developing child. Some defects are caused primarily by the genetic component, while others result primarily from environmental factors such as trauma or a serious infection. Many are the result of the interaction of both genetic and environmental factors.

Anomalies or insults can occur at any stage of fetal development; the timing of such occurrences is critical because it influences the presentation and involvement of the variation. In particular, exposure to drugs or infections during the earliest stages of embryonic development can have the most profound consequences. A number of prenatal, perinatal, and postnatal factors have been identified in the etiology of alterations of congenital origin.

Prenatal Factors

Prenatally, genetic factors are a major source of altered patterns of congenital origin. Aberrations in the structure and number of chromosomes lead to defects such as Klinefelter's syndrome and Down's syndrome. Some disorders are inheritable through basic Mendelian patterns; examples are phenylketonuria and Tay-Sachs disease. Finally, a number of disorders, including spina bifida, result from the interaction of genetic and environmental factors (multifactorial inheritance).

Environmental factors that can have an adverse effect on the developing fetus include maternal infections, such as viruses, rubella, syphilis, cytomegalovirus (CMV), and maternal exposures to radiation and industrial chemicals. Some drugs consumed during pregnancy are known to cause congenital malformations; see Table 11–1. Fetal alcohol syndrome is a recognizable pattern of multiple congenital anomalies seen in infants of mothers with chronic alcoholism (Scheiner 1980).

Extremes of maternal age also place the infant at great risk. Mothers under the age of 17 are at risk for having a child with congenital or gestational problems (Scheiner 1980). Mothers over the age of 35 have a significantly increased risk for having an infant with a chromosomal abnormality. Maternal malnutrition can result in intrauterine growth retardation. Mothers with a metabolic dis-

order such as diabetes also have a greater risk for prematurity and for congenital anomalies in their offspring.

Advanced paternal age has been associated with Down's syndrome, hemophilia A, Marfan's syndrome, and fibrodysphasia ossificans. The effects of exposure to drugs, chemicals, and physical agents remain to be studied. While alcohol use by the mother may lead to fetal alcohol syndrome, very little is known about the effect of alcohol use by the father on the offspring. Agent Orange, a chemical used in Viet Nam, is being studied for its contributions to birth defects among children of soldiers exposed during their tour of duty (Cohen 1986).

Another major environmental factor that can affect prenatal development is maternal socioeconomic level. Women at lower socioeconomic levels are at greater risk for having poor obstetric care, inadequate nutrition, poorer health status, and pregnancies at an earlier age. All these factors may lead to complications during pregnancy and to congenital anomalies (Robinson and Robinson 1976).

Table 11–1. Drugs That May Affect the Fetus

Drugs	Effects on the Fetus
Antibiotics Streptomycin Terramycin Tetracycline	Hearing loss, retarded skeletal growth, cataracts, staining of teeth
Anticoagulants	Increased risk of fetal hemorrhage or death, mental retardation
Alcohol	Small head, facial abnormalities, heart defects, low birth weight, mental retardation
Aspirin and other salicylates	If used in large quantities, may cause neonatal bleeding and gastrointestinal discomfort
Anticonvulsants	Heart defects, mental retardation anomalies such as cleft lip
Barbiturates	Digital and facial anomalies, heart lesions, hypocalcemia
Hallucinogens	Suspected to cause chromosome damage, spontaneous abortion, behavioral abnormalities
Narcotics	Maternal addiction increases risk of premature delivery; fetus often addicted to narcotic agent, which results in a number of complications
Sex hormones	Cardiac defects and limb defects, masculinization of the female fetus, other anomalies
Tranquilizers	Possible cardiovascular defects, may produce respiratory distress in newborns
Nicotine	Growth retardation; increased risk of spontaneous abortion, stillbirth, infant mortality

Perinatal Factors

During the perinatal period, obstetric complications and complications of the birth process may result in serious insults to the infant. Obstetric complications include premature labor, abruptio placentae, cord prolapse, multiple births, toxemia, and breech birth. Maternal factors that may place an infant at risk include a chronic history of abortions, births of infants with congenital defects, stillbirths, and premature labor.

During the birth process, an infant may suffer asphyxia or trauma, resulting in lack of oxygen to vital areas of the brain or in physical injury. Anoxia is a major pathologic mechanism in such disabling conditions as mental retardation and cerebral palsy. Gestational problems such as prematurity, low birth weight, and postmaturity have been associated with greater risk of developmental delay and physical impairments. Premature infants in particular are vulnerable to developing neonatal illnesses such as respiratory distress syndrome that may adversely affect their future development or even place them at risk for permanent impairments.

Postnatal Factors

A number of events occurring in the postnatal period can cause physical or mental impairment of the child. *Trauma*, one of the most common disabling conditions of childhood, can result in a physical impairment such as paraplegia or cerebral palsy. Traumatic injuries to the brain may lead to conditions such as seizure disorders and mental retardation. Serious infections, such as bacterial meningitis and encephalitis, have also been associated with residual impairments to the child; the extent of impairment may vary from a mild ataxia and learning deficit to severe mental retardation, cerebral palsy, blindness, and deafness.

Exposure to environmental toxins is another postnatal factor that can adversely affect a developing child. One of the most serious toxic problems today is lead poisoning. The clinical sequelae of lead poisoning include anemia, behavioral changes, and—in the severest degree—mental retardation, paralysis, blindness, and convulsions (Whaley and Wong 1983).

Living in an impoverished environment can also have a significant impact on a child's ultimate health and development. Children in poor families may not receive adequate health care, nutrition, stimulation, or supervision from adults. In addition, children in such environments are less likely to be exposed to learning activities and parental attention that provide intellectual stimulation and help prepare them for school.

Chronically ill children may also suffer impairments as a residue of their illness that limit their functional abilities. For example, a child with a severe cardiac defect may have limited mobility and self-help skills because of circulatory compromise.

In the following discussion of types of variations and disruptions of congenital origin, the etiology for certain disorders will be addressed more specifically.

TYPES OF VARIATIONS AND DISRUPTIONS OF CONGENITAL ORIGIN

Most of the commonly occurring and serious altered patterns of congenital origin presented in this section are apparent early in life or during the early developmental years. The disorders or disabilities are presented briefly to familiarize the psychiatric nurse with them and their treatments.

Mental Retardation

Mental retardation is one of the most prevalent and yet most misunderstood handicapping conditions in the United States today. In this country, individuals with mental retardation make up approximately 3 percent of the population. The majority of mentally retarded persons are classified as *mildly* retarded; this classification is approximately seven to eight times more common than any other degree of retardation (Whaley and Wong 1983).

Tremendous changes have occurred in attitudes and philosophies regarding care for the mentally retarded. Years ago, mental retardation was treated as an illness, and individuals with this disability were segregated from society, institutionalized at an early age. Today the majority of mentally retarded individuals live in their homes and communities, and the care they receive is individually and developmentally focused. In recent years, federal legislation has been passed guaranteeing the rights of mentally retarded individuals to protection, treatment, and especially education. In addition, there has been growing awareness that mentally retarded children benefit from early intervention and teaching, especially in the home. Early intervention focuses on the teaching of basic life skills, language development, social skills, and fine and gross motor skills.

Changing attitudes toward care have major implications for all health care providers because they are likely to have increasing contact with mentally retarded individuals. Nursing can play a key role in the coordination of care, formulation of care plans, and management of problems associated with mental retardation. For this reason, it is crucial that nurses be knowledgeable in defining mental retardation and in managing its problems, and be sensitive to the needs of individuals and their families.

DEFINING MENTAL RETARDATION According to the American Association on Mental Deficiency (AAMD), *mental retardation* is defined as "significantly subaverage general intellectual functioning existing concurrently with deficits in adaptive behavior and manifested during the developmental period" (Grossman 1973, p. 3). It is important to realize that this definition emphasizes both intelligence and adaptive behavior as inclusive criteria for the diagnosis of mental retardation.

"Significant subaverage intellectual functioning" refers to an IQ of approximately 70 or below. Most standard measures of IQ, such as the Stanford-Binet and WISC, are used to assess intellectual functioning. "Adaptive behavior" refers to the degree to which an individual meets the milestones or standards of personal independence and social responsibility expected for her age within a specific culture (Clifford 1980). At different ages, different skills or tasks are expected for adequate adaptive function. Parents are often the first to notice signs of inadequate adaptive function, such as delays in gross and fine motor skills, late language acquisition, and poor judgment skills. In school-age children, measures of adaptive behavior are viewed in terms of academic performance. For adults, vocational skills, independent functioning, and social skills indicate adaptive functioning.

Five classifications are used to describe the degree of disability and educational potential of mentally retarded individuals. Table 11–2 lists the various classifications according to range of IQ and expected skill level. In counseling parents, it is more important for the nurse to focus on the child's individual abilities, strengths, and skill level than on IQ numbers. Cases of moderate to profound degrees of mental retardation are often associated with other physical disabilities and with chronic illnesses such as seizure disorders. Individuals in this category are likely to have more acute illnesses and to need care for chronic problems and therefore will have greater contact with health care professionals.

The cause of mental retardation is known in only a small percentage of cases—approximately 6 percent. In the majority of cases, the cause is either unknown or not yet classified. The generally recognized sources of mental retardation were described earlier in this chapter.

IMPLICATIONS FOR NURSING: THE CHILD Because of the commonality of developmental disabilities, expanded efforts are needed to identify infants and children who may be candidates for special services.

For many families, the nurse is the primary source of information regarding a child's development and should address two areas of concern: (1) Children should not be labeled "delayed" since this may become a self-fulfilling prophesy, causing parents to lower their expectations and provide less stimulation and fewer learning opportunities; (2) Since considerable controversy exists about the predictive value of scores on infant intelligence tests, these tests might better be seen as an indication of current status and as a means to monitor progress overtime (Yoos 1985).

There are two different groups of developmentally delayed children whose needs vary considerably: those in whom environmental factors such as deprivation are major influences and those who are biologically impaired.

A comprehensive parent interview and past history are essential. A general physical and neurological examination must be done along with a developmental assessment. Intervention programs can then be devised and recommended. Programs for children who are mildly retarded as the result of deprivation are focused around intellectual development and enhancement of the parent-child relationship. For biologically damaged children, programs can, within the constraints of the condition, maximize residual function and prevent secondary problems.

The goal of caring for a mentally retarded person is to promote his optimum development and level of independence as an individual within a family and community. In helping him achieve this goal, it is important for the nurse to understand the learning potential and deficits of the mentally retarded. With a knowledge of the learning problems associated with mental retardation, the nurse can use appropriate teaching methods to train retarded individuals.

The potential for a mentally retarded individual to learn self-help skills, vocational skills, and social skills depends on his functional level and on the appropriateness of the teaching techniques. Mentally retarded learners have marked deficits in their ability to discriminate between two or more stimuli and also have difficulty in areas of abstract thought. Such learners are best taught through concrete instruction and demonstration. Mentally retarded learners also have problems with short-term memory. Because of this, they learn best by simple step-by-step instruction. A teaching technique frequently used with the retarded is *task analysis*, in which a particular task is divided into progressive steps and the child is taught one step before moving on to the next. Because mentally retarded learners may lack motivation for learning a skill, positive reinforcement may be helpful. Techniques of behavior modification are frequently used to help these individuals develop various skills.

Several recent changes have made a significant impact on the habilitation of mentally retarded

Table 11-2. Classifications of Mental Retardation

Category	Preschool (birth to 5 years): Maturation and development	School-age (6 to 21 years): Education and training	Adult (21 years and older): Social and vocational adequacy
Borderline IQ 68-83	Usually has minimal lags in all areas of development. May not be diagnosed until child enters retardation school, usually related to psychosocial causes.	Can achieve regular academic skills with special assistance (education).	Capable of marriage and child rearing. Capable of employment, but vocational choices may be limited to skilled labor. May need additional support during crisis.
Mild (educable) IQ 50-67	Develops normal skills at much slower rate (approximately half) than normal. May have impaired coordination.	Can acquire practical skills, purposeful reading and math skills to fourth-grade level with special education. Achieves mental age of 8 to 12 years.	Functions primarily in sheltered workshop. Capable of vocational skills and independent living. May need much support during times of stress.
Moderate (trainable) IQ 35-49	Marked delays in development. Condition usually associated with disorders such as cerebral palsy, seizures.	Can learn necessary academic, manual, and self-care skills to function in community with supervision. Achieves mental age of 3 to 7 years.	Can perform simple skills in sheltered environment. Is easily frightened and has limited judgment.
Severe IQ 20-34	Severe delays in infancy; little or no communication skills. Associated with other physical disorders or illnesses. Cause usually known.	Can respond to training in self-help skills, such as toileting. Achieves mental age of toddler.	Responds to daily routines and repetitive activities. Needs continuous supervision in protective environment such as home, group home.
Profound IQ 0-20	Gross retardation, infantlike behavior. May walk but may not speak. Associated with other physical disorders or illnesses.	Obvious delays in all areas of development. Training is primarily in areas of developing sensory-motor skills. Achieves mental age of infant.	Needs complete custodial care, which may be provided outside of home.

individuals. *Normalization* is a habilitation principle advocating that services be provided for handicapped individuals in the same manner as for non-handicapped. The goal of normalization is to establish as normal a living pattern as possible for mentally retarded persons. An example of the impact of this principle is the movement of mentally retarded children and adults out of large segregated institutions into small community residences (group homes).

The formation of these group homes has often been a source of controversy among other people in the community. Many are hesitant about having people with mental handicaps in their areas because of the false assumptions that the handicapped are aggressive and dangerous and will disrupt the neighborhood. They also fear that property values will decline as a result.

Another change that parallels normalization is the trend toward *mainstreaming*. The goal of mainstreaming is to place a disabled child in a community school that can provide the least restrictive environment to meet his educational needs. The trend toward mainstreaming has proven to be controversial when the educational programs do not provide the trained personnel and special assistance mentally retarded children need. Many school programs have special classes (EMR class)

with trained personnel and support services to best meet mentally retarded children's needs.

Since many retarded children live in their own homes, respite programs have been developed to provide relief for the family. The aim of such programs is to prevent family breakdown and the institutionalization of the child.

IMPLICATIONS FOR NURSING: THE ADULT Throughout the 1970s, advocacy for people with disabilities brought about new programs, among them the self-help advocacy movement for persons with mental retardation and other developmental disabilities. These groups provide a forum for their members to learn the rights and responsibilities of citizenship, to speak on their own behalf, and to provide support for those who are learning to live in the community. Participation in such a group helps many retarded persons to admit their disability and shed negative self-perceptions that are usually associated with being a member of a stigmatized group (Rhoades et al. 1986).

Problems with normal body functioning may become more prominent in adult years for retarded individuals. Dental health is one area of concern, as years of drug therapy for seizure control can lead to gum hyperplasia and improper placement of teeth. Mouth breathing, grinding of

POSSIBLE NURSING DIAGNOSES FOR VARIATIONS AND DISRUPTIONS OF CONGENITAL ORIGIN

Impaired adjustment
Anxiety
Ineffective family coping
Diversional activity deficit
Altered family processes
Fear
Dysfunctional grieving
Altered growth and development
Altered health maintenance
Impaired home maintenance management
Hopelessness
Total incontinence
Potential for infection
Potential for injury
Knowledge deficit
Impaired physical mobility
Noncompliance
Altered parenting
Feeding/bathing, toileting/dressing self-care deficit
Self-esteem disturbance
Social isolation

The above are the more likely diagnoses related to variations and disruptions of congenital origin. Nursing diagnoses are not limited to the list above. Manifestations of these disorders are individualistic even though certain prevailing patterns are identifiable.

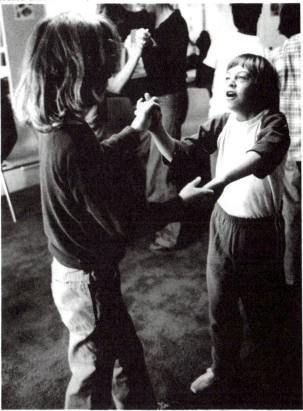

Children with Down's syndrome can live happy lives if they receive affection and encouragement from their companions.
SOURCE: Elizabeth Crews, Stock Boston, Inc.

teeth, and cavity formation from inadequate brushing and poor diet, contribute to the problems. Structured dental programs that involve regular checkups and teaching of good oral care should be stressed.

Weight gain is a problem, as most retarded adults have a tendency toward obesity due to a lack of physical exercise and to the early experiences of receiving candy and food as reinforcers in learning programs. Deviations in posture and stance may become more pronounced. Most are the result of physiological disruptions occurring with the brain damage in earlier years. Corrections may not be possible, but most clients will benefit from a daily program of activity that includes physical exercise to strengthen muscles and reduce weight.

Perceptual handicaps require ongoing evaluation and correction because some retarded adults progress through the aging process more rapidly than would be expected.

There are wide variations in the emotional characteristics of mentally retarded adults. Traits and behavioral responses are usually formed by reactions elicited from others. Aggression may be an unconscious attention-getting mechanism, while withdrawal may be a reaction to anger. Self-abuse becomes a method to relieve boredom and experience sensory stimulation. Elation and embarrassed laughter can come from imitating those who are uncomfortable in conversing with a retarded person.

As mentally retarded persons age, they are faced with changes in living arrangements, transitions from educational to occupational settings, and establishment of new routines. Many have difficulty coping with new experiences and receive less support from parents and siblings. Consequently, they may be subject to anxiety and depression. Mentally retarded persons can benefit from supportive psychotherapy and this should be available and considered (Benchot 1984).

The frequency rate of mental illness in retarded persons ranges from 20 to 35 percent (Hodgins and Monfils 1985). The presence of a dual-diagnosis client, one with retardation and mental illness, provides special challenges to nursing staff in psychiatric hospitalizations. Some of these clients are nonverbal and are unable to express their needs in a conventional manner. This requires nurses to be creative in developing ways of interacting with these clients. If the client is physically capable of communicating verbally, he should be encouraged to talk and given full, careful attention so that he is not frustrated by having to continually repeat the expression.

Special care is required for clients who show self-abuse and aggression. Tolerance and empathy are needed because many clients cannot indicate their needs or concerns. Frequently many of the syndromes of mental retardation dictate allied medical needs that must have attention. A care plan for these individuals must include the deficits and impairments as well as approaches for dealing with inappropriate behaviors. Plans must be made to maintain the optimal level of functioning. This functional level should be developed by involving the client in a full day of educational, vocational, and social programs.

Mentally retarded adults are also at risk to develop substance abuse problems. Studies have reported that 25 to 60 percent of clients in vocational rehabilitation facilities and centers for independent living were abusing alcohol and drugs to the extent that social, mental, and physical functioning were impaired (Greer 1985). One complicating factor for those who are mentally retarded is the prevalence of taking anticonvulsive medications. When taken with alcohol, the sedative effect is compounded. Deinstitutionalization has increased the exposure of the retarded client to the local tavern as a center for socialization where there is a sense of acceptance for the lonely and the isolated.

More research is needed on the continuing development of the mentally retarded adult. Rather than comparing these individuals with normal populations, their uniqueness must be explained. The nursing perspective must emphasize the fostering of independence rather than the need for constant care.

Down's Syndrome

Down's syndrome, one of the most commonly known syndromes associated with a chromosomal abnormality, is actually a multiple system disability characterized by mental retardation and various physical manifestations.

In approximately 95 percent of all cases of Down's syndrome, an extra chromosome 21 produces the alterations in physical and mental development. The extra chromosome occurs as a result of faulty chromosome distribution in the egg or sperm or during division of the fertilized egg. Trisomy 21 is associated with increasing maternal age. The incidence of Down's syndrome increases strikingly as maternal age increases, especially over the

age of 35. In fact, 50 percent of all cases of Down's syndrome occur with maternal age greater than 35. There is increasing evidence that paternal aging can contribute to Down's syndrome as well.

The remaining cases are caused either by a translocation of chromosomes 15 and 21 or a maldistribution that occurs in a later stage of the division of the fertilized egg, called *mosaicism*.

CLINICAL MANIFESTATIONS The classic clinical manifestations of Down's syndrome include flat facial features, flat occiput, epicanthal folds, narrow palate, short broad hands with simian creases, and hypotonia. The accompanying box provides a more thorough list of the physical characteristics. Although the syndrome can be readily diagnosed by these clinical manifestations alone, chromosomal analysis is usually done to confirm the diagnosis.

A number of congenital anomalies and physical problems are associated with Down's syndrome. Approximately 40 percent of the infants born with the syndrome have a significant congenital heart defect. Less frequently occurring anomalies include intestinal atresias, seizures, strabismus, tracheoesophageal fistulas, and atlantoaxial subluxation due to hypoplasia of the odontoid process (Bartoshesky 1980). Various types of leukemia also have increased incidence in children with Down's syndrome. Respiratory and ear infections are common and can be chronic. Because of chronic ear infections and potential middle ear malformations, Down's victims also have an increased risk of hearing impairment. Dental problems are common because of malformed teeth and gum disease. Delays in gross motor ability may occur because of hypotonia.

The most significant feature of Down's syndrome is mental retardation. The majority of affected individuals are mildly to moderately retarded, within the trainable average. Initially, infants with Down's syndrome appear to have normal mental development, but by age two there is a relative decline in performance, and a plateau is reached at about age four. Gross motor delays, visual impairments, and speech delays can all affect various aspects of the child's development. Individuals with Down's syndrome usually perform well on measures of social competence, but behavior disorders can occur.

IMPLICATIONS FOR NURSING In recent years much research has been done on the care of individuals with Down's syndrome. Issues that have been investigated include institutional versus home care and the impact of early intervention. Home care provides many benefits for children with Down's

PHYSICAL CHARACTERISTICS OF DOWN'S SYNDROME

Hypotonia, especially in newborn period
Flat facial features
Flat nasal bulge
Microcephaly
Flat occiput
Inner epicanthal folds
Upward slant of palpebral fissures
Speckling of iris (Brushfield's spots)
Small, malformed ears
Narrow, high, arched palate
Protruding tongue; may be fissured or furrowed
Dental hypoplasia
Short neck with redundant skin
Short stature
Hyperextensible joints
Transverse palmar crease (simian crease)
Short, broad hands
Incurved little finger (clinodactyly)
Characteristic dermal ridge pattern

syndrome. Early intervention programs have encouraged the earlier attainment of developmental milestones for these children.

The potential for the child with Down's syndrome is great if she has the care of a loving, supportive family, early appropriate stimulation and educational programs, and access to advanced medical technology. It is the responsibility of the health care provider to identify the needs, strengths, and weaknesses of the individual and to plan for appropriate comprehensive care to meet these needs.

Learning Disabilities

Learning disability, an alteration in cognitive processes, can be a severely handicapping condition with broad implications for the development of a child's self-esteem, educational achievement, and family life. A *learning disability* is an impairment in one or more cognitive processes, such as attention, memory, visual perception, or written or spoken language (Levine 1980). Manifestations of learning disabilities are seen in problems with reading, mathematics, spelling, or comprehension. Examples of learning disabilities include *dysgraphia* (difficulty writing), *dyslexia* (difficulty reading), and visual-perceptual disorders.

A number of etiologic factors have been known to place a child at risk for developing a learning disability. Such factors include familial patterns, early childhood illness, perinatal injury or stress, environmental deprivations, nutritional deficiencies, and stressful life events (Levine 1980). A child from a lower socioeconomic background may be at greater risk for developing a learning disability because of danger of poor health care, poor nutrition, and lack of parental models to stimulate learning readiness skills.

The severity of learning disabilities may vary at different ages. For this reason, early identification and intervention is crucial for a learning disabled child to achieve academic success. Once a child is identified as having a learning disability, an appropriate school program with special education can be planned and provided.

Commonly associated with learning disabilities is a behavioral condition known as *attention deficit disorder* (also referred to as hyperactivity or minimal brain dysfunction). Attention deficit disorder is a behavioral problem characterized by chronic inattention, overactivity, and difficulty in dealing with multiple stimuli. A number of manifestations have been associated with this disorder—see the accompanying box. For a particular child, the manifestations may be few or numerous, mild or severe, and they will vary at different developmental levels. For example, the behavioral manifestations may be apparent at an early age but the associated learning disabilities will not fully manifest themselves until the child enters school. Many of the characteristics of attention deficit disorder diminish by adolescence, but ongoing emotional difficulties may place the adolescent at risk for developing poor self-esteem, behavior problems, and sociopathic behavior. An individual with continual failures at home, in school, and in peer relationships will have a negative view of himself and of other people.

IMPLICATIONS FOR NURSING Varley (1985), found that 50 percent of children with attention deficit disorders referred to a tertiary care facility had other psychiatric disorders as well: the most common were conduct and adjustment disorders. About 3 percent were mentally retarded. Poor self-concept and feelings of isolation were identified in these children. Many had been subject to frequent discipline and criticism. Treatment focused on helping the children experience success in some arena to develop a sense of self-worth. Counseling also aimed to address the problems of developing and maintaining friendships which coexist with the poor tolerance of their impulsivity.

There are multiple aspects to the management of children with attention deficit disorders. Involved in such management are special education,

---

BEHAVIORAL MANIFESTATIONS OF ATTENTION DEFICIT DISORDERS

Short attention span

Hyperactivity

Distractibility

Impulsivity

Difficulty reaching satisfaction

Difficulty with peer relations

Fatigue

Labile emotions

Sleep problems

Motor skill deficits

Impaired memory

Deficits in communication skills

Perceptual deficits (left/right confusion)

---

family education and counseling, medication, and planned alterations in the environment. Individual psychotherapy may be necessary for a child to modify behavior problems or develop improved self-esteem. Medical research has shown that central nervous system stimulants are often effective in reducing the symptoms of affected children. The most commonly used stimulants are amphetamines, especially methylphenidate (Ritalin) and dextroamphetamine sulfate (Dexedrine).

Learning disabilities associated with attention deficit disorders are complex conditions that require early intervention, ongoing follow-up, and changes in management according to the individual child's needs.

Phenylketonuria

Phenylketonuria (PKU) is a relatively rare autosomal recessive disorder characterized by an alteration in the body's ability to metabolize the essential amino acid phenylalanine (Whaley and Wong 1983). The basic defect is a deficiency in the liver enzyme phenylalanine hydroxylase, which results in an accumulation of phenylalanine in the blood and in urinary excretion of an abnormal by-product, phenylpyruvic acid. This accumulation interferes with normal growth and development of the brain and central nervous system.

CLINICAL MANIFESTATIONS Normally, phenylalanine hydroxylase converts phenylalanine to tyrosine, which is essential for the formation of the

pigment melanin. Because of the tyrosine deficiency that occurs with PKU, affected children have fair skin, blond hair, and blue eyes.

At birth, PKU infants appear perfectly normal. However, if the deficiency goes undetected and the infant ingests milk, increased blood and tissue levels of phenylalanine will develop. This accumulation and its abnormal by-products will result in damaging effects on the nervous tissue and in such common clinical manifestations as developmental delay, failure to thrive, irritability, frequent vomiting, hyperactivity, and unpredictable, bizarre behavior. Seizure activity and abnormal EEGs are common in the severely retarded.

IMPLICATIONS FOR NURSING The need for early identification of PKU victims and immediate therapy is obviously paramount. If the condition is detected in the newborn, treatment can begin immediately and the damaging effects can be prevented. The treatment of PKU is dietary regulation of phenylalanine, which should continue until the child is six to eight years of age.

For mentally retarded children with PKU, dietary restriction can limit the progression of the disorder and improve the child's behavior. Pregnant women with PKU are at risk of having an infant with congenital malformations if they have high levels of phenylalanine.

Primary prevention of mental retardation from PKU involves screening of newborns for abnormal levels of phenylalanine in the blood or of its by-products in the urine. The most commonly used test for screening newborns is the Guthrie blood test. This test is mandatory for all newborns in most states. If parents do have a child with PKU, they should be offered genetic counseling.

Cystic Fibrosis

Cystic fibrosis, the most common fatal genetic disease among white children, is transmitted through an autosomal recessive mode of inheritance. Also known as mucoviscidosis, cystic fibrosis is a disease of generalized dysfunction of the exocrine (mucus-producing) glands. It is a complex disease affecting multiple organ systems in varying degrees of severity, but the majority of children affected have symptoms involving the respiratory system (Schwartz 1978).

CLINICAL MANIFESTATIONS The major clinical manifestations of the disease are gastrointestinal malabsorption related to pancreatic enzyme deficiency, progressive obstructive pulmonary disease, and elevated sweat concentrations of sodium and chloride. The primary mechanism causing these manifestations is a blockage of the organ passages by increased viscosity of mucous secretions. The mucous glands produce a thick mucoprotein that blocks the passages of the pancreas and bronchioles. The significant elevation of sweat electrolytes is related to malabsorption of sodium by the sweat glands.

The pancreatic enzyme deficiency results in impaired digestion and absorption of essential nutrients, especially fats and proteins. Thus, the child with cystic fibrosis has foul-smelling, greasy stools and appears very thin despite a voracious appetite. The pulmonary complications are the most serious threat to survival. The obstruction of the bronchioles and the stasis of mucous in the lungs result in chronic respiratory infections, impaired oxygen/carbon dioxide exchange, and progressive pulmonary dysfunction.

Cystic fibrosis is suspected if one or all of the following are present: history of chronic respiratory disease, positive family history for cystic fibrosis, and reported symptoms of gastrointestinal malabsorption (Larter 1981). Confirmation of the disease occurs with a positive sweat chloride test.

IMPLICATIONS FOR NURSING The care of a child with cystic fibrosis is complex and primarily involves dietary management, replacement of oral pancreatic enzymes, treatment of respiratory infections, and good pulmonary therapy (postural drainage and cupping). Many advances in the management of individuals with cystic fibrosis have increased the life expectancy to young adulthood, but the prognosis remains grim. The goal of caring for an individual with cystic fibrosis is to help the child reach the highest level of functioning at each stage of the disease. Care includes monitoring the individual's psychosocial adjustment, recognizing illness-related emotional problems, and providing the necessary psychosocial support.

Men with cystic fibrosis who live to adulthood have delayed growth and sexual maturation, but the hormonal system is not affected and the libido and secondary characteristics are normal. Sexual performance is also normal, but commonly a developmental abnormality in the reproductive tract prevents the release of sperm into the semen, causing infertility.

Women with cystic fibrosis also have delayed sexual maturation but establish normal menstrual cycles eventually. The fertility rate is reduced because of the viscosity of the cervical mucous, which inhibits sperm penetration, and frequent respiratory problems that contribute to irregularity of anovulatory cycles. Many women with cystic fibrosis can have children. However, the demands of pregnancy place an extra burden on these clients; fluid overload can induce pulmonary complications (Libby 1986).

Cystic fibrosis can produce overwhelming psychosocial problems for the client and the family. The cost of the multitude of medications required each year can result in a financial burden. Fear of suffocation, embarrassment over oderous flatulence and stools, and the almost constant need for bronchial drainage can impede psychological development. Stress management techniques can be of value for these clients (Keller, Guzman, and Culan 1985).

Sickle Cell Anemia

Sickle cell anemia is a genetic disease of hemoglobin abnormalities in the blood. It is found mostly in black persons whose origins are in central Africa.

Sickle cell disease is the result of amino acid substitution in the chain of hemoglobin. Because of this substitution, when the hemoglobin is deoxygenated, it forms long rods that distort the cell, changing it to a sickle shape. To a certain extent, sickling can be reversed when the cell is reoxygenated, but those cells which are continuously distorted eventually have irreversible damage. The rigidity that results impedes the passage of the cells through the circulatory process and the reduction in blood leads to infarction or tissue hypoxia which is called *vaso-occlusive crisis*. The fragility of the cells and the destruction of the abnormal cells by the spleen leads to chronic hemolytic anemia. The life of the sickled red blood cell is about 20 days as compared to the 120 days for normal cells (Hathaway 1984).

CLINICAL MANIFESTATIONS Clients with sickle cell anemia exhibit fatigue, pallor, weakness, and sometimes mild jaundice. The disease may be marked by recurrent crises, systemic pain, blood clots in vital organs, and severe infections. Overwhelming sepsis and spleenic sequestration carry the risk of early sudden death, which is characteristic of the disease.

IMPLICATIONS FOR NURSING Sickle cell anemia is managed conservatively to prevent complications. Health maintenance of the child is of utmost importance and should include continued follow-up. Parents need to be educated as to the early signs of infection and the importance of immunization of the children, especially with the pneumococcal vaccine. Supplementary folic acid therapy is usually given to encourage bone marrow activity and alleviate the anemia. During a crisis, the client should avoid any activity that increases oxygen usage. Sedation can be given along with analgesics for pain, which usually lasts from two to four days.

---

important means of avoiding serious complications of the disease.

Cerebral Palsy

Cerebral palsy is a chronic nonprogressive brain disorder that results in alteration of motor function and coordination. The degree of impairment and involvement of other systems varies among individuals, as does the etiology.

A number of prenatal, perinatal, and postnatal conditions have been known to cause cerebral palsy. Cerebral anoxia resulting from other conditions is the basic pathological mechanism leading to brain damage and subsequent motor impairment. Prenatal factors known to contribute to cerebral palsy include intrauterine infections, brain anomalies, radiation, trauma, and maternal bleeding. Perinatal factors include prematurity, intracranial hemorrhage, birth trauma, cardiopulmonary problems, and hyperbilirubinemia. During childhood, conditions that may result in cerebral palsy include head trauma, cerebrovascular accident, and infections of the central nervous system (Abrams and Panagakos 1980).

Cerebral palsy is usually classified according to the nature and manifestations of the neuromuscular dysfunction. Spasticity is characterized by persistence of primitive reflexes, clonus, hypertonia, and a resistance to rapid movement. Dyskinesia is a disruption of involuntary movement that results from changes to the basil ganglia. This includes slow, writhing, and uncontrollable movements; tremor; and rigidity. Ataxia is incoordination of voluntary movement accompanied by balance and position sense problems stemming from cerebellar dysfunction.

CLINICAL MANIFESTATIONS A primary manifestation of the disorder is significant delay in gross motor development. An infant with cerebral palsy will show delays in all expected motor skills; this is particularly significant if the infant is normal in all other areas of development. Other manifestations include abnormal motor skills (e.g., abnormal crawling), muscle tone abnormalities, abnormal posture, and persistence of primitive infantile spasms (Whaley and Wong 1983).

A number of other impairments may be associated with cerebral palsy. Half of the children with cerebral palsy are mentally retarded, and the greater the brain damage, the higher the likelihood of cognitive involvement (Abrams and Panagakos 1980). Other commonly associated problems include feeding difficulties, seizure disorders, hearing impairments, learning disabilities, attention deficit disorders, and strabismus. As with other

Attempts to modify the hemoglobin distortion or disrupt its formation have not been successful. Autotransfusion (a process in which the client's blood is removed and treated to increase hemoglobinated oxygen, then returned to the client) is showing some promise as a treatment regimen. Partial replacement of the client's blood, called hypertransfusion is usually limited to clients in periods of risk, such as pregnancy and surgery (Pollard 1986).

As a chronic disease, sickle cell anemia offers nurses many opportunities for prevention, management, and education. Practical solutions may be years away. Adequate maintenance is the most

*Normal (left and right) and
"sickled" (center) red blood cells
from a person with sickle cell
anemia.*
SOURCE: R.M. Zucker, B.F. Cameron, and R.C. Leif/BPS

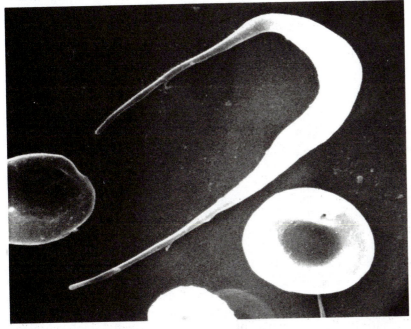

disabled children and adults, cerebral palsy clients are at risk for developing poor self-esteem and psychosocial adjustment problems.

IMPLICATIONS FOR NURSING The management of cerebral palsy is multiphasic and depends on the severity and involvement of the disability. The goal in management of cerebral palsy is to help that individual reach his highest level of potential within the physical limitations of the disability. An important key to successful management is the early identification of involved infants and provision of necessary treatment. Treatment of cerebral palsy focuses primarily on orthopedic care, physical therapy, and occupational therapy. The treatment plans aim at encouraging mobility and self-help skills, correcting orthopedic deformities, and preventing additional deformities that may limit function. Surgery may lengthen muscles to release contractures, prevent more serious deformities and make the gait more normal.

Physical therapy is a crucial component of treatment to facilitate motor development and prevent contractures. Adaptive equipment is needed to position the child properly for mobility and optimal interaction with the environment. Educating parents is of utmost importance. Telling them that their child has cerebral palsy requires patience and sensitivity, as hearing the diagnosis often brings many emotions to the surface. Cerebral palsy is relatively misunderstood. Care should be exercised in discussing the future as accurate predictions cannot be made regarding motor functioning and intellectual ability later in life (Hillquist 1985).

An adult with cerebral palsy may seem more disabled than a child because of chronic contractures and bony deformities that limit function and because of the greater complexity of expected skills. The chronic treatment of cerebral palsy involves ongoing therapy, orthopedic follow-up, and the care of associated disabilities.

Spina Bifida

Spina bifida (meningomyelocele) is a major congenital malformation that affects multiple body systems. Meningomyelocele belongs to the group of neural tube defects that may include anencephaly, abnormalities of the head, and abnormalities of the spine. Meningomyelocele is characterized by a sac-like cyst, protruding through a vertebral defect, that contains the meninges, cerebral spinal fluid, and a part of the spinal cord and its nerve roots. Meningomyelocele results in damage to the underlying nervous tissue and associated neurologic impairment. The associated problems include partial or complete paralysis of the lower extremities, hydrocephalus, bony deformities, impaired lower extremity sensation, bladder incontinence, and bowel incontinence. The degree of involvement depends on the anatomic level of the defect and the size of the lesion.

ETIOLOGY The causes of spina bifida remain unknown, although it is believed to be the result of multifactorial inheritance. In multifactorial inheritance, a defect results from the interactions of genetic influences with factors in the fetal (maternal) environment.

A number of environmental factors have been proposed to cause meningomyelocele. Those include viral infections, maternal fever, and medications such as valproic acid (Myers 1984). Vitamin deficiencies (especially folate) during the first trimester are also thought to contribute to the defect. A number of studies have been conducted to test the hypothesis that early vitamin supplementation may prevent meningomyelocele (Myers 1984).

Although the cause of meningomyelocele is unknown, the pathologic mechanism resulting in the defect is known. Normally, formation of the neural tube begins by the twentieth day of gestation and the tube is fused or closed by the twenty-eighth day. In meningomyelocele, the neural tube fails to close and the surrounding tissues develop abnormally.

IMPLICATIONS FOR NURSING When an infant is born with meningomyelocele, the initial care involves a multidisciplinary evaluation to assess the extent of the disability and the family's need for supportive care and education. Early surgical closure (within the first 24 to 48 hours) of the defect is recommended. Following closure, the infant is monitored closely for the development of hydrocephalus. Surgical shunting procedures are performed to control the progression of hydrocephalus. The majority of children with meningomyelocele and shunted hydrocephalus are of normal intelligence but may experience learning disabilities.

Varying degrees of paralysis and bony deformities of the lower extremities occur as a result of the spinal defect. Because of imbalances between functioning and nonfunctioning muscle groups, clients are at risk for developing contractures and such problems as hip dislocation. The goals in orthopedic management are to reduce and prevent deformities of the lower extremities and to provide mobility. Children with flaccid paralysis can be made functionally mobile with a brace known as the Rochester parapodium. The parapodium allows the paraplegic to view the world from an upright position and to fully explore the environment. Orthopedic care also involves physical therapy and surgical interventions as necessary.

Meningomyelocele also results in impaired sensation in the lower extremities. Affected individuals are at risk for developing decubitus ulcers, burns, and abrasions that may be debilitating.

Urinary incontinence results from abnormal innervation of the bladder and bladder sphincter. Most children with meningomyelocele have a flaccid bladder, which leads to overflow incontinence. A small group have spastic bladders with small bladder capacities and incomplete emptying. In addition to urinary incontinence, bladder dysfunction can lead to recurrent urinary infections and such renal problems as reflux and hydronephrosis. These urologic problems can result in renal damage and renal failure. The goals in urologic management are preservation of renal function and promotion of socially acceptable continence. Today the major method of promoting continence is clean intermittent catheterization (CIC). Clean intermittent catheterization facilitates regular drainage of the bladder, thus reducing overflow incontinence and reflux. The success of CIC depends on compliance with the catheterization at scheduled intervals. Artificial sphincters have also been used to promote urinary continence, alone or with CIC.

Bowel incontinence results from abnormal innervation of the rectum, external anal sphincter, and abdominal muscles. With a dysfunctional anal sphincter, there is uncontrolled passage of stool. Children with a neurogenic bowel are at risk for chronic constipation and fecal impactions. The goals in management are to prevent or manage constipation and promote stool continence (Henderson and Synhorst 1977). Dietary changes (high-fiber bran diets), regular toileting, and the use of stool softeners and laxatives are treatments utilized to address these goals.

Spinal cord dysfunction can also result in impaired sexual function. Males with meningomyelocele may be impotent or may have retrograde ejaculations with significantly reduced fertility. Females with this disability have decreased sensation but normal fertility.

Meningomyelocele is a complex disability that involves multiple body functions. The care of an individual with meningomyelocele requires long-term, comprehensive, coordinated management. The care provider must be sensitive to the ongoing psychosocial needs of the individual and her family and to the developmental needs of the individual. Recent advances in the medical care and habilitation of children with meningomyelocele have provided much hope for successful and satisfying growth through adulthood, although societal attitudes may limit a disabled adult's ability to achieve a satisfying lifestyle. Nursing can play a key role in advocacy for the disabled in the community.

Advances in genetic diagnostics have led to the availability of prenatal diagnosis for parents at risk for having a child with meningomyelocele. The most commonly used techniques are genetic counseling, ultrasound, and amniocentesis. These studies are usually done during the fourteenth to sixteenth week of pregnancy. Through amniocentesis, an elevation in alpha-fetoprotein levels, may indicate the presence of meningomyelocele in the fetus. With open neural tube defects, alphafetoprotein is elevated in both the maternal serum and amniotic fluid. Prenatal evaluation for a neural tube defect allows the family to consider whether to continue the pregnancy. A family going through this process needs much support.

OTHER VARIATIONS AND DISRUPTIONS OF CONGENITAL ORIGIN

Tay-Sachs Disease

Tay-Sachs disease is an autosomal recessive disorder of relatively rare occurrence. This condition involves progressive neurologic deterioration and death before the age of four. Blindness and optic atrophy occur as the degeneration of the nervous system progresses. Varying degrees of mental retardation are associated with the disorder. The pathologic mechanism involved is a disorder of lipid metabolism, with a deficiency in the enzyme hexoaminidase.

Tay-Sachs disease occurs predominantly in Ashkenazic (Eastern European) Jews. Primary prevention of the disorder is possible with carrier screening.

Hemophilia A

Hemophilia is a generic term referring to a group of bleeding disorders that are due to a deficiency or an abnormality in one of the factors necessary for blood clotting. The two most common variants of this disorder are hemophilia A, or classic hemophilia (abnormal clotting factor VIII), and hemophilia B, or Christmas disease (factor IX deficiency). The symptoms are the same for all types of hemophilia, but specific factor deficiencies need to be identified to provide the appropriate replacement therapy.

The primary clinical manifestation of hemophilia is prolonged bleeding anywhere from or within the body. The degree of hemorrhage can vary from individual to individual. The first sign of the disorder can be bleeding from a minor surgical procedure, such as circumcision, or bruising from a slight injury, such as a fall. Another warning sign may be bleeding from the loss of a deciduous tooth. The bleeding may also be internal, especially into a joint, which may result in physically disabling and painful deformities.

The disabling limitations of hemophilia may be minimized with properly administered replacement therapy. For hemophilia A, the treatment involves the administration of blood factor VIII. The frequency and dosage of the therapy will vary with the type of hemophilia and the degree of bleeding. Children and adults are usually taught to administer the replacement factors to themselves. Such home care has proven to be highly successful in the management of hemophilia. Treatment also includes local emergency therapy to control bleeding. Another aspect of treatment is the promotion of a regular exercise program to strengthen muscles and joints.

Children and adults with hemophilia must adjust their physical activity to prevent injury. Successful adjustment to this disorder depends upon an understanding of the illness, a strong support system, ability to cope with limitations, and a positive self-image.

Klinefelter's Syndrome

Klinefelter's syndrome is a congenital defect resulting from an alteration in the sex chromosome makeup of the male cells. In this syndrome, an extra (or possibly more) X chromosome joins to the normal XY pair to result in an abnormal karyotype of XXY (Opitz 1982).

The major impact of this disorder is an alteration in sexual development. The syndrome may be detected in the newborn if his testes are significantly smaller than average, but it is usually not diagnosed until puberty. At that time, the primary manifestations of the disorder are delayed and immature male secondary sex characteristics. Individuals with this syndrome are usually significantly taller than normal males and are infertile. About 15 percent of those affected are mentally retarded (Opitz 1982). Personality disorders, behavioral problems, psychosis, and alcoholism are also common. This syndrome is treated with the administration of male sex hormones, and psychological care is frequently needed. Secondary prevention includes diagnosis by amniocentesis and treatment of the clinical manifestations.

Turner's Syndrome

Turner's syndrome is a classic example of a defect in the sex chromosome makeup of female cells. Instead of the usual sex chromosome pattern of XX, the female with Turner's syndrome has only one X, producing a karyotype referred to as monosomy X.

The characteristics of the disorder include sexual infantilism, short stature, webbed neck, infertility, hearing impairments, and visual defects. Also associated with the syndrome are congenital heart defects that may shorten the life span. The usual treatment includes hormone therapy (estrogen) and administration of anabolic steroids to stimulate growth. Psychological counseling may be necessary to improve self-esteem and to deal with difficulties in body image.

THE IMPACT OF VARIATIONS AND DISRUPTIONS OF CONGENITAL ORIGIN

A child with an altered pattern of congenital origin and his family are continually challenged in coping with the illness or disability. The child's disability affects not only his own but also his family's adaptation skills.

Alterations of congenital origin have an impact on all members of the nuclear and extended family. The basis of the family, the marital couple, faces many stressors that are frequently aggravated by the child's disorder (Battle 1975, Lawson 1977). The birth of a disabled child or an initial diagnosis of disability precipitates profound feelings of grief in the parents (Drotar et al. 1975). The loss of the "perfect" child may lead to a state of chronic sorrow, but dealing openly with this sorrow can augment the parents' ability to raise their disabled child adequately (Olshansky 1962). Siblings often feel resentment, insecurity, and fear of being afflicted with similar condition (Battle 1975, Lawson 1977). Grandparents often suffer feelings of loss similar to the parents' when an infant is born with a congenital defect.

Frequently, the responsibility of caring for the handicapped child rests with the mother, especially if she is a single parent. These women often feel they have failed in their maternal role, not only because of the oneness they felt with the child during pregnancy but because of residual folklore that places primary responsibility for the child on mothers.

Mothers may alter feeding behaviors by feeding their infants for shorter periods of time or when they are not hungry. As a mother anxiously compares her child's feeding habits and weight gain to those of others, she may allow all types of food regardless of nutritional value. Self-feeding may be delayed because the mother insists on doing the feeding and offers the food as a reward.

The mother's identification with her child may be delayed as a mechanism for shielding her from further hurt. The responses of the child cause grief, shock, and confusion and deplete the mother's energy. The lack of positive reinforcement from the infant further erodes the mother's self-image.

At times, unrealistic expectations and an unwillingness to stop searching for a cure prevent the completion of the grieving process. The child may be abandoned or neglected as a result of depression and the inability to work through problems (West 1984).

The health services that provide care for families frequently segregate the mother and disabled child from the rest of the family, since services are usually available at times that are inconvenient for employed family members and school-age siblings (Doernberg 1978). Overshadowing the everyday experiences of the disabled child may be parental uncertainties about the future because of complications associated with the disorder and a possible perception of the child as being vulnerable (Green and Solnit 1964).

Changes in Family Roles

Any chronic illness or disability has a major impact on the family, and sacrifice may become a way of life for various family members. This is true regardless of the identity of the individual who is afflicted, but it is especially true of the congenitally disabled child who enters the family as a newcomer. In such cases, there is no shared experience of love or trust on which to build, for the disabled child is an unknown element who brings overwhelming problems into a family group that is often unprepared for the hardships and adjustments that lie ahead (Griffin 1980).

A child with a congenital disability often becomes pivotal in the life of the family; major proportions of family time and activities tend to revolve around the special child. In some instances, the arrival of a child with a congenital disability may draw the parents closer as they endeavor to console each other. More often, however, a seriously disabled child represents a permanent challenge likely to test the strength of the marital bond and to impose complications on relationships between the parents and healthy children.

At the simplest level, someone has to care for the child around the clock. Thus, parents have less time to spend with each other and with healthy children and less time to pursue their own interests. Furthermore, medical expenses result in less disposable income for everyone. This means changed family habits and reduced amounts of money available for other purposes. Furthermore, the need to care for the disabled child may mean that the mother cannot work outside the home unless foster care can be arranged.

The financial burden of chronic illness is hardest on the middle-class family. Wealthy families can care for their child with minimal sacrifice, and poor families have access to public funds. But middle-income families may well be overcome by a disability of long duration.

A family with a disabled child requires help through the years, and the nature of this need changes as the child and family grow older. Friends and relatives cannot be expected to alter their lives permanently to help the family once the immediate crisis has been met. The parents may become so obsessed with their duties that they lose contact with friends and rarely escape from the pressures at home.

Some communities have established networks of parents whose children share the same disability. These groups are eager to help families with similar problems and to give practical advice, answer questions, and offer emotional support. Such groups are often living proof that parents can face problems that seem insoluble and still survive. Community groups may be affiliated with national organizations devoted to education and research concerning particular diseases or disabilities. These organizations provide additional resources for troubled parents. Many publish informative newsletters or journals that provide practical help to the parents and convey a feeling that they are not alone in their trouble.

A family with a chronically disabled child needs periodic reevaluation of its effectiveness. Adjustments that once strengthened the family may later become dysfunctional. In the first months after learning that an infant is seriously disabled, the mother may give all her time to caring for the child. At the same time, the father may take on more work to reduce family indebtedness. Healthy children called upon for assistance respond to the best of their ability. These first adjustments are usually effective; the baby is cared for, income is increased, everyone is joined in a common goal. Over time these same adjustments may become maladaptive, however. The mother may find she has become the sole caretaker of the child. Since she has been recognized as the expert, family members leave the child in her charge. She feels overburdened but is unwilling to allow her husband or the other children to take over her function. The father is deeply concerned about the child but his life is less dominated by the disability. As he sees his wife becoming more involved with the child he may become jealous and feel excluded. Rather than make more demands on his wife, he may withdraw further, spending more time at work or looking outside the home for companionship. At the same time, the mother may envy her husband's life outside the family. In their zeal to meet the needs of the disabled child, the parents may have caused their functions to be so separate that they have little in common with each other. Meanwhile, the healthy children in the family may be receiving insufficient attention, and their early willingness to cooperate may have deteriorated into indifference or rebellion.

Both father and mother may assign the disabled child the central role in the family. In these circumstances, family life revolves around the lim-

itations of the disabled child, and the needs of other members become secondary. Such overprotection inhibits the child's mental, physical, and psychological growth. The parents are so intent on coping with the disability that they lose sight of the real child. While single-minded attention to the sick child may create a strong partnership between the parents, it is unfair to the healthy children and may even prevent the disabled child from reaching full potential.

A paradoxical form of the sick role develops when the family "scapegoats" the disabled child. In this situation, parents and siblings blame all adversity in family relationships on the ill child. This behavior relieves a family of the difficult task of finding out what is really wrong and trying to correct it. Since the child is unlikely to get better, family problems may never be resolved. Scapegoating the sick child allows all deficiencies to be rationalized. This may be the most pervasive distortion in families with chronically ill children.

A common secondary gain for families with a chronically disabled child is that family relationships are simplified by the routine task of caring for the child. Other gains result from friends' and neighbors' recognition of the family's strength and courage. The mother, in particular, may feel pride in having met and overcome the challenge of caring for the child. It is not uncommon for a mother, after learning to care for her own disabled child, to return to school and become a specialist in caring for others with the same disability. The professionalization of the mother is worthwhile if she is willing and able to give her husband and her other children the attention they need. Otherwise, professionalization is only a sign of her total involvement with the disabled child and her inability to give to other members of her family (Griffin 1980).

The guilt that occurs after the birth of a disabled child can take many forms. Some parents who have produced a defective child feel that they are being punished for their sins. Other parents may try to escape responsibility by blaming each other. Devoted parents may set unreachable standards for themselves, thereby increasing their feelings of guilt and inadequacy. As the child grows older, the parents may be ashamed to be seen with him in public, yet feel guilty for being ashamed. Siblings have similar feelings. They may be reluctant to bring friends home because of embarrassment and may feel guilty because their presence in the home diverts parental attention from the task of caring for the disabled child. Conflicting emotions complicate the lives of every family member.

It is difficult to predict the reaction of relatives to the birth of a disabled child. The disability may frighten relatives and cause them to seem cruel and distant. Some grandparents blame the disability on the in-laws and feel that their own child has been unfairly burdened. Other grandparents may feel guilty, suspecting that their genes may have caused the defect. Relatives may be upset by the birth of a congenitally disabled child, wondering if they, too, will have defective children. These understandable reactions may restrict the amount of help that the stricken family can expect from relatives.

Because of the chronicity of the illness, good relationships between health professionals and the family are important. In addition to a variety of health services, the family needs a primary professional who can coordinate treatment and engage in ongoing assessment and evaluation of the changing needs of the disabled child and other family members.

Stress and Coping

The family has rarely had time to prepare for raising a disabled child. Most families have little previous exposure to such situations to help them develop mechanisms for coping with the stressors they must face.

The stress experienced by a disabled child and her family is described by Sperling (1978) as having two phases: acute and chronic. The *acute* phase is dramatic and intense, occurring when the child is born, during hospitalization, or when there is an exacerbation in the condition. The *chronic* phase is associated with daily coping with the physical limitations caused by a disability.

Factors that may affect stress levels include the developmental stage of the child, the perception of the disability or illness, the support systems available to the family, and the family's coping abilities (Hymovich 1976, Sperling 1978).

MATURATIONAL CRISES Maturational crises occur throughout the development of a child, producing unique stressors for the disabled child and his family.

There are critical transition points for families, which are usually related to stresses encountered throughout the child's life cycle. These stresses are associated with the child's excessive and prolonged dependency, the family's consciousness of being different and anxiety about the future. Early family adjustment is usually predictive of the psychological adjustment of these children.

The child's preschool years are characterized by the family's fears for the child's physical safety and the uncertainty about the diagnosis. As the child enters school, the confinement and financial aspects become more prominent. Mothers are usually unable to take employment outside the home. There are more comments about the child's condition as he gains a wider exposure to others.

In adolescence, the child may have an increased wish for independence, making the teaching of appropriate social skills difficult. Problems with self-care, personal hygiene, aggressive behavior, and frustration from ridicule by peers may be evident. Young adulthood calls for major decisions about the ability to leave home, work, marry, and have children. By this time, parents are cognizant of their own aging and have concerns about their ongoing responsibilities toward the child (Beavers, et. al. 1986).

PERCEPTION OF THE DISABILITY The individual's and family's perception of a disability may affect the amount of stress it produces. If parents overestimate the extent of the disability, they may see the child as vulnerable and become overly protective. The family's socioeconomic level can be a significant factor in the perception of a disability. In higher social strata, for example, the birth of a mentally retarded child may be viewed as a tragic crisis that is frustrating to the aims of the family (Farber 1968). In lower social classes, the birth of a mentally retarded child creates a crisis in role organization, as many parents are unable to meet the needs of the family because of disorganization.

SUPPORT SYSTEMS The amount of stress affecting a family with a disabled child may be reduced by the availability of support systems. Deep religious faith and a community of supportive relatives and friends have been identified as positive coping factors (Farber 1968, Battle 1975). Of particular adaptive value is a good relationship with the maternal grandmother (Farber 1968, Battle 1975, Lawson 1977). Another helpful support system is a multidisciplinary health care team that provides high-quality, affordable care. A community with resources that are responsive to the needs of the disabled or chronically ill is also a valuable support system.

COPING ABILITIES Coping abilities are resources the person uses to adapt to stress. Personal qualities of the child that affect long-term adaptation include maturity, intelligence, and a sense of humor; adaptive family qualities include stability, flexibility, warmth, and commitment (Pless and Pinkerton 1975). A strong marital relationship and financial stability also positively affect adaptation (Battle 1975, Lawson 1977). Another adaptive quality is a positive self-concept as a parent, which is essential for maternal attachment to a disabled infant. For this reason, parents tend to cope better if the disabled child is not their first. Another factor that can help the family adapt to disability is knowledge of the disorder and its expected changes or impact over time. Anticipatory guidance helps a family prepare for crises in the future.

Research about families with retarded children has indicated that higher functioning families had two adults (married or in a supportive relationship) in which the coalition for parenting was strong and each partner felt capable and valued in relation to the special needs of the family. Members of adaptive families were aware of the special needs of the child while still having energy and concern to maintain their interest and satisfaction in other family relationships and activities. There was an impressive give-and-take in these families, with an allowance for each person's views, experiences and the meanings attached to those experiences. Siblings were involved in the concern for the future care of the handicapped child and all members had considerable clarity regarding the functioning capacity of the child. The value system of the family included acceptance of responsibility, meeting and dealing with hardships, and rising to meet challenges.

In less well functioning families, the child and the primary care giver were the center of attention and concern. Uncertainty about the child's ability and lack of methods to deal with deficiencies increased the likelihood of conflict and weakened the coalition of the parents. There were control struggles in relation to the handicapped child and less expectations of a successful outcome. The handicapped child became the focus of the family fears and feelings of inadequacy. Support, flexibility, and respect for the individual was lacking (Beavers, et. al. 1986).

Adapting to Specific Disabilities

The problems facing the child and her family often depend on the specific type of alterations of congenital origin present. Different coping mechanisms are needed for dealing with physical, behavioral, emotional, social, and cognitive alterations.

PHYSICAL ALTERATIONS A major goal in caring for individuals with physical impairments is to address their need for efficient mobility. Mobility is critical to the early development of the child, for through mobility she is able to explore her environment and learn from her interactions. Mobility is also vital for the older child to maintain interactions with her peers.

A physical alteration with major impact on a child's self-esteem is incontinence. As mentioned earlier, incontinence is a common problem with spina bifida. This problem needs to be thoroughly assessed, and interventions should be planned to improve the situation. Incontinence causes a child to be dependent on parents for a longer than normal time, and protective clothing infantalizes the older child. In adolescents, feelings of low self-esteem and anger may decrease compliance with suggested treatments, and the incontinence problem will be magnified. When a child gains control of his incontinence, he will have feelings of achievement and improved self-esteem.

BEHAVIORAL ALTERATIONS Individuals with an alteration of congenital origin are at risk for psychological maladjustment, which is often manifested in behavioral problems. Adolescents who realize the permanence of their disability may experience feelings of anger and denial. Those with attention deficit disorders may react to their feelings of anger and lower self-esteem by engaging in delinquent behavior. Because of negative feelings, compliance with medical treatments and self-care may falter. The vulnerable child who has been overprotected by her parents may become passive and dependent on adults for interactions. In light of these potential problems, it is important to continually monitor disabled children's reactions and feelings and to address them through supportive techniques.

EMOTIONAL ALTERATIONS A disability can have a major impact on the individual's self-esteem. Self-esteem is made up of one's self-image, the reactions of significant others, and the values placed on oneself by others that one integrates. Disabled children and adolescents are at risk for low self-esteem because they view themselves negatively and feel different from others.

In emotionally abusive family situations, parents may downgrade the value of the disabled child and give him ambivalent messages. Such parents may not be able to separate their feelings about the child from those about the disability. Children who receive ambivalent messages are susceptible to feelings of low self-esteem. At the same time, parental reactions of overprotection and permissiveness can result in a dependent, demanding child. Such overprotectiveness is a consequence of guilt, anger, and ambivalent feelings. Parents do not give the child opportunities to develop feelings of initiative, independence, and self-esteem. Instead, the child learns to manipulate the adults in her life, and she interacts poorly with her peers.

SOCIAL ALTERATIONS The disabled or chronically ill child is likely to experience periods of loneliness, often as a result of repeated hospitalizations, social isolation, immobility, or limited peer interactions. Because the disabled child may have few opportunities to develop skills of social interaction with peers, the nurse should explore with the family methods and opportunities for increasing peer activities and other activities of interest.

Changes in societal attitudes and in the treatment of the disabled are making the community more accessible so that the disabled can participate in the mainstream of life. In addition, nursing interventions might include working with the family to improve mobility in the home environment, such as the addition of ramps to provide greater independence for the disabled individual.

COGNITIVE ALTERATIONS Mental retardation and learning disabilities are primary manifestations of many alterations of congenital origin. In other disorders, however, learning problems may be secondary sequelae. Children who are chronically ill may have poor school attendance, leaving gaps in their learning and resulting in academic failures. Emotional and behavioral alterations can also limit a disabled child's ability to function optimally in school. Specific therapy directed at increasing the child's coping abilities can increase his success in educational and social situations.

Sensory and adaptive impairments will dictate special learning needs for disabled children. In those with spina bifida and shunted hydrocephalus, for example, visual-spatial and perceptual difficulties are common. Any child with an alteration of congenital origin should have a thorough assessment of academic skills, intellectual functioning, adaptive skills, vision, hearing, and motor abilities before entering school. Such evaluations should be tailored to meet the specific needs of the individual child. From the data gathered in a preschool assessment, an appropriate educational program can be coordinated.

GENETIC SCREENING AND COUNSELING

Genetic screening is a systematic search for individuals with a given genetic constitution. The purpose of genetic screening is to identify those persons at risk, for themselves or their offspring, of getting a genetic disease. There are two types of screening: presymptomatic, which detects individuals whose own life is threatened (such as those with PKU), and carrier identification, which is done in subpopulations in which carriers of harmful mutant genes are common (such as those with sickle cell anemia).

Genetic counseling consists of accurate information gathering by the counselor to define the particular problem and educating the client to make an informed decision. The goals of genetic counseling are to inform parents of the risk of occurrence when a family member has a genetically influenced disorder and to help prevent serious birth defects in children (Whaley and Wong 1983). Genetic counseling and prenatal diagnostic techniques are recommended for parents who have had a child with a birth defect, who have a family history of a disorder, or who are considering pregnancy at an age associated with increased risk.

Genetic counseling is usually performed by trained specialists who have a comprehensive understanding of genetics and of various inherited disorders, their occurrence, and their risk of recurrence. Teams of experts in genetics are often called upon in delivery of this service. The genetic counseling team usually consists of a nurse, a social worker, trained counselors, a medical geneticist and a pediatrician. This team may refer to consultants that include clergy, specialists in medical ethics, and psychologists.

The primary goal of genetic counselors is to establish a trusting relationship with clients through effective communication of positive regard and empathy (Muir 1983). Most genetic counselors try to communicate facts in a nonjudgmental, neutral manner to better assist parents in their decision-making process.

A major step in the genetic counseling process is to carefully obtain a complete family history, which is recorded in a pedigree chart or family tree. The information necessary for an accurate pedigree chart includes data on the medical histories (diseases and disabilities), abortions, stillbirths, ethnic background, and causes of death for several generations. When the pedigree is completed, a particular problem may be identified and an estimation of risk may be given to the parents.

Both the counselor and the client must understand what the counseling process can accomplish. The purpose is not to direct the client to make certain choices but to provide information that allows the client to make informed decisions.

In the decision-making process, the counselor should remain nondirective. However, some points should be addressed. Choices do exist and a decision does need to be made. Not making a decision is a conscious decision and should be recognized as such. The counselor must explore the options with the couple while not advocating any particular one. Ethical and religious issues are always present. It is of greatest importance that the counselor not impose any value system or ethical standards on any of the clients. Nurses who are involved in direct genetic counseling need to provide psychological support to families in the counseling program. These nurses must have a basic understanding of genetic problems and an awareness of services available to affected families. They especially need to be sensitive to the needs of families and to be available to support them and listening to their concerns.

THE NURSING PROCESS IN VARIATIONS AND DISRUPTIONS OF CONGENITAL ORIGIN

Psychiatric nurses can play an essential role in the care of the individual with variations and disruptions of congenital origin. To care for these clients, the psychiatric nurse must be knowledgeable about the nature of the disabilities, their etiology, their impact on the individual and his family, and appropriate interventions. In addition, nurses working with this population must be particularly sensitive to the needs and feelings of affected families (Tudor 1978).

Nurses interact closely with a number of other health care professionals in planning coordinated, comprehensive care for disabled clients. Physical therapists intervene in areas of gross motor function, mobility, and development. Occupational therapists focus on the areas of adaptive function, fine motor skills, perceptual skills, and self-help skills. Furthermore, nurses from various areas of specialization may share in planning interventions. For example, a pediatric nurse may consult with a psychiatric mental health nurse regarding a hospitalized disabled adolescent who shows signs of depression.

In planning interventions, the care plan should be designed to meet the needs of the particular individual and his family. The client should not be considered alone but rather as a part of a family and community; a holistic approach to care of the client is essential.

Assessment

For disabled children to reach their highest potential, their health status should be monitored and their impairments assessed. Many children with congenital variations and disruptions are at risk for secondary impairments and health problems that may result in reduced functional ability. Observing for complications necessitates an understanding of the child's baseline health status and an awareness of the potential complications for each disorder. For example, a child with hydrocephalus needs to be monitored for signs of shunt failure and progressive hydrocephalus. If the hydrocephalus is uncontrolled, sensory impairment, loss of cognitive ability, motor impairment, and even coma can result.

Psychological assessment is also important. Assessing a child's feelings and understanding may require special techniques, such as play therapy and drawing, based on the developmental level of the child.

The parents', child's, and siblings' knowledge of the disabling condition should be assessed. During the period of initial diagnosis, the family may not hear all the information shared with them. Nurses often need to repeat information about the disorder, its treatments, and its potential complications. It is important that families feel comfortable enough with health care providers to ask their questions and express their concerns.

Another area for assessment is the support systems available to the family. If support systems are lacking, interventions can be planned to meet support needs. For example, the family may be referred to social service agencies, clergy, or parent support groups. Family assessment should occur in the home environment and, when needed, in the school environment.

Planning

Setting realistic goals for their disabled child may be a difficult task for parents. It is therefore important to help parents realize the strengths, potentials, and needs of their child. Realistic goal setting is influenced by the parents' perception of their child and by the child's degree of disability. Short- and long-term goals will be significantly different for a profoundly retarded two-year-old than for a school-aged child with mild motor impairment, for example. It is vital for parents to have hope for their child's future, but their expectations must be correlated with their child's actual potential. Providing parents with feedback regarding their child's abilities and impairments will help to reinforce a realistic perception of the child's future.

Parents of physically disabled children frequently look forward to the time when their child will reach adulthood and independent living. But physically disabled adolescents are often ill-prepared to meet the challenges of independent living. Preparation for independence should begin when a child is very young, and it needs continual reinforcement. A physically disabled child should be encouraged to be as independent as possible at each developmental age. As the child develops, his skills should be cultivated to reach his highest level of potential.

Implementation

Tudor (1978) has outlined goals for interventions with developmentally disabled infants, but these goals can be modified to meet the needs of children or adolescents of any age:

1. In times of crisis the family must be supported and provided with resources to adapt and meet the total needs of the family.

2. The individual child must be helped to reach the highest level of health, development, and independent function within her potential and degree of disability. Each child is an individual with unique strengths, abilities, potential, and needs. The family may need guidance to identify these strengths and set realistic goals.

3. The disabled or chronically ill individual must become a loved, integrated member of the family and community.

A few major interventions are necessary to help meet these goals, including family intervention, realistic goal setting, coordination of comprehensive care, health assessment, and genetic counseling.

A nurse may interact with an affected family during any phase or stage of the disabling condition. Therefore, it is vital for the nurse to evaluate the individual family members' strengths, coping mechanisms, and reactions to the disabled member and to the disability. To understand the needs of a family and how they may respond to suggested interventions, the nurse must assess the impact of the disability on each family member, including parents, siblings, and extended family members. Fathers are often overlooked because mothers most frequently interact with the child's health care providers. It is essential for fathers to be included in all assessments and planning interventions.

Major requirements of effective family intervention are being available, willing to listen, and sensitive to the particular needs of a family. Each family will respond differently to the stresses and crises associated with a disabling condition. Some families will adapt rapidly to a new crisis; others will respond more slowly and need more time and intervention. In situations of maladjustment and major crisis, families may need intensive crisis intervention, individual therapy, or family therapy.

For a family to adjust and regain equilibrium, each family member must be supported and involved in the planning process. Supporting the disabled child may involve helping him reduce his feelings of being different. The child needs to understand the disability and realize his strengths and interests. He should be encouraged to share with disabled peers, to mobilize his coping abilities, and to verbalize his concerns. Allowing the child control of aspects of his life will also improve his feelings of self-esteem.

Child and parent education regarding the disability is an essential intervention in the maintenance of health status. The child and parents need to know the potential complications and necessary interventions, including therapies, medications, and special care needs.

Evaluation

Nurses can play a key role in the coordination of care of individuals with variations and disruptions of congenital origin because of their understanding of the medical care and the multiple disciplines that may be involved. It is the lack of coordination that frequently makes treatment implementation difficult. The role of the nurse as coordinator requires continuous evaluation. Nurses are also involved in the day-to-day management of the problems facing a family with an affected child. With their knowledge of family needs, they have a unique perspective that is necessary to coordinate family-focused interventions. Coordination of care, is essential to avoid miscommunications, duplication of care, and gaps in service. The health care team for a particular child may include the pediatrician, school nurse, teacher, specialty care providers, and therapists. Establishing lines of communication with all these providers and the family is an important function.

Modern care of the developmentally disabled often centers around established, coordinated, interdisciplinary teams. Some teams function primarily to diagnose needs and obtain services. Other multidisciplinary teams provide ongoing evaluation and treatment, such as spina bifida clinics, cystic fibrosis centers, and hemophilia centers. Each program should have the disciplines necessary to meet the needs of the population.

SUMMARY

The health care of a child with a physical or mental disability has experienced many changes over the years. Many such children are now treated in communities and in their homes rather than in institutions. This has resulted in greater numbers of nurses and other providers being involved with the care of these clients.

A number of prenatal, perinatal, and postnatal factors have been identified in the etiology of variations and disruptions of congenital origin. Genetic and environmental influences interact to produce the physical, mental, and behavioral characteristics of the developing child. The most common disorders of congenital origin include mental retardation, Down's syndrome, learning disabilities, phenylketonuria, Tay-Sachs disease, cystic fibrosis, hemophilia, sickle cell anemia, cerebral palsy, spina bifida, Klinefelter's syndrome, and Turner's syndrome.

It has been the goal of this chapter to help prepare psychiatric nurses for the care of individuals with altered patterns of congenital origin. The individual affected by a disability or chronic illness *(Text continues on page 303.)*

A CHILD WITH DOWN'S SYNDROME

The Hazlett family consists of Tim and Michelle Hazlett, their six-year-old daughter, Betsy, and their two-year old son, James, who was born with Down's syndrome. James has demonstrated several developmental lags and has required constant medical care and personal attention since birth. Most of the responsibility has fallen on Michelle. Her husband helps with the household chores but not with the care of his son. In the last two years, Betsy has become his joy and solace. Father and daughter are very close; Tim spends most of his evenings reading to her or playing games with her. Betsy attends school during the day, which provides her with playmates and relieves the load on her overburdened mother.

ASSESSMENT

During the initial interview, it was noted that although the family had been coping, the distance between husband and wife had been widening. Michelle had become increasingly resentful toward her husband. Tim, for his part, was repelled by the services his son needed and could not bear to observe the boy closely. Michelle sensed this, although it was never discussed, and she became reluctant to ask Tim for assistance in caring for James. She also felt excluded from the happy times that Tim and Betsy shared in the evenings. In her loneliness, Michelle began to feel that she and James were both rejects. She also spent a great deal of time wondering why their child had been born retarded and if it were inherited from her family or from her husband's.

The following diagnoses were made:

Nursing Diagnoses

Altered parenting
(related to overinvolvement of mother with son, father with daughter, lack of father's participation in care)

Diversional activity deficit
(related to lack of adult social activities for parents, time for self for mother)

Impaired home maintenance management
(related to burden of care of disabled child)

Knowledge deficit
(related to lack of information concerning occurrence of Down's syndrome)

Multiaxial Psychiatric Diagnoses

Axis I   V61.10 Marital problem
            V61.20 Parent-child problem
Axis II   318.10 Severe mental retardation
Axis III   Down's syndrome
Axis IV   (for the child) Chronic life-threatening illness, enduring circumstance. Severity: 4 (for the parents) Serious chronic illness in child, enduring circumstances. Severity: 5
Axis V   Current GAF for family: 40
            Highest GAF in past year: 50

PLANNING

The family was visited regularly by a nurse practitioner from the local chapter of the Association of Retarded Persons. It was to her that Michelle turned for help. Although the nurse had been concerned primarily with helping Michelle cope with James, she was aware of problems within the marital relationship. The first nursing goal was to reduce the excessive involvement between mother and son and to encourage the interaction between father and son. In this way, the nurse hoped to relieve the burden carried by Michelle and to encourage a family structure that did not fragment parent and sibling relationships. Secondly, there was a need to arrange for open discussion between husband and wife concerning the causes of, and probability of the occurrence of, Down's syndrome.

IMPLEMENTATION

The primary objectives for interventions were to reduce Michelle's preoccupation with James and to simplify his care, to modify the relationship between Tim and Betsy to include Michelle, and to strengthen the marital partnership by encouraging communication and shared activity between husband and wife.

The first intervention the nurse made was to provide practical advice. As an expert in mental retardation, she was knowledgeable about special chairs, feeding aids, adaptive devices, and other labor-saving techniques. Michelle had some equipment, but James could obviously use more. By arranging to visit in the evening, the nurse was able to involve Tim in helping to simplify James's care.

The nurse commented on Michelle's need for adult company and suggested that the couple plan for some recreational activities together. She gave

Nursing Diagnoses	Goal	Nursing Actions	Outcome Criteria	Outcome Evaluation
Altered parenting	Involvement between mother and son will be reduced, father's participation in care will increase.	Visit during evening, to include father. Encourage communication of feelings of frustration regarding son's disability.	Parents will share responsibilities for care.	Father remained reluctant to care for his son's physical needs but did agree to read to him. Total acceptance may be unrealistic.
Diversional activity deficit	Outlets for mother and activities for mother and father together will be provided.	Assist in obtaining qualified babysitters to allow for social times in evenings. Encourage participation in support groups.	Parents will spend time with each other; will benefit from shared experiences of parents with similar problems.	Parents were able to enjoy an occasional evening out together. The mother became involved in support groups but the father chose not to participate. He needed more time to adjust to the situation.
Impaired home maintenance management	Care of child will be easier for both.	Provide advice on care giving, assist in obtaining special equipment.	Home care schedule will be simplified by reorganization, demands on mother will be decreased.	Labor-saving devices were obtained which gave the mother more time to share in activities with her husband and daughter; time for herself will be available.
Knowledge deficit	Parents will understand their influence in the occurrence of Down's syndrome.	Arrange for visit to genetic counselor.	Accurate information will open communication and resolve suspicions on both sides.	Parents responded well to informational session, were able to share feelings and concerns.

them a list of qualified babysitters endorsed by the local retardation chapter. Because Tim resisted the idea of joining a group of parents with children like James and needed more time to work through his feelings, the nurse put only Michelle in touch with a parents' group. Even though Tim did not accompany her, Michelle needed to meet with other parents who might alleviate her feelings of isolation.

It was suggested that the couple visit a genetic counselor to obtain more information about the occurrence of Down's syndrome. It was hoped that this would lead to better communication on the issue. Both Michelle and Tim agreed to this.

EVALUATION

Because James's disability was permanent, evaluation, like assessment and planning, was ongoing. Helping the father adjust to his son's disability was likely to be a protracted process that might never be wholly successful. However, it was possible for the nurse to ascertain that the first primary objective had been accomplished. James's routine care was simplified and the demands made on his mother's time and energy were eased. Regular communication with parents who were experiencing similar problems helped reduce Michelle's sense of isolation, even though her husband resisted the idea of participation. With more time at her disposal, Michelle was able to devote additional attention to her daughter. The closeness between father and daughter

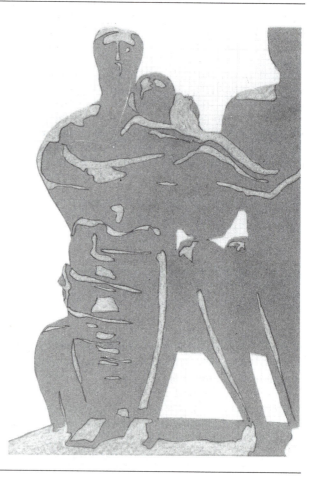

continued, but Michelle began to share in some of the games and activities from which she had previously been excluded.

Tim remained reluctant to undertake James's physical care, but he did agree to read to his son at bedtime and stay with both children when Michelle wished to attend meetings of the parents' group. Recruiting qualified babysitters allowed both parents to go out together occasionally, a welcome change for them. It allowed Tim to see Michelle as a wife and companion rather than as a harassed, preoccupied caretaker. Michelle began to realize that her narrow world could expand to include her husband and healthy daughter as well as her disabled son.

Both were enlightened at the information given them by the counselor and were then able to share their own suspicions about the cause. This relieved some of the tension between them.

---

is at risk for maladaptation to the situation. Many challenges and stressors affect a disabled person and his family. Their understanding of the disorder, their social supports, and their coping abilities will influence their adaptation to the disability. Because psychiatric nurses may be called upon to intervene at various stages of a disability, they should be sensitive to the behavioral, emotional, social, and cognitive effects of the disability on the individual and his family. Armed with this sensitivity and a knowledge of disabilities, psychiatric nurses can serve as advocates for the disabled in their community. By being role models for others, they can help improve social attitudes toward the disabled and their acceptance in the community.

Review Questions

1. Compare and contrast genetic and environmental causes of variations and disruptions of congenital origin.

2. Describe the influence of the home environment on children with disabilities.

3. Describe the degrees of mental retardation and suggest appropriate nursing interventions for each.

4. Discuss the critical components of family intervention.

5. Describe the process of realistic goal setting for a child with a variation or disruption of congenital origin.

Research Report

Maternal Psychological Conflicts Associated with the Birth of a Retarded Child.

This study was undertaken to learn more about the feelings of mothers who had given birth to retarded children, with special attention to the troublesome quality of those feelings. Fifty mothers were interviewed during the child's first year of life.

Most of the mothers experienced guilt, thinking they had done something to cause the problem. Many described feelings of denial, inferiority, dishonor, disgrace, and shame. Many needed to blame others for the problem. The author concludes that support for these mothers is essential immediately after delivery when the mother is informed of the retardation and again, three weeks following the birth, when feelings of depression, decreased self-concepts, and marital difficulties may be experienced.

R.E. Childs. *Maternal-Child Nursing Journal.* 14, no. 3 (Fall 1985):175–182.

Suggested Annotated Readings

Blackwell, M. *Care of the Mentally Retarded.* Boston: Little, Brown & Co., 1979.

This book presents the full spectrum of special needs of retarded persons that require nursing attention. Emphasis is given to theories and technical skills important to caregivers of various backgrounds who work with the mentally retarded.

Fagin, C. *Nursing in Child Psychiatry.* St. Louis: C. V. Mosby, 1972.

The content of this book is intended as source material for nursing students. It provides an overview of child psychiatric nursing and covers several areas in depth. The principles of behavior modification are applied to various conditions.

Hall, D., and H. Jolly. *The Child with a Handicap.* Boston: Blackwell Scientific Pub., 1984.

Written for those working with children as well as their parents, this book discusses behavior problems and their modification. Parents are seen as vital members of the team helping the child to achieve optimal capabilities.

Shanks, S. J. *Nursing and the Management of Pediatric Communication Disorders.* San Diego, CA: College-Hill Press, 1983.

This text, designed for multidisciplinary use, demonstrates how vital the nurse's collaboration is in the management of children's communication disorders. It discusses practical aspects of patient management, utilizing the nursing process with a wide variety of communication problems.

Steele, S. *Health Promotion for the Child with Long Term Illness.* Norwalk, Conn: Appleton-Century-Crofts, 1983.

The author focuses on health promotion in order to compensate for deficits that are already present or which may occur in chronically ill children. Guidelines are presented for children and families for promoting healthy behaviors that can result in improved health status for these children.

References

Abrams, I., and D. Panagakos. "The Child with Significant Developmental Motor Disability." In *The Practical Management of the Developmentally Disabled Child.* A. Scheiner and I. Abrams, eds. St. Louis: C. V. Mosby, 1980.

American Academy of Pediatrics. *Official Statement to the Committee on Children with Handicaps.* Washington, D.C.: The Developmental Disability Council, U.S. Department of Health, Education and Welfare, 1979.

Bartoshesky, L. E. "Genetics and the Child with Developmental Disabilities." In *The Practical Management of the Developmentally Disabled Child.* A. Scheiner and I. Abrams, eds. St. Louis: C. V. Mosby, 1980.

Battle, C. "Chronic Physical Disease: Behavioral Aspects." *Pediatric Clinics of North America* 22 (1975):525–533.

Beavers, J., R. Hampson, Y. Hulgus, and W. Beavers. "Coping in Families with a Retarded Child." *Family Process* 25 (1986):365–378.

Benchot, R. "The Mentally Retarded Adult: A Nursing Perspective." *Journal of Community Health Nursing* 1 (1984):235–246.

Bergsma, D., ed. *March of Dimes Birth Defects Compendium,* 2d ed. New York: Alan R. Liss, 1982.

Clifford, T. "Cognitive Development of the School-ager." In *The Process of Human Development: A Holistic Approach.* C. J. Schuster and S. S. Ashburn, eds. Boston: Little, Brown, 1980.

Cohen, F. L. "Parental Contributions to Birth Defects." *Nursing Clinics of North America* 21 (1986):49–63.

Doernberg, M. "Some Neglect Effects on Family Integration of Health and Educational Services for Young Handicapped Children." *Rehabilitation Literature* 39 (1978):4.

Drotar, D., A. Baskiewicz, N. Irvin, J. Kennel, and M. Klaus. "The Adaptation of Parents to the Birth of an Infant with a Congenital Malformation: A Hypothetical Model." *Pediatrics* 56 (1975):710–717.

Farber, B. *Mental Retardation: Its Social Context and Social Consequence.* Boston: Houghton Mifflin, 1968.

Green, M., and A. Solnit. "Reactions to the Threatened Loss of a Child: A Vulnerable Child Syndrome/Pediatric Management of the Dying Child, Part 3." *Pediatrics* 34 (1964):58–66.

Greer, B. G. "Substance Abuse among People with Disabilities." *Journal of Rehabilitation* 46 (1985):72–77.

Griffin, J. Q. "Physical Illness in the Family." In *Family Focused Care.* J. R. Miller and E. H. Janosik, eds. New York: McGraw-Hill, 1980.

Grossman, H. J. *Manual on Terminology and Classification in Mental Retardation.* American Association on Mental Deficiency, Special Publication, No. 2. Baltimore: Garamond Pridemark Press, 1973.

Hamburg, B. "Chronic Illness." In *Developmental Behavioral Pediatrics,* M. Levine et al., eds. Philadelphia: W. B. Saunders, 1983.

Hathaway, G. "The Child with Sickle Cell Anemia: Implications and Management." *Nurse Practitioner* 9 (1984):16–22.

Henderson, M., and D. Synhorst. "Bladder and Bowel Management in Child with Myelomeningocele." *Pediatric Nursing* 3 (1977):24–31.

Hillquist, J. M. "Cerebral Palsy." *Physician's Assistant* 5 (1985):55–82.

Hodgins, D. M., and M. J. Monfils, "Nursing Care and Treatment of the Retarded Mentally Ill." *Journal of Psychosocial Nursing* 23 (1985):31–33.

Hymovich, D. "Parents of Sick Children: Their Needs and Tasks." *Pediatric Nursing* (Sept/Oct 1976):9–13.

Keller, S., C. Guzman, and L. Culan. "Psychological Intervention for Adults with Cystic Fibrosis." *Patient Education and Counseling* 7 (1985):263–274.

Larter, N. "Cystic Fibrosis." *American Journal of Nursing* 81 (1981):527–531.

Lawson, B. "Chronic Illness in the School-Aged Child: Effects on the Total Family." *American Journal of Maternal Child Nursing* 2 (1977):49–56.

Levine, M. "The Child with Learning Disabilities." In *The Practical Management of the Developmentally Disabled.* A. Scheiner and I. Abrams, eds. St. Louis: C. V. Mosby, 1980.

Libby, L. S. "Cystic Fibrosis and Genetics." *Respiratory Therapy* 16 (1986):13–16.

Mattsson, A. "Long-Term Physical Illness in Childhood: A Challenge to Psychosocial Adaptation." *Pediatrics* 50 (1972):801–811.

Muir, B. *Essentials of Genetics for Nurses.* New York: John Wiley & Sons, 1983.

Myers, G. "Myelomeningocele: the Medical Aspects." *Pediatric Clinics of North America* 31 (1984):165–175.

Olshansky, S. "Chronic Sorrow: A Response to Having a Mentally Defective Child." *Social Casework* 43 (1962):190.

Opitz, J. "Klinefelter's Syndrome." In *March of Dimes Birth Defects Compendium*, 2d ed. D. Bergsma, ed. New York: Alan R. Liss, 1982.

Pless, I., and P. Pinkerton. *Chronic Childhood Disorders: Promoting Patterns of Adjustment*. London: Henry Kimptom Pub., 1975.

Pollard, G. "Sickle Cell Anemia." *Physicians Assistant* 6 (1986):76–84.

Rhoades, C. M., P. L. Browning, and E. J. Thorin. "Self-Help Advocacy Movement." *Rehabilitation Literature* 47 (1986):2–7.

Robinson, N., and H. Robinson. *The Mentally Retarded Child*. New York: McGraw-Hill, 1976.

Scheiner, A. "High-Risk Mother and Infant." In *The Practical Management of the Developmentally Disabled*. A. Scheiner and I. Abrams, eds. St. Louis: C. V. Mosby, 1980.

Schwartz, R. "Cystic Fibrosis." In *Principles of Pediatrics: Health Care of the Young*. R. A. Hoekelman, ed. New York: McGraw-Hill, 1978.

Sperling, E. "Psychological Issues in Chronic Illness and Handicap." In *Psychological Aspects of Pediatric Care*, E. Gellert, ed. New York: Grune & Stratton, 1978.

Summit, R. "Turner's Syndrome." In *March of Dimes Birth Defects Compendium*, 2d ed. D. Bergsma, ed. New York: Alan R. Liss, 1982.

Tudor, M. "Nursing Intervention with Developmentally Disabled Children." *American Journal of Maternal Child Nursing* (Jan/Feb 1978):25–31.

Varley, C. K. "A Clinical Nurse Specialist's Role in the Comprehensive Management of Attention Deficit Disorder." *Child Health Care* 3 (1985):139–142.

West, M. "The Mother, The Developmentally Disabled Child and the Nurse." *Topics in Clinical Nursing* 6 (1984):19–29.

Whaley, L., and D. Wong. *Nursing Care of Infants and Children*. St. Louis: C. V. Mosby, 1983.

Yoos, L. "Assessment and Management of the Developmentally Delayed Infant in Primary Care." *Nurse Practitioner* 10 (1985):24–36.

12

Degenerative Variations and Disruptions

Learning Objectives

After reading this chapter, the student should be able to:

1. Differentiate between acute variations and disruptions in mental function and chronic variations and disruptions of degenerative origin.

2. Describe clinical manifestations of variations and disruptions due to degenerative processes.

3. Examine nursing responsibilities and approaches in caring for clients experiencing variations and disruptions of degenerative origin.

4. Discuss nursing responsibilities toward families of clients with variations or disruptions of degenerative origin.

Overview

Variations and disruptions of degenerative origin lead to changes in all spheres of an individual's life. A degenerative disruption has a profound impact physiologically on the client and psychologically and socially on the client, his family, and his social network. The earlier parts of this chapter deal with some of the major adaptive and maladaptive responses to variations and disruptions of degenerative origin exhibited by individuals. Nursing approaches often make the difference between clients' coping and not coping with degenerative processes. These approaches are outlined in a later part of this chapter. Because degenerative variations and disruptions usually rob the client of independence and the ability to think rationally, much of the work of the nurse involves the client's family, especially in the later stages of the disorders. Family-focused nursing interventions are therefore an important consideration in dealing with the client affected by a degenerative disorder.

Until recent years, little was known about the etiology, courses, treatment, or management of most variations and disruptions of degenerative origin. Because many of these degenerative disorders are primarily found in elderly individuals, they were regarded as inevitable outcomes of aging. As a result, there was little interest in either the clinical or research arenas until demographic shifts toward larger numbers of older people prompted scientific and societal concern.

In every field of clinical practice, nurses are called upon to work with individuals suffering from degenerative disorders. General medical and surgical units are increasingly filled with older clients, and these individuals often present with cognitive disruptions of a short-term nature (delirium) superimposed on a degenerative disorder such as Alzheimer's disease. Acute disruptions are commonly due to electrolyte imbalance, dehydration, and the physiological and psychological stresses of trauma and surgery, medications, pain and sleep deprivation. These same clients are often found in critical care units, where distinguishing the behavioral effects of delirium from those of the underlying degenerative disruption is a complex and important nursing function.

Degenerative variations and disruptions are the major problems of persons occupying our country's nursing home beds. Nurses working in long-term care settings find that care of individuals with degenerative variations and disruptions constitutes a large part of their clinical practice. Contrary to popular mythology, the majority of individuals with a degenerative disorder are cared for at home by family members, and community health nurses are often involved in providing services to these families.

DEFINITION OF KEY TERMS

For purposes of this chapter, the term *variations and disruptions of degenerative origin* will be used to describe processes reflecting an underlying organic etiology that results in permanent disruption of central nervous system functioning. This distinguishes degenerative disruptions from functional disruptions, which result from either psychic conflict or psychological factors with no demonstrable brain damage or disturbance in brain tissue function (Pasquali et al. 1981, Wang 1973). Here *degenerative variation and disruption* and *degenerative disorder* will be used interchangeably.

Delirium Delirium is a transient organic mental disorder with an acute onset that is characterized by global cognitive dysfunction due to impairment of cerebral metabolism. The term is often used interchangeably with acute confusional state, acute brain syndrome, metabolic encephalopathy, toxic psychosis, and acute brain failure. In some cases, the delirium may be persistent and result in irreversible brain impairment (Liston 1984).

Acute disruptions in mental function versus chronic degenerative disruptions. Acute disruptions in mental function (delirium) are generally reversible or amenable to curative intervention, and they usually have a sudden onset. Degenerative disruptions tend to have a slow, insidious onset; their progression is not amenable to treatment, and inevitably leads to death (Richardson and Adams 1980). Degenerative disruptions are characterized by permanent, irreversible damage to the central nervous system caused by a gradual, relentlessly progressive wasting away of neurons or disruption of neuronal function. Some common degenerative disruptions include Alzheimer's disease, Parkinson's disease, and Huntington's chorea.

It is important to recognize that a person may suffer from both an acute disruption in mental function and a chronic degenerative disruption simultaneously, as in the case of a person with Alzheimer's disease who develops a delirium due to metabolic effects of pneumonia.

Organic mental (brain) syndrome Organic mental syndrome is a term used to describe a group of psychological or behavioral signs and symptoms without reference to etiology (American Psychiatric Association 1987). A diagnosis of organic brain syndrome is appropriate when the etiology of a brain disorder is unknown. Examples of organic brain syndrome include delirium of unspecified etiology, dementia of unknown etiology, and organic delusional syndrome.

Organic mental disorder. DSM-III-R defines organic mental disorder as an organic mental syndrome in which the cause is known or presumed. The presence of a specific factor judged to be etiologically related to the abnormal mental state must be demonstrated by means of history, physical, or laboratory tests. Examples of organic mental disorders are multi-infarct dementia, alcohol-withdrawal delirium, and primary degenerative dementia.

Dementia. Dementia is defined as an acquired, persistent compromise in intellectual function, with impairments in at least three of the following spheres of mental activity: language, memory, visuospatial skills, personality, and cognition, including abstraction, judgment, and mathematics (Cummings 1984). The fact that more than one sphere must be compromised helps to differentiate dementia from neuropsychological disorders such as aphasia that affect only one type of mental activity. Dementia is persistent and does not happen abruptly, as does an acute confusional state.

TYPES OF DEMENTIAS

Two patterns of mental deterioration can be distinguished in clients with dementia; those that affect the cerebral cortex and those that affect the structures below the cortex (subcortical) (Shapira et al. 1986).

The two types of dementias differ in the manifestations of the disabilities. Clients with cortical dementia have markedly disturbed memory and lose the ability to learn new information. Their language is abnormal in that they use words incorrectly in speaking and writing but their ability to speak remains intact. Impaired cognition is manifested by declining judgment, impaired abstract thinking, and inability to calculate. Behavior may be apathetic or disinhibited but changes in mood are not usually shown. Depression, if present, is often in the early stages but is mild and transient. Movement abnormalities do not occur until late in the disease; normal neurological signs are a clinical feature.

By contrast, clients with subcortical dementias have problems recalling information but do not have amnesia; they can learn new information. There are many mechanical difficulties with speech: the articulation, volume, and timing of speech are abnormal. Impaired cognition is manifested by loss of problem solving ability. Depression is a cardinal symptom and does not necessarily correlate with the degree of disability. With the subcortical dementias, there is a movement abnormality accompanied by bradykinesia from altered muscle tone (Shapira et al. 1986).

Although their ability to speak and write remains intact, their language is abnormal in that they use words incorrectly.

Dementia must be distinguished from pseudodementia, a syndrome in which dementia is mimicked by a functional psychiatric illness, most often depression (Wells 1979). The time course of both the onset and remission of features of the illness can help to differentiate between depression and dementia. Pseudodementia has a rapid onset, usually noted by the family in the early stages. By contrast, the family is often unaware of organic illness for a long period of time because the client conceals or compensates for the losses that take place. In dementia, the cognitive losses precede the depressive symptoms whereas the reverse is true in pseudodementia. In pseudodementia, a history of previous psychiatric illness is common while this is unusual in clients with dementia.

A distinguishing feature that facilitates a correct diagnosis is the client's attitude toward the cognitive losses. In pseudodementia, the client complains of failing memory and can recount instances in which memory loss occurred. By contrast, the demented client will attempt to conceal the problem and may be unaware of readily observable deficits. In response to questions, the organic client will volunteer an answer or confabulate responses, while the clients with pseudodementia will state that they do not know. Memory loss in pseudodementia may be for specific periods of time and may be more circumscribed than it is in organic disease. Accentuation of the dysfunction at night is common with dementia but rare in pseudodementia.

It is of primary importance that clients be appropriately diagnosed because treating individuals who have a reversible cognitive disorder as though they were demented is one way to ensure senility (Fopma-Loy 1986). The differences in the presenting clinical features are presented in the box on page 311.

Another form of dementia that is appearing with increasing frequency is a neurological disorder called AIDS dementia complex. The symptoms, such as severe memory deficiency and confusion, may become clinically evident at the same time as, or before, overt AIDS. This dementia, also referred to as *subacute encephalitis* or *encephalopathy*, is often overlooked, as it may be attributed to reactive depression or overshadowed by concurrent systemic illness.

The syndrome consists of a distinct constellation of cognitive, motor, and behavioral impairment. The client may show signs of cognitive difficulty and slowed thinking. Writing and walking may be clumsy because fine motor control is slow. Steady progression of the problem leads to ataxia

and paraparesis within a few months: the client becomes mute, bedridden, and incontinent. Although male homosexuals and intravenous drug users present with a risk background, the increase in heterosexual transmission places these clients at risk for misdiagnosis and delays in proper treatment (1987).

About one in ten AIDS clients develops dementia or another neurological problem as the first signs of the disease and sometimes dies without ever showing the more common physical symptoms. Researchers were slow to recognize that AIDS itself could be the cause of the mental decline often observed in AIDS clients. The memory loss and reasoning difficulties were attributed to the shock of the diagnosis.

The finding of the virus in the brain of AIDS clients has presented tremendous ramifications for the health care system. Most hospitals are equipped to handle the acute medical problems of AIDS but not the long-term help that demented clients need. In addition, almost none of the nation's 19,000 nursing homes will accept clients with AIDS.

The presence of the virus in the brain also complicates efforts to develop an effective treatment for the disease, since any drug to be effective has to penetrate a protective barrier, located between the blood vessels and brain tissue, which allows only vital blood components to pass into the brain. AZT, the first and only drug available to date for extending the lives of clients with AIDS, can cross the hurdle, but whether or not it is effective once it gets into the nervous system is still unclear.

The addition of dementia to the many manifestations of AIDS has compounded the dilemma about what and how much to tell the AIDS client. This information has a shattering effect on the lives of clients who have received the diagnosis. For many, physical symptoms are problem enough but the prospect of losing one's mind is too much to bear (Goode and Silberner 1987).

THE RELATIONSHIP BETWEEN AGING AND VARIATIONS AND DISRUPTIONS OF DEGENERATIVE ORIGIN

Although we have recently come to understand that aging itself is probably not the cause of degenerative disorders, the process of aging does result in neuronal changes in many individuals. These changes are the backdrop against which the cellular and biochemical pathology of degenerative alterations must be viewed. The neurobiology of aging begins with neuronal changes and results in decreased transmission of neurochemicals (see Figure

---

FEATURES OF PSEUDODEMENTIA AND DEMENTIA

Pseudodementia	Dementia
Course of disease	
Family aware of problem and severity	Family often unaware
Defined date of onset	Diffuse onset
Rapid progression of symptoms	Slow progression of symptoms
History of psychiatric illness	No history of psychiatric illness
Behavior	
Complaints of cognitive loss	No complaints of cognitive loss
Detailed complaints	Vague complaints
Emphasizes disability	Conceals disability
Makes little effort to perform	Struggles to perform
Early loss of social skills	Social skills retained early on
Accentuation at night	No accentuation at night
Attention and concentration present	Attention and concentration faulty
Answers "Don't know"	Answers with confabulation
Short- and long-term memory loss severe	Short-term memory loss more severe than long-term
Variability on task performance	Consistently poor performance
Communicates severe distress	Appears unconcerned

SOURCE: Adapted from S. Berman and M. Rappaport (1985).

12–1). In addition to the neuronal alterations, senile plaques and neurofibrillary tangles develop during the aging process. *Senile plaques*, which consist of abnormal extracellular protein, are associated with decreased neuronal functioning. *Neurofibrillary tangles* (tiny nerve fibers tangled upon themselves and lying in the cytoplasmic space of nerve cells) lead to decreased functioning by interfering with intracellular transport; this results in permanent changes and impaired functioning. Both senile plaques and neurofibrillary tangles are thought to be implicated in some as yet unknown way in the development of Alzheimer's disease (Stewart 1982).

Wang (1973) has stated that aging is similar to a chronic illness in that it progresses with little remission until the final outcome of death. Successful adaptation to changes that accompany aging depends on the following:

1. Maintenance of identity and self-esteem.
2. Acceptance of inevitable losses and positive use of life experiences to compensate for losses.
3. A sense of satisfaction with life experiences.

Failure to adapt to inevitable situations exerts a strong influence on the development of degenerative disorders in the elderly. This psychological influence must not be overlooked when considering the physiological etiology of organic mental disorders.

MAJOR DEGENERATIVE VARIATIONS AND DISRUPTIONS

The three best-known degenerative disruptions are Alzheimer's disease, Parkinson's disease, and Huntington's chorea.

Alzheimer's Disease

Alzheimer's disease was once called "the silent epidemic" but is now believed to be the big disease of the future because of the number of people who will develop and die from the syndrome. This disease alone accounts for 75 percent of dementia in the elderly. Definitive diagnosis can only be made on autopsy, but through exclusion of a variety of other factors, a diagnosis can usually be made in a living client (Powell 1985).

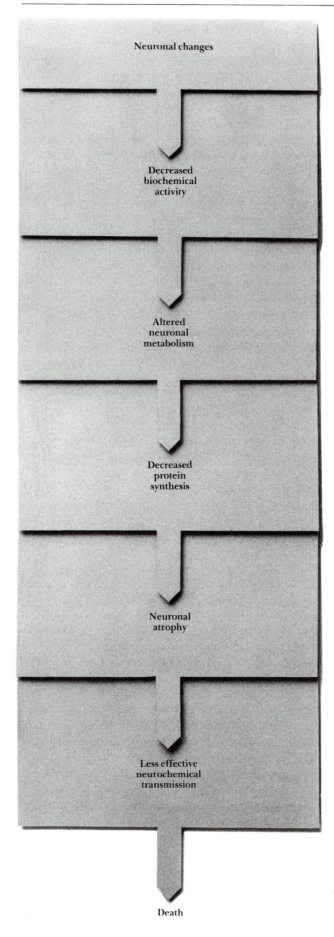

Figure 12–1. *The neurobiology of aging.*

Recently, scientists have identified what could be the first fully accurate diagnostic indicator of Alzheimer's in living people. This indicator, A-68, is a protein found in the brains of Alzheimer's victims, which also appears in the spinal fluid of living clients thought to have the disease. It is not known if the protein plays a causal role in the illness, but its presence is unique to Alzheimer's. The development of a diagnostic test (which may be available soon) would discriminate between true Alzheimer's cases and those that are currently misdiagnosed, such as stroke, malnutrition, and depression. In addition, the protein could be used to diagnose Alzheimer's while the client's dementia is still reversible. If a cure is found in the next few years, early diagnosis would save many lives (Levine 1986).

Alzheimer's disease is characterized by certain neuropathologic changes that are exaggerations of the degenerative changes seen in normal aging. In this condition, the junctions between neurons develop deposits of amyloid, a starchlike protein (Charles, Truesdell, and Wood 1982). This complex is referred to as a *neuritic plaque*. Plaque and neurofibrillary tangles interfere with transmission of electrochemical signals between neurons, eventually disrupting intellect and memory, depending on the number, location, and size of the plaques and tangles (Palmer 1983). Most of these lesions occur in the cerebral cortex and eventually lead to diminished brain mass. In the initial stages, atrophy is greatest in the frontal and temporal lobes. In advanced Alzheimer's disease, over half of the cerebral cortex may be atrophied (Charles, Truesdell, and Wood 1982).

Another finding is a decline in the enzymes choline acetyltransferase and acetylcholinesterase in the cortex of the brain, an area important to memory function. This decrease in enzyme levels results in impaired utilization of the neurotransmitter acetylcholine (Palmer 1983, Comfort 1984).

Several causal theories of Alzheimer's disease have been advanced over the years, and research in this area has expanded. Some of these etiologic theories include (1) heredity, (2) increased brain aluminum concentration, (3) slow virus infection, (4) autoimmune disorder, (5) head injury. Although there are indications to support all these theories, none have been proven conclusively (Wolanin and Phillips 1981, Olsen and Mather 1985).

STAGES OF THE DISEASE Three stages of Alzheimer's disease have been identified in the literature. The first stage, known as the forgetfulness phase, can last from one to ten years. Recent memory is impaired; clients tend to forget where things are placed and

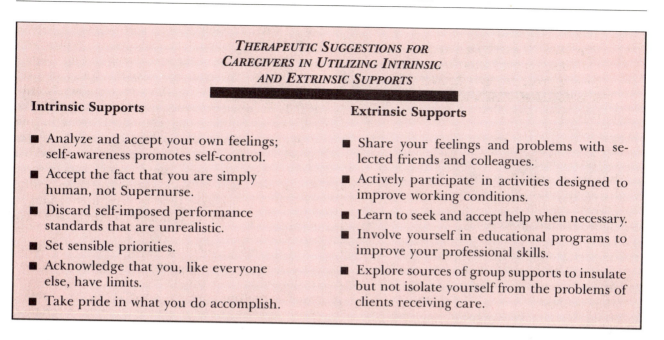

THERAPEUTIC SUGGESTIONS FOR CAREGIVERS IN UTILIZING INTRINSIC AND EXTRINSIC SUPPORTS

Intrinsic Supports

- Analyze and accept your own feelings; self-awareness promotes self-control.
- Accept the fact that you are simply human, not Supernurse.
- Discard self-imposed performance standards that are unrealistic.
- Set sensible priorities.
- Acknowledge that you, like everyone else, have limits.
- Take pride in what you do accomplish.

Extrinsic Supports

- Share your feelings and problems with selected friends and colleagues.
- Actively participate in activities designed to improve working conditions.
- Learn to seek and accept help when necessary.
- Involve yourself in educational programs to improve your professional skills.
- Explore sources of group supports to insulate but not isolate yourself from the problems of clients receiving care.

have difficulty remembering names. Often the client will begin to write things in order to remember them. The client appears absentminded, has difficulty concentrating, is emotionally unstable at times, and becomes careless in actions and appearance. There is a tendency to blame others for the increasing inability to perform everyday tasks efficiently. Transitory delusions of persecution may arise in an attempt to project inadequacies on others.

Nursing care of clients in the first stage consists primarily of emotional support and individual counseling with the client. Most are still at home and expectations of family and friends need to be modified. Clients are aware that something is happening to them and can become overwhelmed and frightened. Clients and their families must be informed and educated about the nature of the disease; they should be encouraged to talk to each other and express their concerns and fears.

As clients begin to deteriorate, problems develop in daily living. When memory fails and attention span decreases, writing daily tasks and times for performing them may help alleviate stress and confusion. Limiting activities and avoiding sudden changes in routine can also reduce irritation. Safety hazards in the environment should be identified and modified as motor deficits occur. Teaching the family basic interventions as soon as possible will facilitate the coping process.

The second stage, the confusional phase, may extend over one to ten years. The client forgets recent and remote events and becomes completely disoriented as she loses the ability to comprehend. There is increased aphasia and failure to attach meaning to sensory impressions (agnosis). Abstract thinking declines and the client becomes less able to discern common themes or use good judgment. Learned socially accepted behaviors are forgotten and are evidenced by poor grooming and inappropriate eating and toileting habits.

Increased muscle tone (hypertonia) and unsteady gait become apparent, accompanied by the inability to read and write (agraphia), to do simple arithmetic tasks (acalculia) and to perform simple skilled movements (apraxia). There is an increased need for oral stimulation. Clients may chew anything that is available, and the appetite becomes insatiable without significant weight gain.

Clients who enter this stage can no longer live alone and must be assisted in making decisions about supervised placement, whether with family or friends or in an adult home. Family roles should change. Family counseling should be encouraged to help relatives deal with feelings of anger, depression, and guilt. Because of the problems that occur in simple daily activities, the strain on the family can be overwhelming. Family members need to find time for themselves and get away for periods of time. Although the client will never regain skills that are lost, he may still be able to perform portions of the task. Families should know the importance of encouraging the activities and skills that are still present.

Safety needs become more important as the client's restlessness and wandering behavior increases. Doors should be locked with locks placed in hard-to-reach places. Medications should be kept in a locked cabinet, and the client should not be permitted to smoke alone.

Structured cuing that stimulates long-term memory and evokes habitual patterns of functioning

<table>
<tr><td>

POSSIBLE NURSING DIAGNOSES FOR CLIENTS WITH VARIATIONS AND DISRUPTIONS OF DEGENERATIVE ORIGIN

Activity intolerance
Impaired adjustment
Anxiety
Chronic pain
Impaired verbal communication
Ineffective individual coping
Diversional activity deficit
Altered family processes
Fear
Altered growth and development
Altered home maintenance management
Altered health maintenance
Hopelessness
Total functional/reflex incontinence
Potential for infection
Potential for injury
Knowledge deficit
Impaired physical mobility
Noncompliance
Altered nutrition
Powerlessness
Bathing/dressing/feeding/toileting
  self-care deficit
Self-esteem disturbance
Impaired skin integrity
Social isolation
Potential for violence

The above are the more likely diagnoses related to variations and disruptions of degenerative origin. Nursing diagnoses are not limited to the list shown above. Manifestations of these disorders are individualistic even though certain prevailing patterns are identifiable.
</td></tr>
</table>

can be used to encourage independence in daily care. New activities for the family to do together need to be devised. Listening to music, walking, going for a drive in the car, visiting a shopping center may still be possible at this stage and should be encouraged to provide stimulation without frustration. Loud and disruptive environments tend to overwhelm the client and can produce disruptive behaviors.

Nutrition and elimination can become problematic. Offering nourishing finger foods assists the clients in feeding themselves. Incontinence develops because the clients forget where and how to use the toilet.

Sexual intimacy should be maintained as long as possible. The disease varies in its effects on sexuality: some clients become demanding, while others lose interest. Although clients may still have the desire and ability to have intercourse, they may

forget what happened as soon as they are finished. At times, drug side effects, paranoia, combativeness, and hallucinations make sexual contact impossible.

As this phase progresses, the focus of care should be on preserving the caregiving family unit. Family needs such as increasing support networks, preserving physical and emotional strength, and dealing with financial problems become the center of interactions. Respite care should be provided and families may need "permission" to take some time for themselves. Day care centers can be helpful to give the caretaker time to earn money and to place the client in the company of others who have similar problems.

Continuous medical monitoring is important to prevent minor illnesses from developing into major additional problems. Since clients may be unable to communicate what is wrong, families need to learn the signs and symptoms of common problems that may develop: urinary tract infections, side effects of medications, and skin integrity breakdown.

The third stage, the dementia phase, finds the clients in a constant state of severe and significant decline. All symptoms become more pronounced and the clients eventually become bedridden, mute, and unresponsive. This stage is considered terminal because clients do not usually live more than a year after progressing to this phase. By this time, clients usually have lost the unique personality traits that defined them as individuals. A Kluver-Bucy-like syndrome occurs in which the clients attempt to touch every object in sight and have lost any emotions.

Family members must be assisted to make decisions as they try to balance the responsibility of caring for the client and the need to maintain the strength of the family. When home management is no longer feasible, the family needs help in dealing with anger over its loss and feelings of guilt for abandoning the client. Relatives must have an opportunity to mourn the loss of the demented family member. The family may need help in releasing its caregiver role and becoming re-involved in their former recreational activities (Berman and Rappaport 1985, Williams 1986).

TREATMENT MODALITIES Although there is no known cure for Alzheimer's disease, drug therapy for palliative treatment may be used to relieve signs and symptoms as the disease progresses. Vasodilators such as cyclandelate have been used to improve cerebral blood flow and improve mental functioning. Antidepressants and antipsychotics must be used with discretion because their side effects may worsen the already impaired cognition. Several drugs are being investigated for use to improve memory (Cutler and Narang 1985).

Special care units are being utilized in some facilities to accommodate the clients' perceptual problems and segregate these clients from others whom they irritate. Low-stimulus units, which have no television, telephones, or intercom systems, reduce confusion. Care schedules are followed consistently so that clients have the same activity at the same time each day (Wagner 1987, Schafer 1985, Hall 1986).

Group therapies have been introduced into the care of the demented client. Reality orientation, the continued reinforcement of who the client is, where he is, what day it is, and so forth, may be performed individually and in groups. Remotivation is a group method used with confused and withdrawn clients to stimulate the senses (Schwab et al. 1985).

One of the most successful approaches is establishing a group identity in milieu therapy (Cox 1985). The milieu gives individuals and groups the opportunity to socially experience, explicitly recognize, and cope with the real and feared consequences of Alzheimer's disease. Open communication is fostered to develop and maintain trust. By encouraging interpersonal contact at meetings and during meals clients come to share in a group process and identity.

Community meetings, group therapy, and one-to-one sessions are used to promote an atmosphere of acceptance and lessen individual anxiety. Standards of acceptance are set by the clients and as trust increases, clients take greater risks in sharing their losses and fears. The source of power in the milieu is the experience of having personal deficits confronted and accepted by the group. The goal of the program is to further the adjustment process in response to loss.

Rather than seeking to change behavior by restructuring personality, as in traditional psychiatric treatment, this approach builds on the existing personality structure. Defense mechanisms are supported and therapeutically manipulated to strengthen existing coping strategies. Clients experience the pain of loss and emerge with heightened emotional integrity. The environment reinforces risk taking and enables members to develop new attitudes and practice coping skills in response to their losses.

As the incidence of Alzheimer's disease continues to increase, nurses in all areas of practice will come in contact with these clients. Although specialized skills may be necessary for working with these clients on a daily basis, nurses in general must have an understanding of the effects of the disease and methods for coping with the process to help clients hold on to what little they have left.

DSM-III-R Classification of Variations and Disruptions of Degenerative Origin

Organic Mental Disorders

Dementias Arising in the Senium and Presenium
Primary Degenerative Dementia, Alzheimer's type, senile onset
   290.30 with delirium
   290.20 with delusions
   290.21 with depression
   290.00 uncomplicated

Code in fifth digit: 1 = delirium, 2 = delusions, 3 = depression, 0 = uncomplicated

   290.1x Primary Degenerative Dementia of the Alzheimer's type, presenile onset
   290.4x Multi-infarct Dementia
   290.00 Senile Dementia, not otherwise specified
   290.10 Presenile Dementia, not otherwise specified

Organic Mental Disorders Associated with Axis III Physical Disorders when Etiology is Unknown

   293.00 Delirium
   294.10 Dementia
   294.00 Amnestic disorder
   293.81 Organic delusional disorder
   293.82 Organic hallucinations
   293.83 Organic mood disorder
   294.80 Organic anxiety disorder
   310.10 Organic personality disorder
   294.80 Organic mental disorder not otherwise specified

Parkinson's Disease

Parkinson's disease is a progressive degenerative neurologic disorder, which first presents as a motor disorder in which clients gradually develop rigidity, tremor, slowness of movement, and problems maintaining balance (Strub and Black 1981). The symptoms of bradykinesia or akinesia make the initiation of any movement difficult. The individual often exhibits a shuffling (fenestrating) gait and may "freeze" in place for several moments, unable to move her feet. There are also problems with fine motor movements of the fingers, which lead to difficulties with buttoning clothes and writing. Impaired muscle function eventually leads to development of the masklike faces of Parkinson's disease. The person's face appears dull and without expression even under conditions of considerable emotional arousal. Bradykinesia involving the muscles used in speech and swallowing results in dysarthria, dysphagia, and drooling. The client's voice becomes decreased in volume, high-pitched, monotonous, and often unintelligible.

Muscular rigidity, another manifestation of Parkinson's disease, may eventually cause muscular aches, cramps, and diffuse bone pain (Langan 1976).

While all muscles may be tightened, the flexor muscles in particular produce contracture due to disuse of the joints.

The other classic symptom of Parkinson's disease is tremor at rest, which is due to alternating contractions of antagonistic muscle groups. The tremor usually begins in an upper limb, moves to the lower limb on the same side, then spreads to the opposite side, head, and mouth. The tremor will stop when purposeful movement is initiated and when the client sleeps. The "pill rolling" tremor is the result of rhythmic movements of the thumb and first two fingers; it may involve one or both hands (Topp 1987). Eventually the bradykinesia, rigidity, and tremor of the disease make even the most simple movement excruciatingly difficult to initiate or sustain.

Early studies of Parkinson's disease focused little attention on associated mental changes. Recently, there has been convincing documentation of the presence of a true dementing process in the later stages of the illness. It is important to remember that mental deterioration does not appear until the disease has been present for several years. It is often difficult to determine the extent of the dementia because the client's physical symptoms and deficits in communication make adequate testing of cognitive function problematical (Strub and Black 1981). Despite these diagnostic obstacles, it is likely that a sizeable percentage of clients with Parkinsonism (25 to 80 percent) develop a degenerative mental disorder as the disease progresses (Strub and Black 1981). The manifestations of the degenerative disorder include a general lack of arousal that prevents normal cognition and social behavior, impairment of problem solving and concept formation, poor judgment, and apathy.

Parkinson's disease is thought to be due to a deficiency of the neurotransmitter dopamine in the corpus striatum, globus pallidus, and substantia nigra. These areas of the brain are responsible for the control of posture and voluntary muscular action. Diagnosis is difficult because there are no definitive tests for the disease, although urine samples may show a decreased excretion of dopamine. Therefore, diagnosis is based primarily on the client's history and motor symptoms (Langan 1976).

The use of phenothiazines over a long period of time can cause Parkinsonism, which is usually relieved when the drug is discontinued. Other factors that may lead to a decrease in dopamine are manganese or carbon dioxide poisoning, trauma, neurosyphilis and hypoxia (Topp 1987).

TREATMENT MODALITIES Treatment for Parkinson's disease revolves around replacement of dopamine to near-normal levels by the use of levodopa, a precursor of dopamine. Unfortunately, the drug has several side effects including nausea, vomiting, decreased motility, hypotension, and dyskinesia. Mental changes may include agitation, confusion, short-term memory loss, hallucinations, and delusion.

Also used to treat the disease are anticholinergic drugs, such as Cogentin and Artane, whose action is to potentiate the effect of any dopamine present. Behavioral alterations are a side effect, as are urinary retention, glaucoma crisis, cardiac arrhythmias, and inability to control body temperature by sweating (Topp 1987).

Recently a surgical procedure has been developed that relieves the symptoms of Parkinson's disease. Tissue from the adrenal glands, which produce dopamine, is transplanted to the brain. Since the cells are the client's own, there is no danger of rejection by the immune system; they are accepted by the brain and begin producing the needed dopamine. How long the effects of the surgery will last is still unknown.

IMPLICATIONS FOR NURSING Client and family education regarding the use of drug therapy and the course of the disease are primary responsibilities for nurses caring for clients with Parkinson's disease. Nurses need to monitor clients closely and know the signs of the disease, expected outcomes of drugs, dose ceilings, side effects, and symptoms of overdose.

Because of the slow progression of the disease, clients experience a gradual decline in activity and change in family roles. Nursing interventions should be directed toward facilitating the clients' residual capacities. This can be achieved by providing activities that yield success and increased self-esteem.

Many clients are embarrassed by their tremors and may be able to arrest them with a slight movement of the limb. However, the tremor reoccurs after a few minutes when the limb is at rest. Tremors of the hand will disappear while the client is walking if he swings his arms; it will also disappear if the client holds something in his hands.

Deformities and contractures can be prevented if clients walk as far as they can and avoid standing still for long periods of time. Range of motion and balance exercises should be initiated. Shuffling gait and festinations can be reduced if clients are taught to walk with high steps and count while concentrating on listening to their feet hit the floor. Longer strides also facilitate walking.

Communication problems can be a source of frustration. Encouraging clients to speak slowly and read aloud provides opportunities for verbal exchange. Depression is frequently seen in these clients as they react to changes in body image and experience a decrease in self-esteem. Interventions should be directed toward setting realistic goals, encouraging self-care, and discussing feelings about loss of function, self-esteem, and sexuality. If depression is severe, antidepressant drugs may be indicated.

Support groups are available for these clients and their families. The American Parkinson Disease Association maintains informational centers and publishes newsletters in many areas of the country.

Parkinson's disease presents challenges to nurses because of its insidious onset and long-term disabling effects. Working closely with clients and families can help them benefit from all sources that are available to them for care and support (Topp 1987).

Huntington's Chorea

Huntington's chorea is an autosomal dominant genetic disease that combines progressive dementia with bizarre involuntary movements (*chorea*) and odd postures. Autosomal dominant genetic transmission implies that the disease can be passed along to offspring by one parent, with each child having a 50 percent chance of eventually developing the disease (see Figure 12–2). The disorder usually becomes apparent between the ages of 30 and 50; the remaining life expectancy is approximately 15 years. Usually, symptoms do not occur until after the childbearing years, when potentially afflicted individuals may have already borne children likely to develop the disease in later life. Thus, much research is focusing on detecting the disease prior to the childbearing years (Wells 1972, Richardson and Adams 1980, Wilson and Carron 1980).

The onset is insidious. Impairments slowly develop in problem solving, alertness, and concentration.

Impulsive behavior, a result of mental deterioration, may lead to such behaviors as alcoholism, drug addiction, and sexual promiscuity. As intellectual losses progress, the individual is no longer able to care for himself and becomes totally dependent (Stipe, White, and Van Arsdale 1979).

The neuropathologic changes of the disorder consist of cortical atrophy with ventricular dilatation. No specific cause of neuronal loss has been determined, but anatomic and pharmacologic discoveries indicate that the chorea that occurs in Huntington's disease is due to excess amounts of dopamine in relation to the acetylcholine and GABA within the caudate nucleus. Restoration of the balance among these three neurotransmitters may lessen choreiform movements (Stipe, White, and Van Arsdale 1979).

The characteristic choreiform movements of Huntington's disease consist of uninhibited, involuntary writhing and twisting movements of the facial muscles and extremities. Psychological stress increases these movements. Because of involvement of facial and neck muscles, speech is impaired to the degree to which it is unintelligible, and swallowing becomes difficult. The later stages of the disease are characterized by physical helplessness with complete dementia and nearly constant writhing movements, leaving the client exhausted, emaciated, and often bedridden (Pinel 1976). Huntington's chorea itself is not fatal, but death occurs from secondary complications, usually cardiac or respiratory in nature (Wells 1972).

IMPLICATIONS FOR NURSING Nursing care for clients with Huntington's chorea should be directed toward helping the clients maintain their independence for as long as possible. The choreiform movements make eating and dressing problematic. Nonslip mats under plates and foam-wrapped utensils will be of assistance. Use of velcro closures instead of zippers and buttons facilitate dressing. Because the energy output of these clients is high, attention to caloric intake and nutrition is important.

Figure 12–2. Inheritance pattern for Huntington's chorea, an autosomal dominant disorder. If one parent has the disorder, offspring have a 50-50 chance of developing the disorder.

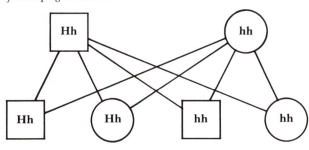

H = Gene for Huntington's chorea
h = Normal gene
Hh = Affected individual
hh = Nonaffected individual

☐ = Male
◯ = Female

Since part of the deterioration in Huntington's chorea is related to environmental deprivation associated with the client's restricted experience, participation in occupational, recreational, and physical therapy should be encouraged to the fullest extent. Music therapists report that these clients are capable of active musical expression on several levels.

Exercises, daily walks, and deep breathing can be helpful to maintain function. The drug of choice for these clients is tetrabenazine, which helps reduce choreic movements by balancing the neurotransmitter levels and inhibiting a certain degree of excitation. Antidepressants and phenothiazines may be administered to calm the clients, but these drugs have a limited use.

Currently, there is no known cure for Huntington's disease. At-risk families, having seen relatives die from the disorder, may use denial, withdrawal, or even suicide to escape the problem. Counseling which focuses on the realities of the situation and working through of feelings and fears is a necessity (Small 1986).

Table 12–1 compares the etiologies, neuropathology, manifestations, and treatment approaches for Alzheimer's, Parkinson's, and Huntington's diseases.

IMPACT OF DEGENERATIVE VARIATIONS AND DISRUPTIONS ON THE CLIENT

Common problems in the nursing care of clients with variations and disruptions of degenerative origin include memory and cognitive impairment, behavioral alterations; impaired reality testing, judgment, communication, self-care ability, and social skills.

Memory Impairment

Memory deficits common to degenerative disorders interfere with the client's ability to learn new material and to recall previously learned information. At first, memory deficits have their greatest impact on complex activities such as reading, balancing a checkbook, finding directions, and engaging in complicated conversations. Eventually, even the most basic tasks involved in eating, dressing, bathing, and toileting will become difficult for the client to perform independently because of his inability to remember the sequence of steps involved.

Early in the degenerative process, the client should be encouraged to continue as many normal activities as possible and to avoid situations that may prove too complex for him to handle. Routines should be established and followed as closely as possible. The client should be provided with an identification necklace or bracelet in case he becomes lost or disoriented (Mace and Rabins 1981). Memory aids such as lists of tasks and prominently displayed clocks and calendars may be helpful. Familiar objects should be left in the same places after each use so that the client can easily locate them again. The client should not be expected to generalize knowledge from one situation to a similar one; each new situation will require direction and supervision, with tasks broken down into simple steps given one at a time. Hayter (1974) suggests that repetition of an activity will increase retention of the pattern of functioning. The client who does not respond to verbal direction may be capable of continuing an activity that another person has initiated for him.

Memory loss in the early stages of a degenerative disorder is often accompanied by a marked increase in anxiety as the client finds himself unable to fulfill social and occupational expectations. As

Table 12–1. Comparison of Degenerative Alterations

	Alzheimer's Disease	Parkinson's Disease	Huntington's Chorea
Etiology	Unknown; suspected causes: trace minerals, virus, autoimmune, genetic	For idiopathic Parkinson's, unknown; may be drug-induced (by major tranquilizers)	Genetic
Neuropathology	Structural changes: neuritic plaques, neurofibrillary tangles, loss of dendritic spines, ventricular dilatation	Deficiency of dopamine in the corpus striatum, globus pallidus, and substantia nigra	Progressive atrophy of basal ganglia and cerebral cortex
Classical manifestations	Memory loss, disorientation, impaired judgment, decreased cognitive abilities	Bradykinesia, tremor, rigidity; mental impairment in later stages	Involuntary muscular movements, mental impairment, emotional changes
Medical treatment	None specific; tranquilizers, cortisones sometimes therapeutic	Dopamine replacement with precursor, levodopa; anticholinergic drugs	Palliative; dopamine antagonists

memory loss progresses, the world becomes an unfamiliar and frightening place for the client, and he may respond with agitation, paranoia, delusions, and violence.

Assessing memory may sometimes be difficult. In the early stages of deterioration, a client may compensate for memory deficits. One of these coping behaviors is *confabulation*, the filling in of amnesic gaps with imaginary stories. *Circumstantiality*—avoiding a topic by talking around it—is also employed to cover memory losses. Both of these behaviors can be viewed as assets; they are attempts to adapt to a threatening situation (Pasquali et al. 1981). If not identified and dealt with, indications of memory deficits can also cause a client to become anxious and to question his competence (Mahoney 1980).

Cognitive and Behavioral Disruptions

The progressive dementia common to degenerative disorders leads to bizarre and irrational behaviors that may be difficult for the client, the family, and the nurse to understand and manage. Some of these behaviors include clinging to those with whom the client feels secure, hoarding, perseveration (repetition of behaviors and words), repeated fidgeting, and relocating and fondling of objects in the environment (Beam 1984). The affected individual may follow trusted caregivers around continually but is often suspicious and demanding.

Because these clients are not able to carry a thought long enough to complete a purposeful movement, they exhibit a variety of repetitive activities such as opening and closing pocketbooks, packing and unpacking clothing.

Sleep problems are frequent because of the change in cognition which upsets habitual and other diurnal cues and alters energy levels.

The most common difficulty is multiple awakening at night, which can be the result of an overall decrease in the need for sleep or increased daytime napping (Reisberg et al. 1986).

These odd behaviors lead to problems for both client and caregiver. Bizarre activity may cause caregivers to become exasperated, exhausted, or fearful of the client, and they may cope by withdrawing from her. For the community-resident client and family, these behaviors may lead to social isolation, as neighbors and friends find themselves unable to deal with the client's irrational acts and threatening physical alterations, such as incontinence, movement disorders, and inattention to personal hygiene and grooming.

Clients with degenerative disorders frequently display paranoid and delusional ideation. Since they are unable to recall the whereabouts of objects, a common delusion is that someone is hiding or stealing from them. As this delusion becomes more prominent, clients begin to believe that people are coming into the home to steal and the clients speak or listen to the intruders. As a result of cognitive deficits, these clients no longer recognize their homes and continuously request to be taken back to where they live. They may pack their luggage and attempt to leave. Similarly, they no longer recognize their former caregivers and believe that they are imposters who are conspiring to institutionalize them. These insecurities often lead to the conviction that the caregivers are unfaithful, sexually or otherwise.

Clients may hallucinate and see intruders or dead relatives in the home. They may hear the intruders, particularly when they are alone (Reisberg et al. 1986).

The client with a degenerative disorder is at great risk for injury in any setting. Potential hazards include lookalike objects (a container of apple juice and a full urinal), forgotten cigarettes, lit stoves, and wandering outdoors in unfamiliar settings or inclement weather (Beam 1984). For the client, coping with these hazards presents a constant frustration and challenge to her diminished physical and mental abilities. For the caregiver, the need for perpetual vigilance and foresight becomes burdensome and frightening.

Because of decreased cognitive ability, the client with a degenerative disorder has difficulty managing large amounts of stimulation. This inability to process incoming information may lead to a "catastrophic reaction," brought on by the client's fear of not reacting according to personal and social expectations. Wolanin (1981) describes catastrophic behavior as characterized by somatic and observable manifestations, such as sympathetic activation, apathy, anxiety, withdrawal, and confusion. If severe enough, the catastrophic reaction may lead the client to assaultive or self-destructive behavior.

In situations where behavioral alterations threaten the safety of the client and those around her, small doses of psychotropic medications may be indicated. Drug usage must be tailored to the client's disorder and her response to these medications. Most of the major tranquilizers are highly *lipidophilic*, meaning that most of the drug is bound to fat. Since the elderly have a higher body fat proportion than younger people, lower doses of these drugs should be used with older clients. The highest therapeutic success with the fewest side effects has been reported with thioridazine (Mellaril), haloperidol (Haldol), molindone (Moban), and loxapine (Loxitane) (Dellefield and Miller 1982).

For Parkinson's clients, it is essential to avoid drugs associated with extrapyramidal side effects, which mimic Parkinsonian features of rigidity and tremor. These clients are likely to respond better to thioridazine and other drugs of the piperidine class (mesoridazine, piperacetazine) because they are relatively less likely to induce extrapyramidal side effects.

Impaired Reality Testing

The client with a degenerative disorder is apt to withdraw from reality, thus decreasing his awareness of the world around him. Confusion, which is increased by anxiety, interferes with the client's ability to test reality accurately. Disorientation may be increased at night by the lack of sensory stimulation and the client's diminished perceptual acuity. Placement in an unfamiliar environment may lead to prolonged disorientation to time, place, and person. Going along with the client's misperceptions to avoid upsetting him only adds to his insecurity and confusion, since he is then unable to trustingly test reality with those who represent security and sources of reliable feedback.

Reality can be reinforced by use of 24-hour reality orientation techniques, which incorporate environmental cues (such as reality orientation boards, signs, clocks, and calendars) and frequent reminders of time, place, and person. It is often helpful to reinforce time by associating reminders with daily activities such as breakfast, lunch, dinner, and bedtime. Reminiscing with the client about his past experiences helps to reaffirm his sense of past identity. Keeping some of the client's personal items, especially photographs, in his environment is also beneficial.

The degree of reality orientation can be assessed by asking the client questions regarding time, place, and person. The client must be given enough time to respond to questioning. If he is hurried, his anxiety will increase and probably interfere with his response. In an institutional setting, responses to questions regarding orientation should be evaluated in light of the impact of the institution's milieu on the client's perception of time, place, and person. It may be unrealistic to expect even the mildly impaired client to know day, date, and clock time if he has limited access to newspapers, radio, television, watches, or windows with an outside view. In a similar vein, settings that allow for frequent changes of caregivers and other personnel make it difficult for the client to retain orientation to person.

Impaired Judgment

Another outcome of degenerative disorders is impaired judgment. The client becomes unable to objectively examine her behavior and its effects on herself and others, so she is likely to exhibit socially unacceptable behavior. One type of socially unacceptable behavior that commonly occurs is assaultiveness. The client may not be purposefully assaultive; however, she may be assaultive without knowing what she is doing. The client should always be approached slowly and within her line of vision in order to avoid startling her and perhaps provoking an assault. Touch should be used judiciously; some clients will become combative if touched, while others respond positively to touch that indicates genuine acceptance and support.

Impaired judgment may also lead to inappropriate displays of sexual behavior, such as public masturbation or exposure. Caregivers need to be aware that the client's sexual needs persist despite the disease process. Affection and caring are more effective than scolding and guilt inducement. The anticipation of needs and use of distraction may divert inappropriate sexual activity without provoking anger (Beam 1984).

Impaired Communication

Most clients with degenerative disorders suffer from impaired communication. Communication problems may arise from impairment of facial and neck muscles (as in Huntington's chorea and Parkinson's disease) or from decreased intellect (as in Alzheimer's disease). As dementia progresses, comprehension may also be affected. It is impossible to accurately determine the exact degree of a client's comprehension. Therefore, caregivers must talk to a client as if he is capable of understanding. Relatives should be advised to continue to talk to the client as well. Every client has the ability to communicate, even if only on a limited, primitive level. Communication, both verbal and nonverbal, must be maintained. Caregivers should avoid administering physical care without talking to the client. Such behavior negates the client's existence and decreases his motivation to remain connected to reality. Encouraging the client's efforts to communicate and praising his success will increase his ability and foster his self-esteem. If the client's communication problems are dealt with ineffectively, however, catastrophic reactions may result. Frustration over inability to communicate needs is a frequent precipitant of assaultive behavior, particularly in an institutional setting.

Dementia clients are extremely sensitive to nonverbal cues and tend to respond to and mirror the affective behaviors of those around them. Caregivers must be role models to help soothe these clients. Arguments should be avoided as the clients are reasoning by a different set of rules, and the arguments will usually result in aggravation for both the clients and the caregivers. Desired behavior should be praised meaningfully and undesirable behavior ignored as long as this is safely feasible. One of the most troublesome behaviors is the frequent repetition of questions. It is not necessary to respond to each question; many times the repetition is a sign of anxiety or want of attention, not a need for information. Caregivers should respond to the feeling of the communication and develop sensitivity to hints of anxiety, fear, and anger. If the client's verbal communication does not make sense, the emotional message should be assessed and responded to (Thornton 1986).

When communicating with someone whose mental abilities have deteriorated, it is important to pick out his meaningful comments. Often the meaning of the client's behavior is misunderstood. Teaching those caring for him about the problems associated with degenerative diseases is essential for improving the quality of client care. The family also needs adequate explanation of client behaviors to facilitate their adaptation (Hayter 1974, Dewis and Baumann 1982, Hayter 1982).

Understanding the context of the client's communication may help the caregiver to interpret it. This is one of the most convincing arguments for consistent assignment of caregivers and routines. When the caregiver knows the client well, he or she can often "fill in the gaps" in the client's incomplete or incoherent messages.

The simple act of a handshake can be of clinical value in caring for these clients. A handshake helps to focus the clients' attention; it is a dominant stimulus and a familiar, nonthreatening one. The handshake also reinforces the nurse's attentiveness (Dawson et al. 1986). A handshake can aid in the process of care, as it may indicate the presence of a grasp reflex. If the clients do not let go of the hand, they are displaying a reflexive neurological response over which they have no control, rather than showing resistance, anxiety, or aggression.

When the client with a degenerative disorder is having difficulty with word finding (anomia), it may be helpful for the caregiver to supply the word for him or attempt to guess the content of his communication while checking with the client for accuracy of interpretation. Referral to a speech therapist and utilization of common speech therapy techniques for enhancing communication may also be helpful.

When the client cannot communicate, it is necessary to establish a regular routine for checking on his comfort and safety (Mace and Rabins 1981). Caregivers should systematically assure that the client's basic human needs for adequate nutrition,

elimination, mobility, respiration, ambient temperature, and environmental stimulation are being met.

The diminished hearing and vision accompanying normal aging can compound the communication problems inherent in degenerative disorders. Referral to appropriate specialists for hearing and vision evaluations and prostheses may help to maintain adequate communication. In addition, communication techniques such as those in the box below should be consistently employed by those who interact with the client.

Self-Care Deficits

As mentioned previously, the cognitive deterioration associated with degenerative alterations ultimately leads to either partial or complete inability to perform basic activities of daily living. Loss of these abilities acquired so early in life is extremely upsetting to the client, especially at the beginning of the disease process. It is important that these

---

COMMUNICATING WITH CLIENTS

When communicating with clients who have alterations of degenerative origin, use the following techniques (Mace and Rabins 1981):

1. Eliminate distracting noises or activities. If possible, communicate with the client in a quiet, secure, well-lit environment.

2. Look directly at the client and be sure she is in a position to see your face and hands.

3. Lower the tone of your voice.

4. Use short words and short, simple sentences.

5. Ask only one question at a time.

6. Speak slowly and wait for the client to respond.

7. Use signals other than words to reinforce verbal information. Point, gesture, demonstrate, and guide the client with your own hands.

8. Physical demonstrations of caring may be understood when all else fails. Don't be afraid to hug, hold hands, or just sit companionably with the client if other methods of communication are no longer effective.

self-care deficits be handled sensitively and in a matter-of-fact manner to avoid further distressing the client with shame or performance anxiety.

Their cognitive decline puts clients at risk of acquiring excess disability, which is a reversible deficit that is more disabling than the primary disability. This condition exists when there is greater disturbance in functioning than can be accounted for by the basic illness. The encouragement of self-care activities helps to prevent excess disability. Many self-care activities are overlearned skills that can be retained longer if their use is continued. Assessment must be made to determine what types of self-care the client can initiate on her own, imitate after demonstration, and complete after initiation (Dawson et al. 1986).

Rehabilitation nursing texts are excellent sources of information on coping with self-care deficits. Referral to physical, occupational, and recreational therapists may also prove beneficial in determining ways to preserve maximum self-care ability. Specially adapted tools for bathing, feeding, ambulation, and toileting are growing more available; many of these items are now sold by nationally known mail-order catalogue firms.

Incontinence is a problem deserving special mention when considering the self-care deficits of the client with a degenerative disorder. Incontinence is one of the major precipitants for institutional placement of a person with a degenerative disorder. Because of our deeply ingrained ideas about the implications of inability to control one's bladder and bowels, many caregivers respond to the problem of incontinence with shame, disgust, or neglect. Any problem with incontinence requires thorough medical evaluation to rule out and correct treatable causes, such as infection, prostatic obstruction, cystocele, rectocele, and fecal impaction. Caregivers need to understand the reasons for incontinence and its management. In cases of incontinence for which no physical cause can be determined, it is important to develop consistent toileting schedules and to use incontinence management devices, such as a collecting apparatus and protective clothing, which minimize both embarrassment for the client and work for the caregiver. Above all, the caregiver must communicate to the client that her incontinence in no way diminishes her dignity or worth as a human being.

Social Disruptions

The client with an altered pattern of degenerative origin and his family face a difficult and uncertain future clouded by the knowledge that the client's losses are progressive and irreversible. The client and family need help to begin the process of ac-

cepting the chronicity of the disorder. They also need to learn how best to manage the impact of the disorder so that it does not overwhelm and distort the workings of the entire family system and social network. The nursing goal in caring for the client and family is to assist with this adaptation.

Successful adaptation has been identified as the client's ability to live with himself and his condition. The client's acknowledgment of the disease and its limitations is evidence of the final stage of acceptance.

According to Hayter (1982), families of relatives with irreversible degenerative disorders have many needs that are not being met adequately. Many need more information about the causes, treatment, and prognosis of the disorder. Families often state that they received comfort from knowing a specific diagnosis; the unknown is extremely frightening to them. The nurse must provide explanations in order to counter the myths and inaccurate information that abound about degenerative disorders.

One way to insure that families obtain accurate and up-to-date information about degenerative disorders is to refer them to the Alzheimer's Disease and Related Disorders Association (ADRDA). Most metropolitan areas now have a local chapter of the ADRDA, which conducts self-help support groups for families of clients with degenerative disorders. Initially, the group provides the information crucial to coping with the diagnosis of the disorder. Many ADRDA groups promote networking of families who are in close proximity and in similar situations. These networks help with problems of anticipatory grief and isolation. They also offer practical and tested techniques for dealing with clients' problem behaviors (Gwyther and Matteson 1983).

During the time that the individual with a degenerative disorder lives at home, the nurse needs to be sensitive to threats to the client's self-esteem. The client should be encouraged to express what kind of care is acceptable to her (Dewis and Baumann 1982). The family should also be involved in discussions of care, for they are often the primary caregivers in the early degenerative stages.

Relatives often have negative feelings about the client's behavior. The disorder may necessitate role changes that are disruptive to the family. Relationships are altered as the client is transformed from an independent person to a dependent one. A husband may be forced to retire while the wife goes to work and becomes the major provider. A parent may become dependent on her child. Such changes result in family tension and resentment, particularly if some family members feel burdened by additional responsibilities. Ambivalent feelings about the client's impending death, role reversal, and competition and greed among siblings are all thorny family issues that may arise as the client's illness progresses (Lansky 1984). The nurse must be sensitive to these issues while facilitating frank discussion and acknowledging that such painful feelings are to be expected.

Emotions of the caregivers can range from denial, to shame, embarrassment, fear, and frustration. Understanding anger as a reaction to frustration is important to help the caregiver deal with the situation in an appropriate way. Anger is a constructive force when it mobilizes caregivers to protect and assert themselves when necessary. It becomes destructive when anger is directed toward the clients in response to actions they are no longer able to control and for which they are not longer accountable. Caregivers can become self-destructive and limit their capacity to help the clients when anger replaces the loving feelings of the past. Caregivers can learn to manage and use their anger in the interest of survival, but they must first be able to understand their own needs (Powell 1985).

Family members may employ many coping mechanisms, including projection, denial, and reaction formation (Hirschfeld 1976). Utilization of reaction formation (that is, focusing on caring for the client in an attempt to negate the negative feelings that her behavior evokes) can be especially maladaptive. As Hayter (1982) points out, "The nurse can help the family find a balance between responsibility to themselves, their relative with Alzheimer's disease, and the remainder of the family" (p. 85).

As the degenerative alteration progresses, the client usually requires institutionalization. Often after the client has been institutionalized, the relatives experience feelings of relief mixed with guilt. This guilt may be alleviated somewhat by the nurse's acknowledgement of what the family members have done for the client. Also, the nurse can emphasize the unique role family members can play with an institutionalized relative. They can provide the client with love and affection (Hayter 1982). The family may need to be encouraged to visit the client because his lack of response can alienate them.

IMPACT OF DEGENERATIVE VARIATIONS AND DISRUPTIONS ON THE NURSE

Caring for clients who are cognitively impaired is difficult and, at times, frustrating for the nurse. The nurse may become discouraged to see a client for whom he is caring continue to deteriorate. It is important for the nurse to remember that sometimes improvement in function is impossible. Car-

ing for clients who are unable to improve means remembering that they remain human beings worthy of respect.

The caregiver must initially evaluate his own feelings about cognitive loss. Our society values intellectual achievement, and degenerative mental disease carries a social stigma (Hirschfeld 1976). Through self-awareness, the nurse may realize that he is negatively biased toward an individual whose intellect is impaired. An increase in self-awareness can lead to empathy and greater understanding of what the client is experiencing.

The chronicity of degenerative disorders may also affect the nurse's reactions. As Butler (1977) has stated: "Chronicity is often used as an excuse for not doing anything when there may be many treatment techniques that could comfort, support, and even greatly increase the functioning of brain-damaged individuals" (p. 78). Once the brain damage has occurred, there is no return to a normal physical condition. However, functioning may be improved by treating some of the client's emotional and physical symptoms. The nurse working with the client who has a degenerative disorder must be able to derive satisfaction from small improvements or even just maintenance in the client's functional ability. When this is no longer possible, she must realize the tremendous value of helping another human being face deterioration and, ultimately, death with as much dignity as possible.

THE NURSING PROCESS IN THE CARE OF CLIENTS WITH VARIATIONS AND DISRUPTIONS OF DEGENERATIVE ORIGIN

Assessment

To help the client with a degenerative alteration reach or maintain his highest level of function, the nurse must be proficient in assessing both the client's deficits and his remaining strengths. Often, maximizing strengths helps the client to maintain feelings of adequacy and self-esteem despite ravaging losses in other abilities. For example, the client who can no longer remember what he ate for lunch may still be able to engage in meaningful social interaction by relating valuable experiences and insights gained over decades of living and coping successfully.

Assessment begins with gathering information about the life history of the client. How has the client coped with adversity in the past? What have been his sources of support and guidance? Who are the significant people in the client's life, and are they still available for support? Is his religious faith an asset? What losses has the client experienced, especially recently? When assessing losses, the nurse should include health factors as well as social and emotional losses (Wolanin 1981).

The next area to be assessed is the client's environment. According to Wolanin (1981), environments should be assessed to answer two questions:

1. What in the client's environment facilitates his ability to function optimally?
2. What in his environment prevents this client from functioning optimally?

Both of these questions must be answered in terms of available human resources and the structure of the client's physical environment.

It is also important to assess how the client interacts with others. Here, it is necessary to observe how the client and family relate to one another. Does the family overprotect the client and inadvertently assign him the role of passive receiver of care? Or does the family expect too much of the client in view of his diminished capacities? Is the relationship between client and family warm and loving, or is it fraught with conflict from old, unresolved problems or new difficulties associated with the client's condition? Does the family understand the nature of the client's disorder and its long-term implications?

Thorough assessment of the client with a degenerative alteration mandates use of holistic nursing assessment techniques. Self-care deficits and abilities must be carefully determined by direct observation of the client's functioning in activities of daily living. Special attention should be given to the integrity of the client's sensoriperceptual abilities. A comprehensive mental status exam is of primary importance in planning care. It may be helpful to refer the client for psychological testing to determine functioning in attention, memory, orientation, constructional ability, judgment, and abstract reasoning (Strub and Black 1981).

Planning

Realistic goals should be established on the basis of the client's known assets and liabilities. Planning care for the client with a degenerative disorder requires that the nurse have a good understanding of the expected course of the degenerative processes involved. This understanding must also be imparted to family members who serve as caregivers. Initially, planning focuses on the client's memory deficits and resulting anxiety. Caregivers should help the client organize his activities so that daily events are consistent and predictable. Provi-

sion must also be made for the client's safety needs as her judgment and reality testing abilities decline..

Caregivers must plan for the reality of the client's increasing dependency on others for physical care. While the client is still a community resident, it may be useful to put families in touch with appropriate community health and service organizations. These agencies can help to arrange for personal care assistance, recreation, and transportation. It may also be possible to obtain respite care for families who need an occasional break from caregiving burdens.

As the degenerative disorder progresses, the issue of institutional care may become a major focus of planning. Nursing homes and other long-term care facilities are still viewed as negative options by many clients, families, and nurses. However, when the client reaches the later stages of a degenerative disorder, it may be impossible to continue to provide for his many needs at home. It is important for everyone involved in the placement decision to understand that not all long-term care facilities are the substandard places depicted in the media and that it is possible to find a facility where care is provided skillfully and compassionately. The nurse can provide an invaluable service at this time by assisting client and caregivers in carefully exploring placement alternatives. Most facilities welcome inquiries and will arrange nonobligatory interviews and tours for interested parties. The client should be as involved in this exploratory process as his physical and mental capabilities will allow.

Ultimately, planning revolves around assuring a comfortable and dignified death for the affected client. This involves attention to planning for the client's physical comfort as well as his psychological ease. Throughout the long course of illness and disability, the client and caregiver should be supported in their decisions about the extent of treatment desired and the setting in which the client's final days will be lived.

Implementation

Throughout this chapter, interventions have been suggested for various problems associated with degenerative disorders. Table 12–2 summarizes many of these interventions and lists others that may be indicated in the care of clients with degenerative disorders.

Evaluation

Evaluation of the effectiveness of nursing interventions in the care of the client with a degenerative alteration is based on the degree to which established goals are attained. Since the degenerative process usually progresses over an extended period

Table 12–2. The Nursing Process in Degenerative Alterations

Client's Problem	Goal	Nursing Interventions
Memory impairment	Provide safe environment; promote self-esteem	Maintain structured environment with a regular schedule of activities. Provide memory aids (lists, frequent reminders). Encourage reminiscing and ventilation of anxieties.
Cognitive impairment	Provide safe environment; maximize self-care ability	Encourage self-care in areas where client is capable of continued independence. Teach families about anticipated problems with the client's cognitive function. Minimize stimulus overload. Remove potential hazards from the client's environment.
Behavioral alterations	Provide safe environment; prevent injury to client and others	Teach families about potential behavioral alterations. Use psychotropic medications judiciously. Use distraction instead of confrontation. Break down tasks into simple steps.
Impaired reality testing	Maintain orientation to time, place, and person; provide safe environment; decrease anxiety	Use 24-hour reality techniques and teach them to the family. Provide for consistent scheduling of caregivers. Maintain consistent routine. Keep client's treasured personal possessions in the environment.
Impaired judgment	Provide safe environment; decrease anxiety	Approach client cautiously and within her line of vision. Avoid scolding and criticism for irrational behavior. Positively reinforce desired behaviors. Remove potential hazards from the environment.
Impaired communication	Meet client's basic physical and emotional needs	Provide consistent routines and caregiver assignments. Refer client for speech and hearing evaluation. Minimize distractions in the environment. Use good communication techniques.
Self-care deficits	Promote maximum independence in ADL's; maintain client's self-esteem	Communicate about self-care problems in a matter-of-fact manner. Obtain tools and products to maximize self-care ability. Refer client to occupational therapy, physical therapy, or recreational therapy. Provide family with information on personal care services and products.
Social alterations	Maintain client in community setting as long as possible; maintain client's relationship with family and friends	Care for the family as well as the client. Encourage discussion of the effect the client's illness has on others in the family and social system. Provide nonjudgmental support. Educate the client and family regarding the course of the disorder. Refer family to self-help groups such as ADRDA.
Deciding on institutional care	Maintain health of family members caring for client; meet client's needs for physical care; decrease family members' guilt feelings; decrease client's feelings of abandonment, relocation trauma	Facilitate discussion of institutional care, if appropriate. Provide information about placement alternatives. Support the family's decision. Provide support for dealing with guilt, role reversal, and anticipatory grieving.

of time, periodic reassessments and adjustments of goals and interventions should be conducted. Sometimes a goal that was initially thought to be achievable may have to be revised because of unanticipated declines in the client's ability brought on by intercurrent acute illness or psychosocial stressors. In other instances, goals may need to be revised upward because the client responds more positively than expected to planned interventions.

In broad terms, evaluation of nursing care for the client with a degenerative disorder should be based on two parameters: the attainment of maximum functional ability and the achievement of the greatest possible comfort for the client and family. The nurse's evaluation of the effectiveness of care in promoting functional ability may be supplemented by evaluations from other professionals, such as occupational and physical therapists. Assessment of success in promoting both physical and emotional comfort is more difficult; the best sources of feedback are frequent observations of the client's behavior and regular, open discussions with his significant others.

(Text continues on page 328.)

CLINICAL EXAMPLE

HUNTINGTON'S CHOREA: A FAMILY AND INDIVIDUAL PROBLEM

George Harris is a 62-year-old male who was becoming disabled by Huntington's chorea. He was being cared for at home while he received outpatient care at a medical facility and was visited regularly by a community health nurse. George lived with his wife, Elaine, his 20-year-old daughter, Leslie, who worked as a teacher, and his 23-year-old son, Tony, who worked as an engineer for a local firm.

When he was simply sitting in a chair, George gave little indication of his disability. However, when he attempted to move from one place to another, George's gait was not purposeful but was characterized by wide, lurching movements that made it seem as if he was in imminent danger of falling. His arms and legs swung widely as he moved in the general direction of his destination. Although others watched with apprehension, George was usually able to navigate without colliding with objects or falling.

As his disease progressed, George's problems gradually became more pervasive. His coordination was so impaired that he could not eat without smearing his hands and face and spilling food on his clothing and the floor. George knew that family members found his eating habits repulsive, so he asked not to eat with the family.

The main burden of caring for George fell on Elaine, who became more frightened and resentful as her duties increased. George felt himself in the grip of a great force that he could not control. He saw his family moving away from him, recognized the strain on his wife, and saw the horror and dismay of his children as they witnessed his erratic behavior. Try as he might, George was unable to control his movements and to reduce the amount of help he needed. His speech became increasingly impaired. When he tried to talk with his wife and children, sometimes he could make no sound at all. At other times, animal-like noises came from his mouth. If people were patient enough, George, with great effort, could form words that approximated human communication.

The atmosphere in the Harris home was one of sadness. When Leslie was at home, she spent most of her time in her room. Tony arranged to be out of the house as much as possible, except for meals. Mrs. Harris generally felt isolated with only herself and her husband, although the community health nurse was a welcome visitor from the outside world.

Elaine had a vague memory of her husband's father dying of a mysterious malady that seemed to resemble her husband's, but her father-in-law had died a few years before her marriage, and the details of his illness were unclear.

ASSESSMENT

The community health nurse who was visiting the family noted the devastating effects on family members as George's chronic illness took its course. She saw the isolation of family members who had been close and loving not long before. As circumstances in the family changed, the nurse decided that additional help was indicated. She saw that Leslie and Tony were frightened young people using flight behavior in order to avoid dealing with their father's illness. They resisted any interaction with the nurse and did not acknowledge their father's plight or the burden on their mother. The nurse realized that Leslie and Tony needed help in accepting the realities of the situation. Because of the genetic etiology of their father's illness, it was important for the children to become aware of the implications for their own futures.

The following nursing and psychiatric diagnoses were made:

Nursing Diagnoses

Ineffective individual coping
(related to cognitive and communication losses)

Ineffective family coping
(related to excessive responsibilities of the wife and flight behavior of the children)

Fear
(related to lack of knowledge and unexpressed anxiety concerning the father's illness and its implications for the whole family)

Self-esteem disturbance
(related to the feelings of worthlessness and being a burden to the family)

Multiaxial Psychiatric Diagnoses

Axis I   290.21 Primary degenerative dementia with depression
Axis II   None

Axis III Huntington's chorea
Axis IV Serious chronic illness, enduring circumstances. Severity: 5
Axis V Current GAF: 34
Highest GAF past year: 40

PLANNING

The nurse explored George's social security status and learned that he was eligible for care in a community day treatment center as long as he was ambulatory and had some capacity for self-care. She arranged a family meeting with the parents and children and explained to them that George could apply for admission to the day treatment center and attend three days a week while continuing to live at home. A chairmobile could be provided by the supplementary social security funds to transport him.

At the meeting, the illness of George's father was mentioned and the nurse asked for more information. George was able to recall some facts, and for the first time Leslie asked the question that had been troubling her for weeks: "Is this illness hereditary?" The nurse gave an affirmative answer but disclaimed any special expertise in this area. She suggested that Leslie and Tony make an appointment to see a genetic counselor at the medical center where George's care was being coordinated. The nurse then began to guide the family toward a series of immediate goals:

1. Arrange an intake interview at the day treatment center to determine George's suitability for admission to its program.
2. Divide the day-to-day responsibilities for George's care among all three members of the family. Leslie agreed to do weekly shopping for groceries and to help with the laundry. Tony agreed to be available when his father needed help with bathing and shaving.
3. Accept George's illness as a family problem and begin to learn more about the disorder that frightens all of them so much.

IMPLEMENTATION

With George out of the house three days a week, his wife felt a sense of relief. She was able to visit friends occasionally and to invite them to her home. Because she was experiencing some respite from her responsibilities, she was more patient with George when he was at home. Attending the day treatment center gave George a sense of social involvement. Staff members accepted his disability without making him feel rejected. The fact that he was still ambulatory enabled him to perform small services for other clients in wheel chairs and this, too, increased his feelings of self-worth.

The interview with the genetic counselor was difficult for Leslie and Tony. They learned that Huntington's chorea was transmitted by a dominant gene, that one or both of them might develop the illness later in life, and that any children they had might be affected. Shock and dismay drew Leslie and Tony closer. Neither was presently involved in a serious relationship, but both realized that difficult decisions regarding marriage and children lay ahead for both of them.

EVALUATION

The nurse knew that George's placement in the day treatment center was a temporary measure and that the time would come when hospitalization would be indicated. Fortunately, the family had access to a range of services to which George's status as a disabled person entitled them. For the present, the family had adjusted as well as possible. George was less depressed attending the day center where he felt like "one of the guys." He knew what the future held for him, but for the moment the quality of life had improved. Elaine

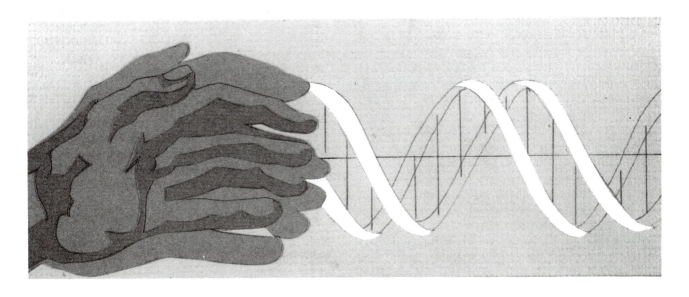

now felt that her problems were manageable and that help would be forthcoming when the family required it. Leslie and Tony were somewhat bitter, but their bitterness was not directed toward their parents. Several meetings with the genetic counselor and some independent readings had made them better informed. The realization of their situation was stark and frightening, but they supported each other. They also found that knowledge felt better than ignorance and that working together as a family was better than being alone.

Nursing Diagnoses	Goal	Nursing Actions	Outcome Criteria	Outcome Evaluation
Ineffective individual coping	Client will maintain communication and socialization at present level of disability.	Provide activities, increase social involvement and opportunities to utilize present level of functioning.	Client will participate in a day center program.	Client was able to be involved in the center programming that could compensate for his disabilities.
Ineffective family coping	Children will be involved in care, wife will be relieved of total responsibility.	Divide responsibilities for care among family members; discuss the need for future placement.	Care will be undertaken by children as well as mother; family will explore placement options to prepare for future.	Wife was able to have some social contacts when husband was at day center; son and daughter agreed to share some aspects of care.
Fear	Client will reduce knowledge deficit, accept implications.	Refer children to genetic counselor for accurate information and guidance.	Children will understand the implications of the disease for themselves and their future offspring.	Both children became better informed but were still understandably frightened of the future; sibling relationship grew closer.
Self-esteem disturbance	Client will increase sense of self-worth.	Explore services that client can do for others at the center.	Success at small tasks will provide sense of accomplishment.	Client's sense of self-worth improved by doing things for others; quality of life improved for the present time.

SUMMARY

In nearly every arena of practice, nurses are increasingly challenged to provide knowledgeable and effective care for the burgeoning number of clients with variations and disruptions of degenerative origin. Nurses are the primary caregivers for this population. If they are to adequately fulfill their role, they must increase their knowledge regarding the degenerative disorders and their management.

Degenerative variations and disruptions affect every sphere of client and family function. Physical disruptions such as movement disorders, sleep disturbances, and incontinence interact with the problems of memory and communication impairment, cognitive deterioration, behavioral disruptions, impaired judgment, faulty reality testing, and social disruptions. Nursing goals for clients with these disorders include promotion of self-esteem, provision of a safe environment, prevention of injury to self and others, maintenance of orientation and physical integrity, and reduction of anxiety. Goals involving the family include maintaining the health of family caregivers, increasing the knowledge of family members regarding the causes and treatments of degenerative disorders, and reducing family members' frustration and guilt feelings.

The care of clients with degenerative disorders demands all of a nurse's skills in providing for both physical care needs and psychosocial requirements. Knowledgeable nursing care for the client with a degenerative variation or disruption allows the client to function as well as he can with as much comfort as possible.

Review Questions

1. Describe the relationship between aging and variations and disruptions of degenerative origin.

2. Design a nursing care plan for a client with memory impairment.

3. Discuss the importance of genetic counseling for children of clients with Huntington's chorea.

4. Explain why degenerative disorders are irreversible.

5. Describe three areas that the nurse must assess when caring for a client with a variation or disruption of degenerative origin.

Research Report

Measuring Improvement in Patients with Dementia

Poor memory, which is often associated with old age, affects the functional capacity in activities of daily living. This study was undertaken to measure improvement in memory, communication, and self-care in men receiving lecithin and physostigmine. A tool was used to assess the clients' ability to perform activities of daily living, their orientation, communication, and behavior before and after receiving the drugs. Scores on the evaluation tool improved after therapy for six of the nine men. The results indicated that at least some clients can improve moderately in memory, communication, and behavior, as the result of care.

M. Antoine, C. Holland, and B. Scruggs. *Geriatric Nursing* 7 (July–August 1986):185-187.

Suggested Annotated Readings

Horton, A. M. *Mental Health Interventions for the Aging*. South Hadley, Massachusetts: J. F. Bergen Publishers, Inc., 1982.

Designed for interdisciplinary audiences, this book provides contrasting viewpoints on the interaction of the patient, his environment and his behavior. Traditional psychotherapy approaches are discussed as well as newly evolved ones with a specialized focus. Included are a geriatric bibliography, behavior therapy, and reality orientation. Horton discusses the ability of mental health professionals to contribute solutions to the problems of the aged.

Kaplan, O. J. *Psychopathology of Aging*. New York: Academic Press, 1979.

This series of essays on selected topics in geriatric psychiatry includes problems that were formerly considered those of the young and are now

prominent in the elderly. Sociopathy, drug abuse, sexual deviations, and alcoholism are included. Research and learning needs in this field are defined.

Werner-Beland, J. A. *Grief Responses to Long-Term Illness and Disability*. Reston, Virginia: Reston Pub. Co., Inc., 1980.

The aim of this book is to increase nurses' understanding and ability to deal with grief responses in those who continue to live in spite of having suffered a severe assault to their well-being. Psychoanalytic and attachment theories are reviewed and attention is given to family members and significant others who also grieve losses of the patient. The author presents hope as the opposite of grief and shows nurses ways they can be instrumental in fostering hope and responding to stress.

Wolanin, M. O., and L. R. Phillips. *Confusion: Prevention and Care*. St. Louis: C. V. Mosby, 1981.

The title topic of this book is applied primarily to the elderly client but is not limited to that group. The authors begin with confusion as a nursing diagnosis and as a phenomenon that confronts caregivers in working with elderly people. Physiological, sensoriperceptual, and interactional factors that contribute to confusion are examined. Reasons for labeling the nonconfused as confused are analyzed and high-risk patients are identified. The book utilizes a holistic approach.

References

American Psychiatric Association. *Diagnostic and Statistical Manual of Mental Disorders*, 3d ed., rev. Washington, D.C., 1987.

Beam, I. M. "Helping Families Survive." *American Journal of Nursing* 84 (1984):229-231.

Berman, S., and M. Rappaport. "Social Work and Alzheimer's Disease: Psychosocial Management in the Absence of Medical Care." *Social Work in Health Care* 10 (1985):53-70.

Butler, R. N., and M. I. Lewis. *Aging and Mental Health: Positive Psychological Approaches*, 2d ed. St. Louis: C. V. Mosby, 1977.

Charles, R., M. Truesdell, and E. L. Wood. "Alzheimer's Disease: Pathology, Progression and Nursing Process." *Journal of Gerontological Nursing* 8 (1982):69-73.

Comfort, A. "Alzheimer's Disease or 'Alzheimerism'?" *Psychiatric Annals* 14 (1984):130-132.

Cox, K. "Milieu Therapy." *Geriatric Nursing* 6 (1985):152-154.

Cummings, J. "Dementia: Definition, Classification and Differential Diagnosis." *Psychiatric Annals* 14 (1984):85–92.

Cutler, N., and J. Narang. "Drug Therapies." *Geriatric Nursing* 6 (1985):160–163.

Dawson, P., K. Kline, D. Wiancko, and D. Wells. "Nurses Must Learn to Distinguish between Excess and Actual Disability to Promote the Patient's Competence." *Geriatric Nursing* 7 (1986):229–230.

Dellefield, K., and J. Miller. "Psychotropic Drugs and the Elderly Patient." *Nursing Clinics of North America* 17 (1982):303–318.

Dewis, M. E., and A. Baumann. "Alzheimer's Disease: The Silent Epidemic." *The Canadian Nurse* (July-August, 1982):32–35.

Fopma-Loy, J. "Depression and Dementia." *Journal of Psychosocial Nursing* 24 (1986):27–29.

Goode, E., and J. Silberner. "AIDS: Attacking the Brain." *U.S. News and World Report* 103 (Sept 7, 1987):48–49.

Gwyther, L., and M. Matteson. "Care for the Caregivers." *Journal of Gerontological Nursing* 9 (1983):92–95.

Hall, G., M. Kirschling, and S. Todd. "Sheltered Freedom—An Alzheimer's Unit in an ICF." *Geriatric Nursing* 7 (1986):132–137.

Hayter, J. "Patients Who Have Alzheimer's Disease." *American Journal of Nursing* 74 (1974):1460–1463.

——. "Helping Families of Patients with Alzheimer's Disease." *Journal of Gerontological Nursing* 9 (1982):81–86.

Hirschfeld, M. "The Cognitively Impaired Older Adult." *American Journal of Nursing* 76 (1976):1981–1984.

Langan, R. "Parkinson's Disease: Assessment Procedures and Guidelines for Counseling." *Nurse Practitioner* 2 (1976):13–16.

Lansky, M. "Family Psychotherapy of the Patient with Chronic Organic Brain Syndrome." *Psychiatric Annals* 14 (1984):121–129.

Levine, J. "A Test for Alzheimer's." *Time* 128 (November 17, 1986):83.

Liston, E. H. "Diagnosis and Management of Delirium in the Elderly Patient." *Psychiatric Annals* 14 (1984):109–118.

Mace, N., and P. Rabins. *The 36-Hour Day*. Baltimore: Johns Hopkins University Press, 1981.

Mahoney, E. "Alterations in Cognitive Functioning in the Brain-Damaged Patient." *Nursing Clinics of North America* 15 (1980):283–292.

Olsen, E. J., and J. H. Mather. *Dementia Guidelines for Diagnosis and Treatment*. Veteran's Administration Department of Medicine and Surgery. Washington, D.C., Oct 10, 1985.

Palmer, M. H. "Alzheimer's Disease and Critical Care: Interactions, Implications, Interventions." *Journal of Gerontological Nursing* 9 (1983):86–90.

Pasquali, E. A., E. G. Alesi, H. M. Arnold, and N. DeBasio. *Mental Health Nursing: A Biopsychocultural Approach*. St. Louis: C. V. Mosby, 1981.

Pinel, C. "Huntington's Chorea." *Nursing Times* 72 (1976):447–448.

Powell, L. S. "Alzheimer's Disease: A Practical, Psychological Approach." *Women and Health* 10 (1985):53–63.

Reisberg, B., J. Borenstein, E. Franssen, E. Shulma, G. Steinberg, and S. Ferris. "Remediable Behavioral Symptomatology in Alzheimer's Disease." *Hospital and Community Psychiatry* 37 (1986):1199–1201.

Richardson, E. P., and R. D. Adams. "Degenerative Disease of the Nervous System." In *Harrison's Principles of Internal Medicine*, 9th ed. K. I. Isselbacher et al., eds. New York: McGraw-Hill, 1980.

Schafer, S. C. "Modifying the Environment." *Geriatric Nursing* 6 (1985):157–159.

Schwab, M., J. Rader, and J. Doan. "Relieving the Anxiety and Fear in Dementia." *Journal of Gerontological Nursing* 11 (1985):8–15.

Shapira, J., R. Schlesinger, and J. Cummings. "Distinguishing Dementias." *American Journal of Nursing* 86 (1986):699–702.

Small, O. "Huntington's Chorea." *Nursing Times* (April 9, 1986):32–33.

Stewart, C. M. "Age-Related Changes in the Nervous System." *Journal of Neurosurgical Nursing* 14 (1982):69–73.

Stipe, J., D. White, and E. Van Arsdale. "Huntington's Disease." *American Journal of Nursing* 79 (1979): 1428–1433.

Strub, R. L., and F. W. Black. *Organic Brain Syndromes: An Introduction to Neurobehavioral Disorders*. Philadelphia: F. A. Davis, 1981.

Thornton, J. E., H. Davies, and J. R. Tinklenberg. "Alzheimer's Disease Syndrome." *Journal of Psychosocial Nursing* 24 (1986):16–22.

Topp, B. "Toward a Better Understanding of Parkinson's Disease." *Geriatric Nursing* 8 (1987):180–182.

Wagner, L. "Nursing Homes Develop Special Alzheimer's Units." *Modern Health Care* 17 (1987):40–46.

Wang, H. S. "Special Diagnostic Procedures: The Evaluation of Brain Impairment." In *Mental Illness in Later Life*, E. W. Busse and E. Pfeiffer, eds. Washington, D.C.: American Psychological Association, 1973.

Wells, C. "Pseudodementia." *American Journal of Psychiatry* 136 (1979):895–900.

Wells, R. W. "Huntington's Chorea: Seeing Beyond the Disease." *American Journal of Nursing* 72 (1972): 854–956.

Williams, L. "Alzheimer's: The Need for Caring." *Journal of Gerontological Nursing* 12 (1986):21–28.

Wilson, R. S., and D. C. Carron. "Psychological Features of Huntington's Disease and the Problem of Early Detection." *Social Biology* 27 (1980):11–19.

Wolanin, M. O., and L. R. Phillips. *Confusion: Prevention and Care*. St. Louis: C. V. Mosby, 1981.

——. "Another Aspect of AIDS." *Emergency Medicine* 19 (1987):44–46.

13

Adaptational Variations and Disruptions

Learning Objectives

After reading this chapter, the student should be able to:

1. Describe Alexander's specific conflict theory and Dunbar's specific personality theory.

2. Explain the general adaptation syndrome described by Selye.

3. Discuss the role of the autonomic nervous system in activating the general adaptation syndrome.

4. Discuss the physiological and psychological factors present in gastrointestinal responses to stress.

5. Compare the behavioral traits of type A and type B personalities.

6. Analyze the impact of aggression levels and control levels in clients exhibiting skeletomuscular, cardiovascular, and gastrointestinal stress responses.

7. Identify the physiological, psychological, and cultural influences exhibited by the anorexia nervosa client.

8. Enumerate the major components of a holistic health care plan for clients with a stress-related disorder.

Overview

Stress and the effects of stress on the human organism have been given a great deal of attention in this century. Numerous investigators have explored the nature of stress, its consequences, and its varied manifestations. One of the pioneers in stress research, Hans Selye, described the stress of pleasure and fulfillment, but also noted the stress that accompanies pain and frustration. It was Selye who coined the word *eustress* for the stress of pleasure, and reserved the word *distress* for the stress of pain and frustration. According to Selye, stress is virtually unavoidable; that is, the only way to avoid stress would be to do absolutely nothing. However, the experience of doing nothing day after day, hour after hour would produce excruciating stress for most of us. What we must hope for is to discover what our optimal level of stress is. In other words, we must try to preserve in ourselves and in our clients the stress level that challenges but does not exhaust the mental, physical, and emotional powers that all of us possess in varying degrees.

Almost every disorder to which people are susceptible can be affected, positively or negatively, by emotional states. It is our emotional state that determines whether the stress we encounter in daily life takes the form of distress or eustress. Here, as in so many instances, it is not what happens that is of paramount importance, but the interpretation we give to what happens. In this chapter we discuss some of the variations and disruptions that arise when stress levels are

extremely high or unduly prolonged. In the first part of this chapter relationships between mind and body are described, using different perspectives. Theories of stress and adaptation are covered next. The remainder of the chapter is devoted to some of the specific consequences of stress. Suggestions are included for nursing approaches designed to reduce stress levels for clients, colleagues, and ourselves.

In early times little was known about the causes of human dysfunction, and supernatural influences were blamed. As a result, available therapeutic measures were concerned with the whole person, mind, body, and spirit. Strangely enough, this holistic viewpoint narrowed as frontiers of knowledge enlarged. Searching for causes of dysfunction became more specific and more physiological. With the development of lenses, scientists became interested in the physical world that had just become visible, and this included the study of the body. Human beings gradually came to be regarded as triadic (three-part) entities consisting of mind, body, and spirit. With specialization the order of the day, the human spirit or soul became the realm of theologians; the mind, the realm of philosophers and teachers; and the body or *soma*, the realm left to physicians and scientists. Little attention was given to spiritual influences on the physical self, and physical symptoms of illness were the objects of greatest concern. Divisions between mind, body, and spirit prevailed from the fifteenth through the nineteenth centuries. It was not until the twentieth century that the interactive and holistic aspects of human existence were truly accepted once more.

Unified, holistic views of human function and dysfunction have proliferated in recent years. Nurses and other providers of health care have come to realize that separating physical illness (the traditional realm of medicine) from psychological and social factors (the traditional realms of psychology and sociology) is not desirable. Any variation or disruption of function, whether physiological, psychological, or social in its nature, is a disorder of the whole person, not of any one part.

The term *psychosomatic* was part of the standard psychiatric terminology until 1968, when it was replaced with the term *psychophysiological*. Somewhat later the term *biopsychosocial* was applied to certain patterns. This term has been widely accepted and has effectively expanded the duality implied by the earlier terminology. In the DSM-III-R the terms *mental disorder* and *physical disorder* are used, but a cautionary statement is included that the use of these terms does not mean that mental disorders are unrelated to physical or biological processes (DSM-III 1980, DSM-III-R 1987).

THEORIES OF STRESS AND ADAPTATION

Biopsychosocial research has demonstrated that emotional states can inhibit or accelerate the defenses of individuals against a wide range of disorders. Impressive numbers of research studies indicate that almost every disorder to which people are susceptible can be affected positively or negatively by emotional factors (Collins 1983). For example, Rahe (1974) found a correlation between health problems of a population sample and the life changes experienced in the period immediately preceding the onset of the problems. Jones (1977) found that positive emotions are associated with immunity or rapid recovery from certain physical disorders, while other researchers have found that negative emotional states induce or aggravate some physical disorders (Williams and Holmes 1978, Coelho, Hamburg, and Adams 1980). These and similar findings are important because they reinforce holistic approaches to health promotion, restoration, and maintenance.

Some theorists have tried to link specific disorders to particular conflicts or personality traits. Franz Alexander (1960) proposed that specific conflicts are likely to produce dysfunction or deterio-

ration in particular organs or organ systems. For example, an individual who is conflicted between a wish for closeness and a fear of closeness might express the conflict somatically by developing a neurodermatitis, such as psoriasis or eczema. A related hypothesis was offered by Dunbar (1943, 1954), who compiled psychosocial data on over 1,600 individuals and developed personality profiles linked to specific disorders in which mind and body factors could be identified. Using individual and family data, behavior patterns, personality traits, living habits, and situational factors, Dunbar formulated a specific personality theory to explain the etiology of certain disorders. Persons with rheumatoid arthritis, for instance, were described as quiet, affable individuals whose pleasant exterior concealed considerable hostility.

Alexander's specific conflict theory and Dunbar's specific personality theory are now considered simplistic and reductionistic, but personality profiles still enjoy some credibility. Meyer Friedman and Ray Rosenman (1974) developed a classification of personalities to explain some of the etiologic factors of cardiac disorders. Their work was based on prospective as well as retrospective data; that is, their samples contained persons who had already suffered a myocardial infarction or coronary artery deficits as well as persons who had not at the time the study began. According to their typology, those with *type A* personalities are competitive, striving individuals, driven by a sense of urgency and a need to achieve.

Type A's are at greater risk for developing heart disease than those with *type B* personalities. Friedman and Rosenman described type B persons as less impatient, less competitive, and less easily angered than type A persons. Laboratory studies have shown that type A individuals have significantly higher levels than type B individuals of serum cholesterol, triglycerides, and abnormalities in lipoprotein ratios. In a prospective study, these three laboratory findings were significant predictors of heart disease, but the behavioral patterns of the subjects were the most important predictive factor. Some studies question the accuracy of this personality categorization and dispute the association between personality types and susceptibility to heart disease. Specific characteristics such as hostility and distrust have been cited as more accurate predictors of heart attacks than global personality generalizations. There is now considerable support for the idea that ambition and competitiveness in themselves may be less detrimental than was once supposed (Tierney 1985).

Other theorists have taken a more general approach to the question of what role mind-body relationships play in the etiology of diseases. In the nineteenth century, long before the concept of stress was introduced, the French physiologist Claude Bernard noted that the internal environment of any living organism must remain constant despite external changes to which it might be exposed. About fifty years later an American physiologist, Walter Cannon (1932), applied the word *homeostasis* to the steady state that must be maintained within an organism if healthy functioning is to continue. It was Cannon who laid the foundation for a scientific analysis of the adaptive mechanisms that are necessary for the preservation of life.

In a series of animal experiments, Selye found that stimuli or irritants such as cold, heat, infection, trauma, noise, and overcrowding all produced the same kinds of physiological changes. He used the broad term *stressors* to encompass stimuli that precipitate similar physiological and psychological reactions, and he referred to the clusters of physiological responses to various stimuli as *local*

CHRONOLOGICAL DEVELOPMENT OF ADAPTATIONAL CONCEPTS

Cannon (circa 1927)
■ Demonstrated the physiological effects of emotion and the role of the autonomic nervous system.

Alexander (circa 1934)
■ Discovered that symptoms occurred only in organs and organ systems activated by the autonomic nervous system.

■ Found that symptoms resulted from prolonged physiological processes that were activated by psychological needs and that in turn acted on the autonomic nervous system.

Dunbar (circa 1936)
■ Stated that a specific personality configuration is associated with specific adaptational disorders.

Selye (circa 1945)
■ Believed that individuals respond to stress through the general adaptation syndrome. The general adaptation response is activated by the autonomic nervous system, and involves the endocrine system.

SOURCE: Adapted from Kaplan (1980).

---

adaptation syndromes and *general adaptation syndromes* (Selye 1974, 1976).

When stressors produce a local injury that seems not to affect the whole organism or even an organ or organ system, a localized response is elicited. The endocrine glands, especially the pituitary and adrenal glands, produce hormones in order to contain the infection or trauma. The adaptive hormones present in local reactions may be anti-inflammatory or pro-inflammatory, but their purpose is to limit the damage to the organism. Perhaps the most important adaptive hormone is *adrenocorticotropic hormone* (ACTH), which is produced by the pituitary gland, ACTH stimulates the adrenal cortex to produce *corticoids*. The corticoids include glucocorticoids, such as cortisone, which decrease inflammatory processes, and mineralocorticoids, which promote inflammatory processes.

Sometimes deficient or excessive amounts of corticoids create *systemic reactions*. This might occur if excessive secretions of a pro-inflammatory hormone, produced in response to localized trauma, damage tissues unrelated to the original injury. When this happens, the local adaptation syndrome gives way to general adaptation reactions that may initiate or aggravate disorders affecting organs or organ systems. A localized reaction to an insect bite might, for example, precipitate a systemic reaction in very sensitive individuals.

The general adaptation syndrome (GAS) identified by Selye (1976) consists of three stages of response to stressors; alarm, resistance, and exhaustion. In the first stage, the autonomic nervous system is called into action; in the second and third stages the endocrine system becomes involved. When stress is prolonged or extreme, the anterior portion of the pituitary gland, influenced by the hypothalamus, causes the adrenal cortex to release hormones into the bloodstream. One group of hormones, the glucocorticoids, are involved in sugar metabolism and have contradictory effects. They increase the amount of blood sugar available for energy and facilitate blood circulation, but they also reduce resistance to infection and reduce the ability of the body to repair tissue damage. The effects of the glucocorticoids include the following:

■ Inhibition of new tissue formation around wounds
■ Reduction in the formation of antibodies
■ Reduction of the number of circulating white cells
■ Depression of thyroid activity
■ Reduction in production of reproductive and sexual hormones

STAGES OF THE GENERAL ADAPTATION SYNDROME

Stage One: Alarm

The body is exposed to an adverse stimulus or stressor and immediately mobilizes to offer resistance in the form of compensatory behavior. For example, extreme cold produces shivering, which in turn increases body heat.

Stage Two: Resistance

Alarm and mobilization give way to resistance when the stimulus is excessive or prolonged. For example, in the presence of extreme cold, shivering may give way to fever or hypothermia.

Stage Three: Exhaustion

When exposure to the stressor continues, energy is depleted and the body becomes weakened and exhausted. Exhaustion may be either reversible or irreversible. Selye differentiated *superficial energy*, which is accessible and renewable, from *deeper energy*, which is inaccessible to regeneration or restoration.

The accompanying box describes the three stages of the GAS.

A great many physiological processes are part of the general adaptation syndrome. The autonomic nervous system is the instigator of the reactive process and is involved throughout. Influenced by the hypothalamus, the emotional switchboard of the body, the pituitary gland stimulates hormonal production by the adrenal glands located just above the kidneys. Also involved is the thymus gland, a lymphatic organ in the chest, and lymph nodes in the cervical, axillary, pelvic, and other regions of the body (see Figure 13–1). The interaction of so many structures helps explain the importance of the general adaptation syndrome in the occurrence of dysfunctional alterations of organs and organ systems.

Once the general adaptation syndrome is activated, intervening factors help determine which organ or organ system is likely to be affected. Certain organs or organ systems seem more vulnerable than others, even though every part of the body is involved in the general adaptation response.

One question Selye sought to answer was, why does the same amount of exposure to the same stimuli elicit responses of different intensity among different individuals? The explanation he offered was that different intrinsic and extrinsic factors in different people alter the intensity of their responses. Intrinsic factors might be related to genetics, age, or gender. Extrinsic factors might include environmental conditions, family or group influences, or personal habits. Any of these factors helps determine whether an individual can tolerate and overcome the effects of stressors or whether the stressors will lead to dysfunction.

Individual responses are also influenced by perceptions of events. One person's debilitating stress is another person's exciting challenge. In addition, some physiological reactions are the legacy of premodern times. Like our primitive ancestors, we react to perceived danger by stimulating the heart to send increased blood supply to the brain, legs, and trunk. In the physically dangerous world of our early ancestors, these and other changes activated by the autonomic nervous system were essential. Our forebears resorted to *flight* behavior to escape danger or *fight* behavior to overcome danger. Substances produced in the alarm state promoted vigorous activity and were dissipated. In present-day life, people often feel threatened but cannot resort to flight or fight behavior. Present-day stressors are likely to be symbolic rather than physical, yet the human body continues to respond as if the dangers of the modern world were primarily physical. The mobilization of the cardiovascular system, skeletomuscular system, and nervous system that was once so essential to survival now operates to predispose individuals to stress-related alterations (Miller, Ross, and Cohen 1982, Day 1984). Figure 13–2 illustrates the general adaptation response.

A prevailing belief is that stress is always an undesirable, uncomfortable condition. However, Selye (1980, 1974) explained that stress is not always painful. Some stressors, or *eustressors*, are rewarding and even pleasurable. The problem for most people is not the experience of stress but the management of it. Selye believed that it is possible to modify one's responses to stress in order to cope with the conditions of everyday life and to enjoy the eustress that accompanies satisfactory accomplishment.

To understand stress, it is necessary to accept the concept of *homeostasis*. When stressors intrude, they upset the natural balance of the individual. Individuals are usually able to adjust only partially to stress; failing to adapt completely, they continue to exist in a subjective state of *distress* (Coyne and Holroyd 1982).

It is difficult to measure the impact of a particular stressor in absolute terms, although Holmes and Rahe (1967) did assign numerical values to life change events (see Chapter 3). Although Holmes and Rahe posited that the higher the numerical

Figure 13–1. *The physiological pathways of response to stressors.*

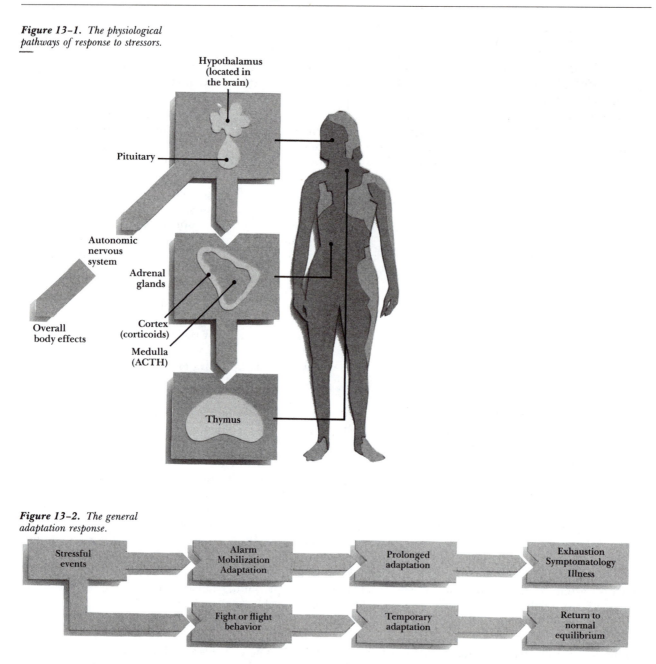

Figure 13–2. *The general adaptation response.*

value of a particular event, the greater the likelihood of developing an illness or sustaining an injury within a relatively short period of time, they established only correlations. Despite the assigned values given to life changes, no causal relationships were established.

Current views of the quantitative nature of stressful events were summed up by Wilder and Plutchik (1985), who noted, "When dealing with humans, it is evident that one cannot measure the stressfulness of life events in terms of physical dimensions, such as decibels and volts, and that almost no life event is a stressor to all individuals exposed to it. With humans, a complex mediation process occurs between the life event and the biolog-

ical responses of the body. This mediation process involves a cognitive interpretation of the event in the light of one's past history and experiences, an emotional reaction, and an attempt at coping. To understand an individual's stress responses, all these elements need to be identified and evaluated."

Stressors and the feelings they produce are cumulative. Life changes, work pressures, and family problems might be manageable if they arrived singly, but they become overwhelming if they occur within a brief period. It is helpful, then, to eliminate stressors that are avoidable and to learn to cope with those that are not. To accomplish this, a number of guidelines have been suggested as techniques to help people maintain a steady state as they adapt to conditions of the world they inhabit (Selye 1974):

1. Ascertain your natural tolerance to stress. This is important because individuals vary in the amounts and kinds of stress they can manage. These individual differences are influenced by a variety of psychological, physiological, and social factors. Analyzing and accepting one's limitations are essential to the management of personal stress levels.

2. Learn to be both selfish and unselfish. Altruism, compassion, and desire for recognition may be sources of satisfaction and pride, provided your real needs for self-esteem and self-actualization are not sacrificed along the way.

3. Consider whether an objective is worth the struggle involved, in light of the situation in which you must function. Fight and flight behaviors are two extreme alternatives, but a middle course may be more advisable.

4. Confront problems promptly instead of procrastinating when a task is necessary but difficult. Delay due to procrastination tends to aggravate stress.

5. Contain or minimize stress by concentrating on actions likely to improve conditions. Blaming yourself or others, or ruminating about the painful aspects of a situation without engaging in active problem-solving tends to increase stress.

DISORDERS OF ADAPTATIONAL ORIGIN

Stress is a recurring theme in certain disorders believed to have a major psychological component. There are exceptions to this—some of the same disorders may occur in the absence of known stressors. However, emotions play a part in the onset and continuation of virtually all human dysfunction, especially alterations that are thought to be directly related to stress, hyperactivity of the autonomic nervous system, and the general adaptation response (Brody 1983). Some stress-related disorders that affect organs and organ systems include the following:

- Gastrointestinal responses to stress, such as peptic ulcer and ulcerative colitis
- Respiratory responses to stress, such as asthma
- Cardiovascular responses to stress, such as hypertension and coronary artery disease
- Skeletomuscular responses to stress, such as rheumatoid arthritis

---

POSSIBLE DIAGNOSES RELATED TO ALTERED PATTERNS OF ADAPTATIONAL ORIGIN*

Altered health maintenance

Impaired home maintenance management

Impaired physical mobility

Self-care deficit

Activity intolerance

Diversional activity deficit

Altered nutrition: less than body requirements

Altered nutrition: more than body requirements

Altered tissue perfusion (cerebral, cardiopulmonary, renal, gastrointestinal, peripheral)

Sleep pattern disturbance

Pain

Chronic pain

Knowledge deficit

Self-concept disturbance

Altered family processes

Impaired social interaction

Altered sexuality patterns

Impaired adjustment

Ineffective individual coping

Ineffective family coping

Spiritual distress

*The above are the more likely nursing diagnoses related to altered patterns of adaptational origin. Nursing diagnoses are not limited to the list above. Manifestations of these disorders are individualistic even though certain prevailing patterns are identifiable.

- Behavioral responses to stress, such as obesity, anorexia nervosa, and bulimia
- The remainder of this chapter is devoted to the role of stress in the development of various disorders that represent adaptation to stress.

Figure 13–3 shows the hypothetical relationships between physiological tendencies, psychological traits, situational stress, and the formation of peptic ulcers.

Gastrointestinal Responses to Stress

UNDERSTANDING THE CLIENT WITH PEPTIC ULCER
The term *peptic ulcer* includes both gastric ulcers and duodenal ulcers. Ulcers result from excessive production of acidic digestive juices, which erode the lining of the stomach and upper part of the small intestine, causing a lesion. Although multiple factors are involved, it is believed that worry, anger,

Figure 13-3. *Multiple factors that play a role in the etiology of ulcer formation.*

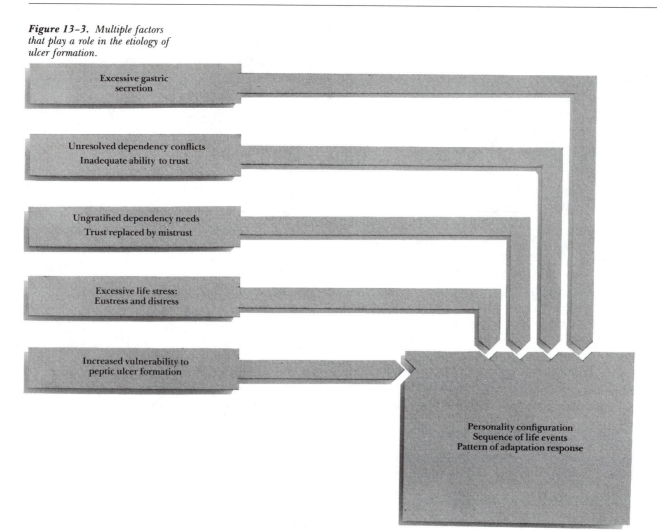

anxiety, and other negative emotions tend to stimulate production of digestive secretions beyond normal levels, thus creating conditions likely to cause ulcers (Robinson 1983, 1984).

Some studies support the idea that persons with unfulfilled dependency needs and difficulty in trusting or relying on others are especially prone to ulcer formation.

In one early study (Weiner et al. 1957) more than 2,000 army draftees were classified as maximum or minimum gastric secreters. Membership in one group or the other was sufficient to predict those who were at risk for peptic ulcer formation. Furthermore, a series of psychological tests not only predicted which subjects were maximum and which were minimum secreters, but also identified which maximum secreters were most likely to develop ulcers. Test results showed that subjects at greatest risk were those with severe dependency conflicts compounded by frustration and suppressed hostility. The dependency of all vulnerable individuals may not be readily apparent at the behavioral level. Indeed,

many dependent persons behave in independent or counterdependent ways. The dependency needs become apparent only by means of psychological testing, or systematic, ongoing assessment of the meaning of behaviors being displayed. The important contribution of the Weiner study was that neither high gastric secretion levels *nor* dependency needs *alone* led to peptic ulcer formation. In combination, they caused a vulnerability that, activated by the stress of army life, resulted in the formation of peptic ulcers.

Engel and Schmale (1964) found it possible on the basis of psychological traits to identify which individuals produced high amounts of gastric secretions. They studied subjects who did not have ulcers and found that many of them had a physiological predisposition to ulcer formation based on the association of high gastric secretion levels with psychological profiles denoting vulnerability. From the data the investigators inferred that physiological predisposition and certain psychological traits, compounded by stressful life events, interact to generate ulcer formation.

Based on research concerning the needs of a client who has peptic ulcers, it is reasonable for nurses to assume that there may be an underlying problem of dependency, regardless of how the client behaves (Putt 1970, Rosenbaum 1980). If clients are using the defense mechanism of reaction formation, they may seem to reject assistance and will need reassurance that accepting help will not threaten their autonomy in any way. The person who has a peptic ulcer is suffering from a physical problem that requires attention, but nurses can do much to aid him besides monitoring medical treatments. The basic need is the establishment of a relationship that meets but does not reinforce dependency, and nurses are in a position to provide a therapeutic approach that enhances the client's sense of comfort and security. The client needs to learn that everyone must be dependent at times and that warm, caring relationships are important regardless of one's physical condition.

Nurses should encourage clients to share their thoughts and feelings verbally and directly, rather than behaviorally or covertly. Clients with a peptic ulcer may be either very demanding or very undemanding. Some of them are quiet and self-effacing, expecting nurses to guess their needs. They should be encouraged to state their requests, to have reasonable requests granted, and gradually to assume responsibility for their own care. Some of these clients, especially those who seem passive-dependent, exhibit regressive behavior. Tendencies to regress should be counteracted by fostering client participation in self-care activities. Some clients may resist taking responsibility for self-care because they are afraid of losing the attentions of staff and family members. It is useful to remind them that being independent does not mean that others stop caring, that dependency is acceptable in some situations, and that there are acceptable ways to interact besides enacting the sick role.

In a nursing research project, Putt (1970) studied three groups of peptic ulcer clients who received different kinds of nursing care while hospitalized. One group of clients were offered psychological support in the form of unstructured interactions with nurses, which gave clients the opportunity to verbalize their feelings and to participate in self-evaluation and treatment. Minimum emphasis was given to diet or medication for this group. A second group of clients were involved in an instructional program about their disorder and its management. A third group received only the routine nursing care given to all persons with peptic ulcers.

After discharge, subjects were interviewed to learn the effects of the three types of nursing care. Those in the instructional group were more knowl-edgeable about their problem than those in the other two groups, and those in the psychological support group had learned more than those who had received routine nursing care. It was also found that the instructional approach was most effective in reducing discomfort after admission to the hospital, in improving the rate of healing, and in reducing the length of the hospitalization. The data implied that the teaching activities of nurses are especially valuable for persons with a peptic ulcer and that health teaching should be part of the therapeutic regimen. Putt concluded that, for clients with a peptic ulcer, psychological support alone is less effective than a combination of instruction and psychological support, because the latter meets only the immediate needs of the client and does not encourage anticipatory planning. The proven success of the instructional program was attributed to teaching clients how to deal with future as well as with immediate problems.

This study included subjects between the ages of 21 and 71, so the findings are applicable to many age groups. This is important because peptic ulcer is most common among adults in the third and fifth decades of life.

Hospitalization with an enforced period of respite from the daily routine is beneficial psychologically as well as physiologically because, without producing excessive guilt, it permits the client to fulfill his desire to be dependent. Diet, antacids, and surgery are frequently employed, but the care plan should also include cognitive instruction, psychological support, and environmental manipulation to reduce stressful conditions. The hospitalization experience can be crucial to outcomes for clients with peptic ulcer; after leaving the hospital, clients must draw on what they have learned about the disorder and about themselves as they reenter their usual environment. The accompanying box summarizes the principles underlying the care of persons with peptic ulcers.

Most persons who have been treated for peptic ulcer benefit from health teaching that is cognitive and supportive in nature. Because the physiological predisposition will persist, they need to learn new ways of eating, living, and behaving. One of the primary considerations is helping these clients to monitor their stress levels in order to avoid a worsening of their problem. Most persons with peptic ulcers require high-protein, low-carbohydrate diets supplemented with vitamins. A referral for dietary consultation is indicated so that the food needs and food preferences of the client can be reconciled. Unless this is done, dietary considerations become another source of frustration for the client. In addition to the dietician, a psychiatric nurse specialist, social worker, and the family should be involved in

NURSING PRINCIPLES IN THE CARE OF PEPTIC ULCER CLIENTS

■ Nursing interventions significantly influence the progress of clients hospitalized because of peptic ulcer.

■ Interactions with nurses significantly alter the client's perception of her problem.

■ Psychological support is an important addition to the care of the ulcer client but is not the only effective intervention.

■ Instructional programs that increase the client's cognitive understanding of the disorder may be more effective than psychological support alone.

■ An encompassing approach that includes cognitive learning as well as psychological support is beneficial in promoting healing, reducing discomfort, and preparing the client to cope with future as well as current demands.

the care plan. The primary nurse not only coordinates the efforts of various professionals, but, as the person most closely involved in providing care, can do much to explain and reinforce what is being taught (Feikert 1987).

UNDERSTANDING THE CLIENT WITH ULCERATIVE COLITIS Ulcerative colitis is an inflammatory disorder of the colon, primarily of the rectum and sigmoid colon. Clinical manifestations of the disorder include protracted diarrhea and bleeding that can be quite debilitating and even fatal. Diagnosis is sometimes difficult because other disturbances may simulate the disorder or coexist with it. Although the etiology is unclear and epidemiological data are inconclusive because of diagnostic difficulties, research has pointed to four areas of causation: infection, genetic factors, immunological factors, and psychological factors.

One unproven hypothesis is that the disorder may be caused by a viral agent. Genetic factors may play a part because the disorder is more common among Caucasians than among members of other racial groups and the incidence is higher among blood relatives than among conjugal or unrelated persons.

Some researchers postulate a consistent personality configuration typical of the persons with colitis, but replication of the studies and validation of the findings have not been very successful. Although methodological deficiencies may account for the confusing results, there is evidence for both opposing views about whether a typical ulcerative colitis personality does exist. Weiner (1977) found evidence to support the belief that a typical personality does exist but added that persons with ulcerative colitis differ from each other in degree and possess a range of sensitivities that recede or emerge depending on life events and environmental conditions. The lack of agreement on this question indicates need for additional research performed by investigators with no previous bias.

Despite a lack of consensus and the need to consider multifactorial explanations, there are certain attributes that recur in the psychological profiles of persons with ulcerative colitis (see Table 13–1). Engel (1972), Bloom, Asher, and White (1978), and Stroebe and Stroebe (1983) looked at interpersonal rather than intrapsychic influences.

Conflict about control was expressed behaviorally through rumination, indecision, passive compliance, extreme conscientiousness, hypervigilance, and excessive self-restraint.

Other personality traits that have been associated with persons who have ulcerative colitis include obsessive-compulsive behaviors, perfectionism, and inflexibility combined with a strong desire for approval (Engel 1954, 1972).

In meeting the needs of the client with ulcerative colitis, the nurse should give attention first to the physical discomfort of the individual. The struggle to control diarrhea and colonic bleeding is especially distressing for clients as fastidious and conscientious as are the majority of persons with ulcerative colitis. Nurses must monitor the amount

Table 13–1. Common Characteristics of Persons with Ulcerative Colitis and Suggested Nursing Interventions

Client Characteristics	Nursing Interventions
Perfectionism	Encourage lower self-imposed standards of behavior.
Rumination	Offer substitute activities to interrupt unproductive rumination.
Indecision	Simplify choices to facilitate decision making.
Inflexibility	Promote tolerance of alternative ways of thinking and acting.
Passive compliance	Encourage participation and self-care to increase the client's sense of control.
Vigilance	Reassure client by providing an interpersonal climate of trust and security.
Self-restraint	Reinforce verbal expression of thoughts and feelings, positive or negative.
Lack of insight	Encourage client to reflect on thoughts and feelings in an accepting way.

and quality of the client's excreta in a matter-of-fact way that does not contribute to the client's feeling of self-disgust. Like the person with a peptic ulcer, the client who has ulcerative colitis needs a benevolent, accepting relationship that does not threaten his self-image and that allows him to control as much of the therapeutic regimen as possible.

Ulcerative colitis is a disorder for which there is no specific cure, and the symptoms are distressing enough to make life miserable for the clients. Managing the discomfort is time-consuming and difficult. Sometimes the discomfort can be alleviated partly through client education and compassionate nursing care. At one time these clients were considered psychologically unstable, and psychiatric evaluations were routine. A more usual care plan at present is to approach the problem from several standpoints. If the client seems to have problems in coping or suffers from low self-esteem, counselling is recommended, with particular emphasis on stress reduction and raising the client's self-image. Sometimes these clients add to their problems by making excessive demands on themselves and by trying to meet impossible standards (Bullock and Rosendahl 1984). Their perfectionism sometimes causes these clients to deny themselves the relaxation and rest they need. Many of them have to be shown how to relax, using simple rhythmic breathing exercises or more elaborate techniques such as meditation or yoga (Schaefer 1986). An effective intervention is to suggest that the client keep a diary of what he eats, what activities he engages in at home and at work, stressors he has encountered, and his physical and emotional reactions to stress. The diary serves more than one purpose. First, it gives the client a sense of control over his actions and health status. Second, it helps make connections between events and their aftermath. The diary also helps to evaluate the results of the medical regimen that is being followed. Clients with this disorder are often unaware of how unrealistic their performance goals are. Data supplied by the diary offers the nurse a powerful tool to help clients reshape a view of themselves and their reactions to stress.

Irritable bowel syndrome, sometimes called spastic colon, is another gastrointestinal disorder thought to be stress-related. It is more common than ulcerative colitis; Schaefer (1986) suggests that it may be as prevalent as the common cold. Differential diagnosis to rule out ulcerative colitis, diverticulosis, and colon cancer is made by means of diagnostic tests. At one time it was thought that all persons with irritable bowel syndrome were highly anxious and stressed. At present, dietary measures and anticholinergic drugs are used to reduce intestinal spasm and cramps. Persons who respond poorly to physiological measures and whose symptoms are not controlled are usually referred for counseling that includes stress-reducing techniques. As with the ulcerative colitis client, the person with irritable bowel syndrome requires medication, dietary instruction, and stress management that involves lifestyle changes as well as relaxation techniques.

Respiratory Responses to Stress

UNDERSTANDING THE CLIENT WITH ASTHMA Bronchial asthma is a recurrent disorder of the bronchial airways characterized by constriction of the airways, edema, and excessive secretion. Wheezing and apnea, the dominant manifestations of an asthma attack, result from physiological changes caused by infection, allergens, and psychological factors (Knapp 1980). Studies of persons with asthma have pointed to four major psychological precipitants: anger, anxiety, depression, and excitement associated with pleasure (Falliers 1978).

Alexander, French, and Pollock (1968) tried to explain the interaction that leads from emotional disturbance to organic dysfunction. However, no psychological tests or research investigations have satisfactorily shown that asthma has an association with a specific conflict or personality configuration.

Another etiological hypothesis is that asthma represents learned ways of expressing distress. For example, infants or young children who receive little response from parents when they cry may learn over a period of time that gasping, coughing, or wheezing behaviors elicit immediate attention. Even in these instances, however, a physiological predisposition is thought to exist. The multifactorial model developed by Mattson (1975) proposes that for asthmatics physiological vulnerability in the form of bronchial hyperactivity is present. Infectious, allergic, or psychological stimuli interact with physiological conditions to produce airway constriction. Unfortunately, recurrent asthma attacks often lead to repercussions within the family, which in turn aggravate the respiratory distress of the asthma sufferer and heighten the stress of other family members. Figure 13–4 illustrates the interactive explanation offered by Mattson for the etiology of asthma attacks, particularly among children.

The most credible hypothesis is that a variety of stressful stimuli, emotional states, and behavioral patterns are contributing factors. In most persons with asthma, especially children, there seems to be a fundamental allergic predisposition, and if the allergy potential is low, individuals are able to tolerate more stress without experiencing an attack (Knapp 1980).

CLINICAL VIGNETTE

BIOPSYCHOSOCIAL APPROACH FOR A SALESMAN'S STRESS-RELATED PROBLEMS

When Victor sought help, he was a car salesman in a high-pressure job where his salary depended on the commissions he earned. His sales record was the best in the agency, but lately Victor's record had deteriorated. Whenever he encountered sales resistance from a customer, Victor would be gripped with severe abdominal pain and sudden diarrhea that made him rush to the lavatory. At other times he had bouts of constipation that were relieved with laxatives. Victor tried a number of patent medicines to relieve his symptoms. When he noticed blood and mucus in his stool, he finally consulted his physician. The physician examined Victor briefly and prescribed Donnatal. When Victor's discomfort persisted, his physician hospitalized him for diagnostic tests. An upper GI x-ray series, a colonoscopy, a barium enema, and a hematest indicated that Victor had an irritable bowel with potential for ulceration.

Knowing the demands that were made on Victor at work, and unable to give the time that Victor's problems required, his physician referred Victor to a gastroenterologist whose office staff included an adult health nurse practitioner. The gastroenterologist ordered Valium and Librax to reduce Victor's anxiety and decrease the motility of his irritable bowel. In his practice the gastroenterologist relied greatly on the nurse practitioner to spend time with clients in order to deal with symptoms for which there was no single treatment regimen.

In meeting with Victor, the nurse assured him that his symptoms should respond to good care, but the process might take time. The nurse asked Victor to record what foods he ate that seemed to cause discomfort, and what events at work or home seemed to bring about pain and diarrhea. Another aspect of Victor's life that the nurse explored was his diet. High-fiber foods were suggested to control the alternating diarrhea and constipation; Victor was advised to drink fluids in ample amounts, preferably between meals to avoid feeling of bloatedness. Gradually a dietary regimen was developed that made Victor more comfortable.

With some direction from the nurse, Victor recognized behaviors that added to his feelings of stress. In his zeal to be the champion salesman, Victor overscheduled appointments and worked long hours. He considered every missed sale a personal failure, even though the goals he set for himself were impossible to achieve on a daily basis. The nurse realized that it would be hard for Victor to stop behaving in his usual fashion. Instead of specifically urging changes at work, the nurse suggested that Victor introduce some leisure-time activities into his life. Victor denied himself even a full lunch hour and a nap after work. At the nurse's suggestion, Victor joined a health club where he could work out. Although he couldn't accept the idea that progressive relaxation or meditation might be helpful, he did permit the nurse to teach him rhythmic abdominal breathing. Victor's discomfort was alleviated but not eradicated by treatment. He accepted some but not all of the measures that were suggested, refusing, for example, to give up cigarettes and alcohol. He did stop overscheduling and derived enjoyment from using the gym. The gastroenterologist and the nurse were convinced that the lifestyle changes were more beneficial to Victor than the medication prescribed. However, Victor firmly believed that any relief he experienced was due only to the medication and not to behavioral or dietary modifications.

Among chronic child asthmatics the mortality rate is from 1 to 2 percent, and asthma accounts for 10 percent of the nonviolent deaths of children. A report of childhood deaths attributed to chronic asthma indicated the existence of depression in the child, lack of family support for the child, and tendencies of the child to deny the severity of symptoms despite frequent attacks requiring medication and/or hospitalization. In adults with asthma, depression and pessimism have been identified as prominent characteristics. Increased cholinergic activity has been associated with depression; increased cholinergic activity has been found to cause bronchoconstriction; and anticholinergic medication is sometimes used to control asthma symptoms. Thus, depression and asthma have in common some degree of neurotransmitter imbalance (Fritz, Rubenstein, and Lewiston 1987).

Often family members of the child with asthma do not provide consistent, timely care. They rarely

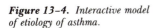

Figure 13-4. Interactive model of etiology of asthma.

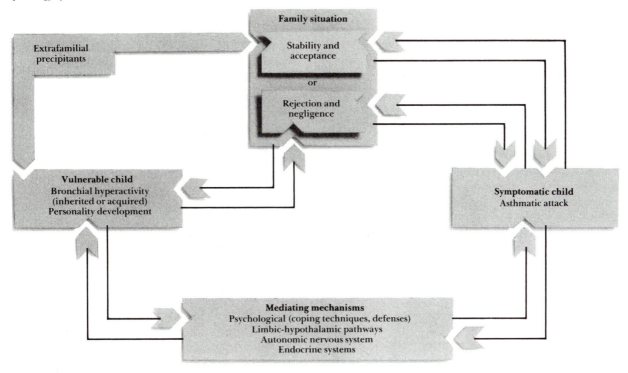

encourage the child to care for himself, nor do they promote relaxation techniques to manage symptoms. Asthma frequently becomes complicated with other issues in the family, so that the asthma symptoms are used by the family to divert attention from other internal conflicts (Fritz, Rubenstein, and Lewiston 1987). Parents may be overprotective even when the child is asymptomatic; overprotection may increase the child's fears, erode her self-confidence, and create petulance that isolates her even more from the age-appropriate activities of her peers. Additionally, asthma may lead to sibling rivalry when the parents become preoccupied with the asthmatic child. Conversely, parents may harbor unconscious resentment and hostility toward the child who seems to threaten the stability of the family. Even apparently devoted parents may express covert feelings of hostility and believe that the child is using the illness to manipulate family members.

Caring for an individual with asthma is a collaborative effort by all members of the health care team. Persons who have asthma often demonstrate one of two behavioral polarities:

- Behaviors that indicate a strong wish for protection, security, and special privileges

- Behaviors that ignore or deny a wish for protection and security, substituting competitive actions and struggles to excel

Two forms of asthma are thought to exist: extrinsic and intrinsic. The *extrinsic* form is characterized by reactions in response to such allergens as pollen, dust, and certain foods. Extrinsic asthma is more common in children and adolescents, many of whom seem to outgrow the disorder. Persons with *intrinsic* asthma are usually adults in whom sensitivity to allergens is less pronounced. This type of asthma often follows a pulmonary infection and is likely to be perennial rather than episodic. Adults who are severely affected may develop *status asthmaticus*. For these persons, medication is relatively ineffective and acute paroxysms continue. Frequent periods of *status asthmaticus* can lead to emphysema, resulting in dehabilitation that makes the individual highly dependent on significant people in the family or in the health care system.

To help control the condition, an individualized program that combines physical, environmental, and social factors should be made available. Medication, behavior modification, and hypnosis have been used with varying success. Systematic muscle relaxation techniques seem to lessen constriction of the air passages and lower anxiety levels. Intervention that includes family members is a useful approach. Improving family relationships and teaching family members to understand the physiological processes at work facilitate the adjustment of the individual with asthma. This is especially important if the person with asthma is a child or adolescent. When working with children who have asthma, health team members often seem quite willing to adopt a more holistic approach to care than when they work with adult clients. There is a tendency on the part of health professionals to dismiss adult clients once the most urgent physical symptoms have been controlled. This is unfortunate, for persons with asthma need a multidimensional approach to care regardless of age.

School nurses and community health nurses are often called upon to help persons with asthma maintain a normal existence. During acute episodes, oxygenation is a major need, and medications are available for self-administration. Bronchodilators in the form of oral medication or inhalators may be used on a selective basis. An understanding of the physiological processes involved can make an attack less frightening to the client.

In general, nurses caring for persons with asthma may be guided by the following facts and principles:

1. No typical personality configuration has been associated with this disorder.

2. Persons with asthma frequently seem to have a strong need for comfort, security, and protection.

3. Although asthma has been attributed to separation anxiety, especially separation from the mother, no single pattern of mother-child interaction has been identified.

4. Persons with asthma often engage in extreme behaviors: either they organize their lives around the disorder or they try to ignore its existence.

5. Caring for the client with asthma requires a careful balance between overprotectiveness on the one hand and neglect or denial on the other.

Primary, secondary, and tertiary levels of intervention in the care of clients with asthma are discussed in the accompanying box. Table 13–2 identifies behaviors frequently seen in clients with asthma and suggests appropriate nursing interventions.

Cardiovascular Responses to Stress

UNDERSTANDING THE CLIENT WITH HYPERTENSION Hypertension is one of the most prevalent health problems in modern life. Under normal conditions, the heart beats regularly and evenly; visceral organs are adequately nourished by blood circulation. Under adverse conditions, blood vessels supplying visceral organs contract. This contraction makes the heart beat more rapidly and more forcefully, thereby increasing diastolic and systolic blood pressure. For most people the increase is temporary; when conditions improve, blood pressure returns to normal levels. However, for some people the elevated blood pressure continues. Many persons with hypertension are not aware of their disorder because it produces discomfort only in severe cases. It is difficult to identify precise causes or preexisting factors; the term *essential hypertension* has been coined to indicate that the causes are unknown (Byassee 1977, Day 1984). The condition has been linked to emotional stress, job pressures, life changes, and diet. Essential hypertension is twice as common among blacks as among whites, and is more common in lower socioeconomic groups

---

PRIMARY, SECONDARY, AND TERTIARY LEVELS OF INTERVENTION IN THE CARE OF ASTHMATIC CLIENTS

Primary Level of Nursing Intervention
Identify specific allergens.

Instruct the client and the family in avoiding food and environmental allergens.

Explore behaviors, events, and situations that precede an asthmatic attack.

Give permission to verbalize feelings, including doubts and fears.

Maintain a balance between overprotectiveness and denial of the disorder.

Secondary Level of Nursing Intervention
Provide relief for wheezing and apnea during the attack through prescribed measures.

Offer support and reassurance to reduce anxiety.

Involve family members in supportive and instructional interventions.

Tertiary Level of Nursing Intervention
Help families cope with problems arising from the chronic illness of a family member.

Explore the possibility of secondary gain derived by the asthmatic client or by a family member from the illness.

Encourage clear communication between all family members.

Introduce the client and family members to community resources, especially self-help groups.

CLINICAL VIGNETTE

ETIOLOGICAL FACTORS IN THE DEATH OF AN ASTHMATIC CHILD

Leroy, a 12-year-old black boy, had experienced severe asthma attacks since the age of six months. Throughout his life he had been hospitalized once or twice every year and was a frequent visitor to emergency departments. Leroy was in foster care; because of his physical problems foster families became unwilling to care for him for very long. Therefore new placements often had to be found for the boy. As a result there was little continuity in the medical care Leroy received. Little was known of Leroy's parents or siblings except that Leroy's mother had a hospital record of asthma, which was discovered at the time of Leroy's birth. In addition to asthma, Leroy had atopic dermatitis and allergic rhinitis.

Leroy's foster mother reported that his school progress was unsatisfactory and that he constantly quarrelled with two other youngsters in the foster home. A psychological workup was done that showed Leroy to be very depressed, with periods of passive withdrawal interrupted by aggressive, attention-seeking acts. A sleep study showed increased insomnia, usually precipitated by wheezing. Because Leroy's foster mother was unwilling to continue to care for him, a decision was made for him to enter a residential home for children with chronic illnesses. After entering the home Leroy showed some improvement in mood, behavior, and compliance with treatment measures.

His caseworker was a black man with whom Leroy developed rapport. Since Leroy had no understanding of what asthma was or how to take care of himself, the caseworker instituted an educational program for Leroy so that the boy would learn that it was possible to control his symptoms. Attendance was arranged at a local allergy clinic where, for the first time, adequate followup care was given. The caseworker realized that Leroy was still depressed but believed that enough progress had been made to reduce their contacts. Staff at the home were of the opinion that Leroy had made a good adjustment, although all were aware that his asthma remained severe enough to be frightening for him at times. He no longer engaged in angry outbursts, and was cooperative but slightly guarded with staff members. The most meaningful person in Leroy's life was his caseworker, who continued to see the boy, but at infrequent intervals. One day, about a week before a scheduled appointment with his caseworker, Leroy came home from school wheezing. The staff member in charge excused Leroy from his afternoon chores and told the boy to lie down for a nap. Leroy slept until suppertime. When a roommate came to call Leroy for supper, the boy was in great distress. Paramedics were called. Because their resuscitation efforts were unsuccessful, Leroy was rushed to the nearest emergency room. By this time cardiopulmonary arrest was in progress, and Leroy was pronounced dead on arrival.

Table 13–2. Common Behaviors of Persons with Asthma and Suggested Nursing Interventions

Client Behaviors	Nursing Interventions
Dependent, fearful, clinging	Offer support and reassurance without fostering dependency.
Helpless, hopeless	Instill hope by teaching.
Lacking confidence and self-esteem	Emphasize client's strengths, abilities, and accomplishments.
Noncompliant and denying dysfunction or distress	Formulate with the client alternative activities and program modifications acceptable to her.
Behaving rebelliously or delinquently	Encourage verbal rather than behavioral expression of feelings.

(Eyer 1979). Figure 13–5 compares normal and abnormal blood pressure responses to stimuli. The dysfunctional responses are characteristic of persons with essential hypertension.

The usual psychological explanation for hypertension is that it is related to unexpressed anger, but this is too simplistic. Some persons with hypertension seem to be type A personalities (competitive, hard-working achievers whose tension is evident in their behavior). There are, however, masked type A people whose outward behavior conceals inner tension and striving. Additional research is needed in order to identify the many psychological, physiological, and behavioral variations among the large number of persons with hypertension.

Figure 13-5. Functional and dysfunctional hypertensive responses.

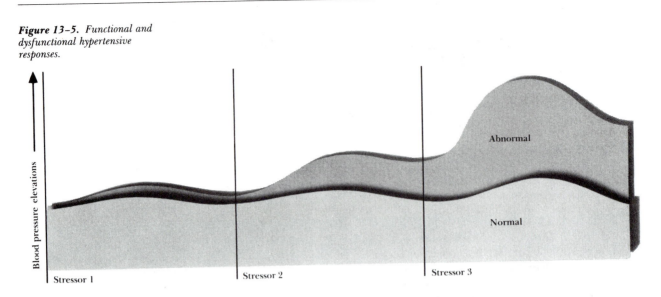

Thus far, the search for a specific personality or conflict associated with hypertension has been unrewarding. Some researchers allege that hypertensives are inwardly angry and outwardly pleasant, concealing hostility in order to be liked (Lipowski, Lipsitt, and Whybrow 1977). No evidence of unexpressed hostility was found in a population sample whose hypertension was discovered in a routine screening. Correlations but not causal relationships have been found between hypertension and anxiety; no correlations have been established between hypertension and depression (Hayman et al. 1988).

In a careful study of well-controlled, well-adjusted hypertensive individuals, two nurse researchers looked at critical factors that determined outcomes of this disorder (Powers and Jaloweic 1987). They found that health care regimens, job performance, and sexual function were variables that predicted physiological and psychosocial adaptation. The client's involvement in health care, satisfaction with health care, and feelings of control also indicated the likelihood of positive outcomes. Other factors associated with favorable outcomes were available social supports and the client's understanding of hypertension as an incurable but controllable disorder. Out of their research the investigators constructed a profile of the controlled, well-adjusted hypertensive client.

NURSING INTERVENTIONS Nursing approaches to the control of hypertension are guided by four objectives:

1. Detecting essential hypertension as soon as possible
2. Helping clients reduce and maintain lower blood pressure levels

---

COMBINED PROFILE OF THE CONTROLLED, WELL-ADJUSTED HYPERTENSIVE CLIENT

Blood pressure was under control

Complied with dietary and medical regimen

Understood side effects of medication and how to deal with them

Realized that hypertension was a chronic disorder with no single cure

Accepted considerable responsibility for self-monitoring and self-care

Was willing to examine and accept alternative solutions to problems

Did not handle stress in destructive ways (overeating, drinking, smoking)

Preferred social support to solitary withdrawal when feeling stressed

Remained optimistic regarding ability to manage health status

Considered overall quality of life to be satisfying

SOURCE: Adapted from Powers and Jaloweic (1987).

---

3. Helping clients modify habits contributing to hypertension
4. Encouraging compliance with the total care plan

Because many persons with hypertension have no symptoms, there is a tendency for them to discount the seriousness of the condition, leading to noncompliance. Pharmacological treatment is effective but is often complicated by undesirable side effects such as depression, loss of sexual desire, and sexual dysfunction. Nurses concerned with establishing a therapeutic relationship should endeavor to be supportive and informative without increasing anxiety in the client. Interpretations and confrontations are unlikely to be helpful since such interventions are likely to produce reactions that elevate blood pressure levels even more.

If drug therapy is instituted, nurses should be alert to the possibility of frequent or severe depressive reactions. Reserpine, methyldopa, and propanol are among the blood pressure regulatory agents that may cause depression. Ongoing assessment of hypertensive clients on medication is important; there have been reports of suicide attempts by persons suffering from unrecognized depression produced by antihypertensive medication.

The client who is hypertensive requires a comprehensive care plan that includes cognitive information, emotional reassurance, and support. For hypertensive clients a therapeutic relationship is not a substitute for but an adjunct to other methods of managing the disorder. Medication, exercise, relaxation, biofeedback, modification of diet, and lifestyle are all important components of the care plan that can be coordinated by the generalist nurse. Because smoking constricts tiny blood vessels and exacerbates the problem, hypertensives should be made aware of the health risks posed by this habit.

Almost all individuals respond to frustration with elevated blood pressure and rapid heartbeat. If they are permitted to express their feelings verbally or through motor activity, there is usually a return to normal functioning. When no outlets for expressing frustration are available, there is far slower return to normal functioning. Therefore, in addition to other objectives, the nursing care plan should be designed to help hypertensive individuals express frustration and discharge tension through verbal and motor channels.

Relaxation Techniques Management of responses to stress can help reduce discomfort due to everyday tensions. Some mental health professionals advocate biofeedback training as part of stress management programs. *Biofeedback* is a technique by which bodily functions often thought to be involuntary, such as blood pressure and heartbeat, can be consciously regulated. Biofeedback equipment, which operates on the same principles as polygraph devices, measures various physical changes in the body that occur in response to greater or lesser amounts of accumulated tension. Individuals can use biofeedback methods to record and monitor

blood pressure and to incrementally lower their blood pressure at each session. With biofeedback, lowering blood pressure becomes much like losing weight; gradual, measured progress is made toward the client's goal.

Although helpful in many instances, biofeedback is not essential to learning relaxation techniques. *Progressive relaxation* is a technique that involves deliberate muscle relaxation as a means of reducing the discomfort caused by accumulated stress and tension. To relax muscles progressively one begins by tensing and then relaxing the major muscle groups of the body, concentrating on one group at a time. Consciously tensing and relaxing the muscle groups makes one aware of what happens in the body during states of tension and relaxation. Instructions for progressive relaxation are provided in the accompanying box. The muscle groups of the head, face, neck, and shoulders are primary sites of tension. Other muscle groups that are often involved are those of the arms, hands, chest, back, stomach, legs, and feet.

Relaxation simply means doing nothing with the muscles, neither assisting, resisting, nor participating in any form of movement or gesture. Progressive relaxation is not difficult to learn, nor is the

---

INSTRUCTIONS FOR PROGRESSIVE RELAXATION

Progressive relaxation involves all the major muscle groups of the body. Begin by tensing the entire body. Maintain a state of tension for five seconds. Then exhale slowly and silently. Command yourself to relax and let go. As you slowly exhale, try to experience a sense of calm and serenity as the whole body becomes slack and at ease. Next, tense one part of the body while leaving the other parts limp and relaxed. Keep one part of the body tense for a few seconds, then relax, breathing out slowly while allowing the tense part of the body to go limp. Follow this procedure for the head and neck, arms and hands, chest, back, stomach, legs, and feet.

With sufficient practice, progressive relaxation techniques can become almost automatic in promoting tension reduction throughout the day without interfering with the daily routine. In fact, the sense of well-being that accompanies mastery of the technique is likely to enhance one's ability to cope with everyday life.

technique spectacular or dramatic. All that is required is awareness of what it feels like when a group of muscles is tensed or poised for action and when the same group of muscles is at rest.

Progressive relaxation can be practiced at various times of the day, whenever a few moments are available. Alternate states of tension and relaxation can be attained while waiting for an elevator or for a red light to change, typical situations that trigger tension in many individuals. Once an individual learns to recognize rising tension, he may use progressive relaxation to induce a less stressful internal environment. Stress is not eradicated by this technique, but its management can be improved.

Additional research is needed to learn how, why, and to what extent progressive relaxation methods work. There is some agreement that positive physiological and psychological benefits are derived in the form of decreased activity of the sympathetic nervous system and increased activity of the parasympathetic nervous system. Even though research data are inconclusive, it is reasonable to assume that relaxation teaching of clients is a valid nursing intervention, especially since subjective observations by nurses and clients indicate positive effects.

UNDERSTANDING THE CLIENT WITH CORONARY ARTERY DISEASE Every year, more Americans succumb to heart disease than to any other disorder, even though such deaths have declined about 20 percent in recent decades. This decline in mortality rates is attributed to dietary changes, reduced smoking, and more emphasis on physical fitness.

Stressors such as job pressures, time urgency, frustration, and feelings of dissatisfaction with one's life have been associated with heart disease. For some persons, stress seems to be a natural way of life. They seem to transform everyday events into enormous ordeals and contests. This is certainly true of the type A personalities described by Friedman and Rosenman (1974). A prospective study by these investigators showed that type A persons were susceptible to coronary artery disease and were more likely to die after a heart attack. Autopsy examinations showed that type A heart attack victims had narrower arteries than other victims of fatal heart attacks.

Current studies aim at identifying the aspects of type A behavior that constitute the greatest risk. Early results indicate that persons with extreme amounts of hostility are most at risk. The kinds of challenges to which type A persons are exposed also seem to be influential. For example, type A personalities seem far more responsive than type B personalities in the way they handle cognitive tasks.

On the other hand, few differences are found in the responses of type A and type B individuals to physical tasks (Turkington 1984).

In a study of type A and type B behavior in kindergarten children, Brown and Tanner (1988) found that children identified as type A showed more cardiovascular response to challenges than did their type B counterparts. Less conclusive results were obtained by Hayman et al. (1988) who found no significant association with type A behavior and physiological cardiovascular risk factors in a study of grade school children. Since atherosclerotic processes begin early in life, research into relationships between psychological and physiological cardiovascular risk factors continues to receive attention.

A recent study done over a twelve-year period examined survival rates of men who had suffered a heart attack and found that the death rate among type A men was only 58 percent as high as that of type B men. While early studies found that type A people were more likely to have a heart attack than relaxed type B people, they were also more likely to recover after a heart attack.

Friedman continues to emphasize the importance of personality types in heart disease, but it is evident that the concepts of type A and type B personalities need further refinement (Brody 1988). Additional studies of personality types and related behavior have shown that type A individuals have a need to feel in control and an eagerness to tackle difficult situations. Moreover, they set high standards for themselves but generally worked to achieve them in more realistic ways than do persons with less need for control. Thus, the same forces that may increase the vulnerability of type A individuals to heart disease may facilitate recovery once an acute attack has occurred.

Although substantial evidence points to personality as a factor in heart disease, lifestyle and age remain important risk factors, as well. Males between the ages of 39 and 49 are six times more likely to experience coronary artery disease than all the type A personalities in the general population (Matthews 1982). Perhaps the heavy responsibility and the pursuit of success that characterize the fourth decade for most men heightens their vulnerability to heart disease.

Even though the impact of type A behaviors is upheld by some theorists and discounted by others, psychological counseling remains an important adjunct to the care of anyone who has suffered a heart attack. Counseling should be directed toward curbing the sense of urgency, competitiveness, and easily aroused anger of type A individuals. In one three-year study, psychological counseling was found to be far more effective than any other intervention in preventing a second heart attack (Brody 1983). Because type A behavior is viewed as a risk factor, efforts should be made to help such individuals modify their behavior. In this area behavioral approaches are often effective and may be attempted by generalist nurses. Behavior modification can be directed toward stress management and lifestyle modification. Stress management involves learning relaxation, identifying stressful situations, and moderating the impact of stressful situations. Nurses are in a position to advise these clients on nutritional regimens that are likely to reduce serum cholesterol levels and maintain normal weights. In addition, individuals should be encouraged to change daily habits that are stressful and to reduce personal feelings of competitiveness, time urgency, performance standards, and hostility.

The nurse should offer support and information to the families of recovering cardiac clients, as well as to the client. Marital counseling may be especially needed in situations where the spouse is very attentive, even overprotective, yet resentful of the demands being made on her. Supportive nursing interventions combined with teaching help the client and the family plan for the future rather than dwell on the recent past. Sexual counseling for the recovering cardiac client and the spouse should be available routinely before discharge from a hospital.

The families of heart attack victims, especially the spouse, are subject to anxiety, fatigue, irritability, sleeplessness, and depression. Often their distress is overlooked by caregivers preoccupied with the client. Returning a cardiac client to a living arrangement where the spouse is worried and dysfunctional is unlikely to promote recovery.

Many recovering cardiac clients worry about sexual activity but hesitate to introduce the subject. Sometimes they reveal anxiety by joking about sexual matters or acting in a "macho" manner. It is a good idea to deal with unspoken anxiety by including a discussion of sexual activity in the health teaching content. A fact sheet may be used to open discussion and is a reference point for the client and the partner. In some cardiac rehabilitation programs a protocol has been developed to answer pertinent questions. In other settings the fact sheet may have to be formulated for each client, with input from nursing and medical persons involved in care. Some of the questions that clients want to know but are afraid to ask include the following:

Is it safe for me to have sex?

When is it safe for me to have sex? In a few weeks? In a few months? In a year or so? What time of day is safest for me to have sex?

What effect exactly does sexual intercourse have on my heart?

What are the warning signs that my heart is being strained by intercourse?

What can I do to protect my heart when I am having intercourse?

Does the medication I am taking have any effect on my sexual ability?

I have not been interested in sexual intercourse since my heart attack, but my partner is. How can I satisfy my partner?

I am interested in resuming sexual activity, but my partner is concerned about the effect on me. What can I do or say to reassure my partner?

The attitudes of health team members are important factors in a client's recovery. Because a heart attack is a frightening experience, clients and their families are usually receptive to information and guidance. It is not unusual for wives of men who have suffered a heart attack to become overprotective and extremely concerned. Some wives feel guilty and blame themselves for having contributed to the heart attack in some way. They keep their worries and resentment to themselves for fear of causing another attack. Overall, this makes them very solicitious, to the point of forbidding their husbands to engage in permissible activities. In such cases the behavior of the wife takes on punitive overtones. The husband faces a dilemma. He feels that his illness is a burden on his wife and that he has an obligation to get well quickly. At the same time he receives a message that he must be cared for, guided, and protected from his own actions. When such a pattern develops in the marital relationship, nursing intervention should be directed toward having the client take primary responsibility for his recovery, with the wife enacting a supportive but not preemptive role.

During the recovery and rehabilitative phase of a heart attack, communication between team members is just as important as communication with the client and the family. Health care teams composed of a cardiologist, a primary care nurse, a physical therapist, a dietitian, a psychiatric-mental health nurse, and perhaps a consulting psychiatrist can offer a coordinated approach to meeting the biopsychosocial needs of the cardiac client.

Skeletomuscular Responses to Stress

UNDERSTANDING THE CLIENT WITH RHEUMATOID ARTHRITIS Rheumatoid arthritis is a condition that has been associated with life stresses for many years. In the nineteenth century Sir William Osler, the renowned physician, identified worry, shock, and grief as precursors of rheumatoid arthritis (Garfield 1979).

There is also evidence that rheumatoid arthritis may be an autoimmune disease. Current research suggests that an unspecified antigen probably stimulates the production of antibodies. The body then reacts to these antibodies as if they were foreign substances. The pathophysiological response of the immune system to the body's own antibodies, the *rheumatoid factor*, is present in some, but not all, persons with rheumatoid arthritis (Silverman 1980). For some years the rheumatoid factor was thought to be the cause of the dysfunction, but this explanation has been discarded. The rheumatoid factor, when present, is now believed to perpetuate the problem but not to cause it. The rheumatoid factor consists of reactive antibodies that may be present in various other conditions, such as hypertension. It has been hypothesized that stress and distress activate the immunological system in nonspecific ways, one of which leads to the presence of the rheumatoid factor.

A number of investigators agree that persons with rheumatoid arthritis tend to overcontrol their aggressive impulses (Robinson 1983, Coleman, Butcher, and Carson 1984). Studies using different population samples have described persons with rheumatoid arthritis as self-sacrificing, hardworking, conforming, and, frequently, interested in physical activities until they are incapacitated. These studies are suggestive rather than definitive.

Persons with progressive arthritis undergo restrictions and losses that threaten body image, role performance, mobility, and independence. As the disorder advances, the losses and restrictions increase. Gross (1981) and Sperger, Erlich, and Glass (1978) cited the tendency of arthritis clients to use subtle deceits and socially desirable responses to pretend to themselves and others that their lives were still "normal." Many of them refused to acknowledge the significance of their handicap in order to protect significant others who might not be able to cope and might eventually reject the person with arthritis. In a study that compared self-reports of arthritis clients with psychological assessments by caregivers, Muhlenkamp and Joyner (1986) found that caregivers overestimated client's levels of anxiety and depression, and underestimated their levels of hostility. These findings are consistent with other data indicating unwillingness of many of these clients to admit to anxiety and depression, or to express anger.

One study attempted to identify specific stress responses in persons with essential hypertension and others with rheumatoid arthritis. Persons with rheumatoid arthritis reacted more to stress in their joints and muscles than did hypertensives. On the other hand, the blood pressures of persons with hypertension did not return to normal levels when stressors were removed as quickly as did the blood pressures of those with rheumatoid arthritis. These findings seem to support theories of specific response patterns that precipitate, perpetuate, or at least are present in certain disorders. The results are clouded by the fact that the population sample consisted of subjects identified as already having hypertension or rheumatoid arthritis; the presence of a certain form of dysfunction may intensify reactions in the organ system already affected (Silverman 1980).

Persons who have rheumatoid arthritis tend to move less because of a natural wish to avoid pain. The desire to avoid pain is often coupled with a wish to regress, give up, and be cared for. These feelings are opposed by a desire to remain functional and independent. Awareness of these conflicting feelings in the client enables nurses to suggest compromises that can help the client cope with her contradictory feelings and alterations in structure and function.

Although there is no single personality configuration common to persons with rheumatoid arthritis, their families often describe them as having been vigorous, athletic, and competitive before the onset of dysfunction. Comparative psychological tests given to men with hypertension, rheumatoid arthritis, and peptic ulcer have shown that subjects with rheumatoid arthritis exhibit high levels of aggression and high levels of control, a combination very likely to induce anxiety and tension because the individual has aggressive impulses but feels that they must be strongly controlled. Table 13–3 summarizes levels of aggression and control in subjects with three types of stress-related disorders.

The emotional sensitivities of clients with rheumatoid arthritis require special consideration. Loss of mobility, loss of function, and body image changes are hard for clients to accept, especially if they previously thrived on activity. They may react

Table 13–3. Psychological Features of Persons with Stress-Related Disorders

Type of Disorder	Level of Aggression	Level of Control
Rheumatoid arthritis	High	High
Hypertension	Low	High
Peptic ulcer	Low	Low

SOURCE: Adapted from Cobb et al. (1969).

with inward anger, which can worsen their discomfort. Supportive nursing interventions may be as valuable as physiotherapy or medication in relieving their physical and emotional distress. A structured, predictable, sustained relationship with a nurse can be helpful to the client striving to remain as independent as possible for as long as possible.

Any client with rheumatoid arthritis eventually becomes very familiar with the health care system and may lose faith in the system and in the benefits of therapeutic measures if her condition doesn't improve. She may feel anger toward family members and caregivers who have not fulfilled her expectations yet fear to express that anger toward those on whom she must depend. Usually the client can determine what kinds of physical efforts she is able to attempt. Unless the nurse encourages the client to indicate the extent of her abilities, the nurse may have a tendency to do things for the client or to neglect activities that exhaust the client unless she is helped. A meaningful dialogue between the client, family, and care providers will help ensure that the client's needs will be perceived accurately and will be met. Table 13–4 presents some basic needs of the client with rheumatoid arthritis and suggested nursing interventions.

Rheumatoid arthritis runs a chronic course characterized by remission, alleviation, or progressive incapacitation. Assessment and planning must be flexible enough to adapt to the changing status of the client. The immediate goals are the management of pain and the enhancement of mobility. Long-range goals include the maintenance of a normal, fulfilling existence, the prevention of musculoskeletal deformity, and the fulfillment of psychological and social needs. The client and family members should understand the reason for certain procedures that may be uncomfortable, because they may tend to become discouraged when procedures are unsuccessful and relief does not come easily. The care of the client with rheumatoid arthritis often requires complex exercises and physiotherapy measures that are costly in terms of time and energy. A coordinator should oversee the various aspects of the plan and assume responsibility for continual assessment of the psychological and physical status of the client and family members who carry much of the burden of daily care. Depression and giving up are common in clients with this dysfunction. Such behaviors should be identified promptly so that relief can be provided through pharmacologic and supportive psychological intervention.

Table 13–4. Needs of the Client with Rheumatoid Arthritis and Suggested Nursing Interventions

Client's Needs	Nursing Interventions
Reduced mobility	1. Allow the client time to adjust to loss of mobility without forcing the issue. 2. Encourage the client to be realistic in accepting methods and devices that will promote or maintain mobility. 3. Help the client enhance the quality of his life even though special arrangements may be needed for him to engage in such activities as seeing a film or eating in a restaurant.
Social isolation and feelings of alienation	1. Explore whether the isolation is self-imposed or caused by the indifference of friends and family members. 2. Help the client and the family plan activities that include one or two other people. 3. Introduce the client and the family to community groups and resources.
Pain and physical discomfort	1. Clients know more about their tolerance for pain than anyone else; permit the client to be the teacher in this area. 2. Respect the client's preferences for rituals and procedures that alleviate subjective discomfort.
Anger toward care providers (often displaced or suppressed)	1. Avoid being defensive. 2. Explain reasons for events and decisions; focus on specifics.
Anger toward family members (often displaced or suppressed)	1. Include family members in supportive and instructional nursing actions. 2. Try to change or moderate specific causes for anger, whether generated by family members or by professional care providers.
Preoccupation with oneself	1. Promote participation in self-care as much as possible; accept the occasional need of the client to regress and be dependent, without fostering regression and dependency. 2. Accept and be attentive to verbal expressions of anger, pain, and discouragement.

CLINICAL VIGNETTE

PROVIDING CARE FOR A CLIENT WITH RHEUMATOID ARTHRITIS

Neil Brown was a middle-aged, successful lawyer, prominent in community activities, and a good provider for his family. Neil and his wife, Bess, are devoted to each other and to their son and daughter. During the Viet Nam War, Neil's son, Rick, was drafted into the Army immediately after his college graduation. When it was time for Rick to leave, his mother and sister, Gail, dissolved in tears, but Neil was composed as he embraced his son. Rick's tour of duty was to last two years.

For several years before Rick's departure Neil had been complaining of pain in his shoulder muscles. He was annoyed at times because the pain had caused his golf game to deteriorate. Cortisone injections relieved the pain temporarily, but physiotherapy had little effect. During this time discomfort had remained at tolerable levels and sometimes even disappeared, but during the months after Rick's departure the pain became much worse. Even more worrisome was the fact that the pain was no longer confined to one area. Before long, other joints were affected; his hands and knees became inflamed, and he was constantly in pain. For a time Neil continued to play golf with his friends, but he soon felt that his disability robbed him of enjoyment of the game. He dropped out of the foursome that had played golf together over the years. As months passed Neil's range of motion became more and more restricted. His family physician diagnosed the condition as rheumatoid arthritis and referred Neil to a specialist when the discomfort proved unresponsive to conservative treatment.

Soon Neil was no longer able to drive his car or walk more than short distances. A whirlpool tub was installed in his home, and a community health nurse visited daily to help Bess with the complicated treatments that Neil required. The community health nurse helped simplify Neil's home care. He also helped Neil and Bess learn more about rheumatoid arthritis and offered them both emotional support. Although Neil received the best possible care, his condition continued to deteriorate. Neil exhibited some of the characteristics and lifestyle patterns seen in other persons with rheumatoid arthritis. He could not recall any close relative with the same disorder but knew that his father and grandfather had, in their later years, suffered from gout, a condition that also affects the joints. Neil was a loving father whose wife and children were

the center of his life. Quiet spoken and hard-working, Neil was a man well respected in the community.

Even before Rick was drafted Neil was experiencing localized arthritic discomfort but the disease process was exacerbated after his son left.

The community health nurse observed that Neil had unrealistic hopes that the return of his son would produce a remission. The nurse voiced some doubts about sudden, miraculous cures but did not confront Neil and Bess directly, continuing instead to help the family manage Neil's care and live as normal a life as possible.

After serving his two-year tour of duty, Rick returned safely from Viet Nam. The family had chosen not to tell Rick of the extent of his father's disability until he returned home, so Rick was unprepared for what he found. He was shocked to see his vigorous, capable father now confined to a wheelchair and his mother acting as a nurse. The only family member who had not changed greatly was Gail, and Rick derived comfort from the conversations with his sister. The reunion of the family was a happy event, but no recovery followed. Even though Neil did not improve much, the family was strengthened by Rick's return. His sister had someone near her own age in whom she could confide. His mother had someone on whom to lean when she was tired and discouraged. Neil was especially pleased when Rick indicated a desire to enter law school and eventually join his father's firm.

Even though Neil's condition was unchanged, the atmosphere in the family home was brighter. The momentum of Neil's disorder was slowed by competent medical treatment, good nursing care, and psychological support for the couple. The community health nurse continued to be involved with the family, teaching Neil and Bess, suggesting household arrangements that were more convenient, and offering supportive counseling.

The care plan developed for Neil consisted of the following interventions either implemented or coordinated by the community health nurse, who visited daily:

1. Assist Neil with bathing, dressing, and grooming, encouraging as much self-care as he seems capable of performing.

2. Teach Bess how to help Neil move from bed to chair to bathroom with minimum exertion for them both.

3. Provide honest answers and reading material to increase the couple's understanding of Neil's problems.

4. Watch for signs of discouragement in Neil and for signs of fatigue in Bess and respond supportively but realistically. Refer the couple for counseling if signs of depression or friction appear.

5. Inform the family of community agencies and self-help groups for arthritic clients and their families.

6. Coordinate the health care plan with the physician, physiotherapist, and mental health counselor who are involved.

7. Establish on ongoing relationship with the parents as members await Rick's return, without encouraging or dismissing their hopes for a miraculous cure.

8. Encourage Neil to focus on the activities and diversions he is capable of enjoying rather than dwelling on his limitations.

Behavioral Responses to Stress

Behavioral responses to stress may take the form of eating disorders, such as obesity and anorexia nervosa.

UNDERSTANDING THE CLIENT WITH OBESITY Obesity is popularly defined as an excessive accumulation of fat in the body. Usually obesity is said to exist when body weight exceeds 20 percent of the ratios given in standard height and weight tables, but it should be remembered that definitions of obesity and reactions to it are to a great extent culturally determined. In societies where food is scarce, fatness is a sign of status, whereas in affluent societies it is "in" to be thin. Social pressures in the United States encourage eating too much, yet those who become obese are reproached. Youthfulness is highly valued in Western society, and slenderness is often equated with looking young (Bruch 1973).

The first generation of American immigrants are likely to become overweight as they avail themselves of ample food. The second generation adopts the attitudes of mainstream America toward being overweight, and the prevalence of obesity drops drastically from the first to the second generation. Variables that affect the occurrence of obesity are listed in Table 13–5.

Some obese persons report that they overeat not only when they are emotionally upset but also when they feel happy and well-adjusted. Such eat-

---

BEHAVIOR MODIFICATION IN OBESITY

Advantages

- The dropout rate is low.

- Emotional reactions such as anxiety and depression are infrequent.

- Persons whose obesity began in childhood are more responsive to behavior modification than to traditional weight loss methods.

Disadvantages

- Weight losses obtained through behavior modification are modest, seldom exceeding 15 pounds.

- Weight loss as a result of behavior modification is regained just as easily as weight lost through customary methods.

---

ing patterns suggest that obese persons may be excessively responsive to any external stimulus that induces eating and quite unresponsive to internal feelings of hunger or satisfaction. Of those who consume abnormally large amounts of food, many are women whose food intake occurs at night. This nocturnal pattern may be due to stressful conditions encountered during the daytime. Nocturnal overeating differs from bulimia (binge eating) in that the latter is more episodic whereas the former is ongoing. Both eating patterns are often followed by agitation and self-recrimination and both are attributable at least in part to stress.

Social factors have a powerful influence on the prevalence of obesity in the United States and around the world. In earlier times it was unusual for an entire population to have enough to eat, and this is still true in many third world countries. In many parts of the world to be well fed, even obese, is a status symbol, since abundant food is regularly available only to the privileged classes. The opposite is true in the United States where different conditions prevail.

Table 13–5. Demographic Variables Affecting Obesity Prevalence

Variable	Prevalence
Age	Obesity is most prevalent among those between 20 and 50.
Gender	Obesity is more common among women in all age groups.
Socioeconomic status	Obesity is more prevalent in lower socioeconomic groups.
Social mobility	Obesity is more prevalent among the socially mobile (those moving from one social class to another).

One of the major influences on obesity prevalence is socioeconomic class. Among women, obesity is six times more prevalent in low socioeconomic groups. Similar but less extreme tendencies are characteristic of men in the same socioeconomic class. Age is another influence on obesity prevalence; prevalence increases markedly between ages 20 and 50, at which time there is a sharp decrease. One reason given for decreased obesity prevalence after age 50 is the high mortality rate of overweight men in later life (Stunkard 1985).

Excess food intake and sedentary habits play a part in the development of obesity, but the entire etiological picture is unclear. A major difficulty experienced by dieters is the lowered rate of metabolism that occurs when they restrict calorie intake. This means that the body responds to reduced intake by reducing its need for food. The only known recourse at present is to encourage dieters who reach a weight plateau to increase their physical activity, since it has been established that physical exercise increases metabolism, and that metabolic rates remain high for several hours after the activity has been discontinued. Recent studies by reputable scientists suggest that obese persons may be born with a handicap in the form of slow metabolic rates. To compound the problem, obese persons sometimes have normal metabolic rates only when they are grossly overweight. When they lose weight, their metabolism reverts to slower than average, thus making it easy to regain weight (Kolata 1988).

Many obese persons admit that they overeat when they feel tired or emotionally upset. Bruch (1973) noted that obese persons overeat because they do not differentiate feelings of hunger from other forms of discomfort such as boredom or anxiety. Because many obese persons lack or disregard internal signals to eat or not to eat, strong external signals must be provided. These might take the form of diaries kept by the client of cues that trigger eating, or schedules negotiated with the client that are enforced and reinforced. Along with nutritional guidance, activity regimens, and behavior modification, attention should be paid to how the obese client interprets and responds to somatic signals, particularly to what "feeling hungry" means to the client.

Increased physical activity, combined with dietary measures, is essential to weight reduction. Physical activity should be taken up gradually by those who have been sedentary, and large amounts of weight loss should not be attempted except under carefully supervised conditions. Self-help groups for obese persons have proliferated in recent years. The best known are the nonprofit TOPS (Take Off Pounds Safely) and the profit-making Weight Watchers groups. Subjective reports indicate that the programs are helpful, but little objective information is available. The dropout rates are high, but so are the reentry rates. The programs do offer a rational approach to weight loss and for that reason merit attention.

Behavior modification is used often in the care of obese persons, but, again, there is little evidence of actual effectiveness. Although there is some disagreement on this issue, consensus has been reached on the points covered in the accompanying box.

One advantage of behavior modification in weight control is the fact that the procedures are clear and specific. Behavioral tasks can be assigned and forms given to help clients record their calorie intake and note their progress. When weight is lost, the client receives instant recognition and approval from the leader and from other members if the program involves a group. Group and individual behavioral approaches can be inaugurated by nurses working in schools, clinics, and health maintenance organizations. These programs can be individualized and multidimensional as nurses apply their knowledge of physiological, psychological, and interpersonal processes to help the obese adult or child.

UNDERSTANDING THE CLIENT WITH ANOREXIA NERVOSA *Anorexia nervosa* is the extreme aversion to food that results in life-threatening weight loss. The disorder is considered to be present if the client has lost 20 percent of her body weight, if there is no known reason for the weight loss, if she has a great fear of regaining weight, and if she has a gross distortion of body image. Until recently the disorder was presumed to be limited to adolescence and young adulthood. It is now realized that the disorder may extend into later years, as women continue to be so obsessed with the need to be thin that they refuse to give up their starvation diets no matter how much weight they have lost. Indeed, for most anorectic persons reactions of joy rather than regret accompany the loss of pounds.

Anorexia nervosa is often accompanied by *bulimia*, a separate but related disorder in which the individual consumes enormous amounts of food and then deliberately vomits it. The bulimic person often resorts to harsh laxatives so that no nutritional value is obtained from any residual food. Unlike the obese person, the bulimic individual is frequently able to maintain normal weight because binge eating is counteracted by vomiting and laxatives.

Statistics on the prevalence of anorexia and bulimia among different age groups are limited because the disorders are concealed as long as possible, especially by bulimic persons. A survey by the National Association of Anorexia Nervosa and

Related Disorders indicated that among 1,400 respondents who admitted to being anorectic or bulimic or both, 1.8 percent were over fifty, 5 percent were over sixty, 2.7 percent were between forty and forty-nine, and 20.5 percent were between thirty and thirty-nine. Thus, 70 percent of the respondents were under thirty years old (Brozan 1983).

Eating disorders are most prevalent among women, and their onset seems to coincide with physiological changes unique to women. When excess amounts of body weight are lost, the adolescent girl may feel more able to return to her carefree childhood years, especially if, as often occurs, weight loss is accompanied by cessation of menstrual periods. Bruch (1973) reported that pregnant women sometimes cannot tolerate the idea of having a large abdomen, and by means of fasting they manage to lose weight even during pregnancy. In some instances morning sickness was transformed into bulimia. For older women anorexia nervosa and bulimia seem to be connected with life stresses and transitions in work, marriage, or emotional relationships (Neuman and Halverson 1984).

Eventually, during repeated fasting, the transmission of physiological messages signaling hunger seems to be lost. Anorectic behavior then moves beyond conscious control and becomes resistant to change. In some respects, the term anorexia is misleading; although anorectic persons deny themselves food, they do not actually lose their appetites until the condition has advanced to severe stages. In earlier stages the person is preoccupied with food, often collecting recipes and cooking for others but not ingesting food herself.

Control of one's life seems to be an important concern for anorectic persons. Eating is one area in which they can exert control, and food thus becomes a substance they fear and avoid. Initially, control of appetite takes the form of occasional dieting, such as is common among women. The anorectic, however, goes on to engage in a prolonged course of self-destruction that may end in death. Among the intelligent, highly motivated achievers who are most prone to anorexia nervosa, emaciation becomes a new accomplishment and an enormous source of satisfaction.

Exercise patterns of these clients are equally individualistic, but often increased physical activity accompanies decreased caloric intake. Sometimes clients "earn" craved foods by engaging in extremely vigorous exercise. They sleep or rest to a very limited extent, often using caffeine or other stimulants to maintain the constant activity.

The deprivation to which anorectic persons subject themselves causes the same physiological changes that would appear in any starving person. Some of the changes are described in the following box.

PHYSIOLOGICAL CHANGES IN ANOREXIA NERVOSA

Loss of subcutaneous fatty tissue

Dry, inelastic skin, sometimes with a yellowish tinge

Bruises and petechiae due to capillary fragility

Bradycardia, low blood pressure, and low body temperature

Lanugo (fine hair) may appear on the face and extremities

Fluid and electrolyte imbalance

Hypokalemia (decreased blood potassium), and hypochloremic (decreased blood chlorides) alkalosis

Cardiac arrhythmias

Cerebral atrophy as shown on CAT scan

The etiology of this disorder remains controversial but external pressures are thought to play a role, particularly the high value placed on slimness in Western society. According to Bruch, anorectic persons display three characteristics: (1) distorted body image, (2) distorted perception of sensations of hunger and fatigue, and (3) underlying sense of being ineffective. Bruch attributed the disorder to parental neglect or inappropriate response to the child's needs. The parents may be overcontrolling and/or overprotective, causing the child to doubt her own value and competence. As a consequence of the control imposed by parents, the child comes to experience herself and her body in a distorted way (Bruch 1973, 1983, 1988).

Another proponent of the external etiological approach is Minuchin, who found that families of anorectic children are overly involved with each other. He described the following factors as contributing influences in the appearance of anorexia nervosa in a young family member (Minuchin, Rosman, and Baker 1978).

In addition to the above factors, Minuchin observed that families of an anorectic child tend to emphasize food and body functions such as digestion and elimination. With this emphasis, it is not too surprising that a child whose maturing need for autonomy has been frustrated might turn to anorexia as a weapon which allows her to control the family which is bent on controlling her. Since autonomy represents a condition that attracts and terrifies the child, anorexia permits her a measure of autonomy without severing family involvement. Investigators proposing a biological explanation for

---

FAMILY INFLUENCES IN THE ETIOLOGY OF ANOREXIA NERVOSA

Family enmeshment: All members are overly involved with each other.

Family rigidity: Family has a compulsive need to maintain appearances at all cost.

Family conflict avoidance: Family avoid but rarely resolves disagreements.

Family authority: Family discourages autonomy in the child so that child's social skills and peer relationships are impaired.

---

anorexia have not been markedly successful (Johnson 1982). There is a school of thought that attributes the disorder to hypothalamic disturbance. Other investigators have looked at pituitary, thyroid, and adrenal function, all without definitive results. Most experts believe that the hypothalamic dysfunction and amenorrhea present in anorexia result from malnutrition, and are the result rather than the cause of the disorder.

Management of Anorexia Nervosa

In life-threatening situations nutrition therapy may be administered by drip or pump into the stomach. When nutritionally complete liquids are given in this way, care must be taken to avoid overfeeding, since this may cause gastric dilation or a paralytic ileus. Edema frequently occurs when adequate nutrition is restored. This may be very distressing to the client, so anticipatory information about fluid accumulation is warranted. When it is necessary to hospitalize an anorectic person, the therapeutic regimen varies with the facility. In some facilities the client is allowed to choose any foods on the hospital menu to meet nutritional goals. In other programs strict rules are established about what is to be eaten. If the client refuses solid food, a liquid supplement is substituted. The client may drink this in the usual manner but in some cases is fed by tube. Whatever the program consists of, the client must have a clear understanding of what is mandatory and what is negotiable. Nursing care is of paramount importance. Every nurse dealing with the client must adhere to the principles agreed upon by the care providers and the client. Adherence to rules and schedules by all personnel avoids unnecessary power struggles between staff members and the client.

The immediate need of the client with anorexia nervosa is the restoration of nutrition and weight to a point where life can be sustained safely. When emaciation, dehydration, and electrolyte disturbance are severe enough to be life-threatening, hospitalization may be needed to provide the client with a regulated environment. The nursing care of persons with severe anorexia nervosa begins with total bed rest, augmented with behavior modification programs that use positive reinforcement to produce change. As the client begins to gain weight, total bed rest and other restrictions are gradually modified. Positive reinforcement might consist of increased physical activity, visiting privileges, and social outlets in return for gains of specified amounts of weight. At times, negative reinforcement in the form of isolation, tube feeding, and withdrawal of privileges may be necessary. Nursing interventions helpful in caring for anorectic clients are described in Table 13–6.

The physical care of a client with anorexia nervosa is only part of the therapeutic regimen. Family counseling is often necessary for younger clients and marital counseling for older ones (Brozan 1983). Clients with anorexia nervosa need

---

Table 13–6. Nursing Interventions with Anorectic Clients

Nursing Interventions	Rationale
Have client weigh each morning after she has voided and before liquids are ingested.	To prevent the client from creating the illusion of weight gain by drinking copious amounts of water and not emptying her bladder
Record daily intake of food and fluids and output of excreta; record quality and amounts.	To prevent dehydration, renal damage, and electrolyte imbalance
Restrict bathroom privileges for two hours after meals unless client is supervised.	To control self-induced vomiting
Prohibit laxatives; give stool softeners if needed.	To prevent misuse of laxatives (if diarrhea occurs, the client may be using laxatives secretly)
Offer small feedings about six times a day rather than three large meals.	To prevent stomach distention and circulatory overload after prolonged fasting
Develop a comprehensive care plan to be followed consistently by all staff members.	To reduce tendencies of the client to control others through manipulation

help in realizing that control over their lives is possible without jeopardizing their existence through starvation. Depression is often a complicating factor when clients are very undernourished, and occasionally antidepressant medication may be used. Almost invariably, clients with anorexia nervosa require long-term psychological help, and the prognosis is better for younger than for older clients. The long-range goal is to enable these clients to stop judging themselves and the world in terms of pounds lost and calories not consumed.

Understanding the Client with Bulimia Nervosa

Bulimia is an eating disorder that consists of gorging on food, followed by self-induced vomiting. This behavioral disorder may be part of anorexia nervosa or may constitute a distinct, separate syndrome. In discussing eating disorders the following distinctions should be made:

Bulimia: gorging and vomiting without starvation

Bulimarexia: gorging and vomiting accompanied by starvation

Gorging: eating abnormally large quantities of food (food binging)

The bulimic person is usually aware of abnormal eating habits, and fears not being able to control her eating. The binging episodes are followed by efforts to control weight through dieting, fasting, or purging. After an episode of binging the bulimic individual feels depressed and worthless.

Bulimia develops in 40 to 50 percent of anorectic persons, and it also seems to be increasing among women of normal weight (Orleans and Barnett 1984). Because it is a secret disorder (bulimic persons go to great lengths to avoid discovery) the real incidence is unknown. As a rule, the bulimic person is older than the anorectic one, appears well-adjusted, and is socially adept. She is rarely as seriously disturbed as an anorectic person, and is more insightful about her problem (Worthington-Roberts 1985). Often she engages in excessive eating to reduce feelings of anxiety. Temporary relief of anxiety is followed by vomiting to relieve bloated feelings and avoid having the food turn into body fat. As binging, vomiting, and purging continue some people lose control altogether, and are at the mercy of this inescapable cycle.

Beyond the psychological consequences of bulimia, there are physiological consequences, the most serious of which are listed in the accompanying box.

PHYSIOLOGICAL CONSEQUENCES OF BULIMIA NERVOSA

Hypokalemia (decreased blood potassium); electrolyte disturbances

Loss of gastric contractility

Renal problems and urinary infections; gastrointestinal problems

Dental erosion due to regurgitation of acidic gastric contents

Parotitis (inflammation and infection of salivary glands)

Esophagitis (infection of esophagus)

Cardiac arrhythmia and dysrhythmia (resulting from hypokalemia)

MANAGEMENT OF BULIMIA NERVOSA The condition is usually managed on an outpatient basis. Interventions are directed first to stopping the cycle of binging, vomiting, and purging. The client is encouraged to discover better ways of coping with feelings of anxiety and depression. Therapy centers on the idea that it is one's own distorted thinking that engenders bad feelings about oneself, rather than the actual situation. Long-term counseling helps the client develop better feelings about herself, and reinforces belief that she has the power to change her behavior. Antianxiety or antidepressive medications are sometimes used. Besides individual counseling, support or self-help groups are beneficial. Bulimic persons are accustomed to using deceit and secrecy in their dealings with others, partly to hide the behavior of which they are ashamed. Establishing trust with these clients and helping them to trust other people are appropriate therapeutic goals. Behavior modification may be used to change eating habits by substituting other activities for binging and vomiting. Cognitive therapy to help correct the emotional, behavioral, and thought distortions that perpetuate the cycle, is also relevant for these clients.

SUMMARY

Almost a century after recognizing the influence of mind and spirit on physiological processes, health professionals are beginning to understand some of the mechanisms that influence the onset and course of human dysfunction. Researchers have established significant associations between emotions, the central

(Text continues on page 362.)

CLINICAL EXAMPLE

AN EFFECTIVE REGIMEN FOR A YOUNG WOMAN WITH ANOREXIA NERVOSA

Heidi Baxter is a 20-year-old married woman who was admitted to an inpatient psychiatric unit of a general hospital. At 5'5" and weighing 78 pounds, Heidi was about 40 percent under a desirable weight. When Heidi was 11 years old her menses began. At age 14 she was hospitalized for possible appendicitis; her chief complaint was of severe abdominal pain. When tests proved negative, Heidi was discharged without surgery. The family was stable but had moved several times as Heidi's father progressed in his career as a college teacher. Heidi is the middle of three children. She described her father as capable and hardworking, and considered her mother good-natured but not very competent.

Heidi has been married for a year. On admission to the hospital she said that she was determined not to gain weight after her marriage. She admitted having a good appetite and to indulging in food binges at times. After a binge of overeating, she often tried to induce vomiting and was usually successful. About six months before the hospital admission Heidi became very weight-conscious. She said she felt fat and was afraid of getting fatter. She restricted her eating to very small portions of vegetables, used a laxative every day and an enema several times a week. At the same time she took great interest in cooking, collected gourmet recipes, and prepared delicious meals for her husband. Of late she had noticed decreased interest in sex and sleep disturbance. When she was unable to sleep, she would get up and exercise or begin some housekeeping task. At age 19, when Heidi got married she weighed 98 pounds. She described her husband as loving and easily pleased. She had known him for several years and reported with pride that they had never had a disagreement.

ASSESSMENT

When Heidi was in high school she put on considerable weight, reaching 160 pounds. Although the weight was well distributed and Heidi was tall enough to carry it, other students teased her about her plumpness. In her senior year in high school she dieted until she weighed 105 pounds. Her friends were very complimentary and her social life was active. Heidi was pleased with the results of dieting and continued not to eat much. After her marriage she gained a few pounds and became frightened that she would never be able to stop gaining weight. She reduced her food intake drastically and steadily began to lose weight. When she weighed about 85 pounds her menstrual periods ceased.

Heidi described herself as a perfectionist in everything she did. She was a good student, an obedient daughter, and now wanted to be a model wife. Her parents encouraged her to marry; two brothers had already left home and Heidi believed that her parents were looking forward to independence at this stage of their lives. She said that her wedding day was the happiest day of her mother's life. As emaciated as Heidi was, she did not consider herself "too thin." She showed some regret because her husband was worried about her and some concern because she was not menstruating. She said that she and her husband hoped someday to have a child but that neither of them felt ready.

Nursing Diagnoses

Altered nutrition: less than body requirements (related to drastic dieting)

Altered sexuality pattern (related to lowered sex drive)

Body image disturbance (related to feelings of being fat despite emaciation)

Sleep pattern disturbance (related to problems falling asleep and remaining asleep; related to habit of exercising and working when unable to sleep)

Psychiatric Diagnoses

Axis I   307.10 Anorexia nervosa

Axis II   No diagnosis

Axis III   No diagnosis

Axis IV   Code 3 Moderate psychosocial stressors

Axis V   Global assessment of functioning (GAF) Code 40 Moderate impairment

PLANNING

Psychotherapy was needed to reduce Heidi's denial and resistance. The primary therapist caring for Heidi assured her that the proper treatment regimen would solve the two aspects that seemed to distress her (the cessation of menses and her problems in sleeping). Heidi was also told that her obsessive behavior around food and weight prevented her from accomplishing some goals that were important to her, such as having a happy marriage and eventually having a child. Because Heidi's dysfunctional behavior actually started about five years earlier, the health team decided that hospitalization was the only way to interrupt her behavior patterns. The health team also realized that the first goal was to repair the effects of extreme emaciation, since it was unwise to begin psychotherapy or behavioral modification until Heidi's physical condition had improved. The program that was instituted involved individual psychotherapy, marital counseling, and behavioral modification.

IMPLEMENTATION

Individual psychotherapy dealt with helping Heidi make connections between her actions and her failure to accomplish some things that were important to her. Attention was directed toward her conflict about growing up and her extreme fear of failure in any undertaking. Cognitive therapy was used to persuade Heidi that her deep need to control herself and others was unnecessary and potentially harmful.

Behavioral therapy followed operant conditioning principles. Positive reinforcement contingent on weight gain consisted of rewards such as home visits and recreational privileges. In the initial hospitalization period bed rest was imposed and progressively lifted through a reward system that operated as Heidi gained weight. Heidi received immediate rewards for weight gain as well as less frequent reinforcement that was contingent on accumulated gains. For Heidi a weight gain of two to three pounds a week was considered desirable. She was required to be in the day room under staff observation for two hours after each meal to forestall self-induced vomiting.

EVALUATION

During hospitalization Heidi slowly gained weight. Her target weight was 120 pounds, and she was discharged when she reached 100 pounds. In therapy sessions Heidi was able to gain some insight into her need for control and perfectionism in everything she undertook. She made it clear that she did not want to continue to gain weight and rejected her target weight as excessive. Negotiation with her outpatient therapist enabled Heidi to accept a target weight of 110 pounds. It was important to her that she still maintain weight that was less than average.

As an outpatient Heidi maintained weight between 105 and 108 pounds. Her husband participated in some of her counseling sessions to help him gain an understanding of Heidi's problems. Eighteen months after her hospitalization, menstruation resumed. She and her husband reported a satisfactory sexual relationship and said they plan to have a child within the next three years.

Heidi was fortunate because her anorexia did not become severe until early adulthood, at which time prompt diagnosis, family support, and comprehensive treatment measures were available to her.

Nursing Diagnosis	Goal	Nursing Action	Outcome Criteria	Outcome Evaluation
Altered nutrition (less than body requirements)	Client will reach target weight of 120 pounds.	Encourage bed rest and permit increased activity as client gains weight.	Client will gain 2 to 3 pounds weekly.	Client is slowly gaining. Agreement reached that client will be discharged at 100 pounds.
Altered sexuality pattern	Client will regain interest in sexual activity.	Give cognitive explanation of physical and psychological effects of extreme dieting and emaciation. Invite husband to participate in joint counseling sessions.	Client and husband will resume sexual interest and activity. Husband will attend counseling sessions.	Couple report improvement in their sexual relationship.
Body image disturbance	Client will adopt normal weight standards.	Set target weight with client. Agree upon expected weekly weight gain.	Client will gain 2 to 3 pounds while hospitalized.	Weekly goal maintained during hospitalization. Client now weighs 100 pounds.
Sleep pattern disturbance	Client will sleep 6 to 8 hours nightly.	Arrange quiet activities before bedtime. Client will take bedtime snack. If sleepless, client will read or listen to music.	Client's difficulty in getting to sleep and staying asleep will moderate.	Client is fearful that sleeping at night will cause more weight gain; client has increased daytime activities to prevent this.

and autonomic nervous systems, hormonal levels, and immunological response systems. Early investigations between emotional states and physiological dysfunction tended to be simplistic. The specific personality theories of Dunbar and the specific conflict theories of Alexander have been replaced by multifactorial explanations for the etiology of various disorders. Research in this area has moved from specific to generalized explanations.

The formulation of the general adaptation syndrome by Selye contributed to popular acceptance of the role of stress as a predisposing factor in various dysfunctional alterations of physiological processes. Human responses to any stress or stressors are individualistic and are greatly influenced by the meaning that events have for the individual. What one person perceives as overwhelming stress may be an exciting challenge for another. There is no panacea for stress-related problems, but it is possible to identify stressors that are especially harmful and to modify their effects.

Medical research has been devoted primarily to the understanding and treatment of physical illness, while social and behavioral research has been limited to the study of psychological and social factors. Both perspectives are inadequate, particularly for nurses who are concerned with providing holistic care in three dimensions, mind, body, and spirit. A number of physical disorders have traditionally been associated with stress and with psychological influences. These disorders have been linked to stress, to hyperactivity of the autonomic nervous system, and to the general adaptation response. Current research, however, points to the fact that virtually every dysfunction to which human beings are susceptible can be influenced, positively or negatively, by psychological states. Therefore, the studies strongly suggest that teaching, counseling, and behavioral techniques should be included in any comprehensive nursing care plan.

Most nurses are committed to holistic approaches to health care, and an understanding of the interactive nature of cognitive, emotional, and physiological processes is the point at which holism begins. In times past a limited number of disorders were categorized as psychosomatic, a term that was later changed to psychophysiological. In recent years both terms have been discarded, as was the limited number of disorders considered to be psychologically induced. The current belief is that mind, body, and spirit are inseparable, and that the terms *psychosomatic* and *psychophysiological* imply a dichotomy that simply does not exist. In addition, there are probably no disorders that are not related in some way to stress and influenced by biopsychosocial conditions. The review of disorders presented in this chapter is by no means complete and merely represents part of the vast array of conditions in health and illness that require a multidimensional approach.

Review Questions

1. Explain how the development of scientific instruments contributed to a fragmented view of health and illness.

2. Differentiate the specific conflict theory from the specific personality theory of stress-related alterations.

3. Describe appropriate nursing interventions for the client categorized as a type A personality.

4. Select a representative disorder and explain the multifactorial theories concerning its etiology.

5. Name the principles that should form the basis of a nursing care plan for a client with peptic ulcer.

6. Explain the rationale for the following statement: "When psychological issues contribute to the clinical manifestations of dysfunction, psychological intervention will repair the dysfunction."

7. Trace the psychological, physiological, and cultural influences that contribute to the prevalence of anorexia nervosa.

8. Identify some common stressors in modern life and suggest ways in which nurses can help clients deal with these stressors.

9. Identify some common stressors confronted by nurses in their professional role, and suggest ways a nurse might effectively cope with these stressors.

10. Explain the following statement: "A holistic approach to health care requires a three-dimensional perspective."

Research Report

Human Responses to Chronic Illness: Physiological and Psychosocial Adaptation

Adaptation to chronic illness is a complex process involving numerous physiological and psychosocial variables, one of which may be a personality characteristic known as "hardiness." The investigator proposes that persons who cope adaptively with chronic illness have the stress-resistant personality trait of hardiness, a set of attitudes toward stress that mediates their responses. Hardy individuals are presumed to see change as challenge and are committed to influencing events and outcomes.

The study dealt with three client groups, each with specific disorders: rheumatoid arthritis, diabetes mellitus, and hypertension. The basic hypothesis was that persons with the hardiness trait would display more adaptive behavior in physiological and psychosocial ways. Sixty male and female adult subjects comprised the sample; each diagnostic group had 20 subjects. Measures of physiological adaptation included specific symptoms and laboratory values, with an absence of complicating factors as determined by experienced clinicians. A health-related hardiness scale developed by the author was used, supplemented with items from existing scales measuring control, commitment, and challenge. Psychosocial adjustment was self-reported, using a four-point scale covering role function, family, social environment, and intropsychic function.

Relationships between hardiness and psychosocial adaptation, and between hardiness and physiological adaptation were tested for the whole sample and for each diagnostic group. Significant relationships for the whole group were not found between hardiness and physiological adaptation. When diagnostic groups were differentiated, the following results were obtained.

Rheumatoid arthritis group: Hardiness was not significantly related to psychosocial or physiological function. No significant relationships were found between psychosocial and physiological adaptation.

Diabetes mellitus group: Hardiness was significantly related to both psychosocial and physiological function. Significant relationships were found between psychosocial and physiological adaptation.

Hypertension group: Hardiness was significantly related to physiological function but not to psychosocial function. Significant relationships were not found between psychosocial and physiological adaptation.

N.B. In general, physiological and psychosocial adaptation were found to be two separate, independent domains. This is important because each disorder imposes different conditions and requires different coping patterns if optimal adaptation is to be achieved.

Pain and loss of mobility, for example, were concerns of rheumatoid arthritis clients, but not of clients in the other groups. Control of one's health status is a greater possibility for clients with diabetes or hypertension than for most clients with rheumatoid arthritis. Based on their experiences with pain and reduced mobility, arthritic clients in the study rejected the concept of control. This was not true of the concept of challenge, which seemed to be a positive factor for all subjects, regardless of diagnosis.

The study found that hardiness may not have a direct effect on adaptation to chronic illness but is likely to facilitate psychosocial adjustment, thus indirectly fostering adaptation to chronic illness. Hardiness as a personality characteristic does not safeguard individuals against illness, but it does affect adaptation once illness develops. Differences between specific chronic disorders seem to be as at or greater than the commonalities they share.

Susan E. Pollock. *Nursing Research* 36, no. 2 (March/April 1986):90–95.

Suggested Annotated Readings

Axiak, Lynne-Marie. "Whatever Happened to the Right to Refuse Treatment." *Nursing 89* 19, no. 1 (January 1989):64.

In this article a nurse records her regret for following orders that denied a dying man his last wish. In refusing the client's small request, the nurse blames herself for violating his trust. Though terminal, the man was rational and knew the consequences of disobeying explicit medical orders. Since he accepted a degree of risk, the nurse now wishes she had had the courage to do the same.

Carr, Judith A, and Marjorie J. Powers. "Stressors Associated with Coronary Bypass Surgery." *Nursing Research* 35, no. 4 (July/August 1986):243–246.

The purpose of this investigation was to evaluate the severity of stressors experienced by 30 men recovering from bypass surgery, and to assess concordance between patient's rating of stressors and nurses' ratings of stressors felt after bypass surgery. The most interesting part of the report is the ratings given by the men themselves. Highest stress ratings were given to the experience of having cardiac surgery. Resuming one's lifestyle received the second highest stress rating. This was considered more stressful than fear of dying, which was ranked fourth. Pain and discomfort were ranked third by the men and second by their nurses. Restriction on visitors was ranked lowest by the men and by their nurses, in terms of causing stress. Significant differences were found between stressor ratings of the patients and of their nurses.

Geach, Barbara. "Pain and Coping." *Image* 19 no. 1 (Spring 1987):12–15.

This sophisticated article makes a number of interesting points. Many people do not experience pain until late in life. Although they may have faced stress and suffering, and have acquired some good coping skills, pain is a new experience for these people, and they may need time and direction to transfer their coping skills to deal with it. The author suggests using the term *pain work* in much the same way that the term *grief work* is used. Grief work, as a descriptive term, removes any hint of stigma or value judgment from the mourner. In the same way, the term pain work would discourage caregivers from moralizing or stereotyping behaviors. Even well-intentioned nurses may comment that one client is dealing with pain "like a soldier" while another is crying "like a baby." Nurses caring for persons in pain are asked to listen carefully to the clients' words but not to infer the clients' psychological state from the words used. In particular, nurses are asked not to patronize persons in pain, but to treat them as colleagues and valuable informants, since the clients are experts in the matter of their own pain.

Gibson, Jo. "A New Approach to Better Medication Compliance." *Nursing 89* 19, no. 4, (April 1989):49–51.

A hospital nurse, over some objections from physicians and other nurses, instituted a self-medication program for hospitalized clients. The program works as follows. The client, a family member, and a nurse fill out a bedside medication record, and a three-day supply of medication is placed in the client's bedside drawer. The author reports improved bedside teaching, more family involvement, and increased compliance after discharge from the hospital.

Fleetwood, Janet. "Bioethical Dilemmas: A Practical Approach." *Nursing 89* 19, no. 3 (March 1989): 62–64.

This article offers guidance for nurses dealing with a person who is not going to recover to the extent of functioning normally, and who wishes to die. The article does not concern itself so much with philosophical matters as with confronting a genuine problem that needs resolution. The dilemma is that of nurses, since the individual client has already made a decision. Nurses are advised to follow these steps. First, investigate to determine whether the client understands fully the diagnosis, prognosis, and probable course of his illness. Next, review the two ethical considerations of autonomy (the client's) or benefit (the client's) and determine which carries more weight in this particular situation. Third, explore all options. Among the options are forcing treatment on the client, persuading him to accept treatment, discontinuing treatment, or challenging his competency in a court of law. Having consulted with family members, other caregivers, a chaplain, an attorney, and agency administrators, nurses are then in a position to make a decision that will be supported by most persons who have been involved in the decision-making process. Once a decision has been made it should be reviewed before and after it is implemented. Clients and families may change their minds; while the client lives the decision can be changed. After the client dies, the decision should again be reviewed to determine the effect of the decision on the quality of care given to the client. This is indeed a practical approach to an ethical dilemma, and one that emphasizes the danger of any nurse's making a decision alone in such a serious matter.

Miller, Sister Patricia, Richard Wikoff, Margaret McMahon, Mary Jane Garret, and Kathleen Ringel. "Influence of a Nursing Intervention on Regimen Adherence and Societal Adjustments Postmyocardial Infarction." *Nursing Research* 37, no. 5 (September/October 1988):297–302.

Over one hundred postmyocardial infarction clients participated in a cardiac rehabilitation program while hospitalized. In addition, the experimental group received an intervention program consisting of data assessment, problem identification, and goal setting. All subjects were visited at home 30 and 60 days after discharge. No differences were found between experimental and control groups in adherence to their regimen or in societal adjustment. There was a significant decrease in mean scores of all subjects in compliance, attitudes toward prescribed medication, coping methods, and beliefs of others regarding compliance. The decrease came during the first 30 days after hospitalization; there was no further change from 30 to 60 days post-hospitalization. The investigators stated that attitudes of clients and their perception of the beliefs of others were significant factors that should be included in any cardiac rehabilitation program.

Orbach, Susie. *Hunger Strike: The Anorectic's Struggle as a Metaphor for Our Age.* New York: Norton, 1986.

The feminist author of this book sees cultural obsession with thinness as part of a pervasive repression of women. The anorectic person is engaged in a struggle for autonomy over her own body that sometimes culminates in death by starvation. Ms. Orbach is a psychotherapist who works with women who are anorectic and bulimic. Psychoanalytic and social influences play a part in the behavior of women who use eating in response to cultural demands to stay thin and by definition are alienated from their own bodies and their own needs. Readers may not agree with the arguments of the author but their understanding of anorexia nervosa will increase.

Smith, Carol E. "Assessing Bowel Sounds; More than Just Listening." *Nursing 88* 18, no. 2 (February 1988):42–43.

Although aimed at nurses with good physical assessment skills, this article uses steps of the nursing process to review salient points. Included are suggestions of salient questions to ask when clients complain of abdominal distress. Hyperactive bowel sounds may indicate gastroenteritis, bleeding, diarrhea, allergic reactions, or emotional turmoil. Hypoactive bowel sounds may be caused by bloating, distention, or reduced food intake. Some procedures described are beyond the capabilities of many nurses but the significance of some bowel sounds should be familiar to all nurses.

Walker, Barbara. "Give Him Control." *Nursing 88* 18, no. 1 (January 1988):50–52.

Controlling clients are difficult for every nurse because such clients seem to interfere with the nurse's implementation of the health care plan. Often controlling clients manage to frustrate and intimidate the most caring of nurses. This case study recounts the experience of a group of nurses who mobilized a client's need to control by sharing information and giving him a form of control that entailed taking responsibility for his own progress and recovery. While this would not be effective for every client, it worked well with the knowledgeable, capable, and controlling man whose progress is described here.

Woods, Nancy, Bernice C. Yates, and Janet Primomo. "Supporting Families during Chronic Illness." *Image* 21, no. 1 (Spring 1989):46–50.

Although the individual "has" the illness, the entire family is affected, one way or another. This article reports on individual and family support when an adult has been diagnosed with heart disease, diabetes, or cancer. Support extended to families must match the current demands of the illness. A distinction is made between informational support, emotional support, and instrumental (practical) support; all are indicated at different points and to different degrees. It is futile to give one kind of support when another is needed more. Regardless of the source of support (family, professional, or community networks), it is the nature, timing, and appropriateness of support that qualitatively influences health outcomes for individuals and their families confronting chronic illnesses.

References

Alexander, F. *Psychosomatic Medicine: Its Principles and Application*. New York: W. W. Norton, 1960.

Alexander, F., T. M. French, and G. H. Pollack. *Psychosomatic Specificity*. Chicago: University of Chicago Press, 1968.

Bloom, B. L., S. J. Asher, and S. W. White. "Mental Disruption as a Stressor: A Review and Analysis." *Psychological Bulletin* 85 (1978):867–894.

Brody, J. E. "Emotions Found to Influence Every Human Ailment." *The New York Times* (May 24, 1983).

——. "Type A Men Fare Better in Heart Attack Study." *The New York Times* (January 14, 1988).

Brown, M. S., and C. Tanner. "Type A Behavior and Cardiovascular Responsivity in Preschoolers." *Nursing Research* 37, no. 3 (May/June 1988):152–155.

Brozan, N. "Anorexia: Not Just a Disease of the Young." *The New York Times* (July 18, 1983).

Bruch, H. *Eating Disorders: Obesity, Anorexia Nervosa, and the Patient Within*. New York: Basic Books, 1973.

——. "Psychotherapy in Anorexia Nervosa and Developmental Obesity." In *Eating and Weight Disorders*, R. K. Goodstein, ed. New York: Springer, 1983.

——. "Anorexia Nervosa: Therapy and Theory." *American Journal of Psychiatry* 1, no. 138 (1988):12–14.

Bullock, F. L., and P. P. Rosendahl. *Pathophysiology: Adaptations and Alterations in Function*. Boston: Little, Brown, 1984.

Byassee, J. E. "Essential Hypertension." In *Behavioral Approaches to Medical Treatment*, R. B. Williams and W. D. Gentry, eds. Cambridge, Massachusetts: Ballinger, 1977.

Cannon, W. B. *The Wisdom of the Body*. New York: W. W. Norton, 1932.

Cobb, S., S. Kasl, E. Chen, and R. Christenfeld. "Some Psychological and Social Characteristics of Patients Hospitalized with Rheumatoid Arthritis, Hypertension, and Duodenal Ulcer." *Journal of Chronic Diseases* 22 (1969):295–298.

Coelho, G. V., D. A. Hamburg, and J. E. Adams, eds. *Coping and Adaptation*. New York: Basic Books, 1980.

Coleman, J. C., J. N. Butcher, and R. C. Carson. *Abnormal Psychology and Modern Life*, 8th ed. Glenview, Illinois: Scott, Foresman, 1984.

Collins, G. "A New Look at Anxiety's Many Faces." *The New York Times* (January 24, 1983).

Coyne, J. C., and K. Holroyd. "Stress, Coping, and Illness: A Transactional Perspective." In *Handbook of Clinical Health Psychology*, T. Millon, C. Greene, and R. Meagher, eds. New York: Plenum, 1982.

Day, S. B. *Life Stress*. New York: Von Nostrand Reinhold, 1984.

Dunbar, F. *Psychosomatic Diagnosis*. New York: Harper & Row, 1943.

——. *Emotions and Body Changes*, 4th ed. New York: Columbia University, 1954.

Engel, G. "Studies of Ulcerative Colitis: Clinical Data Bearing on the Nature of the Somatic Process." *Somatic Medicine* 16, no. 3 (1954):496–499.

———. *Psychological Development in Health and Disease*. Philadelphia: W. B. Saunders, 1972.

Engel, G., and A. H. Schmale. "Psychoanalytic Theory of Somatic Disorder." *Journal of the American Psychoanalytical Association* 15 (1964):344–365.

Eyer, T. "Hypertension as a Disease of Modern Society." In *Stress and Survival*, C. A. Garfield, ed. St. Louis: C. V. Mosby, 1979.

Falliers, C. J. *Psychiatric Aspects of Asthma*. New York: Ciba-Geigy, 1978.

Feikert, P. M. "Gastric Surgery: Your Crucial Pre- and Post-Op Role." *RN* (January 1987):24–34.

Friedman, M., and R. Rosenman. *Type A Behavior and Your Heart*. New York: Knopf, 1974.

Fritz, G. K., S. Rubenstein, and N. J. Lewiston. "Psychological Factors in Fatal Childhood Asthma." *American Journal of Orthopsychiatry* 57, no. 2 (April 1987): 246–252.

Garfield, C. A. *Stress and Survival*. St. Louis: C. V. Mosby, 1979.

Gross, M. "Psychosocial Aspects of Osteoarthritis: Helping Patients Cope." *Health and Social Work* 6, no. 3 (March 1981):40–46.

Hayman, L. L., J. C. Meininger, E. E. Stashinko, P. R. Gallagher, and P. M. Coates. "Type A Behavior and Physiological Cardiovascular Risk Factors in School-age Twin Children." *Nursing Research* 37, no. 5 (September/October 1988):290–296.

Holmes, T. H., and R. H. Rahe. "Social Readjustment Scale." *Journal of Psychosomatic Research* 11 (1967): 213–215.

Johnson, C. "Anorexia Nervosa and Bulimia." In *Promoting Adolescent Health*, T. J. Coates, A. C. Peterson, and C. Perry, eds. New York: Academic Press, 1982.

Jones, R. A. *Self-fulfilling Prophecies: Social and Psychological Effects of Expectancies*. Hillsdale, New Jersey: Erlbaum, 1977.

Kaplan, H. I. "History of Psychosomatic Medicine." In *Comprehensive Textbook of Psychiatry*, 3d ed., H. I. Kaplan, A. M. Freedman, and B. J. Sadock, eds. Baltimore: Williams & Wilkins, 1980.

Knapp, P. H. "Current Theoretical Concepts in Psychosomatic Medicine." In *Comprehensive Textbook of Psychiatry*, 3d ed., H. I. Kaplan, A. M. Freedman, and B. J. Sadock, eds. Baltimore: Williams & Wilkins, 1980.

Kolata, G. "Studies Point Strongly to Low Metabolism Rate as Cause of Obesity." *The New York Times* (February 25, 1988).

Lipowski, Z. J., D. R. Lipsitt, and P. C. Whybrow. *Psychosomatic Medicine: Current Trends and Clinical Applications*. New York: Oxford, 1977.

Matthews, K. A. "Psychological Perspectives on Type A Behavior Patterns." *Psychological Bulletin* 91 (1982): 293–323.

Mattson, A. "Psychological Aspects of Childhood Asthma." *Pediatric Clinics of North America*. (February, 1975).

Miller, L. H., R. Ross, and S. I. Cohen. "Stress." *Bostonia Magazine* 56, no. 4 (1982):11–16.

Minuchin, S., B. L. Rosman, and L. Baker. *Psychosomatic Families*. Cambridge, Massachusetts: Harvard University Press, 1978.

Muhlenkamp, A. F., and J. A. Joyner. "Arthritis Patients' Self-reported Affective States and Their Caregivers' Perceptions." *Nursing Research* 35, no. 1 (January/February 1986):24–27.

Neumann, P. A., and P. A. Halverson. *Anorexia and Bulimia: Handbook for Counselors and Therapists*. New York: Van Nostrand Reinhold, 1984.

Orleans, C. T., and L. R. Barnett. "Bulimarexia: Guidelines for Behavioral Assessment and Treatment." In *The Binge/Purge Syndrome*, R. C. Hawkins, W. J. Fremouw, and P. F. Clement, eds. New York: Springer, 1984.

Powers, M. J., and A. Jaloweic. "Profile of the Well-Controlled, Well-Adjusted Hypertension Patient." *Nursing Research* 36, no. 2 (March/April 1987):106–110.

Putt, A. "One Experiment in Nursing Adults with Peptic Ulcer." *Nursing Research* 19, vol. 6 (1970): 484–494.

Rahe, R. H. "Life Changes and Subsequent Illness Reports." In *Life Stress and Illness*, K. E. Gunderson and R. H. Rahe, eds. Springfield, Illinois: Charles C. Thomas, 1974.

Robinson, L. *Psychiatric Nursing as a Human Experience*. Philadelphia: W. B. Saunders, 1983.

———. *Psychiatric Aspects of the Care of Hospitalized Patients*. Philadelphia: W. B. Saunders, 1984.

Rosenbaum, J. "Peptic Ulcers." In *Comprehensive Textbook of Psychiatry*, 3d ed., H. I. Kaplan, A. M. Freedman, and B. J. Sadock, eds. Baltimore: Williams & Wilkins, 1980.

Schaefer, K. M. "Easing the Torment of an Irritable Bowel." *RN* (April 1986):34–38.

Seyle, H. *Stress Without Distress*. New York: McGraw-Hill, 1974.

———. *Guide to Stress Research*, Vol. 1. New York: Van Nostrand, 1980.

———. *The Stress of Life*, 2d ed. New York: McGraw-Hill, 1976.

Silverman, A. J. "Rheumatoid Arthritis." In *Comprehensive Textbook of Psychiatry*, 3d ed., H. I. Kaplan, A. M. Freedman, and B. J. Sadock, eds. Baltimore: Williams & Wilkins, 1980.

Sperger, P., G. E. Erlich, and D. Glass. "The Rheumatoid Arthritic Personality: A Psychodiagnostic Myth." *Psychosomatics* 19, no. 2 (February 1978):79–86.

Stroebe, M. S., and W. Stroebe. "Who Suffers More? Sex Differences in Health Risks of the Widowed." *Psychological Bulletin* 93 (1983):279–301.

Stunkard, A. J. "Obesity." *Comprehensive Textbook of Psychiatry*, 4th ed. Baltimore: Williams & Wilkins, 1985.

Tierney, J. "Type A's, Maybe Now You Can Relax." *Science 85* (June 1985):12.

Turkington, C. "Physical Factors Explored in Dieting, Type A Behavior." *Monitor* (February 1984):24.

Weiner, H. F., M. Thaler, M. F. Reiser, and I. A. Mersky. "Etiology of Duodenal Ulcer: Relation of Specific Psychological Characteristics to Rate of Gastric Secretion." *Psychosomatic Medicine* 19 (1957):1–10.

Weiner, H. *Psychology and Human Disease*. New York: Elsevier, 1977.

Wilder, J. F., and R. Plutchik. "Stress and Psychiatry." In *Comprehensive Textbook of Psychiatry*, 4th ed. H. I. Kaplan and B. J. Sadock, eds. Baltimore: Williams & Wilkins, 1985.

Williams, C. C., and T. H. Holmes. "Life Change, Human Adaptation, and Onset of Illness." In *Clinical Practice in Psychosocial Nursing*, D. Longo and R. Williams, eds. New York: Appleton-Century-Crofts, 1978.

Worthington-Roberts, B. "Eating Disorders in Women." In *Focus on Critical Care* 12, no. 4 (August 1985):32–31.

C H A P T E R

14

Sexual Variations and Disruptions

Learning Objectives

After reading this chapter, the student should be able to:

1. Delineate the physiological responses to sexual stimulation and explain changes that occur as one ages.

2. Examine the intrapersonal and interpersonal dimensions and cultural forces affecting sexual expression.

3. Differentiate between adaptive sexual expression, alternative sex role enactment, sexual abuse, and sexual dysfunction.

4. Recognize the need for sex education for clients with debilitating chronic illnesses and sexually transmitted diseases.

Overview

Although nurses have been leaders in advocating a holistic approach in health care, they have often ignored their clients' sexuality. Some nurses are uncomfortable discussing sexual concerns with clients or have insufficient information about sexual physiology and psychology. Some believe common myths and misconceptions about sexuality. Others believe that there is only one "right" way to express sexuality. Such attitudes constitute a nontherapeutic approach to helping clients deal with sexual variations and disruptions as well as healthy sexual activities. The caring continuum dictates that nurses recognize their own value system while accepting the values of others.

Nurses need to acquire accurate information and examine their own values and beliefs about sexuality before attempting to assist clients with their problems.

This chapter gives a brief overview of sexual anatomy and physiology, examines behavioral factors in sexuality, and describes alternative styles of sexual expression. The roles of sexual activities in aging and physical illness are discussed as well as sexually transmitted disease, sexual dysfunction and deviance. Nursing implications are presented and counseling techniques are delineated.

Physiological Aspects of Human Sexuality

Many people in our culture have received negative conditioning about the sexual parts of their bodies from earliest childhood. People learn to think of the genitals as something "down there" or the "privates," which are not to be looked at, touched, or discussed. Particularly for women in our culture, the genitals are a source of embarrassment; they are often considered shameful and dirty. This sense of shame may not remain limited to one's genitals but may extend to the whole body. One result of such negative attitudes about the body is that often people have little knowledge about their own anatomy and how it works. An important aspect of caring for clients with variations and disruptions of sexuality is to clear up any misconceptions they may have about their bodies and to provide them with information about sexual anatomy and physiology.

Anatomical Structures

The female external genitals, or *vulva*, consist of several structures (see Figure 14–1). The *mons veneris* is the fatty tissue over the pubic bone that is richly supplied with nerve endings; touch and pressure in this area can produce pleasurable sensations. The *labia majora* are the outer lips and the *labia minora* are the inner lips of the vulva. The labia minora join at the *clitoral hood* and can vary considerably in size, shape, and color from one woman to another. The *clitoris* consists of a *glans* and *shaft*, which contains two cavernous bodies called the crura (stalks) that extend internally. Although the clitoris is small, it has the same number of nerve endings as the male penis and is highly sensitive to sexual stimulation. The remaining structures are the *urethral opening* and the *introitus* of the vagina.

The internal structures of the female consist of the ovaries, Fallopian tubes, uterus, cervix, and vagina (see Figure 14–2). The *vagina* has a very rich blood supply, and in a nonaroused state it is about three to five inches in length. During arousal, the vagina changes in size and shape and is capable of lubrication, which is related to the vasocongestion of the area. The existence of an area known as the *Grafenberg spot*, or *G-spot*, has been the subject of controversy in recent years. Advocates of this structure believe that it is located on the front wall of the vagina and surrounds the urethra midway between the cervix and the top of the pubic bone. This area is about the size of a dime in the unaroused state, but when a woman is sexually aroused it doubles in size. It is thought that this tissue is the female counterpart to the male prostate gland and arises from the same embryonic tissue. Some women find that direct stimulation of the G-spot is pleasurable and brings about a rapid orgasm. There have been some reports of a female ejaculation associated with G-spot stimulation, but it is not known how common a response this is (Barbach 1982, Crooks and Baur 1983).

The male sexual organs are more visible than the female genitals. The *penis* consists of the *glans*, which contains many nerve endings, and the *shaft*. In the shaft of the penis are spongy areas of erectile tissue called the *corpora cavernosa* and *corpus spongiosum*, which become engorged with blood during sexual arousal, causing the penis to stiffen into an erection. Many men are concerned about the size of their penis. There is a great deal of variation in

Figure 14–1. *Female external genitals.*

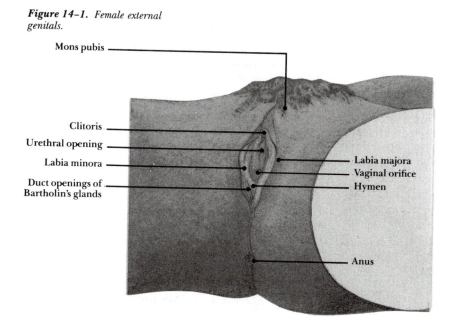

Mons pubis

Clitoris
Urethral opening
Labia minora
Duct openings of Bartholin's glands

Labia majora
Vaginal orifice
Hymen

Anus

Figure 14-2. *Female internal reproductive organs.*

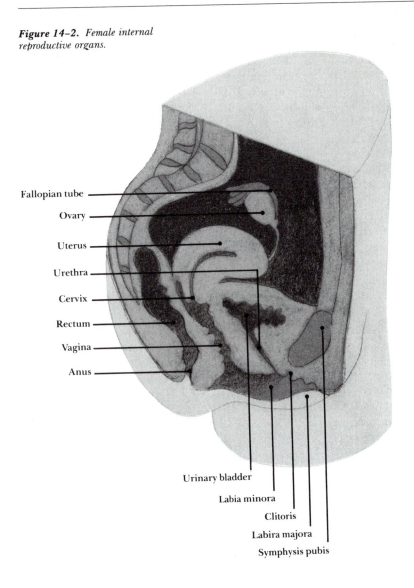

Fallopian tube

Ovary

Uterus

Urethra

Cervix

Rectum

Vagina

Anus

Urinary bladder

Labia minora

Clitoris

Labira majora

Symphysis pubis

penis length in the flaccid state, but erections in all men are about 5 to 7 inches long. Penis size is not related to body build, skin color, or sexual ability.

The two *testicles*, which are located in the *scrotum*, produce sperm (see Figure 14–3). From each testicle, the sperm travel through the *epididymis* and up through the *vas deferens*, whose terminal end forms a storage compartment called an *ampulla*, where sperm are held until ejaculation. The vas deferens and the *seminal vesicle* join to form the *ejaculatory duct*, which runs inside the *prostate gland* and joins with the urethra. The *seminal vesicles* are small glands that provide a fluid rich in fructose sugar, which activates the vigorous movement of sperm cells after ejaculation. The prostate gland contributes a thin, milky, alkaline fluid to the *semen*. The *Cowper's glands*, which are located below the prostate, secrete a clear, alkaline fluid into the urethra during sexual excitement. A small drop or two may be seen at the urethral orifice just before

ejaculation (Haeberle 1981, Crooks and Baur 1983). During ejaculation, the sperm, suspended in semen, are expelled through the urethral orifice. The smooth muscle sphincter at the base of the bladder is closed due to the higher pressure in the urethra caused by expansion of the corpus spongiosum, preventing the expulsion of urine during ejaculation.

Physiological Responses

Sexual arousal and response in humans is influenced by many factors and is a complex interaction of biological, psychological, and cultural components. Our understanding of the physiology of sexual arousal has been expanded by the work of William Masters and Virginia Johnson (1966). They used a variety of direct observation techniques in a laboratory setting to study human sexuality. According to Masters and Johnson, the

Figure 14–3. *Male reproductive system.*

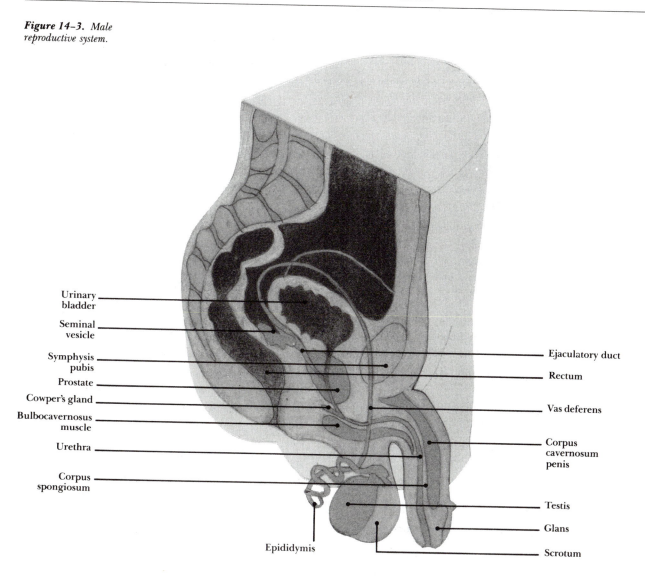

Urinary bladder

Seminal vesicle

Symphysis pubis

Prostate

Cowper's gland

Bulbocavernosus muscle

Urethra

Corpus spongiosum

Epididymis

Ejaculatory duct

Rectum

Vas deferens

Corpus cavernosum penis

Testis

Glans

Scrotum

human sexual response occurs in four phases: excitement, plateau, orgasmic, and resolution. The initial arousal is referred to as the *excitement phase*, during which physiological changes tend to build rapidly. Muscle tension, respiration, heart rate, and blood pressure increase. Vasocongestion produces erection in the penis and swelling and hardening of the clitoris. Nipple erection occurs in both sexes. In the *plateau phase* (also called the *charge phase*), the physiological reactions continue, but at a less rapid rate. Sexual tension builds but may fluctuate. During the *orgasmic phase*, sexual tension is released in a spasmodic response centered in the pelvic region. Muscle spasms usually occur throughout the body, and a series of muscular contractions pulsate through the pelvic area. In males, orgasm is accompanied by ejaculation. Whether females experience a similar discharge during orgasm remains controversial. In the *resolution phase*, the body returns to the prearoused state. In males, there is a refractory period during which another orgasm is impossible. Table 14–1 summarizes the physiological changes that occur during the sexual response cycle.

INTRAPERSONAL AND INTERPERSONAL DIMENSIONS

Human sexuality is made up of a combination of biological, cultural, and psychological factors that are interwoven so intricately that it is almost impossible to isolate any one of them. The brain has been called the most important sex organ because it mediates the influence of these three elements. Physiologically, our five senses send messages to the brain, which then sends its neural messages via the spinal cord to produce the sexual responses of erection, lubrication, and orgasm. Our culture defines what is sexual or not sexual, so it thereby defines which incoming sensory messages the brain interprets as erotic. Sexual fantasies are a psychological

Table 14–1. The Sexual Response Cycle

Phase	Female Response	Male Response
Excitement	Myotonia (increased muscle tension) gradually increases. Moderate increase in pulse and blood pressure occurs. Clitoris becomes erect. Vaginal lubrication begins. Vagina increases in length and width and changes color to a deeper purple. Labia majora increase in size and flatten to expose vaginal opening. Labia minora enlarge to double or triple their size. Uterus pulls upward. Nipples become erect and entire breast begins to swell.	Myotonia gradually increases. Moderate increase in pulse and blood pressure occurs. Penis becomes erect. Scrotal tissue thickens and testicles pull upward toward abdomen by spermatic cord contraction. Nipples become erect.
Plateau	Myotonia, both voluntary and involuntary, becomes more pronounced. There may be facial grimaces. Pulse, blood pressure, and respiratory rate continue to increase. Sex flush may appear. Lubrication continues. The outer third of the vagina becomes congested with blood, which narrows it by about 33%. This is called the *orgasmic platform*. Labia minora continue to darken. Clitoris retracts under its hood. Breasts reach greatest expansion and nipple erection may subside.	Myotonia, both voluntary and involuntary, becomes more pronounced. There may be facial grimaces. Pulse, blood pressure, and respiratory rate continue to increase. Sex flush may appear. Testicles swell and continue to elevate. Cowper's glands secrete a few drops.
Orgasm	Muscular and nervous tension is suddenly released with involuntary muscle spasms. Sphincter muscles contract. Pulse, blood pressure, and respiration rate reach highest levels. Outer third of vagina contracts. Uterus contracts. Clitoris remains retracted under its hood.	Muscular and nervous tension is suddenly released with involuntary muscle spasms. Sphincter muscles contract. Pulse, blood pressure, and respiration rate reach highest levels. Ducts, urethra, and penis contract. About 1 teaspoon of semen is usually ejaculated. Orgasm and ejaculation are different processes and may occur independently of each other.
Resolution	Myotonia decreases. Pulse, blood pressure, and respiration rate return to normal. Nipples lose their erection. Sex flush disappears. Congestion in outer third of vagina disappears. Labia return to former shape and size. Clitoris reemerges from its hood. Uterus descends. No, or mild, refractory period, when no amount of stimulation will result in orgasm, occurs.	Myotonia decreases. Pulse, blood pressure, and respiration rate return to normal. Nipples lose their erection. Sex flush disappears. Penis loses erection. Testicles return to former shape and size. Refractory period occurs.

process in the brain that stimulates a physiological response. Each of the three factors can be short-circuited by the brain itself. For example, feelings such as guilt, anger, anxiety, and fear will prevent the brain from sending the appropriate signals for sexual response.

It is important to recognize that sexuality is conditioned by an individual's cultural setting, or milieu. The social conditioning of sexual expectations and norms is very subtle, which often leads people to believe that their feelings and behaviors are innate. The range of acceptable sexual norms is very diverse. In some countries, such as the United States, there is a mix of acceptable norms; a single pattern of "American sexual behavior" does not exist.

Sexuality is an integral part of people's self-concept and as such is intrinsically related to body image and self-esteem. Thus, it is an important aspect of all feelings and behavior. Most people, regardless of sexual preferences, have a need for sexual self-validation—that is, validation of their masculinity or femininity. The sexual self, like other aspects of the self, needs to be constantly reinforced and supported. Sexuality is potentially a rich source of pleasure, but for many people it can also be a source of guilt, frustration, and conflict. They must resolve their sexual conflict and guilt in order for sex and sexuality to enhance their feelings about themselves and to help them relate more comfortably and positively to others.

Socially Conditioned Sexual Expectations

Each society dictates what is appropriate and inappropriate sexual behavior and thus strongly shapes its members' attitudes and expectations. Some of these socially conditioned expectations can interfere with people's sexual functioning and enjoyment because they rob sexual expression of freedom and spontaneity. Also, people may feel bewildered, hurt, or rejected when their partners are unable to meet their expectations. The socialization process is so subtle that many people are unaware of the impact of a number of unspoken expectations about sex. These expectations include (Kaplan 1974, Siemens and Brandzel 1982):

EXPECTATION 1 Sexual behavior should be instinctual. This assumption confuses sexual drive, which is innate, with sexual behavior, which is learned. Through the socialization process one learns what behavior is acceptable and what is unacceptable at each stage of life. Sexual drive changes throughout life as a person develops new sexual tastes and habits, and experiences changes in sexual frequency needs. The belief that sexual behavior should be instinctual leaves little room for teaching and learning to occur within a relationship.

EXPECTATION 2 Sexual performance is all-important. American culture is an achievement-oriented society, and people tend to evaluate themselves and each other by their sexual achievements. Sexual activity tends to become work if goals are set for intercourse and orgasm and little attention is paid to the process of lovemaking. Our language reflects such attitudes, for example, in the use of the word "foreplay." Such a term indicates that this activity is only meaningful when it is a preliminary to genital intercourse. Such expectations can contribute to anxiety, which in turn may block physiological responses. When a person becomes a spectator of his or her own sexual performance, the stage is set for sexual dysfunction. The high value some areas of our culture place on work and the low value placed on pleasure lead to the assumption that activities are important only if they are productive and that pleasure-oriented activities are selfish and unimportant. It is difficult for many people to set aside time for pleasure. Frequently, pleasurable activities such as sex are sacrificed in order that all other tasks for the day be accomplished.

EXPECTATION 3 Sex equals intercourse. This expectation minimizes the importance of all the touching, holding, and manual and oral stimulation that also compose sexual activity. Such an assumption allows people to consider themselves "virgins" even though they have participated in every sexual activity except intercourse. It can also lead to unrealistically high expectations about intercourse and to disappointment when it does occur. A couple's exclusive focus on the penis in the vagina may rob them of a great deal of pleasure and warmth. Such an exclusive focus also requires the attainment and maintenance of a penile erection for a long period, which is not always easy or possible.

EXPECTATION 4 Men are responsible for sexual activity. Men are expected to be more interested in sex, to initiate and direct the sexual act. Satisfaction for both partners is considered the man's responsibility. Women are expected to remain passive, innocent, and unknowledgeable. This expectation places an unfair burden on the man and discounts the woman's responsibility for satisfying herself and her partner. Because of this expectation it is difficult for many men to passively allow their partners to stimulate them and give them pleasure. Many men are also afraid to ask their partners about their sexual preferences for fear of being thought ignorant or unmanly. Women hesitate to tell men their preferences for fear of hurting their egos. A woman believes that if her partner loves her he will be able to divine her wishes. Thus both men and women are victims of this cultural conspiracy of silence.

EXPECTATION 5 Men are always ready for sex and should be able to get an erection with anyone, anywhere, at any time. This expectation dismisses the highly complex psychological and physiological processes that can short-circuit sex in both men and women. This misconception is often fueled by another—that men, by nature, have a stronger sex drive than women. Such unrealistic expectations frequently lead to disillusionment for both partners.

EXPECTATION 6 All physical contact should lead to sexual intercourse. Couples who hold this belief see touching and holding only as preliminaries to intercourse, not as acts valuable or pleasurable in their own right. Such couples may cease to touch and hold each other when sexual intercourse is neither desired nor feasible. They lose a valuable means of expressing warm, tender, and intimate feelings.

EXPECTATION 7 Intercourse should always end in orgasm for both partners. In reality, the orgasmic reflex can be triggered or inhibited by many physiological and psychological factors. While under most circumstances both partners may wish to achieve orgasm at some point during sex, it is possible for one or both partners to enjoy intercourse without orgasm. Some couples strive for simultaneous orgasm as the "right" way to have intercourse and thus are disappointed when it does not occur. Individuals vary widely in the amount of time and stimulation they need to achieve orgasm. It is unrealistic to expect simultaneous orgasm. Focusing on the orgasm tends to diminish pleasure in sex and to increase concern about performance. Other aspects of sexual activity become neglected. Yet concentrating on the process of sexual interaction—touching, holding, caressing, meeting the partner's needs—is usually more rewarding than concentrating solely on having an orgasm.

EXPECTATION 8 Sexual activity requires an erection. This is closely related to the assumption that sex equals intercourse. Expecting an erection becomes another source of pressure and frequently results in a failure to maintain or achieve an erection. A couple needs to remember that the penis is not the only part of the man's body involved in lovemaking and that there are many other sexual activities they can try. It is unfortunate when couples forego all pleasure when erectile difficulties occur.

EXPECTATION 9 Sexual activity should be spontaneous. This expectation rests on the belief that both partners should be in the mood for sex before any activity should be initiated. In reality, it is common for one partner to initiate sex and the other partner to get in the mood as lovemaking proceeds. With the busy schedules many people have, couples need to make "dates" to ensure they have enough intimate time together. Rather than a detriment to the mystique of sexual activity, planning can become a source of pleasurable anticipation that can enhance time together.

EXPECTATION 10 Women should have orgasms during intercourse and be able to achieve multiple orgasms. Expecting the woman to have frequent and multiple orgasms has become a measure of the liberation of the wife and of the sexual competence of the husband. Unfortunately, this obsession can interfere with sexual pleasure. Some women are unable to communicate their needs and preferences, particularly about other modes of stimulation be-

sides genital intercourse. Research has shown that there is no "normal" orgasm and no "right" way to have orgasms (Masters and Johnson 1966). The majority of women, in fact, have difficulty reaching orgasm solely by penetration of the penis.

Sexual Activity as a Coping Mechanism

Although the purposes of sexual activity are usually thought to be reproduction and the expression of affection, it may also be viewed as a coping mechanism. Whether it is an adaptive or maladaptive coping mechanism depends on two criteria: (1) how well an activity serves its intended purpose, and (2) whether it harms anyone.

Self-affirmation may be one of the greatest benefits of sexual activity. Feeling accepted and being able to give and receive pleasure are emotionally valuable consequences of sexual activity. They help counterbalance the self-doubts and disappointments inherent in living. However, when the need for reassurance reaches such extremes that even frenetic sexual activity cannot fulfill it, then sexual activity can become a maladaptive response.

Sexual activity may also be used to relieve anxiety, since orgasm discharges tension fairly reliably. Many people use sexual activity as a kind of tranquilizer, especially during times of temporarily increased stress. However, extremes of anxiety can result in erectile failure or nonorgasmic response, consequently increasing anxiety.

Although a decrease in sexual activity is usually associated with depression, an increase in activity may be seen in the milder depressions. This coping mechanism is an effort to counteract the depression through stimulation and personal contact.

Pleasure and excitement are human needs that must be met for optimal well-being, and sexual activity is one source of pleasure and emotional stimulation in people's lives. Sexual enjoyment can help people bear the difficult times that inevitably occur in life. But when sex becomes the sole source of excitement or cannot provide enough excitement to meet a person's needs, it can become a maladaptive response.

Some people view sex as a way to obtain love, but there is a great difference between sex as an expression of love and sex as a plea for love. The more manipulative a sexual activity is, the more maladaptive it becomes and the more painful its consequences can be. Some people may engage in sexual intercourse to obtain body contact and touching, but, again, the distinction must be made between sex as an expression of physical affection and sex as a plea for human contact.

The exercise of power over another person is another manipulative use of sex that is unlikely to have satisfactory consequences. People who feel dependent and helpless may believe their only means of wielding power is with sex. If an individual does not feel he has the power to gain what he wants directly, he may use sex as a reward or the withholding of sex as a punishment to get what he wants indirectly. Withholding sex can have a powerful effect. The partner not only ends up feeling inadequate as a lover but is also deprived of pleasure. Thus, what began as a coping mechanism may end up harming the couple's relationship.

Sexuality and Aging

The expectation that has perhaps the most widespread and inhibiting implications is the myth that sexuality is only for the young. Denial of the sexual needs of aging persons and discomfort when faced with the evidence of their sexual activity is still present, even among health care providers.

Although cultural bias has tended to define older people as asexual, physiological, psychological, and sociological data indicate that older people are indeed sexually active or have the potential to be so (Steinke and Bergen 1986). The ability to be sexually active in later years appears to be dependent on frequent sexual activity when one is younger. Sexual activity in later life helps maintain normal function and dilutes some of the involutional changes caused by decreased amounts of naturally produced sex steroids. Changing sexual responses in advancing years do not indicate the end of sexual functioning, and awareness of such changes can prevent anxiety reactions that cause sexual withdrawal and dysfunction.

Both sexes experience changes in sexual arousal and orgasm with age. These differences are displayed in Table 14–2. The physiological changes that occur can be compensated for to allow successful experiences for both men and women into the eighth and ninth decades of their lives. Most of the decrease in sexual activity can be attributed to attitudes that were developed earlier. A significant factor in sexual disinterest is the monotony of the marital relationship when individuals have made little effort to each other's needs. Other facets of aging, such as decreased self-esteem, long-standing resentments, and the cultural set that sex is for the young, can contribute to sexual apathy. Mental fatigue and decreased communication among couples can also play a role.

Fear of failure is the most crucial factor in withdrawal of older men from sexual activity. The shattering experience of impotency, even once, can lead the man to avoid repeating the act for fear of further inadequacy.

Both men and women may need to be counseled regarding the normal changes that occur with aging and the necessity for prolonged stimulation.

Table 14–2. Age-Related Changes in Sexual Arousal and Orgasm

Women	Men
Arousal Shortening of vagina, delayed and reduced expansion; decreased vaginal secretions; less enlargement and less elevation of uterus	*Arousal* Longer time to ejaculate; firmness of penis decreases; shorter ejaculatory sense
Orgasm Fewer contractions Occasional painful spasms	*Orgasm* Shorter, less forceful ejaculation; volume of fluid decreases
Postorgasm Vaginal irritation from trauma; cervical os not dilated	*Postorgasm* Rapid loss of erection; longer refractory period
Extragenital Less increase in breast volume; less engorgement of areolar; nipples retain erection longer; few rectal contractions; bladder and urethral irritability, leading to need to urinate	*Extragenital* Few rectal sphincter contractions; less elevation of testes; less swelling and erection of nipples

SOURCE: Adapted from William H. Masters (1986).

It should also be emphasized that sexuality needs can be met by other means than sexual intercourse. Touching, holding, and sharing of feelings are needs that do not change with age (Masters 1986).

Although sexual activity can remain a source of enjoyment for men and women throughout their lives, the occurrence of a chronic, debilitating illness can alter the options available. Impediments to sexual response and necessary adaptations are discussed in the next section.

Sexuality in Illness

Chronic and terminal illness places a strain on any relationship. Some couples are able to adapt to the added stress and can continue to support one another. Others, however, may withdraw from each other emotionally and sexually for a variety of reasons.

A couple's ability to cope with significant trauma is a function of the strength and stability of the relationship. Some couples grow closer in a crisis situation; others are barely able to maintain marginal support; and some relationships cannot survive the stress.

Physical illness may be used as a reason to withdraw completely from sexual relationships. For some of these clients, sex was not a highly valued activity prior to the physical complications. As a result, the illness becomes a pretext for avoiding all sexual involvement. Sensitive and accurate client education can play a distinct role in helping couples to maintain their expression of love and comfort for each other, particularly when the illness brings a sense of deprivation and fear to a sexual relationship that was meaningful and important. Physical illnesses in one or both partners may require adjustment and modification of sexual activity. The following section of this chapter provides some suggestions that nurses can use when counseling clients who have developed a variety of chronic debilitating conditions.

CARDIOVASCULAR DISEASE The occurrence of cardiovascular disease can have a profound impact on client and partner alike. A lack of appropriate information has led many clients to refrain from all sexual activities for fear that the increased physical exertion will lead to death during intercourse. The sexual response creates an increase in both heart rate and blood pressure which lasts for less than a minute. Anger and anxiety raise the blood pressure much more than sexual activity. Clients can safely have intercourse as soon as they can comfortably climb two flights of stairs (Renshaw 1986).

Clients with hypertension can take advantage of the supine position to utilize the effects of postural hypotension. Medications frequently prescribed for hypertension have sexually inhibiting side effects. Adjusting the timing of the dose to occur after sexual activities may be helpful.

When a client has experienced a cardiovascular accident, sexual capacity and functioning are usually maintained. Previous sexual activities can usually be resumed after discharge from the hospital. There will be sensory changes on the affected side of the body as well as muscular weakness, which can be dealt with by communicating about sensations and using physical supports such as pillows during sexual intercourse (Renshaw 1986).

CHRONIC LUNG DISEASE Sexual dysfunction as a result of activity intolerance and shortness of breath are often seen in clients with chronic obstructive pulmonary disease. The fear of dyspnea can keep clients from pursuing sexual activities and result in a decreased desire for sex, less frequency, and feelings of worthlessness and isolation. Sexual encounters may also cease because of the coughing, sputum production, and mouth odor that accompany lung disease. Variation in position may facilitate sexual intercourse. Partners should be made aware that both oral sex and kissing will be difficult for the client with lung disease because of dyspnea.

The use of bronchodialators before and during sexual activity may be helpful. A recommendation should be given to precede intercourse by a rest period (Cooper 1986).

CANCER Meeting the sexual needs of the client with progressive cancer should begin long before the final stages of the illness. Losses for people with cancer are serial in nature, resulting in chronic grief. Such losses include parts of the body, bodily functions, reproductive organs, fertility, potency, and libido. In addition, there are repeated losses associated with the metastases and deterioration. Permission must be given clients to grieve to enable them to validate their feelings. Anger may be an appropriate emotion as a response to loss, uncertainty, helplessness, and vulnerability. Family members and health care providers should be aware that such expression is helpful to clients and is not a personal attack on them.

Symptoms associated with cancer and its therapy all affect the client's self-image. Clients with cancer must adjust to monumental changes in their body image. Unless the client is aware of the multiple ways that sexuality can be expressed, the focus will be on the changes rather than on the client as an individual with sexual needs. Support from partner and family can be of great assistance in adapting to the changes in body image.

The self-esteem of the client with cancer suffers tremendously when the ability to fulfill prescribed roles diminishes. Changes in sex role can lead to feelings of worthlessness and problems justifying their existence. Sharing intimacy and giving pleasure can increase a personal sense of worth (MacElveen-Hoehn and McCorkle 1985).

DIABETES Physical sexual response changes in men with diabetes include initial severe metabolic compensation that is associated with impotence; this usually resolves once the metabolic control is attained. Over time, sexual function is affected by the duration of the illness and the presence of autonomic neuropathy. Neither men nor women with diabetes are likely to experience any change in sexual desire. Impotence may develop gradually in men as a result of damage to blood vessels and nerves supplying the genitals. Women experience decreased amounts of vaginal secretions and may have a tendency to develop vaginal infections. Many diabetic women have a marked increase in sensory threshhold for orgasm and require greater and longer periods of stimulation (Manley 1986).

ALCOHOLISM Since moderate consumption of alcohol frequently facilitates sexual exchange by lowering inhibitions, many people believe that alcohol is a stimulant and that it promotes sexual liberty. In actuality, alcohol is a depressant which, after the initial period of euphoria, causes drowsiness, delayed or partial erections, or delayed ejaculations.

As a chemical depressant in the brain, alcohol directly inhibits sexual response and affects the sexual cycle in both sexes. Peripheral neuropathy, a side effect of alcohol, can cause impotence (Renshaw 1986). Counseling for clients with alcoholism should include the effects of alcohol intake on sexual activity. Approaches for these clients can be found in Chapter 10.

SPINAL CORD INJURIES Spinal cord injuries usually result in loss of mobility, and alteration in function is severe. Until recently, these clients were viewed as asexual beings, but now paralyzed clients and their partners are receiving sex education and therapy. Erection and ejaculation are controlled by spinal nerves. Despite a cord lesion, some men experience a bypass sympathetic erotic erection as well as reflex erection. Other paraplegic men however, have only unpredictable, nonerotic reflex erections that are not under control and may not be sexually useful. Some clients with spinal cord injuries are fitted with silicone penile prostheses to enhance their sexual performance. Others develop alternative methods (oral, manual) for sexual satisfaction with their partners. Women with paraplegia can become pregnant and have painless vaginal delivery. Intercourse remains satisfying even though legs and pelvic muscles are unable to provide the contractions of orgasm (Renshaw 1986).

MENTAL RETARDATION Mentally handicapped individuals are frequently treated as if they had no sexual identity. This occurs not only in institutional settings but in group homes, workshops, school, and in the home. Parents who are afraid to teach the mentally handicapped about sexuality ignore the issue. Attempts to involve parents of these clients in sex education workshops have been unrewarding.

Although mentally handicapped individuals are being integrated into communities and are trying to become involved, society has only accepted that it is "allowable" for the mentally retarded to be sexually active but has not advanced further than that. The biggest problem for these clients is sexual exploitation and, because of their increased freedom in the community, they are being taken advantage of at a high rate (Peakman 1986).

TERMINAL ILLNESS The terminally ill client is at risk for severe sexual deprivation. Sexuality is a normal part of all stages of life, including dying. It is important to remember that all persons are sexual beings, including the dying client. Clients and their loved ones (who are usually their caretakers) can be assisted in maintaining their sexuality in different ways. Assistance in grooming and special attention to small aspects such as perfume or after-shave can help the client deal with feelings of uncleanliness and being untouchable. Attention should be given to signs of neglect in the appearance of the caregivers as this may indicate fatigue and frustration on their part.

The need to touch and be touched is one of the greatest of human needs. At times caregivers can become so involved in the actual physical care that the need for close and intimate touching gets forgotten. Fear of hurting the client or intimidation by the disease process can also result in depriving the client of physical contact. At times clients who are dying have a strong desire to engage in sexual activity. They may not have the strength or energy to do so, but they may have the desire to try. They should be given permission to engage in any form of sex that is satisfying to them if at all possible (Caruso 1986).

Implications for Nursing In concern for the client who is experiencing difficulties with physical illness, the ramifications of the influence of chronic illness on the client's partner are often overlooked. Supporting the partner may be one of the most important goals in the nursing care plan. The sexual self-image of the client is likely to be a reflection of the partner's overt or covert perceptions. Communication must be facilitated to aid in the adjustment process. The reaction of the partner must be considered. Some may feel helpless; others, angry or guilty. They may be confused or misunderstand the reactions of the client to the illness, not knowing whether the client's anger or depression is due to the illness or something they have done. They may not know how to respond to their ill partner; false reassurances and cheerfulness are less than helpful.

Partners are faced with conflicting demands. Often the need to maintain outside role performance yet meet the additional supportive needs of the client can cause difficulties. Partners have many opportunities for guilt—they feel guilty for being angry and resentful at the disruption in their lives, often wishing they did not have to cope with the problem. They may also feel guilty about their own health and their own unmet needs (MacElveen-Hoehn 1985).

Frequently sexual health is omitted from a client's care plan. Healthy sexual adaptation is just as important as any other adjustment to a physical illness. Education in sexual health should be integrated with professional care at all levels. Nurses practicing in any area need to teach clients to deal with sex and their sexuality in an open and healthy way. It is important to ask clients how they feel about themselves as men or women and assess the self-concept related to sexuality.

If sexual issues are a part of the problem for mentally ill clients, it is necessary to identify the clients' problems and strengths. The clients must be given permission to talk about sexuality. One of the best means of facilitating the discussion is for the nurse to provide a role model, displaying comfort in talking about the subject (Stewart 1986).

This section has delineated the need for sexual guidance during physical illnesses unrelated to sexual behavior. In addition, there is a need for recognition and counseling for those clients who become ill as a direct result of their sexual activities. The next section describes sexually transmitted disease and recommended nursing interventions for those clients.

SEXUALLY TRANSMITTED DISEASES

Infectious diseases that are spread through sexual contact were identified early in the history of the human race. The incidence and prevalence of these infections have varied in different periods of time. Concern about venereal disease was less evident during the 1960s and 1970s in part because of the use of antibiotics which have been successful in treating these conditions. However, with the advent of the sexually transmitted disease AIDS (acquired immune deficiency syndrome), interest and research efforts have increased dramatically. Unfortunately, some of the other infections that have been controlled in the past are now developing strains that are resistant to antibiotics. There is concern among health care providers that the continued emphasis on AIDS is causing some neglect of other infections that need attention at this time.

Although there are a wide variety of sexually transmitted infections, this section only describes the most common ones and their implications. Syphilis has always been a common disease that is distributed worldwide, with the largest concentration in major cities. From 1956 to 1987 incidence of this disease increased five-fold. Reported cases are believed to represent only a tip of the iceberg (Smith 1987). The disease has, to a large extent, gone underground and should be exposed. Syphilis is caused by a spirochete called *Treponema Pallidium*, and penicillin is the drug of choice for treatment.

Gonorrhea is the most common reportable sexually transmitted disease and has been endemic in the world for centuries. The disease reached epidemic proportions in the 1960s in the United States. This infection is caused by *Neisseria gonorrhoeae*, which has developed resistant strains to both penicillin and tetracycline. The most recently recommended treatment for the gonococcus is a cephalosporin antibiotic (Hook 1987). Clients may contract gonorrhea many times. Many infections are asymptomatic. Gonorrhea, along with Chlamydia infections, is one of the most common causes of pelvic inflammatory disease in women and a major cause of infertility and ectopic pregnancy.

Chlamydial infection was described as early as 2700 B.C., by the Chinese. It was prevalent in the Middle Ages and during the Napoleonic Wars but has only recently been identified and classified (Larson and Nachamkin 1985). Infections are caused by two species: *Chlamydia trachomatis* and *C. psittaci*. Persons who use barrier methods of contraception such as condoms with spermicide, have less risk of infection. Penicillin does not cure chlamydia, but the infection can be treated with tetracycline or erythromycin (Loucks 1987).

Over the past ten years, there has been a pronounced increase in the number of cases of genital herpes. The disease is caused by the herpes simplex virus type 2 but genital infection with type 1, usually associated with cold sores, is seen with increasing frequency. One of the most distressing features of this infection is its tendency to recur on a continuing basis.

Implications for Nursing Case finding and follow up of contacts have been a function of nurses in public health for many years. Nurses practicing in other areas need to be aware of the continuing threat of venereal disease. Clients should be educated concerning the spread and infectivity of the disease, and the need to follow the prescribed medical regimen. Counseling for clients with venereal disease should include permission to verbalize feelings that are common when the realization of having contracted a venereal disease begins. Anger at the sexual partner, shock, and disbelief are frequent reactions. In order to avoid frightening the client away from health care, the client's beliefs about sexually transmitted disease should be explored to dispel myths and provide accurate information. Clients should be encouraged to have their partners seek care also. The benefits of using a condom and/or spermicide should be explained and encouraged to prevent future infections. Clients should be aware of the lack of immunity, resistance to drug therapy, and large number of asymptomatic infections. Since stress is believed to be a major factor in the recurrence of herpes, stress management should be included in any counseling of these clients.

ACQUIRED IMMUNE DEFICIENCY SYNDROME AIDS was first identified in 1981 in California when two patients died from a pneumonia that seldom killed anyone. The pneumonia was lethal in these cases because the immune system in these individuals was suppressed. Since that time, the knowledge of the disease, related research efforts, and education aimed at containment of the syndrome have expanded at a rapid rate. Because of the acceleration in research and epidemiological findings, it is difficult to make an assessment of the present and future impact of this syndrome. Any published material should be constantly updated to obtain an accurate picture of AIDS.

It is now recognized that AIDS is an infectious disease caused by a retrovirus, human T lymphotropic virus type III (HTLV-III LAV) (Redfield 1986). There are three stages of the disease: the first stage, when the client is infected but has no symptoms; the second, known as Aids Related Complex, in which the client experiences weight loss, swollen glands, fever, and night sweats; and the third, which is characterized by Kaposi's sarcoma and pneumocystis carinii pneumonia. AIDS was originally thought to be a disease of homosexuals, particularly gay men. However, it is now known that AIDS can be transmitted by sexual activity between males and females as well. AIDS may also be contacted from blood transfusions (this is becoming a remote possibility, due to screening), sharing IV drug apparatus, and from mother to the unborn infant.

Because control of this disease may be several years away, the response of the general public has included extensive educational campaigns. The predominant message has been "safe sex" for both men and women, advocating the use of condoms for all sexual encounters to reduce the spread of the syndrome. Spermicidal gels also increase protection. The nation's homosexual community has become unified as never before. Support groups are established, and high-risk behavior has been reduced. The advent of AIDS may well bring about a revolution in sexual practices for both sexes.

Implications for Nursing The physical and psychological ramifications of AIDS and the AIDS Related Complex provide what may be the greatest challenge in many years to the health care professions. Individual providers are concerned for their own safety and the number of interventions they must perform.

AIDS has brought out both the best and the worst in all members of the health care team. There have been instances of refusal to give care as well as

dedicated, concerned nurturance to the AIDS victim. In the hospital setting, caregivers can protect themselves by following the same blood and body fluid precautions as they would for a patient with hepatitis B. Artificial respiration can be given with artificial airways and Ambu bags. Mouth-to-mouth contact should be avoided since the AIDS virus is present in saliva (Webster 1987).

Families should know these same precautions when they care for the client at home. Nurses should recognize and address personal feelings and values about homosexuality, drug abuse, and death in order to give unconditional, positive regard to the AIDS patient. They should spend time with clients to open communication. Eye contact and therapeutic touch help to minimize the effects of distancing.

AIDS has created one of the greatest crises for families that they may ever face. They must learn to cope with their grief and shame. They also must cope with their anger at the AIDS victim. Because of the disease's association with homosexuality and drug abuse, families feel stigmatized, secretive, and afraid of contamination and of the unknown (Walker 1987).

Support groups established in a variety of forms are available for family referral. Churches, gay groups, and volunteers are all working to provide a network for clients and their families.

Psychiatric team members should be aware of the depression, delirium, and denial that may be present in the AIDS client.

Countertransference problems can develop in caregivers to the extent that they fear contagion and have a tendency to stereotype the client on the basis of being a member of a high-risk group. Emotional distancing can deprive the client of the empathetic relationship appropriate for a client with a fatal disease (Perry and Markowitz 1986).

The presence of clients with AIDS-related dementia on a psychiatric unit requires changes in the therapeutic milieu. Clients with HIV-related dementia are challenging because of their need for physical care. The fluctuating cognitive abilities, loss of self-care functions, and the disfiguring symptoms of Kaposi's sarcoma and emaciation all exacerbate the client's sense of isolation. Touch, often contraindicated in psychiatry, is an essential part of daily care.

Clients with other diagnoses may have difficulty responding and interacting with the client with AIDS-related dementia because they have trouble understanding that young people can be demented. Some may incorporate the AIDS client in their delusional system and express fears of contagion.

Demented clients are unable to respond to limits set to promote change in behavior in therapeutic milieus. Decreasing memory, increasing impulsiveness, and perseveration make behavior modification techniques minimally effective. Establishing routines for meals, toileting, and recreation can be of some assistance in minimizing new stimuli.

Infection control guidelines need to be developed and followed meticulously. Protective coverage is necessary if the client becomes assaultive and requires restraint, to minimize the contact with bodily secretions.

The need for, and response to, psychoactive medication changes as the mental status changes. Demented clients are susceptible to side effects and toxicity. Clients with progressive neurological impairment due to HIV may not require ongoing medication, and if such therapy is given, it should be in low doses.

Since it is difficult for AIDS clients to participate in the larger therapeutic milieu, staff must make decisions regarding the involvement of these clients on a case-by-case basis. The tendency to encourage physically healthy clients into the milieu and allow those with dementia to withdraw must receive continued attention (Baer et al. 1987).

ALTERNATIVE SEX ROLE ENACTMENT

Much of the material in the preceding sections of this chapter apply to both homosexual and heterosexual couples. However, homosexual individuals and persons who enact other sex roles often have needs and problems that differ from those of heterosexual individuals.

Homosexuality

The word *homosexual* is used to describe the sexual orientation of men and women who find their primary emotional and sexual fulfillment with people of the same sex. Homosexuality is only an aspect of personality, as is heterosexuality. Identifying people solely by their choice of sex partners tends to belittle them; it conveys the impression that homosexuals' only interest is in sex. Other aspects of an individual's personality tend to be ignored when sexual labels are applied, so such labels should be used carefully and with the understanding that the only basic difference between heterosexual and homosexual people is in their preference of sexual partners.

Our culture's negative attitude toward homosexuality has been strongly influenced by religious teachings that hold homosexuality to be sinful and by psychoanalytic theory, which has traditionally held that homosexuality is an emotional disorder caused by arrested psychosexual development. According to traditional psychoanalytic theory, homosexuality can be attributed to an unresolved masochistic attachment to the pre-Oedipal mother, a distant relationship with the father, a defense against castration anxiety, or an immature ego (Bell and Weinberg 1978, Carrera 1981). Other unproven theories about the causes of homosexuality include a fetal hormonal imbalance, peer pressure, and learning processes. (It is perhaps revealing that theorists have not tended to address the broader question of what causes *any* sexual orientation, whether homosexual or heterosexual. Until this broader question is answered, the causes of homosexuality cannot be fully understood.)

Homophobia, a strong, irrational fear of homosexuals or the fear of homosexual feelings within oneself, is so widespread in our society that many homosexuals are robbed or assaulted by people who feel they "deserve" to be punished. Homosexuals are often regarded as safe targets by criminals because they may be reluctant to press charges out of fear of exposure and publicity. In one study (Bell and Weinberg 1978), one third of homosexual men reported that they had been assaulted and robbed at least once in connection with their homosexuality. It was also found that 25 percent of homosexual men and women had been threatened with blackmail about their sexual preference.

MYTHS ABOUT HOMOSEXUALITY

Widespread ignorance about homosexuality in this country leads to the perpetuation of many myths. Nurses, as professionals, have a responsibility to counteract these myths with accurate information. The following are some of the common myths about gay people:

You can tell gay people just by looking at them.

Homosexual people are pretty much alike.

They could change if they really wanted to.

They make poor parents.

In a relationship, one plays the part of the woman and the other plays the part of the man.

Gay teachers will persuade young people to become gay.

Gays are sexually attracted to children.

Homosexual people are responsible for the majority of sexual violence.

In our culture, men appear to be more homophobic than women and more threatened by male than female homosexuals. Behaviors that demonstrate homophobia are making "queer" jokes, disparaging homosexuality, and verbally or physically assaulting homosexual people. Homophobic men tend to have rigid gender role stereotypes lest they be thought of as homosexuals. They avoid behavior that might be seen as homosexual by others, such as choosing "feminine" professions, hugging friends and relatives of the same sex, and engaging in oral-genital sex or manual-genital contact, even with their wives.

Homosexual behavior has been decriminalized in many countries, but most states in America still have laws against homosexual behavior. The sodomy laws make persons engaging in oral sex and anal intercourse subject to arrest and trial. Homosexuals are often also arrested for loitering to solicit and for disorderly conduct. Police officers at times use entrapment by posing as decoys soliciting sex. Homosexual people also have their civil rights infringed on in the area of housing and employment. They are discriminated against in the areas of credit, insurance coverage, divorce, child custody, and adoption. Because there cannot be a legal marriage, they have difficulties with tax benefits and property and inheritance rights.

A more liberal attitude toward homosexuality is beginning to emerge as churches reexamine their traditional attitudes and psychologists offer new studies and opinions. Alfred Kinsey's studies in 1948 and 1953 demonstrated that millions of Americans had engaged in homosexual behavior. His surveys showed that 50 percent of men and 28 percent of women had had some homosexual experience during their lives. These studies made it very clear that a person's sexual preference is not fixed and that sexual orientation can be seen as a continuum. Kinsey developed a six-point scale that rates people from "entirely heterosexual" to "entirely homosexual." He found that nearly half of people fell between these two end points. Kinsey's studies support the view that there is a natural variation of sexual expression among humans.

Traditionally, therapists working with homosexual clients have tended to assume homosexual persons would like to relinquish their sexual orientation if they could. However, it has been shown that many homosexual men and women have no regrets about being homosexual. Homosexual adults who have come to terms with their sexual orientation don't regret it; they can function sexually and socially and are no more distressed than heterosexual adults (Bell and Weinberg 1978).

Homosexual people are generally thought to be very unstable in their work situations due to emotional instability. There is no evidence of greater job instability for homosexuals than for their heterosexual counterparts.

Homosexual relationships are often thought to follow rigid patterns, but in reality they are as varied as heterosexual relationships, with the same joys, sorrows, commitments, and breakups. Researchers have identified four basic homosexual relationship styles to which 71 percent of the sample could be assigned. In a *close-couple* relationship the partners are closely bound and relate in a quasi-marital style. These couples seldom go out to gay bars or baths, report fewer sexual problems and have fewer partners than other homosexuals, and they report little regret over their sexual orientation.

Open-couple relationships are also quasi-marital, but individuals in these relationships tend to have more partners, to have more sexual problems, and to participate in more "cruising." (Cruising is the act of frequenting known gay establishments in hopes of finding new sexual partners.)

Persons considered to have a *functional* style of homosexuality are "single" people who have a number of partners, a high level of sexual activity, little regret about their orientation, and few sexual problems. Functional homosexuals are more overt about their homosexuality and more energetic and optimistic than other types.

The last type of homosexual behavior is *asexual*. These people are more covert than those in the other groups, are not coupled, have few partners, and describe themselves as lonely. They also have a lower level of sexual desire and activity than those in the other groups.

Stereotypes of homosexual men as being highly promiscuous and homosexual women as interested in a permanent "marriage" correspond with general sex stereotypes that men focus on sex and women on affection and commitment. It is true that men—straight or gay—are more easily able to separate sex from affection and that they tend to evaluate themselves by their sexual prowess. Therefore, it is no surprise that homosexual men tend to have more partners than homosexual women and are more apt to have sex with a stranger.

Another myth is that homosexual couples take on sex roles in their relationships, one person being dominant ("the man") and the other submissive ("the woman"). Although this may happen at times, homosexual couples are actually less likely to embrace dominant and submissive roles than are heterosexual couples. The homosexual couple could well serve as a model of equality for heterosexuals.

Another common assumption is that certain sexual behaviors and practices are exclusively homosexual. In reality, homosexual people make love in much the same way as heterosexual people, except that they do not engage in penis-vagina intercourse. Homosexual couples kiss, caress, and stroke each other. In descending order of frequency, men use oral sex, hand-genital stimulation, and anal intercourse. Homosexual women use hand-genital contact most often, followed by oral sex and body rubbing. Contrary to popular belief, only 2 percent of homosexuals use dildos in their lovemaking. None of these practices is exclusive to the homosexual population (Bell and Weinberg 1978, Crooks and Baur 1983).

Homosexual people are often thought to be consumed by their uncontrollable desire for sexual activity. Some heterosexuals fear that homosexuals lie in wait to proposition them in public restrooms, movie theaters, or parks. But 40 percent of homosexual men do no cruising at all, and those who do usually do it in the safer setting of a gay bar or bath. Most homosexual activity takes place in the privacy of homes (Bell and Weinberg 1978).

Homosexual men and women are also more likely to have more close friendships than heterosexual people. Perhaps this is because family commitments take priority over friendships among heterosexuals. Gay people tend to have both heterosexual and homosexual friends. Very few heterosexuals report that they have one or more friends of the same sex whom they know to be homosexual (Bell and Weinberg 1978).

Homosexuality and Psychiatry

The official position of the American Psychiatric Association in 1980 was that homosexuality in itself was not a disease. DSM-III described ego-dystonic homosexuality as a disorder. A person in this category was one who wished to become heterosexual and whose homosexual arousal was a persistent source of distress.

Subsequently the DSM-III-R has eliminated this category because most people who are homosexual go through a phase in which their homosexuality is uncomfortable (American Psychiatric Association 1987). Homosexuality is still used in the ICD-9CM codes, however.

Perhaps no other aspect of human sexual behavior is as controversial today as homosexuality. It is to be hoped that knowledge and understanding of homosexual behavior will help the public reach a more tolerant view.

Bisexuality

Many people fall on the continuum between exclusive heterosexual behavior and exclusive homosexual behavior. *Bisexuality* is defined as erotic attraction to and sexual fulfillment with people of both sexes. This definition excludes homosexual people who are married to maintain a pretense of hetero-

sexuality or those who choose partners of other than the preferred sex when partners of the preferred sex are not available. Kinsey (1948, 1953) found that 18 percent of the men in his study and between 4 and 11 percent of the women had had as much homosexual as heterosexual experience. Bisexuality is as real an orientation as heterosexuality or homosexuality.

There are variations among the lifestyles of bisexual people just as there are among homosexual and heterosexual people. Bisexuality may be classified as transitional, historical, sequential, or concurrent. A *transitional* bisexual person is in movement from either heterosexual or homosexual preference to the opposite preference. During the time of transition, the person appears to be bisexual. The person who is *historically* bisexual had sexual experience in the past that was the opposite of his or her basic orientation. *Sequential* bisexuality occurs when a person is involved in heterosexual and same-sex relationships at different times. The number of such relationships varies among individuals (Klein 1978). *Concurrent* bisexuality occurs when a person engages in simultaneous sexual relationships with both women and men.

Bisexuality has received less attention in the medical literature than homosexuality until very recently. The persistent belief that people are either heterosexual or homosexual and never in between has left this sexual orientation poorly researched and understood. It has been difficult for scientists and laymen alike to believe that people can feel desire, gratification, and delight with members of both sexes. Bisexuals are frequently viewed with contempt by both heterosexual and homosexual people. It is commonly thought that the bisexual person has not yet arrived at his or her true preference or that the bisexuality is a fearful compromise. Therefore it is quite common for the bisexual person to feel alienated and oppressed by both homosexual and heterosexual people. At the time of this writing there are very few support systems available for bisexual individuals, but as more "come out," support systems will emerge, just as they have for homosexuals.

Celibacy

Celibacy is a voluntary choice not to engage in sexual activity with other people. A person may choose celibacy either temporarily or permanently. There are many reasons a person may choose to be celibate, including dedication to a religious vocation, postponement of sex until marriage for moral or religious reasons, unavailability of one's partner, avoidance of sexually transmitted diseases, disappointment in past sexual relationships, or the protection of a newly developing relationship. For some people, celibacy may be a temporary necessity when other aspects of their lives assume precedence. Celibacy can be a beneficial choice for some people. It can enable them to conduct emotional self-exploration or regrouping apart from the conflicts of a sexual relationship. Sexual frustration need not occur during the time of celibacy because sexual pleasure through self-stroking and masturbation often provides an acceptable alternative to the individual.

Transvestism

A *transvestite* is usually defined as a person who finds sexual stimulation in cross-dressing, or wearing clothing of the opposite sex. Most transvestites are male heterosexuals. A minority of male homosexuals also cross-dress, but primarily to parody women with misogynistic intent (Freedman, Kaplan, and Sadock 1976). Female impersonators differ from transvestites in that they cross-dress to entertain rather than to express their female gender identity. The form of transvestism can vary from one individual to another. Cross-dressing may be limited to an article or two of women's underwear or may consist of an entire outfit, including makeup and a wig. Some transvestites cross-dress only occasionally and have no gender identity conflict. At the other end of the continuum are men who cross-dress as often as possible and who maintain their masculine identity with less conviction.

The transvestite cross-dresses to create the illusion of femininity—that is, "to pass" as a woman. Cross-dressing is not a vehicle for satire at women's expense; it is done primarily for sexual arousal. Some men move beyond the fetishistic stage and are no longer sexually excited by cross-dressing. These men go on to a more total form of female "passing" and take their aspirations to femininity seriously. They make genuine attempts to behave as well as to dress as women. The transvestite can live and work as a man without anyone knowing about his obsession. He is rarely effeminate in his male role (Ackroyd 1979).

Cross-dressing is not harmful in itself, nor is it dangerous to other people. Its most distressing result may be the disapproval of family members. Some transvestites hide their cross-dressing from their wives in fear of being misunderstood or rejected. Some wives who discover that their husbands are transvestites mistakenly assume that their husbands are homosexual. Other wives feel that their own sexuality and sexual identity are placed in doubt. After their initial surprise, many wives are eventually able to understand and accept their husbands' needs to cross-dress. Some transvestites are able to share this component of their personality with other family members, while others keep it hidden from them. There are societies for transvestites in many countries, and support groups are becoming active in this country. The Human Outreach and Achievement Institute in Boston is an educational group that offers informational programs for the helping professions and services for those concerned with gender issues.

Transsexualism

Gender is a person's biological maleness or femaleness; *gender identity* refers to a person's inner psychological conviction of feeling male or female. *Gender roles* are culturally determined rules about tasks, expectations, and feelings considered appropriate for each gender. Cultural rules determine what is considered "normal" and "abnormal" within a culture. *Transsexualism* is considered a disorder of gender identity: a person born as a biological male or female believes that he or she was born with a body that does not match his or her internal identity. Transsexualism is a lifelong cross-gender identification that can be traced back as far as early childhood.

Chemical, family, and social factors have been proposed as causes of transsexualism. The most likely cause appears to be hormonal. Transsexualism appears to be related to two syndromes of genital malformation. *Testicular feminization syndrome* occurs when a biochemical defect prevents testosterone from developing the genitals of a genetically male fetus; from birth the child is considered female. *Adrenogenital syndrome* occurs when a genetically female fetus produces large amounts of androgen so that it develops almost normal male genitals. It has been postulated that transsexualism is an incomplete testicular feminization or adrenogenital syndrome. In the male fetus, the genitals differentiate earlier. In a transsexual male, there may have been insufficient androgen to masculinize the sex-specific areas of the hypothalamus at the critical time. In a female transsexual, the androgenic influences may have been high at the critical time of hypothalamic development although not at the time of genital formation. This biological determinant theory is yet to be confirmed by research (Klein 1978, Carrera 1981).

Since transsexualism is a life-long characteristic, these people know that they are different very early in life. Some are fearful that they are "insane" and do not discuss their feelings out of fear. Others may marry in hope of adjusting to accepted standards of sexual behavior. Male transsexuals who desire relationships with heterosexual males do so not because they consider themselves homosexual but rather because they consider themselves female.

Because gender identity is fixed at a very early age for all people, the mind of the transsexual cannot be adjusted to the body; there is no evidence of cures by psychotherapy. It therefore seems appropriate to adjust the body to the mind with surgery. There are gender identity clinics at many major hospitals and universities where the transsexual can undergo medical tests to determine his health status and psychological tests to determine his emotional stability. For a period of one to two years the transsexual must live the life of the intended sex and prove that he can survive socially, financially, and emotionally in his new role. Hormone treatment is begun during this period. Anatomical males receive estrogen, which increases breast development, decreases erections and body hair, and softens the skin. Electrolysis may be used to remove unwanted facial hair, and the person may take voice training. Anatomical females receive androgen, which deepens the voice, coarsens the skin, increases body hair, causes hypertrophy of the clitoris, and stops menstruation. The transsexual continues in counseling during this phase of the treatment program.

The final phase of treatment is surgery, which merely confirms what has already occurred in the social and work life of the person. In the male-to-female transsexual, the penis is amputated and the testicles are removed. A vagina is created and is lined with skin from the penis. Breasts are augmented and the laryngeal cartilage may be reduced. In the female-to-male transsexual, the breasts are reduced and a hysterectomy and oophorectomy are performed. A penis is constructed, using a tube flap of skin from the lower abdomen, and the clitoris is embedded in the new penis. A urinary conduit is run through the penis and a prosthesis may be implanted to allow for erections. The vaginal opening is closed, and a scrotum is fashioned from labial tissue with insertion of plastic testicles. Postoperative transsexuals are heterosexual in their orientation and are able to function sexually with partners. Both males and females maintain their orgasmic ability (Hogan 1980).

After surgery the transsexual must apply to the courts for a name change and then follow through with changes in licenses, social security, and passports. Some states will issue a new birth certificate, but others will not. Insurance companies discriminate against transsexuals, and it is very difficult for them to obtain health and life insurance.

When the transsexual makes the decision to have sex-change surgery there may be a great deal of family distress. Spouses may feel bewildered, shamed, guilty, or angry. They may need counseling to work through the feelings aroused by their partner's decision. Likewise, children of the transsexual will need counseling and support, as it may be very difficult for them to comprehend the situation. It is hoped that a meaningful future relationship can be developed and that the transsexual is not castigated for his or her behavior.

SEXUAL DYSFUNCTIONS

Sexual problems can result from psychological, sociological, spiritual, or physical distress, or a combination of these sources. Sexual dysfunctions can take many forms, including decreased or increased sexual interest, inhibitions, orgasm difficulties, and problems with satisfaction.

Decreased Sexual Interest

A decrease in sexual interest can occur in one or both sexual partners. Unless there is interest in sexual activity, arousal usually will not occur even in situations of intense stimulation. However, a desire for sex can vary; it is not usually an all-or-none phenomenon. Most people can recall times of illness, fatigue, preoccupation, or anger when their interest in sex was reduced. If both partners are similarly uninterested, there is no problem in the relationship. The disparity of needs, not the frequency of sexual activity, determines whether a lack of interest is dysfunctional.

Decreased sexual interest is most frequently situational and acquired, but it may be generalized or inherent. A combination of factors may contribute to the problem. Sometimes a decrease in intimacy occurs in a long-standing relationship. People become so involved in work, childrearing, and household management that their communication often becomes shallow and goal-oriented. A decrease in interdependency may lead to loss of feelings of closeness and a decreased interest in sexual interaction. A related complaint is that sex has simply become boring. Early in a relationship sexual activity involves discovery, novelty, and excitement. As relationships progress, some people feel they have explored all the alternatives and are bored with the same techniques and partner.

A change in self-perception may also precipitate decreased sexual interest. A person may believe that she has become less physically attractive with age and doesn't wish to "force herself" on her partner. The belief that older people lose interest in sex may also become a self-fulfilling prophecy. A person's self-image may be altered by illness or surgery and may produce feelings that are incompatible with sexual excitement. Likewise, a person who has been conditioned to consider the body dirty and shameful and sex as sinful may have difficulty in becoming interested in physical intimacy.

Situational disturbances may also interfere with sexual desire. These may include such things as loss of a job, financial worries, job dislike, or difficulties with children. The depression that often accompanies these disturbances is likely to lead to a significant decrease in sexual interest. Marital dissatisfaction is, of course, an obvious source of declining interest in sexual relations. Partners who are angry, bitter, or hurt are unlikely to want to share sexual intimacy. Any other type of sexual dysfunction may also reduce the interest of one or both partners. Since failure is emotionally painful, the person may begin to avoid sexual activity in order to avoid failure.

Increased Sexual Interest

An increase in sexual activity and interest frequently accompanies manic episodes in persons who are subject to bipolar disorders. As the person's mood elevates, there is an increase in gregariousness and an inflation of self-esteem. The person begins to seek not only more sexual activity but also a variety of partners, with little regard for the results of this behavior. At the height of a manic episode, the person may actually experience a paradoxical decrease in sexual activity. This occurs because the person is so busy trying to seduce everyone he or she meets that there is no time to consummate any of the relationships. When the manic episode ends, the person's sexual interest and activity return to normal.

Poorly integrated sexual activity, a high number of sexual partners, and little concern for the consequences of such behavior may also occur in the person with antisocial personality disorder. It is thought by some that this type of person functions with a hypomanic mood level much of the time, which may explain the variety of partners and activities.

Inhibitions

Erectile inhibition, or the inability to achieve an erection, is caused by insufficient vasocongestion. It may be either primary (never able to maintain an erection) or secondary (presently unable) and can occur in either heterosexual or homosexual men. The term commonly applied to this condition is *impotence*, but that term is pejorative since it implies that the man is weak, powerless, and ineffectual. The term erectile inhibition is now preferred to describe erectile difficulty objectively.

Situational erectile failure is often related to fatigue, anxiety, anger, or too much alcohol. Such episodes can lead to secondary erectile failure if the man experiencing them does not accept them as normal occurrences.

Although physiological causes are uncommon, a man with erectile inhibition should be assessed for drug use, diabetes, endocrine problems, and vascular or cardiopulmonary disease. Psychological factors related to primary erectile failure may include a sexually repressed upbringing, life experiences that have decreased the man's ability to trust and love, or a traumatic failure during his first attempt at sexual intercourse. Performance anxiety and interpersonal problems may also contribute to erectile failure. A homosexual male in a heterosexual marriage may develop erectile difficulties because of the conflict between his homosexual desires and the heterosexual stipulations of marriage. Some argue that the women's liberation movement has increased the incidence of erectile failure. However, an emotionally healthy man is not threatened by a woman who is assertive and active in the lovemaking process. Most men delight in women who enjoy and accept some of the responsibility for sexual activity (Hogan 1980).

Inhibition of vaginal lubrication, like erectile inhibition, is due to insufficient vasocongestion. Lubrication is the woman's first physiological response to sexual arousal. A variety of factors, including anger, fear, conflict, and decreased estrogen levels, may be the cause. Insufficient vaginal lubrication may cause aching, burning, and itching of the vagina during intercourse and may also cause pain for the male. It is important for women to know that vaginal lubrication naturally decreases during prolonged coitus. A water-soluble lubricant may be helpful in such cases.

Vaginismus is a strong, involuntary contraction of the muscles in the outer third of the vagina that makes penile penetration impossible. A woman does not consciously cause vaginismus. It is a conditioned, involuntary response to frightening, painful, or conflicting situations. A woman suffering from this dysfunction can learn to prevent these contractions through various relaxation techniques and behavior modification.

Orgasm Difficulties

In the past, nonorgasmic women were commonly referred to as *frigid*, but like "impotence," frigidity is an emotionally laden term that denigrates a woman's personality without specifically describing her difficulty with sexual response and enjoyment. Some women are *preorgasmic*, that is, they have never experienced orgasm by any means. Other women may be *secondarily nonorgasmic* in that they have experienced orgasm in the past or with a different partner. They may experience interest, arousal, lubrication, and enjoyment but their response stops before orgasm. Physiologically, the difficulty may be related to fatigue or to neurologic or vascular damage. A more common cause is psychogenic; it may be related to lack of knowledge, ineffective techniques, a negative attitude about sex, lack of feelings of intimacy, traumatic life events, fear of pregnancy, fear of losing control, or homosexual conflict (Hogan 1980).

Rapid ejaculation may be defined in a variety of ways, but usually as ejaculation that is so quick that the man or his partner experience decreased enjoyment. This common male problem may be caused by anxiety, anger, or the tendency to hurry in early experiences, which has led to a conditioned response.

Ejaculatory inhibition is the inability to ejaculate during intercourse. This is a relatively rare problem and may be primary or secondary. Possible organic causes are drugs and neurologic conditions. Psychogenic explanations may be fear of causing pregnancy, guilt, interpersonal problems, or a compulsive personality that is afraid of losing control during orgasm.

Problems with Satisfaction

A person may be dissatisfied with sexual activity even though able to achieve arousal and orgasm. Disappointments about the length of time of lovemaking, the frequency of sexual activity, or the quality of satisfaction are common. The following conditions are important for a person to achieve fulfillment.

1. His or her personal rights should not be violated through the use of manipulation or force.
2. His or her experience should be compatible with his or her value system.
3. The relationship with his or her partner should be sensitive, caring, and tender rather than aggressive, competitive, or controlling.
4. He or she should be able to relate to his or her partner in a variety of ways.

Sexual health, then, is a process rather than a goal. It may be defined as the ability to relate responsibly with a partner in an intimate, fulfilling, and mutually pleasing manner that is compatible with one's chosen lifestyle.

SEXUAL DEVIANCE

In DSM-III-R, *paraphilia* is used to refer to deviant sexual behavior in which unusual acts or fantasies are required for sexual arousal or sexual satisfaction. Sexual imagery often plays a part in sexual acts performed by consenting adults, but the term paraphilia is usually applied to fantasies that are acted out in some bizarre fashion. In order for sexual behaviors to be labeled deviant, psychological rather than physiological factors must play a major etiologic role. Disorders that have an organic cause may lead to psychological consequences, but they are not considered paraphilias. Transsexualism, for example, is not considered a paraphilia. The recognized forms of paraphilia include fetishism, zoophilia, pedophilia, exhibitionism, voyeurism, and necrophilia.

Fetishism

Fetishism is the achievement of sexual excitement by the substitution of an inanimate object (such as a glove or a shoe) or parts of the body (such as a lock of hair) for a sexual partner. Orgasm is achieved by fondling the fetish object, by looking at it, by masturbating onto it, or by having sexual intercourse with a partner in its presence. Usually the fetish object is associated with some childhood experience; the need for the fetish may begin in adolescence and continue into adulthood.

This extreme attachment to certain objects occurs more often in men than women, and it is possible that fears of mature genital expression may be alleviated by the symbolic meaning or reassurance conveyed by the fetish object. Many forms of fetishism are harmless; innumerable people find themselves aroused by a certain melody or aroma, for example. Other forms, however, require a nonconsenting donor who may be frightened even if not seriously harmed. Some behavioral modification programs may be helpful, and psychotherapy is sometimes recommended to explore the symbolic meaning of the fetish. The motivation of the fetishist and the possible victimization of others are crucial considerations in deciding whether treatment is indicated and what form it should take.

Zoophilia

Zoophilia is the use of animals as sexual objects or partners. It is probably more common in rural communities where people are isolated from human companionship for months at a time. Sometimes zoophilia stems from isolation and sexual frustration. When continued, the person practicing zoophilia may eventually respond sexually only to animals rather than humans. The custom is not always restricted to farm animals and their lonely keepers. Occasionally household pets may be trained to lick or rub against their human owners in a manner that generates sexual excitement and orgasm in the human partner.

Frotteurism

Recurrent sexual gratification derived (usually by males) from touching or rubbing against a nonconsenting person (usually female) is called *frotteurism*. Acts of frottage occur most often between 15 to 25 years; after these ages urgency and frequency of episodes decrease. Acts are accompanied by fantasies of a sexual relationship with the nonconsenting person. Perpetrators are often distressed by their own behaviors and feel ashamed and guilty.

Unlike exhibitionists, who seem to want to be discovered, frotteurists operate in crowded places such as buses or theaters, where they can rub against a selected person without the action's being noticed. Even the person they rub against may assume the contact was accidental and hesitate to object.

Pedophilia

Pedophilia, or the use of children as sex objects and sex partners by adults, is quite common, although it is one of the least acceptable forms of deviance. A pedophile may be either heterosexual, bisexual, or homosexual. A bisexual or heterosexual pedophile is more likely to be attracted to prepubescent children, usually girls between the ages of eight and ten. Homosexuals usually choose older children of the same sex. It is possible for women to commit sexual abuse of male and female children, but the socialization of women for centuries has encouraged sublimation of female sexuality, which may explain why relatively few women make sexual advances to children. A number of lesbian groups have made official statements opposing the sexual exploitation of children by any adult, regardless of sexual preference (Finkelhor 1979).

The sexual act may be limited to fondling, but penetration of a child by an adult male can be extremely traumatic, physically and psychologically, to the child. Current estimates show that ten times as many girls as boys are molested, but projected estimates indicate that if present trends continue, 25 percent of all girls born today will be molested before reaching age thirteen, and 10 percent of all boys born today will be molested in childhood by an adult (Rush 1980).

Exhibitionism

Exhibitionism is the morbid compulsion to expose the genitals to a member of the opposite sex. Usually the exhibitionist is a male who wishes to affirm his manhood by startling the viewer. The exhibitionist rarely represents a genuine danger to others. This behavior is repetitive and compulsive; the exhibitionist frequently returns to the same neighborhood, exposes his genitals, and, by witnessing the fear of his audience, may become aroused and orgasmic. Exhibitionists are often apprehended because they repeat their behavior in the same vicinity. Treatment is mandated by the courts. Often exhibitionists suffer from a deep sense of inadequacy. Their prognosis for change is only fair. As with most forms of sexual deviance, motivation to change is a significant factor in recovery.

DSM-III-R CLASSIFICATIONS

The following disorders discussed in this chapter are classified under Sexual Disorders.

Paraphilias

302.40 Exhibitionism
302.81 Fetishism
302.89 Frotteurism
302.20 Pedophilia
302.83 Sexual masochism
302.84 Sexual sadism
302.30 Transvestic fetishism
302.82 Voyeurism
302.90 Paraphilia not otherwise specified
　　　　(necrophilia, zoophilia)

Sexual Dysfunctions

302.71 Hypoactive sexual desire
302.79 Sexual aversion disorder
302.72 Female sexual arousal disorder
302.72 Male erectile disorder
302.73 Inhibited female orgasm
302.74 Inhibited male orgasm
302.75 Premature ejaculation
302.76 Dyspareunia
302.51 Vaginismus
302.70 Sexual dysfunction not otherwise
　　　　specified
Other disorders previously classified under sexual disorders are now found under Disorders Usually First Evident in Infancy, Childhood, and Adolescence.

Gender Identity Disorders

302.60 Gender identity disorder of childhood
302.50 Transsexualism
302.85 Gender identity disorder of
　　　　adolescence or adulthood,
　　　　nontranssexual type
302.85 Gender disorder not otherwise
　　　　specified

Voyeurism

Voyeurism is the practice of obtaining sexual gratification by observing persons who are naked, disrobing, or engaging in sexual acts. A certain amount of voyeurism is present in almost everyone, and the books we read, the films we see, and the magazines we buy testify to this human tendency. Many voyeurs watch but do not seek out sexual contact with the person or persons they observe. The voyeur may engage in masturbation while watching and derive satisfaction in this fashion. Sometimes the mere knowledge that the person being observed would feel humiliated if the presence of a "peeping Tom" were disclosed is in itself satisfying enough for the voyeur.

Necrophilia

There is a great deal of mythology surrounding *necrophilia*, or "love of the dead." Although no longer included in the list of paraphilias, this term is sometimes still used. For example, claims were made by both sides in the Viet Nam War that dead bodies were defiled sexually. It is also possible that necrophilia is a factor in crimes that involve murder and sexual mutilation, but it is difficult to find reliable, objective data.

SEXUAL ABUSE

Sexual abuse may be defined broadly as an act of a sexual nature that harms someone. The act can involve either verbal or physical mistreatment, and the person hurt may or may not consent to the abuse. Forms of sexual abuse include sadomasochism, incest, and sexual harassment.

Sadomasochism

The term *sadism* is derived from the name of the eighteenth-century French writer the Marquis de Sade, while the term *masochism* comes from the name of the nineteenth-century Austrian writer Leopold von Sacher-Masoch.

Sadomasochism is a paradoxical combination of pain and pleasure. The pain may be verbal (abusive language, threatening, humiliation) or physical (hitting, slapping, whipping). Both sadism and masochism tend to be chronic behaviors. Some people stay at the same level of activity; others need to gradually escalate the behavior to achieve sexual excitement.

Sadomasochistic activity is not the same as the nibbling and biting that some couples do in the height of sexual excitement. Such acts are not deliberate attempts to create pain or humiliation. People who have sadomasochistic fantasies that they do not act out are not considered sadomasochists.

Sadomasochistic activity may range from mild inclinations to extreme forms. Bondage and discipline are usually mild forms that use various types of restraint and verbal humiliation. Bondage is frequently symbolic rather than real, and pain is not usually a component of the act. It may be playful and harmless if done carefully and with a consenting partner. Sadomasochism becomes a deviance when inflicting or experiencing pain becomes a substitute for or the main source of pleasure during sexual activity. It is the exclusive mode of sexual functioning for some people. At the extreme end of the continuum is the sexual sadist who inflicts extensive and possibly fatal injury on a nonconsenting person. A person with this severe disorder may rape, torture, and even kill victims.

It appears that there are fewer sadists than there are masochists, but generally one does not exclude the other and a person is likely to alternate between the two variations. Some sadomasochists believe that somehow it is better to be punished than to impose pain, and they are even willing to pay people to inflict pain on them. Both heterosexual and homosexual people engage in sadomasochism, although one study showed that 90 percent of sadomasochistic activity is among heterosexual persons (Carrera 1981).

The causes of sadomasochism are not understood. One theory is that the sadistic person may have been taught as a child to loathe anything sexual. The guilt aroused during sexual activity is thought to be projected onto the partner so that the sadist is able to experience pleasure. The masochist is thought to believe that sex is sinful. To relieve guilt over any pleasure she may feel, she inflicts punishment on herself. Another theory is that the sadist suffers from feelings of inferiority that are alleviated by inflicting pain on others. The masochist may act out feelings of insignificance and dependency. Some theorists believe that sadomasochistic activity is a replaying of childhood trauma. Violent sexual activity may also be a way of indirectly acting out anger. For some, it tends to be an exaggeration of traditional sex roles and allows the person to give up responsibility for his acts during sex. For others, it is a means of pretending to be a different person, for example, a powerful, successful man who can humiliate a "slave." Yet others may find sadomasochism alluring because it is unconventional.

Pain is not the main goal of sexual sadomasochism but rather a part of the drama, which may be structured or unstructured. The pain is usually controlled enough that it does not interfere with erotic feelings. It is believed that the muscle tension that accompanies the suspense increases sexual arousal. Most sadomasochistic people choose a trusted partner who will play the sadist's role within mutually agreed-upon limits. A partner who turns out to really enjoy sadistic acting out could become very dangerous. Some prostitutes offer sexual theater as a specialty. The drama includes not only a "script" but also various props such as blindfolds, restraints, handcuffs, collars, diapers, and whips. Sadomasochism is becoming more open, and there are special clubs, bars, and magazines available for interested people.

Incest

Incest, or sexual relations among family members, is the most common form of sexual abuse of children. It may occur between siblings, or with parents, grandparents, uncles, or aunts. Incestuous activity can range from caressing and fondling to masturbation, oral sex, and intercourse. Today, incest is an almost universal taboo, but in the past it was condoned among royal or rich families in some cultures as a way to conserve power and wealth. In the United States incest is illegal in every state.

It is difficult to determine the incidence of incest because of fear of punishment, cultural inhibitions, and shame and guilt help hide the problem. It is also difficult for professionals to recognize the incestuous family. Incest occurs in all socioeconomic classes and is usually ongoing rather than a one-time event. Father-daughter incest is most commonly reported and the best understood. Brother-sister incest is the most frequent type, but it is seldom discovered. Some professionals believe that brother-sister incest is the least damaging form because it is usually transitory and generally a form of experimentation rather than exploitation. Mother-son, father-son, and mother-daughter sexual interactions have not been well studied. The strongest cultural taboo is against mother-son relationships, and these are the least commonly reported (Schlesinger 1982).

Incest between a father and daughter usually begins before the child understands the meaning of the acts. It may start with playful romping and progress to genital touching, oral or manual stimulation, and intercourse. The father tends to avoid emotional attachments with adults; he may abuse alcohol, and he may have been sexually molested as a child himself.

Sexual abuse of children is a symptom of a dysfunctional family (Janosik 1984). It is a misguided attempt to preserve the continuity of the family. The family tends to be either a closed system with few outside relationships or a loosely orga-

nized system that has not accepted the taboo against incest. Five family factors promote the breakdown of the incest barrier:

1. Role development is confused and distorted: the daughter replaces the mother as the central female figure and substitute wife.

2. The parents experience sexual dissatisfaction. This may be accompanied by severe marital conflict and spouse abuse.

3. The father doesn't seek a sexual partner outside of the home as a way of maintaining a stable family facade.

4. The entire family fears disintegration and is willing to go to extreme lengths to protect and maintain the family.

5. The nonparticipant mother gives an unconscious sanction. She may not "notice" the incest or may deliberately go out and leave the father and daughter alone. This covert sanction is of key importance in the development of incest. The mother usually remains quiet because of shame, fear of reprisals by her husband, fear of her husband's going to jail, or fear that she might have to resume sexual relations with her husband if the situation is discovered.

Various forms of coercion may be used against the child. The father may tell the daughter that he is teaching her, that he is doing something good for her, or that he is expressing his love for her. Bribery and pressure are other tactics to maintain secrecy. The child may be told that it will be her fault if other people find out and bad things happen to the family. Threats such as "Daddy would go to jail," "Mommy would get upset and sick," or "You would be taken away from us" may be used. With such pressure, the child feels isolated and afraid to tell anyone for fear of being blamed, punished, or disbelieved. Later, it may be difficult for the child to break a well-established pattern of incest with the father.

Incest is emotionally damaging to both parties according to all available data. It has a negative effect on family relationships while binding the individual members together in a secret coalition that restricts other social relationships. Girls suffer from decreased self-image, guilt, shame, anger, and a sense of alienation from others. They may have difficulty in forming intimate adult relationships. Boys suffer from anxiety, guilt, and depression. Parents feel guilt and face criminal action, humiliation, and the risk of family disintegration (Carrera 1981, Crooks and Baur 1983).

The strong cultural taboo against incest does not prevent its occurrence but hinders its recognition and treatment. Treatment for incest should consist of an in-depth family evaluation and, if possible, family therapy from a systems perspective. Strong modeling of parental roles should also be a part of the therapy. The victims need education about sex and their own sexuality to alleviate their sense of guilt. A self-help group called Parents United has been established in some parts of the country for individuals and families who have experienced child sexual molestation in any form. A division of this group for children between the ages of five and eighteen is known as Daughters and Sons United.

Sexual Harassment

Sexual harassment is often a subtle but very real form of sexual abuse. A research and resource center, Working Women United Institute, defines it as any form of unwanted attention of a sexual nature from someone in the workplace that creates discomfort or interferes with the victim's job performance. It is a very common problem.

Legally, harassment may be either verbal or physical. Persons may be subjected to obscenities or made the target of sexual jokes. Some victims are expected to perform sexual acts for their superiors or for customers. Persons not complying risk losing a promotion, receiving a demotion or a decrease in pay, having vacation preferences denied, getting fired, or receiving poor references. Some people are too intimidated to reject unwanted advances, some try to ignore them, and some try to refuse politely. Those who cannot afford to risk losing their jobs, fear peers' responses or fear being labeled a troublemaker may acquiesce.

The emotional harm to the victim can be serious. She may feel embarrassed, degraded, helpless, humiliated, angry, and even guilty (if she feels somehow at fault). Stress-related illnesses may even develop (Strong and Reynolds 1982).

Sexual harassment is a serious problem that is finally being brought out into the open and being dealt with in the courts (Strong and Reynolds 1982). Companies can be held liable for sexual harassment that occurs at the workplace. Large monetary payments have been awarded through the judicial system for victims of sexual harassment (Crooks and Baur 1983). A good initial strategy is for the victim to tell the abuser that his behavior is harassment and that it will not be tolerated. Usually there is an in-company protocol for filing a complaint. A complaint may also be filed with the Human Rights Commission or with the Equal Employment Opportunity Commission. If actual or attempted rape has occurred, criminal charges may be filed.

COUNSELING

Whether sexual problems are the main reason for seeking the help of a psychiatric mental health nurse or whether such problems are discovered only in the course of therapy, premarital, marital, and sexual counseling often fall within the scope of a nurse's clinical practice.

Premarital Counseling

When couples marry they frequently experience a conflict in expectations about the "right" roles for men, women, husbands, wives, parents, and children. These expectations have been absorbed unconsciously in the family of origin and determine how people feel and behave and how they expect their mate to feel and behave. The greater the discrepancy between the expectations of the parties, the less likely each is to have his needs met, and the more likely that the anger, frustration, and conflict between them will undermine their intimacy. One task of a couple who seeks premarital counseling is to integrate two designs for family living, two sets of expectations for the relationship, and two dreams for the future into a healthy marriage in which both people are able to cope constructively with their differences. If couples are unable to do so, each person will attempt to reform the other, an approach that is doomed to fail.

Modern life in this country requires that an adult be assertive, independent, and self-reliant, but the traditional concept of femininity has made many women unable to behave in these ways. On the other hand, an adult is also required to be able to relate to other people, to be sensitive to their needs and concerned about their welfare, and to be able to depend on them for emotional support. Frequently, the traditional concept of masculinity keeps men from responding in such "feminine" ways. Men are expected to be competent, aggressive, logical, emotionally unexpressive, insensitive to the feelings of others, interested in math and science, and not very talkative. Women are expected to be the opposite: helpless, unaggressive, intuitive, emotionally expressive, sensitive to others' feelings, uninterested in math and science, and talkative. These stereotypes limit both men and women. Couples may be constrained by roles that neither person really wants yet each has difficulty changing. Sex role stereotyping may make it difficult even in an intimate relationship to relate to a partner as a human being rather than as a role player. However, some couples find traditional sex roles comfortable and useful because they allow the couple to avoid conflict.

Counseling may be needed in those cases where rigid gender role expectations block the couple's growth and their ability to be intimate with each other. In premarital counseling, *androgyny* is presented as flexibility in gender role and the acceptance of those positive human qualities that legitimately belong in the repertoire of both men and women. Karen Fontaine of Purdue University has developed a role assessment tool to be used during premarital counseling sessions (see Figure 14–4). Each partner receives a checklist and independently identifies who should be usually responsible for each behavior. Each person also stars those items that he or she would not be willing to do except under extraordinary circumstances. The partners then compare lists and discuss which expectations have been placed on them because of their gender, which they accept or defy, and which areas are likely to cause conflict between them. This tool is helpful in prompting discussion regarding areas that might cause problems later on. At six months and at one year after the marriage, the couple should recheck the lists and assess how the relationship has developed in terms of role expectations and identify any new problems that need to be solved.

Communication is a key factor in a successful, creative sexual relationship. Premarital counseling should include both sexual and nonsexual forms of communication. Many people find it difficult to

Figure 14–4. *Role assessment tool.*

Please indicate on the line if you believe: the husband (H) should have the major responsibility for the area or job; the wife (W) should have the major responsibility for the area or job; or they both (B) should share the area or job equally. Please answer according to your beliefs and preferences, NOT what you think your partner believes or prefers.

Religious roles
____ prayer life
____ church attendance
____ degree of involvement in church activities
____ amount of money given to church
____ religious education of children
____ if couple is of different faiths, who determines which church couple and children will attend

Occupational roles
____ job outside the home
____ higher income
____ if both work, who takes off if a child is home

Family roles
____ changing diapers
____ bathing child
____ feeding child
____ cuddling child
____ disciplining child
____ taking child to activities
____ reading to child
____ putting child to bed
____ attending PTA meetings
____ helping with homework

Household responsibilities
____ ironing
____ laundry
____ dishes
____ mopping floors
____ cleaning bathroom
____ vacuuming
____ cooking
____ grocery shopping
____ mending clothes
____ making bed
____ washing windows
____ washing car
____ car maintenance
____ changing a tire
____ shoveling snow
____ mowing lawn
____ planting flowers
____ gardening (trimming shrubs, hoeing, etc.)
____ taking garbage out
____ cleaning gutters
____ high ladder jobs
____ moving furniture around
____ painting inside
____ cleaning garage

Sexual roles
____ initiating lovemaking
____ determining positions and frequency of lovemaking
____ deciding method of birth control
____ verbalizing likes or dislikes about lovemaking activities
____ sex education of son
____ sex education of daughter

Emotional roles
____ verbalizing feelings (sadness, anger, hurt, joy, love)
____ crying
____ deciding on family therapy
____ deciding how to handle problems with parents and in-laws
____ initiating intellectual discussions
____ showing assertive behavior
____ showing self-reliance
____ showing affection

Financial roles
____ paying bills
____ preparing income tax
____ making day-to-day decisions about expenditures
____ making big decisions about expenditures
____ making decisions about use of credit cards
____ developing a budget
____ spending money on self
____ having most life insurance

Social roles
____ organizing a party
____ preparing for a party (cleaning, cooking)
____ cleaning up after a party
____ inviting relatives to visit
____ writing letters to family and friends
____ deciding on recreational activities
____ deciding on vacations
____ having a friend of opposite sex (nonrelative)
____ having a night out with women or men friends
____ choosing friends as a couple
____ deciding on living location (area, near job, etc.)
____ making arrangements for moving to new house or apartment

reveal their inner feelings to others, especially concerning emotions and deeply held beliefs. For some it is not easy to verbally express love, intimacy, or even concern. In a sexual relationship such expressions count almost as much as physical contact. Whereas communication about sexuality has generally become more open over the past two or three decades, the intimate sexual communication of most couples has not followed suit.

Most couples develop nonverbal signals that indicate their interest in sexual activity. This is appropriate if the signals are clearly understood by each partner, but ambiguous signals can lead to hurt feelings and unmet expectations. An example of unclear signals is provided by a woman who was unable to tell her husband directly that she was interested in making love, so she would take a shower whenever she wanted sexual contact. Almost every time she took a shower her husband went into the bedroom expecting her to be sexually receptive, but discord arose whenever she took a shower for cleanliness. When the couple realized how ambiguous the signal was, they decided to state more clearly to each other their needs and expectations. It is equally important to establish clear signals when sexual activity is not desired. Many people interpret their partners' refusal to have sex as a personal rejection. They can easily accept their partners' refusal to eat out or go to a movie but not a refusal to have sex. Couples need to communicate openly and honestly so that a negative response is seen merely as a refusal at that particular time.

Many people also expect their partners to intuitively perceive their needs and desires, especially during sexual activity. This unrealistic expectation may be expressed in many ways: "If she doesn't know what I want, then she must be insensitive," "If he loved me, he would know what I want," and "If I have to ask for something, it detracts from my pleasure." Often a person does to his partner what he wishes to have done to him. Such means of indirect communication usually fail. In premarital counseling couples can be taught how to diplomatically assert their needs. Couples should be taught to avoid "you" language, which evokes a defensive response and leads to arguments (Satir 1967, Watzlawick, Beauvin, and Jackson 1967). The recipient of a "you" statement feels accused, inadequate, and guilty. As she tries to defend herself the argument becomes a win-lose situation. Whoever wins the quarrel, the relationship always loses, and the power struggle escalates. To prevent such a situation, the couple should be advised to use "I" language, in which each person relates his or her own thoughts, feelings, and beliefs. The following are

some examples of responsible "I" statements and accusatory "you" statements.

"I" language

"I am really too tired to make love tonight but I enjoy your interest in me."
"I miss all the little hugs and caresses we used to do spontaneously."
"I would like you to rub my clitoris more gently."
"I am unhappy with the way our sexual life is going."

"You" language

"You always wait until I'm too tired to approach me sexually."
"You only touch me when you want sex."
"You clumsy oaf—that hurts!"
"What you need is a sex therapist."

Learning to recognize and identify one's own feelings is not always an easy process. Individuals should assume responsibility for their own feelings and support each other as their communication skills improve. It takes time and practice before a person can satisfactorily express his or her sexual feelings and requests. If this process can begin early in the relationship, the couple will receive more pleasure and enjoyment throughout their sexual relationship.

Marital Counseling

Marital counseling focuses on promoting the growth of a relationship by broadening and deepening a couple's marital interaction. The counselor can help the couple define issues and establish goals in behavioral terms by asking questions such as: "What behaviors of yours and your partner's have to be changed in order for this relationship to work out?" or "Give me a word picture of what you will be like as a couple when your relationship has improved." The goals, or expected outcomes, are written down and revised as assessment and intervention continue. The couple is viewed as a system and counseling as a joint effort to help them find meaningful, cooperative interdependence.

Part of the counseling process consists of helping a couple clarify their attitudes toward each other and their problems. The counselor should identify any self-destructive attitudes, such as anxiety, anger, guilt, resentment, or fear of failure. At the same time, the counselor should identify positive attitudes, such as good self-esteem, joy, creativity, and openness to change. Attitudes are learned in interactions with other people, and therefore they are open to modification.

As the counseling proceeds, past events should be analyzed in context. Individuals adapt in order to protect themselves. Couples should not be asked why they behaved as they did but rather where, with whom, under what circumstances an event occurred, and how it affected the other person. As each individual begins to understand the process of their interactions, he also begins to see how a situation is perceived by the other person. With this understanding a couple can seek alternative actions to solve relationship problems.

As in premarital counseling, marital counseling should address the questions of sex role stereotyping, unspoken expectations, and identification and expression of feelings. The couple may need to learn assertiveness techniques, such as the use of "No" and "I" language to express needs, wants, and feelings. Male-female cotherapy teams can be very effective in modeling the suggested behaviors.

Marital counseling is an opportunity for the growth of both the individuals and the relationship. It is not an easy cure but rather hard work for both persons. Their reward is the development of more effective relating skills, which will serve them in good stead when future difficulties arise.

Sexual Counseling

Sexual dysfunctions are considered shared disorders, and the relationship, not the individual presenting with the symptom, should be the focus of attention in sexual counseling. There are many possible causes of sexual problems, from a mere absence of sexual happiness to severe distress in the marital system. Some couples are able to get along sexually but not in any other context of their relationship.

Most typically, sexual counseling is done with a male-female therapy team, which enables the therapists to serve as models for effective and mutually satisfying relationships. Modeling is especially effective for people who grew up without marriage models or whose models were maladaptive. The examples of support and freedom the cotherapists demonstrate may teach a couple far more about interpersonal relations than what they actually say. A female-male team also permits the therapists to serve symbolically as gender role models for the couple.

The initial one or two sessions should consist of data collection and assessment of the identified problem. Complete sex histories and complete medical histories should be obtained. If an organic problem is suspected, the client should be referred to his or her physician for a complete physical examination. Frequently the counselor will recommend books from which clients can learn new sexual techniques. Couples should also be assured that masturbation and fantasy are normal sexual practices. The aim of counseling is not to change clients' value systems but rather to have clients explore the source and the validity of their value systems.

Sexual counseling should help promote both insight into behavior and behavioral change. Many people consider the ability to perform sexually as a mark of their manhood or womanhood and thus create a great deal of performance anxiety. One of the goals of counseling is to redefine the purpose of sexual activity as a way of giving and receiving pleasure. Negative attitudes toward sex, ambiguous methods of communication, and behaviors that are destructive to the sexual relationship should all be discussed. Couples should be encouraged to learn to recognize the positive rather than just focus on the negative in their interactions.

Homework may be assigned at each session to help clients analyze their interactions, identify problem areas, and take responsibility for changing their own behavior outside the therapeutic relationship. Such assignments require that the couple cooperate and share their thoughts. Each should be instructed to seek to understand his or her partner's needs, preferences, and moods.

The homework usually consists of a process called *sensate focusing*, which helps the partners learn to give and receive pleasure by touching (Kaplan 1974). In the beginning there is a ban on breast and genital touching and on intercourse. These restrictions free a couple from fear of failure and allow them to direct all their attention to the pleasure of touching. The exercise redefines the meaning of touching. It becomes not a demand for intercourse but an expression of affection and an opportunity to learn about oneself and one's partner.

The couple is instructed to spend 30 minutes a day doing the sensate focus homework at a time when they are not tired, angry, or anxious. During the first week many couples are surprised to discover that they seldom spend time alone together because of the many interruptions they allow to intrude. They are encouraged to make the time for each other, because the more frequently they practice, the more quickly their sexual relationship will improve. One partner gives and one receives pleasure for 15 minutes, and then they switch roles for another 15 minutes. Giving and receiving simultaneously is discouraged because a person cannot fully enjoy either experience when he or she is trying to concentrate on both processes at the same time. Initially, some people are uncomfortable in the passive role, but as they learn that they have a right to pleasure, this discomfort eases.

The giver is instructed to hold, kiss, stroke, and massage the partner's entire body in order to learn what is pleasurable and arousing to the other person. He or she is asked to experiment with various types of touch and to focus on his or her own feelings during the touching. The receiver is instructed to relax and enjoy the experience and pay attention to his or her own feelings of pleasure and arousal. The receiver should tell the partner which kinds of touch are not enjoyed and which kinds he or she would like to have done during the exercise. Communication, through words and sounds, is extremely important because one's own arousal depends greatly on seeing and hearing one's partner becoming aroused. "I" language is encouraged as the preferred mode of communication.

The couple is also encouraged to experiment with massage oil, powder, lotions, or touching in the shower because these all give different sensations. It is important to "touch" the partner's mind by expressing caring and affection before touching the body in order to involve the whole person in lovemaking. The couple is encouraged to cultivate all five senses by using loving words, sensual whispers, music, the sound of a crackling fire in the fireplace, suggestive movements, sensual clothes, dim or colored lights, a favorite meal, a glass of wine, a favorite perfume. As couples experiment,

they find that their sex life becomes less boring and more pleasurable.

Each person is directed to complete a homework sheet after the exercise and not to share the sheet with each other until the next counseling session. On these sheets they rate only their own enjoyment and arousal in both giving and receiving, not what they think their partner felt (see Figure 14–5). The more specific they can be in their descriptions and comments, the more helpful the information will be to each partner and to the counselors in revealing strengths and identifying problems.

As the couple progresses, they move to breast and genital touching, and finally to sexual intercourse. Throughout each stage total body touching remains a part of lovemaking. About the third or fourth week, each partner is asked to choose a day when he or she will plan a surprise sensual or erotic evening for the partner. This could involve such things as moving the stereo into the bedroom, having the children out of the house, having a candlelight dinner, buying a vibrator, burning incense, going out for dinner and dancing, or whatever each thinks the other might enjoy.

Sexual therapy tends to be short-term therapy unless there is severe marital distress causing the sexual dysfunction. If that is the case, the marital

Figure 14–5. Example of a homework sheet for recording sensate focusing activities.

Sensate Focus Homework Sheet

Name _____ Date _____ 1 2 3 4 5 6 7 week (circle one)

Make your comments in "I" language. Record your *own* reactions and observations about your partner: negative, positive, questions, thoughts, etc. Be specific about the activity, for example, "touching face." Report each time sensate exchange took place.

Day	Activity done to me	Enjoyment on a scale of 1–10	Sexual arousal on a scale of 1–10	Comments	Day	Activity done to me	Enjoyment on a scale of 1–10	Sexual arousal on a scale of 1–10	Comments

issues need to be dealt with either first or concurrently with the sexual problems. Depending on the presenting dysfunction, other techniques are taught to the couple, such as squeezing the penis to prevent rapid ejaculation or self-stimulation to help the preorgasmic woman achieve climax. Detailed description of these methods can be found in many textbooks on sexual therapy.

THE NURSING PROCESS IN SEXUAL HEALTH CARE

Sexual health care is an important component of holistic nursing. As with other types of health care, the delivery of sexual health care should be based on the nursing process. First, the nurse must assess her own beliefs, values, and attitudes that affect how she deals with people. In particular, the nurse should assess her values and biases about human sexuality and make sure she does not project them onto her clients in her professional practice. She should remember that clients have the right to determine their own values and views.

Another aspect of self-assessment is the examination of one's professional practice. A question the nurse might ask is, "Do I deny, inhibit, or allow for the sexuality of my clients?" The nurse must consider whether the topic of sex is incorporated in the history taking and in client teaching. Even in the face of peer disapproval, has the nurse been able to function as a client advocate about sexual issues? Have appropriate referrals been made for clients suffering from sexual problems? In conjunction with this, it is important to develop an awareness of how one is perceived by others. If the nurse realizes that few or no clients discuss sexual concerns during nursing interactions, the next question is, "Do the clients I come in contact with have no or few sexual questions, or am I sending nonverbal messages that discourage people from discussing these issues with me?" The nurse should then evaluate how comfortable she is in discussing sexual concerns with clients. Most clients quickly perceive a nurse's discomfort and react accordingly. In order to confer with a client on the topic of sexuality the nurse must undergo a desensitization and resensitization process, discarding her own hangups and becoming sensitive to the client's feelings. This new sensitivity will help prevent hasty and judgmental responses to clients.

The nurse should appraise the extent of her knowledge of sexual physiology and psychology throughout the life cycle. Confidence in doing sexual counseling, as in all other kinds of counseling, is based on a thorough knowledge of the subject. It is very important that the nurse not convey incorrect information, misconceptions, or stereotypic values to her clients.

Interpersonal communication skills are important threads throughout the nursing process. Good interviewing skills and the ability to talk openly and nonjudgmentally about sex should be cultivated. Creating a comfortable atmosphere is essential; the nurse who is embarrassed or anxious only augments these reactions in the client. Managing one's own feelings and responding appropriately to those of the client are essential to good nursing practice.

The nursing process begins with the collection of data necessary for determining the sexual health status of a client. These data should include a physical assessment, a general sexual history, medical diagnosis, laboratory tests, and previous treatment regimens. A detailed sexual history is not appropriate unless it is indicated by the other data. The nurse needs to recognize that any alteration in a person's physical or emotional state may affect various aspects of his life pattern—including sexual activity. The nurse must refrain from making assumptions that will distort the process of gathering data, such as that all clients are heterosexual, that married clients are sexually active, and that single clients, especially older people, are sexually inactive.

The next step in the nursing process is the interpretation of the data to formulate a nursing diagnosis. Some of the possible nursing diagnoses are listed in the accompanying box.

Once the nursing diagnoses have been formulated, the nurse can help the couple formulate measurable expected outcomes or goals. This process should include the couple lest the nurse impose his own biases and expectations on the pair.

The nurse's role as teacher is very important when dealing with clients' sexual concerns and needs. Many problems can be solved simply with accurate information. The nurse should also be prepared to counsel the client in how to utilize new knowledge to develop a satisfactory and accountable lifestyle. The sexual effects of medications and disease changes and alternate modes of sexual activity are among the most important in nurse teaching. The nurse must also be able to support the couple as they struggle with making adaptive changes. A nurse should have additional education and supervision in order to be able to intervene in the advanced level of sexual therapy. If a client is in need of sexual therapy and the nurse is not competent in this area, she should refer him to an appropriate professional.

Nurses may also function at the primary level of prevention by teaching sex education in schools,

---

**POSSIBLE NURSING
DIAGNOSES FOR SEXUAL PROBLEMS**

Fear related to returning to sexual activity after recent myocardial infarction or other medical problem

Anxiety related to unrealistic performance expectations

Knowledge deficit of sexual physiology

Ineffective family coping related to unresolved anger between the couple

Ineffective individual coping related to past history of incest

Disturbance in self-concept or body image related to body and coital shame

Disturbance in self-concept or self-esteem related to ego-dystonic homosexuality

Disturbance in self-concept or role performance related to disparate gender role expectations of husband and wife

Disturbance in self-concept or personal identity related to transsexualism

Alterations in patterns of sexuality, such as organic erectile failure, related to colostomy or other surgical procedure

Alterations in patterns of sexuality, such as retrograde ejaculations, related to neuropathy of diabetes or other chronic illness

Alterations in patterns of sexuality, such as rapid ejaculation, related to a conditioned response

Alterations in patterns of sexuality, such as nonorgasmic response, related to lack of knowledge of sexual anatomy and physiology

---

The above are the more likely diagnoses related to clients with sexual problems. Nursing diagnoses are not limited to the list shown above. Manifestations of these disorders are individualistic even though certain prevailing patterns are identifiable.

SUMMARY

Understanding and responding positively to human sexuality is essential for a caring approach by nurses. There is no other aspect of human experience that is so subject to conflict. Through negative social conditioning, women are often taught to regard sexual organs as unclean, while men often learn to equate sexual performance with competence and mastery in other areas of life. Nurses need to acquire accurate information about male and female sexuality in all its variations to develop an awareness of their own values and to avoid making moralistic criticisms of attitudes unlike their own.

Social and cultural variables have considerable influence in determining people's sexual expectations and in perpetuating myths about male and female sexual behavior. Nurses are in a unique position to dispel myths and to help individuals deal with their own sexual needs and limitations.

Review Questions

1. Discuss the role of self-perception and self-image in sexual response.
2. Describe male and female sexual anatomy.
3. List the four phases of the human sexual response and the major characteristics of each.
4. Discuss ways in which sexuality is influenced by cultural settings. Include the ramifications for the elderly population.
5. List some of the unspoken expectations regarding sexual relationships and discuss the influence of these expectations on sexual response.

Research Report

Sexual Counseling with Women with Coronary Heart Disease

This study was undertaken to gather data that would help nurses increase their awareness of the need for sexual counseling of women with coronary

in classes for adults, or with groups of adolescents who are struggling with sexual questions and values. Interventions may also take the form of client advocacy, such as removing the barriers to sexual expression in nursing homes and long-term care facilities.

Evaluations of nursing interventions in sexual health care should be based on how well the expected outcomes have been achieved. If the outcomes have not been met, the nurse must determine which step or steps of the nursing process must be modified in order to most effectively assist the client.

(Text continues on page 401.)

CLINICAL EXAMPLE

SEXUAL DYSFUNCTION IN A YOUNG COUPLE

Connie and Tom Hulburt were referred for sexual therapy from an alcohol rehabilitation program; their chief complaints concerned decreased sexual interest and disparity of sexual desire. They are a couple in their early thirties, married for five years, with one child, age three. Both Connie and Tom are intellectual, articulate, and well-educated professionals. At the initiation of treatment, Connie, the alcoholic spouse, had been sober for four months and was active in Alcoholics Anonymous. Tom had been active in Alanon for two years. Connie's alcoholism had not yet seriously interfered with her work; nor had she become abusive or neglectful with her family.

ASSESSMENT

When Tom was ten years old, his father deserted the family. His mother took a job outside the home, and Tom was left in charge of his two younger sisters. He described his home life as very happy in spite of the fact that he had to "grow up rapidly." His family was both verbally and physically expressive, and sex was openly discussed. As an adult, Tom believed that he had to be the perfect husband and father at the expense of meeting his own needs. He had difficulty in doing good things for himself and in expressing anger. He was able to express other emotions easily. One of his chief complaints was that he had had a greater interest in sex than Connie throughout the marriage and that he believed he usually had to initiate sexual activity. He stated that he felt hurt and rejected when Connie refused sexual interaction.

Connie had two siblings, a younger brother and sister. Her family of origin was not demonstrative either verbally or physically. Neither feelings nor sex were openly discussed. As an adult, Connie was emotionally stunted in her development. Her intellectual capacities had served her well in most areas of life, but not in the relational area. She had compulsive traits, which were her way of defending herself against chaos and loss of control. Whenever she felt anger, she suppressed it by telling herself, "It serves no good purpose to respond with anger. I would rather talk it out logically." Connie also did not recognize her dependency needs. She had always seen herself as a strong person who was in control.

Both Tom and Connie used a great deal of "you" language during the initial session, such as, "You never initiate sex," "You are the one with the problem," and "You read too much psychology stuff." Before entering therapy, both Tom and Connie were aware that the decreased sexual interest might have an organic basis related to the toxic effects of alcohol.

The following diagnoses were made:

Nursing Diagnoses

Knowledge deficit
(related to sexual anatomy, physiology, and psychology)

Impaired verbal communication
(related to inability of both clients to share expectations and feelings)

Anxiety
(related to performance expectations)

Self-esteem disturbance in Connie
(related to role performance)

Self-esteem disturbance in Tom
(related to decreased self-esteem)

Sexual dysfunction
(related to decreased sexual desire, disparity of sexual desire)

Multiaxial Psychiatric Diagnoses

Axis I   V61.10 Marital problem
           302.71 Hypoactive sexual desire disorder
Axis II   None
Axis III   Alcoholism
Axis IV   Psychosocial stressors—chronic alcoholism
           with current sobriety. Severity 3: moderate
           (predominantly enduring circumstances)
Axis V   Current GAF: 70
           Highest GAF past year: 75

PLANNING

Based on the clinical presentation of Tom and Connie, plans were made for couple counseling sessions to explore the issues of their sexual difficulties, with emphasis on communication techniques. Both needed education about normal sexual response and a better awareness of their own sexual expectations. They needed assistance in expressing their thoughts and feelings about sexual issues and in learning to use "I" statements rather than "you" language.

IMPLEMENTATION

During the sessions, Tom and Connie were given reading assignments, and discussions were held about the physiology of sexual response. The counselor helped them to identify their own bodies' responses and to express their expectations about sex. With the help of the nurse, they analyzed the ways in which unspoken expectations led to disappointments and hurt feelings, and they were instructed to share an expectation a day with each other. The nurse expressed support of Tom and Connie's interest in changing the relationship.

The use of "I" instead of "you" language was taught in the sessions by the identification of "you" language and by the practice of restating expressions in "I" language. The nurse modeled both types of expression and discussed ways in which the pain caused by "you" language can lead to defensive behavior.

Some of the sessions were devoted to discussion of the importance of touch, particularly how touching was regarded in both their families of origin and how the expectations that touching would lead to intercourse increased anxiety and decreased the frequency of physical contact. Tom practiced asking

Connie to simply hold him, using "I" language. Both of them were taught how to say "no" in an acceptable manner without feeling guilty.

Gradually Tom and Connie were taught sensate focus and progressed through the various stages to help them redefine the purpose of their sexual activity as a way of giving and receiving pleasure. The nurse also helped them discuss their personal fears about the expression of angry feelings. They began to realize that avoiding conflict created a situation where anger might be expressed in other ways, such as decreased sexual interest or alcohol abuse.

EVALUATION

Tom and Connie stated that the reading assignments were helpful in teaching them about sexual functioning and in prompting discussion about sexuality. Connie was able to articulate that her sexual desire decreased when there was a lot of stress at work. Tom was able to acknowledge that at such times, his requests for sex must have felt like more work to Connie. At the end of therapy, they were continuing to seek alternative ways to meet the needs of each.

At the beginning of therapy, both had expressed the belief that they spent a great deal of time together. By the second week, they had discovered that very little of this time was "private" time, and they decided to restructure some family activities and make "dates" with each other. Tom and Connie were typical of many couples in that they had minimal communication about sexual activity at the beginning of therapy. They gradually learned to share their expectations prior to interacting sexually, and they learned to extend this skill to other areas of their lives, such as discussing expectations for leisure activities. They learned how to compromise on those issues and therefore experienced fewer hurt feelings related to unmet needs.

Tom and Connie were able to reframe the expression of their thoughts and feelings into "I" language, first during sexual interactions and later in other areas of their lives. Prior to therapy, Tom had been minimally verbal during lovemaking and Connie had been the silent partner. At first during sensate focus she was uncomfortable with talking and making pleasurable noises. She became more comfortable when she discovered that her communication was sexually stimulating to Tom. Tom was able to increase his communication, which was stimulating to Connie.

After they agreed that it was acceptable to hug and touch without the expectation of intercourse, their physical contacts increased. Connie initiated more caring behavior. They completed the stages of sensate focus in seven weeks and were able to experiment with various types of pleasurable activities that were satisfying to both of them. Connie was beginning to have an increase in her sexual drive and her responses continued throughout therapy. Tom and Connie were relieved to know that Connie had no organic dysfunctions. The couple terminated treatment pleased that most of the expected outcomes had been achieved.

Nursing Diagnoses	Goal	Nursing Actions	Outcome Criteria	Outcome Evaluation
Knowledge deficit—sexual anatomy, physiology, psychology	Clients will understand sexual anatomy, physiology, psychology.	Give reading assignments. Discuss with both clients the physiology and psychology of their own responses.	Reading assignments will teach and facilitate discussion about clients' sexuality and sexual needs at this stage of their cycle.	Connie was able to articulate that sexual desire decreases with stress at work. Tom was able to acknowledge that his requests for sex seemed like more work for Connie. Both were able to understand their individual responses.
Impaired verbal communication	Clients will more readily express thoughts and feelings about issues.	Teach use of "I" language by restatement and role modeling.	Clients will use "I" language and identify negative and positive feelings, deal with those appropriately and rationally.	Both learned to reframe expression of thoughts and feelings into "I" language during sexual interaction and in other areas of their lives.
Anxiety regarding performance expectations	Clients will identify body responses and expectations about sex.	Analyze the ways unspoken expectations lead to disappointments and hurt feelings.	Clients will verbally share one expectation and/or reaction each day.	Both learned to share expectations prior to interacting sexually and extended this to other areas of their lives, including leisure activities, which were restructured to allow for "private time."
Self-esteem disturbance in role performance	Clients will become comfortable with themselves as sexual partners.	Reinforce other areas of competence. Teach importance of touch, explore how touching was regarded in family of origin.	Physical contact without expectation of intercourse will lead to more caring behaviors and decrease tension for both clients.	Physical contacts increased. Agreement to hug and touch without expectations of intercourse led to relief of tension, comfort with newly established roles. Connie no longer felt the need to perform. Tom did not feel his image was affected if intercourse did not take place.
Sexual dysfunction	Pleasurable activities will be established for both.	Give instruction in sensate focus.	Clients will complete stages of sensate focus in seven weeks. Connie will have increased sexual desire.	Both Connie and Tom were able to verbally communicate during lovemaking, which was sexually stimulating for both. Connie was beginning to respond more frequently.

disease. Appropriate sexual counseling can facilitate the client's return to prehospitalization levels of sexual activity. Fifty-eight women were interviewed within a few days of planned hospital discharge and were questioned about living arrangements, sexual activity before hospitalization, feelings about being sexually active, and reasons for lack of activity. An assessment was made of the occurrence of sexual counseling—when, how, from whom, and how helpful it was. About half of the women reported sexual activities; those who did not attributed the lack to not having a partner or disinterest from the partner. Only one third had received sexual counseling, but the majority asked for written information and felt that health care professionals should routinely initiate discussions about sexual activity.

J. Baggs and A. Karch. *Heart and Lung* 16, no. 2 (March 1987):154–158.

Suggested Annotated Readings

Ables, B. *Therapy for Couples*. San Francisco: Jossey-Bass, 1977.

This book is directed toward creating a couple-treatment approach distinct from individual therapy that works with couples whose discomfort lies with their interactions. The focus is on the work of the therapist rather than on the kinds of individuals or marriages with whom or which the therapist works. The reader can apply a variety of theoretical frameworks to the material presented.

Hammer, S. *Women, Body and Culture*. New York: Harper & Row, 1975.

The essays in this anthology explore some of the ways in which body and culture affect, separately or together, the sexual lives of women in our society. Sexuality was chosen as a focus because it remains poorly understood and is central to every woman's experience of herself. The processes of identity formation, puberty, menstruation, menopause, sexual arousal, and childbirth are explored.

Kaplan, H. *The New Sex Therapy*. New York: Brunner/Mazel, 1974.

The modality of sex therapy is described as having the primary objective of relieving the sexual symptom. Sex therapy relies heavily for its therapeutic impact on erotic tasks which the couple do at home. This book describes treatment for sexual disorders and clarifies the basic underlying concepts of relating this material to the theory of psychopathology and psychiatric treatment.

Klemer's Counseling in Marital and Sexual Problems. R. Stakmann and W. Heibert, eds. Baltimore: Williams & Wilkins Co., 1977.

The goal of this book is to bring together information, ideas, and guidelines of use to marriage counselors. The approach is dyadic and interactional. It gives information on specific types and systematic considerations in premarital, marital, and sexual counseling.

Sager, C. *Marriage Contracts and Couple Therapy*. New York: Brunner/Mazel, 1976.

The central concept of this book is that each partner in a marriage brings to it an individual, unwritten contract, a set of expectations and promises, conscious and unconscious. These individual contracts may be modified during the marriage but will remain separate unless the two partners are fortunate enough to arrive at a single joint contract that is agreed to at all levels.

References

Ackroyd, P. *Dressing Up*. New York: Simon & Schuster, 1979.

American Psychiatric Association. *Diagnostic and Statistical Manual of Mental Disorders*, 3d ed. Washington, D.C.: American Psychiatric Association, 1980.

_____ . *Diagnostic and Statistical Manual for Mental Disorders*. 3d ed., rev. Washington, D.C.: American Psychiatric Association, 1987.

Baer, J. W., J. M. Hall, K. Holm, and S. Lewitter-Kochler. "Challenges in Developing an Inpatient Psychiatric Program for Patients with AIDS and ARC." *Hospital and Community Psychiatry* 38 (1987):1299–1303.

Barbach, L. *For Each Other*. New York: Anchor Press/Doubleday, 1982.

Bell, A., and M. Weinberg. *Homosexualities*. New York: Simon & Schuster, 1978.

Carrera, M. *Sex*. New York: Crown Publishers, 1981.

Caruso, D. M. "Sexuality and the Terminal Patient." *Caring* (October 1986):68–71.

Cooper, D. "Sexual Counseling of the Patient with Chronic Lung Disease." *Focus on Critical Care* 13 (1986):18–20.

Crooks, R., and K. Baur. *Our Sexuality*. Menlo Park, CA: Benjamin/Cummings, 1983.

Finkelhor, P. *Sexually Abused Children*. New York: Free Press, 1979.

Freedman, A. M., H. I. Kaplan, and B. J. Sadock, eds. *Modern Synopsis of Psychiatry*. Baltimore: Williams & Wilkins, 1976.

Haeberle, E. *The Sex Atlas*. New York: Continuum, 1981.

Hogan, R. *Human Sexuality: A Nursing Perspective*. New York: Appleton-Century-Crofts, 1980.

Hook, E. W. "Gonococcal Infections: A Continuing Diagnostic and Therapeutic Challenge." *Infectious Disease Journal* 36 (1987): 48–53.

Janosik, E. *Crisis Counseling*. Boston: Jones and Bartlett, 1984.

Kaplan, H. S. *The New Sex Therapy*. New York: Bruner/Mazel, 1974.

Kinsey, A. et al. *Sexual Behavior in the Human Male*. Philadelphia: W. B. Saunders, 1948.

_____ . et al. *Sexual Behavior in the Human Female*. Philadelphia: W. B. Saunders, 1953.

Klein, F. *The Bisexual Option*. New York: Arbor House, 1978.

Larson, E. L., and I. Nachamkin. "Chlamydial Infections." *American Journal of Infection Control* 13 (1985): 259–268.

Loucks, A. "Chlamydia: An Unheralded Epidemic." *American Journal of Nursing* 87 (1987):920–922.

MacElveen-Hoehn, P., and R. McCorkle. "Understanding Sexuality in Progressive Cancer." *Seminars in Oncology Nursing* 1 (1985):56–62.

Manley, G. "Diabetes and Sexual Health." *The Diabetes Educator* 12 (1986):366–369.

Masters, W. H. "Sex and Aging: Expectations and Reality." *Hospital Practice* 21 (1986):175–198.

Masters, W. H., and V. E. Johnson. *Human Sexual Response*. Boston: Little, Brown, 1966.

Peakman, J."Sexuality and the Psychiatric Patient." *Psychiatric Nursing* 16 (April 1986):7.

Perry, J. W., and J. Markowitz. "Psychiatric Intervention for AIDS-Spectrum Disorders." *Hospital and Community Psychiatry* 37 (1986):1001–1006.

Redfield, R. R. "Heterosexual Transmission of Human T Lymphotropic Virus Type III: Syphilis Revisited." *Mt. Sinai Journal of Medicine* 53 (1986):592–597.

Renshaw, D. C. "Sexuality: Making Adjustments for Illness, Disability and Age." *Consultant* (1986):81–107.

Rush, F. *The Best-Kept Secret: Sexual Abuse of Children*. Englewood Cliffs: Prentice-Hall, 1980.

Satir, V. *Conjoint Family Therapy*. Palo Alto: Behavior Books, 1967.

Schlesinger, B. *Sexual Abuse of Children*. Toronto: University of Toronto Press, 1982.

Siemens, S., and R. Brandzel. *Sexuality: Nursing Assessment and Intervention*. Philadelphia: J. B. Lippincott, 1982.

Smith, J. L. "Syphilis Underground." *Journal of Clinical Neuro-ophthalmology* 7 (1987):17–19.

Steinke, E. E., and M. B. Bergen. "Sexuality and Aging." *Journal of Gerontological Nursing* 12 (1986):6–10.

Stewart, R. "Sexuality and the Psychiatric Patient." *Psychiatric Nursing* 16 (1986):5.

Strong, B., and R. Reynolds. *Understanding Our Sexuality*. St. Paul: West Publishing, 1982.

Walker, L. A. "What Comforts AIDS Families." *The New York Times Magazine* (June 21, 1987).

Watzlawick, P., J. Beauvin, and D. Jackson *Pragmatics of Human Communication*. New York: W. W. Norton, 1967.

Webster, M. L. "Are AIDS Patients Getting Better Nursing Care?" *Nursing Life* (January/February 1987):48–53.

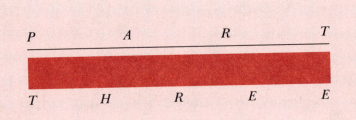
CRITICAL TASKS
AND
TRANSITIONS

15

Maturational Variations and Disruptions

Overview

The following section deals with maturational and situational crises, and presents guidelines for crisis counseling. The subject of this chapter is maturational crises that arise at various developmental stages of the life cycle. Maturational crises are inevitable and anticipated, but the way in which they are confronted may be functional or dysfunctional, depending on the responses and resources available to individuals and families as they react to change.

The chapter describes therapeutic nursing approaches that may be employed during four life cycle stages: childhood, adolescence, adulthood, and old age. Selected theories that enhance our understanding of maturational stages and critical tasks are explained, and examples given of their clinical application. In the chapter the terms *maturational crises* and *critical tasks* are used interchangeably. Maturational or developmental tasks are considered critical because of their importance to human growth and fulfillment. Unless maturational tasks are resolved in a functional, adaptive manner, they tend to deteriorate into genuine crises.

During the lifetime of every person, changes take place as one moves from infancy to childhood to adulthood and old age. The occurrence of these changes is predictable, but their characteristics are altered by multiple forces bearing on the person concerned. While maturational changes always introduce new conditions to which individuals and families must adapt, occasionally they produce conditions that seem distressing and insurmountable. Maturational changes that are dealt with adaptively are discussed in this chapter as well as some variations that prove disruptive. Four theorists have been chosen to illustrate some facet of maturation: Erik Erikson, Lawrence Kohlberg, Jean Piaget, and Evelyn Duvall. Erikson has a wide-ranging theory of psychosocial development. Kohlberg looks at moral development, and Piaget looks at cognitive development. Duvall places individual development in the context of family life. Carol Gilligan objected to conclusions drawn by Kohlberg; these objections are presented in the chapter. The work of Thomas and Chess on childhood temperament, and some implications of their data are reviewed. Together, the contributions of these important theorists direct us to a holistic understanding of maturational tasks and transitions.

ERIKSON'S PSYCHOSOCIAL TASKS

Stage 1. Trust versus mistrust
Stage 2. Autonomy versus shame and doubt
Stage 3. Initiative versus guilt
Stage 4. Industry versus inferiority
Stage 5. Ego identity versus role diffusion
Stage 6. Intimacy versus isolation
Stage 7. Generativity versus stagnation
Stage 8. Ego integrity versus despair

DEVELOPMENTAL THEORY

Psychosocial Theory

Erik Erikson (1963) divided the human life span into eight stages and suggested that each stage brings with it a specific critical task (see Chapter 2). Successful resolution of a maturational crisis means that the critical task for that stage has been accomplished. The achievement of the critical task results in the acquisition of desirable personality traits and in social adjustment, but failure to accomplish the task results in undesirable traits and maladjustment. However, if one fails to accomplish a critical task during the appropriate life stage, it is still possible to accomplish it later because subsequent events might present new opportunities. The box above summarizes the critical tasks that accompany maturational change.

Erikson's first three stages encompass early childhood. During the initial stages of *trust versus mistrust*, the infant learns that someone will meet her needs for food, warmth, shelter, and love. If the infant's needs are not met regularly and adequately, she will develop a mistrust of others that will continue into adult life. The second stage, that of *autonomy versus shame and doubt*, is characterized by demands for independence as the child begins to display qualities of willpower and self-direction. If the critical task of autonomy is not mastered, the child develops inhibitions that lead to diminished self-confidence and reluctance to develop new skills later in life.

Initiative, the critical task of stage 3, is concerned with the resolution of the child's ambivalent feelings of love and hate for his parents. During this stage, the child begins to imitate behaviors of authority figures. An inner sense of direction and purpose is the desirable outcome resulting from successful mastery of this stage. If the critical task of this stage is not successfully achieved, the result may be a lack of spontaneity and the appearance of a harsh and controlling conscience.

The fourth stage, which occurs in middle childhood, is centered around the critical task of *industry versus inferiority*. During this stage, the child is actively involved in learning and practicing skills. As the child moves through this stage, she develops a sense of pride and accomplishment in completing tasks. In addition she develops the ability to set realistic goals for herself. The successful outcome of this stage is a sense of competence. Lack of success results in feelings of inadequacy and inferiority.

Stage 5 occurs during puberty and adolescence, from ages 12 to 20. Termed the period of *ego identity versus role diffusion*, it is a time when the individual is confused about his identity and asks such existential questions as "Who am I?" It is also a time when sexual identity and sexual preferences are being expressed. Often the young person discovers and identifies with a role model. A positive self-image is the desired result of this stage, accompanied by the traits of devotion and fidelity. Problems with sexual identity and delayed selection of an occupation are common manifestations of failure to resolve the critical task of stage 5.

The sixth stage, lasting from ages 20 to 40 is the stage of *intimacy versus isolation*. The task of these years is to be able to commit oneself to meaningful, loving relationships with others. When intimacy is not achieved, the individual avoids or retreats from emotional commitments in various ways, such as being aloof, fleeing relationships as soon as they become intense, or being promiscuous so that no relationship is meaningful. Avoidance behaviors may take diverse forms, but they all have the effect of isolating the individual from closeness.

The task of the seventh stage, which lasts from ages 40 to 60, is the mastery of *generativity versus stagnation*. In this period the individual shows concern for younger generations, usually by offering them guidance and support. Besides her own children, she may express a global concern for generations yet unborn. Although many adults experience a heightened sense of productivity and creativity at this time, those who have not accomplished the critical task may enter a period of stagnation, characterized by an inability to care for the needs of others. The stagnated person has an exaggerated self-interest, often manifested in preoccupation with somatic complaints or indifference to conditions except as they affect her.

The eighth and last stage, occurring after the age of 60, is Erikson's period of *ego integrity versus despair*. The final developmental task is to accept one's life and its meaning. Wisdom, altruism, and solace are attributes acquired by the individual who is successful at this task of the life cycle. Those who cannot arrive at a state of satisfaction or contentment with themselves and their entire existence often desire to relive their lives in order to do things differently. These persons engage in wistful longing for the past, express deep regrets about the course their lives have taken, and frequently have a profound fear of death.

Moral Development Theory

Lawrence Kohlberg (1968) is a social scientist and educator who has proposed a theory of moral development that sees the individual as going through a fixed series of states. This theory is based on a longitudinal study of males ranging in age from 10 to 28. Data collection procedure consisted of reading the subjects stories that depicted moral dilemmas, asking them to solve them, then questioning subjects about their reasons for arriving at particular solutions. Kohlberg's emphasis was on the subjects' reasoning processes in solving the moral dilemmas, not on the solutions themselves. A coding and scoring system was used that allowed researchers to classify and analyze the proposed solutions. As a result of this long-term investigation, Kohlberg identified three levels of moral development, each of which is further divided into two stages (called orientations), making a total of six. The accompanying box outlines the stages and levels of moral development proposed by Kohlberg.

One of Kohlberg's basic assumptions is that the progression of moral development does not vary in any way. That is, each individual must proceed through each of the given stages in sequence and cannot omit a stage while advancing to higher levels of moral development.

Each stage of moral development has its own particular orientation; ambiguity arises as individuals begin to question their present orientation stage. This questioning is resolved as individuals move to the next stage and find that the new orientation settles or reconciles their previous questions. If a person finds that his present stage is not adequate to resolve a moral dilemma, he will gravitate toward the next highest stage.

THE PRECONVENTIONAL LEVEL Kohlberg described the first level, or *preconventional level*, as one at which the child is responsive to cultural labels of good and bad, right and wrong, but interprets these labels in terms either of the physical or psychological consequences of action (punishment, reward, exchange of favors) or of the physical power of those who enunciate the rules and labels. This level describes most children up to the age of early adolescence; however, some adults are fixated at this level, too. At this first level, actions are judged according to expected consequences.

Fear governs the actions of a person at stage 1 of the preconventional level called the punishment and obedience orientation. Kohlberg's theory would explain the antisocial actions of criminals as behaviors of a stage 1, preconventional level. Kohlberg called stage 2 the instrumental relativist orientation. At this stage a person decides issues based on what satisfies her own needs and sometimes considers the needs of others. Persons operating at stage 2 of the preconventional level perceive society as made up of others like themselves, and they believe that if they extend help to others, they are likely to be helped in return. Because the person at this stage believes that all people are alike, she will begin to question why one person should have more rights than another. Thus, stage 2 marks the beginning of a sense of fairness. Nonetheless, self-interest remains important, and fear of authority is reduced. To obtain compliance from persons at this stage, it may be necessary to demonstrate how they will benefit from a given situation or transaction.

THE CONVENTIONAL LEVEL The move from the preconventional level to the *conventional level* is accompanied by acceptance of group values and recognition of the importance of group rules and sanctions. The personal consequences of an action are no longer the only criteria by which to judge its goodness or morality. Instead, an action is judged by how well it meets the standards or expectations of others in a group or social order. When individuals identify with a group, the esteem and approval

---

KOHLBERG'S MORAL DEVELOPMENT STAGES

Preconventional Level

Stage 1. Punishment and obedience orientation
Stage 2. Instrumental relativist orientation

Conventional Level

Stage 3. Interpersonal concordance or good boy/nice girl orientation
Stage 4. Law and order orientation

Postconventional Level

Stage 5. Social contract legalistic orientation
Stage 6. Universal ethical principle orientation

of others begin to displace tangible rewards as the dominant motivator of behavior. One aspect of the conventional level is *cohesiveness*, or the feeling of belonging to and valuing a group. People at the conventional level adopt standards of group conformity and loyalty to justify the group not only to others but to themselves.

Most teenagers operate at stage 3, the interpersonal concordance orientation. Their concentration on heroes, idols, and fads is just one indication of the overwhelming importance they give to group identity and group approval. As a result, an appeal to group values is likely to have an impact on adolescents.

Once individuals become fully aware that society is composed of divergent groups with opposing value systems, the usefulness of broader laws, rules, and behavior codes becomes more apparent. It is at this point that individuals move on to stage 4, which Kohlberg called the law and order orientation. Individuals at this stage believe they are acting correctly when they show respect for authority and comply with rules and laws.

Because the law is considered to be the guardian of social order, no individual or group is thought to be above it. Kohlberg contends that the majority of adults remain permanently at this stage of moral development.

THE POSTCONVENTIONAL LEVEL With advancement to the *postconventional level* comes the first hint of independent or autonomous judgment. Prior to this level, behaviors are directed by fear of punishment (stage 1), expectation of pleasure or reward (stage 2), group norms (stage 3), or adherence to law (stage 4). Individuals who have progressed to stage 5 can make up their own minds about behaviors that are right or wrong. Instead of merely judging actions according to existing principles established or enforced by others, persons at the postconventional level consider what principles the individual and society *should* follow.

Those who have reached stage 5 (the social contract legalistic orientation) believe that individuals have a right to personal values, beliefs, opinions, and behaviors, provided they do not harm others. The person at this stage makes a clear distinction between areas of personal freedom and areas of public welfare. In areas where individual actions may affect the lives of others, he recognizes the need for legislation and regulation. This viewpoint represents a radical departure from the belief that law is fixed and unchangeable.

A person functioning at stage 5 may be critical of the status quo, but does not think this constitutes a license to be arbitrary or anarchistic. He believes that existing and proposed legislation may be sub-jected to scrutiny and questioning but that laws cannot be discarded simply because they are personally objectionable.

The sixth and highest stage of moral development is the universal ethical principle orientation. The individual at this advanced stage of moral development is guided not by fixed rules and regulations but by abstract principles compatible with internal values. These internalized standards include respect for the rights of everyone and devotion to principles of honor and justice. When the individual fails to live up to these principles, feelings of guilt and self-recrimination follow. Therefore, the individual will go to great lengths to avoid violating the self-imposed principles, even when adherence is followed by unpleasant consequences. A conscientious objector who refuses to bear arms and is willing to suffer imprisonment for his views exhibits behavior characteristic of this stage. Kohlberg believes that this stage represents an ideal that is often sought but seldom reached.

GILLIGAN'S MORAL DEVELOPMENT THEORY It has been noted that the sample population of the longitudinal study on which Kohlberg's theory is based included no females. Critics of this work assert that a comprehensive theory of moral development should give balanced attention to both sexes. Gilligan was involved in formulating Kohlberg's theory (Kohlberg and Gilligan 1971) but was concerned because females were excluded from the sample. She also called attention to the brevity of Piaget's mention of girls in his work (see next section) and his assumption that the word *child* really referred to boys. The preoccupation of theorists with male cognitive and moral development led to one developmental standard, so the females whose progress did not conform to the accepted standard were labeled deviant and by implication, inferior. Gilligan argues eloquently that there are not one but two modes of moral reasoning and decision making. One mode is based on logic, justice, and rights; the other is based on caring, responsiveness, and context (Gilligan 1982, 1983).

One moral dilemma devised by Kohlberg is a situation in which a man with a sick wife cannot afford to buy a life-saving drug. The question Kohlberg asked is whether the man should steal the drug after the druggist refuses to adjust the price. Gilligan presented this dilemma to two eleven-year-old children, Amy and Jake. She found, as she had discovered in larger investigations, that the boy and girl followed two different response patterns. What she found was that the boy answered the question that was asked (Should the man steal the drug?), but the girl answered a different, unasked question. Amy was not interested so much in *whether* the man should steal the drug, but rather in *how* he should *behave* in this predicament.

Gilligan identified two distinct moral languages that are gender-related; the language of logic preserves separation and the language of responsiveness preserves attachment. Moral development as defined by Kohlberg maintains independence at the expense of interdependence and even fosters indifference to the circumstances of others.

From her research Gilligan concluded that men are likely to define themselves in terms of autonomy and achievement, and women in terms of relationships. Even if one disagrees with Gilligan, her work is important for two reasons. First, it reminds us of the complexity of human development, moral or otherwise. Second, it looks at the important influence of gender in moral development. Men and women inhabit the same world, but their experience of the world is "genderized" regardless of their preferences or aptitudes. The full range of moral development and of gender-related priorities in moral dilemmas has yet to be mapped.

Cognitive Development Theory

Jean Piaget was a Swiss psychologist who conducted extensive observational studies of children in an attempt to understand their stages of intellectual and cognitive development. On the basis of observation, interviews, and experiments, Piaget postulated four stages of cognitive development in children, lasting from birth to the beginning of adolescence. Although he gave normative ages to the stages, Piaget (1969) emphasized the range of individual differences in rates of development and therefore presented chronological ages simply as a guide (see Table 15–1).

SENSORIMOTOR STAGE Piaget termed the first stage of cognitive development the *sensorimotor stage*. During the first 18 months of life, an infant uses her senses to learn about the world. By means of sight, hearing, taste, touch, and smell the infant explores her environment. Eventually she learns patterns of behaviors and looks for ways to test and replicate these patterns, and she gradually learns to predict actions based on the consequences of previous actions. For example, she may learn that dropping a bottle on the floor causes adults in the vicinity to retrieve the bottle and return it to her, an action that she finds gratifying. Such primitive sequences of cause and effect behavior are the foundation for future problems solving and lead to more complex intellectual development.

PREOPERATIONAL STAGE During the *preoperational stage*, the thinking of the young child is quite rigid and inflexible, partly because the child is *egocentric* and unable to appreciate ideas and viewpoints that differ from his own.

At this age, the child comes to realize that even though he cannot see a hidden object or a person who has left the room, the object or person continues to exist. Thus, he attains *object permanence*, the understanding that people and objects exist apart from the self. To the child in the sensorimotor stage, people or objects that are out of sight have disappeared permanently as far as he is concerned. Therefore, when a toy is taken away from him and concealed, he will not look for it. The child at the preoperational stage, on the other hand, will search for a concealed toy, demonstrating object permanence.

Another characteristic of the preoperational stage is the use of symbols in the child's thinking and communication. At this stage the child realizes that a single word or sign can represent more complex ideas and meanings. Bringing a ball to father is an invitation for father to play with the child; putting on a coat signifies a desire or readiness to go outdoors. Pumpkins signify Halloween and the flag signifies one's country. From such basic signs, the child learns the significance of symbols.

Table 15–1. Piaget's Cognitive Development Stages		
Stage	**Age**	**Characteristics**
Sensorimotor	Birth–18 months	Child learns about self and surroundings through sensory and motor exploration and experience; learns through trial and error.
Preoperational	18 months–7 years	Child develops language skills, acquires understanding of symbols, recognizes object permanence, learns to separate and classify.
Concrete operational	8 years–11 years	Child uses and manipulates numbers, understands spatial relationships, learns to think logically and to reason.
Formal operational	12 years–Adulthood	Adolescent understands abstract concepts, expands ability to think logically and to reason, formulates and tests hypotheses.

CONCRETE OPERATIONAL STAGE Between the ages of 8 and 11, the child is in the *concrete operational stage*. During this stage the child can use and manipulate numbers and begin to understand spatial relationships. These are the years when the concept of moral judgment begins to develop and when the cognitive skills of the child are burgeoning, although abstract thinking is not yet present. When asked to explain the meaning of the proverb "Never change horses in the middle of a stream," the child will give a literal interpretation, explaining that a rider changing horses in the middle of a stream would fall in and get wet. The child would be unlikely to generalize the meaning to other situations or to extract the message that anyone who starts a project and changes the original plan risks failure.

FORMAL OPERATIONAL STAGE The fourth stage of cognitive development, the *formal operational stage*, begins at about age 12. This is the most sophisticated cognitive level. The individual becomes capable of abstract thinking and is able to formulate and test hypotheses. Problem solving at this stage is sequential and orderly, and reasoning processes are logical and usually consistent.

Cognitive development theory has been enriched by investigators representing various disciplines and views; a few of their observations deserve mention here.

Just as socialization begins at birth, so does learning. Newborn infants respond to visual patterns and prefer complex, three-dimensional and moving patterns to plainer, two-dimensional, or stationary ones. Newborns also react to sound and can localize its point of origin. Babies at one week of age have learned to imitate an "adult's fluttering her eyelashes or opening or closing her mouth." Thomas (1981) also cited other research that documented movement of the child in precise rhythm with adult speech.

Furthermore, as is true with attachment processes, this learning process involves both infant and adult caretaker. The infant's responses influence the adult's activities with the child. Elkind (1974) identified children's attachment to their parents as the stable foundation from which children venture forth to learn about the world. Because of this fundamental role of adults, their understanding or lack of understanding of how children learn is crucial to their children's experiences.

Adults tend to think of children as being miniature adults. Thus, adults expect that children will learn only while they are sitting quietly and listening. In truth, children learn by getting actively involved with their environment and manipulating

various parts of it. Forcing a preschool child to "be quiet and learn this" paves the way to resentment.

In keeping with the erroneous idea of the child as a miniature adult, parents attribute adultlike understanding and intention to their young child's use of "dirty words," swear words, expressions of contempt, or wishes that a person were dead. At most, the child realizes that such words or phrases are powerful in some way. Understanding is based on the reactions of others rather than on understanding of the meaning of the words.

From age two on, children ask many questions if they are permitted to do so. By age four they want to know the origin and purpose of things around them. "Where did it come from?" or "What is it for?" are questions they ask repeatedly. At this age children begin to be concerned about death. "What is death?" and "Why do people die?" At this age children do not see death as final.

At some time between ages five and nine, children come to realize that death is final. However, they also personify death and therefore, they feel that death can be outwitted and eluded. This concept still locates death as being outside the person. Thus, children's perception of death is gradually modified by cognitive development. Very young children view death as temporary and when confronted with the death of a loved one believe that the person will return at some future time. School-aged children recognize the difference between life and death but tend to believe that only other people die. By eight or nine years of age, children are aware of personal mortality but perceive death as possible rather than inevitable. Magical thinking is often used by children to ward off threats of illness or injury. Some youngsters take reckless risks to master their fears. They may accept dares and challenges that permit them to scoff at danger and deny their growing awareness of sharing the destiny of all living things.

In explaining death to children, it is advisable to be factual and honest. Euphemisms and evasions tend to confuse children. Statements to the effect that "Grandpa is happier where he is now" seem strange when uttered by weeping family members. Preparing children to deal with death can be facilitated by candid discussion of the cyclical nature of human existence. Such discussion is a form of anticipatory guidance that may be painful for adults but helpful for children, whose cognitive and experiential understanding of death is limited. When any family member dies, the reminiscing and mementos that ease mourning for adults can be adapted to help children accept and understand.

Entry into the stage of concrete operations occurs at about age 7 or 8 and this stage persists until about age 11. To their parents' delight, children's intense question asking is over. Their thinking is now more adultlike in that they can deal with two elements or relationships of a situation at the same time. Furthermore, in their mastery of recognizing classes of things, children can complete the primary school exercise of inspecting several items and picking out the one that does not belong—that is, the item not in the same classification as the others. However, in their new ability to think in these ways, children are not able to clearly separate what they think from what they perceive. If facts contradict hypotheses that they have formulated, children reject or adjust the facts (Elkind 1974).

Family Development Theory

The developmental frameworks described thus far have been concerned primarily with individuals, although social considerations are sometimes mentioned. The developmental framework of Evelyn Duvall (1967, 1971) focuses on the family life cycle, dividing it into eight stages, each centered around specific tasks and based on the age of the oldest child (see Figure 15–1). The eight tasks that determine the family's developmental stage are: (1) physical maintenance; (2) allocation of resources; (3) division of labor; (4) socialization of family members; (5) reproduction, recruitment, and release of family members; (6) maintenance of order; (7) placement of members in the larger society; and (8) maintenance of motivation and morale. Like the other developmental theorists, Duvall believes that specific tasks must be accomplished if the biological, psychological, and social needs of every family member are to be met. (For a more detailed discussion of critical family tasks, see Chapter 19.)

When children are quite young, the primary family task is to meet the children's needs for physical, emotional, and social nurture. At the same time, parents must also attend to their own needs for intimacy and privacy; the marital relationship must be sustained within the family relationship. As children enter school, parents must begin to concern themselves with the educational progress of their children and with the children's adjustments to the larger society, represented by school and community functions. When children become teenagers, parents must manage the delicate balance between being supportive and fostering independence. At the time when children leave home to launch their own lives, the parents must readjust to the contraction of family size. During the last stages of the family life cycle, parents must adjust to being a couple again as they adapt to retirement and aging.

In functional families, each individual member is supported in the accomplishment of individual critical tasks as the family as a whole adjusts to the changing needs of its members. The result is a system in which no member is unfairly exploited and in which the family continues to modify its operations in order to function adaptively.

STRESS AND ADAPTATION IN THE FAMILY Growth and maturational processes inevitably bring changes to individuals and families. These universal changes, even when predictable and anticipated, produce conditions of stress. Similar events can produce different reactions in different people (Barry 1984). Thus, it is not the event itself that is the crucial factor but the response of the individual or the family. Most people are consistent in their manner of responding to stressful situations. Some usually respond with anger, while others use avoidance tactics. In addition, people vary in their ability to tolerate stress. Some people have little tolerance, while others appear to cope well.

In an ideal situation, the needs of the individual are compatible with the needs of the family; what seems beneficial for individual members coincides with what is deemed beneficial for the family. However, in the everyday world of real families there is frequent disagreement and incompatibility between what is good for the family and what is desired by individual members. The resulting conflict may be detrimental to the resolution of individual and family tasks. When a family member is working through a particular task, an optimal resolution would be to reconcile family needs and individual needs so that neither is achieved at the expense of the other. Unfortunately, this is not always easy to accomplish.

EXTERNAL FAMILY INFLUENCES In a sense, maturational tasks are rites of passage that mark the transition from one phase of life to the next. These rites of passage are influenced by the values of the family, which in turn are shaped by the larger social order. Some families are fortunate enough to feel that they truly belong in the community in which they live, but other families feel that they have been transplanted from a familiar, more comfortable environment to a new community where they feel like strangers.

When this happens, the family is perceived as deviant by others in the community, and this becomes a source of stress, especially for children and adolescents, who feel strong pressure to conform to the norms of the larger society. Customs concerning childrearing, socialization, and parental expectations then became a source of contention among family members. Since some transactions between such families and the community cannot be avoided, a way must be found to accommodate the values of traditionalist family members who are reluctant to adopt the values of the surrounding community.

Figure 15–1. *Duvall's eight stages of the family life cycle.*

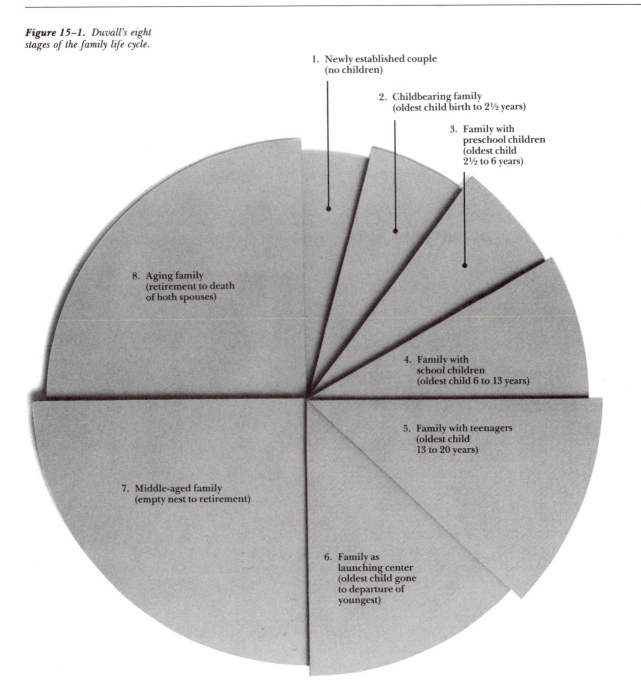

1. Newly established couple (no children)
2. Childbearing family (oldest child birth to 2½ years)
3. Family with preschool children (oldest child 2½ to 6 years)
4. Family with school children (oldest child 6 to 13 years)
5. Family with teenagers (oldest child 13 to 20 years)
6. Family as launching center (oldest child gone to departure of youngest)
7. Middle-aged family (empty nest to retirement)
8. Aging family (retirement to death of both spouses)

Issues concerning independence and individuality must be settled by every family, but they often become problematic for families transplanted from one culture to another. Independence and individuality are highly regarded in American culture, but these attributes are often viewed with fear and suspicion by ethnic families who fear a drastic break with old customs (Feretta, Rivera, and Lucero 1981).

INTERNAL FAMILY INFLUENCES Stress may be induced by factors generated within the self or by factors within the social environment. As the first social unit that molds personality, the family is a powerful influence on the young child. Family dynamics can be either constructive or destructive. For example, a mismatch between the temperament of a child and the expectations of the parents can be detrimental to the child's development. A highly organized, perfectionist parent may be disappointed with the behavior of a child who is careless or indifferent about projects such as homework. Outgoing parents may become impatient with a shy, retiring child, whereas quiet, reticent parents may feel overwhelmed by a boisterous, aggressive child. Such incongruity may inhibit the development of the child (Chess and Thomas 1982).

As integral components of the environment that the child inhabits, the child's parents bring their goals, attitudes, and values to bear on her. Their responses to the child depend in part on compatibility of the youngster's temperament with their expectations (Thomas and Chess 1977, 1980).

Temperament may be defined as a description of behavioral style evident at a given point in time. The origins of behavioral style lie with genetic factors which are reinforced by the environment, and with early prenatal and neonatal influence by the parents. Later in children's lives, environmental factors play a role in accentuating or changing temperament. Environmental or cultural expectations are conveyed to children by the behavior and attitudes of their parents and siblings, their peers, older children, and other adults, including extended family members, neighbors, and teachers.

It is clear that a child's temperament interacting with certain environmental circumstances can precipitate a crisis, such as the disruption of the relationship between a parent and child.

Thomas and Chess were interested in seeing whether behavioral problems of their subjects in late childhood and adolescence could be predicted on the basis of temperament; they found that the most important predictor of adjustment or maladjustment was not the temperament of the child but the "fit" or "consonance" between the child and the family environment. Consonance was considered present when parental expectations and demands were in accord with the child's capacities, motivation, and behavioral style. For example, a boy might have a constellation of behaviors that earned him the label of "difficult" by the investigators, but if his parents accepted that his behaviors were different from those of an "easy" child and rose to the challenge without rejecting their son, the child's adjustment would be eased. Also important was compatibility between the family standards of acceptable behavior and those of the school attended by the child.

Nursing Implications

Of the theoretical frameworks presented here, Erikson's psychosocial theory probably has received the greatest acceptance by nurses, perhaps because the contributions of Kohlberg and Piaget are more limited in focus. Nevertheless, these two theorists have a place in the assessment of human development. To illustrate, Kohlberg's identification of the search for group identity in adolescence helps nurses recognize the powerful impact of peer group influence. The nurse who can recognize the group standards of dress, diet, and conduct that influence the adolescent client is then able to use this information to devise interactions acceptable to the client. In the same way, a nurse who can determine whether a client is guided by fear of punishment, by a wish for social approval, or by an internalized value system will find it easier to collaborate with the client in setting mutually acceptable goals.

Piaget's theoretical framework can be useful to nurses trying to teach, reassure, and care for children of various ages, whatever the setting. Knowing that a young child cannot use or understand symbols will remind nurses to interact in a fashion appropriate to the child's age and cognitive abilities. The use of games, dolls, and puppets to explain various procedures to hospitalized children is one example of the application of Piaget's ideas. His framework is also helpful in understanding why separation from the mother is particularly distressing for children in the sensorimotor stage, who believe that absent persons and objects cease to exist.

There is no guarantee that every individual will proceed to the highest levels of cognitive and moral development. The capacity of individuals for growth is affected by innumerable factors; moral and cognitive growth are no exception. However, the frameworks independently determined by Kohlberg and Piaget provide normative guidelines that are worthy of consideration.

In using Duvall's developmental framework to assess a family, a nurse might begin by asking questions designed to identify discordant areas in the operation of the family and the lives of its members. A nurse assessing the cause of maturational difficulties might well superimpose the individual tasks conceptualized by Erikson onto Duvall's framework. Formulating nursing interventions that help reconcile both individual and family critical tasks is one way of promoting adaptive functioning. The failure of any members to resolve maturational tasks may be a means of preserving family equilibrium, but the price is maladaptive behavior that neglects or exploits one or more family members. For example, a protective mother may be a necessity for young children but a detriment for older children as they begin to search for identity and intimacy outside the home.

When using a combined individual/family approach to assess maturational progress, the nurse might include the following points of investigation:

1. What is the developmental stage of the family?
2. What is the primary critical task of the family at this point?
3. What is the developmental stage of each family member?
4. What is the primary critical task of each family member?
5. What critical tasks of the family and of individual members are being achieved in an adaptive, compatible way?

SEVERITY OF PSYCHOSOCIAL STRESSORS SCALE: CHILDREN AND ADOLESCENTS

Code	Term	Examples of Stressors	
		Acute events	**Enduring circumstances**
1	None	No acute events that may be relevant to the disorder	No enduring circumstances that may be relevant to the disorder
2	Mild	Broke up with boyfriend or girlfriend; change of school	Overcrowded living quarters; family arguments
3	Moderate	Expelled from school; birth of sibling	Chronic disabling illness in parent; chronic parental discord
4	Severe	Divorce of parents; unwanted pregnancy; arrest	Harsh or rejecting parents; chronic life-threatening illness in parent; multiple foster home placements
5	Extreme	Sexual or physical abuse; death of a parent	Recurrent sexual or physical abuse
6	Catastrophic	Death of both parents	Chronic life-threatening illness
0	Inadequate information, or no change in condition		

SOURCE: American Psychiatric Association DSM-III-R (1987).

6. What critical tasks of the family and of individual members are not being achieved in an adaptive, compatible way?

7. What are the sources of maladaptation and incompatibility?

8. How can incompatibility be reduced while attending to the needs of individual members and preserving the integrity of the family?

9. How have individual members of the family dealt with developmental issues in the past?

VARIATIONS AND DISRUPTIONS OF CHILDHOOD

Stresses in the life of the parents can greatly affect their ability to offer sustained affection and nurturing. Changes in the marital relationship, in the financial status of the family, or in the health of family members may have considerable impact on the parent-child relationship. Because young children have few channels other than crying to communicate distress, they tend to express anxiety, anger, and fear behaviorally in the form of sleep disturbances, eating problems, and excretory difficulties.

The temperament and responses of the child also play an important part in the attachment process. Children differ greatly in their behavior patterns, and the child who is demanding and difficult to care for will arouse negative emotions in even the most devoted parents.

Sleep Disturbances

At birth the infant does not distinguish the self from the environment. In effect, the self is merged with the surroundings and the infant makes no distinctions between persons who give care. At about six to eight months of age, the infant begins to make distinctions between what is strange and what is familiar. Because the familiar is associated with mother, food, and security, what is familiar becomes welcome and what is strange becomes something to be avoided. Usually it is the mother's absence that produces the greatest fear, followed by the appearance of strangers (Bowlby 1969, 1973, 1979). Prolonged separation from the mother can be highly traumatic during this crucial period.

Fear of separation from the mother (*separation anxiety*) is often manifested in sleep disturbances, such as refusal to sleep. When this happens the parents may be deprived of their own rest; fatigue then heightens the reactions of parents and fosters anxiety in them. In addition, when parents themselves are anxiety prone, their anxiety is sensed by the infant, who then becomes more anxious and less likely to sleep.

SLEEP DISORDERS

Parasomnias

307.47 Dream anxiety disorder (Nightmare disorder)
307.46 Sleep terror disorder
307.46 Sleepwalking disorder
307.40 Parasomnia NOS

SOURCE: American Psychiatric Association DSM-III-R (1987).

In infants, poor sleep patterns often have a physical cause, such as hunger, colic, itching, binding clothing, or a room temperature that is too hot or too cold. Treatment requires adjustment of the specific cause of the problem. Observant nurses who take the time to investigate can often discover the cause of the sleep difficulty. A formula may have to be changed, or the parents may need help in learning how and when to offer nourishment to the infant. Sometimes parents lack understanding of the sleep patterns of normal infants and need to be better informed about childhood patterns of growth and development.

The sleep disturbances common in childhood may take the form of resistance to sleep, restless sleep, nightmares, night terrors, sleepwalking, and wakefulness. These sleep disturbances are apt to have more varied etiology than the sleep disturbances of infancy. Parents who are inconsistent in the sleep routine they establish are the most likely to encounter sleep disturbances in their children. Although it is unwise for parents to permit the bedtime ritual to become too elaborate, a familiar routine can be reassuring to a child.

Fearfulness may keep a child awake or may contribute to restless sleep. Fear of the dark is a common phenomenon in young children. Their imagination can easily convert sounds and shadows into sinister agents, especially if they are alone in the dark. Unsuitable movies, violent television programs, and ghost stories told before bedtime can intensify what began as mild discomfort. A child may also be anxious and fearful about tangible problems either at home or in school. School worries may be related to peer acceptance or to academic performance.

Talking in one's sleep is a common occurrence among children, although their speech is usually mumbled and unintelligible. Occasionally, sleep talking is followed by screaming and crying.

The response to sleep disturbances requires correction of any underlying physical cause and appropriate changes in bedtime routines. After an active or exciting day, children need a period of time to "wind down" before falling asleep. Bedtime stories and lullabies were invented for just this purpose.

Children's fears and anxieties, however trivial, should not be ignored or carelessly dismissed but responded to in a caring, attentive manner. Another remedial approach is to explore the parents' attitudes toward the sleep patterns of their children. It is not useful for naptime or bedtime to amount to a state of warfare between parents and child. Equally inadvisable is the habit of sending children to bed as a punishment for unacceptable behavior.

Nurses can give helpful advice to parents whose children have developed sleep disturbances. Warm baths and warm, nonstimulating beverages have been good inducers of sleep for many generations. A storytelling period when the child is lying in bed or a short interval when the child can talk in a relaxed way with a parent may be an enticement that helps prepare the child for sleep. It may also prove helpful to provide parents with information and education regarding the normal range of children's sleep behaviors and the individual differences in children that account for the wide variation in their sleep requirements.

Nightmare, or Dream Anxiety Disorder as it is named in the DSM-III-R, is not uncommon in children. Nightmares may occur any time during the sleep cycle but are more common toward morning. The content of the dream is frightening, and there may be a recurrent theme. During the dream there is little physical movement because the sleeper is usually in an REM sleep stage, where muscle tone is relaxed, but there may be agitated movement as the sleeper wakens. The dream is usually remembered upon awakening and in the morning. Nightmares in children are generally not associated with serious psychiatric disorder; in adults their occurrence is more apt to indicate psychiatric disturbance. In half the instances onset is before 10 years of age. However, children outgrow the disorder and daytime adjustment is rarely impaired. The cause may be a stressful event or changes in sleep environment or routine. Childhood illnesses and medications may bring on an episode of nightmare. The experience is vivid and terrifying to the child, since what he remembers is a dream that threatened his security or safety. The child needs help in getting back to sleep and needs comfort and reassurance from a trusted person.

Sleep terror disorder is often mistaken for dream anxiety, but there are important differences. In sleep terror disorder there are repeated episodes of awakening, and no detailed dream is recalled. Epileptic and other forms of seizures during sleep are possible; the occurrence of sleep terror episodes should instigate a physical workup that includes an electroencephalograph.

Sleepwalking usually begins between ages 6 and 12 and may take place rarely or every night. The problem may last several years, but tends to disappear by late adolescence. When the onset is delayed until adulthood, the problem is apt to be more chronic. Typically, the sleepwalker seems calm and purposeful and is capable of opening doors, climbing stairs, eating, or going to the bathroom. Yet the sleepwalker is unresponsive to efforts to communicate or be awakened. Some of them awaken spontaneously and are confused about where they are and how they got there. Others return to bed without ever wakening and have little or no recall of the episode the next day. Even though they seem to be aware of objects in their path, sleepwalkers have poor coordination. They are liable to stumble or fall during the episode and may take routes that are quite dangerous. The major complication of sleepwalking is the possibility of accidental injury; vigilance and protective measures are called for until the child outgrows the problem. The episodes seem to be associated with daytime stress and extreme fatigue; these conditions should be controlled as much as possible.

Sleep problems can be a cause of great concern for parents, and repeated manifestations should be investigated to rule out organic causes or psychopathology. Reassurance, protection, and comfort are usually sufficient to deal with the problem in children. Inevitably there are situations where sleep disturbances resist the usual remedies. If the nurse suspects that a differential diagnosis is needed or that the sleep problem is a sign of psychological distress, referral for extensive evaluation is in order.

Eating Disturbances

Poor appetite in children is a complaint that frequently troubles parents. Although many infants exhibit a lessening of appetite toward the end of the first year, poor eating rarely becomes a problem before age two. During the first year, physical growth is dramatic; on the average, birth weight is tripled. After that the average weight gain from ages one to five is about five pounds annually. The rate of weight gain is sporadic, and months may pass without any appreciable gain. As a result, the need for food is correspondingly lower in the preschool years and appetite is diminished. Parents who do not understand the reasons for this lessened appetite show their concern by pleading, coercing, or cajoling their child to eat. The discrepancy between parental expectations and the child's physiological needs may lead to eating disturbances during childhood and later (Bruch 1973, 1978).

EATING DISORDERS

307.10 Anorexia nervosa
307.51 Bulimia nervosa
307.52 Pica
307.53 Rumination disorder of infancy
307.50 Eating disorder NOS

SOURCE: American Psychiatric Association DSM-III-R (1987).

Between the ages of one and five, the child is in the process of developing independence. By resisting parental direction and by demanding to do things differently, the child is differentiating himself from others. Sometimes this means that the child refuses to eat when the parents want him to. By insisting that the child eat when and what they choose, parents lay the groundwork for an ongoing battle over food and eating. In such instances mealtime often signals the acting out of a struggle for dominance between parents and child (Sanger and Cassino 1984).

Another parental behavior contributing to eating disturbances is continuing to feed a child who is capable of self-feeding. Although a mother may feel that it is neater and quicker to feed the child, her actions may frustrate the child and lead to a test of wills, resulting in refusal by the child to eat or to be fed. Parents who are rigid and inflexible about their child's diet may offer the child a way to annoy them merely by breaking or defying rules and schedules. Once established, patterns like this can become fixed and difficult to change.

Because many eating problems are either initiated or worsened by parental attitudes and behaviors, some primary prevention approaches are in order. From infancy onward, the surroundings for eating should be pleasant and free from irritating distractions. Schedules for mealtime should be regular without being excessively rigid. Children should be encouraged to feed themselves as soon as they show an interest in doing so and should be gently instructed in the proper use of eating utensils. Small portions of food should be served to the child, and parents would be wise not to insist that every morsel on the plate be eaten. If a child expresses a strong dislike for a certain food, it should be removed and reintroduced at a later time or in another form. Parents and other family members should avoid announcing their food biases, especially their dislikes, in the presence of a young child. By setting a tone of relaxation and anticipation about meals and by avoiding the temptation to bribe or reward children for eating, parents can do much to reduce the potential for conflict on this issue.

Pica is an altered eating pattern sometimes encountered by community health nurses visiting in the home and by nurses working in pediatric clinics. The altered behavior consists of persistent eating of nonnutritive substances such as paint, plaster, string, or hair. Most children with pica remain willing to eat normal foods as well. The eccentric eating behavior may begin in late infancy and usually ceases during childhood, although in some cases it continues into adolescence. The behavior is sometimes displayed by pregnant women but to a lesser extent than that shown by children.

As a rule, the behavior stops without causing long-term impairment. There is always a possibility, however, that the ingested substances may cause damage. Lead poisoning may follow ingestion of paint chips or paint-covered plaster. Frequent ingestion of hair may lead to intestinal obstruction; and ingestion of dirt, soil, or feces may cause toxic reactions. When children exhibit behaviors typical of pica, nursing intervention should include testing for lead poisoning and parental guidance if the nurse observes that the children are neglected, malnourished, or inadequately protected.

Urinary and Excretory Disturbances

Because the etiology of urinary and excretory disturbances in children may be physiological, this possibility should be investigated first so that proper corrective measures can be taken. A thorough physical examination of the child, accompanied by a family and social history, is essential before exploring the potential emotional sources of such problems. Common urinary and excretory disturbances include enuresis, constipation, and encopresis.

Enuresis is the involuntary discharge of urine, either during the day (diurnal) or at night (nocturnal), after the age of four. There are many possible physiological causes, including congenital abnormality of the urinary tract, diabetes mellitus, diabetes insipidus, and seizure disorders. All such possibilities must be thoroughly investigated.

Enuresis tends to be nocturnal and may occur every night with some children. For most children with this problem, nocturnal bladder control has never been achieved. When bedwetting takes place, the child rarely wakens even though the amount of urine voided may be quite large.

In some cases simple adjustments can alleviate nocturnal enuresis. Limiting or eliminating the amount of fluids ingested after the evening meal may have beneficial effects. Behavior modification procedures are sometimes effective. One procedure is for the child to sleep on a mattress on which the first few drops of urine trigger an alarm bell that wakens the child and inhibits further voiding in bed. Such conditioning techniques inhibit reflex voiding but overlook emotional factors.

The emotional causes of enuresis are multifactorial, ranging from family interactions characterized by anxiety and hostility, to insecurity and resentment engendered in the child by the birth of a new sibling, to developmental or maturational lags in the child due to emotional problems.

When enuresis is the response to a new baby in the home, it is often part of a generalized regression that includes petulance, whining, thumbsucking, temper tantrums, baby talk, and demands to drink from a bottle or to be diapered. Because these regressive behaviors indicate feelings of insecurity and resentment, solicitude and reassurance are needed. Extra attention, in the form of special time with mother and father, will help allay these feelings and encourage a return to age-appropriate behaviors.

Constipation is an excretory disturbance characterized by infrequent or difficult evacuation of feces. In an infant, the cause tends to be physiological, such as a redundant colon or a diet too low in roughage or too high in calcium. When constipation is habitual in older children, emotional factors deserve consideration. The attitude of the parents toward defecation and constipation may be a contributing factor. When the mother pays great attention to the time of evacuation and the appearance of stool, the child will sense the potential for conflict with and control over her mother. If enemas, suppositories, or cathartics are used to any great extent, habitual constipation is almost inevitable.

Encopresis is involuntary defecation after three years of age that is not related to dysfunction of the bowel. This condition is less common than enuresis and occurs more often in boys, especially between the ages of six and twelve. Initial intervention should include assessment for possible physiological causes, followed by a professional study of dietary habits in order to eliminate foods causing or exacerbating the condition. Because many children who are encopretic are also constipated, both conditions should be the object of study.

Treatment of encopresis requires physiological and psychological measures. In dealing with the psychological aspects of encopresis and enuresis, parents and professionals should be cautioned against employing rigid, compulsive actions that threaten the child's sense of confidence and self-control. Shame tactics should be strictly avoided. Shaming or humiliating the child is unlikely to be effective in curbing the behaviors and may in fact intensify emotional problems.

(Text continues on page 421.)

ELIMINATION DISORDERS

307.70 Functional encopresis
   Specify: primary or secondary type
307.60 Functional enuresis
   Specify: primary or secondary type
   Specify: nocturnal only, diurnal only, nocturnal and diurnal

SOURCE: American Psychiatric Association DSM-III-R (1987).

CLINICAL EXAMPLE

MATURATIONAL REGRESSION IN REACTION TO A NEWBORN SIBLING

Mark Evans is six years old and the middle child in a family of three children. His sister, Connie, is eleven and he has a new nine-week-old brother. Connie had eagerly looked forward to the baby's arrival and is excited to have a new brother. She is old enough to realize that she is still the only girl in the family, and her mother reinforces this feeling by making Connie her official helper as far as the boys are concerned.

Mark had reacted to the news of his mother's pregnancy by becoming more clinging, but he seemed to accept the situation as time went on. For the first two weeks after the birth of the baby, Mark was quiet but gave no serious indication of maladjustment. Then he began soiling himself at home after school. Realizing that Mark might be having problems accepting the new baby, his mother tried not to overreact to the episodes. She simply changed his clothing, gave him a hug and a cookie, and tried to overlook the incidents. It was more difficult for Mark's mother to remain casual when the soiling began to happen during the school day. Whenever Mark had an "accident," his teacher sent him to the school nurse, who made him as comfortable as possible until his mother arrived with a change of clothing. Because Mark seemed upset and reluctant to return to the classroom, his mother took him home. She usually left the baby with grandma or a neighbor, so the episodes of soiling gave Mark time to be with his mother without competing for attention.

Within a week or two the "accidents" in school became more frequent, while those at home subsided. Mark's teacher was annoyed by the disruptions to class routine, and the other children teased him constantly, but Mark did not seem overly distressed by the commotion. When the behavior showed no signs of improving, the school nurse suggested a physical examination and the possibility of getting psychological help if there was no physical explanation for Mark's problem. Mark's mother followed the nurse's recommendation and took him to the family pediatrician, who could find no physical explanation. Knowing that Mark had complete bowel and bladder control until his little brother was born, the pediatrician suggested an evaluation at a child guidance clinic.

ASSESSMENT

Mark's symptomatology accomplished a number of things. When he soiled himself in school, his mother left the new baby and came to the rescue. She then provided the care Mark had received and enjoyed as a much younger boy. Mark and his mother had always been extremely close, but when the new baby was born, she seemed preoccupied with him and Mark felt rejected. Assessment led to the following diagnoses being made:

Nursing Diagnoses

Anxiety
(related to separation from mother)

Ineffective individual coping
(related to encropresis and manipulative tactics)

Ineffective family coping: compromised
(related to role changes and discord)

Multiaxial Psychiatric Diagnoses

Axis I   309.21 Separation anxiety disorder
          307.70 Functional encopresis: secondary
                 type
Axis II   V61.20 Parent/child problem
Axis III None
Axis IV   3 Moderate
Axis V   GAF 50: Current
          GAF 80: Highest in past year

PLANNING

Mark's encopresis was attributed to changes in the family caused by the entry of a new baby. Although Mark and Connie had been prepared for the arrival of the new brother or sister, there were safeguards for Connie that did not exist for Mark. Because of her age and gender, Connie was able to move into a new role as family helper without losing her special position as the only girl. Her closeness with her father was enhanced rather than threatened by the baby brother, and a new closeness was developing between Connie and her mother. Mark, on the other hand, had lost his special relationship with his mother and had found nothing to take its place. It was therefore considered important for Mark's father to build closer ties with the boy in order to compensate Mark for what he thought he had lost. When there were only two children, it was possible for the family to function with alliances between mother and Mark, father and Connie. The new baby changed the family balance. It became essential that the father form a new alliance that included both older children and that the mother reinforce Mark's important status as the older brother.

IMPLEMENTATION

Although Mark's encopresis was the presenting problem, this family had been divided for some time. Dysfunction was not evident because the division in the family was equitable and the alliances satisfied all family members. However, the alignment between his mother and Mark and between Connie and her father meant that each child was uninvolved with one parent. The birth of a new baby allowed Connie to move closer to her mother without jeopardizing her special relationship with her father.

Mark, on the other hand, was ousted from his special position with his mother and yet continued to be excluded from closeness with his father. His soiling episodes at school were covert attempts to renew his previous relationship with his mother.

The counselor at the child guidance clinic assured Mark's mother that encopresis was unlikely to become chronic regardless of the emotional component but indicated that some family changes would be helpful. Since the changes required the father as well as the mother, both parents were asked to attend several sessions. The need for new family alliances was pointed out to Mark's father, and a strong recommen- dation was made that Mark be included in the closeness that existed between Connie and her father. This

could be done by arranging activities that included both children, in addition to those that included only Mark and his father.

Mark's mother was advised to bring a change of clothing but not to take Mark out of school whenever he had an "accident". Mark's teacher and the school nurse were informed of this recommendation and agreed to co-operate. At home, Mark's mother began to rely on him to perform small services in order to encourage a sense of autonomy and self-esteem in him. This also had the effect of removing from Connie the role of the parenting child, a development that had further eroded Mark's self-esteem.

EVALUATION

Mark's episodes of encopresis gradually ceased over a six-month period. Mark's father made a conscious effort to establish a positive relationship with him and Mark proved receptive. Closeness with the father was facilitated because Connie continued to be involved with her mother and the baby. Both parents had learned the importance of including every child and excluding no child from parental attentiveness. Both had been devoted parents, but each had performed parenting functions as a solo act. Aware now of the reciprocal nature of parenting and the importance of operating as a dyad, the parents were committed to the ideal of equitable treatment of all three children.

Nursing Diagnosis	Goal	Nursing Action	Outcome Criteria	Outcome Evaluation
Anxiety	Client will be more willing to leave mother. Client's feelings of sibling rivalry will decrease.	Suggest mother spend time alone with client. Suggest father arrange shared activity with client.	Client will be less enmeshed with mother and more involved with father.	Mother now spends half hour with client before bedtime. Mother now spends half hour with daughter before bedtime. Father tends to infant while mother is with the older children.
Ineffective individual coping	Client's episodes of encopresis will diminish.	Refer client for physical workup. Refer client to child guidance clinic for evaluation. Suggest client remain in school after soiling episodes and return to class after change of clothing.	Client will not return home after encopresis. School nurse will assist client and enable him to finish the school day.	Client's physical workup was negative. Encopresis has declined: only 2 episodes in last 6 weeks. Evaluation at child guidance clinic was encouraging. Parents were seen twice for counseling and direction.
Ineffective family coping: compromised	Family equilibrium will be restored as new baby is integrated into family life.	Consult with child guidance clinic regarding evaluation. Interpret meaning of client's behavior to his parents. Encourage parents to involve client with the baby. Suggest parents point out to client that baby reacts to him by smiling and making friendly sounds.	All family members will be involved in tending to baby at mother's discretion. Client will not be excluded from any subsystem that includes sister and/or the baby. Parental subsystem will attend to the different needs for all three children.	Family routine had stabilized. Client and sister have begun to form a subsystem, calling themselves "the big kids." Client now talks about what a big brother can teach a little one.

Fears and Phobias

Fear is a warning sign that a threat or danger is near. Because fear, especially realistic fear, is something of a necessity, it is not advisable to teach children that fear should be avoided; rather, they should be reminded that fear can sometimes be a protection against danger. Fears can be aroused by objective (external) or subjective (internal) stimuli. Examples of objective stimuli include things that can be seen, heard, or felt, such as loud explosions or growling dogs. Subjective stimuli are often affected by earlier experiences and by what an individual has been told or has imagined.

Between the ages of two and five, many children are afraid of anticipated and imagined dangers. Fear of the dark is common among preschoolers, many of whom also fear being left alone or abandoned by loved ones. Thus, separation anxiety may become linked with fear of the dark. When fearful children are called upon to endure darkness in isolation, a dread of imaginary creatures may also appear. Causal factors linked to fearfulness in children include (Kashani et al. 1981):

■ Unusual constitutional sensitivity to fear-producing stimuli

■ Undermining of feelings of adequacy and security by an early trauma, such as accident, illness, or loss

■ Exposure to unfamiliar surroundings such as a hospital or a new school

■ Excessive warnings of the dangers of the world communicated to the child

■ Repeated experiences with failure, reinforcing the child's feelings of inadequacy and inability to cope

■ Inadequate interpersonal relationships extending beyond the family

As children enter and progress through school, fear of failure and fear of the unknown may become joined in their mind. For some children the primary fear is of parental disapproval or of failure to attain satisfactory academic standards. Children whose parents are less concerned with academic performance, may fear not making friends or not being accepted by the group.

Childhood fears may continue into adolescence and adulthood, but this is not the prevailing outcome. As children become older and have more opportunities for social interaction, they are likely to encounter corrective experiences. Behavior modification procedures (including desensitization and assertiveness training) and experiences that promote autonomy and confidence help to eliminate childhood fears (Carstens 1982).

In treating irrational fears, it is initially necessary to understand what the child fears. If the identified fear involves an imminent event, anticipatory guidance may be offered. The sequence of steps leading up to the feared event and the circumstances surrounding the event itself may be discussed with the child. This mental rehearsal, combined with reassurance and encouragement, does much to diminish fear of what might happen. If what the child fears is a repetition of a previous, painful event, she can practice repeating the experience in a safe atmosphere. This technique is appropriate for a shy child who is afraid of speaking or of being noticed in public.

It is important to distinguish between a fear and a phobia. A phobia has little or no basis in reality and therefore originates in subjective, internal stimuli. The identifying feature of a phobia is that the phobic person recognizes the irrationality of the feelings but cannot alter them. Thus, the unreasonable, unwarranted fears that surround the phobia continually intrude on conscious awareness. Perhaps the most common example of phobia in children is school phobia, also known as avoidant behavior about school, which is generally thought to be related to fear of separation from the mother. The restrictions that some phobias place on the life of any individual can be severe enough to require intensive measures. Behavior therapy may be used to help children and adults incapacitated by phobia, as may insight therapy that seeks to uncover the emotional basis of the problem. Sometimes both approaches are used in conjunction (Atkinson, Quarrington, and Cyr 1983).

Childhood Autism

Autism in childhood is a condition that begins in infancy and is marked by the inability to form interpersonal attachments, by obsessive-compulsive behavior patterns, and by conspicuous peculiarities of thought and language. Although the onset occurs within the first year of life, it may not be noticed until the child is about two years old. Unlike childhood schizophrenia, which is rarely manifested before age seven, autism cannot be said to make children regress. Instead, children with autism do not begin to develop according to cognitive, affective, or behavioral standards or norms. It has been said that schizophrenic children appear to develop normally for a time and then withdraw from the world, whereas autistic children never really enter the world. As infants, autistic children seem undemanding and this contributes to delayed recognition

---

PERVASIVE DEVELOPMENTAL DISORDERS

299.00 Autistic disorder
        Specify if childhood onset
299.80 Pervasive developmental disorder
        NOS

---

of the problem. The following behaviors are characteristic of these children (Bettelheim 1972a, 1972b).

Behavioral Patterns of Autistic Children

- Lack of interpersonal contact: manifested by failure to cuddle and avoidance of eye contact

- Insistence on sameness: manifested by rituals, repetitive actions, and intolerance of change or interruptions

- Speech and language peculiarities: manifested by patterns ranging from muteness to delayed speech development, to idiosyncratic speech such as babbling, echolalia, perseveration, and irrelevancy

There is a wide range of intellectual ability among autistic children. They are difficult to test, but usually score higher on performance than on verbal items on standardized tests. They may be retarded in some testing areas and normal to superior in others. Prognosis for these children is not good across the board. The systematic use of behavior modification techniques facilitates the management of these children and gives parents a sense of helping to alleviate a very distressing situation. Autistic children whose intelligence is near or above normal may reach their potential with special schooling and psychotherapy.

The families of autistic children need support and understanding from caregivers, for the condition is long-lasting. During adolescence and young adulthood the behavior patterns begin to resemble those of schizophrenia, even to the extent of gross delusions and hallucinations. Organic workups and neurological testing are necessary for these children, as well as individual testing of intelligence and motor skills. Speech therapy is advisable and should begin as early as possible. Aggressive and self-destructive actions are managed with appropriate medication, behavior modification, and psychotherapy. Sometimes the children are very resistant to psychotherapeutic intervention, but a therapeutic environment and consistent, caring people can

make a difference over time if the programs are developed in response to the needs and behaviors of each child.

Many autistic children can frustrate and try the patience of their caregivers. Like others with intractable behaviors, autistic children have been subjected to restraint, seclusion, and electric shock. These interventions may have assuaged caregivers, but not these troubled children.

Working with Children

Childhood is often romanticized by adults. They like to think of children as living in a protected world where their needs are met, playtime is joyous, and happiness abounds. This is not wholly true, for in even the best of environments a child also lives in an inner world of uncertainty and apprehension, which may be aggravated by urgent maturational tasks. Because infants and young children must depend on parents or parent surrogates to meet their needs, teaching parents about maturational tasks and children's developmental progress can serve as primary prevention aimed at avoiding dysfunctional behavior patterns in children. Many altered maturational patterns are created or worsened by unrealistic parental expectations. When parents do not recognize the time frame of development and growth in children, they either hasten or impede processes that may already be within the normal range.

If behavior problems have already become apparent, a nurse can utilize principles of secondary prevention. If assessment indicates that a parent is the instigator of the problem, the nurse might arrange opportunities to model effective adult-child interactions. By explaining and demonstrating basic concepts of stimulus, response, and reward, the nurse can indicate those adult actions that initiate or reinforce undesirable behavior in children. The difference between discipline and punishment is a subtle one for parents who rely only on scoldings or spankings to alter the behavior of their children. Of prime importance is the need to show parents the effectiveness of positive reinforcement in bringing about improved behaviors. For some parents praise is more difficult to bestow than disapproval. Such parents need to be assured that approving gestures will not necessarily threaten discipline or erode their authority.

Most parents tend to repeat the kind of parenting practices they themselves experienced. A nurse who recognizes a generational cycle of parenting behavior that is contributing to dysfunction may have to begin by introducing alternative ways of talking to and interacting with the children. Often parents resist the nurse's interventions until she has gained their confidence and trust by acknowledging

ADDITIONAL DISORDERS OF CHILDHOOD AND ADOLESCENCE

Specific Developmental Disorders

Academic skills disorders
315.10 Developmental arithmetic disorder
315.80 Developmental expressive writing disorder
315.00 Developmental reading disorder

Language and speech disorders
315.39 Developmental articulation disorder
315.31 Developmental expressive language disorder
315.31 Developmental receptive language disorder

Motor skills disorder
315.40 Developmental coordination disorder
315.90 Specific developmental disorder NOS

Other Developmental Disorders

315.90 Developmental disorder NOS

Disruptive Behavior Disorders

314.01 Attention-deficit hyperactivity disorder

Conduct disorder
312.20 Group type
312.00 Solitary aggressive type
312.90 Undifferentiated type
313.81 Oppositional defiant disorder

Anxiety Disorders of Childhood or Adolescence

309.21 Separation anxiety disorder
313.21 Avoidant disorder of childhood or adolescence
313.00 Overanxious disorder

Gender Identity Disorders

302.60 Gender identity disorder of childhood
302.50 Transsexualism
    Specify sexual history:
    asexual, homosexual, heterosexual, unspecified
302.85 Gender identity disorder of adolescence or adulthood, non-transsexual type
    Specify sexual history:
    asexual, homosexual, heterosexual, unspecified
302.85 Gender identity disorder NOS

Tic Disorders

307.23 Tourette's disorder
307.22 Chronic motor or vocal tic disorder
307.21 Transient tic disorder
    Specify: single episode or recurrent
307.20 Tic disorder NOS

Speech Disorders Not Elsewhere Classified

307.00 Cluttering
307.00 Stuttering

Other Disordance of Infancy, Childhood, or Adolescence

313.23 Elective mutism
313.82 Identity disorder
313.89 Reactive attachment disorder of infancy or early childhood
307.30 Stereotype/habit disorder
314.00 Undifferentiated attention-deficit disorder

SOURCE: American Psychiatric Association DSM-III-R (1987).

---

that parenting is a difficult, complicated task for which most people are not fully prepared.

VARIATIONS AND DISRUPTIONS OF ADOLESCENCE

Adolescence is generally recognized as a turbulent period of life. The individual is maturing physically, intellectually, socially, and sexually at a rapid rate. In an interval of about seven years, the individual travels the territory between childhood and incipient adulthood. It is a strange and intense journey over an unknown terrain (Erikson 1968). Most adolescents progress without undue difficulties, although the period is often stressful for parents as well as children. Perhaps the major task for adolescents is the establishment of identity as they move away from their family of origin. In the process of establishing a separate identity, they sometimes acquire problematic behaviors.

Identity Confusion
The task of creating a separate identity is complicated by the fact that most adolescents must accomplish it

while continuing to live with their family of origin, on whom they are likely to be financially dependent. At this point the adolescent is asking himself such existential questions as "Who am I? What shall I do with my life? Where will I fit in?" While the adolescent is asking these questions and differentiating from his family, his peer group assumes a position of great importance. Fads, stereotyped activities, and group-approved behavior become highly influential, often more than parental viewpoints.

A pattern of antisocial behavior can sometimes be discerned early in life. Between the ages of five and ten, the child begins to show signs of excessive defiance, temper tantrums, unruliness, and hostility. One of the consistent findings in the lives of delinquent adolescents is a constellation of unfavorable family characteristics. Parents of teenagers who display antisocial behaviors have a higher than average history of alcoholism, criminality, and marital conflict. The mothers frequently lack close emotional ties to their children and tend to ignore the delinquent behavior. The fathers tend to be strict and to use physical forms of punishment. Although disorganization is common in the families of delinquents, it is by no means a requirement. Antisocial behavior is expressed by adolescents from all socioeconomic levels, from intact nuclear families and one-parent families. In short, there is no clear-cut, simple formula to identify delinquent-producing families (Webster-Stratton 1985, Hartman, Burgess, and McCormack 1987).

When an adolescent engages in antisocial behavior, the entire family can probably benefit from counseling. Family issues are likely to be complex and to require the intervention of a skilled counselor. Just as no single cause precipitates antisocial behavior, so no single strategy is likely to rectify the situation. Approaches to intervention are varied. When facilities and staff are adequate, special schools, special programs, and specially prepared teachers can be of assistance. The major goals are to help adolescents learn about the world and themselves, to advance their education, and to teach them marketable skills. It is essential that peer group influences be directed toward resocialization rather than continuation of delinquent practices. Behavior techniques are usually part of programs designed to change maladaptive learned behaviors.

Residential institutions are dubious places for young people whose actions would not be considered criminal if committed by an adult. These would include such actions as running away from home and being sexually active. For this category of juvenile offenders, institutionalization might intensify rather than alleviate the problem. Institutionalizing juvenile status offenders along with persons who have committed violent antisocial acts places them under the influence of malevolent peers. However, failure to institutionalize young people who have committed violent crimes may be a disservice to society and to the young people themselves. A progressive step would be to remove felonies and misdemeanors committed by young people from the broad classification of juvenile delinquency and to formulate subgroups of offenses based in the seriousness of the juvenile's action as well as the age of the offender.

Body Image Distortion

Most adolescents are intensely preoccupied and concerned with their body image. They monitor the somatic changes in themselves and make comparisons with the bodies of peers and with the physical ideals of society. In some adolescents, especially females, attention to one's body takes on compulsiveness that far exceeds the established limits of normalcy. One particular expression of body image distortion is the condition called *anorexia nervosa.*

Anorexia nervosa is a physiological disorder, psychogenic in origin, that is accompanied by self-induced dieting that eventually exceeds the boundaries of conscious control and becomes compulsive. The syndrome includes episodes of fasting, gorging, vomiting and purging, a compulsive preoccupation with food, weight, and dieting that is demonstrated in a never-ending struggle with the environment and with persons in the environment. Because the condition is sometimes a maladaptive reaction to stress, psychological or social, it is discussed from a different perspective in Chapter 13.

The anorectic young woman believes that there is little she can do to experience feelings of mastery, so she looks for one area that she can control. Ultimately she discovers this mastery by controlling what she eats. As the disorder progresses she no longer experiences sensations of hunger yet continues to be preoccupied with preparing and discussing food (Halmi, Falk, and Schwartz 1981). Most anorectic clients are high achievers in school and display compulsive behaviors regarding academic achievement. The relationship between the anorectic young woman and her mother is thought to be highly significant. The mother of the victim is seen as a domineering perfectionist who is often dependent on her own mother yet displays controlling attitudes toward her daughter.

A behavior related to anorexia nervosa is bulimia, in which the person gorges on junk food, then initiates vomiting and excessive use of laxatives. Bulimia may exist in conjunction with anorexia nervosa or as a separate syndrome. Extreme weight

CLINICAL VIGNETTE

IDENTITY ACHIEVEMENT IN AN ADOLESCENT

Jenny is the oldest child in a conservative, devout, middle-class family. Her father is a prosperous corporate lawyer and her mother is an active club woman and avid golfer. Jenny did not question family values until she left home and became a college freshman. The college she chose was known for liberal thinking of its faculty and students, many of whom were political activists. At college Jenny was influenced by the opinions of the people around her. Gradually she stopped attending church services because she no longer found them relevant. She became involved in a number of student organizations that took a strong stand on controversial issues, and she began marching in demonstrations, chanting, carrying signboards, and engaging in sit-ins. When she went home at vacation time, Jenny argued heatedly with her parents, who were shocked by most of the causes Jenny supported. She, in turn, criticized her parents for their affluence, their smugness, and their indifference to poverty and social injustice. Her school performance suffered because of her new interests, providing another source of contention between Jenny and her parents.

Relations between Jenny and her parents were strained until the beginning of her junior year, when she informed them that she had decided to go to law school after graduation. However, she warned her father that she was not at all interested in corporate law because such lawyers were "social parasites." Instead,

Jenny would become a lawyer who protected the rights of the poor and humble, even if this was less profitable than corporate law. Although her parents did not agree with their daughter's extremism, they were relieved that she had chosen an occupation that seemed acceptable.

Jenny herself was satisfied with her decision, and the family conflict abated. There were even times when she and her father could discuss legal matters without becoming enraged at each other. In effect, Jenny had resolved a maturational crisis, even though the resolution was a stormy, tumultuous time for the family. She had challenged her parents' outlook on politics, religion, and occupational choice. The sessions with her parents were difficult for everyone, but the questioning process undertaken by Jenny was important to her identity achievement as she identified and became committed to a value system of her own. The sequence Jenny followed in her search for identity can be summarized in six steps:

1. Group influences at College
2. Challenge to family values
3. Acquisition of new values
4. Family crisis
5. Commitment to individual values
6. Achievement of individual identity

---

loss is not usually a symptom of bulimia unless anorexia is also present.

Reliable statistics on the prevalence of bulimia are unavailable because the disorder is concealed by the individual, who manages to maintain normal weight despite the practice. It is now believed that the disorder is less widespread than was once thought. The DSM-III-R defines bulimia as binge eating followed by self-induced vomiting at least twice weekly. A large study of bulimia showed that only 1 percent of college women and 0.2 percent of college men were bulimic compared to a previous estimate of 19 percent prevalence rates among college women. It is believed that previous definitions of bulimia were too vague and included many women who engaged in binge eating followed by

self-induced vomiting only on occasion and not regularly (Drewnowski, Hopkins, and Kessler 1988). Unfortunately, bulimic behavior is often linked to anorexia nervosa, which can be dangerous and life-threatening.

Working with Adolescents

Erikson (1968) wrote that the adolescent engages in forms of fantasy and introspection that were suppressed in childhood and will again be suppressed in adulthood. He called adolescence a time of leaning over precipices and cautioned adults against overreacting to the role experimentation that adolescents engage in as they strive for identity. Whether or not the adolescent moves forward or regresses depends on the opportunities and rewards available in the family, in the peer group, and in society at large.

During adolescence, joys and sorrows are experienced intensely and turbulently. Occasionally, adults take a casual attitude toward the intensity of adolescents, underestimating the pain and uncertainty of the adolescent experience. Because most teenagers are able to detect this attitude, they become less willing to share their feelings with adults. Professionals who belittle or misunderstand the seriousness with which adolescents view life are rarely given a second chance to be helpful.

In working with adolescents, nurses have the opportunity to offer primary prevention. Children and teenagers are accustomed to regarding nurses as experts and as sources of reliable information. Thus, one of the interventions nurses can provide is accurate information about the physical changes associated with adolescence and the normal range of changes. Nurses can reassure adolescents that the physical changes are natural and are part of becoming an adult. Nurses are also in a position to note when normal concern about the physical changes becomes maladaptive, as in the case of anorexia.

There is no need for a nurse to demonstrate to adolescents that it is possible to solve all their problems quickly and easily. Merely listening reflectively to a teenager's problems and to the solutions that have been attempted can be reassuring and can help the teenager trust the adult world.

Because peer groups are so influential with adolescents, group work can be highly effective. Meeting regularly with others of the same age who are experiencing the same difficulties is extremely beneficial for adolescents.

VARIATIONS AND DISRUPTIONS OF ADULT LIFE

Most persons reach adulthood after successfully negotiating the transitions of childhood and adolescence and make a commitment to career and family. This means that the maturational crises of adults are likely to revolve around career and family.

Career Crises

Children are asked so often what they want to be as adults that they soon learn that career choice is a serious matter. As they become teenagers they are pressured to choose an occupation compatible with the ambitions of their parents, even at the expense of their own preferences. Directly and indirectly, children are given the message that identity and status will largely depend on what they do for a

living. Many young people believe they must select an occupation while they are still in school. This means that some of them make a career choice based on a limited knowledge of opportunities and their own capabilities.

Even for individuals fortunate enough to have made a good career choice there are inevitable periods of occupational stress. This is true not only for persons performing menial jobs at minimum wages but for highly successful professionals as well.

Although occupational stress cannot be wholly eradicated, there are ways of dealing with it. The first step is to recognize the existence of stress and to identify the cause. Many clerical, technical, service, and industrial workers suffer stress because of the repetitive monotonous nature of their work (McLean 1980). Restrictive and regulated working conditions are also stressful, especially if production quotas are imposed. Workers' perceptions of themselves and their jobs can be a source of stress. Two factors are involved: quantitative and qualitative overload. *Quantitative overload* means having too much to do. Workers with this type of overload tend toward excessive drinking, low self-esteem, poor motivation, and high absenteeism. *Qualitative overload* means having tasks that are too difficult to do. Workers with this type of overload experience high levels of tension and job dissatisfaction, accompanied by a loss of confidence. Similar emotional reactions have been reported by workers who perceive that their abilities exceed the demands of the job.

Workers who experience occupational frustration have several available alternatives. Many workers are now asking that the conditions of their employment be less restrictive and more fulfilling. When workers are unable to obtain modification of undesirable working conditions, they may resort to retraining, additional education, early retirement, or passive resistance in the form of absenteeism or lowered efficiency. Occupational stress may be a contributing factor in psychophysiological dysfunction; the crucial issue is the interaction between the worker's temperament and the work situation. Any job that is characterized by rapid change and unrealistic performance standards will be stressful for most workers, but the perception of conditions and reactions to conditions are highly individualized. In some instances, it is the worker who must endeavor to change, and counseling may be indicated. If the worker makes extreme demands on himself, the focus of counseling might be to encourage more realistic performance standards. However, if many workers share similar feelings of frustration, modification of company standards might be a group goal.

CLINICAL VIGNETTE

REORGANIZATION IN A THREE-GENERATIONAL FAMILY

Viola Briggs and her husband Jim are the parents of three children, two boys and a girl. When their daughter and older son were high school students and the younger boy was in fifth grade, Viola and Jim were beginning to look forward to a few years of relative freedom as the older children prepared to enter college. Their dreams were interrupted when Jim's father died after a long illness and his mother came to live in their home. Jim's mother was in relatively good health, but she was a querulous, demanding woman with whom Viola had quarreled in the past. Unfortunately, there was not enough money for Jim's mother to live independently even if she had wished to do so. Viola was reluctant to accept Jim's mother as a permanent resident but felt she had no choice. Jim's only sister was married to an engineer whose work made it necessary to live overseas.

Always very talkative, Jim's mother constantly intruded when family members brought friends home to visit. She was critical of her daughter-in-law's housekeeping and child rearing methods. With the children of the family she was controlling and intrusive. In a short time the grandchildren stopped bringing their friends home and began socializing elsewhere. This added to Viola's resentment. She complained a great deal to Jim, who reacted by becoming distant and withdrawn. A previously happy household became contentious and discontented.

Viola had a girlhood friend, a social worker, who could see the problems objectively. When Viola confided in her, the friend suggested counseling for Viola and Jim in order to deal with a situation that seemed to grow worse every day. Counseling sessions gave the couple an opportunity to express their feelings without becoming angry and dysfunctional. Viola was surprised to learn how guilty Jim felt for placing the burden of caring for his mother on his family. Until Jim openly expressed his feelings about having sole responsibility for a parent he had never been close to, Viola believed that her husband and his mother had forged an alliance that excluded her. The positive feelings that Viola and Jim had for each other and their wish to do what was right while regaining family harmony were hopeful signs.

Counseling sessions focused on how to integrate Jim's mother into family life so that her presence would not be disruptive. Practical arrangements were attended to first, since these were easy to solve. Jim indicated that his sister was far more affluent than he, and could contribute to the support of his mother if she chose. However, she had not volunteered to do so and Jim had not asked for help. Since this aspect of the situation was especially hard for Viola to endure, the counselor suggested that they might approach the sister and directly tell her that financial help for mother's care would be welcome. Jim and his sister negotiated the details, and it was arranged that his sister would send mother an allowance, out of which she would pay a small sum to Jim and Viola. This arrangement was extremely valuable. It removed some pressure from the son and daughter-in-law, and it gave the mother a sense of independence that alleviated her tendency toward self-pity and martyrdom.

Viola had been planning to take a job as a salesclerk to help with the older children's college expenses. When her mother-in-law came to live with her, Viola no longer felt free to do this. Yet Jim's mother was in fairly good health and did not require full-time care. Jim, with encouragement from the counselor, assured Viola that she could carry out her plan. Viola was ambivalent because she feared that if she took a job her mother-in-law would take complete charge of the household. Acknowledging that this was a possibility, the counselor suggested that family meetings be held to establish ground rules for everyone when Viola started her job.

The meetings were surprisingly effective. With Jim as family spokesman, Viola's role as mother, homemaker, and decision-maker was reinforced. The older children could see advantages for them in having more money available and promised their cooperation. The younger boy, who rather liked grandma, said that it would be nice to have someone in the house to greet him after school. The person who was most receptive to the idea was Jim's mother, who saw that the family reorganization would give her a place where her contributions would be needed.

Of course there were times when Jim's mother was difficult. Viola and Jim had to remain united as household heads in order to prevent the older woman from taking over. The reorganization worked because the self-esteem of the members was no longer jeopardized by the presence of the grandmother in the home. Receiving a regular allowance from her daughter allowed Jim's mother to be independent and even generous at times to her grandchildren. Together Viola and her mother-in-law prepared the week's menus; because she prepared the evening meal, Jim's mother received a small sum from Viola. The older woman continued to pay for room and board because, as she explained, "I can have more to say about planning the meals."

Because Jim and Viola had a functional marriage they were able to use the limited counseling sessions to advantage. After talking with each other, they found the courage to impose rules for all family members and to set limits for Jim's mother that benefited everyone involved. This was a caring family, but they were not accustomed to sharing feelings, nor to attacking problems directly. In changing their behaviors, Viola and Jim modeled a new way of dealing with each other that eventually modified the behaviors of other family members, including Grandma.

Parental Crises

Although some couples are choosing not to have children, the majority of married couples become parents. In Eriksonian terms, the conscious choice to produce a child is an expression of creativity and generativity. Once children enter the family, the parents face years of hard work and sacrifice. Time, energy, and money must be expended to meet the physical and emotional needs of the children. New mothers speak of chronic fatigue, overwhelming domestic chores, and a decline in outside interests and activities. Mothers who gave up enjoyable employment to be home with their children frequently yearn for the stimulation of outside work, while mothers who must return to work feel guilty and unhappy at leaving their children. New fathers also report increased fatigue, greater worries over money, and a decline in social activities. Both parents feel a loss of privacy and a decrease in sexual activity (Green 1980).

As children grow older, parental time previously spent on the physical care of children is devoted to supervising and arranging school and community activities. The onset of adolescence brings new problems and concerns. The questioning of parental values that teenagers engage in as they pursue a separate identity is a cause of worry for many parents. The tendency of many teenagers to experiment with drugs, alcohol, and sex is another source of ongoing tension.

When adolescents continue their education in colleges or universities, they remain financially dependent on parents, and the costs of a college education can be extremely burdensome. At this time mothers who have never worked outside the home may have to look for paid employment. For some women this may prove a source of pride and accomplishment; for others it is an unpleasant reminder that the father is not adequately fulfilling the role of provider. In such instances additional strain may be brought to bear on the marriage.

Working with Adults

One approach a nurse can offer adults experiencing a maturational crisis is guidance in setting realistic, achievable goals. Many adults have an ideal

SEVERITY OF PSYCHOSOCIAL STRESSORS SCALE: ADULTS

Code	Term	Examples of Stressors	
		Acute Events	**Enduring circumstances**
1	None	No acute events that may be relevant to the disorder	No enduring circumstances that may be relevant to the disorder
2	Mild	Broke up with boyfriend or girlfriend; started or graduated from school; child left home	Family arguments; job dissatisfaction; residence in high-crime neighborhood
3	Moderate	Marriage; marital separation; loss of job; retirement; miscarriage	Marital discord; serious financial problems; trouble with boss; being a single parent
4	Severe	Divorce; birth of first child	Unemployment; poverty
5	Extreme	Death of spouse; serious physical illness diagnosed; victim of rape	Serious chronic illness in self or child; ongoing physical or sexual abuse
6	Catastrophic	Death of child; suicide of spouse; devastating natural disaster	Captivity as hostage; concentration camp experience
0	Inadequate information or no change in condition		

SOURCE: American Psychiatric Association DSM-III-R (1987).

FACTS ABOUT THE ELDERLY IN AMERICA

The number of Americans over the age of 65 is greater than the entire population of Canada.

To meet the expected need for nursing homes for the elderly, 40 facilities per month must be built.

Every day in the United States, 18 babies are born to fathers over 55 years of age.

Older people are more likely than any other age group to say they like the way they look.

Most women experience menopause without major physical or psychological distress and even welcome the onset of postmenstrual freedom.

SOURCE: Adapted from Tavris (1987).

of how they would like their lives to be, and most feel they have fallen short of that ideal. When adults feel disappointed in themselves or in their families, they need assistance in identifying the positive achievements in their lives. When they measure their achievements against impossible standards or set objectives that cannot be reached, they may need help in modifying or reordering their priorities. Thus, a man who is not promoted may need to be reminded of how far he has already advanced in rank and how much he is loved by his family and respected by the community. Such interventions represent a cognitive approach that counteracts the tendency of many adults to cling to impossible dreams.

Many well-adjusted people experience a temporary state of disequilibrium when they or a family member confronts a maturational crisis. For such individuals, referral to a *support group* may be helpful. Support groups are available for people dealing with various problems, maturational and situational. There are support groups for single parents, for the unemployed, and for the newly divorced or widowed, to name but a few. When there is no available group to meet specific needs, a nurse might use her skills to help individuals organize their own group. Support groups are widely used on a local and national level by persons with similar concerns. They serve an important purpose in a mobile, transient society, offering acceptance and understanding to their members. Additionally, such groups present an opportunity for members to aid newer members, once their own problems have abated. This is a therapeutic aspect of the group experience, as was noted by Maslow (1970),

who wrote that mature adults need to be needed. Support groups for adults in a maturational crisis are thus an avenue for the expression of generativity as well as a source of aid.

The age at which adolescence ends and adulthood begins is subject to wide variation. Some individuals marry, or become job holders and parents before reaching the age of 20, thereby avoiding the postadolescence, preadulthood stage that Keniston (1974) characterized as *youth*. Other individuals, chronologically the same age, remain students, dependents, or rebels well into their twenties. Despite the range of differences in lifestyle, young adults confront a series of choices whose outcomes will affect their entire lives. Geographic and social mobility have scattered the extended family and isolated the nuclear family. As a result marital partners and other family members must find outside help in difficult times. Many couples and families are reluctant to seek professional help, but are often receptive to suggestions from nurses already assisting them in various ways. In particular, nurses offering preventive health services to children, home health care to adults, or perinatal care to expectant families should be sensitive to opportunities for additional counseling when indicated. Without appropriate intervention many individuals simply proceed in the same old manner, even when irritations and dissatisfactions continue to accumulate. Regardless of the clinical setting where care is provided, the maturational issues of adulthood should respect the value system and social context of the adult client, whose energies and abilities are sometimes overmatched by problems and responsibilities.

VARIATIONS AND DISRUPTIONS OF LATER LIFE

More and more people are living well into their seventies, eighties, and even nineties. More importantly, they are enjoying life. Many conditions once attributed to aging have been found to result from poor nutrition, lack of exercise, social isolation, and treatable physical ailments. There are some attributes—such as reasoning ability, spatial ability, and verbal comprehension—that do seem to decline with age, but the extent of decline may be overstated. Researchers have found that when the same subjects were followed from adulthood into old age, the amount of decline was far less than that found in studies that compared two different population groups, one in middle adulthood and the other in old age. As one researcher wrote, "The greatest difference in sexual activity—or any other aspect of aging—is not between the young and the old, but between individuals" (Tavris 1987).

The maturation crises of the elderly are intensified by the way society regards old age. Youthfulness is highly valued in American society, and fear of aging is reinforced. Many individuals see in the elderly the prediction of their own future, fear their own aging, and try to avoid accepting the later stages of the life cycle until they must. This is unfortunate, because planning for the final life cycle stage can help avoid or ameliorate some of the problems.

Adjustment to recurrent loss is a prevailing theme in the lives of older people. In addition to the loss of youthful strength and vigor and of friends and loved ones, the elderly suffer role losses as their children become independent, and as retirement arrives.

The *empty nest syndrome* refers to feelings of loneliness and depression experienced by many parents, especially mothers, after their last child has left home. Although the concept of the empty nest has been given considerable public attention, it is possible that the problem has been exaggerated and that it is experienced by a relatively small percentage of parents. The key factor in adjusting to the empty nest seems to be the number of options available to the parents. The absence of dependent children may be distressing to a woman who has treasured the role of mother beyond all else but not for the woman whose role as mother has already been supplemented by other roles. Some women work throughout the years that their children are dependent and suffer no great distress when all the children are gone. Even women who chose to be homemakers may see the empty nest period as an opportunity to enter the paid labor force, to continue their interrupted educations, or to become involved in community activities.

The effect of the empty nest on fathers has received less attention than the effect on mothers. Farrell and Rosenberg (1981) did examine fathers' reactions to the departure of their children as part of a larger examination of men at midlife. They found a number of conflicting feelings among men whose children were in the process of leaving home.

For large numbers of older people, the empty nest is a mirage. Middle-aged and older adults are having to cope with even older parents, who are no longer able to live independently. A recent study showed that the average age of relatives caring for elderly parents was 57 years, and a third were over 65 years. Long-term care for persons unable to manage on their own is not covered by Medicare, and the cost is out of reach for all but the wealthy.

Almost always the person who takes care of elderly relatives is female. One extensive survey showed that seven out of ten primary caretakers were unpaid females, friends or relatives, and an average of 16 hours a week was devoted to providing care. Primary caretakers who were male reported spending five hours a week. In these days of expanded opportunities for women, many of them looked forward to living in an empty nest that would finally allow them time to develop interests and talents, either as volunteers or late-blooming careerists. Instead, many women have found themselves caught between the demands of a job and the arduous task of caring for a parent who is less than competent (Wood 1987).

While the federal government tries to deal with the problem of how to bear the cost of caring for the elderly, the burden continues to be assumed by family members, especially the women. An important precept to remember is that caretakers need relief, and the relief should be periodic, frequent, and available. Support services should be utilized throughout the caretaking process, not merely in times of crisis or when the primary caretaker is on the verge of collapse. Many families lack information about support services and respite care. This is an area where nurses can make appropriate suggestions and referrals (Neidrick 1988).

Another way in which nurses can help these families is to encourage them to take care of their own needs as well as the needs of the dependent relative. Sometimes the caretaker feels guilty about spending time away from the relative or blames herself for not being able to halt the inroads of time. Here nurses can assure the caretaker that caring for herself is an important aspect of caring for the relative. As long as family members continue to provide most of the care needed by elderly relatives, there is little incentive for government or other agencies to become very involved. There is a strong case to be made for voters to exert pressure on elected officials to integrate long-term health care, in the home or in institutions, into the reimbursement system (Quist 1989).

Retirement Crises

Retirement has been defined as the socially sanctioned withdrawal from one's occupation in order to cope with changes in health or occupational status or to enjoy more leisure and freedom. Retirement includes the notion that the individual is entitled to stop working after being in the labor force for many years. However, in many important respects, retirement represents a multiple loss. It is a loss of worker identity, a loss of power and privileges that accompanied the role of provider, and often a loss of income in the absolute terms (Atchley 1984).

Another loss associated with retirement is the disruption or severing of friendships or associations with colleagues and fellow workers. This can be a substantial loss that exacerbates feelings of loneliness and rejection. Reisman (1979) referred to friendships initiated and perpetuated in the workplace as associative friendships. Although the persons involved feel friendly toward one another, the friendship is dependent on the occasional association and the roles they play. When the occupational roles change because of promotion, transfer, or retirement, the friendship attenuates or ceases to exist. Although promises may be exchanged to continue the friendship, this rarely happens when one of the participants leaves. Persons who remain employed generally replace the lost associates with others at the workplace.

The loss of associative friendships is keenly felt by retirees unless they have a network of more enduring relationships based on more than shared occupational interests. These friendships, called *friendships of reciprocity* (Reisman 1979), help the retiree maintain social involvement after retirement as well as before. However, in order to sustain the same level of social involvement, a retired person must cultivate new friendships over the years to replace meaningful persons who move away or die. Given the circumstances of retirement, this may not be easy. After one has lost a number of beloved friends, the inclination is to retreat from new friendships to avoid the pain of further loss. This means that social contacts of older retirees may consist of depersonalized encounters with medical, nursing, or social agency personnel and of interactions with shopkeepers and other such service providers.

Adjustment to retirement is also affected by the extent of preretirement planning, but only a minority of the labor force has access to preretirement planning programs. These programs are often limited to an explanation of the employer's obligations and benefits extended to retirees (Silberstein 1981). Such programs are likely to include information about pensions, social security payments, and similar matters. This is essential data, since adequate income has been identified as the single most essential element for successful retirement (Lamb and Duffy 1979). Nevertheless, preretirement planning should not be limited to finances. Among other important issues to include in planning programs are use of leisure time, support networks and groups, and health-related matters.

Health-Related Crises

The inroads of physical decline represent another form of loss confronted by the elderly.

Although every system of the body ages, the rate of aging varies from person to person and from organ system to organ system. For example, an individual's gastrointestinal system may be healthy and resilient while her cardiovascular system may be degenerating. Therefore, chronological age is not a reliable predictor of the rate of aging, even though every individual undergoes the aging process over time.

When older people feel hurried or under pressure, their anxiety further slows their reaction time and performance. One way to lessen this anxiety is to slow one's own movements and speech to match the pace of the elderly person. This relatively simple alteration in tempo will reduce the elderly person's anxiety and increase his comfort.

There are a number of ways in which an elderly person's environment can be modified to accommodate his physical changes. Handrails near toilets and bathtubs compensate for impaired balance. Chairs with arms or with seats that lift or tilt compensate for a lack of muscle strength or coordination. Improved lighting arrangements can help remedy decreased visual acuity and poor night vision. Sensory losses can be offset in part by hearing aids, eye-glasses, large type, and the use of bright or contrasting colors for doors and stairways.

An important aspect of alleviating adverse changes associated with aging is the maintenance of proper nutrition. Studies show that the diets of older people are likely to be too high in sugar, refined grains, and cholesterol, and too low in fiber, minerals, niacin, thiamine, and vitamins A and C (Tavris 1987). These deficiencies preclude optimal metabolism and promote physiological changes associated with aging. Improving the elderly person's diet is an area in which nurses can make a substantial contribution (Hall 1987, Weg 1978).

There is a strong social component in the eating habits of the elderly. People living alone, as many of the elderly do, often eat poorly or irregularly because there is no social impetus to prepare a meal or to eat. Few people, regardless of age, like to eat alone. Without the social exchange between individuals, much of the desire to eat abates.

Terminal Crises

Death is repeatedly encountered by elderly people, who must deal with the loss of loved ones as well as the impending end of their own lives. The deaths of significant persons create crises that are difficult for the elderly to resolve. Each loss tends to reactivate memories of earlier losses and to remind the elderly of what lies ahead for them.

At the turn of the century, only 4 percent of the population lived to age sixty-five, compared with the current rate of 11 percent. At one time infectious diseases, childbirth, accidents, and poor sanitation claimed the lives of people of all ages, so that death was not exclusively associated with old age (Atchley 1980). Today, however, death is considered a concomitant of old age, and the death of a young person is considered an untimely tragedy. This thinking allows people to deny death until their own accumulated years force awareness upon them.

Death is denied in the way Americans treat and react to their dead. In previous generations, people died at home and adults knew how to treat a dead body (Feifel 1973). Today the care of the deceased is almost the exclusive domain of professional morticians and undertakers. With fewer people dying at home there is less opportunity to see someone die or to view an unembalmed body. Such lack of contact with the physical remains helps people to keep death at arm's length.

One of the most painful encounters with death is the demise of a spouse, for this means the loss of a companion, confidant, friend, and lover. Because women tend to live longer than men and to marry men who are somewhat older, they are more likely than men to face widowhood. Of course, not all marriages are happy and not all partners find the role of husband or wife congenial or central to existence. Allowing for these variations, the dissolution of a marriage by death still brings strong feelings of grief and regret. Some widows and widowers may idealize the deceased, forgetting his or her faults and weaknesses. This may be disconcerting for those who have a more accurate recollection of the deceased, but idealization is part of the grief process, and distortion need not be corrected. When the strengths and weaknesses of the deceased are accurately perceived by the mourner, it is likely that his or her grieving has been completed. (For additional discussion of grief and grieving, See Chapter 8)

Working with the Elderly

One of the basic needs of all persons is recognition of their human dignity, and this need does not disappear with age. One way that human dignity finds expression is through the maintenance of activity and independence. It is therefore important to permit the elderly to feel useful and in control as much as possible. All too frequently, people live in progressively restrictive environments as they age. Although some restrictions may be necessary, the elderly should be allowed control over their possessions and should be given choices as long as they are able to make reasonable decisions. Until the moment of death, people need to feel that their wishes and preferences will be respected whenever possible. Although independence is valued by the aging person, interdependence is also a human need. To be interdependent means to be involved in a mutually rewarding exchange with one or more other people. Interdependence means giving and taking and sharing. Forming interdependent relationships is one way

of preserving human dignity and maintaining the quality of life in old age.

One of the objectives of nurses working with elderly persons is to help them maintain their self-esteem despite the multiple losses that accompany old age. Self-esteem can be maintained in a number of ways. Some people are able to see themselves as useful and competent individuals by means of positive self-affirmation of their own value. The person who believes in himself or herself can preserve self-esteem in the face of disappointment and reverses. Another way of maintaining self-esteem is to receive affirmation or validation from others, in the form of recognition, reinforcement, and reassurance. Even a person with good intrapsychic supplies can suffer a loss of self-esteem, especially after experiencing an illness or loss. Interventions from nurses and from others in the environment can be helpful in replenishing intrapsychic supplies. Lowered self-esteem that is not restored or replenished may lead to depression.

A nursing intervention that is often helpful for elderly persons is the life review process (Butler 1963). Life review involves reflecting on past experiences and accepting the success and failures of a lifetime. Sometimes the life review process may engender feelings of anxiety, depression, and even despair, but more often it is beneficial, particularly if the listener refutes destructive interpretations of events. By participating in the life review process as a sensitive listener, an empathic nurse can facilitate a therapeutic adjustment to aging and impending death. There may be times when a person engaged in a life review decides that her life has been useless. When this happens, nursing responses should be directed toward showing the client that this is an inaccurate perception that overlooks the client's strengths and accomplishments.

Developmental tasks have been described as individual adjustments to the changing self (Erikson 1963), while adaptational tasks have been described as adjustments to changing individual and cultural expectations. Thus, development and adaptation require accommodation between individual capacities and cultural expectations. The critical adaptational tasks associated with aging have been identified as follows:

1. Recognition of aging and its consequent limitations
2. Redefinition of physical and social life space
3. Substitution of alternative sources of satisfaction
4. Readjustment of criteria for self-evaluation
5. Reintegration of life goals and values

(Text continues on page 434.)

CLINICAL VIGNETTE

NURSING HOME PLACEMENT OF AN ELDERLY PARENT

The Grady family consisted of the parents, Gus and Jean Grady, five adolescent youngsters, one of whom was in college, and Grandpa Bennett, who had moved in after the death of his wife eight years previously. Until the last two years, Grandpa had been a resourceful, self-sufficient family member, always willing to stay with the children when his daughter and son-in-law wanted a night out. Shortly after his eightieth birthday, Grandpa began to change in ways that were subtle at first but became blatant. Previously a light eater, he became a habitual refrigerator raider, especially at night when the family was asleep. Always a reticent, quiet man, he was now very garrulous. When other family members entertained friends, he was intrusive and repetitive.

Because Grandpa was her father, Jean Grady was inclined to be rather tolerant of his idiosyncrasies. More and more often she found herself in the position of trying to restrain her father while apologizing to her husband and children for his behavior. As time passed, Grandpa became increasingly unmanageable. He began wandering through the neighborhood, getting lost several times and being returned by neighbors or the police. Occasionally he was incontinent, especially after he had generously helped himself to forbidden alcohol. One morning when Jean was working in the garden, Grandpa accidently started a kitchen blaze, which firemen had to extinguish.

Gus Brady was an easygoing man, but as Grandpa began to need constant supervision, Gus issued an ultimatum to Jean: "Either your father leaves this house within the next month, or the kids and I will." His ultimatum regarding Grandpa was partly motivated by selfish interests, but he was also worried about the strain on his wife and the estrangement of his children. Having taken a stand, Gus then became very supportive of Jean and promptly began to investigate facilities in which Grandpa might be placed. There were times when Jean felt angry as they visited various facilities, but secretly she was a little relieved that a difficult decision had been made for her.

Jean had a close friend who was a nurse and who was willing to accompany the couple on their observational tours. Following the advice of her friend, Jean compiled a checklist of things to look for on her visits. The checklist included the following considerations:

- Environmental factors
- Costs and accreditation
- Nursing care
- Medical supervision
- Dietary considerations
- Programs and activities
- Social amenities
- Philosophy and policies

The facility eventually chosen was a skilled nursing home supervised by the county health department and located two miles from the Grady residence. Grandpa was taken by the family to see his new quarters a week before placement was to occur. He was told of the impending change and reassured that the family would be very near. Grandpa seemed to understand that he was leaving the family home, but talked vaguely of just going on a visit. Jean was very distraught during the week that her father was due to leave. Because she became tearful every time she thought of the prospect, Gus prevailed on her not to go with them when her father was admitted. Grandpa was accompanied by Gus, Jean's friend, and two of his grandchildren. When the time for departure came, Jean clung to her father, and the family members were glad she had been spared the ordeal of escorting her father to the facility. At the suggestion of the nursing staff, Jean agreed to wait a day or two before visiting so that the staff could help her father accept his new surroundings. There was no doubt that his physical and behavioral deterioration had increased the tensions within the family system. Even a daughter as loving and conscientious as Jean was unable to supervise his regimen, and Grandpa's regressive actions were hastening his own decline. Jean admitted to feeling a sense of relief after her father left the household. The care facility had been carefully chosen and was near enough for all family members to visit frequently. There was no doubt that the nursing staff could monitor Grandpa's physical problems more efficiently than Jean. Reality orientation and resocialization techniques seemed for the present to have arrested further cognitive deterioration for Grandpa.

The Grady family regained equilibrium shortly after Grandpa was placed in a long-term-care facility, but his long-term adjustment remained an unknown.

Successful adaptation does not mean that the elderly person must enjoy the limitations brought about by age, but merely that limitations must not be denied. With advancing age, control over one's social environment is threatened. Personal space becomes circumscribed as certain activities and roles are no longer accessible. Searching for alternative interests is part of adaptation, and individuals who cannot give up total autonomy or accept some dependency fail to adapt well to aging. Readjustment of criteria for self-evaluation means that various criteria for self-evaluation must be modified, unrealistic standards of performance must be lowered, and that self-esteem must no longer be based on autonomous functioning or the managerial ability of the elderly person. Finally, reintegration of goals and values necessitates revision of the aspirations of older people so that they can find meaning and purpose in life as it presently exists for them.

SUMMARY

Every person experiences predictable crises during the span of the life cycle. Each stage of the life cycle ushers in a maturational or development task that must be confronted and resolved. These critical tasks have been viewed in different ways by different theorists. Erikson has posited eight life cycle tasks in the context of a psychosocial developmental framework. Kohlberg formulated a theory of moral development that assumes individuals follow a fixed sequence as they move from simplistic to complex moral reasoning. Piaget contributed a framework of cognitive development that traces the thinking of children from early sensorimotor levels to formal operational levels. Duvall presented a sequence of family development tasks that, when combined with Erikson's individual tasks, permit the identification of conflict areas between the family and its individual members. The work of Kohlberg on moral development has been supplemented by the studies of Gilligan on gender-related differences in moral development. Thomas and Chess in their investigations of childhood temperament emphasized the interactive nature of family life and the importance of parental acceptance of a child's temperamental characteristics.

Familiarity with the maturational tasks of individuals and families helps nurses assess whether progress is being impeded or prematurely hastened.

Sometimes maturational tasks are resolved adaptively, but often adaptive patterns are altered in various ways that may result in disturbances characteristic of a particular life stage. Among children these alterations may take the form of attachment disorders, sleeping and eating difficulties, excretory problems, fears, and phobias. In adolescence identity confusion, antisocial behavior, and body image distortions are among the manifestations of maladaptive maturational alteration.

Crises of adulthood most often involve problems with one's career, marriage, or parenting. Crises of occupational origin may be caused by premature career choices, by stressful conditions on the job, or by a combination of family- and job-related factors. The stresses caused by dual-career marriages are an example of the impact of combined family and occupational problems. In later adulthood the empty nest syndrome, retirement, physical decline, and death are among loss-related crises. Increased longevity has introduced a new form of loss into the lives of adults. Very elderly parents now live long enough to experience declining competence in daily life. As a result, middle-aged adults find themselves functioning as primary caretakers at a time when they anticipated freedom to pursue their own dreams and ambitions.

The nursing implications of maturational crises are multiple and diverse. Most of the predictable maturational crises cannot be evaded, but there are ways to help individuals and families respond adaptively. A nurse can provide primary prevention by assuring people of the universality of a particular maturational task and by encouraging them to engage in anticipatory planning, if possible. Many clients find solace in learning that they are neither alone nor unique in the worrisome situations they face. Simply explaining the normal, customary aspects of the task at hand helps people understand their reactions and examine possible outcomes. Advance knowledge of the possibilities inherent in a situation helps allay the anxiety generated by a maturational crisis. If an individual is already experiencing a maturational crisis, nurses can provide secondary prevention by offering intervention based on knowledge of the life cycle stage of the client and on the probable critical tasks, and by being effective referral agents when the situation requires intervention beyond their own competence.

Review Questions

1. In what ways does Kohlberg's theory of moral development explain the decision-making process of adults?

2. In what respects do the developmental frameworks of Erikson and Duvall complement each other?

3. How does a teenager's reference group affect the resolution of the maturational tasks of adolescence?

4. What are some crucial issues to be considered when recommending institutionalization for an adolescent delinquent?

5. In what ways can the personality traits of a youngster influence parent-child relationships?

6. What aspects of moral development are explained by Gilligan?

7. What modern phenomenon has replaced the empty nest in the lives of adults?

8. How can Erikson's theory be used to explain the situation of an elderly person who is in good health but is lonely, isolated, and friendless?

Suggested Annotated Readings

Bird, C. "The Jobs You Do." *Modern Maturity* 31, no. 6 (December 1988/1989):40–46.

The official magazine of the American Association of Retired People sponsored a survey on second careers to which 35,000 people responded. The survey explored respondents' attitudes toward the primary jobs of their lifetimes, as well as the second careers to which they turned after retirement. Written in an anecdotal style, the article is reinforced with facts and figures about jobs and wage earning before and after retirement. Even though more women expressed interest in second careers, they constitute only 41 percent of all employed persons over 55 years of age. Of women still working after age 62, only 4 percent have private pensions, compared to 68 percent of men in a comparable group. For more information, write to AARP Senior Employment Service Department, 1909 K Street N.W., Washington, D.C. 20049.

Desrosiers, M. C. "A Nursing Response to the Teen Pregnancy Epidemic." *RN* (April 1989):22–24

A number of school districts across the country have established student health clinics within high schools, where students have access to services that they might not otherwise seek. Staffed by nurse practitioners and part-time physicians, the clinics usually accept referrals from school nurses, teachers, parents, and the students themselves. The school-based clinics utilize support services of school guidance counselors, nutritionists, psychologists, and of community health care providers. Most of the clinics provide services ranging from emergency care to physical assessment, immunization, counseling, and followup supervision. Infor-

mation on school-based clinics is available from the Support Center for School-Based Clinics, 5650 Kirby St., Suite 242, Houston, Texas 77005. The Support Center is underwritten by the Center for Population Options, Washington, D.C.

Jessee, E. H., G. J. Jurkovic, J. Wilkie, and M. Chiglinsky. "Positive Reframing with Children: Conceptual and Clinical Considerations." *American Journal of Orthopsychiatry* 52, no. 2 (April 1982):314–322.

"Reframing" is the name applied by the authors to *relabeling*. Relabeling is a therapeutic tactic in which behaviors and actions with negative aspects are reframed to emphasize positive aspects of the behavior. The authors see the tactic as a management strategy for hospitalized children and also as a way of raising their self-esteem. Children's resistant behaviors were interpreted as bids for closeness; peer conflict was interpreted as an expression of caring and a wish for involvement. The authors report success with the device of reframing but caution that staff members must be accepting and knowledgeable about how and when to use reframing. Additionally, reframing interventions must be carefully tailored to the emotional and cognitive levels of the children participating in the interactions.

Moore, B. F., C. W. Snow, and G. M. Poteat. "Effects of Variant Types of Child Care Experience on the Adaptive Behavior of Kindergarten Children." *American Journal of Orthopsychiatry* 58, no. 2 (April 1988):297–303.

The adaptive behaviors of children who had experienced day care was compared with the adaptive behaviors of kindergarten children who had not experienced day care. No significant differences were found among groups in measures of adaptive behavior, communication skills, daily living skills, motor skills, or socialization skills. The data suggest that day care centers, family day care, and at home care were all appropriate options for parents with preschool children. The authors warned that despite their findings quality day care is essential to desirable outcomes, as is compatibility of day care standards and values with parental standards and values.

Quist, J. C. "Helping a Caregiver Keep Up the Good Work." *RN* (April 1989):88–91.

This sensitive article describes the dilemma of families whose lives are disrupted by the 24-hour-a-day care of aged family members. Support for the primary caregiver is strongly advised. Since the article is intended chiefly for community health nurses, considerable space is devoted to the need for respite care. A very helpful list of local and national resources that may be called upon to help beleaguered families is included. Support groups are also mentioned as potential sources of help. A condensed list of some national resources follows. For additional information, local voluntary associations and agencies may be consulted.

Alzheimer's Disease & Related Disorders Association
800-621-0379 (in Illinois 800-572-6037)
70 East Lake Street
Suite 600
Chicago, Ill. 60601

American Association of Homes for the Aging
1129 20th St., N.W.
Suite 400
Washington, D.C. 20036

AARP
1909 K St., N.W.
Washington, D.C. 20049

Foundation for Hospice and Homecare
519 C St., N.E.
Stanton Park
Washington, D.C. 20002

Gray Panthers Project Fund
311 S. Juniper St.
Philadelphia, Pa. 19107

Hospice Association of America
519 C St., N.E.
Washington, D.C. 20002

Make Today Count
National Office
514 Tama Building
Burlington, Idaho 52601

The National Association of Area
Agencies on Aging (N4A)
600 Maryland Ave., S.W.
Suite 208-W
Washington, D.C. 20024

National Association for Home Care
519 C St., N.E.
Stanton Park
Washington, D.C. 20002
(202) 547-7424

National Cancer Institute
NIH Publications List
Office of Cancer Communications
Building 31, Room 10A-18
Bethesda, Md. 20892

National Institute on Aging
Federal Building, 6C12
7550 Wisconsin Ave.
Bethesda, Md. 20814

The Self-Help Center
1600 Dodge Ave.
Suite S-122
Evanston, Ill. 60201

The National Self-Help Clearinghouse
c/o City University of New York
33 W. 42nd St.
New York, N.Y. 10036

National Support Center for
Families of the Aging
P.O. Box 245
Swarthmore, Pa. 19081

Schecter, A. "Learn the Art of Retirement." *Modern Maturity* 31, no. 6 (December 1988/January 1989): 12–13.

The author states that retiring is like being a parent; you only learn how to do it after it happens. The Center for Creative Retirement based at the University of North Carolina at Ashville has developed programs to ease the transition from productive work to productive retirement. Seminars, forums, and courses are available to help senior citizens return to their communities as political, economic, and cultural leaders of projects designed for retirees. The Center is receptive to visits and inquiries, and has a rapidly expanding developmental program of its own. For information, write North Carolina Center for Creative Retirement, Owen Hall, Ashville 28804-3299 UNC.

Watson, J. "Human Caring as a Moral Context for Nursing Education." *Nursing and Health Care* 9, no. 8 (October 1988):423–430.

The author calls for a new "moral context" in nursing education and asks that knowledge and technical competence not supersede "knowledgeable caring." Among the objections raised in the article are the following:

■ Treating student nurses as objects

■ Using mechanical or industrial terms such as "products"

■ Emphasizing competency at the expense of compassion

■ Focusing only on cognitive/technical outcomes

■ Limiting education to behavioral goals, facts, and techniques

This is a radical article in some respects, and it may arouse controversy in many quarters. It deals with specifics as well as generalities; it makes recommendations to improve the depth and quality of nursing education from entry level onward. The importance given to the caring aspects of nursing and to the need for more liberal, humanistic ways of preparing nurses deserves thoughtful consideration. Many of the opinions expressed in the article complement the material contained in this textbook, although the textbook authors are less critical of contemporary nursing education.

References

Atchley, R. *Social Forces in Later Life*, 3d ed. Belmont, California: Wadsworth, 1980.

——. *Aging: Continuity and Change*. Belmont, California: Wadsworth, 1984.

Atkinson, L., B. Quarrington, and J. Cyr. "School Refusal: The Heterogeneity of a Concept." *American Journal of Orthopsychiatry* 55, no. 1 (1983):83–101.

Barry, P. *Psychosocial Nursing: Assessment and Intervention*. Philadelphia: J. B. Lippincott, 1984.

Bettelheim, B. *Love is not Enough*. New York: Avon, 1972a.

——. *The Empty Fortress*. New York: Free Press, 1972b.

Bowlby, J. *Attachment*. New York: Basic Books, 1969.

——. *Separation*. New York: Basic Books, 1973.

——. *The Making and Breaking of Affectional Bonds*. London: Tavistock, 1979.

Bruch, H. *Eating Disorders: Obesity, Anorexia Nervosa and the Person Within*. New York: Basic Books, 1973.

——. *The Golden Cage: The Enigma of Anorexia Nervosa*. Cambridge, Massachusetts: Harvard University Press, 1978.

Butler, R. "The Life Review: An Interpretation of Reminiscence in the Aged." *Psychiatry* 26 (1963):50.

Carstens, C. "Behavior Treatment of Functional Dysphagia in a Twelve-Year-Old Boy." *Psychosomatics* 23 (1982):195–196.

Chess, S., and A. Thomas. "Infant Bonding: Mystique and Reality." *American Journal of Orthopsychiatry* 52 (1982):213–222.

Drewnowski, A., S. Hopkins, and R. Kessler. "The Prevalence of Bulimia Nervosa in the United States College Student Population." *American Journal of Public Health* 78, no. 10 (October 1988):1322–1325.

Duvall, E. *Marriage and Family Development*, 3d ed. Philadelphia: J. B. Lippincott, 1967.

——. *Marriage and Family Development*, 4th ed. Philadelphia: J. B. Lippincott, 1971.

Elkind, D. *Childhood and Adolescents: Interpretative Essays on Jean Piaget*. New York: Oxford University, 1974.

Erikson, E. H. *Childhood and Society*. New York: W. W. Norton, 1963.

——. *Identity, Youth, and Crisis*. New York: W. W. Norton, 1968.

Farell, M., and S. Rosenberg. *Men and Midlife*. Boston: Auburn, 1981.

Feifel, H. *Dealing with Death*. Los Angeles: University of Southern California: 1973.

Feretta, F., G. Rivera, and A. Lucero. "The Chicano Family: Myth and Reality." In *Understanding the Family: Stress and Change in American Life*, C. Getty and W. Humphreys, eds. New York: Appleton-Century-Crofts, 1981.

Gilligan, C. "New Maps of Development: New Visions of Maturity." *American Journal of Orthopsychiatry* 52, no. 2 (April 1982):199–212.

——. *In a Different Voice*. Cambridge, Massachusetts: Harvard University Press, 1983.

Green, E. "Losses in the Family System." In *Family-Focused Care*, J. R. Miller and E. H. Janosik, eds. New York: McGraw-Hill, 1980.

Hall, T. "Cravings: Does Your Body Know What It Needs?" *The New York Times Good Health Magazine* (September 27, 1987):22, 23, 62–65.

Halmi, K. A., J. R. Falk, and E. Schwartz. "Binge Eating and Vomiting: Survey of a College Population." *Psychological Medicine* 11 (1981):697–706.

Hartman, C. R., A. W. Burgess, and A. McCormack. "Pathways and Cycles of Runaways: A Model for Understanding Repetitive Runaway Behavior." *Hospital and Community Psychiatry* 38, no. 3 (March 1987): 292–298.

Kashani, J. H., K. K. Hiodges, J. F. Simonds, and E. Hilderband. "Life Events and Hospitalization in Children: A Comparison with the General Population." *British Journal of Psychiatry* 139, no. 6 (1981):221–225.

Keniston, K. *The Uncommitted: Alienated Youth in American Society*. New York: Basic Books, 1974.

Kohlberg, L. "Moral Development." In *International Encyclopedia of Social Science*. New York: Macmillan, 1968.

Kohlberg, L., and C. Gilligan. "The Adolescent as Philosopher: The Discovery of Self in a Postconventional World." *Daedalus* 100 (1971):1051–1086.

Lamb, T., and D. Duffy. *The Retirement Threat*. Los Angeles: J. P. Tarcher, 1979.

Maslow, A. H. *Motivation and Personality*, 2d ed. New York: Harper & Row, 1970.

Neidrick, D. J. *Caring for Your Own: Nursing the Ill at Home*. New York: John Wiley & Sons, 1988.

Piaget, J. *The Origin of Intelligence in Children*. New York: International Universities Press, 1969.

Quist, J. C. "Helping a Caregiver Keep Up the Good Work." *RN* (April 1989):97–90.

Reisman, J. *Anatomy of Friendship*. Lexington, Massachusetts: Lewis, 1979.

Sanger, E., and T. Cassino. "Eating Disorders: Avoiding the Power Struggle." *American Journal of Nursing* 84, no. 1 (1984):30–33.

Silberstein, C. "Nursing Role in Occupational Health." In *Community Health Nursing: Keeping the Public Healthy.* L. Jarvis, ed. Philadelphia: F. A. Davis, 1981.

Tavris, C. "Old Age is Not What It Used to Be." *The New York Times Good Health Magazine* (September 27, 1987):24–25, 91–92.

Thomas, A. "Theory and Review: Current Trends in Developmental Theory." *American Journal of Orthopsychiatry* 51, no. 3 (1981):580–609.

Thomas, A., and A. Chess. *Temperament and Development.* New York: Brunner/Mazel, 1977.

——. *Dynamics of Psychological Development.* New York: Brunner/Mazel, 1980.

Wallerstein, J. S. "Children of Divorce: A Preliminary Report of a Ten-Year Follow-Up of Young Children." *American Journal of Orthopsychiatry* 54 (1984):444–445.

Webster-Stratton, C. "Comparison of Abusive and Non-Abusive Families with Conduct-Disordered Children." *American Journal of Orthopsychiatry* 55 (1985):59–69.

Weg, R. *Nutrition and the Later Years.* Los Angeles: University of Southern California, Andrus Gerontology Center, 1978.

Wood, J. "Labors of Love." *Modern Maturity* 30, no. 4 (1987):28–34, 90–94.

16

Situational Variations and Disruptions

Learning Objectives

After reading this chapter, the student should be able to:

1. Discuss the contributions of various theorists in the development of situational disruption concepts.

2. Discuss suicide as a response to variations and disruptions in life style.

3. Discuss the characteristics of the perpetrator and victim of violence.

4. Formulate basic principles for assessing suicide and violence potential.

5. Determine the appropriate elements of the nursing process in response to suicide and violence.

Overview

Nurses often find themselves working with both the victim and the perpetrator of situational variations and disruptions. This chapter contains the theoretical background, appropriate nursing responses, and nursing process approaches for four situational disruptions that nurses frequently encounter in their practice: the disruption of suicide, the disruption of violence, the disruption of rape, and the disruption of the violent family.

Situational disruptions occur in the lives of everyone, regardless of age, sex, race, and socioeconomic characteristics. The severity and intensity of reactions to such disruptions varies with the person's ability to adapt and resolve the problem. Situational disruptions are often externally imposed, chance events that are unpredictable for the victim. These disruptions often demand solutions that the victim is unable to achieve, and they elicit an emotional strain that calls for additional resources or adaptive behavior. The individual's response depends on such factors as personality, perception of the event, social and cultural influences, and past experience dealing with stress. The situational disruptions with the greatest social ramifications are suicide, violence, and rape.

THE DISRUPTION OF SUICIDE

Suicide is a denial of the human being's most urgent need: self-preservation; it is a contradiction of the value placed on human life that is implicit in social and democratic ethics. Yet there is recorded evidence that suicides occurred more than 4,000 years ago, and there is good reason to believe that people have been killing themselves since civilization began.

Although suicide is condoned in some cultures, most societies have condemned it. In ancient Greece and Rome, suicide was considered a crime against the state. In England during the Middle Ages, bodies of people who committed suicide were dragged through the streets and hung naked upside down in public view. The punishment was actually directed at the surviving family and was intended to be an example for others.

Suicide is considered a crime in several American states. Although legal action is not taken against the family, society's judgmental attitude is reflected in other ways. For example, the bodies of suicide victims may not be interred in the cemeteries of some churches, and it is difficult for families to collect insurance payments if the insured person committed suicide within two years of the inception of the policy.

Interest in the field of suicide and suicide prevention has shown a dramatic upsurge in recent times. The number of community suicide prevention centers has grown, and suicide research has expanded in new directions. Statistics concerning suicide are not totally reliable since it is impossible to tell whether many "accidental" deaths, especially those by car accidents, may have been intentional. Also, because of persistent cultural taboos and financial pressures, some families and communities refuse to admit that a suicide has occurred.

Most suicides occur in urban areas, and there is an upward trend in suicide among minority groups. Suicide most commonly occurs in April and May, with December having the lowest rate except around the Christmas holidays. Although one might expect that the autumn season with the coming of winter would be a more likely time for depression and discouragement, spring apparently brings feelings of rebirth and renewal that render some individuals unable to cope. Suicides are more likely to occur on Friday, Sunday, and Monday. People seem to feel loneliest at those times, and loneliness is one of the major causes of suicide.

Three times more women than men attempt suicide, but three times more men actually succeed. Women may use attempts as a way to express their distress, while men may be less able to until the pain becomes too great.

There are sex differences in the methods chosen: men are more likely to commit suicide with a gun, while women usually resort to barbiturates and other less violent methods. Some experts feel that women use these methods because they fear disfigurement or because society does not sanction violence on the part of females. People who attempt suicide also use the means most accessible to them. For example, while only 3 percent of all suicides on the national average are the result of jumping from high places, the rate is 33 percent in New York City, where there are many tall buildings.

Some people destroy their lives in subtle, less deliberate ways. Examples include the man with a lung condition who continues to smoke, the diabetic who won't take insulin, and the alcoholic who won't seek help for her drinking problem. There are others whose actions might also be considered suicidal, including reckless drivers, stunt people, and racing car drivers who continually take unnecessary chances with their lives.

People do not have to be mentally ill to commit suicide. Of course, some people who take their lives *are* mentally ill, and many are clinically depressed. Suicide occurs 500 times more often among people with serious depressive reactions than among the general population. Nurses who are working with depressed clients therefore need to be alert to the possibility of self-destructive acts by these people.

Many suicide victims have feelings of loneliness, helplessness, and hopelessness that often have been aggravated by a loss. Suicides occur more frequently among divorced people than among single people and among single people more frequently than among married persons. For the survivors, suicide is a highly personal tragedy that produces feelings of pain, guilt, remorse, and bitterness.

Theoretical Approaches

Theorists from many disciplines have offered explanations for the phenomenon of suicide. The theories with the greatest implications for nursing care of the suicidal client are the sociological, psychological, communicative, social-psychological, and bio-chemical theories. None of these explanations should be considered alone, however; a multifaceted approach that draws from several theories is a preferable way to understand this complex problem.

SOCIOLOGICAL THEORIES Emile Durkheim (1897) believed that suicide could be explained only with reference to the social structure in which the individual exists. He proposed three categories of suicide:

egoistic, altruistic, and anomic. *Egoistic* suicide results from the lack of integration of the individual into society. The more intensely individuals are forced to rely on their own resources in a society, the higher the suicide rate.

Durkheim also found egoistic suicide in cases where individuals were not integrated into family life. The greater the concentration of families, the greater the immunity to suicide. In communities, the suicide rate fell in periods of crisis because society was more strongly integrated and the individual participated actively in social life.

Altruistic suicide occurs when the individual's life is rigorously governed by custom and habit. The individual takes his or her own life because of higher commandments, either religious sacrifice or unthinking political allegiance. Egoistic and altruistic suicides are symptomatic of the way in which the individual is structured into society—in the first case, inadequately, and in the second case, overadequately.

Anomic suicide, the third type, is due to the loss of the regulation imposed by the group to which the person has become accustomed. When horizons are suddenly broadened or contracted, anomic suicide increases. Sudden wealth, for example, can stimulate suicide, as the newly rich person is unable to cope with new opportunities. In the case of divorce, marriage no longer exercises its regulatory influence, and the likelihood of suicide increases. According to Durkheim, this anomic situation affects men more severely than women because men have profited more from the regulative influence of marriage.

Sociologists after Durkheim have included a multitude of variables in their attempts to isolate indicators of suicide. Suicide has been related to age, sex, marital status, socioeconomic status, occupation, and urban living. The inadequacy of these explanations has been pointed out by Beall (1969). To attempt a sociological explanation omits the basic internal struggle of the individual and fails to explain why only some individuals commit suicide. Psychological explanations are needed to provide additional insights.

PSYCHOLOGICAL THEORIES Freud (1917) viewed suicide as a failure to externalize aggressive feelings, which are instead turned inward upon the self. He believed that suicide is a reaction to the loss of an ambivalently loved object. Menninger (1958) thought suicide represents the translation of a wish to kill into a wish to be killed and finally a wish to die. Zilboorg (1935) saw suicide as an attempt to thwart frustrating external forces, to gain immortality, and to maintain the ego rather than destroy it.

In psychoanalytic approaches, suicide has often been associated solely with depression and schizophrenia. Although suicide is frequently found with the affective disorders, it is not limited to depressive conditions, nor do all depressed persons commit suicide.

Some theorists have seen suicide as an attempt to solve an identification conflict (Wahl 1957). Litman (1964) considered suicide an attempt to restore lost identification with a symbiotic union. He suggested that suicide is likely to occur when there is a fusion of the self with the lost object.

COMMUNICATIVE THEORIES In their book *The Cry for Help* (1961), Farberow and Shneidman called attention to the communication of messages in suicide. They suggested that all suicides represent an indirect form of communication. Meerloo (1962) described suicide as a form of mental blackmail in which the individual unconsciously attempts to punish a disappointing person. Karon (1964) also saw some forms of suicide as attempts to hurt someone else through the fantasy that killing oneself is an effective aggressive retaliation. Wahl (1957) considered suicide a magical attempt to solve a conflict and achieve comfort by relieving one's own guilt and inducing it in others.

SOCIAL-PSYCHOLOGICAL THEORIES Social psychologists have been concerned with the precipitating role of unsatisfactory interpersonal relationships or the breakup of an adaptive relationship. According to social-psychological theories, suicide is the outcome of the process of social interaction rather than the result of a specific type of psychopathology. Suicide attempts and communication of intent are efforts to solve problems of living—they are pleas for help from others. Whether or not suicide is committed depends on the response from the environment (Hattem 1964, Kobler and Stotland 1964).

BIOCHEMICAL THEORIES Recently a deficiency of a specific chemical—serotonin—has been identified in the brains of some people who are prone to take their own lives when faced with difficulties. Serotonin is a neurotransmitter that, along with others, is instrumental in regulating certain brain activities, including emotion.

The current understanding is that serotonin deficiency occurs in people more prone to impulsive violence and, when they become depressed, they are more likely to commit suicide. The combination of serotonin deficiency and depression increase the risk of suicide more than either factor alone (Goleman 1985).

MYTHS CONCERNING SUICIDE

Over the years, a variety of myths have grown around the subject of suicide (Freedman, Kaplan, and Sadock 1976). Nurses should be aware of these myths and examine their own beliefs to provide adequate care of the potentially suicidal client.

- Myth 1. People who talk about suicide don't do it. *Fact*: Eight out of ten clients who kill themselves have given warnings about their intentions.

- Myth 2. Suicide happens without warning. *Fact*: The suicidal person gives many clues—they are just unrecognized or disregarded.

- Myth 3. Suicidal people wish to die. *Fact*: Most are ambivalent about dying and are gambling with death, hoping others will save them.

- Myth 4. Once a person is suicidal, he or she is always suicidal. *Fact*: Persons are suicidal only for short periods of time.

- Myth 5. Improvement after a crisis means the risk is over. *Fact*: Suicides commonly occur about three months after improvement, when people have the energy to put thoughts into actions.

- Myth 6. Suicide is inherited and runs in families. *Fact*: Suicide is an individual experience.

- Myth 7. Suicidal persons are mentally ill. *Fact*: Although suicidal persons are extremely unhappy, they are not necessarily mentally ill.

Table 16–1. Comparison of Theoretical Approaches to Understanding Suicide

Type of Theory	Approach
Sociological	Suicide is related to position in and interaction with the social structure.
Psychological	Act is the result of aggression turned inward, loss of a love object, or loss of self-identity.
Communication	Act is a form of communication, a way of relieving guilt, a form of aggressive retaliation.
Social-psychological	Act is the result of unsatisfactory interpersonal relationships or breakup of adaptive relationships.
Biochemical	Act is the result of serotonin deficiency combined with depression.

suicidal person. Many caregivers believe that suicide is a justifiable act in some instances. Occasionally the terminally ill client who is suffering immensely is seen as having the right to end that painful existence. While such beliefs are subject to debate, it is the caregiver's duty to preserve life whenever possible. Therefore, interventions must be directed toward helping the client through difficult periods, after which the client's feelings may indeed change. Conversely, at times caregivers become overwhelmed by their own rescue fantasies and take personal responsibility for suicidal clients. Assuming such an inappropriate obligation can soon lead to discouragement and frustration.

During the crisis period, the client needs to be able to depend on the therapeutic relationship with the nurse. However, nurses should be aware that this dependency can become overwhelming to

The five main types of theoretical approaches are summarized in Table 16–1. When working with a suicidal client, nurses should attend to all these theoretical approaches by assessing the social structure, the presence of psychopathology, the client's need to communicate, and the nature and quality of the client's interpersonal relationships. Any or all of these variables may be influencing an individual's suicidal expression.

Nursing Attitudes

Because working with suicidal clients can be taxing and draining, it is important for caregivers to examine their own feelings toward suicide and the

POSSIBLE NURSING DIAGNOSES FOR SUICIDAL CLIENTS

Impaired verbal communication
Ineffective individual coping
Fear
Dysfunctional grieving
Hopelessness
Potential for injury
Powerlessness
Self-esteem disturbance
Social isolation
Potential for self-directed violence

The above are the more likely diagnoses related to suicidal clients. Nursing diagnoses are not limited to the list above. Manifestations of these disorders are individualistic even though certain prevailing patterns are identifiable.

them and destructive to clients if it is allowed to continue over an extended period of time. A gradual increase in clients' responsibility for their own decision making must be fostered with appropriate timing. Because the clients' dependency needs tend to be difficult for the nurse, continual objectivity is of paramount importance. Many times the support of colleagues or a supervisor will help the nurse maintain this attitude.

High Risk Groups

Nurses have extensive contact with a wide variety of clients and are in a primary position to assess people at risk for suicide. Certain groups of persons have been identified as being at higher risk than others.

The following groups of clients are at higher risk of suicide than the general population:

1. Alcoholics and drug abusers. These clients frequently mix drugs, which can result in lethal doses. In addition, many clients are depressed and lack judgment when under the influence of a substance. Impulsive behavior becomes more likely at these times.

    Additional information is found in Chapter 10.

2. The elderly. Overall rates of suicide are highest among the elderly (Goleman 1985). Old age is a time of loss—of self-worth, of role performance and of significant others. The perception that life is no longer meaningful becomes a reason for ending that life. Displacement from job-related roles and family roles may produce a feeling of hopelessness and uselessness. Widows and widowers are particularly vulnerable, especially in the first year following the death of a spouse.

    Social isolation is another contributing fac-

tor. Women tend to have a greater chance for survival because of the contact with friends and the responsibility for integrating kinship groups.

Disabling physical illness may impair functioning and change one's self-image. A loss of independence increases isolation. Mental illness, particularly depression, is the most common syndrome in people over 65 years of age (Hirst, Brockington, and Sheesley 1985).

3. Physicians. Psychiatrists in particular have a much higher rate of suicide than the general population. Perhaps this results from believing that they are the ones other people look to for solutions and they cannot see anyone to help them with their own problems.

4. Children and adolescents. Of the estimated 400,000 teenagers in the United States who attempt suicide each year, 10,000 succeed (Hodgman 1986).

    Unfortunately, self-destructive acts on the part of children and teenagers are often thought to be accidental when in fact they are not. Children under the age of 15 are bright enough to know the consequences of some of their actions. They have already learned about dangerous situations in the environment and know what will happen in many instances but may not comprehend the permanence and irreversibility of death. Children who attempt suicide often come from disturbed families with discord and abuse; they may have experienced a loss of self-esteem and are often depressed.

    Depression is a common element in adolescent suicidal behavior. Many times this is overlooked or not taken seriously by caregivers. Impulsive behavior is also seen frequently, and hopelessness is a primary factor. Many teenage victims have shown borderline states that are marked by shifting identities, confused attachments, and changing moods.

    The most important factor when working with adolescents is to let the clients know that they are being taken seriously. All too often, the behavior of teenagers is treated as normal acting-out behavior or a hysterical response that does not warrant attention.

5. Previous attempters. Although it is commonly believed that clients who frequently attempt suicide will never actually complete the act, a previous attempt is actually one of the strongest indicators of potential suicide. For some, the aborted attempt is but another example of failure, increasing feelings of hopelessness and worthlessness.

DSM-III-R CLASSIFICATIONS

The suicidal client may receive various DSM-III-R diagnoses, depending on the perceived etiology of the suicidal potential. The following are examples from Axis I:

Major Depression

296.2x   Single episode
296.3x   Recurrent
300.40   Dysthymia
312.39   Impulse control disorder
309.00   Adjustment disorder with
           depressed mood

The Nursing Process and the Suicidal Client

In order to properly assess a client's potential for suicide, the nurse must be alert to several aspects of the client's presentation (Farberow and Shneidman 1961).

The suicidal plan is probably the most significant of the criteria. Four main elements should be considered: the lethality of the planned method, the means to use the method, the thought and detail of the plan, and preparations for death. Planning to use a gun or hang oneself is more lethal than planning to take pills or slash one's wrists because the latter methods leave time for rescue. A threat of shooting oneself is more serious if the client has a gun than if no guns are available. If the client mentions specific details of the plan, such as when, where, and how, and if she has made preparations such as making a will and giving away cherished possessions, the seriousness of the plan rises markedly.

Current stressors must be evaluated, along with the client's ability to cope and adapt. Loss of a loved one, of a job, or of money, status, health, or body image can precipitate suicidal feelings. Impending surgery, with resultant fear and increased anxiety, can increase suicide potential.

Verbal clues to suicidal intent can be direct or indirect. Direct messages include "I want to die," and "I can't stand living any longer." Indirect statements are more subtle and take the form of "I won't be here when you get back," "This is the last time I will be here," or "I'm not worth much anymore." Behavioral clues can also be direct or indirect. The clearest example of direct behavioral communication is a suicide attempt, or "practice run."

The current psychological state of the client can also manifest suicidal tendencies. The most common suicidal states are depression, psychosis, and agitation. Evidence of severe depression can be elicited with questions about sleep, loss of appetite, weight loss, withdrawal, loss of interest, and apathy. Psychotic states characterized by delusions, hallucinations, disorientation, and confusion can cause loss of control of suicidal tendencies. Agitated states are evidenced in tension, anxiety, guilt, shame, rage, hostility, and thoughts of revenge. Of most significance is the state of agitated depression, in which the client may feel unable to tolerate the pressure of feelings and anxieties and feels the need to act in some way to obtain relief.

The client's feelings about the suicidal thoughts are important to know. The client who is afraid of the thoughts and wants to make them go away is at less risk than the client who is comfortable with them.

The client's environmental resources are often critical in determining whether he or she will live or die. Inquiry must be made into resources that can be used for support, such as family, relatives, friends, clergypersons, or social agencies.

The client's medical status may give additional information for evaluating suicidal potential. The client with a chronic debilitating illness that has caused considerable changes in self-image and self-concept may be at high risk. The client suffering from fears of a fatal illness may have a preoccupation with death and dying.

No single criterion for assessing suicide potential should be considered excessively alarming, with the exception of a lethal and specific plan for action. The assessment should be based on the general pattern of all the indicators related to the individual case. It is as important to assess the client's strengths and resources as it is to evaluate the negative aspects of the picture. Sometimes a client will present with alarming negative feelings and behaviors, but these negative aspects will be defused by a number of positive features within the situation.

PLANNING The goals of caring for the suicidal client are directed toward providing protection from self-destruction until the client is able to assume that responsibility himself. It will be necessary to assist the client to express feelings of aggression and hostility constructively and outwardly rather than focusing them destructively and inwardly. During this time, the client must be assisted to meet her physical needs, as she may be so preoccupied with self-destructive thoughts that she neglects other necessities. The long-range goal is to help the client achieve a more realistic and positive self-concept so that her feelings of self-esteem, self-respect, acceptance by others, and belonging are enhanced.

Clients with high suicidal potential who appear out of control will require hospitalization. In addition, clients without external support systems may need short-term hospitalization until supports can be established. The current laws permit commitment of clients who are a danger to themselves or others; nurses should be familiar with the commitment proceedings of their particular state.

Most clients, however, can be treated on an out-patient basis, either by establishing a trusting relationship with close monitoring of the client's status or by referral to another suitable agency, depending on the need.

Several resources can be used in planning the client's care. The client should be encouraged to discuss his problems with the family if possible. If it is considered desirable for someone to be with the client during the crisis, a family member should be called and apprised of the situation even if the client may be reluctant to have this done. The family must accept responsibility for the emergency and help the client get the recommended treatment. Close friends can often be utilized in the same way. If the client belongs to a church group, the clergyperson may be of assistance. The police should be used only in cases of clear and immediate emergency, such as when a suicide attempt is about to occur or has occurred. The client may need prompt medical attention, and the police are the ones who can procure that treatment most quickly.

IMPLEMENTATION Suicidal clients on an inpatient unit should be closely observed at all times, especially in the bathroom, where there are objects that can be harmful or where the client may attempt suicide by drowning. Some hospitals require that suicidal clients have someone with them on a one-to-one basis until the danger of suicide is believed to be past. During the period of close observation, the nurse has an excellent opportunity to assist the client to unburden himself and talk out his feelings. The need to be accepted, respected, and appreciated is paramount for such clients. Acceptance and respect penetrate even the most deeply depressed person if the communicating person is sincere. An attitude of hopefulness on the part of nursing personnel conveys reassurance of the client's worth.

It is important to determine what is meaningful to the client at the moment and to avoid imposing one's own feelings. Sensitive listening is important, but the client needs to be reminded that suicide is not the only choice. The nurse can suggest alternative actions and work with the client to implement them. Disturbed thoughts cannot be forgotten until they are replaced with other thoughts. The client needs to know that seemingly insoluble problems can somehow be worked out. The client must be granted permission to make suicidal threats whenever there is a need. It is important not to argue with these threats and to take them seriously. The client needs to know that it is permissible to discuss suicidal ideation or intent and that caregivers are committed to helping.

When suicidal clients are serious about their intent, they are going to become actively suicidal no matter what preventive measures are taken. The environment must therefore be checked for potential hazards. Anything sharp or potentially injurious, such as scissors, knives, razors, glass, neckties, sashes, and cleaning fluids, should be removed. Paper plates and plastic eating utensils are a good alternative to chinaware and metal utensils.

During the day, a therapeutic schedule should provide the client with tasks that will increase feelings of usefulness. Interaction with others should be encouraged. Adequate nourishment and physical care measures to induce rest and sleep are needed. Suggested nursing interventions are provided in Table 16–2. The nurse is the key person in providing liaison activities between the suicidal person and those who can give the continuing support and direction essential for the emotional recovery.

Because death is no easy escape from misery, the suicidal person approaches this finality with ambivalence. Even in deep despair and hopelessness, the depressed person longs to be rescued from his deadly inclination and usually communicates this longing to those around him. The prevention of suicide consists of knowing the potential signs and responding when they appear. One of the most dangerous times is when a serious depression is lifting and the client now has the energy to mobilize his suicidal plan. The individual coming out of a depressed state may also commit suicide out of fear of having to reexperience such deep depression. Unfortunately, this may occur after the client has been discharged from the hospital. The early

Table 16–2. Nursing Interventions for Suicidal Clients

Client's Problems	Nursing Interventions
Potential for self-destruction	1. Observe client closely at all times and reduce environmental hazards. 2. Supply nourishment and physical care as needed until client can assume responsibility for himself. 3. Take suicidal threats seriously; do not argue with client about them. 4. Use measures to induce sleep and rest. 5. Remind client that there are alternatives to suicide. 6. Be alert for signs of acting-out behavior. 7. Observe client closely during recovery from depression, as danger of suicide may increase at this time.
Feelings of aggression toward self	1. Show interest in client and seek her out; encourage interaction with others. 2. Assist client to express feelings of aggression constructively and outwardly; help client to unburden herself and talk about feelings. 3. Provide a busy schedule; plan diversional activities. 4. Encourage client to make decisions for herself whenever possible.
Loss of self-esteem, self-respect	1. Listen to client to determine what is meaningful to him. 2. Be sincere and honest, making efforts to bolster client's confidence in himself. 3. Do not tell client he is getting better. Wait until he can make that observation for himself.

establishment of a trusting therapeutic relationship and supportive environment is therefore of extreme importance.

EVALUATION Nurses may not be helpful to clients unless they are able to perceive the clues to suicide and to recognize the implications of related behaviors and verbal communications. Remaining uninvolved and indifferent prevents nurses from responding to the client's cry for help. Telling the client that she seems better rather than waiting for her to discover that for herself will convey an attitude of not understanding the client's pain. Failing to convince a client that he really wants to live may be due to the nurse's refusal to accept the fact that the client wants to die. Another attitude on the part of the nurse that is nonproductive is interpreting suicide as a sinful or illegal act, which only adds distance to the nurse-client relationship and decreases its therapeutic effectiveness.

The reaction of others in the client's environment should also be evaluated. Significant others may be nonhelpful or even injurious. If they reject the client and deny the suicidal behavior, the client may withdraw physically and psychologically from continued communication. Sometimes significant others resent the client's increased demands and insistence on gratifying dependency needs. In other cases, they may act helpless and indecisive, giving the suicidal person the feeling that help is not available, thereby increasing his feelings of despair. To help the situation, treatment for the significant others may be indicated as well.

THE DISRUPTION OF VIOLENCE

Violence, whether between individuals or societies, has been present since the beginning of humankind. As a nation, the United States has used violence to attain its ends and has sanctioned the use of violence within certain contexts, such as war and civil control. The prevalence of violence in the media, especially on television and in motion pictures, provides exposure to violent acts for all age groups. Against this background of acceptable violence, it is little wonder that the management of violence between individuals and within families is one of the most difficult problems facing caregivers today. The remainder of this chapter deals with these aspects of violence: the violent individual, the rape victim, and the violent family. Because research has shown that alcohol use is frequently associated with violent behavior, the implications of alcohol use will be discussed for both the individual and the family.

The Violent Individual

At times nurses find themselves working with clients who exhibit violent or acting-out behavior. This violence may be deliberate or may occur because the client has lost control. In order to function adequately, it is important for nurses to be aware of their own reactions to such clients. Knowledge and skill in working with violent clients will help nurses to overcome fear reactions that may prevent them from responding appropriately. Being afraid of someone who can potentially cause harm is a natural human reaction. The recognition and acceptance of this fear is the first step toward actions that will benefit the client and safeguard the personnel.

According to Haber et al. (1982), several categories of clients may be prone to acting-out behavior. The client experiencing an acute attack of paranoia, either from a functional disorder or organic brain syndrome, sees his environment as hostile and threatening. Such distortions force the client to use destructive acts to protect himself. Clients suffering from organic brain syndrome may have distorted thinking and loss of reality testing, which can lead to a sudden onset of violent behavior with little warning for the staff. Often the client has had no history of assaultive behavior and has been unable to communicate his fears. Clients with temporal lobe epilepsy may have a history of rage reactions that result in violent fights with little or no provocation. Frequently such clients do not remember the incidents. Certain physiological conditions, such as metabolic or endocrine disorders, drug withdrawal, and space-occupying brain tumors, increase the likelihood of acting-out behavior in clients who tend to react violently to uncomfortable situations.

Other clients who act out in a violent fashion may have personality disorders (see Chapter 9) or problems with impulse control. Such individuals tend to have a low tolerance for frustration and an impatience to get needs met; they lack guilt feelings for the results of their behavior—a lack that psychodynamic theorists attribute to inadequate superego development. This arrested development is thought to be due to inadequate or traumatic parenting, which has prevented the client's internalization of concepts of right and wrong. The explosive client, in contrast, does have a sense of guilt at having harmed others but lacks proper impulse control. This lack of control may be a result of inadequate socialization techniques or inappropriate role models during development. A wife beater, for example, may have learned this behavior by watching his father physically abuse his mother.

Whatever the cause, it is important for nurses to maintain a certain vigilance and awareness of possible violent behavior and to be able to intervene for their own protection and the safeguarding of the client. The best nursing interventions are directed toward reducing the rage and calming the client so that more extreme measures, such as the use of restraints, can be avoided.

The Nursing Process and the Violent Individual

Aggression becomes destructive and negative when it is not channeled or expressed in appropriate ways. The resulting behavior is usually harmful. Causes of such acting-out behavior may be fear, frustration, reality testing, intrusion of personal space, feelings of inferiority, and grief.

It is important that nurses do not take the verbal or physical attacks from clients personally. Although aggressive behavior has many meanings, most frequently nurses are only the convenient targets for the collected emotions of the client.

ASSESSMENT Making an accurate assessment of a potentially violent client can enable the nurse to defuse the situation before the client becomes out of control. Taking an accurate history of past violent behavior and drug use will provide clues to a client's potential for violence. A past history of violence is the single most reliable predictor of future violent behavior. In addition, clients will often give a number of behavioral clues to accelerating anger. Any distinct behavior change should be regarded as an indication of a potential flare-up. A client who has been under control may begin to pace, bite his nails, and appear anxious and jumpy. The client may engage in verbal abuse and threatening gestures, such as throwing objects or pounding his fists into furniture. Conversely, a very active client may suddenly become quiet and withdrawn before an explosion. Nurses need to develop an observational ability about these clients that enables them to sense the acceleration and know at what point the client will strike out. The client who is actively hallucinating and who is confused and disoriented is also at high risk to act out.

PLANNING Once the potential for violent behavior has been determined, the nurse should plan the possible interventions. The short-term goals are to protect the client from self-harm and from acting out impulses until she is able to assume responsibility for herself. It will be necessary to help the client express her feelings of hostility in a safe and acceptable manner. To facilitate the exploration and ventilation of hostility, it is necessary to let the client know that she will not be judged or retaliated against. Initially, an effort should be made to talk calmly to decrease her anger. If this effort fails, plans must be made to restrain the client until she is able to regain control.

IMPLEMENTATION Morton (1986) offers a variety of techniques that can be used to subdue emotional intensity. Psychologically disarming the client is a first and most crucial step. It is important to acknowledge the client's distress and never minimize the seriousness of the problem by making light of events. As emotions rise, people have difficulty in paying attention; prefacing any statements with the person's name is an effective way of getting attention.

Specific directions must be given when talking with staff; members should address clients in short, simple statements because dysfunctional emotional levels cause slower ability to receive and organize information.

If clients are told exactly what is expected of them, their sense of security and control will be increased. Arguing or defending should be avoided at all costs because these will only escalate a problem. Voice tones can be useful tools in helping to control a potentially violent episode. A softer than normal tone can be effective in getting attention and de-escalating the situation if emotions are not yet too high. When emotional levels are severe, a louder than normal voice and slower speech can establish communication; shouting, however, is never indicated. If emotions have erupted, a normal and monotonous tone, using bland, repetitive statements, may calm and reassure the client.

Attention should be given to the effect of body language on a potentially explosive situation. Not only should nurses be aware of the personal gestures of the client that indicate changes of behavior, but they must also recognize their own body language. A threatening body position can precipitate a violent reaction in a client. Clenched fists, hands on hips, tense or angry facial expressions, and quick movements should be avoided. Clients should be approached from an angle instead of straight on, which is perceived as being a threat and confrontation.

Lastly, it is important to respect the client's personal space and ask permission to enter that space whenever possible. Most people claim a certain amount of space around them as personal territory. Invading this space may provoke physical aggression. Psychotic clients may have an exaggerated sense of personal space and need more room and distance from others.

When the client shows threatening, angry behavior, it is necessary to remove other clients from the immediate area for their own protection and to reduce distractions. The nurse should keep a safe distance from the client, allowing him to remain in his present position without feeling pushed or attacked. The client needs space between himself and others. The next step is to help the client identify the anxiety that is causing the behavior and to reassure him that he will not be allowed to lose control. The client generally senses when he is about to lose control and needs to know this will not happen. At this point, an appropriate intervention would be "You seem really upset, and I'm afraid you may injure someone if you throw that vase." The nurse should provide reassurance with statements such as "I want to help you control your behavior. I cannot allow you to lose control." The nurse can provide the client with alternatives with suggestions such as "Let's have a cup of coffee to talk this over." The nurse should also encourage verbalization of the anger rather than acting out: "Whatever happened to make you so angry?"

Many times this nursing approach will subdue the anger and relieve the situation. However, if this approach does not work, it may be necessary to restrain the client. The first step is to provide a show of strength or force, which consists of at least five people approaching the client from a side-front angle (not directly from the front, as this can be perceived as an attack). Such a show of force will usually subdue the client without having to actually restrain him.

If physical restraint is necessary, at least five people are needed; one to hold each limb and one to be available to administer intramuscular medication. Each member of the team must know what he is doing in order to prevent injury to himself. Eyeglasses and sharp objects should be removed before approaching the client. Once the client is medicated and restraints have been applied, the client should have someone in attendance to provide physical care and an opportunity to talk about the episode whenever the client is ready. Restraints should be removed one at a time at intervals to massage the limb and to check skin condition. When the medication has taken effect and the client is calmer, restraints may be removed. Helping the client to return to the area with other clients must be handled with care, as the client will most likely be embarrassed and will need assistance to regain assurance.

EVALUATION After an incident of restraining a client, the staff should meet and discuss what happened and how the problem could have been prevented. A nursing staff that is insecure at functioning in such situations may have been part of the problem. Clients can sense fear in others, and this fear only accelerates their own misgivings that the episode will get out of control. The reaction of the staff and their feelings during the restraining process need to be honestly explored to promote better performance and to decrease fear.

Van Rybroek et al. (1987) have described a natural aggression cycle that takes place after a client has been brought out of seclusion or restraints. Because the staff is fearful that the aggressive client will become violent again, they tend to avoid the aggressor in a pattern of social distancing. Staff are hesitant to interact with the client because of the potential for physical harm. This social distancing further enhances the client's reputation as an aggressor and deepens staff countertransference feelings of fear and anger. This cycle of aggression, seclusion, fear, and social distancing will repeat itself if conditions that minimize interaction and contact with the client remain unchanged. Negative attention from staff and other clients caught in a culture of fear and avoidance can anger the clients and precipitate further aggressive behavior.

A summary of nursing interventions for the violent client is provided in Table 16–3.

RAPE

According to statistics, rape is the fastest growing crime of violence in the United States, but opinions differ as to whether rape is actually increasing or whether simply more rapes are being reported than in the past. It has been estimated that only one out of every ten rape offenses is actually reported (Rada 1978).

Motivation to Rape

It is a widely accepted concept that rape is not a sexual act but an act of aggression (Sadock 1972). The major motive of the rapist is a desire to control another person, and the means for gaining this control is the act of rape (Rada 1978). In many instances, the intercourse itself is the least important part of the event. Emphasis is placed instead on the plan, the tension built up, and the apprehension of the victim. Although the sex act may be of secondary importance, the reason for assaulting in a sexual manner is that rape represents to the rapist a violation of the most sensitive personal control that a woman has. By forcing the victim to submit, he deprives the victim of control over her intimate privacy (Rada 1978). Consequently, if the victim submits without a struggle, the rapist is left with a diminished sense of control and feelings of unfulfillment (Rada 1978).

Reactions of Rape Victims

During the rape experience, the woman is in a state of panic in which she must make a quick decision on how much to resist. Her main concern is to stay

Table 16–3. Nursing Interventions for the Violent Client

Client's Problems	Nursing Interventions
Impending violent behavior	1. Allow client to remain in present physical position; give space and keep some distance. 2. Observe client while placing self between client and door; do not turn your back, and move slowly and deliberately. 3. Ask other clients to leave the area. 4. Identify the client's feeling of anxiety and encourage verbalization. 5. Offer alternatives, provide reassurance, and set limits.
Need for physical restraints	1. Assemble equipment and appropriate number of staff members. 2. Prepare a private room that is free of potentially dangerous items. 3. Explain to client that staff is going to help him control his behavior. 4. Approach the client slowly but deliberately, being careful to prevent injuries both to client and staff. 5. Once the client is restrained, have someone with the client at all times; medicate as ordered. 6. Take vital signs at least every half hour; observe extremities for lack of circulation or pressure. Offer snacks and fluids; give mouth care p.r.n. 7. Encourage client to express thoughts and feelings about the incident; explore the situation that caused the client to lose control. 8. Allow other clients who may have observed the incident to ventilate their feelings or concerns about the client or about their own potential for loss of control.
Loss of impulse control	1. Explore the violent episode and loss of control with the client; identify why this act was done at this time; was there a relief of tension and frustration? 2. Help client learn to identify the precipitating factors that led to the loss of control. 3. Validate the client's appropriate responses to anger and frustration; explore alternative modes of expression. 4. Work with family if possible so they may understand client and support new coping methods.

POSSIBLE NURSING DIAGNOSES FOR VIOLENT INDIVIDUALS, VICTIMS, AND FAMILIES

Anxiety
Impaired verbal communication
Ineffective individual coping
Ineffective family coping
Potential altered parenting
Altered family processes
Fear
Hopelessness
Potential for injury
Rape trauma syndrome
Self-esteem disturbance
Potential for violence, directed at others

The above are the more likely diagnoses related to individuals, victims and families that experience violence in their lives. Nursing diagnoses are not limited to the list shown above. Manifestations of these disorders are individualistic even though certain prevailing patterns are identifiable.

persist in extreme form for several years, complicating the victim's interpersonal relationships.

Following the rape, the victim has a sense of living in a dangerous, unpredictable world, and she may become preoccupied with her own feelings of victimization and vulnerability. Some women are unable to resume normal sexual relationships with their chosen partners, either because of sexual revulsion or because of feelings of unworthiness. The ability of the victim to work through the trauma of rape and adapt to the changes in her life as the result of the rape depends to a large extent on the attitudes of caregivers, law enforcement officers, and the significant persons in her life.

Attitudes toward Rape

The rape victim needs acceptance and empathy from health professionals and from the significant persons in her life. Hints by family members, friends, or professionals that the victim's own behavior encouraged the rape will intimidate and prolong self-recrimination. The most detrimental attitude of all is for others to believe the myth that the rape victim is a seductive woman who has misled the unsuspecting male or that she is a manipulative female who is shouting "Rape!" in order to deny her culpability for a sexual encounter. The feminist movement has done much to eradicate such myths and to help ease the ordeal faced by

alive. Since the rapist is usually physically stronger than she is, it is fairly easy for him to enforce submission. Regardless of how much resistance she offers, the aftermath of the rape finds the victim humiliated, confused, fearful, and enraged. These reactions do not abate quickly and may in fact victims who wish to bring charges against alleged rapists. The recruitment of policewomen as regulatory agents has also done much to assist rape victims and to raise the consciousness of other police personnel.

Nurses need to develop an awareness of their own feelings about the victim of a rape. If the nurse inwardly believes that the rape is the fault of the woman and that rape cannot happen to "nice women," the victim will sense this attitude and a therapeutic relationship cannot result. Overidentification with the victim can be equally detrimental. Nurses should work through their own experiences and feelings about sex and rape in order to be helpful to rape victims.

Rape is a traumatic event with great potential for precipitating crises in victims and in their significant others. Because the reactions of family members and significant others are varied and unpredictable, it may not be advisable to notify anyone until the victim has given permission to do so. Many rape victims need time to deal with their own feelings before being intruded on by well-intentioned friends and relatives. The reaction of the victim's sexual partner is of particular importance. If the partner is concerned primarily with the emotional state of the victim and offers unquestioning support, a state of disequilibrium in the victim may be averted. But if he interprets the rape not as a crime against the victim but as a violation of his own rights, the needs of the victim will not be met.

Most towns and cities now have rape crisis centers or hotlines that function around the clock to provide services to victims. Professional staff working in hospital emergency departments collaborate with rape crisis teams and act as liaison agents when a rape victim is brought in for treatment. Close work relationships between rape crisis workers and hospital staff members prevent the destruction of important evidence during the post-rape examination and provide continuity of care for victims.

The Nursing Process and the Rape Victim

ASSESSMENT The initial interview of the rape victim is of paramount importance in assessing the client's amount of psychological distress and in determining a plan of care. The purpose of the interview is to learn as much as possible about the incident and about the victim's reaction to it.

Attention should be given to the victim's nonverbal responses. Her general appearance tells how she feels about herself, which helps to assess the severity of the distress and the loss of coping skills. It is also important to determine whether any physical problems need attention. A medical and gynecological examination may be indicated as part of follow-up care.

The circumstances of the rape, the characteristics of the assailant, and the events that happened during the rape will all influence the victim's reaction. When and where was the victim approached? Where did the rape occur? Was the assailant known to her? Was she threatened? Did he have a weapon? Did she struggle? Guilt feelings about not resisting may add complications to the client's recovery process. What type of sex was demanded? For many women, the sexual aspect of the rape is highly distressing, especially if they have been forced to commit acts that are repulsive to them.

In order to provide appropriate treatment, it is necessary to determine the meaning of the sexual assault to the woman and her feelings about sex in general. The rape may create difficulties in the victim's present relationships and may stimulate doubt and fear about the possibility of future relationships.

The client's help-seeking behavior should also be explored. Where did the woman go for help? What was the encounter with the police like for her? How was she treated at the hospital? Is she considering pressing charges against the rapist? Who is available to help her? Who can she confide in? Who is she willing to tell about the experience? The social support systems of the victim can make the difference between successful resolution and continued fear and guilt.

PLANNING When planning care for the rape victim, the following goals should be considered:

1. To help her work through the experience and settle the crisis.
2. To help her resume her normal style of activity as soon as possible.
3. To assist her in making decisions about seeking someone to talk with, about informing friends and family, and about prosecuting the assailant.
4. To help her repair any estranged family and social relationships.
5. To attend to measures to regain her physical health.
6. To help her repair the emotional damage and overcome fear of future relationships.

IMPLEMENTATION Because of the severity of the crisis of rape, the victim should be encouraged to seek counseling to assist her in regaining control and in resolving the issue. Counseling should be directed toward suppressing anxiety and reestablishing the

DSM-III-R CLASSIFICATION FOR VIOLENT CLIENTS AND FAMILIES

Any physiological conditions resulting in violent behavior are classified according to the individual syndrome. For example, organic mental disorders and substance abuse. The acting-out character disorder is classified as a personality disorder on Axis II.

Other diagnoses that may apply are the following:

Conduct Disorders

312.20 Group type
312.00 Solitary aggressive type
312.90 Undifferentiated type
313.81 Oppositional deficit disorder

Impulse Control Disorders

312.34 Intermittent explosive disorder
312.39 Impulsive disorder not otherwise specified

Family violence may be classified under V Codes for conditions not attributable to a mental disorder that are a focus of attention or treatment.

V61.10 Marital problem
V61.20 Parent-child problem
V62.81 Other interpersonal problem
V61.80 Other specified family circumstances

victim's sense of worth and value. The counseling sessions should help the victim talk about her fear that she may have unwittingly contributed to the rape. In order to proceed with her life, she must be helped to express her feelings. Talking about the rape helps to settle the experience. Depending on the reaction of significant others, couple or family counseling may be indicated.

Informing the victim of her legal rights, helping her talk about the experience, and enlisting her cooperation in apprehending and prosecuting the rapist are measures that reduce feelings of helplessness. Even when the rapist is not apprehended immediately, participating in the activities of law enforcement agencies distracts the victim from ruminating about the experience. A common fear is that the rapist will try to retaliate in some manner.

The nurse should encourage the victim to work with the police on this issue to determine whether this fear is substantiated by concrete data.

The victim should be encouraged to resume her normal style of activity as soon as possible, since delays only lead to difficulties later on. The nurse should help the victim explore alternative actions and express her feelings about these alternatives. She needs to be assisted in making decisions about whom and when she is going to tell about the experience and who will make up her support system. By using available support systems, she can begin to regain the self-confidence needed to resume her normal lifestyle.

EVALUATION The victim has most likely come to terms with the rape when her memories are less frequent and when the pain of the memories has decreased. A good sign is the resumption of a normal lifestyle. Not all women will be able to settle the crisis completely or to attain the same level of acceptance. If progress stagnates, it may be necessary to reevaluate the available support systems to determine some of the difficulties the woman is encountering.

THE VIOLENT FAMILY

From 1939 to 1969, the *Journal of Marriage and the Family* did not contain any reference to family violence. Such violence was believed to be an isolated problem in disturbed couples that fulfilled the masochistic needs of the wife and was necessary for family equilibrium. Keeping family violence a private rather than a public problem enabled professionals to treat symptoms rather than to identify the real occurrence (Hilberman 1980).

But what was thought to be a relatively rare problem is actually one of epidemic proportions. Researchers such as Richard Gelles (1974) and Lenore Walker (1979) cite the incidence rate of violence between American couples to be as high as 60 percent.

Data from the early 1980s indicates that between 20 and 25 percent of adult women—12 to 15 million—have been physically abused at least once by a male intimate (Kissel 1986).

The problem of family violence is obviously not a new one. What *is* new is that it is just beginning to be recognized as an important social problem. Violence in the family is a multifaceted phenomenon encompassing wives, husbands, children, and even pets. More recently, abuse of elderly parents has begun to receive attention as well.

Family violence is a widespread and complex phenomenon. As it becomes stripped of its pseudo-justification, it is exposed and thereby accessible to study and to identification of possible intervention approaches. The increasing volume of literature attests to the researchable quality of the situation and the rising interest of many academic disciplines.

Spouse Abuse

Although family violence is often thought to be associated with lower socioeconomic groups, studies are showing that wife battering transcends all ethnic groups and social classes. DeLorto and La-Violette (1980), who operate a shelter for battered wives in Long Beach, California, found their clients to be 62 percent white, 20 percent black, 13 percent Chicano, 3 percent Asian, and 2 percent other and the husbands to represent almost every profession and occupation. It is currently believed that battering *appears* to be more prevalent in the lower socioeconomic classes because families at this level more often come to the attention of service organizations and law enforcement officials (DeLorto and LaViolette 1980). When wealthy or middle-class husbands beat their wives, the behavior stays hidden because wives are often too embarrassed to let people know.

Wife abuse exacts a high physical, psychological, and social price. Abused wives frequently receive physical injuries requiring medical attention or hospitalization.

Why do husbands beat their wives? In recent years, a number of theoretical approaches have been advanced by various disciplines. Each emphasizes certain aspects as the most crucial for understanding spouse abuse. Nurses should use concepts from many theories to form their own basis of understanding and to develop a framework from which to plan their care of the battered wife.

INTRAPSYCHIC THEORIES Traditional explanations of wife battering rest on Freud's (1959) theory of feminine masochism. According to Freud, the masochist wants to be treated like a little, helpless, dependent *naughty* child. The true masochist always holds out a cheek whenever there is a chance of receiving a blow. The maintenance of suffering is all that matters; punishment is used to try to erase feelings of guilt. In the Freudian view, this self-destructive behavior results from a failure to resolve the female version of the Oedipal complex. The girl is competitive with her mother for her father's attention but fears loss of her mother's love. In order to show she is not interested in her father, she unconsciously provokes paternal aggression, which assures her that she has forsaken her father

ADVOCACY FOR BATTERED WIVES

The organized movement against wife beating started in England in 1971, when Erin Pizzey opened a rundown house to which local women could flee from violent husbands. Within a few years, a network of refuges was developed throughout the United Kingdom, and a Parliamentary investigation of marital violence was begun.

In 1972, an organization called Women's Advocates, Inc., in St. Paul, Minnesota, began a telephone information and referral service for women, and in 1974 it opened the first U.S. shelter for battered women. About this time, the first studies concerned with violence in the home began appearing in the sociological journals. It was not until 1976 that the first presentation of the problem was available to the general public through the book *Battered Wives*, by Del Martin of the National Organization for Women.

and thereby reduces the guilt feelings associated with her desire for her father. This pattern persists in adult relationships.

Shainess (1979) also saw battered wives as masochistic but incorporated sociocultural circumstances in her explanation. She postulated that violent men use violence as an ego-enhancing technique. Violent men play violent games because their nonviolent repertoire is restricted and limited. These are the kind of men to whom masochistic women relate. In this way, masochism can be considered in terms of developmental and cultural influences. The person has been influenced not only by persons who have become harsh but by significant adults who were harsh and cruel in earlier years.

According to psychoanalytic theorists, other factors, such as helplessness, plasticity, and long periods of dependency, make infants vulnerable to the masochistic process. The masochistic person is afraid to resist, refuse, offend, or insist on limits. In addition, sociocultural circumstances—awareness of superior masculine strength and lack of control in reproductive processes—have shaped submissiveness in women. Cultural acceptance of brutality to women has also caused women to play the role that will avoid the most conflicts.

The psychoanalytic stance has been attacked from several perspectives. Based on clinical observations, Symonds (1979) has attacked the idea of the victim's masochism and attributes its popularity in part to society's need to reject and blame the victim. She and Martin Symonds (1978) suggest that violent marriages can be divided into two groups: those in which violence precedes the marriage and those in which the violence develops within the marriage.

In the first group, violence is brought into the marriage by a man with a history of violence. His violence-prone characteristics usually erupt early in the courtship and get progressively worse. He uses violence to handle any conflict and to express a pervasive feeling of powerlessness. His violence is ego-syntonic and his aggression is poorly controlled. He has a history of early and prolonged exposure to family violence and was usually an abused child as well. Alcohol is frequently associated with his expression of violence.

Why do wives stay with such husbands? According to Symonds and Symonds, women react to their situation in three phases: impact, traumatic psychological infantilism, and depression. The second phase is crucial to understanding the battered wife. In this phase, she is reduced to coping mechanisms from her early childhood; she becomes obedient and cooperative, doing anything her husband wishes in a desperate effort to save her life. Later, when she discovers there is no outside support system that can help her, isolation and hopelessness set in. The violence is not provoked by the wife; she is a convenient recipient of poorly controlled violent behavior.

In the second group of violent marriages, the violence comes as a last resort when all other attempts at communication have failed. These are marriages with a neurotic interaction in which the behavior of one partner threatens the psychological defenses of the other, and each projects his or her feelings and shortcomings onto the other. The occurrence of violence makes both partners feel worse, not better. These relationships usually improve with therapy or marriage counseling.

Susan Steinmetz (1978) also believes that psychoanalytical theories blame the victim for being abused. She points out that these theories suggest that certain types of women are prone to be victims because of their psychological defects or because they avoid taking steps to resolve their own problems. Research describing personality characteristics of battered wives often leaves the impression that these victims have permitted the violence to occur. The woman is seen as having few resources and as being fearful, isolated, dependent, helpless and trapped, overcome by anxiety, depressed, and full of guilt and shame. It is often suggested that violence can be reduced by changing the woman's social and economic resources, increasing her education and job skills, teaching her to be less submissive, and so on. These approaches tend to emphasize the ability of a woman to control her environment, an ability many women lack. Thus, a profile emerges of a woman, who, by her own weakness, allows herself to be victimized.

Based on an examination of case studies of battered women, Steinmetz suggests that there is a need to reformulate this thinking about wife battering. Contrary to the notion that certain women are at risk to be beaten because of personality traits, she suggests that the dynamics of beatings are what produce these traits. She believes that the dynamics involved in severe chronic battering syndrome are analogous to those used in brainwashing. Brainwashing is made possible by isolating individuals from their usual supports and rewards. This isolation results in hypersuggestibility and increased receptivity to introduction and reinforcement of new values and behaviors. The only validation of the person's worth is that offered by the individuals enforcing the isolation. Inconsistent, confusing, threatening treatment that is interspersed with kindness produces the effects of brainwashing.

In another attempt to explain the psychology of battered women while rejecting the psychoanalytic approach, Lenore Walker (1979) has utilized Martin Seligman's theory of *learned helplessness*. According to Seligman (1975), people who are exposed to negative reinforcement unrelated to their actions learn that their voluntary behavior has no effect on controlling what happens to them. As a result, they learn to be helpless, their "survival" instincts are extinguished, and they become depressed. Walker believes that this sort of process occurs with battered wives.

Walker has also integrated the patriarchal nature of society into her theory. She believes that the very fact of being a woman automatically creates a situation of powerlessness. Women are systematically taught that their personal worth, survival, and autonomy do not depend on effective and creative responses to life situations but rather on their physical beauty and appeal to men. Having been trained to be second best, women begin marriage with a psychological disadvantage, since marriage in our patriarchal society does not offer equal power to men and women. The law seems to perpetuate the historical notion of male supremacy. Cultural values and beliefs, marriage laws, economic realities, and physical inferiority all teach women that they have no direct control over the circumstances of their lives.

SOCIOLOGICAL THEORIES In developing a sociological approach to family violence, Straus and Hotaling (1977) have noted the myth of family non-violence, which is the culturally promulgated image of the family as a place of love and gentleness. Concurrently our culture maintains a set of norms that legitimize and at times encourage the use of violence between family members. The features of family life that contribute to intimacy also facilitate the occurrence of a high rate of family violence.

Adding to these variables is the widespread occurrence of violence in the United States as a society, which produces the norm that violence is an acceptable way of dealing with problems. The approval of violence in other spheres of life cannot help influence what goes on in the family. Indeed, there is evidence to show that it is a circular process: the violence occurring in the family is one of the things that makes for a violence-approving society in other spheres of life (Straus 1974).

Gelles (1974) has devised a structural theory of violence based on the assumption that deviance is unevenly distributed in the social structure, being more common among those occupying lower socioeconomic positions. He postulates that people in certain structural positions suffer greater frustrations and deprivations and that a common reaction to this situation is violence. This reaction is legitimized in some segments of society and is seen as an appropriate response to stress and frustration. Thus, violence may be more common in these social segments.

Gelles has listed several factors that play a role in the occurrence of family violence. They include: (1) the family of orientation, (2) forms of socialization, (3) family structure such as unwanted children and religious differences, (4) structural stresses such as unemployment and health problems, (5) social isolation, (6) situational factors such as gambling and drinking, and (7) norms and values that regulate violent behavior.

Gelles emphasizes that "it takes two"; that is, acts of family violence are not sporadic outbursts of irrational violence. Rather, the role of the victim is an important and active one, with the victim commonly serving as verbal tormentor.

Straus (1973) has developed a general systems theory of family violence. This theory attempts to account for violence by viewing the family as a goal-seeking, purposive, adaptive system. Straus sees violence as a system product or output rather than as a product of individual pathology. He points out positive feedback processes that can produce an upward spiral of violence, such as sexual inequality and society's acceptance of violence, and negative feedback processes that serve to maintain or dampen the present level of violence, such as low community tolerance levels and diminished power of the aggressor relative to the victim. Straus's theory seeks to identify the processes that account for the *continuing* presence of a given level of family violence.

Maria Roy (1977), social worker and founder/director of Abused Women's Aid in Crisis, New York City, has developed a broad perspective that encompasses historical, present-day, and future implications of wife abuse. She believes that the wife-beating phenomenon is cyclic—that it is passed from one generation to the next—and that it could be prevented by a gestalt approach involving societal, educational, and legislative changes. According to Roy, in a violent society all members are capable of violence against one another. Where violence is condoned and victims are blamed, all members tolerating the violence are potential perpetrators, and men, women, and children learn that physical aggression can be a useful tool. Roy asserts that city, state, and federal governments, organized religion, and the media must be held accountable and must respond to the problem with new programs, new laws, new interpretations of the marriage contract, and responsible television and radio programming.

The subject of wife battering is still in the early stages of research and understanding. More research is needed to isolate causal factors. Generally established treatment is not available, due in part to the fragmentation of the theoretical background. Most important have been the changes over the last ten years that have made spouse abuse a visible issue and its recognition as a dysfunction that requires help rather than punishment.

Child Abuse

For many centuries abuse of children was justified by the belief that severe physical punishment is necessary to maintain discipline, and that parents, because their children are their property, have the right to inflict any action deemed necessary to enforce control (Helfer and Kempe 1968). In various cultures, such practices as clitoridectomy, castration, and the ultimate abuse, infanticide, have been routine. Children have been misused in the workforce to the extent of slavery, and they have been abandoned in times of war and crises.

Concern about harmful treatment of children led to the founding of the Society for Prevention of Cruelty to Children, in New York City in 1871. Other cities followed this example, and dedicated individuals began to force upon the public conscience the awareness of the plight of many children. In the early 1960s, Henry Kempe introduced

THE FEMINIST VIEWPOINT

In the last two decades the feminist movement has done a great deal to publicize the plight of the battered woman. Jane Roberts Chapman (1978) has written about the economic implications of the victimization of women. She believes that economic factors are an integral part of victimization and that limited resources are often a significant factor in a woman's ability to extricate herself from a violent situation. Some victimization is thus made possible or prolonged by female economic dependency. The battered woman must consider not only the economic problems caused by the specific crisis but also her means of financial survival if she decides to leave her abuser. Many wives are ill-prepared to be breadwinners, and remain in abusive situations because they cannot afford to do otherwise.

Even when women attempt to control their lives and maintain economic independence, Chapman maintains, they do not escape the prospect of victimization because they can be victimized by men in authority positions in the world outside their families. Sexual assault, sexual harassment, and medical exploitation are examples. Chapman mentions sexual advertising, pornography, and prostitution as methods used by society as a whole to promote and maintain the victimization of women.

Coming from an equally strong feminist viewpoint is Del Martin (1977), who states that every institution in our society is designed to keep marriages intact, regardless of the danger involved. Violent behavior is excused by inaction committed to maintaining the status quo of male supremacy within the home and society. Women are described as too aggressive, too passive, too passive-aggressive, too masochistic, too assertive, too well educated, or "too" anything in order to justify the situation they are in. The husband is described as pathological as well, but the tone is different. He is under too much stress, he is unemployed, or he is drunk, and the behavior is excused.

Martin believes that men beat wives because they are permitted to do so and nobody stops them. She says women are beaten because they are trained, enforced, and maintained into dependence. Women are caught in a double bind. In a patriarchal society that depends on the subjugation and control of women, rules and roles are defined and enforced by male-dominated institutions.

Marriage is a means by which women are routinely cast in the role of victim. They are taught from birth that their ultimate goal should be marriage and motherhood, or they forgo fulfillment. To catch a husband, a woman must be feminine and adopt the characteristics of a subordinate, passive, dependent, and permissive female. She submerges her own personality to be "normal and well adjusted." Patriarchy then legitimizes the inequality. Her passivity makes her a doormat that provokes her husband's abuse. If she "steps out of line," she is again abused to "put her back in her place." She is in a "no win" situation.

---

the term "battered child syndrome" and conducted a well-attended symposium at the American Academy of Pediatrics in 1961 that was the stimulus for the beginning of present-day interest in the problem of child abuse.

Child sexual abuse is defined as engaging developmentally dependent, immature children and adolescents in sexual activities that they do not fully comprehend or for which they are unable to give informed consent (Kempe 1978). The child is left powerless and is victimized by a lack of choice. Frequently, sexual activities are obtained through bribing or coercion. The offender is often known to the child.

Long-term effects that may occur for a child who has been sexually abused are aggressive personality, avoidance of men, eating problems, neglect and abuse of one's own children, splitting of affection and sexual behavior, impaired ego integration and fragmentation (Greenberg 1979).

Many caregivers tend to believe that child abuse occurs only among the disadvantaged and the poor. This is simply not true. Parents who abuse their children come from all socioeconomic strata. They live in large cities, in small towns, and in rural areas, their educational achievement ranges from grade school to postgraduate degrees, and they represent a variety of religious affiliations and ethnic groups (Helfer and Kempe 1968).

CONTRIBUTING FACTORS IN CHILD ABUSE A number of contributing factors are thought to play a role in child abuse, including characteristics of the abusing parent, of the nonabusing parent, and of the child.

Characteristics of the Abusing Parent Although abusing parents do not usually have overt psychopathology that distinguishes them from nonabusing parents, there are some characteristics they commonly display. These parents tend to be depressed at times and expect and demand a great deal from their children. Their expectations are usually beyond the ability of the child to comprehend and to react to appropriately. Abusive parents deal with their children as if they were older than they actually are, often feeling insecure and unloved themselves and looking to the children as a source of reassurance, comfort, and support. For the child abuser, infants and children exist primarily to satisfy parental needs, and the children's needs are unimportant. Kaufman (1966) has described these parents as projecting their own problems onto their children and feeling that the child is the cause of all their troubles. They attempt to relieve their anxiety by attacking the child instead of facing their own problems.

In many cases parents who abuse their children are re-creating the pattern of their own upbringing. They experienced abuse and a sense of intense and continuous demand from their own parents. Accompanying this demand was a sense of constant parental criticism, with their performance always seen as inadequate and inept. Everything was oriented toward the parent.

Helfer and Kempe (1968) suggested that abusing parents have not been able to develop the ability to adequately parent because they lacked a satisfying, confidence-producing relationship with their own parents. This lack of a significant emotionally satisfying experience with their own parents has created a disbelief in the possibility of a parental relationship, which persists into adult life. Relationships for these persons tend to be distant, meager, and unfulfilling. Lack of confidence originating in inadequate parenting in infancy is reiterated in adult life experiences and plagues marriages and other relationships. Left with a conviction that needs can never be met by parents, spouse, or friends, the person looks toward his or her children as a last, desperate attempt to get comfort and care (Helfer and Kempe 1968).

Contribution of the Nonabusing Parent Usually only one parent actually attacks the child, but the other parent contributes either by openly accepting the abuse or by ignoring it. If the nonabusing parent shows undue attention and interest toward the child, feelings of envy and resentment may lead to abusive behavior in the other parent. Any rejection from the nonabusing partner is a stimulus to attack, as the abusing parent's needs are neglected and rebuffed. In some cases, one parent is the active perpetrator and the other is the cooperator. These tendencies become obvious when one parent tries to change and the other one then becomes abusive. Sometimes the child is a scapegoat for conflict between the parents. Inability to solve frustrated dependency needs results in turning to the child for comfort that the child cannot give.

Contribution of the Child Although innocently and unwittingly, the child may contribute to his own abuse. Unwanted infants are common targets for abuse. So are infants who do not live up to their parents' idealized image of them. Parents who expected an active child may be disappointed when the child is placid, and vice versa. Children who are fussy and cry a lot may threaten the parents' self-esteem; they may feel that the baby is not responding normally because they are not parenting adequately. Other potential targets of abuse are children born with some type of congenital defect that requires considerable attention and that may be a drain on the family finances.

Care of the Abused Child
The potential for encountering and identifying battered children is found in all areas of nursing practice, particularly in emergency rooms and in the community. Nurses should know whether the state in which they are practicing has permissive or mandatory legislation on reporting suspected abuse. Persons who report in good faith are granted immunity from court action. The failure to report suspected child abuse hurts not only the child but also the parents, who are in need of help.

ASSESSMENT The nurse can make observations that may lead to a diagnosis of child abuse. Children should be observed for unusual marks on the body, such as scars and unexplained bruises. Certain behavioral characteristics may also offer clues. These include a passive response to pain; fear and withdrawal, especially around the parent; flinching and withdrawal from touch; and violent and aggressive play. Parents should be assessed for the presence of factors that may place them at risk for being abusers.

PLANNING Among goals that should be considered is protecting the child from further pain, fear, and neglect. The parents need support in adopting methods that will limit their potential for abusing the child. Appropriate referrals should be made to groups or agencies that will assist the parents in adopting new coping mechanisms and that will provide the parents with support.

IMPLEMENTATION Suggested nursing interventions for helping abused children and their parents are provided in Table 16–4.

EVALUATION If the child is to remain in the custody of the parents, it is important to establish support systems and to be sure that the parents are aware of how to contact helping persons when they are needed. Referrals should be made for family or individual therapy. Other problems, such as alcohol and drug abuse, must be attended to in the long-term planning.

In some instances, it may be necessary to remove the child to temporary placement in a foster home until the parents can receive the help they need. Nurses have a role in helping both the child and the parents to accept this plan, which is necessary for safety of the child.

Child abuse is a long-standing problem in many families and will, unfortunately, continue to be so. Public recognition of and attention to the situation will help increase available facilities and services to aid abused children and to help parents develop their parenting potential and to stop the abuse. Rather than seeing these parents as uncaring and criminal, it is important for caregivers to see them as individuals in need of help and care. Without this help, abusive behavior will continue and may be passed on to their children, who may in turn become abusers.

Elder Abuse

The abuse of the elderly population is beginning to receive public attention.

Abuse of the elderly can be manifested by (1) physical abuse in which the older person is beaten, shoved, or physically restrained for long periods, (2) psychological abuse, such as infantilization, exclusion from conversation, and isolation, (3) financial exploitation in which the elder is forced to sign over property, and (4) neglect, such as inadequate food and medical treatment.

Abuse toward the elderly may be a result of stressors imposed on a family caring for an impaired older person, a reaction to the dependency of the older person from the younger caretaker. Abuse may also be a part of a pattern of transgenerational violence (Anderson and Thobahen 1984).

Care of the Abused Elderly

To successfully intervene in actual or suspected cases of elder abuse, nurses need knowledge about the demographic variables, possible etiology, availability of community resources, and normal aging processes.

ASSESSMENT In contacts with older persons, nurses should be aware of the possibility of abuse. Bruises, fractures, malnourishment, and confusion should not be attributed to the normal consequences of aging. The possibility of abuse should be evaluated

---

Table 16–4. Suggested Nursing Interventions for Child Abuse

Client's Problems	Nursing Interventions
Child's need for protection from injury	1. Monitor visitors. Note reaction of child when around significant others. 2. Make referrals to social service departments for continuous monitoring.
Child's difficulties in adjustment	1. Encourage child to talk about feelings; avoid judgmental comments. 2. Provide drawing materials, as children often depict their feelings through art. 3. Provide other play materials for expression of feelings. Do not probe. 4. Give comfort by holding and rocking, and make note of child's reactions.
Child's need for relationship with parents	1. Be aware of your own feelings and nonverbal messages. Maintain composure and refrain from implied criticism or rejection. 2. Consider asking parents to keep a daily diary of their feelings and situations in which they feel stress. Ask them to identify the triggers that set off a chain of events. 3. Help parents to talk through their feelings and start plans for family therapy. 4. Let parents know that you really care about them and that other parents share their feelings and frustrations.
Poor parent-child relationship	1. Help the parents to enjoy their child. 2. Point out lovable attributes of the child and introduce them to the pleasures of reading to and playing with their child. 3. Ask the parents to join you and the child in simple games. 4. Teach the parents about normal growth and development, giving them realistic expectations. 5. Demonstrate how limits can be set without harsh punishment. 6. Reinforce any attempts to nurture and express affection. 7. Reassure parents that they have rights and needs, too.

through a thorough history and assessment of daily living situations and the family's level of functioning. Any unusual evidence of fear shown by the older person in the presence of her caregiver should be noted. A caregiver may react with hostility to questions assessing abuse potential; care and tact must be used to obtain information about the family relationships. Most abused elderly will not report the abuse for fear of retaliation, exposure of children to community censure and legal action, and the fear of being removed from the only home they know.

PLANNING When planning interventions, nurses need to know the legal constraints and conditions for reporting abuse in their particular state. The issue of client competency must be addressed. If the client is competent and chooses to remain in the home, the nurse must yield to that decision after counseling the client. If the client is incompetent, the nurse should begin appropriate guardianship procedures.

INTERVENTIONS Interventions should be directed at alleviating the stress of care demands at home. Obtaining home services, providing respite and referral, and exploring the possibility of support groups are the first steps to relieve the tension. Giving the family some guidance about the normal aging processes and methods of providing care help to sustain a family relationship and provide safe maintenance of the elderly in their homes. Table 16–5 summarizes suggested nursing interventions for elder abuse.

Table 16–5. Suggested Nursing Interventions for Elder Abuse

Client's Problems	Nursing Interventions
Elder's need for protection from injury	1. Make referrals for continuous monitoring. 2. Note interactions between elder and caregiver. 3. Evaluate physical status and take corrective measures if indicated.
Dependency on caregiver	1. Obtain home services to alleviate stress. 2. Provide guidance in giving physical care. 3. Explore activities for elder to relieve continued reliance on caregiver for all needs. 4. Provide education for caregivers concerning normal aging processes.
Fear of caregiver	1. Encourage elder to talk about feelings and assessment of situation. 2. Provide information about ways to obtain immediate help.

EVALUATION If the elder client is to remain in the home, continued follow-up and appropriate referrals for support care are necessary. Nurses can develop interdisciplinary protocols and emergency hotlines. Educational programs for families may be of assistance (Anderson and Thobahan 1984).

The Nursing Process and the Violent Family

Nurses are greatly concerned with family dynamics, as the family is the context in which health is maintained or illness develops. Today, with the old psychoanalytical notions of female masochism falling by the wayside, nurses must develop an eclectic theoretical framework within which to formulate effective intervention stratagems. This framework should incorporate the approach that is unique to nursing—the advancement of health and the reinforcement of wholesome client attributes.

ASSESSMENT Several areas need to be examined to provide a baseline from which to plan and develop interventions.

What factors are present in the family of origin that would lead to violence? What does the use of physical violence symbolize within the family? Did the forms of socialization within the family include coercive tactics? If the family did indeed provide the training for violence as a means of problem solving, what factors are present that can be used to facilitate learning other ways? How strong is the parental influence, and can it be overcome?

Components of the family structure need to be evaluated. What are the family's financial resources? Were the children planned or unplanned? What stressors are currently acting on the family? Are religious differences or ideologies contributing to the justification of violence? Is there evidence of drinking, gambling, intense jealousy, or infidelity? Are these factors amenable to change? Are other health problems evident? Are any family members emotionally isolated? What emotional demands are placed on the marriage? Total dependency of one spouse on the other provides fertile ground for dysfunctional relationships. How can this be changed? What other areas can be reinforced to provide relief? The norms and values in the family system are of primary importance. If the violence is justified and rationalized, the problem can take on different dimensions.

Assessment of the wife needs careful attention, especially if she has left home and is seeking assistance. Her coping style, strengths and weaknesses, and readiness for change and the availability of social supports need to be evaluated to plan appropriate courses of action.

The man who abuses his wife or children must, of course, receive attention in the assessment. If alcohol use is a problem, it may have to be treated before other interventions can be made. It is important to obtain an understanding of the man's point of view of the battering incidents and of the family situation as a whole. Making the assumption that he enjoys the results of his behavior can lead to inappropriate interventions. Many men are upset by their behavior and can be open to change. It is important to perceive the man as an individual who is also in pain rather than as one who deserves only punishment.

The influence of the child on the family needs attention. Does the child cry a lot? How do the parents manage the child's crying? Do the parents get upset when they are unable to comfort the child? Is the mother upset when she is left alone? Has she ever been afraid to be alone with her baby? Can she call someone for help at these times? Does she become anxious when someone watches her care for the baby? Does she feel others are critical of her parenting skills? When do the parents think that children are old enough to understand what is expected of them? How well do the parents feel their children understand expectations now?

During a family interview, the nurse should observe the body language of both parents and children. Do the parents hold their child at a distance? Does only one parent hold the child? Does the child cringe or show overt fear of a parent? Or is the interaction one of trust?

Obtaining a picture of the violence based on these factors will provide a baseline for planning interventions.

PLANNING In planning to institute change in the family, nurses need to utilize exchange theory. If the costs of violence continue to be less than the rewards, the violence will continue. The rewards for nonviolent methods of problem solving must therefore be increased. The nurse can help by assisting the client to determine what is gained by the violence and to find other ways to reach the same ends. Goals must be reachable and realistic to the particular family setting.

Depending on the situation, individual, couple, family, or group therapy can be used. If the family is still intact, marital counseling may be the treatment of choice. Through this method, the communication problems and neurotic components of the marital relationship can be explored. Behavioral approaches can also be used, as they lend themselves readily to evaluation of effectiveness. In family therapy, emphasis must be placed on the relationship between the parents, as emphasis on the child may increase a parent's feelings of rejection and of having his needs cast aside in favor of the child's needs.

When planning action for battered wives, it is important to keep several factors in mind. The abused woman should not be encouraged or urged to leave her partner until she is ready. She will not leave him until she has developed enough self-confidence and trust in the community at large to be able to do so. With opportunities now available for women to seek shelter from the abuse at battered women's centers, there are more alternatives that she can consider. Initially, the woman may need help recognizing that she has alternatives. After becoming involved in counseling, during which self-esteem is fostered, the woman may be more able to carry out structured plans.

Because the battered wife is usually ambivalent about her abusing spouse, it is important that the nurse not berate or deride him. There is a need to acknowledge the woman's ambivalence by recognizing the pain in being abused by a man who is at other times loving and sensitive to her needs. If the ambivalence is not dealt with openly and with support, she may feel further alienated and misunderstood.

Planning should take into account the woman's ability to face problems realistically. Factors to be aware of include (1) her sensible and concrete planning about income, shelter, and legal services, (2) her concern for herself as a person, and (3) her acceptance of the fact that the abuse is a long-standing pattern and not merely an isolated episode.

Many battered women resist treatment in a psychiatric setting for a variety of reasons. Some fear reprisal from their partners, while others do not see the value of a "talk session" when their lives continue to be a terrifying existence. Some women may also not wish to have the label of mental patient attached to all the other negative labels they already have. It is important for health caregivers to engage these resistances in order to provide effective interventions for these women (Weingourt 1985).

Group work with battered women and with the men who batter is becoming and effective mode of intervention. Therapy groups for women should focus on increasing the understanding of the situation and providing a sense of control. One of the goals for the group interaction is to assist the client to relate to others and thereby decrease the sense of isolation. Sharing of stories and concerns can provide both emotional and informational support. Group members need to learn to master their own anger and get in touch with their angry feelings. As therapy progresses, the emphasis should be placed on rebuilding their lives to eliminate destructive ways of relating to men and elevate self-esteem to decrease the possibility of abuse (Weingourt 1985).

Group therapy aims at assisting women to validate their own existence and strengthen their belief in their responsibility for themselves. Grief work helps members deal with the impending losses of the safety of the victim role, the protector and the protection of invisibility.

Therapy groups for men who batter are being formed through a variety of sources. Although these men are very difficult to engage in treatment, referrals for therapy are now being instituted by the criminal justice and court systems as well as by counseling agencies. The emphasis of the group interaction is on the responsibility of the perpetrator; the excuse "she made me do it" is neither condoned nor tolerated. The man uses violence because he has learned that this is an acceptable way of getting needs met and hitting his partner is something he chooses to do.

Because many of these men feel intimidated by other men in a group and are reluctant to share feelings, the group focuses on role modeling, first by the therapist and later by other group members. The men are also encouraged to keep a diary to document and describe their angry feelings and utilize "time out" periods as they learn to identify when their anger is liable to reach intense proportions (Nikstaitis 1985).

IMPLEMENTATION Interventions based on assessment and planning can be instituted by nurses at all levels of prevention. Suggested interventions are listed in Table 16–6.

Primary prevention can be done through early recognition of the signs of family violence as well as identification of couples at risk. In working with clients, nurses can use their knowledge to discern communication problems and to identify predisposing family backgrounds and existing structural elements that may act to increase the likelihood of violence. Early interventions can alter many of the existing problems to prevent further complications.

Of equal importance is the involvement of the nurse in premarital counseling to help clients explore their expectations of marriage and to identify potential problems shown by incongruencies in the plans and aspirations of the couple. Teaching appropriate ways of communicating can provide a better foundation for problem solving within the marriage.

Another area in which nursing can play a preventive role is in genetic counseling. Realization of risks and potential difficulties that can occur with a child who has a congenital alteration or illness can help reduce stress that could lead to violence.

Table 16–6. Suggested Nursing Interventions for Helping a Battered Wife

Client's Problems	Nursing Interventions
Potential for injury	1. Provide clients with information concerning ways to obtain immediate help. 2. Help clients work through the need to leave the situation for safety if necessary.
Ambivalence toward abusing spouse	1. Encourage ventilation of feelings. 2. Allow expression of both the anger and the feelings of affection. 3. Respect the client's need to remain with the spouse until self-confidence allows different choices. 4. Be wary of alienating client by deriding her spouse. 5. Explore possibility of marital counseling to facilitate communication.
Isolation	1. Encourage group therapy to provide support.
Helplessness	1. Provide appropriate referrals for legal and financial aid. 2. Explore possibilities for job training, career counseling, continued education.

Secondary prevention can involve crisis intervention for the violent family. Emphasis may be placed on helping the battered wife develop a realistic perception of her situation and decide whether to leave the home temporarily or permanently. Protection for the wife and her children should be considered. Current ways of coping with the violence should be studied and new methods taught. During a crisis situation, the client's readiness for change will be enhanced and can be utilized to teach her new and more adaptive behaviors.

The family as a whole may be guided to seek professional help. When a history of violence has preceded the marriage, the focus of intervention may be placed on intrapsychic change. When violence has erupted as a result of conflict generated by the marriage, the focus of intervention may be on interpersonal issues.

In years past, the family was considered a unit of production. As the economic focus shifted to the husband/father being the individual wage earner, and as more goods became available for family use, the family became a unit of consumption. Currently, with the majority of wives working, the family is again returning to being a unit of production. Such change may be accompanied by economic pressures, role changes, separation, and individuation that create feelings of disenchantment and disillusionment among family members. Nursing interventions should be directed toward exploring such feelings. Communication therapy is indicated when meaningful exchanges and understanding of feelings are disintegrating. In dysfunctional families, abuse may be a substitute for or a method of communication.

Tertiary prevention for nurses involves encouragement of the family and referral to available resources. Nurses need to know what options are available to battered families, how to counsel them, and when and how to refer families to available community resources, including law enforcement agencies. Referrals are a vital part of preventing recurrence of injuries, as women and children need reassurance from professionals that they are victims of a crime, that others suffer similar abuse, and that they do not have to tolerate it and can get protection. Referral to such organizations as Alcoholics Anonymous and Parents Anonymous can supplement ongoing therapy to address issues that will help families rebuild their lives.

EVALUATION Determining the effectiveness of nursing interventions can be done subjectively and objectively. Wives and families may feel they are getting better even if change is not evident to the observer. Likewise, nurses may be able to see changes occurring without the clients being able to identify them. For objective evaluation, realistic goals must be established as measures for determining whether desired changes have occurred. These goals are dependent on the nature and position of the individual family and on the use of violence within that family.

Implications for Nursing

As awareness of the inequities between the sexes increases, as women enter the legal and health professions in greater numbers, and as feminist organizations identify problems common to women, family violence will be reported with greater frequency. It is an issue that demands social, legal, medical, and nursing intervention. As the problem of family violence comes out of the closet, the issue will become more prevalent for nurses. Awareness of the potential for violence in families must be part of case finding and identification of problems. Nurses in all settings need to be aware of the patterns of abuse so they can look for these patterns when assessing families.

Community health nurses are in perhaps the best position for case finding and recognition of the problem. These nurses have access to the setting in which the abuse is most likely to occur. The nurse in the emergency room needs to be aware of abusive injuries that may be presented as "accidents"

for emergency treatment. Likewise, the nurse in the general hospital setting may be able to identify victims and to make the first steps of progress by assessing the problem, providing a safe environment, helping the client begin to trust the helping professions, and making the proper referrals. The pediatric nurse is in a position to detect child abuse, which may be an indication of generalized violence in the family. Psychiatric nurses, especially those involved in family therapy, will find family violence to be a prevalent presenting problem.

Nurses are in a unique position to be of assistance to the battered family. Unlike many of the other health services professions, nursing is concerned with the broad spectrum of physiological, social, and psychological aspects of patient care. In addition to having a substantial base of knowledge for understanding illness, nurses possess a holistic view that enables them to place needed emphasis on the psychosocial areas. Nursing is concerned with identifying what is right, whole, and functioning in clients, whether they are sick or well, and it attempts to maximize the clients' strengths, assets, and potentials for optimal levels of health, comfort, and self-fulfillment. By maximizing the client's existing strengths, nurses can provide comprehensive care in the battering situation.

SUMMARY

Clients with situational disruptions frequently come to the attention of mental health nurses because of the emotional strain imposed on these clients and their need to find additional resources to help them adapt. Four events likely to cause strain in people's lives are suicide, violent families and individuals, and rape.

While certain populations are at higher risk for suicide than others, the phenomenon itself is very democratic, with little discrimination regarding race, color, creed, age, or sex. Various explanations of suicide have been offered, but the theories that have the greatest implications for nursing are sociological, psychological, communicative, social-psychological, and biochemical.

Nurses should be acquainted with these approaches to formulate plans for accurate assessment and interventions.

Violence presents itself to caregivers in a variety of forms. One of the most frightening is the individual who is no longer in control of his behavior and threatens staff members, other clients, and himself. The ability to perceive the potential for

(Text continues on page 466.)

CLINICAL EXAMPLE

HELP FOR A POTENTIAL CHILD ABUSER

Patsy is an 18-year-old unmarried mother of a 2-year-old boy. Paul, the boy's father, is a 35-year-old construction worker who is married and the father of three daughters. Although he has no intention of leaving his wife, Paul is very fond of the little boy. He visits Patsy often and regularly contributes to the support of his only son.

The relationship between Patsy and Paul has been intense and stormy. He often accuses her of being unfaithful to him, and she is extremely jealous of the time Paul spends with his legitimate children. She shows her resentment by sending her son to stay with a girlfriend when Paul is likely to visit. She often leaves her son alone at night and goes to taverns, where she drinks and socializes. On occasion, she meets men and goes to their apartments or invites them home overnight. She taunts Paul about these episodes; he reacts with fury because of jealousy and worry about his son being left alone.

The battles between Paul and Patsy have been loud and violent. Often police officers have been called by neighbors hearing the uproar. The police have usually tried to soothe the couple and have treated the incidents as minor domestic squabbles, even when Patsy has obviously been bruised and Paul has been obviously intoxicated. When the little boy has been present, he has stared wide-eyed and frightened at his battling parents.

On one occasion Paul came to the apartment in Patsy's absence. Finding his little boy alone, Paul took him to the home of a neighbor woman, whom he paid to look after the child indefinitely. Meanwhile Patsy arrived home with a male companion. Both of them had been drinking and were engrossed in each other. It was not until her male companion left in the morning that Patsy realized her son was gone. Her first reaction was that kidnappers had snatched her son, and she was very upset.

When she called the police, the officers who arrived were already acquainted with the household situation. They phoned Paul, who promptly admitted having taken custody of his neglected child. The police left after telling Patsy there was little she could do except negotiate with Paul. After their departure she became hysterical. In a rage, she slashed the curtains, bedding, and clothing with a knife. She broke mirrors and windows and loudly threatened to throw herself out of a window. The police officers returned but were unable to calm Patsy, whose hands and feet were badly cut. Their recourse was to take her to a psychiatric facility for evaluation and treatment. She was admitted to an inpatient facility for a period of ten days in order to reduce her stress and implement plans for her and her son.

ASSESSMENT

During the initial interview with Patsy on the inpatient unit, the nurse saw a disheveled, wide-eyed, frightened-looking woman who used an abundance of makeup. She verbalized her intention not to talk with the nurse, stating that no one could help her anyhow, her life was a mess, and she wanted "out." She paced rapidly around the room; her speech became louder and her thoughts rambled. After waiting quietly until Patsy seemed to decrease her anxiety by expending physical energy, the nurse was able to calm her and to begin to take a history of the events leading to hospitalization.

During the interview, the nurse learned that Patsy had been an illegitimate child who was abandoned by her mother when she was three years old. She had been raised in a variety of foster homes with adults who had little interest in her and who at times had abused her. When she met Paul, she thought that she had at last found someone who would take care of her, despite the fact that he was already married. When her expectations were not met, she relived her childhood experiences of fear of loneliness and rejection. Although she was knowledgeable about birth control methods, she chose to get pregnant in hopes that this would cause Paul to leave his wife and marry her. Because of the pregnancy, Patsy had not completed high school and had no marketable skills. She was living on welfare and child support.

Based on the history that Patsy supplied and the clinical picture that she presented, the following diagnoses were made:

Nursing Diagnoses

Ineffective individual coping
(related to unfulfilled needs for love and attention, reliance on dramatic tactics to get needs met)
Fear
(related to loneliness and fear of abandonment)
Altered parenting
(related to inability to give love and support to son)

Self-esteem disturbance
(related to discomfort with self, unresolved issues from childhood, and lack of marketable skills)

Potential for violence
(related to possibility of violence toward son)

Altered family processes
(related to ineffective communication, manipulative behavior by both to achieve needs)

Social isolation
(related to lack of supportive, constructive relationships)

Multiaxial Psychiatric Diagnoses

Axis I	309.40	Adjustment disorder with mixed disturbance of emotions and conduct.
Axis II	301.5	Histrionic personality disorder
Axis III	None	
Axis IV		Psychosocial Stressors: relationship disorder, being a single parent. Severity: 3 — Moderate (predominantly enduring circumstances)
Axis V		Current GAF: 50 Highest GAF past year: 60

PLANNING

The mental health team decided that the primary focus for Patsy's treatment should be related to her loneliness, isolation, and unfulfilled dependency needs. Individual therapy that would emphasize building self-esteem was planned. Her suicidal gestures needed further evaluation, but the team felt that the need to

act out in this manner would decrease as Patsy became more comfortable with herself. This acting-out behavior would be explored in individual sessions. Attention was given to her lack of vocational skills and her inability to parent. In her isolated world, Patsy did not have any outlets for developing supportive, constructive relationships and was unable to see much hope for change in the future. Consequently, all her energy was directed toward obtaining the love and attention of someone to care for her rather than finding ways to care for herself.

The need to establish a peaceful, adult relationship with Paul was of paramount importance, for the safety of both her and her child and to provide for better communication between the two in order to arrive at a workable plan for the child's future contacts with them.

IMPLEMENTATION

The nursing diagnoses were helpful in identifying the areas in which Patsy needed the most help. Because of her inability to cope with her life situation and her feelings of being unloved, she was unable to give love and support to her child. She was encouraged to enroll in a parenting class, which was to be supplemented by supervisory visits by a community health nurse to assess Patsy's progress and give additional guidance. Because of Patsy's potential violence toward her son, the nurse's observations of the continued interaction would be used to determine whether the child should remain with Patsy.

In order to help Patsy begin to control her life, she was evaluated for vocational training and plans were made for her to finish her high school education. To facilitate this and to allow her time for herself and to develop new social outlets, her son was placed in a day care center for three days a week. This placement had the added advantage of giving him a healthy environment where he could be with other children.

Couple therapy was provided for Patsy and Paul to improve their communication and arrive at a mutually acceptable plan for visiting the child. This therapy complemented the individual sessions to enable Patsy to decrease her dependence on Paul while beginning to establish new patterns for her life. Paul contracted with the therapist not to see Patsy or her son outside the hospital until an agreement was reached.

EVALUATION

The complexity of Patsy's problems dictated coordination of efforts by multiple caregivers. Interventions could not be directed toward Patsy's problems alone; it was necessary to attend to her son's and Paul's needs as well. Once the safety of all involved was assured, emphasis could be placed on growth and change through vocational guidance and psychotherapy.

Patsy needed to resolve the issues of her childhood and gain an understanding of their influence on her current behavior. Once her desperate need for love and attention was understood, further change could occur to build a more successful, independent life with less reliance on dramatic tactics to get needs met. By providing social outlets through schooling, Patsy had the opportunity to meet others and expand her contacts. This helped decrease her isolation and continued feelings of abandonment.

Nursing Diagnoses	Goal	Nursing Actions	Outcome Criteria	Outcome Evaluation
Ineffective individual coping	Client will increase ability to understand and cope with life situation.	Explore acting-out behavior in individual sessions.	Client will understand her use of various behaviors and her desperate need for love and attention.	Client was beginning to find ways to care for herself and have less reliance on others. Continued therapy was indicated.
Fear	Client will decrease feelings of loneliness and abandonment.	Relate childhood experience to current situation.	Client will understand how her childhood losses are affecting her fears and behaviors.	Client was able to see some hope for the future and realize how her past influenced her present feelings. She was able to devote less energy toward seeking love and attention.
Altered parenting	Client will establish parenting skills.	Enroll in parenting class, supplement with supervisory visits from public health nurse.	Energy will be directed toward her son's needs rather than only her own.	Client showed growth in the area of sensitivity to son's needs. Times of frustration resulted in reverting to past behavior of leaving son alone; visits needed to be continued by nurse.
Self-esteem disturbance	Client will increase comfort with self.	Arrange for evaluation for vocational training.	Client will finish high school education.	Client enrolled in a school program. Support during this period had to continue.
Potential for violence	Client will eliminate violent episodes.	Enroll son in day care center to allow time for self, observe interactions with son to determine need for alternate placement.	Constructive time for client will facilitate interactions between mother and son, enhance parenting skills.	Time for self allowed development of new social outlets and placed son in healthy environment with other children.
Altered family processes	Client will establish effective communication and decrease manipulative behavior.	Couple therapy to arrive at workable plan for child's future contacts with father.	Beginning steps at communication will allow a respite for couple until agreement can be reached.	Paul contracted with therapist not to see client or son outside the hospital until agreement was reached.
Social isolation	Client will develop constructive relationships and a wider support system.	Decrease dependency on Paul through couple sessions, encourage new relationships at school.	Client will develop a more successful, independent life with less reliance on dramatic tactics to get needs met.	Opportunity to meet others expanded client's contacts, helped decrease isolation and feelings of abandonment. Continued support was needed.

violence and to defuse a situation before control is lost is an important one for nursing personnel. Of equal value is the ability to subdue an individual who is out of control in a therapeutic manner and to use that incident for learning, both for the client and for the nurse.

The victims of violence, particularly the rape victim, provide a different challenge to nurses. Rape is a traumatic event that calls for a successful resolution of the emotional as well as the physical trauma involved.

The violent family, with its components of spouse abuse and child abuse, demands the ability of nurses to assess the complex interactions, determine contributing factors, and plan for change while safeguarding all family members.

Perhaps the most important aspect of working with clients who are in situational disruptions is nurses' insight into their own feelings and behaviors in relation to these clients. Self-assessment is a necessary prelude to successful therapeutic relationships.

Review Questions

1. Explain your understanding of the interplay between sociological, psychological, communicative, biochemical, and social-psychological variables that may culminate in suicide.

2. When confronted by a potentially violent client, what interventions should nursing personnel use to defuse or control behavior?

3. What aspects need to be considered when helping a rape victim?

4. Based on the various theories of wife abuse, outline your own theory and understanding of the factors involved.

5. Describe the elements that should be considered in the assessment of the violent family.

Research Report

Suicide Attempts

This study was conducted to examine the common themes expressed as reasons for suicide attempts, to describe the extent to which clients communicated their intent and the feelings of the clients both before and after the event. Subjects were interviewed four days after admission to the hospital for a suicide attempt. Three key themes were evident in the responses pertaining to the purpose of the attempt: some clearly wanted to die, others were ambivalent, and a third group wanted to influence their significant others. Over half of

them communicated their intent verbally, usually to family members and therapists. The feelings surrounding the event were contentment, hopelessness, anger or depression prior to the overdose, and happiness, anger, and indifference afterwards. Of special interest is the fact that 85 percent of the subjects overdosed on prescription drugs that were either their own or belonged to family members.

L. Pallikkathayil and A. McBride. *Journal of Psychosocial Nursing* 24, no. 8 (August 1986):13–17.

Suggested Annotated Readings

Davidson, T. *Conjugal Crime: Understanding and Changing the Wifebeating Pattern*. New York: Ballantine Books, 1978.

This book explores such questions as "What kind of man beats his wife?", "What kind of woman becomes a battered wife?", and "How does he get away with it?". Historical precedents for the toleration of wifebeating are presented and the effect of spouse abuse on children is discussed. Guidelines are given to help battered wives, wifebeaters, children, friends, and family.

Graham, H. D., and T. R. Gurr. *Violence in America: Historical and Comparative Perspectives*. New York: Bantam Books, 1970.

Written by the nation's leading scholars and historians, this report is a searching look at violence in America. It explores patterns and the extent of violence by private individuals and groups in the United States and makes comparisons to Western Europe. Historical conditions that have contributed to the different kinds of violence in America are analyzed and the relevance of the immigrant experience, the frontier, and vigilante traditions are discussed. The book provides examples of conditions that give rise to violence and of the extent to which private violence, public force, concession, and nonviolent group responses to discontent can lead to the resolution of those conditions.

Rada, R. T. *Clinical Aspects of the Rapist*. New York: Grune and Stratton, 1978.

The purpose of this book is to present previous knowledge and new developments in the biology, psychology, sociology, treatment, and legal aspects of the rapist. Although it is written primarily for the mental health professional directly involved in the diagnosis, treatment, and rehabilitation of the rapist, professionals in allied fields will find the material useful, particularly for developing strategies for the prevention of a crime that causes considerable physical and emotional suffering.

Reynolds, D. K., and N. L. Farberow. *Suicide Inside and Out*. Berkeley: University of California Press, 1976.

This book is based on a study of suicidal patients and of suicide observation. The data was collected by an anthropologist who entered a hospital under the assumed identity of a depressed, suicidal patient. The result is a very personal account of a researcher-patient. A broad framework for understanding suicides during and shortly after psychiatric hospitalization is offered, and suggestions for preventions are presented.

References

Anderson, L., and M. Thobahen. "Clients in Crisis." *Journal of Gerontological Nursing* 10 (1984):6–10.

Beall, L. "The Dynamics of Suicide: A Review of the Literature, 1897–1965." *Bulletin of Suicidology* (March 1969):6–16.

Chapman, J. R. "The Economics of Women's Victimization." In *The Victimization of Women*. J. R. Chapman and M. Gates, eds. Beverly Hills, California: Sage Publications, 1978.

DeLorto, D., and A. LaViolette. "Spouse Abuse." *Occupational Health Nursing* (1980):17–19.

Durkheim, E. *Suicide: A Study in Sociology*. Glencoe, Illinois: Free Press, 1951 (originally published in 1897).

Farberow, N. L., and E. S. Schneidman. *The Cry for Help*. New York: McGraw-Hill, 1961.

Freud, S. "Mourning and Melancholia." In *Collected Papers*, Vol. IV. London: Hogarth Press, 1948 (originally published in 1917).

——. "The Economic Problem of Masochism." In *Collected Papers*. New York: Basic Books, 1959.

Gelles, R. J. *The Violent Home*. Beverly Hills: Sage Publications, 1974.

Goleman, D. "Clues to Suicide: A Brain Chemical Is Implicated." *The New York Times* (October 8, 1985).

Greenberg, N. H. "The Epidemiology of Childhood Sexual Abuse." *Pediatric Annals* 8 (1979):296.

Haber, J., A. Leach, A. Schudy, and B. Sideleau. *Comprehensive Psychiatric Nursing*. New York: McGraw-Hill, 1982.

Hattem, J. V. "The Precipitating Role of Discordant Interpersonal Relationships on Suicidal Behavior." *Dissertation Abstracts* 25 (1964):1335–1336.

Helfer, R. E., and C. H. Kempe. *The Battered Child*. Chicago: University of Chicago Press, 1968.

Hilberman, E. "Overview: The Wifebeater's Wife Reconsidered." *American Journal of Psychiatry* 137 (1980): 1336–1347.

Hirst, S. P., W. Brockington, and L. Sheesley. "Suicide among the Aged: Concern for Care Givers." *Dimension in Health Service* 62 (1985):25–27.

Hodgman, C. H. "Suicide in the Young. How to be Helpful before It's too Late." *Consultant* 26 (1986): 71–81.

Karon, B. "Suicidal Tendency as the Wish to Hurt Someone Else and Resulting Treatment Techniques." *Journal of Individual Psychology* 20 (1964):206–212.

Kaufman, I. "Psychiatric Implications of Physical Abuse of Children." In *Protecting the Battered Child*. Denver: American Humane Association, 1966.

Kempe, C. H. "Sexual Abuse: Another Pediatric Problem." *Pediatrics* 62 (1978):382.

Kissel, S. J. "Violence in America: An Emerging Public Health Problem." *Health and Social Work* 11 (1986): 153–155.

Kobler, A. L., and E. Stotland. *The End of Hope: A Social Clinical Study of Suicide*. New York: Free Press, 1964.

Litman, R. E. "Immobilization Response to Suicidal Behavior." *Archives of General Psychiatry* 11 (1964): 282–285.

Martin, D. "Society's Vindication of the Wife Beater." *Bulletin of the American Academy of Psychiatry and the Law* 5 (1977):391–410.

Meerloo, J. A. *Suicide and Mass Suicide*. New York: Grune and Stratton, 1962.

Menninger, K. A. *Man against Himself*. New York: Harcourt Brace, 1958.

Morton, P. G. "Managing Assault." *American Journal of Nursing* 86 (1986):114–116.

Nikstaitis, G. "Therapy for Men Who Batter." *Journal of Psychosocial Nursing* 23 (1985):33–36.

Rada, R. T. *Clinical Aspects of the Rapist*. New York: Grune and Stratton, 1978.

Roy, M., ed. *Battered Women*. New York: Van Nostrand Reinhold, 1977.

Sadock, V. A. "Special Areas of Interest." In *Comprehensive Textbook of Psychiatry*, 2d ed. H. E. Kaplan, A. M. Freedman, and B. J. Sadock, eds. Baltimore: Williams & Wilkins, 1972.

Seligman, M. E. *Helplessness: On Depression, Development and Death*. San Francisco: W. H. Freeman, 1975.

Shainness, N. "Vulnerability of Violence: Masochism as a Process." *American Journal of Psychotherapy* 33 (1979): 174–188.

Steinmetz, S. "Wife Beating: A Critique and Reformation of Existing Theory." *Bulletin of American Academy of Psychiatry and the Law* 6 (1978):322–334.

Straus, M. A. "A General Systems Theory Approach to a Theory of Violence between Family Members." *Social Science Information* 12 (1973):105–125.

————. "Cultural and Social Organizational Influences on Violence between Family Members." In *Configurations: Biological and Cultural Factors in Sexual and Family Life*. New York: Lexington Books, 1974.

Straus, M. A., and G. Hotaling. *The Social Causes of Husband-Wife Violence*. Minneapolis: University of Minnesota Press, 1977.

Symonds, A. "The Myth of Masochism." *American Journal of Psychotherapy* 33 (1979):161–173.

Symonds, M. "The Psychodynamics of Violence-Prone Marriages." *American Journal of Psychoanalysis* 38 (1978): 213–222.

Van Rybroek, G. J., T. L. Kuhlman, G. J. Maier, and M. S. Kaye. "Preventive Aggression Devices (PADS): Ambulatory Restraints as an Alternative to Seclusion." *Journal of Clinical Psychiatry* 48 (1987):401–404.

Wahl, C. W. "Suicide as a Magical Act." *Bulletin of the Menninger Clinic* 21 (1957):91–98.

Walker, L. *The Battered Woman*. New York: Harper & Row, 1979.

Weingourt, R. "Never to Be Alone. Existential Therapy with Battered Women." *Journal of Psychosocial Nursing* 23 (1985):24–29.

Zilboorg, G. "Suicide among Civilized and Primitive Races." *American Journal of Psychiatry* 92 (1935): 1347–1369.

Crisis Guidelines in Nursing Practice

Learning Objectives

After reading this chapter the student should be able to:

1. Differentiate *crisis* from *emergency*.

2. Describe the role of anxiety and stress in the emergence of crisis.

3. Discuss the effects of emotional, cognitive, and behavioral distortion in crisis.

4. Identify the psychological effects of natural and economic disasters on individuals and communities.

5. List the major factors included in crisis assessment.

6. Describe the basic principles of crisis theory and intervention.

7. Define the term *compound crisis* and describe its manifestations.

8. Explain how primary, secondary, and tertiary prevention levels might apply to crisis assessment and intervention.

Overview

Regardless of the setting in which they practice, nurses frequently encounter persons who are in crisis. In this chapter, as elsewhere, crisis is defined as a biopsychosocial response to conditions of stress and change that overwhelm the individuals, families, and communities that are involved. Crisis theory and practice have become increasingly important in health care delivery, and the crisis intervention model may be applied at all three levels of prevention. Primary prevention measures may be used to help people avoid the onset of crisis. Examples of this are the behavioral and physical alterations that a community health nurse teaches to pregnant teenagers in preparation for parenthood. When the emotional or psychological resources of a family are inadequate to deal with the crisis of serious illness and hospitalization, caregivers' interventions are examples of secondary prevention. Here efforts are made to meet the urgent needs of the person who is ill and minimize the disruptive effects of the illness on family life. Tertiary prevention consists of helping clients improve their coping ability after the immediate problems have been alleviated, and of encouraging them to learn from the events that preceded and followed the onset of crisis.

There are several reasons for the attention currently given to crisis theory and practice. First, the crisis intervention model provides caregivers with a focus that illuminates clients' reactions to life changes. A focused perspective directs the attention of caregivers to the immediate situation that a client faces. This enables caregivers to help clients deal with "here and now" circumstances before tackling long-range problems that may be very complex. Persons in crisis are usually overwhelmed by the situation at hand, and are therefore unable or unready to look far into the future. This introduces the second advantage of using the crisis intervention model. The resources of most health care systems are limited, and the crisis intervention model permits caregivers to formulate time-limited strategies that mobilize clients to deal realistically with current problems. A third advantage of crisis theory and practice is that the model may be used in many settings and with a variety of clients. Crisis may occur anywhere and everywhere—homes, schools, hospitals, and the workplace. It is no respecter of persons, regardless of age, gender, geographic location, or socioeconomic class. Since crisis is a universal and inevitable part of life, a working knowledge of its basic theory and practice is both sensible and necessary.

Crisis has its own particular claim to holism. Not only individuals and families, but whole communities must sometimes deal with crisis in the form of natural disasters (such as flood or earthquake) or economic disasters (such as industrial closings). No one discipline or school of thought can claim crisis theory as its own, for the theory is derived from several sources. The result is an eclectic therapeutic model that is limited in its aims and potential, but can yield excellent results when adapted by a knowledgeable caregiver to the needs and abilities of the client.

DEFINITIONS OF CRISIS

There is a body of theory that is applicable to many crisis situations, and at one time principles of crisis theory were considered appropriate to use with all persons in crisis. Early work on crisis intervention tended to be limited to the circumstances surrounding the crisis. At the present time crisis counselors try to consider not only the circumstances of the crisis but also the characteristics of the person and persons involved. The strong emphasis in nursing on the importance of individualized care means that nurses should adopt a comprehensive approach that assesses the crisis, the skills and resources of the people in crisis, and their reciprocal interaction. Every individual, family, and community has a breaking point at which crisis becomes imminent, but the forces bearing on them and their reactions to those forces vary greatly. It is these unique and individualized differences that must be included in crisis assessment and intervention.

In modern life there are innumerable pressures that predispose people toward the state of social and psychological disorganization known as crisis. Crises are so prevalent and widespread that a therapeutic modality has been formulated that is the treatment of choice for people recognized as being in crisis. Recognition that an individual is in crisis is a prerequisite for offering crisis assessment and intervention. It is essential then to understand just what a crisis is so that its presence may be identified and help offered.

NATURE OF CRISIS

For a crisis to be present, a problem or threat, real or perceived, must exist. People respond to crises in a variety of ways, expressing themselves through biological, psychological, and social channels. They try to deal with the threat by employing methods that have worked for them in the past. When customary coping techniques fail, disorganization, or disequilibrium, follows. Disorganization is an internal, subjective experience that, in effect, constitutes a state of crisis.

Two nurse authors, Loomis and Wood (1983), developed a classification of actual or potential health problems, any of which may precipitate a crisis. The categories of health problems they identified are:

- Developmental life changes
- Acute health deviations

- Chronic health deviations
- Culturally induced stressors
- Environmentally induced stressors

There is no actual or potential health problem that cannot be assigned to one of these five categories. In reacting to such health problems, individuals, families, and communities may use more than one response system. Acute or chronic illness, for instance, may elicit biological, psychological, and social responses. Culturally induced stressors, on the other hand, may evoke psychological and social responses primarily.

A broader categorization of crises differentiates developmental crises from situational crises. Every individual experiences developmental crises periodically during the life cycle. Even for those fortunate individuals who are able to move tranquilly through life, every new experience, whether developmental or situational, contains the potential for crisis if customary coping methods prove inadequate and alternative methods are not found.

Interpreting crisis as a human response to actual or potential life problems helps to reduce the mystery surrounding crisis theory and practice. Identifying the response systems used by clients and assessing the usefulness of the responses helps nurses construct a multifactorial assessment model that recognizes the nature of the crisis and identifies the response systems that are involved. Such an assessment model leads to the problem-solving activities that are the core of crisis intervention (deChesnay 1983).

CHARACTERISTICS OF CRISIS

A pioneer in the development of crisis theory was Gerald Caplan (1964), whose work contributed greatly to the community mental health movement and validated the concepts of primary, secondary, and tertiary prevention described in Chapter 1. Caplan described crisis as the result of frustration caused by impediments to the attainment of life goals. Preceding any crisis is an event or hazard that is perceived as a threat to one's fulfillment, aspirations, or even existence. The threat may not be real or seem important in the eyes of others, but it is very real and very distressing to the person or persons involved. It may take the form of the loss of a significant person (Engel 1964) or of a challenge to competence, growth, or self-esteem (Glazer 1981). The type of threat often influences the response that follows. Losses are likely to produce grief reactions or depression. Threats to security may cause anxiety. Challenges to maturity or self-esteem may result in feelings of inferiority unless the challenges can be overcome.

Several factors must be present for a crisis to develop. First, a precipitating or hazardous event must intrude on the life of an individual, family, or group, causing an uncomfortable inner state of tension. Second, the person experiencing the tension tries to deal with the event or hazard by using customary coping measures. If the coping measures successfully relieve tension, an internal state of equilibrium is preserved and crisis is avoided. If the coping measures are not successful in reducing tension, the person is propelled into the state of disequilibrium known as crisis.

During the disequilibrium of crisis, people do not behave in their usual fashion. Their internal discomfort increases to the extent that there is disorganization and distortion—emotional, cognitive, and behavioral. The disorganization, confusion, and distortion further reduce their problem-solving abilities and coping skills. At this point they feel overwhelmed and may turn to friends or professionals for assistance.

Opportunities in Crisis

Crisis is a phenomenon that combines danger with the possibility of growth. The disequilibrium of crisis provides opportunity for growth and for expanding one's repertoire of coping skills. This is a time when the person initially tries to search for solutions, either alone or with help from others. The search is impeded by the distortions and disorganization that accompany crisis. Sometimes the attempted solutions are functional and sometimes they are not. Dysfunctional solutions include denying or avoiding the hazardous event, being indecisive, ruminating endlessly, or becoming depressed and angry. In such cases the danger surrounding crisis outweighs the opportunities for growth. Inability to cope in a functional way not only hinders current problem solving but also affects future problem solving adversely.

In dealing with a crisis, people tend to cling to preferred or accustomed ways of behaving. Some individuals will experiment with one solution after another, trying new ways of coping as soon as an earlier one fails. Other individuals procrastinate and do little or nothing to deal with the crisis. Often the person is angry and projects personal feelings of inadequacy onto the crisis worker, who is then labeled inept or unhelpful. Others in crisis suffer a sense of personal failure and blame themselves for events, even when the situation is beyond their power to control. Self-blame is counterproductive

because it intensifies feelings of helplessness and hopelessness.

During the disequilibrium of crisis, dysfunctional behaviors often are variations on one of four patterns: fight-flight behavior, conflicted behavior, helpless behavior, and hopeless behavior. Table 17–1 shows how these patterns of behavior might be expressed during a period of crisis.

Many persons in crisis, however, are able to seek help and to engage in a search for alternative behaviors that bring the crisis to a successful resolution. In the process of responding to the crisis, individuals learn new ways of coping that will be available to them in the future. The new coping methods may enable them to avoid future crises or to respond more effectively in crisis situations if and when they recur. Table 17–2 illustrates the three possible outcomes of crisis resolution in the situation of a demanding elderly woman, unable to continue living alone, who moves in with her married daughter.

Crisis and Emergency

Everyday annoyances are commonly but inaccurately referred to as crises. There is a tendency, for example, to confuse a *crisis* with an *emergency*, but it is not difficult to distinguish between the two (Parad and Resnik 1975). A working mother whose babysitter suddenly becomes unavailable and must make other arrangements might call this a "crisis." Actually, what the mother must deal with if she wants to get to work that day is an emergency. If the situation occurs repeatedly and the mother is unable to find a reliable babysitter, she may lose the job she needs so badly. If this should happen, the mother may then find herself facing a genuine crisis. On the other hand, if the mother can make arrangements that permit her to get to work regularly and on time, she has dealt with the emergency and has avoided crisis. Only if the mother

Table 17–1. Characteristic Behavioral Patterns in Disequilibrium

Behavior Pattern	Characteristics
Fight-flight behavior	Blaming others (fight) or avoiding responsibility (flight)
Conflicted behavior	Accomplishing tasks partially but not fully; behaving inconsistently; showing indecision
Helpless behavior	Placing responsibility on other people; showing childish, incompetent behavior
Hopeless behavior	Surrendering all autonomy; becoming passive, apathetic, and unresponsive

Table 17–2. Alternative Outcomes in a Family Crisis

The problem: a demanding elderly woman, no longer able to continue living alone, moves in with her married daughter and the daughter's family.

Type of Solution	Coping Strategy	Outcome
Functional	Relocation of the mother is discussed by the daughter, her husband, and the children. Agreement is made that family life will go on as usual, with all members taking some responsibility for Grandma. The daughter and husband share results of the family conference with the elderly mother. Common expectations are discussed.	*Improved coping skills*: Preliminary agreement and planning prepare the family for change. Future turmoil and dissension are avoided.
Questionable	Daughter tries to interact with family as if nothing has changed. She does this by placating her mother, her husband, and her children, as she has always done. Her motto is "Peace at any price" even if this requires considerable self-sacrifice on her part.	*Unchanged coping skills*: Family equilibrium is preserved. The family and elderly mother are comfortable. Daughter feels entrapped by her mother's demands and her family's needs, as she often has since her marriage.
Dysfunctional	Daughter aligns herself with her mother and against her family. She struggles to satisfy all her mother's whims and argues constantly with her husband. Eventually her husband moves out of the house; the marriage is in serious trouble. The family is in crisis.	*Impaired coping skills*: Family is in a state of disequilibrium. The children are enraged, and the husband is estranged. Grandma is content, but her daughter is unhappy.

cannot locate a reliable babysitter despite her best efforts and loses the job she needs to support her child has the emergency situation deteriorated into a crisis.

Emergencies are sudden, distressing events in which prompt action is needed. The persons involved may or may not take steps to help themselves, but unless some remedial action is taken quickly, an emergency may have serious, even life-and-death, consequences. Nevertheless, most emergencies respond to almost any active intervention, such as reassurance, explanation, distraction, control, or rescue.

A *crisis* is often less immediate and less urgent than an emergency. Entering school, relocating, and marrying are not emergencies, but circumstances surrounding these events may introduce hazards that can lead to either emergencies or crises, depending on conditions and the responses of the persons involved. Some theorists believe that an emergency exists if immediate intervention is warranted. If the persons in distress can wait 24 hours for help, a crisis rather than an emergency is present (Caplan 1964).

Duration of Crisis

All crises are of limited duration, usually ending by six or eight weeks; at this time the subjective distress and disequilibrium lessen. Whether or not the problem has been effectively solved, the state of crisis abates. It is thought that crisis has a natural termination regardless of outcomes because it is impossible for people to tolerate the subjective distress and disequilibrium of crisis for very long. In other words, the severe disorganization of crisis must eventually diminish in order for people to endure and survive.

Although the state of crisis may be time-limited, the manner in which the crisis has been handled has long-term consequences, in that coping skills may have improved or deteriorated. Such changes in coping skills in turn influence future responses to crises.

An emergency situation is apt to induce reactions of shock, disbelief, distress, and anxiety. Intervention at the time of an emergency may result in relief or rescue so that the emergency situation does not assume the proportions of a crisis. However, an emergency situation often deteriorates into a crisis if the immediate intervention produces only temporary or questionable relief.

Stress and Crisis

The term *stress* is sometimes used interchangeably with the term *crisis*, but the two are not the same. Stress is an interactive process in which people respond to conditions shaped by themselves or others. Stress is a broad term that includes all responses individuals make in striving to maintain equilibrium while dealing with environmental or social demands. It is a complicated stimulus-response situation that is influenced by many intervening variables. Breier (1988) noted that the effects of stress are similar to the effects of exercise

(Text continues on page 475.)

CLINICAL VIGNETTE

CRISIS OF UNRESOLVED GRIEF

Bill Bennett and his wife, Laura, had raised two sons on a farm that had been in the Bennett family for three generations. As youngsters, the boys had joined 4-H clubs and enjoyed entering their animals in state fair competitions. Because Laura and Bill had always assumed that the sons would eventually take over the farm, they were surprised when the sons announced that they would not attend an agricultural college. The older boy wanted a career as a chemist, whereas the younger was interested in pursuing a career in music. Reluctantly the parents acceded to the boys' request that they be allowed to attend the colleges of their choice.

After the boys left for college, Bill and Laura hired farm hands and tried to keep things going even though their hard work exacted a toll. Laura in particular began to show signs of strain. When she suffered a strep throat that first winter, an antibiotic was injected to which Laura proved allergic. She suffered a severe anaphylactic reaction at home; in spite of heroic measures by her physician and the local rescue squad, Laura died without regaining speech or consciousness. The boys came home for the funeral, were contrite and miserable, but did not offer to stay on the farm permanently. After the funeral they returned to their respective colleges.

For a while friends and neighbors were quite attentive. Bill was invited out for meals, the minister called, and church women brought over homemade soups and casseroles. Even with this attention Bill became more and more morose. He described himself as an old horse who had reached the time of being put out to pasture. Bill missed Laura, with whom he could discuss signs of changing weather and make decisions about when to plow or plant. It was a different existence for a man who loved the earth and the changing seasons but had always shared his thoughts and questions with Laura. The winter was slow in passing, but Bill hoped he would feel less discouraged in the spring. The boys were due to come home for a few weeks, and Bill had the visit to anticipate.

While his sons were home, the three of them worked together on the farm. As they went about accustomed tasks, things seemed almost as they had always been. Only at mealtime was the absence of Laura painful for the boys, but out of consideration for their father they did not mention their grief to him. During the evenings, the boys were restless, talking

animatedly to each other about subjects that were unintelligible to Bill. Only when Bill was not present did they discuss their mother.

After the boys returned to school, the farm seemed lonelier than ever. Bill kept busy but it seemed harder for him to concentrate on what had to be done. For years Bill had risen with the birds, but now it was difficult to get out of bed in the mornings. Following Bill's example, the hired men became more lax in their work, and as weeks passed the farm began to take on a neglected look. Bill became so irritable and taciturn that his two helpers turned resentful, packed their gear, and left the farm without giving notice. Finding himself completely alone, Bill became more despondent. One early morning after feeding the animals and cleaning the barn, Bill took out his rifle and shot himself in the head. A few days later he was found in the barn by his minister, who had missed Bill at church services. A note was discovered saying that the farm was to be sold and the proceeds divided between his two sons, whom he wished well in their chosen occupations. "The farm was only important to my wife and to me," he wrote. "Without her the farm is nothing and I am nothing."

The indifference of his sons to the family tradition of farming was a blow to Laura and Bill that they concealed from their sons. When Laura became ill, Bill blamed himself and his devotion to the farm for her untimely death. An inarticulate man, he shared little of his feelings with others but was devoted to Laura. After her death, he began to hate the farm and to believe that the farm had robbed him of his wife and his sons. When Laura died, Bill experienced an inhibited grief reaction. He shared his deep sorrow and self-recrimination with no one, and his sons lacked the insight to help their father express his feelings. Feeling guilty, they protected themselves by avoiding open discussion of their mother's death and their own pain. As a result of mutual avoidance, Bill's feelings found no outlet. He held his emotions within, and as time passed, the inhibited grief reaction became a chronic depressive state.

Bill was in a state of crisis as a result of the death of his wife and separation from his boys. Even though his minister, his sons, and his neighbors tried to be helpful, no one realized the acute distress Bill was experiencing. Isolated on the farm, showing little outward emotion, unwilling to burden his sons or confide in anyone, Bill sent no clear warning messages.

For a while he was sustained by the prospect of seeing his sons again, but when the reunion ended, Bill's wish to join Laura in death was far stronger than his wish to live. In his suicide, as in most matters, Bill discussed his plan with no one. And as usual, he carried his plan to completion without consulting anyone.

---

on a muscle. The proper amount increases strength; too little causes atrophy, and too much results in excessive wear and tear, or injury. Thus, the effects of stress may be benign or malignant.

Two primary factors determine whether stress will be malignant or benign. One relates to the biopsychosocial capacities of the individual; the second relates to the nature, strength, and duration of the stressors impacting on the individual. Any stressor that can be controlled by the individual is less likely to have adverse effects than one that cannot. Animal studies have demonstrated that when stress agents are under control of the animals, mortality rates decline and biopsychosocial deficits are less prominent. Investigators have also found that exposure to controllable stress agents prepares animals to cope better with future exposure to stress agents. This "toughening" process has been widely recognized.

In experiments with people similar discoveries have been made. When identical levels of stress, controllable and noncontrollable, were exerted on human subjects, only the uncontrollable stress caused maladaptive functioning. Such findings indicate that successful coping and control of events leads to more adaptive behavior and greater ability to deal with later occurring stress (Breier 1988). In addition to control of stress agents, another variable is an individual's evaluation of his own performance and his appreciation of the rewards available in the stressful situation. For example, nurses working on a spinal cord injury unit might be able to deal with the demands made on them by frustrated clients, and try valiantly to meet their needs. Some nurses may feel sufficiently rewarded when they see bitter, discouraged clients make progress toward rehabilitation and improved function. If, however, the physical and emotional demands are excessive, or if a nurse hasn't the temperament to continue working in such a setting, the stress may prove intolerable. The result in the latter instance is that the nurse becomes exhausted or "burned out." When demands of the workplace are not reduced to acceptable levels, burnout can become severe enough to be considered a crisis. Although demands of the workplace may be distributed equally among all workers, they will not affect everyone equally. Stress and the meaning of stress, as well as the rewards of working under stressful conditions, are interpreted differently by different people.

Stress itself, therefore, does not constitute a crisis, but it may be a precipitating or hazardous event that leads to crisis (Haack and Jones 1983).

PATTERNS OF CRISIS BEHAVIOR

Knowledge of how people react in crises has been enhanced by the work of Lindemann (1944), who studied the grief responses by survivors of events in which loved ones were lost. Lindemann found both similarities and differences in the way people reacted to the loss of a loved one. When survivors were able to grieve or mourn for the one who was lost, they proved eventually able to accept the loss, to disengage from the lost person, and to begin to form new relationships. However, such losses became crises for people who were unwilling or unable to proceed with grief work or mourning.

Belief that the process of grieving has a beginning and an end is prevalent among theorists and clinicians in the health field (Kubler-Ross 1969, Collison and Miller 1987). A variation of this viewpoint is that the crisis of grief is rarely resolved once and for all but is only partially resolved or is reactivated periodically in ways that may even generate another crisis. For many survivors the period of grieving may last for years, but most of them learn to live with the burden of loss as they try to integrate the experience into their lives and readjust.

People who have suffered the loss of a loved one are not the only ones entitled to be called survivors. Individuals who have undergone major surgery or have recovered from a serious illness may be regarded as survivors, as may those people who have lived through disasters such as fire or flood, or experiences such as war or internment in a prison camp. By understanding the effects of a survival experience, nurses can help people use the experience as a way of expanding rather than restricting coping skills (Smith 1979, Cohen 1987).

When the experiences of people who have recovered from a serious illness are compared with those of people who have survived a common disaster, certain differences emerge. Whenever a shared disaster occurs, there is considerable social support in the form of external rescue efforts and internal common interests. This is not generally the case with severe illness, where support networks may not extend beyond the family (McNett 1987).

Even so, the survivors of serious illness and shared disasters exhibit some similar reactions.

COMMUNITIES IN CRISIS

As communities advance technologically, they become more distant from their environment and more dependent on the organization of complex systems. In a disaster situation, this dependence can aggravate problems. Disasters cause individual disorganization, family disorganization, and community disorganization in the form of confusion and fragmentation. Each form of disorganization intensifies the others, for individuals and families find restoration of equilibrium more difficult in the face of community breakdown. The emergence of a crisis after disaster follows the sequence of other crises. There is a hazardous event or stressor, failure of usual coping measures, and disorganization, followed by recovery or reorganization.

Ambiguity concerning the outcome of disaster causes anxiety, which is exacerbated when customary behaviors prove inadequate. The unexpectedness of a disaster and the inexperience of the inhabitants in coping with disaster can drastically alter the outcomes. People who live where landslides are common become practiced in preventive and restorative measures. The same is true of inhabitants of arid regions where a brush fire can become a conflagration of terrifying proportions.

People living in a disaster situation cannot comprehend immediate instructions very well because of the cognitive distortion that anxiety brings. Three months after a flood one elderly person was discovered living alone in a trailer, incapable of understanding the financial aid forms that had been left by a community worker. He had received instructions at the time of the disaster, but was not at that point able to comprehend nor later to remember what he had been told to do with the papers.

Natural Disasters

There is some evidence that personal commitments may take precedence over community duties in times of disaster. One dedicated director of a children's home did not participate in community rescue efforts following a flood until she had loaded the children in her charge on a bus and driven them to another area. This evacuation was accomplished even though the children were in no immediate danger and she had never before driven a bus. Once the children were transported, their protector was able to participate in rescue operations.

Disasters impose internal strains on family role enactment because members are not sure what is expected of them nor what the future will bring. When central family members, such as parents, cannot meet their own role expectations in protecting and caring for the family, the result is role strain accompanied by feelings of personal inadequacy.

Separation anxiety is a universal human experience; loss of loved ones, loss of possessions, and loss of comforting routines are examples of separation that produces feelings of helplessness and hopelessness. In these circumstances, community workers can reduce anxiety wherever possible by providing information about other family members and missing possessions. For many survivors, uncertainty is harder to tolerate than the actual knowledge of events.

Young children are apt to regress and cling to parents or favorite possessions that have been rescued. Such regressive behaviors should be tolerated

---

POPULAR MYTHS ABOUT CRISIS INTERVENTION

- *Myth One:* Crisis intervention is appropriate only for psychiatric emergencies.

- *Myth Two:* Crisis intervention is limited to a single therapeutic session.

- *Myth Three:* Crisis therapy is practiced only by paraprofessionals.

- *Myth Four:* Crisis intervention offers only temporary stabilization until more lasting help can be given.

- *Myth Five:* Crisis intervention can be considered only a primary prevention method.

- *Myth Six:* Crisis intervention requires no special knowledge or expertise if the clinician is experienced in more traditional therapeutic approaches.

SOURCE: Adapted from Burgess and Baldwin (1981).

and understood. Adolescents may display uncharacteristic behavior by becoming withdrawn or belligerent. Either manifestation should be met with consideration coupled with limit setting. Encouraging adolescents to assume responsibilities that are constructive but not unduly demanding may help restore age-appropriate behavior. For adults in the family, loss of home and possessions is a bitter blow. Realization that the rewards of a lifetime of hard work have been swept away may cause depressive reactions with accompanying somatic complaints.

For some survivors, short-term crisis intervention may be insufficient. There are always a number of people who cannot cope with disaster despite relief measures. These individuals do not resolve crisis adaptively but relive their experiences in the guise of nightmares, flashbacks, or intrusive rumination. Some of them react by withdrawing and decreasing their attachment to the living.

In analyzing human responses to disaster, economic, physical, and psychological effects should be evaluated. At present there is a tendency to measure the severity of a disaster in quantifiable terms, such as financial losses or number of fatalities. Comparatively little attention has been directed to social or psychological impairment following disasters. Lately there has been some recognition of the need to include mental health counseling in relief programs organized for disaster victims, and judgments have been made that on-site crisis intervention is probably the most efficacious approach. Data accumulated thus far indicate that relatively few disaster victims experience long-term emotional damage even though substantial numbers report transitory difficulties around problems of everyday living. The value of traditional psychotherapeutic intervention offered in clinical settings is questionable for crisis victims who were functioning adequately before the disaster experience (Black 1987). One of the most important elements of crisis work is acknowledgement that people in crisis are not ill, but simply people in need for whom the community has a responsibility. Community crisis intervention does not adhere to traditional methods of history taking and scheduled appointments in a clinical setting but can be undertaken by professionals or paraprofessionals working wherever disaster conditions exist.

Economic Disasters

For people old enough to remember the Great Depression of the 1930s, massive economic decline and unemployment constituted a disaster that has not been forgotten even after years of relative affluence. Those were days of humiliating economies for some families and of great suffering for many more. The American dream of prosperity and upward mobility was tarnished. Men blamed themselves for their inability to provide for their families, and housewives existed at less-than-subsistence levels in order to offer more food to their children. Whenever there are more workers than jobs, the concept of equal opportunity receives minimal attention. During the Great Depression, people lucky enough to be employed allowed themselves to be exploited in order to retain their precarious jobs.

Some economic disasters are national in scope and have a rippling effect that carries economic consequences beyond national borders. The Great Depression was a worldwide phenomenon and probably contributed to the upheaval that led to the outbreak of World War II. Lesser economic disasters are more circumscribed, and their impact is felt only in one region or by one segment of workers. A single-industry town may become a disaster area as a result of a corporate decision to relocate a factory. Technological changes or reduced demand for certain products may cause large-scale layoffs of workers, some of whom must retrain or relocate in order to become employable.

Being laid off even temporarily is an awesome experience for contemporary workers, for it is a dramatic reminder that the individual is expendable. Even the fortunate workers who retain their jobs when others are laid off fear that their luck will not last.

The furloughed worker with no assurance of being called back to work exists in limbo, for there is reluctance to accept a less satisfactory job if any hope remains of being rehired. It is not only the unemployed worker but the entire family who endures the crisis of unemployment. Loss of employment frequently causes workers to blame themselves for decisions they had taken earlier. They begin to wish they had chosen another occupation, pursued more education, or moved to another part of the country. The self-recrimination of unemployed workers means that worried wives must deal with the depression and guilt of their husbands in addition to managing financial retrenchment. Sometimes a wife who had preferred being a homemaker becomes a reluctant wage earner, or a wife whose job provided small luxuries for the family finds herself the major breadwinner. This role shift is difficult for couples even in families in which there is little emphasis on gender-differentiated role enactment.

When the parents are feeling uncomfortable with the role changes in the family, the children are invariably affected. A child who was fairly well adjusted at home and at school may begin to fail academically, withdraw, or become obstreperous. Well-meaning parents may try to shield children from the facts by glossing over or not explaining the problem. This avoidance makes it difficult for children to understand the reason for family tension. The result is that they may engage in fantasies of separation or family dissolution that are more frightening than the reality from which they are being protected. Even when this fantasizing does not happen, the children feel excluded rather than part of a family system in which every member must adapt to new conditions.

Whenever there is widespread economic adversity, mental health facilities report an increase in the number of people seeking help. Massive unemployment can precipitate community disruption in the form of vandalism, riots, and looting. Family conflict is a by-product of troublesome economic conditions. Not only is marital maladjustment more prevalent, but parents and children seem to have more difficulty with each other. In Hartford, Connecticut, one out of eight workers laid off by an aircraft factory reported that their marriage deteriorated as a result, and 15 percent reported more quarrels with their children (Pines 1982). The same source observed that every notice of job furlough or termination should be accompanied by a surgeon general's warning that the notification may be hazardous to your health.

Like natural and environmental disasters, economic adversity is likely to be evaluated primarily in financial terms. A British sociologist challenged the use of income as an indicator of the deprivation suffered by individuals and families during economic decline, calling this evaluative measure a remnant of Victorian thinking that restricted basic human needs to food, shelter, and clothing. Since human beings are social as well as biological entities, deprivation should be measured in more than monetary terms. A deprivation index was compiled that included social indices of economic decline, such as not inviting people to the house, not having birthday parties for the children, not taking vacations, and not having money for recreation or other amenities. The premise is that the accumulated deprivation that accompanies lowered income eventually reaches a level at which people can no longer function as social beings. When, for example, parents must keep their children home from school because there is no money for athletic equipment or school outings, neither the parents nor the children are able to perform their socially accustomed roles. Communities have definite expectations of families in various socioeconomic strata, and the families have certain expectations of themselves. These expectations cannot be fulfilled in

periods of severe economic decline, and the result is family disequilibrium expressed in discord between spouses, between parents and children, and between families and community institutions, such as school, business, and the legal system (Rattner 1982).

Loss of morale and feelings of deprivation characterize families faced with indefinite periods of employment. Crisis counseling cannot produce jobs but can help make the period of unemployment less bleak. Group counseling programs for unemployed workers, for their wives, and children are perhaps the best form of supportive work. These programs can range from vocational retraining for workers whose skills are obsolete to emotional support for workers who blame themselves for being unemployed. Shared unemployment in a community tends to reduce the guilt and self-blame of the workers but perhaps intensifies their feelings of powerlessness. Unemployed men usually feel a loss of role and status within the family, particularly if authority was dependent upon the man's economic contribution. Abandoning the meaningful family role of provider adds to the frustration of the unemployed worker even when family affection is strong and role flexibility can be accomplished within the system.

Even though there is comparatively little loss of life attached to economic disasters, there is loss of roles and of family stability. When unemployment affects large numbers of workers in the community, there is a collective interpretation of the situation that may help affected families. Usually families of unemployed workers tend to externalize blame, and this externalization is less destructive than the self-blame of workers or the scapegoating of a family member. However, anger should not be allowed to continue to the extent of immobilizing the problem-solving potential of the family. General precepts of crisis intervention that permit catharsis before moving on to productive problem solving can reduce confusion and depression. Assessment of family resources in terms of marketable skills and willingness to relocate can help the members focus on strengths rather than weaknesses.

Epidemiology, with its interactive components of agent, host, and environment, provides a framework for understanding the development of community crisis (see Figure 17–1). Equilibrium represents a balance between host factors and agent factors operating in a dynamic environment. When environmental conditions shift the balance in favor of the host, the likelihood of disequilibrium and ensuing crisis decreases. If environmental conditions favor agent factors, the result is a shift toward increased probability of disequilibrium and crisis. Host factors that influence the relative susceptibility of individuals include such variables as age, sex,

Figure 17–1. *Epidemiology of Disaster Crises*

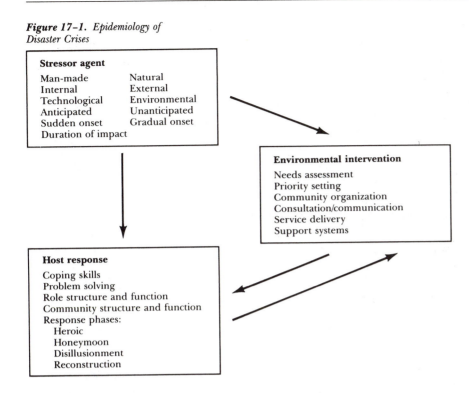

race, occupation, and marital status. The response of individuals to agent factors depends on their levels of functioning, previous experiences, present needs, and future goals. Agent factors include any stressors of sufficient intensity and duration to produce disequilibrium in the host.

HELPING DISASTER VICTIMS

Disaster conditions disrupt patterns of role performance established over the years. Under ordinary circumstances, role performance is distributed between family, job, and social responsibilities. In times of disaster, additional demands are made at all three levels of role performance. When individuals must choose between meeting the responsibilities of one role at the expense of other roles, the result is ambivalence and role conflict. For example, an ambulance attendant working round the clock in the aftermath of a disaster must decide whether to remain on the job or look after the well-being of his own family. It is natural at such moments for personal considerations to intrude on the decision. Members of police and fire departments usually continue in their occupational roles and endeavor to meet community demands that for them supercede personal obligations. Balancing family tasks against community needs is less a choice of one over the other than a need to maintain communication between family members and the community worker. A fireman's knowledge that

his own family is relatively safe erases his reluctance to fulfill community responsibilities and facilitates his external role performance.

Some researchers have made a point of separating the traumatic event from the reactions that follow it (Eth and Pynos 1985). The impact of a disaster often causes conflicting feelings in survivors that interfere with adaptive grieving. Parks and Weiss (1983) contrasted survivors' responses to sudden, untimely death with responses to anticipated death and found that sudden losses produced psychological impairment that made the experience harder to bear.

Crisis workers have observed a wide range of behaviors in people who have experienced losses as a result of catastrophe. Many such persons seem to avoid learning details of the disaster and caregivers have been advised not to disclose detailed information until survivors show readiness to listen. When they realize the extent of their losses, many engage in angry outbursts. For some, apathy follows anger, and they keep other people, especially caregivers, at a distance. As they come to realize their losses, sensory misperceptions emerge. They may lose touch with reality to the point of having hallucinations or delusions.

Survivor's guilt may surface in the aftermath of disaster. Even persons who acted heroically may blame themselves for not having done more. From efforts to help survivors of disaster, certain facts emerged in a study by Cohen (1987). The major findings are described below.

- After the traumatic event many victims were reluctant to seek details and used approach-avoidance behaviors in facing reality.

- The first emotions were distress and anxiety; sadness and grief appeared later.

- Anxiety was expressed first through somatic symptoms; verbalization of emotions such as fear, disorientation, and confusion came later.

- Primitive defenses such as denial, rumination, guilt, and magical thinking were prominent.

- The onset of genuine grief was often delayed; in some instances apathy and detachment preceded grief work.

- Caring and commitment on the part of workers was often met with irritation on the part of victims; this negativism combined with the distress of victims created difficulties for the workers, many of whom suffered burnout.

- Consultation and support for workers was essential to helping them accept and understand the conflicting messages and confusing behaviors of disaster victims. (Cohen 1987)

In their desire to relieve the physical and psychological discomfort of survivors, nurses should not overlook the growth potential inherent in having survived a life-threatening illness or disaster. In caring for survivors, experts recommend the following nursing interventions:

1. Encourage people to talk about their experience and about any changes in their personal values, without suggesting what those changes should be.

2. Encourage people to realize that others have had similar experiences, although the dimensions of the experience are unique for each individual. Speak of the whole range of human experience without belittling the individual experience in any way. Recognizing the universality of the experience may help people to live through it without feeling so overwhelmed by it.

3. Encourage survivors to talk with others who have had similar experiences, especially with others who are at various stages of distress or recovery. This is particularly important for survivors whose experience has been solitary rather than shared.

CRISIS COUNSELING PRINCIPLES

Crisis intervention is directed toward mobilizing and channeling the client's own problem-solving and coping skills. Because people in crisis are in a state of disequilibrium, reducing the inner turmoil is a prerequisite for problem solving.

The fundamental goal of crisis counseling is restoration of the client to functioning levels equal to or surpassing those that existed before the onset of crisis. This does not mean that the client necessarily returns to the same state of psychological and social well-being that existed earlier. The loss of a loved one, illness, divorce, relocation, and retirement are examples of events that may cause permanent changes in a client's outlook even when the accompanying crisis has abated. Restoration of function means that the cognitive, emotional, and behavioral distortions of crisis have been corrected to the point that the client is no longer in a condition of disorganization and disability. Restoration of function also means that the client, however slowly, has regained energy to meet the basic demands of everyday life and is beginning to enjoy some simple pleasures without being overcome by guilt or regret (Parkes and Weiss 1983). The crisis counselor who keeps this realistic goal in mind should find the following suggestions useful (Weiss 1987).

- Accept the client's feelings about the current situation even if they seem excessive or inappropriate. Offer assurance that the feelings are understandable without commenting on how the client should feel. For example, the crisis counselor might comment on the difficulty of making decisions or just getting through the day when the client is so upset.

- Explain to the client why he or she feels so overwhelmed. Many clients in crisis wonder why they cannot function; some of them even worry that they may be "crazy." For example, the crisis counselor might review the sequence of events the client has experienced, and indicate that this is the reason the client feels helpless and inadequate.

- Instill hope in the client by stating that the present emotional distress need not last forever. It can be useful to describe gradual stages of recovery that are likely to follow initial distress. For example, the crisis counselor might say, "After an experience like yours many people say it takes a long time to get readjusted and even longer before they can manage as well as they did before."

- Give the client permission to recover and move toward normalcy and restored function. Some clients feel that loyalty to a lost person or place, or resentment at changes or injuries suffered

(Text continues on page 482.)

CLINICAL VIGNETTE

CRISIS OF RAPE TRAUMA

Becky Walker had dinner with three female friends at a country inn. Because she was late for her appointment, Becky neglected to lock her car before meeting her friends. After finishing dinner she walked alone to the parking lot as her friends drove away. A man hiding in her car forced Becky at gunpoint to drive to a side road, where he raped her. In addition, she was forced to engage in acts of sodomy and fellatio. When her attacker finally left, Becky managed to drive her car home. Disheveled and hysterical, she told the story to her husband.

George Walker was shocked at his wife's condition but reluctant to report the incident to the police. He believed that Becky's failure to lock the car made her partly responsible and that her general behavior had been careless. Without saying it directly, George implied that Becky was at fault for allowing the rape to occur. His attitude prevented the intervention that both of them needed, and seriously impaired the marital relationship.

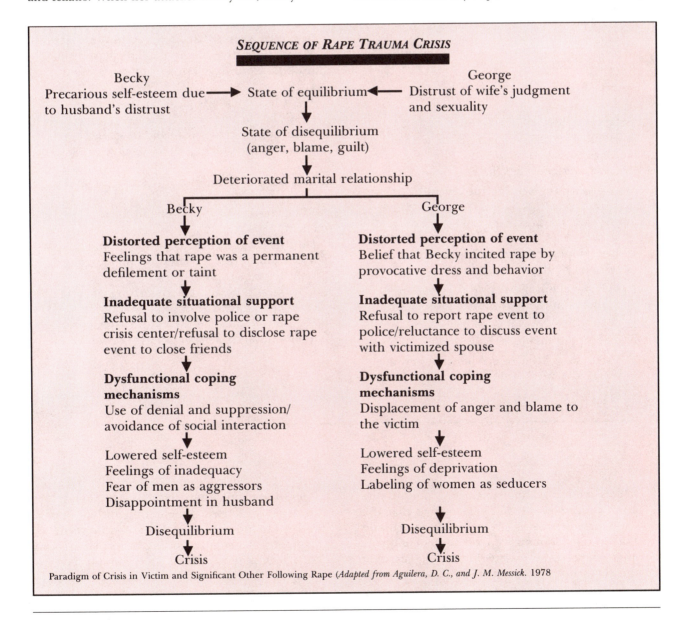

SEQUENCE OF RAPE TRAUMA CRISIS

Becky
Precarious self-esteem due to husband's distrust → State of equilibrium ← George
Distrust of wife's judgment and sexuality

↓

State of disequilibrium
(anger, blame, guilt)

↓

Deteriorated marital relationship

Becky

Distorted perception of event
Feelings that rape was a permanent defilement or taint

↓

Inadequate situational support
Refusal to involve police or rape crisis center/refusal to disclose rape event to close friends

↓

Dysfunctional coping mechanisms
Use of denial and suppression/ avoidance of social interaction

↓

Lowered self-esteem
Feelings of inadequacy
Fear of men as aggressors
Disappointment in husband

↓

Disequilibrium

↓

Crisis

George

Distorted perception of event
Belief that Becky incited rape by provocative dress and behavior

↓

Inadequate situational support
Refusal to report rape event to police/reluctance to discuss event with victimized spouse

↓

Dysfunctional coping mechanisms
Displacement of anger and blame to the victim

↓

Lowered self-esteem
Feelings of deprivation
Labeling of women as seducers

↓

Disequilibrium

↓

Crisis

Paradigm of Crisis in Victim and Significant Other Following Rape (*Adapted from Aguilera, D. C., and J. M. Messick.* 1978

CRISIS ASSESSMENT TOOL

Initial Steps

1. Collect data that indicate the dimensions of the problem, using various sources of information.
2. Formulate a dynamic hypothesis concerning the problem and the coping responses of the client.
3. Assess the problem in terms of intrinsic and extrinsic factors and determine a therapeutic approach.
4. Involve the client in problem-solving activities.
5. Negotiate a contract that sets clear, reachable goals.
6. Explain that treatment will be terminated according to the terms of the contract.

General Procedures

1. Obtain demographic data.
2. Define the problem in realistic terms. Assess the mental, physical, and psychosocial status of the client(s).
3. Assess coping skills of the client(s).

Coping Skills Assessment

1. How does the client deal with anxiety, tension, or depression?
2. Has the client used customary coping methods in the current situation?
3. What were the results of using customary coping methods?
4. Have there been recent life changes that interfered with customary coping methods?

5. Are significant persons contributing to continuation of the problem?
6. Is the client considering suicide or homicide as a way of coping? If so, how? When?
7. Has the client attempted suicide or homicide in the past? Under what conditions?
8. Assess the extent of suicidal or homicidal risk presented by the client. Hospitalization may be necessary as a protective measure.

Planning and Problem Solving

1. Is the present crisis new or a reenactment of similar events that occurred in the past?
2. What alternative methods might have been used to avoid development of the present crisis?
3. What new methods might be used to resolve the present crisis?
4. What supports are available to strengthen new problem-solving methods?

Anticipatory Guidance

1. What sources of stress remain for the client?
2. How might the client deal with problematic issues in the future, based on the current repertoire of coping skills?
3. How might the current repertoire of coping skills be maintained or expanded?
4. With termination of the contract for crisis intervention, is further referral or follow-up care necessary?

makes recovery impossible. For example, the crisis counselor should acknowledge that the client may proceed at his own pace, but should not become immobilized because of guilt or anger. The counselor might also suggest that the client not only needs to begin to function again, but has the right to recover and move on.

■ Help the client interpret recovery as simply a return to effective functioning rather than a return to the status quo. Indicate that recovery is not the same as forgetting or forgiving, both of which may be a long time coming. For example, the crisis counselor might describe recovery in the following way:

Recovery from crisis does not mean forgetting what happened.

Recovery from crisis does not mean that you and your life are unchanged.

Recovery from crisis means a return of energy for everyday living.

Recovery from crisis means a resumption of attachment to others.

Recovery from crisis means renewed ability to feel satisfaction, even joy.

Recovery from crisis means that distress is not fixed or endless. It may, however, return from time to time, triggered by an anniversary, a memory, or a chance remark.

One of the first steps in crisis work is to explore the meaning of the crisis to the person or persons involved. Often the client perceives the significance of events as far greater than outsiders perceive it. The nurse or other crisis worker begins by accepting the reality of the client's distress, inasmuch as the situation may have a symbolic meaning to the client that is not immediately apparent. For example, an ambitious man passed over for promotion may in his disappointment discount his impressive accomplishments and may become discouraged and depressed so that he is no longer able to function well at work. The same man, if promoted to a position he has sought, may feel doubtful of his ability to meet the new demands made on him. He may become anxious and unable to concentrate, sleep, work, or relate to other people.

The essential element of crisis work is that it represents a shift in emphasis from the intrapsychic life of the individual to interaction of the individual with others or with the environment.

Every crisis involves an individual, a family, or a community that responds in a particular way to particular circumstances. During the crisis contract, the nurse, in words and actions, acknowledges the existence of a compelling problem that is causing distress. The focus of crisis work is on the search for a solution to the immediate problem.

The contract for crisis counseling is usually short-term, lasting for the six- to eight-week duration of acute crisis. The counseling sessions may vary in length from 15 minutes to an hour. Frequency of meetings is decided jointly by the client and the nurse. If distress is extreme, if the client has poor impulse control and may be destructive to himself or others, daily meetings may be necessary. The nurse may consider it appropriate to give the client a phone number where she can be easily reached. If the client has a reliable support network,

weekly or biweekly meetings may be sufficient. During the sessions, the crisis caregiver is actively involved but does nothing for the client that the client is able to handle himself. Some clients may become dependent on the nurse or other crisis worker, but the dependency is not too worrisome because crisis intervention and the period of the therapeutic contract are brief (Sifneos 1980).

Sometimes nurses working on a long-term basis with a family or individual will observe that a crisis situation has developed. It may be necessary for the nurse to alter the approach being used and to become more active in order to facilitate resolution of the crisis. Then the nurse may have to resume her previous approach in which involvement was less intense. One way to accomplish this is to introduce other professionals into the care plan, so that any dependency on the nurse can be gradually reduced.

For nurses engaged in helping clients in a crisis, a primary rule is not to make decisions *for* them but to become involved in making decisions *with* them. Restoration of equilibrium through improved coping behavior is the maximal goal of crisis work. A minimal goal is to help the clients return to at least precrisis levels of functioning, but there are occasions when even this lesser goal is not achieved.

DEALING WITH DISTORTIONS In dealing with persons in crisis, the nurse should use an approach that considers three major forms of distortion that may be present. After exploring the nature of the crisis and its meaning to the client, the nurse should endeavor to identify and encourage correction of *cognitive, emotional,* and *behavioral* distortions.

People in crisis find it difficult, if not impossible, to think clearly and rationally. This means that their ability to deal realistically with events, to plan, and to make decisions is greatly reduced. Often these individuals are easily distracted, incoherent, and tangential. Because of their cognitive distortions, they are overreactive emotionally. The emotional distress they experience may lead to such somatic symptoms as insomnia or anorexia. Behaviors are not goal-directed but may take the form of apathy or of pointless, unproductive activity.

An early task of the nurse engaged in crisis intervention is to go over with the client the sequence of events that led to the crisis, asking questions about what happened, when, and to whom. It is also necessary to ask what efforts were made to cope with the crisis. The exploration yields important information and also helps the client begin to put events into perspective. Often, people in crisis cannot make a cognitive connection between the hazardous event, unsuccessful efforts to deal with the event, and the eventual disequilibrium. Therefore, tracing the sequence of events clarifies the situation for the client and sometimes leads to a more realistic view of what actually happened. In discussions with the client about what led to the crisis, the nurse should convey confidence in their ability to find a solution together.

Emotional or affective distortions are also present. The cognitive exploration is often helpful in reducing emotional reactivity to manageable proportions, but some people in crisis need to be allowed a period of emotional ventilation, or catharsis. In the first sessions, free emotional expression should be permitted and even encouraged. It is advisable, however, to call attention to extreme emotional reactions as soon as possible, since prolonged outbursts are likely to impede problem solving. The nurse may offer empathy by making statements about how difficult things must seem to the client but should add that the situation will not always seem as overwhelming as it does now. In other words, the nurse should offer hope and set limits, along with providing empathy.

Behavioral distortions should also be confronted—not only distortions in the client's own behavior but also in the client's interpretation of the behavior of others. Blaming oneself or others is dysfunctional; emphasis should be placed not on past errors or misjudgments but on making the future better.

Emphasis on cognitive processes should continue throughout the duration of the therapeutic contract. Behavioral and emotional distortions can be modified by introducing additional social or professional resource people into the picture. Persons in crisis are reassured by the contributions of an expanded support network. These other contributions not only reduce dependency on the nurse but also convince the client that others care and will help.

DEALING WITH ANXIETY Anxiety has the ability to generate energy, but when levels of anxiety are high, energy becomes undirected and disintegrative (Freud 1936, Peplau 1952). Sullivan (1953) used the word "euphoria" to describe the absence of anxiety and described anxiety as perhaps the most unpleasant human experience. *Mild* anxiety releases energy that can be used for problem solving. *Moderate* anxiety usually decreases efficiency, while *severe* anxiety leads to frustration and distortion. When anxiety rises to panic levels, available energy is directed toward escape. In the disequilibrium of crisis, anxiety hovers between severe and panic levels. The nurse who is dealing with a client in crisis must assess the level of anxiety being experienced and endeavor to reduce anxiety so that coherent communication between nurse and client can take place. Table 17–3 shows the various levels, characteristics, and appropriate interventions for anxiety.

For persons in crisis, anxiety is pervasive and retards the restoration of equilibrium. Therefore, the nurse should offer enough reassurance to foster a sense of safety and hopefulness. Such general statements as "I think it was wise for you to come for help" indicate to clients that their disorganization is not total. Excessive solicitude is apt to foster regression, but clients will respond to a nurse who seems confident that a solution can be found. Fostering an attitude of hopefulness increases the client's motivation and problem-solving skills. Delineating the outlines of the crisis and exploring problem-solving efforts of the past help the client to reduce anxiety to manageable levels. Because mild levels of anxiety are facilitative, a central challenge for the crisis worker is to help the client tolerate mild anxiety and direct it into constructive problem-solving behaviors.

DEALING WITH VIOLENCE During the entire course of crisis counseling but especially in the first

Table 17–3. Levels, Characteristics, and Interventions for Anxiety

Level of Anxiety	Characteristics	Nursing Interventions
Mild anxiety	Alertness and vigilance	1. Reconcile demands of the situation and the expectations and perceptions of the individual.
Moderate anxiety	Reduced perception and attention; subjective distress	1. Trace connections between the causes and symptoms of anxiety.
Severe anxiety	Selective perception and attention; subjective distress	1. Encourage motor activity. 2. Promote cognitive expression (talking, thinking). 3. Permit emotional expression (crying, talking).
Panic	Gross perceptual distortion; inability to communicate; inability to function	1. Offer firm structure and direction until panic recedes.

SOURCE: Adapted from Peplau (1952) and Sullivan (1953).

sessions, any homicidal or suicidal thoughts should be appraised. Clients should be asked if they are thinking about suicide or if they have any urge to harm others. If the answer to either question is affirmative, additional questions should probe the seriousness of the thought, the details of any plan, and the availability of the means to carry out the plan. There is a popular myth that bringing up the topic of suicide or violence toward others may put ideas in the client's head. This myth attributes more power to the clinician than actually exists. If a clinician is reluctant to ask such questions and to discuss them openly, the client will tend to conceal intentions.

If the client has a well-thought-out suicide plan and available means, hospitalization may be indicated unless the client has reliable social supports. Suicidal persons who seek professional help are likely to be ambivalent about carrying out an attempt. This means that they are likely to respond to a caring, concerned nurse who is accessible to them at any time during the acute phase of suicide intention.

Crisis intervention is effective for suicidal persons who are ordinarily stable but who have been thrown into disequilibrium by sudden, stressful events. The end of a romantic relationship or failure to pass final examinations may induce suicidal feelings that will not be acted on if other people are available who care and want to help. Chronically depressed persons, alcoholics, psychotic clients, and withdrawn, socially isolated individuals are not good candidates for crisis intervention because they usually require help for longer periods of time.

Many suicidal persons require a long-term relationship with a supportive clinician. Such persons may regard the short-term crisis contract as another abandonment and need additional help.

Violent and assaultive individuals are usually brought to emergency departments by the police. For safety reasons staff members may be more comfortable when police or security guards are present, but they should be excluded as soon as trust has been established between staff members and the client.

If, however, there are grounds for believing that the client cannot remain in control, the presence of police or security guards is warranted. Some persons verbalize a wish to harm others but have not previously carried out their threats and seem unlikely to do so. As with suicidal clients, the presence of a detailed plan for violence plus access to the means of activating the plan is a significant sign of actual intent. Occasionally clients will lose control without warning, but it is likely that a crisis of violence has been foreshadowed by previous behaviors.

Persons experiencing delusional or hallucinatory thoughts are often capable of unpredictable actions and therefore require vigilant supervision. If a client has a history of committing violent acts, or if the current situation is complicated by addiction, antisocial behavior, or severe neurological or psychiatric disorders, crisis intervention is not appropriate. As a rule, violent, assaultive persons need emergency treatment followed by long-term treatment. Prolonged assessment is necessary in order to discover whether assaultive behaviors are directed toward a specific target, are generated by particular events, or are global in nature. Disposition and follow-up care are guided by the client's history and prognosis, the wishes of the family, and the safety of the community.

INTRUSION OF OLD CRISES

The term "compound crisis" has been coined to describe the experience of some clients currently experiencing a traumatic event whose problems are intensified by memories of previous losses that had receded from consciousness until reactivated by present circumstances (Horsley 1988). Many nurses who are not practicing in mental health settings will encounter the phenomenon of compound crisis in clients facing illness or injury of themselves or a family member, whose inability to cope is related to unresolved events of the past. The memory of past crises intrudes on the present; the difficulties of the present situation are compounded by old griefs; so that the energy needed to deal with the new problem is depleted and recuperative powers are doubly threatened (Worden 1982). Clients dealing with a compound crisis often are extremely sensitive to incidents that seem trivial to staff members. They may become withdrawn or very demanding, or apparently uncooperative. With such clients, the nursing staff should call upon a psychiatric nurse specialist who will help staff members deal with their reactions to the difficult client and in some instances explore with the client the meaning of the maladaptive behaviors.

Clients displaying extreme reactions to current situations may or may not be suffering compound crisis. Exploration of past events in the life of the client helps determine whether unresolved grief is present. Sometimes there is no history of previous trauma or loss. At other times there have been previous crises, but the client is able to discuss them with appropriate emotionality, showing neither uncontrolled nor deficient reactions. When clients are dealing primarily with the current situation, they may be upset and anxious but they are able to think

(Text continues on page 486.)

C L I N I C A L   V I G N E T T E

COGNITIVE AND BEHAVIORAL DISTORTION IN CRISIS

Joel Benson, aged 35 years, married, and the father of three children, was attacked and beaten savagely by unknown persons on a city street at about 2 A.M. His wallet and car were taken by his assailants. Joel was left unconscious on the street, his inert body soon concealed by falling snow. The next morning he was found by the police and taken by ambulance to a nearby hospital, where he was pronounced dead on arrival. Joel's body lay unclaimed in the city morgue for two days until his brother arrived to make an identification.

Family grief for Joel's death was intensified by the circumstances in which he died. A police investigation revealed that Joel had been on his way home after being with another woman. Because of the severe beating he suffered, his body was badly mutilated, so much so that no family member except his brother viewed the body before burial. This decision was made jointly by Joel's wife and his brother. Despite the discovery of Joel's extramarital affair and the sordid circumstances of his death, Joel's wife mourned for her husband. Unlike Joel's wife, his mother was told no details of her son's death except that he had been robbed, knocked unconscious, and died of exposure. The two women closest to Joel, his wife and his mother, remained separate and self-contained in their grief, but both of them appeared to overcome the acute crisis of loss successfully. Joel's wife, in particular, comforted and was comforted by the presence of her children.

About six months after the tragedy, Joel's mother began to behave strangely. Even though she had attended the funeral service and seen the casket interred, she began to question whether her son was really dead. Within a short time she became convinced that her son was still alive. She reasoned that the blow on his head had caused amnesia and that Joel was somewhere in the city waiting for her to find him. Her daughter-in-law and her surviving son tried vainly to persuade her that Joel was actually dead. She began to see men on the street, in shops, and in automobiles who resembled her lost son. She followed men who reminded her of her son, sometimes trying to engage them in conversation until closer contact showed them to be strangers. Eventually her actions became so bizarre that she was referred to a community mental health center for help.

The initial interview with Joel's mother indicated that she was using massive denial to avoid acknowledging that her son was dead. It was not hard for her to do this because her protective family had not permitted her to learn the true circumstances of Joel's death. The funeral service had convinced her for a while that Joel was dead, but she rejected the finality of her loss. Her strong wish to eradicate awareness of Joel's death caused her to reshape painful events in her own mind. Since she had not seen her son dead, she did not have to refute the evidence of her own senses.

The goal set for Joel's mother was to help her recognize the death of her son, to experience the pain of permanent loss, and to immerse herself in active grieving for a time. Only then would she be able to complete the detachment process. The well-meant protection of her family was interpreted as an influence that helped perpetuate her denial. In addition, the subterfuge of the family contributed to her accurate conviction that important information was being withheld from her.

A time-limited crisis model was used to facilitate grief work for Joel's mother. All the adult members of the Benson family were invited to a series of six weekly meetings coordinated by a crisis worker. At these sessions Joel's death was discussed frankly and openly. Family members explained their motives for not being candid with Joel's mother and admitted that their decision was ill-advised. During the meetings the family talked and wept together. Joel's widow talked about the bitterness she felt toward her husband, even though she grieved for him. Joel's brother described the battered body of his brother and his own lonely ordeal of going to the city morgue to identify the corpse. The sixth meeting of the series was attended by the entire family, including Joel's children. Encouraged by the crisis worker, the family arranged to meet at the cemetery on a sunny day. Together they planted flowers on the grave as Joel's mother began the painful work of acknowledgment, detachment, and restitution.

CLINICAL VIGNETTE

CRISIS OF DECISION

Jennifer was a college junior who arranged counseling at a mental health center after she discovered she was pregnant. Although she lived off campus with her boyfriend, Jennifer planned not to marry until she finished her program in journalism. Her boyfriend, Dave, was an accounting student who had already been admitted to a graduate school of business. The pregnancy had not estranged the couple, but both of them were worried about school, money, and the reaction of their parents. Dave said he would marry Jennifer if she was willing. At the same time he assured her that he would "see her through" an abortion if that was what she wanted. Dave's accommodating attitude meant that the decision weighed heavily on Jennifer. Although ambivalent, she had already visited an abortion clinic and had met twice with one of the counselors. Since Jennifer was two months pregnant, there was some urgency about making a decision. During her interview at the mental health clinic, Jennifer said, "Things are happening so fast. I feel as if Dave and everybody else is pressuring me to get rid of this baby and I'm just not sure. What I need is time to think it all through. One mistake is bad enough. I don't want to make another one."

Within the next few days Jennifer and Dave visited the counselor together. The couple had already talked over their options at considerable length. During the interview, Jennifer was able to tell Dave that she did not want an abortion and that she was sure their respective families would support this decision. Influenced by Jennifer's convictions, Dave said that he thought they should be married immediately and that a way could be found for Jennifer to graduate. He expressed willingness to borrow money or find a part-time job if necessary. As the couple began to plan, both of them seemed to grow less tense. It was apparent that they had many resources, among which were maturity, mutual affection, and shared family values.

There is probably no crisis more difficult than deciding whether to terminate or continue an unwanted pregnancy. Advocates of elective abortion and its opponents are equally sustained by their principles, but it is imperative that professional counseling on this issue be supportive rather than coercive or even persuasive. Counselors who hold strong views will deal more fairly with clients if they affiliate with or work out of an agency that does not violate their principles. Pregnant women who come to an organization like Birthright have virtually made a decision to carry to term, and this decision must be respected. Pregnant women who contact facilities where abortions are performed may or may not have made a decision. These are the clients who need freedom to choose, and no choice is more intimate than this nor more far-reaching in its consequences. Time factors compound the difficulties present in this extreme crisis of decision. If time constraints are pressing, frequent preliminary sessions should be arranged in order to promote decision making. A model for conflict resolution has been formulated to be used in deciding pregnancy outcome.

1. Acknowledgement of the pregnancy and the emotions it evokes
2. Formulation of alternatives and possible actions
3. Consideration of merits and disadvantages of various alternatives
4. Commitment to the decision made, with opportunity provided for emotional catharsis

The initial counseling sessions should deal with issues categorized as retrospective, immediate, and prospective. For each category certain relevant questions should be asked:

Retrospective issues

What were the circumstances surrounding the pregnancy? Is the pregnancy the result of rape or incest? Were the partners involved in a long-term relationship?

Immediate issues

Is the putative father still involved with the expectant mother? What are his feelings about the pregnancy? Is he pro-abortion, anti-abortion, or neutral?

What is the most compelling reason for considering abortion? Fear of parenthood? Financial worries? Commitment to career goals?

What is the most compelling argument for or against abortion? Religious beliefs? Parental disapproval? Other emotional entanglements?

Prospective issues

What are the most formidable aspects of carrying the pregnancy to term? What would it be like to deliver the baby and keep it? What would it be like to deliver the baby and give it up for adoption?

What are the most formidable aspects of abortion? Physical fears? Emotional consequences? Anxiety? Guilt? Remorse? Relief?

By asking the foregoing questions the counselor will be able to ascertain some of the client's feelings about the pregnancy. The woman will begin to clarify her feelings and correct distortions that intrude on the actual situation. Some unplanned pregnancies are merely inconvenient. Some inappropriate pregnancies are consciously or unconsciously desired by one or both partners. Other pregnancies are indeed intolerable in the sense that social, financial, and psychological resources are deficient. Asking matter-of-fact questions about the pregnancy decreases emotionality and facilitates constructive and corrective reassessment of the crisis by the client.

During sessions the counselor observes the reactions and language employed by the pregnant woman. Referring to the fetus as a baby indicates that she considers the fetus to be human and viable. Suggesting, as Jennifer did, that abortion might be another "mistake" signifies reluctance as well as ambivalence. When a decision for or against abortion is made, the client will require support. This remains true if a decision has been reached to proceed with the pregnancy. An early therapeutic intervention consists of the statement that regardless of the decision, there will be occasions when the client will fervently wish she had made an opposite choice. This statement needs amplification, for there inevitably will be moments of regret for any decision made. Predicting periods of regret helps clients to cope with this reaction when it does arise. Unless warned, the client will become frightened by the disquiet and sadness that accompany regret. Once a decision is made to abort, intervention consists of preparing the client cognitively and psychologically for the procedure. Telling the client what to expect, helping her arrange for aftercare, and offering to be available for counseling after the procedure are interventions well within the crisis model of treatment.

Young single people who are active sexually need help in learning to deal with sex rationally rather than emotionally. All women, single or married, are most receptive to counseling about responsible sexuality just after delivery or an abortion procedure. It is a disservice to end counseling at the time of delivery or abortion and lose the opportunity to help during a period when the individual is most receptive.

---

about the future. When clients are dealing with compound crisis they are more apt to respond to the present situation with depression, apathy, or surrender, rather than anxiety. In offering nursing intervention to these clients a suggested model is available for nurses working in collaboration with a psychiatric nurse specialist.

■ Examine the current situation to determine what factors in the present crisis have evoked past experiences of trauma or loss.

■ Search for similarities and differences between the present and past.

■ Focus on past and present stressors in ways that reinforce the client's strengths.

■ Help the client identify his preferred methods of coping, now and in the past.

■ Utilize cognitive interventions to help the client understand the influence of the past on his current reactions.

■ Help the client reduce the intensity of any memories of previous crises to acceptable levels by expressing grief and sorrow for the past.

■ Provide time-limited intervention that encourages the client to move from the past to the present.

■ Refer the client for follow-up counseling if previous losses cannot be dealt with adequately in the time allowed.

■ Interpret the client's behavior as an indication of compound crisis rather than a desire to be troublesome.

STAFF BURNOUT AS CRISIS

Burnout has been described as a state of physical and emotional exhaustion that produces a poor self-concept, poor job attitudes, and deficient concern for clients (Pines and Kanner 1982). Burnout may manifest itself in somatic complaints, such as headache, backache, and general malaise, and in such behaviors as neglecting one's assigned tasks, becoming angry over minor matters, and coming to work late and leaving early. It may also be expressed in cognitive ways, such as forgetting details, making errors, and using poor judgment. From this description it is easy to recognize the emotional, behavioral, and cognitive distortions that are the hallmark of crisis.

(Text continues on page 490.)

C L I N I C A L   V I G N E T T E

COMPOUND CRISIS

Mrs. Franklin was hospitalized on a surgical unit for a radical mastectomy. She was 45 years old, the wife of a prominent businessman and the mother of three teenage children. She had handled her ordeal extremely well in the opinion of her surgeon and the nursing staff. Her demands on staff were minimal and she was regarded as an ideal patient. The Franklin family was a close one, and the children visited daily after school. Mr. Franklin was unable to visit every day because of business pressures, but he came in several times a week. His wife's room was full of gifts and flowers sent by the family and friends. Only the immediate family was permitted to visit, at Mrs. Franklin's request, and she had asked not to have her phone connected. Although her primary nurse was concerned about Mrs. Franklin's withdrawal, she was reassured by the fact that her client seemed bright and animated whenever her husband and children visited.

As the days passed the nurse became more and more concerned. When it was suggested that Mrs. Franklin walk a little to regain her strength, she complied but walked only within her own room. She kept her door closed, spoke politely to staff, but initiated no conversation except with her own family. The primary nurse was experienced enough to recognize signs of deepening depression and was not surprised to find her cooperative client crying bitterly one morning. Mrs. Franklin said she was merely tired after a sleepless night, but when her nurse suggested that Mrs. Franklin might like to talk with a mental health nurse, the client agreed.

When the nurse specialist visited, she expected Mrs. Franklin to talk about her changed body image and misgivings about her sexuality. Introducing these topics caused Mrs. Franklin to smile ruefully and dismiss the subject with a wave of her well-manicured hand. It was only when the nurse specialist introduced the topic of the Franklin children that the client's defenses began to crumble. The nurse realized that this was an area that needed to be explored and asked about the children's reaction to their mother's surgery. The question caused the client to talk about her fears of dying and abandoning her children at a time when they still needed her. She said that she had grown up in a motherless home and it was the last thing she wanted to happen to her own children. She described her feelings as a child of ten when her mother had died. She remembered being the object of much solicitude that had quickly diminished as people were caught up in their own affairs. Her grandmother, a stern and straightlaced woman, had come to live with Mrs. Franklin, who was an only child. She remembered being told that she mustn't cry for her mother because her father would be unhappy and he was doing his best to be both mother and father. Mrs. Franklin also had memories of being dressed in a funny, old-fashioned way as a child, of never having a birthday party, and of being more restricted than other youngsters her age.

As a result of her own childhood, Mrs. Franklin had resolved to make her husband and family as comfortable and happy as possible. She had evidently succeeded, for the devotion shown by her husband and children was remarkable. From her remarks it was evident that Mrs. Franklin was reliving her own emotionally barren childhood and foreseeing the same fate for her children. The nurse specialist recognized that Mrs. Franklin was suffering a compound crisis related to her own surgery and to her memories of a mother who had died.

Listening to Mrs. Franklin talk about her mother's death, the nurse specialist realized that the client's emotional reactions stemmed from her painful association of her current situation with the past. While accepting the reality of the client's feelings about her mother's death, the nurse specialist pointed out the differences in the two situations. Mrs. Franklin's mother had succumbed to pneumonia at a time when antibiotic drugs were unknown. The client's condition was discovered by mammography at a very early stage and the prognosis was excellent. The only real similarity in the two situations was that two mothers, a generation apart, had become ill. The energy that Mrs. Franklin had devoted to being a wise and giving mother was still there and could be used to assist her own recovery. In addition, the energy of the Franklin family was available to be mobilized on her behalf if she chose to use it. The nurse specialist suggested that shutting herself off from friends and showing only her heroic side to her family deprived everyone of an opportunity to be supportive. The nurse specialist met several times with Mrs. Franklin. In the meetings the client grieved openly for her mother and even began to smile at her grandmother's quirks and demands. The nurse specialist continued to emphasize the importance of dealing with the present situation. She pointed out to the client that she had been strengthened as well as weakened by her childhood experiences, and that the present situation could be dealt with more easily if it were not clouded by bitterness about the very different circumstances of the past.

Burnout can be a devastating experience for the professionals who experience it and for the clients receiving care. One of the prevailing features of burnout is decreased productivity. Burned out staff members often call in sick or simply perform poorly when they do come to work. Dissatisfaction with the job increases. Complaining and arguing increase among staff members, and sometimes clients are pulled into the patterns of nontherapeutic communication. When one or two staff members are burned out, the responsibilities of the rest of the staff become heavier, thereby increasing the probability that burnout will become epidemic (Potemka et al. 1986).

In addressing the problem of burnout among nurses, two acknowledgments must be made. The first acknowledgment is that inadequate staffing is a relatively common problem for nurses. The second is that the nurses who become burned out are often those who contribute most to client care, sometimes at the expense of their own well-being. Nurses without genuine commitment to their profession are unlikely to experience burnout, because they are rarely ignited or motivated by a genuine desire to give the best possible care to their clients. In short, nurses suffering burnout are well worth salvaging and indeed may have been the most energetic workers on the staff (Chenevert 1978, Pines and Kanner 1982).

Burnout need not be a permanent condition, but the question is: How can it be reduced or alleviated? There are some measures that sound simplistic but can be highly beneficial. All nurses should try to develop the introspective skills to ascertain signs of burnout in themselves and in their co-workers. Forsyth and Cannady (1981) have provided excellent guidelines for assessing burnout signs and symptoms:

1. Be aware of your own emotional reactions. Recognize what you are thinking and feeling. If your reactions are negative, identify the cause or target so that you don't displace these reactions onto innocent bystanders.

2. Analyze your usual coping patterns. For example, if an unpleasant episode occurs at work, do you take it home with you? If an unpleasant episode occurs at home, do you bring it with you to work and burden yourself and others with it during the working day?

3. Develop new methods of coping if your behavioral analysis reveals questionable patterns. Persons who work hard and conscientiously need adequate rest and relaxation. Rescheduling home responsibilities may be necessary to get you off the treadmill of rushing home to take on new chores without any respite (Hutchinson 1987).

4. Develop the ability to say no to tasks that are exploitive. Burned out people behave aggressively, but people who are assertive enough to say no when the situation demands it are more likely to avoid getting burned out.

When a large number of staff members on a unit are burned out, a mutual support group may be the answer. Peer support can do a great deal to assuage the tension and fatigue of burnout. Specific problems can be dealt with more effectively when the entire staff is involved in a discussion. A support group for nurses who feel the effects of burnout can also be a place to share feelings and ideas, to delineate themes of interest to all, and to solve common problems. Topics of interest might include the use of assertive techniques instead of aggressive exchanges, and the management of household responsibilities in single-parent or dual-career homes.

One of the perennial complaints of people who are burned out is that they are unappreciated and their hard work is unrecognized. A support group might be a place where peer recognition can be given and where misunderstandings can be erased.

In organizing a support group to prevent or alleviate burnout, it is important to establish a well-defined contract and to agree upon group goals. Without such preparation the group sessions are likely to deteriorate into forums for airing complaints and reviving old disputes. Leadership should be democratic and egalitarian, but some form of leadership is essential. Group leadership might be conferred on a nurse with special knowledge of group theory and process, or it might be shared among members on a rotating basis. There are also advantages in having the group meet outside the borders of the actual unit or facility so that an atmosphere of collegiality and neutrality can be established (Pines and Kanner 1982).

Caregivers involved in helping victims of trauma and disaster are also subject to crisis reactions. Often these crisis reactions take the form of burnout. Feelings of burnout reduce caregivers' feelings of competence. To protect their professional self-image caregivers begin to blame others for their feelings of inadequacy. They may blame fellow workers and even the victims. Blaming the victims for their injuries is especially frequent when victims fail to recover, thus adding to the uneasiness of caregivers. The global blaming by caretakers further diminishes their self-esteem and erodes their confidence in the work they are doing. The sequence of crisis development in caregivers is shown in Figure 17–2.

MARITAL CRISIS

At the time of selecting a mate or sexual partner, young adults are facing what Erikson (1963) calls the intimacy crisis. After progressing through prior stages of independence and identity, individuals begin to think of themselves as ready to form a meaningful union with another person in which there is space to share activities of career, procreation, and recreation. Most individuals marry, even though there have been social changes in the last few decades that permit cohabitation without marriage, homosexual alliances, and communal living. One contemporary change in marriage is the increase in dual career marriages, in which both partners work outside the home. With both husband and wife committed to jobs or careers, there are heavy demands on the marriage, especially if there are children. Even in childless marriages many demands are placed on the relationship. Conflicts over communication, sex, money, fidelity, and changing interests are frequent causes of marital discord. Although causes vary, the end result is alienation, separation, or divorce. In the past, prohibitions against divorce were stronger and many unhappy couples remained married, but this is less true today.

The dissolution of a marriage by divorce is an emotional experience that affects not only the couple but also their friends, children, and other relatives. In-laws who have come to care for a son-in-law or daughter-in-law feel upset and confused. Married friends see in the troubled marriage a reflection of their own problems and are frightened. Children are angry and bitter, frequently blaming themselves. The experience of divorce has been compared to experiencing another's death without the comfort of formal rituals. And the aftermath of divorce must be endured without the social support given to those who have lost a husband or wife through death.

The intricate pattern of establishing a second marriage remains largely an unexplored area of research. Because most divorced persons are also parents, remarriage introduces tasks of blending the two families and enacting new roles as stepparents. Forming a stepfamily challenges all concerned. Each individual comes to the new family with a different set of expectations and with memories that must be integrated into the new arrangements. A period of testing and uncertainty is almost

Figure 17–2. Sequence of Crisis Development in Caregivers of Trauma Victims

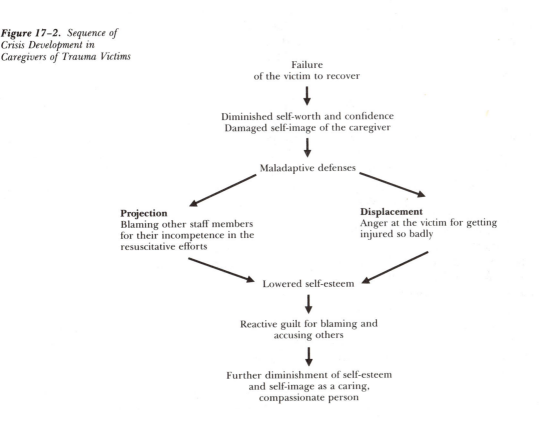

Failure
of the victim to recover

Diminished self-worth and confidence
Damaged self-image of the caregiver

Maladaptive defenses

Projection
Blaming other staff members
for their incompetence in the
resuscitative efforts

Displacement
Anger at the victim for getting
injured so badly

Lowered self-esteem

Reactive guilt for blaming and
accusing others

Further diminishment of self-esteem
and self-image as a caring,
compassionate person

inevitable. Three problems that may surface in second marriages have been identified:

1. The new partner who has chosen to marry a single parent may be reluctant to accept the children as part of the package.

2. Former mates may accept the remarriage of a spouse but dislike the idea that their children have a stepparent.

3. Children may continue to entertain fantasies that their natural parents will reconcile in spite of the remarriages of the parents.

CRISIS GROUPS

Crisis intervention may be offered on a one-to-one basis or on a group basis. The crisis group is an alternative treatment for clients who are in some distress but retain the ability to interact in a group milieu. Many individuals are so overwhelmed by crisis that they cannot deal with the demands and interpersonal dynamics present in groups. For these persons, a crisis group will not be a positive experience and should not be recommended. Nevertheless, people in crisis are usually amenable to environmental manipulation, and a group enlarges the interpersonal experience of clients. The crisis group is a social, rather than physical, form of environmental manipulation, for crisis groups are uniquely able to give members a sense of community. Feelings of belonging are important to crisis-ridden persons, as is the opportunity to give help as well as receive it.

Crisis groups are open-ended and ongoing, with each member agreeing to attend for no more than six to eight weeks. During this brief period when crisis is present, members are motivated and willing to engage. The brevity of the group experience creates an urgency that is catalytic. With members constantly joining and terminating, cohesiveness may be a problem. Group cohesiveness may be increased by selecting members who have similar problems or similar characteristics. For example, adolescents, new widowers, or newly divorced persons have common interests that cause the group to coalesce even though problems brought to the group are not identical. In preliminary sessions before referral to a group is made, prospective members are interviewed for assessment purposes. During this screening process, the presence of a hazardous event is recognized, and agreement is reached that the individual will be helped by group intervention.

Like all crisis workers, the group leader is an active teacher, interpreter, and regulator. Group pressure is used to bring about change, but the leader is the guardian of the group contract and remains mindful of group goals. Leaders of crisis groups insist that members adhere to the agreement that only crisis issues will be discussed. Members may wish to digress to irrelevant matters, but time constraints can be cited as reasons for staying with the task. The number of members in a crisis group should be limited to eight; entry and termination of members should be arranged so that group composition changes gradually. Goals are specific, and termination is not an issue to be negotiated after the group experience begins.

Group work may be an adjunct to individual crisis work or it may be the only treatment offered. The group leader should be knowledgeable about crisis theory and group process, but crisis group work is restricted to symptomatic aid. Chronic problems or deep-seated concerns cannot be treated within the temporal and contractual limits of crisis group work. One advantage of a crisis group is that it may be acceptable to individuals who reject individual counseling or avoid group psychotherapy. Within the group, self-help is emphasized and regressive tendencies are strongly discouraged. Group interaction is invoked to help members express themselves and search for new coping methods (Aguilera and Messick 1978). Crisis groups demand careful selection of members, are limited in what they try to accomplish, but operate on several levels: cognitive, affective, behavioral, and interpersonal.

Crisis groups can supplement or replace individual work in instances in which the client seems able to tolerate group interaction. Preliminary screening is essential because many clients are overwhelmed by the crisis and cannot benefit from group work. Leaders of crisis groups follow the general outlines of individual crisis intervention. The groups are time-limited, goals are specific, and leaders insist on adherence to the group contract.

CRISIS HOT LINES

Crisis intervention by telephone is a contemporary development that has won widespread support. The sponsors of crisis hot lines may be official or voluntary agencies, large or small in terms of size and resources. Counseling agencies, drug programs, poison control centers, psychiatric facilities, and general hospitals often organize and administer their own crisis phone service. In some cities, one phone number is publicized as a "lifeline" to be used regardless of the nature of the emergency or crisis. Phone calls to the central number are answered, screened, and referred to appropriate channels.

Crisis hot lines, which usually operate 24 hours a day, are used by individuals with a wide range of problems. Runaways, battered wives, disappointed lovers, jobless workers, and pregnant teenagers are a cross-section of the worried people who turn to crisis hot lines for help. The individual using a crisis phone service may prefer to remain anonymous, although serious efforts are made to obtain correct identification and to follow up on the calls. One explanation for the proliferation of crisis hot lines is the accountability and careful preparation of volunteers or staff members answering the calls. Virtually all agencies require their volunteers and staff members to undergo thorough preparation for this demanding work. Persons answering a crisis phone are usually required to keep a log that fully reports every conversation. The caller may refuse to give a name or address, but the time and details of the call are recorded, the problem described, and the response of the worker noted. A preceptor or senior staff member reviews the log carefully, usually on a daily basis. If the interventions of the worker are deemed inadequate, they are discussed and remedied when possible. In cases in which a referral has been made, a preceptor or worker may check to see whether the caller has followed through. Confidentiality is absolute unless there is clear danger to the self or others. In contemporary society, where families move frequently and social support is absent, the crisis hot line fills a pressing need. Crisis treatment cannot be fully accomplished by phone, but the crisis hot line is a mechanism that attracts troubled people and moves them to a point where they may receive further help.

LEVELS OF CRISIS PREVENTION

Primary Crisis Prevention

Primary crisis prevention may be defined as crisis work that deals with variables affecting people at risk. The assumptions on which primary crisis prevention is based depend on clinical, investigatory, and epidemiological studies that indicate the incidence (new cases) and prevalence (total cases) of crisis in certain populations. In primary crisis prevention, the aim is to reduce the incidence of crisis in populations at risk by modifying external variables and reinforcing internal coping strengths.

Primary crisis prevention provides intervention before the arrival of change through counseling or teaching that emphasizes anticipatory planning. Some life changes arrive without warning, but other impending changes allow time for advance preparation. Populations at risk for crisis are found in perinatal clinics, hospitals, schools and colleges, nursing homes, and facilities for the elderly. Primary crisis prevention may be offered on an individual, group, or community basis. Through anticipatory guidance, people are given the opportunity to select and practice behaviors that are likely to be helpful in the imminent situation.

The premise of anticipatory guidance is that knowledge is strength and that individuals facing crisis are better equipped if they have an idea of what may lie ahead. Increasingly the docile, submissive patient is recognized by health professionals as a person who may have a relatively difficult adjustment to illness. More demanding patients who ask insistent questions about their condition and seek information about proposed treatments frequently achieve a better adjustment than do patients who appear acquiescent or passive (Glazer 1981). Childbirth education classes that include both of the prospective parents are an example of widely accepted anticipatory guidance. A primary prevention approach used by community nurses working with potential child abusers is to teach parents about the developmental progress of young children. In this way the unrealistic expectations of the parents are reduced and appropriate responses to natural childish behavior can be rehearsed in advance.

Research on attachment and separation between mothers and their young children has led to more involvement of parents with their hospitalized children even when treatment schedules must be adjusted. The substitute grandparents program is another primary prevention program that benefits old and young people and reduces the prevalence of crisis stemming from intergenerational distrust. Other examples of primary prevention include premarital counseling by the clergy, bedside teaching by nurses, and orientation programs offered by colleges.

Primary crisis prevention often follows Maslow's hierarchy of needs (1962) by including in its purview physical resources that are necessary for survival, such as food and shelter; psychological resources that are necessary for self-esteem, such as love and security; and social resources that encourage the self-actualization necessary for fulfillment.

Secondary Crisis Prevention

Secondary crisis prevention consists of early intervention with persons in crisis in order to restore equilibrium promptly and reduce the severity of distress. During periods of crisis people feel helpless, and their motivation to find solutions is high. Unless remedial crisis counseling is offered early, people tend to "muddle through" until they reach a state of reequilibrium that is no longer susceptible to therapeutic intervention. It is during the acute stage of crisis that the influence of the crisis worker is greatest.

During secondary crisis intervention, the disorganization of the individual is obvious. What may be less obvious is the effect of the crisis on the entire family. Secondary crisis prevention should include an assessment of strengths and weaknesses of the family system since it is the family context in which the crisis has developed and must be resolved. After the extent of the crisis has been defined, and cognitive, affective, and behavioral distortions have been identified, the plan of action is developed jointly by the crisis worker and the client. Here the crisis worker may be as active as necessary, but no more so. Suggestions may be made, but coercive direction is not advisable. Solutions must be acceptable to the family and not merely to the crisis worker. One of the most valuable services a crisis worker can provide is instillation of hope within people who are distraught. Since every crisis inevitably comes to a conclusion, this assurance can be given without reservation.

Throughout the intervention process, attention is paid to whatever abilities the individual and family possess. Preoccupation with defeat and failure dampens hope. However, reassurance should not be unrealistic, nor should the crisis worker endeavor to dispel all anxiety. The presence of some anxiety can be a propelling force toward adaptive problem solving, provided anxiety does not become overwhelming.

Even though secondary prevention involves persons who are already in crisis, group and community programs can be used advantageously. Parents Anonymous is a group program for actual and potential child abusers. Gamblers Anonymous is a group program for compulsive gamblers trying to overcome the habit. These programs are similar to Alcoholics Anonymous, which combines group support with a ritualized format. Pregnant teenagers comprise another population that is frequently the recipient of secondary prevention measures. For this population, the most effective programs are those that offer primary and tertiary prevention, in addition to secondary measures needed during the immediate crisis of pregnancy. Postnatal counseling concerning responsible sexuality, motherhood, and educational guidance fall under the rubric of primary and tertiary crisis prevention (Ellison, Hughes, and White 1989).

Tertiary Crisis Prevention

Tertiary crisis prevention endeavors to reduce the amount of residual impairment that follows the resolution of some crises. Because the emphasis of crisis work is on functionality rather than on personality, it is possible to educate persons outside the health professions to the need for primary and tertiary intervention and to involve them to a con-

siderable degree. Teachers, scout leaders, and athletic coaches are examples of people who can learn to identify and help persons embarked on a crisis course. These informal care providers can also help individuals who have recently moved from a crisis state to restored homeostasis. If community agents are sensitized through training programs, the media, or ongoing communication with health professionals, they become important adjuncts in crisis prevention.

All forms of crisis prevention benefit from program planning with a community orientation. Crisis is so prevalent in contemporary life that only a small percentage of persons in need find their way to professional help. Therefore, crisis prevention programs should receive the attention their importance deserves. At present there are reliable hypotheses about the nature and prevalence of crisis in various populations. It is possible to predict some manifestations of crisis, to make assumptions about populations at risk, to avert certain crises, and to minimize residual impairment through judicious use of the three forms of crisis prevention: primary, secondary, and tertiary.

SUMMARY

Nobody can escape the emergence of crises at recurrent points of the life cycle, and most people are called upon at some time to intervene in crisis situations in the lives of others. The range of crisis theory includes the precipitating event, the person's response systems, and the results of responses to the precipitating event. If the responses elicited by the hazardous event are adequate and functional, the person is not propelled into the state of disorganization known as crisis. But if the person's responses to the hazardous event are inadequate and dysfunctional, a state of crisis follows.

The development of crisis theory is fairly recent, but in practice crisis intervention is as ancient as the human race. Families, friends, and communities have always sought or extended help in conditions of crisis. Whenever one distraught, confused person turns to another for help or advice, a form of crisis intervention takes place. Nurses working in acute care settings, in birthing centers, in schools, in outreach clinics, in homes, and in hospices all participate formally or informally in the problem-solving activities on which crisis intervention is based.

Sometimes it is difficult to apply strict standards to the selection of crisis clients, for in many respects this population is self-selected. The problem is compounded by the fact that many generalist nurses without advanced preparation in psychodynamics and without access to consultation services are called upon to offer crisis counseling in the context of their professional practice. It is important, then, for all nurses to have an understanding of crisis work and of the ways in which it can augment other treatment approaches.

At times crisis work is supportive and limited to the immediate event. At other times, depending on the characteristics and motivation of the client, the crisis worker may decide that it is advisable to explore issues beyond the current crisis and to consider the client's general coping patterns in addition to the behaviors necessary to resolve the current crisis. These exploratory approaches demand greater psychological strength from the client and greater psychodynamic knowledge from the clinician.

During the period of acute disequilibrium that accompanies crisis, clients experience high levels of anxiety. Reduction of anxiety and subjective distress is the initial goal of crisis intervention, even if a decision is ultimately made to refer the client for exploratory psychotherapy. At this point the generalist nurse should indicate to the client the need for help from other practitioners qualified to offer more intensive forms of psychotherapy.

The phenomenon known as *compound crisis* occurs when individuals and families face a current trauma that reactivates memories of a previous loss or injury that has not been fully resolved. When a client is able to speak appropriately of past crises and to show concern about future adjustments, she is probably not suffering from compound crisis. Clients who refuse to acknowledge or plan for a current crisis, who become depressed and withdraw, or are angry and demanding may be experiencing one crisis superimposed on an earlier one. The result of compound crisis is lack of energy or desire to meet the challenge of the current situation.

No one is exempt from the threat of crisis, including nurses and nursing staff. Staff burnout is a group crisis that can be alleviated either through self-help measures or the intervention of a psychiatric nurse specialist or group leader. Group intervention is one way of providing crisis counseling, but the selection criteria for members must be strict. Some persons in crisis cannot tolerate group interaction and their distress would increase if they were urged to join a crisis group prematurely.

Community crises may result from disasters that affect large segments of the population. Disasters are diversified in nature, and a number of typologies can be used to differentiate forms of disaster, even though distinctions are sometimes blurred. Disasters may be expected or unexpected, recurrent or unprecedented. They may be natural occurrences or the result of man-made decisions about the environment. Some disasters are generated by forces external to the community; others are the result of internal community forces.

Economic disasters possess a uniqueness that warranted their discussion as separate phenomena. As in all disasters, role enactment is affected by massive economic adversity. Families in which role flexibility can be maintained are more likely to adapt successfully to conditions of severe economic deprivation. A recommended form of primary prevention would require employers to give advance warning of layoffs or shutdowns so that workers could adjust, relocate, or retrain during periods of economic decline.

Because crises are so widespread and are part of the life experience of people of all ages, there is a place in crisis work for all three levels of prevention: primary, secondary, and tertiary.

Review Questions

1. In sequential order, list the progression that leads to the disorganization and disequilibrium of crisis.

2. Crisis represents both danger and opportunity. What is meant by this statement?

3. What are the major differences between an emergency and a crisis?

4. What forms of distortion are present in a crisis? How might the nurse deal with these distortions?

5. Define the term *burnout* as a professional risk for nurses.

6. Describe two possible methods of dealing with burnout experienced by nursing staff.

7. Describe the emotional and behavioral consequences of sudden, traumatic events.

8. Explain how crisis workers should deal with behavioral and emotional distortions of survivors after a disaster.

Suggested Annotated Readings

Gavalya, A. S. "Reactions to the 1985 Mexican Earthquake: Case Vignettes." *Hospital and Community Psychiatry* 38, no. 12 (December 1987): 1327–1329.

The Mexican earthquake of September 1985 caused severe damage. Loss of life was extensive, as were physical and emotional trauma in an area already suffering economic, political, and social problems. The social disintegration that might be expected to follow a disaster of this magnitude did not occur. Instead, the inhabitants surmounted the experience, managed relief measures effectively, and began the reintegration process almost immediately. The focus of this article is primarily clinical, as the author portrays by means of selected case examples the reactions and behaviors of individuals and families when they rallied after the earthquake. Suffering is neither minimized nor exaggerated, and the vivid case examples should prove helpful to crisis workers in general.

Hahn, N. "The Assessment of Coping, Defense, and Stress." In *Handbook of Stress: Theoretical and Clinical Aspects.* L. Goldberger and S. Breznitz, eds. New York: Free Press, 1982.

This is one of a number of useful articles in this handbook. It differentiates coping from defensive behaviors. More than a response to trauma, coping is an effort to resolve difficulties by searching within and outside oneself for solutions. The author goes on to state that any self-protective mechanism, regardless of its nature, if adopted consciously and used with awareness, could be considered an adaptive coping response. It is the context that determines whether an action is a coping response or merely defensive. The philosophical overtones offered here provide much food for thought.

"Mark's Rehabilitation Was a Labor of Love." Nursing Grand Rounds. *Nursing 88* 18, no. 3 (March 1988):58–64.

This nursing grand rounds report was presented by a panel of four nurses, a physical therapist, and an occupational therapist. Coordinated by a nurse supervisor, the report deals with a quadriplegic whose wife was three months pregnant when a motor accident severed his spinal cord between C6 and C7. The rehabilitation team describes the program that was instituted for the paralyzed client. Three levels of crisis prevention were implemented by the health care team. Beyond implementing a rehabilitation program, the young man's caregivers adjusted his schedule so that he could attend Lamaze classes with his wife. The positive attitudes of the health team motivated the client so that his progress was impressive. Although he was confined to a wheelchair, arrangements were made for him to help his wife during labor and to be present during delivery. The article is truly inspiring, even though no miracles were reported. However, this case example demonstrates the results of commitment and mutual caring by client, family, and caregivers.

Murphy, S. "Mental Distress and Recovery in a High-Risk Bereavement Sample Three Years after Untimely Death." *Nursing Research* 37, no. 1 (January/February 1988):30–35.

This is a report of a longitudinal study of postdisaster bereavement one year and three years after the traumatic event. After the Mount St. Helens eruption 119 control and bereaved subjects were studied. Findings suggest that persons who experience high distress levels one year after a disaster that caused the untimely death of a loved one can be predicted to experience high distress levels three years after the event. Demographic factors, current absence of life stress, and social support seem to have relatively little impact on distress levels. The author concludes that changes are necessary in thinking about the bereavement process, and rejects the denial-anger-bargaining-acceptance sequence formulated by Kübler-Ross. Instead, the bereavement process is lengthy and complex, being influenced by many factors, such as the importance of the lost one and beliefs that the deaths were preventable. Future studies are recommended to increase our knowledge of bereavement so that interventions might be offered to meet needs of survivors that change in nature but persist over time. In particular, durable bonds between survivors and the deceased deserve attention directed to understanding the qualitative changes in attachment bonds that take place over time.

Ravenscroft, K. "Psychiatric Consultation to the Child with Acute Physical Trauma." *American Journal of Orthopsychiatry* 52, no. 2 (April 1982):298–307.

Psychological management of young trauma victims emphasizes primary prevention through family morale and cohesiveness during emergency care, and rehabilitation. While lifesaving procedures have priority, support for parents, siblings, and the victim is essential. Explaining the purpose of necessary procedures reinforces the importance of self-control and maturity in family members. Young victims over the age of one year also benefit from explanations of present and future treatment. Unless parents are obviously upset, their presence is a source of reassurance for the victim. If parents cannot be present, a caring, supportive nurse may become a surrogate for a time. Consistent, stable caretakers bring order to the chaotic world the young victim has entered. Intensive care units often produce a psychotic state, especially in frightened children. Nightmares and anxiety attacks are common and may be due to repressed memories of the traumatic event. This commonsense article has a strong theoretical base and is recommended for all nurses who find it essential to know why certain measures are beneficial.

References

Aguilera, D. C., and J. M. Messick. *Crisis Intervention: Crisis Theory and Methodology*, 3d ed. St. Louis: Mosby, 1978.

Black, J. W. "The Libidinal Cocoon: A Nurturing Retreat for Families of Plane Crash Victims." *Hospital and Community Psychiatry* 38, no. 13 (December 1987): 1322–1326.

Breier, A. "Stress Isn't Always Bad." *Hospital and Community Psychiatry* 39, no. 6 (June 1988):591.

Burgess, Ann W., and Bruce Baldwin. *Crisis Intervention Theory and Practice*. Englewood Cliffs, New Jersey: Prentice Hall, 1981.

Caplan, G. *Principles of Preventive Psychiatry*. New York: Basic Books, 1964.

———. *Support Systems and Community Mental Health*. New York: Behavioral Science Press, 1974.

Chenevert, M. *Special Techniques in Assertiveness Training*. St. Louis: C. V. Mosby, 1978.

Cohen, R. E. "The Armero Tragedy: Lessons for Mental Health Professionals." *Hospital and Community Psychiatry* 38, no. 12 (December 1987):1316–1321.

Collison, C., and S. Miller. "Using Images of the Future in Grief Work." *Image* 19, no. 1 (Spring 1987):9–11.

deChesnay, M. "Problem Solving in Nursing." *Image* 15 no. 1 (1983):8–11.

Ellison, J. D., D. H. Hughes, and K. A. White. "An Emergency Psychiatry Update." *Hospital and Community Psychiatry* 40, no. 3 (March 1989):250–260.

Engel, G. "Grief and Grieving." *American Journal of Nursing* 64 (1964):93–96.

Erikson, E. *Childhood and Society* 2d ed. New York: W. W. Norton, 1963.

Eth, S., and S. R. Pynos. "Interaction of Trauma and Grief in Childhood." In *Post-Traumatic Stress Disorder in Children*. S. Eth and S. R. Pynos, eds. Washington, D.C.: American Psychiatric Association, 1985.

Forsyth, D. M., and J. Cannady. "Preventing and Alleviating Staff Burnout through a Group." *Journal of Psychosocial Nursing and Health Services* 19, no. 9 (1981): 35–38.

Freud, S. *Problems of Anxiety*. New York: W. W. Norton, 1936.

Glazer, G. "The Good Patient." *Nursing and Health Care* 2 (1981):144–146.

Haack, M., and J. W. Jones. "Diagnosing Burnout Using Projective Drawings." *Journal of Psychosocial Nursing and Mental Health Services* 21, no. 7 (1983):8–16.

Horsley, G. "Baggage from the Past." *American Journal of Nursing* 88, no. 1 (January 1988):60–63.

Hutchinson, S. "Self-Care and Job Stress." *Image* 19, no. 3 (Winter 1987):192–196.

Kübler-Ross, E. *On Death and Dying*. New York: Macmillan, 1969.

Loomis, M. E., and D. J. Wood. "Cure: The Potential Outcome of Nursing Care." *Image* 15, no. 1 (1983):4–7.

Maslow, A. *Toward a Psychology of Being*. New York: Van Nostrand, 1962.

McNett, S. C. "Social Support, Threat, and Coping Responses and Effectiveness in the Functionally Disabled." *Nursing Research* 36, no. 2 (March/April 1987): 98–103.

Parad, H. J., and H. L. Resnik. "The Practice of Crisis Intervention in Emergency Care." In *Emergency Psychiatric Care and Management of Mental Health Crises*, H. L. Resnik and H. L. Rubin, eds. Bowie, Maryland: Charles Slack, 1975.

Parkes, C. M., and R. S. Weiss. *Recovery from Bereavement*. New York: Basic Books, 1983.

Peplau, H. E. *Interpersonal Relations in Nursing*. New York: Putnam, 1952.

———. "Some Reflections on the Earlier Days of Psychiatric Nursing." *Journal of Psychosocial Nursing and Mental Health Services* 20, no. 8 (1982):17–23.

Pines, A. M., and A. D. Kanner. "Nurse Burnout: Lack of Positive Conditions and Presence of Negative Conditions as Two Independent Sources of Stress." *Journal of Psychosocial Nursing and Mental Health Services* 20, no. 8 (1982):30–35.

Pines, M. "Recession Is Linked to Psychological Harm." *The New York Times* (April 6, 1982).

Potemka, K., M. Lopez, C. Reid, and L. Lawson. "Chronic Fatigue." *Image* 8, no. 4 (Winter 1986):165–169.

Rattner, S. "Poverty Is More than Being Flat Broke." *The New York Times* (April 11, 1982).

Sifneos, P. E. "Brief Psychotherapy and Crisis Intervention." In *Comprehensive Textbook of Psychiatry*, 3d ed., H. I. Kaplan, A. M. Freedman, and B. J. Sadock, eds. Baltimore: Williams & Wilkins, 1980.

Smith, D. W. "Survivors of Serious Illness." *American Journal of Nursing* 79 (1979):441–445.

Sullivan, H. S. *The Interpersonal Theory of Psychiatry*. New York: W. W. Norton, 1953.

Weiss, R. S. "Principles Underlying a Manual for Parents Whose Children Were Killed by a Drunk Driver." *American Journal of Orthopsychiatry* 57, no. 3 (July 1987): 431–440.

Worden, W. J. *Grief Counseling and Grief Therapy: A Handbook for the Mental Health Practitioner*. New York: Springer, 1982.

P A R T

F O U R

THERAPEUTIC GUIDELINES IN NURSING PRACTICE

18

Behavior Guidelines in Nursing Practice

BEHAVIOR MODIFICATION
 Classical Conditioning
 Operant Conditioning

BEHAVIOR MODIFICATION TECHNIQUES
 Systematic Desensitization
 Aversion Techniques
 Operant Techniques

BASIC GUIDELINES FOR THE USE OF BEHAVIOR
 MODIFICATION

LIMITATIONS OF BEHAVIOR THERAPY

IMPLICATIONS FOR NURSING

Learning Objectives

After reading this chapter, the student should be able to:

1. Integrate concepts of behavior modification into the nursing process.

2. Formulate appropriate assessment and intervention strategies for use with behavior modification.

3. Discuss the implications of providing behavior therapy for clients.

Overview

Regardless of philosophical orientation, the ultimate goal of all therapeutic approaches is to introduce functional change. The client has, over the course of time, developed some undesirable ways of dealing with internal and external stress. Therapy is aimed at helping the client find more desirable strategies to take their place. Unlike some other psychotherapeutic approaches, behavior modification, or behavioral therapy, concerns itself, not with the causes of undesirable behaviors, but rather with the behaviors themselves.

The behavioral therapist concentrates exclusively on helping clients unlearn troublesome behaviors and learn new, more adaptive ones. This chapter will help the student learn to understand the ways in which a problem may be conceptualized behaviorally and to apply techniques that may be used to change behavior.

How do individuals develop ineffective strategies for dealing with stress? What is necessary to change these strategies? These are questions around which all psychotherapeutic approaches have arisen. For example, Freud's psychoanalytic theory proposes that unconscious conflicts, usually of a sexual or aggressive nature, are at the core of an individual's psychological problems. Using techniques such as free association, interpretation, and analysis of the transference neurosis, the psychoanalyst can probe the client's unconscious mind to bring the conflict into conscious awareness, where the individual can begin to deal with it. Once the client is aware of unmet sexual or aggressive needs, he or she can endeavor to meet those needs in socially acceptable ways. The basic objective in psychoanalytic therapy is to help clients develop new behaviors that begin to meet their needs, rather than frustrate them.

Carl Rogers's client-centered therapy is based on the idea that it is normal for people to grow, to actualize their potential, to evolve into the fullness of their being. Unfortunately, individuals often encounter obstacles along the way and misperceive their needs and direction in life, which hinders their growth. In client-centered therapy, the therapist assists the client in discovering the obstacles to growth and removing them so that the self-actualization process may continue. The therapist does this by creating an atmosphere of total acceptance so that the client feels free to explore any aspect of her personality without fear of rejection. This attitude of therapeutic acceptance is called *unconditional positive regard*. By trying to identify with the client during the exploration, the therapist can help the client clarify her needs and feelings. Facilitating self-actualization thus also produces behavioral change.

Behavior modification, or *behavioral therapy,* does not concern itself with unconscious conflicts, obstacles to self-actualization, or other subjective inferential concepts. Its central concern is simply with human behavior and learned changes in behavior (Franks 1969). According to this school of thought, all behavior, both appropriate and inappropriate, is *learned*. The behavior modifier, armed with principles of learning that have been observed, replicated, and validated under controlled experimental conditions, helps clients unlearn troublesome behaviors and learn new, more adaptive behaviors in their place.

This represents quite a deviation from other therapeutic approaches. The *content* of what a client has learned previously is of little or no importance to the behavioral therapist. For instance, if Mr. Jones has a fear of flying, the therapist seeks no symbolic meaning for his distress, looks for no issues of self-doubt, sexual inadequacy, or death wish in devising a treatment plan. Rather it is the *process* of learning that is central to the resolution of the problem. In Mr. Jones's case, the inappropriate behavior is considered to be an avoidance response to a stimulus. The essential questions to be answered are: What principles of learning are keeping Mr. Jones's ineffective behavior entrenched? What principles and techniques must be used to bring about the desired behavior change? Behavioral therapy is a direct attack upon symptoms because it is the symptoms that are seen as the problem.

BEHAVIOR MODIFICATION

The principles of behavior modification have been derived from careful observations and have been validated by experimental data. Although scientific methods have been applied to the study of behavior since the nineteenth century, the most influential studies were done early in this century by Ivan Pavlov (1927), the Russian physiologist, and B. F. Skinner (1972), the American psychologist. Their two models of conditioned learning, classical conditioning and operant conditioning, respectively, form the basis upon which the modern school of behaviorism rests.

Classical Conditioning

Ivan Pavlov (1849–1936) was a Russian professor of physiology originally interested in doing research on digestion and the automatic reflexes associated with it, including the salivation response. However, chance observations in the course of this research sent him on a new track of study, and he ultimately demonstrated and introduced a model of learning that has come to be known as *classical conditioning*.

It was in 1904 that Pavlov noticed that a dog being used in digestion experiments began to salivate not only when food was in its mouth but also at the very sight of food. Salivation when eating is a reflexive, unlearned response, so Pavlov called it an *unconditioned response* (UCR). But salivation at the mere sight of food was a new, learned response, which Pavlov named a *conditioned response* (CR).

Pavlov went on to explore and examine how this conditioned response might have been learned. In his experiments, the dog was securely strapped in place. A bowl into which meat powder was automatically dispensed was placed in front of the dog. The dog's salivary gland was connected to a device that measured salivary flow.

At the start of the experiment, a neutral stimulus, such as a tone from a tuning fork, was presented to the dog. The stimulus had no previous control over or association with food. Then several trials were made in which the tone was quickly followed by the presentation of food. As the dog ate, its natural salivation response was recorded.

The procedure was then changed again. This time the tone was presented, but without food. Pavlov found that the dog salivated in response to the tone, even in the absence of food. A new association had been made between a neutral stimulus (the tone) and an old response (salivation). In short, Pavlov demonstrated one way that *learning* (stimulus-response links) can take place. He showed that when a neutral stimulus is repeatedly paired with another stimulus (unconditioned stimulus, UCS) that already elicits a given response (unconditioned response, UCR), the neutral stimulus (conditioned stimulus, CS) will become connected with that response (now termed the conditioned response, CR) and become capable of eliciting the response on its own. This model of learning, called classical conditioning, is diagrammed in Figure 18–1.

Using variations of this basic experiment, Pavlov made some fundamental behavioral discoveries. Each pairing of the CS and UCS was called a *trial*; and, generally speaking, the more trials, the stronger the association. The recorded weakening of the new CS–CR bond when the tone was no longer followed by food demonstrated a process called *extinction*. But even after the CR was extinguished, Pavlov found that, days later, a rested animal again presented only with the tone would begin to salivate. This recurrence of the CR after extinction is referred to as *spontaneous recovery*. Initially, the animal might respond to any tone, no matter what the pitch. This responding to any and all similar stimuli is called *stimulus generalization*. By hearing different pitched tones, an animal could learn, under proper training, that only one tone would be followed by food, and would learn to salivate to only that tone. This ability to distinguish between stimuli is called *stimulus discrimination*.

Operant Conditioning

Classical conditioning is helpful in explaining how an existing response (such as salivation) can come under the control of a new stimulus (such as a tone), but it tells us nothing about how new behaviors or habits are learned. For example, what unconditioned stimulus is needed to induce a rat to run a maze? Or to teach a bear to ride a motorcycle in the circus? Whereas Pavlov's paradigm occurred with a passive subject (the dog) from which an involuntary autonomic nervous system response was obtained, most actions in life involve an active organism emitting voluntary responses (without any identifiable controlling stimulus) that are followed by consequences. The process of learning brought about by a reinforcing stimulus or consequence following a response is called *operant conditioning*.

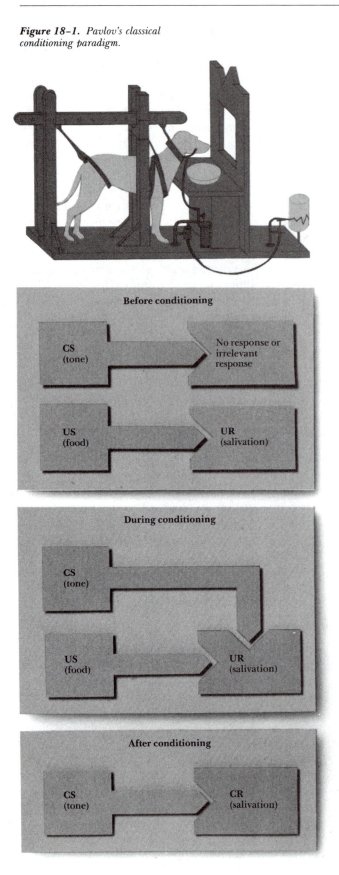

Figure 18–1. Pavlov's classical conditioning paradigm.

Before conditioning

CS (tone) → No response or irrelevant response

US (food) → UR (salivation)

During conditioning

CS (tone)

US (food) → UR (salivation)

After conditioning

CS (tone) → CR (salivation)

Edward R. Thorndike's (1911) *law of effect* was the starting point for B. F. Skinner's development of operant conditioning. The law of effect states

that behavior is a function of its consequences. *Reinforcement* is any stimulus that increases the probability of the recurrence of a response that it follows. A *positive reinforcer* is any stimulus that, by its *presence*, increases the probability of the recurrence of a response. A *negative reinforcer* is anything that, by its *absence*, increases the probability of the recurrence of a response. Giving a child a piece of cake (positive reinforcer) for finishing dinner increases the probability of his finishing dinner the next time. If Mr. Smith stays home, his wife nags him. If he goes out, he escapes the nagging. Therefore, his "going out" behavior is strengthened by the absence of the nagging (a negative reinforcer).

Some inherently desirable stimuli are naturally reinforcing and do not have to be learned. Such *primary reinforcers* include food, water, and sex. Other stimuli are not in themselves reinforcing but have become learned reinforcers for us. Money has no natural inherent reinforcing value, but it can buy things that have reinforcing value. Therefore, money is a learned, or *secondary reinforcer*.

To help control stimulus-response contingencies, Skinner devised an experimental "box" that has come to be associated with his name. The *Skinner box* is a small animal cage with a lever or pecking disk on the inside that, when depressed by the animal, dispenses food. The Skinner box creates an easily measured dependent variable that is usually automatically recorded: the number of presses. The box is usually equipped with a small light located close to the lever or disk. Independent variables that can be manipulated by the experimenter might include the type of food (reinforcer), the time interval between pressing and the dispensing of the food, the hours of food deprivation in the animal before the trial, the type of animal, or the schedule of reinforcement (the interval or number of responses preceding reinforcement). In a typical operant conditioning experiment, the experimenter waits for the desired behavior to occur spontaneously, immediately after which the animal receives reinforcement. After this procedure is repeated many times, the frequency of the recurrence of the desired behavior will have significantly increased over its preexperiment base rate.

SHAPING An important behavioral concept demonstrated in Skinner's work is *response discrimination*, more popularly known as *shaping*. If a rat is placed in a Skinner box, some time may elapse before the rat presses the bar and is rewarded. The experimenter may choose to save some time and "shape" the rat's behavior by trying to break down the lever-pressing behavior into its component parts and reinforcing successive approximations that resemble the desired behavior. For example, if the experimenter wishes to have a rat press a lever with its left front paw only when a red light is on, he may first reward any movement that the rat makes *toward* the bar. As the rat begins to spend more time near the bar, the animal may next be rewarded if he stops *in front of* the bar. The next step might reward the rat when it accidentally hits the bar with any leg. When the rat begins to hit the bar in many different ways, it is rewarded each time. Then the experimenter may decide only to reinforce the rat for pressing the bar with its front paws. Once that response is established, the experimenter may decide to reinforce only *left paw* pushes. Finally, left paw pushes might be rewarded only *when the red signal light above the bar is lit*. A great deal of learning has taken place—complex learning that could not have occurred within the context of a classical conditioning model.

MODELS The establishment and maintenance of connections between stimuli and responses can be made in several different ways depending on how reinforcers are dispensed (Ferster and Skinner 1957). These various methods, or models, can help one analyze a given situation and thus can have therapeutic implications. The simplest is the *reward model*, whose goal is to strengthen behavior. For the rat in the Skinner box, the lever-pressing response is followed by the presentation of a reward, food, which makes the rat more likely to press the lever in the future. The child who finishes his dinner to receive his cake is another example of the reward model.

A second model aimed at strengthening behavior employs a negative reinforcer. If a rat is placed in a Skinner box where the floor is electrified, and if, when the rat presses the lever, the shock stops, then the termination of the shock is said to be a negative reinforcer. A model that uses a negative reinforcer is called an *escape model*. The husband who avoids the company of his nagging wife is another example of the escape model.

A third model of operant conditioning is the *avoidance model*, in which a response by the organism can prevent the presentation of a negative event. For example, a rat that is given 10 seconds to press a lever and prevent 30 seconds of shock will quickly learn to push that lever. A diabetic who takes insulin is also demonstrating a learned avoidance behavior.

A fourth model is *punishment*, in which the goal is not to strengthen a response but to suppress one already in existence. If a rat that seems to enjoy exercising in its running wheel is shocked every time it enters the wheel, the rat will eventually be less likely to enter it. For the behavioral therapist, the punishment paradigm is generally the last re-

---

BEHAVIORAL TERMINOLOGY

- *Stimulus.* An internal or external event
- *Response.* An internal or external reaction to stimulus
- *Unconditioned response.* A reflexive, unlearned response
- *Conditioned response.* A learned response
- *Conditioned stimulus.* An internal or external event that is the result of learning
- *Extinction.* The abolition of a given behavior
- *Spontaneous recovery.* The recurrence of a response after it has been extinguished
- *Stimulus generalization.* The same response to similar stimuli
- *Discrimination.* The ability to distinguish among stimuli
- *Positive reinforcer.* A stimulus whose presence increases the probability of the recurrence of a behavior
- *Negative reinforcer.* A stimulus whose absence increases the probability of the recurrence of a behavior
- *Primary reinforcer.* An unlearned, naturally occurring reinforcer
- *Punishment.* An undesirable reinforcement given to suppress a behavior

---

sort considered in trying to change a behavior. Aside from being unpleasant for the client, the procedure has certain drawbacks: The behavior is only suppressed, not extinguished, and often it is only suppressed in the presence of the punishing agent. Too severe a punishment can create a need for revenge on the part of the recipient. These are two important aspects of punishment of which every parent should be aware.

BEHAVIOR MODIFICATION TECHNIQUES

Arnold Lazarus (1967), a behavioral researcher and therapist, has promoted what he terms a "broad spectrum" behavioral approach to therapy. This broad spectrum is an eclectic and pragmatic approach to helping people change their behaviors with whatever means produces the desired result.

Concepts such as insight, rapport, and interpretation are important in certain situations, and they should not be excluded simply because they do not fit neatly into a behavioral paradigm. But the broad spectrum behavioral therapist has access to a broad repertoire of clinical tools that includes behavioral techniques in addition to traditional techniques.

The behavioral point of view itself can be a useful tool in assessing a person's problems. Sometimes a client can overwhelm a caregiver with difficulties, and no behavior modification technique appears to be immediately appropriate or applicable. How can a therapist begin to understand the problems, let alone select a treatment technique? If the therapist thinks in terms of maladaptive learned responses, the reinforcers that are holding them in place, and the appropriate behaviors that could take the place of the inappropriate ones, then a useful framework is available to conceptualize the problem. Frequently, therapeutic strategies (behavioral or otherwise) will become apparent from such an analysis.

With the behavioral perspective in mind, it becomes possible to understand and explain three major types of behavior modification: systematic desensitization (counterconditioning), aversion therapy, and general operant procedures.

Systematic Desensitization

In the 1950s, Joseph Wolpe devised a technique specifically for treating what may be the most common neurotic symptom: *maladaptive anxiety*, in which an inappropriate connection has been learned between a stimulus and anxiety. The therapist's task is to break that connection. One possibility is extinction; that is, helping the client face the anxiety-producing stimulus. If no terrible consequence were to follow, the anxiety response would weaken and eventually disappear. Although extinction paradigms might work on people with low to moderate levels of anxiety, a person troubled enough to seek therapy is unlikely to stay in the presence of a feared object long enough for extinction to occur.

Wolpe (1958) believed the way to treat such a conditioned fear is through *counterconditioning*, or associating a new, antagonistic response to take the place of the anxiety response (see Figure 18–2). This new response would inhibit the anxiety response (the principle of *reciprocal inhibition*) and weaken it. Counterconditioning has the added benefit of reducing the client's avoidance behaviors toward the feared object. It increases the likelihood of her coming into contact with the object without negative consequences and thus facilitates extinction.

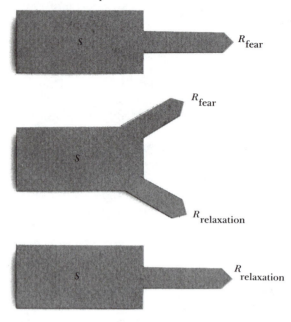

Figure 18–2. In counterconditioning, a fear response to a stimulus is replaced with a relaxation response.

Wolpe adopted Jacobson's (1938) deep muscle relaxation procedure because he believed the relaxation response is incompatible with anxiety. By having a client systematically tighten and loosen the various muscle groups in his body, the physiological and muscular components of anxiety could be decreased. Wolpe found that after a couple of weeks of practice, a client became capable of relaxing deeply in a very short period of time. Wolpe found that other counterconditioning responses could be used as well. For example, a young retarded woman who had difficulty learning the relaxation response was scheduled for therapy at noon and was asked to bring her favorite lunch to the session. Food was used as a primary reinforcer. The therapist had her think of anxiety-arousing situations while she was experiencing the pleasant sensations associated with eating.

In vivo desensitization is possible (using the feared object itself as the stimulus during treatment), but it can be difficult to control and is often overwhelming for the client. Therefore, Wolpe asked his clients to imagine scenes involving the feared object and to arrange these scenes from the least anxiety-provoking to the most (in a *hierarchy* of anxiety). An important behavioral rationale is at work here. Attacking the most feared scene first would be impossible, but starting with a low-anxiety scene increases the chances that the strong relaxation response will replace the anxiety. Working up the ladder step by step is a form of shaping.

Success at the lower levels of the hierarchy tends to generalize, making success at the higher levels more likely.

Once the client has acquired the learned relaxation response and has described the hierarchy, the desensitization procedure begins. The client is asked to relax and is given a few minutes to do so. The first item from the hierarchy is read, and the client is asked to imagine the scene and to signal the therapist when she begins to feel anxious. At that point, the client is told to wipe the scene from her mind and to take a minute or so to get relaxed again. The same item is presented until two trials can occur (perhaps 60 seconds and 90 seconds, although timing is optional) without the client's signaling that the scene is producing anxiety. At this point, the therapist moves on to the next item of the hierarchy, repeats the procedure for two successive successful trials, and then continues up the ladder until the hierarchy is completed.

The extinction paradigm for anxiety, or *implosion therapy*, is a technique by which the client is graphically talked through his hierarchy of anxiety-provoking stimuli, literally bombarded with scenes involving the feared object (Stampfl and Lewis 1967). As the client relives the anxiety-producing scenes in his imagination, the therapist attempts to extinguish the future influence of the material over the client's behavior and feelings and to replace previous avoidance responses with more appropriate responses. Implosion presents more risk and discomfort to the client than does desensitization, especially when severe anxiety is present, but it may be quicker than systematic desensitization and a quite effective method for mild or moderate anxieties. It should not be used with clients who have a history of depression or attempted by a therapist inexperienced with the technique.

Aversion Techniques

The goal of *aversion therapy* is to suppress an undesirable response by using escape-avoidance paradigms to train the client in a new response. It is used most commonly to treat problems such as alcoholism and sexual deviance—behaviors the client finds undesirable but, at the same time, reinforcing. The alcoholic with three DWIs (driving while intoxicated) who has lost his job and family may see the destructiveness of his behavior, but the immediate gratification that accompanies alcohol is a strong reinforcer for his alcoholic behavior pattern. Likewise, the man with a shoe fetish may be appalled by it, but when the sight of six-inch spiked heels is followed by the primary reinforcement of sexual arousal, the result is a strong habit formation and maintenance.

Aversion therapy may be seen in one of two ways: as an attempt to associate an undesirable behavior pattern with unpleasant stimulation (the classical conditioning model) or as an attempt to establish the expectation of an unpleasant stimulus as a consequence of undesirable behavior (operant conditioning). Drugs, shock, and learned nausea (taught much as relaxation training is taught) are three possible ways of inducing unpleasant stimuli in conjunction with inappropriate behavior.

Overt sensitization is the use of naturally noxious stimuli (such as shock or drugs) to weaken a response. An alcoholic is given an injection of a drug that produces nausea and vomiting. After the injection, she is shown pictures of alcohol as she begins to feel sick and vomits. After she vomits and begins to feel better, the pictures are removed. This classical conditioning paradigm is forming a new association between drinking (a conditioned stimulus) and the nausea and vomiting (the conditioned response).

Disulfiram (Antabuse) is a drug that induces respiratory distress and gastrointestinal response in the person who drinks after taking it. The alcohol is followed not by the usual high but by a very punishing experience. The aim is to weaken the old stimulus-response bond. Unfortunately, most alcoholics are wise enough to stop taking the Antabuse pills a few days before they drink. If they stay on the drug, however, they experience an avoidance paradigm: the "not drinking" response is followed by the prevention of a negative experience and is therefore strengthened. Giving alcoholics a mild electrical shock when they reach for a drink is also an attempt to punish their response to alcohol and weaken it.

Covert sensitization produces an aversion response indirectly with imagery rather than directly with pain or nausea. A man with homosexual tendencies who wishes to be heterosexual in his behavior might use covert sensitization as part of his treatment (Gold and Neufeld 1965). With training, a person can be taught to produce a mild feeling of nausea without the aid of chemicals in response to undesirable behavior. The advantage of this response is that it is directly under the client's control. The technique can be taken out of the therapy session and into the real world.

With covert sensitization the client would also be taught the relaxation response and be asked to produce a hierarchy. For example, the client could be given a set of pictures showing males in different stages of undress. He would be asked to select ten to fifteen pictures and arrange them in order from least sexually arousing to most. Once the hierarchy is set and the client has mastered the relaxation and nausea responses, the covert sensitization procedure can be begun.

In the case of the homosexual client, he first would be told to get himself relaxed. Then he would be instructed that, upon opening his eyes, he would see the first picture from his hierarchy. He would be told to signal the therapist as soon as he feels sexually attracted to the picture. At that point, the nausea response would be induced for 10 to 15 seconds in the presence of the picture. Then the picture would be withdrawn and the client would be told to take a few seconds to get relaxed again. After he completed two trials without indicating feelings of sexual attraction, the next picture would be shown, and so on, up the hierarchy. Upon conclusion of the procedure, the attraction to males should be weakened by the association of the unpleasant stimulus with the once arousing stimuli.

This procedure would be only *one part* of a total treatment program for such a client. Inquiry might reveal that the man is anxious around females. In that case, desensitization to females might also be in order. A client might also lack appropriate behaviors necessary to interact successfully with women. Failure to interact would punish him for attempting new heterosexual behaviors, and he might revert to his old homosexual patterns. Therefore, role playing and assertion training would be used to help him acquire the new behaviors necessary for success with women.

Another approach might be shaping, or breaking down complex behaviors to smaller components, with appropriate reinforcement at each step to encourage generalization and to make the next step easier. For example, a young man with a history of homosexual inclinations and experiences who wants to be heterosexual might express early in therapy that he would like to test his new inclinations upon completion of therapy by going to a prostitute. Such an encounter would put him at the top of his hierarchy of anxiety-provoking heterosexual interactions (the most anxiety-producing), where his likelihood of success would be the lowest. Instead, he should be taught the smaller steps along the way to intercourse: how to ask a woman out on a date, what to talk about, how to hold hands, and how to kiss her goodnight. Success at each of these levels would be more likely to get him to the top of his hierarchy without major setbacks.

Operant Techniques

Techniques based on principles of reinforcement include time out (an extinction paradigm), assertion training (a complex process involving role playing, modeling, feedback, and other social reinforcers), and token economics (a reward paradigm that often produces dramatic results in chronic psychiatric clients).

TIME OUT A good example of how inappropriate behavior is learned and how it can be analyzed behaviorally is a three-year-old's temper tantrum. Suppose Bill, a ten-year-old, has been watching television when his three-year-old brother, Erik, comes in and wants to turn the channel to watch cartoons. Dad is in the kitchen trying to prepare supper and entertain the baby. Suddenly, he hears Erik screaming and kicking. Bill runs into the kitchen and tells Dad that Erik is throwing a tantrum. He tells Bill to go back and watch his program and to ignore his brother.

Fifteen minutes later, Erik is still screaming; Bill is yelling at his brother because he can't hear his show; supper is burning; the baby has joined in the hysteria; and Dad feels a migraine on the way. Finally, out of desperation, he tells Bill to let Erik change the channel. Bill goes off to his room and closes the door; Erik is quiet now that he has gotten his way; the baby settles down; and, finally, there is peace and quiet. What has this experience taught the participants?

1. Erik has found a behavior (or behavior pattern) that works for him. The tantrum was rewarded, so he is more likely to throw a tantrum the next time he desires something.

2. Dad has learned that giving in to the tantrum is followed by a pleasant event: peace and quiet. So he is also more likely to give in when Erik acts up again.

3. Bill learned that telling Dad didn't solve his problem, so next time he may try something else, such as hitting his brother or throwing a tantrum of his own.

A better solution to the tantrum would have been to isolate Erik in another room until he remained silent for a few minutes. This isolation procedure is called "time out," meaning "time out from reinforcement" (Ferster 1958). What is the reinforcement Erik is being denied by isolation? *Feedback*, for one. Watching Dad, brother, and the baby getting agitated during a tantrum is reinforcing because it is a sign that the behavior is working. During time out he is denied this reinforcement and also the reinforcement of interacting with other people and of moving freely.

Once begun, time out must be followed through to completion. If, after thirty minutes, Erik is still having a tantrum in isolation, and Dad gives in, he will have learned something worse than before: if he keeps a tantrum up long enough, it will eventually work. He must learn that it doesn't *ever* work. Also, the good behavior modifier (in this case, the father) should think in terms of reinforcing *competing* responses. If Erik does *not* cause a scene, this competing behavior should be reinforced with praise or a promise to have his turn watching the TV in a half hour. This kind of positive approach, in conjunction with time out, will be doubly effective.

ASSERTION TRAINING *Assertion training*, or teaching people how to stand up for their rights in ways that do not violate the rights of others, is another operant technique. Unassertive people tend to feel taken advantage of by others. They can't say no when they want to, and they tend to avoid people and potentially conflicting circumstances as a defense. Assertion training is aimed at teaching such persons the behavioral repertoire needed to successfully interact with others.

Assertion training is generally taught in two parts: relaxation training and role playing. For example, if Mary knows exactly how to say no to sex with her boyfriend but is too anxious at the time to get the words out, she may end up doing something she doesn't want to do. Relaxation training alone may be enough to help her control her anxiety (if it is mild or moderate) so that she can assert herself. If her anxiety level is high in such situations, desensitization might be a necessary adjunct to therapy.

Role playing might also be employed in Mary's case. The therapist could act as a high-pressure salesman to whom Mary is trying to say no. If role playing is conducted in a group (as is usually the case), Mary could get *feedback* (social reinforcement) from other members on her performance. She would be encouraged to practice both in the group and outside of it, but in a controlled way, saying no in low-level anxiety situations first and then working her way up to highly anxiety-provoking situations with her boyfriend. This shaping procedure increases the likelihood of success, and the generalization effect and history of reinforcements will make each step easier.

TOKEN ECONOMIES *Token economies* are operant programs that have produced dramatic successes with long-term inpatient psychiatric clients (Ayllon and Azrin 1968). *Tokens* are secondary reinforcers that are given to a client contingent on his performing certain desired behaviors. The tokens can be exchanged for food, snacks, library time, or any other reinforcers. One key to success is finding something that is reinforcing for a given client. One person might do anything for a candy bar; for another, 15 minutes alone might be highly valued. A second factor important to success is total staff cooperation. Each person interacting with the client must understand what the targeted behavior is, what reinforcers are being used, how and when they are being administered, and what the details of the treatment program are. If the goal is to get Mr. Smith to make his bed, a plan must be devised and understood by the whole staff so appropriate and timely reinforcement can be made. The first week, for example, the goal must be set low enough so that Mr. Smith will be reinforced and get a "taste" of success. Aside from leaving his bed unmade, Mr. Smith also throws his pillow around, so the contingency of reinforcement for the first week might be a token every day the morning nurse comes in and finds the pillow anywhere on the bed. After that behavior is occurring consistently, the program changes as the shaping procedure continues: the pillow must be at the head of the bed for Mr. Smith to receive the token. The next step might be to have Mr. Smith pull up the sheet and blanket, and so on. As each step becomes more demanding, manipulations can also be made with the tokens: more or less can be given at each occasion, and they can buy more or less as time goes by. Initially, every appropriate behavior should be promptly rewarded with a token that is immediately redeemable for the backup reinforcers. A variable ratio schedule (rewarding him only occasionally for making the bed) might later be introduced to encourage the long-term performance of the new behavior.

Stickers are a good reinforcer for children. Toilet training a child, for example, can be made a lot easier by thinking operantly and using shaping and reinforcing behaviors. A parent might start by giving the child a sticker for every time she asks to sit on the potty. After that behavior becomes common, a sticker might be awarded only if she urinates in the potty, and two stickers if she has a bowel movement in the potty. An additional sticker might be awarded if her pants are dry when she asks to use the potty. Then, a sticker might be awarded only every couple of times or every day she remains dry. The behavioral framework can help a parent (or therapist) attack almost any behavioral problem.

One complaint leveled against the use of stickers or other such secondary reinforcers is that they are bribes and that desirable behavior cannot and should not depend on bribes indefinitely. The behavior modifier responds with this advice: giving the sticker, candy, or token should be accompanied by social reinforcement. In the case of the child, the parent should tell her how proud he is of her.

"Bribes" can help shape an appropriate behavior into existence. Backup up such "artificial" reinforcers with social reinforcement makes them less important to the maintenance of the behavior. They can eventually be phased out, and the appropriate behavior can continue to be reinforced solely by praise or other signs of approval.

SOCIAL SKILLS TRAINING A large proportion of psychiatric outpatients suffer from social skills problems and associated anxiety. Social Skills Training (SST) is an approach that has recently evolved for treating such difficulties. This technique involves teaching clients new forms of social behavior by rehearsal of such behavior during sessions and by performance of appropriate social tasks, or "targets," between sessions.

Brady (1984) discussed the implications of this treatment for clients with chronic schizophrenia. Social skills deficits in hospitalized clients are usually severe and quite prevalent. The high recidivism rate of these clients is in part due to their lack of ability to interact appropriately with others. Various degrees of ineptness and isolation are common features of the promorbid adjustment of schizophrenic clients. The experience of severe and frightening perceptual distortions and cognitive dysfunctions impede the resocialization after the psychosis is resolved and the recovery of social skills is lost by lack of practice. The manner in which the social environment responds to the behavior of the psychotic client further shapes the behavior that may make the behavior even more alien. After long-term hospitalization, the client usually leaves with residual problems—depression, lack of motivation, and lingering cognitive deficits, which limit the capacity for relearning and maintenance of social skills.

The psychosocial and socioenvironmental programs which have demonstrated improvement in the posthospital course of schizophrenic clients have large social skills training components. Recognition of the pervasive nature of the limitations of these clients has resulted in the development of social skills training with broader elements that include learning other essential skills, such as personal hygiene, money management, selection and preparation of food, and use of community resources.

BASIC GUIDELINES FOR THE USE OF BEHAVIOR MODIFICATION

In setting up any behavioral treatment program, the behavior modifier prefers to use a *reward* paradigm whenever possible. Aversion techniques have a place only if a reward approach fails or is impractical. Using the toilet training example, the good behavior modifier thinks in terms of rewarding the correct toilet behavior, not of punishing the wetting or soiling. As mentioned earlier, punishment is not only unpleasant for the subject, but also it only suppresses, *not* extinguishes, a response. Suppression may occur only in the presence of the punisher (in this case, the parent). The punisher ends up associating himself and the whole toilet training experience with unpleasantness. Equally important, the suppression of an inappropriate response does not ensure the learning of a more appropriate response to take its place.

Sometimes a combination of reward and punishment can be helpful, however. The five-year-old who continually runs into the street without looking puts his life in danger, and a mild punishment (such as withdrawal of permission to play on the sidewalk) when he does so may be in order. But it makes a great deal of behavioral (and common) sense to show him the proper way to safely cross a street and to reinforce this appropriate behavior when it occurs. Suppressing the inappropriate response while at the same time rewarding the good one is a reasonable approach in such a case.

Since most therapists prefer reward over punishment, it stands to reason that desensitization is likely to be used more frequently than implosion for treating anxiety. In the case where implosion seems to be the treatment of choice, the procedure must be understood and agreed upon by the client in advance.

When speaking of punishment, an obvious ethical question arises: What right does a therapist have to shock a person or to induce physical illness? One must remember that aversion techniques are used with people (alcoholics, sexual deviants, homosexuals) who have shown little ability to change their behaviors with conventional treatment modalities. Such clients should be told that a technique is available that might help them but that it involves a low-level shock, a chemically induced reaction, or a self-induced discomfort response. It is important to explain the procedure, to ascertain whether the client understands what will happen to him, and to tell him that treatment can be terminated at any time he chooses. Given the strong positive reinforcement associated with the behaviors mentioned, the aversive approach may be the most appropriate means of changing them. Most behavior modifiers have no qualms about offering aversive therapy as a choice.

However, even in cases where aversive therapy is used, the therapist should employ more than just punishment, to increase the probability of success.

The therapist should verbally reinforce the client throughout treatment for her hard work and motivation. New behaviors should be shaped and reinforced to replace the suppressed ones. The client should become a partner with the therapist, making suggestions, constructing hierarchies, and doing homework.

The behavior modifier should also think like a scientist. A simple observation that a client seems to be doing better after a therapeutic intervention is no real proof of the intervention's effectiveness. Although one can't expect laboratory controls in the therapist's office, some care can be taken to objectively assess a program's effectiveness. In the case of the tantrum thrower, the first step should be to clearly define the problem behavior. His parents should be sent home to get a *base rate*, that is, to describe how often in a given time period (say two weeks) the child throws a tantrum. Time out can then be explained to the parents, and, as they implement it, they should continue to keep track of tantrums. Baseline data are vital to assess the effectiveness of the technique as time goes by. Charting progress can also be a real reinforcement to the parents, who can see actual reductions in the inappropriate behavior and are thus encouraged to continue behavior modification.

LIMITATIONS OF BEHAVIOR THERAPY

Dramatic results have been demonstrated in the shaping of behaviors with behavior modification in chronic psychotic clients confined to hospital wards. These techniques are no more a "cure" for psychosis than any other treatment approaches, but they have proven quite successful in helping to alter neurotic, anxiety-related behaviors. They are especially effective with simple phobias but less so with more complex problems, such as obsessive-compulsive disorder. They have made inroads in controlling serious behavior problems such as alcoholism and sexual deviations, with which most other treatment modalities have failed. Treatment programs based on behavioral principles have also been used successfully with problems as diverse as obesity, anorexia nervosa, stuttering, tics, enuresis and encopresis, delinquent behavior, and smoking.

The simpler the problem behavior involved, the more effective the behavioral technique is likely to be. Unfortunately, the complexities of human behavior are usually the results of years of reinforcement, multiple conditioning, and complex contingencies. Cognitive learning theorists hold that looking at stimulus-response connections is too simplistic. As Kanfer and Phillips (1970) have

stated, the human capacity for language and thought provides behavioral capacities to bypass simple conditioning arrangements. Researchers such as Julian Rotter (1954) have made important contributions by trying to apply learning theory to the complexities of human social behavior.

The good therapist knows that there is no specific behavioral technique that will prove effective with every problem behavior with which a client may present. Therefore, the therapist may choose to restrict services to a specific kind of clientele (such as phobics). Or, the therapist may adapt Lazarus's broad spectrum behavior therapy approach, using behavioral techniques where appropriate as well as giving support and developing the therapeutic relationship. This does not mean that the therapist should stop thinking behaviorally, only that she not be so naive as to believe that she has all the answers at her fingertips. Most practitioners would agree (some grudgingly) that rapport is still an important factor in therapy, that a good history is essential (especially a history of the problem behavior), and that an assessment of the client's behavioral strengths and weaknesses is invaluable.

IMPLICATIONS FOR NURSING

A broad-based behavioral model which incorporates the role and importance of cognitions and self-image can provide a conceptual framework for nursing practice. The behavioral model embodies the practices of careful observation and assessment, target seeking, treatment planning, outcome evaluation, and reformulation of plans. It offers a structure on which to build these treatment plans. A behavioral cognitive model offers an explanation of and a way of dealing with problems of everyday living. These problems can be seen in the context of disturbed behavior or as responses to occupational stress or bereavement. Cognitive behavioral approaches have been applied to the management of chronic pain. Adjustment to the disability of chronic illness may be enhanced by these strategies.

This model provides a structure on which to build a set of plans for action and it demands active involvement in decision making (Wilson 1986).

SUMMARY

Learning, or the acquisition of relatively permanent new behaviors, has become a central area in the study of psychology. The behaviorists have described the relationships between stimuli and

(Text continues on page 511.)

CLINICAL EXAMPLE

BEHAVIORAL THERAPY FOR A CLIENT WITH A PHOBIA

Jim Short is a 35-year-old who works for an engineering consulting firm and is advancing rapidly within the corporate structure. His latest promotion has placed him in a position that demands frequent travel, most of which must be done by air because of the distances involved. He is terrified of flying, specifically the take-off. Once airborne, he is able to relax, but during take-off he at times hyperventilates and occasionally loses consciousness, which causes him much embarrassment. He presented for therapy to help him overcome his fear of flying.

ASSESSMENT

The therapeutic interview showed an otherwise psychologically healthy man with a clear-cut, simple phobia. He functioned well in all other areas of his life, and his phobia was of limited proportions in that only one stimulus (take-off) elicited the anxiety response.

Nursing Diagnosis

Fear
(related to plane take-off)

Multiaxial Psychiatric Diagnoses

Axis I   300.29 Simple phobia
Axis II   None
Axis III None
Axis IV   None; no acute events or enduring circumstances that may be related to the disorder
Axis V   Current GAF: 80
          Highest GAF past year: 85

PLANNING

In collaboration with a behaviorally oriented clinician, plans were made to teach Jim the Jacobson relaxation technique with the following sequential hierarchy:

1. You look at your calendar and notice that you have an upcoming business trip for which you must fly to your destination.
2. You call the airlines and make your reservation.
3. You wake up and realize this is the day of the trip.
4. You get dressed and specifically pick out loose-fitting clothes so that you will not feel constricted on the trip.

5. You call a taxi and are on the way to the airport.
6. You get out in front of the airport at your designated airline.
7. You walk to the airline desk, check your luggage and obtain your boarding pass.
8. You walk through the metal detector device and proceed to your gate of departure.
9. You sit in the gate area, waiting for your flight to be called.
10. Your flight is called and you proceed through the gate and walk along the jetway.
11. You enter the plane and find your seat.
12. You put your briefcase under the seat.
13. You take your seat and fasten your seatbelt.
14. You read a magazine until the plane begins to taxi.
15. The plane taxis to the runway.
16. The plane waits for take-off.
17. The plane begins its acceleration and leaves the ground.
18. The plane reaches cruising altitude.

IMPLEMENTATION

Jim was seen twice a week during the desensitization stage, going through the hierarchy about three times a session. After approximately four weeks, the hierarchy was completed, and he felt confident about his ability to remain calm during take-off.

EVALUATION

Jim came back after his next business trip with a smile on his face. Although he didn't like the take-off, his maladaptive anxiety responses (the hyperventilation, excessive sweating, and avoidance responses) were gone.

Aspects of the feared stimuli had been paired with a response incompatible with anxiety. This weakened the maladaptive stimulus-response connection enough to allow Jim to approach the feared experience and to discover that it didn't have the punishing consequences that he had feared. This would make it easier for him the next time, and each successive trial without anxiety would continue to weaken the fear and maybe even make it disappear totally.

Nursing Diagnoses	Goal	Nursing Actions	Outcome Criteria	Outcome Evaluation
Fear	Client will be able to fly without symptoms of anxiety.	Teach relaxation techniques utilizing desensitization and sequential hierarchy.	Client will complete treatment and remain calm during take-off.	Client was able to experience take-off without maladaptive anxiety responses. Continued trials were expected to further weaken the fear.

responses and the principles that result in the acquisition, strengthening, or extinction of learned responses.

Ivan Pavlov demonstrated that if a conditioned stimulus (CS) is paired with an unconditioned stimulus (UCS), the CS will become capable of eliciting the response that was once under the control of the UCS. This model of learning has been called respondent, or classical, conditioning. It explains how autonomic nervous system responses become associated with different stimuli.

B. F. Skinner's operant conditioning model addresses the issue of how new behaviors are learned. According to Skinner, behavior is a function of its consequences, and reinforcement becomes the key to new stimulus-response bonds. Through his painstaking research and his emphasis on observation and experimental procedures, Skinner has amassed a wealth of data that demonstrate such concepts as extinction, generalization, spontaneous recovery, and schedules of reinforcement—concepts and principles that have applications to humans as well as to the animals used in psychological studies.

Behavior modification represents a collection of techniques that have some basis in laboratory study. The most commonly applied techniques include desensitization, aversion therapy, time out, assertion training, and token economics. These techniques are used in the real world by therapists of diverse backgrounds with different theoretical and philosophical orientations. They share a tendency to think in terms of reinforcements and contingencies, but they also generally realize that the complexities of human behavior defy simple applications of specific behavioral techniques in every circumstance.

Review Questions

1. Make a list of secondary reinforcers that operate daily in our lives and keep us doing the day-to-day tasks that must be done.

2. Explain why a reward paradigm is generally preferred to a punishment model in helping a person modify a behavior.

3. In systematic desensitization, why does the hierarchy begin with the least anxiety-provoking scene?

4. The parents of a ten-year-old have been using a "time out" procedure to suppress their son's habit of slapping his younger sister whenever he becomes angry. Although the slapping has dramatically decreased, they are concerned that their son has now become more withdrawn and apparently unhappy. What have they overlooked in their program?

5. Twelve-year-old Gina barely passed last semester. Her parents want her to do better this semester. Thinking in terms of shaping, what component parts make up "getting better grades," and how might these steps be reinforced along the way?

Suggested Annotated Readings

Barlow, D. H. *Behavioral Assessment of Adult Disorders.* New York: Guilford Press, 1981.

The purpose of this book is to provide up-to-date descriptions of assessment procedures and strategies for the most common adult clinical problems. It describes the relationship between behavioral assessment and the DSM-III, reviews strategies for behavioral assessment, and presents areas that should be assessed for selected problems.

Cull, J. G., and R. E. Hardy. *Behavior Modification in Rehabilitation Settings.* Springfield, Illinois: C. C. Thomas Pub., 1974.

This collection of papers considers the whole field of social and rehabilitation services as they are related to settings in which the magnitude of work is done in the field of rehabilitation. It explores basic concepts of behavior modification principles that are applied in rehabilitation work. Techniques for use in token economies, with the mentally retarded, disadvantaged, delinquent, mentally ill, and alcohol abusers are presented.

Lichstein, K. L. *Clinical Relaxation Strategies.* New York: John Wiley & Sons, 1988.

The purpose of this book is to organize a broad sampling of relaxation procedures to allow access to a variety of techniques. The integration of relaxation with other therapy techniques and systems is discussed as well as history, theory, basic and clinical outcome research.

Russell, M. L. *Behavioral Counseling in Medicine.* New York: Oxford University Press, 1986.

This book is written for allied health personnel who want to learn how to conduct health-related behavioral counseling with medical patients. The author aims to provide a basic understanding of this counseling process and present applications of behavioral counseling to specific health-related behavioral problems.

References

Ayllon, T., and H. Azrin. *Token Economy: A Motivational System for Therapy and Rehabilitation.* Englewood Cliffs, New Jersey: Prentice-Hall, 1968.

Brady, J. "Social Skills Training for Psychiatric Patients: Clinical Outcome Studies." *American Journal of Psychiatry* 141 (1984):491–497.

Ferster, C. B. "Withdrawal of Positive Reinforcement as Punishment." *Science* 126 (1958):509.

Ferster, C. B., and B. F. Skinner. *Schedules of Reinforcement.* New York: Appleton-Century-Crofts, 1957.

Franks, C. M., ed. *Behavior Therapy: Appraisal and Status.* New York: McGraw-Hill, 1969.

Gold, S., and I. Neufeld. "A Learning Theory Approach to the Treatment of Homosexuality." *Behavior Research and Theory* 2 (1965):201–204.

Jacobson, E. *Progressive Relaxation.* Chicago: University of Chicago Press, 1938.

Kanfer, F. H., and J. S. Phillips. *Learning Foundations of Behavior Therapy.* New York: John Wiley & Sons, 1970.

Lazarus, A. "In Support of Technical Eclecticism." *Psychological Reports* 21 (1967):415–416.

Pavlov, I. P. *Conditioned Reflexes.* London: Oxford University Press, 1927.

Rotter, J. B. *Social Learning and Clinical Psychology.* Englewood Cliffs, New Jersey: Prentice-Hall, 1954.

Skinner, B. F. *Beyond Freedom and Dignity.* New York: Random House, 1972.

Stampfl, T. G., and D. J. Lewis. "Essentials of Implosive Therapy: A Learning-Theory-Based Psychodynamic Behavior Therapy." *Journal of Abnormal Psychology* 72 (1967):496–503.

Thorndike, E. L. *Animal Intelligence.* New York: Macmillan, 1911.

Wilson, L. "A New Era?" *Nursing Times* 82 (January 1, 1986):48–49.

Wolpe, J. *Psychotherapy by Reciprocal Inhibition.* Stanford, California: Stanford University Press, 1958.

19

Family Guidelines in Nursing Practice

Learning Objectives

After reading this chapter, the student should be able to:

1. Explain the viewpoint that the dysfunction of an identified client *originates in* the family and is a symptom of family problems.

2. Describe major approaches in family theory and the significant concepts of each approach.

3. Identify and describe the following tools used in gathering and organizing family data: family mapping, family geneogram, family chronology, family sociogram.

4. Describe types of dysfunctional communication and explain the purposes they serve in family life.

5. Discuss the influence of role function and role expectations in traditional and nontraditional families.

6. Describe appropriate behaviors by nurses in an initial family meeting, in the working sessions, and in the termination sessions.

Overview

The family is the primary group in human life. It is the most influential group to which people belong. Whether we accept or reject family values and customs, we continue to feel their influence. The presence of family life shapes us from the moment of birth, just as an absence of family life also shapes us, since we must find other groups and other customs to fill the void in our lives. Family life has been studied in all its variations by many investigators representing various disciplines. Their findings are interesting but are sometimes contradictory and confusing. Family investigation methods and data are quite varied and inconclusive, so that it is almost impossible to do justice to all of them. Therefore, in this chapter certain concepts and principles are selected from the broad scope of family study. Although family study is often a means of understanding individual behavior, in this chapter it is the family unit that is the focus rather than individual members.

In discussing the family unit, theories are explained that are relevant for nurses applying family guidelines to their practice. To guide discussion in this chapter, we turn to an interrelated group of questions. First, does the family we are assessing interact in harmony or in conflict?

In other words, what is happening to make some families exist in a constant state of war, while others exist in peace? Second, why do some families manage to cope well under adverse conditions while other families cannot cope even under the most favorable conditions? In addition, why do some harmonious families seem incapable of making group decisions while other families that are always in conflict, nevertheless manage to reach a consensus on what should be done, and proceed to do it? Along the same line of inquiry, why do some quarrelsome families survive while apparently harmonious families are shattered by separation, divorce, or alienation?

These are complicated questions, and the answers are not immediately apparent. The search for answers is facilitated by the contributions of family theorists and clinicians whose work is described in this chapter. Family theory is based on the premise that the problems of a client usually originate in the operations and interactions of family life and reflect dysfunction within the family, of which the client's problems are merely a symptom. Family therapy carries this premise even further and is interested not only in the family *of* the client but in the family unit *as* the client (Carter and McGoldrick 1980).

HISTORICAL INFLUENCES

No family exists in isolation, for every family constantly interacts with larger social institutions (see Figure 19–1). The interactions are reciprocal; by this we mean that the family is both a cause and a consequence of social change. As society changes so do the structure and functions of the family unit. When economic, political, and religious conditions alter over time, so do the family arrangements that support them. In traditional, unchanging times, family roles and values tended to be fixed and constant. In a dynamic, nontraditional, pluralistic society family roles and values are constantly changing. At present in Western society there is no uniform pattern of family life to which everyone conforms. What has developed in this century is an assortment of patterns of family life that includes unbroken extended and nuclear families, single parent families, stepparent families, married and unmarried couples who may be heterosexual or homosexual but consider themselves to be authentic family units. There are many explanations for the vast changes that have taken place in family life. The women's movement, reliable contraception, permissive divorce laws, the secularization of society, and geographic and economic mobility are only a few of the social trends that have had notable impact on family life.

One of the most significant developments in modern families is the disappearance of the family as a working unit. At the present time it is the individual rather than the family that constitutes the work unit. Production and distribution are now in the hands of vast corporations far removed from families' everyday life. The geographic mobility of the work force exceeds anything previously known. Workers often commute many miles between home and job; others repeatedly relocate their families in regions far from cherished relatives and familiar places. The consequence of mobility is a loss of continuity and security. Lacking their usual supports, members of the nuclear family turn to one another for support. This creates a high level of intensity and emotional involvement in the family, as members rely on each other in unaccustomed ways. The intensity places a burden on some of the family members, particularly when unrealistic expectations are not met.

Two other family functions have changed, and that is control of sexuality and of reproduction, perhaps because the two are no longer interdependent. The long period of adolescence imposed on young people caused sexual frustration in times past, but this is less true today. Dependable contraception has weakened prohibitions against premarital and extramarital sex. Recently the spectre of AIDS has produced public demands for "safe" sex. It remains to be seen whether fear will permanently alter sex habits. If so, the long-term, monogamous pairing on which the nuclear family depends might be strengthened.

FAMILY COLLABORATION

Although many health care professionals allege that families should participate in the care of their members, many of them act in ways that make families feel like intruders. This habit of saying one thing and behaving in a contradictory way shuts client and staff off from possible sources of support. When families are treated like enemies by caregivers, they do not become allies. Even when families behave in a manner that is detrimental to the client, they are unlikely to change without guidance.

The most favorable opportunity to enlist a family's cooperation is at the time of a nurse's initial contact. This is the point at which family members

Figure 19–1. *Forces operating on families and members.*

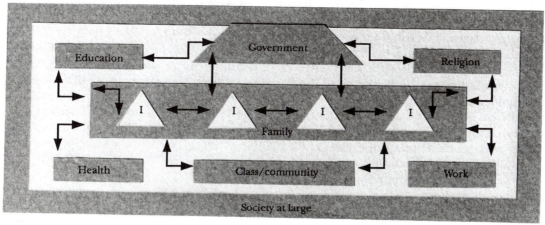

look for direction. The occasion might be hospitalization, admission to a nursing home, or the first clinic appointment. Even though they may be anxious or upset, the first visit is a time when families are receptive to expressions of caring and solicitude not only for the client but also for the entire family (Wright and Leahey 1984). Family interviewing and family assessment are within the ability of any nurse who has completed a basic program, provided the nurse has acquired necessary assessment and communication skills. This assumes that the nurse has sufficient knowledge of normal family development to recognize the presence of various factors. It also assumes that the nurse will not go beyond her own powers and will acknowledge family patterns that require the skills of a clinical nurse specialist or other health professional with graduate level preparation.

If a generalist nurse has the ability and experience to engage in family intervention in addition to assessment, the interventions should be relatively straightforward and uncomplicated, and should deal with social and environmental change rather than intrapersonal alteration. In 1978 the Department of Health, Education, and Welfare recognized the American Association for Marriage and Family Therapy as the accrediting body for family therapy programs. The National League for Nursing is the accrediting body for graduate nursing programs, most of which have a family theory and practice component. Certification programs related to psychiatric nursing require master's level preparation plus two years of clinical experience before nurses are considered to be advanced clinical specialists. Family therapy *per se* should be restricted to such nurses or to nurses working under the close supervision of a clinical specialist.

ORIGINS OF FAMILY THEORY AND THERAPY

During the 1950s, family theory was concerned primarily with interactional patterns in the families of schizophrenic clients, especially young persons with schizophrenia. There were a number of reasons for this interest. To begin with, these families offered an accessible laboratory for study and investigation. In addition, young clients with schizophrenia were usually at a developmental point where family factors contributing to dysfunction could be identified. Studying the families of these clients offered some possibility for primary prevention of schizophrenia in other families at risk and for promoting secondary and tertiary prevention in families already dealing with the disorder (Cohen, Younger, and Sullivan 1983). Family theory and fam-

ily therapy thus developed in tandem. Theoretical concepts were applied to clinical situations, and an innovative, significant treatment modality was born.

Although family theory and family therapy were initiated by clinicians working with psychiatric clients, many concepts derived from their work proved applicable to families without identified psychiatric disorders. Even in the absence of psychiatric illness, certain interactional patterns seem to differentiate functional from dysfunctional families.

The early family theorists believed that the family is a social unit in which all members interact with each other, and this belief has been supported by sustained observation. The interdependent, reciprocal quality of family life has led some theorists to claim that there is a cause-and-effect relationship between family interactional patterns and the dysfunction of the client. Other family theorists have asserted that family interactional patterns might increase a client's dysfunction without necessarily causing it.

No less a person than Florence Nightingale is among those who have attributed psychological distress to flawed family interaction. With her mother and sister united against her determination to lead a useful life, Nightingale wrote, "The family uses people, not for what they are, nor for what they are intended to be, but for what it wants them for—its own uses. It thinks of them not as God made them but as the something which it has arranged that they shall be. If it wants someone to sit in the drawing-room, then that someone is supplied by the family, though that member may be destined for science or for education . . . This system dooms some minds to incurable infancy" (Payne 1983).

Not all families attempt to frustrate the ambitions of nonconforming members, and such extreme bitterness is not characteristic of all rebellious members, particularly successful ones like Nightingale. Nevertheless, many family theorists, even those who do not accept causal connections between client dysfunction and family interaction, believe that family patterns often influence the development and the course of dysfunction in one or more members.

Family therapy may be offered in one of several ways, depending on the needs of the family, the availability of staff, the preferences of the therapists, and the policies of the agency where care is given. Table 19–1 indicates different forms of family therapy.

CONCEPTUAL APPROACHES

Family theory is relatively new, and many of the innovators in this area have worked independently

Table 19–1. Forms of Family Therapy	
Form of Therapy	**Characteristics of Therapy**
Conjoint family therapy	The family meets with one therapist or a pair of cotherapists. This is the most usual form of family therapy, especially for marital counseling or nuclear family meetings that include parents and children.
Multiple impact family therapy	The family or subgroups of the family meet with several therapists simultaneously or concurrently. In this form of family therapy the impact of treatment is increased by the teamwork of a group of therapists working with the family.
Network family therapy	A nuclear family is joined by the extended family group and by significant friends and neighbors to meet with a therapist or a pair of cotherapists. This form of therapy reduces the isolation of a small family unit and mobilizes a strong supportive network.
Multiple family therapy	A number of families meet together with one or two therapists. Families with common problems or shared interests profit from this form of therapy, in which group leadership tactics are used by the therapists.

of one another, which has led to a certain amount of conceptual confusion. This redundancy, added to the undeniable complexity of family life, makes the body of family knowledge seem formidable to beginners. One way to simplify the task of describing theories and concepts is to categorize them according to conceptual approach. Although such categorization may seem arbitrary, it does produce a degree of order out of disorder.

Specific conceptual approaches help the practitioner recognize and describe family structure and function. Having mastered basic family theories and concepts, a nurse should be able to assess obvious strengths and weaknesses in the family, to distinguish between functional and dysfunctional interactions, and to plan appropriate interventions. Initially, a nurse may prefer to rely on a single conceptual approach, gradually drawing on others as needed. Whether used in a pure or in an eclectic manner, a conceptual approach guides the selection and organization of observable data, thereby facilitating assessment of family dynamics.

Some conceptual approaches are more widely used than others, but most have a unique contribution to make to family theory. In this section, a number of different conceptual approaches will be described. As each approach is presented, representative theorists will be identified and their concepts will be explained in terms of family theory.

Developmental Concepts

The developmental approach views families from a life cycle perspective; families are seen as changing not only from day to day but also from year to year. An important contributor to family developmental theory was Evelyn Duvall (1977), who formulated an eight-stage model of the family life cycle, similar to the eight-stage model of individual development offered by Erikson (1963) (see Table 19–2). Duvall divided family development into two broad phases:

Table 19–2. Comparison of Duvall's Family Critical Tasks and Erikson's Individual Critical Tasks	
Family Stages and Critical Tasks	**Individual Critical Tasks**
Marital stage: Establishing a marriage	Trust versus mistrust
Childbearing stage: Adjusting to parenthood and maintaining a home	Autonomy versus shame and doubt
Preschool stage: Nurturing children	Initiative versus guilt
School-age stage: Socializing and educating children	Industry versus inferiority
Teenage stage: Balancing teenagers' freedom and responsibility	Identity versus role confusion
Launching stage: Releasing children as young adults; developing postparental interests	Intimacy versus isolation
Middle-aged stage: Reestablishing the marital dyad; maintaining links with older and younger generations	Generativity versus stagnation
Aging stage: Adjusting to retirement, aging, loneliness, and death	Ego integrity versus despair

SOURCE: Adapted from Duvall (1977) and Erikson (1963).

expanding family life and contracting family life. The expanding period lasts from the establishment of the marital dyad until the children are grown and launched. Contraction begins when the first child leaves home and ends with the death of the surviving spouse. Figure 19–2 illustrates the family life cycle formulated by Duvall.

By contrasting the eight stages of Duvall's family life cycle with the eight stages of Erikson's individual life cycle, it is possible to recognize hazards related to the negotiation of family and individual life cycle tasks. According to Erikson, each critical or developmental task is related to the preceding

Figure 19–2. *Phase, stages, and critical family life cycle tasks.*
SOURCE: Adapted from Duvall (1977).

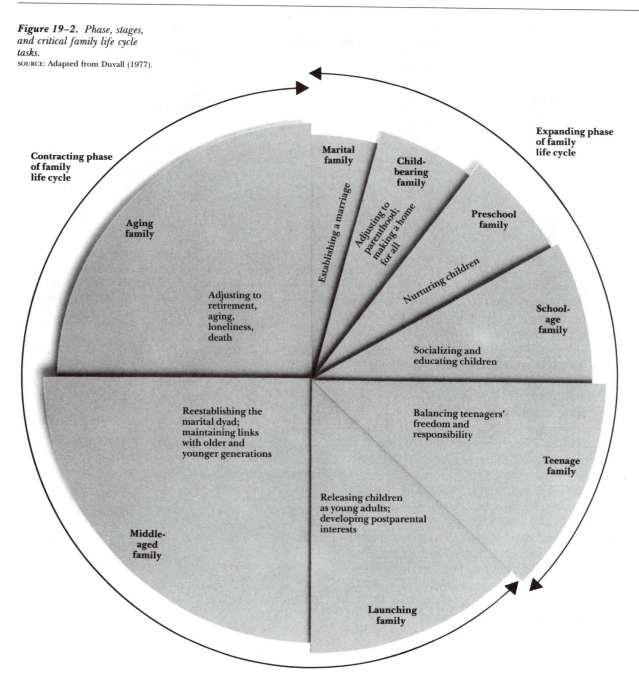

ones, and there is a time of "ascendance" during which a specific task can be performed most effectively. This time of ascendance is determined by the physiological maturation of the individual, by psychological impulses, and by cultural expectations.

Sometimes it is difficult for a family to integrate the individual tasks of all its members into the developmental scheme of family life. For example, the resolution of the identity crisis requires that an adolescent begin to separate from parental influence. This separation may take place at a rate unacceptable to parents who are unwilling or unready to exchange the characteristics of a teenage family for those of a launching family. Reluctance to move into the next stage of family life may also be apparent in the behavior of a couple moving uneasily from the relatively carefree activities of a marital dyad to the responsibilities of a childbearing family. Unless this couple can be assisted and reassured as they enter early parenthood, their young children may be impeded in moving toward trust and autonomy, the first two individual tasks in Erikson's life cycle model.

Ideally, the family adjusts to the changing needs of its members so that individual critical tasks may be resolved. In families that are inflexible, the needs and aspirations of individual members may meet with resistance because the family unit fails to advance to its next developmental stage. A nurse using the developmental approach to assess families begins by identifying the appropriate life cycle stage of the family as a whole and then notes the progress being made by individual members in achieving their critical tasks. If the attainment of individual tasks has been or is being impeded, it may be possible to recognize the source of the impediment and to assess the seriousness of the situation. Sometimes merely teaching families the importance of stage-appropriate developmental tasks is enough to reduce family resistance. At other times the nurse may decide not to intervene directly but to make a referral if conditions are serious enough to warrant extensive family therapy. In some instances a generalist nurse may remain involved with the family and work collaboratively with the family therapist.

Systems Theory Concepts

Von Bertalanffy (1974) described the family unit as a *system* whose components engage in mutual interactions according to rules and patterns developed over time so that the system may survive. As a system, the family is composed of separate but interdependent components separated from the external environment by *boundaries*. Boundaries are an indispensable part of family systems. They surround individual family members and groups or subsystems composed of family members, and they surround the entire family unit. Individual boundaries help family members maintain their separate identities, other boundaries determine who belongs to the family system, who is placed in family subsystems, and how and with whom various members may interact inside and outside the family unit.

Depending on the characteristics of its boundaries, a family system may be totally open, totally closed, or somewhere in between. Energy, in the form of tension within the system, preserves the interdependence of the components. All families, functional or dysfunctional, contain a certain amount of tension generated by the emotional connections among members. Although excessive tension may cause strain on the system, a family without tension would cease to be a viable system.

BOUNDARIES In order to accomplish their life cycle tasks families need a degree of stability, or *homeostasis*. Homeostasis is a state of balance that maintains family stability but also permits families to change in response to internal and external conditions. Stability should not be confused with stagnation, for a capacity of families to adapt to changing

circumstances is essential to their survival (Kraft and DeMaio 1982). For example, the adaptation of families in a launching stage is unlike that of families in earlier stages. Launching-stage families must deal with separation issues; earlier stage families must deal with nurturing children and integrating them into family life.

Boundaries enable families to regulate the amount of input or feedback into the family from external sources. Family systems whose boundaries are partially open and penetrable have the best chance of remaining functional. Such systems are capable of responding to input from their external surroundings and can discharge internal tension across their boundaries in the form of output. In closed systems there is little likelihood of discharging tension except on other family members. This behavior results in rising internal tension that increases the dysfunction of the system.

The concept of family boundaries may be used by nurses to assess and diagnose some forms of family dysfunction. Family boundaries that are too easily penetrated threaten family equilibrium by fostering a climate of instability. An example of family boundaries that are too open occurs in some upwardly mobile families who hastily discard old customs in order to imitate the behaviors of a higher socioeconomic group regardless of their relevance or appropriateness. On the other hand, family boundaries that cannot be penetrated prevent the transmission of input from outside that might improve the family's ability to cope. An example of close or impenetrable boundaries is seen in some immigrant families in which parents resist the influence of the mainstream culture and try to preserve accustomed values despite opposition from their children.

Awareness of family boundaries helps nurses understand puzzling family behaviors and the origin of certain types of conflict. Family growth can be promoted by helping families maintain protective but penetrable boundaries. Functional families can adjust to changing conditions within the system and in the outside environment. Dysfunctional families, on the other hand, tend to oppose change and growth in their members. In dysfunctional families, inflexible rules are used to maintain the status quo, regardless of the cost to individual members.

FEEDBACK *Feedback* is an important concept in systems theory. By means of feedback the family transmits output to the environment in the form of emotional and behavioral responses. The surrounding environment, in the form of neighborhood, church, or school, reacts by sending responses (input) to the
(Text continues on page 521.)

CLINICAL VIGNETTE

PROBLEM SOLVING IN AN EXPANDING FAMILY

Kay Lockwood was a healthy 25-year-old woman, married to Don and the mother of two girls, one aged 3 years and the other aged 20 months. The deliveries of the two girls were simple and uncomplicated. Kay was a farm girl, the oldest of four sisters. Before her marriage she attended college for two years with the intention of becoming a teacher. Leaving college to marry Don, she was happy fulfilling the roles of wife and mother. The Lockwoods recently learned that Kay was pregnant with twins; the delivery date was about six months in the future. The disclosure that she was to have twins explained Kay's rapid weight gain and reduced her fears that there was something wrong with her pregnancy. It also meant that the family faced some unexpected problems.

Don Lockwood was a self-employed farmer who enjoyed excellent health. Working with his two brothers, he operated the family farm and managed a profitable farm produce business. Don's father was deceased; his mother was living but was engrossed in caring for Don's two sisters, both of whom had Down's syndrome. The disability of Don's sisters worried him and Kay before their little girls were born, but genetic testing before birth showed that their children were normal. Similar testing was scheduled for Kay in this pregnancy, but the couple still found it hard to deal with the issue of abortion if a genetic defect was found.

Don and Kay found it fairly easy to accept the prospect of a larger family although the pregnancy was unplanned. However, both of them realized that Don considered himself responsible for helping his mother and sisters, even though his brothers shared this commitment with Don. Recently Don and Kay had purchased an old house and moved it to the family acreage. Money had been put aside to renovate the house without taking into account a rapidly expanding family.

Kay was upset and worried about her ability to carry twins to term, especially if she had to spend much time in bed. She knew from conversations with her physician that this was a possibility in the last weeks of her pregnancy. She also worried about continuing to give her little girls the attention they needed. Don was a devoted family man, but Kay wondered what impact her pregnancy would have on their relationship. She was not sure that she could meet all the demands that soon would be made on her. She was concerned about coping after the twins arrived and about managing the household.

The rural visiting nurse was referred by the family physician, and began discussion of how the family would cope with the arrival of twins in terms of available time, space, and money. Much of the discussion was tentative. For example, could plans for renovating the house be adapted to accommodate the new family members? What was the possibility of obtaining a mother's helper before and after delivery? Would it be possible to enroll the oldest child in a nursery school two or three mornings a week? What arrangements could be made so that Kay and Don would have some time to themselves? Beyond discussing future arrangements, the nurse reinforced Kay's need for prenatal care and for frequent contact with her obstetrician.

With encouragement from her husband and the nurse, Kay began setting priorities for herself. She spent less time with housekeeping tasks in order to concentrate on taking care of herself while meeting the needs of her young daughters. A part-time housekeeper was found to help with heavy cleaning. Plans for remodeling the house were changed so that the basement became a laundry room and spacious play area for the children. The room previously planned as a playroom became a den/bedroom for Don and Kay. A young woman from Ireland was found who was willing to live in as a mother's helper for a year. The older daughter was enrolled in a nursery school. This helped Kay realize that family life was not static, and that children soon grew up enough to move gradually into the world. Don expressed concern about draining the family's nest egg, but as Kay pointed out, they were spending the nest egg on their nest. Don was confident, on the whole, of his ability to continue helping his mother while providing for Kay and his children. "We've changed some of our plans, but I expect to have a good growing season. Kay and I are used to large families so we'll manage," he said. Don's cooperation in making plans for the future and his devotion to family values was crucial to Kay's equilibrium. Their discussions and adjustments added a new dimension to their relationship.

environment they inhabit. By analysis and feedback nurses can identify the characteristics of family boundaries and, if necessary, work to increase a family's awareness of their actions and of community norms. When input from the community indicates that a family should modify its behavior, the community feedback is negative. When input from the community indicates that the family should continue its present behavior, the feedback is positive. Whether positive or negative, feedback is helpful in promoting adaptive family functioning. Figure 19–3 shows circular feedback.

An advantage of using a system theory approach to family assessment and intervention is the avoidance of heaping blame on one or another of the family members. If the family is perceived as a system in which parents, children, extended family members, and the community influence one another reciprocally, then interactions become a shared responsibility. Systems theorists contend

Figure 19–3. *Circular feedback. The action of A influences the actions of B and C, who then interact with each other and with A, who initiated the circular feedback.*

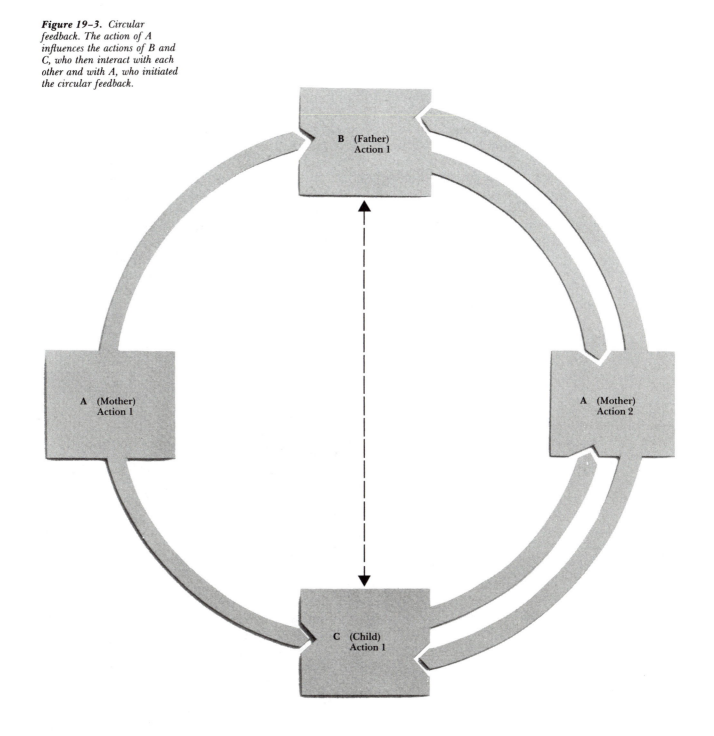

that alterations in one part of the family inevitably lead to alterations in other parts of the family. Health care professionals who adopt a systems approach tend to see family strengths as well as weaknesses. They try to reinforce the confidence and competence of family members, especially the parents, so that they can learn to provide an internal climate in which everyone can flourish without exploiting individuals or subgroups in the system (Collins 1984).

EFFECTS OF DIVORCE The effect of divorce on children has been studied extensively (O'Leary and Emery 1984, Wallerstein and Kelly 1980, Heckerton, Cox, and Cox 1985). Many investigators have proposed that sons are more adversely affected by parental divorce than are daughters but this is not uniformly substantiated by research of gender differences in children's reactions to parental divorce. Zaslow (1989) rejected a global view of gender differences and suggested that boys do not always respond more negatively. In some circumstances girls may respond more negatively, although their responses differ from those of boys. Emery, Heckerton, and Di Lalla (1985) differentiated "externalizing" reactions that are more prevalent in boys from "internalizing" reactions that are more prevalent in girls. When reactions to divorce are externalized, the result is likely to take the form of aggressive, undercontrolled behaviors. When reactions to divorce are internalized, the result is likely to take the form of withdrawn, dependent rather than disruptive behavior. Even though there is little consensus on gender distinctions, there is agreement that intense reactions to parental divorce occur in both sons and daughters, and persist for years. When investigators compared stepfather families with intact families, they found depressed, withdrawn behavior in both boys and girls who had stepfathers, but the behavior was more pronounced in girls. Additional research points to lasting difficulties in establishing heterosexual relationships among adolescents and young adults who have lived through parental divorce, with the postdivorce problems more pronounced among girls (Kalter 1984). These findings are not conclusive, but they indicate that parental divorce is a critical event for children. Because parental divorce is a significant event in the family of origin, it is a fact to be included in the assessment of youngsters, even though their feelings on the issue seem to be resolved. The concept of internalized and externalized behaviors helps caregivers to understand reactions of children to parental divorce.

The traditional family life cycle consisting of major stages of expansion and contraction is not experienced by those adults who confront successive stages of estrangement, separation, divorce,

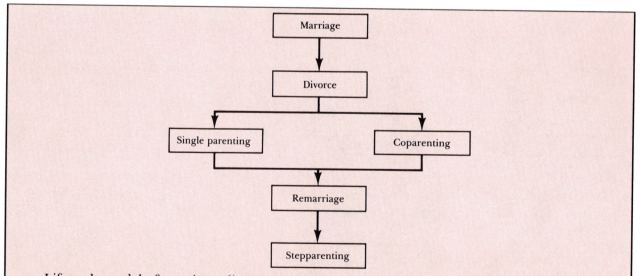

Life cycle model of marriage, divorce, and remarriage. Social uncertainty and social isolation are common during the aftermath of divorce. Divorced women complain that they are seldom included in the activities of married couples, who consider invitations to unattached females to be awkward. Although divorced men enjoy the relatively desirable status of unattached males, many of them feel uncomfortable with the unfamiliar role of bachelor. However, dissolution of a marriage seems to be a more difficult adjustment for women, perhaps because being married is more central to the identity and socialization of women (Bohannon 1980).

single parenting or coparenting, remarriage, and stepparenting. Transitional stages between the ending of one marriage and the beginning of another have received scant attention from investigators and clinicians even though divorce rates have risen steadily in the last three decades (Weingarten 1986).

Nearly half the divorces in the United States involve persons with minor children, and it is estimated that before reaching eighteen years of age, 40 percent or nearly one out of every two children will live in a one-parent or stepparent family at some point (Messinger and Walker 1981). Two thirds of all divorced women are under 30 years of age, and most of these are mothers of young children. The possibility of a woman's becoming head of a single-parent household is far greater than that of a man. Desertion, death, and the decisions of never-married women to raise their children alone have added to the numbers of households headed by women. In such homes, responsibilities of the woman are apt to be overwhelming, especially if financial resources are inadequate and the mother must work long hours outside the home.

Despite soaring divorce rates, faith in the rewards of marriage prevail. Proof of lasting belief in marriage is reflected in the number of divorced persons who remarry. An estimated 80 percent of divorced spouses marry again, most of them within three to five years following divorce.

The sweeping changes introduced by divorce cause disequilibrium compounded by feelings of failure even when the decision is a mutual one. Children of a dissolving marriage react with confusion, fear, anger, and guilt. Relatives who have become fond of a daughter-in-law or son-in-law are conflicted, and many divorced persons find they have lost not only their partners but significant others as well. Similarity between divorce and the death of a loved one was noted by Weiss (1979), who deplored the lack of mourning rituals for newly divorced persons, adding that the dignified finality of death is impossible for individuals who must continue to interact with former partners during and after legal proceedings. Except that there is no provision for interment and no ceremonial grieving, divorce gives rise to the acute separation anxiety evoked by any irrevocable loss. The paradox of divorce is that the marriage may be ended legally, but the relationship persists, especially when children are involved (Zigler and Black 1989).

Psychodynamic Concepts

The founder of the psychodynamic approach was Sigmund Freud. During his long career, Freud revised his early belief that childhood sexual trauma was the cause of neurosis and became more attentive to constitutional factors. In other words, Freud came to believe that many individuals become dysfunctional not because of external sexual trauma but because of their own internal drives and impulses. His preoccupation with constitutional factors caused him to overlook the contributions of parents and families in the development of psychological disturbance in their children. Although in some respects he was a skeptic who questioned prevailing beliefs of his day, Freud seemed to accept the idea that parents love their children in benign ways and that psychological problems are largely attributable to constitutional drives (Freud 1949, Thompson 1957, Brown, 1967).

At first Freud believed that the frequent accounts by his patients of having been sexually assaulted in childhood were factual. Later he reported that such accounts were not substantiated, and he considered them to be fantasies representing patients' unconscious wish fulfillment of forbidden impulses. This reversal in Freud's thinking continues to arouse controversy today. Feminists assert that the Freudian position has made it difficult for women and children to establish their credibility as victims of sexual trauma. Among other writers, Masson (1984) suggests that Freud's failure to uphold his initial conviction reveals a lack of moral courage. It must be acknowledged that Freud's original views on this subject met with public disapproval, and Masson alleges that when Freud labeled the traumatic reports of his patients as fantasies or wishful thinking he was intellectually dishonest. There is no way to reach a definitive conclusion on this issue, but Freud continues to be held responsible for encouraging distrust by establishment figures, such as physicians and lawyers, toward self-reports by women and children of traumatic sexual experiences.

Freud made other, more acceptable observations regarding families. He suggested, for example, that there exists within each family a collective psychological life that is simultaneously created and shared by the family members. The family's collective psychological life may be compared to the psychological processes of individual members, but the family psyche possesses unique dimensions of its own. Through the intrapsychic life of the family, older generations, living and dead, can transmit family values and attitudes to newer generations. Although Freud was referring primarily to the transmission of dysfunctional neurotic behaviors, his formulations emphasized the presence of a collective psychological life in every family, functional or dysfunctional.

(Text continues on page 525.)

CLINICAL VIGNETTE

APPLYING SYSTEMS THEORY TO A MARITAL RELATIONSHIP

George and Dolly Mann were professional musicians in their late thirties. They were employed in an urban orchestra, had been married 12 years, and were childless by choice. The orchestra was often on tour; as a result the Manns spent considerable time traveling from city to city. One day the intake worker at the community mental health center in the neighborhood where they lived received a call from Dolly who sounded excited and desperate. "You have to do something about my husband. I can't stand living with him another minute. I must talk to someone before I kill myself." The intake worker succeeded in calming Dolly and obtained enough information to make an appointment for Mr. and Mrs. Mann to be seen that evening. Both appeared promptly to keep the appointment.

During the assessment interview it was disclosed that Dolly had been terminated by the orchestra about two months earlier. She had become less and less able to play her violin because of an arthritic problem in her hands. When she was informed by the orchestra manager that she was not employable, Dolly was filled with despair. She accused her husband of being indifferent to her predicament and reported that life with him was intolerable. She said that he constantly found fault with her, yelled at her that she should find another job right away. In turn, George accused his wife of screaming at him, throwing things, and physically attacking him.

As the interview progressed, it was obvious that the couple agreed on only one detail—that Dolly had lost her job. They bickered over every fact, each contradicting and interrupting the other. The mental health worker realized that husband and wife were in a period of severe stress, and tried to review the chronology of their relationship in order to assess their customary interaction patterns. This approach elicited more arguments and grievances. Each reported that the other was always dissatisfied and looking for a fight. There was no indication that they had ever interacted in any other way, nor that they were distressed by their interactional pattern until Dolly lost her job. The job loss had produced a crisis, and they wanted someone to do something immediately to relieve their distress.

The couple agreed to attend five marital sessions with the agreed-upon goal of helping Dolly calm down and begin looking for some kind of job that she could do in spite of her physical impairment. In the sessions the couple examined conditions in which arguments began, and ways in which insults and accusations could be avoided. Rules were developed for discussing issues calmly and for focusing on the real cause of their disagreement. Instead of issuing ultimatums, George was instructed to use the phrase "it seems to me" when trying to explain his viewpoint to his wife. This simple phrase reduced contention because it gave Dolly an opportunity to describe how things seemed to her. At the end of the session contract George stated that there was less fighting at home and that his practice schedule did not give him time to continue the meetings. Dolly agreed that they were fighting less and could discontinue sessions even though she still had not found a job.

A week later Dolly called the clinic requesting to renew the sessions. She had a sense of unfinished business and wanted to understand her part in maintaining the conflict in her marriage. She wanted to define and modify her own behavior in her relationships with her husband and other people. With assistance from the mental health worker, Dolly began to look at her own behavior. While she had observed and criticized her husband's actions for years, Dolly had spent no time examining her own actions. She learned that she presented herself in such a way that other people, including her husband, thought her helpless and barely competent. Due to the arthritis in her hands, she could not perform as a professional musician. In fact, she could no longer do needlework, which was a pastime she always enjoyed. Since her husband used the car, she could not go anywhere during the day. She was afraid that she could no longer drive alone and must depend on her husband to take her.

The mental health worker did not make suggestions or give specific advice about how Dolly might solve her problems. That would have prolonged the pattern of dominance versus dependency that the client said she wanted to change. Instead of making suggestions which Dolly would probably reject, the mental health worker helped the client search for alternative behaviors. What had Dolly thought of trying?

What had she done to solve her problems in the past? What had other people done in circumstances similar to hers? What sounded reasonable to attempt? There were times in the sessions when Dolly accused the counselor of being uncaring and indifferent, but within a few months she had figured out how to drive the car herself. This was her first step in realizing that she tried to get other people, especially her husband, to help her, and then resented their interference. She recognized that there were many things she could do by herself. This led to her considering what she was capable of and what she needed to achieve. Once she made some decisions, she began to put her plans into effect. She decided to teach music to children. Although she could no longer play well enough to perform, she was enough of a musician to give lessons.

During the sessions the counselor explained about family systems and how they work. As Dolly moved toward independent functioning, the mental health worker predicted some strong reactions from George, who had learned to deal with his wife's anger but not her autonomy. This helped prepare Dolly for her husband's responses to her changed behavior. He was furious when she first suggested he form a carpool to get to work so that she could have the car three days a week. She did not retreat and finally he agreed. After some months she told the mental health worker that the orchestra was going on tour. She would be traveling with her husband for a time but would continue to teach her pupils on her return. She said that she still became upset when her husband was angry with her, but instead of fighting back, she tried to avoid an argument without giving in completely.

To summarize the outcome, once the immediate situation improved the husband dropped out of treatment. His wife, who was in more distress, was not satisfied with minimal results but wanted to change the interactional pattern of her marriage. She was willing to make changes in her own behavior. Even though her husband resisted change, his wife's actions led to alterations in the marital system. Inevitably, her altered behavior influenced the interactional patterns of the couple in ways that the wife welcomed and the husband came to accept. He found disadvantages as well as advantages in having a more independent partner, but overall, family functioning improved.

Certainly the idea of the transmission of family attitudes and values can be seen in families in which there is a collective, intergenerational commitment to certain occupations, such as teaching, or a collective disregard of certain goals, such as accumulating material possessions. The idea of a collective family psyche has implications for nurses working with families because it recognizes the impact of family traditions on individual members regardless of whether they adopt or challenge these traditions. In many families there is a long-standing tradition for members to choose a particular field of endeavor or to enter a family business upon reaching adulthood. The member who deviates is likely to arouse negative reactions within the family and to seek support outside.

PSEUDOMUTUALITY AND PSEUDOHOSTILITY Psychodynamic theory is concerned with conflict between the wish of individuals to be cared for and nurtured and their opposing urge to be separate and assertive. Some families nurture their members but are unwilling to permit the formation of a separate identity. In more dysfunctional families, individual differences are not tolerated at all, and family members are expected to conform to family standards even if personal identity is sacrificed.

Wynne et al. (1958) described a form of family interaction in which any deviation from family standards was thought to threaten family survival. In this type of family interaction, a surface harmony is maintained even if it required a denial of identity and selfhood by one or more members. A family characterized by false harmony, or *pseudomutuality*, tends to be rigid, inflexible, and intolerant of change or individual differences among its members. The result is a family unit in which compliance is valued more than individuality. Family harmony may appear to be preserved, but growth is sacrificed. Pseudomutuality is maintained, but some members may be exploited in order for the family to continue just as it is.

Wynne et al. (1958) used the term *pseudohostility* to describe families that habitually engage in bickering and rancor in order to avoid intimacy or closeness. Unlike pseudomutual families, where closeness is highly regarded, pseudohostile families go to considerable lengths to avoid harmonious involvement. Even though conflict and argumentation are prominent in family interactions, the genuine conflict is seldom identified and resolved. Resolution of a conflict may pave the way for closer relationships, which is what pseudohostile families are trying to avoid. Pseudomutuality and pseudohostility are equally destructive methods for dealing with the universal human difficulty of relating to others while maintaining a separate identity.

In applying the concepts of pseudomutuality and pseudohostility to family situations, the nurse might first identify the prevailing style of family interaction. If the family displays apparent harmony but has unresolved problems, the nurse might try to analyze whose rights are being ignored in order to preserve peace. Not infrequently, the family member who is being exploited or neglected becomes the identified client, or the family "problem." For example, open marital discord can sometimes be avoided if parents unite in their behavior toward a school-aged child who is a chronic bedwetter or an adolescent who is rebellious. Even when the parents disagree on how to treat a problem child, their disagreement about the child helps them avoid dealing with marital issues.

In families where there is a great deal of quarreling and disagreement, the issues to be resolved are: What is the true nature of the conflict and what are the real goals of the contenders? Are the participants confronting each other honestly, or are other family members forced to choose sides and join the hostilities? Are genuine problems being addressed, or are peripheral issues being used to avoid dealing with more crucial matters? One example is the husband who is excessively preoccupied with his career and indifferent to the delinquent behavior of his son. This indifference incites rage in the mother, but whenever the father does attempt to talk with his son, his wife intervenes. As the pivotal member of the household, she interprets each of them to the other; this gives her the power to isolate the two. She secures the allegiance of her son by protecting him from his father. But because her son's behavior is upsetting to her, she occasionally berates him. At the same time she avoids taking responsibility by blaming her husband for not being a more attentive father. At first glance the mother may seem justified, but further assessment shows the pseudohostility that conceals the mother's inconsistent behavior toward her son and her desire not to share her son with his father despite her protestations to the contrary (Frias and Janosik 1980).

RUBBER FENCES In some dysfunctional families, the boundaries are neither clear nor stable but instead expand and contract in ways that are inconsistent and unpredictable. The term "rubber fences" has been used to describe such undependable, elastic boundaries. Persons living in a family with such boundaries find themselves in an emotional field in which behaviors and rules change continually. As a result, most of the members are bewildered and confused about what is acceptable or unacceptable within the family. Secrecy, inconsistency, and disorder characterize family interactions, and very little that goes on in the family has a rational basis (Wynne et al. 1958).

MARITAL SCHISM AND MARITAL SKEW The early family theorists were interested in tracing the etiology of various psychiatric disorders, especially schizophrenia, to questionable interactional patterns in the family. Few theorists alleged that families actually *cause* schizophrenia; rather, they suggested that dysfunctional patterns of interaction are found in many families with a schizophrenic member (Lidz and Lidz 1949, Lidz, Fleck, and Cornelison 1965).

Lidz found two specific interactional patterns to be conspicuous in the families of persons with schizophrenia. The first pattern is that of a dominant spouse whose specific ideas on what a family should be like are followed by the less dominant partner. This family is superficially compatible, but there is an underlying hostility that is not directly expressed. Lidz labeled these families as *skewed* and found the skewed family arrangement to be more common in families with a schizophrenic son. In families that Lidz labeled *schismatic* there is open dissension and acrimony. In these families it is usually a daughter who becomes the identified patient.

In skewed families the mother is usually dominant and intrusive, especially in her son's affairs. She resists her son's efforts to separate and looks to him, rather than her husband, for gratification of her needs. Because of his passivity, the father does not actively intervene on his son's behalf. He either tolerates the excessively close relationship between mother and son or else adopts siblinglike behavior and competes with his son for his wife's attention. The dominance of the mother and the passivity of the father deprive the son of a positive role model with which to identify. The result is a stunting of personality development in the son, sometimes to the extent of psychiatric illness.

In schismatic families the father generally dominates while the mother is aloof and detached. Although the mother may appear affectionate toward her daughter, her behavior is covertly antagonistic. Since the daughter finds it difficult to identify with a mother who subtly rejects her, she may turn to her father for affection. The father often cooperates in this because his marital relationship is so unrewarding. The psychoanalytic explanation for the girl's dilemma is that she has failed to resolve the Electra conflict (the female counterpart of the Oedipal conflict). The daughter cannot renounce her father and identify with her mother because she is trapped by the hostility of the parents toward each other. She cannot entirely please one parent without risking loss of the other. Regressive behaviors, in the form of truancy, delinquency, withdrawal, or defiance may seem to be the only solution available to her (Lidz 1958, Lidz, Fleck, and Cornelison 1965).

Parents in skewed and schismatic families have the power to scapegoat a child. Although the interactions of the parents are self-destructive, their status in the family enables them to continue to function, but their self-centered behaviors impair their children's psychological growth. When a son or daughter is especially vulnerable, a process of loneliness, withdrawal, distrust, and regression may eventually lead to psychiatric illness.

Structural Concepts

Every family is organized along structural lines that reveal relationships among family members. Within the family, patterns develop governing how, when, and to whom family members relate. This patterning of relationships helps reduce frustration and inefficiency, because family members know what interactions are likely to be acceptable at a particular point in time. Of course, family structure is altered whenever family members join or leave the unit.

Family *subsystems* are divisions within the family based on age, gender, and responsibilities (Minuchin 1974). Families begin with a marital dyad that becomes the parental subsystem when children enter the family. The children form a sibling subsystem. In large families there may be several sibling subsystems, and in many families female members form one subsystem and male members another. In general, any one family member belongs to several subsystems that help the family operate in a relatively orderly fashion.

In some families homeostasis is maintained by exploiting one of the children. Disagreements between the parents may be avoided by displacing conflict to a particular child who performs the function of family scapegoat. It is not unusual for the scapegoated child to develop psychological, physiological, or behavioral symptoms. Conflict between the parents can be avoided or detoured as the parents become preoccupied in dealing with the child, who may actually serve the function of preserving the family unit.

Boundaries that are clearly defined uphold family and subsystem functioning. When boundaries between members are extremely rigid, family members remain separate and disengaged from one another. When boundaries between members are weak or diffuse, there is little differentiation or separation of members. In families where boundaries are diffuse the members are so close that they become enmeshed with each other. The members may enjoy a sense of belonging, but they sacrifice their individuality and autonomy.

Structural family therapists use a technique called family mapping to help assess characteristics of the family system. The family map can help nurses identify possible goals and can be used to demonstrate spatial and organizational relationships to family members. Table 19–3 shows the symbols most commonly used in family mapping.

Table 19–3. Mapping Family Structure

Organizational Structure	Symbol	Organizational Consequences
Clear boundaries	– – – –	Differentiation and autonomy
Diffuse boundaries	....	Enmeshment and over-inclusiveness
Rigid boundaries	———	Disengagement and isolation
Detouring	——→	Displacement of conflict and problems to another family member
Subsystems	▭	Natural family subdivisions
Conflict	⊐╎╎⊏	Hostility between two or more family members or subgroups

SOURCE: After Minuchin (1974).

The foremost exponent of structural family intervention is Salvador Minuchin (1974), who advises clinicians to enter the family system in order to restructure family relationships and alter positions in the family. To accomplish this restructuring, the therapist may (1) strengthen individual boundaries to increase separation and individuation of members who are enmeshed, (2) reinforce natural subsystems such as the parental subsystem and sibling subsystems by suggesting age-appropriate behaviors and tasks, and (3) strengthen the parental subsystem by emphasizing parental responsibilities and by challenging inappropriate alliances that weaken the parental subsystem.

In a family where the mother and father are distant and disengaged from each other, the parental subsystem may have ceased to function as a dyad. The mother or father may have given a selected opposite-sex child the position in the parental subsystem that rightfully belongs to the spouse. The result may be family dysfunction in which the misplaced child is exploited and in which left-out siblings are resentful. In such an instance the structural therapist would intervene to alter distances and closeness between various members in an attempt to reestablish communication between the spouses and return the child to the subsystem with the other siblings.

ROLES AND ROLE ENACTMENT Role theory contains concepts that are part of family *structure* and concepts that are part of family *function*. If roles relate to family positions, to closeness and distance between family members, then roles are part of family structure. However, when role enactment is being considered, it is role theory and family function

(Text continues on page 529.)

CLINICAL VIGNETTE

STRUCTURAL REALIGNMENT IN A MULTIGENERATIONAL FAMILY

Rosalie was a teenage mother who chose not to marry the father of her child. Because Rosalie wanted to finish high school, she lived at home and relinquished the care of her baby to her mother. Rosalie was a good student who was eager to return to school and to resume some of the social activities she had enjoyed before the birth of the baby. At the same time she was dismayed to find that her mother took full charge of the infant, making all decisions and indicating to Rosalie that the girl was incapable of taking proper care of the baby. Rosalie had expected that having a baby would make her more mature and independent. Instead she discovered that both she and her baby were being treated as children. The conflict between Rosalie and her mother over the baby became evident to the nurse in charge of the well baby clinic where the health of the infant was supervised. Aware of the struggle, the nurse began to deal with Rosalie's mixed feelings about motherhood and with the reluctance of the older woman to accept her proper place as grandmother and relate to Rosalie as the baby's mother.

When Rosalie brought the baby to the clinic, the nurse tried to reinforce her confidence in handling the baby. At the same time the nurse acknowledged the contribution that Rosalie's own mother was making. Because the grandmother had moved into the position of mother to her granddaughter as well as to Rosalie, positions in the family were confused. Generational boundaries were unclear because the grandmother related to the baby in a way that excluded Rosalie, who needed help in order to finish high school but resented the price her mother exacted. It became the objective of the clinic nurse to define responsibilities in the family in order to reduce conflict. In attempting this the nurse supported the contributions of the grandmother as teacher and advisor for Rosalie. The nurse also encouraged Rosalie to perform mothering tasks while seeking guidance and support from her mother. The nurse's interventions produced some structural changes in the family that are illustrated in the accompanying family maps.

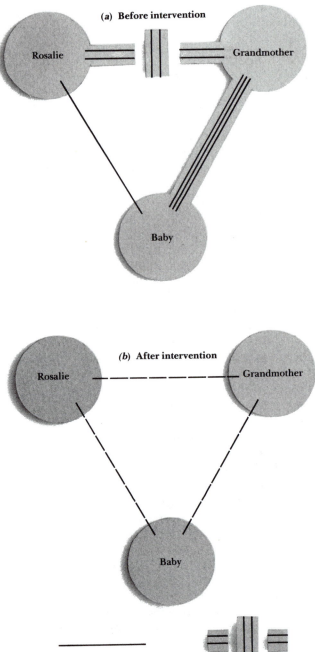

(a) Before intervention

Rosalie   Grandmother

Baby

(b) After intervention

Rosalie   Grandmother

Baby

Disengagement (rigid boundaries)

Conflict

Enmeshment (diffuse boundaries)

Clear boundaries

that are connected. This ambiguity means that role theory is a bridge between family structure and family function.

Roles are an important aspect of family theory. Roles can be analyzed in terms of status or position (structure) and performance or enactment (function). In families roles may be assigned or ascribed to certain individuals by reason of the position they hold in the family. The husband/father role is assigned to the person who completes the marital dyad and sires the children. A number of functions are expected from the person who fills this role. Not too many years ago, it was a common expectation that the husband/father would be the primary breadwinner and that major family decisions would be his to make. In present-day families the husband/father may or may not be present in the home. When he is physically absent, many role functions formerly assigned to him are discharged by the mother, perhaps with the help of older children. When role functions are performed by family members not usually associated with enactment of that particular role, this is called *achieved* rather than *assigned* role performance (Parsons 1951, Lambert and Lambert 1984).

Variations in the structure of contemporary families have lessened emphasis on assigned roles in favor of achieved roles. This pattern may be necessary, but it often introduces new problems. One danger is that a single parent trying to fill two roles may become overwhelmed by responsibility.

Another danger is that immature family members may be pushed into achieved roles for which they are not ready, and resolution of critical life cycle tasks may not be handled as well as they might be. Maturation, readiness, aptitude, and experience are factors that affect adequate role performance. These considerations are sometimes overlooked in single-parent families, dual-career families, and families where the partners are not in agreement concerning role expectations. Men who have grown up in traditional families of origin where tasks were assigned on the basis of gender differentiation may cling to familiar patterns in households where both partners hold jobs outside the home.

In family coping efforts it is important for members to agree on what the family problem is. Only after defining the problem can family members begin solving problems. Problem solving may require new role distribution and new uses of family resources. The effectiveness of family problem solving determines whether the family moves in the direction of equilibrium or disequilibrium, as shown in Figure 19–4.

THE SICK ROLE Individuals in the family, their internal relationships, and their willingness to receive external aid influence their response to illness or

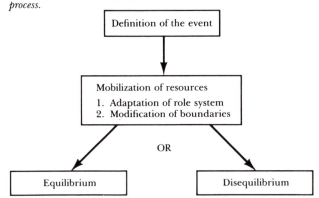

Figure 19–4. Family coping process.

disability. In more traditional times life and death, health and illness were considered to be one continuous process. All outcomes were attributed to the will of God, and the promise of eventual reunion with the deceased somewhat relieved the grief of survivors. In contemporary life, such comfort is less widespread. Furthermore, for marginal families who already have little control over their existence, the onset of illness or disability constitutes another reminder of their limitations. Failure to deal well with stress or crisis then becomes part of a familiar experience of feeling overwhelmed.

Marginal families are sometimes slow to recognize serious disturbance in a member, but after acknowledging the symptoms, they make an effort to respond (Minuchin 1974, Minuchin et al. 1967). Many of these families first try random solutions and intrafamily consultation before searching for professional help. After accepting care from health professionals, an ailing family member is expected to enact the sick role with its accompanying exemptions and obligations. Depending on the identity of the family member and the life cycle stage of the family, obligations of the sick role occupant may outweigh exemptions. This pattern is especially true when it is the wife and mother who becomes ill. Because the mother is crucial to carrying out daily family routines, immediate readjustment is necessary when she is the ailing member. When it is the husband and primary provider who falls ill, economic deprivation may be an early consequence. In two-parent households, reallocation of tasks is feasible, but role flexibility is a luxury unavailable in single-parent homes, which comprise a sizable number of all households in the United States.

It was Talcott Parsons (1951) who conceptualized various aspects of the sick role and noted that the nature of illness or disability influenced how the role was enacted. Specifically, Parsons outlined certain major privileges and responsibilities that accompany enactment of the sick role.

(Text continues on page 531.)

CLINICAL VIGNETTE

FAMILY CONFLICT DUE TO DIVERSE VALUES

Flora and Jay grew up in the same neighborhood and attended the same schools and church. Flora was the oldest of eight children; her father was a truck driver and the undisputed boss of the family. Flora's mother worked in a fast food restaurant. When her mother was at work, Flora was expected to look after the younger children and soothe the uneven temper of her father when he was at home. The household was noisy, crowded, and disorganized in spite of Flora's efforts to maintain order.

Flora was an attractive girl, quiet, unassuming, and busy with school and her tasks at home. While in high school, she began dating Jay, whose home life was as orderly as Flora's was disorderly. Jay's mother was a school teacher before marrying, and Jay was her only child. His father was a plumber who earned a good living; Jay's mother did not work outside the home but was active in community affairs. She was a meticulous housekeeper who spent a great deal of her time with Jay. Even in grade school Jay showed academic promise, which his parents tried to cultivate. They had high ambitions for Jay and were disappointed when he began dating Flora, particularly when she left high school before graduating.

During Flora's senior year her father was ill for a time and could not work. As a result the family could not pay its debts. The money earned by Flora's mother was not enough to feed and clothe a large family, so Flora dropped out of school to work with her mother as a waitress. When her father recovered, Flora tried to return to school, but she became discouraged when she realized how far behind she was. Flora attended her high school prom with Jay and she accompanied his parents to graduation where she watched her former classmates receive their diplomas.

The friendship between Jay and Flora continued while he was in college in spite of the objections of his mother, who thought that he should look for a college girl instead of wasting his time with "that dumb little waitress around the corner." Jay usually listened to his mother, but showed no signs of giving up Flora. They were married shortly after he finished college. At that point Jay had a fellowship for graduate work and was self-supporting.

The years in graduate school were rewarding for Jay, but less so for Flora. Since all their friends were struggling to make ends meet, their lack of money did not bother Flora. What bothered her was her discomfort with the wives of other graduate students. It was easier after her son was born for then she had more in common with some of the other wives who had children.

In this marriage the husband and wife came from working class families, but Jay's family was upwardly oriented whereas Flora's was not. There was more stability and affluence in Jay's family. As an only child he received a great deal of parental attention, especially from his mother who had many middle class values. By means of higher education Jay had clearly moved into the middle class and identified with middle class attitudes toward career and family. Flora now lived in a middle class neighborhood but retained the lower class values that made her more comfortable. Five years after the birth of her son, Flora found herself in a suburban home with four bedrooms, landscaping, and no close friends. She was close to her mother and sisters, whom she visited several times a week, taking her son with her to the old neighborhood. These visits were the only times when Flora felt relaxed and comfortable. Although she attended company functions with Jay, these were stressful events that often left her with a throbbing headache.

The headaches were relieved only when she lay down in a darkened room while Jay or a baby sitter cared for her son. At Jay's insistence Flora visited an internist, who told her she suffered from migraine headaches. She also saw a gynecologist because of her concern that she was unable to become pregnant. Neither the internist nor the gynecologist found a physiological basis for the headaches or her infertility. Jay became impatient as Flora's headaches increased in frequency. She was often unable to attend company functions. Their sex life, which had been gratifying to them both, began to deteriorate. Jay worried about the welfare of their little boy when Flora was "out of it," as he described her headaches. Noting the strain in the couple's relationship, the internist referred Flora to a psychiatrist.

After an assessment of Flora and several conjoint interviews with the couple, the psychiatrist suggested marital counseling. It was concluded that Flora's problems originated in her feelings of inferiority, her loneliness as a corporate wife, her husband's immersion in his career, and her inability to ask him for emotional support. Jay was devoted to Flora and willingly involved himself in marital counseling. Counseling sessions helped him appreciate the stress that social and economic advancement had brought to Flora. This understanding of his wife's feelings made him more supportive of her efforts to fit into his world. Learning of her need to see her family of origin, he was more willing to see them often. His increased interest was reassuring to Flora and made her more willing to find a place for herself in the environment he had chosen. Flora progressed enough to accept a recommendation that she join a group for mothers of preschoolers that dealt with personal and parenting issues. Communication between the spouses was enhanced by marital counseling and their own high motivation.

Exemptions of the sick role occupant in physical disorders

- Exemption from responsibility for being ill
- Exemption from customary role obligations

Obligations of the sick role occupant in physical disorders

- Obligation to accept competent assistance
- Obligation to cooperate in the recovery process
- Obligation to be dependent, submissive, compliant

Observation of the ways that families respond to serious illness or disability reveals interesting variations. When a family member becomes chronically or terminally ill without hope of recovery, other persons in the family are unlikely to look for help with their own emotional problems, either because they do not relate their problems to the illness or because they hesitate to blame the person who is ill. When illness continues without remission for a protracted period, families become enmeshed in the schedules necessitated by the illness and are unwilling to delegate tasks. At the same time there may be deep resentment for having to be so attentive at the expense of individual fulfillment. Occasionally a family member will withdraw from those in the family who are well, fulfilling personal needs to protect and nurture the ill member, ultimately becoming dependent on enacting the caretaker role. When families are preoccupied with illness or disability, life cycle tasks, such as separation, that are chronologically suitable for younger family members may be delayed because of the burden of caring for the ill member (Collings 1981).

A number of characteristics of the sick role are more relevant to acute illness than to chronic and terminal illness. For example, the chronically or terminally ill person must adjust to affliction rather than strive for full recovery. Since other family members must make a parallel adjustment, complex group dynamics will be called into play.

Enactment of the sick role is affected by factors other than the prognosis of the illness. Insufficient attention has been given to variations of sick role behavior among different populations and families. This neglect may be due in part to the ethnocentricity of practitioners, who represent the mainstream of society, or to a sincere but misguided wish to avoid stereotypical judgments. One study of sick role expectations held by hospitalized women found only a single area of agreement between the subjects' perception of sick role behavior and Parsons's model (Segall 1972). The emphasis of Parsons is that in order to conform to the sick role, patients must be willing to relinquish many ordinary activities, become dependent on others, and utilize professional treatment facilities.

When Parsonsian concepts of the sick role are applied to mental illness, other discrepancies become apparent. In effect, enactment of physical and psychiatric sick roles are contradictory in the exemptions and obligations extended to the occupants. In general, role concepts are more readily applied to physical illness than to psychological disorders. In other words, viewing individuals as suitable occupants of the sick role is unlikely when the illness is not considered fully somatic in origin and expression. Whenever a purely somatic disorder is present, the patient is not held responsible for being ill. When the disorder has overt psychological overtones or is thought to be the result of deviant social behavior such as alcoholism, the sick role occupant may be held accountable for causing as well as coping with the disorder.

Exemptions of the sick role occupant in psychiatric disorders

- Partial responsibility for being ill
- Partial exemption from customary role obligations

Obligations of the sick role occupant in psychiatric disorders

- To accept competent assistance
- To cooperate in the recovery process

■ To be adaptive, interactive, and self-directed
■ To accept the stigma of a psychiatric label

It is evident from this discussion that enactment of the sick role is not consistent or unidimensional. The nature of an illness, the identity of the ailing family member, and the context in which the illness develops are factors that determine how the sick role is enacted and how other family members relate to the role enactment of the afflicted member.

Enactment of the sick role is affected by factors other than the prognosis of the illness. Insufficient attention has been given to variations of sick role behavior among different populations and families.

Functional Concepts

Many functional aspects of family life have been dealt with by Murray Bowen (1971, 1974, 1976), who originally described his approach as part of systems theory but later became attentive to the emotional unity of the family. However, Bowen continued to accept the idea of the family as an operating system in which forces and counterforces are always present. Bowen's theory is directed toward the emotional functioning of families. He (1971b) delineated eight major concepts that may be applied to the assessment of family function: the nuclear family emotional system, differentiation of self, triangles, multigenerational transmission, family constellation, family projection, emotional cutoff, and societal regression.

NUCLEAR FAMILY EMOTIONAL SYSTEM Bowen used the terms *undifferentiated ego mass* and *fusion* to describe nuclear families in which members do not see themselves as separate individuals but rather as joined or fused to each other. When emotional fusion exists among family members, it is difficult for them to distinguish between thinking and feeling. As a consequence, they manage rational processes rather poorly. Irrationality then impairs their ability to handle life's problems.

DIFFERENTIATION OF SELF Central to Bowen's theory is the importance of *self-differentiation*, which requires that individuals distance themselves from the emotional system of their family of origin. Self-differentiation does not forbid ongoing interaction between adult family members and their family of origin, but it does mean that the emotional forces of the original family do not dominate members.

In explaining the concept of differentiation of self Bowen made a distinction between "solid self" and "pseudoself." He developed a continuum called the *Differentiation of Self scale*, with the solid self at one end and the pseudoself at the other (see Figure 19–5). All individuals fall at some point on the continuum, depending on the amount of self-differentiation they have attained. One's position on the continuum is not static but may move in either direction during a lifetime.

The solid self is made up of rational, firmly held principles and attitudes that are deeply ingrained. The solid self evolves gradually and may change as an individual learns or fails to learn from life experiences. Because the solid self depends on rational thinking and is an intrinsic part of the personality, it does not succumb to pressure from external sources. The pseudoself, on the other hand, lacks intrinsic values and therefore must

(Text continues on page 536.)

Figure 19–5. Bowen's Differentiation of Self scale.

Low differentiation of self

High differentiation of self

Pseudoself

Automatic responses
Subjective reactions
Emotional dependence
Low self-identity
High vulnerability to stress
High incidence of illness
Prone to recurrent crisis

Solid self

Self-directed
Objective reactions
Rational
Flexible
High self-identity
Good coping skills
Lower incidence of illness

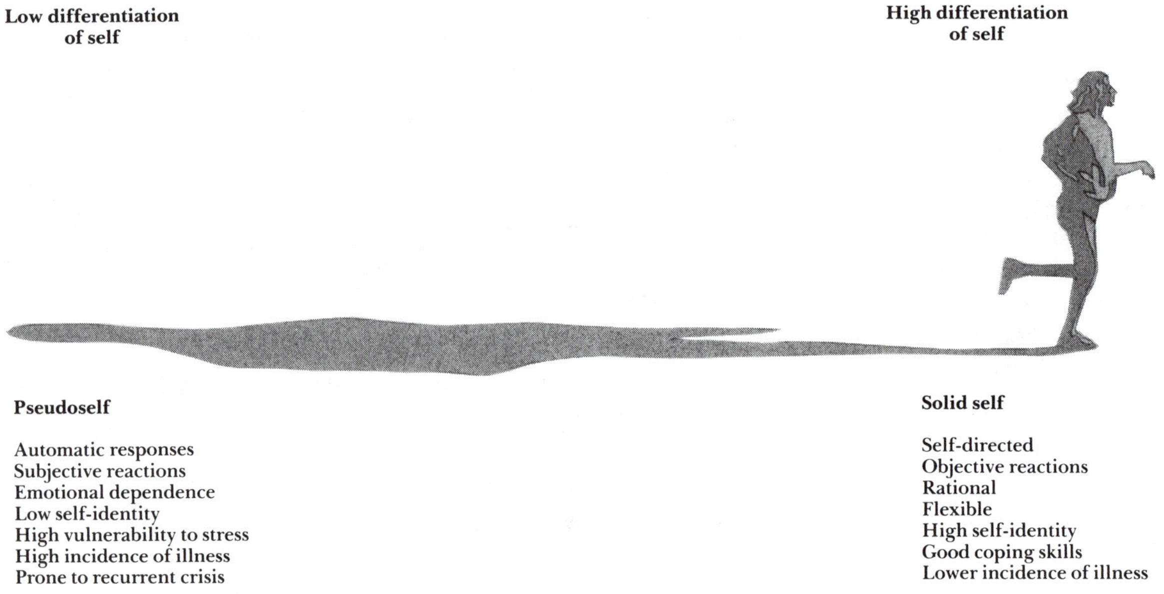

FAMILY ASSESSMENT TOOL

	Antecedent past	Here and now	Anticipated future
Characteristics of individual members 1. What members comprise the nuclear family? 2. What members comprise the families of origin? 3. Which member is the identified patient or patients? 4. What signs of equilibrium or disequilibrium are apparent in the identified patient? 5. What signs of equilibrium or disequilibrium are apparent in other members? 6. What signs of equilibrium or disequilibrium are apparent in the family system?			

Characteristics of internal family communication
1. How does each family member communicate and interact with other members of the nuclear family?
2. How does each family member communicate and interact with members of the families of origin?
3. How are decisions made in the family?
4. How is conflict handled in the family?
5. What are the prevailing communication patterns in the family?
    Specific?
    Consistent?
    Ambiguous?
    Tangential?
    Contradictory?
    Placating?
    Blaming?
    Confusing?			

Characteristics of external family communication 1. Are family boundaries open or closed to external influence? 2. Is the family integrated into the social mainstream? 3. Is the family isolated from the social mainstream? 4. How does the family relate to larger systems, such as school, church, or community? 5. How do individual family members relate to external systems?			
Psychological characteristics of the family 1. Whose needs are being met in the family? 2. Whose needs are being ignored in the family? 3. Where is the locus of power in the family? 4. Who is the task leader in the family? 5. Who is the socioemotional leader in the family? 6. Is leadership invested in both parents, one parent, or neither parent? 7. Are family alliances based on natural distinctions of age, gender, and generational roles? 8. Are family alliances based on coalitions that transcend age, gender, and generational roles?			
Socioeconomic/environmental characteristics of the family 1. Are family and socioeconomic resources sufficient for basic needs? 2. Is there harmony between material resources and family expectations? 3. Are the hopes and expectations of family members realistic? 4. Are the hopes and expectations of family members unrealistic? 5. Are conditions present that are likely to promote class advancement? 6. Are conditions present that are apt to promote class slippage? 7. Are external socioeconomic resources available to the family? 8. Are external socioeconomic resources acceptable to the family?			

SOURCE: Family Assessment Tool (*Adapted from Howells, J. G.* Principles of Family Psychiatry. *New York: Brunner/Mazel, 1975.*)

CLINICAL VIGNETTE

DYSFUNCTIONAL SICK ROLE ENACTMENT

The White family consisted of Pamela, a 51-year-old woman, and her husband, Jim, who was a few years older. The couple lived in a single-family home in a suburban neighborhood. Paul, their only child, was married and lived with his wife in an apartment complex about 15 miles away. Three years earlier, Pamela had been diagnosed as having uterine cancer. She had received no radical treatment, and in the intervening time her condition had deteriorated greatly. There was widespread metastasis to other organs.

INTERNAL COMMUNICATION CHARACTERISTICS

When Pamela was first told her diagnosis she decided on no drastic medical or surgical treatment, despite the advice of her physician. Her rationale for the decision was "I don't want chemotherapy because my hair will fall out. I don't want my body cut by surgeons. I've prayed and asked for guidance. My Bible gave me the answer. I shall simply trust in the Lord." Jim had little influence on her decision but did not protest much, saying "It's her choice. When she makes up her mind, no one on earth can influence her." Their son Paul was not consulted when these decisions were being made, and he was not deeply involved with his parents. Neither Pamela nor Jim talked much about Paul or seemed to expect him or his wife to help care for Pamela. When asked about Paul, Pamela would say, "He's busy with his own life, and I don't want to bother him." Several photographs of Paul during his growing-up years were on display in the house, but his name was mentioned infrequently. Pamela and Jim attended the same church, and this was one of the few activities they shared as a couple. Until her condition worsened, Pamela had been an active participant in church affairs. Paul had changed his religious affiliation when he married and converted to his wife's faith.

Emotional distance impeded communication between Pamela and Jim. Even before Pamela became ill, conversation between the partners was superficial and minimal. As the malignancy progressed, the implications of Pamela's condition and the possibility of her death were not mentioned. When the two did talk together, discussion took the form of argument and recrimination, with Jim's leaving the house in a controlled rage. Even though Pamela's illness was the dominant force in their relationship, it was never alluded to by either of them.

EXTERNAL COMMUNICATION CHARACTERISTICS

The White family was virtually a closed system that avoided external input whenever possible. When their only son married, he was extruded from the family and no longer was an integral part of the family unit. Both partners believed themselves to be disciplined and self-controlled, but they operated on an emotional rather than a rational level. Pamela based her decisions on what she intuitively felt was right. She refused to justify her decisions or explain them to her husband. Jim was unable to articulate his beliefs or base his opinions on logic or reason and usually followed Pamela's dictates even when he was not in agreement. He had always had a few male friends with whom he played cards until Pamela's illness took up all his free time. Jim admitted to his friends that he felt tied to the house and his sick wife, but he took no initiative to institute change.

Even before Pamela became so ill, this family resisted external relationships that were intimate. Ties with the community were maintained through Pamela's friendships in their church. A few friends from church called to see Pamela or offered help, but she usually put them off with some pretext. Because of the conspiracy of silence surrounding Pamela's illness, neither her pastor nor her friends were able to provide much assistance. By default Jim became the sole provider of care. A physician visited to give medical treatment of a supportive nature only.

PSYCHOLOGICAL CHARACTERISTICS

The locus of control in the family resided with Pamela. Even though terminally ill, she used her condition to manipulate and control Jim. If she allowed others to attend her, Pamela thought that Jim would be free to pursue his own life and interests. Much of her behavior was motivated by a wish to punish Jim. He desperately wanted some respite from attending to Pamela but was not able to make any direct requests for himself. A brief extramarital affair that existed at the time of Pamela's diagnosis three years before had ended, but the relationship left a residue of guilt for Jim. Even though he often felt victimized, Jim would say, "How can I turn away from a sick woman. And besides I owe her this."

SOCIOECONOMIC AND ENVIRONMENTAL CHARACTERISTICS

By exerting heroic efforts, Jim endeavored to meet Pamela's needs. All his time and attention when he was not at work were spent making her as comfortable as possible. In the three years since the original diagnosis, Pamela's health and energy steadily declined. She became inactive in the home and withdrew from the church activities that had been her only pleasure. Jim gradually took over all the household chores, such as shopping and cleaning, in addition to working full-time at his job. Pamela spent her time listening to religious programs on the radio and reading her Bible. Even when she was still capable of walking, she preferred to stay in bed. Jim moved out of the bedroom and slept in Paul's old room in order not to disturb Pamela, but his sleep was interrupted frequently to answer her bell. Nothing he did for her ever seemed to satisfy Pamela. "He takes so long to help me to the bathroom at night. . . . He cooks food I dislike. . . . He is clumsy in everything he does." Pamela also complained that her physician was incompetent, even though she was not compliant in following the suggested regimen regarding analgesic medication.

PLANNING AND INTERVENTION

Some time before Pamela died, her physician insisted on making a referral to a hospice program. At this time Jim was spending all his time shuttling between his job and his home. He would leave work several times during the day to attend to Pamela and was the only person caring for her at night. He had not played cards with his friends for more than a year. When he tried to work for brief intervals in his woodshop, Pamela complained bitterly of being neglected. Even though Jim was soft-spoken and unassertive, there were enormous amounts of unexpressed bitterness in him. The punishing schedule he maintained began to take a physical toll; Jim lost weight, slept poorly, and showed other signs of depression.

It was obvious to hospice staff members that Pamela was using her condition to make Jim share her suffering. From the beginning of her illness, she had taken no responsibility for her own welfare, and she encroached on Jim's life as much as possible. Even though she was terminally ill, Pamela was strong enough to use her condition as a weapon against her husband. An initial step in planning was to elicit from the partners what each saw as their major problem.

The hospice workers realized that Pamela would need more care in the weeks ahead, and this need was the presenting problem perceived by Pamela and Jim. Talking about meeting Pamela's needs more effectively was an indirect method of moving toward granting Jim some relief from his wife's hostility and her incessant demands.

It was already too late to alter the long-standing dysfunction in this family, but it was thought that Pamela's discomfort would be lessened if she agreed to accept help from the hospice staff. With the encouragement of the physician, a hospice worker began to visit daily and to refer openly to Pamela's condition. The worker saw Pamela's religious faith as a strength and was attentive to the sick woman's explanation of her religious beliefs. An oncology nurse who also visited was able to suggest some procedures to make Pamela more comfortable. All the members of the hospice staff recognized the strain Jim was under, his depression, and his need to ventilate his pent-up feelings. Individual counseling was offered to Jim to provide emotional support in the final weeks of Pamela's illness and help him work through his guilt and grief during the time of bereavement.

A significant meeting was held at which Pamela, Jim, the physician, an oncology nurse, and a hospice worker were present. At this meeting Pamela's prognosis was discussed and family needs were prioritized. All agreed that the most urgent need was to provide the best possible care for Pamela. Regular visits by an oncology nurse were scheduled and supplemented by a home health aide. Pamela had always resisted medication, but she was advised to take her analgesic every three hours rather than wait until she found the pain unbearable. The importance of other procedures was explained, and Pamela was told that she should take some responsibility for her own comfort. Occasional visits from some of her friends were suggested during the day and in the evenings. Instead of complaining whenever Jim left her or expecting him to leave work to take care of her, Pamela was persuaded to allow some old friends from church to visit and help. This arrangement gave Jim a few precious hours for himself. Since he was less exhausted, it was easier for him to get up with Pamela at night. A referral to a male social worker on the hospice staff was made for Jim, who was very responsive to this part of the plan.

FAMILY EVALUATION

The interventions implemented for this family were considered successful even though Pamela died about a month after entering the hospice program. She was relatively free from pain during those weeks and found solace in the visits of friends who shared her religious views, even though she had initially resisted their attention. Jim was able to play cards a few times with his friends when his wife had company. A productive therapeutic relationship was established between Jim and his social worker that continued for a time after Pamela's death.

In responding to the crisis of this family, an approach was utilized that considered the family's most pressing needs but did not exclude either member. For Pamela only the secondary and tertiary levels of care were appropriate; the relief offered Jim included primary, secondary, and tertiary measures. Pamela's passive-aggressive actions toward Jim prevented her from receiving the care she needed. Her regressive tendencies were expressed in her unwillingness to take any responsibility for her own care, and her dependency needs were directed into religious channels. As death approached, her religious beliefs helped support her and finally induced her to reach out again to her church. The therapeutic relationship established between Jim and his social worker employed anticipatory guidance so that grief work could begin. Meetings with the social worker for a short period after Pamela's death facilitated the expression of Jim's feelings and reduced the need to atone for his infidelity. After Pamela's death Jim mentioned his wish to see his son from time to time, and the social worker encouraged him to renew communication.

depend on and respond to external emotional influences. Individuals who have managed to separate only slightly from domination by the emotional system of their family of origin are likely to be located near the pseudoself end of the differentiation of self continuum. They react emotionally rather than cognitively and exhibit greater degrees of emotional fusion with others. Thus, in appraising relative amounts of solid self and pseudoself in individuals, Bowen first determines whether individuals react on a feeling or a thinking level.

Use of the differentiation of self scale is helpful in assessing individuals and family units. Having made an assessment of self-differentiation (even though this is an impressionistic rather than an exact measurement), the practitioner can begin to develop goals to help family members separate themselves from the emotional fusion and undifferentiation that contribute to dysfunction. Bowen points out that the differentiation of self scale should be used to examine family patterns over extended periods rather than to assess at a particular point in time.

It is useful to obtain a complete family history to ascertain the extent of self-differentiation in individuals and in the family. For this reason it is advisable for the family therapist to construct a *geneogram* that traces family events over several generations. Demographic data regarding family illnesses, longevity, occupations, and lifestyles all help the practitioner develop a geneogram that is informative and helpful in developing goals for clients who have failed to differentiate from the family of origin. A sample geneogram is shown in Figure 19–6.

FAMILY PROJECTION In *family projection*, the anxiety of one or both parents is transmitted or projected to a child. The selected child is made the focus of attention, with one parent becoming overly protective and involved. Although the child may continue to function after a fashion, his or her psychological development is endangered, because it is difficult for the child to separate and differentiate from the parent who is so close. Even when the child's psychological development is not seriously impaired,

Figure 19–6. *Example of a geneogram.*

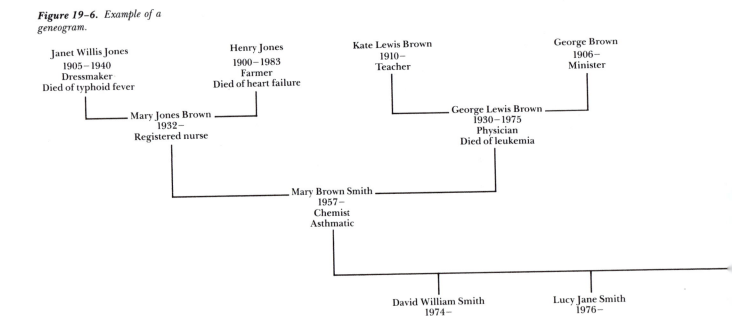

the closeness of one parent may cost the child the affection of the second parent and the acceptance of siblings who resent the special position conferred on one of their number. An inevitable consequence of the family projection process is that the selected child does not remain in the sibling subsystem but is "triangled" or drawn into the parental subsystem in order to absorb the parents' negative feelings toward each other. Family projection is used by immature parents with poor self-differentiation in order to avoid dealing with actual issues. Bowen believes that children on whom parental anxiety and conflict are projected may be unable to move in the direction of establishing a solid self.

EMOTIONAL CUTOFF Bowen used the concept of *emotional cutoff* to describe the detachment from one's family of origin that individuals must try to accomplish. When deep attachment to the family of origin continues even after the individual has established a new family of procreation, conditions of pseudoselfhood continue. This pattern of prolonged attachment and emotional dependency on the family of origin can become a source of contention between marital partners and can threaten the existence of the family of procreation. Bowen does not advise individuals to abandon their families of origin but rather to develop a solid sense of self that allows them to be autonomous in thoughts and actions without feeling anxious and disloyal.

TRIANGLES According to Bowen, the triangle is the basic "molecule" of the family. Whenever the relationship between two people in a family becomes difficult, one person will pull in, or "triangle," a third party in order to relieve tension. A wife who sees her husband as detached or uncaring may turn to a son in order to fulfill her unmet needs. This exploits the son in many ways but reduces the anxiety of the mother and permits the father to continue his behavior. Often the father in such a situation is content with the status quo. Sometimes, however, the father resents his isolated position and moves toward the son, thereby becoming his wife's rival for the son's affection.

Triangulation is not confined to family members. The married man who takes a mistress has constructed a classic triangle, and the man who devotes most of his energy to his job creates a different kind of triangle. So has the woman who turns to alcohol to relieve marital boredom. In one case the apex of the triangle is the husband's job; in another case the apex of the triangle is the wife's alcoholism.

The solution to the dysfunctional family triangle is *detriangulation*. Bowen suggests that this be done by showing clients the difference between responding (acting in a manner that meets their own needs) and reacting (acting in a manner that meets the needs of others). For Bowen, reacting means being manipulated by others, whereas responding means being free to recognize the perspectives of other people but not to be ruled by this alone.

MULTIGENERATIONAL TRANSMISSION The concept of *multigenerational transmission* was anticipated by Freud in his description of the collective emotional life of families as allowing certain values to be perpetuated across generations. As postulated by Bowen, movement toward one extreme or the other on the differentiation of self continuum can occur from one generation to the next. Progression

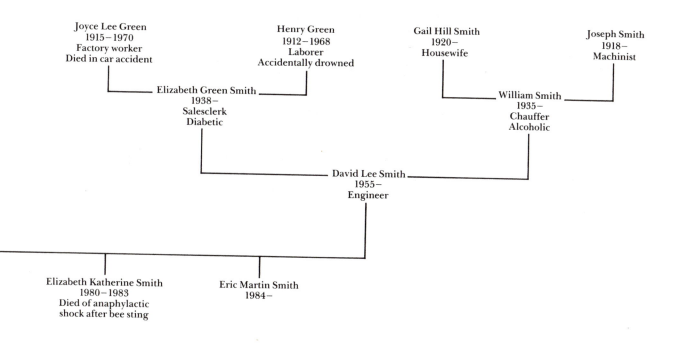

Joyce Lee Green
1915–1970
Factory worker
Died in car accident

Henry Green
1912–1968
Laborer
Accidentally drowned

Gail Hill Smith
1920–
Housewife

Joseph Smith
1918–
Machinist

Elizabeth Green Smith
1938–
Salesclerk
Diabetic

William Smith
1935–
Chauffer
Alcoholic

David Lee Smith
1955–
Engineer

Elizabeth Katherine Smith
1980–1983
Died of anaphylactic
shock after bee sting

Eric Martin Smith
1984–

or regression in one generation has an effect on succeeding generations, which also have the ability to reverse direction. After several generations of decreasing self-differentiation in families, mental disorders may become apparent in offspring made vulnerable by dysfunctional family triangling or projection.

FAMILY CONSTELLATION The effects of sibling rank and order in the family were recognized by Toman (1976), who suggested that sibling positions, gender differences, and family configurations influence the personality characteristics and social tendencies of offspring. Toman listed eight significant positions in addition to being an only child or one of twins:

Oldest brother of brother(s).

Youngest brother of brother(s).

Oldest brother of sister(s).

Youngest brother of sister(s).

Oldest sister of sister(s).

Youngest sister of sister(s).

Oldest sister of brother(s).

Youngest sister of brother(s).

Each of these positions is thought to be accompanied by certain behavioral and personality qualities.

The concept of sibling position does offer clues to the understanding of certain predispositions. One assumption is that children who are oldest siblings tend to feel responsible and to be somewhat directive, whereas those who are youngest siblings are apt to feel dependent and to accept direction. This concept is a broad generalization, however, and does not take into account relevant family events, past and present. As part of a tentative or provisional appraisal, the concept may be helpful, but careful validation is needed to recognize discrepancies and exceptions. Toman's work on family constellations and sibling positions may be used in assessing families, and his concepts have been incorporated into Bowen's formulations.

In constructing a family geneogram it is useful to ask what sibling position the spouses held in their respective families of origin, what responsibilities and privileges were attached to various sibling positions, and what emotional reactions were aroused in them and in their siblings by these responsibilities and privileges. The wife who grew up as the oldest girl in a family with five younger boys is apt to have a different perception of family life than her husband who was the baby brother of five doting older sisters. Helping the partners to resolve discrepancies in their early experiences of family life is possible only after identifying the discrepancies. Utilizing the concept of sibling position can be an effective way of introducing this issue.

SOCIETAL REGRESSION Bowen suggested that society itself is an emotional system resembling the family. Just as families must struggle to deal with rationality versus emotionality, so society must work to avoid regressive behavior. Under stressful conditions such as illness or loss, families become

---

SOCIETAL REGRESSION DURING THE GREAT DEPRESSION

The unemployed had been put to work on certain road jobs, to be paid by the towns with a certain amount of state aid. The towns had no money, and state money would not be available until sometime in December. The result was that some of the men had as much as $300 due in back pay! In some towns the school teachers were actually on relief. Some of them hadn't received any money since last January. And before that their pay had been cut down to practically nothing. In one town they were going to close the schools, but the teachers, having no place to go and no way to earn a living, said they preferred to keep on working—for food orders. Their offer was accepted . . .

Largely because it was handled by public officials who were inexperienced and unsympathetic in their attitude, the relief administration in some places was awful. Weekly food orders were written out by men who apparently hadn't the slightest idea of the food needs of a family. Nor its other needs. It had never occurred to some of them that people need soap, for instance. One food order . . . contained, in fact, practically nothing except starch, a little fat, and a little molasses.

SOURCE: Richard Lowitt and Maureen Beasley, eds., *One Third of a Nation* (Chicago: University of Chicago Press, 1981).

dysfunctional. Under stressful conditions such as crop failure, economic fluctuation, and environmental pollution, society becomes dysfunctional. The consequence is that legislative and administrative decisions are made on an emotional rather than a rational basis, so that problems are worsened rather than solved.

The concept of societal regression is important because all families are affected by conditions of the society in which they exist. Poverty, bureaucracy, occupational and industrial obsolescence are only a few of the negative aspects of society that transform functional families into dysfunctional ones. As advocates for families and as care providers, nurses should be informed about social and political developments in communities where they practice and should make informed judgments about the logic and rationality of legislative and administrative actions.

Communication Concepts

Several theorists have devoted themselves to the application of communication concepts to family work. Communication theorists rarely conceptualize personality except in terms of communication and interaction. Their central purpose is to improve the ways in which families communicate, nonverbally as well as verbally. *How* messages are sent and received is just as important to communication theorists as the content of the messages that are transmitted.

DOUBLE BINDS A classic paper titled "Toward a Theory of Schizophrenia" proved to be of considerable importance in family theory and family therapy (Bateson et al. 1956). In this paper, Gregory Bateson and his colleagues made a distinction between situations in which it is possible to choose one course of action over another and situations in which options seem to be offered but no choice is available. The term they coined for these latter situations is *double bind*.

In a double bind transaction, a primary command or message is given followed by a secondary command or message that contradicts the first. The recipient of the message is in essence told, "Do not take this action or you will suffer consequences," followed by "Do take this action, for if you do not you will suffer consequences." For double bind messages to create the greatest harm to the recipient, the practice must occur repeatedly and the recipient must be unable to escape the situation.

Although the double bind concept grew out of observations of families with a schizophrenic member, this phenomenon is also evident in many families that might appear to be quite functional; it is only after study of family interactional patterns that the double binding of one or more members is revealed. Because of their immaturity and dependency, children are often the target of double bind messages, although it may also be one of the spouses who is victimized in this fashion.

The secondary message in the double bind is often communicated nonverbally. For example, a mother might ask her young son to come to her for a kiss and then proceed to ward off his attention because his face or hands are dirty. Another example is provided by parents who consider themselves permissive, assuring their children that they are free to choose any occupation they wish, and who then show disappointment when a preference is expressed.

What do people do when they are constantly subjected to double binds? First they suspect that something mysterious is happening to them that they could figure out if they just tried hard enough. But the more they ruminate about their situation, the more confused they become. Some of them adopt the attitude that since nothing makes sense, why bother trying to understand anything. Others react by becoming rigid and literal in their thoughts and actions as they try to obey every command given them, no matter how paradoxical the commands become. Still others give up so completely that they withdraw from interpersonal involvement, thus avoiding confusion and entrapment.

The concept of the double bind has proven quite useful in family therapy (Wynne 1978). Because double bind transactions are often beyond the awareness of family members, senders and receivers alike, caregivers are in a position to identify contradictory messages and to offer feedback to correct the confusion. Recognizing double binds and helping families clarify messages are activities within the scope of nurses who have had sufficient opportunity to observe and assess family communication patterns.

A frequent interactional pattern in families is *equifinality*. This refers to the proposition that often the same assessment of a family will be made regardless of when the assessment is done. Take, for example, a marriage in which the wife is at first a reckless spendthrift and the husband is a frugal planner. Over time, the behavior of each partner changes so that the partners' attitudes toward spending become reversed. After decades together, the husband and wife have exchanged positions, but family homeostasis has been maintained because the marriage continues to consist of a spendthrift and a saver. The frugality of one partner perpetuates the extravagance of the other, regardless of the identity of either partner. Equifinality thus reveals the reciprocal nature of family transactions. In other marriages the passivity of one partner makes possible and reinforces the dominance of the other.

One therapy technique advocated by Jackson (1968) is *relabeling*. This strategy consists of taking behavior that is considered negative by the family and emphasizing its positive aspects. For example, in a family with a school nonachiever whose parents are angry and impatient, the therapist might interpret the child's behavior as a self-sacrificing effort to distract the attention of parents from their disillusionment with each other. In another context, a violent argument between husband and wife might be interpreted as a dysfunctional attempt to get closer to each other.

Virginia Satir (1967) has assessed communication and interaction in families and has focused on the way family members feel about one another. Satir's approach brings an empathy to family work that is absent from the work of many other communication theorists. This empathetic quality makes her interventions very compatible with the nursing process.

It is Satir's contention that the husband and wife are the architects of the family and that the causes of dysfunction lie in their relationship. Assessment therefore begins with the marital dyad. Satir's assumption is that at one point in their lives the partners both thought their mutual needs would be met through their relationship. Therefore, it is important to take a family history or chronology dealing with how the partners met, what their expectations of marriage were, and what memories they have of their early years together. Gathering a family chronology has two benefits: it traces the divergent memories and expectations of the partners, and diverts the partners from current feelings of hostility as they recall happier times (Satir, Stachwiak, and Taschman 1977). A sample chronology is provided on page 542.

SELF-ESTEEM A basic tenet of Satir's approach is that low self-esteem is the fundamental problem in dysfunctional marriages, not sexuality. In relationships where the self-esteem of one of the partners is threatened, rising levels of anxiety and aggressiveness appear in their transactions. Children are often brought into the world as a way of increasing the self-esteem of the parents. This may become a heavy burden for the child who cannot live up to unrealistic parental expectations.

In order to acquire adequate self-esteem, children need physical care, continuity of relationships, parental consistency, and reassurance that they are valued for themselves rather than for their accomplishments. If these qualities were markedly deficient in the family of origin, they are likely to be deficient in the family of procreation as well.

Three ideas are basic to Satir's approach to family assessment and intervention:

1. Everyone wants to survive, to grow, and to be close to other significant people. All behavior, however bizarre it may seem, is directed toward these ends.

2. Behavior that appears to be "sick" or "crazy" is usually an effort to transmit distress signals to others.

3. Thoughts and emotions are closely connected; to understand thinking one must get in touch with what oneself and others are feeling.

COMMUNICATION PATTERNS One result of failure to maintain the self-esteem of family members, particularly between the partners, is that unclear, ambiguous communication patterns develop.

According to Satir, family members should be able to express their needs and feelings openly but with regard for the needs and feelings of other members. She has identified several dysfunctional ways in which families communicate. These are described in Table 19–4.

In order to assess family communication patterns, Satir uses a *sociogram*—a technique for noting the frequency and direction of messages sent between family members. After a family meeting has ended, the health professional can diagram the spatial positions of family members, who spoke to whom and how often, and who failed to speak to

Table 19–4. Types of Dysfunctional Communication

Type	Purpose
Blaming	Family members are fearful of being blamed and therefore attribute responsibility for error or failure to others.
Placating	Family members adopt a pretense of being inadequate but well meaning in order to preserve peace at any price.
Generalizing	Family members make global statements using terms like *always* and *never* instead of dealing with specific issues or problems.
Computing	Family members emphasize cognitive and literal transactions, ignoring emotional issues in order to appear in control and fully reasonable.
Distracting	Family members introduce irrelevant details into problematic issues in order to avoid functional problem solving.

SOURCE: Adapted from Satir (1967).

other family members. An example of a communication sociogram is shown in Figure 19–7. This tool can be used for evaluation as well as assessment purposes. If a sociogram is developed soon after every family session, it is possible to note changes in communication patterns that occurred as family intervention proceeded.

Although sociograms are helpful in permitting the professional to recall communication direction and frequency more accurately, they have some deficiencies. Unless the sessions are videotaped and later analyzed or there is a skilled observer taking notes, total accuracy is impossible. As an impressionistic measurement, however, the sociogram has definite advantages.

Sociograms can also be used as reminders of the qualitative differences in family communication. The following qualitative aspects of family communication should be part of the assessment process:

1. How are messages transmitted in the family? Directly? Indirectly?

2. How are disagreements dealt with in the family? By avoidance? By confrontation? By negotiation?

3. What subjects are not discussed by the family?

4. What issues absorb the attention of the family?

Communication theorists believe that communication can be a major assessment, implementation, and evaluation tool in working with individuals and families—a belief that has particular applicability for nurses. Any message, verbal or nonverbal, that occurs in the presence of another person reveals something about the nature of their relationship. Only the more sophisticated professionals need decide whether power, emotion, or cognition is the most significant influence in family communication. The generalist nurse can be effective merely by using and understanding basic principles of communication theory and by learning to observe carefully and listen actively to the multiple levels on which communication takes place.

Learning Theory Concepts

Social learning is an ongoing process in which people teach others how to behave. The teaching is accomplished through reward and punishment methods that have the power to perpetuate or alleviate dysfunctional behavior. Although strict behaviorists believe that behavior can be reduced to simple stimulus-response patterns, most learning theorists are more apt to recognize the impact of intervening influences.

Human beings have the capacity to interpret events in an individualistic manner. This means that the same event will be perceived differently by different people, because people who share the same physical environment inhabit an internal symbolic environment that is entirely their own (Mead 1933, Speigel 1971). Human beings also have the capacity to analyze their own actions and to understand the reactions of other people. This

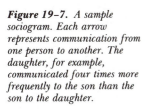

Figure 19–7. A sample sociogram. Each arrow represents communication from one person to another. The daughter, for example, communicated four times more frequently to the son than the son to the daughter.

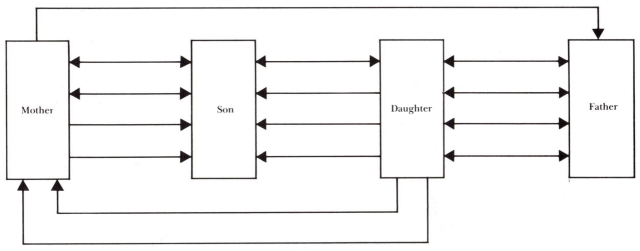

FAMILY CHRONOLOGY

1950–1973 Richard Grant was born and raised in California. He has two older sisters. His father is a practicing lawyer and his mother manages a dress shop.

1955–1973 Rosemary Cooper was born and raised in Cleveland, Ohio. After high school she attended a business college, where she earned an associate degree. Her father died the year Rosemary found her first job. Rosemary is an only child.

1973–1975 Richard graduated from college and began working for an insurance company. He attended a sales conference in Cleveland, where Rosemary was working as a secretary. The couple met when Rosemary was assigned to help Richard finish a report.

1975–1977 Rosemary and Richard corresponded and saw each other as much as possible. They were married in June 1977 and moved to California.

1978 Rosemary's mother had a stroke and she returned to Cleveland to look after her mother. The stay lasted eight months and although he visited occasionally Richard became increasingly unhappy with the separation.

1979 Rosemary became pregnant and agreed to return to California if her mother could come live with her. Twin boys were born in November 1979. The first year after the birth was hectic but the couple managed well by sharing parenting tasks.

1981 Richard left the insurance company to go into business for himself. The move was financially successful, but Richard was absent from home much of the time.

1982–1983 Rosemary and her mother, who still lived with the couple, formed a coalition that excluded Richard. Rosemary often felt torn between her mother and her husband, who did not get along well with each other. She felt lonely at times, was impatient with her sons, and resented Richard's absences from home. Richard was proud of the way he had provided for his family, was devoted to his sons, was resentful of his mother-in-law's presence, and worried about Rosemary, who did not seem like the bright, confident young woman he had married.

1984 At Richard's insistence, the couple went to a marriage counselor to try, in Richard's words, to "revitalize the marriage."

means that people can predict the behavior of others at least some of the time and can modify their own behavior based on these predictions. To understand how this operates one has only to compare the behavior of school-children when an experienced, organized teacher is present and the behavior of the same children when an unfamiliar, insecure substitute teacher enters their classroom.

In attempting to promote change in families, the nurse enacts a social learning role not simply by teaching appropriate behaviors but by modeling them. Instead of telling the family how to interact, the nurse can demonstrate desirable ways of interacting with one another. In family meetings the nurse should not become the ally of any single coalition or subsystem but should recognize the existence of all subsystems and coalitions. The nurse may agree or disagree with family members, indicating by these actions that it is acceptable to express one's opinions. Without relying on verbal directives, the nurse models a more functional way of interacting.

As has been noted by various family theorists, a great deal of human behavior is learned in the family of origin and transferred to the family of procreation. If conditions in the more recently established family are such that the old behaviors are rewarded, there is no doubt that they will continue. If in the family of origin an action taken in response to certain stimuli has been rewarded, similar stimuli will tend to produce the same behavior. For example, a young woman who becomes accustomed to functioning in a managerial role in her family of origin and who has enjoyed a reputation for competence will try to perform the same role in her family of procreation, especially if she receives positive rewards from her husband and children. If, however, her executive functions are resented by her new family, she will undoubtedly be disappointed. Disappointment over not being rewarded may lead her to modify her managerial tendencies, but this is likely to happen only if family members are able to express their feelings and she is willing to listen. If she does not receive expected rewards, she may react with anger and disapproval. Such feelings may lead to avoidance of appropriate role enactment or to retaliation against family members who have not provided the expected rewards. If she is aggressive enough, she will retain the executive role in the family, but other members will experience mounting tension in the form of unexpressed resentment.

In this example, the young woman becomes accustomed to enacting a role that was rewarded in her family of origin. In other words, she learns to behave in a way that was appreciated and therefore reinforced in that family. The most powerful reinforcers in family life are social. For most people a smile, an expression of approval, an embrace, or a touch is enormously effective in promoting social learning. Single episodes of reinforcement are unlikely to have sustained impact, but repeated reinforcement can have profound effects on human expectations and behavior (Patterson 1975, Bandura 1977).

Table 19–5 summarizes the learning approach along with the several other approaches to family theory that have been discussed in this chapter.

FAMILY-CENTERED CARE

This chapter has presented an overview of major approaches to assessing and assisting families. Some of the concepts are quite sophisticated, but many are relatively simple and can be used safely by generalist nurses. Assessment of family needs is within the scope of every nurse, but it is essential for generalist nurses to consult with colleagues prepared on the graduate level before offering family intervention. If consultation and supervision are available, an experienced generalist nurse may undertake family intervention around a specific problem. Otherwise a referral for family intervention is more appropriate.

Family theory is a fairly new field, and systematic and clinical investigation continues at a rapid rate. Nevertheless, there are some established guidelines to help nurses as they begin to enter this complex field.

THE INITIAL INTERVIEW Families who seek professional help have already made a difficult decision. They are anxious and confused, and they are afraid of what may be revealed in family sessions. A good rule is for the nurse to discover first what the family's perception of the problem is. This should be one of the goals of an initial family meeting.

The initial interview is primarily a time for getting acquainted with the family members who are present, for observing their interactions with one another, and for trying to reduce the levels of anxiety that are present. It is important to know who initiated the referral. Was a recommendation made by another professional or by a relative or neighbor, or was the contact initiated by a family member? If the family behaves as if there is an identified patient who is the family problem, this is important to know.

The nurse should tell the family the purpose of the meeting and disclose enough identifying information to decrease the family's fears of the nurse as a powerful, intrusive stranger. It may even be appropriate for the professional to share some personal feelings regarding the family meeting. While trying to establish a calm, unhurried atmosphere, the nurse should also bring up contractual matters, such as how often they will meet and how long the sessions will last. If the family can tolerate exploration at the initial meeting, the nurse might ask what the members would like to accomplish as a result of the sessions. Usually some but not all the family members will respond to this request.

ORGANIZING DATA A great deal goes on at family meetings, and a number of tools have been suggested to organize data in a coherent way. The family map suggested by Minuchin, the geneogram adapted by Bowen, and the family chronology and sociogram devised by Satir are all useful mechanisms for data organization, especially in the early sessions.

When family members give inaccurate information, their distortion may not be deliberate but rather may indicate feelings of embarrassment or anxiety. Distortion can be reduced considerably if the nurse carefully avoids indications of shock or disapproval as information is given. Emotionally charged words should be avoided. Instead of asking what the family problem is, the nurse should simply ask, "What has been happening in the family to bring you here?" It is permissible and even desirable to refer to what was discussed at the previous meeting. Very often the most important data are not revealed until the very end of a session. Referring back to such unresolved issues is an excellent way to provide continuity from session to session and to demonstrate to the family that what they say is important.

WORKING PHASE As families begin to trust their therapist, they move into the working phase of the therapy. Even then hazards persist, and many families find the prospect of change so difficult that they drop out of treatment. For families who continue to meet, it is necessary to continue to word questions carefully. Interpretations of statements and challenges of actions should be done in the form of suggestions or reflective comments. Examples of this strategy are: "How have things changed in the family since we've been meeting?" "You both may be right, but there is another way of looking at what happened." "I wonder whether you were really as hurt as you say you were. Is it possible that you were hurt and angry, too?"

During the working phase the family is likely to reveal their dysfunctional interactional patterns. Feelings of bitterness and anger are expressed, and

Table 19–5. Approaches to Family Theory

Conceptual Approach	Representative Theorists	Concepts	Nursing Process Actions
Developmental theory	Erikson Duvall	Individual life cycle tasks Family life cycle tasks	1. Identify stage-specific individual tasks. 2. Identify stage-specific family tasks. 3. Recognize impediments to resolution of individual and family tasks. 4. Help families identify and reduce impediments to individual and family task resolution.
General systems theory	Von Bertalanffy	Interdependence boundaries feedback	1. Emphasize interdependence of all members to avoid placing blame on any one member. 2. Help families acknowledge circular effects of their actions on all members. 3. Promote boundary maintenance that protects the family from excessive input from external sources. 4. Promote boundary maintenance that allows the family adequate input from external sources. 5. Encourage families to recognize the reciprocal effects of their actions on all members.
Psychodynamic theory	Freud Wynne Lidz	Collective family psyche Pseudomutuality Pseudohostility Rubber fences Marital schism and skew	1. Identify significant family attitudes and values. 2. Differentiate genuine harmony from surface harmony (pseudomutuality). 3. Differentiate conflict around authentic issues from conflict used to avoid authentic issues (pseudohostility). 4. Help families establish consistent, functional family boundaries. 5. Discourage excessive closeness between a parent and a selected child. 6. Strengthen the relationship between the partners.

Structural theory	Minuchin	Boundaries
		  Clear
		  Rigid
		  Diffuse
		Subsystems
		  Parental
		  Sibling
		Scapegoating
		Family mapping
			1. Use a family map to show emotional closeness and distance between members and family organizational structure.
			2. Identify boundary characteristics.
			3. Promote clear, functional boundaries between members.
			4. Help the family realize that the symptoms of the identified client may be keeping the family together.
			5. Encourage family members to reduce their preoccupation with the symptoms of the identified client.
			6. Restructure family positions so that parents form a parental dyad and children form a sibling subsystem.

Functional theory	Bowen
	Toman
		Family emotional systems
		Differentiation of self
		  Pseudoself
		  Solid self
		Geneograms
		Family projection
		Emotional cutoff
		Multigenerational transmission
		Family constellation
		  Sibling position
		Societal regression
			1. Promote separation and individuation of members in nuclear families.
			2. Encourage rational rather than irrational thoughts and behaviors.
			3. Attempt to modify inappropriate family triangles.
			4. Help families avoid placing any child in a special position in relation to a parent.
			5. Assess family direction across generations toward or away from developing a solid self (rational) or pseudoself (irrational).
			6. Teach families the effects of age, gender, and rank order on the behavior and development of adults and children.

(continued)

Table 19–5. *Continued*

Conceptual Approach	Representative Theorists	Concepts	Nursing Process Actions
Functional theory (cont'd)			7. Encourage encounters with family of origin that foster autonomy and differentiation of adult members. 8. Help families cope with stressful environmental conditions such as unemployment, poverty, overcrowding, and environmental pollution. 9. Formulate a geneogram showing marriages, births, deaths, and other events across generations.

Communication theory	Bateson
	Jackson
	Lederer
	Haley
	Satir
		Double binds
		Equifinality
		Symmetrical relationships
		Complementary relationships
		Dysfunctional communication
		  Blaming
		  Placating
		  Generalizing
		  Distracting
		  Computing
		Self-esteem
		Family chronology
		Family sociogram
			1. Reinforce self-esteem of all members.
			2. Use relabeling techniques to interpret behaviors in a positive way.
			3. Analyze communication in terms of cognition (thinking), power (control), and emotion (feeling).
			4. Encourage specific, clear messages.
			5. Help families identify behaviors that reinforce or complement each other (dominant wife/passive husband).
			6. Help families identify behaviors that are symmetrical or parallel (spouses compete for nurture/spouses compete for dominance).
			7. Formulate a family chronology or history of events.
			8. Develop family sociograms showing the frequency and direction of communication between members.

Learning theory	Skinner Mead Parsons	Stimulus-response Interactional symbolism Role expectations Role performance Rewards	1. Use operant behavioral concepts to modify behavior. 2. Identify and apply intervening variables to reinforce or reduce socially learned behavior. 3. Help families recognize how inappropriate role expectations and role performance increase family dysfunction. 4. Teach families appropriate ways of rewarding desirable behaviors.

even experienced nurses are apt to be dismayed by the atmosphere. Here nurses may find support in a theoretical model entitled "Levels of Marital Conflict" (Weingarten and Leas 1987). The model helps organize data and conceptualize family dissension patterns. Having identified the conflict level at which the family is functioning, the family therapist tries to reduce emotional intensity by de-escalating the conflict and promoting problem solving (see Tables 19–6 and 19–7). The five levels of conflict are identified by prevailing behaviors in the family. Each behavior level is more destructive than the one preceding it.

A warning should be heeded by generalist nurses giving family-centered care to clients operating at levels 3, 4, or 5. At these dysfunctional levels a generalist nurse should seek consultation or supervision from a clinical specialist whose knowledge of family theory and practice augments the skills of the generalist nurse. Knowing one's limitations and obtaining backup expertise are prerequisites in this complex sphere of endeavor.

TERMINATION SESSIONS Sometimes the family terminates the meetings prematurely and without the concurrence of the therapist. Even the most adept therapist cannot change the family. The therapist can only offer the family an opportunity to change; it is the family that decides whether or not to grasp the opportunity. A wide gulf may exist between what the family is willing to change and what the therapist would like to see changed. When there is discrepancy between the therapist's and the family's views on what should be altered, some agreement must be reached.

Table 19–6. Levels of Conflict

Behavior Level	Behavior Pattern	Therapeutic Approach
1. Problem Solving	Effective interaction dealing with tasks and decisions even in difficult situations.	Support customary adaptive interaction of the family.
2. Disagreeing	Saving face and not being hurt are more important than solving problems; outside advice may be sought; members disagree but are not wholly antagonistic	Offer support and protection to entire family; avoid becoming part of a family triangle; insist that members be clear, specific, and focused on problems.
3. Competing	Anger and resentment surface; self-protection is less important than getting even.	Outline communication rules; explore separate goals and experiences of members; use a cognitive approach; construct a geneogram to defuse anger and promote sharing of information among members.
4. Fighting/Fleeing	Goals and basic issues are forgotten in attempts to hurt other members either through confrontation or withdrawal.	Conflict has produced an impasse; set rules for communicating; search for issues where a degree of agreement is possible.
5. Waging War	Injury and revenge are a way of life; spouse and child abuse may be present; victim and victimizer are locked in a life-threatening struggle.	At this level reconciliation is not an immediate goal; suggest a period of separation to control family violence; utilize legal and protective services.

SOURCE: Adapted from Weingarten and Leas (1987).

Table 19–7. Levels of Conflict

Behavior Level	Major Objective	Emotional Climate	Interaction Style	Clients' View of Practitioner
1. Problem solving	Solve or resolve the problem.	Hope and optimism	Open, direct, focused communication; little or no distortion of content; recognition of common interests	Advisor and objective facilitator; resource person and expert
2. Disagreeing and arguing	Protect oneself. Comprise if necessary.	Uncertainty and vigilance	Vague, unfocused communication; cautious and calculated discussion	Mediator, enabler, intermediary
3. Competing and contending	Win or lose the competition.	Frustration and resentment; fear of losing	Distorted communication; personal attacks and manipulation	Arbiter, referee, judge
4. Fighting and/or fleeing	Injure the other person. Ignore the other person.	Hostility, antagonism, alienation	Stubborn unwillingness to change self or opinions; distorted perceptions; mixed messages; refusal to take responsibility for self or situation	Ally or enemy
5. Waging all-out war	Eliminate the other person by any means possible.	Revenge and destructiveness; retaliation and vindictiveness	Extreme volatility; no recollection or understanding of issues; self-righteous, compulsive driven behavior	Rescuer or destroyer

SOURCE: Adapted from Weingarten and Leas (1987).

During the earlier family meetings, specific goals must be formulated so that the family has a sense of direction and a sense of achievement if the goals are reached. Without specific negotiated goals, neither the family nor the therapist has standards by which to evaluate progress.

SUMMARY

Family theory and family therapy are based on the premise that dysfunction originates in the family rather than in the client. Family therapy is a treatment modality that has developed within the last few decades and is widely used, but it demands special preparation from practitioners. However, a number of family concepts are available that may be used to advantage by generalist nurses adopting a family-focused approach to health care.

Because many of the early family theorists and therapists worked independently of one another, there is considerable overlap in their conceptual approaches. Some approaches are more compatible with the nursing process than others, but most of them have some unique contribution to make. Six conceptual approaches were described in this chapter: developmental theory, psychodynamic theory, general systems theory, functional theory, communication theory, and learning theory.

Although early family theorists worked mostly with families that have a schizophrenic member, many of the dysfunctional patterns found in these families are present in families without any identified psychiatric disorder. Among the notable concepts from psychiatric theory that have contributed to the understanding of dysfunctional family dynamics are the double bind, rubber fences, pseudohostility, pseudomutuality, equifinality, and schismatic and skewed families.

The communication theorists offer concepts that are especially compatible with the nursing process, since effective communication is a skill well within the scope of the generalist nurse. Communication principles are extremely compatible with nursing process and nursing interventions. Especially the empathic qualities of Satir's approach.

A number of methods have been devised to help professionals working with families collect and organize data. Minuchin developed the technique of family mapping to show the structural characteristics of family organization. General systems theorists emphasized the influence of circular feedback and the interdependence of the family as an operating system. Bowen, a theorist who viewed the family as an emotional system, proposed eight concepts that support his insistence on personal autonomy and emotional separation from the family of origin.

Learning theory augments the contributions of other conceptual approaches to family work. Changing role expectations and structural variations in present-day families help explain some causes of conflict in families. Assessment of role expectations and structural organization can help nurses understand reasons for conflict when people raised in traditional families of origin find themselves in nontraditional families of procreation.

Family therapy requires advanced preparation from its practitioners, but family interventions are within the scope of generalist nurses who have a basic knowledge of family theory. Attrition rates are high in family therapy, but the nurse who can sustain a climate of nonjudgmental acceptance is more apt to forestall premature termination. Even the most experienced family therapist cannot alter family interactional patterns unless the family is willing to change. When there is disagreement between the family and the therapist regarding goals, accommodation is necessary to resolve areas of dispute. Without specific goals being set, neither the family nor the therapist has a sense of direction or standards by which to evaluate progress.

Family therapy is an accepted but complex treatment modality that requires graduate preparation and supervised clinical experience from those who practice it. It is a multidisciplinary approach, and practitioners are drawn from medicine, nursing, psychology, and social work. It is also an interdisciplinary modality, in that co-therapists often represent more than one health care profession. Nurses who perform family therapy should possess at least a master's degree in psychiatric mental health nursing. Even though extensive family therapy may not lie within the competence of the generalist nurse, this is not true of family assessment and planning. Nurses and other care providers who exclude family considerations from their care plan limit their effectiveness and jeopardize the welfare of clients.

Review Questions

1. How might individual and family life cycle tasks be used as a basis for assessment?

2. Describe what is meant by the interdependence of family members, using systems theory terminology.

3. Explain the difference between pseudomutuality and pseudohostility in families.

4. Using a diagram, illustrate clear boundaries, rigid boundaries, and diffuse boundaries in a family. What are the effects of these diverse boundaries on family members?

5. What is a family subsystem? What function do subsystems perform in a family?

6. What are the major differences between pseudoself and solid self? Which is considered more functional?

7. Explain the concept of triangling. Give an example of a family triangle.

8. What is a double bind? How does it affect family members?

Suggested Annotated Readings

Fenton, Mary V. "Development of a Scale of Humanistic Behaviors." *Nursing Research* 36, no. 2 (March/April 1987):82–85.

The subject of this report is the humanistic behaviors extended by nurses toward clients; the subject is especially relevant for nurses basing their practice on rational caring. The author, using research methodology, developed a scale of humanistic health care based on the replies of 316 nurses working in four hospitals: public, private, community, and university-affiliated. The eventual scale that was developed yielded four areas of humanistic nursing behavior: shared decision making and responsibility, holistic selves, status equality, and empathy. The area called holistic selves refers to the inclusion of all aspects of a client's life in providing health care. This exploratory study showed that measures of humanistic nursing behavior may be used diagnostically in comparing health care agencies. The scale of humanistic nursing behaviors may be used to help nurses identify and incorporate humanistic behaviors into their practice.

Lindblad-Goldberg, Marion, Joyce Lynn Dukes, and John H. Lasley. "Stress in Black Low-Income, Single-Parent Families: Normative and Dysfunctional Patterns." *American Journal of Orthopsychiatry* 58, no. 1 (January 1988):104–120.

Stressful life events and the influences of demographic and social network factors were studied in 50 clinic-referred and 76 nonclinic-referred families. All families were urban and black; 70 families were classified as functional and 56 as dysfunctional. In all families the biological mother was the single parent living at home with her children. There were no serious health problems in any of the children of participating families. As expected, demographic factors such as low income, unemployment, and poor education were distinct aspects of stress. Unexpectedly, social network support *per se* did not significantly alleviate stress. More important were the family's perception of stressful events and the resources that were available within the family unit.

Mercer, Ramona T., Katharyn A. May, Sandra Ferketich, and Jean De Joseph. "Theoretical Models for Studying the Effect of Antepartum Stress on the Family." *Nursing Research* 35, no. 6 (November/December 1986):339–345.

The report of this research study is significant because the whole family is included in the study, not merely the marital or the parent-child dyad. A developmental approach is used and the family is described as a dynamic system. Pregnancy produces internal and external change in the family. Internal change occurs in family structure and function; this internal change affects the way the family interacts with larger systems. Theoretical models identify relationships among complex family factors. The models offer guidance in designing family research. More importantly, the article utilizes many family concepts that are explained in the preceding chapter.

Murphy, Susan. "Family Study and Nursing Research." *Image* 18, no. 4 (Winter 1986):170–174.

This comprehensive article reviews the history of family study and nursing research. It acknowledges that nursing sometimes clings to an individual focus and deplores the lack of nursing research that is truly family-oriented. Although many nursing studies deal with families, most are deficient in some respects. Either they overlook the family as a unit, or they ignore the relationship of the family unit to larger social structures. The author calls on nurses to build on what has already been done and to collaborate with other disciplines. Inclusion of naturalistic studies of functional and dysfunctional families in their own environments is also recommended.

Shachnow, Jody. "Preventive Intervention with Children of Hospitalized Psychiatric Patients." *American Journal of Orthopsychiatry* 57, no. 1 (January 1987):67–77.

The premise of the study is that children are affected by the psychiatric hospitalization of a parent in ways that are not well understood. For such children the situation is a psychological crisis, especially since most of them have been living with a disturbed parent. The study endeavored to identify reaction patterns of the children, develop suggestions for brief intervention, and recommend areas for future study and practice. The investigative site was a psychiatric inpatient unit where the average patient stay was 90 days. Over a twenty-month period 36 children were seen with cooperation from the well parent. Much of the sample fell into two distinct subgroups representing opposite poles of adjustment. The two groups were made up of children described as "compromisers" or as "copers."

The children who coped all possessed a number of attributes. They were older and had an empathic adult in their lives to give them direction and hope. If empathic adults can act as buffers for these children at risk, two clinical recommendations follow. Professionals working with such children must be empathic and sensitive to the profound emotional turmoil the children are experiencing. They also need to use a family approach that includes the child, the hospitalized parent, and the well parent. Crisis intervention with these children should remove the mystery from the hospitalization and thereby help deal with the terror that even coping children feel as they try to rise to the challenge.

References

Bandura, A. *Social Learning Theory*. Englewood Cliffs, New Jersey: Prentice-Hall, 1977.

Bateson, G., D. D. Jackson, J. Haley, and J. H. Weakland. "Toward a Theory of Schizophrenia." *Behavioral Science* 1 (1956):251–264.

Bohannon, P. "Marriage and Divorce." In *Comprehensive Textbook of Psychiatry*, 3d ed., H. I. Kaplan, A. M. Freedman, and B. J. Sadock, eds. Baltimore: Williams & Wilkins, 1980.

Bowen, M. "Family and Family Group Psychotherapy." In *Comprehensive Group Psychotherapy*, H. I. Kaplan and B. J. Sadock, eds. Baltimore: Williams & Wilkins, 1971a.

——. "The Use of Family Theory in Clinical Practice." In *Changing Families*, J. Haley, ed. New York: Grune & Stratton, 1971.

——. "Toward the Differentiation of Self in One's Family of Origin." In *Georgetown Family Symposia: A Collection of Selected Papers*, F. Andres and J. Loria, eds. Washington, D.C.: Georgetown University, 1974.

——. "Theory in the Practice of Psychotherapy." In *Family Therapy*, P. Guerin, ed. New York: Gardner, 1976.

Brown, J. A. C. *Freud and the Post-Freudians*. Baltimore: Pelican Books, 1967.

Carter, E. A., and M. McGoldrick, eds. *The Family Life Cycle*. New York: Gardner, 1980.

Cohen, M. W., R. Younger, and J. M. Sullivan. "Treating the Family of Chronically Emotionally Impaired Adults." *The Family Therapist* 4, no. 1 (1983):2–12.

Collings, G. "Families Deal with Chronic Illness." *The New York Times* (October 12, 1981).

Collings, G. "A Dean of Pediatricians Looks at Today's Family." *The New York Times* (May 28, 1984).

Duvall, E. M. *Marriage and Family Development*, 5th ed. Philadelphia: J. B. Lippincott, 1977.

Emery, R. E., E. M. Heckerton, and L. F. DiLalla. "Divorce, Children, and Social Policy." In *Child Development, Research, and Social Policy*, H. Stevenson and A. Siegal, eds. Chicago: University of Chicago Press, 1985.

Erikson, E. H. *Childhood and Society*. New York: W. W. Norton, 1963.

Foley, V. D. *An Introduction to Family Therapy*. New York: Grune & Stratton, 1974.

Frias, C., and E. H. Janosik. "Mental Illness in the Family." In *Family-Focused Care*, J. R. Miller and E. H. Janosik, eds. New York: McGraw-Hill, 1980.

Freud, S. *Outline of Psychoanalysis*. New York: W. W. Norton, 1949.

Heckerton, E. M., M. Cox, and R. Cox. "Long-Term Effects of Divorce and Remarriage on the Adjustment of Children." *Journal of American Academy of Child Psychology* 24, no. 3 (March 1985):518–530.

Jackson, D. D. *Communication, Marriage, and Family*. Palo Alto, California: Science and Behavior Books, 1968.

Kalter, N. "Conjoint Mother-Daughter Treatment: A Beginning Phase of Psychotherapy with Adolescent Daughters of Divorce." *American Journal of Orthopsychiatry* 54, no. 2 (February 1984):490–497.

Kraft, S. P., and T. J. DeMaio. "An Ecological Intervention with Adolescents in Low-Income Families." *American Journal of Orthopsychiatry* 52, no. 1 (1982):131–140.

Lambert, V. A., and C. E. Lambert. "Role Theory and the Concept of Powerlessness." *Journal of Psychosocial Nursing* 11, no. 1 (1984):11–14.

Lidz, R. W., and T. Lidz. "The Family Environment of Schizophrenic Patients." *American Journal of Psychiatry* 106 (1949):332–345.

Lidz, R. W., S. Fleck, and A. Cornelison. *Schizophrenia and the Family*. New York: International Universities Press, 1965.

Lidz, T. "Intrafamilial Environment of Schizophrenic Patients: Marital Schism and Skew." *American Journal of Psychiatry* 114 (1958):241–248.

——. *The Origin and Treatment of Schizophrenic Disorders*. New York: Basic Books, 1973.

Masson, J. M. *The Assault on Truth: Freud's Suppression of the Seduction Theory*. New York: Farrar, Straus, 1984.

Mead, G. H. *Mind, Self, and Society*. Chicago: University of Chicago Press, 1933.

Messinger, L., and R. N. Walker. "From Marriage Breakdown to Remarriage: Parental Tasks and Therapeutic Guidelines." *American Journal of Orthopsychiatry* 51, no. 5 (October 1981):429–438.

Minuchin, S. *Families and Family Therapy*. Cambridge, Massachusetts: Harvard University Press, 1974.

Minuchin, S., B. Montalvo, B. Guerney, B. Rosman, and F. Shumer. *Families of the Slums*. New York: Basic Books, 1967.

O'Leary, K. D., and R. E. Emery. "Marital Discord and Child Behavior Problems." In *Middle Childhood: Development and Dysfunction*, M. D. Devine and R. P. Satz, eds. Baltimore: University Park Press, 1984.

Parsons, T. *The Social System*. New York: Free Press, 1951.

Patterson, G. R. *Families: Applications of Social Learning to Family Life*. Champaign, Illinois: Research Press, 1975.

Payne, K., ed. *Between Ourselves: Letters of Mothers and Daughters*. New York: Houghton Mifflin, 1983.

Satir, V. *Conjoint Family Therapy: A Guide to Theory and Technique*. Palo Alto, California: Science and Behavior Books, 1967.

Satir, V., J. Stachwiak, and H. Taschman. *Helping Families to Change*. New York: Jason Aronson, 1977.

Segall, A. *Sociocultural Variations in Illness Behavior* (Ph.D. dissertation). Toronto: University of Toronto, 1972.

Speigel, J. *Transactions: Interplay Between Individual, Family, and Society*. New York: Science House, 1971.

Sullivan, H. S. *The Interpersonal Theory of Psychiatry*. New York: W. W. Norton, 1953.

Thompson, C. *Psychoanalysis: Evolution and Development*. New York: Grove Press, 1957.

Toman, W. *Family Constellation*. New York: Springer, 1976.

Von Bertalanffy, L. "General Systems Theory in Psychiatry." In *American Handbook of Psychiatry*. New York: Basic Books, 1974.

Wallerstein, J. S., and J. B. Kelly. *Surviving the Breakup: How Parents and Children Cope with Divorce*. New York: Basic Books, 1980.

Weingarten, H. "Strategic Planning for Divorce Mediation." *Social Work* 31, no. 3 (March 1986):194–200.

Weingarten, H., and S. Leas. "Levels of Marital Conflict: A Guide to Assessment and Intervention in Troubled Marriages." *American Journal of Orthopsychiatry* 3, no. 57 (July 1987):407–416.

Wright, L. M., and M. Leahey. *Nurses and Families*. Philadelphia: Davis, 1984.

Wynne, L. *Beyond the Double Bind*. New York: Brunner/Mazel, 1978.

Wynne, L., I. Rykoff, and S. I. Hirsch. "Pseudomutuality in Family Relations of Schizophrenics." *Psychiatry* 21 (1958):205–220.

Zaslow, M. T. "Sex Differences in Children's Response to Parental Divorce: Samples, Variables, Ages, and Sources." *American Journal of Orthopsychiatry* 59, no. 1 (January 1989):118–141.

Zigler, E., and K. B. Black. "America's Family Support Movement: Strengths and Limitations." *American Journal of Orthopsychiatry* 59, no. 1 (January 1989):6–19.

Group Guidelines in Nursing Practice

Learning Objectives

After reading this chapter, the student should be able to:

1. Trace the historical development of group methods as a therapeutic modality.

2. Differentiate between primary, secondary, and reference groups.

3. Classify group development according to the stages and dominant issues characteristic of each stage.

4. Identify the primary and secondary tasks of groups and relate them to leadership styles and functions.

5. Present guidelines for organizing, leading, and observing groups.

Overview

Nurses often work with groups, whether for purposes of psychotherapy (group therapy) or for purposes of accomplishing interpersonal, cognitive, or behavioral change (therapeutic groups). Group therapy and therapeutic groups are contrasted. Steps in organizing groups are described in the context of nursing process. The chapter explores leadership as an interaction between the leaders and group members. Variations in leadership styles are identified, along with their probable effects on the group membership. Issues of coleadership are presented, and the advantages and disadvantages of coleadership are compared.

A section on curative factors present in groups directs attention to factors likely to facilitate progress toward group goals. Evaluation of progress toward group goals begins by recognizing the developmental stage at which the group is functioning. Identifying the prevailing behaviors of the group helps to determine the maturational stage that has been reached. Record keeping in the form of checklists or anecdotal accounts of each meeting simplifies evaluation activities. More sophisticated measures are available for those who wish to move from impressionistic evaluation to systematic analyses in the form of group research.

THE CARING CONCEPT IN GROUP WORK

Structured group interaction is an effective method of promoting positive change in people. Positive change produced by means of structured group interaction may be in the form of behavioral change, cognitive change, emotional change, or any combination of the three. When carefully organized, group interaction offers competent caregivers an efficient way to teach and influence clients and families. Group experiences can modify members' actions and reactions in positive ways when a safe, regulated environment is established and maintained.

Nurses have worked with groups for many years, especially with families. Although only nurses with advanced preparation are qualified to lead therapy groups the aim of which is deep personality change, every nurse will function from time to time as a group leader. Nursing process, with its emphasis on assessment, planning, implementation, and evaluation, can be relied upon by any nurse leading a group. At the same time, group leadership makes special demands on caregivers. It is important then to review some aspects of leadership that contribute to the welfare of group members and avoid hazards that careless or impatient leaders might cause.

A classic study of group leadership shows that certain leadership styles correlated with severe, persistent, adverse effects on some group members. In trying to learn what leadership characteristics were beneficial, the investigators identified four basic leadership styles, as follows:

- Emotional stimulation and confrontation
- Caring, supporting, and nurturing
- Explaining and attributing meaning
- Executive and managerial actions

The group leaders who achieved the most positive changes in members were those who provided high amounts of caring and explaining, combined with only moderate amounts of managerial actions or emotional stimulation and confrontation. A high level of confrontation by a charismatic but aggressive leader seemed to bring about the greatest incidence of psychological trauma in group members. Leaders with flamboyant, intrusive personalities tended to seek premature change in members, and therefore exerted excessive pressure on the group. Although it is true that different groups require different leadership styles and that the interventions of the leader must be adapted to the needs

of the group, there is no group that does not require caring, thoughtful leadership (Yalom and Lieberman 1972, Lieberman, Yalom, and Miles 1973).

Building on the findings of these researchers, nurse-theorist Maxine Loomis suggested that the four leadership styles designated above could be used to formulate leadership guidelines for different kinds of groups (Loomis 1979). Table 20–1 shows various types of groups likely to respond well to a particular leadership style.

Contemporary society has been described as an age of alienation, characterized by geographic mobility and the breakdown of traditional family, neighborhood, religious, and social-support systems. Nurses have often viewed illness in a social context, providing care while understanding the ramifications of illness to family and community. As traditional support systems have become unavailable, nurses have expanded their practice to fill this void. Their role expansion frequently has taken the form of leadership of small supportive and educational groups such as those for preoperative patients, post-partum mothers, and diabetics (Bernikow 1986). Today's health care system provides challenges and opportunities for nurses to assist groups, families, and communities to prevent illness and to restore health.

Group therapy and therapeutic groups have become very important in the health care system, especially in the field of mental health. In this chapter a distinction is made between group therapy and therapeutic groups. *Group therapy* (or group psychotherapy, as it is sometimes called) is a treatment modality in which selected clients with psychiatric problems meet in a group led by a qualified therapist for the purpose of reducing intrapsychic distress or modifying personality

Table 20–1. Styles of Leadership and Types of Groups

Leadership Style	Type of Group
High in caring	Support
High in executive function	Task/educational
High in caring and executive function	Socialization/reality orientation
High in meaning attribution and executive function	Behavior modification
High in emotional stimulation and meaning attribution	Sensitivity group/ consciousness raising group
Moderate in emotional stimulation, moderate in executive function, high in caring, high in meaning attribution	Psychotherapy

traits. *Therapeutic groups* is a broader term that includes formal or informal group meetings in which some form of positive change is sought on interpersonal, cognitive, or behavioral levels, but in which deep psychological alteration is not an objective.

A number of factors have enhanced the opportunities available to nurses wishing to engage in group work (Lancaster 1982). The sense of isolation felt by many persons in contemporary life is one factor. Another factor is the soaring cost of health care and the quest for cost-efficient treatment modalities. Equally important is the current emphasis on community rather than institutional treatment, the trend toward distributive rather than episodic care, and the commitment to the three levels of prevention (primary, secondary, and tertiary) introduced by Caplan (1964, 1970). Even though generalist nurses rarely function as group psychotherapists, they lead groups that address the three prevention levels. Examples of therapeutic groups directed at various levels of prevention are shown in Table 20–2. The examples include groups with a professional leader, self-help groups without a professional leader, and groups where leadership is shared among members on a rotating basis.

CATEGORIES OF GROUPS

There are three major categories of groups: primary, secondary, and reference. Everyone belongs to each of these groups in a lifetime, though membership in any specific group may change over time. Membership may be inherited, as in a family group, or acquired, as in an occupational group.

Membership defines who is and who is not included in the sphere of influence of the group. Members of a group are expected to conform to certain attitudes and behaviors, which may be clearly defined or vaguely implied, depending on the group. Membership is contingent on the eligibility and attraction which the group has for the potential member. It is one thing to be acceptable to a group and quite another to wish to join the group. Therefore, membership is determined by eligibility or noneligibility and by negative or positive attractiveness.

Nonmembership has interesting ramifications. The nonmember who is independent and eligible but who refuses to join a group may threaten group integrity by refusing to acknowledge the group. This phenomenon is exemplified in the actions of certain political leaders who refuse to join social clubs that exclude ethnic and racial minorities. Another uncertain and difficult situation involves the nonmember who wishes to be accepted but is currently ineligible.

Both primary and secondary groups have two major functions: maintaining the members' interpersonal needs and accomplishing the group's task. The importance of these two functions may vary, though both functions are vital to the life of the group and are influenced by the leader. For example, the family, as a primary group, must meet the socioemotional as well as the material needs of its members. These two types of needs may be provided by one or both parents. The health team, as a secondary group, may have a major external role in the management of a patient's illness, but it also must provide internal respect and cooperation to insure the morale of its members. As a rule, nurses whose identity is shaped by professional activities regard their professional organization as a reference group rather than a secondary group. Reference groups are characterized by powerful racial, religious, ethnic, or occupational affiliations. A minority with negative self-image and powerlessness may use reference-group affiliation as a form of affirmative action. Within recent decades, minority memberships have gained reference-group strength with slogans such as "Black Is Beautiful" and "Women Are Equal." One can accept or deny minority

Table 20–2. Therapeutic Groups at Three Levels of Prevention			
Level	**Goal**	**Leadership**	**Example**
Primary prevention	Reduce incidence of illness or dysfunction	Designated leader(s)	Childbirth education; premarital counseling
Secondary prevention	Decrease prevalence of illness or dysfunction	Designated leader(s) or shared leadership	Alcoholics Anonymous, Parents Anonymous, hypertensive groups, weight reduction groups, smoking cessation groups
Tertiary preventions	Diminish impairment due to illness or dysfunction	Designated leader(s) or shared leadership	Vocational rehabilitation groups, cardiac rehabilitation groups, resocialization groups

group membership. Denial of reference-group allegiance causes one to identify with what the reference group is not. Interracial and interreligious marriages often represent a repudiation of inherited reference-group affiliation (Tsui and Schultz 1988).

Adopting a new reference group carries the potential for redefining oneself, creating conflict between one's personal values and group values, or dividing oneself between the old and new reference groups. In short, changing reference groups can be constructive or destructive in terms of self-definition, role adjustment, and self-esteem.

Group interaction takes place between individuals protected by psychological boundaries that are more or less penetrable. Such boundaries tend to inhibit full comprehension by observers of what is taking place. Individual boundaries encircle each person in the group, while larger boundaries surround the group itself. The nurse who is a leader or participant-observer must transcend protective individual boundaries to some extent. An outside observer must transcend both group and individual boundaries in order to assess group phenomena.

The term *boundaries* is subject to interpretations that concern the extent of individual involvement with others and the extent of group involvement with the environment. Individual boundaries may be described as outer limits within which selfhood is contained. In group terminology, boundaries consist of rules and role expectations that define which persons belong to the group and how they function as group members. Boundaries facilitate group development by separating the group from external systems in order to promote task accomplishment. At the same time the boundaries of individual members function to prevent excessive loss of self as group forces begin to emerge. Usually there is more interaction or energy exchange inside individual or group boundaries than across these boundaries.

Probably the most influential group in the life of an individual is the *primary group*, or the family. This is the group that shapes one's identity, influences one's values, and provides emotional support.

Secondary groups are limited in time and purpose. They exert less influence on their members than the primary group, but they may incite intense loyalty and generate extensive interaction for a while. Some secondary groups, such as a committee charged with a specific task, have a very brief life. Others, such as a board of directors that meets intermittently for many years, develop a quasi-permanent status.

Reference groups are formal or informal groups that influence the attitudes, values, and behaviors of those who consider themselves members. Membership in a reference group implies that the individual has identified with the group, so aspects of selfhood are evaluated according to the standards of the reference group (Marram 1978). Some reference groups are based on occupation, race, national origin, or religion. Membership in a reference group may be constructive or destructive, depending on the values perpetuated by the group and the stigma or pride that accompanies membership. A reference group for one person may be only a secondary group for another. For example, for some alumni graduation means the end of their association with their college. For others, this association continues to influence them throughout their lives.

HISTORY OF GROUP WORK

The use of groups within the health-care system was first introduced by a Boston internist, Dr. Joseph Pratt, in the treatment of despondent tuberculosis patients. Pratt met regularly with groups of patients and, in an atmosphere of support and reassurance, taught them about diet and hygiene. While the primary task of these groups was educational, Pratt may have been aware of other therapeutic ingredients at work within these groups, such as a mutual sharing of concerns in a supportive environment. He continued to use auxiliary-group treatment at his Boston clinic for many years.

Pratt organized group meetings for his patients in 1905, a time when tuberculosis patients were isolated from their families for many months and ostracized by the community. He lectured groups of 20 to 30 patients once or twice a week about the course, treatment, and prognosis of their disease. Patients who had progressed satisfactorily were invited to tell the group about the success of their treatment. In this atmosphere of hope and encouragement, very ill patients could identify with those who were recovering, much as alcoholics do today in meetings of Alcoholics Anonymous (Perez 1986). Difficult patients who resisted the therapeutic regimen were seen individually by a nurse called a "friendly advisor."

The first to employ group methods with mentally ill clients was L. Cody Marsh, a psychiatrist and clergyman. Like Pratt, Marsh called his meetings "classes" and referred to patients as "students." Lectures were given on a range of mental disorders as students took notes. Attendance was taken, homework was assigned, and examinations were given. Students who did poorly were assigned a tutor or were required to repeat the course. Marsh

GROUP TERMINOLOGY

Term	Definition
Primary group	An all-encompassing group such as the family, which shapes identity and values of its members
Secondary group	A group limited in time and organized for a specific purpose
Reference group	A formal or informal group that contributes significantly to its members' sense of self
Participant-observer	A person in an interaction who participates but retains objectivity and detachment; one who observes even as he acts and reacts in a social interaction
Play therapy	A therapeutic mode in which children or others with minimal verbal skills reveal their feelings by manipulating toys or other props
Psychodrama	Impromptu enactment of a real-life problem, using clients as actors and audience. Those witnessing the drama make suggestions, react, and may gain insight into their own problems. The therapist acts as director of the drama
Group dynamics	Forces and counterforces that produce changes in a group
Group pressure	Influence exerted by the group as a whole or by subgroups on the group members
Encounter groups	Emotionally charged groups in which free expression is encouraged; catharsis is used to achieve self-actualization and self-knowledge
T-groups	Training groups organized to improve members' ability to handle interpersonal problems, especially in the workplace
Role differentiation	Patterned behaviors of group members that can be observed and identified
Role specialization	Consistent or repeated adherence of an individual member to the same behavior patterns
Group rules	Explicit group standards, either written or verbal, that are imposed on all group members
Group norms	Implicit, incompletely defined group standards that evolve gradually during the life span of the group; norms are unwritten and are rarely applied equally to all group members

was one of the first mental health professionals to realize the importance of the transactions between patients and the staff of a psychiatric facility. He included physicians, nurses, social workers, and aides in discussion groups with patients. In effect, he was one of the first persons to consider a psychiatric facility a therapeutic community (Sadock 1980).

Another pioneer in the introduction of group treatment methods was Trignant Burrow. In 1927 Burrow, an American psychiatrist, applied the term "group analysis" to meetings in which persons with psychiatric disorders were encouraged to share their thoughts and feelings with each other. Burrow emphasized the role of the *participant-observer*—that is, the individual who observes while participating. He insisted that most emotional experiences are universal and that sharing emotions with others in a group reduces feelings of loneliness and isolation. Burrow did not think of group members as sick people being treated by a healthy leader; rather, he thought of all those present as participants in a shared experience.

Samuel Slavson (1964, 1974), an engineer, conceived of the idea of *play therapy* by watching the behaviors of children at play. He initiated a form of play therapy in which groups of children were encouraged to act out conflicts spontaneously un-der the supervision of a permissive therapist. Slavson's approach allowed children to discharge aggressive impulses in a secure environment. Using toys as props, the children improvised spontaneous domestic dramas that revealed their feelings about significant people in their lives. The premise was that the children would become aware of their feelings, would realize that others had similar feelings, and would learn that there were appropriate and inappropriate ways to express feelings. According to Slavson, similar group techniques may be used to teach withdrawn, fearful, and even psychotic children new ways of behaving.

The fact that Slavson was an engineer and not a physician helped open the field of group work to nonmedical practitioners. The American Group Therapy Association, which Slavson helped establish in 1948, remains an interdisciplinary group concerned with sharing information and maintaining professional standards and qualifications among the practitioners of group work. A minimum of master's level preparation in an appropriate discipline has been endorsed by the AGTA for persons undertaking group therapy leadership.

Psychodrama, a variation of group treatment, was introduced into the United States in 1925, although it had been used in Europe more than ten years earlier. Jacob Moreno, a psychiatrist, introduced psychodrama as a therapeutic tool. He used a method of role playing called "the theater of spontaneous man," in which patients acted out problem situations for the purpose of gaining insight into their own problems. In psychodrama the therapist (the "director") encourages a client (the "protagonist") to enact extemporaneously a problem or conflict drawn from her own experience. Other members of the group (the "alter egos") make suggestions concerning the drama being portrayed and frequently connect their own feelings and experiences to the events unfolding before them (Coleman, Butcher, and Carson 1984).

Kurt Lewin, a social psychologist, introduced the idea that a group consists of more than the sum of its parts. He coined the phrase *group dynamics* to describe forces, counterforces, and changes within a group. He used the phrase *group pressure* to describe influences exerted by the group on its members, which he believed could alter behavior. It was Lewin's contention that each member wields influence in a group and that groups function as interdependent units even though they are composed of separate individuals (Lewin 1957, Anthony 1971).

Group work advanced during World War II, when the number of psychiatrists was inadequate to deal with the emotional trauma suffered by Allied soldiers. American and European psychiatrists working at a military center in Northfield, England, discarded army rules and regulations in order to adopt innovative group treatment methods. One innovation was the *community network*, which consisted as much as possible of friends and family members who had significant relationships with the clients at the onset of the breakdown. The experiments in group treatment at Northfield were forerunners of today's therapeutic communities and milieu therapy.

After World War II, many disciplines became interested in group therapy and practice. Programs in sociology, psychology, education, psychiatry, nursing, and social work added courses in group methodology to their curriculum. Wellesley College was the first institution to introduce group theory in a nursing program in 1952. In order to ease the entry of Wellesley College freshmen into the nursing role, the group experiences of students were explored. As masters programs in psychiatric nursing proliferated, sensitivity training was introduced to enhance the self-awareness of students. By means of groups, students learned to analyze their own feelings and reactions in the context of group dynamics.

Industry and government soon realized the importance of understanding how groups operate and provided financial support for the application and study of group theory. In 1947, the National Training Laboratory for Applied Behavioral Science was established. The purpose was to acquaint corporate and industrial executives with the effects of group dynamics on human relationships. The National Training Laboratory used training groups, or *T-groups*, to increase the members' ability to handle difficult interpersonal situations and to transfer this ability to the work place.

During the prosperous years after World War II, there was intense popular interest in achieving self-actualization and personal fulfillment. In this period, lower level needs, as outlined by Maslow (1968), were easily met, and popular yearning grew for "peak experiences" to overcome the tedium and boredom of everyday life. Although Maslow did not equate self-actualization with peak experiences, the ideas seemed to merge in the public mind. This contributed to enormous interest in groups whose goal was a vaguely defined but emotionally exciting experience. The demand for self-actualization was the impetus for the *encounter groups* of the 1960s and 1970s. Many diverse groups, led by both qualified and unqualified leaders, fell into the broad classification of encounter groups; most sought to fulfill people's need to be loved and to belong. Encounter groups were based on the belief that the open expression of feelings is an end in itself. For a time the encounter group movement was regarded as a cure-all for emotional alienation, but systematic studies eventually questioned its worth. One study of encounter groups suggested that, while the groups did provide opportunity for self-expression, they produced few lasting positive changes in members and negative effects in some (Lieberman, Yalom, and Miles 1973).

Psychodynamic Issues

Nurses do not often lead psychoanalytically oriented groups that attempt to promote personality change, but they do utilize a number of concepts contributed by psychoanalytic theorists, sometimes without being aware of the source. Since various psychoanalytic concepts are likely to surface in therapeutic groups as well as psychotherapy groups, a brief discussion of psychodynamic issues is included in this section.

There are two general ways of examining a group experience (see Figure 20–1). To psychoanalytic theorists, a group is a replication of the early family experience, and members bring to the group residual feelings and behaviors from their family of origin. Although this perception of the members is seldom conscious, they react to the

Figure 20–1. *Two ways of looking at groups.*

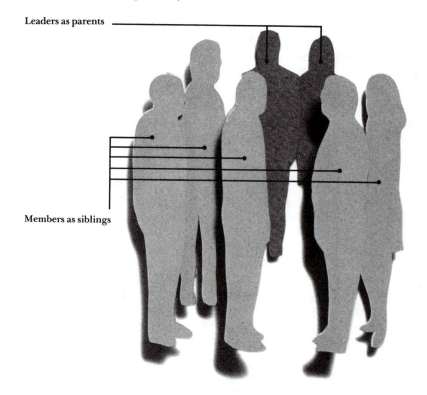

Group as family

Leaders as parents

Members as siblings

leaders as if they were surrogate parents and to the other members as if they were siblings. The corrective reenactment of experiences that first occurred within the original primary group is thought to modify emotional conflicts and dysfunctional defenses developed in early life (Maluccio 1981).

The other view of group dynamics is less psychoanalytic. In this perspective, the group is seen as a microcosm of society. Interactions between members are thought to reduce feelings of alienation, to clarify communication, and to teach alternative ways of acting and reacting. Regardless of whether the group is perceived as a family or as society in miniature, a number of psychodynamic phenomena are likely to become evident, including transference, countertransference, resistance, acting out, and insight.

Transference is an unconscious distortion in which individuals transfer to others the wishes and fears associated with significant persons in early life. For example, a group member who was "Daddy's little girl" in the original family configuration may continue to enact that role, especially with a male group leader. If the underlying dynamics of the behavior are recognized by the leader and by other members, the urge to behave like "Daddy's little girl" may be replaced by more mature actions.

The leader and the group thus have the potential to correct transference.

Countertransference is an unconscious distortion in which the group leader transfers to one or more members wishes and fears associated by the leader with people in his early life. A group leader who becomes enraged by the actions of a member may be responding to his internal distortion rather than to the reality of group events. Like other mortals, group leaders may not always be aware of the underlying causes of their reactions and may engage in denial, rationalization, or other defensive maneuvers. But if the leader is aware of countertransference, she can more easily control it. The leader is a powerful person in the eyes of group members, and only a mature group will be able to deal directly with countertransference issues. This is one reason why supervision, observation, and consultation are important for all group leaders but are crucial for psychotherapy groups, whose members are likely to be very vulnerable.

Resistance is unwillingness on the part of members to relinquish distortions or to turn their attention to accomplishing the purpose for which the group was formed. Resistance may be individual or collective, open or hidden, conscious or unconscious. Some indications of resistance are inattention,

Group as social microcosm

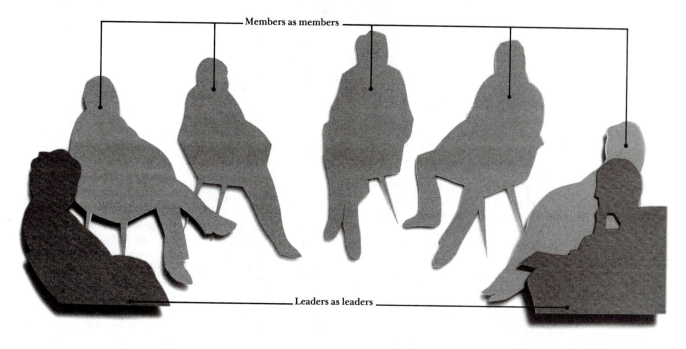

flippancy, superficiality, anger, tardiness, or absences. Like transference and countertransference, resistance can be a complex issue. It may be directed toward the leader or toward group members in ways that are not immediately identified but that sooner or later become apparent.

Acting out is often confused with simple acting up, although the latter is usually a sign of resistance. Acting out is more profound, for it means that a member is expressing internal conflicts through symbols or actions instead of openly. An example of acting out is the behavior of a member who is very frightened that confidentiality will be broken and therefore avoids personal disclosure. The unresolved conflict may center on issues of trust versus mistrust (Erikson 1963). Acting out behavior is usually unconscious, and in therapy groups it should be confronted by the leader or other members who notice it. If the behavior is confronted or interpreted, the acting out member may reject the meaning but later may come to accept its accuracy, and thus take a step toward insight.

Insight is the conscious connection ultimately made between one's behavior and one's underlying motives. Acquiring insight is often a slow process of which intellectual understanding is only the beginning. Gaining insight into the meaning of one's acting out behavior is a long process that requires a state of readiness and a willingness to work through the connections between behavior and motives. Without emotional as well as intellectual readiness,

genuine commitment to change will not be made. This is one of the reasons that group psychotherapy devoted to the goal of promoting intrapsychic change is of long duration (Robinson 1983).

Individuals who are part of a group may feel that their personal identity has merged with that of the group. This loss of separateness means that they may be less rational and responsible. Mature, well-organized groups can restrain the impulsiveness of individual members in order to reach the objectives of the group. Less mature and less organized groups may permit and even encourage aggressive, regressive, frivolous, or erotic behavior on the part of some individual members so that the purpose of the group as a whole is neglected.

Under the influence of the group, individuals are capable of heroic actions that place the welfare of the group before their own. In such instances a sense of being part of the group supersedes the individuality of the members. Psychoanalytic theory uses the term *ego ideal* to describe an idealized image of what one wants to be. *Espirit de corps* seems to make the ego ideal of the group and the ego ideal of the hero become one. The outcome may, on the one hand, be a deed of courage. On the other hand, group pressure and the merging of the individual with the group may sometimes provoke questionable actions, at least when an immature, disorganized group acts in a manner that suggests the absence of group responsibility (*group superego constraints*). When a group gives free rein to aggressive behavior, merging with the group may

CLINICAL VIGNETTE

PSYCHOANALYTIC ISSUES IN A MOTHER'S SUPPORT GROUP

A supportive group for mothers of preschool children was organized by an elementary school principal and led by Debbie, a community health nurse, and Jane, a psychiatric mental health nurse. The school was located in a stable working-class neighborhood, and the group was sponsored by the adult education division of the local school board. Preschool children accompanied their mothers to the school and engaged in supervised play in the next room while their mothers met. The group met weekly for a period of five months, and there were two group objectives. Didactic information was presented on the developmental tasks of young children, and the mothers were encouraged to express their feelings about themselves and their roles in the family. Both nurses were experienced group leaders. Jane was an older, married woman with grown children, and Debbie was single and childless. During the first meetings the members showed deference toward Jane (*idealization of the leader*) and indifference or distrust toward Debbie (*negative transference*). Jane's contributions to the meetings were warmly received, while Debbie's were ignored, except when a member would refer sarcastically to Debbie's free and childless state, it was apparent that Jane represented a mother figure to the group, while Debbie was treated like a schoolgirl.

Jane and Debbie responded to the problem by allocating the tasks of the group between the two of them. Debbie was described to the group as the undisputed authority on all child-rearing subjects. When a question on this topic was directed to Jane, she pleaded ignorance, asserting that she couldn't remember the time when her own children were toddlers, but that Debbie would know the answer (*leader transparency*). After a while the status denial practiced by Jane had an effect. Debbie began to be asked questions and to be heard. After one helpful response by Debbie a mother commented, "You remind me of my sister. She doesn't have any kids either, but she teaches school and thinks a lot. Sometimes she can help me figure things out" (*positive transference*).

Altering the negative transference to Debbie did not altogether lessen the positive feelings the members had for Jane, but it did make them more realistic. With Debbie's expertise established, Jane was able to use her leadership role to elicit interactions among the members themselves and reduce her own centrality. The group became cohesive as the mothers began to share ideas, recipes, and life experiences. One of the members gave birth to a baby during the months that the group met. The baby became a great source of excitement and interest (*empathy*). As a group, the members collected money for a gift and visited the new baby. Both leaders were excluded from these activities, and the group spokesperson explained, "We didn't ask Jane and Debbie to join in. They're both so busy and it's not like they're really part of the gang" (*group maturation*).

After this shared activity there was less reliance on the leaders for guidance and greater spontaneity among the members. During the first group meetings the mothers repeatedly left the group to see how their children were. As the mothers became more comfortable with each other, this behavior decreased. Eventually the mothers became so engrossed in the group discussions that when children tapped on the door to see their mothers, they would be told firmly not to bother Mommy when she was busy.

As termination neared, one session was devoted to evaluating the group experience. The group was pronounced a success, so much so that the members planned to meet in each other's homes. The judgment was that "Jane and Debbie helped us some, but they haven't answered all our questions. And since all of us are in the same boat maybe we can help each other" (*identification and insight*).

---

threaten an individual member's mature ego integration. A decrease in feelings of autonomy and personal responsibility may, for example, incite group members to such violent acts as looting, rape, or assault. Although psychoanalytic concepts grew out of work with individuals, many group theorists apply Freudian topographic (*conscious* and *unconscious mental activity*) and structural (*id, ego, superego,* and *ego ideal*) formulations to the study of groups (Freud 1957).

Sometimes membership in durable, established groups mitigates the impact of primitive groups. Primary and reference groups may effectively counter an individual's wish to merge with a secondary group. An exchange student from Britain reported being able to resist the aggressive tendencies of an unauthorized encounter group on a college campus by reminding himself that "Englishmen do not behave in that fashion."

At times a group experience may arouse neither heroism nor antisocial behavior but rather apathy or aimlessness. In an account of a blizzard that immobilized Kennedy Airport, stranded passengers relapsed into listless dependency (Hammerschlag and Astrachan 1971). No cohesiveness developed among persons suffering the same predicament, except within certain nuclear families. Even though there was no actual danger, hoarding behaviors appeared among those marooned together. There were fantasies of an unknown, omnipotent rescuer who would appear and lead everyone to safety. Neither panic (*flight*) nor effective mobilization for action (*fight*) was exhibited. Breakdown of the organizational system at the airport and the absence of outside resources created social immobility. The travelers were too numerous to constitute a small group, although it is possible that within the crowd smaller constellations were formed whose members engaged in sharing behaviors. The general mood of dependency and helplessness, however, precluded the formation of group measures to decrease discomfort or find rescue.

The previous examples indicate some possible effects of group pressure: (1) heroism and self-sacrifice on behalf of the group; (2) guilt-producing (ego-alien) acts committed in collusion with the group; and (3) apathy and helplessness, which prevent interdependence and utilization of group resources. A number of group theorists have attempted to explain these and similar phenomena in psychoanalytic terms.

ORGANIZING THE GROUP

There are occasions when prospective members become aware of their own needs and can organize a group that meets their requirements. More often, however, prospective members lack the resources or are ignorant of the possibilities of using a group approach to health care. Therefore, it is usually a nurse or other health professional who must identify a target population and begin to consider the needs (Marvin 1982). Nurses who determine that the needs of certain clients can be met through group methods can turn to nursing process for direction.

Before organization can begin, prospective leaders should have a clear idea of the purpose of the group and of the priorities to be set. Although leaders should be responsive to the needs of members, no group can be all things to all people. Adherence to a stated group purpose offers protection to leaders and to members and therefore should remain a reference point throughout the life span of the group. Inevitably, needy or manipulative members will try to alter the original purpose of the group. This can only be countered if leaders have a clear idea of the scope of the group and its designated purpose. Alcoholics Anonymous, an international movement with a proven record of success, shows how important fidelity to the group purpose can be. AA is concerned with maintaining sobriety and limits intervention to those aspects of life that threaten sobriety. Personality change and insight are secondary to the overriding behavioral consideration.

(Text continues on page 563.)

REQUIREMENTS FOR GROUP ORGANIZATION

According to Freud (1957), there are five basic requirements for group organization:

- First there must be continuity of existence in the group: The same individuals must be together for some time or the same fixed positions must exist even though occupied by successive individuals.

- Individual members should have a definite idea of the nature, functions, capacities, and composition of the group in order to develop emotional relationships to the group as a whole.

- The group should be brought into some interaction, perhaps in the form of rivalry, with other groups similar in some respects but differing from it in other respects.

- The group should possess traditions, customs, and habits, especially those that determine the relation of its members to one another.

- The group should have a definite structure, expressed in the specialization and differentiation of the functions and roles of its members.

CLINICAL VIGNETTE

TASK ADHERENCE IN A STUDENT NURSES' GROUP

The basic course in psychiatric mental health nursing was required of all seniors in a baccalaureate nursing program. As part of the clinical component of the course, 10 of the senior nursing students were assigned to an acute care psychiatric inpatient facility for three months. In previous years students complained that this particular clinical placement was stressful. Some students assigned to the facility proved unable to fulfill the clinical requirements and had to repeat the course the following year. A few students with otherwise satisfactory records dropped out of the nursing program during this clinical placement.

The nursing faculty considered the problem a serious one. On the one hand, the acute care facility offered a rich learning experience and the majority of the students were able to take advantage of it. On the other hand, the placement evidently made demands that some students were unable to meet. Despite careful selection of students and good clinical teaching, there were always students who performed poorly and became discouraged. The problem was discussed at length by the nursing faculty. They concluded that the students were psychologically unprepared for this clinical experience and that no organized support was available to them. The nursing faculty decided to ask Mrs. Beck, a team leader at the acute care facility, to meet weekly with the students assigned there. Mrs. Beck was a nurse accustomed to leading short-term, task-oriented groups that helped prepare patients for discharge.

Participation in the meetings was voluntary. The leader was selected for her leadership skills and because she was an authority figure for the students. Group confidentiality was pledged, especially with regard to nursing faculty and hospital administration. The stated group purpose was to give anticipatory guidance to help students deal with their feelings about psychiatric illness and psychiatric nursing. As planned by the nursing faculty and implemented by Mrs. Beck, the group was a form of primary prevention.

Hour-long weekly meetings were scheduled for eight weeks and were held in a conference room at the psychiatric facility. At the first meeting Mrs. Beck expanded on the rationale for the group and disavowed any connection between herself as group leader and the nursing faculty or personnel. The crisis intervention format was described, and the group leader then began to disclose her own feelings about working in the psychiatric facility, describing how her feelings had changed over time. She suggested that members might like to discuss methods of adjustment that had worked for them in other clinical placements and to look for ways to adapt these to the present clinical setting.

Group cohesion was evident even in the first meeting because of relationships already present among the students and because of shared feelings about the clinical placement. The first four meetings were effective in uncovering some of the students' concerns. Under Mrs. Beck's leadership the group began to problem-solve together. In the second meeting Kitty Sawyer confided that she had grown up with a manic-depressive brother and described the reactivation of old feelings when she had to interact with a manic patient. Kitty's uncertainty about her ability to get through the clinical placement elicited advice from the group. Among the suggestions made by her classmates was the possibility that expanding her knowledge of manic-depressive illness might make this problem less upsetting to her. During the fourth meeting Jennie Brice, a student with an alcoholic mother, talked of feelings that made her unable to be therapeutic in her interactions with alcoholic patients in the unit, particularly females. Again the group was supportive and concerned. At this point Mrs. Beck noted a lowering of anxiety among most of the students (*content consistent with group goals*). During the first meeting Mrs. Beck told the group that the nursing faculty realized that not every student could work with every psychiatric patient, and she suggested that Kitty and Jennie could request assignments to patients with whom they felt comfortable.

Clara was an interested, participating member in the first meetings but was silent in the session when Jennie talked about her mother's alcoholism. Early in the next meeting Clara told the group she had a personal matter to discuss. Although Clara was usually composed, her manner of speaking became hesitant and agitated. Because the group had responded so warmly to Kitty and Jennie, Clara said she felt brave enough to talk about her problem. After a few false starts Clara blurted out the information that she was uncomfortable with her sexual identity and was contemplating transsexual surgery so she could live as a male. She said she had tried lesbian relationships, but they were not satisfying. She considered them inadequate and unnatural, although there were several women whom she had loved. Furthermore, the revelations of Kitty and Jenny had made her feel very protective toward them, and this in turn had aroused a sexual response in her. "This is a real problem for me," Clara went on. "I know it's a heavy thing to lay on the group but I love all of you so much. You people are so beautiful that I want to tell the truth to you. It feels good to be able to take off the mask" (*content inconsistent with goals*).

There was stunned silence for a few minutes after Clara's remarks, but the group rallied. Members asked questions about Clara's family and personal life, which she answered with growing ease. It seemed to Mrs. Beck that in spite of Clara's turmoil she was deriving satisfaction from being the center of attention. After a short time the leader intervened, choosing her words carefully. "I feel very sympathetic about Clara's dilemma and I think she has been courageous in talking about it. However, I am not sure this group is able to deal with such a complicated problem. We are limited to three more meetings and our agreement is to discuss feelings related to this clinical placement. If we try to help Clara it means we can't meet our commitment to the group. It also means we are not being fair to Clara, who needs more help than this group can provide. I'd like to ask Clara and the rest of the group to trust me to find help for Clara while she considers this important decision. We can talk about this later, Clara, and I promise to be available to you. Now perhaps we can use the remainder of the meeting to finish the work we have started—how to get the most out of this clinical placement" (*redirection to group goals*).

The leader's deliberate intervention was received with signs of relief from the group. One student said she felt bad for Clara but knew she was out of her depth in trying to give advice. Another member confessed to mingled sympathy and resentment toward Clara, saying, "This is too heavy a burden to put on us. At first I was just angry at Clara. I didn't know what to say and I was glad when Mrs. Beck got us off the hook. Right now I don't feel angry with you, Clara. I just feel sorry and hope you get the help you need."

Mrs. Beck followed this by commenting on the honest emotions the group was able to express. "This is a sign we trust each other and that we have grown. Let's use this trust to return to our original purpose, since there are people better qualified than we to help Clara. Clara has trusted us and we can help her most by remembering that we are pledged to confidentiality. She and I will meet later to consider other sources of help" (*structure for the group; reassurance for Clara; adherence to the group purpose*).

Assessing Needs and Resources

The process of organizing a group should begin by asking whether the prospective leaders are equipped by temperament and preparation to act as leaders. The answer to this question depends to a large extent on the kind of group that is being considered. Nurses are accustomed to working on health teams, teaching families, and interacting with groups of clients in hospital and community settings. Basic nursing programs emphasize self-awareness and usually provide students with some knowledge of group dynamics, but it is important for generalist nurses to realize their limitations. If the proposed group involves psychotherapy, the prospective leaders should meet the standards of the American Nurses' Association, which state that psychotherapy groups should be led by nurses with graduate preparation at least at the master's level. The availability of qualified supervision, the group composition, and the group objectives should also be considered when deciding whether a nurse can lead a group safely and effectively.

Before deciding that a group is needed, the status of the target population should be reviewed in relation to existing resources and services. It is important to decide whether the needs of the target population are already being met by existing services. If so, there is no need to organize a new group. For example, a community health nurse concerned with the problem of child abuse might attempt to discover what groups are available for parents who are potential abusers. If programs such as Parents Anonymous are already active in the community, the nurse might refer troubled parents to this support group. If no appropriate group is found, the nurse might, with the approval of the employing agency, take steps to organize a support group or activate a chapter of Parents Anonymous. The degree of support of the sponsoring agency can be a significant factor in a group's success (Loomis 1979).

Planning the Group

Experienced group leaders stress the importance of advance planning in ensuring successful outcomes. Before interviewing prospective members, the leader or leaders should decide what the selection standards will be. Group objectives must be clearly stated and conveyed to the members so that the understanding of leaders and members coincides. The formulation of specific goals also reassures members about what they may expect and later permits an adequate evaluation of group outcomes.

Authorities on group work disagree on whether homogeneous groups are consistently superior to heterogeneous groups. Some feel a degree of homogeneity may be beneficial in helping members relate to one another, but others claim that heterogeneity in a group helps members to learn from one another (Yalom 1975). Some groups benefit from homogeneity of problems and interests among members—groups of substance abusers, for example. But in virtually all groups a certain amount of heterogeneity is inescapable. Individual differences in defenses, coping mechanisms, and interactional styles persist in all groups.

It is impossible to predict with total accuracy whether a particular individual will do well in a group because the success or failure of the experience may depend less on the characteristics of the client than on the characteristics of the group itself. Each group, whether it is considered group therapy or a therapeutic group, will develop its own constellation of relationships, behaviors, and values based to a large extent upon the composition of the membership and the orientation of the leader.

In selecting and preparing prospective group members, Marvin (1962) recommended that the following questions be considered:

What specific needs does this client have?

Can her needs be met effectively through a group experience?

Will the client tolerate the anxiety engendered by a group experience?

What previous experience has the client had with primary, secondary, and reference groups?

Is there evidence of willingness to participate in the group?

Is the client motivated to work on achieving group goals?

Group cohesion—the sense of belonging in the group—constitutes a powerful factor in maintaining a viable group. Group cohesion can be promoted by choosing members on the "Noah's Ark" principle, which states that the isolation felt by any group member will be decreased by the presence of another member with similar characteristics who can serve as his compeer, or companion. Age, gender, occupation, and interests are among the characteristics that may be used in matching group members. Examples of unfortunate group selection would include a solitary male or female member, a middle-aged member among a group of adolescents, or a young, vigorous member among a group of elderly, infirm retirees.

During the process of selecting and preparing members for the group experience, a group contract or agreement should be discussed. The group contract should be clearly stated and agreed to by

the leader(s) and members. Provisions of the contract, once accepted, should be carefully followed as originally outlined. If it becomes necessary to alter provisions of the group contract, the decision should be made jointly by the members and leader(s).

Negotiating the group contract requires collaboration and open communication between leaders and prospective members. Provisions of the contract should also be shared with members of the sponsoring agency. Sharing general information about group goals and the contract can be done without betraying confidentiality, and it encourages support from the sponsoring agency. When prospective members are interviewed, they should be asked whether they understand and accept the group contract. In some cases the leader may devise a written contract that is cosigned by members and leaders. If used, the written contract should note the time and place of the meetings, the agreed-upon goals for the group, and the commitments and expectations shared by members and leaders. Although it is not mandatory and not always appropriate, a written contract reduces any discrepancy between what members would like the group to be and what the leader has promised.

The length and frequency of group sessions may vary according to the time frame and the goals of the group. A psychotherapy group might meet twice a week for an hour or once a week for an hour and a half. A teaching group for hypertensive or for diabetic clients might meet for only 45 minutes at weekly or biweekly intervals. A group for recovering cardiac clients and their spouses might meet daily for 30 minutes over a period of several months. In all cases, the surroundings in which the group meets should be as comfortable as possible, and sessions should convene at the same place and at the times designated during the preparatory period.

Group size depends on the composition of the group and the nature of the group goals. There is little agreement on the optimal size for a group, but there is consensus on the optimal range of group size. The generally accepted range for small groups is from five to fifteen members. Groups with fewer than five or more than ten members are unlikely to generate maximum therapeutic exchange. Groups of more than ten members tend to form subgroups; groups of less than five members are inclined to be inhibited in their participation. Therefore, groups with five to ten members fall within the ideal range, although these are not hard and fast rules but merely guidelines. A nurse contemplating group work with an elderly population might limit the group to three or four members if reality orientation is the objective. If the proposed group is designed to promote reminiscing or life review for elderly members, the leader might be advised to increase the number of members. One shortcoming in the field of group research is the lack of systematic investigation needed to correlate successful outcomes with group size (Burnside 1984).

Another issue to be decided is whether a group is to be closed or open to new members. There are arguments supporting both decisions. Closed groups tend to become more cohesive, but groups that admit new members at specified times benefit from the orienting activities extended by senior members toward new arrivals. Another decision that must be made is whether to allow members to leave the group if they feel they have made sufficient progress or to insist that termination be collectively experienced by all members. These are decisions that should be made during the preparatory phase of organizing the group.

Early in the group sessions the question will arise as to whether group members should meet outside the scheduled sessions, and this is an issue that leaders should consider even before the sessions begin. There is no denying the fact that outside meetings between two or three members may fragment the group and impede group progress. Nevertheless, there will be times when group members have an affinity for other members and therefore arrange meetings that do not include the entire group. One solution is to acknowledge the possibility that such meetings will take place but insist that they not be kept secret from the rest of the group. This suggestion may not satisfy purists who believe, with some justification, that group interaction should be confined to meetings at which all members are present. Since it is almost impossible for the leader to enforce prohibitions against meeting outside the scheduled sessions, the suggested compromise may be the answer.

JUDGMENTAL VERSUS NONJUDGMENTAL NURSING BEHAVIORS

- *Moral Judgments:* Forms of blaming that have no place in nursing theory or practice.
- *Speculative Judgments:* Untested choices that may contribute to nursing theory but prove risky in nursing practice until validated.
- *Pragmatic Judgments:* Decisions based on practicality and on recollection of what measures proved effective in the past.
- *Professional Judgments:* Optimal judgments that integrate tested theoretical formulations, situational factors, and clinical and ethical considerations with nursing process and role.

SOURCE: Adapted from Doona (1979).

TYPE OF GROUP AND RECOMMENDED SIZE

Type	Number of Members
Support group	Up to 12 Up to 6 members if regressed or unstable
Reality orientation group	8 to 10 Up to 4 if confused or grossly impaired
Remotivation group	Up to 12
Reminiscing group	Up to 8
Psychotherapy group	6 to 9
Didactic (educational) group	Up to 20 Up to 15 if task is complex

---

Implementing the Plan

Once assessment and planning have been completed, implementation of the group can proceed. Usually private screening interviews, consisting of two or three meetings are arranged to select and prepare each member. Questions directed to prospective members should be based on the objectives of the group. If mastering cognitive knowledge, changing behavior, learning new skills, or promoting insight is a major goal, the interviewees should be appraised for their potential capacity to achieve this goal.

In these preparatory meetings the leader should be prepared for questions and challenges from the interviewees. The prospect of a group experience is apt to evoke some anxiety, and candidates are entitled to have their questions answered at this time. Interviewees often ask the leaders about their qualifications and previous group experiences. Essentially what is being asked is whether the leader can guarantee that the group will be a safe place for the members. Questions about the leader should be answered truthfully and without resentment. Before requesting a prospective member to decide about joining the group, time should be allowed for mutual consideration.

Evaluating Group Progress

Evaluating group progress of the whole group and of individual members allows leaders to determine the effectiveness of their interventions and of the group experience. In evaluating group progress, the stated goals are a good standard of measurement, especially if the goals have been expressed behaviorally and if adequate records have been kept. Judging the extent to which group goals have been met helps evaluate group outcomes, but this is not always easy to do. Members' subjective impressions of the progress they have made are of questionable reliability and validity, but these factors can be increased if pretests and posttests are used. These questionnaires are more helpful if the items are ranked so that quantitative comparisons are possible. Figure 20–2 illustrates what is meant by ranking questionnaire items. Ongoing observation of group development in terms of movement from dependence to interdependence is another subjective way of evaluating the effectiveness of the group. Later in this chapter, group development is described in terms of observable behaviors that emerge at various stages of the group life cycle.

Evaluation of group progress is facilitated by using a log or journal to record changes noted in the group by the leader or by observers. Some results of the group experience are indisputable, even though external variables may intrude. Losing 10 pounds, getting a job, maintaining normal blood sugar readings, or reducing blood pressure readings provides tangible evidence of a successful group experience.

Evaluation of group progress can be difficult. This is one reason for using a coleadership model in which two leaders can compare observations, engage in validation, and correct false impressions. Any systematic method of observing and recording group data will make evaluation easier. One-way mirrors and electronic taping, either audio or audiovisual, can be helpful. All observation and recording methods must be disclosed to prospective members during contract negotiations, and written consent must be obtained in advance from every member. Observers or supervisors can review group proceedings with the leader while events are recent and give immediate feedback to the leader in a postsession.

In the absence of electronic taping or live supervision, a log or journal of the sessions may be substituted. This record should be made as soon as possible after a session and should identify group themes, describe interventions, and note the impact of interventions on individual members and on whole-group interaction. Although less objective than other methods, the log enables the leader to review group events, recall sequential actions, analyze interactions, and clarify relationships within the group.

STAGES OF GROUP DEVELOPMENT

Group development refers to the changes that occur in the life cycle of a group, from a tentative beginning into a productive phase, and eventually to the end. Some groups enjoy a full and vigorous life span; some do not survive infancy; still others reach maturity without ever achieving their potential. Most groups go through stages in which conflict arises around various issues that are characteristic of the developmental stage of the group. Accepting the idea that groups go through stages of development helps leaders and observers interpret various tumultuous group events as constructive rather than destructive.

There is some danger in taking the stages of group development too literally. Groups resemble individuals in that they are prone to periods of progression and regression. Realizing that groups do not always progress steadily and without interruption helps eliminate disappointment or surprise when "settled" issues are revived in the group and must be dealt with again. It is also important to recognize that few groups move as a single unit through developmental stages. Some members may be more willing than others to confront the group task. Usually a group does not become productive until a majority of members indicate readiness. Although group development has been described in many ways, one of the simplest and most useful divisions of group development is into an initial stage, a middle, or working stage, and a final stage.

Initial Stage

In the early stage of group development the dominant issues are dependency and authority. The leader is assumed to possess great power and may be perceived by members as a parental figure. Feelings of rivalry may exist in the group, with members wishing to be the favorite of the leader but fearing exclusion by other members if the wish is realized. All members hope for a safe and secure place in the group but may be afraid of giving up too much individuality in order to be accepted. In this early period politeness and conformity are used by the members to control anxiety. Because silence often heightens anxiety, there is a tendency on the part of leaders and members to avoid silences at any cost. Controversy and differences also generate anxiety, so the members search for similarities and common interests among themselves.

After most of the members have managed to become part of the group without sacrificing too

Figure 20–2. Sample items showing quantitative rank order. These items deal with self-reported distress of a client. Items are given a numerical value of one to four, with one indicating the lowest index of distress and four representing the highest index. By means of rank order it is possible to compare individuals or groups of individuals.

Name _____ Age _____ Sex _____ Date _____	1. Never or rarely	2. Some of the time	3. Much of the time	4. Most or all of the time
I feel downhearted, blue, and sad				
I find it hard to make decisions				
I have crying spells or feel like crying				
I have trouble sleeping through the night				
I get tired for no reason				

much of their individuality, a struggle against the leader may follow. Now the members begin to assert themselves and to challenge the authority of the leader. In this period of competition some members are more active than others. The movement of group members from attitudes of dependency to struggles for power is an indication that the group is beginning to mature. Rather than resenting the growing strength and autonomy of the group, the leader should tolerate and even encourage questions and criticisms that represent challenges to authority and renunciation of dependency by the members (Mills 1967).

Mills described five stages of group development based on the prevailing group activities recognizable at each stage. Mills paid special attention to the final stage of the group, which he called separation. During the separation stage, members deal with termination and the approaching death of the group by reviewing the impact of the group experience and dealing with feelings about separating. According to Mills this period features behaviors that symbolize a search for a "benediction" before the group ends. Members may review the history of the group and reminisce about its successes and failures. Another group theorist (Tuckman 1965) found that groups in general, regardless of their purpose, undergo a predictable sequence from immature phases of testing and conflict to mature phases of work and accomplishment. Tuckman's developmental sequence resembles that of Mills,

except for the omission of a final phase of separation. Tuckman's sequence assumes that in mature groups productivity remains high until the group dissolves.

The group's challenge to the leader requires a rational and careful response. For example, a head nurse whose staff meetings are disrupted by criticisms about work assignments or complaints about time schedules may decide not to consider the validity of the objections that are raised and choose instead either to ignore or dismiss the opinions of staff members. The head nurse could then continue the usual practice of making unilateral decisions about staffing, thereby retaining full control in this matter. On the other hand, the head nurse might decide to rotate responsibility for assignments and schedules among the nurses working on the unit. By sharing power with the group, the head nurse would foster self-direction and independence among the nursing staff. As they experience leadership responsibility, staff members should realize how many factors intrude when assignments are made. The result in most cases would be growing maturity of the staff members and greater respect for the designated leader.

Another example of therapeutic response when leadership is challenged might occur in a psychiatric day treatment center where clients habitually deface bulletin boards with graffiti. Instead of invoking punitive measures, the nurse administrator might arrange to set aside one bulletin board for the clients. At a community meeting they could be told that one bulletin board is theirs on which to write whatever they choose. This concession would make the problem of defacing informational bulletin boards no longer the focus of prolonged discussion at community meetings.

The initial stage of group development may be divided into a dependency phase and a power phase. The first phase represents the willingness of individual members to become part of the group, the second represents the reluctance of individual members to merge fully with the group. In group terminology the first part of the initial stage deals with dependency and inclusion; the second part deals with power and authority (Schutz 1966).

Middle Stage

By the end of the initial stage of group development, problems of dependency and power should be resolved for the most part. At this stage cohesion has developed among the members and the group should be ready to undertake productive work. Some tension and anxiety may be present, because members must now confront the task for which the group was organized, even though they may hesitate to do so.

A group in the working stage has accumulated a shared history. Group norms have evolved, and members have formulated standards that define which behaviors are acceptable and which are unacceptable. There is a marked difference between group rules and group norms. *Group rules* can be established by the leader or agreed upon by the leader and the members even before the group

---

MILL'S PERIODS OF GROUP DEVELOPMENT

Period 1. Encountering

Period 2. Boundary testing and role modeling

Period 3. Establishing norms

Period 4. Working and producing

Period 5. Separating

TUCKMAN'S STAGES OF GROUP DEVELOPMENT

Stage 1. Forming: stage of testing and dependency

Stage 2. Storming: stage of conflict and emotional expression

Stage 3. Norming: stage of establishing norms and becoming cohesive

Stage 4. Performing: stage of task accomplishment and relatedness

---

VARIATIONS IN GROUP LEADERSHIP ROLE ENACTMENT

■ *Leaderless groups:* Most experienced member functions as leader; leadership is shared; leadership resides in commitment to a creed or goal.

■ *Leaderless sessions:* Alternate meetings are conducted without the presence of a designated leader.

■ *Leader as a background figure:* Leader functions mostly behind the scenes in that his or her influence is felt but presence is subtle and unobtrusive.

■ *Leader as a foreground figure:* Leader is dominant presence in the group: directs, stimulates, extends, interprets.

SOURCE: Adapted from H. I. Kaplan and B. J. Sadock (1975).

---

begins to meet. *Group norms* cannot be imposed but rather emerge gradually as the group begins to move toward interdependence and task performance. One example of the difference between rules and norms is the fact that the leader may enforce a rule that no member who is more than five minutes late will be admitted to a session. This is an explicit rule that is part of the group contract and that has been in effect since the first meeting. Because of the rule all of the members are punctual. Gradually a group norm develops that the members consistently arrive 15 minutes early to have coffee together. Group rules are generally enforced for everyone, but norms may not be applied uniformly. For instance, a member who works irregular hours might not be expected to be part of the premeeting socializing (a norm) but is expected not to be late for the session (a rule). Norms are usually unwritten and may not even be verbalized; rules are usually verbalized and are more explicit and well-defined than norms.

The working stage is usually a satisfying time for the members. Each of them has moved toward achieving a position in the group that feels comfortable. Problems will inevitably arise that require decisions and solutions. Anxiety and resistance to the task may be evident from time to time, but the general direction of the group is progressive. The leader may be less active than in the initial stage but continues to intervene to help resolve problems, to protect the exploitation of weaker members by stronger ones, and to monitor the anxiety level of the group so that no member is overwhelmed.

Final Stage

As in every therapeutic interaction, the process of termination begins with the first meeting. It may already have been discussed during preparatory interviews with group members in terms of how long the group will meet. In open-ended groups, members may terminate individually; in close-end groups, the group terminates as a unit. Premature termination occurs when a member drops out or when a group disbands without completing its primary task. Even though termination has been mentioned during negotiation proceedings and alluded to during meetings, it usually seems to come as a surprise to members. The element of unexpectedness that surrounds termination is a form of denial, especially if the group has become meaningful to members.

Often it is the more successful groups that have the most difficulty with termination, and this is true of leaders as well as members. It is helpful to divide termination into two phases: disengagement and actual dissolution. The period of disengagement, which precedes dissolution, is a time when members begin to recognize the fact that the group will end soon. Problems of dependency and authority may reappear. Members may display anger, perhaps because anger is a less painful emotion than grief (Rubin 1981). Avoiding discussion of termination is dysfunctional, and members should be encouraged to talk about the history and meaning of the group. Appropriate leadership tactics during termination include reminiscing, review of group themes, and discussion of group outcomes. It is also useful if leaders and members can identify authentic feelings of sadness at the end of the group experience. Termination is an important part of the group life cycle and should neither be denied, avoided, nor ignored.

There is danger that group leaders and observers who use a chronological, stage-specific model will note only conspicuous clusters of behavior and ignore subtle changes in the group. However, dividing group development into stages helps in the assessment of group progress. The work of a number of group theorists has dealt with stage-specific behaviors. Schutz (1966) conceptualized group conflicts likely to appear at various stages; Tuckman (1965) formulated a well-known sequence of group behaviors that has the advantage of being recalled easily. The sequential nature of group development is even more obvious when the psychosocial framework of Erikson (1963) is superimposed. Table 20–3 synthesizes the concepts of these three theorists and applies them to developmental group stages.

LEADERSHIP IN GROUPS

Marram (1978) differentiated leadership functions from leadership interventions. *Leadership functions* are essential responsibilities that the leader does not delegate or share with members. Leadership functions include providing a safe environment within the group, fostering autonomy and maturation of the group, and meeting the needs of members in a growth-enhancing manner. *Leadership interventions* refer to specific acts or behaviors that facilitate progress toward the group task, and these may be delegated or shared among group members.

Groups have primary and secondary tasks. The primary task is the purpose for which the group was formed. The secondary task is group maintenance so that the group survives long enough for the primary task to be accomplished. The existence of a primary and secondary group task means that group leaders always have two functions: to meet the emotional needs of the members so that the group is preserved and to mobilize abilities and resources within the group so that the primary task can be completed. If a group has only one leader, she must perform both. The most important consideration is that the primary task (achieving the purpose of the group) cannot be met if the secondary task (maintaining and preserving the group) is neglected or left to chance.

In order to fulfill leadership functions an individual must possess a working knowledge of content and process. *Content* is the substantive, explicit factual material that is brought up in a group, in other words, *what* is said or done in a group meeting. *Group process* is less easily observed; it includes covert, subtle, implicit forces present in the group. Process deals with *how* and *why* interactions develop in the group. Questions that help a leader understand group process are: How do the members relate to each other? How do the members and the leader interact? Why do group interactions take the form they do?

The importance of analyzing both content and process cannot be overstated, for the two are equally significant. Analyzing group content permits the leader to uncover recurrent themes and patterns in the group. Analyzing content also helps the leader understand process and make assumptions on which to base interventions. By observing and analyzing group process a leader is better able to understand and meet the needs of group members. Monitoring group process requires attention to both nonverbal and verbal messages, as well as sensitivity to subtle behaviors that indicate the needs of the group. In most group meetings one or more themes dominate or recur, and they can be identified. A leader who analyzes a group session by identifying the dominant themes can then explore the substantive content of the theme in order to recognize the process factors that were present in the session. Table 20–4 shows how identifying a group theme can be a prelude to understanding group process.

Leadership Styles

The style of leadership is determined primarily by the group's needs, of composition, and goals. The preferences and personal characteristics of the leader also influence the style of leadership. One of the first issues to be determined by a leader is whether to choose an autocratic, democratic, or laissez-faire style of leadership. An *autocratic* leader is clearly in charge of group proceedings, guiding and directing the members and holding them to the group task. A *democratic* leader remains responsible for the well-being of group members during the sessions and may remind members of the group task but shares leadership functions with them by permitting considerable autonomy. The *laissez-faire* leader may monitor group proceedings but offers little guidance, allowing the group members to shape the group sessions without interventions or reminders from the leader. Even though the first consideration should be the needs of the group, the personal biases of the leader have a way of intruding. If, for example, a leader believes that most people do not enjoy working and need to be harnessed to the task, that leader will likely be autocratic. On the other hand, if the leader believes that most people are willing to work and are capable of

Table 20–3. Stages of Group Development

Stage	Schutzian Conflict Issues	Eriksonian Tasks	Tuckmanian Sequence
Initial	Dependency Authority	Trust vs. mistrust Autonomy vs. shame and doubt Initiative vs. guilt	Storming Forming
Middle	Intimacy Cooperation Productivity	Industry vs. inferiority Identity vs. role confusion Intimacy vs. isolation Generativity vs. stagnation	Norming Performing*
Final	Disengagement Dissolution	Ego integrity vs. despair	

*Tuckman assumes that groups remain productive until their termination. A number of clinicians have observed the contrary and would add a *mourning* stage, characterized by increased group emotion and decreased attention to the group task.

Table 20–4. Theme, Content, and Process Analysis in Group Sessions

Group Theme	Content Analysis	Process Analysis
Cardiac clients in an outpatient health teaching group during their rehabilitation program	Protracted discussion and indecision about time, place, and agenda for future meetings	Covert ambivalence about being in the group, resistance to accepting a changing lifestyle, and a need to be in control
Diabetic clients in a health education group that emphasizes dietary control and general measures of coping with a chronic illness	Complaints about spouses, relatives, and physicians who don't have diabetes and therefore don't understand what it's like to live with so many prohibitions	Covert dissatisfaction with the leader, partial denial of the severity of the illness, anger about being ill, and skepticism about the value of the group
Recent nurse graduates in a staff orientation program preparing them for their first professional positions	Discussion of their residences, how near or far they live from work, commuting problems, car accidents, driver's licenses	Covert fear of giving up student status, of enacting the professional role, and of making errors
Pregnant teenagers in a childbirth education class dealing with labor and delivery, as well as care of the newborn	Ridicule directed to the leaders' emphasis on nutrition, coupled with refusal to give up favorite junk food for a balanced diet	Covert expression of unmet needs for nurturance, reluctance to give up adolescent attitudes and accept responsibility in the new role soon to be thrust upon them

self-direction, that leader is likely to be democratic and to engage in collaborative efforts.

Autocratic or authoritarian leadership seems to result in greater productivity but lower morale compared to democratic leadership. Hostility, scapegoating, and aggression have been found to be significantly greater in groups with an autocratic leader.

Democratic leadership has been found to result in less productivity, but groups with such leadership are more cohesive, self-directed, and better able to mobilize group resources on their own. Laissez-faire leadership has been found to be the least effective in terms of productivity and morale.

Tables 20–5 and 20–6 compare the characteristics and the results, respectively of the three leadership styles.

Flexibility on the part of the leader is necessary, and the choice of leadership style should be determined by the situation. For many groups a direct, authoritative approach is advisable. This is very true of groups where the members are acutely anxious, adolescent, elderly and confused, or even marginally out of touch with reality. Other situations that require authoritarian leadership include the following:

1. When the group is on the verge of dissolving prematurely and an immediate decision must be made if the group is to remain viable. In a scout troop where attendance has become erratic, the leader may issue an ultimatum that members who miss more than three meetings are barred from attending the midsummer camping jamboree.

2. When the task is very structured, and few, if any, alternative approaches are available. A class of nursing students practicing a technical procedure may be limited to step-by-step actions that are needed to ensure safe practice. In this instance the instructor (leader) would not allow deviation or improvisation, regardless of group pressure to accept alternative behaviors.

Table 20–5. Comparison of Characteristics of Three Leadership Styles

Democratic	Autocratic	Laissez-faire
Member-oriented	Leader-oriented	Diffuse orientation
Problem-solving approach	Persuasive approach	Style drifts and changes
Member-defined goals	Leader-defined goals	Few clear goals
Facilitates participation	Limits participation	Unclear participation
Group gauges process and progress by extensive feedback and activity	Limited feedback	Little evaluation of process; minimal feedback; decreased effectiveness
Leader influences group and may share leadership functions	Leadership retained by one or two designated persons	Leadership neither centralized nor distributed
Complex approach	Direct approach	Confused approach
Diversity encouraged	Limited tolerance of diversity	Diversity neither encouraged nor discouraged

SOURCE: Adapted from White and Lippitt (1953), Shaw (1976), Sampson and Marthas (1977), and Lego (1978).

Table 20–6. Comparison of the Results of Three Leadership Styles

Democratic	Autocratic	Laissez-faire
Increased member participation	Decreased participation	Decreased cooperation
Increased member enthusiasm, cohesiveness, morale	Decreased morale, cohesiveness Decreased innovation	Decreased morale, emotional satisfaction, cohesiveness
Increased member commitment	Highest productivity level	Increased scapegoating
Increased productivity, but less than autocratic	Consistent surveillance Increased dependency	Decreased productivity
Increased initiative	Decreased individuality	Decreased learning of leadership skills
Leadership skills learned by members	Restricted conversation	Decreased quality of work
Self-corrective feedback, maximizing member's potential	Task related discussion and conformity Increased uniformity Repressed aggression leading to scapegoating, resentment, passive-aggressive, acting-out behaviors	Increased requests for information

SOURCE: Adapted from White and Lippitt (1953), Shaw (1976), Sampson and Marthas (1977), and Lego (1978).

3. When members desire and expect a strong, central leader and are unwilling or unable to accept a share of leadership. A group of pregnant teenagers preparing in childbirth education classes for labor and delivery is likely to respond to a kind but knowledgeable leader who accepts and does not delegate leadership functions to members.

Situations in which democratic leadership is more suitable include the following:

1. When there are several alternatives in the way the task may be accomplished. In health team meetings where client care is being planned, discussion should be free and open. The suggestions of each team member should receive consideration.

2. When the members are capable of and can benefit from increased self-direction and responsibility. A group of recovering alcoholics engaged in planning a Christmas party may well benefit from permission to take charge of the arrangements with minimal supervision from the leader.

3. When there is need to alter attitudes and opinions as well as promote behavioral change. High school students who are studying the adverse consequences of drug abuse are more likely to believe an instructor who listens to their views and does not reject or discount their opinions.

A group leader is often the target of ambivalent feelings on the part of members. In the early stages of group development the leader is thought to possess enormous power. She is assumed to be wise and kind but is also considered a taskmaster. This contradictory perception of the leader creates problems for groups that want the leader to be human but also larger than life. Dependent members in particular exaggerate the leader's abilities and minimize their own. Other members may also wish to receive care and attention from the leader but resent the wish. The members become assertive or even aggressive toward the leader, dealing with their conflict by becoming counterdependent.

Coleadership Issues

There are advantages and disadvantages to adopting a coleadership model. Data collection regarding content and process is facilitated by the observations, validation, and feedback that occur between coleaders. Mutual support may lower leader anxiety and increase the reserves of leader energy. Group continuity is assured should one of the leaders become ill or go on vacation. The fact that every group requires two leadership functions—socioemotional responsibility and task responsibility—produces a natural distribution of leader functions when this model is used. Coleadership is an arrangement that demands respect, compatibility, and trust between the leaders. If rivalry exists between the leaders, a power struggle that inhibits group development may ensue. Before organizing the group, coleaders must discuss relevant issues and reach agreement. A protocol must be developed that distributes leadership responsibilities and determines procedural matters. If one leader has more experience than the other, a choice must be made as to whether an egalitarian relationship will exist between them during group sessions or

(Text continues on page 574.)

CHARACTERISTICS OF SELF-HELP GROUPS

- The members share a common interest, problem, situation, or experience.

- The groups are largely self-governing, self-regulating, and self-supporting.

- The groups cooperate with professionals but rely primarily on fellowship among members.

- The groups conform to a particular organizational code for conducting meetings, accepting members, integrating new members, and accomplishing the group task.

- The groups frequently emphasize commitment and responsibility to other members, expressed through visitation and phone services that are available to all without charge.

- The groups disregard or blur strict distinctions between consumers, professionals, and boards of directors, combining and exchanging functions in order to serve the membership at large.

- There are a wide variety of self-help groups in the United States; the number appears to be growing, and they greatly augment professional and community resources.

SOURCE: Adapted from Burnside (1984).

C L I N I C A L   V I G N E T T E

INCONSISTENT LEADERSHIP IN A GROUP FOR DIABETIC CLIENTS

In a long-term group sponsored by an outpatient medical clinic, six female diabetics met twice a month after their clinic appointments. The group leader was Ruth Allen, a clinical nurse specialist. All the group members were married homemakers between the ages of 30 and 50 who had been invited to join the group because their disease was either labile or only recently diagnosed. The group was open-ended, with members joining and terminating as indicated by the stability of their physical condition. The purpose of the group was to help provide continuity of care in a supportive interpersonal setting in which didactic material could easily be presented.

The senior group member was Mrs. Drew. A grossly overweight woman, Mrs. Drew had been attending the medical clinic for 10 years, but had recently been invited to join the group because her diabetes was unstable. In their one-to-one interactions relationships between Mrs. Drew and the group leader had been cordial. Ruth Allen, therefore, was surprised to find that Mrs. Drew had become a problem member of the group. Even though her diabetic condition was uncontrolled and her obesity excessive, Mrs. Drew seemed to compete with Ruth for leadership of the group. She constantly contradicted and challenged Ruth's professional judgment and expertise. In meetings Mrs. Drew conveyed the idea that because she was a diabetic, her views were more reliable than Ruth's, whose knowledge came from books. Although Ruth tried to avoid open arguments, she feared that her sound teaching was being undermined and other members misled by Mrs. Drew's pose as the real expert on diabetes.

Because she believed that the group was jeopardized by the contest for leadership, Ruth asked help from a staff consultant on group dynamics. The consultant, a clinical nurse specialist, agreed to observe sessions through a one-way mirror. Because this was not part of the group contract, Ruth presented it to members for their approval. She explained that this was her first experience in leading a group and that she wanted consultation to improve her skills. The members agreed, although Mrs. Drew said that it wasn't necessary to bring in an outsider because the group members could probably point out Ruth's weaknesses (*seeking recognition and status*).

In observing the group sessions the consultant confirmed her own initial suspicion that Ruth in some way was contributing to Mrs. Drew's behavior. The consultant noted that Ruth's interventions were inconsistent in ways that reinforced Mrs. Drew's behavior. By the time the consultant began her observations, Ruth could barely conceal her anger toward the problem member. Ruth felt that her status and credibility were under attack, and she could only see Mrs. Drew as a malicious person rather than a needy group member (*blaming and judging harshly*). The first objective of the consultant was to depersonalize the bitter power struggle and place it in an interpersonal context so that Ruth could accept Mrs. Drew's actions as part of the total group interaction. Based on the observations she made after viewing several group sessions, the consultant presented the following assessment:

1. Although she gave an impression of being powerful and controlling, Mrs. Drew was actually embarrassed by being the oldest member and the one who had accomplished the least. She had been attending the clinic longer than any other member and had been diagnosed as diabetic when she was in high school. Although she seemed indifferent, the instability of her diabetes frightened her and her obesity was a source of humiliation.

   Despite her extensive knowledge of diabetes, she was afraid that the other group members did not respect her. This made her feel anxious and ashamed. Her anxiety and low opinion of herself caused her to attempt an alliance with the group leader rather than with group members, because she thought they were more likely to reject her. Her aggressive behavior was motivated not by rivalry but by a wish to be close to Ruth and win her respect (*isolation from other members; affiliation with the leader*).

   Ruth acknowledged feeling angry with Mrs. Drew, but she was professional enough not to declare war on the member. Because she was inexperienced as a group leader, she did not explore group dynamics in order to understand the underlying meaning of Mrs. Drew's behavior (*discarded objectivity*).

2. Although angry at Mrs. Drew, Ruth seemed to be relieved to be sharing the leadership responsibility

with her. When the group members fell silent, Ruth sent nonverbal messages to Mrs. Drew requesting her to take over. The nonverbal messages included nodding, smiling, and glancing at Mrs. Drew whenever Ruth was unsure of what to say next. This allowed Mrs. Drew to think that Ruth welcomed her contributions (*inconsistent leadership*).

3. Mrs. Drew was exploited by the other group members, who rewarded her verbosity and used it to avoid becoming more involved with each other. The members frequently referred to Mrs. Drew's extensive knowledge and experience with diabetes (*placating*).

4. Although Ruth was glad to relinquish leadership to Mrs. Drew at times, she generally resented doing this. When Mrs. Drew assumed leadership, Ruth doubted her own ability to sustain the group. Ruth gave many double messages to Mrs. Drew. On one level she signaled to Mrs. Drew for assistance. On another level she considered Mrs. Drew an intruder. After trying unsuccessfully to be consistent, Ruth became angry with Mrs. Drew (*ambiguous communication*).

Since the purpose of meeting was to help members handle their diabetes, the consultant suggested that Ruth distribute leadership functions among all the members, rather than continue turning to Mrs. Drew. Competition between two persons is a form of pairing which often interferes with the group task. To weaken the pairing with Mrs. Drew, Ruth asked all the members to identify for the group their most urgent concerns. At the suggestion of the consultant, Ruth told the group that she had depended too much on Mrs. Drew and needed to hear more from other members (*feedback*). Ruth also explained that having diabetes did not, automatically, make one an expert, and asked members to confirm this through their own experiences. She stressed that bringing their concerns to the group was the best way to learn and to work together (*fostering cohesion*).

Because Mrs. Drew found the group experience anxiety-provoking, she tried to protect her self-image. This caused her to avoid involvement with fellow members and to align herself with Ruth, whom she trusted. With the aid of the group consultant, Ruth became aware of the mutual anxiety which motivated the struggle between herself and Mrs. Drew. Interventions were planned to restore Mrs. Drew's self-confidence and to make Ruth's leadership consistent. Ruth explained to group members that diabetes mellitus was a disease with many ramifications, and that no one was a failure because the disease was not stabilized. Once Ruth accepted Mrs. Drew's interpersonal needs as sincere, she was able to modify the leadership inconsistencies which came from her own insecurity. By looking at the reciprocal nature of communication and interaction between Ruth and Mrs. Drew, the consultant helped Ruth to plan interventions that persuaded Mrs. Drew that interpersonal security lay in group membership rather than in a contest for leadership.

---

whether one will be the senior and the other a junior partner. Similarly, the prospective leaders must decide whether one will be responsible for socioemotional issues and the other for task issues, or whether these two essential functions will be shared or rotated. As much attention should be devoted to the matching of coleaders and the resolution of coleadership issues as to the selection and preparation of group members.

MEMBERSHIP ROLES IN GROUPS

Role enactment refers to the behavioral patterns exhibited by individual group members during the life span of the group. Role enactment is usually the result of the personal characteristics and emotional needs of the individual combined with the complex relationships that develop in the group. Role enactment is expressed behaviorally in the form of sustained verbal and nonverbal communication patterns. Usually role enactment is explicit and durable enough to permit leaders and observers to identify the roles that various members assume.

Regardless of its purpose, a group tends to adhere to a constellation of roles that evolve gradually over successive meetings. The role enactment of some members may promote group development, whereas the role enactment of other members may impair group development. Every role enacted in a group produces shared expectations that make group events predictable and understandable. Thus, the member who assumes a certain role in the group may find that the group will not permit that member to relinquish his role. Enacting a certain role in the group may give a member an identity, but it also burdens him with fulfilling the inflexible expectations that others have formed.

An obligation of the leader is to unlock fixed or inflexible role enactment that is detrimental to any member or to the group as a whole. This may be done by leader interventions based on meaning attribution (*explaining*) and supportive nurture (*caring*). For example, a single group member may become the target of hostile, negative remarks by other members. The leader might intervene by giving the member some positive recognition. Pointing out similarities between the member under

GROUP FUNCTIONS AND LEADER RESPONSIBILITIES

Essential Group Functions	Leader Responsibilities
Primary Meeting Instrumental or Task Needs	Working to achieve the major purpose for which the group was organized
	Mobilizing the resources of the group; harnessing the abilities of the group to the group task
	Adhering to the major task of the group
	Maintaining the group until the major task is achieved
Secondary Meeting Socioemotional or Psychological needs	Maintaining an environment within the group that is safe for all members
	Promoting interpersonal exchanges that facilitate positive change
	Assuming responsibility for fragile or vulnerable members when subjected to hostile attack
	Fostering group cohesion and meaningfulness

attack and other members with more status is an indirect but effective intervention that protects one member without blaming others.

Group roles have been classified along the following lines (Marram 1978):

1. Task roles that are essentially administrative and goal oriented
2. Maintenance roles that enhance group participation and interaction
3. Egocentric roles that express individual emotional needs

Egocentric roles are not directed toward maintenance or task accomplishment but are enacted to fulfill personal needs and express inner conflicts. Members who enact egocentric roles often act against the best interests of the group, and their behaviors may become problematic for the group leader. The accompanying box presents a comparison based on role enactment classified as task, maintenance, or egocentric.

A number of roles commonly enacted in groups deserve explanatory comments and basic definitions. *Role differentiation* is the patterned behavior of group members that can be distinguished and identified. *Role specialization* is the result of the adherence of individual members to persistent and consistent patterns of behavior. Among the commonly encountered role specialists is the member who becomes the group *seducer*. No sexual connotations are attached to this label, for the group

seducer is merely the member who is least afraid of interpersonal closeness and therefore weakens group defenses against intimacy. At times the seducer can be a very effective group member, but if attempts to become close are made too early in the life of the group, other members may become frightened. The counterpart of the seducer is the *aggressor*. This role is enacted by a member who fears intimacy and self-disclosure and therefore resorts to distancing maneuvers of one kind or another. Humor, superficiality, or anger may characterize the behavior of the aggressor who feels safe only at a distance.

Many groups need a *scapegoat*, and the member enacting this role often performs a constructive function, even though appearances may belie this fact. The scapegoat may begin by being a seducer or an aggressor, but as time passes he begins to express feelings that other members would like to express but dare not. When group members hear the scapegoat say what they have been refusing to express, they deny their own feelings by attacking him. At times a leader may assume the role of the scapegoat deliberately in order to protect a candid member from group hostility and to demonstrate that negative opinions are not forbidden. As groups mature and settle down to the task, they have less need of a scapegoat. At this point, the scapegoat, in turn, may find it less necessary to express negative or opposing views.

The group *deviant* is a member who performs a constructive function in the group, even though

GROUP ROLE SPECIALIZATION

Task Roles

Initiator—Defines problem, proposes solution, mobilizes group toward problem solving

Elaborator—Illustrates ideas, predicts, and plans

Information and opinion seeker—Requests data, opinions, ideas related to problem

Information and opinion giver—Brings own experiences, opinions, and suggestions regarding group goals and values

Coordinator—Clarifies ideas, offers suggestions to demonstrate relationships between them, harmonizes activities of members

Evaluator—Measures group decisions and achievements against group standards and goals

Energizer—Stimulates group to perform at a higher level

Orienter—Summarizes discussion, raises questions regarding group's direction

Liaison—Performs bridging function between group and external authorities, communicates group needs and concerns

Maintenance Roles

Encourager—Accepts ideas with understanding, approval, and praise

Diplomat—Mediates group conflicts and relieves tension, is sensitive and tactful

Process observer—Reflects observation of group process back to group

Communication facilitator—Uses skillful communication to enhance consensual validation, encourages other members to participate

Follower—Is passive member, frequently an audience in decision-making situations

Egocentric Roles

Aggressor—Expresses behavior that reduces the status and contributions of others, attacks the group or its task

Seducer—Engages in openness and self-disclosure that promote group intimacy but, if premature, may inhibit group progress and increase the anxiety of some members

Blocker—Uses resistive, negative behavior; returns to issues that have been rejected or discarded previously

Humorist—Displays lack of concern and involvement through "horseplay," joking, or other irrelevant behavior

Monopolizer—Assumes responsibility for maintaining communication; dominates group, creating group hostility

Recognition seeker—Attempts to gain admiration and attention by boasting of accomplishments, dressing flamboyantly, arriving late

Scapegoat—Experiences criticism and/or rejection in the group by doing or saying what other members may wish to do or say but dare not

Deviant—Reinforces group standards by opposing rules and norms, thereby demonstrating what is and is not acceptable to the group

Silent member—Remains silent for a variety of reasons, such as anxiety, fear of self-disclosure, or desire for attention, but often participates nonverbally

Rescuer—Acts as self appointed protector of other members

Isolator—Remains separate and uninvolved with group experience

SOURCE: Compiled from Benne and Sheats (1948), and Kreigh and Perko (1979).

she appears to be disruptive. The positive function performed by the group deviant is to define, reinforce, and strengthen group norms by separating acceptable from unacceptable behaviors. In a vague way the group majority seems to recognize the value of the deviant, for the group exerts considerable effort trying to convince the deviant to accept group norms. The deviant therefore receives much attention from other members and is often persuaded to comply. Occasionally the deviant may drop out of the group rather than accept group standards, and the group majority may eventually expel a deviant who fails to conform to a satisfactory extent.

Another member whose behavior may seem disruptive is the group *monopolizer*. This is usually a garrulous member who demands that all attention be paid to his personal needs. He may also operate as an unofficial group leader, dispensing advice and information to other members. The motivation of the monopolizer varies, and it is important for the leader to assess whether the monopolizing behavior stems from anxiety, self-centeredness, fear of closeness, fear of inadequacy, or rebellion against authority. If possible, the leader should not intervene directly to silence the monopolizer, for this may be interpreted by other members as an indication that the leader does not welcome participation. A better tactic is to label monopolizing behavior so that it appears to be constructive. The leader might comment to the group that the monopolizer is doing all the work for other members while they remain aloof, safe, and silent. Such an intervention conveys to other members that their participation is invited but does not display to the group the stark power of the leader.

Another individual with whom leaders have difficulty is the *silent* member. As in the case of the monopolizer, the motivation of the silent member may vary. Silence may be an attention-getting ploy, or it may indicate anxiety, fear of self-disclosure, or difficulty in verbalizing. The leader might begin by speculating on the meaning of the silence and soliciting the help of the group in identifying the underlying feelings of the silent member. It must be remembered that many nonverbal members are actively participating and getting something out of the interaction of other members. While the leader may comment on the behavior of the silent member, allowances should be made for individual differences. It is necessary to accept the fact that all members may not be equally ready to speak and that excluding silent members prohibits any possibility of their verbalizing in a later session.

In addition to the roles enacted by single members, role pairing often appears in a group. Two members may enact the paired roles of *lovers* who are lost in mutual admiration of each other and therefore are joined in their resistance to change. Another common pairing is that of *enemies*; this emerges when two members oppose each other regardless of the issue involved or the cost to themselves or the group. These are members whose decisions are not determined by logic or reason but are controlled by a need to frustrate the opposing member, who is enacting the role of enemy.

CURATIVE FACTORS IN GROUPS

Yalom (1975) described group curative factors as interpersonal experiences or transactions that propel individual members and the group toward productivity, competence, and a sense of well-being. Certain curative factors have been identified as present in groups to varying degrees. The curative factors identified by Yalom are listed in the accompanying box.

Group leaders often use verbal and nonverbal language to encourage the emergence of various curative factors. This may be done by modeling clear, direct communication or by commenting on interactions between members in which certain curative factors were present. For instance, one member might reveal difficulties he is experiencing in a personal relationship. The leader might refer to a similar problem previously revealed by another member and solicit help from that member. Such an intervention would promote the factors of universality and group cohesion. If one member is observed giving support or encouragement to another member, recognition of this by the leader would reinforce the curative factor of altruism and promote imitative behavior from other members. Curative factors are helpful even when members do not call attention to their presence, but are usually more beneficial if attention is directed to them. Cognitive and emotional understanding of what is happening in the group strengthens members' positive reactions (Brabender 1983).

(Text continues on page 579.)

ROLE PAIRING IN GROUPS

Role Pairing	Characteristic Behaviors
Members as lovers	Mutual admiration and praise for each other
Members as rivals	Mutual opposition and competition with each other
Members as enemies	Mutual dislike and antagonism toward each other
Members as collaborators	Mutual commitment to work, achievement, and rewards
Members as comrades	Mutual commitment to work, achievement, and emotional fulfillment

CLINICAL   VIGNETTE

ROLE DIFFERENTIATION AND
SPECIALIZATION IN A SUPPORT GROUP

A support group for single parents met one evening a week at a community mental health center. It was a closed, three-month, time-limited group consisting of seven members who were either widowed or divorced. Selection for the group included the following criteria:

Referral by a staff member of the mental health center

Single parenthood (male or female)

Household consisting of the parent and at least one child under 18 living at home

The primary task of the group was to help members with parenting responsibilities and offer support as they redirected their lives toward personal independence and fulfillment.

The group was led by Bill, a psychiatric nurse who was married and a father. In the first few meetings the members were guarded with one another but polite, frequently making sympathetic remarks. The group's most recently widowed member was Debbie, a 23-year-old secretary who was struggling to raise two toddlers, manage a household, and work part-time. She was shy and timid, and seldom initiated comments during meetings. Debbie usually sat next to Marcia, a middle-aged, attractive divorcee whose only son was about to graduate from high school and join the Navy in spite of his mother's protests. Marcia seemed to take Debbie under her wing like a fledging sparrow, sometimes answering for her, protecting her from making decisions by patting her hand and telling her, "You have plenty of time to think about that. You have your whole life ahead of you." Marcia soon began transporting Debbie to and from meetings because "It's a good way for Debbie to save money, and the poor child needs it."

As the second month of meetings started, group members interacted less and less with Debbie, perhaps annoyed by her lack of participation and by the closeness between her and Marcia. About this time Bill had to have emergency surgery and was absent from meetings for several weeks. Another staff member, Jack, whom the members did not know, was delegated to act as group leader until Bill returned. The group received the leadership change with little comment,

although they expressed annoyance when they learned that Jack was a bachelor. One member, Harry, said that since he was a single parent he would be glad to help lead the group if Jack would split the fee. The suggestion was greeted with laughter and applause by the group.

For the following two weeks attendance was erratic and the group seemed unable to attend to its tasks. Conversation was superficial and socially focused. Marcia, as the most verbal and assertive member, assumed increasing command of the group, suggesting that the group plan a party to celebrate Bill's return the following week. Jack seemed unable or unwilling to direct the sessions to focus on group goals. When Bill did return, he apologized for his inability to prepare them for his absence and began to explore what it had meant to the group to have had yet another loss imposed on them at a time when they were struggling to deal with their marital losses. Marcia replied that she was relieved to see him return, as "the other leader, 'what's his name,' really couldn't understand us."

The following roles are evident in this example. Debbie, the passive, silent member, quickly became the isolate, although she did pair with the more assertive Marcia. Marcia was an aggressor and also a rescuer, both for Debbie and the group as a whole. She changed her role into one of assumed leadership—when the group's dependency needs for a caring leader emerged during Bill's absence. The disturbing issue was the group's fear for safety precipitated by the loss of its assigned leader. The group's anger was denied (lack of comment regarding Bill's initial absence) and then displaced on the substitute leader,

---

ROLE DIFFERENTIATION*

Debbie	Silent Member/Follower
Harry	Playboy/Humorist
Marcia	Aggressor/Rescuer
Bill	Facilitator/Diplomat
Jack	Deviant/Scapegoat

*An individual may enact more than one role at a time, as did Jack and Debbie. An individual may discard one role and assume another, as did Marcia. Roles often change with group needs.

a less threatening or effective person (Jack as deviant), Harry, the group humorist, attempted to alleviate the members' fears by jokingly offering himself as leader. Debbie's individual needs for protection were expressed in her passivity and acceptance of Marcia's attention, which then cast her into the role of silent member. In a reciprocal way, Marcia was able to deny her forthcoming loss of the mother role by providing surrogate mothering for Debbie. Neither one was able to escape the role lock, and, as a pair, were unable to contribute to the group's task function of sharing parenthood concerns and initiating a more independent lifestyle.

GROUP RESEARCH ISSUES

Group research, like other aspects of group work, can be extraordinarily complex, especially if undertaken in a clinical setting. General guidelines were offered by Loomis (1979), who listed the following sources of group data:

- Individual group members
- Group leaders or coleaders
- The group as a whole
- Significant persons in the lives of members
- Group observers and supervisors

Relying on these sources of data does not guarantee reliability or validity, because reports from any of these sources may be highly subjective. Some nurse leaders compare data by using pretests and posttests. However, even carefully designed instruments may not accurately reflect group dynamics or group outcomes. Members and leaders alike may overestimate or underestimate the outcomes of the group experience. Reports of changes observed by significant others may be equally unreliable.

Even though group research can be formidable, nurses are beginning to look beyond customary clinical approaches and to subject their work to more rigorous examination. Nurses starting to organize a group project can easily incorporate a research tool that will elevate their work from the level of intuition to the realm of theory building.

An essential decision is to decide what aspect of group work can be included in the research process. Will the research be focused on leadership versus membership behaviors? Will process or content be studied? Will group productivity or emotional satisfaction be compared?

Having determined the scope of the study, the nurse must begin to formulate clear, concise hypotheses based upon the defined goals set for the group. An illustration of a goal-related hypothesis is "Elderly members of a daily reminiscing group will demonstrate lower depression levels as measured by a valid and reliable self-evaluation scale." To

GROUP CURATIVE FACTORS

- *Guidance*. Experiences in the group that include suggestions and advice on the modification of destructive social attitudes and behaviors
- *Altruism*. Actions that demonstrate mutual caring and concern among members
- *Cohesion*. Shared belief that the group is meaningful to members and that members are meaningful to the group
- *Catharsis*. Therapeutic ventilation and expression of feelings, both positive and negative, within the group
- *Identification*. Adoption of functional behaviors and problem-solving techniques patterned after those of the leader or other group members
- *Family reenactment*. Reliving early family experiences in a conscious, corrective manner
- *Interpersonal learning: input*. Activities related to having events or experiences explained, described, or interpreted by others
- *Interpersonal learning: output*. Activities related to explaining, describing, or interpreting events and experiences to others
- *Universality*. Recognition that one's problems, fears, and emotions are not unique
- *Insight*. Understanding the causes and sources of conflicted attitudes and behaviors
- *Instillation of hope*. Growing belief that one's problems can be solved
- *Existentialism*. Accepting the need for self-direction and self-determination, in order to improve the quality of existence

(Text continues on page 581.)

CLINICAL VIGNETTE

DISPUTED ISSUES OF COLEADERSHIP

Carol Roberts, the nursing staff development coordinator at a general hospital, initiated an assertiveness training group and invited Howard Stewart, a respected team leader of an inpatient unit, to join her as coleader. Carol believed that Howard would augment her own skills and help validate her perceptions of the group. Because of Howard's experience as a team leader, Carol was sure he would be a good role model and reinforce the group's attention to the stated goal of assertiveness training.

Both leaders had prior experience leading patient groups and health team groups. Each approached the task with enthusiasm and confidence. A joint decision was made by the coleaders to limit the group to eight members and to meet for 1½ hours a week for 10 weeks. The majority of group members were female staff members. The first two group sessions were primarily didactic and proceeded according to plan, utilizing role-playing and group exercises. In the second and third sessions the group began to follow Howard into discussions of individual needs and concerns and to disengage when Carol introduced exercises in assertive behavior. Before long Carol began to experience frustration and to reveal her impatience with Howard's tendencies to promote unstructured "rap" sessions and group avoidance of assertive training. In addition, Howard used interventions with group members that focused on socioemotional issues and distributed leadership among various members. This was contrary to Carol's expectations, and she felt that she was losing control of group leadership and goals. Her sense of powerlessness reduced her self-confidence and level of participation. She attributed the group's obvious affection for Howard as evidence of male-female attraction and to cultural stereotypes of male aggression and female passivity.

Carol realized that assertiveness training is based on a structured format and wished to use exercises that followed a specific sequence. She believed that the relatively unstructured climate fostered by her coleader converted the assertiveness training meetings into group therapy sessions. She attributed the conflict between Howard and herself to his violation of the group contract and considered his tactics detrimental to group development. After several frustrating sessions, Carol proposed to Howard that they set aside a time to discuss the progress of the group and clarify its focus.

They decided to meet informally on neutral ground (in the hospital coffee shop). After sharing their perceptions of the group, Carol commented, "We seem to be pulling and tugging in opposite directions rather than working together at leading the group." This brought a nod of agreement from her coleader. Howard then voiced his own frustration at the lack of member participation in assertiveness training and expressed his wish to meet the socioemotional needs of individual members by encouraging honest, open discussion of various issues. He also expressed commitment to the distribution of leadership among the group members. It was apparent from the discussion that both leaders were feeling a loss of power because of their unresolved disagreement and were experiencing threats to their competency. When confronted by Carol, Howard admitted attempting to deal with the disagreement by covertly changing the contract and discarding principles of assertiveness training in favor of his preference for psychotherapy. Carol told him she was uncomfortable with the group's direction, but admitted that she had taken his acceptance of assertiveness training for granted.

The need for each leader to clarify and validate the manner in which executive roles would be enacted had not been included in early discussions. Other disputed issues included the degree to which leadership would be distributed, the level of structure required to meet the goal of assertiveness training, and the divergent commitment of the leaders to the group contract. The different expectations, dynamic characteristics, and security operations of the coleaders altered the group interactions and negatively affected group development.

Both Howard and Carol found their open discussion helpful. The members' indifference to assertiveness training stemmed chiefly from the incongruent messages transmitted by the two leaders. Carol and Howard realized the hazards of using the group as an arena for their own differences. They decided that it was essential to participate in ongoing presession and postsession discussions in order to compare group progress and clarify disputed issues before they became detrimental to group progress. Commitment of both leaders to the contracted goals was reinforced. At the same time Carol was persuaded to deal with members' socioemotional needs and to share leadership functions. She became more willing to delegate responsibility for the assertiveness exercises among the group members.

make comparisons that will prove or disprove the hypothesis, pretesting and posttesting are necessary.

As in any research study, the protection of human subjects is of great importance and agency policies must be strictly followed. How well these requirements have been fulfilled may be determined by asking the following questions:

- Is there an explicit hypothesis based on the goals?

- Is the hypothesis compatible with the goals and composition of the group, and with the leadership style that has been selected?

- Will the addition of systematic data collection impair group progress and affect group outcomes?

- Is the group membership adequately protected from intrusiveness or invasiveness resulting from data collection?

- Is the sponsoring agency in agreement with data collection procedures?

- Have proper procedures been followed to secure permission for data collection from the members, from the sponsoring agency, and from the appropriate human subjects research committee, if one exists?

SUMMARY

Group work may be divided into therapy groups and therapeutic groups. The first category includes groups that deal with intrapsychic and intrapersonal problems, while the latter includes groups concerned with interpersonal, cognitive, or behavioral change. Nurses have been working with groups and families for many years in a variety of settings, but only nurses who possess advanced degrees are considered by the American Nurses Association to be qualified to function as group psychotherapists.

Joseph Pratt, a Boston internist, is credited with being the founder of group work as a treatment modality. Samuel Slavson, an engineer, used play therapy as a method of dealing with the problems of children. Slavson was instrumental in founding the American Group Therapy Association, an interdisciplinary organization that opened group work to disciplines other than medicine. The use of psychodrama was introduced by Jacob Moreno, who used spontaneous dramatization of life experiences as a way of dealing with the life problems of the actors and the audience.

A number of psychoanalytic concepts are evident in groups even though the group may be devoted to here-and-now events. According to psychoanalytic theory, the group represents a corrective reenactment of the original family experience. A less psychoanalytic view is that the group is a social microcosm.

In organizing a group, nurses are advised to follow the nursing process, devoting sufficient attention to assessing the needs of a target population, planning group objectives and negotiating a group contract, implementing the design, and evaluating the impact of the group experience.

Assessing and evaluating the effectiveness of the group experience is facilitated by dividing group development into three stages: initial, middle, and final. Each stage is likely to be dominated by clusters of behaviors, some of which may appear to be disruptive to group progress and troublesome to the leader.

Group leadership involves two major functions: maintaining the group and accomplishing the purpose for which the group was formed. In addition, the leader should analyze group content and group process in order to base interventions on the needs of the group. Several leadership styles are available, each of which has certain advantages and disadvantages. Choice of a leadership style is determined by the needs of members and the goals of the group.

A number of egocentric roles may be enacted by group members. Some seem to impede group progress but in fact do not. Among the egocentric roles are those of group seducer, aggressor, scapegoat, and deviant. Group leaders should analyze the reasons members enact these roles and formulate interventions accordingly.

A number of curative factors are present in groups to varying degrees. Knowledge of the curative factors enables the leader to recognize some of the forces that are operative in the group. In addition, identification of the curative factors present in groups may become the basis of systematic investigation by generalist nurses and others who wish to incorporate research in their clinical practice.

Review Questions

1. What characteristics make a reference group different from a secondary group?

2. Explain what is meant by the *Noah's Ark Principle*.

3. List the dominant issues that are likely to emerge in the first stage of group development.

4. In helping members deal with termination of the group, what interventions might prove facilitative?

5. Describe the characteristics of different leadership styles and their probable effect on the group.

6. What are the advantages of using coleadership?

7. Define the term *role specialization* and give examples of task role enactment, maintenance role enactment and egocentric role enactment.

Suggested Annotated Readings

Boyd-Franklin, N. "Group Therapy for Black Women." *American Journal of Orthopsychiatry* 57, no. 3 (July 1987):394–401.

This article describes a therapeutic group for blacks led by a female black clinical psychologist. A major theme of the meetings was relationship problems, especially with men of their own race. Mother-daughter relationships were also a recurrent topic, as were family relationships in general. Religion and spirituality were focal points, as members expressed a strong desire for individuality that seemed to challenge the influence of strict church beliefs. Sisterhood and common ground promoted group cohesion and erased socioeconomic differences among the members.

Constantino, R. E. "Comparison of Two Group Interventions for the Bereaved." *Image* 20, no. 2 (Summer 1988):83–87.

Levels of depression and socialization measures were done on subjects in three groups: at an intake interview, at six weeks, and at intervals of three months, six months, and nine months. The subjects were divided into three groups. One hundred and seventeen subjects constituted the sample; one third of the sample received no group intervention. One third received crisis intervention in a group setting, and the other third received guided social activities. The crisis group leader was active and directive; the social activities leader was inactive and more peripheral. Most favorable results were found in bereavement group members, whose depression levels decreased and socialization levels increased significantly. Findings suggest that a group led by a caring person helps members deal with their grief. Interestingly, the bereavement group fostered socialization more than the activities group, whose members showed more depression and less socialization after participating in the group.

Kanas, N., P. Stewart, and K. Haney. "Content and Outcome in a Short-term Therapy Group for Schizophrenic Outpatients." *Hospital and Community Psychiatry* 39, no. 4 (April 1988):437–439.

This report describes a group of schizophrenic outpatients that met weekly for one hour; two psychiatrists led the group and a psychiatric nurse evaluated the sessions. The two primary goals were to help members cope with reality and to improve their personal relationships within and outside the group. Leaders were active, directive, and supportive. The nurse observer recorded topics discussed and categorized them. At termination and four months later members were contacted and questioned about the effectiveness of the group. They were also asked to rate the topics discussed in regard to their helpfulness. All five group members termed the experience somewhat or very helpful. Four months after termination four of the five members reported an improvement in interpersonal relationships. Two of the five reported improvement in their ability to cope with visual and auditory hallucination. The methodology used here is questionable and the sample is small, but the results are interesting and demonstrate that research can be built into a small group experience.

Lombardo, B., L. A. Cave, S. Naso, and D. Bernadino. "Group Support for Derm Patients." *American Journal of Nursing* 88, no. 8 (August 1988):1088–1090.

This is a report of a support group for inpatients and outpatients with serious dermatological problems. Organized and led by nurses, weekly meetings permit members to share their feelings with fellow sufferers through discussion and role play exercises. Identified group themes include poor self-image, stress, loss, and concern with medical aspects of care.

Mack, S. A., and L. C. Berman. "A Group for Parents of Children with Fatal Genetic Illness." *American Journal of Orthopsychiatry* 58, no. 3 (July 1988):397–404.

The authors describe a long-term, open-ended group established for parents of children with progressive genetic disorders, such as Tay-Sachs. Instigated by the mother of a child who had died with a genetic disorder, the group met in the evening at a community setting. Themes expressed by parents were guilt, grief, and mutual understanding. The article compellingly describes how parents coping with death or advanced deterioration in their children reached out to help fellow members who were just embarking on the same hard road.

Masterman, S. H., and R. Reams. "Support Groups for Bereaved Preschool and School-age Children." *American Journal of Orthopsychiatry* 58, no. 4 (October 1988):562–570.

Here various models of support groups for preschool and school-age children who have suffered parental death are discussed, and some specific intervention strategies are described. A week-by-week account is given of group themes that emerged over the course of eight weeks. School-age children talked about loss, change, denial, ambivalence toward the group, and fears about the future. Sessions included a 15-minute recess for physical activity in the school-age group.

Group sessions for preschoolers had two 15-minute recesses. These children were from three to six years old. Themes in the preschool sessions centered on anger, powerlessness, and guilt for not being "good enough." Parents expressed positive feelings about the effects of the group on their children.

Oerlemans-Bunn, M. "On Being Single, Gay, and Bereaved." *American Journal of Nursing* 88, no. 4 (April 1988):472–476.

Group membership comprised seven gay men who had lost significant partners to AIDS. They were a high-risk group and their own futures were uncertain. Meeting weekly in a bereavement group for a year, the men saw themselves as temporary survivors. This fact prolonged and intensified their grief; the author reports that at the time of writing group members were still experiencing difficulties in rebuilding their lives. Members reported such feelings as preoccupation with the lost lover, survivor guilt, and irrational anger at the paranoia and ostracism surrounding AIDS.

References

Anthony, E. J. "The History of Group Psychotherapy." In *Comprehensive Group Psychotherapy*. H. I. Kaplan and B. J. Sadock, eds. Baltimore: Williams & Wilkins, 1971.

Bair, J. P., and B. K. Greenspan. "Teams: Teamwork Training for Interns, Residents, and Nurses." *Hospital and Community Psychiatry* 37 (1986):633–634.

Benne, K. D., and P. Sheats. "Functional Roles of Group Members." *Journal of Social Issues* 4, no. 2 (1948): 41–49.

Bernikow, L. *Alone in America: The Search for Companionship*. New York: Harper & Row, 1986.

Brabender, V. "A Study of Curative Factors in Short-Term Group Psychotherapy." *Hospital and Community Psychiatry* 34 (1983):643–644.

Burnside, I. *Working with the Elderly*, Second Edition. Boston: Jones and Bartlett Publishers, 1986.

Caplan, G. *Principles of Basic Psychiatry*. New York: Basic Books, 1964.

——. *Theory and Practice of Mental Health Consultation*. New York: Basic Books, 1970.

Coleman, J. C., J. N. Butcher, and R. C. Carson. In *Abnormal Psychology in Modern Life*, 7th ed. Glenview, Illinois: Scott Foresman, 1984.

Doona, M. E. *Travelbee's Intervention in Psychiatric Nursing*, 2d ed. Philadelphia: Davis, 1979.

Erikson, E. H. *Childhood and Society*. New York: W. W. Norton, 1963.

Freud, S. "Group Psychology and the Analysis of the Ego." In *Standard Edition of Complete Psychological Works of Sigmund Freud*, Vol. 18. London: Hogarth Press, 1957.

Hammerschlag, C. A., and B. M. Astrachan. "The Kennedy Airport Show." In "An Inquiry into Intergroup Phenomena." *Psychiatry* 34 (August 1971): 301–308.

Kaplan, H. I., and B. J. Sadock, eds. *Comprehensive Group Psychotherapy*. Baltimore: Williams & Wilkins, 1975.

Kreigh, H. Z., and J. E. Perko. *Psychiatric and Mental Health Nursing: A Commitment to Care and Concern*. Reston, Virginia: Reston, 1979.

Lancaster, J. "Communication as a Tool for Change." In *The Nurse as Change Agent*, J. Lancaster and W. Lancaster, eds. St. Louis: C. V. Mosby, 1982.

Lego, S. "Group Dynamic Theory and Application." In *Comprehensive Psychiatric Nursing*, J. Haber et al., eds. New York: McGraw-Hill, 1978.

Lewin, K. *Field Theory in the Social Sciences*. New York: Harper & Row, 1957.

Lieberman, M. A., I. D. Yalom, and M. B. Miles. "Encounter Groups: The Leader Makes the Difference." *Psychology Today* 6, no. 10 (1973):69–76.

Loomis, M. K. *Group Process for Nurses*. St. Louis: C. V. Mosby, 1979.

Maluccio, A. N. "A Task-Based Approach to Family Treatment." In *Understanding the Family*, C. Gelty and W. Humphrey, eds. New York: Appleton-Century-Crofts, 1981.

Marram, G. W. *The Group Approach in Nursing Practice*. St. Louis: C. V. Mosby, 1978.

Marvin, L. K. "Group Organization: Selection Criteria, Member Preparation, Contractual Issues." In *Life Cycle Group Work in Nursing*, E. H. Janosik and L. B. Phipps, eds. Boston: Jones and Bartlett Publishers, 1982.

Maslow, A. *Toward a Psychology of Being*. New York: Van Nostrand, 1968.

Mills, T. M. *The Sociology of Small Groups*. Englewood Cliffs, New Jersey: Prentice-Hall, 1967.

Perez, J. F. *Counseling the Alcoholic Group*. New York: Gardner, 1986.

Robinson, L. *Psychiatric Nursing as a Human Experience*. Philadelphia: W. B. Saunders, 1983.

Rubin, S. "A Two-Track Model of Bereavement: Theory and Application in Research." *American Journal of Orthopsychiatry* 51, no. 1 (1981):101–109.

Ruch, J. C. *Psychology: The Personal Science*. Belmont, California: Wadsworth, 1984.

Sadock, B. J. "Group Psychotherapy, Combined Individual and Group Psychotherapy, and Psychodrama." In *Comprehensive Textbook of Psychiatry*, 3d ed., H. I. Kaplan, A. M. Freedman, and B. J. Sadock, eds. Baltimore: Williams & Wilkins, 1980.

Sampson, E., and M. Marthas. *Group Process for the Health Professions*. New York: John Wiley & Sons, 1977.

Schutz, W. C. *FIRO: A Three-Dimensional Theory of Interpersonal Behavior*. New York: Holt, Rinehart, and Winston, 1966.

Shaw, M. E. *Group Dynamics: The Psychology of Small Group Behavior*. New York: McGraw-Hill, 1976.

Slavson, S. R. *A Textbook in Analytic Group Psychotherapy*. New York: International Universities Press, 1964.

——. *Child-Centered Guidance of Parents*. New York: International Universities Press, 1974.

Tsui, P., and G. L. Schultz. "Ethnic Factors in Group Process: Cultural Dynamics in Multi-Ethnic Groups." *American Journal of Orthopsychiatry* 58, no. 1 (January 1988):136–142.

Tuckman, B. W. "Developmental Sequence in Small Groups." *Psychological Bulletin* 63 (1965):384–389.

White, R., and R. Lippitt. "Leader Behavior and Member Reaction in Three Social Climates." In *Group Dynamics, Research, and Theory*, D. Cartwright and A. Zandeu, eds. Evanston, Illinois: Row Patterson, 1953.

Yalom, I. D. *Theory and Practice of Group Psychotherapy*. New York: Basic Books, 1975.

Yalom, I. D., and M. A. Lieberman. "A Study of Encounter Group Casualties." In *Progress in Group and Family Therapy*, C. J. Sagaw and H. I. Kaplan, eds. New York: Brunner/Mazel, 1972.

Community Guidelines in Nursing Practice

Learning Objectives

After reading this chapter, the student should be able to:

1. Define the term *community* and differentiate the community dimensions of group, place, and culture.

2. Identify communication problems that arise in transcultural nursing and nursing interventions likely to resolve such problems.

3. Explain the importance of transcultural issues in providing holistic nursing care.

4. Explain the term *risk factor* as applied to populations.

5. Define epidemiological terms related to community health.

6. Identify variables important to the evaluation of community health programs.

7. Contrast models of mental health care delivery. List advantages and disadvantages of each model.

8. Describe the effect of deinstitutionalization on nursing roles.

Overview

Because the concept of community means different things to different people, it is important to know exactly what is meant when the term is used. Three dimensions of community are described in this chapter: community as group, community as place, and community as culture. Community as culture receives particular attention. An important focus of the chapter is transcultural nursing and the challenges it presents to nurses as they try to meet the health needs of clients and families from other cultures. Perhaps no health care profession is more sensitive to the needs of minorities than is nursing. This does not mean that the challenge is always met but it does mean that nurses are sensitive to the challenge and through education, practice, and research attempt to meet the challenge.

Epidemiology contributes to community theory and practice, and provides terminology that helps explain community phenomena. Epidemiology also provides language and concepts that facilitate community assessment, program planning, and program evaluation. In responding to community conditions, nurses are usually perceived as experts and resource persons. Therefore, they need extensive knowledge of health problems that once existed in the community, that presently exist, or are likely to arise in the future. Such information facilitates the practice and increases the effectiveness of community nurses, whether they function as generalists or as psychiatric nursing specialists.

DIMENSIONS OF COMMUNITY

In order to discuss community mental health, it is necessary first to determine what the word *community* means. *The American Heritage Dictionary* defines community as "a group of people living together in the same locality and under the same government; the district or locality in which they live; a social group or class having common interests." Thus, the term community may be applied to a variety of settings, interests, and groups.

Community can mean different things to different people. Communities may be geographic areas, such as neighborhoods, contained within spatial limits. Communities may consist of individuals drawn together for special reasons. Students may be part of a school community for only a few years, while teachers may be part of the school community for their entire working lives. The school community demonstrates that community membership not only has different time frames for various members but also imposes different role expectations for members who serve in different capacities: Any school community expects one set of behaviors from students and another set from teachers (Stuart 1981).

Common experiences or shared cultures may lead to the formation of a community. Religious orders are communities created around shared missions and values. Membership in a particular ethnic group with a common history establishes another kind of community. Belonging to the black community in the United States does not depend on geography but is based on shared experiences, historical and contemporary. Thus, a community may not always be the place where one lives but may be a collective way of life or state of mind.

There are also communities within larger communities. One area may contain several subdivisions or enclaves existing within the larger community of neighborhood. Essential to the meaning of community is the idea that individuals and families are not solitary but exist in relation to other individuals and families. Because community is an ambiguous term, it is crucial that one understand clearly what is meant when the word is used (Greenblatt 1980).

When it comes to community mental health, the term *community* also has a specific political meaning. Recall that the enabling legislation dealing with mental health centers defines a community as a *catchment area* delineated by geographic boundaries that cut across established neighborhoods and social class differences. Homogeneity was not an important consideration in setting up catchment areas. More important considerations included the range of the catchment population in terms of size, income, and social class. Heterogeneity within a catchment area was thought to be more desirable than homogeneity. Thus, although community mental health nurses work within a specific geographic area, they come into contact with, and must be knowledgeable about, communities that vary along the dimensions of group, place, and culture.

Community as Group

Any ethnic or racial group with shared values and a common culture may be regarded as a community regardless of whether members reside close to one another. Hispanics living anywhere in a city are apt to consider themselves part of the Spanish American community when issues such as education or employment are involved.

The community mental health nurse must be sensitive to the customs and habits of clients being served and to changes, obvious and subtle, that take place in community groups. Just as individuals and families change over time, so do the communities they form. What happens outside the community may have profound effects within the community. Sometimes change is so extreme that the quality of community life is altered beyond recognition.

There is a danger, even among well-intentioned caregivers, to make generalizations about various groups that ignore important subgroup differences. For example, the course of Asian immigration to the United States took various forms and involved some groups who shared only the characteristic of being Asian. Asia is a huge continent inhabited by unique and ancient groups whose national identities are proud and well-defined. It offends members of various Asian peoples to be consigned to a national group of which they are not a part.

In addition to national differences among Asian groups, there are differences based on when the family immigrated. In the nineteenth century Asian immigration was comprised mostly of relatively uneducated workers and farmers. Immigration quotas of the twentieth century encouraged the immigration of professional groups.

Similarities and differences based on group history and experience exist between Puerto Rican and Mexican American families who are so often grouped under the single adjective "Hispanic." The same is true of black families in America who present an infinite number of variations and challenges. In offering care to black families, nurses should minimize color distinctions and attend closely to socioeconomic factors and family lifestyle, for these variables are closely intertwined.

■ Within each racial and ethnic group, there are subgroups that resemble and differ from one another in various ways.

■ Within each racial and ethnic group are families who adjust to mainstream culture in different ways and at different rates.

■ Within each family, regardless of racial or ethnic origin, are members who adjust to mainstream values in different ways and at different rates, depending on the importance they place on stability versus progress.

SOCIAL CLASS VARIABLES Social class differences can have marked effects on attitudes toward health and illness. Admittedly, there is some danger in consigning clients to a specific socioeconomic category since there are many variations within each category. Many individuals and families are inconsistent, in that they may seem to belong in one socioeconomic category on the basis of some characteristics and to another category on the basis of other characteristics. For example, a couple who belonged to the middle-class socioeconomic level most of their lives may in later life have the financial resources of a lower socioeconomic level but continue to adhere to middle-class values.

It is often hard to determine the social class of an individual, family, or group because numerous indicators may be used to classify social class, including income, occupation, and education. In addition, where a family happens to live may influence designation of social class. Depending on the cost of living, a family in one city might exist at a lower-class level while another family with the same income in another city might be considered middle-class. In many instances it is the individual's or family's perception of its social class that proves the determining factor, since this is the class with which they identify and whose values they adopt.

Difficulties may arise when parents are moving from one class to another. Values and expectations of different socioeconomic classes may create confusion and dissension in the family. Families that are upwardly or downwardly mobile may suffer loneliness and confusion along the way. Nurses working with such families may serve as resource persons as the family decides which values and behaviors should continue and which should be discarded in view of their transition from one socioeconomic class to another (Miller and Janosik 1980).

Community as Place

In the United States the management of community affairs is largely accomplished at the local level, although there may be input in the form of regulation or financial support from state and federal agencies. The mental health nurse viewing community as a place must consider a number of variables, beginning with geographic location and physical environment. Among other important considerations are the geographic and environmental factors listed in Table 21–1. These factors contribute to community assessment because of their impact on the physical and mental health of the residents and on the quality of life in the community. In turn, the quality of life experienced by residents has

Table 21–1. Variables in Assessing Community as Place

Variables	Assessment Data
Size	What are the boundaries of the community? What is the total population? What is the population density (how many people per square mile or acre)?
Climate	Is the community located in a tropical, temperate, or arctic zone? Are there seasonal changes in climate? If seasonal changes occur, are there two seasons (dry and rainy) or four seasons?
Basic characteristics	Is the community rural, suburban, urban, or a mixture? Is the community homogeneous or comprised of several racial or ethnic groups?
Natural resources	Is the water supply adequate and safe? Is the community in a mountainous area, in a valley, or in an area that encompasses mountains and valleys? What vegetation, if any, grows in or near the community?
Hazards	Are natural hazards present, such as rivers that flood or dry areas where widespread fires occur? Are hazards present in the form of air, soil, or water pollution?
Housing	Is adequate housing available at reasonable prices for families of various sizes and income levels?
Transportation	Is adequate and appropriate transportation available for workers living in the community? Is more than one means of transportation available?
Recreational facilities	Is there diversity in the types of recreational activities available? Is there diversity in the cost of recreational activities available?
Industry	Is there a single source of employment or several industries that contribute to income of residents?
Health Care Systems	Is the health care delivery system adequate to serve the population? Is the health care delivery system responsive to the needs of the population? What health care resources and personnel are available in the community?

considerable influence on the promotion and maintenance of mental health. Population density, housing, and environmental hazards, whether natural or of human origin, are factors that profoundly affect the lives of community residents.

Community as Culture

Culture may be described as the total of socially determined characteristics handed down from one generation to the next. The United States is a pluralistic society made up of many different groups, each with a different historical past, each with different traditions and priorities. Although some of them are concentrated in particular neighborhoods, many families prefer to live in heterogeneous communities even though their cultural heritage may not conform to their neighbors'.

At the beginning of the twentieth century the disappearance of cultural and ethnic diversity was predicted as newcomers tried to become "Americanized." More astute observers argued to the contrary, and for some years there has been resurgent interest in searching for one's cultural roots. Indeed, cultural inheritance has become a positive force and a statement of individual and collective worth. Minority status and cultural values seem to require less apology than in the past. In the present climate of cultural and ethnic assertiveness, it is not enough for nurses to be open-minded and accepting of people who are different. They must also be aware of historical, anthropological, and sociological factors that affect cultural attitudes toward health and illness.

The concept of community as culture is so complex that a subspeciality has developed called *transcultural nursing*. Transcultural nursing was developed by nurse anthropologists such as Madeline Leininger (1973, 1978). Anthropologists and sociologists, some of whom are nurse scientists, have a great deal to offer community nurses.

Leininger studied the health beliefs of a Spanish-speaking community living in an urban center in the western part of the United States. The group consisted of 550 people living in a circumscribed area that was popularly known as "the Spanish community." Within a 22-year period, this group had moved from a rural setting to a semirural setting and finally to an urban setting. Leininger found that the group members retained many of their customary attitudes toward health, illness, and treatment. It became apparent that the world of modern medicine was alien to the group culture, and only under threatening conditions were modern methods accepted.

Professional caregivers are often unaware of the extent to which their particular cultural orientation influences the way they present themselves to clients and families. An important fact to remember is that each of us interprets our experience in an individualistic way but that we continue to be influenced by the culture in which we were socialized when young. Nurses must therefore be sensitive to the effects of their own cultural biases as well as those of clients. In addition to sensitivity, nurses dealing with cultural or ethnic groups different from their own need to know about how members of the particular culture eat, sleep, and interact with others in order to communicate effectively with clients from that culture.

If nurses become more knowledgeable about and more attentive to cultural differences, clients from such subcultures may seek professional help before conditions become extreme. The successful nurse is the one who respects cultural values, however unusual they appear, and who can provide care that is compatible with the cultural beliefs and lifestyle of clients.

Nurses can also benefit from the following:

- Knowledge of the historical experience, recent and long-term, of ethnic groups composing the community.
- Demographic data that include family size, socioeconomic status, and future expectations characteristic of diverse ethnic groups.
- Recognition of folk beliefs and cultural attitudes toward health and illness, including sick role behaviors, use of folk healers, and folk remedies.
- Awareness of the nature of problems encountered by ethnic group members when they enter the health care system. Problems include fear and distrust of new methods, language barriers, and discrimination by caregivers.

Such information is important to the nurse's understanding of why cultural differences prevail and how they affect behavior.

CULTURAL IDEOLOGY The ideology of a culture includes beliefs about the nature of health and illness, and investigators have found that culture-specific beliefs in these areas continue to be held over time, to be transmitted across generations so that they last beyond the immigrant generation. Some ethnic groups accept and adopt practices from folk medicine lore and from mainstream health care systems, using the two simultaneously. A more common custom is for an ethnic group member to seek help from mainstream health care systems only when folk medicine treatment has failed (Leininger

1978). It is probably fair to say that most care providers, regardless of their own ethnic, racial, or cultural background, are thoroughly indoctrinated into the mainstream health care system and rarely function outside the framework of Westernized (mainstream) health care (Sue 1981).

Every one of us carries a heavy load of cultural baggage, and nurses are no exception. An important step in transcultural nursing is to look at all groups in relative terms, believing that few customs are altogether good or bad. When the client and the caregiver represent groups that have a long history of mutual mistrust, it may be more difficult and more time-consuming to establish rapport. Knowledge of other cultures and belief systems helps caregivers avoid the documented tendencies of European and American psychiatrists to over-diagnose schizophrenic disorders and underdiagnose affective disorders among the Afro-American clients they serve. It is very likely that these tendencies are increased by the clinicians' ignorance of Afro-American beliefs and communication patterns.

Unless the nurse has some knowledge of cultural norms of the client's group, the accuracy of the assessment may be threatened. For example, a member of a charismatic religious sect might respond to questions about auditory hallucinations by saying in a matter-of-fact way, "Sure, I hear God's voice talking to me. Doesn't everyone who takes the time to listen?" The beliefs of Puerto Ricans that they live in a world peopled by invisible spirits, and the beliefs of many Asians concerning the influence of their ancestors on everyday life may seem irrational and even psychotic to the uninformed caregiver. Trancelike states and altered consciousness levels are other cultural phenomena that may be misinterpreted and thus introduce error into the assessment.

TRANSCULTURAL COMMUNICATION When a nurse and a client come from different ethnic or racial backgrounds, additional time must be made available for their interactions, especially in the first stages of the therapeutic relationship, when each may be puzzled by aspects of the other. In order to maintain a reassuring, unhurried atmosphere, it is wise to allow almost twice as much time as would ordinarily be arranged.

Transcultural nursing introduces complicating factors into the health care picture. The client may be an individual for whom English is a secondary language. As a result, communication becomes more challenging for everyone involved. Some clients may be able to report factual details in their second language but be unable to deal with emotions, abstractions, or subtle distinctions. The stress of the clinical encounter, especially if the client is depressed, anxious, or has a thought disorder, will further impair the ability to communicate. Westermeyer (1987) reported that some clients seem to be more confused and disorganized when using a second language because their knowledge of the acquired language is less extensive than their knowledge of their original tongue. Conversely, it has been noted that other clients exhibit less confusion and disorganization when using a second language. In these instances, less knowledge of the language is thought to lend them greater control of disturbing thought and ideas. Since it is difficult to predict what the repercussions will be when selecting the language to use in interviewing such clients, it might be advisable to validate information by communicating with the client in both the primary and secondary language on separate occasions.

The use of translators is an important issue when dealing with clients who are not fluent or comfortable in the caregiver's language. The basic question is whether to use a translator at all, and if one is used, what characteristics are important in the translator? Some Spanish-speaking clients reported more satisfaction when a professional translator was present during psychiatric interviews. However, caregivers in the same study were less satisfied when a professional translator was present and reported that clients who were interviewed in the presence of a translator seemed less "appreciative" and were less likely to return for subsequent visits. The disparity in the reactions of clients and in the reactions of caregivers suggests that the clients felt more at ease with a translator present, but caregivers found the presence of a third party intrusive and unproductive. The reactions of the caregivers were supported in part by higher attrition rates that followed the presence of a translator (Grosjean 1982, Westermeyer 1987).

Translators who are inexperienced or psychologically uninformed may be reluctant to ask questions about sex, violence, suicide, or finances unless they have been prepared in advance for the content areas that will be explored. Sometimes professional translators are unavailable, and the caregiver will try to facilitate communication and/or decrease the client's anxiety by asking a friend or relative to be present. Sometimes this works well, but often it does not. Unfortunately, these persons are rarely objective. As a result they tend either to minimize or exaggerate the client's problem, depending on what they consider relevant. They may selectively omit data or distort what the client is actually saying. Sometimes it is necessary to depend on a professional translator or a client's friend or relative,

CLINICAL VIGNETTE

UTILIZING CULTURAL IDEOLOGY IN MEETING THE NEEDS OF A SCHOOLCHILD

Dolores is a 10-year-old schoolgirl who is a member of a Mexican-American family living in a Los Angeles barrio. She is an active, happy child who was found by the school health team to have a moderately severe case of scoliosis. The school nurse sent a note to this effect to Dolores's mother, asking her to come to the school to discuss the problem. Although the note was friendly, there was no response except that Dolores and her brothers and sisters all stopped coming to school. The nurse and the children's teachers were puzzled by the unexplained absences. None of the children's classmates seemed to know what had happened. After two weeks elapsed, the nurse decided to visit the barrio to discover what was going on. When the nurse asked Dolores's best friend to show her where Dolores lived, the child became upset and said that she wasn't allowed to see Dolores any more. Other children also refused to assist the nurse. As an Anglo, the nurse knew that she was considered an outsider by residents of the barrio, so she decided to approach the barrio priest for help. Together the nurse and the priest visited Dolores's home, and discovered it was the note that had caused the problem. The nurse had written the note in English, using the school's letterhead. Because Dolores's parents could not read English well, they had asked a neighbor for help. The neighbor translated the word *scoliosis* as "tuberculosis," which was a disease greatly feared in the barrio. Word that Dolores had tuberculosis was circulated, resulting in community ostracism of the family. Dolores's parents were afraid that the child would be removed from the home and hospitalized. Thoroughly alarmed, they decided to keep all their children at home so that interfering officials would not take Dolores away.

It did not take long to reassure the parents that they were unnecessarily frightened. Following this, relatives and neighbors were invited in to hear the explanations of the nurse. The explanations were substantiated by the priest, whose word was seldom questioned in the barrio. In the days that followed Dolores's parents were persuaded to visit the school and meet with the nurse to make plans for helping Dolores. As the head of the household, the father was given the opportunity to hear the plans and give his approval. He was inclined to attribute the misunderstanding to the ineptness of women in general—the nurse, his wife, and the neighbor woman. In his opinion, Anglo women were no wiser than Mexican women, but with his help and that of the priest Dolores would soon be well.

---

but in all cases it is essential to discuss one's expectations with the translator. Preliminary preparation helps the translators to avoid making their own interpretations and places them in the auxiliary role where they belong.

Even when a translator is considered unnecessary, an uncomfortable client may feel more at ease if an ethnic companion is permitted to be present in early interviews. A good way to increase the client's comfort is to begin by asking how the client feels about the encounter and what his expectations are. Clarification of what is said and what is meant must be undertaken repeatedly during the interview to ensure that client and caregiver understand the viewpoints of each other.

Direct, probing questions should be used with much care and sensitivity so that the client does not become defensive. By asking open-ended questions and expressing empathy for the client, the caregiver will facilitate progress. Cultural taboos against self-disclosure vary from group to group, and the caregiver should expect some reluctance to share embarrassing information until trust has developed. Initially, the nurse should ask questions in ways that allow the client some choices in replying. Questions that permit the client to avoid premature revelations without being compelled to tell lies help develop a therapeutic relationship that will eventually enable the client to share more information. Inevitably, in some situations a client may be a source of harm to himself or others. In these cases, the indirect, time-consuming approach is not appropriate. More often, however, nurses working in a transcultural situation will be more effective if they take the time to work within racial and ethnic guidelines (Pederson, Sartorius, and Marsalla 1984).

Confrontation is another communication technique that may be seen by the client as a form of criticism or accusation, and therefore should be employed carefully, if at all. A better technique for the nurse is not to confront but to point out apparent contradictions or discrepancies and ask for clarification. An example might be to comment, "You said your husband was a good provider who works hard for the family. But you said he often misses work and yells at the kids. Tell me more about that so I can understand how things are for you and your family."

TRANSCULTURAL ASSESSMENT AND TESTING Whenever cultural differences between client and caretaker hamper assessment based on observation and interpersonal communication, there is increased need for objective laboratory testing and for psychometric testing that does not rely on reading or verbal skills. Drug testing, blood work, endocrine and metabolic tests should be ordered more readily if a comprehensive history cannot be obtained from the client. Furthermore, if the client is a recent arrival, the caregiver should be cognizant of common clinical conditions in the client's native country. The possibilities here are enormous, ranging from malaria to nutritional dementias, to the autoimmune syndrome (AIDS).

Psychometric testing can be a means of supplementing available information about the client, but it must be approached with caution when the client comes from a group or background unfamiliar to the caregiver. Any fully or functionally illiterate client will be unable to perform on a pencil-and-paper test. If the client is literate but was educated in one language and later learned a second language, a test in either language may place the client at a disadvantage. Despite such problems, it is possible to select cross-cultural psychometric tests that are relatively valid. The Draw-A-Person Test, the Bender Gestalt Test, the Rorschach Test, and the Thematic Apperception Test do not require literacy or fluency in any particular language. For literate clients who are not fluent in English, the Minnesota Multiphasic Inventory (MMPI) and the Zung Depression Scale, among others, have been translated into several languages. Cross-cultural psychometric testing is possible if the measurement instruments are selected with the client's limitations in mind. In addition, accurate results will depend to a large extent on the test administrator's skill in clarifying instructions and putting the client at ease (Williams 1987).

EPIDEMIOLOGICAL CONCEPTS

Epidemiology is the study of disease occurrence in human populations. Epidemiologists are concerned with disease patterns in particular populations, such as those living in a particular place or those representing a particular age, gender, or ethnic group. Initially epidemiologists were concerned primarily with communicable diseases, but their interests have expanded to include other phenomena, such as congenital, degenerative, and chronic health problems in various populations. Investigators who analyze patterns of births in the United States have learned, for example, that the number of babies born with some physical or mental defect has doubled over the last 25 years. Identification of this alarming trend will give direction to a search for the causes (Lyons 1983). Reliable epidemiological studies show that a positive association exists between physical and psychiatric disorders and that the strength of the association varies among different populations. Again, the epidemiological findings help researchers and funding sources establish priorities to guide future investigations into suspected biochemical, psychodynamic, or sociocultural factors.

Host, Agent, and Environment

Three concepts are important in understanding epidemiological approaches to health and illness: host, agent, and environment. These concepts emerged with the development of epidemiology as a scientific endeavor. During the nineteenth century, environmental factors such as poor sanitation and filth were acknowledged as contributing to the development of illnesses. The growing field of bacteriology substantiated these beliefs and directed attention to finding the actual causative *agents*. In the twentieth century, immunology, or the study of the resistance or vulnerability of certain individuals and groups to various disorders, led to investigation of *host* factors or characteristics influential in the occurrence, nonoccurrence, or prognosis of an illness. At present the term "host" may refer to an individual, a family, a community, or any segment of the population. Investigation of agent factors and host factors led naturally to interest in environmental factors that might explain variations in the interactions between agent and host. The modern epidemiologist examines the balance between host factors and agent factors within a changing environment. Figure 21–1 shows the trifactorial balance that concerns the epidemiologist.

Environmental factors are instrumental in maintaining a balance between host and agent factors. When there is a shift in the environment that produces imbalance in favor of the host, both the *incidence* (number of new cases) and the *prevalence* (total number of cases at a given point in time) of the illness decrease. When the environment shifts in favor of agent factors, the host's susceptibility to

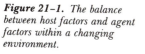

Figure 21-1. *The balance between host factors and agent factors within a changing environment.*

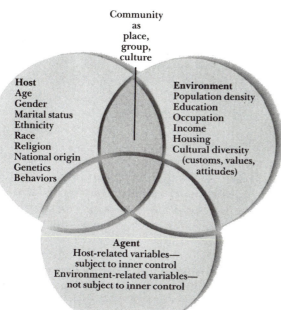

Community as place, group, culture

Host
Age
Gender
Marital status
Ethnicity
Race
Religion
National origin
Genetics
Behaviors

Environment
Population density
Education
Occupation
Income
Housing
Cultural diversity
(customs, values, attitudes)

Agent
Host-related variables—
subject to inner control
Environment-related variables—
not subject to inner control

the illness increases; consequently both incidence and prevalence are likely to grow. Examining relationships between host, agent, and environment not only expands knowledge of causative agents but also permits manipulation of host, agent, and environment variables to reduce the incidence and prevalence of a disorder.

If community is conceptualized as a place, an epidemiologist might begin by examining environmental factors of the area inhabited by the population being studied, then move to agent factors and to host factors. If an outbreak of encephalitis developed in a region during summer months, for example, the epidemiologist would realize the connection between the illness and a certain type of mosquito and would begin investigating the presence of environmental factors such as swamps or stagnant waters where mosquitos breed. If community is conceptualized as a group, an epidemiologist might be concerned about high levels of alcoholism among recruits in an army base. Here investigation might well begin by looking at the characteristics of the recruits; demographic data such as age, marital status, and education would be important, in addition to data as to whether the recruits were draftees or volunteers. Agent factors might include discovering whether the recruits had any control over where they were sent and how severe the training conditions were. Environmental factors might include food, housing, and recreational outlets available to the recruits.

Community conceptualized as culture might be the perspective from which to begin an epidemiological investigation of hypertension. Here the investigation might begin by identifying stressors characteristic of a particular culture, followed by identification of host characteristics, then by a study of environmental conditions such as isolation, overcrowding, or time pressures that influence host and agent factors.

Epidemiological Terminology

Epidemiology is largely a quantitative science that applies statistical tools to data about populations and patterns of illness. A major concern of epidemiologists is to "find and enumerate appropriate denominators (variables) in a useful and meaningful way" (Friedman 1974). Epidemiologists can often use relevant data to obtain probabilities regarding frequency, risks, and prognoses for particular disorders in a population.

Community mental health nurses need to understand basic epidemiological terminology in order to evaluate research in the field and to describe characteristics of a population in knowledgeable terminology. Some of the most commonly used terms are defined in the accompanying box. These terms can be used to demonstrate a number of different phenomena.

Risk Factors

Risk factors are important not only to epidemiologists but to all health care providers, regardless of discipline. Risk factors are interrelated and may be biological, psychosocial, or environmental. Risk factors may also be differentiated according to the place, group, or culture being discussed. When identified, risk factors can assist in planning for populations most likely to suffer illness or injury. This is rarely a simple matter, for in clinical practice the interrelationships among biological, psychosocial, and environmental factors may be difficult to distinguish.

Among risk factors of biological origin are genetic traits that make certain individuals, families, and groups susceptible to particular disorders.

Techniques have been developed that enable scientists to understand the genetic code that transmits human traits. Prenatal screening can already detect genetic errors and predict whether the fetus is likely to suffer specific ailments or defects, a few of which can even be treated in utero. Future discoveries may lead to diagnosing disorders before they develop, thus giving primary prevention a whole new direction (McAuliffe and McAuliffe 1983).

Psychosocial risks include developmental or situational events occurring at a point in the life cycle

COMMON EPIDEMIOLOGICAL TERMS

■ *Rate.* A quantitative measure used to describe phenomena in a group or to compare similar phenomena in different groups. Comparing suicide rates of Afro-Americans and of Asian Americans is an example of using a rate for comparisons.

■ *Incidence.* A quantitative measure used to describe the number of new cases of a disorder or phenomenon in a group. The daily incidence of assaults in an American city, for example, is a matter of great concern to individuals, families, and communities.

■ *Prevalence.* A quantitative measure used to describe the total known number of cases of a disorder or phenomenon in a group at a particular point in time. In discussing prevalence, the time frame, whether a year or a decade, should be clearly stated.

■ *Mean rate.* A quantitative measure used to describe the average rate of occurrence of phenomena in a group.

when individuals are especially vulnerable. Adolescents, for instance, have a high suicide rate, and jobless workers are prone to depression, illness, and marital conflict. A sociological study at Johns Hopkins University reported that a community that experiences a 1 percent increase in the unemployment rate can expect to have 5 percent more suicides, 3 to 4 percent more hospitalizations for mental illness, 4 to 6 percent more homicides, 6 to 7 percent more admissions to prisons, and a 2 percent increase in the overall death rate (Bird 1982).

Some population groups are at greater risk than others because they are more likely to live under unfavorable environmental conditions. Disparity between income and employment opportunities for black Americans and white Americans has not changed greatly since the 1960s. In 1959, 66 percent of blacks under age eighteen lived in households at or below poverty level as defined by the federal government. By 1981 this proportion had declined to 45 percent. Among young whites, 21 percent lived at or below poverty levels in 1959; by 1981 this proportion had declined to 15 percent. Thus, despite gains, young blacks remained three times more likely to live in poverty than their white counterparts. The result is that many black children continue to be affected by living in impover-

ished environments characterized by high population density and poor housing (Herbers 1983). These statistics underline the interrelated risk factors encountered by the black community across the United States. The same data point to psychosocial stress when individual and family hopes are unfulfilled.

Sometimes environmental factors are not restricted to one group or segment of the community but endanger all inhabitants. Flood, earthquake, and nuclear contamination are not discriminatory in their choice of victims, yet even here, characteristics of the host operate to safeguard some residents and endanger others. Whenever a nuclear reactor accident happens, for example, vigorous efforts are made to remove young children and pregnant women from the vicinity as quickly as possible because of their excessive vulnerability to radiation.

Mental health nurses are aware of the unity of mind-body interactions and realize that mental distress is not confined to persons with identified psychiatric diagnoses but is so widespread that identifying risk factors for emotional problems can be extremely complex.

ROLE OF THE COMMUNITY MENTAL HEALTH NURSE

During the deinstitutionalization era of the community mental health movement, leaders of the nursing profession disagreed about who should care for the mentally ill in the community. Because this was an autonomous role, Mereness (1963) argued that nurses with graduate-level preparation in psychiatric nursing were the most appropriate providers of care for mentally ill persons in the community. Another viewpoint was expressed by Wolff (1964), who said that the needs were so great and the supply of adequately prepared psychiatric nurses so limited that community health nurses already skilled in providing family and community care were qualified to serve mentally ill persons living in the community. As more nurses completed graduate work in mental health and community health, the problem of supply and demand became less pressing, and collaboration between mental health nurses and community health nurses proved to be the answer.

Today, a community mental health nurse may be employed by a state or local psychiatric hospital or by a community mental health center. A community mental health nurse who works with individuals, families, or groups as a primary therapist or a cotherapist should have a master's degree. Other nurses who work under closer supervision may use the title of community mental health nurse but lack advanced preparation. In any case, the community mental health nurse works with clients having a range of psychological problems and is concerned with clients' stress levels, adaptation, and coping abilities. According to Sheehy (1976), helping individuals and families anticipate the course of events is a preventive measure that is quite effective. Consumer participation is actively encouraged in developing policies and in evaluating the services provided by the community mental health nurse and related personnel.

The role of community mental health nurse is one that carries considerable independence, even though the nurse has support resources in the person of other professionals who are available as consultants. In addition, the community mental health nurse often functions as a consultant to others, professional and paraprofessional. She may, for example, act as client advocate in a supervised residence where client needs are not being met adequately, or she may become a consultant and guide for families who must place an aged relative in a long-term care facility. A community mental health nurse may function as a counselor for individuals or groups or may be a liaison between clients and community agencies.

Home care for persons with psychiatric problems may be administered by community mental health nurses or by community health nurses working in various home health agencies where a psychiatric nurse specialist is available to generalist nurses for consultation. In addition, the generalist nurse maintains contact with the referring physician, documents care, and may recommend psychiatric hospitalization or follow-up, if either is warranted. Because the client is seen in the home, nurses have found it helpful to establish boundaries, to preserve a professional identity, and not to slip into the role of the client's "good old friend." Setting mutual goals, adhering to time frames, and evaluating progress periodically are ways of keeping one's professional identity. Encouraging clients to do as much for themselves as possible avoids fostering dependency and therefore makes termination smoother.

The principles of relationship therapy are the same regardless of whether therapy takes place in a hospital or home setting. The home setting is advantageous in allowing the nurse to observe first-hand how the client is applying what has been learned. The home setting is disadvantageous in that it may promote intimacy that is counterproductive for the client unless the nurse stays within the professional role. Intimacy is a problem for many clients with psychiatric disorders, who appear to invite closeness but then are frightened by

it. Remaining in the professional role is helpful for nurses and for clients (Lesseig 1987).

Nurses working in mental health clinics perform a variety of functions, although they are usually considered generalists, not specialists, unless they have a master's degree. Medication clinics managed by nurses are offered in most mental health centers. Here stabilized clients are seen monthly by the nurses and by a physician. The care plan is reviewed jointly by nurse and physician; care plans and medication orders are changed as needed. The working relationship between nurses and physicians in mental health centers is a collaborative one in which nurses enjoy considerable autonomy.

COMMUNITY HEALTH CARE DELIVERY

In the United States health care delivery is implemented by persons, agencies, and organizations working in one of three sectors: private, voluntary, or public. As the terms imply, the *private sector* is maintained largely by private funding and the *public sector* by public funding. *Voluntary* organizations are supported by their own fund-raising drives or share in the resources obtained by community fund raising. Some voluntary organizations are not wholly health-related but have an interest in or support health causes to some extent. Other voluntary organizations limit themselves to specific health problems, such as cancer or heart disease, in order to concentrate their resources. One example is the American Cancer Society; another is Compeer, a group with a single mission: to provide lonely psychiatric clients with suitable volunteers who befriend the client and reduce interpersonal isolation.

In the public sector, health care delivery is carried out at federal, state, and local levels. The federal government regulates some medical services, personnel, and facilities, in addition to providing financial support. Direct service from the federal government is available to American Indians, veterans, military personnel, merchant seamen, and, in a limited way, migrant workers. The involvement of the federal government is coordinated through state agencies and is carried out by local agencies.

States have the responsibility for inspecting public areas such as state parks, for licensing professionals, for licensing hospitals and other health care facilities, and for controlling the spread of communicable disease. The states maintain institutions for the care of the mentally ill and the physically disabled who cannot be cared for elsewhere. At the local level, the official health department is charged with providing direct care in homes, clinics, and other facilities. The nursing staff of a health department delivers many of the direct services offered by the department and cooperates with official agencies such as child protection units and with voluntary agencies such as shelters for battered women.

Client advocacy has been accepted as a necessary part of the nursing role. In order to be effective advocates at the local level, nurses are becoming more involved with community planning and community organization. The best way for nurses to prepare for an influential role in the community is, as always, to start with a knowledge base. It is useful to identify the components of the community as a social system, to identify relationships among the components, and to explore popular opinion, especially on controversial issues.

Usually a nurse will have little difficulty learning what problems the community considers important. It may be more difficult to discover how and where decisions are made regarding community health issues. Often decisions are not made by the officially designated health agency or its board of directors. It is not cynical, but only realistic, to say that decisions announced by designated persons may have originated elsewhere. Knowing as much as possible about how the social system of a community operates and where power is vested can be invaluable to nurses trying to meet consumer needs.

Nurses practicing in the community have the opportunity to judge the value of various health programs and to observe deficiencies. When major change seems to be needed, nurses should observe how the health care system is influenced by individuals and groups in the community. What value do most community residents place on physical and mental health needs? What mandate has been given to elected officials concerning the scope and cost of health care services in the community?

Relationships between health care delivery and other aspects of the community social system are constantly changing. The needs and expectations of health care consumers also change. A majority of people now believe that health care is less a privilege than a right, but the costs of health care are burdensome for many communities. Advanced technology and scientific developments have made life-saving measures possible, and this has fostered governmental interest in the policies and actions of health care agencies. The increased longevity of Americans has introduced new problems, both economic and ethical. With medical costs escalating, there is greater emphasis on primary prevention and on holistic health care than on medical care alone.

COMMUNITY PROGRAM EVALUATION

Most nurses have learned to evaluate specific goals met by clients and families with whom they are working. Evaluation of community goals and program outcomes is more complicated but is essential to determining the success or failure of a program. *Progress* evaluation analyzes the degree to which program implementation has reached or approached stated goals. For example, a community concerned with the prevalence of teenage pregnancies in the local high school and the frequency of teenage mothers dropping out of school might consider offering a program in which the following goals are outlined:

- Pregnant teenagers enrolled in the school will receive prenatal care.
- Prenatal care will include preparation for labor and delivery in addition to instruction on child development and child care.
- After delivery, babies will be admitted to a day care facility with services that permit the teenage mothers to return to school.
- Counseling will be provided by school personnel during pregnancy, after delivery, and upon the mothers' return to school.
- Teenage mothers in the program will acquire marketable job skills.
- The rate of school dropout among the teenage mothers will decrease.
- The incidence of second teenage pregnancies among the mothers will decrease.

With these measurable goals clearly defined, a program could be planned and inaugurated to achieve them. By comparing data collected before the program and at regular intervals during it, progress toward goal achievement could be ascertained.

A program such as this would be both costly and controversial. Thus, evaluation of the program should include *efficiency* measures to determine whether program progress and outcomes are justifying the expenditure of time, money, and resources. It would be possible to ascertain the immediate effects of the program in terms of how many teenage mothers remain in school and obtain job skills. However, it would take somewhat longer to discover how many mothers in the program avoid a second teenage pregnancy and even longer to learn how many of them enter the labor force as stable workers. Only if it could be shown statistically that teenagers in the program finish school, do not become pregnant again within two years, and find jobs rather than join welfare lists could the program be justified in terms of efficiency or cost effectiveness. Another long-term way of evaluating program cost effectiveness would be to compare the health of babies born to teenage mothers in the sample and the health of babies born to mothers in a control population with similar characteristics, even though the health of the babies is not a primary consideration.

Subjective changes resulting from the program, such as increasing the self-esteem of the young mothers and improving the quality of life for them and their babies, are rarely part of community program evaluation. These outcomes are important, of course, but community programs are concerned with target populations and with social change rather than with individual change, important as the latter may be.

Community programs are often continued in the absence of solid evidence that they are helping the target population and contributing to the well-being of the community as a whole (Monro 1983). In fact, traditional evaluation has often depended on subjective responses rather than on concrete evidence. If the deinstitutionalization process were to be evaluated, for example, the results would depend on the attitudes of the respondent. In order to avoid subjectivity, evaluation of community programs should incorporate the following questions:

1. What stated goals have been achieved, and to what extent?

2. How effective has the program been in terms of cost effectiveness; that is, do the results justify the expenditures?

3. What impact has the program had on the target population and on the community as a whole?

POSTINSTITUTIONAL IDEOLOGY

The holistic goal of the community mental health nurse is to assist individuals to live in the community, to anticipate and manage stress, and to learn to cope with the anxieties and frustrations of everyday life.

Originally it was alleged that returning to community living would of itself make the lives of clients more rewarding and pleasurable, but for many this has not proved to be true. Institutional care for persons with mental disorders answered many of their needs for food, shelter, psychiatric, and medical care. It also imposed on them an identity as sick people and defined institutional norms to which they were expected to conform. Unlike institutionalized clients, the new deinstitutionalized population may or may not choose to enact the role of patient. They reject identity as patients and either cannot or will not conform to social norms. Minkoff (1987) stated that persons with mental disorders must adapt to their disability whether they are cared for in hospital or community settings. What is called for is a new ideology that helps clients adapt to a chronic or intermittent disorder by also adapting the treatment program to the client. Minkoff suggests several principles upon which to build a benevolent and effective postinstitutional ideology.

Principle 1: *Individualize treatment planning by recognizing the variety and uniqueness of persons suffering mental disorders.* Planning client care as if clients were a homogeneous population is a relic of institutional thinking.

Principle 2: *Offer comprehensive biopsychosocial assessment, planning, and treatment.* Mental health personnel in general and nurses in particular must be prepared and socialized to see beyond the psychiatric diagnosis and perform assessments that consider the entire range of a client's strengths and coping styles.

INTANGIBLE ASPECTS OF DEINSTITUTIONALIZATION

Deinstitutionalization and the community mental health movement have achieved mixed results, depending on the demands made of the community for aftercare and the cost of meeting the demands. One result of deinstitutionalization is seldom mentioned, and that is the opening up of large mental hospitals so that clients and staff are not enshrouded in medieval darkness. Having become aware of patterns of chronicity and dependency, nurses and other staff members are using corrective rather than custodial approaches. Remotivation, resocialization, reality orientation, and recreational groups have introduced a new social interest on the part of clients and greater expectation on the part of staff members that improvement is possible after all.

Principle 3: Emphasize that the nurse's acceptance of the client's individuality and uniqueness and the client's acknowledgement of a chronic disorder for which help is indicated are the primary therapeutic tasks in the early phase of building a relationship.

Principle 4: Provide and suggest a number of mental health care alternatives within the health care delivery system. Postinstitutional ideology, unlike the ideology of deinstitutionalization, does not label institutions as inherently bad. All health care is supplied by some kind of institution, although these institutions vary in the extent of their protectiveness and restrictiveness. The revolving door swings faster when hospitalizations are too brief. An alternative to lifelong institutionalization or excessively short hospitalization is inpatient stays that are long enough for clients to reach a point where community care will be sufficient.

Principle 5: Coordinate substance abuse programs and traditional mental health care programs. Creative two-pronged programs are needed for the many persons with substance abuse problems superimposed on a mental disorder. Clients often use alcohol or other substances for self-treatment. They also prefer being known as alcoholics or drug abusers to accepting the identity of mental patients. Some mental health workers ignore substance abuse and concentrate on the mental disorder. Conversely, substance abuse workers tend to be unprepared to deal with persons suffering major psychiatric disturbances.

Principle 6: Involve families in the care program. In the postinstitutional era clients are not automatically separated from their families. Even if it is inadvisable for families to be closely involved for one reason or another, they deserve support and explanation. Like the clients, their families must learn to live with the presence of mental illness in their lives.

Principle 7: Emphasize the concept of adaptation rather than treatment, relapse, and recovery. The major goal is to build a trusting relationship that will persuade clients to accept continuity of care. One rationale for deinstitutionalization is that it encourages clients' independence and self-determination. The postdeinstitutional era is beset with problems, but the solution is not for clients to resume classic sick role enactment. The solution is to develop methods that help clients acknowledge needs while adapting to living in the community despite chronic mental disorders.

SUMMARY

Assessing community needs is not an easy task, but deciding how the term community is being used in a specific instance helps organize the many variables included in a comprehensive community assessment.

In this chapter community is described along three dimensions: group, place, and culture. The idea of community is complex, for the term can be used in different ways at different times. Therefore, presenting it as a three-dimensional term clarifies its meaning and implications.

Socioeconomic factors affect the lifestyle and value system of the group, and contribute in positive and negative ways to group culture. However, socioeconomic factors influence but do not constitute a group dimension, as the term is applied in this chapter. Within a single geographic area or place several social classes may be living in proximity to one another. Adverse socioeconomic conditions tend to preserve ethnic stability by perpetuating group segregation. As ethnic group members rise from lower- to middle-class status, they frequently move from segregated neighborhoods into the mainstream of the dominant culture, where assimilation processes are accelerated.

Transcultural nursing is an important subdivision of nursing and has received even more attention in recent years as holistic health care has become the standard to which the profession is committed. A knowledge of cultures other than their own enhances the effectiveness of nurses and helps them understand the underlying meaning of a client's behavior. When nurse and client come from different backgrounds, factors intrude that may impede the nursing process. There are specific techniques and methods available that help nurses build a transcultural bridge where client and nurse can meet and therapeutic work can begin. A number of facilitating techniques and methods have been described in this chapter.

Epidemiologists employ the concepts of agent (causes), host (population), and environment (surroundings) to explain the presence or absence of illness. Initially, epidemiologists were concerned with communicable disease, but their interests have expanded to include congenital, degenerative, and chronic health problems. Quantitative measures developed by statisticians and others enable health professionals to describe and compare health-related phenomena within a particular group or between groups.

The evaluation of community programs is relatively complex but is essential. In evaluating these programs, progress toward achieving the stated goals should be measured. The efficiency or cost effectiveness of the program should be evaluated to determine whether the outcomes justify expenditures *(Text continues on page 601.)*

CLINICAL EXAMPLE

EASING THE TRANSITION OF IMMIGRANT FAMILIES

Francesca Weissman is a nurse practitioner who was charged with organizing a program to serve families of Spanish-speaking cannery workers in northern California. Because her mother was of Spanish descent, Francesca was somewhat acquainted with the customs and heritage of the families she hoped to serve. To her surprise, Francesca found that her middle-class upbringing made it hard for her to reach her working-class clients. Even though her grandmother was a Mexican-American, Francesca's parents had lost touch with Spanish culture and values. Moreover, Francesca's father belonged to a family that had lived in California since the gold rush days. Although her parents were sympathetic toward Spanish-speaking people who had arrived recently in the United States, time and a new lifestyle had eroded their memories of what it was like to adjust to a new culture. Within a short time Francesca found that good intentions were not enough to see her through. In order to develop and implement an effective health program for Spanish-speaking workers and their families, Francesca soon realized that she must devise formal and informal learning experiences for herself. Without background knowledge of the people she hoped to serve, any program she established was likely to be unprofitable for all concerned. Using nursing process as a guide, Francesca began to deal with deficiencies in her own experience by learning as much as possible about the experiences, past and present, of the population for whom the proposed program was intended. Francesca already cared deeply about the people she hoped to help. What she lacked was an informed understanding of their values and customs so that her efforts on their behalf would not be rejected. In addition to reading about the Spanish experience in California, Francesca used her grandmother as a resource person. Through her grandmother, she contacted other persons of Spanish lineage who were valuable teachers and informants. With adequate background knowledge at her disposal, Francesca organized the data necessary to plan her health care program for the Spanish-speaking workers. In doing so, she followed the steps of nursing process.

ASSESSMENT

When trying to understand the transition of the Spanish-speaking cannery workers to the United States, Francesca included in her study a number of issues: political, familial, social, and psychological. As a result of her study, she found some experiences that were shared by all recent immigrants, and some that were especially applicable to Spanish-speaking populations. Whether general or specific, knowledge of the immigrant experience increased her ability to serve an ethnic population.

POLITICAL ISSUES

As a community nurse serving a neighborhood populated by recent Spanish-speaking arrivals, Francesca explored the political and economic conditions that impelled these families to immigrate. Most were from Cuba, Nicaragua, or Mexico, countries where political or economic unrest are common. The majority of workers at the cannery had experienced difficulties in their homelands, and these hardships intensified their distrust of official and governmental agencies. All persons transplanted from one culture to another face drastic adjustments. Often their adjustment is complicated by upheavals they endured before coming to the United States. Francesca learned that the cannery workers had been farm laborers before immigrating. Accustomed to rural villages, they now lived in a crowded city where the tempo of life was fast, and crowded housing conditions added to their stress. Most of the cannery workers were uneducated and impoverished, and were content to take any kind of a job. A few among them were educated and had enjoyed considerable status in their homelands. Most of these were political refugees who had to adjust to menial work and loss of privileged status. Regardless of their previous status, all now had to deal with strange conditions in a new, perplexing land.

FAMILY INFLUENCES

As soon as they arrive in the United States, immigrant parents find that their authority is diminished. The children are more adaptable to outside influences, perhaps because they are exposed to the mainstream culture at school and are more receptive to change. Moreover, they have the ability as well as the opportunity to learn English more rapidly than their parents. The adults, therefore, learn about the society they live in from their more knowledgeable children. This opposes accustomed patterns wherein children learn what they need to know from their parents.

In most Spanish-speaking households the man has considerable authority but this is challenged in the United States by the opportunities available to immigrant women. Because of high demand for their services, the women easily find jobs as domestic servants or as child care workers. Except for manual labor, the men cannot obtain jobs easily. Those men who dislike such work cannot afford to leave their jobs, and this adds to their frustration and discontent. As a result of the imbalance between the availability of jobs for women and the scarcity of jobs for men, relationships between husbands and wives tend to be unstable and precarious. In her work with these families, Francesca found that weekend drinking was a major problem for the men.

Another difference between the homeland and the new environment is in the prevailing attitudes toward physical punishment. In the homeland the man may have used physical force to control his children and his wife as well, but these tactics are less acceptable in the United States. When the man persists in such practices, he is apt to find himself in trouble with his neighbors or the police. Again, he may turn to drugs or alcohol to compensate for his lost authority and power, thus aggravating his problems.

SOCIAL PROBLEMS

In talking with the staff of local health agencies, Francesca learned that many cannery families were reluctant to seek or even accept help from outside sources. Based on their experiences in their homelands, they valued anonymity and low visibility. Language deficits were a serious problem; they neither trusted nor understood the agencies nor the people who delivered care. Another problem was the reluctance of immigrant families, especially poorly educated ones, to accept the American commitment to compulsory education for children. The cannery workers did not insist that their children attend school regularly and often kept them home to help out or interpret. Erratic school attendance by the children had already attracted unfavorable attention from school personnel.

PSYCHOLOGICAL PROBLEMS

Many members of the cannery families felt guilty as well as homesick, particularly if relatives had been left behind. Some of them felt that conditions in the United States were no better than those at home. The bitter memories of the past mingled with the disappointments of the present, so that many of these families felt they had sacrificed a former identity without finding a new one. Living arrangements were seldom adequate; space was at a premium; noise and overcrowding were inevitable. Money was in short supply, so the families lived in the least desirable part of town. With parental authority curtailed, the children were restless. And the adults suffered from a sense of rootlessness and alienation.

PLANNING

In planning for the health needs of these immigrant families, Francesca asked two questions: (1) "What are the most urgent needs of this population?" and (2) "How can this population be induced to use the health services that are available?" In some respects, the second question is more important, for persuading immigrant families to utilize services is a basic problem.

Building trust is a primary goal. Employing caregivers who can speak the clients' language will do much to lower ethnic barriers and reduce suspicion on the part of potential clients. Many traditional families are slow to develop personal relationships, and this holds true in interactions with caregivers. Unless the families can communicate with caregivers, they cannot begin to trust them. Without trust, they are not likely to seek or even accept assistance.

Communication is a two-way channel. Caregivers, Francesca realized, have an obligation to become acquainted with the culture of the growing ethnic populations, and of their diverse subgroups. By becoming informed and by conveying respect, caregivers can make interactions with immigrant families less frightening and more productive. Awareness of the economic climate and other conditions in the place of origin helps caregivers recognize that the suspiciousness of immigrant families toward officials may not be wholly irrational.

A family approach to health care is recommended for immigrant groups. If the whole family can be involved in the health care program, the individual members are likely to be less fearful. Family-oriented programs may begin with pragmatic advice about the neighborhood: locations of grocery stores, where to apply for food stamps, and how to look for work. Any programs developed for immigrant families must be offered at convenient times and places because they may not have the knowledge or resources to travel freely in their new community.

IMPLEMENTATION

In her program planning, Francesca included personnel in local schools and churches.

Because education is mandatory for children in the United States, schools are the first institutions that immigrant families know. The schools are also places where the health problems of children are likely to be noticed. Therefore one of the most significant caregivers for immigrant families is the school nurse. Linking the school health program to the overall health needs of immigrant families is an excellent way to expand utilization of existing services. Immunization programs for children are promoted or available in most city school systems as are dental, hearing, and vision screenings. Collaboration between the school nurse and the community nurse is a way of encouraging parents to be more health-minded.

To introduce her program and herself to the community, Francesca offered a series of afternoon and evening programs at a local elementary school and in a church hall. The topic was "Getting to Know Your Community," and content dealt with community resources. A neighborhood woman, fluent in Spanish, assisted Francesca. Refreshments were served and childcare was provided. Husbands were invited to all meetings, since many of the cannery workers did not wish their wives to attend unaccompanied. In addition to holding the orientation meetings, Francesca explored the possibility of sponsoring English language classes for adults, again utilizing the school and the church hall. She realized that even though schools and churches cannot provide a full range of health and social services, they can be entry points directing immigrant families to various sources of aid.

EVALUATION

In developing a health program for the cannery workers and their families, Francesca established quantitative goals. The goals included immunizations for preschool and school-age children, perinatal care for pregnant women, dental, and well-baby clinic visits. Even with these clearcut goals, program evaluation is not a simple matter because many factors such as cost and consumer satisfaction must be weighed. For immigrant families, evaluation of a program is unusually difficult because the primary issue is how to persuade a reluctant group to accept services that are available. Since school is an information source for many immigrant families, Francesca developed good working relationships with school personnel. As a result, she used school attendance and the academic progress of the children as one evaluation measure. Another measure was the number of adults who came to community orientation meetings or English language classes when these were offered. Appointments kept at clinics by members of the families of cannery workers offered and additional data for evaluating the effectiveness of the health program she developed. These are quantitative measures, but Francesca considered qualitative measures equally important. The receptiveness of mothers when she made home visits, and their growing willingness to ask questions indicated that Francesca's background knowledge of this ethnic population and her awareness of the problems encountered by most immigrant groups enhanced her effectiveness and gained acceptance for her program.

of time, money, and resources. The impact of the program on the target population and on the community at large should be included in the evaluation process.

Deinstitutionalization was implemented in the hope of achieving the following goals:

- To save clients from the debilitating effects of lengthy, restrictive periods of hospitalization.
- To return the client to home and community life as soon as possible after hospitalization.
- To maintain the client in the community for as long as possible thereafter.

Deinstitutionalization remains a controversial issue with its share of supporters and critics. Many communities have found their municipal resources drained by large numbers of discharged mental patients living with little supervision or follow-up care.

Review Questions

1. Define the following epidemiological terms: *agent, host, environment.*
2. Briefly describe the relationship between agent, host, and environment in the incidence of illness in a community.
3. Give an example of a biological risk factor and explain its significance.
4. Give an example of an environmental risk factor and explain its significance.
5. What sectors are involved in the delivery of community health care?
6. Identify three causes for the failure of deinstitutionalization in some communities.
7. What considerations are important in transferring clients from institutional to community care?
8. In what ways does community program evaluation differ from evaluation of health care provided to individuals and families?

Suggested Annotated Readings

Coles, Robert. "Civics." *Readings: A Journal of Reviews and Commentary in Mental Health* 3, no. 2 (June 1988):10–12.

In reviewing a book on the schooling of interned Japanese Americans during World War II, the author notes that other groups at other times have been the target of American hostility and prejudice. Coles reminds readers that majority populations can often be swayed by demagogues who play upon our fears of people who look, think, or speak differently from ourselves.

Comas-Diaz, Lillian, and Ezra E. H. Griffith, eds. *Clinical Guidelines in Cross Cultural Mental Health.* New York: John Wiley & Sons 1988.

This book deals with the most significant sociocultural factors that prevail in various ethnic populations of the United States. The descriptions of important sociocultural differences should go far toward sensitizing caregivers. In addition to presenting salient differences, the book offers guidelines for assessment, intervention, and evaluation of intervention.

Ho, Man Keung. *Family Therapy with Ethnic Minorities*. Beverly Hills, California: Sage, 1987.

A treatment approach is described that considers language, biculturalism, and family systems theory. The minorities discussed are American Indians, Native Alaskans, Asian Americans, Afro-Americans, and Hispanic Americans. The book undoubtedly will make caregivers more aware of the experience of people who inhabit two cultures simultaneously, even if the populations they serve are not included in this interesting book.

Mallison, Mary B. "Exactly Like A Nurse." *American Journal of Nursing* 88, no. 5 (May 1988):629.

The editor of a nursing journal searches for metaphors because it is so hard to define just what nurses are and do. Although the word *caring* is not applied, it resonates in every sentence. This is a short but inspirational article to give nurse readers a lift on a bad day.

Marculescu, Gail L. with commentary by Patricia Benner. "Early Warning." *American Journal of Nursing* 87, no. 12 (December 1987):1556–1558.

Experienced nurses are often expert at recognizing "warning signs" in a client's condition, but sometimes status inequities prevent nurses from speaking out strongly, and from being heard when they do speak. This anecdotal account indicates that tensions arise when a nurse challenges a physician's clinical judgment. Even though nursing roles have expanded, those nurses who act as diagnostic monitors may encounter resistance. The commentary at the end of the article attempts, somewhat unsuccessfully, to reconcile the positions of the nurse and physician involved.

Smith, Gloria R. "More Power to You." *American Journal of Nursing* 89, no. 5 (March 1989):357–358.

The author deplores the powerlessness of community health nurses and attributes this to the fact that community health agencies are organized like hospitals, where a nonnurse administrator holds disproportionate power. Uncertain about the boundaries of their profession, community health nurses are content to work under state and county health departments that are rarely headed by a nurse. Even when nurses are equipped by temperament, education, and experience for administrative duties, they limit their goals. This article calls on community health nurses to focus on power acquisition within the health care delivery system.

Taylor, Steven J., Douglas Biklen, and James Knoll, eds. *Community Integration for People with Severe Disabilities* New York: Teachers College Press, 1987.

This collection of papers by various caregivers shows how deinstitutionalization has grown into a hope for full community integration for disabled clients. Issues discussed include staff commitment, flexibility, relationships, and community participation. The book is stimulating and rewarding; unfortunately, reality does not always measure up to the dreams of the caregivers.

References

Bird, G. "Joblessness Scars Deeper than Simple Totals Tell." *The Plain Dealer* (Cleveland, Ohio) April 10, 1982.

Friedman, G. D. *Primer of Epidemiology*. New York: McGraw-Hill, 1974.

Greenblatt, H. R. "Psychopolitics." In *Comprehensive Textbook of Psychiatry*, 3rd ed., H. I. Kaplan, A. M. Freedman, and B. J. Sadock, eds. Baltimore: Williams & Wilkins, 1980.

Grosjean, F. *Life in Two Languages: An Introduction to Bilingualism*. Cambridge, Massachusetts: Harvard University, 1982.

Herbers, J. "Income Gaps between Races as Wide as in 1960." *The New York Times* (July 18, 1983).

Leininger, M. *Transcultural Nursing: Concepts, Theories, and Practices*. New York: John Wiley & Sons, 1978.

——."Nursing in the Context of Social and Cultural Systems." In *Concepts Basic to Nursing*, P. Mitchell, ed. New York: McGraw-Hill, 1973.

Lesseig, D. Z. "Home Care for Psych Problems." *American Journal of Nursing* 87, no. 10 (October 1987): 1317–1320.

Lyons, R. D. "Physical and Mental Disabilities in Newborns Double in 25 Years." *The New York Times* (July 18, 1983).

McAuliffe, K., and S. McAuliffe. "Keeping Up with the Genetic Revolution." *The New York Times Magazine* (November 6, 1983).

Mereness, D. "The Potential Significant Role of the Nurse in Community Mental Health Services." *Perspectives in Psychiatric Care* 1, no. 34 (1963):18–22.

Miller, J. R., and E. H. Janosik. *Family-focused Care*. New York: McGraw-Hill, 1980.

Minkoff, K. "Beyond Deinstitutionalization: A New Ideology for the Post-institutional Era." *Hospital and Community Psychiatry* 38, no. 9 (1987):945–950.

Monro, B. H. "A Useful Model for Program Evaluation." *Journal of Nursing Administration* (March 1983):23.

Pederson, P. B., N. Sartorius, and A. J. Marsalla, eds. *The Cross-Cultural Context*. Beverly Hills: Sage, 1984.

Sheehy, G. *Passages: Predictable Crises of Adult Life*. New York: Dutton, 1976.

Stuart, G. W. "Role Strain and Depression: A Causal Inquiry." *Journal of Psychosocial Nursing and Mental Health Services* 19, no. 12 (1981):20–28.

Sue, D. W. *Counseling the Culturally Different: Theory and Practice*. New York: John Wiley & Sons, 1981.

Westermeyer, J. "Clinical Considerations in Cross-Cultural Diagnosis." *Hospital and Community Psychiatry* 38, no. 2 (1987):160–164.

Williams, C. L. "Issues Surrounding Psychological Testing of Minority Patients." *Hospital and Community Psychiatry* 38, no. 2 (1987):184–189.

Wolff, I. "The Psychiatric Nurse in Community Health: A Rebuttal." *Perspectives in Psychiatric Care* 2, no. 11 (1964):10.

22

Integrated Guidelines in Nursing Practice

Learning Objectives

After reading this chapter, the student should be able to:

1. Describe the various therapeutic modalities used in delivering health care to clients with maladaptive variations and disruptions.

2. Discuss the implications and usefulness of various therapeutic approaches and their relevance for psychiatric nurses.

3. Compare the strengths and limitations of specific therapeutic modalities.

Overview

Integrated psychotherapy involves the selection and application of traditional methods augmented by current approaches to specific clinical situations. The integrated approach matches the clinical methods most suited to the needs of specific clients and takes into consideration indications and contraindications in determining what is appropriate for individual clients. This chapter presents various psychotherapeutic approaches that may be used alone or in combination, depending on the needs of individual clients, in the context of the nursing process. Countless new types of therapeutic approaches for emotional problems have emerged in the United States and Europe since the 1950s and 1960s. Usually, new therapies are associated with a single therapist who is identified as the founder and who often claims to obtain spectacular cure rates. Torrey (1972) wrote that the effectiveness of new approaches may be due to the fact that the founder transmits to clients an utmost faith in the new methods and this certainty increases their expectations of being helped.

It is difficult to determine absolutely the effectiveness of specific therapies for several reasons. For one thing, therapists are seldom purists, and they usually employ more than one type of therapy at a time. Typically, physiological, psychosocial, and group milieu therapies are used together in the hope of achieving optimum results. No school of psychology has the complete answer to all problems accompanying emotional disorders, and no single method of treatment is universally applicable and successful. Furthermore, there is a wide range of competence among mental health practitioners, and methods employed for evaluation of the success or effectiveness of therapy are often inadequate. Because it is impossible to control for differences in therapists and the effects of combinations of various therapeutic approaches, it is often difficult to identify which factors produce which effects.

The choice of a therapy seems to be influenced by various cultural, philosophical, and religious values. In addition, therapeutic goals may reflect the basic values held by the therapist. Also, a client's choice of therapist tends to reflect the client's beliefs about the causes of his or her psychological discomfort. If a client believes psychic pain is caused by traumatic childhood experiences, that client is likely to choose a therapist whose beliefs are compatible. Compatibility of beliefs and the client's perception of the adequacy of a therapist's credentials and preparation may also contribute to the client's expectations of being helped.

The value placed on society on the ability to think rationally, to be responsible and independent, and to work and be productive is reflected in the therapeutic approaches used in the United States today. Since there is no consensus in psychotherapy, an eclectic approach broadens the resources available to caregivers as they adapt various forms and aspects of psychotherapy to specific situations. The therapies discussed in this chapter are summarized in Table 22–1.

Table 22-1. Comparison of Various Approaches to Therapy

Therapeutic Approach	Basic Premise
Reality therapy	People should engage in responsible behavior in order to enhance their sense of self-worth.
Rational emotive therapy	People tend to engage in irrational, immature thinking that is essentially dysfunctional. This form of thinking should be replaced with logical thought patterns.
Implosive therapy	A process called *flooding* is used to reduce anxiety precipitated by a dreaded object or situation. Flooding involves repeated intense exposure to feared objects and situations under controlled conditions.
Primal therapy	People who experience unmet needs and conditional acceptance by parents and significant others develop unhealthy defenses that must be discarded if people are to become aware of their true selves. Regression is sought in order to help clients abandon maladaptive defense patterns.
Milieu therapy	A therapeutic environment is provided that involves staff members and clients in planning and decision making. Unity, group cohesiveness, participation, and mutuality are emphasized.
Client-centered therapy	Therapy is a journey of self-discovery embarked on by the client, with the therapist functioning as guide and companion.
Relationship therapy	Clients are encouraged to express feelings and needs within a therapeutic relationship with the nurse or other caregivers. Clarification, validation, affirmation, and reinforcement are offered in an accepting relationship that utilizes communication constructively.
Transactional Analysis	Transactions are analyzed between clients to ascertain the nature of the stimulus and response—Parent, Adult, Child. Freedom of choice and acceptance of responsibility for self are basic premises.

REALITY THERAPY

Reality therapy reflects many of the current values in our culture. William Glasser (1965), the founder of reality therapy, emphasizes the importance of *responsibility*, which he defines as the ability to fulfill one's needs in a way that does not deprive others of the ability to fulfill their own needs. Glasser believes that people do not act irresponsibly because they are ill; rather, they are ill because they act irresponsibly. It follows from this premise that responsible persons behave in functional ways that enhance their sense of self-worth.

According to Glasser, two basic psychological needs of most people are the need to love and be loved and the need to be valued by oneself and others. Difficulties arise when an individual is unable to meet these basic human needs. He adds that in order to feel worthwhile, one must maintain a socially acceptable standard of behavior. Adherence to society's standards, values, and ethics help individuals maintain their sense of self-worth. Rejecting important social values results in societal disapproval or rejection and leads to a sense of being unloved, unappreciated, and devalued.

In reality therapy, responsibility for one's actions is equated with mental health, and irresponsibility is equated with various manifestations of mental illness. In order to be effective, the reality therapist must promote responsibility and self-determination. Although the reality therapist should be warm, sensitive, caring, and emotionally involved, she must also be willing to allow the client to experience the consequences of any irresponsible behavior. Hostility is never encouraged, and acting out impulsively or irresponsibly is believed to compound problems. This approach helps motivate clients to try out new, more responsible patterns of behavior that are therefore more likely to produce rewarding consequences.

Another premise of reality therapy is that frustration or unhappiness does not justify irresponsible behavior. The reality therapist does not accept or excuse irresponsible behavior or allow the client to blame parents or other people, past circumstances, or the present situation for his actions. The therapist should focus on the present and on ethical values and morality as critical issues. The past should be regarded as history that cannot be changed. Parents or significant other persons are neither censured nor blamed, no matter how irresponsibly they may seem to have acted in the past. Because the past cannot be changed, the client should be encouraged to find ways to live responsibly with or without the influence of significant others.

Avoiding responsibility may help the client feel better temporarily, but ultimately it causes him to cling to dysfunctional behaviors and to become disillusioned with treatment. In reality therapy it is thought that merely listening to a recital of a client's problems provides a measure of comfort, but the client eventually discovers that talking about problems does nothing to alleviate them. The reality therapist focuses on *what* the patient is doing, not *why*.

At the same time, the therapist focuses on the client's strengths and on the areas in which the client behaves responsibly. The reality therapist explores the client's range of interests by discussing many different topics, including politics, marriage, sex, religion, sports, and hobbies, always focusing on values, standards, and responsibility as underlying issues. In this way, the client is reminded that he is a part of the world and his confidence in his ability to cope with the world is reinforced.

The function of the therapist is to become involved with the client and to encourage acceptance of reality, as painful or problematic as it may be. The therapist then helps the client deal with reality and learn better ways of meeting needs through more adaptive patterns of behavior. Reality therapy emphasizes the therapist's role as an educator and as a role model of responsibility.

Reality therapy can be the basis of interventions with clients on a daily basis. The nurse's attitude of genuine concern and involvement permits gentle encouragement of the client to be more responsible. A client who believes that she is being pursued by foreign agents can be reminded that the nurse has no reason to believe this is so, but the nurse also acknowledges it must be frightening to harbor this belief.

A nurse may support the client experiencing the discomfort of chronic mental illness yet find ways to foster more appropriate interactions with others. For example, the nurse may have to suggest to a client who hears internal voices that it is unwise to respond to them in public places such as the checkout counter in a grocery store. The nurse denies the reality of the voices but acknowledges the reality of the client's experience with the voices. At the same time the nurse reinforces the necessity of behavioral controls. Reality therapy focuses on the client's daily activities as they relate to social standards regarding what is acceptable or unacceptable. The client is taught alternative patterns of behavior and alternative ways of relating to others. Reality therapy encourages involvement that will contribute to a greater sense of self-worth and to an increased ability to give and receive love, so that ultimately the client feels more valued and more fulfilled.

RATIONAL EMOTIVE THERAPY

Albert Ellis, a clinical psychologist, formulated *rational emotive therapy* (RET) in 1955 after he found psychoanalysis to be ineffective with many clients. According to Ellis, no matter how much insight a person may gain into his early childhood experiences and their connection with his current emotional state, he can seldom overcome his present distress solely by gaining insight. On those rare occasions when presenting symptoms are eradicated, new disturbing traits tend to surface.

Ellis maintains that virtually all serious emotional dysfunction results from magical, superstitious, immature thinking and asserts that if disturbing thoughts are rigorously disputed and principles of logical thinking are emphasized, the disordered thought processes can be eliminated. The unwarranted dogmatic, irrational, and unexamined beliefs are not thought to be related to reality and therefore are expected to dissolve if they are carefully and logically attacked (1973).

The theoretical premises of RET may be described as the ABC's. "A" stands for *activating event*. Some event occurs and the individual reacts. "B" represents the individual's *beliefs* about "A." "C" represents emotional and behavioral *consequences*. According to RET, traumatic occurrences at point A do not automatically cause depression or strong feelings of deprivation at point C. Rather, one's beliefs about the event at point B result in the feelings of depression and sense of deprivation, or consequences, at point C. This is illustrated in Figure 22–1.

For example, if the traumatic occurrence is the loss of a love relationship, and an individual believes that the loss of this relationship is intolerable, not just unfortunate, then the consequences might include feelings of horror, worthlessness, panic, and profound depression. If, on the other hand, the loss of the relationship is viewed as unfortunate (but not intolerable), then the consequences would tend to be sadness (but not profound depression) and regret (but not panic). The sense of being a worthwhile individual would remain intact.

Once an individual accepts that external events influence her feelings but do not cause them, her control over her own emotions is significantly increased and she is less likely to give in to profound depression, hostility, panic, and self-belittling thoughts and feelings. When an individual accepts the fact that not an event but her perception of an event gives rise to her feelings, she has taken a step toward controlling her feelings.

The therapist then searches for irrational perceptions, statements, and conclusions that distort reality and make situations seem worse than they actually are. Detrimental perceptions of events are termed *masturbatory ideologies* (Ellis and Grieger 1977). An example of a masturbatory ideology is the feeling that "I must excel and win approval for my performance or else I am a mediocre person." Major supporting ideas for this notion are:

1. I must have sincere love and approval almost all the time from all the people I find significant.

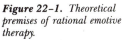

Figure 22–1. *Theoretical premises of rational emotive therapy.*

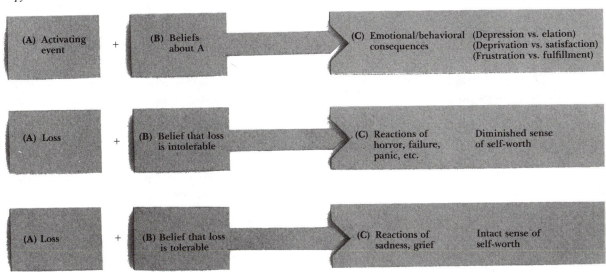

2. I must prove myself thoroughly competent, adequate, and achieving, or at least have real competence or talent at something important.

3. My emotional misery comes almost completely from external pressures that I have little ability to change or control. Unless these pressures change, I cannot help making myself feel anxious, depressed, belittled, or hostile.

4. If events occur that put me in real danger or that threaten my life, I have to react by making myself exceptionally preoccupied with and upset by them.

5. My past life has influenced me immensely and remains all-important. If something once strongly affected me, it has to keep determining my feelings and behavior today. My early childhood gullibility and conditionability still remain, and I cannot surmount them and think for myself.

6. I must have a high degree of order or certainty in the universe around me to enable me to feel comfortable and to perform adequately.

7. I desperately need others to depend on. Because I shall always remain so weak, I also need some supernatural power on which to rely, especially in times of crisis.

8. I must understand the nature or meaning of the universe in order to live happily in it.

9. I can only rate myself as good or worthy if I perform well, do worthwhile things, and have people generally approve of me.

10. If I make myself depressed, anxious, ashamed, angry, or disturbed in response to people and events, I perform incompetently and shamefully. I amount to a thoroughly weak, rotten person if I react in such ways.

11. Beliefs held by respected authorities or by my society must be correct and I have no right to question them in theory or action; if I do, people have a right to condemn and punish me, and I cannot bear their disapproval.

Another masturbatory ideology is the belief that "others must treat me with consideration, in exactly the way I want them to treat me. If they fail in this, they should be severely blamed, damned, and punished for their unkindness to me." Major supporting ideas for this notion include:

1. People must treat others in a fair and just manner; if they act unfairly or unethically, they amount to rotten people and deserve severe punishment. The universe will almost certainly see that they get this kind of retribution.

2. If others behave incompetently or stupidly, they are idiots and ought to feel ashamed of themselves.

3. If people have the ability to do well but actually choose to shirk and avoid their responsibilities, they are worthless and should feel ashamed of themselves. People must achieve their full potential for happy and worthwhile living or else they have little or no value as humans.

This is an incomplete but representative list of irrational, self-defeating, and dysfunctional beliefs that, according to Ellis, release individuals from responsibility for changing unrewarding ways of thinking and acting.

RET proposes that the tendency to think, emote, and behave in irrational ways has an innate, biological basis as well as an acquired one. Because of the genetic or biological nature of this characteristic, a vulnerable individual is naturally inclined toward self-defeating or self-destructive tendencies and has difficulty modifying them. As a result, a sense of personal worthlessness prevails, and social relationships or productive goals are impeded.

Basic to RET is the belief that individuals are born with a potential to be rational as well as irrational in their thinking. Other inherent potentials include predispositions toward creativity language, self-preservation, organization, self-actualization, sexuality, love, and belonging. Paradoxically, individuals also have opposing tendencies toward self-destruction, hedonism, irresponsibility, procrastination, hatred, callousness, superstition, intolerance, perfectionism, and grandiosity. Also, most individuals tend to repeat their mistakes and frequently fail to anticipate future consequences of their current behavior.

The RET approach is cognitive, directive, and discipline-oriented. The RET therapist does not believe that involvement or warmth between the client and the therapist is necessary to achieve personality change. The RET therapist does believe that rapport and unconditional acceptance of the client are desirable. While the therapist may criticize dysfunctional behavior, the client is seen as a fallible but forgivable human being. The therapist refuses to disparage the client even when the client disparages himself. The therapist accepts the client without necessarily extending great warmth or showing high regard for the client's behavior.

Implementation of rational emotive therapy requires debating, challenging, disputing, and debunking each of the client's irrational beliefs. The therapy helps clients differentiate between what they want and what they actually need. The goal of the rational emotive therapist is to help clients gain control over irrational beliefs and modify their overreactive emotions and behaviors. This approach allows a more objective, realistic assessment of events, beliefs, and responses, which helps the individual let go of previously incapacitating behavioral consequences. According to Ellis, real and lasting changes can occur through habituation, or repetition and practice, in a conscious, action-oriented effort.

RET is a useful therapeutic tool that, with preliminary preparation, can be implemented by psychiatric nurses for use with specific client populations. In general, the attitude of the nurse should be one of acceptance of the client as a fallible human being. The client herself should not be criticized, but maladaptive behaviors may be examined in light of the activating event (A), beliefs about the event (B), and the emotional/behavioral consequences (C). This approach can be implemented in an individual or group setting.

The masturbatory ideologies to be avoided can be printed on posters and placed in group or individual therapy rooms as continual reminders of the human tendency to overreact to certain life events. A variety of impersonal therapeutic aids may also be used, such as films, didactic discussions, activity-oriented homework assignments, and approaches that are not essentially empathetic or sympathetic. A combination of behavior therapies such as desensitization, assertiveness training, and operant conditioning may be employed to help the client make a compelling cognitive change.

Persons susceptible to disorders with strong psychological components, such as peptic ulcer, coronary artery disease, hypertension, and migraine headaches, may find this form of therapy especially helpful in reducing excessive reactivity to life stresses and keeping such stresses in perspective.

IMPLOSIVE THERAPY

As explained in Chapter 18, *implosive therapy* is based on the general behavioral principle that a person can overcome maladaptive anxiety elicited by situations or objects by approaching the feared situation while in a psychophysiological state that inhibits anxiety. Implosive therapy is used specifically for persons disabled by phobias and anxiety. The patient is desensitized to anxiety-producing stimuli by intense exposure to fear-producing situations, either through imagination or through actual exposure to the fear-producing situation. This process of repeated intense exposure is called *flooding*. An important difference between flooding and traditional behavior modification procedures is that exposure to feared objects or situations is repeatedly intensified in flooding. Relaxation training and medication are sometimes used to facilitate implosive techniques and shorten the process.

Flooding means that the client confronts the anxiety-producing object or situation at full intensity for prolonged periods of time. This results in the client's being allowed to experience anxiety rather than being protected from overwhelming discomfort. For example, a client who fears heights might be brought to the top of a tall building and required to remain there long enough for excessive anxiety to dissipate. Anxiety tends to diminish to lower levels within the first 25 minutes of the initial intense exposure. Subsequent sessions would be held, preferably within an interval of a few days. In the second session the anxiety level would be lowered more quickly. With repeated exposure to the feared situation, less effort would be required for the client to reach a state of calmness. The flooding process would be repeated until little or no anxiety was experienced. To prevent a return of previous levels of anxiety, additional sessions would be held, with longer periods of time elapsing between each session, until the client was able to remain calm and be aware of a sense of mastery. The entire treatment of flooding usually requires from 5 to 20 sessions, depending on the severity and durability of the problem.

One disadvantage to using flooding techniques is the extent of discomfort produced in the client. Therefore, the flooding approach is suitable only for carefully selected clients. Persons who have a history of cardiac problems or hypertension would certainly not be candidates for this form of therapy. Clients who are susceptible to extremely generalized rather than focused anxiety are inappropriate for this form of therapy. For such clients a psychotic reaction in which contact with reality is lost might be triggered by the induction of overwhelming anxiety. Thus the vulnerability, actual or potential, of any client may preclude the adoption of this form of therapy.

An alternative form of implosive therapy that avoids flooding a client with anxiety is *graded exposure*, which is similar to flooding except that the feared object or situation is introduced gradually.

Imagery is an approach that can be used to help clients cope with fear-inducing measures such as chemotherapy or other painful treatments. When faced with unpleasant experiences, the client is encouraged to detach emotionally from what is happening and to focus on another, more pleasant memory. This approach encourages the client to achieve greater control over emotional and physiological fear responses. Imagery is based on the theory that people are able to modify, through processes of self-monitoring and self-reinforcement, physiological activity or processes of consciousness (Tart and Fadiman 1975). By means of imagery (for example, visualizing heartbeats or the pressure with which blood moves through veins and arteries) clients can voluntarily control some autonomic functions that previously had been thought beyond voluntary control. A principle underlying the effectiveness of imagery is the psychophysiological principle proposed by Green, Green, and Holmes (1980), which states that each change in physiological conditions is accompanied by commensurate changes in cognition and emotions, conscious or unconscious. Conversely, every change in the mental-emotional state is accompanied by commensurate changes in the physiological state of the individual, conscious or unconscious.

Human beings have a biological but not conscious awareness of their physical state down to the level of a single cell. In essence, this means that physiological activity of a single cell induces a reactive response in other cells. It is possible to control the direction and flow of nerve impulses throughout the body and to monitor physiological functioning to some extent. Because the mind is capable of controlling some of the physical activity of cells, it follows that some diseases may even originate in mental processes. Health is affected by stresses largely because the mind confronts situations that are perceived as threatening and that cannot be coped with effectively (Brown 1980).

The belief that physical and psychological processes are interdependent can help clients deal with painful and feared procedures and can assist them in contributing to their own recovery by monitoring their own cognitive and emotional responses.

Imagery and visualization approaches have proved successful in a variety of health problems thought to have strong psychological components, such as migraine headaches, hypertension, peptic ulcers, and asthma. It must be acknowledged that considerable systematic research in the form of controlled studies must be undertaken to validate and evaluate the effectiveness of imagery and visualization techniques.

PRIMAL THERAPY

Primal therapy, originated by Arthur Janov (1970), is based on the idea that infants are born without symptoms of neurosis or psychosis but that when needs for food, tenderness, and acceptance are unmet, difficulties arise. Unmet needs create pain, and the pain continues until the infant separates his needs from his painful feelings and suppresses or disconnects himself from his feelings in an effort to avoid feeling pain. In time, suppressed needs contribute to a continuous state of tension, which, in later life, can be acted out in a variety of behaviors ranging from disrupted sleeping patterns to sociopathic disorders.

The neuroses, or anxiety disorders, are seen as dysfunctional feeling responses that are symbolic substitutes for the original unmet needs. Experiences in which basic needs go unmet may not necessarily be sudden, overwhelming, traumatic events. Instead, they may be subtle and occur insidiously over a period of time. Janov's examples include being forced to say "please" and "thank you," not being allowed to complain or cry when unhappy, being left with an insensitive babysitter too often, or being asked to recite poetry, perform, catch a ball, or solve abstract problems before one is able. Whatever the demands, the child learns that to be loved or to receive approval, she must comply with whatever she is asked to do. The feeling that love is conditional and is withheld unless parental expectations are met produces intolerable feelings of hopelessness and distress. The child's attempt to please the parents is called *the struggle*. This endless struggle prevents the child from feeling hopeless but rather makes her strive ever harder to meet self-imposed standards of high performance. These activities are undertaken in an effort to be loved. Eventually, the behaviors become automatic or unconscious, and the person believes them to be a part of her real self. Although the struggle begins with trying to please the parents it is later generalized to trying to please everyone. The wish to please controls and motivates the person's activities from then on. The real self, as defined by Janov, is the person one is before discovering that such a person is not acceptable to one's parents. A person is born real, but the authentic self is lost in the struggle to please.

The injuries resulting from the accumulation of unmet needs are stored in what Janov calls the *primal pool*. Because substitutes for unconditional love are never fully satisfying, the resulting frustration is acted out through a variety of behaviors that may be symbolic of the pain. Such behaviors may take the form of overachievement, obesity, substance abuse, anxiety, or phobias, depending on the personality traits of the individual.

The primal therapist believes that the real self is disconnected and, along with the original feelings of pain, is encased in a protective shell. When the defense behaviors of the struggle are not present, as during a vacation, the individual may feel strange or unreal. In some vulnerable individuals the absence of the struggle may lead to psychiatric disability.

Janov's "shell" differs from the Freudian defense system. A strong defense system, according to Freudian theory, helps maintain a functional, integrated personality. In contrast, Janov believes that the person who is well-defended is likely to be dysfunctional or "unreal." According to Janov, the healthy, well-integrated person is the one without defenses. Troubled persons reject the real self in favor of the unreal self. At the same time most persons continue to wish to be real. This conflict, according to Janov, results in disruption of the endocrine system, causing strain on other organ systems. Thus, the troubled individual does not function smoothly or normally on physiological and psychological levels.

The troubled individual can be freed from his or her unreal self by reexperiencing the original *primal pain* through primal therapy, which is described as a systematic assault on the unreal self. Janov believes that feeling the original agony of unmet needs eventually results in discovery of the real or true self. Experiencing primal pain is severe enough to cause the individual to react by expressing *primal screams*; the unmet needs of the individual will be fulfilled, paradoxically, when the defenses are removed and the pain is felt. The unreal self is destroyed and the real self can emerge.

The therapeutic approach involves reliving key early events, or *primal scenes*. The client feels the distress of primal hopelessness once again. By reliving the agony and feeling the pain completely, the individual can give up the unreal hope of being loved for what she is. When the unrealistic hope of unconditional love is given up, the individual can then give up the struggle to please, which has caused so much anguish.

Because defenses against pain are viewed as unhealthy, the goal of therapy is for the client to

---

THE PHENOMENON OF PRIMAL THERAPY

Arthur Janov, the originator of primal therapy, reported that his therapeutic approach grew out of an experience in a psychotherapy group of which he was the leader. Upon being asked to call out for "Mommy" and "Daddy," a group member became increasingly agitated; his body trembled and his movements became convulsive. Finally the member uttered a piercing scream, followed by subjective feelings of clarity and understanding. Janov began using similar techniques with other clients and noted that the sequence of agitation and an anguished scream was followed by greater capacity for insight. By using variations of his methods with large numbers of people, Janov formulated a theory to explain the impact of the approach known as primal therapy. The detractors of this approach consider it to be a cathartic emotional experience rather than a rational, proven form of psychotherapy.

relinquish defenses that prevent recalling and experiencing the pain of early hurts. In primal therapy, the client is isolated in a hotel room for 24 hours before the first session. Customary activities, such as reading, smoking, watching television, and making phone calls, which may provide outlets for release of tension, are prohibited. Some individuals who are especially well defended might be asked to remain awake all night. Sleeplessness is thought to break down the defenses, partly because dreaming, a usual outlet for tension, is prevented. With his defenses weakened and his pain threshold lowered by isolation, the client is brought closer to a primal experience.

During the first three weeks of primal treatment, the therapist works intensively with the client. Later, the client usually becomes a part of a primal group that emphasizes reliving painful early scenes. The primal group ordinarily meets for a period of six to nine months.

Treatment usually takes place in a soundproof office where clients lie supine in a defenseless position. Some patients may complain of tight feelings in the throat and chest or may begin to gag and retch in early sessions. As the clients are encouraged to name the pain they feel, they may writhe and thrash about. The therapist continues to encourage the clients to let their feelings out; often a client screams with utterances of "Daddy, be nice!" or "Mommy, hurt!" or just "Hate!" or "Help!" A client may clutch his abdomen and fall to the floor convulsing. The scream is described as a liberating event, orgasmic in nature and involuntary. It represents a reenactment of experiences from the past.

Primal screaming may take place by the third day of the therapy. Sometimes it may not take place for weeks. When it does occur, it is believed that barriers between thought and feelings are broken. The person becomes open to feelings and may have spontaneous primal experiences outside therapy sessions. This is considered an indication that the client is on the way to health. Many more primal experiences may occur over a period of months, each one diminishing the unreal self and expanding the real self, until the client is free of distress.

The goal of the therapist is to evoke pain in order to produce a functioning, feeling person. As the primal process continues, the client may regress into childhood or infancy, speaking with a lisp or using infantile manners as the primal scenes are relived. Some clients have been reported to relive the traumatic birth experience itself.

Being cured means that an individual is able to feel, without outside help, whatever feelings are present. Defenses are relinquished and therefore not available to hide feelings or to cause acting-out behaviors. Total happiness is not the goal of primal therapy, and clients who are cured will have moments of pain. Because they are able to feel what is happening in the here and now, events may upset the postprimal client, but neurotic behavior induced by tensions does not return, and the results are said to be lasting. The struggle is no longer necessary, so life is made easier and the client is able to enjoy life without artificial aids, such as chemicals.

Advocates of primal therapy allege that other forms of therapy that treat only symptoms ignore the totality of the psychophysical self and actually continue fragmenting the self. Tension, they believe, continues and disturbs the client's emotional and physical well-being. Primal therapy is thought to provide a unifying experience that makes the individual whole again.

Primal therapy advocates claim to have discovered the definitive cure for mental disorders and state that it cannot be integrated with other therapeutic approaches. Janov (1972) wrote that all other forms of therapy are obsolete and invalid and that primal therapy is the only valid approach to treating neurotic and psychotic clients. Primal therapy is therefore rarely used in an integrated way.

TRANSACTIONAL ANALYSIS

Transactional Analysis was developed originally by Dr. Eric Berne as a method of group therapy. It is based on the premise that clients are responsible for what happens in the future regardless of what has happened in the past. Advocates of this therapy believe that it enables persons to change, to establish self-control and self-direction and to discover the reality of freedom of choice. The vocabulary of Transactional Analysis is thought by some to be in a language that anyone can understand, as opposed to vague concepts in other theories. The language identifies things that really are, the reality of experiences that really happened in the lives of people who really existed.

The basic unit of analysis in this system is the transaction between two or more people. It is a method of examining a verbal exchange wherein one person's utterance and another's response are based on which part of a multiple nature of individuals those persons are "relating from." The three parts of this multiple nature are Parent, Adult, and Child.

Observations by TA therapists have supported the assumption that these three states exist in all people: the same little person they were as a three-year-old, a reasoning and logical grown-up adult, and a combination of one's own parents.

The Parent is a collection of recordings in the brain of unquestioned or imposed external events perceived by persons in the early years, usually the first five years of life. Because small children are unable to apply meanings to words, they cannot modify, correct, or explain the external stimuli, but instead record the data without any editing. All admonitions, rules, and laws that the children hear from their parents are recorded in the Parent. They range from the earliest parental communications, transmitted nonverbally through tone of voice, facial expression, and cuddling to the more elaborate verbal rules and regulations set forth by parents.

While external events are being recorded in the Parent, another recording of internal events is being made simultaneously—the responses of the children to what they see and hear. Since children do not have extensive vocabularies during the critical time of early experiences, most of the reactions are on a feeling level. Because the process of becoming civilized is frustrating, the predominant by-product of these years is negative feelings. This is the result of being a child, the situation of childhood itself. It is not the intentions of the parents which produce the problem. The child is also the storehouse of positive data—creativity, curiosity, and discovery; but the uncomfortable feelings far outweigh the good.

The Adult is concerned with transforming stimuli into pieces of information, and processing and filing that information on the basis of previous experience. The Adult examines the data in the Parent to determine if it is still true and applicable and studies the Child to determine if the feelings are appropriate to the present. The Adult is necessary for survival; it compiles the probabilities that are essential for dealing effectively with the outside world.

The goal of TA is to enable a person to have freedom of choice, to change at will, and to change responses to recurring and new stimuli. Restoration of freedom is accomplished by knowing the truth about what is in the Parent and the Child and how this data feeds into present day transactions (Harris 1967). The goal is achieved by teaching the individual to recognize, identify, and describe the Parent, Adult, and Child in themselves and others. This type of therapy is accomplished best in a group setting.

The central technique of this therapy is to analyze a transaction to discover which part of a person—Parent, Adult, or Child—is originating each stimulus and response. Transactions can be complementary or crossed. If complementary, communication will proceed smoothly and indefinitely, as in gossip (Parent to Parent), problem solving (Adult to Adult), or playing together (Child to Child or Parent to Child). Communication is disrupted when a crossed transaction occurs. The

most common one and the one which causes most of the social difficulties in the world is originated as an Adult to Adult and responded to as a Child to a Parent. For example, a wife says to her husband, "Maybe we should find out why you have been drinking more lately," and her husband responds with, "You're always criticizing me, just like my mother."

One of the key concepts in TA is that of Games, which are ongoing complementary ulterior transactions progressing to a well-defined, predictable outcome known as the pay-off. The games are unconsciously played by people engaged in duplex (two-sided) transactions that form their social life; these do not necessarily imply fun or enjoyment. Every game is basically dishonest and has a dramatic outcome. A game that is frequently seen in a therapy setting is "Why Don't You, Yes But" in which a client will present a problem to the group and continually reject any solutions proposed by the other group members. The game is not played to receive information or problem solve but to keep the client in a child state, being inadequate to meet the situation. The other group members become Parents who are anxious to dispense their wisdom for the client's benefit. The purpose of the game is not to get suggestions but to reject them. Group members who respond to the game of "Why Don't You, Yes But" begin to play "I'm Only Trying To Help You" in which continued suggestions are given and rejected, leaving the players increasingly frustrated with their efforts. The bewilderment of the Parents at the ingratitude of the child for all their efforts is the payoff.

To therapeutically respond to someone playing "Why Don't You, Yes But," the leader and group members refuse to become parents and to play by placing the responsibility back on the client with a response such as "That is a difficult problem; what are you going to do about it?" (Berne 1964).

Within the group setting, games and transactions are analyzed to help clients view their relationships responsibly. The participant format utilizes a language that forms the basis for client-to-client and client-to-therapist transactions that facilitate examination of all aspects of behavior and feelings regardless of their nature. The members act as both restraining and supporting influences to each other.

MILIEU THERAPY AND THE THERAPEUTIC COMMUNITY

In *milieu therapy* the maintenance of an atmosphere that encourages recovery or optimal functioning is stressed.

Milieu therapy is defined by Cummings and Cummings (1962) as "the scientific manipulation of the environment aimed at producing changes in the personality of the patient" (p. 5). Nurses and other caretakers are not supervisors of work but are co-workers and participants with clients. Designated tasks take into account the ability of the individual. Since overexpectations may be harmful, initial expectations of performance should be modest, and work should be broken down into simple steps. Milieu therapy uses the entire environment, physical and social, therapeutically, and no psychiatric limitation is considered a complete barrier to graded activity (Almond 1974).

Milieu therapy represents a major change from the authoritarian administration of traditional institutions. This approach provides for a more rational, flexible, and democratic decision-making process among those persons affected by the consequences of the decisions. It is thought that clients who have a voice in making rules are more likely to conform to them, so client government is an important part of milieu therapy. It allows clients to develop constitutional by-laws, hold regular meetings, and elect officers to leadership positions that are recognized by clients and hospital administrators alike. Ward meetings are attended by clients, staff, and the unit administrator, but by no one higher in the administrative hierarchy. Clients are permitted to vote on issues and to make suggestions and recommendations to hospital authorities based on the consensus of the client population rather than on any one person's opinion. Clients can organize, assign, and carry out unit duties and can urge changes in unit rules. They can organize and carry out social activities or related projects, such as editing a hospital newsletter. Committees can be formed by clients for the betterment or beautification of the treatment facility. But above all, the client government is responsible for making and enforcing most of the unit rules and regulations.

The concepts of the *therapeutic community* is similar to that of milieu therapy. Both emphasize the importance of using all aspects of the clients' hospital experience in a therapeutic manner. The major difference, according to Almond (1974), is that milieu therapy adheres more closely to the medical model; the psychiatrist heads the treatment team and instructs unit staff about the approach to be used with each client. The therapeutic community is less likely to be organized along hierarchical lines, and planning and implementation of the therapeutic regimen are usually delegated to members of an interdisciplinary team.

Like milieu therapy, the therapeutic community stresses group treatment, group activities, and joint decision making by both clients and staff.

Community meetings, client government meetings, activities programs, job training, planning meetings, social and recreational groups, psychodrama, and family group meetings are all part of the therapeutic community. Democratic processes and egalitarianism are greatly emphasized.

Any therapeutic community should promote a sense of belonging, of shared membership, and of responsibility toward others in the community. Behavioral expectations should be made clear, as is shown in the box below.

According to Jansen (1980), in the therapeutic communities there is a transmission of healing, which can be shared by members and experienced even by newcomers. A therapeutic community provides a communal experience that fosters open communication and promotes intrapsychic and interpersonal adjustment to the maximum potential of each individual.

The therapeutic aspect of the community environment serves as an adjunct to individual therapy, medication, and group and activities therapy. Social therapies, behavior therapy, individual psychotherapies, or eclectic approaches may also be incorporated to meet individual needs of clients.

The introduction and expansion of milieu therapy has had a profound effect on psychiatric nursing. Prior to its introduction, nurses were delegated the responsibility of managing a safe, secure psychiatric unit. With the advent of milieu therapy, the role of the nurse changed from custodial to therapeutic and rehabilitative. Instead of taking charge *of* clients, nurses could now focus on involvement in goal-directed activities *with* clients.

BEHAVIORS EXPECTED FROM CLIENTS IN A THERAPEUTIC COMMUNITY

1. To try to control their own behaviors
2. To engage in social interactions
3. To attend meetings, activities, and therapy sessions
4. To speak out in community and group meetings
5. To trust the staff and client members of the therapeutic community
6. To talk about their problems with staff, among themselves, and with significant others
7. To care about others and to value community interests
8. To show concern for others in the community

The nurse in the therapeutic community plays an active part in making the decisions affecting the community. The nurse's comments, opinions, and suggestions about medication choices and dosages and about client discharge and placement receive serious consideration. Because the nurse is in close touch with and has extensive data on clients, the opinions and observations of the nurse are greatly respected by others on the mental health team.

One responsibility of the nurse in a therapeutic community is to help clients express feelings and conflicts appropriately and to help them find healthier ways of relating to others. The focus is on helping clients to function at their optimum capacity and thus avoid further regression. Limits on client behavior are set whenever necessary to help the client maintain control. The nurse may also use permissive approaches when appropriate and endeavor to provide protection and support when necessary.

Since a substantial portion of the nurse's energies are directed toward various group activities within the therapeutic community, the nurse must be knowledgeable about group dynamics and skilled in group process. A basic assumption in the therapeutic community is that clients have strength and potential, and therefore should be actively involved in developing the treatment plan. This concept of client participation is consistent with the basic assumptions of the nursing process.

CLIENT-CENTERED THERAPY

Originated by Carl Rogers in the 1940s, *client-centered therapy* is concerned with developing the client's potential. It focuses on present rather than past experiences. The therapist offers a caring, listening presence. The therapist's knowledge and technical skills are not emphasized. Instead, three attitudes are considered necessary to effect a change in the client: (1) empathy, or understanding, (2) genuineness, or congruence, and (3) non-possessive caring. An individual's growth is thought to be enhanced by a relationship with a caring, nonjudgmental, empathetic, helping individual. The therapist endeavors to understand the client's experience, and to monitor his or her feelings.

The therapist's unconditional regard for the client's individuality facilitates the process of self-actualization as the client discovers appropriate directions to take. The client-centered therapist does not give advice or direction but rather functions as a companion and guide for the client's journey of self-discovery.

Any techniques that place the therapist in control rather than the client (such as formal psychological testing, manipulation, or the use of specialized language) are avoided. Control or criticism by the therapist is thought to undermine the client's confidence in his ability to discover and mobilize his own resources. Other therapeutic techniques that place the therapist in the role of expert and reduce the client's reliance on personal resources, such as rational emotive therapy or primal therapy, are also avoided. The Rogerian model of therapy emphasizes trust in the client's rational, orderly progress toward growth and fosters constructive behaviors that are conducive to self-fulfillment.

A major goal of client-centered therapy is to facilitate self-discovery and the abandonment of masks, disguises, or facades. Rather than trying to be what others think they should be, clients are helped to reveal themselves, to accept themselves, and to value themselves for what they are. As a result of therapy, clients gradually allow themselves to be more open to experiences and more aware of their inner feelings and attitudes. Clients are also helped to replace their stereotyped views of events with more realistic perceptions that are more flexible and more tolerant of ambiguity. Clients learn to trust their own perceptions of themselves more, and to look less to others as models for behaviors, choices, values, and standards to live by. They learn to accept free choice and to judge their lives by whether they are living in a satisfying and expressive way (Rogers 1960).

The Rogerian approach has a wide range of usefulness in nursing, counseling, social work, and education. It is effective with many types of clients, ranging from relatively functional to chronically dysfunctional. It is especially applicable to individuals living in stressful situations in which they feel insecure, inferior, or trapped. When used by caregivers, this approach helps reduce feelings of loneliness, isolation, and alienation. Nurses can actively transmit positive regard to the client by reflecting or rephrasing the client's words and by communicating acceptance. This allows the client to become aware of any self-image distortions. The nurse should avoid interpreting, explaining, or changing the client. Consistent use of a client-centered approach can be effective in establishing a positive relationship, which in turn can be beneficial in enhancing the client's sense of self. With Rogers' approach, therapy becomes a journey into self-understanding in which the nurse is a trusted companion rather than a leader.

RELATIONSHIP THERAPY AS NURSING PROCESS

Relationship therapy combines the therapeutic nurse-client relationship and nursing process in a therapeutic plan whose purpose is to facilitate the development of more adaptive responses in the client. The therapeutic relationship differs from a social or friendly relationship in that both nurse and client enter into the relationship for the purpose of helping the client and the relationship is time-limited and goal-oriented. Although the nurse is warm, genuinely caring, and accepting of the client, the relationship must remain professional in order for it to be therapeutic. A social relationship develops spontaneously in response to mutual needs; a therapeutic relationship is planned in order to meet the needs of the clients. A social relationship has no time limits expressed or implied, and verbal exchanges are limited by society's norms. In a therapeutic relationship, the client is encouraged to express feelings and thoughts that might not be acceptable in social settings, although an ultimate goal might be to help the client develop socially acceptable expressions of feelings and thoughts.

Communication is the basic tool of relationship therapy and of the nursing process. It is a complex, dynamic process through which people send and receive verbal and nonverbal messages in order to understand and be understood by others, respond to the environment, and transmit ideas to one another (Lippincott 1982). Communication in a therapeutic relationship is monitored by the nurse, who consciously develops and employs communication skills. Superficial social conversation is limited, and communication is directed toward assessment of client needs, identification of goals, and implementation of therapeutic nursing interventions.

Communication skills facilitate the nursing process and the therapeutic relationship. By active listening, the nurse communicates respect for the client. Eye contact and occasional nods or comments indicate that the client has been heard and understood. Broad opening statements and open-ended questions encourage verbalization of relevant information. General leads, such as "Go on . . ." or "And . . ." indicate the nurse's wish for the client to continue. Restating what the client has just said encourages clarification. Validation of perceptions reduces the chance of misunderstanding or misperception by either the nurse or the client. Opportunity should be provided for the client to validate or dispute the nurse's observations. Since communication is a two-way process, feedback from the nurse is also important. Feedback provides the client with information regarding the effect the client's behaviors may have on the interviewer. Focusing and selective reflecting encourage communication of specific information. As relationship therapy progresses, the nurse guides communica-

tion in order to help the client remain on important issues or themes the nurse has identified.

Silences during an interaction can be valuable in providing opportunities for both the client and the nurse to reflect upon what has been said. However, some silences indicate anger or resistance on the part of the client. Some silences can become awkward and provoke anxiety, especially if the nurse or client believes that interactions must be filled with conversation. However, a silence may also indicate resolution of one topic and readiness to bring up other issues.

Reassurance is sometimes used inappropriately to reduce the nurse's anxiety, in which case it may cause a breakdown in communication. On the other hand, sincere reassurance can contribute to a sense of security or provide positive reinforcement, affirmation, or validation of the client's thoughts, feelings, and behaviors.

Throughout a therapeutic interaction, it is important for the nurse to maintain an awareness of his or her own feelings in order to serve the client's best interests. Communication of the nurse's own values or judgments in the form of lectures or "pep talks" is countertherapeutic because such messages belittle the significance of the client's own values and experiences. Judgmental attitudes can block communication and increase anxiety in the client. A nurse may convey stereotyping or prejudice by means of subtle innuendo and phrasing. Clients are often aware of negative attitudes in the nurse even though these attitudes have not been directly communicated. Psychiatric clients are often acutely sensitive to others and soon recognize when a nurse is not wholly accepting. Since negative responses do nothing to promote an effective helping relationship, it is the nurse's responsibility to engage in sufficient introspection so as to develop an awareness of negative personal feelings and to discuss them with an experienced staff person. Once recognized, these problem feelings can be dealt with and their influence diminished.

Offering advice is also counterproductive for most clients. It indicates that the nurse believes the client's decision-making abilities are inadequate, and it places the client in a dependent position and weakens the client's confidence and self-esteem. The client's interests are better served by an approach that encourages clients to make their own decisions once they have had the opportunity to explore their options. In this way, the client's problem-solving abilities are emphasized. Because the client is encouraged to choose a course of action, the responsibility for decisions remains with the client.

Therapeutic use of the nurse's own personality is an integral part of relationship therapy. Qualities that have been identified as helpful include those described by Carl Rogers: empathy, genuineness, and warm regard. These promote therapeutic interaction and contribute to the attainment of mutually agreed-upon goals.

Showing empathy rather than sympathy is in accord with the general principle that the nurse should refrain from doing for clients what they are able to do for themselves. In offering empathy, the nurse feels *with* the client not *for* the client. Sympathy tends to make the nurse assume excessive responsibility for providing relief and reduces the client's potential for growth.

Genuineness implies sincerity and open, authentic communication. Throughout relationship therapy, the nurse strives to understand the client's feelings, remain professionally involved, and become aware of her own feelings that might threaten the therapeutic quality of her relationship with the client.

Involvement, another therapeutic quality, entails caring for another and standing by that person through difficult situations, while doing something with and for that person. The nurse should be involved with clients as a caring human being, but at the same time, her involvement must be shaped by the professional role. Clients who have difficulty relating to others can benefit from a human relationship that models skills in communication and interpersonal transactions. Involvement, however, is different from identification; objectivity is retained even though the client is perceived as a unique individual. Nurses must be able to respond first to the needs of the client, not to their own needs for control or approval.

Both the nursing process and the therapeutic relationship are collaborative processes directed toward the development of adaptive coping mechanisms and behavioral change in the client. The therapeutic relationship can be separated into four sequential phases: (1) the introductory or orientation phase, (2) the testing phase, (3) the working phase, and (4) the termination phase. These parallel the four steps of the nursing process: assessment, planning, implementation, and evaluation.

Assessment in Relationship Therapy (The Introductory Phase)

During the first phase of the therapeutic relationship, the *introductory* or *orientation phase*, the nurse and client become acquainted and reach an agreement on the time, place, and initial goals of their interactions. Together they discover relevant information that helps identify needs, formulate nursing diagnoses, and establish initial goals. During this initial phase, rapport is established between nurse and client. Unless the client begins to develop trust

in the nurse, the prospect of a successful outcome is diminished. They discuss expected length of time needed to meet defined goals, the nature of their relationship, and their respective responsibilities.

During the first phase of the therapeutic relationship, the client's behaviors are assessed and her strengths and vulnerabilities are identified. Maladaptive patterns of behavior (those that compound rather than relieve the client's problems) are the focus of interventions. The client's strengths and functional behaviors can serve as the basis for developing alternatives to maladaptive behavior patterns.

In assessing a client, the nurse must first recognize those behaviors that are self-defeating, ineffective, or inappropriate. Second, the nurse might assess those factors that preceded or seemed to precipitate the problem behavior. She should attempt to identify reinforcing events that encourage the continuation of the problem behavior. One goal is to prevent, if possible, the recurrence of those events that reinforce negative behaviors and to replace them with events that reinforce more constructive cognitive, affective, and behavioral responses. This should be done with the client's consent.

The nurse should also suggest that the client undergo physical assessment to rule out any physiological basis for maladaptive behaviors. Thyrotoxicosis, brain or adrenal tumors, and withdrawal from drugs or alcohol are only a few of the disorders that can mimic conditions of psychiatric disorganization.

Assessment for side effects of psychiatric medications should continue throughout the nurse-client relationship. The psychiatric nurse must also remember that clients may become ill with any disorder that affects the general population. Certain physical conditions may prohibit the use of specific medications designed to relieve psychiatric symptoms. Mental and physical health are interrelated, each one affecting the other. Thus, assessment of client needs must be done on a comprehensive and continuing basis.

Sources of data for assessing maladaptive responses are numerous. The primary source is the client, but the family or other significant persons in the client's life may also contribute information that can be utilized in the plan of care. Here again the client must assent.

Planning in Relationship Therapy (The Testing Phase)

Arriving at a treatment plan is the second step in the nursing process. At this point, the nurse should encourage the client's participation in recognizing and assessing his own maladaptive responses. The origin, perpetuation, and consequences of the client's self-defeating behaviors should be cooperatively determined, and the client should continue to be involved in the problem-solving process.

Goals should be collaboratively developed, mutually agreed upon, and stated in behavioral terms and in language that can be understood by the client. Vague abstractions are not useful in describing goals because clients are often unable to understand abstract, ambiguous concepts.

Goals may be differentiated into long-term and short-term ones. Long-term goals are those that resolve the problems that led the client to become involved in relationship therapy. Short-term goals are the intermediate steps required to meet the long-term goals. Discharge, or outcome, goals that will lead to the termination of therapy should be identified at the beginning of the relationship. This can be done by evaluating progress, anticipating the client's future needs, and identifying specific behaviors needed for more independent living. The entire nursing process should be aimed at encouraging the highest level of adaptation possible within the limits of the client's capabilities.

As the relationship evolves into the second phase, the nurse should expect considerable testing of the relationship. The client who lacks self-esteem and who cannot conceive of another's genuine concern for her may try to prove that the nurse is not trustworthy. The client may miss appointments if she feels especially vulnerable or fearful. The client may be late for an appointment and then covertly try to determine whether the agreement to set aside a specific period of time for her was sincere. It is important at this critical time for the nurse to demonstrate her trustworthiness by not turning to other activities when a client fails to keep an appointment. The nurse should simply wait for the client. If the client appears for the meeting, the nurse can remind her of the agreed-upon starting time in order to encourage punctuality. Even when a client is late, the interaction should be terminated according to the initial time frame. In this way limits are reinforced. Most clients feel more secure when given clear limits. The nurse demonstrates acceptance of the client but at the same time sets limits on unacceptable behaviors. Consistency is an essential aspect of relationship therapy and should extend to other matters, as well.

During early phases of the relationship, the client is usually allowed considerable freedom in introducing topics to discuss. Typically, the client will begin by revealing factual information on an intellectual level. Good interviewing skills are helpful in eliciting information about the client's emotional level. This helps the nurse to assess the client's needs and establish nursing diagnoses. The

nurse should promise confidentiality but must not agree to withhold information from others on the health team.

Achievement of goals can lead to a sense of accomplishment in the client. Therefore, care should be taken to avoid establishing goals incompatible with the client's abilities, values, or level of functioning. It is preferable intially to set goals the nurse and client feel reasonably capable of fulfilling. The nurse may then use positive, low-key reinforcement to increase the client's confidence and self-esteem. Higher-level goals are usually introduced after lower-level goals have been met. Unrealistic goals only frustrate the nurse, discourage the client, and compound the client's feelings of inferiority and worthlessness.

Intervention in Relationship Therapy (The Working Phase)

Implementing relevant nursing actions, the third step in the nursing process, parallels the third phase of the therapeutic relationship, the working phase. It is during this phase that the client verbalizes her feelings most readily and the nurse can suggest adaptive behaviors to take the place of maladaptive or problematic responses. This is usually the longest and most productive of the four phases of the therapeutic relationship. By this time, the nursing care plan has undergone considerable change. The care plan has been evaluated in terms of goal outcomes, and additional information concerning the client has led to modifications of the chosen therapeutic approaches.

During the working phase, the tendency is toward open expression of feelings. Self-defeating or maladaptive responses expressed by the client may be analyzed cooperatively by the client and nurse. Therapeutic approaches are formulated by the nurse or the mental health team. The selection of suitable approaches is made on the basis of an ongoing assessment of the client and an evaluation of the client's progress.

During the working phase, the nurse should anticipate plateaus where little progress is observed. These may take the form of resistance to therapy manifested by the rejection of or hostility toward the nurse, avoidance behaviors, or denial of issues related to the client's maladaptive responses. The nurse can respond by facilitating the client's expression of feelings and identifying possible issues that appear to threaten the effectiveness of the relationship therapy. However, the client, not the nurse, must take responsibility for controlling undesirable or maladaptive responses. The nurse can only provide opportunities for trying out alternative behaviors and help the client work through the anxiety that change often brings. Throughout the therapeutic relationship, the client's gains should be positively reinforced by the nurse.

It is not necessary to cling to a narrow approach in relationship therapy. For example, clients who express aggression in inappropriate or maladaptive ways may need a therapeutic milieu that provides security both for them and for the intended objects of their aggression. Group meetings in the milieu setting provide the opportunity for the clients and staff to discuss their reactions and feelings about others' excessively aggressive behaviors. In meetings, disputes resulting from inappropriate expression of aggression can be confronted and resolved, and agreement can be reached on the consequences of aggressive acts. In a therapeutic community the client can be exposed to peer pressure and to role modeling in learning how to deal with aggressive impulses.

Another approach to dealing with the client who expresses aggression in maladaptive ways might draw from reality therapy. The nurse could emphasize to the client that it is possible to satisfy one's needs without acting irresponsibly toward others. He could emphasize the client's needs to love, to be loved, and to feel worthwhile. The client could be told that in order to fulfill these needs he must maintain satisfactory standards of behavior. The client would not be allowed to project blame for her aggressiveness on early childhood experiences or a traumatic event. Reality therapy thus would attempt to foster in the aggressive client a sense of responsibility for her behavior.

A nurse using rational emotive therapy with an aggressive client would point out the error of believing that *desires* for love, approval, or success are *needs*. The nurse would criticize dysfunctional aggressive responses, yet accept the client as a fallible human being. The ABC's of RET would be applied to aggressive acts. The event that activated the aggressive act would be identified, and the client would be asked to share her beliefs about the activating event. It would be emphasized that the activating event alone did not result in the aggressive act but that the client's *beliefs* about the activating event resulted in her aggressive responses. As the client learned to accept that an activating event may influence responses but not truly cause them, she could attain greater control over her emotions and behaviors. The client would be encouraged to realize that it is not necessary to yield to feelings of anger, hostility, or depression. The client would then be helped to detect her irrational beliefs that distort reality and make situations seem worse than they actually are. Irrational beliefs might cause a sense of worthlessness, or difficulty with interper-

sonal relationships or self-actualization. Each of the irrational beliefs would be debated and disputed. The client would be encouraged to differentiate between her needs and desires and to modify her ineffectual responses by controlling and managing them. The goal of rational emotive therapy would be the development of a more objective, realistic assessment of events, beliefs, and responses.

Should acts of aggression be thought to result from a fear-producing situation, the technique of implosive therapy might be utilized. In implosive therapy, the client would be encouraged to see the relationship between the fear stimulus, his feelings, and the act of aggression that follows. If desensitization is the chosen route, relaxation training could be begun with the client. Sessions with the therapist may be supplemented with tape-recorded procedures that would enable the client to practice self-relaxation on his own.

As relaxation techniques were mastered, an escalating list of anxiety- or fear-producing situations would be prepared and rank ordered, with the least fearsome situation placed in a graded sequence with more fearsome situations. Then the relaxation skills would be used while the client is exposed to the prepared fear scenes. The client, while in a deeply relaxed state, would be encouraged to imagine vividly the least fearsome situation. When he could do so with minimal anxiety, he would progress to the next situation, until, after several sessions, he could imagine the most fearsome situation and experience only minimal anxiety. The client would then be ready to encounter fear-producing situations in real life. The expectation or goal would be that the client would be able to tolerate the actual life situations without experiencing the anxiety or fear that previously precipitated aggressive feelings and actions. Implosive therapy would have the additional advantage of helping the client gain insight into the events and feelings that led to his aggression.

Evaluation in Relationship Therapy (The Termination Phase)

Evaluation, the fourth step in the nursing process, determines the degree to which goals have been met. Evaluation data may also be used to revise goals and intervention strategies as needed. All responses to interventions should be assessed according to the stated goals. Should the interventions be evaluated as having successfully met the identified goals, then termination of the therapy is undertaken.

Termination, the fourth phase of the therapeutic relationship, is often the most poorly planned and executed of all the phases of the relationship.

Ideally, the nurse and the client will mutually determine the date of the last interaction, having reviewed the list of goals and determined whether they have been successfully completed. Typically, during this phase the client may regress to an earlier communication style and exhibit resistance to planning for the future. This is often due to the client's reluctance to end the therapeutic relationship. Reactions of clients to termination vary greatly, depending on circumstances of previous terminations, the type of treatment approach used, and the length and strength of the relationship. The longer the relationship, the longer the time required for termination. The more meaningful the relationship is to the client, the more likely he is to show grief, anger, or a mixture of both. During the termination phase, the nurse should encourage the client to explore and evaluate the course of the relationship therapy and to express his feelings regarding termination. Accomplishments should be reviewed cooperatively. Sometimes a client will have made great progress but will deny having profited from the therapeutic relationship. Other clients will claim progress that may not be apparent to the nurse. Such issues should be examined by the nurse and the client.

Grief reactions to the impending loss of the therapeutic relationship should be anticipated. Feelings of sadness and hostility may be expressed, and earlier maladaptive responses may threaten to return. Denial of termination may be revealed by a lack of emotional response that actually represents a profound reaction to the expected loss. Both nurse and client can be expected to react to impending termination with a degree of grief. The ability of the nurse to recognize and discuss his own thoughts and feelings can serve as a role model for the client. Successful termination of a therapeutic relationship is the result of a well-planned and carefully executed process orchestrated by the nurse and experienced by both parties.

SUMMARY

There is much to be learned about the causes of psychiatric disorders and the effectiveness of different forms of treatment. No school of psychology has the complete answer to all emotional disorders, and no single method of treatment is universally applicable and successful. Combinations of available therapeutic modalities in an eclectic approach are most likely to result in successful outcomes in the clinical situations encountered by nurses.

Reality therapy is based on the assumption that people need to love and be loved and that in order to fulfill these needs people must maintain satisfactory standards of behavior. Clients are taught appropriate patterns of behavior that will increase their acceptance by others and therefore result in an enhanced sense of their own worth.

Rational emotive therapy is based on the belief that virtually all serious emotional illnesses result from magical, superstitious, invalid thinking, and that if the disturbing thoughts are regularly and rigorously disputed and principles of logical thinking are emphasized, the disordered thought processes can be eliminated.

Implosive therapy is based on the principle that a person can overcome maladaptive anxiety elicited by situations or objects by approaching the feared situation while in a psychophysiological state that inhibits anxiety.

Primal therapy is based on the idea that unmet childhood needs for food, tenderness, or acceptance result in a primal pain that later causes an individual to encase his real self in a protective shell. Primal therapy is a systematic assault on the protective shell. It is believed that feeling the original agony of unmet needs eventually results in discovery of the real self and, therefore, mental health. Primal therapy advocates claim that this approach cannot be integrated with other therapeutic approaches.

Transactional analysis is based on the premise that clients are responsible for what happens to them and utilizes the analysis of transactions to determine complementary and crossed communications that determine the results of social interactions.

Milieu therapy is the maintenance of an atmosphere that encourages recovery or optimal functioning. It is based on group treatment, activities geared to the abilities of individual clients, and joint decision making by both clients and staff.

Client-centered therapy is based on the belief that an individual's growth is enhanced by a caring, nonjudgmental, empathetic relationship with a helping individual. A major goal of this type of therapy is to facilitate the abandonment of facades and to help the client learn to accept and value herself for what she is.

Theoretical concepts of the therapeutic relationship and the nursing process are strikingly similar and virtually inseparable in actual practice. Yet the simultaneous application of these therapeutic tools would not be effective without the use of facilitative skills of communication, acute awareness of one's own feelings and attitudes, and authentic personal qualities of warmth, acceptance, and genuine concern.

(Text continues on page 624.)

CLINICAL EXAMPLE

INTEGRATION IN RELATIONSHIP THERAPY

Vince is a 20-year-old man who was hospitalized as the result of a violent outburst during which he attempted to injure his mother and grandmother, with whom he lived, by attacking them with a meat cleaver. Vince's father had deserted his mother when the boy was a baby, and his present whereabouts were unknown. Vince had been restrained forcibly by the police and hospitalized involuntarily. Shortly after hospitalization, Vince was quiet but unresponsive to overtures from the staff or other clients on the unit. He spent most of his time sitting in the day room chain-smoking cigarettes, most of which he begged from other clients. When asked, he would give no reason for his behavior toward his mother and grandmother except to say that they were always "bugging" him. His only visitor was his 18-year-old girlfriend, who came every day to see him.

When Vince's girlfriend visited, the couple were very affectionate toward one another. It was obvious that their embraces and kisses were upsetting to other clients. A nurse mentioned this to Vince and suggested the couple modify their demonstrations of affection or at least meet in a less conspicuous corner of the day room. Vince responded that the other clients were just jealous of him. When his girlfriend next visited, their behavior was even less inhibited than before. Another client objected to their lovemaking and accused Vince of being a "pimp." This evoked a verbal tirade from Vince that caused his girlfriend to say goodbye hurriedly and leave the unit. As soon as she was gone, Vince picked up a glass ashtray, broke it in half and went after the client who had criticized Vince's actions with his girlfriend. Before staff members could bring the situation under control, Vince had lacerated the other client severely and bruised several staff members. By shielding themselves with a mattress from one of the beds, some staff members were able to wrest the broken ashtray from Vince and place him in seclusion. He pounded the walls and swore bitterly before falling asleep. While secluded, Vince was visited regularly by staff members, as required by hospital regulations. The house physician was called to evaluate Vince and his adversary. Vince was released from seclusion the next morning and was allowed to go to the dining hall, provided he remained in control of himself. He complied and joined the other clients for breakfast, although many of them avoided him. The injured client was able to come to the dining room and was the focus of solicitude from the other clients.

ASSESSMENT

The incident involving Vince was discussed at the health team meeting the next morning. The history taken shortly after Vince was admitted to the hospital had shown that Vince's girlfriend had been pregnant a few months earlier and had had an abortion at the insistence of her parents and Vince's mother and grandmother. The girlfriend had not opposed the wishes of the female relatives regarding the abortion. Interviews with Vince's mother and grandmother had persuaded staff members that the older women, especially the mother, were intrusive yet rejecting toward Vince. His mother showed excessive interest in her son's social and sexual life, boasting, "I know more about Vince than he knows about himself."

It was the consensus of the staff that Vince had been victimized by his mother, who was sometimes overinvolved with him and sometimes quite indifferent. Because his mother's attitude toward him was ambivalent and inconsistent, Vince had not learned to develop self-control or to verbalize his emotional reactions. He eagerly sought affection from women because his mother had been so withholding of love and approval. The following diagnoses were made:

Nursing Diagnoses

Potential for violence directed at others
(related to uncontrolled outbursts)

Ineffective family coping
(related to inability to separate from mother)

Impaired social interaction
(related to inability to trust, form friendships)

Multiaxial Psychiatric Diagnoses

Axis I   312.34 Intermittent explosive disorder
Axis II   301.50 Histrionic personality disorder
Axis III None
Axis IV   Family arguments, mother-son difficulties, enduring circumstances. Severity: 3 moderate
Axis V   Current GAF: 55
          Highest GAF past year: 60

PLANNING

A treatment plan was developed, based on Vince's needs. The plan drew from a number of different therapeutic approaches.

Reality Therapy Goals

Vince will begin to modify tendencies to blame others for his problems.
Vince will begin to develop internal sources of control.

Rational Emotive Goals

Vince will utilize a cognitive review of events in order to establish connections between his thoughts, motives, and actions.

Implosive Therapy Goals

Vince will use relaxation techniques and imagery to distance himself from anxiety-provoking situations in order to increase his self-control.

Milieu Therapy Goals

Vince will attend client government meetings regularly, initially as an observer, if he prefers, but later as a participant as his comfort increases.

Relationship Therapy Goals

Vince will begin to trust others as a result of consistent staff behaviors.
Vince will begin to express negative feelings verbally instead of behaviorally.

IMPLEMENTATION

In order to foster trust, Vince was assigned a mature male nurse who functioned as a companion, mentor, and guide. The primary nurse led Vince through the following stages:

Initial Stage. In this stage, efforts were devoted to increasing Vince's trust in staff members, particularly his primary nurse. Rules were made clear and were enforced firmly but not punitively. Vince became dependent on his primary nurse for direction and explanation. This dependency was permitted temporarily in the belief that Vince needed time to develop trust necessary for him to move toward autonomous functioning and internal control. Appropriate behaviors were acknowledged and rewarded; inappropriate behaviors were also acknowledged, but the client himself was never made to feel unworthy or "bad."

Working Stage. During this stage, Vince became an active participant in therapy groups, member government, and occupational therapy activities. He remained dependent on his primary nurse and often became angry and belligerent when his primary nurse had a day off. Various methods were used to oppose these regressive tendencies. Anticipatory guidance was used to explain to Vince the work schedule of his primary nurse. The nurse assigned to care for Vince in the absence of the primary nurse was introduced to

him, and he accompanied the primary nurse in activities involving Vince. None of these methods were effective; other staff members found themselves dreading the absences of the primary nurse. Vince's primary nurse brought up the issue with Vince, and a search for a solution began. A strategy gradually evolved of leaving Vince some object or article that he and the primary nurse had shared. This transitional object could be compared to a security blanket or teddy bear carried by a small child who needs reassurance that the world is stable and predictable and that valued persons who are absent will return. The transitional objects were carefully selected and were always approved by Vince. Sometimes the object was a book or picture that Vince and the nurse had discussed together. The transitional objects were trivial in themselves, but they represented a powerful connection to the rational world that Vince was learning to live in.

During the latter part of the working stage, Vince was encouraged to move from dependency to greater autonomy. Other staff members became more active in his treatment. His girlfriend was encouraged to visit; family meetings were held to help Vince's mother deal more constructively with her son and to tolerate the possibility of separation.

Termination Phase. During this period, Vince was given time to mourn the imminent loss of the primary nurse, who had, in effect, become his "good mother." There was no sudden separation, and it was agreed that occasional communication between Vince and the primary nurse would be beneficial, provided they were integrated into the follow-up plan for care. Because of the long-standing problems between Vince and his mother, and because separation was an appropriate life-cycle task for someone who was 20, plans were made for Vince to enter a halfway house rather than return home. There he would have the advantage of some staff supervision, peer support, and the opportunity to test the new coping methods he had learned. A mature male outpatient therapist was found to continue the consistent, accepting relationship established with the primary nurse while Vince was hospitalized.

EVALUATION

The outcome evaluation of Vince's progress was facilitated by the previous establishment of specific goals. Evaluation was subjective, but there was agreement between Vince and the staff members who worked with him that, in the two months of hospitalization, Vince had discarded his extreme tendency to blame others for his problems, even though it was true that his mother had often provoked Vince's violent outbursts. Vince gradually became able to verbalize his negative feelings rather than act on them, although his mother continued to provoke aggressive reactions from him. Vince used relaxation techniques to monitor his internal reactions to such episodes with his mother and others. As a result of his increased ability to relax and to trust, he was able to make friends more easily and to keep the friends he made. This development also reduced his vulnerability to his mother. Relationship therapy, supplemented by other treatment modalities, was very therapeutic for a young man who had never before encountered a wholesome, constructive, accepting relationship with another human being.

Nursing Diagnoses	Goal	Nursing Actions	Outcome Criteria	Outcome Evaluation
Potential for violence directed at others	Client will have increased self-control, will express negative feelings verbally.	Acknowledge and reward appropriate behaviors, teach relaxation, utilize milieu for constructive activities.	Client will be able to control his own reactions to episodes with his mother and others.	Client was able to verbalize negative feelings rather than act them out, but problems with mother needed further attention.
Ineffective family coping	Client will achieve separation from mother.	Hold family sessions to help mother and son relate more constructively.	Client will achieve greater levels of autonomy.	Client switched dependency to primary nurse. Arrangements were made to find an outpatient therapist to continue relationship, work on establishing independence. Alternate placement arranged to decrease involvement with mother.
Impaired social interaction	Client will learn to trust others and use new coping methods.	Arrange relationship with primary nurse to provide acceptance security for trying new behaviors.	Client will be able to make and keep friends, establish healthy relationship with girlfriend.	Ability to trust and relax was facilitated in halfway house with environment conducive to trying new behaviors.

Review Questions

1. Which of the integrated therapeutic approaches would you feel comfortable using with a particular client? Support your choice with rationale based on chapter content.

2. How can the various integrated therapies be applied by nurses? Give examples from your own experience.

3. How could the nurse benefit a client in a general nursing situation other than a psychiatric setting with:
   a. the various integrated therapeutic approaches discussed in the chapter?
   b. relationship therapy?

4. Which of the integrated approaches lend themselves to group involvement? Which do not and why?

5. Which of the integrated approaches are applicable to stresses of everyday life encountered by the general population? Give examples of how these therapeutic approaches can be implemented to counteract stress.

Suggested Annotated Readings

Berne, E. *What Do You Say After You Say Hello?* New York: Bantam Books, 1972.

This book outlines new developments in thinking and practice in transactional analysis. The writing of life scripts is demonstrated and readers can determine what kind of life script they have. The author delineates how people follow their scripts, (which were written in early childhood) compulsively throughout their lives. Scripts dictate what kind of person one will marry, how many children one will have, and whether one is a winner or a loser. The author shows ways destructive scripts can be changed.

Bloomfield, H., M. Cain, D. Jaffee, and R. Kory. *TM: Discovering Inner Energy and Overcoming Stress.* New York: Delacorte Press, 1975.

The interrelation and interaction between meditation and stress are examined by studying their impact upon the crisis of modern life, techniques involved in contacting pure awareness, the physiology of consciousness and the objectively demonstrable bodily and mental changes associated with transcendental meditation. The effects of TM as a means of therapy and the use of this technique for developing creative intelligence and thereby approaching a solution to personal and social problems are explored.

Cumming, J., and E. Cumming. *Ego and Milieu*. Chicago: Aldine Pub. Co., 1962.

This book analyzes that relation between the hospital and treatment environment and the character of mental illness. Recent years have brought much evidence that the onset, symptoms and recovery rates of major psychiatric illness are decisively influenced by the environment within which the patient is observed and treated. There is no patient "untreated" by his environment—only patients "treated" well or ill.

Fagan, J., and I. Sheperd, eds. *Gestalt Therapy Now*. New York: Harper & Row, 1970.

This collection of essays on Gestalt therapy is intended to bring historical works into focus and present the most recent thinking with a sampling of techniques and application of the therapeutic modality. It is intended for therapists and for lay people interested in ways of feeling, relating, and behaving other than those offered by a work-ridden, past-oriented life.

References

Almond, R. *The Healing Community*. New York: Jason Aronson, 1974.

Berne, E. *Games People Play*. New York: Grove Press Inc., 1964.

Brown, E. *Supermind: The Ultimate Energy*. New York: Harper & Row, 1980.

Cummings, J., and E. Cummings. *Ego and Milieu*. Chicago: Aldine, 1962.

Ellis, A. "Rational Emotive Therapy." In *Current Psychotherapies*. R. Corsini, ed. Itasca, Illinois: F. E. Peacock, 1973.

Ellis, A., and R. Grieger, eds. *Handbook of Rational-Emotive Therapy*. New York: Springer, 1977.

Glasser, W. *Reality Therapy*. New York: Harper & Row, 1965.

Green, K. W., W. B. Green, and D. W. Holmes. "Speech Reading Abilities of Young Deaf Children." *American Annals of the Deaf*, 25 1980:906–908.

Harris, T. A. *I'm OK, You're OK*. New York: Harper and Row, 1967.

Janov, A. *Primal Scream*. New York: Putnam's, 1970.

——. *The Primal Revolution: Toward a Real World*. New York: Simon & Schuster, 1972.

Jansen, E. *The Therapeutic Community*. London: Croon Helm, 1980.

Lewin, K. K. *Brief Encounters*. St. Louis: Green, 1970. *Lippincott Manual of Nursing Practice*. Philadelphia: J. B. Lippincott, 1982.

Rogers, C. R. *On Becoming a Person*. Boston: Houghton Mifflin, 1960.

Tart, C., and J. Fadiman. "The Case of the Yellow Wheatfield: A Dream Style Exploration of a Broadcast Telepathic Dream." *Psychoanalytic Review*, 61 (1975): 607–618.

Torrey, E. *The Mind Game*. New York: Emerson Hall Publishers, 1972.

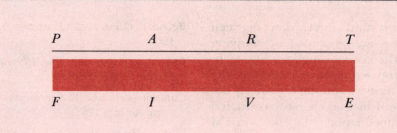

TRENDS AND ISSUES IN PSYCHIATRIC NURSING

23

Mental Health Care Delivery Systems

DEINSTITUTIONALIZATION

MODELS OF COMMUNITY MENTAL HEALTH CARE
Health Maintenance Organizations
Nursing Centers
Programs for Chronically Mentally Ill Clients
Walk-In Services
Vocational Rehabilitation
Care for the Developmentally Disabled

IMPLICATIONS FOR NURSING

Learning Objectives

After reading this chapter, the student should be able to:

1. Analyze the impact of deinstitutionalization process on clients and communities.

2. Describe the effects of deinstitutionalization on nursing roles.

3. Contrast models of mental health care delivery and list advantages and disadvantages of each model.

Overview

Since individuals and families are assumed to have the right to participate in their own health care, who has the responsibility for the health of a community, especially in regard to issues as vast and urgent as those concerning mental health? The question arouses dissension among health professionals and health care consumers. Deinstitutionalization was initiated by groups who were concerned with civil liberties of institutionalized clients on one hand and the costs of institutional care on the other. The result was the formation of an ideology that failed to foresee the effects on clients, families, and communities of speedy deinstitutionalization without intermediate preparation and ongoing follow-up care. A return to institutional care is suggested in quarters where communities struggle with the problems of those persons with mental disorders who receive little or no care.

This chapter examines the movement of deinstitutionalization and its effects on communities. Models for care delivery are presented with emphasis on the role of nursing in the changing environment.

DEINSTITUTIONALIZATION

When state asylums or mental institutions were originally founded, they were perceived by society as humane refuges for persons who could not manage on their own. More recently, society has become disenchanted with such institutions. Basuk and Gerson (1978) wrote that "the reform movement, having seen its original objectives apparently accomplished, had ceased to be a significant influence. By early in this century the network of state mental hospitals, once the proud tribute to an era of reform, had largely turned into a bureaucratic morass within which patients were interned, often neglected, and sometimes abused" (p. 47).

Disenchantment with the system of state mental institutions coincided with the emergence of the community mental health movement. The result was *deinstitutionalization*, or the discharge of large numbers of hospitalized psychiatric clients into the community.

During the 60s and 70s deinstitutionalization was a highly regarded process; more recently questions have been raised as to its ethical and pragmatic value. The force behind deinstitutionalization was the community mental health movement itself. The movement began as a response to poor conditions in state hospitals. The second influence was the technological advances within psychiatry—the open door system, milieu treatment, and the introduction of the phenothiazines. Concurrently the civil liberties movement advocated treatment in less restrictive environments, an end to involuntary commitment and the right to refuse treatment.

The final issue was economic in nature. With the provisions of Medicaid, Medicare, and Supplemental Security Income, states were able to shift funding to federal and local sources. The resulting deinstitutionalization was comprised of two parts: the shift of clients from institutional to community settings and the blockage of new admissions into institutions with the intention of not having anyone else become chronically institutionalized (Talbott 1984).

The process of deinstitutionalization represented a stunning change in the care of persons with psychiatric disorders, who for centuries had received care behind closed doors that were seldom open to public scrutiny. The rationale for the deinstitutionalization movement can be summarized as follows (Minkoff 1987).

■ The nature and character of institutions, especially state hospitals, are untherapeutic and therefore should be eliminated or minimized in the care of persons with chronic mental disorders.

■ If institutions are bad for chronic patients, then deinstitutionalization and a return to community life must be good.

■ Institutionalization promotes an inflexible bureaucracy that enforces regimentation of clients rather than individualized care.

■ Return to the community and freedom of choice are more beneficial than restrictions of institutional life that foster dependency and regression.

Deinstitutionalization is a dramatic example of the impact that one health care trend can have on communities. When the community mental health movement undertook the task of returning large numbers of psychiatric clients to the community, the results were mixed. Many persons who had supported deinstitutionalization in principle became opposed to it in fact when it became evident that discharged psychiatric clients might become their neighbors. Deinstitutionalization aroused fears among established residents, particularly when they were not informed or reassured about the presence of discharged psychiatric clients in their midst. Some people interpreted deinstitutionalization as a legitimate wish by society to free individuals from confinement and restraint; others saw it as neglect and abandonment of chronic psychiatric clients (Coleman, Butcher, and Carson 1984).

In theory, deinstitutionalization seemed workable. It was believed that the staffs of the newly organized community mental health centers would be equal to the task of providing adequate follow-up care and that government costs would be less than were needed to support state mental institutions. But despite the best efforts of many well-intentioned professionals and lay persons, unexpected problems arose. According to one source, "The needs of chronic patients had no place in the original federal mandate for the community mental health center" (Pepper and Ryglewiecz 1982, p. 389).

Lamb (1979) observed that problems arose because there were so many different kinds of chronic mental health patients, and they varied so greatly in the extent to which they could be rehabilitated. Many persons discharged to the community found it difficult, if not impossible, to adjust to community living. Apparently, community mental health centers were better equipped to help clients during acute episodes of psychological impairment than to deal with chronic impairment.

One critic of deinstitutionalization used the example of a young male client who had been admitted to psychiatric hospitals or wards 31 times in eleven years (Smith 1981). Between hospital admissions, the client was arrested more than a dozen times. He was assaulted, beaten, and raped. He made numerous suicide attempts by jumping off bridges, slashing his wrists, and taking drug overdoses. The revolving door through which this client and others move is a consequence of current methods of dealing with the mentally ill. These methods include limited hospitalization and permissive forms of confinement in which clients are relatively free to wander about in the community. According to Smith (1981), the policy of trying to care for mental patients in the community has not meant better or more humane care but only recurrent worry and frustration for clients, their families, and the community. Others have pointed out that perhaps deinstitutionalization and return to the community were oversold and that benefits were lost because of the inability of the mental health care system to adjust to sudden changes in the delivery of mental health services (Bachrach 1980, Estroff 1981, Larson 1983).

Pepper and Ryglewiecz (1982) have expressed concern regarding another population, referred to as the "uninstitutionalized." They describe them as persons who in the past might have been institutionalized for lengthy periods but who now spend just enough time in an institution to be stabilized and are then returned to the same stressful community conditions that they left.

The 1980s were, in effect, the postinstitutional era, during which questions have been raised about the entire deinstitutionalization process. The plight of the homeless, many of whom suffer from mental disabilities, is only one of the community issues for which no easy solutions have been found.

Homeless people make comfortable citizens less comfortable; the sight of bag ladies and of people sleeping on steam grates or bathing in public lavatories has raised a cry for reinstitutionalization. Yet some investigators regard homelessness as a fluctuating stage rather than a permanent condition. Goldfinger and Chavetz (1984) found that only 10 percent of high-service users were homeless on every admission. Appleby and Desai (1987) found that homelessness among the mentally disturbed has risen over the last decade and is much higher than the rate in the general population. However, they describe "residential instability" as the end point of a continuum that is associated with frequent mobility of residence as well as with homelessness.

It really does not matter whether individuals are called "homeless" or "residentially unstable."

Regardless of terminology, they "do not fit in or accommodate easily; instead they drift away from established services. They are not readily motivated to seek other services, in spite of multiple programs; they do not link up with aftercare programs. They do not show up for appointments or schedules on time, nor do they seem to benefit greatly from case management activities. A cycle of avoidance-noncompliance-rejection has been initiated and it is reinforced at intervals in the process" (Appleby and Desai 1987, p. 522).

Deinstitutionalization is a major issue in New York City, as it is in many large urban areas. Concern over the large numbers of homeless people is growing, and this population constitutes an enormous drain on municipal resources. Since the deinstitutionalization process was initiated over two decades ago, the inpatient population of publicly supported mental hospitals in general has been reduced by 70 percent (Lehman, Possidente, and Hawker 1986).

Mental patients are returning to the community with only the most severe aspects of their illness under control (Westermeyer 1982). Such people need a slow, gradual introduction to the activities of daily living and a step-by-step return to independence, living for a time in facilities where food, clothing, and medications are supervised before moving back with their families or finding housing of their own. Yet most patients are not provided with this intermediate stage.

Several problems were highlighted as the result of deinstitutionalization. Funding has not followed clients from hospitals to community settings. There has been no continuum of care that would enable clients to move from the most restrictive to the least restrictive setting in a step-wise, graded way. Adequate housing, job opportunities, and rehabilitation services are in short supply. Family involvement in caring for chronic mental clients has been sporadic and poorly planned (Talbott 1984).

In order for clients to be kept in their homes, several general conditions must be met: (1) the clients must have a home, (2) clients must have persons who are willing to assume responsibility for them and who can provide care, (3) organization and interpersonal relationships in the client household must be such as not to impede or prevent recovery, (4) families must have sufficient understanding of the clients' illness and expected behaviors, (5) the behaviors must be such that the presence of the client in the home does not produce undue hardships, and (6) medical, psychiatric, and nursing services must be accessible to meet the changing needs of the client and the family. Obviously, few clients' situations meet these criteria, yet clients are consistently being released into the community with little attention paid to their ultimate destinations (Moffett 1988).

The policy of deinstitutionalization has placed great demands on families and on the health care system, partly because the benefits of the policy were oversold and the need for support services underestimated. Current demands for a quick return to the former system are equally ill-advised. A number of organizational and mental health care delivery schemes have been proposed to mitigate the impact of deinstitutionalization not only for the homeless but for all clients who lack social supports and prefer a nomadic life to conformity and stability.

MODELS OF COMMUNITY MENTAL HEALTH CARE

In spite of the obvious problems, some investigators support the concept and practice of deinstitutionalization. Braun et al. (1981) concluded that selected clients receiving care in a community in controlled, experimental programs do no worse than hospitalized clients, and in some instances demonstrate outcomes superior to them. Nevertheless, reliable data concerning the outcomes of deinstitutionalization are hard to find, partly because the target population is transient and elusive.

Health Maintenance Organizations

Health maintenance organizations (HMOs) offer an alternative to traditional health insurance coverage and health care delivery in a comprehensive package that is based on cost containment and quality care. Professional roles are defined to maximize the capabilities of all members of the health care team in the delivery of services. These services include 24-hour emergency care, health screening, preventive health care, specialty services, and inpatient care. Because they are committed to intervention on an ambulatory basis, many HMOs are based on a model of primary health care. In this model, physicians and nurses collaborate in the delivery of services and the clients identify a physician and nurse team as their health care providers.

Within the HMO model, the autonomy of each collaborative practice must be supported by management. Usually a nurse-manager serves as a unit manager, administrative problem solver and planner as well as a role model. The nurse manager carries a part-time clinical practice; he or she carries out supervision and policy-making in collaboration with a physician chief, and both report to an associate medical director.

PRINCIPLES FOR SUCCESSFUL DEINSTITUTIONALIZATION PROGRAMS

1. Identify target chronic clients.
2. Integrate treatment and social services through broad-based planning.
3. Offer a full range of services so that community care is not inferior to institutional care.
4. Provide services, including social casework and crisis intervention, on a 24-hour basis.
5. Take cultural and ethnic group attitudes into consideration.
6. Prepare staff members so that they recognize stresses and problems encountered by clients in the community.
7. Maintain a liaison with psychiatric inpatient facilities so that readmission is facilitated when needed.
8. Continue internal evaluation and review processes in order to monitor program effectiveness.
9. Utilize an organizational structure that maintains agency standards but promotes decentralized decision making and staff flexibility.
10. Utilize the following strategies as needed:
    Leveling: Orient staff to prevention and crisis detection measures.
    Forecasting: Plan in advance for peak demands and needs (weather, disaster).
    Rationing: Assign priority to certain clients or situations (suicide, child abuse, violence).
    Buffering: Use community resources to buttress care (inpatient facilities, emergency departments, clinics, home care agencies).

SOURCE: Adapted from Bachrach (1980), Reinke and Greenley (1986).

Although practices are shared between physician and nurse, clients fall into four categories: (1) nurse clients, (2) physician clients, (3) shared clients, and (4) complex clients. Nurse clients have needs that rarely require physician intervention, such as social and environmental needs, education needs, chronic illness problems that require regular follow-up, and management through community resources and episodic illnesses that require lifestyle modification. Physician clients have diagnoses or recurrent symptomatology that go beyond the expertise of nurses. Shared clients require the interventions of both team members, and nurses and physicians may alternate visits or see clients together.

Problem clients have complex medical, social, and psychological needs that are so intertwined that it is necessary to address all areas in order to influence one. As the need arises, primary care nurses in HMOs collaborate with a variety of health care professionals, such as psychologists, nutritionists, and lawyers. When settings for care are changed, as with hospitalization, the team works with hospital personnel for continuity of care (Zander 1980).

Nursing Centers

As changes have occurred in the need for community services, health care options have been devised to provide services without compromising quality of care. One such option is the community based nursing center. Such a center in Brooklyn, New York, was perceived as an alternate "care-sphere" in which clients and significant others could participate with a multidisciplinary health team to achieve mutually determined health-related goals. Three groups provide nursing and health-supporting services through the nursing center: employed and volunteer paraprofessionals, nursing and social work preprofessionals, and professionals from nursing, social work, and other disciplines. A physician, podiatrist, and psychiatrist provide consultation, home visits, and care as the need arises. Direct and indirect care are provided to clients, families, and caregivers, both at the center and in the home. Referrals and networking are crucial components of the system to provide needed services and comprehensive care (Gloss and Fielo 1987).

Another example of nurses meeting community needs is the Wellness Center, described by Utley (1988). It was established to help clients stay well, cope with the developmental tasks of older adulthood, and learn to live with chronic conditions that are often a part of growing older. The Center is cosponsored by the town and the school of nursing of a large university and is staffed by nurse practitioners and university students. Most clients utilizing the center have their own physicians and see the nurses as offering something unique and different. Practitioners listen, offer suggestions for self-care, provide education on diet and exercise, do assessments and act as liaisons with other health care providers.

Programs for Chronically Mentally Ill Clients

Some community mental health programs are working satisfactorily. In Madison, Wisconsin, an integrated program has been developed to stabilize chronic mental clients in the community and to improve their quality of life. Hospital admissions are discouraged through crisis intervention, extensive community support services, work programs, and independent living arrangements. This program was developed by the director of a community mental health center who realized that clients living in the community were becoming disoriented and were being rehospitalized repeatedly.

Introduction of the program followed a three-year systematic investigation of clients in both community and hospitalized settings. One group of clients consisted of 65 persons seeking admittance to a state psychiatric institution for the sixth time. Instead of being admitted, they were treated in the community for twelve months and were followed every four months for two years. A control group of 65 clients similar in age, sex, and illness were hospitalized in the state facility until well enough for discharge. Concerted efforts were made to offer mental health services to the clients treated in the community. Hospital staff members were placed in a house in the community, where they worked in shifts so that someone was always available to the clients. The staff accepted the task of doing whatever seemed necessary to keep the clients in the community. That included negotiating with landlords, shopping with clients in stores near their homes, and teaching them to cook and to take care of their personal needs. At the same time, neighbors and shopkeepers were educated about the actions and behaviors in which the clients sometimes engaged. It was explained to them that dressing and acting differently from the majority is permitted in a free society as long as laws are not broken and no one is victimized.

The results of this experiment were significant. Of the 65 clients in the control group, 58 were rehospitalized within one year. Of the 65 clients in the sample population, only 12 were rehospitalized in the same period. These results led to modification of the mental health care system in Madison. In that city all public funding for mental health is given to community-based programs, which then pay state institutions whenever any of their clients needs hospitalization (Smith 1983).

The Wisconsin community-approach programs were analyzed by Reinke and Greenley (1986), who found three different models of care delivery: The caseworker model; the paraprofessional-extender model; and the team model.

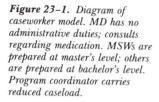

Figure 23–1. Diagram of caseworker model. MD has no administrative duties; consults regarding medication. MSWs are prepared at master's level; others are prepared at bachelor's level. Program coordinator carries reduced caseload.

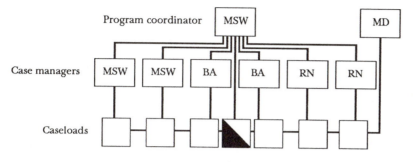

MD has no administrative duties; consults regarding medication. MSWs are prepared at master's level; others are prepared at bachelor's level. Program coordinator carries reduced caseload.

THE CASEWORKER MODEL The caseworker model is shown in Figure 23–1. Here each caseworker is responsible for a specialized caseload. One caseworker handles geriatric clients, one handles young chronic clients, and so forth. Each worker is expected to establish rapport with each client, to meet on a one-to-one basis for support and problem solving, and to lead activity and social skills groups. Clients usually come to the caseworkers' office, but home visiting and outreach are important aspects of the program. Caseload specialization permits a wide range of clients to be served; all caseworkers are expected to do whatever is needed to maintain clients. Because the model does not require much coordination among staff members, most of their time is given to direct care. Disadvantages of the model are (1) the inclination of staff to use rationing and buffering when demands on them are excessive, (2) staff members' heavy responsibility, and (3) their frequent isolation from colleagues. As a result of these disadvantages, adherence to agency standards suffers from deficient monitoring and reinforcement. Investigators have also noted indications of low morale among staff.

PARAPROFESSIONAL-EXTENDER MODEL The prototype of this model studied by Reinke and Greenley and illustrated in Figure 23–2, served a rural, 3000-square-mile area with scant population spread over three Wisconsin counties. Because of a shortage of professional workers, nonprofessional workers are trained and paid to help maintain clients in the community and also to improve community attitudes about mental disorders. The clients served are for the most part cooperative and most of them had been institutionalized for more than 10 years. The program coordinator depends on indigenous residents in each small town, who are designated as "supervisors." Each supervisor has in turn recruited from the area a "worker," who is assigned to one client. Supervisors and workers are part-time

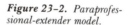

Figure 23–2. Paraprofessional-extender model.

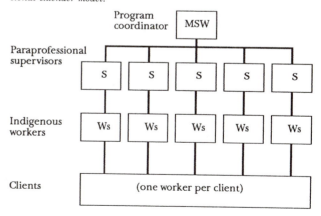

Mental Health Center Professionals

employees who spend most of their paid time working directly with clients, coming to the central office once a month for a staff meeting.

Routine tasks such as helping clients with daily activities are performed by supervisors and workers; the program coordinator makes clinical decisions and provides guidance and reassurance to the supervisors. All clients must be seen regularly by a mental health professional, usually a psychiatrist, at the center. The numbers served by the program are small, averaging about 45.

The program works well for cooperative, stable clients, and the cost is not great. One disadvantage is that there are no facilities for dealing with disruptive, crisis-prone clients, who can only be assessed and transferred elsewhere. Because they work so closely with clients, supervisors and workers come to know their clients well and can increase their involvement when clients are under stress. A genuine disadvantage is the lack of formal communication channels to ensure the flow of adequate information between workers, supervisors, and the program coordinator, even though the availability of the program coordinator is emphasized to the indigenous workers. The monthly meetings are devoted to the personal growth of paraprofessionals by means of the theme that they cannot make "mistakes, only discoveries" (p. 628). The success of programs like this one depends on the interpersonal skills and professional expertise of the program coordinator. Also important is the fact that the clients develop trusting relationships with the paraprofessionals and the health care system they represent.

THE MENTAL HEALTH TEAM MODEL The treatment program studied as a prototype of the mental health team model was a replication of the well-known Program for Assertive Community Treatment, or PACT. The program center serves about 80 persons, who represent the county's most challenging clients and who live in a medium-sized community. The staff operates as a single team out of one large common room. All staff members engage in all types of tasks, except for dispensing medications, which is legally regulated. One-to-one staff-client relationships are discouraged. Medication compliance is stressed, and clients are required to come to the program office daily for medication. This is less demanding than it sounds because clients live nearby. Staff frequently visit in the community to monitor clients and to ease their adjustment to it. Clients' progress is reviewed at daily meetings to keep the entire team informed.

The organizational model reflects a lack of staff specialization (Figure 23–3). This is believed to make all staff members sensitive to crisis prevention and early detection. Considerable control over clients is exercised; staff members are quickly aware of missed appointments, noncompliance with prescribed medication schedules, and clinical changes in general. Lack of specialization by staff means that the workload can be shared more readily. As a result, buffering and rationing are seldom needed. The model is especially effective for resistant, refractory clients, but it necessitates large amounts of internal communication and staff members who accept program norms of tight control and close case management. The program is costly in regard

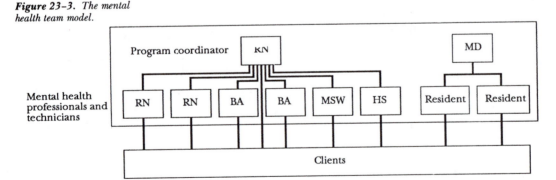

Figure 23–3. *The mental health team model.*

Note: The RN is a program coordinator and supervises mental health technicians. The MD, who is one-third time, functions as a co-equal to the program coordinator and supervises two psychiatric residents on six-month rotations.

to time and energy expended by staff members, yet the team attitude of sharing responsibility for clients preserves staff morale as members go about serving a difficult clientele.

Each organizational model offers advantages and disadvantages. As one compares the three models, two important facts emerge. One is that each model serves different clienteles. The impersonal control that characterizes the PACT approach would not meet the needs of a stable, cooperative group of clients living in sparsely populated rural areas. The paraprofessional-extender model would be inadequate for difficult clients who require more organization and structure. And the caseworker model, while efficient, allocates great individual responsibility to staff members without giving them the opportunity to redistribute caseload pressures. In effect, this would cause morale problems if the clientele comprised only recalcitrant and difficult clients. Thus, each organizational model seems to work equally well if the first criteria are client needs and characteristics.

The second important fact that emerges is that, regardless of the model chosen, nurses play an integral part. Nurses function as administrators in some instances, as coordinators, as case managers, and as purveyors of direct care.

Walk-In Services

Among the many innovations introduced to meet the needs for immediate and comprehensive mental health care are day hospitals, home treatment services, suicide prevention centers, and psychiatric emergency care. One example of an emergency service is the walk-in clinic at Massachusetts Mental Health Center. Without advance categorization-,preselection, or waiting lists, each new client is given an initial interview in which the interviewer tries to focus on the issue which caused the client to seek help. At the end of the interview, a disposition is made to a wide range of services, such as day hospital, inpatient care, long- and short-term outpatient therapy, group therapy, further diagnostic evaluation, or referral to appropriate resources (Shader 1970).

Vocational Rehabilitation

America is a work-oriented society, and disabled clients, particularly psychiatrically disabled clients, have always had problems in obtaining and maintaining employment. Clients with psychiatric disabilities have a poor chance of being vocationally rehabilitated even though their need to work is so great. The mental health care system has never given high priority to the vocational rehabilitation of severely disabled clients. These clients often lose their jobs, not because of their inability to perform job tasks

but because of deficits in interpersonal skills. Clients who lose their jobs often do not possess the skills necessary to obtain new employment. Disincentives to working, such as loss of social security benefits, Medicaid, and food stamps, cannot be ignored.

The goal of psychiatric rehabilitation is to assure that a person who has a psychiatric disability can perform the physical, emotional and intellectual skills needed to live, learn, and work in the community. The process has three phases: diagnosis, planning, and intervention. When a rehabilitation diagnosis is developed, clients must accept their diagnosis; this differs from traditional treatment where clients are rarely helped to understand diagnostic labels. The psychiatric rehabilitation diagnosis assumes that all clients have unique assets and assures that the client's own perspective, assets, and deficits are addressed.

After the diagnostic process, a plan is developed to identify appropriate interventions and specifies how client skills or environmental resources will be developed. Intervention may include direct skill teaching, skill programming, resource development, career counseling, work adjustment training, and career placement (Anthony, Howell, and Danley 1984).

Care for the Developmentally Disabled

As a result of the closing of many large public institutions, admission of persons with mental retardation to these facilities occurs only under exceptional circumstances. The need for health care services for developmentally disabled persons living in the community is pressing. Because of their many handicapping conditions, only a small fraction of these clients can be treated by primary care physicians alone.

A community-hospital-based program of coordinated health services for mentally retarded persons in the community has been developed in Morristown, New Jersey. This center provides comprehensive medical and dental evaluations, primary health services, education, and inpatient medical care; it also coordinates planning for clients being transferred to community living arrangements. The model, utilizing nurse practitioners under the supervision of a developmental pediatrician and internist, provides a regional resource for evaluation, case management, and ongoing medical care.

The capacity to treat adult clients with mental retardation and serious behavioral impairments in the community is problematic. It is an issue that has increasing impact on the current rate of transfer of clients from institutions. In most instances, community mental health systems are ill-prepared to deal

(Text continues on page 639.)

A COMMUNITY-ORIENTED APPROACH IN A NURSING FACILITY FOR THE ELDERLY

A nursing home for the elderly is a community in more than one sense of the word. For elderly persons residing in a nursing home, the daily routine represents a collective lifestyle based on the customs and traditions of the facility. The implications of being placed in a nursing home are painful for family members and for the elderly person. Placement is a statement that the elderly person is no longer considered fully competent. When an elderly person enters a nursing home, personal preferences must be left behind, privacy is invaded, and personal freedom is greatly limited.

A particular nursing home was owned and operated by a corporation that wanted a fair return on its investment but also wished to provide good care. In order to raise the standards of care, a nurse gerontologist was hired. Some budgetary restrictions were placed on the gerontologist, but otherwise she was given a free hand. In accepting the position, the gerontologist made it clear to the owners that certain needs of staff members should be taken into account if the needs of the elderly residents were to be met satisfactorily.

The nurse gerontologist did not immediately make changes but spent a number of weeks studying records and observing the daily routine of the nursing home. Her assessment of the facility, of staff members, and of the residents was comprehensive and detailed.

ASSESSMENT
The Facility

The three-story building was located within city limits but was surrounded by several acres of lawn, shrubbery, and woods. Parking for visitors was adequate. On the first floor was an entrance lobby and two large day rooms that were used for meetings of administrative staff and for occupational therapy. The first floor also had a dining room that was spacious and bright but that provided few amenities. Windows were curtainless, table covers were dark brown vinyl, and eating utensils were plastic.

The nursing home had a capacity of 100 residents. Some of the rooms were private and had one occupant; other rooms were shared by two occupants. Each room had its own toilet and bath.

The second floor had a room that opened onto an open deck or porch with a low, ornamental railing. The room adjoining the deck was called the solarium. Although residents had access to the solarium, the

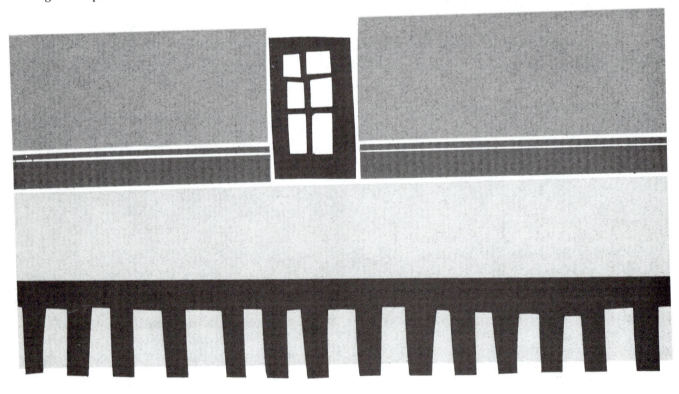

doors to the deck were locked. Because the railing was low, staff members were afraid to allow residents to use the deck even in the best of weather.

The Staff

The nursing home complied with legal standards that required a ratio of registered nurses to be employed on all three shifts. Most of the needs of the residents were met by health aides with varying amounts of preparation. The health aides, dietary staff, and other paraprofessionals were paid minimum wage rates, with very few exceptions.

Turnover rate among employees was very high, even for registered nurses, who were paid more than other employees. Registered nurses were employed in supervisory capacities and did little bedside nursing. Except for giving medication and talking occasionally with family members, record keeping occupied most of their time.

The Residents

The gerontologist realized that the elderly, as a group, are subject to distress related to acute and chronic illnesses, loss of loved ones, decreased physical strength, social isolation, financial reverses, and low self-esteem. She noted that the needs of the elderly clients were not being fully met in the nursing home. Among the needs she identifed were:

Care and attention based on individual needs

Respect from care providers

Comfortable sleeping quarters with some privacy

Nutritious, balanced, attractive meals

Single-purpose day rooms for occupational activities/diversional activities, reading or letter writing, and conversation or TV watching

Regular, consistent medical care, including foot care, eye care, and dental care

Maintenance of normal motion and activity to the fullest possible extent

PLANNING

Some obvious changes could be made in the facility without incurring great expense. One of the two large day rooms, used infrequently for administrative meetings, could be divided in two, creating a room that could be used by small groups of residents for reading, playing cards, or writing letters. The dining room could be brightened by adding colorful table coverings and bouquets of artificial flowers. Replacing plastic eating utensils with stainless steel ones would enable the residents to cut their own meat instead of asking an aide for help.

The gerontologist strongly recommended that a protective railing be installed around the deck so that residents could sit outside in good weather. One or two aides could be assigned to remain in the deck area while it was being occupied by the residents.

Many of the practices that had developed in the nursing home were objectionable to the nurse gerontologist. Some of the problems were attributable to underpaid staff aides who had little or no understanding of the special needs of the elderly. An obvious deficiency was the impatience staff members showed with the slow movements of elderly residents. In

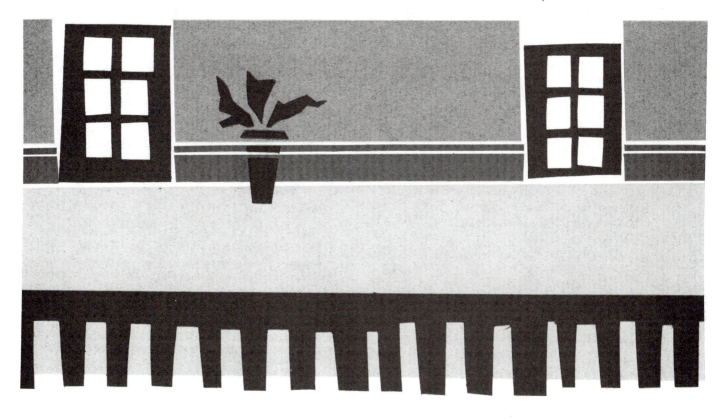

helping clients get dressed, staff members did not take the time to fasten garments properly or comb hair attractively. The result was that the residents looked clean but unkempt, except when family members assumed some of the grooming tasks. Another problem was that residents who were not ambulatory were rarely taken from their rooms, even though their beds were modern, on wheels, and easily moved.

Perhaps the most disconcerting feature of the nursing home routine was the excessive use of restraints. Residents who were even slightly confused were restrained in bed or, if they were ambulatory, in a chair. The reason given was fear of the staff that confused residents might fall or wander into neighboring rooms. Even in the early weeks of observation and assessment, the gerontologist could see the deterioration of restrained residents, who received little sensory input, whose limbs stiffened from lack of use, and who became incontinent because the staff was inattentive to their requests to be taken to the bathroom.

The gerontologist saw no evidence of mistreatment of the residents, but there were signs of thoughtlessness. In general, the routine followed in the nursing home seemed to encourage regression in the residents and indifference in staff members.

IMPLEMENTATION

In presenting recommendations to administrative staff, the gerontologist shared her observations concerning the facility, the staff, and the residents. The following recommendations were presented, voted upon, and implemented by the corporation:

The Facility

Purchase new table covers and stainless steel eating utensils for the dining room. Decorate the room for various holidays.

Divide the day room area into three rather than two rooms.

Provide a safety railing for the deck; assign staff members to supervise the area; transport bedridden residents to the deck in good weather.

Construct safety railings in all corridors to facilitate movement of ambulatory residents.

Place large signs with the occupant's name on the doors of bedrooms.

The Staff

Offer an intensive inservice and orientation program for staff members to help them understand the needs of the elderly.

Arrange regular meetings between administrators and all staff members in order to share ideas and information.

Establish a career ladder within the facility so that staff performing well or staff with seniority can be recognized. Recognition could be in the form of merit increases, commendations, and job titles that indicate higher status.

Develop routine assignments for each shift so that every staff member is aware of specific responsibilities to the residents.

Adopt a system of team nursing so that the residents are given care each day by the same person or group of persons.

The Residents

Residents should be addressed by their proper surnames and titles, such as *Mr.*, *Mrs.*, or *Miss*, except in unusual circumstances.

Current visiting hours (1 to 3 P.M. and 7 to 8 P.M.) restrict family visits. Therefore, new visiting hours should be arranged, lasting from 10 A.M. to 8 P.M.

Family members should be permitted to join residents for meals by paying a nominal sum.

Registered nurses working in supervisory roles should make rounds three times in each eight-hour shift to check the appearance, general condition, and comfort level of each resident.

An ombudsman, or "troubleshooter," should be available to clients and families, functioning as a liaison between care providers and care consumers.

Confused residents who are ambulatory should be restrained as little as possible. When restraints are considered necessary, the resident is to be restrained for no more than 30 minutes without being freed from restraints in order to eat, walk, or go to the bathroom with the help of a staff member.

A system of 15-minute rounds should be established, and staff members should be assigned to make rounds for an hour at a time. When a second staff member takes over the assignment, an accounting of the whereabouts of all residents should be given by the person previously assigned rounds. This method of professional watchfulness would eliminate much of the need for physical restraints.

EVALUATION

The recommendations of the gerontologist required some additional expenditure of funds but were within the allocation that had been agreed to by the corporation. In objective measures, the following outcomes were attributed to the recommendations of the nurse gerontologist:

■ Decreased staff turnover due to greater involvement and recognition

■ Greater satisfaction expressed by family members

- Measurable improvement in the mobility of residents
- Reduced self-care deficits in residents
- Enhanced reputation of the nursing home in the area

- Greater willingness of family and physicians to use the facility for placement purposes
- Fewer indices of depression, regression, and apathy of residents

with a population of "dual diagnosis" clients—those with both mental retardation and mental illness (Ziring et al. 1988).

Implications for Nursing

Mental health care delivery has undergone major changes in the past decades. Nurses should examine their own beliefs as to society's responsibility to the mentally ill and in particular, the role of the nurse in providing such care. The chronically mentally ill in the community are vulnerable individuals in need of a variety of services that nurses can give. Nursing has subscribed to a "care versus cure" model in identifying its area of expertise. The reality for many of the mentally ill is that no cure is available. Nursing must focus on making the lives of the chronically mentally ill as pleasant and productive as possible within the limits of current reality.

Nurses must assume a strong advocacy position for these clients. Although the mass exodus of long-term psychiatric clients from institutions assumes they will be cared for by community mental health programs, most of these programs exclude the long-term clients. The nursing profession must become more involved in responding to the needs of this neglected population.

SUMMARY

The Community Mental Health Center legislation passed by Congress in 1963 supported mental health centers in all 50 states and was an enabling force in the deinstitutionalization process that returned thousands of mental patients to the community. This process represented a shift in the locus of care for the mentally ill from long-term hospitalization to flexible, community-based care. Deinstitutionalization was implemented in the hope of achieving the following goals:

- To save clients from the debilitating effects of lengthy, restrictive periods of hospitalization.
- To return the client to home and community life as soon as possible after hospitalization.
- To maintain the client in the community for as long as possible thereafter.

Deinstitutionalization remains a controversial issue with its share of supporters and critics. Many communities have found municipal resources such as shelters drained by large numbers of discharged mental patients living with little supervision or follow-up care. On the other hand, experimental programs that are based on proven principles have shown that deinstitutionalization can work in practice as well as in theory. Until now, little systematic research has been directed to the study of deinstitutionalization, and evaluations have been largely subjective (Altman 1984).

A variety of models for delivery of mental health care in communities have been devised. Nursing plays a crucial role in the delivery of services to the chronically mentally ill and developmentally disabled clients. Continued advocacy for these clients is needed.

Review Questions

1. What sectors are involved in the delivery of community health care?
2. Identify three causes for the failure of deinstitutionalization in some communities.
3. What considerations are important in transferring clients from institutional to community care?
4. Describe the basic features of mental health care delivery models.
5. Delineate your perception of the role of nursing in providing care to the chronically mentally ill.

Suggested Annotated Readings

Ehrenreich, J. and B. *The American Health Empire: Power, Profits and Politics*. New York: Vintage Books, 1971.

This book is the collective product of the staff of the Health Policy Advisory Center who analyzed the politics of a city's health system. A need for democratic restructuring of American institutions is explored with the premise that health care is not a priority in America.

Mirabi, M. *The Chronically Mentally Ill Research and Services*. New York: Spectrum Pub. Inc., 1984.

This book focuses on emerging trends and developments in the field of chronic mental illness and offers comprehensive coverage of methods of diagnosis, evaluation, and treatment of this population. Mirabi discusses current concepts in diagnosis and treatment of schizophrenia, depression, chronic alcoholism, mental retardation, and mental illness relating to aging.

Rothman, T. *Changing Patterns in Psychiatric Care*. New York: Crown Pub. Inc., 1970.

This volume traces the historic background of psychiatric therapies and presents a series of contributions of current happenings in psychiatric care. Hospitals in transition, community mental health programs, and walk-in services are described. A series of research studies with emphasis on pharmacological treatments are presented.

References

Altman, L. E. "New Focus on World Health." *The New York Times* (January 17, 1984).

Anthony, W., J. Howell, and K. Danley. "Vocational Rehabilitation of the Psychiatrically Disabled." In *The Chronically Mentally Ill: Research and Services*, M. Mirabi, ed. New York: Spectrum Publishers, 1984.

Appleby, L., and P. Desai. "Residential Instability: A Perspective on System Imbalance." *American Journal of Orthopsychiatry* 57, no. 4 (October 1987):515–523.

Bachrach, L. L. "Overview, Model Programs for Chronic Patients." *American Journal of Psychiatry* 132 (1980): 1023–1031.

Basuk, E. L., and S. Gersons. "Deinstitutionalization and Mental Health Services." *Scientific American* 238, no. 2 (1978):46–53.

Braun, P., G. Kochansky, R. Shapiro, S. Greenberg, J. E. Gudeman, S. Johnson, and M. Shore. "Overview: Deinstitutionalization of Psychiatric Patients: Critical Review of Outcome Studies." *American Journal of Psychiatry* 138 (1981):736–749.

Coleman, J. C., J. N. Butcher, and R. C. Carson. *Abnormal Psychology and Modern Life*. Glenview, Illinois: Scott, Foresman, 1984.

Estroff, S. *Making It Crazy*. Berkeley: University of California Press, 1981.

Gloss, E., and S. Fielo. "The Nursing Center: An Alternative for Health Care Delivery." *Family and Community Health* 10 (1987):49–58.

Goldfinger, S., and L. Chavetz. "Developing a Better Service Delivery System for the Homeless Mentally Ill." In *The Homeless Mentally Ill*, H. R. Lamb, ed. Washington, D.C.: American Psychiatric Association, 1984.

Lamb, H. R. "Roots of Neglect in the Long-Term Mentally Ill." *Psychiatry* 42 (1979):201–207.

Larson, R. "The Deinstitutionalized Environment: A Case for Better Planning." *ORB* 3 (May 1983):126–130.

Lehman, A. F., S. Possidente, and F. Hawker. "The Quality of Life of Chronic Patients in a State Hospital and in Community Residences." *Hospital and Community Psychiatry* 37, no. 9 (September 1986):901–907.

Minkoff, K. "Beyond Deinstitutionalization: A New Ideology for the Post-institutional Era." *Hospital and Community Psychiatry* 38, no. 9 (September 1987):945–950.

Moffett, M. J. "Evaluation of Psychiatric Community Care." *Journal of Psychosocial Nursing* 26 (1988):17–20.

Pepper, B., and H. Ryglewiecz. "Testimony for the Neglected: The Mentally Ill in the Post-deinstitutionalized Age." *American Journal of Orthopsychiatry* 52 (1982): 388–392.

Reinke, B., and J. R. Greenley. "Organizational Analysis of Three Community Support Programs." *Hospital and Community Psychiatry* 37, no. 6 (June 1986):624–629.

Shader, R. "The Walk-In Service: An Experience in Community Care." In *Changing Patterns in Psychiatric Care*, T. Rothman, ed. New York: Crown Publishers, 1970.

Smith, S. "Arrests, Suicide Tries, and a Frustrated Family." *Times Union*. Rochester, New York (April 28, 1981).

——. "How an Idea Works in Wisconsin." *Times Union*. Rochester, New York (November 7, 1983).

Talbott, J. A. "The Chronic Mental Patient: A National Perspective." In *The Chronically Mentally Ill Research and Services*, M. Mirabi, ed. New York: Spectrum Publishers, 1984.

Utley, Q., J. Hawkins, J. Ignou, and E. Johnson. "Giving and Getting Support at the Wellness Center." *Journal of Gerontological Nursing* 14 (1988):23–25.

Westermeyer, J. "Bag Ladies in Isolated Cultures, Too." *Behavior Today* 13, no. 21 (1982):1–2.

Zander, K. S. *Primary Nursing*. Germantown, Maryland: Aspen Systems Corporation, 1980.

Ziring, P., T. Kastner, D. Friedman, W. Pond, M. Barnell, E. Sonnenberg, and K. Strassburger. "Provisions of Health Care for Persons with Developmental Disabilities Living in the Community." *Journal of the American Medical Association* 260 (1988): 1439–1443.

24

Case Management, Liaison, and Consultation

Learning Objectives

After studying this chapter, the student will be able to:

1. Compare and contrast the functions of nurses as case managers in team and in primary nursing.

2. Describe the process of consultation and its implications.

3. Discuss collaboration among nurses, and between nurses and other health professionals as a way of increasing overall effectiveness of case management.

4. Describe the implications of the referral process.

Overview

The delivery and management of nursing care in mental health settings has experienced several changes throughout this century. Different models of nursing care delivery have been implemented at various times, such as the functional and team models. Currently, the primary care model is popular because of its value in comprehensive care planning and its accountability.

Along with these changes, the delivery of health care in general has become interdisciplinary and has expanded to include several types of client services. The role of the psychiatric nurse in the health care setting has expanded to include liaison and consultation work, both in the mental health arena and in the psychiatric and medical-surgical settings.

This chapter describes types of nursing care delivery models and the structure of the health care team, with emphasis on the necessity of collaboration and coordination for health care. The expanded role of the psychiatric nurse in the consultation and liaison process and the use of referral systems are also discussed.

HEALTH CARE TEAM STRUCTURE

Three types of teams are commonly used to deliver health care. A *unidisciplinary* team is composed of members of the same discipline, as exemplified by team nursing. A *multidisciplinary* team is composed of members of different disciplines who each provide discipline-specific services to the same client, but with no formal arrangement for interaction between the members; no one is required to give up power, authority, or territory. An *interdisciplinary* team is made up of members from different disciplines all involved in a formal team arrangement, which facilitates opportunities for educational interchange and delivery of service. Challela (1979) describes an interdisciplinary health team as one in which responsibility for assessment, decision making, delivery of services, and evaluation is shared among the health professionals on the team.

The role of the leader is to help team members resolve disagreements and conflicts related to planning and providing care. The leader's role is also to foster effectiveness of the team as a mechanism of achieving optimal client care (Crawshaw and Key 1961). Regardless of which team member assumes the official leadership role, each discipline retains specific responsibilities to the client based on his or her particular educational and clinical expertise.

The role of the nurse as an interdisciplinary team member differs from the role of the nurse as a person charged with responsibility for total client care. As an effective team member, the nurse is guided by the need to understand and respect the contributions and expertise of others on the team (Mereness 1951). Identifying with the team as a whole minimizes the problems of hierarchy, status, and communication (Crawshaw and Key 1961). Benfer (1980) emphasized that each team member should display communication skills along with maturity, trust, professional confidence, and problem-solving ability. Each team member collects relevant information that is then combined with information obtained by other team members in order to form a data base that assures development of a comprehensive care plan.

Challela (1979) raised four issues that the nurse must acknowledge and deal with as a member of an interdisciplinary team: (1) defining the nursing role to achieve role identity, (2) recognizing the need for overlap between disciplines, (3) knowing what other disciplines can do, and (4) developing influence and sharing in the power distribution. Other issues for consideration include communication problems among team members and personal characteristics of team members as a potential barrier to effective functioning of the team.

Nursing care is usually delivered within an interdisciplinary context. However, the way in which care is given can vary from setting to setting, depending on the model of nursing care delivery being utilized.

MODELS OF NURSING CARE DELIVERY

Historically, four major models of nursing care delivery have been identified and utilized: the case method, functional nursing, team nursing, and primary nursing. The *case method* was the earliest type used by nurses. In this model, one nurse planned and administered total care for one client for the entire time the nurse was on duty. The case method is still used in acute care settings, such as intensive care units, that demand continuity of care and that involve complex nursing care. However, private duty nursing in the home, hospital, or other care facility such as a nursing home is rarely used in our present-day system of health care delivery (Langford 1981).

Functional nursing evolved from the industrial concepts of division of labor that were popular from the 1920s through the 1940s. The result was a fragmentation of nursing care, and the client had no identified nurse to provide care for the whole person. Some aspects of functional nursing, such as assigning a medication nurse to pass all medications on one unit for each shift, are still used in some nursing care settings, but otherwise this model is rarely used.

Team nursing began in the post-World War II years, when hospitals were flooded with technical health care workers, such as nurse's aides and vocational nurses, and there was a lack of registered nurses. Team nursing is based on a hierarchical structure, with the most prepared caregiver, the registered nurse, placed in the role of team leader. In this model, team members are assigned groups of clients and tasks according to their ability and to the acuteness of client needs, while the team leader is responsible for guiding and supervising all aspects of nursing care provided to that particular client group. Clients are assigned to one nursing team for the duration of their hospital stay, and the same team members are responsible for their care. A major disadvantage of team nursing is that the supervisory functions of the team leader detract from the time spent delivering care; consequently, the person best prepared to provide direct care, the nurse team leader, is least available to do so.

The most recently developed model of nursing care delivery is *primary nursing*, in which one nurse is assigned a client for the duration of the client's hospitalization. This model is similar to the case method in the one-to-one aspect, but rather than being responsible for only an 8-hour shift, in primary nursing the nurse's responsibility extends for 24 hours a day, every day, throughout the client's hospitalization. The primary nurse assesses the total client needs and collaborates with the client and other health care providers in developing a comprehensive care plan. A secondary nurse (also called an associate nurse) is assigned to the client when the primary nurse is not on duty. However, the primary nurse retains responsibility and may even be called at home during off-duty hours to make a decision regarding the client's nursing care. The requirements of autonomy, authority, and accountability that characterize primary nursing are thus ensured (Marram, Schlegel, and Bevis 1974). In this model, head nurses and supervisors function as nursing care consultants and do not interfere with the primary nurse's responsibilities.

The function of nurses as case managers in team nursing and in primary nursing merit discussion. *Case management* refers to the nurse's responsibility for delivery of comprehensive nursing care to more than one client. Benfer (1980) outlined six basic case management functions of the psychiatric nurse:

1. Collecting data and making a nursing assessment
2. Implementing planned interventions
3. Meeting client needs through environmental change
4. Meeting client needs through health teaching
5. Coordinating client activities to maximize therapeutic effects
6. Predicting and altering maladaptive behaviors

The next two sections describe how these functions are performed in both team and primary nursing.

Team Nursing in Mental Health Settings

The first and most basic nursing function is obtaining a client history and making a nursing assessment. For the assessment to be adequate, inclusion of family issues is essential. A comprehensive assessment culminates in conceptualization of an appropriate nursing diagnosis and development of a care plan that can be implemented, documented, and evaluated. In team nursing the team leader is responsible for seeing that all clients are the focus of ongoing nursing assessment and planning. If the team includes paraprofessional mental health aides, the team leader will delegate the responsibility for assessment and planning to other nurses on the team or will personally assume these tasks. When the health team approach is used, nurses may be writing nursing diagnoses and developing care plans on clients for whom they are not primary caregivers.

The second basic function is implementing planned interventions, evaluating effects, and documenting client responses to the interventions used. In team nursing, individual nurses carry out this function on their assigned shift only and do not maintain this responsibility 24 hours a day as primary nurses do. Consistency in implementing the care plan depends on how clearly specific nursing approaches are described in the care plan and are understood by all team members. Evaluation of outcomes depends greatly on the quality of documentation in the client's nursing record. Continuity of care and consistency among health team members are necessary for successful outcomes in team nursing. Since the case manager in team nursing may not have responsibility for providing direct client care on a continuing basis, outcomes may be unclear unless documentation of interventions and clients' responses are provided for all team members.

The third basic function is determining how the needs of the client can be met within the surrounding milieu. This requires maintenance of a therapeutic environment in which clients are helped to achieve adaptive interpersonal coping skills by means of structured and unstructured group and individual transactions. An aspect of this function includes the impact of significant events in the milieu, such as seclusion of an assaultive client. As an effective case manager, the team nurse will explore the client's response to the seclusion and devise strategies for encouraging ventilation of feelings. In team nursing, the case manager is responsible for planning strategies that help the client cope with the experience of seclusion.

The fourth function is client teaching, including such topics as communication skills, stress management, and the rationale for the use of psychotropic medications. Client education should not be delegated to one discipline alone but should be assigned to all caregivers involved with the client's plan of care. Nurses are frequently in the ideal position to act as coordinators of the client's education.

The fifth function is coordination of client activities. The nursing team conference is a useful means of evaluating the client's behavior in the milieu. Interdisciplinary conferences provide data regarding the patient's behavior in off-unit activities.

The team leader integrates data obtained from all caregivers into the care plan and arranges conferences to discuss needed revisions.

The sixth function is prediction and prevention of maladaptive client behavior. This function is particularly important when the client has a history of suicidal or homicidal behavior. The team nurse will need to be cognizant of such impulses and alert for patterns of behavior that indicate beginning loss of control. Knowledge of risk factors predictive of suicidal and homicidal behavior is necessary in order for the team nurse to identify early warning signs and to share observations with other team members.

For all six nursing functions, there is sharing of responsibility and delegation of tasks among nursing team members. The team leader is expected to be able to guide and supervise the team members in executing all these functions for every client assigned to the team. Ciske's (1974) observation that shared responsibility and accountability often results in *no* responsibility or accountability is a caution worthy of consideration. The team leader is ultimately responsible for ensuring that the needs of all clients are met to the utmost possible extent.

Primary Nursing in Mental Health Settings

Primary nursing in mental health settings also entails Benfer's six functions. Since the first function is obtaining a client history and making a nursing assessment, the primary nurse initiates an admission history, including a family assessment, and writes the initial nursing diagnosis. The primary nurse makes ongoing nursing assessments during each nurse-client interaction and revises the nursing diagnoses if indicated. The primary nurse is accountable for the development and documentation of a care plan designed to meet the client's needs over a 24-hour time frame. The primary nurse develops this plan collaboratively with the client.

The second function is implementing planned interventions, assessing the effects of interventions, and documenting client behavior. The primary nurse implements the care plan when on duty and maintains communication with the secondary nurse to assure continuity of care when off duty. The primary nurse documents the specific interventions used and describes the client's behavioral response. During off-duty hours, the primary nurse is available by telephone to discuss questions about implementation of the plan with secondary nursing staff. Specific aspects of nursing implementation may be delegated to the secondary nurse.

The third function is determining how to meet the needs of the client within the milieu. The primary nurse needs to analyze the environment and its potential supports and stressors in terms of the client's specific needs. This analysis includes examination of the milieu during all three shifts. For example, if a client goal is to increase skill in initiating conversation in groups, the primary nurse may assign the client the task of initiating at least one topic during each evening community meeting. If the primary nurse works days, he or she may have the secondary nurse on evening duty follow up with the client after the community meeting to provide him with feedback.

Regarding the fourth function, the primary nurse is responsible for assessing the client's learning needs and for developing a comprehensive teaching plan to meet these needs from admission until discharge. This includes teaching the client and the family adaptive coping mechanisms to facilitate the client's reentry to family and community. The primary nurse should monitor and evaluate the client's responses to the teaching interventions and revise approaches as needed.

The fifth function, coordinating client activities, is enhanced by use of interdisciplinary conferences. The primary nurse may function as leader of such conferences or may develop a collegial relationship with the psychiatrist to present client data and recommendations for care from their respective viewpoints. Coordination includes designing strategies to involve the family in the client's care. The interdisciplinary conference is an appropriate time to identify the collaborative functions of the various disciplines in carrying out this important aspect of care. For example, the primary nurse, the psychiatrist, and the social worker may all decide to participate jointly in one or more family meetings. To ensure comprehensive and ongoing coordination of care, the primary nurse may plan a home visit before or after discharge.

Primary nursing facilitates implementation of the sixth function of the psychiatric nurse, the prediction of behavior and prevention of problems. Because the primary nurse is familiar with the client's past behavior and because the client's history includes documentation of known precipitants of the current hospitalization, the primary nurse is in a position to watch for early signs of potential problems. Included in the data are identification of the client's usual coping mechanisms, both adaptive and maladaptive, in response to stressors. With this data base, the primary nurse is able to identify and describe high-risk situations that the client may encounter during hospitalization and to collaborate with interdisciplinary team members to develop contingency plans to be implemented as needed. Again, the 24-hour availability of the primary nurse to consult with secondary nurses about potential behavioral problems lessens the risk of clients' engaging in behavior destructive to themselves or others.

Table 24–1 summarizes the similarities and differences between nursing functions within the two delivery systems, team nursing and primary nursing.

The Growth of Primary Nursing

Nursing literature shows that primary nursing effects positive client outcomes. Researchers have found that primary nursing is a significant agent of change whereby the system is not an end in itself but rather a very effective means of achieving the end desired by all nurses—a model of professional nursing practice.

Zander (1985) has described the agenda and the challenge for the second generation of primary nursing. First generation practitioners of primary nursing helped define the concepts and correct misinterpretations related to the system. Primary nursing distinguishes between task responsibility and case-outcome accountability. The worth of the nurses is determined, not by their efforts, but by the clients' achievements.

Table 24–1. Nursing Functions in Team and Primary Nursing

Function	Team Nursing	Primary Nursing
Benfer's basic functions		
1. Collecting data and making assessments	Assigned team nurse is responsible for 8-hour shift assessment. Team leader is responsible if team member not qualified.	Nurse is responsible for admission history and for ongoing assessment.
2. Implementing planned interventions	Team member or team leader initiates individual written care plan.	Nurse is responsible for written nursing care plan to cover client needs on 24-hour basis; client is involved in planning.
	Team member or team leader implements plan.	Nurse may implement plan or delegate.
	Team leader is responsible for 8-hour shift.	Nurse is available to guide decisions regarding nursing care on a 24-hour basis.
	Team nurse is responsible for documentation of client behavior and nursing interventions.	Nurse is responsible for documentation of client behavior and nursing interventions.
3. Meeting clients' needs in the environment	Team maximizes use of therapeutic milieu.	Nurse analyses therapeutic benefits available in total milieu and communicates this to other nurses.
	Each team member is responsible for 8-hour shift.	Nurse is responsible for 24-hour care plan.
4. Client teaching	Team member or team leader assesses learning needs and develops, implements, and evaluates teaching plans.	Nurse is responsible for assessment of learning needs and for developing, implementing, and revising teaching plans.
5. Coordinating client activities	Each member is responsible for 8-hour shift.	Nurse considers client needs over 24-hour time frame, every day.
	Team members participate in nursing team conference; team leader leads nursing team conference.	Nurse participates in and leads client-centered nursing conference.
	Team member or team leader collaborates with other disciplines to provide family-focused nursing care.	Nurse collaborates with other disciplines to provide family-focused care.
6. Predicting and preventing maladaptive behaviors	Members identify and document adaptive and maladaptive behavioral responses to stressors observed during 8-hour shift.	Nurse documents client's usual adaptive and maladaptive responses to stressors, identifies high-risk situations client may encounter during any 24-hour period, and collaborates with team members to develop contingency plan.
Quality of care functions		
1 Accountability	Team leader is accountable for team members' nursing care.	Nurse is accountable for all aspects of nursing care.
2. Continuity of care	Not consistent; team stable but leaders may vary.	Continuity is built into delivery system; same primary or secondary nurse is assigned to client throughout hospital stay.
3. Communication lines	Vertical, hierarchical.	Triangular, collaborative.

Primary nursing does not require an all-RN staff but does demand enough RNs to divide the census into manageable caseloads. Primary nursing highlights the differences between RN's and LPN's and is an opportunity to redefine a department's level of practice.

Twenty-four-hour accountability does not mean 24-hour availability; it is not in-the-home private duty nursing. Continued availability is unmanageable for staff and the individual's work life and is also inappropriate. Nurses practicing primary nursing have the luxury of working in ready-made "group practices." With good management, there is no need for the primary nurses to be available for longer than their normally scheduled hours.

Primary nurses can be individually accountable yet share the care with other nursing personnel. Shared care does not mean returning to team nursing. Tasks and functions are carried out by any capable individuals but the accountability for the outcomes of that care rest with the primary nurses. Caregivers can be interchangeable but primary nurses cannot.

Physicians accept primary nursing when they realize that clients are getting the same or better level of care and they receive better information about their clients when they request it.

Primary nursing can also be adapted to long-term care. Since extended-care clients stay for long periods of time, the primary nursing assignments need to be time-limited (three to six months) to allow nurses to change assignments if they so desire. The utilization of primary nursing can be helpful with confused elderly clients because it provides a continuous person in the environment that clients can relate to. Institutions that have nursing assistants have found that, if properly trained, these individuals can be used effectively as associate caregivers. The technical skills that a nursing assistant can perform can be delegated as a 24-hour responsibility for those skills. The nursing assistants then know that they have 24-hour accountability for that aspect of the clients' care (Jones 1986).

There is a place for every type of staff member in the primary nursing system. Primary nursing is an opportunity to revitalize and redefine nursing practice.

CONSULTATION AND LIAISON WORK

According to Caplan (1970), *consultation* is a process of interaction between two professionals: the *consultant*, who is a specialist, and the *consultee*, who seeks the consultant's help in regard to a current work problem. The consultee accepts the fact that the work problem falls within the consultant's area of specialized competence and solicits assistance. In Caplan's model, the consultant accepts no direct responsibility for implementing remedial action for the client, and professional responsibility for the client remains with the consultee. The consultee is free to accept or reject all or part of the consultant's advice. In addition to helping the consultee with the work problem, the consultant endeavors to add to the consultee's knowledge and to decrease areas of misunderstanding so that in the future the consultee will be able to cope independently with similar problems.

According to Lipowski (1974), *liaison* involves a linking of groups for the purpose of effective collaboration. The groups are usually a liaison team (consisting of one or more psychiatrists, a psychologist, a psychiatric nurse, and a psychiatric social worker) and a health care team on a general hospital unit. The teaching of mental health concepts and care to the medical and surgical staff on general hospital units is an accepted component of liaison work (Kimball 1979, Pasnau 1982). A major goal of liaison work is to enhance the quality of psychological care provided to the medically ill (Strain and Grossman 1975).

Consultation and liaison in nursing have developed in parallel with consultation and liaison in psychiatry. Consultation in nursing was first reported in the literature by Johnson (1963), who described a cross-service consultation program developed at Duke University in response to nursing requests for assistance on complex client care problems. The nursing consultants were experienced head nurses, nursing supervisors, and instructors and included a psychiatric nurse who had primary responsibility on a psychiatric unit but could be called to consult on medical/surgical units. The expectation was that the consultants would not work directly with clients; their focus was to assist the nursing staff (consultees) to solve problems and to become sensitive to the psychological needs of clients and the influence these needs played in the client's response to altered health states (Nelson and Schilke 1976). As the consultant role evolved, the model of an ongoing relationship between the consultant and the consultee became established, and this model was eventually labeled *psychiatric liaison nursing*.

Davis (1983) has compared consultation and liaison nursing models on three parameters: type of contact, determination of concerns, and responsibility for the care of clients (see Figure 24–1). In the consultation model, contact between consultant and consultee is episodic, sporadic, formal, and initiated by the consultee. The consultant has brief

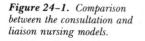

Figure 24–1. *Comparison between the consultation and liaison nursing models.*

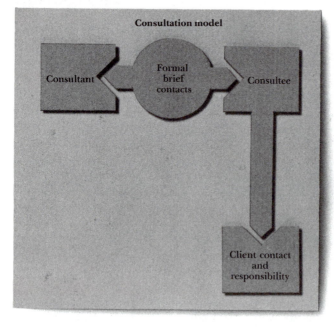

contacts with the consultee, provides suggestions, and leaves the setting. In the liaison model, contact is ongoing, is informal, and may be initiated by either consultee or consultant. The liaison nurse becomes part of the health team and attends staff rounds and conferences. Whereas the consultee determines the focus for consultation work, in the liaison model the consultant may raise issues related to the care of clients or identify clients who need intervention. Finally, in the consultation model responsibility for the care of clients remains largely with the consultee, whereas in the liaison model the consultant may collaborate with the consultee throughout the process and therefore share responsibility to some extent.

Types of Mental Health Consultation

Caplan (1970) described four types of consultation: client-centered case consultation, consultee-centered case consultation, program-centered administrative consultation, and consultee-centered administrative consultation.

Client-centered case consultation, also called direct consultation, focuses on the client's immediate problem. The primary goal is to communicate to the consultee how the client can be helped. A secondary goal is to enhance the nurse's ability to apply the same concepts to similar problems in the future. *Consultee-centered case consultation*, also called indirect consultation, focuses on trying to understand the nature of the nurse's (consultee's) diffi-

culty in working with a client, and the goal is to improve the consultee's functioning.

A consultant is not an all-knowing expert, capable of solving all problems, but is a specialist who has advanced knowledge and a broad range of skills in a clinical specialty area. The consultant develops collaborative approaches to problem solving.

Program-centered administrative consultation focuses on development of a program for nursing staff. An example of this type of consultation is teaching assertiveness skills to a group of nurses as a way of improving interdisciplinary communication. The program could be run as a series of hour-long workshops or as a day-long conference. *Consultee-centered administrative consultation* focuses on helping nurses with administrative or organizational structure, such as consulting to a group of head nurses who will be guiding their staff in changing from team to primary nursing.

Implementation of Consultation and Liaison Work

Lewis and Levy (1982) have delineated five basic steps in the consultation process as applied to psychiatric liaison nurses: (1) request consultation, (2) define the problem, (3) diagnose the consultation issues, (4) make recommendations, and (5) develop the interventions and evaluate. These steps are the same whether the setting is a general hospital unit or a community setting such as a school or visiting nurse service.

THE GOALS OF CONSULTATION

Lewis and Levy (1982) have identified the goals of case consultation in psychiatric nursing as follows:

1. Demonstrating and teaching mental health concepts and their application to clinical nursing practice.
2. Effecting appropriate psychiatric and nursing interventions.
3. Supporting nurses to continue to provide high-quality nursing care.
4. Promoting and developing the professional and personal self-esteem of the nurse.
5. Encouraging tolerance among the nursing staff for situations that preclude immediate or effective intervention or resolution.

Lewis and Levy describe the process of consultation as egalitarian, while Caplan (1970) sees the relationship between consultant and consultee as coordinate, meaning there is no inherent hierarchial authority, which tends to decrease tension throughout the process. Freedom to accept or reject the consultant's suggestions increases the consultee's willingness to consider and to adopt any ideas that seem useful. As part of the overall consultation process, the nurse consultant should develop a contract with the consultee, regardless of setting or context. A contract clarifies mutual expectations and may be verbal or written.

In the first step of the consultation process, the consultant is invited by the consultee to participate in problem solving. Such a request may be made by a nurse, a physician, or another health care provider. One of the next tasks is to set up communication with the nursing staff before and after the actual consultation. Initial communications begin with the head nurse and other involved nursing personnel. Communication is necessary to establishing and maintaining a viable relationship with the nursing staff, an essential element in the consultation process. Face-to-face contact with key individuals early in the process serves to introduce the liaison nurse (the consultant) and to define the scope of consultation. The nurse consultant can instill hope in the consultee group during the initial phase of contact by explaining the consultant's role. In one study, visibility was found to be more important than availability in terms of the utilization of psychiatric nurse consultants (Zahaurek and Morrison 1974). However, development of a trusting relationship between the consultant and the consultee is strengthened by both availability and visibility.

Another early task is building channels of communication between the nurse consultant, the nursing staff, and other involved health care providers. Identification of a staff member who will serve as a gatekeeper, transmitting messages between staff and consultant and among staff members, is an essential aspect of building a communication network (Caplan 1970). Larkin and Crowdes (1976) described this gatekeeper as an individual who controls the consultant's access to the workers and the workers' access to the consultant. The consultant should develop a trusting relationship with the person acting as a gatekeeper and must ensure that the gatekeeper is a person who has ready access to significant staff and to the authority system (Fife 1983).

The second step of the consultation process is to define the problem. Although a consultation request often indicates a concern for some aspect of client care, such as management issues or staff attitudes and feelings, the actual problem may be covert. Application of Caplan's concept of theme interference is helpful in understanding such covert problems. Caplan described *theme interference* as loss of objectivity by the consultee because of unresolved present or past problems that are unconsciously displaced onto the work situation. Such unresolved problems block the nurse's ability to use knowledge and skills effectively. For example, if the nurse consultee believes that all alcoholics are hopeless and resistant to help, he or she is less likely to refer a client to an alcoholism treatment program or AA. Referrals are more likely if the caregiver believes that alcoholics can be helped even though they may have relapses. To reduce theme interference, Caplan (1970) suggests initially accepting the consultee's care plan and later helping the consultee reexamine the data to allow the consultee to see that some favorable outcomes are possible, thus encouraging a more objective approach. For instance, the consultant may use an analogy such as "I worked with a man like your client last year, and with the aid of an AA member who visited after discharge the client became willing to join AA." This type of intervention will cast doubt in the consultee's mind about the "doomed to failure" viewpoint that operates to the disadvantage of the client.

During this period of defining the problem, the consultant must keep in mind that the focus of the consultation is always the care of the client, not the personal dynamics or problems of the consultee. The role of the consultant is not to provide therapy to the consultee but to address client needs. During this phase, the consultant may need to collaborate with other disciplines. For example if psychotropic medication is indicated, the nurse consultant will work with the psychiatrist or encourage nursing staff to do so (Lewis and Levy 1982).

The third step in the consultation process is diagnosing the total consultation. Stanton and Schwartz (1954) found that on a psychiatric unit clients frequently act out conflicts originating among the professional staff, and Bursten (1963) noted that this phenomenon also occurred on general hospital units. Such findings provide a rationale for the nurse consultant to engage in diagnosing the total scope of consultation problems.

Many consultation requests that are stated in terms of client behavioral problems are symptomatic of more complex processes involving clients, nurses, physicians, and the social system of the unit (Bursten 1963). Because distrust, misunderstanding, and lack of meaningful communication between staff and clients interfere with optimal care and with the therapeutic functioning of the hospital unit, it is important to assess staff and client interactions (Lipowski 1974, Pasnau 1975).

Assessment of the client and the system as one integral unit has been described as a "comprehensive consultation" by Barton and Kelso (1971). Comprehensive consultation is accomplished by assessing: (1) the consultation request, (2) the unit nurse and physician, (3) the client's chart, (4) the family and unit culture, (5) the client's medical illness, and (6) client interviews. These assessments facilitate identification and understanding of the overt and covert consultation problems and help clarify expectations of the consultee. From this assessment the consultant can also decide whether direct or indirect consultation will be more beneficial and what types of intervention are indicated.

The fourth step involves interventions and recommendations based on the comprehensive consultation. At first, suggestions need to be as simple and as nonintrusive as possible; they may be increased in complexity if necessary. Suggestions must also be practical and realistic in terms of the limits of the clinical setting; otherwise they will be inappropriate to the setting or unacceptable to the consultee. If the consultee perceives the suggestions as increasing the work load rather than relieving stress, the suggestions will be ignored or attempted in a half-hearted manner. The consultant needs to avoid use of excessive psychiatric jar-

gon in making suggestions and to refrain from statements that might be taken as criticisms.

Client behavior that results in a consultation request is often behavior that consultees believe is beyond the range of their clinical skills or that has not responded to interventions already tried. Usually the identified behavior is actually or potentially disruptive to unit functioning or to client care. The introduction of an expert such as a nurse consultant who can help manage problem behavior has been shown to reduce tension on a unit. A nurse consultant who is willing to accept ongoing involvement with a clinical problem may serve to change the consultee's attitudes, which in turn may lead to more therapeutic interactions with clients. During this phase of the consultation process, the nurse consultant observes and evaluates both client and consultee responses to interventions and makes recommendations as indicated while retaining a focus on client needs.

The fifth and final step is follow-up and reassessment. The nurse consultant should encourage feedback from the consultee and other significant caregivers in order to evaluate the situation. The consultant will want to find out whether suggested interventions have been tried, and if so, what the results were. The consultant will also want the consultee to consider whether interventions suggested in a particular case can be generalized to similar cases in the future. As part of follow-up procedures, the nurse consultant may look for documentation in the progress notes and care plans to evaluate consistent implementation of suggestions among all the nursing shift rotations. Poor communication among members of different shifts may indicate lack of acceptance of or resistance to the consultant's suggestions.

Another aspect of follow-up is evaluation of the teaching of mental health principles to consultees, since this is one of the goals of consultation. The consultee may have implemented the consultant's recommendations and the client may have improved, yet the learning needs of the consultee may not have been met. To illustrate, if a consultant repeatedly receives requests for consultation on terminally ill patients even when staff members usually implement recommendations with good results, the consultant might surmise that the staff's learning needs related to issues of death and dying should be addressed through consultation or education for the staff.

This final step in the consultation process provides data to the consultant about what has been learned about the client, the consultee, the setting, and the recommendations made. These data are useful in stimulating the consultant's professional growth and expertise. It is important that the consultant remain visible for a time after the consultation, so that the consultee does not feel prematurely abandoned. Support can be provided by means of a phone call if a personal follow-up visit is not possible. Requests for future consultation will depend on the consultant maintaining communication with the consultee.

The question of accountability of the nurse consultant has relevance for the consultation process in a clinical setting. Nursing literature emphasizes that the nurse consultant in a general hospital should be based in the department of nursing (Garant 1977, Lewis and Levy 1982). The power and influence derived from this base are an important support when problems arise as part of providing psychiatric liaison nursing service. In some hospitals the nurse consultant may participate as a team member of the department of psychiatric liaison but maintains alliance and accountability to nursing.

Since psychiatric nurses began, some 20 years ago, to provide consultation to nurses on medical and surgical units in a general hospital, practitioners have recognized the need for development of a theoretical framework around which to organize their clinical work. Such a framework is still evolving, but most nursing literature currently emphasizes synthesis and application of theoretical models from nursing, psychiatry, systems theory, crisis theory, adult learning theory, and group process (Hendler, Wise, and Lucas 1979, Lewis and Levy 1982).

Implications of Consultation and Liaison Work

Nursing literature on consultation contains many descriptions, mostly anecdotal, of the outcomes of consultation work. The most common outcome has been an increased awareness by staff nurses of the psychological needs of clients hospitalized on general medical/surgical hospital units. One study of a program of mental health nursing consultation in a general hospital found that at the end of three years more collaboration was occurring among nurses, physicians, and ancillary staff in achieving care goals and in increasing the satisfaction and well-being of clients and families (Hedlund 1978). Among the identified benefits were more effective counseling practices by nurses, increased respect for psychosocial aspects of client care, and enhanced staff interest in developing competency in this area. Nurses also demonstrated greater recognition of counseling and teaching as important functions.

There are many descriptions in the literature of specific and creative interventions developed by nurse consultants to improve the ability and willingness of nurses to provide psychological care to clients on general hospital units. In developing a consultation program, Langman-Dorwart (1979) focused on Caplan's four categories of work problems: lack of knowledge, lack of skills, lack of self-confidence, and lack of professional objectivity. In addressing these problems, Langman-Dorwart used an assertiveness training program that emphasized role-play of situations encountered by nursing staff. For example, nurses on a unit had felt powerless with physicians and behaved either nonassertively or aggressively in their interactions with physicians. After the nurses were taught assertive communication skills, they became more self-confident and adopted alternative ways to negotiate problematic work issues with physicians.

Another useful program developed by consultants has been an inservice model to help staff nurses cope with grief (Baker and Lynn 1979). It is commonly believed that confronting the death of a client is the most devastating problem nurses must face. Nurses experience feelings of helplessness, despair, and anger when dealing with the anticipated or actual death of a client; they need a way to ventilate these feelings so as to develop an understanding of their emotional responses and to build a supportive network among themselves. Baker and Lynn found that nurses who participated in the inservice program on death and grieving scored lower for depression on Zuckerman's multiple affect adjective checklist than did a control group of nurses not participating in the inservice program.

Another example of the application of liaison psychiatric nursing principles was a pilot project designed to improve undergraduate nursing students' ability to integrate principles of psychiatric mental health nursing in clinical areas outside the psychiatric setting (Jansson 1979). Using Caplan's consultee-centered approach, senior students functioned as nursing consultants to junior students. This was a collaborative situation in which the junior students retained responsibility for direct client care. Jansson found that consultees' skill in coping with "difficult" clients improved, leading to better nurse-client relationships and client care.

An essential aspect of the nurse consultant role is education. The examples of inservice programs on assertiveness and grief illustrate two models of educational strategies. Other opportunities for teaching arise during interdisciplinary health team conferences, nursing staff conferences, Kardex-rounds, walk rounds, and formal workshops. Informal teaching also occurs by means of modeling interviewing skills during unplanned staff contacts on the unit. As the nurse consultant helps nursing staff develop a therapeutic environment on general hospital units, the quality of client care will generally improve. Consultation often leads to increased awareness of the stress and anxiety experienced by clients as a result of hospitalization and illness.

Psychiatric nurse consultants have advocated the use of support groups to prevent staff burnout and to minimize stress in nursing staff (Lewis and Levy 1982, Tringali 1982). Nurses in special care settings, such as renal dialysis units, intensive care units, and burn units, are at risk for burnout because of the constant high level of stress in such environments. Because psychiatric nurses have greater understanding than psychiatrists of the demands and conflicts experienced by staff nurses working on such units, the psychiatric nurse consultant is well qualified for this type of consultative work (Barton and Kelso 1971).

There is impressive evidence for the belief that nurse-to-nurse consultation has advantages over consultation from outside experts, such as psychologists or psychiatrists (Stickey, Moir, and Gardner 1981, Fife 1983). The nurse consultant possesses first-hand understanding of the personal and professional stressors that nurses experience. This knowledge enhances the nurse consultant's ability to identify consultee strengths as well as needs. In addition, a trusting relationship may more easily be achieved in a nurse-to-nurse consultation because both view client care from a holistic perspective. It has been found when psychiatric nurse consultants establish credibility with staff and have the support of the nursing administrator, their effectiveness in planning and coordinating improved client care is impressive (Barbiasz et al. 1982).

Psychiatric nurses with consultative qualifications and skills offer a marketable product to primary health care and independent practice settings. Since small health care agencies cannot keep full-time experts on staff, the consultation process has become a popular and economical method of extending health care.

Industry is fast becoming the psychiatric consultant's major client. The liaison nurse can assist the organization to gain insight into its processes by utilizing role clarification, communication processes, stress management techniques, and interpersonal and group dynamics. They can also serve as consultants to the occupational health nurses in the promotion of wellness programs for employees. Psychiatric nurse consultants have the ability to integrate the principles of wellness for the promotion of total health care. To prevent the development of territorial issues with other professionals offering the same services, nurses should clarify their unique contributions. This clarification will also facilitate appropriate use of their services (Alexander 1985).

THE REFERRAL PROCESS IN PSYCHIATRIC NURSING

Hospitalization and illness evoke a variety of emotional responses in clients. Thus, any person receiving care in a general hospital is a potential referral for psychiatric mental health consultation (Marcus 1976). The psychiatric nurse consultant in a general hospital functions in a variety of ways. For example, the consultant may act as a member of a psychiatric liaison consultation team or as part of a crisis team that offers help on demand (Hart 1982). Consultation may also be offered through a service-based system, such as assignment to a burn unit or a renal dialysis unit.

Sequence of Referrals

Who initiates referrals to psychiatric nurse consultants? Any member of the nursing staff may initiate such a referral, as may members of any other discipline. However, nurses are sometimes reluctant to seek nursing consultation and may instead call psychiatrists or psychologists to consult on a nursing problem. Polk (1980) offers two explanations for this paradox. One explanation is related to the socialization of women, which encourages them to depend on men for authority. Since nurses are primarily female and psychiatrists are primarily male, nurses who are socialized in this manner are more inclined to request a psychiatric consultation than a nursing consultation. The other explanation comes from the way nurses are socialized into the profession itself. Nurses are frequently made to believe that they should know everything about nursing, and so they consider it an inadequacy to have to ask another nurse for guidance.

In setting up a referral system, three administrative steps are needed. First is the development of a *referral protocol* (Burch and Meredith 1974). This includes formalizing such things as who may make the request, what channels of communication should be used, who contacts the consultant, when the consultant is available, and how soon to expect the consultant to respond. An important aspect of the referral protocol is to ensure that the head nurse sanctions the consultant's entry into the hospital unit. The head nurse is the most powerful person on the unit, and her support is necessary if the consultant is to be successful. On units with primary nursing, the primary nurse may initiate the nurse consultant request, but the primary nurse collaborates with the head nurse in making the referral (Hart 1982). The referral protocol should include development of a written referral form that includes reasons for the request and a definition of the problem (Hart 1982). Such a form (see Figure 24–2) helps organize data for the consultant and helps the consultee think through the purpose and goals for the consultation request.

The second step is publicizing the nurse consultation service to all involved hospital units in the general hospital, and the third step is to devise a system to assure feedback to the consultee. A written report, documentation in the client's chart, a phone call to the staff, or a conference to evaluate the interventions—all are different ways this feedback can be provided (Burch and Meredith 1974).

Themes of Referrals

From this discussion of the referral process, two main themes emerge, one involving nursing education and the other involving nursing research. Basic content in undergraduate nursing programs includes some content on the consultation process, on the role of the psychiatric nursing consultant, and on types of appropriate referrals. More research is necessary to identify the types of clients and the staff issues that might benefit from ex-

Figure 24–2. Sample consultation request form.

Request for Consultation

Date: _____ To: _____

Client's name: _____

Location: _____

Identified problem: _____

_____

_____

_____

Assistance required/expected outcomes: _____

_____

_____

_____

Preferred date and time of initial consultation:

_____

Requested by: _____

Name: _____

Department: _____

panded nursing consultation services. Other research is needed to determine which interventions are most effective in specific consultation situations and how referrals to nurse consultants can be evaluated.

The occasional need arises for a psychiatric nurse consultant to refer a medical client for psychotherapy. Although crisis intervention is an accepted aspect of consultation/liaison work, if long-term therapy is indicated, the consultant may not be able to assume this responsibility because of policy or time constraints. Additionally, if a client has a complex medical illness and also requires psychotropic medication, a psychiatric referral may be appropriate. Such complexities do not rule out a psychiatric nurse providing psychotherapy for the client if the nurse has adequate preparation and is allowed to offer such services by the employer. In such cases the medical and psychiatric aspects of care must be carefully coordinated.

The psychiatric nurse consultant can play an important role in preparing a medical client for a psychiatric referral. The consultant may do so directly by working with the client or indirectly by working with the client's primary nurse or team leader. Clients invariably have fears about psychotherapy and believe it denotes they are crazy or incurable. A nurse can play a major role in fostering acceptance of psychotherapy regardless of who provides such therapy.

On a psychiatric inpatient unit, the discharge plan often calls for referrals to support networks, such as a day treatment program, a medication clinic, or a halfway house. To preserve confidentiality, the nurse must obtain the client's permission to make such referrals. Most hospitals use a standardized release of information form for referral purposes. When referrals are made between different departments within the same hospital, a written release may not be required; however, the client's verbal agreement for the nurse to initiate such a referral is indicated and should be documented.

When making referrals to another service or agency, the referring nurse must be assured that this agency provides services to meet the client's needs, that it is accessible to the client, that the care providers are competent and qualified, and that payment for service can be made by third-party coverage, private funds, or other means. It is helpful to provide more than one choice of agency or care provider wherever possible, in order to increase the client's sense of control over his or her life (Litwack, Litwack, and Ballou 1980). It is also necessary to be direct in explaining to the client the reason for the referral, such as saying, "You have told me you have no friends and you stated that one goal of hospitalization was to strengthen your social supports, so I am recommending we make a referral to the volunteer companion service." Litwack, Litwack, and Ballou (1980) noted that it is important to counsel the client about the limitations as well as the advantages of the service or agency to which the client is referred.

COLLABORATION AND COORDINATION IN HEALTH CARE DELIVERY

Collaboration refers to the process whereby health care providers share feelings, ideas, and information within a noncompetitive atmosphere focused on the general goal of providing optimal client care (Lewis and Levy 1982). Collaboration involves sharing responsibilities for the client. It occurs between two colleagues, each of whom is expected to carry out role-appropriate behaviors (Caplan 1970). Nurses collaborate with one another and with clients as well as with other professionals. The purpose of collaboration is to utilize various skills of the mental health team members to provide the most effective and comprehensive client care (Wilson and Kneisl 1983).

Nurses may collaborate with each other on a one-to-one basis or within team conferences, whether unidisciplinary or interdisciplinary. For example, the psychiatric nurse consultant may assess a female client for abnormal grief after a mastectomy, whereas the primary nurse evaluates the client's performance of arm muscle strengthening exercises. The nurse colleagues would then meet to discuss client needs and goals and then plan intervention strategies.

An example of collaboration between a psychiatric nurse and another health care provider would be a psychiatric nurse and a dietitian working with an anorectic depressed client who has lost 20 pounds in six months. While the dietitian and client meet to determine food likes and dislikes and to develop a specific meal plan for one week, the psychiatric nurse simultaneously sets up a plan with the client for progressing from eating one meal a day to eating three meals a day in the dining room in the presence of others.

The psychiatric nurse on a primary nursing unit may refer a client with a history of poor medication compliance to a community health nurse for follow-up after discharge. The two nurses would then collaborate in the development of an approach to ensure medication compliance. The psychiatric nurse might review therapeutic and possible side effects of the medication with the client and the family prior to discharge, and the community health nurse would monitor compliance through weekly medication counts at home with the client after discharge.

Coordination is the organizing activity necessary to assure delivery of comprehensive health care. The psychiatric nurse, whether the primary nurse or team leader, generally assumes the coordinating role during the client's hospitalization. Coordination frequently involves seeing that the client's basic daily needs, such as food and safety, are not only met but are delivered in an individualized and timely fashion. If, for example, the client's favorite dish of lasagna is served cold because it was late arriving on the unit, the nurse will call the dietary department to ensure that future meal delivery will be on time. Coordination of higher-level needs, such as self-esteem and creativity, may be implemented by developing an activity schedule that allows extra time in music and art if these are meaningful to the client. In this case, the primary nurse would meet with the activities therapist and plan for coverage of the client's extra time in art and music.

Coordination of the planning for psychiatric follow-up care is a critical task for the psychiatric nurse. The nurse must ensure that the client has an appointment with the outpatient therapist, has the therapist's phone number, and knows how to get to the psychiatric clinic or office. Providing the client with a list of emergency phone numbers before discharge is also a coordination task. The local crisis intervention hotline and the psychiatric emergency department should be on such a list, along with the client's medical care provider and any other relevant support services, such as a transportation service. The coordination of activities related to discharge planning is a responsibility assumed by the psychiatric nurse because he or she is knowledgeable of the client's needs and the services available to support the client in the community. Knowledge of community health care systems will aid the nurse in delivering optimal health care to the client and will facilitate the client's effective interaction with the system.

SUMMARY

This chapter has examined the role and functions of psychiatric nurses as members of health care teams within the two delivery systems of team nursing and primary nursing. The process of consultation as currently practiced by psychiatric nurses emphasizes consultee-centered and client-centered types of consultation within the general hospital. These are exemplified by the psychiatric nurse's
(Text continues on page 657.)

CLINICAL EXAMPLE

PSYCHIATRIC CONSULTATION IN THE CONTEXT OF PHYSICAL DISABILITY AND COGNITIVE DEFECTS

Mr. Thompson, age 82, is a widower and the father of one daughter. He was living in his own apartment until he was hospitalized for bowel cancer and had a colostomy. Subsequently, he was an inpatient on the surgical unit of the local general hospital.

ASSESSMENT

During his hospitalization, it became apparent that Mr. Thompson had moderately severe cognitive impairments. As a result he was diagnosed as having primary degenerative dementia. Every day he talked about wanting to return home to his apartment. He insisted he would be fine and that he did not need any help. He had been shown how to irrigate his colostomy but was unable to remember the steps in the procedure and could not handle the equipment. However, he said he was sure that once he got home he would have no trouble irrigating his colostomy.

Mr. Thompson's daughter approached her father's primary nurse, saying that she knew her father could not manage at home alone but she couldn't face up to telling her father this. The daughter had always looked up to her father for guidance and advice, and she said that she fell apart even thinking of confronting her father with the fact that he couldn't return home alone. Mr. Thompson had been a widower for 20 years and had been fiercely independent, always making his own decisions and taking care of himself.

In addition to coping with discharge plans for her father, the daughter was shocked at the diagnosis of dementia. She couldn't understand how it seemed to show up so suddenly. She stated that she had not noticed any change in her father's functioning except that he had decreased his usual outings with friends and had been asking his daughter to shop for him in the past few months. The daughter was decreasing the frequency and length of her hospital visits because she didn't know how to respond to her father's pleas to go home.

While hospitalized, Mr. Thompson showed a great deal of agitation, calling out for his daughter and ringing the call bell frequently. He was not sleeping well at night and was found wandering in the hall, disoriented as to time and place. After talking with Mr. Thompson's daughter, his primary nurse decided that a request for a psychiatric nursing consultation would be helpful to plan interventions in response to Mr. Thompson's changed behavior and to develop a discharge plan for the client with the daughter's involvement. The primary nurse reviewed the referral with the head nurse, who agreed this was a good idea, and the primary nurse filled out the formal referral form.

Based on the history and the clinical presentation, the following diagnoses were made:

Nursing Diagnoses

Ineffective family coping
(related to daughter's inability to cope with changes in her father)

Knowledge deficit
(related to the daughter's lack of understanding of the ramifications of dementia)

Self-care deficit
(related to the father's inability to care for himself)

Sleep pattern disturbance
(related to the father's agitation and unrest in the hospital)

Multiaxial Psychiatric Diagnoses

Axis I   290.00 Uncomplicated primary degenerative dementia of the Alzheimer's type, senile onset
Axis II None
Axis III Cancer of the colon
Axis IV Serious chronic illness, enduring circumstances
         Severity 5, extreme
Axis V   Current GAF: 50
         Highest GAF past year: 70

PLANNING

After receiving the consultation request, the psychiatric nurse went to the surgical unit. Initially she arranged a meeting with the primary nurse and then reviewed the client's chart. She met again with the primary nurse and together they discussed the interventions to decrease Mr. Thompson's agitation and improve his orientation. The nursing consultant then met with the head nurse and the primary nurse and suggested that an interdisciplinary team conference with the surgeon and social worker would be beneficial to develop a comprehensive care plan for the client's discharge. This strategy was agreed upon, the primary nurse contacted the other involved team members, and the conference was held the next day.

The primary nurse opened the meeting; then the psychiatric nurse consultant encouraged the members to focus on identifying their unique contributions to the client's care. The surgeon stated that Mr. Thompson would not require further treatment for his cancer and she would see him in surgery ambulatory clinic for routine follow-up visits. The team then developed a list of disposition options, including nursing home placement, home care with 24-hour aides in Mr. Thompson's own apartment, and moving in with his daughter, with aides during the day and the community health nurse visits every week to monitor the overall health and colostomy irrigation and function. The psychiatric nurse consultant and the social worker arranged to meet together with the daughter to discuss these options and to be supportive figures to her. In addition, the consultant counseled the daughter about dementia and its usual course.

IMPLEMENTATION

The psychiatric nurse consultant met with the head nurse to suggest a series of four weekly inservice meetings to focus on the care of clients with dementia and their families. Information on support services available in the community for the daughter, such as the group for Alzheimer's clients' family members, and an adult day care program was presented to the staff, along with specific teaching about dementia and communication techniques used to decrease client anxiety and to convey empathy to the client.

EVALUATION

These interventions led to the following outcomes in one week: Mr. Thompson's agitation and calling out decreased, his sleep improved, and his daughter was able to make the decision to place him in a nursing home. The consultant then met with the daughter and primary nurse for short visits every afternoon for one week to help her work through her grief about the loss of her once intact, independent father.

As a result of this consultation, the primary nurse felt more confident to plan future interventions to cope with Mr. Thompson's cognitive impairments and was more aware of how the daughter's feelings had affected her. The nursing staff felt better prepared to cope with clients like Mr. Thompson in the future, and they acquired increased awareness of the psychological impact of dementia on the client and the family.

Nursing Diagnoses	Goal	Nursing Actions	Outcome Criteria	Outcome Evaluation
Ineffective family coping	Daughter will become less fearful about father's condition.	Involve daughter in treatment plan. Provide individual counseling to work through grief.	Daughter will develop coping skills for dealing with her own feelings and relating to her father.	Daughter was beginning to understand her reactions to her father's illness; continued support was indicated.
Knowledge deficit	Daughter will understand dementia and be aware of available community resources.	Educated daughter in the manifestations of dementia and support services available to her.	Daughter will know course and consequences of disease, expectations for future.	Daughter began to realize the ramifications of dementia; would need further support in the future.
Self-care deficit	Appropriate discharge plans will be developed to compensate for deficits.	Involve daughter in plans, present options.	Daughter will be able to make informed decision regarding placement.	Daughter was able to make decision about nursing home placement.
Sleep pattern disturbance	Father's agitation and disorientation will decrease.	Provide inservice to staff on the management of cognitively impaired adult, methods to decrease client's anxiety.	Staff will be able to provide interventions to decrease agitation and sleeplessness.	Client's sleep improved and agitation decreased in one week.

consultant/liaison role. Referral and collaboration among nurses and between nurses and other health professionals should follow sequential steps. The process of nursing consultation is facilitated by a formal written referral, by the visibility and accessibility of the nurse consultant, and by careful documentation and record keeping. Ongoing use of consultation makes nurses more sensitive to the psychosocial needs of clients and promotes effective coordination of care and collaboration between nurses and between nurses and other care providers.

Review Questions

1. Discuss the components of the consultation process.

2. Describe the four models of nursing care delivery and the advantages and disadvantages of each.

3. Describe the role of the primary nurse in a mental health setting.

4. Compare and contrast the consultant and liaison models in nursing.

5. Review the steps of the referral process as exemplified in the clinical example.

Suggested Annotated Readings

Ashley, J. *Hospitals, Paternalism and the Role of the Nurse*. New York: Teachers College Press, 1976.

The author gives her account of how men in medicine, health care, and hospital administration have kept nurses powerless and inhibited the growth of nursing as a caring profession. The contribution of the competition between the two professional nursing associations—the ANA and the NLN—is explored, and suggestions for change and unification are presented.

Caplan, C. *The Theory and Practice of Mental Health Consultation*. New York: Basic Books Inc., 1970.

In one of the most complete books written on mental health consultation, the author presents the development of the consultation process in the community setting and emphasizes that mental health consultation is a way of communicating, not a new profession. Caplan describes the manner in which a small number of mental health professionals can exert a widespread influence. The methods are specific and expressly relevant to the practice of community psychiatry.

Lewis, A., and J. Levy. *Psychiatric Liaison Nursing: Theory and Clinical Practice*. Reston, Virginia: Reston Publishing Company, Inc., 1982.

The theme of this book is that liaison nursing is a complex activity requiring identification of clients' needs and the utilization of a broad range of interventions and skills. Some attention is given to the research potential in liaison nursing to validate nursing practice.

Mundinger, M. *Autonomy in Nursing*. Germantown, Maryland: Aspen Systems Corp., 1980.

The author describes the uniqueness of nursing in a straightforward way along with her concepts of independent nursing practice. The settings are varied but the components of individual decision making are the same.

Rosenbaum, C. P., and J. E. Beebe. *Psychiatric Treatment, Crisis and Consultation*. New York: McGraw-Hill, 1975.

This book presents a variety of theories and suggestions for treatment to help new clinicians get started. Experience with patients is linked to clinical evaluation and new frameworks. Crisis work, outpatient approaches, medical treatment, and consultation are explored. Psychiatry, physical illness, and issues around use of drugs with psychotherapy are discussed.

References

Alexander, S. "The Consultative Role of the Psychiatric Nurse Clinician: From General Health Care to the Industrial Setting." *Occupational Health Nursing* 33 (1985):567–571.

Baker, B., and M. Lynn. "Psychiatric Nursing Consultation: The Use of an Inservice Model to Assist Nurses in the Grief Process." *Journal of Psychiatric Nursing* 17, no. 5 (1979):15–19.

Barbiasz, J., et al. "Establishing the Psychiatric Liaison Nurse Role: Collaboration with the Nursing Administrator." *Journal of Nursing Administration* 12, no. 2 (1982):14–18.

Barton, D., and M. S. Kelso. "The Nurse as a Psychiatric Consultation Team Member." *Psychiatry in Medicine* 2, no. 2 (1971):108–115.

Benfer, B. A. "Defining the Role and Function of the Psychiatric Nurse as a Member of the Team." *PPC* 18, no. 4 (1980):166–177.

Burch, J. W., and J. L. Meredith. "Help with Problem Patients: Nurses as the Core of a Psychiatric Team." *American Journal of Nursing* 74 (1974):2037–2038.

Bursten, B. "The Psychiatric Consultant and the Nurse." *Nursing Forum* 2, no. 4 (1963):6–23.

Caplan, G. *The Theory and Practice of Mental Health Consultation.* New York: Basic Books, 1970.

Challela, M. "The Interdisciplinary Team: A Role Definition for Nursing." *Image* 11, no. 1 (1979):9–15.

Ciske, K. L. "Primary Nursing: An Organization That Promotes Professional Practice." *Journal of Nursing Administration* 4, no. 1 (1974):28–31.

Crawshaw, R., and W. Key. "Psychiatric Teams: A Selective Review of the Literature." *Archives of General Psychiatry* 5 (1961):397–405.

Davis, D. S. "Psychiatric Mental Health Nursing Consultation in the General Hospital: Liaison Nursing." In *Handbook of Psychiatric Mental Health Nursing*, C. Adams and A. Macione, eds. New York: John Wiley & Sons, 1983.

Fife, B. "The Challenge of the Medical Setting for the Clinical Specialist in Psychiatric Nursing." *Journal of Psychiatric Nursing* 21, no. 1 (1983):8–13.

Garant, C. A. "The Psychiatric Liaison Nurse—An Interpretation of the Role." *Supervisor Nurse* 8, no. 4 (1977):75–78.

Hart, C. A. "Psychiatric Mental Health Nursing Consultation: A Two-Model System in a General Hospital." *Issues in Mental Health Nursing* 4, no. 2 (1982):127–147.

Hedlund, N. L. "Mental Health Nursing Consultation in the General Hospital." *Patient Counseling and Health Education* 1, no. 2 (1978):85–88.

Hendler, N., T. N. Wise, and M. J. Lucas. "The Expanded Role of the Psychiatric Liaison Nurse." *Psychiatric Quarterly* 51, no. 2 (1979):135–143.

Jansson, D. P. "Student Consultation: A Liaison Psychiatric Experience for Nursing Students." *Perspectives in Psychiatric Care* 17, no. 2 (1979):77–94.

Johnson, B. S. "Psychiatric Nursing Consultation in a General Hospital." *Nursing Outlook* 11 (1963):728–729.

Jones, C. P. "Adapting Primary Nursing to Long-Term Care." *Geriatric Nursing* 7 (1986):87–89.

Kimball, C. P. "Liaison Psychiatry: Approaches and Ways of Thinking about Behavior." *Psychiatric Clinics of North America* 2, no. 2 (1979):201–210.

Langman-Dorwart, N. "A Model for Mental Health Consultation to the General Hospital." *Journal of Psychiatric Nursing* 17, no. 3 (1979):29–33.

Larkin, M., and N. E. Crowdes. "Nurse Consultation: The Instilling of Hope." *Supervisor Nurse* 7, no. 11 (1976):54–58.

Lewis, A., and J. S. Levy. *Psychiatric Liaison Nursing.* Reston, Virginia: Reston Publishing, 1982.

Lipowski, Z. J. "Consultation-Liaison Psychiatry: An Overview." *American Journal of Psychiatry* 131 (1974): 623–630.

Litwack, L., J. M. Litwack, and M. B. Ballou. *Health Counseling.* New York: Appleton-Century-Crofts, 1980.

Marcus, J. "Nursing Consultation: A Clinical Specialty." *Journal of Psychiatric Nursing* 14, no. 11 (1976):29–31.

Marram, G. D., M. W. Schlegel, and E. O. Bevis. *Primary Nursing: A Model for Individualized Care.* St. Louis: C. V. Mosby, 1974.

Mereness, D. "Preparation of the Nurse for the Psychiatric Team." *American Journal of Nursing* 51, no. 5 (1951): 320–322.

Nelson, J. K. N., and D. A. Schilke. "The Evolution of Psychiatric Liaison Nursing." *Perspectives of Psychiatric Nursing* 14, no. 21 (1976):60–65.

Pasnau, R., ed. *Consultation-Liaison Psychiatry.* New York: Grune & Stratton, 1975.

Pasnau, R. "Consultation-Liaison Psychiatry at the Crossroads: In Search of a Definition for the 1980s." *Hospital and Community Psychiatry* 33 (1982):989–1005.

Polk, G. C. "The Socialization and Utilization of Nurse Consultants." *Journal of Psychiatric Nursing* 18, no. 2 (1980):33–36.

Stanton, A. H., and M. S. Schwartz. *The Mental Hospital: A Study of Insitutional Participation in Psychiatric Illness and Treatment.* New York: Basic Books, 1954.

Stickey, S., G. Moir, and E. Gardner. "Psychiatric Nurse Consultation: Who Calls and Why?" *Journal of Psychiatric Nursing* 19, no. 10 (1981):22–26.

Strain, J., and S. Grossman. *Psychological Care of the Medically Ill.* New York: Appleton-Century-Crofts, 1975.

Tringali, R. "The Role of the Psychiatric Nurse Consultant on a Burn Unit." *Issues in Mental Health Nursing* 4 (1982):17–24.

Watson, L. J. "Psychiatric Consultation-Liaison in Acute Physical Disabilities Setting." *American Journal of Occupational Therapy* 40 (1986):338–342.

Wilson, H. S., and C. R. Kneisl. *Psychiatric Nursing*, 2d ed. Menlo Park, California: Addison-Wesley, 1983.

Zander, K. "Second Generation Primary Nursing: A New Agenda." *Journal of Nursing Administration* 15 (1985): 18–24.

Zahaurek, R., and K. Morrison. "Help with Problem Patients: Mental Health Nurses and Consultants to Staff Nurses." *American Journal of Nursing* 74 (1974): 2034–2036.

Ethics, Legality, and Advocacy

Learning Objectives

After studying this chapter, the student should be able to:

1. Discuss the interplay of values, ethics, rights, and the law in the practice of nursing.

2. Outline the rights of clients guaranteed by the U.S. Constitution and the Patients' Bill of Rights.

3. Describe the implications of standards of practice and peer review for professional accountability and liability.

4. Describe the ethical problems peculiar to the psychiatric setting and delineate the interaction between these problems and clients' rights.

Overview

This chapter examines the interplay of ethical values, clients' rights and responsibilities, and legal issues in the practice of mental health nursing. It explores the unique rights of psychiatric clients as well as problems specific to the area of psychiatric nursing. Concerns for the elderly population in long-term care institutions and the need for DNR orders for psychiatric clients are discussed. Finally, the chapter examines the role enactment of the psychiatric nurse as client advocate and promoter of a professional climate that respects the rights and needs of clients with mental health problems.

Values, ethics, human rights, and the law are inextricably intertwined. *Values* represent the ideals, customs, and institutions for which individuals have enormous regard. Values that address human relationships at the level of society are called ethics. *Ethics* are guiding principles that define what individuals should do in relation to one another on the basis of general values held by most members of the society. These principles in their abstract form are considered essential to the maintenance and promotion of a moral and just society. In effect, the principles delineate the societal member's right to individuality, freedom, and self-determination in behavior and decision making. The legal system defines in a formal and less abstract way what members of society may or may not do according to prescribed doctrine or law. Law is created within society to make explicit the rights of the members according to an ethical value system; the law, then, serves society in protecting the individual's autonomy and rights through formal judgments and actions (see Figure 25–1).

NURSING AND ETHICS

The professional nurse experiences situations that have ethical ramification in all areas of practice. Such issues as when to tell the client the truth when this may in itself be harmful, who to give health care services to and in what priority, and when to withdraw treatment are but a few of the dilemmas facing nurses today.

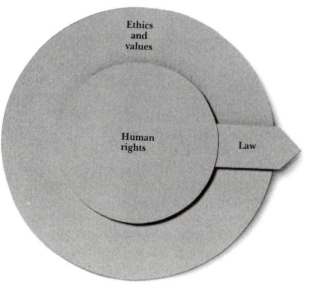

Figure 25–1. *The interrelationship of values, ethics, human rights, and the law.*

Ethics is concerned with our conduct toward each other and the environment, our obligations and what we ought to do, not necessarily what we do in actual practice. Nurses engage in ethical reasoning when they reflect on what should be done in a systematic way and substantiate decisions and conclusions before taking action.

Many situations that nurses face raise complex issues that cannot be answered by professional knowledge and expertise alone. Several of these problems arise in our society because of the major emphasis on individual freedom of choice. Because of the new and unprecedented range of choices that are now available due to new technologies, a field of bioethics has emerged to assist in decision making for complex problems in health care (Aroskar 1985).

The moral principles of ethics include autonomy and self-determination based on respect, beneficence (doing good), malfeasance (avoiding harm), veracity (truth telling), promise keeping and justice in equality, or equal access to health care. Any or all of these can cause conflict in real-life situations and may be enhanced or negated by the decisions made by nurses in their variety of practice settings.

Ethical analysis is a decision making process that requires the nurse to separate ethical problems from legal or communication difficulties. A sound knowledge base concerning all the facts of any given situation is essential. An analysis of involved ethics is imperative to ascertain the issues at stake, examine responsibilities and obligations, and provide a rationale for decisions (Aroskar 1985).

Nursing has special obligations to society in regard to ethics, human rights, values, and the law. Members of the nursing profession are charged with a responsibility for performing in a way consistent with the ethics and guiding principles of the society, as well as consistent with accepted formal standards of practice and conduct set for and by the profession.

The same law that protects the rights of all members of society is applicable to the professional practice of nursing. This law demands that professionals practice their discipline in such a manner that the rights of the client are never unreasonably compromised. Should professional practitioners violate the ethical code and the standards of professional practice derived from that code, they are accountable to the larger society under the law.

Individual practitioners of a profession therefore reflect the ethical values of their society and their profession in their philosophy of professional practice and their basis for decision making. Internal consistency among the various levels of values—social, legal, professional, and individual—enhances the development of a discipline. When individual or professional values are not congruent with prevailing social values, one result is a potential for creating change in the society (Chinn and Jacobs 1983). Another result is the potential for creating change within the profession.

The nursing profession upholds the larger society's ethical values for the protection of basic human rights. This is evident in the Code for Nurses (American Nurses' Association 1976), which identifies the general duties, powers, and obligations of members of the profession regarding clients' rights (see the accompanying box). This code guides the nurse in the performance of professional duties in such a way that the rights of the client are explicitly valued and protected.

In addition to seeing that the practice of nursing is aligned with society's ethics, the ethical code provides direction, self-regulation, and self-evaluation for the members of the profession. "The Code and the Interpretive Statements together provide a framework for the nurse to make ethical decisions and discharge responsibilities to the public, to other members of the health team, and to the profession" (American Nurses' Association 1976, p. 1).

Nurses today face an ethical tension between the obligation to benefit the individual and the obligation to benefit society (Fry 1985). Professional codes of ethics speak to both areas by holding nurses accountable for providing services that are individual and unique to the client yet emphasizing the responsibility of nurses to promote the aggregate good. The mandate to promote the individual over the aggregate is limited because of the impossibility of meeting every individual's needs. The aggregate good is also limited by the considerations that need to be given to the individual.

Nurses are becoming increasingly accountable for justifying the promoting of one good over the other and for specifying reasons for limiting the provision of the good in some situations.

The Rights of Mental Health Clients

Webster's defines *right* as "that which is due to anyone by just claim." The Constitution of the United States sets forth specific rights for all individuals in accordance with the ethical values held by the larger society; these rights are protected by civil laws and are accepted and assumed as expected outcomes. While the protection of civil rights for all is generally assumed, much attention has recently been given to the protection and enforcement of the rights of individuals seeking or requiring health care. A number of professional policy-making organizations, associations, and accrediting groups have taken the issue of patients' rights beyond mere

assumption and have devoted special policy statements or publications to this important issue (American Hospital Association 1975, Joint Commission on Accreditation of Hospitals 1983). A Patient's Bill of Rights devised by the American Hospital Association is reproduced in the accompanying box.

Psychiatric illness presents particular threats and challenges to the assumptions that underlie client rights. Psychiatric clients are often stereotyped in a manner that is a direct affront to individuality and uniqueness. The psychiatric client is commonly considered to be incompetent and therefore incapable of exercising autonomy in behavior and decision making. The right to legal counsel, the right to refuse medicine that may be prescribed to control behavior, and the right to oppose involuntary hospitalization are a few of the civil rights threatened in care of the psychiatric client.

In caring for the mental health client, the health professional is often faced with the fact that acknowledging a client's civil rights may mean the withdrawal of a treatment, which ultimately will have an impact on the client's well-being. Conversely, to medicate or restrain a client in order to promote ultimate health and well-being can be interpreted as an infraction of the client's rights. The distinctions between what is ethical, what is legal, and what is needed to safeguard the psychiatric client's rights are not always apparent.

In psychiatry, the ethical problems for all members of the health care team are substantial. The controversial procedures—electroshock, behavior modification, and psychosurgery—are of special concern. These treatment modalities have been adopted because they work, not because they have a rich and rational theoretical basis. At times, clients' rights have been violated because informed consent was not obtained. Since there are now methods available for imposing major psychological transformations on clients, the right to do these procedures must be bound by legislation that guards against cruel and unusual punishment and by a morality that respects the right to be different (Flanagan 1986).

Institutional Responsibilities Regarding Client's Rights

The institution or agency and health care providers share the responsibility of explaining to individuals their rights as clients in that facility. It is expected that the clients' rights will be explained to them in a manner that they can understand. In the explanations of rights, it is necessary to inform clients of the facility's rules or regulations that have an impact on their conduct and behavior. Clients should be assured of their right to impartial access to

ANA CODE FOR NURSES

1. The nurse provides services with respect for human dignity and the uniqueness of the client unrestricted by considerations of social or economic status, personal attributes, or the nature of health problems.

2. The nurse safeguards the client's right to privacy by judiciously protecting information of a confidential nature.

3. The nurse acts to safeguard the client and the public when health care and safety are affected by the incompetent, unethical, or illegal practice of any person.

4. The nurse assumes responsibility and accountability for individual nursing judgments and actions.

5. The nurse maintains competence in nursing.

6. The nurse exercises informed judgment and uses individual competence and qualifications as criteria in seeking consultations, accepting responsibilities, and delegating nursing activities to others.

7. The nurse participates in activities that contribute to the ongoing development of the profession's body of knowledge.

8. The nurse participates in the profession's efforts to implement and improve standards of nursing.

9. The nurse participates in the profession's efforts to establish and maintain conditions of employment conducive to high-quality nursing care.

10. The nurse participates in the profession's effort to protect the public from misinformation and misrepresentation and to maintain the integrity of nursing.

11. The nurse collaborates with members of the health profession and other citizens in promoting community and national efforts to meet the health needs of the public.

SOURCE: Used with permission of American Nurses' Association.

treatment and should receive care that respects their personal dignity. Providers should make it clear to clients and families that an individualized treatment plan will be instituted and mutual planning will establish the therapeutic goals.

Clients and their families must be informed about the care and treatment being given. Clients should be told about who is responsible for their care, the professional status of caregivers, and their role in the health care team of the treatment facility. If there is a change in the professional team responsible for the client, or if a transfer to another facility or ward is necessary, this must be explained to the client in understandable terms. Informing clients about the personnel ultimately responsible for their care may seem to be simplistic and elementary, but in large teaching facilities it may not be clear to clients just who is responsible for various aspects of their care.

Health professionals should pay attention to clients' preferences for and reactions to their treatment. Information concerning the benefits, side effects, and risks of treatment should be explained. Alternate treatment options should also be made clear and presented in such a manner that clients can make an informed choice for themselves and their families.

With the increasing involvement of clients in institutional and individual research, special emphasis must be given to the rights of clients as research subjects. All clients must be informed and must give written consent for participation in research projects. What is more, such consent should be obtained without coercion, unfair inducements, or persuasion on the part of the health care provider (Watson 1982). Written consent is also required for the use of audiovisual equipment in the treatment process, for the performance of surgical procedures, for invasive diagnostic procedures, for electroconvulsive therapy, and for the use of any unusual medication. If the client is unable to give consent or is incompetent, the next of kin or legal guardian must give consent prior to implementing the procedure or treatment.

The issue of consent for care is of particular concern when working with elderly clients. In long-term care facilities, professional decisions must be made that are appropriate for the clients' conditions and wishes. However, at times elderly clients are unable to make informed decisions about their care. Families may be nonexistent or live at too great a distance to become involved. A team of professionals may then be placed in the position of acting "in loco parentis," which necessitates merging the obligations toward the clients with obligations toward the family, the state, and the facility.

Traditionally, many infirm elderly clients have been placed in the position of having "parents," either the family or the state. When clients are no longer able to actively participate in the decision-making processes, the "parents" impose their "sovereignty." These decisions are usually guided by input from health professionals.

Wilson and Netting (1986) postulate that there is a serious flaw in the parental sovereignty approach because it does not distinguish between clients who are completely dependent and those who are physically incapacitated and have trouble communicating but who are mentally intact. They propose a determining rule, that the level of mental capacity, rather than decisions about physical capacity, should be the deciding factor of competency with regard to treatment. This "mature elderly" doctrine is consistent with the principles of autonomy and the acknowledgment that changes that accompany aging do not necessarily interfere with cognitive competence and the ability to make decisions.

The Right to Refuse Treatment

A major issue in clients' rights is the right to refuse treatment. This right is implied and supported by certain amendments to the Constitution of the United States, including the First Amendment, which protects the freedoms of speech, thought, and expression; the Eighth Amendment, which grants the right to freedom from cruel and unusual punishment; and the Fifth and Fourteenth Amendments, which grant due process of law and equal protection for all.

The Patient's Bill of Rights states that the client has the right to refuse treatment to the extent permitted by law. The "extent permitted by law," however, may vary from state to state. This necessitates being familiar with the mental health laws in the state in which one practices. Statements on clients' rights clearly mandate that health care providers explain to the client what steps the facility will take when refusal of treatment occurs (Joint Commission on Accreditation of Hospitals 1983). These steps may include involuntary commitment and other legal alternatives, such as a competency hearing or discharge of the client.

In psychiatric settings refusal of treatment primarily concerns the administration of psychotropic medication. Advocates of refusal of treatment point out that psychotropic medication alters thought process and controls behavior rather than cures the illness (Davis 1978). Those who are concerned with the ethical implications of psychotropic medication argue that the individuality and autonomy of the client are compromised when drugs are given to make behavior conform with what is considered "normal" (Curtin 1979a).

Some limits have been placed on the psychiatric client relative to the right to refuse treatment. In emergency situations where there is substantial ev-

idence to predict or support the possibility that clients may harm themselves or others, it is admissible to temporarily medicate forcibly (Regan 1981a, Arkin 1983). For inpatients who are involuntary admissions and deemed incompetent, the right to refuse treatment requires intervention from the client's legal guardian or the legal system. Here again it is important to know the laws of the particular county or state and to be familiar with the facility's policy.

The right to refuse ongoing treatment that necessitates residence in an institution has aroused much attention (Bandman 1978). *O'Connor* v. *Donaldson* established that it is unconstitutional to hold persons involuntarily in an institution primarily for custodial reasons (Carroll 1980). Involuntary commitment is a denial of the individual's autonomy and is a direct challenge to the ethical values of our society. If a person's independence is being denied by involuntary commitment, it is crucial that full efforts be directed toward providing therapeutic treatment and not merely custodial care.

Do-Not-Resuscitate

The do-not-resuscitate (DNR) order has become one of the most important issues concerning clients' rights. Rapid advances in technology have given health care professionals a greater ability to monitor and treat critically ill clients. When this intervention only prolongs suffering, however, clients, families, and professionals may consider some limitations. A number of hospitals have responded to these dilemmas by adopting official policies concerning orders not to resuscitate. Other hospitals have recognized the authority of physicians to write DNR orders. Two goals are implicit in these policies: (1) to decide about the appropriateness of resuscitative attempts before they are needed and (2) to consult with the client or the family of an incompetent client to determine their wishes (Evans and Brody 1985).

Although a DNR order essentially means that cardiopulmonary resuscitation will not be used, there is still general confusion among health care givers and many disagree about the type and level of intervention that should be provided to a DNR client. Proposed guidelines recommend specifying the exact nature of treatment to be withheld, documenting the justification of the decision and recognizing that a DNR order does not mean medical or emotional abandonment of the client. The client's wishes, quality of life, probability of success, and medical costs are all criteria for consideration. (Youngner et al. 1985).

Research findings related to the study of clients who have DNR orders are appearing more frequently in the professional literature (Lipton 1986,

A PATIENT'S BILL OF RIGHTS

1. The patient has the right to considerate and respectful care.

2. The patient has the right to obtain from his physician complete current information concerning his diagnosis, treatment, and prognosis in terms the patient can be reasonably expected to understand. When it is not medically advisable to give such information to the patient, the information should be made available to an appropriate person in his behalf. He has the right to know, by name, the physician responsible for coordinating his care.

3. The patient has the right to receive from his physician information necessary to give informed consent prior to the start of any procedure and/or treatment. Except in emergencies, such information for informed consent should include but not necessarily be limited to the specific procedure and/or treatment, the medically significant risks involved, and the probable duration of incapacitation. Where medically significant alternatives for care or treatment exist, or when the patient requests information concerning medical alternatives, the patient has the right to such information. The patient also has the right to know the name of the person responsible for the procedures and/or treatment.

4. The patient has the right to refuse treatment to the extent permitted by law and to be informed of the medical consequences of his action.

5. The patient has the right to every consideration of his privacy concerning his own medical care program. Case discussion, consultation, examination, and treatment are confidential and should be conducted discreetly. Those not directly involved in his care must have the permission of the patient to be present.

6. The patient has the right to expect that all communications and records pertaining to his care should be treated as confidential.

7. The patient has the right to expect that within its capacity a hospital must make reasonable response to the request of a patient for services. The hospital must provide evaluation, service, and/or referral as indicated by the urgency of the case. When medically permissible, a patient may be transferred to another facility only after he has received complete information and explanation concerning the needs for and alternatives to such a transfer. The institution to which the patient is to be transferred must have accepted the patient for transfer.

8. The patient has the right to obtain information as to any relationship of his hospital to other health care and educational institutions insofar as his care is concerned. The patient has the right to obtain information as to the existence of any professional relationships among individuals, by name, who are treating him.

9. The patient has the right to be advised if the hospital proposes to engage in or perform human experimentation affecting his care or treatment. The patient has the right to refuse to participate in such research projects.

10. The patient has the right to expect reasonable continuity of care. He has the right to know in advance what appointment times and physicians are available and where. The patient has the right to expect that the hospital will provide a mechanism whereby he is informed by his physician or a delegate of the physician of the patient's continuing health care requirements following discharge.

11. The patient has the right to examine and receive an explanation of his bill regardless of source of payment.

12. The patient has the right to know what hospital rules and regulations apply to his conduct as a patient.

Bedell 1986, Schwartz and Reilly 1986). However, the psychiatric literature does not evidence equal concern. Since mental illness is not usually fatal, decisions to withhold resuscitation may never arise in treating psychiatric illness. But many institutions treat terminally ill psychiatric clients, and implementing a DNR policy in a psychiatric hospital is a complex issue because of the multiple problems in the lives of a chronically ill client. In contrast to a general hospital for acute care with a defined purpose, a psychiatric hospital has many. When clients have lived in a psychiatric facility for many years and become terminally ill, the institution becomes a substitute for a hospice, a skilled nursing home, a chronic care hospital, or home care for the dying.

DNR orders pose significant problems to psychiatric hospitals. Clients are competent to consent to a DNR order when they are able to understand the nature and severity of illness, the risks and benefits of interventions, and can indicate a preference for one course of treatment over another. Since clients in psychiatric facilities have impaired mental functioning by definition, the issue of competency may be raised in almost every case.

Despite impaired functioning, clients can and do participate in decisions about their own care and should be allowed to make choices. However, there are clinical problems inherent in discussing these issues with psychiatric clients. Little information is available describing how well clients can tolerate these discussions. A vague presentation may leave many questions unanswered, while a general talk may be frightening enough to provoke an anxiety that leaves the client unable to make a rational decision.

When the client is determined to be incompetent, a surrogate decision maker must be found. In long-term psychiatric facilities, the staff, with expertise in psychiatry, may not necessarily be the best qualified to advise others about the medical facts of a client's condition. In many instances, it is difficult to find a surrogate, as many long-term clients do not have families, and the staff of the institution may be closer to the client than anyone else. At times, cases involve court decisions. Usually clinicians do not have the legal background to make appropriate decisions, and many public mental hospitals have limited legal resources for assistance.

It is important to offer psychiatric clients the same level of care as would be provided to any other citizen. When a client becomes terminally ill, the client should be transferred to a general hospital if the psychiatric facility cannot provide the aggressive care that is necessary and/or desired by the client. Hospice care can be given quite competently in a psychiatric hospital if this is congruent with the client's wishes. Comfort and pain control are well within the abilities of a mental hospital, whereas intensive medical care may not be. DNR policies should be developed within all psychiatric institutions for protection of clients and staff alike (Cournos 1986–87).

Restrictive Treatment

Another area of controversy has been the concept of least restrictive treatment. Carroll (1980) pointed out that "the more intrusive or restrictive a technique, the more the person's autonomy is di-

minished" (p. 288). While this may be true, most clinicians would agree that restrictions, at times, do provide necessary controls. The use of physical restraints (the most restrictive form of treatment) may be necessary if less restrictive measures have proven ineffective in providing safety for the client and others (Miller 1982).

With hospitalization, the least restrictive treatment alternatives must be followed. In trying to maintain the least restrictive treatment alternative, it is imperative not to allow the client to become dangerous to himself or to others. While respecting individual rights is important, it is also necessary to respect and assure the safety of everyone concerned. It is unreasonable to think that seclusion or restraints should never be employed. It is equally unreasonable to use seclusion or restraint procedures when other alternatives are available.

Health professionals must make a judgment as to when a restrictive measure is warranted. When a client unexpectedly becomes disturbed and violent, it is the responsibility of the facility and the staff to ensure the safety of the client and others. The nurse should be knowledgeable concerning the policy and procedure of placing a client in seclusion or restraints. In most facilities a nurse may make an independent judgment but must immediately obtain a retroactive physician's order for the restrictive procedure.

It is equally important to know when a client must be released from seclusion or restraint. Most states and most facilities have strict limits on the time that seclusion and restraint measures can be used, even with a written medical order. If the client's behavior no longer warrants seclusion or restraints, he or she should be released immediately. To maintain a person in seclusion or restraints without adequate behavioral justification is subjecting the client to treatment that is a violation of the right to mutually agreed treatment.

Involuntary Commitment

In most states there are specific criteria for involuntary commitment. In general, the criteria are centered on the person's posing a clear danger to himself or others (Roth 1980, Tancredi 1980). With involuntary commitment, the treating facility has a legal responsibility for the client's care and wellbeing. The length of time a commitment is effective varies from state to state, as do the application procedures for commitment.

Many states specify a detention period in which the family or hospital can begin necessary legal proceedings for commitment. When the initial detention period has lapsed and there are no pending legal plans for involuntary commitment, the individual is free to leave the treating facility. Detention after the expiration of the legal time frame is considered false imprisonment (Cazalas 1978).

Once an individual is legally committed to a health care facility, does she still have the right to refuse treatment? The answer is yes; the person who is an involuntary admission does maintain the right to refuse treatment (Regan 1981b). This concept may be difficult to comprehend, as the criteria for involuntary commitment clearly specify that the person must pose a clear danger to self or others. However, the person who has been committed has not lost his or her civil rights. Those rights may only be lost if the person is judged incompetent (Tancredi 1980, Arkin 1983). A hearing for incompetency is separate from a commitment hearing.

To be judged *incompetent* means that the person has difficulty in comprehending the full impact of binding legal transactions and that questionable thinking contributes to impaired judgment. Thus, individuals who are judged incompetent cannot marry, divorce, enter into any contractual agreements, or vote. Their license to operate a motor vehicle is also revoked. Persons who are ruled incompetent have no power to consent to or refuse treatment.

When clients are confined within an institution, they have a fundamental right to receive adequate treatment. Nurses, along with other members of the mental health team, must provide individualized treatment plans that assure a physical, social, and psychological environment that is not below the standards of living of the average free citizen. Active psychiatric care provides not only for services to maintain clients at their level of functioning but also to correct or improve the clients' conditions.

The nursing staff is responsible for the clients' milieu, planning nursing care, providing a safe environment, and coordinating the daily activities. The current focus on self-care and prevention of stress pose a special challenge to nurses. An individualized treatment plan, which should reflect the treatment goals assigned to nursing, is the starting point for active treatment. Whenever possible, the plan should be developed with clients and their families. (Sanders and DuPlessis 1985).

The importance of documentation in the medical record by nurses cannot be overemphasized. Such documentation provides an indication of nursing treatment as well as the quality of nursing intervention.

Nursing Implications of Clients' Rights

The issue of clients' rights has many implications for nursing. One major implication is that nursing

personnel must be knowledgeable about the rights of clients and must be aware of their facility's policies and of procedures concerning client rights. They should also be aware of the mental health laws in their state.

In the administration of medication, the nurse must realize that both inpatients and outpatients have the right to refuse medication (Appelbaum and Gutheil 1980). To forcibly administer medication may result in the client's filing suit for assault and battery. The Supreme Court of Colorado has ruled that an involuntary client has the right to refuse treatment when alert, oriented, and aware of the illness and of what treatment is proposed (Regan 1980). If a client refuses medication, the nurse may try to elicit reasons for the refusal and encourage the client to voice concerns. The nurse may try to persuade the client but should not try to coerce him into taking the medication.

Nursing staff must also learn what constitutes the least restrictive treatment alternatives. They must know what interventions or measures should be taken before more restrictive treatment is instituted. Using the least restrictive form of treatment implies that the client's treatment plan should be individualized and that placement of treatment (as inpatient or outpatient) should be appropriate and responsive to the degree of illness. That is, if the client can be treated on an outpatient basis, then outpatient care is preferable to hospitalization.

The nurse should also be aware of society's ethical values as they apply to the mental health client. Every effort should be made to acknowledge and respect the client's individuality and to promote the client's autonomy to the fullest extent possible. The client should be viewed as an active, not passive, participant in the planning and implementation of care. The nurse must be vigilant concerning the form of care rendered by nursing personnel and by other professionals as well.

There are those who would argue that the practice of mental health nursing provides nurses with insurmountable ethical problems. From the ethical viewpoint, certain measures are contrary to what nurses might prefer if they were free to follow their own values only. The use of behavior-controlling drugs, environmental and mechanical restraints, and other prescribed therapeutic approaches, for example, is sometimes a direct attack on the nurse's belief in the client's right to individuality and autonomy (Curtin 1979a). Nevertheless, nurses must fulfill professional standards of practice that are directed toward helping the client progress to an improved health state.

There are inevitable circumstances in the practice of mental health nursing that necessitate the use of measures that infringe on the client's individuality and autonomy in decision making. The nurse must be clear in the knowledge of state laws and of the ethical rights of the client before implementing these measures. Once they are implemented, every precaution should be taken to see that any restrictive or controlling measures are withdrawn as soon as the safety and well-being of the client will permit. To the extent that the nurse is attentive to professional responsibilities outlined in the Code for Nurses, as well as to the basic rights of her clients, the ethical values of society and the mental health client's well-being will be safeguarded.

Although current emphasis is placed on informing clients of their rights within the health care system, the Joint Commission of Accreditation of Hospitals (1988) advocates that clients be made aware of their responsibilities as well. These responsibilities are reproduced in the accompanying box.

PROFESSIONAL ACCOUNTABILITY AND LIABILITY

Nurses function within an enormously complex system involving a delicate balance between protection of clients' rights and implementation of health care directed at improving the clients' well-being. The responsibility of the professional nurse within this complex system is to maintain the standards of nursing practice. To the extent that the standards of care are violated, nurses can be held accountable and liable for negligence. This section of the chapter deals with nursing accountability and liability for actions that are committed or omitted in care of the psychiatric client.

Laws and Regulations

Our legal system is a complex of laws set forth to govern human conduct, which are enforced by courts or governmental agencies to protect society.

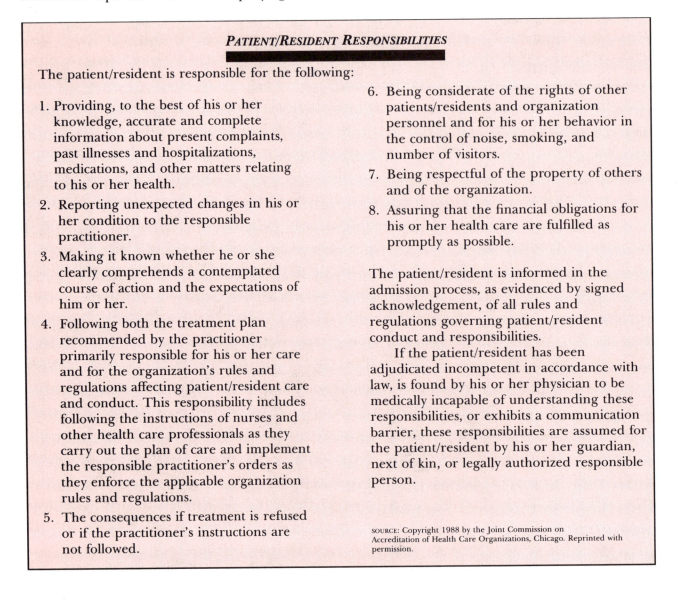

PATIENT/RESIDENT RESPONSIBILITIES

The patient/resident is responsible for the following:

1. Providing, to the best of his or her knowledge, accurate and complete information about present complaints, past illnesses and hospitalizations, medications, and other matters relating to his or her health.

2. Reporting unexpected changes in his or her condition to the responsible practitioner.

3. Making it known whether he or she clearly comprehends a contemplated course of action and the expectations of him or her.

4. Following both the treatment plan recommended by the practitioner primarily responsible for his or her care and for the organization's rules and regulations affecting patient/resident care and conduct. This responsibility includes following the instructions of nurses and other health care professionals as they carry out the plan of care and implement the responsible practitioner's orders as they enforce the applicable organization rules and regulations.

5. The consequences if treatment is refused or if the practitioner's instructions are not followed.

6. Being considerate of the rights of other patients/residents and organization personnel and for his or her behavior in the control of noise, smoking, and number of visitors.

7. Being respectful of the property of others and of the organization.

8. Assuring that the financial obligations for his or her health care are fulfilled as promptly as possible.

The patient/resident is informed in the admission process, as evidenced by signed acknowledgement, of all rules and regulations governing patient/resident conduct and responsibilities.

If the patient/resident has been adjudicated incompetent in accordance with law, is found by his or her physician to be medically incapable of understanding these responsibilities, or exhibits a communication barrier, these responsibilities are assumed for the patient/resident by his or her guardian, next of kin, or legally authorized responsible person.

SOURCE: Copyright 1988 by the Joint Commission on Accreditation of Health Care Organizations, Chicago. Reprinted with permission.

CLINICAL VIGNETTE

REFUSAL OF TREATMENT

Bill Shaeffer, a hospitalized patient, complains that his medication is making him dizzy and that he therefore does not want to continue with the treatment. Bill has a history of severe hypertension and has been diagnosed as having a bipolar disorder, depressed type. On admission his blood pressure was 182/108. He is extremely suspicious of the staff and fears they will harm him.

Although Bill had willingly taken his hypertensive and antidepressant medication for two days, he now refuses all medications and is becoming more withdrawn. Among the relevant questions to be addressed are:

1. Is Bill a candidate for involuntary admission? Yes. With a history of an affective disorder and untreated, uncontrolled hypertension, he is a danger to himself. His judgment at present is impaired.

2. Can Bill be forcibly medicated for his hypertension and not his antidepressant medication? No. Until he is committed for treatment to an appropriate facility or is legally ruled incompetent, he may not be forcibly medicated. If he becomes violent and poses a serious threat to himself or others, he may be medicated; once he has been medicated, the nurse or physician should contact the legal system for guidance.

3. What measures should the nurse take concerning Bill's medication? Until Bill is committed to the facility or is judged incompetent, nursing measures are somewhat limited. The nurse may encourage Bill to verbalize his reasons for refusing the medication but may not coerce him into taking it. The nursing staff should monitor his blood pressure and physical activity frequently, record the results, and inform the physician.

The purpose of the legal system is to provide justice and fairness, protecting the rights of one person from infringement by another. It seeks to establish standards of behavior of how similarly educated and experienced persons would act when under the same circumstances. A primary fundamental assumption is that individuals are responsible for their own actions. Only recently have nurses been recognized as accepting responsibility for their own actions. Physicians are no longer held responsible for the actions of nurses. Consequently, more nurses are being sued today than in the past.

Nurses have struggled to gain professional recognition as being capable of making informed and mature judgments. As a result, they are now being held accountable for making decisions based on education and experience. Nurses are now expected to question medical orders rather than blindly follow them (Feutz 1986).

Standards of Practice

Nursing as a professional discipline has structured its practice principles so that it may (1) judge the competency of its members, (2) evaluate the quality of the services rendered to clients, and (3) safeguard client rights (American Nurses' Association 1973). This structuring is partially represented in the development of nursing practice standards.

Standards of practice are authoritative statements or approved concepts that provide guidance to the profession and its members in the actual delivery of care. Both generic and specific standards for each major division of nursing practice have been developed by the American Nurses' Association.

The Standards of Psychiatric and Mental Health Nursing Practice were developed in 1973. These standards provide guidance and direction in the delivery of care as well as in defining professional roles and expectations for mental health nurses (see Appendix C). Each standard is written with a supporting rationale statement and a list of assessment factors. The assessment factors identify nursing behaviors that, if employed, assure achievement of the standard.

For example, Standard III is "The problem-solving approach is utilized in developing nursing care plans" (p. 3). The rationale states that a nursing diagnosis that encompasses the individual and the environment and the interaction between the two is utilized in the development of a plan of care. This standard gives direction to the specific aspects that must be addressed in the daily delivery of care. The assessment factors specify that attention should be given to the individual in response to the environment, and to behavioral patterns. Not only must these specific elements be observed, but an assessment must be drawn. The statement implies that the assessment process is ongoing. The assessment factors further state that input should be obtained from others who know the client and that the plans of nursing care are shared with other caregivers. These plans of care are used as guides for each client-nurse interaction and are periodically reviewed and revised. Utilization of the assessment factors facilitates the successful attainment of the mental health standard, thereby improving the quality of care. Failure to utilize the assessment factors places the nurse in a vulnerable position that ultimately could lead to a negligence or malpractice suit.

Standardization of nursing care eliminates reliance on individual values and standards, thereby improving the quality of care and consistently defining clear expectations of the professional nurse. Standards of practice facilitate the definition and delineation of standards of care. *Standards of care* have been defined as acts committed or omitted that an ordinary prudent person would have committed or omitted. Standards of care are a measure of what ought to be done in a given situation by a nurse carrying out professional duties and responsibilities. An individual nurse may be judged by peers who compare the nurse's actions with those described by the standards of care. Knowledge of the standards of care is the basis for providing quality care as well as for ensuring against a lawsuit for malpractice.

Peer Review

"Peer review is the process by which nursing care delivered by a group of nurses or an individual nurse is evaluated by individuals of the same rank or standing according to established standards of practice" (Dunkley 1973, p. 17). The process of *peer review* uses the standards of nursing practice as guidelines for evaluating the quantity and quality of nursing care.

The advantages of peer review are many. The degree of peer collaboration and the analysis of the care rendered does much to enhance personal growth and to improve the quality of nursing care rendered. Peer review is a self-regulatory mechanism that should be used as a continual evaluation tool for professional nurses in any setting. It provides an impetus for individual professional growth and accountability and is a mechanism for evaluating and enhancing the quality of nursing care.

Peplau (1980) pointed out that "peer review is more essential in psychiatric nursing practice than in general practice because of the ambiguity of the field" (p. 132). Perhaps the most important aspects of peer review are the disclosure and assessment of clinical data from nurse-client relationships in a supervising review process in which nurse colleagues openly check each other's work. In such review it becomes possible to know whether a nurse is practicing in a way that fosters professional growth, clinical judgment, and personal control. By means of peer review it is possible to note whether the nurse is using theory in considering a range of nurse actions and in foreseeing the probable consequences of actions taken.

Professional Liability

The nurse is held responsible for her nursing judgments and actions and is responsible for the safety and well-being of designated clients receiving care. There are three important legal concepts that every nurse should be familiar with: malpractice, negligence, and liability. *Malpractice* is defined as "professional misconduct, an improper discharge of professional duties, or a failure to meet the standard of care by a professional which results in harm to another." *Negligence* is defined as "carelessness, failure to act as an ordinary prudent person, or action contrary to the conduct of a reasonable person." *Liability* is "an obligation one has incurred or might incur through any act or failure to act" (Cazalas 1978, p. 258).

Although nurses are intellectually aware that a malpractice claim may arise in the course of their practice, most cannot imagine such an event happening to them personally. Many nurses believe that they are protected by their employer's insurance policy. While it is true that the employer may be liable for the actions of its employees (doctrine of respondent superior) and must therefore pay for damages incurred, there is no guaranty that the employer will not file a later claim against the negligent individual to recover damages paid. This practice, called *subrogating the claim*, is quite common.

In order for nurses to protect their professional careers, they should have professional liability insurance. Most people insure possessions they consider valuable, such as jewelry, home, and automobile, but fail to consider their professional career as a valued possession. Professional liability insurance does not absolve accountability for actions; it simply means that the damages awarded in a liability suit are paid by the insurance company and not by the individual nurse. Most individuals would have difficulty paying for the awarded damages and legal fees. Malpractice insurance provides some protection if a suit is brought against an individual practitioner. The payment of damage awards is outlined in the individual policy. In general, liability insurance will pay for the attorney fees and for bond, if the latter is required during an appeal (Creighton 1974).

The insurance contract covers a specified period of coverage. Policy coverage can be either "occurrence" or "claims made." *Occurrence* covers the insured for lawsuits that stem from any incidents that occur during the time of the policy coverage. For example, if a person was insured during an incident in 1980 but the malpractice suit was not filed until 1983 when the person was no longer insured, the person would still be covered since the incident occurred during the time when the policy was active. With *claims made* coverage, the person is insured for any claim that is filed during the policy time frame. If a lapse in coverage occurs, the person is not covered for any events that happen during the lapse in coverage. In this situation the nurse should check on the statute of limitations for client claims for his or her respective state (Trandel-Korenchuk and Trandel-Korenchuk 1980).

The amount payable to the injured party will be no more than the maximum coverage stated in the policy. If the awarded damages are more than the policy's maximum coverage, the individual must pay the difference.

In the conditions section of the insurance policy, the responsibility of the insured to notify the insurance company is spelled out. If there is any indication that a suit may be filed or that an actual injury has occurred, it is the responsibility of the insured to notify the insurance company. There is usually a clause concerning the cooperation of the insured in working with the insurance company. Also included is a clause concerning changes in the policy and cancellation of the policy.

Nurses must realize that they are accountable for their actions at all times. If nurses are provided with liability coverage by their employing agency, they must realize that the coverage is only for the time they are at work. There is no coverage for nonwork hours in which individuals may be volunteering their time to community activities or when a neighbor may seek their help. Individual professional liability insurance provides a broader coverage.

Four requirements for liability are imposed upon a nurse. When the nurse-client relationship is established, a legal duty exists between the nurse and the client. The nurse becomes responsible for the client's welfare and is held accountable for what happens to the client as a result of her actions. This requires a nurse to exercise standards of care in conducting nursing interventions.

A second factor necessary in establishing liability is a breach of existing legal duty, which is negligence. This occurs when nursing actions fall below the standard of reasonably prudent care. For nursing malpractice to occur, it must be established that the intervention or conduct deviated from acceptable nursing practice at the time. A nurse may be negligent in two ways: by direct conduct and by observing negligence on someone else's part and failing to report the same.

The third element for establishing liability is showing that the client sustained an injury as a result of the nurse's negligence. Because of the nature of their work, nurses commit acts of negligence frequently (e.g., medication errors), but most do not result in injury or damage to the client. The last element necessary for liability is damages, which is a monetary award to compensate the client for injuries. If no real damage occurs, the nurse is not held liable.

There are many inherent risks in health care and these are recognized by the courts. However, the courts do require that limits be placed on risk taking. Nurses must recognize these risks and document nursing actions in care plans and progress notes to reduce these risks (Feutz 1986).

Although there is no foolproof way of avoiding the chance of being sued, adherence to nursing standards of practice is one way to decrease the likelihood. No one is totally immune, but knowledge of the facility's policies and procedures and the use of sound nursing judgment will help protect the nurse from litigation and assure clients of the highest quality nursing care.

The nurse's best method of prevention for his own protection is thorough, clear, and accurate documentation that describes the situation and the nurse's interventions, which prove that the actions taken were similar to those any reasonably prudent nurse would take under similar circumstances.

ADVOCACY

Despite general efforts on the part of health professionals and the legal system to safeguard the rights of clients, several issues specific to mental health clients have yet to be addressed. Clients with histories of psychiatric illness have begun to bring violations of their rights by care providers and institutional policies to the attention of legislators, attorneys, and the general public. One of their main grievances is that they are not given the legal representation they require. Prior to a commitment hearing, legal counsel is appointed without the client's consent or knowledge. Such appointed attorneys are often poorly prepared because of lack of time to confer with the client, lack of competence in mental health law, and limited commitment to the client's interests.

Similarly, psychiatrists are called in on short notice to evaluate clients whom they have not previously seen. Their assessment is often made on the basis of a short interview. Yet their judgments and subsequent recommendations are seldom questioned or challenged. Because the appointed lawyer lacks mental health law expertise, his or her only recourse is usually to defer to the psychiatrist. Thus, the client's welfare is placed in the hands of one individual, whose competency in assessing the client may be limited or compromised.

As a result of these and other problems, concerned citizens, health professionals, and even institutions have begun to participate in the client advocacy movement. Concerned individuals and organizations have joined forces to see that care providers, the legal system, and clients themselves join in safeguarding the rights of mental health clients. Many hospitals and health care agencies philosophically or financially support the existence of formal client advocacy systems. People functioning within these formal systems are charged with: (1) informing clients of their rights, (2) advocating and protecting those clients whose rights have been violated, and (3) fostering a public perception of mental health clients that accepts their capacity to challenge the status quo of the health care system and to defend their civil rights.

The Nurse as Client Advocate

"Client advocacy" and "nurse as advocate" are certainly not new terms in nursing. The need for someone to act on the behalf of clients, as well as the feasibility of the nurse's assumption of this role, has emerged as a significant issue in psychiatric nursing. There is no general agreement, however, as to what exactly the advocate's role should be or even as to whether the nurse should act as the client's advocate.

The definition of *client advocacy* within nursing ranges from a broad philosophical interpretation to a more narrow, concrete definition with legal and political implications. Curtin (1979b), for example, defined advocacy as the very essence of nursing. She viewed it as the foundation upon which the nurse and client determine the form of their relationship—child-parent, client-counselor, friend-friend, colleague-colleague, and so on. She suggested that the ideal of advocacy is based on the commonality of the rights and needs of both client and nurse.

In strictest legal terms, advocacy is "the act of defending or pleading the case of another." This definition represents the traditional role of the legal defense counselor—the practice of law within the defense of individual legal rights (Durel 1981). Kohnke (1980) has offered a parallel definition for nursing as the act of informing and supporting a client, who can then make the best possible decisions. Two actions of the advocate are implied here:

(1) informing the client of exactly what his rights are, including supplying the client with information sufficient to make an informed decision, and (2) supporting the client once a decision has been made.

While nursing viewpoints on advocacy vary, all embody the tenets and philosophy undergirding many conceptual frameworks of nursing practice. These frameworks have traditionally emphasized the concept of advocacy without specifically describing it. Holism of the individual, the promulgation of client-centered interaction, and protection of the client's autonomy in determining her health state and in choosing measures to restore, maintain, or advance that health state—all are elements of advocacy that have been described and supported by various conceptual views on nursing practice (Nightingale 1860, Hall 1966, Levine 1971, Cox 1982).

Thus, in principle, the concept of advocacy has long been an integral part of the practice of nursing. As the principles of client advocacy become more visible, they are increasingly subject to intra- and extra-professional scrutiny and to legal interpretation. As a consequence, issues and controversies related to the nurse's assumption of the formal client advocate role have emerged and broadened.

THE PROS AND CONS OF THE NURSE AS CLIENT ADVOCATE Although most nurses agree in principle that the nurse should be the client's advocate, they are divided as to whether the nurse should assume a formal advocate role with clients. Those who would champion the formalized advocate role argue that the nursing profession is particularly well suited to assume this role. First, nurses spend more time with clients than do any other providers and thus are afforded more potential opportunities to learn about the clients as individuals, noting their concerns, strengths, and limitations. Second, nurses have traditionally emphasized client teaching as a primary professional function. In the teaching role, nurses provide clients with knowledge sufficient to enable them to make informed decisions about their health care. This, of course, is a primary function of the advocate (Kohnke 1980, Thollaug 1980).

An additional argument for nurses' assumption of the advocate role comes from their position as employees of a specific agency institution. Internal advocates, as opposed to advocates outside the institution, have a number of advantages. They have greater access to information about the client and are more familiar with the inner workings of the institution or agency. At the same time, they may be seen as a lesser threat to administrators than external advocates would (Willetts 1980).

C L I N I C A L   V I G N E T T E

PROFESSIONAL LIABILITY

John Noth sought admission to a hospital's emergency room where he was well known. Mr. Noth had been discharged the previous day from one of the hospital's psychiatric units. He was seen by Mrs. Warren, one of the registered nurses, for an initial assessment. Mr. Noth stated that he wanted to kill himself. Mrs. Warren noted that both the client's arms had superficial scratches, which he said he put there with a piece of broken glass. Mrs. Warren documented that Mr. Noth was agitated, had rambling, slurred speech, became loud, and cursed frequently during the initial assessment process.

When Mrs. Warren completed her interview, she asked the client to wait for the physician in the emergency room receiving area. Mr. Noth left the examining room and went to the receiving area. The nurse then paged for the psychiatrist on duty to report to emergency. Left unattended in the receiving area, Mr. Noth walked out of the hospital onto a busy street and was hit by an automobile; he died at the scene.

1. At which point did Mrs. Warren fail to use good judgment? When she left Mr. Noth and did not arrange to have him observed by anyone in her absence.

2. Was Mrs. Warren negligent? Yes, because the client stated he wanted to kill himself. She noted this in the medical record but took no precaution to observe or have someone observe the client. With the client's presenting complaints and his behavior during the interview process, the nurse was negligent and her actions were not those of a "reasonable" person.

A final point that provides support for the nurse as advocate is economic. Nursing services within agencies and institutions are, for the most part, not directly reimbursable. Decisions that clients make regarding their health status do not serve as financial incentives for the nurse. Unlike the physician or the attorney, therefore, the nurse in the advocate role is more likely to be client-centered rather than provider-centered (Thollaug 1980). Decisions are more likely to be made for the benefit of the client than to enhance any benefits for the provider.

The same arguments presented as supportive of the nurse as client advocate have been suggested by others to be the very reasons why nurses should *not* assume the advocate role. For example, the fact that the nurse is with the client more than other providers are is thought to set up a dependent relationship that negates the intent of the advocacy role. If the client has to depend on the nurse for basic care, it would seem that clients would come to rely on the nurse for extensive decision making. Because the role of advocate is enacted in order to enable the individual to make independent decisions, potential for conflict between the nurse and client is increased and the risk of invading a client's rights is exacerbated when nurses assume advocacy roles (Castledine 1981).

A second argument against the nurse as advocate is based on educational background. Most nurses have an inadequate knowledge base to support the formalized role of conservator or legal advisor. Although increasing numbers of nurses are preparing themselves for joint nursing-legal careers, they remain in the minority. General nursing education simply has not prepared nurses to enact a formalized advocate role that assumes legal expertise.

A third factor that makes the nurse an undesirable client advocate is that clients would have no choice of who would act as their advocate. If the advocacy role is to be assumed by the nurse charged with the client's primary nursing care—independent of client input—the client's rights have already been violated.

The final argument against the nurse as advocate comes from the constraints placed on the nurse by the institution or authority who employs him or her (Castledine 1981). Very often the major functions of advocacy are antagonistic to the institution. The advocate often acts as "informer" and is labeled a troublemaker or insubordinate if he or she supports the client in a decision that is contrary to the thinking of other health care providers or the institution.

Brown (1986) offers another viewpoint—that clients should not need an advocate. By implying that advocacy is necessary, the client is relegated to the role of the weak and oppressed. Calling nurses advocates is another way of rationalizing and coming to terms with the oppressed existence of nursing.

CLINICAL VIGNETTE

THE NURSE AS ADVOCATE

A number of clients in a mental hygiene day clinic were concerned that their group sessions had become less effective because of the simultaneous participation by several nursing students. While the clients welcomed the students' participation in general, they felt that the introduction of more than one student per session significantly altered the context and character of the group process. The nurse/group leader asked permission from group members to serve as spokesperson to the faculty member in charge of the students. The nurse promised to express their con-cerns exactly as they were presented and to report the results of the discussion with the faculty member at the next group session.

In this example, the nurse was taking a direct advocacy action in that she was serving as the group representative to express concerns on a matter that had implications for institutional policy and practice. If the nurse had arranged a meeting to allow direct confrontation between the faculty person and the clients themselves, it would have been an act of indirect advocacy.

By identifying with the depressed, angry, frustrated client, nurses can account for their own anger, frustration, and depression. The theory of advocacy does not work simply because it is an excuse for being miserable. Rather than use the clients' weaknesses as nursing's strengths, nurses should accept the clients' assertiveness, knowledge of their own needs and capabilities. The role should be one of facilitator to enable clients to present their own cases directly to those who are deciding what treatment to give. Throughout nurse-client interaction, collaborative goals are negotiated. When client advocacy is initiated by the nurse and carried out by the nurse, the importance of collaboration is overlooked. Even in advocacy, the client should be enlisted as a participant if at all possible. Failing this, family members or friends should be involved. In this way, the client is reminded of potential and resources that are available within himself or his support system.

CHARACTERISTICS AND RESPONSIBILITIES OF THE MENTAL HEALTH CLIENT ADVOCATE Despite controversies over the nurse's general assumption of the advocate role, advocacy as a psychiatric nursing function has been clearly described. The psychiatric nurse's advocacy role is not only to defend client rights but to monitor the safety of services rendered to mental health clients. Durel (1981) sees the advocacy role for mental health nurses as a logical blending of professional, legal, and ethical responsibilities. For example, the mental health nurse should monitor whether:

1. Clients' medications are being reduced in order to determine lowest maintenance dosages.
2. Treatment plans are periodically evaluated for their contribution to the patient's well-being.
3. Alternatives to hospitalization are being offered to clients and their families.
4. Safeguards are being provided for those clients who may be unable to communicate effectively.
5. Clients are routinely informed of the potential side effects of psychotropic drugs.
6. Diagnostic labels are used as therapeutic tools rather than applied for bureaucratic or administrative reasons.

Durel has proposed that the mental health nurse as client advocate assumes two types of functions: direct and indirect. *Direct* advocacy includes those actions taken by the nurse to speak as the client's representative to those who have control over the client's treatment. *Indirect* advocacy refers to those nursing actions that place the client in a favorable position to speak for himself to those having the power to satisfy his needs or interests.

In keeping with the basic philosophical tenets of nursing practice, indirect advocacy or a combination of direct and indirect advocacy is often preferred to direct advocacy. Direct advocacy is reserved for those situations that (1) reflect institutional practices or policy, (2) cannot be addressed by the client because of emotional or cognitive limitations, (3) would be ineffectively addressed by the client because of lack of social power, or (4) would potentially elicit negative interpersonal responses from those holding power, resulting in loss of self-esteem for the client (Durel 1981).

Cautions Relative to the Advocacy Role

Caution must be exercised by the mental health nurse in executing the advocacy role. Advocacy acts can be in direct conflict with the traditional image of nursing as a discipline that offers professional expertise. Professional education and experience tend to reinforce the image of "experts" who know what is best for the client and who are paid to make clinically relevant decisions. The tendency, then, is to make decisions *for* the psychiatric client as opposed to supporting the client in making his or her own decisions. Making choices for the client not only violates his or her rights but also places the nurse in the position of being blamed if the choice turns out to have been a poor one (Kohnke 1980).

Another caution concerning advocacy is the potential for conflict of values between the mental health nurse and the client. To faithfully represent the rights and interests of clients without interjecting a personal set of values is difficult, at best. Mauksch (1980) pointed out that at times "fending for" can easily lead to "control of." The mental health nurse must continually ask whether actions taken as advocate represent the interests of the client or actually reflect his or her personal biases and perspectives on the issue.

Clearly, there will be times when clients make decisions that are in direct opposition to the values of the nurse. If possible, however, it is the client's values that should prevail. When compromise is essential to protect the client's health and well-being, the compromise that is most acceptable to the client should be the one enacted.

SUMMARY

The practice of mental health nursing involves an interplay of ethical values, clients' rights, and legal issues. Nurses have obligations to society, their profession, their clients, and themselves. Achieving the proper balance between these obligations necessitates a knowledge of rights and responsibilities of both clients and institutions, of the use of DNR orders and restrictive treatment, of involuntary commitment and the right to care, and of the implications for nursing in these areas.

Because the care of the mentally ill can be overwhelmingly complex, nurses should be aware of their professional accountability and liability when working with these clients. The Standards of Psychiatric and Mental Health Nursing Practice and the peer review process are necessary for establishing guidelines and promoting excellence in care of mentally ill clients.

The complexity of the health care system dictates the need for advocates for clients, especially those who are mentally ill. While there are conflicting views about the amount of involvement that nurses should have in client advocacy, most nurses find themselves in a position of helping clients in obtaining the best care available. It is imperative that nurses be aware of the various roles that they may perform in this capacity. Perhaps the most powerful and influential of these roles is that which promotes change in the larger arena of health care, thereby ultimately benefitting the individual client.

Review Questions

1. What are the major responsibilities of an institution or agency in delineating clients' rights?

2. Under what circumstances would detention of a client be considered false imprisonment?

3. How do DNR policies affect nurses in psychiatric settings?

4. What is the purpose of standards of practice?

5. List three arguments for nurses not to assume the client advocate role.

Suggested Annotated Readings

Chinn, P. *Ethical Issues in Nursing*. Rockville, Maryland: Aspen Pub. Co., 1986.

A variety of essays presents an overview of theoretical and philosophical dimensions of ethics in nursing, with particular emphasis on ethical issues in nursing practice and education. The articles reflect contradictions, inconsistencies, and alternative views inherent in ethical issues.

Hartmann, B. *The Patient's Advocate*. New York: Viking Press, 1981.

The author presents information that nurses as patient advocates need to know about hospital systems and how to play the game to their advantage. The goal of the book is to decrease sources of fear and worry caused by lack of knowledge to allow patients more energy for getting well.

Murchison, I., T. Nichols, and R. Hanson. *Legal Accountability in the Nursing Process*. St. Louis: C. V. Mosby, 1982.

This overall approach seeks to integrate law into the nursing process. Litigated cases demonstrate the level of practice for which nurses are being held accountable. The content is structured to stimulate productive thinking about the law and its relationship to professional nursing.

Quinn, C., and M. Smith. *The Professional Commitment: Issues and Ethics in Nursing*. Philadelphia: W. B. Saunders, 1987.

This book focuses on the similar aspects of clinical and professional ethics, emphasizing that each is a part of broad professional concerns. It provides a slightly different and broader perspective on ethics and professional issues.

Steele, S., and V. Harmon. *Values Clarification in Nursing*. Norwalk, Connecticut: Appleton-Century-Crofts, 1983.

The purpose of this book is to expose the reader to the systematic process of values clarification in nursing. Designed to facilitate the readers' active involvement in the decision-making process, it contains exercises to be completed during the study.

References

American Hospital Association. *A Patient's Bill of Rights*. Chicago: American Hospital Association, 1975.

American Nurses' Association. *Standards of Psychiatric Mental Health Nursing Practice*. Kansas City, Missouri: American Nurses' Association, 1973.

———. *Code for Nurses with Interpretive Statements*. Kansas City, Missouri: American Nurses' Association, 1976.

Appelbaum, P., and T. Gutheil. "Drug Refusal: A Study of Psychiatric Inpatients." *American Journal of Psychiatry* 137 (1980):340–345.

Arkin, H. "Forcible Administration of Antipsychotic Medication." *Journal of the American Medical Association* 249 (1983):2784–2785.

Aroskar, M. A. "Nurses as Decision Makers: Ethical Dimensions." *Imprint* 32 (November 1985):29–31.

Bandman, B. "Some Remarks on the Mentally Disabled Patient's Right to Receive and Refuse Treatment." *Issues in Mental Health Nursing* (Winter 1978):46–50.

Bedell, S. E., D. Pelle, P. L. Maher, and P. D. Cleary. "Do-Not-Resuscitate Orders for Critically Ill Patients in the Hospital." *Journal of the American Medical Association* 256 (1986):233–237.

Brown, P. "Who Needs an Advocate?" *Nursing Times* (August 6, 1986):72.

Carroll, M. A. "The Right to Treatment and Involuntary Commitment." *The Journal of Medicine and Philosophy* 5 (1980):278–290.

Castledine, G. "The Nurse as the Patient's Advocate: Pros and Cons." *Nursing Mirror* 153 (1981):38–40.

Cazalas, M. W. *Nursing and the Law*, 3d ed. Rockville, Maryland: Aspen Systems, 1978.

Chinn, P., and M. Jacobs. *Theory and Nursing: A Systematic Approach*. St. Louis: C. V. Mosby, 1983.

Cournos, F. "Orders Not to Resuscitate and the Psychiatric Hospital." *Psychiatric Quarterly* 58 (Spring 1986-1987):24–31.

Cox, C. "An Interaction Model of Client Health Behavior: Theoretical Prescription for Nursing." *Advances in Nursing Science* 5 (1982):46–57.

Creighton, H. *Law Every Nurse Should Know*. Philadelphia: W. B. Saunders, 1974.

Curtin, L. "The Nurse as Advocate: A Philosophical Foundation for Nursing." *Advances in Nursing Science* 1 (1976):1–10.

———. "Clarity and Freedom: Ethical Issues in Mental Health." *Issues in Mental Health Nursing* 2 (1979a): 102–108.

Davis, J. "The Ethics of Behavior Control: The Nurse as Double Agent." *Issues in Mental Health Nursing* (Winter 1978):2–16.

Dunkley, P. "Accountability: The Implications." *South Carolina Nursing* 21 (1973):7–21.

Durel, S. "Advocacy: A Function of the Community Mental Health Nurse." *Virginia Nurse* 49 (1981):33–36.

Evans, A. L., and B. A. Brody. "The Do-Not-Resuscitate Order in Teaching Hospitals." *Journal of the American Medical Association* 253 (1985):2236–2239.

Feutz, S. A. "Diminishing Liability: Laws and Regulations." *Journal of Nursing Administration* 16 (1986): 12–14.

Flanagan, L. "A Question of Ethics." *Nursing Times* (August 27, 1986):39–41.

Fry, S. T. "Individual versus Aggregate Good: Ethical Tension in Nursing Practice." *International Journal of Nursing Studies* 22 (1985):303–310.

Hall, L. "Another View of Nursing Care and Quality." In *Community of Patient Care: The Role of Nursing*, K. Staub and K. Parker, eds. Washington, D.C.: Catholic University Press, 1966.

Joint Commission on Accreditation of Hospitals. *Consolidated Standards Manual/83 for Child, Adolescent, and Adult Psychiatric, Alcoholism and Drug Abuse Facilities*. Chicago: Joint Commission on Accreditation of Hospitals, 1983.

——. *Long-Term Care Standards Manual for 1988*. pp. 55–56. Chicago: Joint Commission on Accreditation of Hospitals, 1988.

Kohnke, M. "The Nurse as Advocate." *American Journal of Nursing* 80 (1980):2038–2040.

Levine, M. "Holistic Nursing." In *The Nursing Clinics of North America*, L. Germain and G. Alfano, eds. Philadelphia: W. B. Saunders, 1971.

Lipton, H. L. "Do-Not-Resuscitate Decisions in a Community Hospital." *Journal of the American Medical Association* 256 (1986):1164–1169.

Mauksch, I. "Advocacy or Control: Which Do We Offer the Elderly?" *Geriatric Nursing* 1 (1980):278.

Miller, R. D. "The Least Restrictive Alternative: Hidden Meaning and Agendas." *Community Mental Health Journal* 18 (1982):46–55.

Nightingale, F. *Notes on Nursing*. New York: Appleton, 1860.

Peplau, H. "The Psychiatric Nurse Accountable? To Whom? For What?" *Perspectives in Psychiatric Care* 18 (1980):128–134.

Regan, W. "Force-Medicating the Mental Patient: Assault." *The Regan Report on Nursing Law* 20, no. 11 (1980).

——. "Mental Patients and Forced Medication." *The Regan Report on Nursing Law* 21, no. 10 (1981a).

——. "N. J.: No Forced Meds for Mental Patients." *The Regan Report on Nursing Law* 22, no. 6 (1981b).

Roth, L. H. "Mental Health Commitment: The State of the Debate." *Hospital and Community Psychiatry* 31 (1980):385–395.

Sanders, J. B., and D. DuPlessis. "An Historical View of the Right to Treatment." *Journal of Psychosocial Nursing* 23 (1985):12–15.

Schwartz, D. A., and P. Reilly. "The Choice Not to Be Resuscitated." *Journal of the American Geriatric Society* 34 (1986):807–811.

Tancredi, L. R. "The Rights of Mental Patients: Weighing the Interests." *Journal of Health, Politics, Policy and Law* 5 (1980):199–204.

Thollaug, S. "The Nurse as Patient Advocate." *Imprint* 27 (1980):37+.

Trandel-Korenchuk, D., and K. Trandel-Korenchuk. "Current Legal Issues Facing Nursing Practice." *Nursing Administration Quarterly* 5, no. 1 (1980):37–45.

Watson, A. "Informed Consent of Special Subjects." *Nursing Research* 31 (1982):43–47.

Willetts, R. "Advocacy and the Mentally Ill." *Social Work* 25 (1980):372–377.

Wilson, C. C., and F. E. Netting. "Ethical Issues in Long-Term Care for the Elderly." *Health Values* 10 (1986):3–12.

Youngner, S. J., W. Lewandowski, D. H. McClish, B. W. Juknialis, C. Coulton, and E. T. Barttell. "Do-Not-Resuscitate Orders." *Journal of the American Medical Association* 253 (1985):54–57.

26

Nursing Research Issues and Development

Learning Objectives

After studying this chapter, the student should be able to:

1. Discuss clinical opportunities for nursing research.

2. Compare and contrast experimental, quasi-experimental, and survey designs for research.

3. Describe the direction of nursing research in health care.

4. Understand the implications of implementing the Diagnosis-Related Groups (DRG) system for the psychiatric community.

5. Delineate mechanisms that nurses can use to cope within a constrained economic environment.

Overview

In order to continue to grow as a profession, nursing must direct its efforts toward the study and evaluation of the practice of nursing as well as its role in the health care system. The basis for self-evaluation within nursing is the careful and thorough development and use of clinical research by nurses so as to advance the body of knowledge that is nursing theory and practice.

Health care delivery in the United States has become problematic and controversial. Costs are spiraling and access to care is unequally distributed. Changes are being demanded on a national basis and the nursing profession is now in a position to influence these changes and to advance its standing as a profession while offering greater benefits to health consumers.

In order to cope with these changes, nurses need to develop methods of accurately defining their contributions to health care and delineating the cost for quality care based on standards of practice. Quality assurance programs are necessary to evaluate the effectiveness and quality of care given to clients. Such studies are a way of demonstrating that nurses make a difference in client care.

NURSING RESEARCH

Nursing research is a systematic, detailed attempt to discover or confirm facts that relate to a problem in the field of nursing. The goal of nursing research is the provision of scientific knowledge in nursing. Research with the ultimate goal of application of scientific knowledge to improve nursing practice is referred to as *clinical research in nursing* (Abdellah 1970). Research by nurses is just beginning to come into its own. Ever-increasing numbers of nurses are preparing to do research and are doing it. Findings from this research are having an impact on clinical practice, nursing education, nursing administration, and the relationships between nursing and other disciplines in providing health care to all segments of the population. Yet many nurses, particularly staff nurses who are "where the action is" in clinical practice, regard nursing research as something to be avoided. This unwillingness to engage in research is due to many factors: lack of knowledge about conducting research, other demands on available time, fear of attempting something new, and lack of realization concerning the value of nursing research.

Nurses prepared at the masters or Ph.D. level are schooled in sophisticated methods of research, and these nursing scholars are important to the advancement of nursing science through research. But clinical nursing research also needs to be conducted by nurses who are experiencing the everyday problems of delivering nursing care. These are the nurses who can help bridge the gap between theory and practice by contributing knowledge based on hands-on experience. The nurses in clinical practice are in a position to know what does and doesn't work and to share these experiences with others.

The student should keep in mind that research does not have to be complicated and sophisticated to be important. Many times the basic premise and methodology of a study are relatively simple. An example of such a simple project would be evaluating the effects of a patient-teaching program by comparing client knowledge and compliance before and after the instruction.

The problems in delivering good-quality nursing care are painfully evident to all nurses. These problems should be the basis of nursing research. One way to discover the basis for a study is to ask "Isn't there a better way to do . . . ?" The process of discovering, implementing, and evaluating such "better ways" is nursing research.

Historical Perspectives

The first clinical nursing research was done by Florence Nightingale during the Crimean War. Her investigations and use of statistics revealed the deplorable conditions in military and civilian hospitals and brought about widespread reforms (Stewart 1962).

The three schools of nursing that were established in the United States in 1873—Bellevue in New York, Massachusetts General in Boston, and the Connecticut School in New Haven—adhered to the principles of accurate recording and data collection set forth by Nightingale. Unfortunately, later schools did not follow these guidelines. From 1900 to 1930, schools of nursing were established at a rapid rate as hospitals discovered that the easiest and cheapest way to obtain nurses was to have their own school. The bulk of the work was done by students, as most graduates went into private duty. Physicians, the public, and nurses themselves began to think of the practicing nurse as one who followed the directions of physicians and other authority figures. These conditions did not promote the growth of nursing research (Gortner and Nahm 1977).

Practice-related research began again in the 1920s and 1930s, when the need for systematic evaluation of nursing procedures was recognized. Descriptions of nursing care plans and case studies predominated in the literature and reflected a gradual change in emphasis from focusing on case studies as teaching tools to case studies as a method for improving patient care.

During the 1940s and 1950s, as a result of the shortage of nurses that was demonstrated during World War II, research turned to studies of nursing resources (kinds, numbers, and uses of nurses) and of the organization and delivery of nursing services. Studies about the nurse outnumbered studies about nursing practice ten to one.

In 1952 the journal *Nursing Research* was established. It provided an avenue for nurses to publish and share their findings. Concern for improvement of nursing services was particularly acute in psychiatric and maternal-child health nursing at this time. These fields received major research thrusts from federal grant and training programs. Federal funds supported the development of graduate programs in these two areas of nursing, and the Russell Sage Foundation provided grants for studies related to the functioning of psychiatric nurses. Typical of these studies were those by Schwartz and Shackley (1956), which focused on the role of the nurse with the psychiatric patient, and by Stanton and Schwartz (1954), which studied the social context of psychiatric institutions.

The 1960s witnessed an increase in studies related to specific groups of clients, such as dying clients and cardiac clients, and to the areas of geriatrics, ambulatory care, and pediatrics. In 1970, the emphasis turned to the topic of assuring quality nursing practice, with a search for direct cause-effect relationships between the process of nursing care and client outcomes. Practice-related research is gaining momentum because of the interest in increasing the knowledge base for nursing (Gortner and Nahm 1977).

Within psychiatric nursing specifically, the focus of nursing research has changed. Prior to World War II, the emphasis was on the individual as the unit of study. In the 1950s, the conceptualization of illness turned from a "within the person" approach to a "within the relationship" framework, and studies about the nurse-patient relationship came into being. The following decade brought a pattern of collaborative work between social scientists and nurses, producing "within the social system" studies. There was a trend toward the investigation of psychosocial variables related to physical illness states. The interdisciplinary approach to research had begun. Nursing should continue to study what is within its boundaries and to study collaboratively with other disciplines what is within the larger boundaries of health care (Sills 1977).

The Research Process

A research study can range from the simple to the highly complex in its design, management, and analysis. However, certain elements are incorporated in any study. The following section is designed to give the student a basic introduction to the process of research (Polit and Hungler 1978).

In order to understand the research process, the student needs a basic understanding of some terms that are frequently used when discussing research. A brief glossary of terms is provided in the accompanying box.

The research process involves a number of sequential steps: defining the problem, reviewing the literature, defining the variables, formulating the hypotheses, designing the study, collecting the data, analyzing the data, interpreting the results, and communicating the findings.

DEFINING THE PROBLEM Getting started on a research project and defining the problem are frequently the most difficult parts of doing research. Many nurses may wonder what there is to be studied, while others may have a variety of ideas and have difficulty choosing among them. The problem statement may arise from a difficult situation encountered in practice or from the nurse's particular area of interest. For example, a nurse may be interested in remotivation therapy for groups of clients. Her experience indicates that clients who receive remotivation therapy are able to socialize better with other clients on the unit. The nurse would like to determine whether her observations

can be demonstrated to have merit by researching the effect of the therapy on socialization. The research question or problem may become: Does remotivation therapy make a difference in socialization of clients?

Other factors that must be considered when designing the research question are: Is the problem of significance to nursing? Are facilities available to conduct this research? Is there access to enough subjects? Is the cooperation of others needed, and will it be available?

Once the problem is defined, it is stated as the purpose of the study. Using the example of remotivation therapy, the purpose would be stated as:

The purpose of this study is to examine the differences in the amount of time clients spend socializing with other clients and staff before and after receiving ten sessions of remotivation therapy.

REVIEWING THE LITERATURE A review of the literature is necessary as a beginning step in the research process. The researcher needs to be familiar with studies that have already been done in the area that has been chosen for study. The review of the literature can provide (1) a justification for doing the study, (2) a baseline upon which to build the study, (3) a comparison of a variety of views and opinions on the subject, and (4) suggestions for the methodology for performing the study. A comprehensive review of the literature should not be limited to nursing literature, but should encompass such related fields as sociology, psychology, law, economics, and medicine, depending on the subject of the research.

The research should also be linked to a basic theoretical framework. Without a theoretical underpinning to guide it, the research is unlikely to be useful in explaining the phenomenon being studied. The theory need not be complicated or inhibitive for the student. For example, the theoretical framework for the remotivation study might be Sullivan's or Peplau's theories of interpersonal relations, which emphasize the need for interpersonal experiences for the development of self-concept. Or behavioral theory could be used: The researcher might see the positive experiences in group sessions as reinforcers that promote the continued social behavior after the group sessions are finished.

DEFINING THE VARIABLES The next step in the process is to define the variables in a way that they can be measured. In the remotivation study, the independent variable to be manipulated is the remotivation sessions. The purpose, objectives, and content of these sessions should be clearly defined and described. The dependent variable is the socialization scores of the clients after they have experienced ten remotivation sessions.

RESEARCH TERMINOLOGY

- *Design*. A plan for the research that specifies what, who, how, and when.
- *Hypothesis*. The researcher's statement concerning the relationship between the elements being studied; what the researcher expects to find. *Example:* Clients who are given a course of instruction in the use of their medications will have greater compliance in taking the medication than those clients who have not had instruction.
- *Instrument or tool*. The device used for collecting the data. *Example:* a questionnaire.
- *Operational definition*. Communicating exactly what the researcher means by a certain concept used in the research.
- *Reliability*. Consistency of the measurement tool; its ability to perform in a similar manner each time it is used. *Example:* A blood pressure cuff that registers 140/80 is expected to register this same value every time the blood pressure is taken, and the client's pressure remains at that level.
- *Validity*. Measuring what is claimed to be measured. *Example:* Does an instrument designed to measure attitudes toward alcoholism really measure those attitudes, or does it measure something else, such as responding in the expected, usually accepted manner?
- *Variable*. An entity that can take on several values; usually the focus of the study. *Example:* Age is a variable that can range from birth to any number of years.

- *Independent variable*. The variable that is manipulated or changed in the study. *Example:* A teaching program is given or not given to groups of clients.
- *Dependent variables*. Variables to be explained. Values of the dependent variable are the result of the manipulation of the independent variable.
- *Experimental research*. Research in which the researcher makes a change or an intervention and observes the results.
- *Nonexperimental relationship*. Research in which the researcher observes a phenomenon without making an intervention.
- *Population*. The universe available for study. *Example:* All cardiac clients in the United States.
- *Sample*. A representative group of the population. *Example:* All cardiac clients at one hospital treated during a certain time period.
- *Random sampling*. Sampling in which every subject has an equal chance of being assigned to any group.
- *Experimental group*. Group that receives the experimental intervention.
- *Control group*. Group that does not receive the experimental intervention.
- *Descriptive statistics*. Statistics that describe and summarize data. *Example:* means and frequency distributions.
- *Inferential statistics:* Statistics that infer a relationship among variables.

FORMULATING THE HYPOTHESES The hypotheses are statements of the relationship between the variables. A hypothesis is the researcher's interpretation of the outcome of the research. Hypotheses are developed before the study to give the study a direction and to facilitate the interpretation of the data. The hypotheses may be directional or nondirectional; that is, they may or may not specify a direction of the relationship of the variables. In the remotivational study, a directional hypothesis would be most appropriate, since the nurse's first interest in the topic was generated by the observation that remotivation sessions increased the socialization of clients. The hypotheses might be stated:

There will be a positive relationship between attendance at ten remotivation therapy sessions and the socialization scores of the clients.

DESIGNING THE STUDY The research design is the overall plan to obtain answers to the research question. Research can be either *experimental* (in which the researcher makes an intervention with participants and then observes the results) or *nonexperimental* (in which data are collected without making any changes or interventions).

Experimental Designs A true experimental design must have three elements: (1) the researcher must make some kind of intervention with some of the subjects, (2) there must be some control over the research situation, usually provided by the use of a control group, and (3) the subjects must be assigned to either experimental or control groups on a random basis. An experimental design is often considered to be the ideal form of research because direct cause and effect can be hypothesized from it. Unfortunately, much research that is needed in nursing cannot be conducted in this manner. Many times the variables that nurses need to study cannot be manipulated or experimentally controlled. There are also many ethical considerations in this type of research. For example, depriving some clients of treatment or giving controversial treatments to clients could create ethical dilemmas.

In a true experimental design, an experimental and a control group are used. Both are initially assessed, an intervention is made with the experimental group, and then both groups are reassessed. Any changes observed in the experimental group are attributed to the intervention if no change occurs in the control group over the same time.

Quasi-experimental Designs

A quasi-experimental design resembles the experimental design except that one or more of the three essential elements is lacking. Sometimes no suitable control group is available; at other times, randomization is not possible. However, quasi-experimental designs do involve an intervention.

If, in the remotivation study the clients are given a socialization score before the ten sessions and again after the sessions but no control group is used, the study would be quasi-experimental. Without a control group, any changes in the socialization scores may be due to a variety of factors besides the remotivation session—changes in personnel, institution of another program during the same period of time, growth in general comfort level because of increased familiarity with the surroundings, and so on. The use of a control group would help eliminate these alternative explanations.

Survey Designs

Survey research is designed to assess an existing situation within a group of people. Surveys are frequently conducted in all aspects of life. During an election year, surveys are continually made of samples from the population to assess the popularity of various candidates. Mail surveys are commonly used to determine buying preferences of consumers.

Surveys are the most common method of descriptive research. Surveys are often needed to aid in defining a research question or in delineating the pertinent variables. In many instances, it is necessary to find out what *is* before the researcher can decide what needs to be. Various methods can be used for survey designs, including face-to-face interviews, questionnaires, and telephone interviews. Information obtained by surveys is usually relatively superficial, since surveys lack the ability to probe deeply into behavior and feelings. However, this type of research is especially needed in nursing today. Nursing is at a stage where descriptive studies are necessary to define phenomena before progress can be made in experimental research on these phenomena. The practice of nursing is not well understood. Descriptive studies are needed to understand and explain functions and forms of nursing care in meeting the needs of society and in helping individuals regain or maintain health.

COLLECTING THE DATA   Data can be collected in a variety of ways, depending on the design of the research. Some frequently used methods include:

1. Physiological measurements, such as changes in blood pressure, sweat gland activity, and eye blinks.
2. Observational measurements, such as observing behaviors, activities, communication, and the environment.
3. Interviews and questionnaires.
4. Scales and psychological measures, such as Rorschach tests and the Minnesota Multiphasic Personality Inventory.

In the remotivation study, observation measures would be used to compile a socialization score for each client. For a two-week period prior to the sessions, the number of times that a client approached another client or staff member and the length of time of the contact would be noted. The same observations would be made for a two-week period following the sessions. In order to collect the data, the researcher would need the cooperation of a nurse on each shift. The same observations might be made again two months later to assess sustaining effects.

ANALYZING THE DATA   The data collected in a study need to be analyzed to provide meaning to the study. For descriptive studies, statistics such as means and frequency distributions are used. These statistics describe the results; they do not make any references about the relationships between variables. Experimental or quasi-experimental studies frequently make use of inferential statistics, which do make inferences about the relationships between the variables. Inferential statistics provide the means for drawing a conclusion about the population studied based on the results obtained from the sample.

Several statistical tests are available to determine whether the scores obtained by one group are statistically different from scores obtained by another group. Statistical significance means that the differences in scores are probably not due to chance. There will always be some differences in scores, but whether the difference is great enough to be significant can be determined by the statistical tests. In the remotivation study, the scores obtained prior to and after the remotivation sessions could be tested for significance using the T-test for Dependent samples.

The beginning researcher should not be overwhelmed by lack of knowledge about statistics. In most institutions, there are people available who can help with the statistical analysis and interpretation if this is needed. In many instances, basic computation of averages and frequencies will be sufficient.

INTERPRETING THE RESULTS After the data are collected and analyzed, it is the researcher's task to make some sense of the results and to draw conclusions based on the findings. If the findings fit the hypothesis, the explanation is easier. But alternative explanations should also be listed. If the hypothesis is not supported, the researcher must develop some possible explanations, such as that measurement was poor or that the sample was too small. Suggestions for future research should be made.

COMMUNICATING THE FINDINGS In preparing the report of the research, the writer should be as clear and objective as possible, realizing that the reader will not be familiar with the research. Reports will vary in style and length, but the basic format outlined in this chapter should be followed. Many researchers hesitate to report negative findings, perhaps because most journals do not report studies with negative findings. However, in many instances negative findings are as important as positive ones in guiding others for future research. The importance of writing and sharing research findings and ideas with other nurses cannot be overemphasized. Nurse researchers who, after laboriously planning and researching, are hesitant to write up their findings. Their reasons are many and varied, but nurse researchers may be assisted in their writing efforts by keeping the following thoughts in mind that are discussed later in this chapter in the section "The Importance of Writing."

RESEARCH PRIORITIES FOR THE FUTURE

Several gaps in the existing body of knowledge have been identified in the literature. Nursing has not yet reached the stage where one study builds upon another. Replication and follow-up studies are rarely done. A scientific body of knowledge that is uniquely nursing has yet to be defined to provide a basis against which nursing practice can be measured. Without these criteria, nursing practice is one of trial-and-error rather than one of solid scientific foundation.

Many issues relate to the areas of nursing practice and the profession of nursing and lack research and development. Initial studies should take high priority and should include such subjects as improvement of care to high-risk groups, adaptation to chronic illness, interventions to promote health, utilization of new technologies, application of new knowledge to client care, and upgrading and evaluating of curriculum in schools of nursing.

Of particular concern in the current economic environment is the effect of new health care legislation and its ultimate influence on the practice of nursing. Several key issues warrant attention by nurses in their evaluation of nursing practice. One example is the development of new payment systems for health care and its implications for the financial future of nursing.

Prospective Payment Systems

The reality of the escalating costs of health care in the United States has become a major source of concern for consumers, the government, and the providers. In response to these costs, Congress voted for a restructured program to halt and reverse the spiraling expenses. On April 20, 1983, President Reagan signed into law H.R. 1900, the Social Security Amendment of 1983. This legislation established a prospective payment system that allowed for pretreatment diagnosis billing categories. This enactment will permanently alter the nature of health care delivery and has widespread implications for all health care providers, including and perhaps, most especially for nurses. Although the theoretical basis of this reform is that efficiency and quality will be increased while costs are reduced, the beginning experience with this system has sparked vehement debates and concerns from providers. Professionals in the psychiatric arena have discovered a myriad of problems in trying to apply this system to their services.

The concept of Diagnosis-Related Groups (DRGs) was developed at Yale University to define types of cases that could be expected to receive similar amounts of services from the hospital. The length of stay (LOS) was used as a measure of hospital services (Shaffer 1984a, 1984b).

With DRGs, payment for inpatient costs is based on a fixed amount, determined in advance for each case, depending on the diagnostic group. This amount is considered payment in full. If the treatment costs the hospital less than the DRG allotment, the hospital keeps the extra as profit. If the treatment costs more than the specified rate, the hospital must absorb the loss.

The DRG system is expected to provide incentives for efficiency and to decrease the demand for inpatient hospital services. Although the length of stay is not as accurate an indicator as actual costs, it is being used because of its practical availability at a time when cost cutting is required on a near-emergency basis (Plomann and Shaffer 1983).

The DRGs developed for psychiatric illness are shown in Table 26–1.

A study conducted by the American Psychiatric Association in 1985 found that there was very little relationship between a psychiatric DRG payment and the actual resources needed to care for the clients. The system is not accurate for psychiatry and does not have a reliable ability to predict costs (English et al. 1986).

Since applying the current DRG-based prospective payment system to psychiatric hospital care is generally deemed unwise by the psychiatric community of caregivers, a search for alternative systems is underway. Many variables are being identified as contributing to the length of stay in psychiatric facilities. One of the greatest influences on a client's length of stay appears to be the resources available for aftercare and living arrangements in the community. Many clients lose both their homes and incomes during a psychiatric hospitalization and cannot be discharged until these losses are addressed. Some groups of clients can only live in the community if they are placed in highly structured and well-supervised residences and service programs (Caton and Gralnick 1984).

A prospective reimbursement for psychiatry based on variables that are indicative of prognosis (i.e., probability of relapse) has been suggested (de-Figueiredo and Boerstler 1985). Prognosis of mental disorders when assessed in terms of outcome dysfunction such as work or social relations, has been found to be relatively independent of diagnosis. With a system based on prognosis, it is possible to plan for long-term treatment that could cover outpatient services as well as inpatient care. Prognosis-related groups should be developed incorporating such variables as age, self-care, marital status, employment status, having a place to live, and availability of social supports.

By giving the acute-care hospitals an incentive for early discharge of clients, the system of prospective payment has increased the complexity of care demanded by long-term care facilities. Since nursing homes do not have incentives to treat these more acutely ill clients, a system that pays nursing homes according to case mix should be developed. The case mix reimbursement system that appears to have potential as a prototype is the one now being used in New York State known as Resource Utilization Groups (RUGs II).

Table 26–1. Drugs for Psychiatric Illness

DRG #	DRG title
424	Operating room procedures with principle diagnosis of mental illness
425	Acute adjustment reactions and disturbance of psycho-social functioning
426	Depressive neuroses
427	Neuroses except depressive
428	Disorders of personality and impulse control
429	Organic disturbances and mental retardation
430	Psychoses
431	Childhood mental disorders
432	Other diagnoses of mental disorders
433	Substance use and induced organic mental disorders, left against medical advice
434	Substance abuse, intoxication, or induced mental syndrome except dependence or other symptomatic treatment
435	Substance dependence, detoxification, and/or other symptomatic treatment
436	Substance dependence with rehabilitation therapy
437	Substance dependence, combined rehabilitation and detoxification therapy

SOURCE: Adapted from English et al. (1986).

VARIABLES ASSOCIATED WITH LONG-TERM STAY IN PSYCHIATRIC HOSPITALS

Self-destructive, violent behavior
Level of adaptive functioning
Level of ego development
Availability of outside support systems
Prognosis—possibility of relapse
Response to treatment
History of repeated failure of treatment
Level of care required
Complicating physical illnesses

Table 26–2. RUG Categories and Activities of Daily Living Scores

CATEGORY	ADL Index	ADL SCORES	
Rehabilitation A	3–4	Eating	
Rehabilitation B	5-10	Independent	1
Special Care A	5-7	Continuous supervision	2
Special Care B	8-10	Fed by hand	3
Clinically Complex A	3	Tube or parenteral	4
Clinically Complex B	4-6	Transferring	
Clinically Complex C	7-8	Independent	1
Clinically Complex D	9-10	Assistance of one	2
Behavioral A	3	Assistance of two or more	3
Behavioral B	4-7		
Behavioral C	8-10	Toileting	
Physical A	3	Independent	1
Physical B	4	Continuous assistance, does not use toilet	2
Physical C	5-7		
Physical D	8	Incontinent, toileted on a regular basis	3
Physical E	9		

SOURCE: Adapted from Micheletti and Shlala (1986).

The DRGs are of questionable use in long-term care because the data used to develop them did not include long-term care clients. These clients rely more on nursing services than on medical treatments. Long-term care is concerned more with a client's functional ability than with such factors as diagnosis, complications, and surgical procedures. In addition, the weights for DRGs are unrelated to the costs of long-term care: the chronically ill are assigned lower weights, while these conditions involve the highest cost of care in nursing homes.

The RUGs II was developed to determine the resource consumption among nursing home residents and encourage nursing homes to accept more acutely ill clients. It is based on 16 categories arranged in five hierarchical groups: rehabilitation; special care; clinically complex; severe behavior problems; and reduced physical functioning. Clients who fall into these groups are further subdivided by the Activities of Daily Living Index, which consists of scores for eating, transferring, and toileting. Each RUG level receives a different cost reimbursement, and those clients in need of restorative rehabilitation five days a week receive the highest amount. This schema is illustrated in Table 26–2.

Nursing plays a crucial role in the implementation of the RUGs II system. Assignment to a RUG category must be made by a registered nurse who has been certified by the state to make such assignments. Proper payment for nursing homes depends on the documentation in the medical record, which must be clear, concise, and detailed. Since nursing is responsible for the majority of the content in a client's record, there is a need for specific nursing data regarding the functional level of the client.

There are many checks and balances in the New York State system to provide for monitoring the quality of care and the appropriateness of the RUG level assignment. RUGs II presents a variety of challenges to long-term care managers and the nurses employed by such facilities (Micheletti and Shlala 1986).

Implications for Nursing

All nurses should be educated about the prospective payment system. Traditionally, nurses have performed their duties with very little thought about the cost of their care. It will be difficult for some nurses to become cost-conscious and think of their services with a dollar value.

The first task of nursing under the system of DRGs is to define essential nursing services under reduced financial conditions. If monies become less available, nurses will be faced with justifying the necessity of nursing care to top management. Within hospitals, the nursing service is the largest portion of the budget. As a result, nursing will be vulnerable to cost containment policies.

With the implementation of the DRG reimbursement system, nursing faces the challenge of providing quality care within predetermined time frames. The variables that delineate the length of stay per DRG relate only to medical conditions. Any consideration of the intensity and kinds of nursing care required have not been integrated into the system.

Since only nursing can meet the clients' nursing needs, the profession itself must determine the amount and type of care needed for appropriate nursing interventions as well as contact time necessary for each DRG. Without this knowledge, it will not be feasible for nursing to assure that needs are being met, to identify whether enough qualified personnel are available to meet those needs, or to identify nursing's contribution to the costs of client care. If nursing does not accept this task, other departments most likely will; this may not be in the best interests of nursing (McClain and Selhot 1984).

Because hospitals will want to use as few resources as possible, nurses will need good negotiation skills to ensure that resources are obtained for nursing. Up until this time, specific costs for nursing services have never been clearly identified. Nursing services are currently included in the "room rent."

Further studies are needed to cost out nursing services in order to illustrate the importance and effectiveness of nursing care. Several nursing researchers have started to study the problems of the cost of nursing care per specific DRG. The results have indicated that, as suggested, the medically focused DRG classification bears little relationship to the use of nursing resources (Mitchell 1984, Sovie 1985).

Nurses should determine what resources are available and identify what can be done within those limits. Unfortunately, when hospitals need to cut costs, staff reduction will be considered first. However, a number of alternatives should be tried first, such as cutting supply costs through better control, reducing less essential expenses such as continuing education and travel, lowering benefit costs by decreasing benefits, and closing units or programs that lose money.

An alternative to reducing costs is to increase revenue. As inpatient census declines, nursing must shift resources to meet clients' needs in markets outside the hospital. Nursing clinics, nurse preceptorships, contracting with nursing homes to sell clinical specialist services, charging for consultations, are a few possibilities.

Nursing productivity can be increased by providing flexible scheduling to improve morale and eliminate per diem costs. Less skilled employees should be taught to do all that they can safely and effectively to utilize the professional staff to advantage. Nursing rituals such as changing a bed every day should be examined for their necessity in providing good care.

Sovie (1985) offered several strategies for producing "more with no more" for nurses. She suggested that a staff with a high if not total percentage of registered nurses is necessary because of the versatility of the RN in meeting client and family needs. RNs can readily expand their functions and have the knowledge and skills needed to intervene and prevent expensive complications. RNs can supplement the rehabilitation and treatment programs of many other disciplines, lead group sessions, design new programs to meet hospital needs and improve existing ones. A total RN staff also eliminates the necessity for supervising nonprofessional staff which gives more time for client care. Although many hospital administrators presume that a total RN staff costs more, the fact that RN staffing gives more care with less cost has been validated by others (Halloran 1983).

Other time-saving measures that can be implemented include the use of generic care plans with standards of care for clients with the highest volume of admissions. New flow sheets need to be designed to streamline documentation. Teaching programs should be evaluated for use with groups as opposed to only individuals. Nursing inservice programs and information can be packaged as self-learning videotaped modules to decrease instructional time.

Nurses must begin to focus more intensively on the discharge planning process. Because the prospective payment system rewards efficiency, efforts will be made to discharge the client as soon as possible. Effective discharge planning can be an effective means of monitoring quality client care. Discharge planning will be improved by a system which dictates that length of stay is understood at the time of admission. Nurses must become responsible for educating the client and the family at the time of admission about the length of stay and discharge.

Decentralization should be considered by nursing departments. A decentralized structure will diminish the demands made on nursing administration and allow more time for focusing on hospital-wide policy issues. Decentralization moves decision-making authority down the organization and involves staff nurses in making decisions about client care, which often results in greater productivity, more commitment, and better morale.

It is important for nurse managers to develop skills in all management areas. They should learn staffing and scheduling skills, with special attention to client acuity; they should learn cost control and budget preparation; and they should use the full potential of their staff and develop unit and individual objectives. First-time nurse managers are the key figures in facing the challenges of the prospective payment system.

Nurses should become acquainted with the use of computer information systems. Nurses gather and generate large amounts of data that must be utilized accurately and appropriately. Statistics are needed to prepare meaningful reports to top management.

Finally, nursing services must take steps to control nursing staff involvement in nonnursing functions. Under DRGs, nursing services will lose money when providing services other than direct client care. Nonnursing duties should be delegated to appropriate staff.

Hospitals are the primary employers of nurses. Unless nurses can begin to quantify their contribution to client care, autonomy for nursing will not become a reality. If nurses can demonstrate that hospitals can provide quality client care within budget restrictions, nursing will become the key ally for hospital management, and nursing will acquire an increasingly greater responsibility for coordinating client care.

Whatever the strategies, the time is now. The nursing profession must meet the challenge of its changing environment and assure that it receives an adequate portion of resources to deliver quality care. The other side of the problem that must also be addressed is the potential for not having the number of professional nurses to accomplish what must be done even if resources are available. The inevitable shortage of qualified registered nurses that is only beginning to be addressed will have an impact on the entire health care delivery system in ways that cannot even be predicted at this point in time. Difficult times are ahead!

Maintaining the Quality

Because of the implementation of a prospective payment system in most areas of health care services, attention is now being focused on the quality of care. Although quality has always been an issue, heightened interest is emanating from concerns about the effects of the new incentives to control costs.

Quality assurance can be defined as assuring the client of a specified degree of excellence in nursing care through continuously and objectively measuring the structure, process, and outcome components of nursing against pre-established criteria of nursing standards. Data must be collected and critically analyzed, and actions must be taken based on the data to improve the quality of client care (Smeltzer 1983). *Quality assurance* is a systematic inquiry designed to evaluate client care and to identify, study, and correct deficiencies in the client care process. Quality assurance activities are usually aimed at solving immediate problems, and they rely on use of descriptive data. The primary purpose is to change and improve nursing practice. Quality

assurance should not be rigid; there is no right or wrong way to utilize the concept. It can be used to solve everyday problems, to provide data to promote change in procedure and policy, to provide feedback, and to develop a basis for decision making.

The American Nurses' Association (1982) has proposed a conceptual model of quality assurance that provides an overall philosophy and framework. There are five steps in this model:

1. Designing the study
2. Establishing the criteria
3. Gathering the data
4. Interpreting the data
5. Taking action

According to this framework, the process can be entered at any step. If nurses know that a problem exists and have already discovered a possible solution, emphasis should be placed on step 5. After taking action, it may be appropriate to start at step 1 to evaluate the effectiveness of the action. If a study is repeated, the effort goes into the data collecting, interpretation, and action (steps 3, 4, and 5). In other cases, all steps may require a great deal of time and commitment, especially if the problem is great and the topic difficult to define. By using this five-step process, nurses can become more familiar with the techniques and can apply the procedure quickly and accurately to a variety of problems.

A quality assurance program should be composed of assessment of structure, process, and outcome. Three domains of client care: Questions regarding the structure ask whether facilities, equipment, and manpower are sufficient to deliver quality care. The philosophy and objectives of a nursing service are an important aspect of the structure. These factors comprise the working environment and either broaden or constrain performance.

Process questions focus on the nature or sequence of events that take place while care is being given that includes appropriate nurse behaviors. Outcome studies describe the end result or changes in the health of the client. In order to evaluate the quality of nursing care, all three domains must be considered for their interrelationship and influence on nursing practice (Smeltzer 1983).

In the newly imposed cost containment atmosphere, a succesful quality assurance program may be the only defense of quality of services to prevent loss of personnel and other valuable resources. For a QA program to be effective, the nursing staff must work together to provide quality services and the nurses must own the program. Effective quality assurance is done by the staff, not *to* the staff. Involvement and respect for staff are key ingredients since quality assurance activites are often seen as a threat. Monitoring of care can raise the level of anxiety of nurses as they see their practice being scrutinized. If the program is a shared endeavor, its basic premise will be that professionals can learn together and their knowledge will improve client care.

Most published articles about the assessment of quality assurance are at the conceptual level and concern the development of models and standards as well as instruments. Few comparative studies have been done. Single program evaluation has led to a large body of research that does not have generalizability. Comparative studies are needed to determine the relationships among structure, process, and outcome variables. There is also a need for descriptive studies to relate the prevalent patterns of nursing care, describe norms for criteria, and delineate interventions and processes for nursing care. Continued reliability and validity testing should be undertaken to assure proper measurement to guide clinical decisions (Lang and Clinton 1984).

Finally, it may be beneficial to consider individual differences in the approach to nursing care. Quality of care has been shown to be a function of the therapeutic awareness of the nurse rather than of extraneous variables such as unit facilities and ancillary staff support (Kitson 1986).

The Importance of Writing

Not too many years ago, thoughtful nurses working in clinical settings were ready and willing to share their experiences by publishing case studies that were highly personal. These early contributions to nursing literature were important, even though they lacked the sophistication provided by a strong theoretical foundation or competence in research techniques. Most of the early articles followed a familiar theme in which physicians insisted, patients resisted, and nurses persisted until a successful denouement was achieved.

As nursing became more complex, hierarchical ranking became prevalent within the profession. The eventual result was that capable but lower-status nurses who practiced solely in clinical facilities were silenced by their feelings of inferiority. Because they lacked impressive academic credentials, nurses who were working with clients became less willing to compete with colleagues who had advanced degrees but who were more removed from hands-on client care. This hierarchical ranking can be compared to that of the army, in which only generals are encouraged to describe the battles while the silent footsoldiers listen, sometimes in awe and sometimes in disbelief. The paradox in this

arrangement is that soldiers who have served in the front lines may have as much to tell as some of the generals, or more. Unfortunately, nurses directly engaged in delivering care to clients are all too often like the silent soldiers.

The analogy is by no means a denigration of the leadership skills of highly educated nurses attempting to develop a body of theoretical knowledge crucial to our profession. What it does mean is that the work of identifying and testing hypotheses in structured settings is essential but is of little value unless it is validated by nurses practicing in a clinical context. The task of applying theoretical constructs under clinical conditions is one that is well within the scope of the professional nurse with no academic background beyond a baccalaureate degree.

Many of the most important scientific discoveries have stemmed from accidental occurrences that were noted by acute observers. This means that the clinically oriented nurse is in a favorable position to evaluate responses to conceptual innovations presented by nurse theorists, to consider viable modifications, and to disseminate this information by writing and publishing. An eavesdropper listening to a group of nurses talking about their clinical practice would find the perceptiveness and analytic thinking of the nurses remarkable. Humor, independence, compassion, judgment, and intellectual vigor are likely to characterize the attitudes of such nurses in their professional practice. Yet most lack the confidence to put in writing the opinions and ideas they verbalize so easily.

There is no denying that writing is hard work. It is one of the loneliest jobs in the world, for it is a solitary undertaking and there is no audience to give immediate applause. In order to confront the challenge of an empty page, one must first be convinced that one has something important to say. Many nurses in clinical settings must resolve the crisis of confidence that makes them believe they lack the tools for scholarly writing. They do themselves and the profession a great disservice if they fail in this regard.

The schism in nursing that is most detrimental to the growth of nursing research may be the gulf between abstract nursing theory and clinical application. Only by bridging this gulf and by hearing what clinical nurses are doing and thinking can nursing theory be refined and the uniqueness of the nursing process be truly understood. The major tool of clinical scholarship is not research methodology but critical thinking.

The message being transmitted here is an invitation for nurses to exchange their burden of inferiority for the impetus of mastery. Nurses, except for a notable few, tend to underestimate their abilities and contributions. It is possible in any clinical setting to observe phenomena, to use deductive and inductive reasoning in order to accept or question established theory, and to consider new ways of thinking and acting. These behaviors are displayed every day in nursing; the challenge is to make them known to others. Intellectual vigor in the form of inquiry and evaluation exists in nursing to an extent far greater than is commonly acknowledged. Nursing and nursing theory will be enhanced if more nurses become motivated to express their ideas on paper and thus move into the ranks of published authors whose opinions and reactions carry weight within and beyond the borders of the profession.

Every nurse, regardless of predilection or position on the career ladder, has access to information that is interesting and publishable. One does not need extensive academic credentials in order to have knowledge worth sharing. For all nurses interested in personal growth and professional enrichment, the question should not be "Why write?" but rather "Why not write?" This is particularly true of nurses who have not retreated to the groves of academe but who remain closely involved with individual clients and their families.

SUMMARY

The area of clinical research has attracted few nurse researchers until recently, as more nurses are being prepared for and are conducting research. The importance of research done by nurses who are engaged in clinical practice cannot be overemphasized. It is in the everyday, reality-based world that the gap between theory and practice can be closed.

The rising costs of health care have become a concern for everyone. Efforts to control these costs in the past have not been effective. As a result, a new prospective payment system has been legislated which will change the delivery of health care.

This new system based on Diagnosis Related Groups is of questionable value in allocating monies for psychiatric care because of the chronicity of that population. Studies are being conducted to test its accuracy and to find alternative ways to distribute costs to psychiatric facilities. If the present DRG system were to be implemented, there would be a decided effect on access of psychiatric care and the ability to adequately treat these clients.

The new payment system has several implications and challenges for the nursing profession. It is now necessary for nurses to define their professional contributions and delineate their role in client care. The cost of nursing care should be separated from a per diem room and board cost.

Changes will be needed in a cost containment environment and several possibilities have been suggested. While operating under these constraints, nurses should assure that they receive adequate portions of resources to continue to give quality care.

Review Questions

1. Explain the importance of clinical nursing research.

2. Using one of the priorities for nursing research, outline a brief study, including the steps in the research process.

3. How can a staff nurse contribute to the quality assurance process?

4. Discuss ways in which nursing can be influential under the DRG system.

5. What are some dangers to nursing that may be realized under the DRG system?

Suggested Annotated Readings

Diers, D. *Research in Nursing Practice*. Philadelphia: J. B. Lippincott, 1979.

This book examines nursing practice research on problems in patient care. It was designed to be read by nurses—undergraduate, through clinicians and faculty. Research examples range from studies of problems in patient care as perceived by staff nurses through problems in special settings or with patients with special illnesses through problems perceived by nurses in expanded roles.

McCall, R. B. *Fundamental Statistics for Psychology*. New York: Harcourt, Brace and World, Inc., 1970.

This text is designed for undergraduates in the behavioral sciences who are beginning to study applied statistics. It is well-written, clear and concise, with graphic illustrations, examples of concepts, and explanation of rationale.

Selltiz, C. M., L. Wrightaman, and S. Cook. *Research Methods in Social Relations*. New York: Holt, Rinehart and Winston, 1976.

This book focuses on bringing together at an introductory level the considerations that enter into every step of the knowledge-gathering process as it relates to social phenomena. Research is emphasized that contributes to the solution of practical problems with immediate application.

(Text continues on page 694.)

CLINICAL EXAMPLE

CONTINGENCY CONTRACTING FOR WEIGHT LOSS IN AN OUTPATIENT PSYCHIATRIC SETTING

Obesity, or an excess of body weight, has been called the main public health problem in the United States and has received extensive attention from the public at large as well as from the scientific community. Efforts have been made to define, measure, and determine the etiology of this problem and to discover safe, effective means of dealing with it.

Nurses are in a unique position to assist in the treatment of obesity. Not only do they have the ability and skill to assess the individual's psychosocial needs, but they also possess the nutritional knowledge essential to any successful weight reduction program. Their direct and continued client contact allows for an in-depth relationship, creating a more trusting environment in which to implement and evaluate a program.

Obesity, like many chronic conditions, is difficult to control. The reasons for the obese individual's resistance to treatment and the recidivism rate following weight loss still remain quite vague (Wineman 1980). However, a plausible explanation is noncompliance with the prescribed treatment or a failure of the persons to assume an active role in their own treatment (Stalones, Johnson, and Christ 1978, Epstein and Martin 1977, Steckel and Swain 1977).

One approach that has been used to deal with this problem is the use of behavioral techniques. Although it should not be assumed that a behavior modification technique is a complete answer (Jordan and Levitz 1975), several studies attest to the effectiveness of this approach. Some researchers believe that the implementation of positive reinforcement principles is potentially usable to modify outpatient behaviors in their natural life setting (Mann 1972, Steckel 1980). On this premise, several behavior modification techniques have applied to obesity, including contingency contracting and self-monitoring for new behaviors.

The contingency contract is an explicit statement of specified behaviors linked to a terminal goal, whose occurrence would produce specific consequences (Mann 1972). Although multidimensional, contingency contracts have identifiable components, such as increased attention from a therapist; clients' involvement in goal setting and active participation in decision making regarding their therapeutic regimen; incentives for goal achievement; and assistance in applying general information regarding a topic to the clients' own environment or social circumstances (Steckel and

Swain 1977). These components aid in the treatment of obesity because they utilize the principles of self-management so vital in successful weight reduction programs.

Self-monitoring is a technique in which the individual records verbally or in written form specific behaviors to be modified. For example, an individual may contract to slow down his eating time by chewing his food 20 times before swallowing. He therefore monitors the number of times he chews his food and must report his compliance or noncompliance to the researcher.

PURPOSE

The purpose of this study was to determine the effectiveness of a program of contingency contracting for behavior change in order to facilitate weight loss in an overweight outpatient population. Following is the report of a study on application of contingency contracting and self-monitoring in a weight loss program.

METHODOLOGY
Sample

The study took place in an outpatient clinic for psychiatric clients. Participation in this study was strictly voluntary. All male clients over the age of 20 were invited to join a weight control group to be conducted weekly for 20 weeks. Criteria were an expressed desire to lose at least 5–10 pounds and being at least 10 percent overweight using the Metropolitan Life Insurance Company's weight/height charts as guidelines.

Design

The research design was quasi-experimental. In this study each client served as his own control. His weight loss or gain during the first 10-week period, in which the group-oriented client education approach was used, was compared to the loss or gain during the second 10-week period, in which contingency contracting was used. The group-oriented client education consisted of weekly meetings of the weight control group where clients weighed in, had a 10- to 15-minute session of ambulating outdoors or performing basic stretching exercises, and engaged in a 15- to 20-minute discussion/education session. The education consisted of information on basic nutrition, caloric values of food, and suggested modifications of behavior.

Procedures

The study was conducted in two stages. During Stage I, all clients participated in the group with the client education focus. Following these ten weeks, the researcher met with each participant and obtained an eating habit record and a profile of the client's weight history. Self-monitoring was explained to the participants and instruction was given on contingency contracting, reinforcers, goal setting, and the mechanics of keeping a diary.

To facilitate the learning process, trial contracts were written with each participant. This enabled them to set a goal of weight to be lost, help identify problem behavior, and decide on meaningful reinforcers to be used during Stage II.

Stage II consisted of a 10-week period during which all participating clients contracted for some form of new behavior, such as increasing activity by taking the stairs instead of the elevator. By evaluating clients' individual personalities and weight history patterns, the researcher assisted them in choosing the behaviors to be monitored. Terminal and intermediate goals were set and revised as needed. Clients who were able to read and write without assistance contracted for compliance in the written diary recording. Some participants also contracted for verbal reporting to the researcher of self-monitored behaviors, such as eating smaller portions or eating one less dessert each day. The contracts were individually designed and modified regarding the behaviors chosen to be self-monitored as well as the reinforcers used. Each contract used in the study was written, signed, and dated by both the researcher and the participants each week.

Reinforcers included fruit, extra ceramic or other craft projects, special occupational therapy privileges, and calorie-counting books. The participants were required to comply 100 percent with their contract in order to receive their chosen reinforcement.

The dependent variable, the client's weight, was measured and recorded on a flowsheet by the researcher and placed on a graph by the participants on a weekly basis. In addition, each participant submitted his written diary at the beginning of each group meeting for the researcher to review, and the diary was returned at the end of the session. The subjects also met with the researcher for approximately five minutes during group time to give a verbal report of their self-monitored behavior compliance. The researcher recorded all data relating to the contracts and compliance on a flowsheet, which summarized the subjects' weekly compliance and activities. Data were analyzed using T-tests for dependent samples to determine whether any significant difference existed between amount of weight gained or lost during Stage I and Stage II.

RESULTS

Eighteen persons chose to participate in the study, and sixteen completed the 20-week program. Thirteen of the sixteen subjects had gained weight during the control period while three had lost weight. In the research study, two participants gained weight, twelve lost weight, and two remained unchanged. Thus, more participants lost weight under the experimental conditions. The T-test for dependent samples was significant at the .10 level of probability.

DISCUSSION

Before the study was undertaken, the researcher believed that all participants would progress to a point of keeping daily dietary diaries, including calorie counting. By gradually increasing their responsibility for daily recording—first contracting to record three out of seven days, then four out of seven days, and so on—the researcher assumed the subjects could handle the task. In fact, very few individuals were able to progress to this point. Although the exact reasons are not known, one can speculate that the participants' psychiatric disabilities caused a greater impairment than originally thought. They may have either forgotten to complete the diary, felt too much pressure or stress to record all meals, or lacked the confidence to complete the task and the terms of the contract. Clients easily became discouraged when they did not comply with the contract and therefore chose to contract for less diary keeping. Some individuals expressed concern over their writing abilities, which could have been a source of embarrassment and lowered self-esteem. Alleviation of this stress might be accomplished in future studies by developing a diary flowsheet, which would decrease the amount of writing necessary to complete the task.

Interestingly, participants were eager to contract for modification of other problem behaviors, such as eating too quickly, eating too many sweets, or low activity levels. These other self-monitored behaviors were reported verbally rather than in diary form.

When asked for feedback, participants gave these replies: "It made me feel better to accomplish my goals. My self-image improved." "I felt more determined and watched what I ate." "I became more conscious of my nutrition by writing down what I ate." "I felt more in control." "It made me more aware. I didn't realize I ate so much, like when I had nine slices of bread in one day." "Writing the contract and knowing I would get something by following it really helped me stay motivated."

Several individuals became more aware of their eating habits through their attempts to use the diary, however limited that was, and they did lose weight.

LIMITATIONS

There are several areas that should be considered when evaluating the effectiveness of the study. As mentioned in the discussion, the degree of impairment second to psychiatric illness must be more closely evaluated when designing contracts for such clients. Since the subjects in this study all carried a psychiatric diagnosis, a thorough review of their medications and possible side effects should have been conducted. It is a known fact that psychotropic medications and many antidepressant drugs can cause weight gain.

Many of the individuals in this study had expressed a concern about the lack of control they had in deciding on meals served to them. Because of group living situations or uncooperative families, it is possible that those individuals who lost little or no weight during the experimental conditions had a less active role in meal planning than those who lost more weight.

Because of the lack of funding, reinforcement tools were very limited. If the reinforcement had been more desirable to obtain, such as money, a greater change in eating habits and weight loss might have resulted.

Tischler, G., and B. Astrachan. *Quality Assurance in Mental Health*. U.S. Dept. of Health and Human Services. Rockville, Maryland: NIMH 1982.

This text presents a conceptual and methodological framework for implementing quality assurance programs. It gives a working knowledge of the major principles and practices of quality assurance and aims to assist the mental health staff in a variety of settings. Guidelines extend to program monitoring, educational tools, and mechanisms for improving the effective and efficient utilization of staff and fiscal measures.

Treece, E., and J. Treece. *Elements of Research in Nursing*. St. Louis: C. V. Mosby, 1973.

The aim of the authors was to cover all avenues of nursing research on a level suitable for beginning nurse researchers. The book presents the research process against a background of nursing. Examples are taken from the broad world as well as the health field.

References

Abdellah, F. G. "Overview of Nursing Research 1955–1968, Part I." *Nursing Research* 19 (1970):6–17.

American Nurses' Association. "Professional Nurses' Role in Quality Assurance." In *Nursing Quality Assurance Management/Training System*. Kansas City, Missouri: American Nurses' Association and Sutherland Learning Associates, 1982.

Caton, C. L., and A. Gralnick. "A Review of Issues Surrounding Length of Psychiatric Hospitalization." *Hospital and Community Psychiatry* 38 (1977):858–863.

deFigueiredo, J. M., and H. Boerstler. "DRGs and Reimbursement for Inpatient Psychiatry." *Comprehensive Psychiatry* 26 (1985):567–572.

English, J. T., S. S. Sharfstein, O. J. Scherl, B. Astrachan, and I. L. Muszynski. "Diagnosis-Related Groups and General Hospital Psychiatry: The APA Study." *American Journal of Psychiatry* 143 (1986):131–139.

Epstein, L. H., and J. E. Martin. "Compliance and Side Effects of Weight Regulation Groups." *Behavior Modification* 1 (1977):551–557.

Gortner, S. R., and N. Nahm. "An Overview of Nursing Research in the United States." *Nursing Research* 26 (1977):10–33.

Halloran, E. J. "RN Staffing: More Care—Less Cost." *Nursing Management* 14 (1983):18–22.

Jordan, H. A., and L. S. Levitz. "A Behavioral Approach to the Problem of Obesity." *Obesity/Bariatric Medicine* 4 (1975):58–69.

Kitson, A. L. "Indications of Quality in Nursing Care—An Alternative Approach." *Journal of Advanced Nursing* 11 (1986):133–144.

Lang, N. M., and J. F. Clinton. "Assessment of Quality Nursing Care." *Annual Review of Nursing Research* 2 (1984):135–163.

Mann, R. A. "The Behavior-Therapeutic Use of Contingency Contracting to Control an Adult Behavior; Weight Control." *Journal of Applied Behavior Analysis* 5 (1972):99–109.

McClain, J. R., and M. S. Selkat. "Twenty Cases: What Nursing Costs per DRG." *Nursing Management* 15 (1984):26–34.

Micheletti, J. A., and T. J. Shlala. "RUGs II: Implications for Management and Quality in Long-Term Care." *Quality Review Bulletin* 12 (1986):236–242.

Mitchell, M., J. Miller, L. Welches, and D. Walker. "Determining Cost of Direct Nursing Care by DRGs." *Nursing Management* 15 (1984):24–32.

Plomann, M. P., and F. A. Shaffer. "DRGs as One of Nine Approaches to Case Mix in Transition." *Nursing and Health Care* 10 (1983):438–443.

Polit, D. F., and B. P. Hungler. *Nursing Research: Principles and Methods*. Philadelphia: J. B. Lippincott, 1978.

Schaffer, F. A. "A Nursing Perspective of the DRG World, Part I." *Nursing and Health Care* 1 (1984):48–51.

———. "Nursing: Gearing up for DRGs, Part II." *Nursing and Health Care* 2 (1984):93–99.

Schwartz, M. S., and E. L. Shackley. *The Nurse and the Mental Patient: A Study in Interpersonal Relations.* New York: Russell Sage Foundation, 1956.

Sills, G. M. "Research in the Field of Psychiatric Nursing, 1952–1977." *Nursing Research* 26 (1977):201–207.

Smeltzer, C. H. "Organizing the Search for Excellence." *Nursing Management* 14 (1983):19–21.

Sovie, M. D. "Managing Nursing Resources in a Constrained Economic Environment." *Nursing Economics* 3 (1985):85–94.

Sovie, M. D., M. A. Tarcinale, A. W. VanPuttee, and A. E. Stendan. "Amalgam of Nursing Acuity, DRGs and Costs." *Nursing Management* 16 (1985):22–42.

Stalones, P. M., W. G. Johnson, and M. Christ. "Behavior Modification for Obesity: The Evaluation of Exercise, Contingency Management and Program Adherence." *Journal of Counseling and Clinical Psychology* 46 (1978): 463–469.

Stanton, A. H., and M. A. Schwartz. *The Mental Hospital: A Study of Institutional Participation in Psychiatric Illness and Treatment.* New York: Basic Books, 1954.

Steckel, S. B. "Contracting with Patient-Selected Reinforcers." *American Journal of Nursing* 80 (1980): 1596–1599.

Steckel, S. B., and M. A. Swain. "Contracting with Patients to Improve Compliance." *Journal of the American Hospital Association* 51 (1977):81–84.

Stewart, I. M. "Remarks on Research in Nursing." *Nursing Research* 2 (1962):5–6.

Wineman, N. M. "Obesity: Focus of Control, Body Image, Weight Loss and Age-at-Onset." *Nursing Research* 29 (1980):231–237.

A P P E N D I X   A

NANDA APPROVED NURSING DIAGNOSTIC CATEGORIES

(as published in the Summer 1988 *NANDA Nursing Diagnosis Newsletter*)

This list represents the NANDA-approved nursing diagnostic categories for clinical use and testing (1988). Changes have been made in 15 labels for consistency.

Pattern 1: Exchanging

1.1.2.1	Altered nutrition: more than body requirements
1.1.2.2	Altered nutrition: less than body requirements
1.1.2.3	Altered nutrition: potential for more than body requirements
1.2.1.1	Potential for infection
1.2.2.1	Potential altered body temperature
**1.2.2.2	Hypothermia
1.2.2.3	Hyperthermia
1.2.2.4	Ineffective thermoregulation
*1.2.3.1	Dysreflexia
#1.3.1.1	Constipation
*1.3.1.1.1	Perceived constipation
*1.3.1.1.2	Colonic constipation
#1.3.1.2	Diarrhea
#1.3.1.3	Bowel incontinence
1.3.2	Altered urinary elimination
1.3.2.1.1	Stress incontinence
1.3.2.1.2	Reflex incontinence
1.3.2.1.3	Urge incontinence
1.3.2.1.4	Functional incontinence
1.3.2.1.5	Total incontinence
1.3.2.2	Urinary retention
#1.4.1.1	Altered (specify type) tissue perfusion (renal, cerebral, cardiopulmonary, gastrointestinal, peripheral)
1.4.1.2.1	Fluid volume excess
1.4.1.2.2.1	Fluid volume deficit
1.4.1.2.2.2	Potential fluid volume deficit
#1.4.2.1	Decreased cardiac output
1.5.1.1	Impaired gas exchange
1.5.1.2	Ineffective airway clearance
1.5.1.3	Ineffective breathing pattern
1.6.1	Potential for injury
1.6.1.1	Potential for suffocation
1.6.1.2	Potential for poisoning
1.6.1.3	Potential for trauma
*1.6.1.4	Potential for aspiration
*1.6.1.5	Potential for disuse syndrome
1.6.2.1	Impaired tissue integrity
#1.6.2.1.1	Altered oral mucous membrane
1.6.2.1.2.1	Impaired skin integrity
1.6.2.1.2.2	Potential impaired skin integrity

Pattern 2: Communicating

2.1.1.1	Impaired verbal communication

Pattern 3: Relating

3.1.1	Impaired social interaction
3.1.2	Social isolation
#3.2.1	Altered role performance
3.2.1.1.1	Altered parenting
3.2.1.1.2	Potential altered parenting
3.2.1.2.1	Sexual dysfunction
3.2.2	Altered family processes
*3.2.3.1	Parental role conflict
3.3	Altered sexuality patterns

Pattern 4: Valuing

4.1.1	Spiritual distress (distress of the human spirit)

Pattern 5: Choosing

5.1.1.1	Ineffective individual coping
5.1.1.1.1	Impaired adjustment
*5.1.1.1.2	Defensive coping
*5.1.1.1.3	Ineffective denial
5.1.2.1.1	Ineffective family coping: disabling
5.1.2.1.2	Ineffective family coping: compromised
5.1.2.2	Family coping: potential for growth
5.2.1.1	Noncompliance (specify)
*5.3.1.1	Decisional conflict (specify)
*5.4	Health-seeking behaviors (specify)

Pattern 6: Moving

6.1.1.1	Impaired physical mobility
6.1.1.2	Activity intolerance
*6.1.1.2.1	Fatigue
6.1.1.3	Potential activity intolerance
6.2.1	Sleep pattern disturbance
6.3.1.1	Diversional activity deficit

*New diagnostic categories approved 1988
**Revised diagnostic categories approved 1988
#Categories with modified label terminology

6.4.1.1	Impaired home maintenance management
6.4.2	Altered health maintenance
#6.5.1	Feeding self-care deficit
6.5.1.1	Impaired swallowing
*6.5.1.2	Ineffective breastfeeding
#6.5.2	Bathing/hygiene self-care deficit
#6.5.3	Dressing/grooming self-care deficit
#6.5.4	Toileting self-care deficit
6.6	Altered growth and development

Pattern 7: Perceiving

#7.1.1	Body image disturbance
#**7.1.2	Self-esteem disturbance
*7.1.2.1	Chronic low self-esteem
*7.1.2.2	Situational low self-esteem
#7.1.3	Personal identity disturbance
7.2	Sensory/perceptual alterations (specify) (visual, auditory, kinesthetic, gustatory, tactile, olfactory)
7.2.1.1	Unilateral neglect
7.3.1	Hopelessness
7.3.2	Powerlessness

Pattern 8: Knowing

8.1.1	Knowledge deficit (specify)
8.3	Altered thought processes

Pattern 9: Feeling

#9.1.1	Pain
9.1.1.1	Chronic pain
9.2.1.1	Dysfunctional grieving
9.2.1.2	Anticipatory grieving
9.2.2	Potential for violence: self-directed or directed at others
9.2.3	Posttrauma response
9.2.3.1	Rape-trauma syndrome
9.2.3.1.1	Rape-trauma syndrome: compound reaction
9.2.3.1.2	Rape-trauma syndrome: silent reaction
9.3.1	Anxiety
9.3.2	Fear

A P P E N D I X   B

DSM-III-R CLASSIFICATION: AXES I AND II CATEGORIES AND CODES

All official DSM-III-R codes are included in ICD-9-CM. (International Classification of Diseases, 9th Version—Clinical Modification).

A long dash following a diagnostic term indicates the need for a fifth digit subtype or other qualifying term.

The term *specify* following the name of some diagnostic categories indicates qualifying terms that clinicians may wish to add in parentheses after the name of the disorder.

NOS stands for "not otherwise specified."

The current severity of a disorder may be specified after the diagnosis as:

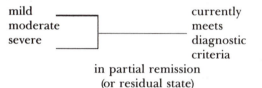

mild
moderate
severe

currently
meets
diagnostic
criteria

in partial remission
(or residual state)
in complete remission

DISORDERS USUALLY FIRST EVIDENT IN INFANCY, CHILDHOOD, OR ADOLESCENCE

Disruptive Behavior Disorders

314.01	Attention-deficit hyperactivity disorder
	Conduct disorder
312.20	group type
312.00	solitary aggressive type
312.90	undifferentiated type
313.81	Oppositional defiant disorder

Anxiety Disorders of Childhood or Adolescence

309.21	Separation anxiety disorder
313.21	Avoidant disorder of childhood or adolescence
313.00	Overanxious disorder

Eating Disorders

307.10	Anorexia nervosa
307.51	Bulimia nervosa
307.52	Pica
307.53	Rumination disorder of infancy
307.50	Eating disorder NOS

Reprinted with permission of the American Psychiatric Association. *Diagnostic and Statistical Manual of Mental Disorders*, 3d edition, revised. Washington, D.C., 1987.

DEVELOPMENTAL DISORDERS
NOTE: THESE ARE CODED ON AXIS II

Mental Retardation

317.00	Mild mental retardation
318.00	Moderate mental retardation
318.10	Severe mental retardation
318.20	Profound mental retardation
319.00	Unspecified mental retardation

Pervasive Developmental Disorders

299.00	Autistic disorder
	Specify if childhood onset
299.80	Pervasive developmental disorder NOS

Specific Developmental Disorders

Academic skills disorders

315.10	Developmental arithmetic disorder
315.80	Developmental expressive writing disorder
315.00	Developmental reading disorder

Language and speech disorders

315.39	Developmental articulation disorder
315.31	Developmental expressive language disorder
315.31	Developmental receptive language disorder

Motor skills disorders

315.40	Developmental coordination disorder
315.90	Specific developmental disorder NOS

Other Developmental Disorders

315.90	Developmental disorder NOS

Gender Identity Disorders

302.60   Gender identity disorder of childhood
302.50   Transsexualism
         Specify sexual history: asexual, homosexual, heterosexual, unspecified
302.85   Gender identity disorder of adolescence or adulthood, nontranssexual type
         Specify sexual history: asexual, homosexual, heterosexual, unspecified
302.85   Gender identity disorder NOS

Tic Disorders

307.23   Tourette's disorder
307.22   Chronic motor or vocal tic disorder
307.21   Transient tic disorder
         Specify: single episode or recurrent
307.20   Tic disorder NOS

Elimination Disorders

307.70   Functional encopresis
         Specify: primary or secondary type
307.60   Functional enuresis
         Specify: primary or secondary type
         Specify: nocturnal only, diurnal only, nocturnal and diurnal

Speech Disorders Not Elsewhere Classified

307.00   Cluttering
307.00   Stuttering

Other Disorders of Infancy, Childhood, or Adolescence

313.23   Elective mutism
313.82   Identity disorder
313.89   Reactive attachment disorder of infancy or early childhood
307.30   Stereotypy/habit disorder
314.00   Undifferentiated attention-deficit disorder

ORGANIC MENTAL DISORDERS

Dementias Arising in the Senium and Presenium

         Primary degenerative dementia of the Alzheimer type, senile onset
290.30   with delirium
290.20   with delusions
290.21   with depression
290.00   uncomplicated
         (Note: code 331.00 Alzheimer's disease on Axis III)

Code in fifth digit:
1 = with delirium, 2 = with delusions,
3 = with depression, 0 = uncomplicated

290.1x   Primary degenerative dementia of the Alzheimer type, presenile onset, _____ (Note: code 331.00 Alzheimer's disease on Axis III)
290.4x   Multi-infarct dementia, _____
290.00   Senile dementia NOS
         Specify etiology on Axis III if known
290.10   Presenile dementia NOS
         Specify etiology on Axis III if known (e.g., Pick's disease, Jakob-Creutzfeldt disease)

Psychoactive Substance-Induced Organic Mental Disorders

         Alcohol
303.00   intoxication
291.40   idiosyncratic intoxication
291.80   uncomplicated alcohol withdrawal
291.00   withdrawal delerium
291.30   hallucinosis
291.10   amnestic disorder
291.20   dementia associated with alcoholism

         Amphetamine or similarly acting sympathomimetic
305.70   intoxication
292.00   withdrawal
292.81   delirium
292.11   delusional disorder

         Caffeine
305.90   intoxication

         Cannabis
305.20   intoxication
292.11   delusional disorder

         Cocaine
305.60   intoxication
292.00   withdrawal
292.81   delirium
292.11   delusional disorder

         Hallucinogen
305.30   hallucinosis
292.11   delusional disorder
292.84   mood disorder
292.89   posthallucinogen perception disorder

         Inhalant
305.90   intoxication

         Nicotine
292.00   withdrawal

         Opioid
305.50   intoxication
292.00   withdrawal

Phencyclidine (PCP) or similarly acting arylcyclohexylamine

305.90	intoxication
292.81	delirium
292.11	delusional disorder
292.84	mood disorder
292.90	organic mental disorder NOS

Sedative, hypnotic, or anxiolytic

305.40	intoxication
292.00	uncomplicated sedative, hypnotic, or anxiolytic withdrawal
292.00	withdrawal delirium
292.83	amnestic disorder

Other or unspecified psychoactive substance

305.90	intoxication
292.00	withdrawal
292.81	delirium
292.82	dementia
292.83	amnestic disorder
292.11	delusional disorder
292.12	hallucinosis
292.84	mood disorder
292.89	anxiety disorder
292.89	personality disorder
292.90	organic mental disorder NOS

Organic Mental Disorders Associated with Axis III Physical Disorders or Conditions, or Whose Etiology is Unknown

293.00	Delirium
294.10	Dementia
294.00	Amnestic disorder
293.81	Organic delusional disorder
293.82	Organic hallucinosis
293.83	Organic mood disorder
	Specify: manic, depressed, mixed
294.80	Organic anxiety disorder
310.10	Organic personality disorder
	Specify if explosive type
294.80	Organic mental disorder NOS

Psychoactive Substance Use Disorders

Alcohol

303.90	dependence
305.00	abuse

Amphetamine or similarly acting sympathomimetic

304.40	dependence
305.70	abuse

Cannabis

304.30	dependence
305.20	abuse

Cocaine

304.20	dependence

305.60	abuse

Hallucinogen

304.50	dependence
305.30	abuse

Inhalant

304.60	dependence
305.90	abuse

Nicotine

305.10	dependence

Opioid

304.00	dependence
305.50	abuse

Phencyclidine (PCP) or similarly acting arylcylohexylamine

304.50	dependence
305.90	abuse

Sedative, hypnotic, or anxiolytic

304.10	dependence
305.40	abuse
304.90	polysubstance dependence
304.90	psychoactive substance dependence NOS
305.90	psychoactive substance abuse NOS

Schizophrenia

Code in fifth digit: 1 = subchronic, 2 = chronic, 3 = subchronic with acute exacerbation, 4 = chronic with acute exacerbation, 5 = in remission, 0 = unspecified.

Schizophrenia

295.2x	catatonic, _____
295.1x	disorganized, _____
295.3x	paranoid, _____
	Specify if stable type
295.9x	undifferentiated, _____
295.6x	residual, _____
	Specify if late onset

Delusional (Paranoid) Disorder

297.10	Delusional (paranoid) disorder
	Specify type: erotomanic, grandiose, jealous, persecutory, somatic, unspecified

Psychotic Disorders Not Elsewhere Classified

298.80	Brief reactive psychosis
295.40	Schizophreniform disorder
	Specify: without good prognostic features or with good prognostic features
295.70	Schizoaffective disorder
	Specify: bipolar type or depressive type
297.30	Induced psychotic disorder
298.90	Psychotic disorder NOS (Atypical psychosis)

MOOD DISORDERS

Code current state of major depression and bipolar disorder in fifth digit: 1 = mild, 2 = moderate, 3 = severe, without psychotic features, 4 = with psychotic features (*specify* mood-congruent or mood-incongruent), 5 = in partial remission, 6 = in full remission, 0 = unspecified

For major depressive episodes, *specify* if chronic and *specify* if melancholic type.

For bipolar disorder, bipolar disorder NOS, recurrent major depression, and depressive disorder NOS, *specify* if seasonal pattern.

Bipolar Disorders

	Bipolar disorder
296.6x	mixed, _____
296.4x	manic, _____
296.5x	depressed, _____
301.13	Cyclothymia
296.70	Bipolar disorder NOS

Depressive Disorders

	Major depression
296.2x	single episode, _____
296.3x	recurrent, _____
300.40	Dysthymia (or depressive neurosis) (230)
	Specify: primary or secondary type
	Specify: early or late onset
311.00	Depressive disorder NOS

ANXIETY DISORDERS (or Anxiety and Phobic Neuroses)

	Panic disorder
300.21	past "panic" with agoraphobia
	Specify current severity of agoraphobic avoidance
	Specify current severity of panic attacks
300.01	without agoraphobia
	Specify current severity of panic attacks
300.22	Agoraphobia without history of panic disorder
	Specify with or without limited symptom attacks
300.23	Social phobia
	Specify if generalized type
300.29	Simple phobia
300.30	Obsessive compulsive disorder (or Obsessive compulsive neurosis)
309.89	Post-traumatic stress disorder
	Specify if delayed onset
300.02	Generalized anxiety disorder
300.00	Anxiety disorder NOS

SOMATOFORM DISORDERS

300.70	Body dysmorphic disorder
300.11	Conversion disorder (or hysterical neurosis, conversion type)
	Specify: single episode or recurrent
300.70	Hypochondriasis (or hypochondriacal neurosis)
300.81	Somatization disorder
307.80	Somatoform pain disorder
300.70	Undifferentiated somatoform disorder
300.70	Somatoform disorder NOS

DISSOCIATIVE DISORDER (or Hysterical Neurosis, Dissociative Type)

300.14	Multiple personality disorder
300.13	Psychogenic fugue
300.12	Psychogenic amnesia
300.60	Depersonalization disorder (or depersonalization neurosis)
300.15	Dissociative disorder NOS

SEXUAL DISORDERS

Paraphilias

302.40	Exhibitionism
302.81	Fetishism
302.89	Frotteurism
302.20	Pedophilia
	Specify: same sex, opposite sex, same and opposite sex
	Specify if limited to incest
	Specify: exclusive type or nonexclusive type
302.83	Sexual masochism
302.84	Sexual sadism
302.30	Transvestic fetishism
302.82	Voyeurism
302.90	Paraphilia NOS

Sexual Dysfunctions

Specify: psychogenic only, or psychogenic and biogenic (Note: If biogenic only, code on Axis III.)
Specify: lifelong or acquired
Specify: generalized or situational

	Sexual desire disorders
302.71	hypoactive sexual desire disorder
302.79	Sexual aversion disorder
	Sexual arousal disorders
302.72	female sexual arousal disorder
302.72	male erectile disorder
	Orgasm disorders
302.73	inhibited female orgasm
302.74	inhibited male orgasm
302.75	premature ejaculation
	Sexual pain disorders
302.76	dyspareunia

306.51	vaginismus
302.70	sexual dysfunction NOS

Other Sexual Disorders

302.90	Sexual disorder NOS

SLEEP DISORDERS

Dyssomnias

	Insomnia disorder
307.42	related to another mental disorder (nonorganic)
780.50	related to known organic factor
307.42	Primary insomnia
	Hypersomnia disorder
307.44	related to another mental disorder (nonorganic)
780.50	related to a known organic factor
780.54	Primary hypersomnia
307.45	Sleep-wake schedule disorder
	Specify: advanced or delayed phase type, disorganized type, frequently changing type
	Other dyssomnias
307.40	Dyssomnia NOS

Parasomnias

307.47	Dream anxiety disorder (nightmare disorder)
307.46	Sleep terror disorder
307.46	Sleepwalking disorder
307.40	Parasomnia NOS

FACTITIOUS DISORDERS

	Factitious disorder
301.51	with physical symptoms
300.16	with psychological symptoms
300.19	Factitious disorder NOS

IMPULSE CONTROL DISORDERS NOT ELSEWHERE CLASSIFIED

312.34	Intermittent explosive disorder
312.32	Kleptomania
312.31	Pathological gambling
312.33	Pyromania
312.39	Trichotillomania
312.39	Impulse control disorder NOS

ADJUSTMENT DISORDER

	Adjustment disorder
309.24	with anxious mood
309.00	with depressed mood
309.30	with disturbance of conduct
309.40	with mixed disturbance of emotions and conduct
309.28	with mixed emotional features
309.82	with physical complaints
309.83	with withdrawal
309.23	with work (or academic) inhibition
309.90	Adjustment disorder NOS

PSYCHOLOGICAL FACTORS AFFECTING PHYSICAL CONDITION (333)

316.00	Psychological factors affecting physical condition
	Specify physical condition on Axis III

PERSONALITY DISORDERS
(Note: These are coded on Axis II.)

Cluster A

301.00	Paranoid
301.20	Schizoid
301.22	Schizotypal

Cluster B

301.70	Antisocial
301.83	Borderline
301.50	Histrionic
301.81	Narcissistic

Cluster C

301.82	Avoidant
301.60	Dependent
301.40	Obsessive-compulsive
301.84	Passive-aggressive
301.90	Personality disorder NOS

V CODES FOR CONDITIONS NOT ATTRIBUTABLE TO A MENTAL DISORDER THAT ARE A FOCUS OF ATTENTION OR TREATMENT

V62.30	Academic problem
V71.01	Adult antisocial behavior

V40.00	Borderline intellectual functioning (Note: This is coded on Axis II.)

V71.02	Childhood or adolescent antisocial behavior
V65.20	Malingering
V61.10	Marital problem
V15.81	Noncompliance with medical treatment
V62.20	Occupational problem
V61.20	Parent-child problem

V62.81	Other interpersonal problem
V61.80	Other specified family circumstances
V62.89	Phase of life problem or other life circumstance problem
V62.82	Uncomplicated bereavement

V71.09	No diagnosis or condition on Axis I
799.90	Diagnosis or condition deferred on Axis I

V71.09	No diagnosis or condition on Axis II
799.90	Diagnosis or condition deferred on Axis II

ADDITIONAL CODES

300.90	Unspecified mental disorder (nonpsychotic)

Axis IV
Severity of Psychosocial Stressors Scale: Adults

		Examples of Stressors	
Code	Term	Acute Events	Enduring Circumstances
1	None	No acute events that may be relevant to the disorder	No enduring circumstances that may be relevant to the disorder
2	Mild	Broke up with boyfriend or girlfriend; started or graduated from school; child left home	Family arguments; job dissatisfaction; residence in high-crime neighborhood
3	Moderate	Marriage; marital separation; loss of job; retirement; miscarriage	Marital discord; serious financial problems; trouble with boss; being a single parent
4	Severe	Divorce; birth of first child	Unemployment; poverty
5	Extreme	Death of spouse; serious physical illness diagnosed; victim of rape	Serious chronic illness in self or child; ongoing physical or sexual abuse
6	Catastrophic	Death of child; suicide of spouse; devastating natural disaster	Captivity as hostage; concentration camp experience
0	Inadequate information, or no change in condition		

Axis IV
Severity of Psychosocial Stressors Scale: Children and Adolescents

		Examples of Stressors	
Code	Term	Acute Events	Enduring Circumstances
1	None	No acute events that may be relevant to the disorder	No enduring circumstances that may be relevant to the disorder
2	Mild	Broke up with boyfriend or girlfriend; change of school	Overcrowded living quarters; family arguments
3	Moderate	Expulsion from school; birth of sibling	Chronic disabling illness in parent; chronic parental discord
4	Severe	Divorce of parents; unwanted pregnancy; arrest	Harsh or rejecting parents; chronic life-threatening illness in parent; multiple foster home placements
5	Extreme	Sexual or physical abuse; death of a parent	Recurrent sexual or physical abuse
6	Catastrophic	Death of both parents	Chronic life-threatening illness
0	Inadequate information, or no change in condition		

Axis V
Global Assessment of Functioning Scale (GAF Scale)

Consider psychological, social, and occupational functioning on a hypothetical continuum of mental health illness. Do not include impairment in functioning due to physical (or environmental) limitations.

Note: Use intermediate codes when appropriate, e.g., 45, 68, 72.

Code

90 | 81	Absent or minimal symptoms (e.g., mild anxiety before an exam), good functioning in all areas, interested and involved in a wide range of activities, socially effective, generally satisfied with life, no more than everyday problems or concerns (e.g., an occasional argument with family members).
80 | 71	If symptoms are present, they are transient and expectable reactions to psychosocial stressors (e.g., difficulty concentrating after family argument); no more than slight impairment in social, occupational, or school functioning (e.g., temporarily falling behind in school work).
70 | 61	Some mild symptoms (e.g., depressed mood and mild insomnia) or some difficulty in social, occupational, or school functioning (e.g., occasional truancy, or theft within the household), but generally functioning pretty well, with some meaningful interpersonal relationships.
60 | 51	Moderate symptoms (e.g., flat affect and circumstantial speech, occasional panic attacks) or moderate difficulty in social, occupational, or school functioning (e.g., few friends, conflicts with coworkers).
50 | 41	Serious symptoms (e.g., suicidal ideation, severe obsessional rituals, frequent shoplifting) or any serious impairment in social, occupational, or school functioning (e.g., no friends, unable to keep job).
40 | 31	Some impairment in reality testing or communication (e.g., speech is at times illogical, obscure, or irrelevant) or major impairment in several areas, such as work or school, family relations, judgment, thinking, or mood (e.g., depressed man avoids friends, neglects family, and is unable to work; child frequently beats up younger children, is defiant at home, and is failing at school).
30 | 21	Behavior is considerably influenced by delusions or hallucinations or serious impairment in communications or judgment (e.g., sometimes incoherent, acts grossly inappropriately, suicidal preoccupation) or inability to function in almost all areas (e.g., stays in bed all day; no job, home, or friends).
20 | 11	Some danger of hurting self or others (e.g., suicide attempts without clear expectation of death, frequently violent, manic excitement) or occasionally fails to maintain minimal personal hygiene (e.g., smears feces) or gross impairment in communication (e.g., largely incoherent or mute).
10 | 1	Persistent danger of severely hurting self or others (e.g., recurrent violence) or persistent inability to maintain minimal personal hygiene or serious suicidal act with clear expectation of death.

CONTROLLED DRUGS

The drugs that come under jurisdiction of the Controlled Substances Act are divided into five schedules. They are as follows:

SCHEDULE I SUBSTANCES
The drugs in this schedule are those that have no accepted medical use in the United States and have a high abuse potential. Some examples are heroin, marijuana, LSD, peyote, mescaline, psilocybin, tetrahydrocannabinols, ketobemidone, levomoramide, racemoramide, benzylmorphine, dihydromorphine, morphine methylsulfonate, nicocodeine, and nicomorphine.

SCHEDULE II SUBSTANCES
The drugs in this schedule have a high abuse potential with severe psychic or physical dependence liability. Schedule II controlled substances consist of certain narcotic, stimulant, and depressant drugs. Some examples of Schedule II narcotic-controlled substances are: opium, morphine, codeine, hydromorphone (Dilaudid), methadone (Dolophine), pantopon, meperdine (Demerol), cocaine, oxycodone (Percodan), anileridine (Leritine), and oxymorphone (Numorphan). Also in Schedule II are amphetamine (Benzedrine, Dexedrine), methamphetamine (Desoxyn), phenmetrazine (Preludin), methylphenidate (Ritalin), amobartital, pentobarbital, secobarbital, and methaqualone, etorphine hydrochloride, diphenoxylate, and phencyclidine.

SCHEDULE III SUBSTANCES
The drugs in this schedule have an abuse potential less than those in Schedules I and II, and include compounds containing limited quantities of certain narcotic drugs, and nonnarcotic drugs such as: derivatives of barbituric acid except those that are listed in another schedule, glutethimide (Doriden), methyprylon (Noludar), chlorhexadol, sulfondiethylmethane, sulfonmethane, nalorphine, benzphetamine, chlorphentermine, clortermine, mazindol, phendimetrazine, and paregoric. Any suppository dosage form containing amobarbital, secobarbital, or pentobarbital is in this schedule.

SCHEDULE IV SUBSTANCES
The drugs in this schedule have an abuse potential less than those listed in Schedule III and include such drugs as: barbital, phenobarbital, methylphenobarbital, chlorallbetaine (Beta Chlor), chloral hydrate, ethchlorvynol (Placidyl), ethinamate (Valmid), meprobamate (Equanil, Miltown), paraldehyde, methodhexital, fenfluramine, diethylpropion, phentermine, chlordiazepoxide (Librium), diazepam (Valium), oxazepam (Serax), clorazepate (Tranxene), flurazepam (Dalmane), clonazepam (Clonopin), prazepam (Verstran), lorazepam (Ativan), mebutamate, and dextropropoxyphene (Darvon).

SCHEDULE V SUBSTANCES
The drugs in this schedule have an abuse potential less than those listed in Schedule IV and consist primarily of preparations containing limited quantities of certain narcotic drugs generally for antitussive and antidiarrheal purposes.

SOURCE: Controlled Substance Act of 1970 as interpreted by United States Department of Justice.

A P P E N D I X D

PSYCHOLOGICAL TEST: PURPOSES AND AGE RANGE OF SUBJECTS

Test	Type	Assesses	Age of Patient
Bayley Scales of Infant Development	Infant development	Cognitive functioning and motor development	1–30 months
Bender Visual-Motor Gestalt Test	Projective visual-motor development	Personality conflicts Ego function and structure Organic brain damage	5 to adult
Benton Visual Retention Test	Objective performance	Organic brain damage	Adult
Catell Infant Intelligence Scale	Infant development	General motor and cognitive development	1–18 months
Draw-a-Person, Draw-a-Family-House-Tree-Person	Projective	Personality conflicts Self-image (DAP) Family perception (DAF) Ego functions Intellectual functioning (DAP) Visual-motor coordination	2 to adult
Frostig (Marianne) Developmental Test of Visual Perception	Visual perception	Eye-motor coordination Figure-ground perception Constancy of shape Position in space Spatial relationships	4–8 years
Gesell Developmental Schedules	Preschool development	Cognitive, motor, language, and social development	1–60 months
Illinois Test of Psycholinguistic Ability (ITPA)	Language ability	Auditory-vocal, visual-motor channels of language; receptive, organizational, and expressive components	2–10 years
Minnesota Multiphasic Personality Inventory (MMPI)	Paper-and-pencil personality inventory	Personality structure Diagnostic classification	Adolescent to adult
Otis Quick-Scoring Mental Abilities Test	Intelligence	Intellectual functioning	5 to adult
Rorschach Test	Projective	Personality conflicts Ego function and structure Defensive structure Thought processes Affective integration	3 to adult
Stanford-Binet	Intelligence	Intellectual functioning	2 to adult
Thematic Apperception Test (TAT)	Projective	Personality conflicts	Adult—TAT
Michigan Picture Stories	Projective	Defensive structure	Adolescent—Mich.

COMPENDIUM OF COMMON DRUGS IN PSYCHIATRIC NURSING

ANALGESIC NARCOTIC MEDICATION

All narcotic analgesics, whether natural or synthetic, are related to opium, which has been used for many centuries. In fact, the term *opiate* or *opioid* is often used as a more accurate and descriptive title for this important group of drugs.

Morphine was the first opium alkaloid to be isolated, and by the latter half of the nineteenth century pure alkaloids of opium were widely used in medical practice. Although more than 20 alkaloids have been isolated from crude opium, only a few are used clinically. A number of semisynthetic opiates, produced by simple modification of the morphine molecule, and true synthetic opiates are also available.

Of the opiate analgesics, morphine is the standard to which all other opiates are compared. The semisynthetic and synthetic narcotics were developed as part of the search for a potent morphinelike analgesic without the addictive and other side effects of the opiates.

Morphine and related drugs are effective against all types and sources of pain, including deep visceral pain.

There is some difference of opinion as to whether morphine actually alters the physiologic sensation of pain or whether it only increases the ability to tolerate painful sensations—that is, raises the pain threshold.

The major effects of morphine on the central nervous system are related to the drug's depressant effects. In addition to analgesia, other manifestations are drowsiness, mental clouding, and sometimes an exaggerated sense of well-being. Although the analgesic effect occurs first, it may not be followed by sleep even though drowsiness, lethargy, and apathy are induced. Morphine has a depressant effect on the respiratory center in the medulla, causing a decrease in rate and depth of respirations. In morphine poisoning, death is caused by complete respiratory failure. Other effects on the central nervous system include pupillarly constriction, depression of the cough center, and stimulation of the emetic zone in the medulla, which may cause nausea and vomiting.

The effects of morphine on the gastrointestinal tract include increased smooth muscle tone in the sphincters, which causes a delay in stomach emptying, and decreased peristalsis. The defecation reflex is depressed, and constipation may result from continued morphine use. Glandular secretions are also diminished, slowing down digestive process. Urinary bladder tone is affected, and this may cause difficulty in voiding. Urinary output may also be decreased.

In therapeutic doses, morphine has no significant effects on blood pressure or heart rate and rhythm. However, the small blood vessels in the head, neck, and chest may dilate, causing a flushed appearance and diaphoresis, even when small dosages are given.

Opiate tolerance varies with individuals and with usage patterns. The more frequently the drug is used, the more frequently the dose must be increased to produce the desired effects. Tolerance develops to the drug's euphoric, respiratory, analgesic, and sedative effects, but not to the gastrointestinal or pupillary effects; hence, an addict will still exhibit contracted pupils and constipation. When a narcotic analgesic is used continually, tolerance may develop in as little as two weeks. Moreover, if a client is addicted to one opiate, he or she will be just as tolerant to another, so that changing the prescription from one narcotic to another will not delay or prevent addiction.

NATURAL OPIUM ALKALOIDS

Generic Name   Morphine sulfate, morphine hydrochloride
Trade Name   MS
Classification   Narcotic analgesic

Action   Depresses cerebral cortex; causes sleep; depresses respiratory center and cough center; causes blood vessel dilatation in face, head, and neck (causes pruritus and sweating); stimulates contraction of ureters, bladder, and other smooth muscles; decreases GI secretions and motility, increases biliary tract pressure; releases ADH and histamine; promotes contraction of bronchial musculature; may cause nausea and vomiting through stimulation of emetic center in medulla.

Indications for Drug   Relief of severe pain, anxiety; preanesthetic agent; relief of pain and dyspnea in myocardial infarction.

Contraindications   Urethral stricture, head injuries, craniotomy, acute alcoholism, bronchial asthma, prostatic hypertrophy, convulsive disorders, undiagnosed abdominal disorders, pancreatitis, ulcerative colitis, hypersensitivity to opiates. Use with caution in clients with reduced blood volume or those with reduced respiratory reserve; in the presence of hepatic or renal insufficiency; toxic psychosis; arrhythmias; in the elderly or very young children.

Forms of Drug Tablets and capsules containing 10, 15, 30 mg; oral solution containing 10 mg/5 ml or 20 mg/5 ml; 1-ml ampules containing 2, 8, 10, or 15 mg/ml; 20-mg vials containing 15 mg/ml; prefilled cartridges containing 2, 8, 10, or 15 mg/ml. Store in light-resistant containers.

Administration of Drug Adults: Oral: 5 to 30 mg every 3 to 4 hours: Frequently used orally as solution or SR tablets. Intramuscular, subcutaneous: 5 to 15 mg every 3 to 4 hours; 10 mg/70 kg for initial dose. Intravenous: 2.5 to 15 mg in 4 to 5 ml of sterile water. Children: 0.1 to 0.2 mg/kg per dose subc; single dose not to exceed 15 mg.

1. For IV route, administer slowly over a 4- to 5-minute period.
2. Assess pupillary size and vital signs, particularly respirations, before each dose. Withhold medication if respirations are below 12 per minute and notify physician.
3. Do not mix with other medications, since morphine is incompatible with many drugs.

Absorption From GI tract, nasal mucosa, lungs, and vascular system. Peak action occurs in: 20 minutes (IV), 60 to 90 minutes (subc, IM). Duration of action is 3 to 7 hours. Crosses placenta and small amounts appear in breast milk.
Distribution Concentrated in the kidneys, lungs, liver, spleen, and skeletal muscles.
Metabolism In the liver.
Excretion Mostly in urine by glomerular filtration. Also in feces via biliary tract (about 7% to 10%).

Side Effects Slow and shallow respirations, coma, pinpoint pupils, cyanosis, hypothermia, weak pulse, hypertension, nausea, vomiting, dizziness, mental clouding, constipation, cough center depression, urinary retention, dysuria, biliary colic, bradycardia, allergic dermatologic reactions. Coma, severe respiratory depression, pulmonary edema, hypothermia, and cardiac arrest occur with acute intoxication.

Interactive Effects Effects are exaggerated and/or prolonged by tricyclic antidepressants, antianxiety agents, phenothiazines, MAO inhibitors, alcohol, general anesthetics, barbiturates, and other sedatives and hypnotics. Morphine can potentiate the effects of other CNS depressants and skeletal muscle relaxants. Narcotic antagonists block the effects of morphine.

Nursing Considerations
1. Assessment and planning
   a. The most effective analgesia is achieved before client's pain becomes intense. Evaluate client's need for medication carefully and be aware that smaller doses are effective in controlling continuous dull pain.
   b. Morphine has a high abuse potential. Clients, except for those who are terminally ill, should be transferred to a less potent analgesic as soon as possible.
   c. Oxygen and narcotic antagonists should be readily available.
2. Assessment and implementation
   a. Instruct client not to ambulate without assistance after receiving drug. Postural hypotension, dizziness, and syncope are common side effects.
   b. Movement and ambulation often enhance the emetic effect of morphine. Client should be instructed to remain supine following administration until effects are ascertained.
   c. Elderly clients may become restless because of paradoxical CNS stimulation.
   d. Bedrails should be instituted for all clients during first few days of morphine therapy and maintained until effects are ascertained.
   e. Intake and output should be monitored and client assessed for urinary retention.
   f. Assess client frequently for abdominal distention, decreased peristalsis, and constipation.
3. Assessment and evaluation
   a. Clients with acute myocardial infarction may experience temporary hypotension after administration.
   b. Possible false-positive results of serum amylase, lipase, and urine glucose with Benedict's solution. May cause decreased urinary vanilmandelic acid excretion and elevated serum glutamic-oxaloacetic transaminase.

Generic Names Codeine, codeine phosphate, codeine sulfate
Classification Narcotic analgesic and antitussive agent

See morphine for contraindications and side effects.

Action Similar actions to morphine, but one-tenth the analgesic activity. Less side effects than morphine (gastrointestinal, pupillary, respiratory). Depresses cough center. Addictive, but tolerance develops much more slowly than morphine. (See morphine.)

Indications for Drug Relief of mild to moderate pain; suppression of cough. Used in patients sensitive to morphine.

Forms of Drug   Tablets containing 15, 30, or 60 mg; vials containing 15, 30, or 60 mg/ml; elixir and syrup for coughs (combination preparation); prefilled cartridges containing 15, 30, or 60 mg/ml.

Administration of Drugs   Adults: 15 to 60 mg po or subc every 3 to 4 hours; Children—3 mg/kg daily.

Interactive Effects   Aspirin and codeine have a synergistic effect. (See morphine.)

Nursing Considerations   Large doses may stimulate nerve center causing restlessness. (See morphine for further details.)

WHOLE OPIUM DRUGS

Generic Name   Opium tincture
Trade Name   Laudanum
Classification   Narcotic (antiperistaltic)

See morphine for contraindications and side effects.

Action   Similar actions to morphine, but contains only 1% morphine (10 mg/ml). Major effect is gastrointestinal (decreases propulsive peristalsis).

Indications for Drug   Diarrhea.

Forms of Drug   Liquid alcoholic solution (combination preparation).

Administration of Drug   0.3 to 1.5 ml po qid.

Nursing Considerations   (See morphine.) Dilute drug in about 50 ml of water before administering. When diarrhea is controlled, drug should be discontinued, since it has addictive potential.

Generic Name   Paregoric
Trade Name   Paregoric
Classification   Narcotic (antiperistaltic)

See morphine for contraindications, side effects, and drug interactions. See morphine and opium tincture for nursing considerations.

Action   Opium with camphor, benzoic acid, and anise oil. Similar actions to morphine, but contains 0.25 mg morphine per milliliter. Major effect is to decrease peristalsis. (See morphine.)

Indications for Drug   Diarrhea.

Form of Drug   Liquid in light-resistant bottle containing 0.25 mg/ml.

Administration of Drug   4 to 8 ml po qid.

SEMISYNTHETIC OPIATES

Generic Name   Diacetylmorphine
Trade Name   Heroin
Classification   Narcotic

Action   Similar actions to morphine, but produces greater euphoria. Highly addictive. (See morphine.)

Indications for Drug   None—illegal.

Generic Name   Apomorphine hydrochloride
Classification   Narcotic (emetic)

See morphine for drug interactions and nursing considerations.

Action   Produced by treating morphine with acids. Has reduced analgesic potency. Stimulates emetic center in medulla, causing vomiting.

Indications for Drug   Oral ingestion of poisons.

Contraindications   Corrosive poison ingestion, shock. CNS depression for any reason.

Forms of Drug   Power; hypodermic tablets containing 6 mg. Packaged in airtight, light-resistant containers. Must be dissolved in sterile water and sterilized before use. Once dissolved, solution deteriorates rapidly. Discolored solutions should be discarded.

Administration of Drug   Acts within 10 to 15 minutes. If first dose does not produce emesis, subsequent doses will be ineffective. Do not repeat dosage. Adults 5 mg subc; Children: 0.1 mg/kg subc.

Generic Name   Hydrocodone bitartrate
Trade Names   Dicodid, Mercodinone (an incredient of Hycodan)
Classification   Narcotic analgesic (antitussive)

See morphine for contraindications and side effects. See morphine and codeine for drug interactions.

Action   Similar actions to morphine and codeine, but with greater antitussive activity. (See morphine and codeine.)

Indications for Drug   Primarily for cough.

Contraindications   Not to be used in patients with glaucoma. (See morphine.)

Forms of Drug   Tablets containing 5 mg; syrup containing 5 mg/ml.

Administration of Drug   Adults: 5 to 15 mg po every 4 hours; always taken after meals. Children: under 2 years: 1.25 mg po every 4 hours; Ages 2 to 12 years: 2.5 to 5 mg po every 4 hours.

Nursing Considerations   (See morphine and codeine.)
1. Addictive liability is greater than for codeine.
2. Warn clients not to operate machinery if drowsiness occurs.

Generic Name   Hydromorphone hydrochloride
Trade Names   Dilaudid, Hymorphan
Classification   Narcotic analgesic

See morphine for contraindications and side effects.

Action   Similar actions to morphine, but five times more effective for pain relief. Less hypnotic effect than morphine. (See morphine.)

Indications for Drug   Relief of moderate to severe pain.

Forms of Drug   Tables containing 1, 2, 3, or 4 mg; ampules containing 1, 2, 3, or 4 mg/ml; vials of 10 or 20 ml containing 2 mg/ml; suppositories containing 3 mg.

Administration of Drug   1 to 4 mg po, IM, subc, or IV every 4 to 6 hours, whenever necessary; Rectal suppository: 3 mg.

Nursing Considerations   (See morphine.)
1. For IV route, administer slowly over a 3- to 5-minute period.
2. Less tendency than morphine to produce nausea, vomiting, and constipation.

Generic Name   Oxycodone hydrochloride
Trade Name   (An ingredient of Percodan and Percocet)
Classification   Narcotic analgesic

See morphine for contraindications and side effects. See morphine and codeine for drug interactions. See codeine for indications for drug.

Action   Similar actions to morphine and codeine. Effective with oral administration. (See morphine and codeine.)

Contraindications   Not to be used in pregnancy or children under 6 years.

Forms of Drug   Tablets (combination preparation).

Administration of Drug   Adults: 3 to 20 mg po every 6 hours, whenever necessary. Children: Ages 6 to 12 years: 0.5 mg po every 6 hours, whenever necessary; Over 12 years: 1 mg po every 6 hours, whenever necessary.

Nursing Considerations   Addictive liability is greater than for codeine. (See morphine and codeine for further details.)

Generic Name   Oxymorphone hydrochloride
Trade Name   Numorphan
Classification   Narcotic analgesic

See morphine for action and side effects.

Indications for Drug   Relief of severe pain.

Forms of Drug   Powder for injection containing 0.5 mg/ml; suppositories containing 2.5 mg. Store in refrigerator.

Administration of Drug   0.75 to 1.5 mg IM or subc every 4 to 6 hours; Rectal suppository: 2 to 5 mg every 4 to 6 hours.

Nursing Considerations   (See morphine.)

1. Less tendency than morphine to produce GI symptoms and respiratory depression.
2. Peak action occurs in 10 to 20 minutes when administered parenterally.

Generic Name   Opium alkaloid hydrochloride
Trade Name   Pantopon
Classification   Narcotic analgesic

See morphine for contraindications and side effects. See morphine and codeine for drug interactions and nursing considerations.

Action   Similar actions to morphine and codeine. Purified opium alkaloids containing about 50% morphine. (See morphine and codeine.)

Indications for Drug   Relief of pain in patients hypersensitive to morphine.

Forms of Drug   Ampules containing 20 mg/ml.

Administration of Drug   5 to 20 mg IM or subc.

Synthetic Opiates

Generic Name   Meperidine hydrochloride, pethidine hydrochloride
Trade Name   Demerol
Classification   Narcotic analgesic

See morphine for contraindications and side effects.

Action   Similar actions to morphine, but one-tenth the analgesic activity. Less hypnotic, antitussive, and pupillary effects than morphine. Less likely to cause nausea, vomiting, or respiratory depression. (See morphine.)

Indications for Drug   Relief of moderate or intermittent pain; preanesthetic agent; obstetric analgesic.

Forms of Drug   Tablets containing 50 or 100 mg; syrup containing 50 mg/5 ml; ampules of 0.5, 1, 1.5, or 2 ml; vials of 30 ml containing 50 mg/ml.

Administration of Drug   Adults: 50 to 100 mg po or IM every 3 to 4 hours, whenever necessary; Children: 6 mg/kg po or IM daily. Intravenous: 25 mg.

1. For IV route, administer very slowly over a 3- to 5-minute period.
2. Demerol solution is not compatible with barbiturate solution; do not mix together.
3. Dilute syrup in water.

Interactive Effects   Amphetamines enhance analgesic effect. (See morphine.)

Nursing Considerations
1. Constipation and urinary retention are unlikely with Demerol.
2. Addictive liability is less than for morphine.

Generic Name   Anileridine, anileridine phosphate
Trade Name   Leritine
Classification   Narcotic analgesic

See morphine for contraindications and nursing considerations. See morphine and meperidine hydrochloride for drug interactions. See meperidine hydrochloride for indications for drug.

Action   Similar actions to meperidine, but three times the analgesic activity. Unlike meperidine, anileridine seldom causes constipation.

Forms of Drug   Ampules and vials containing 25 mg/ml, tablets containing 25 mg.

Administration of Drug   25 to 50 mg po, IM, or subc every 3 to 4 hours; not to exceed 200 mg daily. Intravenous: 5 to 10 mg every 3 to 4 hours.

Generic Name   Diphenoxylate hydrochloride with atropine sulfate
Trade Names   Colonil, Lomotil
Classification   Narcotic (antidiarrhetic)

See morphine for contraindications and side effects. See morphine and meperidine hydrochloride for drug interactions.

Action   Similar actions to meperidine. Strong constipating effect.

Indications for Drug   Diarrhea.

Contraindications   Not to be used for children under 2 years. (See morphine.)

Forms of Drug Tablets and liquid (5 ml) containing 2.5 mg diphenoxylate with 0.025 mg atropine sulfate.

Administration of Drug Adults: 20 mg po daily in divided doses; Children: 0.3 to 0.4 mg/kg po daily in divided doses.

Nursing Considerations (See morphine.)
1. Exempt from restrictions of federal narcotic law.
2. May cause slight sedation with therapeutic doses. In doses over 40 mg/day, client can be expected to exhibit side effects like those of morphine.
3. For children 2 to 12 years, use liquid preparation only.

Generic Name Fentanyl citrate
Trade Name Sublimaze
Classification Narcotic analgesic

See morphine for contraindications, side effects, drug interactions, and nursing considerations.

Action Similar actions to morphine. Analgesic activity is equivalent to 10 mg morphine or 75 mg meperidine. Respiratory depression may last longer than analgesic effect.

Indications for Drug Primarily as preanesthetic agent or anesthetic supplement.

Forms of Drug Ampules of 2 or 5 ml containing 0.05 mg/ml.

Administration of Drug Intramuscular, intravenous: 0.025 to 0.1 mg.

Generic Name Levorphanol tartrate
Trade Names Levo-Dromoran, Methorphinan
Classification Narcotic analgesic

See morphine for contraindications, side effects, drug interactions, and nursing considerations.

Action Similar actions to morphine, but more potent. (See morphine.)

Indications for Drug Relief of severe pain; preanesthetic agent.

Forms of Drug Tablets containing 2 mg; 1-ml ampules containing 2 mg/ml; 10-ml vials containing 2 mg/ml.

Administration of Drug Oral: 2 to 3 mg every 3 to 4 hours; Subcutaneous: 1 to 3 mg every 3 to 4 hours.

Generic Name Methadone hydrochloride
Trade Names Adanon, Amidone, Dolophine, Methadon, Miadone, Polamidon
Classification Narcotic analgesic

See morphine for contraindications, side effects, and drug interactions.

Action Similar actions to morphine, but longer duration of action (up to 72 hours). (See morphine.)

Indications for Drug Relief of pain; treatment of narcotic withdrawal symptoms, heroin users; antitussive.

Forms of Drug Tablets containing 5 or 10 mg; ampules containing 10 mg/ml; vials containing 10 mg/ml; elixir or syrup containing 0.34 to 1 mg/ml.

Administration of Drug
- *Relief of pain:* 2.5 to 10 mg po or IM every 3 to 4 hours.
- *Treatment of narcotic withdrawal symptoms:* 15 to 20 mg po or IM every 3 to 4 hours.
- *Cough:* 1.5 to 2 mg po.

Nursing Considerations Withdrawal from methadone addiction is more prolonged than for other opiates, but symptoms are less severe. (See morphine.)

Generic Name Propoxyphene hydrochloride
Trade Names Darvon, Dolene, Progesic
Classification Analgesic (mild narcotic)

See codeine for contraindications and side effects.

Action Similar actions to codeine, but only half as potent. With aspirin, is as effective as codeine and aspirin. Has no antitussive effect. *High Addiction potential*

Indications for Drug Relief of mild to moderate pain in chronic or recurring diseases.

Contraindications Hypersensitivity; not to be used for children.

Forms of Drug   Capsules containing 32 or 65 mg.

Administration of Drug   65 mg po q4h.

Interactive Effects   Has synergistic effect with aspirin. Has addictive effect with alcohol, tranquilizers, and other CNS depressants.

Nursing Considerations
1. Exempt from restrictions of federal narcotic law.
2. Has very slight addictive liability, but can produce psychic and physical dependence.
3. Client should not drive or operate machinery until effect of drug is evaluated.
4. Drowsiness usually occurs only with very large doses (300 mg or more).
5. Client should not consume alcohol or any other sedatives or hypnotics while taking propoxyphene.

Generic Name   Pentazocine hydrochloride
Trade Name   Talwin
Classification   Analgesic (mild narcotic)

See morphine for side effects and drug interactions.

Action   GI and CNS effects similar to morphine and codeine. Is a weak narcotic antagonist and has no antitussive effect. High doses cause elevation in blood pressure and heart rate. High addiction potential.

Indications for Drug   Relief of moderate pain.

Contraindications   Not be used for children under 12 years. Safety in pregnancy has not been established.

Forms of Drug   Tablets containing 50 mg. (30 mg/ml ampules and vials)

Administration of Drug   Oral: 50 to 100 mg q4h: Intramuscular, subcutaneous, intravenous: 30 to 60 mg q4h. Total dosage should not exceed 600 mg daily.

Nursing Considerations (See morphine.)
1. Exempt from restrictions of federal narcotic law.
2. Do not mix with barbiturates as the drugs are incompatible in solution.
3. May cause dependence in clients with a history of drug abuse.
4. Clients should not operate machinery while taking drug.
5. In respiratory depression produced by pentazocine, narcotic antagonists are not effective. Artificial respiration and respiratory stimulants are preferred methods of treatment.

Generic Name   Butorphanol tartrate
Trade Name   Stadol
Classification   Synthetic opiates (narcotic agonist-antagonist)

Action   Similar actions to morphine; the analgesic potency is 3 to 7 times that of morphine on a per mg basis.

Indications for Drug   Relief of moderate to severe pain; preoperative analgesia.

Forms of Drug   Vials containing 1 and 2 mg/ml

Administration of Drug   Adults: IM 1 to 2 mg (range 1 to 4 mg) may be repeated every 3 to 4 hours as needed. IV 1 mg (range 0.5 to 2 mg) may be repeated every 3 to 4 hours as needed.

Side Effects   Sedation; nausea, sweating, headache, dizziness, confusion.

Interactive Effects   May be an additive effect with other CNS antidepressants.

Generic Name   Nalbuphine hydrochloride
Trade Name   Nubain
Classification   Synthetic opiates (narcotic agonist-antagonist)

Action   Similar actions to morphine; the analgesic potency is equivalent to morphine and is about three times that of pentazocine.

Indications for Drug   Relief of moderate to severe pain; preoperative analgesia.

Forms of Drug   Vials and ampuls containing 10 and 20 mg/ml.

Administration of Drug   Adults: 10 mg SC, IM, or IV repeated every 3 to 6 hours as needed. May be increased up to 20 mg if needed; the total daily dose should not exceed 160 mg.

Side Effects   Sedation; sweating, nausea, vomiting.

Interactive Effects   May be additive effects with other CNS depressants.

NARCOTIC ANTAGONISTS

Generic Name   Nalorphine hydrochloride
Trade Names   Lethidrone, Nalline Hydrochloride
Classification   Narcotic antagonist

Action   Displaces other narcotics from cellular receptor sites. An effective antagonist against depressant effects of all narcotics. Causes abrupt withdrawal symptoms in narcotic addicts. Is not effective against other CNS depressants, barbiturates, or alcohol. May cause respiratory depression when given alone.

Indications for Drug   Acute narcotic toxicity with respiratory depression; diagnosing narcotic addiction; prevention of respiratory depression in newborns after narcotic given to mother.

Contraindications   CNS depression from sources other than narcotics. Not to be used for the treatment of addiction.

Forms of Drug   Adults: Ampules of 1, 2, or 10 ml containing 5 mg5ml; Children: 1-ml ampules containing 0.2 mg/ml. Store in light-resistant containers.

Administration of Drug   Adults: 2 to 10 mg IM, subc, or IV as needed; Newborns: 0.1 to 0.2 mg IM or IV as needed.

Absorption   From tissues after subc injection.
Metabolism   Detoxified in liver.
Excretion   In urine.

Interactive Effects   Can aggravate the effects of barbiturates and other hypnotics on the respiratory system.

Nursing Considerations
1. Exempt from restrictions of federal narcotic law.
2. Respiratory rate and volume and blood pressure should increase within 2 minutes after IV administration in clients with severe narcotic depression. Additional doses may be required to prevent recurrence of respiratory depression.
3. Large doses cause drowsiness, sweating, dysphoria, nausea, and vomiting.
4. When used on narcotic-free clients, effect is similar to that of a small dose of morphine.

Generic Name   Levallorphan tartrate
Trade Name   Lorfan
Classification   Narcotic antagonist

See nalorphine hydrochloride for indications for drug, contraindications, side effects, drug interactions, and nursing considerations.

Action   Similar actions to nalorphine, but ten times more potent. (See nalorphine hydrochloride.)

Forms of Drug   Adults: 10-ml vials containing 1 mg/ml; 1-ml ampules containing 1 mg/ml. Children: Vials containing 0.05 mg/ml. Store in light-resistant containers.

Generic Name   Naloxone hydrochloride
Trade Name   Narcan
Classification   Narcotic antagonist

See nalorphine hydrochloride for indications for drug, contraindications, side effects, and nursing considerations.

Action   Similar actions to nalorphine, but 10 to 30 times more potent. When given alone, does not cause morphinelike effects and does not aggravate respiratory depression of barbiturates and hypnotics. (See nalorphine hydrochloride.)

Forms of Drug   2-ml ampules containing 0.4 mg/ml: 10-ml vials containing 0.4 mg/ml.

Administration of Drug   Adults: 0.2 to 1 mg IM, subc, or IV as needed; Children: 0.02 mg/ml. Dose 0.01 mg/kg repeated at 2 to 3 minute intervals until desired effect.

ANTIDEPRESSANT MEDICATIONS

Two major classifications of antidepressant medications are (1) tricyclic and tetracyclic antidepressants and (2) monoamine oxidase (MAO) inhibitors.

Antidepressant medication is used to alleviate the discomfort of clients with moderate to severe signs of depressed mood and affect and to treat clients experiencing a depressed cycle of manic-depression illness.

TRICYCLIC AND TETRACYCLIC ANTIDEPRESSANTS

Generic Name   Amitriptyline hydrochloride
Trade Names   Amitid, Amitril, Elavil, Endep, SK-Amitriptyline
Classification   Tricyclic antidepressant

Action   Amitriptyline is closely related to the phenothiazines and produces an antidepressant effect without the side effects of MAO inhibitors. Although the exact mechanism of action is unknown, amitriptyline is believed to interfere with the reuptake of brain amines by nerves. It enhances the effects of epinephrine and serotonin; it is a mild CNS depressant. Amitriptyline is an effective mood elevator and promotes mental acuity and an increased level of physical activity. Its sedative effects help counteract insomnia that may accompany any depression.

Indications for Drug   Treatment of depressive disorders and anxiety neuroses.

Contraindications   Acute phase of myocardial infarction, severe renal or hepatic deficiency, concomitant use of MAO inhibitors, glaucoma.

Forms of Drug   Tablets containing 10, 25, or 50 mg; vials containing 10 mg/ml.

Administration of Drug   Adults: 75 mg po or IM daily, usually in divided doses; can be increased gradually to a maximum dosage of 150 mg/day. Geriatrics and teenagers: 10 mg po tid and 20 mg hs; 300 mg/day for inpatients. May get lighter doses when monitored closely.

Absorption   Readily absorbed from GI tract. Peak action occurs in 3 to 4 hours. Half-life is 2 days.
Distribution   Widely distributed in body tissues and plasma proteins.
Metabolism   In the liver.
Excretion   In urine.

Side Effects   Dry mouth, constipation, orthostatic hypotension; allergic reactions; CNS symptoms (extrapyramidal signs, anxiety, agitation, disorientation, hallucinations, ataxia, tremors, seizures); cardiovascular symptoms (arrhythmias, congestive heart failure, stroke); GI symptoms (gastric upset); endocrine and hematologic changes; altered blood sugar, blood dyscrasias, altered hepatic function.

Interactive Effects   Enhances the effects of other CNS depressants, catecholamines, adrenergics, anticholinergics, thyroid hormones, disulfiram, anticoagulants, vasodilators, and central-acting skeletal muscle relaxants. Antagonizes the effects of anticonvulsants, phenylbutazone, cholinergics, clonidine, and guanethidine. Tricyclic effects are potentiated by phenothiazines, methylphenidate, amphetamines, furazolidone, acetazolamide, MAO inhibitors, and urinary alkalizers. Tricyclic effects are inhibited by urinary acidifiers and barbiturates.

Nursing Considerations
1. Assessment and planning
   a. Drug should be discontinued at least 48 hours prior to surgery.
   b. Baseline vital signs, particularly blood pressure, should be determined prior to institution of therapy.

2. Assessment and implementation
   a. Entire daily dose may be prescribed at bedtime since drug is long-acting and has sedative effects.
   b. Monitor blood pressure frequently during initial phase of therapy.
   c. Inform client that the full therapeutic effect may occur 1 to 3 weeks after initiation of therapy.
   d. Instruct client that drug must be taken as prescribed, not merely when needed for depression.
   e. Instruct client to be alert for development of orthostatic hypotension; the elderly are particularly susceptible.
   f. Caution clients to avoid prolonged exposure to sunlight.
   g. Warn client not to drive or use heavy machinery while taking drug, since drowsiness is a frequent side effect.
   h. Instruct client that alcohol will potentiate drug effects, possibly producing extreme drowsiness and ataxia.
   i. Advise client to ingest sufficient fluids, rinse the mouth frequently, and chew gum to relieve the unpleasantness of dry mouth.

3. Assessment and evaluation
   a. Assess suicide risk carefully, since all depressed clients are potentially suicidal.
   b. Observe for slowing of normal elimination processes, since urinary retention and constipation are common side effects.

Generic Name Desipramine hydrochloride
Trade Names Norpramin, Pertofrane
Classification Tricyclic antidepressant

Action It has been theorized that desipramine is the active metabolite of imipramine and so is at least as therapeutic as imipramine (Desipramine may no longer be as effective after a few weeks, which is the amount of time needed for behavioral changes when other tricyclic antidepressants are administered.) (See amitriptyline hydrochloride.)

Forms of Drug Tablets containing 25, 50, 75, 100, or 150 mg; capsules containing 25 or 50 mg.

Administration of Drug Adults: 25 to 50 mg po daily in divided doses; then increase gradually to a maximum dosage of 200 mg/day until desired effect; Maintenance dosage: 50 to 100 mg po daily.

Side Effects May cause hyperthermia or a bad taste in the mouth. (See amitriptyline hydrochloride.)

Generic Name Doxepin hydrochloride
Trade Names Adapin, Sinequan
Classification Tricyclic antidepressant

See amitriptyline hydrochloride for contraindications, side effects, drug interactions, and nursing considerations.

Action Similar to amitriptyline.
(See amitriptyline hydrochloride.)

Indications for Drug Treatment of depression in psychoneurotic patients.

Forms of Drug Capsules containing 10, 25, or 50 mg.

Administration of Drug Adults: 75 mg po daily in divided doses; Maximum dosage: 150 to 300 mg/day.

Generic Name Imipramine hydrochloride
Trade Name Tofranil
Classification Tricyclic antidepressant

See amitriptyline hydrochloride for indications for drug, contraindications, side effects, and drug interactions.

Action Similar to amitriptyline. (See amitriptyline hydrochloride.)

Forms of Drug Tablets containing 10, 25, or 50 mg; vials containing 12.5 mg/ml.

Administration of Drug Adults: Outpatients: 75 mg po or IM daily in divided doses. Hospitalized clients: 100 to 150 mg po or IM daily; can be gradually increased to a maximum dosage of 300 mg/day in divided doses until desired effect; Maintenance dosage 50 to 150 po or IM daily. Geriatrics and teenagers: Initially, 30–40 mg daily, not to exceed 100 mg daily.

Nursing Considerations (See amitriptyline hydrochloride.)
  1. Improvement in behavior may be observed as early as 3 days after onset of therapy.
  2. Full therapeutic effect may not be apparent for 1 or 2 weeks.

Generic Name Nortriptyline
Trade Name Aventyl
Classification Tricyclic antidepressant

See amitriptyline hydrochloride for indications for drug, contraindications, side effects, and drug interactions.

Action Similar to amitriptyline. (See amitriptyline hydrochloride.)

Forms of Drug Capsules containing 10 or 25 mg: concentrate containing 10 mg/5 ml.

Administration of Drug Adults: Initial dosage: 20 to 40 mg po daily in divided doses for the first week: Maintenance dosage: 30 to 75 mg po daily; Maximum dosage: 100 mg/day. Geriatrics: 30 to 50 mg po daily.

Nursing Considerations (See amitriptyline hydrochloride.)

Generic Name Protriptyline hydrochloride
Trade Name Vivactil
Classification Tricyclic antidepressant

See amitriptyline hydrochloride for indications for drug, contraindications, drug interactions, and nursing considerations.

Action Similar to amitriptyline. (See amitriptyline hydrochloride.)

Forms of Drug Tablets containing 5 or 10 mg.

Administration of Drug Adults: Initial dosage: 30 to 60 mg po daily in divided doses; Maintenance dosage 15 to 40 mg po daily.

Side Effects Causes more cardiovascular side effects than other tricyclic antidepressants, but produces less sedation. (See amitriptyline hydrochloride.)

Generic Name Trimipramine maleate
Trade Name Surmontil
Classification Tricyclic antidepressant

Action Trimipramine is a tricyclic antidepressant that increases the synaptic concentration of norepinephrine in the central nervous system by blocking its reuptake by nerves.

Indications for Drug Treatment of depression, depressive neurosis and bipolar disorder, depressed phase.

Forms of Drug Capsules containing 25, 50, or 100 mg.

Administration of Drug Adults: 25 mg po 2 times daily initially then increase as needed up to 200 mg/day for outpatients or 300 mg/day for inpatients.

Absorption Peak levels occur in about 2 hours.
Metabolism and Excretion Metabolized in the liver and excreted in the urine and feces.

Side Effects (See amitriptyline hydrochloride.)

Interactive Effects (See amitriptyline hydrochloride.)

Generic Name Maprotiline hydrochloride
Trade Name Asendin
Classification Istracyclic antidepressant

Action Maprotiline represents a new tetracyclic chemical class of antidepressants. It increases the synaptic concentration of norepinephrine in the central nervous system by blocking its reuptake by nerves. Maprotiline does not block serotonin reuptake.

Indications for Drug Treatment of depression, depressive neuroses and bipolar affective disorder, depressed phase.

Forms of Drug Tablets containing 25 mg, 50 mg, and 75 mg.

Administration of Drug Adults: 25 mg po three times a day initially; then increase gradually up to 225 mg/day as needed and tolerated; may also be given as a single daily dose at bedtime.

Absorption Peak levels occur at about 8 to 24 hours.
Metabolism and Excretion Metabolized by the liver and excreted in the urine and feces.

Side Effects (See amitriptyline hydrochloride.)

Interactive Effects (See amitriptyline hydrochloride.)

MONOAMINE OXIDASE INHIBITORS

Generic Name Isocarboxazid
Trade Name Marplan
Classification Antidepressant (MAO inhibitor)

Action MAO inhibitors interfere with the enzyme monoamine oxidase, which metabolizes norepinephrine. The direct clinical result is a buildup of norepinephrine in the tissues, with all the attendant complications. These drugs affect blood pressure and hepatic function.

Indications for Drug Endogenous depression, manic-depressive psychosis, severe reactive depression. Usually administered only after a trial with tricyclic antidepressants has proven ineffective.

Contraindications Children under 16 years, congestive heart failure, hepatic dysfunction, phenochromocytoma, hyperthyroidism, cardiovascular disease, the elderly, debilitated clients.

Forms of Drug Tablets containing 10 mg.

Administration of Drug Adults: 30 mg po daily in a single dose or in divided doses; Maintenance dosage: 10 to 20 mg po daily.

Absorption Readily absorbed from GI tract.
Metabolism Rapidly metabolized in the liver.
Excretion In urine.

Side Effects Orthostatic hypotension, dizziness, insomnia, GI upsets, headache, arrhythmias, tremors, hypomania, euphoria, confusion, memory loss, ataxia, hallucinations, convulsions, dry mouth, blurred vision, dysuria, impotence, palpitations, edema, weight gain, blood dyscrasias, jaundice, photosensitivity reactions, sodium retention, hypoglycemia, glaucoma, anorexia.

Interactive Effects Potentiates the effects of sympathomimetics, anticholinergics, antihistamines, antiparkinsonian drugs, and antihypertensives. Increases the toxic effects of barbiturates, phenothiazines, and CNS depressants. Causes hypertension excitement, rigidity, hypotension, and coma when used with narcotic analgesics, especially maperidine. Increases the hypoglycemic effects of hypoglycemic drugs and the muscle-relaxing effect of succinylcholine. Interferes with the effect of antiepileptics. Foods containing tyramine (cheese, sour cream, yogurt, beer, wine, yeast, herring, chicken livers, aged meats, tenderizers, licorice, caffeine, chocolate) increase the risk of hypertensive crisis. Reserpine or guanethidine administered IV or IM can cause severe hypertension.

Nursing Considerations
1. Assessment and planning
   a. Drug should be discontinued at least 3 weeks prior to surgery.
   b. Baseline blood and hepatic function tests and blood pressure determinations should be done prior to institution of therapy.
2. Assessment and intervention
   a. Give with meals to reduce GI distress.
   b. Observe client carefully for toxic reactions, which can occur within hours of the first few doses.
   c. Blood pressure should be monitored between doses during initial phase of therapy.
   d. Instruct client to take no other drugs, including OTC preparations, concurrently and for 3 weeks following cessation of therapy.
   e. Instruct client to avoid tyramine-rich foods.
   f. Advise client to change positions slowly to avoid postural hypotension.
   g. Instruct client to report promptly any symptoms suggestive of hypertensive crisis (headache, palpitations).
   h. Client should report any rapid or unusual weight gain or other unusual symptoms.
3. Assessment and evaluation
   a. Observe client for color blindness, which indicates eye damage.
   b. Assess lethality of client's suicidal statements, since client's mood improves with continued therapy.
   c. Since drug is long-acting and may have a cumulative effect, behavioral changes may not be apparent for 1 to 4 weeks.

Generic Name Phenelzine sulfate
Trade Name Nardil
Classification Antidepressant (MAO inhibitors)

See isocarboxazid for indications for drug, contraindications, and drug interactions.

Action Similar to isocarboxazid for indications for drug, contraindications, and drug interactions.

Forms of Drug Tablets containing 15 mg.

Administration of Drug Adults: Initial dosage: 45 mg po daily in divided doses; then gradually increase to a maximum dosage of 75 mg/day, if necessary, until desired effect; Maintenance dosage: 15 mg po every other day.

Side Effects Similar to isocarboxzid, but less likely to precipitate a hypertensive crisis. (See isocarboxazid.)

Nursing Considerations Therapeutic effect can occur after 1 to 2 weeks. (See isocarboxazid for further details.)

Generic Name Tranylcypromine sulfate
Trade Name Parnate
Classification Antidepressant (MAO inhibitor)

See isocarboxazid for contraindications, drug interactions, and nursing considerations.

Action Similar to isocarboxazid, but stimulant effect is stronger. (See isocarboxazid.)

Indications for Drug Intractable depression. Should only be administered when other safer medications have been tried.

Forms of Drug Tablets containing 10 mg.

Administration of Drug Adults: Initial dosage: 20 mg po daily in divided doses for 2 to 3 weeks; then gradually increase to a maximum dosage of 30 mg/day until desired effect; Maintenance dosage: 10 to 20 mg po daily.

Side Effects As the peak effect of this drug occurs much sooner than that produced by the other MAO inhibitors, there is a greater chance of precipitating a hypertensive crisis.

OTHER ANTIDEPRESSANTS

Generic Name Fluoxetine hydrochloride
Trade Name Prozac
Classification Antidepressants

Action Fluoxetine is chemically unrelated to other antidepressants. It increases the synaptic concentrations of serotonin in the CNS by blocking its neuronal reuptake; there are no effects on norepinephrine.

Indications for Drug Treatment of depression.

Forms of Drug Capsules containing 20 mg.

Administration of Drug Adults: 20 mg/day in the morning, may be increased by 20 mg/day at intervals of several weeks up to 80 mg/day as needed. Doses above 20 mg/day should be administered in two divided doses—morning and noon.

Side Effects Headache, nervousness, insomnia, drowsiness, anxiety; nausea, diarrhea, anorexia, sweating, skin rash.

Interactive Effects May enhance the activity of other CNS-active drugs. May prolong the half-life of diazepam. May displace highly protein-bound drugs, resulting in an enhanced effect of the displaced drug (e.g., digoxin, warfarin). There is no data on concomitant use with monoamine oxidase inhibitors so the combination should be avoided. When combined with tryptophan, restlessness, agitation, and GI disturbances may be increased.

Generic Name Trazadone hydrochloride
Trade Name Desyrel
Classification Antidepressant

Action Trazadone is a triazolopyridine antidepressant that is not related chemically to tricyclic or tetracyclic compounds. Its probable mode of action is to increase the synaptic concentration of serotonin in the central nervous system by blocking its reuptake by nerves.

Indications for Drug Treatment of depression with or without anxiety.

Forms of Drug Tablets containing 50 or 100 mg.

Administration of Drug Adults: 50 mg po three times a day initially, then increase by 50 mg/day up to 400 mg/day for outpatients or 600 mg/day for inpatients if needed.

Absorption Peak levels occur in about 1 to 2 hours.
Metabolism Metabolized by the liver and excreted in the urine.

Side Effects Dry mouth, blurred vision, constipation; confusion, tremors, tiredness, weakness; nausea, vomiting, diarrhea; priapism.

Interactive Effects May lead to increased serum levels of phenytoin and digoxin. May antagonize antihypertensive effect of clonidine. Use with caution with monoamine oxidase inhibitors.

Generic Name Amoxapine
Trade Name Asendin
Classification Antidepressant

Action Amoxapine, while chemically different from the tricyclic antidepressants, appears to act in the same manner. It increases the synaptic concentrations of norepinephrine and serotonin in the central nervous system by blocking their reuptake by nerves.

Indications for Drug Treatment of depression, agitated depression, and depressed bipolar disorder.

Contraindications Similar to tricyclic antidepressants. (See amitriptyline.)

Forms of Drug Tablets containing 25, 50, 100, and 150 mg.

Administration of Drug Adults: 50 mg po three times a day initially, then gradually increase as needed and tolerated up to 300 mg/day or up to 600 mg/day in hospitalized patients.

Absorption Peak levels usually occur in about 90 minutes.
Metabolism and Excretion Metabolized in the liver and excreted in the urine and feces.

Side Effects (See amitriptyline hydrochloride.)

Interactive Effects (See amitriptyline hydrochloride.)

ANTIMANIC MEDICATIONS

Generic Name Lithium carbonate
Trade Names Eskalith, Lithane, Lithonate, Lithotabs
Classification Antimanic

Action Precise mechanism is unknown, but seems to act similarly to the sodium ion and enhances the excretion of sodium and potassium. Decreases circulating thyroid hormones, may block renal response to ADH, decreases glucose tolerance, and increases circulating growth hormone levels.

Indications for Drug Some controversy abounds concerning the value of lithium in treating manic-depressive illness. It has been found to be extremely effective in controlling acute manic and hypomanic behaviors, such as hyperactivity, poor judgment, flight of ideas, and aggressiveness. May be used in conjunction with phenothiazines.

Contraindications Cardiovascular or renal impairment, dehydration, clients taking diuretics, clients with sodium depletion, pregnancy, lactation, schizophrenia, organic brain disease. Safe use in children (under 12 years) has not been established.

Forms of Drug Tablets and capsules containing 300 or 600 mg.

Administration of Drug Adults: 300 to 600 mg po tid until desired effect; Maintenance dosage: 300 mg po tid.

Absorption Rapidly absorbed from GI tract. Peak action occurs in 2 to 4 hours. Half-life is 24 hours. Crosses the blood-brain barrier slowly. Crosses placenta and appears in breast milk.
Distribution Widely distributed in body water, with high concentrations in the kidneys and saliva. Some drug is concentrated in bone, muscles, and liver.
Excretion About 75% in urine within 24 hours; alkalization of the urine enhances excretion.

Side Effects Dry mouth, metallic taste, thyroid enlargement, glycosuria, hyperglycemia, weight gain, edema. Lithium poisoning: nausea, diarrhea, diabetes-like symptoms, tremors. More serious symptoms include blurred vision and slurred speech. Dermatologic manifestations may also occur. In acute toxicity, convulsions, shock, coma, and death can occur. (See amitriptyline hydrochloride.)

Interactive Effects Acetazolamide, aminophylline, sodium bicarbonate, and sodium chloride enhance the renal excretion of lithium, thereby decreasing its effect.

Phenothiazines may enhance hyperglycemic effects. Iodine-containing agents and tricyclic antidepressants may enhance hypothyroid effects. Thiazide diuretics, haloperidol, and methyldopa may increase lithium toxicity. Lithium may decrease the effects of amphetamines.

Nursing Considerations
1. Assessment and planning
   a. Since there is no antidote available for lithium poisoning, every effort must be made to prevent it.
2. Assessment and implementation
   a. Careful monitoring is required because there is a narrow margin between therapeutic and toxic dosages. Blood lithium levels should be determined before each morning dose during the initial treatment period and then weekly; therapeutic serum drug levels: 0.6 to 1.5 mEq/1.
   b. Give with meals or immediately after to minimize GI upset.
   c. Emphasize the importance of performing serum lithium determinations as scheduled (monthly).
   d. Stress the need to maintain adequate sodium and fluid intake and to avoid the use of diuretics.
   e. Advise client not to drive or operate machinery, since drowsiness is common.
   f. Lithium intoxication begins to develop when serum levels reach 1.5 mEq/1; if such levels occur, therapy should be discontinued for 1 day and then resumed at a lower dosage.
3. Assessment and evaluation
   a. Therapeutic response is usually evident within 10 days. If no response occurs within 2 weeks, drug should be discontinued.
   b. Client should be weighed daily. Report evidence of fluid retention.
   c. Assess client regularly for symptoms of hypothyroidism and/or thyroid enlargement.

ANTIANXIETY MEDICATIONS

Two major classes of antianxiety medications are benzodiazepines and propanediols. Sometimes called minor tranquilizers, antianxiety agents effectively reduce mild to moderate anxiety and the accompanying neurotic symptoms without interfering with the individual's ability to function at an adequate level.

Antianxiety agents have been especially useful in treating people with high anxiety levels or withdrawal from alcohol intoxication. The use of these drugs is said to enhance the individual's ability to participate effectively in psychotherapy.

BENZODIAZEPINES

Generic Name Diazepam
Trade Name Valium
Classification Antianxiety agent

Action Unlike the barbiturates used as antianxiety agents, diazepam produces only minor circulatory and respiratory depression, while preserving mental acuity even when administered in large dosages. Most of the brain is not depressed, but electrical impulses in the limbic system are inhibited. Diazepam is an effective skeletal muscle relaxant and a powerful anticonvulsant, but its mode of action is not clearly understood. Benzodiazepines depress the polysynaptic reflexes of the spinal cord, which reduces skeletal muscle tension, thereby inhibiting those afferent proprioceptive impulses that might aggravate existing anxiety. Benzodiazepines also inhibit stimulation of the amygdala and the hippocampus structures of the brain, which influence behavior. These drugs therefore have a mild sedative effect but do not alter the level of consciousness or the ability to perform psychomotor tasks.

Indications for Drug Anxiety states of organic or functional origin, such as anxiety due to angina pectoris, asthma, premenstrual tension, or menopause; insomnia; preoperative sedation; relaxation of tension due to arthritis and low-back pain; status epilepticus; withdrawal from alcohol intoxication.

Contraindications Severe psychoses, glaucoma, shock, children under 6 months.

Forms of Drug Tablets containing 2, 5, or 10 mg; vials of 2 to 10 ml containing 5 mg/ml.

Administration of Drug Adults: 4 to 40 mg po, IM, or IV daily in divided doses; Elderly patients require a lower dosage; Children: Over 6 months: 1 to 2.5 mg po tid.

1. IM injection must be deep into gluteal muscle.
2. Do not mix drug with other solutions. Do not add to IV fluids.
3. IV injection should not exceed 5 mg/min. Give into a large vein and avoid extravasation.

Absorption Readily absorbed from GI tract or the bloodstream. Onset of action is: 30 to 60 minutes (po); 15 to 30 minutes (IM). Peak blood levels occur in 2 hours. Half-life is 20 to 50 hours. Crosses placenta and appears in breast milk.
Metabolism Metabolized slowly in the liver; can still be found in the blood 7 days after discontinuation of therapy.

Excretion In urine, with a small amount in stool.

Side Effects Drowsiness, lethargy, ataxia, confusion, headache, syncope, vertigo, depression, stupor, excitement, dry mouth, constipation, urinary retention, blurred vision, hypotension, weight gain, cardiovascular collapse, blood dyscrasias, hypersensitivity reactions, endocrine abnormalities.

Interactive Effects Enhances the depressant effects of alcohol, barbiturates, antihistamines, phenothiazines, and narcotics. Potentiates the effects of phenytoin and skeletal muscle relaxants. Antagonizes the effects of levodopa. Smoking may inhibit the effects of benzodiazepines.

Nursing Considerations

1. Assessment and planning
   a. Since the effect of diazepam is accumulative, therapeutic results may not be apparent for 5 to 10 days after initiation of therapy.
2. Assessment and implementation
   a. Since diazepam is long acting, 1 dose per day is usually sufficient. The dose should be given at bedtime to promote sleep and relieve anxiety throughout the following day.
   b. Observe client for excessive drowsiness or ataxia.
   c. Provide bedrails and assistance with ambulation.
   d. Observe client for signs of developing physiologic or psychologic dependence. As dosage and duration of therapy increase, the risk of dependence increases.
   e. Observe geriatric clients carefully, since they are more likely to develop side effects.
   f. Advise clients not to drink alcohol or take any other CNS depressant.
   g. Instruct client not to drive or operate dangerous machinery.
   h. Instruct client to change position slowly to prevent postural hypotension.
   i. Instruct client not to discontinue drug without medical supervision.
3. Assessment and evaluation
   a. Observe client for signs of drug dependence.
   b. Arrange for periodic blood and liver function tests if drug is given on a long-term basis.

Generic Name Chlordiazepoxide, chlordiazepoxide hydrochloride
Trade Names Libritabs, Librium
Classification Antianxiety agent

See diazepam for contraindications, drug interactions, and nursing considerations.

Action   (See diazepam.)

Indications for Drug   Management of delirium tremens; treatment of anxiety associated with psychosomatic conditions.

Contraindications   Use with caution in addiction-prone clients.

Forms of Drug   Tablets and capsules containing 5, 10, or 25 mg; ampules containing 100 mg of dry powder.

Administration of Drug   Adults: 15 to 40 mg po, IM, or IV daily in divided doses; can be gradually increased to a maximum dosage of 300 mg/day. Geriatrics: 10 to 20 mg po, IM, or IV daily. Children: Over 6 years: 0.5 mk/kg po, IM, or IV daily.

Generic Name   Clorazepate dipotassium
Trade Name   Tranxene
Classification   Antianxiety agent

See diazepam for action, indications for drug, contraindications, and drug interactions.

Forms of Drug   Capsules containing 3.75, 7.5, or 15 mg.

Administration of Drug   Adults: 15 to 60 po daily in divided doses; Geriatrics: 7.5 to 15 mg po daily; Children: Over 6 years: 7.5 to 60 mg po daily in divided doses.

Generic Name   Oxazepam
Trade Name   Serax
Classification   Antianxiety agent

See diazepam for action, indications for drug, contraindications, and drug interactions.

Forms of Drug   Tablets containing 15 mg; capsules containing 10, 15, or 30 mg.

Administration of Drug   Adults: 30 to 120 mg po daily in divided doses.

Nursing Considerations   Monitor elderly clients carefully for the development of hypotension. (See diazepam.)

Generic Name   Temazepam
Trade Name   Restoril
Classification   Antianxiety agent, hypnotic

See diazepam for contraindications and drug interactions.

Indications for Drug   Short-term treatment of insomnia.

Forms of Drug   Capsules containing 15 or 30 mg.

Administration of Drug   Adults: 15 to 30 mg po at bedtime.

Generic Name   Lorazepam
Trade Name   Ativan
Classification   Antianxiety agent

See diazepam for indications, contraindications, and drug interactions.

Forms of Drug   Tablets containing 0.5, 1, or 2 mg; disposable syringes containing 2 or 4 mg/ml.

Administration of Drug   Adults: 2 to 6 mg po daily in divided doses; IM 0.05 mg per kg of body weight up to a maximum of 4 mg for preanesthetic sedation; IV 0.044 mg per kg of body weight or a total dose of 2 mg, whichever is less for preanesthetic sedation.

Generic Name   Triazolam
Trade Name   Halcion
Classification   Antianxiety agent, hypnotic

See diazepam for contraindications and drug interactions.

Indications for Drug   Short-term treatment of insomnia.

Forms of Drug   Tablets containing 0.25 or 0.5 mg.

Administration of Drug   Adults: 0.25 to 0.5 mg at bedtime; in geriatric or debilitated patients 0.125 to 0.25 mg po at bedtime.

Generic Name Alprazolam
Trade Name Xanax
Classification Antianxiety agent

See diazepam for indications, contraindications, and drug interactions.

Forms of Drug Tablets containing 0.25, 0.5, and 1 mg.

Administration of Drug Adults: 0.75 to 4 mg daily in divided doses.

Generic Name Flurazepam
Trade Name Dalmane
Classification Antianxiety agent, hypnotic

See diazepam for contraindications and drug interactions.

Indications for Drug Short-term treatment of insomnia.

Forms of Drug Capsules containing 15 or 30 mg.

Administration of Drug Adults: 15 to 30 mg po at bedtime; elderly patients, particularly those over 70 years should not receive more than 15 mg initially.

PROPANEDIOLS

Generic Name Meprobamate
Trade Names Equanil, Miltown
Classification Antianxiety agent

See diazepam for contraindications and drug interactions.

Action Similar to diazepam in that it reduces anxiety. Meprobamate is a skeletal muscle relaxant and an anticonvulsant. Its action is believed to be similar to phenobarbital.

Indications for Drug Insomnia, simple nervous tension, petit mal epilepsy.

Forms of Drug Tablets and capsules containing 200 or 400 mg; oral suspension containing 40 mg/ml; vials containing 80 mg/5 ml.

Administration of Drug Adults: 400 mg po or IM daily in divided doses. Children: Over 6 years: 100 to 200 mg po or IM daily in divided doses; Maximum dosage: 2.4 g/day.

Nursing Considerations (See diazepam.)
1. Skin rash responds to antihistamines.
2. Drug dependence may develop.

ANTIPARKINSONIAN MEDICATIONS

Drugs that decrease the cholinergic activity in the basal ganglia or restore the inhibitory effects of dopamine receptor stimulation are effective in controlling the symptoms of parkinsonism. Until the late 1960s, only drugs with anticholinergic activity were available; as the client's symptoms progressed, the characteristic tremors could only be controlled by brain surgery. Levodopa, the precursor of dopamine, was released for use in 1970. Both levodopa and anticholinergic drugs are used today.

Anticholinergic agents, such as trihexyphenidyl, are effective in controlling the rigidity and tremors of parkinsonism. Drugs that block the brain's muscarinic receptor sites are particularly effective; unfortunately, these atropinelike drugs cause numerous untoward reactions; including dry mouth, constipation, blurred vision, and urinary retention. When necessary, the long-acting drug benztropine can be injected and is used for clients who are unable to take oral medication. The newer synthetic anticholinergic agents are effective in controlling akinesia, as well as rigidity and tremors.

Antihistamines, such as diphenhydramine, and the phenothiazine derivative ethopropazine have anticholinergic properties and are therefore useful in controlling symptoms of parkinsonism. The effectiveness of antihistamines and ethopropazine seems to be related to their anticholinergic properties. These drugs tend to cause drowsiness and other central nervous system disturbances.

Levodopa increases the amount of dopamine in the basal ganglia. Dopamine is unable to cross the blood-brain barrier, but levodopa can and is converted to dopamine by the nigrostriatal nerve endings. Although parkinsonism symptoms do not improve immediately, continued use of the drug will first result in improvement of akinesia and then rigidity and tremors. Levodopa does not cure the disease, it only replaces a necessary body substance. If the drug is taken regularly, symptoms will reappear. Due to the high incidence of untoward reactions, levodopa treatment is initiated at relatively low dosages and the dosage is then gradually increased every 5 to 7 days until the maximum benefit is obtained with the minimum of untoward reactions, particularly nausea and orthostatic hypotension. As the effectiveness of levodopa varies from individual to individual, dosages are highly individualized.

Carbidopa prevents the degradation of levodopa by body tissues so that larger quantities of intact levodopa molecules are available to cross the blood-brain barrier. Since carbidopa is unable to cross the blood-brain barrier, its action is limited to tissues outside the brain. When carbidopa is administered concurrently with levodopa, lower dosages of levodopa are required to sustain therapeutic drug levels in the blood and therefore the brain.

Amantadine is actually an antiviral agent, but has been found to be effective in treating parkinsonism. Although the exact mechanism of action is unknown, amantadine is thought to stimulate the release of dopamine from nigrostriatal neurons, thus causing increased dopamine levels in the basal ganglia. Amantadine is effective within 2 to 4 weeks and causes few untoward reactions.

Bromocriptine has been found to be a potent stimulator of dopamine receptor sites in the corpus striatum and is therefore useful in the treatment of parkinsonism. Unfortunately, the drug is less effective than levodopa and can induce marked behavioral changes. However, combined therapy with levodopa permits smaller dosages of each drug to be used.

Since the advent of tranquilizers for the treatment of mental disorders, drug-induced extrapyramidal symptoms similar to parkinsonism have become a major concern. Phenothiazines and other tranquilizers block stimulation and dopamine receptor sites by dopamine. The drug effects cause extrapyramidal symptoms similar to parkinsonism.

ANTICHOLINERGIC AGENTS

Generic Name Trihexyphenidyl hydrochloride
Trade Names Artane, Hexyphen, Pipanol, Tremin, Trihexidyl
Classification Anticholinergic agent

Action Trihexyphenidyl, a synthetic tertiary amine, causes relaxation of smooth musculature through a direct action on the muscle tissue and indirectly by inhibiting the parasympathetic nervous system. Its antispasmodic activity is about one-half as effective as atropine; but trihexyphenidyl causes milder secondary effects, such as mydriasis, drying of secretions, and cardioacceleration. The drug is particularly effective in reducing the rigidity associated with all forms of parkinsonism and is effective in treating extrapyramidal disorders caused by CNS drugs, such as dibenzoxazepines, phenothiazines, thioxanthenes, and butyrophenones. It is said to partially relieve some of the depression associated with parkinsonism.

Indications for Drug Drug-induced extrapyramidal disorders, as an adjunct in the treatment of postencephalitic, arteriosclerotic, and idiopathic parkinsonism.

Contraindications Although it is not contraindicated in hypertensive clients, these clients should be assessed frequently for untoward reactions. Use with caution in clients with glaucoma, obstructive disorders of the GI tract, and elderly clients with prostatic hypertrophy. Elderly clients (over 60 years) and clients with arteriosclerosis or a history of drug hypersensitivity may be hypertensive to the drug's action and may require reduced dosages during long-term therapy. Incipient glaucoma may be precipitated.

Forms of Drug Scored tablets containing 2 or 5 mg; elixir containing 2 mg/5 ml; sustained-release capsules containing 5 mg (used after desired dosage has been established).

Administration of Drug Highly individualized. Reduced dosages are required in clients over 60 years.

■ *Drug-induced extrapyramidal disorders:* If the dosage of the causative agent is reduced, less trihexyphenidyl is required to eliminate the extrapyramidal symptoms. Initial dosage: 1 mg po daily after a meal; 1 mg po bid after meals; then 1 mg po tid after meals; then increase by 1 to 2 mg po daily: Dosage range: 5 to 15 mg daily. Dosage may be reduced when the symptoms are controlled for several days.

■ *Idiopathic and Postencephalitic parkinsonism:* Initial dosage: 1 mg po daily after meals; then increase by 2 mg daily every 3 to 5 days; give in 2 to 3 divided doses after meals; Dosage range for idiopathic: 6 to 10 mg daily; Dosage range for postencephalitic: 12 to 15 mg daily. Clients receiving other antiparkinsonian agents, particularly levodopa, may only require 3 to 6 mg daily.

1. Give after meals with a full glass of water.
2. Provide client with a full pitcher of ice water or other measures to control dry mouth.
3. Drug can be given 3 minutes before meals; but may cause nausea.

Absorption Rapidly absorbed from GI tract; may be irritating to GI tract. Onset of action is about 1 hour. Peak action occurs in 2 to 3 hours and duration of action is 6 to 12 hours.
Metabolism Unknown
Excretion By the kidneys

Side Effects Mild secondary reactions such as dry mouth, blurred vision, dizziness, nausea, and nervousness are experienced by 30% to 50% of clients. These symptoms tend to disappear during long-term therapy. Untoward reactions characteristic of atropine, including suppurative parotitis, skin rashes, colon dilation, paralytic ileus, delusions and hallucinations, rarely occur. Dilation of the pupil and increased intraocular tension may progress to angle-closure glaucoma during long-term therapy. GI disturbances, including nausea, vomiting, and constipation, may occur. Urinary hesitancy and retention may occur, particularly in elderly males. Drowsiness, tachycardia, weakness, and headaches may occur. Elderly clients and clients with arteriosclerosis or a history of drug hypersensitivity may develop CNS disturbances, including confusion, amnesia, agitation, paranoid behavior, nausea, and vomiting.

Interactive Effects Concurrent therapy with antihistamines has additive anticholinergic effects and may cause excessive dryness of the mouth, loss of teeth, and suppurative parotitis. Concomitant therapy with amantadine may cause CNS disturbances, such as confusion, agitation, delusions, and hallucinations. The dosage of trihexyphenidyl should be reduced before instituting amantadine therapy.

Nursing Considerations
1. Assessment and planning
   a. Assess the amount of muscular rigidity, drooling, and other symptoms before instituting therapy.
   b. Gonioscopic evaluation and intraocular pressure should be determined before initiating therapy.
   c. Obtain history of drug hypersensitivities and the presence of urinary disturbances, particularly in elderly males.
2. Assessment and implementation
   a. Client may require cool drinks, ice chips, or sugarless gum to control dry mouth.
   b. Assess the type and severity of symptoms daily when drug is first instituted or dosage adjusted.
   c. Assess the presence daily of CNS disturbances in elderly clients when drug is first instituted or dosage is adjusted.
   d. Record intake and output. Notify physician if urinary retention occurs. Advise client to void before taking drug.
   e. Caution client against driving or engaging in other activities that require constant attention until dosage adjustment is complete.
3. Assessment and evaluation
   a. Tolerance to the drug may develop with long-term therapy. Assess the symptoms of parkinsonism regularly.
   b. Instruct client on long-term therapy to report the return of symptoms (muscular rigidity) to the health care provider.

Generic Name Benztropine mesylate
Trade Name Cogentin
Classification Anticholinergic agent

See trihexyphenidyl hydrochloride for contraindications, side effects, and drug interactions.

Action Benztropine exhibits anticholinergic and antihistaminic effects. This drug has the advantage of being injectable and can therefore be used in emergency situations for dystonia. (See trihexyphenidyl hydrochloride.)

Indications for Drug Parkinsonism, drug-induced extrapyramidal disorders, acute dystonia (except tardive dyskinesia).

Contraindications Children under 3 years, angle-closure glaucoma. May aggravate tardive dyskinesia and may cause paralytic ileus.

Forms of Drug Tablets containing 0.5, 1, or 2 mg; 2-ml ampules containing 2 mg/ml.

Administration of Drug
- *Parkinsonism:* Initial dosage: 0.5 to 1 mg po at bedtime; then increase gradually; Usual dosage: 1 to 2 mg daily.
- *Drug-induced extrapyramidal disorders:* 1 to 2 mg IM; then 1 to 2 mg po bid to prevent recurrence.
- *Acute dystonia:* 1 to 2 mg IM or IV; then 1 to 2 mg po bid; may be gradually increased by 0.5 mg/day; Maximum dosage: 6 mg/day.

Absorption Onset of action is: about 1 hour (po); within minutes (IM, IV). Duration of action is about 8 to 12 hours.

Nursing Considerations Protect drug ampules from light. (See trihexyphenidyl hydrochloride.)

Generic Name Biperiden hydrochloride
Trade Name Akineton Hydrochloride
Classification Anticholinergic agent

See trihexyphenidyl hydrochloride for drug interactions and nursing considerations.

Action More effective than atropine in reducing akinesia, rigidity, and tremors. Weak action on intestinal mucosa and blood vessels and little mydriatic activity. Particularly effective in treating drug-induced akathisia, akinesia, dyskinetic tremors, rigidity, oculogyric crisis, and profuse sweating caused by reseperine and phenothiazines. May not be effective for arteriosclerotic parkinsonism.

Indications for Drug   Drug-induced extrapyramidal disorders, parkinsonism, spastic disorders (multiple sclerosis, cerebral palsy, spinal cord injuries).

Contraindications   Hypersensitivity to biperiden preparations. Safe use in children and during pregnancy and lactation has not been established.

Forms of Drug   Scored tablets containing 2 mg.

Administration of Drug   2 mg po tid or quid after meals or with food.

Absorption   Nearly 90% of drug is thought to be absorbed from GI tract.

Side Effects   Dry mouth and blurred vision are common. GI disturbances may occur, particularly when given on an empty stomach. Hypotension and dizziness may occur.

Generic Name   Biperiden lactate
Trade Name   Akineton Lactate
Classification   Anticholinergic agent

See trihexyphenidyl hydrochloride for contraindications and drug interactions. See biperiden hydrochloride for action.

Indications for Drug   Acute episodes of drug-induced extrapyramidal disorders.

Contraindications   Use with caution in clients with arrhythmias or prostatic hypertrophy.

Forms of Drug   Ampules of 1 ml containing 5 mg/ml.

Administration of Drug   5 mg slow IV bolus; may be repeated in 24 hours, or 2 mg IM or IV may be repeated every 30 minutes until resolution of symptoms; maximum dosage: 8 mg/day.

Side Effects   Transient hypotension, confusion, euphoria, and disturbances of coordination may occur.

Nursing Considerations   (See trihexyphenidyl hydrochloride.)
  1. Do not use if solution is discolored or if a precipitate has formed.

2. Monitor vital signs frequently, particularly in elderly and debilitated clients.

3. Have client void before administering drug, when possible.

Generic Name   Chlorphenoxamine hydrochloride
Trade Name   Phenoxene
Classification   Anticholinergic agent

See trihexyphenidyl hydrochloride for contraindications, drug interactions, and nursing considerations.

Action   Mild anticholinergic activity. Particularly effective in controlling rigidity. Tremors may be augmented.

Indications of Drug   All forms of parkinsonism.

Contraindications   Use with caution in clients with narrow-angle glaucoma, arrhythmias, or prostatic hypertrophy.

Administration of Drug   50 to 100 mg po tid or qid after meals.

Side Effects   Blurred vision, constipation, dry mouth, nausea, and vomiting. May cause drowsiness, particularly in the elderly.

Generic Name   Cycrimine hydrochloride
Trade Name   Pagitane Hydrochloride
Classification   Anticholinergic agent

See trihexyphenidyl hydrochloride for nursing considerations.

Action   Less than half as potent as atropine in reducing neuromuscular symptoms and is slightly more toxic. May not be well tolerated or effective in arteriosclerotic parkinsonism or the elderly. Ineffective for drug induced extrapyramidal disorders.

Indications for Drug   Parkinsonism

Contraindications   Safe use during pregnancy has not been established. Use with caution in the elderly and in clients with glaucoma, tachycardia, or urinary retention.

Forms of Drug   Sugar-coated tablets containing 0.25 or 2.5 mg.

Administration of Drug

■ *Postencephalitic parkinsonism:* 5 mg po tid; then increase slowly.

■ *Idiopathic and arteriosclerotic parkinsonism:* 125 mg po tid; then increase slowly; Maximum dosage: 20 mg/day.

Side Effects Blurred vision, GI disturbances, and dry mouth are common. CNS disturbances may occur.

Generic Name Procyclidine hydrochloride
Trade Name Kemadrin
Classification Anticholinergic agent

See trihexyphenidyl hydrochloride for drug interactions and nursing considerations.

Action Relieves spasticity of voluntary muscles. Particularly effective in reducing rigidity, but may not reduce tremors.

Indications of Drug Parkinsonism, drug-induced extrapyramidal disorders, sialorrhea.

Contraindications Angle-closure glaucoma. Use with caution in clients with mental disorders, since psychotic reactions may be precipitated. Use with caution in the elderly and in clients with tachycardia, prostatic hypertrophy, or hypotension.

Safe use in children and during pregnancy and lactation has not been established.

Forms of Drug Scored tablets containing 2 or 5 mg.

Administration of Drug

■ *Parkinsonism:* Initial dosage: 2 to 2.5 mg po tid after meals; then increase slowly; usual dosage: 15 to 30 mg daily.

■ *Extrapyramidal disorders:* Initial dosage: 2 to 2.5 mg po tid after meals; then increase by 2 to 2.5 mg daily until desired effect; Usual dosage: 10 to 20 mg daily.

Absorption Onset of action is about 30 minutes and duration of action is about 4 hours.

Side Effects Low toxicity, but secondary reactions frequently occur with high dosages. Dry mouth, mydriasis, blurred vision, and nausea are common. Suppurative parotitis may occur. Constipation, epigastric distress, and vomiting are relatively common. Allergic skin rashes have occurred. Weakness, confusion, disorientation, agitation, and hallucinations have occurred.

PHENOTHIAZINES

Generic Name Chlorpromazine hydrochloride
Trade Names Chlor-PZ, Promachel, Promapar, Sonazine, Thorazine
Classification Antipsychotic

Action Antipsychotic, antiemetic, hypothermic, sedative, antidopaminergic, and anticholinergic actions. Inhibits release of ACTH, growth hormone, and prolactin-inhibiting factor. Not effective in depression or retarded withdrawal states.

Indications for Drug Psychoses, hiccups, acromegaly, as an antiemetic. Also, during surgery, labor, and delivery, to enhance action of narcotics and hypnotics. In combination with analgesics for severe pain.

Contraindications Pregnancy, coma, glaucoma, prostatic hypertrophy, cardiovascular disease, convulsive disorders, infants under 6 months. Use with caution in women of childbearing age, elderly clients, and children (since they are more susceptible to acute dystonia than adults). Clients with cirrhosis are more susceptible to sedative effects. Clients with the following conditions should be evaluated frequently: renal, hepatic, cardiovascular, or respiratory disease, blood dyscrasias, cardiovascular accidents, hypoparathyroidism.

Forms of Drug Tablets containing 10, 25, 50, 100, or 200 mg; sustained-release capsules containing 30, 75, 150, or 200 mg; ampules of 1 or 2 ml containing 25 mg/ml; 10-ml vials containing 25 mg/ml; syrup containing 10 mg/5 ml; suppositories containing 25 or 100 mg.

Administration of Drug Adults: 30 mg to 1 g po, IM, or IV daily in divided doses; Rectal suppository: 100 mg every 6 to 8 hours. Children: 2 mg/kg po daily in divided doses.

1. Protect skin, eyes, and clothing from contact with drug.
2. When administering IM, drug should be slowly and deeply injected. The pain from injection can be alleviated by massaging the injection site.
3. Do not mix with other drugs.

Absorption Readily absorbed from parental sites; erratic absorption following oral administration. Peak action occurs in 1 to 3 hours, and duration of action is 3 to 6 hours. Half-life is about 6 hours. Crosses placenta and blood-brain barrier.

Distribution Distributed to all body tissues with some distribution to brain. Concentrated in lungs and keratin structures.
Metabolism In the liver.
Excretion In urine and feces.

Side Effects Drowsiness is common; tolerance usually develops in 1 to 2 weeks. Hypotension, evidenced by dizziness and weakness on standing, is common. Extrapyramidal symptoms: uncoordinated spasmodic movements, involuntary motor restlessness, parkinsonism. Tardive dyskinesia, which is characterized by hyperkinetic activity in the oral region and for which there is no effective treatment, may appear after long-term use; has also been reported after low doses given for short periods. Autonomic nervous system effects: dry mouth, blurred vision, constipation, urinary disturbances, weight gain, delayed ovulation, amenorrhea, abnormal lactation, increased libido in women, decreased libido in men. Dermatologic effects: skin rash, skin discoloration on exposure to sunlight, phototoxicity (painful sunburn after brief exposure to sun). Visual changes: corneal and lens opacities. Toxic effects: obstructive jaundice, agranulocytosis, hepatitis, leukopenia.

Interactive Effects Potentiates hypotensive effects of methyldopa, reserpine, and beta blockers; potentiates the anticholinergic effects of tricycle antidepressants and antiparkinsonian drugs. Enhances respiratory depression produced by meperidine. Blocks the hypotensive effects of guanethidine. Lithium trihexyphenidyl, and antacids decrease plasma levels of chlorpromazine. Alcohol and sedatives potentiate sedative effects of chlorpromazine.

Nursing Considerations
1. Assessment and planning
   a. Caution client against activities requiring mental alertness and muscular coordination.
   b. Advise client to avoid alcohol, sedatives, and hypnotics.
   c. Advise client to change position gradually and to dangle legs for 1 minute before getting out of bed.
   d. Because of photosensitivity, client should be instructed to protect himself or herself from exposure to sun.
   e. Encourage high fluid intake and frequent rinsing of mouth.
2. Assessment and implementation
   a. Because orthostatic hypotension is common, the client's blood pressure should be monitored daily.
   b. Observe for dizziness and weakness.
   c. In severe cases of hypotension, put client in Trendelenburg's position and request administration of plasma expanders.
   d. Monitor intake and output; check frequency of bowel movements.

e. Drug should be discontinued at least 48 hours prior to surgery.
f. Protect elderly clients with bedrails; these clients are more prone to develop hypotension.
g. Institute measures to prevent hyperthermia or hypothermia.
h. If client develops extrapyramidal symptoms, reduce sensory stimuli.

3. Assessment and evaluation
   a. Report any visual changes and schedule regular eye examinations.
   b. Report sore throat or elevated temperature.
   c. Observe client for jaundice.
   d. Advise client not to discontinue drug without medical supervision.
   e. False-positive results may occur for urobilinogen, urine bilirubin, and pregnancy tests. May also affect results for urine catecholamines, ketones, and radioactive iodine uptake tests.

Generic Name Acetophenazine maleate
Trade Name Tindal
Classification Antipsychotic

See chlorpromazine for contraindications, drug interactions, and nursing considerations.

Action Acetophenazine has a stronger sedative effect than chlorpromazine. (See chlorpromazine.)

Indications for Drug Management of psychoses in the elderly, such as organic brain syndrome. Large dosages are needed to treat other psychoses.

Forms of Drug Tablets containing 20 mg.

Administration of Drug Adults: 40 to 80 mg po daily: Children: 0.8 to 1.6 mg/kg po daily in 3 divided doses.

Side Effects Produces fewer extrapyramidal symptoms than chlorpromazine. (See chlorpromazine.)

Generic Name Butaperazine maleate
Trade Name Repoise
Classification Antipsychotic

See chlorpromazine for contraindications, drug interactions, and nursing considerations.

Actions Similar to chlorpromazine. (See chlorpromazine.)

Indications for Drug   Treatment of paranoia and chronic brain syndrome.

Forms of Drug   Tablets containing 5, 10, or 25 mg.

Administration of Drug   Adults: 15 to 30 mg po daily in divided doses; can be increased to a maximum dosage of 100 mg/day. Geriatrics: ¼ to ½ of adult dosage.

Side Effects   Extrapyramidal symptoms occur frequently.

Generic Name   Carphenazine maleate
Trade Name   Proketazine
Classification   Antipsychotic

See chlorpromazine for indications for drug, contraindications, drug interactions, and side effects.

Action   Similar to other phenothiazines in the piperazine group. (See chlorpromazine.)

Administration of Drug   Adults: 75 to 150 mg po daily in divided doses; can be increased every 1 to 2 weeks by 25 to 50 mg; Maximum dosage: 400 mg/day. Geriatrics: ½ of adult dosage.

Forms of Drug   Tablets containing 12.5, 25, or 50 mg; concentrate containing 50 mg/ml.

Nursing Considerations   Full therapeutic effect may not be apparent for several months. (See chlorpromazine.)

Generic Name   Fluphenazine enanthate, fluphenazine decanoate
Trade Name   Prolixin
Classification   Antipsychotic

See chlorpromazine for contraindications and drug interactions.

Action   Similar to chlorpromazine. (See chlorpromazine.)

Indications for Drug   Treatment of outpatients whose compliance with the medication regimen is doubtful.

Forms of Drug   Vials of 10 ml containing 2.5 mg/ml; protect from light; if solution is darker than light am-

ber, do not use. Tablets containing 1, 2.5, 5, or 10 mg; protect from light. Elixir containing 0.5 mg/ml; avoid freezing.

Administration of Drug   Adults: 2.5 to 10 mg po daily in divided doses; under close hospital supervision, clients can receive up to 20 mg daily; 25 mg IM every 1 to 3 weeks. Children: 0.25 to 3 mg po daily in divided doses.

Side Effects   This drug is very potent and has a high incidence of extrapyramidal symptoms. (See chlorpromazine.)

Nursing Considerations   (See chlorpromazine.)
1. Antiparkinsonian drugs may be needed to prevent extrapyramidal symptoms.
2. Geriatric clients are at a greater risk of developing extrapyramidal symptoms, especially women who have been medicated with phenothiazines for a long time.

Generic Name   Mesoridazine besylate
Trade Name   Serentil
Classification   Antipsychotic

See chlorpromazine for indications for drug, contraindications, side effects, drug interactions, and nursing considerations.

Action   Similar to chlorpromazine. Not effective in treatment of delirium tremens. (See chlorpromazine.)

Forms of Drug   Tablets containing 10, 25, 50, or 100 mg; 10-ml vials containing 25 mg/ml.

Administration of Drug   Adults: 100 to 400 mg po daily in divided doses; 25 to 200 mg IM daily in divided doses. Geriatrics: ¼ to ½ of drug dosage.

Generic Name   Perphenazine
Trade Name   Trilafon
Classification   Antipsychotic, antiemetic

See chlorpromazine for indications for drug, contraindications, drug interactions, and side effects.

Action   Similar to chlorpromazine, but six times more potent. (See chlorpromazine.)

Forms of Drug Tablets containing 2, 4, or 8 mg; syrup containing 2 mg/5 ml; concentrate containing 16 mg/ml (diluted in 60 ml of fluid).

Administration of Drug Adults: 16 to 64 mg po or IM daily in divided doses.

Nursing Considerations (See chlorpromazine.)
1. May be used IV during surgery for hiccups or vomiting. Should not be given IV as an antipsychotic.
2. Dilute concentrate with water, milk, or orange juice. Do not mix with tea, coffee, cola, apple, or grape juice.

Generic Name Piperacetazine
Trade Name Quide
Classification Antipsychotic

See chlorpromazine for contraindications, drug interactions, and nursing considerations.

Action Similar to chlorpromazine. (See chlorpromazine.)

Indications for Drug Schizophrenia characterized by agitation; most effective in treating acute rather than chronic schizophrenia.

Forms of Drug Tablets containing 10 or 25 mg.

Administration of Drug Adults: 20 to 40 mg po daily in divided doses; can be increased to 160 mg daily in divided doses. Geriatrics: ¼ to ½ of adult dosage.

Side Effects Piperacetazine causes a higher incidence of extrapyramidal symptoms than most phenothiazines. (See chlorpromazine.)

Generic Name Prochlorperazine maleate
Trade Names Combid, Compazine
Classification Antipsychotic, antiemetic

See chlorpromazine for indications for drug, contraindications, drug interactions, and nursing considerations.

Action Prochlorperazine has greater antiemetic activity than most phenothiazines. It is also effective as an antipsychotic agent. (See chlorpromazine.)

Forms of Drug Tablets containing 5, 10, or 25 mg; sustained-release capsules containing 10, 15, 30, or 75 mg; 10-ml vials containing 5 mg/ml; 2-ml ampules containing 5 mg/ml; suppositories containing 2.5, 5, or 25 mg; syrup containing 5 mg/ml; concentrate containing 10 mg/ml.

Administration of Drug
- *Antipsychotic:* Adults: 5 to 10 mg po or IM bid, tid, or qid; the dosage can be gradually increased to 75 to 150 mg daily in divided doses. Rectal suppository: 25 mg bid. Children: Ages 2 years and older: 0.4 mg/kg daily in divided doses.
- *Antiemetic:* Adults: Preoperative: 5 to 10 mg IM 1 to 2 hours before surgery; 5 to 10 mg IV 30 minutes before anesthesia. Postoperative: 5 to 10 mg IM.

Side Effects: The risk of developing extrapyramidal symptoms is greater for prochlorperazine than for other phenothiazines. (See chlorpromazine.)

Generic Name Trifluoperazine hydrochloride
Trade Name Stelazine
Classification Antipsychotic

See chlorpromazine for contraindications and drug interactions.

Action Trifluoperazine is fast-acting and 10 times more potent than chlorpromazine. (See chlorpromazine.)

Indications for Drug Treatment of psychoses where the client demonstrates withdrawal and apathy.

Forms of Drug Tablets containing 1, 2, 5, or 10 mg; 10-ml vials containing 2 mg/ml; concentrate containing 10 mg/ml (dilute in 60 ml of fluid).

Administration of Drug Adults: Oral: 2 to 5 mg bid or tid initially; then increase to 15 to 20 mg daily in 2 to 3 divided doses. Intramuscular: 1 to 2 mg every 4 to 6 hours; can be increased to 6 to 10 mg daily. Children: Ages 6 to 12 years: 1 to 2 mg po daily; Maximum dosage: 15 mg/day.

Side Effects Extrapyramidal symptoms occur frequently. (See chlorpromazine.)

Nursing Considerations The maximum therapeutic effect is reached in 3 weeks and is more prolonged than with chlorpromazine. (See chlorpromazine.)

Generic Name Triflupromazine hydrochloride
Trade Name Vesprin
Classification Antipsychotic

See chlorpromazine for indications for drug, contraindications, drug interactions, and nursing considerations.

Action Similar to chlorpromazine; fast-acting. (See chlorpromazine.)

Forms of Drug Tablets containing 10, 25, or 50 mg; 10-ml vials containing 10 or 20 mg/ml; suspension containing 50 mg/5 ml.

Administration of Drug Adults: Determined individually; up to 150 mg daily. Children: Ages 6 to 12 years: 2 mg/kg po, or 0.25 mg/kg IM daily. Maximum dosage: 150 mg/day po, or 10 mg/day IM.

Side Effects Extrapyramidal symptoms are the most serious. (See chlorpromazine.)

Generic Name Thiopropazate hydrochloride
Trade Name Dartal
Classification Antipsychotic

See chlorpromazine for contraindications, side effects, drug interactions, and nursing considerations.

Action Similar to chlorpromazine. (See chlorpromazine.)

Indications for Drug Psychoses marked by hostility and aggression.

Forms of Drug Tablets containing 5 or 10 mg.

Administration of Drug Adults: 10 mg po tid; Maximum dosage: 100 mg/day.

Generic Name Thioridazine hydrochloride
Trade Name Mellaril
Classification Antipsychotic

See chlorpromazine for indications for drug, contraindications, drug interactions, and nursing considerations.

Action Thioridazine is one of the less potent tranquilizers. It has very little antiemetic activity and does not affect the temperature-regulating mechanism. It is considered to be a useful antipsychotic drug and a good basic tranquilizer. (See chlorpromazine.)

Forms of Drug Tablets containing 10, 25, 50, 100, 150, or 200 mg; concentrate containing 30 mg/ml.

Administration of Drug Adults: 20 to 800 mg po daily; Children: Over 2 years: 1 mg/kg po daily in 3 to 4 divided doses.

Side Effects Produces fewer extrapyramidal symptoms than chlorpromazine. Large doses have reportedly produced pigmentary retinopathy. Sudden death has been reported following long-term use. (See chlorpromazine.)

BUTYROPHENONES

Generic Name Haloperidol
Trade Name Haldol
Classification Antipsychotic, antiemetic

See chlorpromazine for contraindications and drug interactions.

Action Similar to phenothiazines. (See chlorpromazine.)

Indications for Drug Control of hyperactivity that occurs in the manic phase of manic-depressive illness; acute psychiatric problems.

Contraindications Parkinsonism. (See chlorpromazine.)

Forms of Drug Tablets containing 0.5, 1, or 2 mg; concentrate containing 2 mg/ml; ampules containing 5 mg/ml.

Administration of Drug Adults: 2 to 8 mg po or IM daily; can be gradually increased 0.5 to 1 mg every 3 days; Maximum dosage: 15 mg/day.

Absorption Peak action occurs in 30 to 45 minutes.
Excretion Slowly in urine.

Side Effects Generally similar to phenothiazines, but there is a high incidence of extrapyramidal symptoms and less sedation, hypotension, hypothermia, and photosensitivity. Severe depression leading to suicidal tendencies may develop. (See chlorpromazine.)

Nursing Considerations   There is a narrow margin between therapeutic and toxic dosages. (Chlorpromazine.)

THIOXANTHENES

Generic Name   Chlorprothixene
Trade Name   Taractan
Classification   Antipsychotic, antiemetic

See chlorpromazine for contraindications, drug interactions, and nursing considerations.

Action   Similar to phenothiazines, but a more powerful inhibitor of motor coordination and produces fewer antihistaminic effects. (See chlorpromazine.)

Indications for Drug   Schizophrenia, acute depression, neurosis, withdrawal from alcohol, agitation.

Forms of Drug   Tablets containing 10, 25, 50, or 100 mg; vials containing 12.5 ml/mg.

Administration of Drug   30 to 200 mg po or IM daily in divided doses; Children: 30 to 100 mg po daily.

Absorption   Peak action occurs in 30 minutes.

Side Effects   Drowsiness, orthostatic hypotension, and dry mouth occur frequently. Extrapyramidal symptoms, agranulocytosis, and cholestatic hepatitis are less likely to occur. (See chlorpromazine.)

Generic Name   Thiothixene
Trade Name   Navane
Classification   Antipsychotic

See chlorpromazine for contraindications and drug interactions.

Action   Similar to phenothiazines, but a more powerful inhibitor of motor coordination and produces fewer antihistaminic effects. (See chlorpromazine.)

Indications for Drug   Acute and chronic schizophrenia.

Forms of Drug   Capsules containing 1, 2, 5, or 10 mg; concentrate containing 5 mg/ml; vials containing 2 mg/ml.

Administration of Drug   Adults: 6 to 15 mg po or IM daily in divided doses; can be gradually increased to a maximum oral dosage of 60 mg/day or a maximum intramuscular dosage of 30 mg/day.

Side Effects   Insomnia and extrapyramidal symptoms occur frequently. (See chlorpromazine.)

Nursing Considerations   There is a very narrow margin between therapeutic and toxic dosages. (See chlorpromazine.)

DIHYDROINDOLONES

Generic Name   Molindone
Trade Names   Lidone, Moban
Classification   Antipsychotic

See chlorpromazine for contraindications and nursing considerations.

Action   Similar to phenothiazines. (See chlorpromazine.)

Indications for Drug   Acute schizophrenia.

Forms of Drug   Tablets and capsules containing 5, 10, or 25 mg.

Administration of Drug
- *Mild schizophrenia:* Adults: 5 to 15 mg po daily in divided doses.
- *Moderate schizophrenia:* Adults: 10 to 25 mg po daily in divided doses.
- *Severe schizophrenia:* Adults: Up to 225 mg po daily in divided doses.

Side Effects   Clients have experienced profound CNS depression while taking other drugs. (See chlorpromazine.) Excessive weight gain is less a problem. (See chlorpromazine.)

DIBENZOXAZEPINES

Generic Name   Loxapine
Trade Name   Lozitane
Classification   Antipsychotic

See chlorpromazine for contraindications, drug interactions, and nursing considerations.

Action A tricyclic dibenzoxapine-derivative antipsychotic agent with actions similar to the phenothiazines and other antipsychotics. (See chlorpromazine.)

Indications for Drug Treatment of psychotic disorders.

Forms of Drug Capsules containing 5, 10, 25, or 50 mg; oral concentrate containing 25 mg/ml; ampules and vials containing 50 mg/ml.

Administration of Drug Adults: 20 to 100 mg po daily in 2 to 4 divided doses; can be gradually increased up to 250 mg/day until symptom control is obtained; IM 12.5 to 50 mg every 4 to 6 hours.

Absorption Peak serum levels are usually obtained within 2 hours.
Metabolism and Excretion Metabolised in the liver and excreted in the urine and feces.

Side Effects Similar to other antipsychotic agents. (See chlorpromazine.)

BARBITURATE MEDICATIONS

The major action of barbiturates is central nervous system depression. When used within prescribed dosage ranges, the effects can range from mild sedation to coma, depending on the particular barbiturate used, its duration of action, route of administration, and the client's clinical status. When used in high concentrations, barbiturates have a generalized depressant effect on most other body systems. With prompt treatment, these effects are reversible, but the danger of cardiovascular collapse in acute barbiturate intoxication poses a serious threat while the drug is in the body.

Barbiturates also have subtle, long-lasting effects. There is evidence of impairment of fine motor functions and of judgment for as long as 20 hours after ingestion of a sleep-inducing dosage. Many individuals become irritable and/or emotionally labile during this period.

Although all barbiturates have anticonvulsant properties, phenobarbital has a specific effect on the motor cortex when given in small, nonsedative doses. It is most effective for the control of grand mal seizures, alone or in combination with other anticonvulsant drugs.

Barbiturates can produce physical and psychological dependence and tolerance. Physical tolerance develops for two reasons: (1) the production of enzymes in the liver is increased and results in more rapid metabolism of the drug, and (2) the central nervous system adapts to the drug. As tolerance develops, higher doses are required to maintain effective concentrations of the drug. Tolerance to a lethal dose does not increase proportionately, so that as physical tolerance escalates, the gap between the effective intoxicating dose and the fatal dose is narrowed. Another

danger is that barbiturates, alcohol, and many other sedative drugs are cross-tolerant.

Barbiturate overdose produces symptoms that can range from slurred speech to cardiovascular collapse, respiratory depression, and coma and death. The greatest dangers of barbiturate poisoning are circulatory collapse, respiratory insufficiency, and renal failure. Emergency treatment is directed at preventing these complications. Long-term users who are physically dependent on barbiturates will suffer serious symptoms if their drug withdrawal is sudden. Psychoses, convulsions, and even death may result unless withdrawal takes place in a protected, medically safe environment. Despite their potential for misuse, barbiturates have legitimate therapeutic value if carefully administered and supervised.

ULTRA-SHORT-ACTING BARBITURATES

Generic Name Methohexital sodium
Trade Name Brevital Sodium
Classification Barbiturate anesthetic

Action CNS depressant. Induction dose with 1% solution will provide anesthesia for 5 to 7 minutes.

Indications for Drug Induction of anesthesia, anesthetic for short procedures, as a supplement for other anesthetic agents.

Contraindications Known hypersensitivity, severe cardiac disease, hepatic or renal impairment, Addison's disease, myxedema, anemia, asthma, increased intracranial pressure, history of porphyria. May be habit-forming. Use with caution in clients with impaired circulatory, respiratory, endocrine, hepatic, or renal function. Use with caution in pregnancy. Use with extreme caution in status asthmaticus.

Forms of Drug Vials and ampules containing 250 or 500 mg of dry powder.

Administration of Drug 5 to 12 ml (50 to 120 mg) of a 1% solution IV at a rate of 1 ml/5 seconds for induction; then 20 to 40 mg every 4 to 7 minutes for maintenance. Administration must be performed only by qualified anesthetists. Close observation of patient is necessary, since reactions to drug are highly individualistic. Oxygen and resuscitative equipment should be at hand.

Absorption Onset of action is 30 to 40 seconds after IV administration. Crosses placenta.
Distribution Stored in fatty tissues.

Metabolism   In the liver.
Excretion   By the kidneys.

Side Effects   Circulatory depression, arrhythmias, respiratory depression, bronchospasm, nausea, vomiting, twitching, headache, hiccups, hypotension, rash, sneezing, coughing, hypersensitivity reactions.

Interactive Effects   An increase in CNS depression occurs with concurrent use of alcohol, other sedatives, narcotics, antihistamines, phenothiazines, disulfiam, MAO inhibitors, procarbazine, and methotrimeprazine. By interfering with absorption and increasing liver enzyme activity, barbiturates can decrease the effects of oral anticoagulants, corticosteroids, digitalis glycosides, estrogens, oral contraceptives, griseofulvin, lidocaine, phenytoin, carbamazepine, and methyldopa. Sulfonamides increase the effect of barbiturates by inhibiting protein binding.

Nursing Considerations
1. Contact with the nonvascular tissues can cause necrosis. Intra-arterial injection can cause gangrene. Incompatible in solution with lactated Ringer's solution and acid solutions, such as succinylcholine chloride, atropine, and metocurine iodide.
2. Dilute only in sterile water, 5% dextrose, or 0.9% sodium chloride IV solutions.
3. When reconstituted, solution should be clear. If dissolved in sterile water, solution is stable at room temperature for 6 weeks. If dissolved in dextrose or saline, solution is stable at room temperature for 24 hours only.

Generic Name   Thiamylal sodium
Trade Names   Surital, Thioseconal
Classification   Barbiturate anesthetic

See methohexital sodium for indications for drug, contraindications, side effects, and drug interactions.

Action   CNS depressant.

Forms of Drug   Ampules and vials containing 1, 5, or 10 g.

Administration of Drug   3 to 6 ml of a 2.5% solution IV at a rate of 1 ml/5 seconds for induction; then 1 drop/second for maintenance.

Nursing Considerations   Solutions may be stored in refrigerator for 6 days or at room temperature for 24 hours. (See methohexital sodium.)

Generic Name   Thiopental sodium
Trade Names   Intraval, Pentothal
Classification   Barbiturate anesthetic

See methohexital sodium for contraindications, side effects, and drug interactions.

Action   CNS depressant.

Indications for Drug   Control of convulsions following other anesthetics, reducing intracranial pressure during neurosurgical procedures, narcoanalysis and narcosynthesis in psychiatric disorders.

Forms of Drug   Ampules and vials in a variety of dosages.

Administration of Drug   2 to 3 ml (50 to 75 mg) of a 2.5% solution IV for induction; then use a continuous drip of a 0.2% to 0.4% solution for maintenance or additional IV injections of 25 to 50 mg as necessary.

Nursing Considerations   (See methohexital sodium.)
1. Reconstituted solutions should be used within 24 hours.
2. After induction of anesthesia, shivering sometimes occurs because of client's increased sensitivity to cold.

SHORT-ACTING BARBITURATES

Generic Name   Pentobarbital sodium
Trade Names   Nebralin, Nembutal, Pental
Classification   Barbiturate sedative and hypnotic

See methohexital sodium for contraindications, side effects, and drug interactions

Action   CNS depressant. Onset of action is 15 to 30 minutes after oral administration. Duration of action is up to 4 hours.

Indications for Drug   Sedation, hypnosis, preanesthesia, acute convulsive states.

Forms of Drug   Elixir (5 ml unit dose) in pint and gallon bottles (20 mg/5 ml); capsules containing 30, 50, or 100 mg in bottles and unit-dose packages; tablets containing 100 mg; 2-ml ampules; vials of 20 or 50 ml; suppositories containing 30, 60, 120, or 200 mg.

Administration of Drug
- *Sedation:* Adults: 30 mg po tid or qid.
- *Hypnosis:* Adults: 100 to 500 mg IV; 150 to 200 mg IM; 120 to 200 mg rectally.

Dosage is individually adjusted according to age, weight, general condition, and purpose of administration.

Nursing Considerations

1. Assessment and Planning
   a. Client should be warned that mental and/or physical abilities may be impaired for a 24-hour period following dosage.
   b. Oxygen and resuscitative equipment should be readily available when drug is administered IV.

2. Assessment and implementation
   a. Parenteral solutions should be clear.
   b. Extravasation and intra-arterial administration must be avoided, since tissue necrosis can result.
   c. When administering IM, inject into large muscle mass with no more than 5 ml delivered to a site.

3. Assessment and evaluation
   a. Since reactions to drug are highly individualistic, clients should be assessed carefully for adverse effects.
   b. Vital signs should be monitored every 3 to 5 minutes when drug is administered IV.
   c. Some clients, particularly the elderly, may become restless and irritable after administration; appropriate precautions, including bedrails, should be instituted.
   d. Client should be advised that prolonged use can lead to physical and psychological dependence.
   e. Clients on prolonged therapy must be cautioned against discontinuing the drug abruptly, since withdrawal symptoms can be life-threatening.

Generic Name   Secobarbital sodium
Trade Name   Seconal
Classification   Barbiturate sedative and hypnotic

See methohexital sodium for contraindications, side effects, and drug interactions.

Action   CNS depressant. Duration of action is up to 4 hours.

Indications for Drug   Sedation, hypnosis, preanesthesia, acute convulsive states.

Forms of Drug   Elixir in 16-oz bottles (22 mg/5 ml); capsules containing 30, 50, or 100 mg in bottles and unit-dose packages; tablets containing 100 mg; 20-ml ampules (50 mg/ml); suppositories containing 30, 60, 120, or 200 mg.

Administration of Drug
- *Sedation:* Adults: 30 to 50 mg po tid.
- *Hypnosis:* Adults: 100 to 200 mg IV (up to 250 mg); 50 to 150 mg IM; 150 to 250 mg rectally.

Dosages are adjusted for children according to age and body weight.

Nursing Considerations   (See pentobarbital sodium.)
1. Ampules and suppositories must be refrigerated.
2. Aqueous solution must be used within 30 minutes after container is opened. Solution is mixed by rotating vial; do not shake. Solution should be clear.

INTERMEDIATE-ACTING BARBITURATES

Generic Name   Amobarbital sodium
Trade Names   Amytal, Tuinal
Classification   Barbiturate sedative and hypnotic

See methohexital sodium for contraindications, side effects, and drug interactions.

Action   CNS depressant. Duration of action is up to 8 hours.

Indications for Drug   Sedation, relief of anxiety, hypnosis, acute convulsive states, narcoanalysis and narcotherapy in psychiatric disorders.

Forms of Drug   Elixir in 16-oz bottles; capsules containing 65 or 200 in bottles and unit-dose packages; tablets containing 15, 30, 50, or 100 mg. Ampules containing 125, 250, or 500 mg of dry powder; dissolve in sterile water; may dissolve slowly.

Administration of Drug   Oral: 30 to 50 mg tid or 65 to 200 mg in one dose; Maximum dosage: 1 g in adults. Intramuscular: 65 to 500 mg (10% to 20% solution); Maximum dosage: 0.5 g in adults. Intravenous: 1 ml/min. of a 10% solution; must not exceed 1 ml/min.

Nursing Considerations   Aqueous solution must be used within 30 minutes after container is opened. Solution is mixed by rotating vial; do not shake. Solution should be clear. (See pentobarbital sodium.)

Generic Name   Aprobarbital
Trade Name   Alurate
Classification   Barbiturate sedative and hypnotic

See methohexital sodium for contraindications, side effects, and drug interactions. See pentobarbital sodium for nursing considerations.

Action   CNS depressant. Duration of action is up to 8 hours.

Indications for Drug   Sedation, insomnia.

Forms of Drug   Elixir in 16-oz and gallon bottles (40 mg/5 ml).

Administration of Drug   Adults: 5 ml (40 mg) po tid, 5 to 20 ml hs for sedation or insomnia.

Generic Name   Butabarbital sodium
Trade Names   Butisol, Butal, Buticaps, Sarisol
Classification   Barbiturate sedative and hypnotic

See methohexital sodium for contraindications, side effects, and drug interactions. See pentobarbital sodium for nursing considerations.

Action   CNS depressant. Duration of action is 5 to 8 hours.

Indications for Drug   Sedation, hypnosis.

Forms of Drug   Elixir in pint and gallon bottles (30 mg/5 ml); capsules and tablets containing 15, 30, 50, or 100 mg.

Administration of Drug
- *Sedation:* Adults: 15 to 30 mg po tid or qid; 50 to 100 mg preoperatively.
- *Hypnosis:* Adults: 50 to 100 mg hs.

LONG-ACTING BARBITURATES

Generic Name   Mephobarbital
Trade Name   Mebaral
Classification   Barbiturate sedative

See methohexital sodium for contraindications, side effects, and drug interactions.

Action   Duration of action is 10 hours or more.

Indications for Drug   Sedation, acute convulsive states (epilepsy).

Forms of Drug   Tablets containing 32, 50, 100, or 200 mg.

Administration of Drug   Sedation: Adults: 50 mg po tid or qid; Children: 16 to 32 mg po tid or qid.

Nursing Considerations   (See pentobarbital sodium.)
1. Does not generally cause clouding of mental faculties.
2. Possibility of cumulative drug action increases with the long-acting barbiturates. Client should be instructed to be alert for adverse reactions.
3. Drug should not be withdrawn abruptly, but tapered over a period of 1 to 2 weeks.

Generic Name   Phenobarbital; phenobarbital sodium
Trade Names   Eskabarb, Luminal, Solfoton, Sodium Liminal
Classification   Barbiturate sedative and hypnotic

See methohexital sodium for contraindications, side effects, and drug interactions.

Action   CNS depressant. Onset of action is 10 to 60 minutes, and duration of action is 10 to 16 hours. Lowers bilirubin by stimulating production of glucuronyl transferase.

Indications for Drug   Sedation, hypnosis, acute convulsive states, neonatal hyperbilirubinemia.

Forms of Drug   Elixir containing 20 mg/5 ml; capsules (prolonged action) containing 65 or 100 mg; tablets containing 8, 16, 32, 65, or 100 mg. Vials containing dry powder must be reconstituted with sterile water. Solution should be clear; stable for 2 days.

Administration of Drug

- *Sedation:* Adults: 15 to 120 mg po bid or tid; Children: 15 to 50 mg po.
- *Hypnosis:* Adults: 100 to 320 mg po daily; 100 to 300 mg IM or IV daily. Children: 2 to 5 mg/kg IM or IV; 2 to 3 mg/kg rectally bid or tid.

1. Drowsiness may occur during early weeks of treatment.
2. Elderly patients may exhibit restlessness or excitability.
3. When administering IV, dose should not exceed 60 mg/min.
4. When administering IM, inject into large muscle mass with no more than 5 ml delivered to a site.

Nursing Considerations   (See pentobarbital sodium and mephobarbital.)

1. Long-term treatment may cause blood dyscrasias. Be alert for signs of infection or bleeding.
2. Hepatic function tests and blood counts should be done routinely for clients on prolonged therapy.

GLOSSARY

A

abreaction
The process of bringing repressed material to conscious awareness, including the emotional response elicited by the recalled material.

abuse
Actions that mistreat, injure, or threaten oneself or others. Drug abuse inflicts injury on oneself; child abuse inflicts injury on children; spouse abuse inflicts injury on a husband or wife.

accommodation
The process of reorganizing information already known in order to include new information; adjusting to reality and unfamiliar experiences.

achieved role
A role conferred because of special skills or attributes of an individual; sometimes referred to as *assumed role*.

acrophobia
Extreme fear of heights.

acting out
Discharging tension by responding to the present situation as if it were a previous situation in which the response was initiated.

acute alterations
Changes in physiological structure or function characterized by severe symptoms and a relatively short course.

adaptation
Response to change within the organism or outside its boundaries. Adaptation requires mobilization of the organism in addition to processes of assimilation.

addiction
A behavioral pattern of drug use characterized by an overwhelming preoccupation with compulsive use of the drug and securing a supply, and by a tendency to withdrawal symptoms upon abstinence.

adjustment
Modification of various aspects of the self in order to cope with the demands of daily life.

advocacy
See client advocacy.

affect
An emotional or feeling state.

affective disorders
Alterations in mood that may take the form of severe depression or elation.

aggression
Actions performed in order to gratify the need to excel, achieve, or compete within or separate from the group; aggressive actions may be positive or negative in nature.

agitation
Extreme restlessness and excitability.

agoraphobia
Extreme fear of open spaces.

akathisia
Sensations of restlessness and unease often caused by reactions to psychotrophic medication.

alienation
Loss or lack of relationships with others.

alterations of degenerative origin
Changes due to deterioration of physiological structure or function, usually from a higher to a lower level or form.

altered patterns of relatedness
A term used in this textbook to describe behavioral alterations caused by anxiety and personality disorders that adversely affect interpersonal relationships.

altruism
Concern for the well-being of others without regard for personal gain.

Alzheimer's disease
A degenerative neurological disorder characterized by loss of mental powers, disorientation, and motor impairment; thought to be inherited.

ambivalence
Conflict resulting from simultaneous feelings of being attracted to and repelled by the same object, action, or goal; often expressed in approach-avoidance behavior.

amnesia
Loss of memory for events within a certain period of time; may be temporary or permanent.

amniocentesis
Drawing of amniotic fluid from the amniotic sac of a pregnant woman in order to examine fetal cells for chromosomal abnormalities. Down's syndrome, among other disorders, may be diagnosed in utero through this diagnostic technique.

anaclitic separation
Loss of the mother or mother figure by the infant during the first year of life, often resulting in developmental deficits or indications of depression.

anhedonia
Inability to experience pleasure or joy.

anomie
Absence or loss of meaningful relationships with other individuals or groups; absence or loss of social norms and values.

anorexia nervosa
Refusal to eat because of psychological factors such as distorted body image or control issues. May result in extreme emaciation and even death.

anthropology
Branch of social science dealing with the study of humankind.

anxiety
A vague sense of apprehension or dread originating within the individual; it may not necessarily be generated by identifiable external stimuli.

anxiety disorders
A group of disorders manifested in various behavioral patterns that tend to be rigid and fixed; excessive anxiety is present and is handled by the appearance of maladaptive behavioral syndromes.

apathy
Lack of feeling, interest, or initiative.

ascribed role
A role conferred because of status, age, gender, or position and not because of attributes or qualities within the control of the individual.

assertiveness
The ability to express one's needs, goals, or preferences appropriately and effectively in interpersonal transactions.

assimilation
The process of integrating new information or experience into what is already known and understood.

ataxia
Deficient muscular coordination causing difficulty in walking.

attention deficit disorder
A behavioral problem characterized by chronic inattention, overactivity, and difficulty in dealing with multiple stimuli.

authenticity
Acting in accord with one's own attitudes, beliefs, and values.

autism
A disorder of childhood characterized by language deficits and inability to relate to others.

autistic thinking
Preoccupation with private, self-determined thoughts or actions without concern for reality or objective standards shared with others.

autonomic nervous system
The part of the peripheral nervous system that innervates internal organs; is subdivided into the sympathetic and parasympathetic nervous systems.

autonomy
Self-determination and self-reliance, the sense of being individual and independent.

aversion therapy
A form of behavior modification in which a painful stimulus is linked with a pleasurable stimulus, thereby causing dislike (aversion) for the stimulus previously associated with pleasure.

B

behavior modification
A therapeutic modality that uses stimulus and response conditioning in order to alter dysfunctional patterns of behavior.

bestiality
Sexual intercourse with animals; sometimes referred to as zoophilia.

biofeedback
Use of electrical devices to monitor autonomic physiological processes in order to produce relaxation and reduce tension.

biogenic amines
Organic substances that serve as transmitters or monitors of neural impulses.

bipolar disorder
A disturbance of mood and affect in which at least one manic episode can be identified; it may or may not be characterized by depressive episodes.

bisexuality
Sexual attraction toward both males and females.

blocking
Difficulty in thinking or communicating because channels of thought are obstructed or interrupted for emotional reasons.

body image
Internalized impressions and attitudes regarding one's physical self.

bonding
Attachment of a parent to an infant; any process in which individuals make a mutual commitment.

borderline
Personality disorder in which the client displays unstable interpersonal relationships, impulsivity, identity disturbance, chronic feelings of emptiness, and self-destructive threats/behaviors.

brief psychotherapy
Short-term therapy that usually focuses on restoring functioning and providing emotional support.

bulimia
Alternating episodes of overeating (binge eating) and deliberate, self-induced vomiting.

burnout
A reaction to stressful occupational conditions in which workers feel exhausted and depleted; often expressed behaviorally through anger, apathy, depression, or detachment.

C

caring
The act of attending to or being concerned with another person or persons; in a professional sense, the act of providing and being responsible for holistic health care.

case management
A nursing model in which one nurse is responsible for the comprehensive care of several clients, often with the assistance of other nurses accountable to the nurse charged with the case management.

case mix
Proportion of various types of cases or diagnoses in a particular hospital.

castration anxiety
In psychoanalysis, a threat to the masculinity or femininity of individuals.

catatonia
A state of muscular rigidity and inflexibility, often accompanied by symptoms such as tremor, excitability, or stupor.

catecholamines
A group of biogenic amines, including dopamine, epinephrine, and norepinephrine, that affect the neuronal systems.

cathexis
Psychoanalytic term used to describe a bond or attachment.

central nervous system
Neural structures of brain and spinal cord.

cerebral palsy
Partial paralysis and poor muscle coordination due to a defect, injury, or disease of nerve tissue in one or more areas of the brain, often caused at the time of birth because of anoxia, premature or difficult delivery, or blood type incompatibility.

chronobiology
Study of the effect of time intervals on living systems or organisms.

circadian rhythms
Cyclical changes occurring within a period of 24 hours.

circumstantiality
A communication pattern in which tangential, trivial details are given. The purpose is usually to lower the anxiety of the speaker.

clanging
Rhyming speech patterns; often used by persons with schizophrenia.

classical conditioning
A behavioral procedure in which two stimuli are offered simultaneously or close together in sequence. One stimulus evokes a spontaneous response from the subject; the other does not. If the pairing is repeated, the stimulus that previously evoked no response will eventually elicit the spontaneous response from the subject. This conditioned response will appear even without the stimulus that was previously needed to arouse the response.

claustrophobia
Extreme fear of being confined in a small space.

client advocacy
Process in which professionals, para-professionals, and clients themselves attempt to improve the quality of care and protect the rights of persons receiving care.

client-centered therapy
Originated by Carl Rogers, a form of therapy that offers empathy and nonjudgmental acceptance to enable the client to embark on a journey of self-actualization, or self-discovery.

cognition
The act, process, or result of knowing, learning, or understanding.

cohesion
Conditions of attraction among group members and between individual members and the group as a whole.

coitus
Sexual intercourse between persons of the opposite sex.

collaboration
The process of sharing information and working together, usually toward common or mutually acceptable goals.

coma
Deep stupor or loss of consciousness.

commitment
Hospitalization that was not sought by the client but was arranged by family members or by legal or medical officers when the client was considered a clear danger to himself or others.

community
Any group of people living in proximity, sharing certain interests regardless of spatial separation, working toward a common goal, or upholding certain values.

compulsion
An irrational, repetitive act that must be performed in order to control rising anxiety.

concrete operational stage
According to Piaget, the stage at which the child can begin to use and manipulate numbers; thinking tends to be concrete, and the abilities for abstract reasoning are absent or limited.

concrete thinking
Use of literal statements instead of abstract or symbolic forms of communication.

concretization
Loss or decreased awareness of consensually understood words, symbols, or meanings.

confabulation
Filling in lost memory gaps with manufactured details.

confidentiality
The responsibility of professionals to disclose no information about clients except to participating colleagues, and then only with the knowledge and consent of the client.

confirmation
Acts, ceremonial or individual, that verify, validate, or strengthen a person or idea through acknowledgement or approval.

conflict
Discomfort (anxiety) experienced by persons torn between a wish for something and fear of the consequences if the wish is gratified; a clash between opposing intrapersonal or interpersonal forces.

conformity
Agreement, harmony, or accordance with rules, customs, or behaviors.

confrontation
Communication designed to help others engage in reflection and self-examination of their motives and behaviors.

congruence
Agreement between verbal and nonverbal levels of communication.

consensual validation
Reinforcement of meanings and interpretations by evidence and corroboration from others.

consultation
A process in which a nurse or group of nurses seek remedial advice from a person, usually another nurse, who is a specialist in a particular area. The consultant works through the consultees and rarely gives direct, hands-on service.

context
The setting and circumstances in which an event or transaction occurs.

contract
Agreement between client and professional concerning therapeutic goals and regimen; usually developed collaboratively.

conversion disorder
Transformation of anxiety-producing thoughts and feelings into sensory or motor impairment; previously termed a hysterical reaction.

coping
Efforts directed toward managing various problems, events, and stressors.

correlation
Establishing of relationships between variables; a correlation shows connections but not cause-and-effect relationships between variables.

countertransference
A phenomenon in which the person on whom transference thoughts and feelings are projected returns and reinforces the transference.

covert
Concealed; masked; not openly manifest.

crisis
Periods of vulnerability or disorganization that have the potential for growth and maturation.

crisis intervention
Therapeutic intervention designed to restore functioning at or above precrisis levels; usually time limited.

critical task
A developmental milestone that involves the acquisition and mastery of specific behaviors and competence.

culture
Sum of the customs, habits, and traditions of a particular ethnic or social group.

cunnilingus
Oral contact with the vulva and clitoris.

cyclothymia
Condition characterized by alternating moods of elation and dejection.

cystic fibrosis
A congenital general disorder of the exocrine glands resulting in accumulation of thick mucus and excessive secretion of sweat and saliva. The mucus secretion of persons with cystic fibrosis is tenacious and adhesive; the lungs are clogged and bacteria adhere to the tissues. Secretions also impede the flow of digestive enzymes from the pancreas to the small intestine. Infections, usually staphylococcal, recur repeatedly, leading to chronic lung damage. Poor transmission of digestive enzymes leads to malnutrition.

cytochrome
Enzyme produced in excess by alcoholic clients that may be linked to the development of alcoholism.

D

data base
The sum of information collected from which to make inferences, develop hypotheses, assess needs, and evaluate outcomes.

day hospital
Facility offering a therapeutic program for clients who attend during the day and return home at night; a form of partial hospitalization.

decompensation
Disorganization of the personality or ego during periods of overwhelming stress.

defense mechanisms
Unconscious intrapsychic processes used to reduce anxiety and emotional conflict.

deinstitutionalization
Return to community living of persons previously hospitalized for long periods; a movement emphasizing community aftercare rather than institutional care for clients.

déjà vu
A sense of having experienced new events previously.

delinquency
Legally prohibited actions committed by a juvenile or minor.

delirium
Impairment of mental processes to the extent of confusion and disorientation, usually caused by a specific agent or stressor.

delirium tremens
State produced by withdrawal from alcohol, characterized by tremors, hallucinations, and occasionally convulsions.

delusion
A false belief maintained despite the absence of factual or corroborating evidence.

dementia
Absence, impairment, or reduction of cognitive and intellectual abilities.

dementia praecox
Outmoded term once applied to schizophrenia.

denial
Refusal to acknowledge the reality of certain events, thereby protecting the

individual from the unwelcome recognition of such events.

dependency
The tendency to rely on others.

depersonalization
Feelings of unreality and disconnection from the self occurring as a result of personality disorganization.

depression
A psychological state characterized by dejection, lowered self-esteem, hopelessness, helplessness, indecision, and rumination.

desensitization
The reduction of intense reactions to various stimuli by repeated exposure to the stimuli in milder forms.

desocialization
Withdrawal from interaction with others, often attributable to autistic patterns of thinking and acting.

desymbolization
Loss of the ability to derive commonly understood meanings from well-known symbols; it often accompanies concrete thinking and the inability to think in abstract terms.

detoxification
Elimination of a toxic agent from the body via natural physiological processes or with the aid of medical and nursing measures.

deviance
Noncompliance with norms established and upheld by the group.

Diagnostic Related Group (DRG)
A group of disorders of similar severity that are deemed to require a stipulated number of hospital days for treatment and recuperation.

discrimination
Ability to differentiate between and respond differently to two or more stimuli.

disengagement
An interactional process characterized by withdrawal. The withdrawal is often reciprocal, as in the case of interactions between the elderly and society or in family situations where members maintain distance from each other.

disorientation
Confusion and impaired ability to identify time, place, and person.

displacement
A transfer of emotion or behaviors to an unrelated person or event; substituting one target of emotions or behavior for another target.

dissociative disorders
Reactions that protect the self from awareness of anxiety-producing stimuli. Amnesia, somnambulism, fugue states, and multiple personality are examples of dissociative reactions.

dizygotic
Term usually applied to fraternal twins derived from more than one fertilized ovum (Zygote).

dysthymia
Any abnormal affective state, usually applied to depressive moods.

Do-Not-Resuscitate (DNR)
Orders that specify the nature of treatment to be used or withheld upon impending death of a client.

double bind
Communication in which a positive command is followed by a negative command; the recipient cannot obey both commands and therefore feels confused and trapped.

Down's syndrome
A form of mental retardation associated with chromosomal abnormalities.

drives
In psychoanalytic theory, instinctual urges and impulses arising from biological and psychological needs.

drug abuse
See abuse.

drug dependence
Physiological or psychological dependence on a chemical substance.

dyad
A two-person group.

dynamic formulation
Synthesis of a client's traits, values, behaviors, and conflicts for the purpose of explaining, understanding, and helping the client.

dynamics
Interactive forces within the individual, usually unconscious, that are manifested in thoughts, feelings, behavior, and symptomatology.

dyslexia
Impaired ability to read.

dyspareunia
Painful sexual intercourse. It occurs in both sexes but more often in women.

dystonia
Muscle spasms of the face, head, neck and back; usually an acute side effect of antipsychotic medication.

E

echolalia
Automatic repetition of words and phrases recently heard.

echopraxia
Repetition of movements and actions recently observed in others.

ecology
Branch of science dealing with relationships between living organisms and their environment.

ego
In psychoanalytic theory, the aspect of the personality that mediates between demands of the id and the superego; the aspect of the personality that deals with reality.

ego-dystonic (ego-alien)
Thoughts, feelings, impulses, and acts that are unacceptable to the ego and therefore produce anxiety.

ego ideal
The internalized image of the self as one would like to be.

ego-syntonic
Thoughts, feelings, impulses, and acts that are acceptable to the superego and therefore do not produce anxiety.

electroconvulsive therapy (ECT)
Therapeutic seizures produced by means of electric current applied to the temporal areas under controlled conditions.

electroencephalogram (EEG)
A graphic record of the electrical activity of the brain obtained by means of electrodes applied to areas of the head.

empathy
The ability to understand the feelings of others and respond sensitively to their perceptions of experience.

encopresis
Soiling of the clothing by feces.

endocrine glands
Ductless glands that secrete hormones directly into the lymphatic or circulatory system.

endogenous
Originating in internal sources and causes.

endorphins
Opiumlike substances produced by the brain in response to stimulation of the pituitary glands and other areas.

eneuresis
Involuntary discharge of urine.

enmeshment
A maladaptive pattern of overinvolvement and intensity seen in families.

epidemiology
The study of the distribution of physical and mental disorders in a given population.

episodic
Tendency of events, conditions, symptoms, and disorders to abate and recur intermittently.

ethics
A system of professional standards, moral conduct, and accountability adhered to by an individual or group.

ethnocentrism
The belief that one's own group, race, or culture, is superior to any other.

ethnology
Branch of anthropology dealing with comparative customs and characteristics of various groups and cultures.

etiology
The systematic study of the cause of disorders.

eudaemonistic
Conditions of high-level health, emotional stability, and potential for growth.

eugenics
Utilization of selective breeding methods for the purpose of improving the species.

euphoria
An exaggerated sense of well-being and pleasure.

exclusion
Acts, ceremonial or individual, that reject, ban, denigrate or shut out a person, group, or idea through refusal to acknowledge, admit, share, or approve.

exhaustion
The final stage of the general adaption syndrome; the organism no longer has the resources to react adaptively to stress. In extreme cases, exhaustion may result in death.

exhibitionism
Sexual gratification obtained through public exposure of the genitals.

exogenous
Originating in external sources or causes.

extended family
All persons related by birth, marriage, or adoption.

extinction
The gradual disappearance of a condition response; it occurs when the response is no longer reinforced.

extrapyramidal effects
Side effects of antipsychotic medication that resemble the symptoms of Parkinson's disease.

F

family therapy
A treatment modality that focuses on relationships within the family system.

fantasy
Unrealistic mental images based on conscious or unconscious wish fulfillment.

feedback
Process by which functioning is monitored, corrected if necessary, and maintained if appropriate.

fellatio
Oral sexual contact with the penis.

fetal alcohol syndrome
Fetal irregularities such as low birth weight, cardiac problems, and other congenital abnormalities caused by maternal alcohol ingestion during pregnancy.

fetish
An object or a part of the body to which sexual significance or meaning is attached.

fixation
Attachment to immature levels of thinking and acting instead of progressing developmentally.

flashback
Recurrence of an experience, often drug-induced, without further use of the substance; memory traces of intense experiences that continue to intrude on the individual and cause emotional discomfort.

flight of ideas
Rapid movement from one topic to another in response to stimuli from outside and from within the individual.

folie à deux
Interpersonal relationship in which two participants show psychotic characteristics; the irrational behavior of one person reinforces the irrational behavior of the other.

forensic psychiatry
The branch of psychiatry that deals with legal issues surrounding mental disorders.

formal operational stage
Piaget's final stage of cognitive development, during which abstract thinking exists, mental problems are often solved by sequential steps, and hypotheses may be formulated and tested.

free association
Psychoanalytic technique in which the client communicates whatever thoughts come to mind without interference from the therapist.

frustration
Curtailment of gratification by conditions of external reality or by internal controls.

fugue state
A mental state characterized by physical flight from the immediate surroundings and by total or partial amnesia.

G

games
Ongoing complementary interpersonal transactions, usually progressing to a predictable outcome.

gamete
Either of two cells: the female ovum or the male spermatozoon.

gender identity
Psychological awareness of being male or female.

gender roles
Culturally determined rules about tasks, expectations, and feelings considered appropriate for each gender.

geneogram
A technique used in family counseling to record accurately and in some detail the intergenerational data of the original families of the partners.

general adaptation syndrome (GAS)
Physiological and structural changes produced in response to stress; the stages are alarm, resistance, and exhaustion of the organism.

generalist
A person whose expertise encompasses an overall sphere of knowledge and/or practice.

genetic screening
Systematic search for individuals with a given genetic constitution to identify persons at risk for themselves or their offspring of getting a genetic disease.

genetics
The science of heredity.

geriatrics
The study and treatment of disorders associated with aging.

gerontology
Study of the aging process.

Gestaltists
Persons concerned with existentialism or self-determination. They emphasize human potential and authentic or genuine emotional expression.

goals
The ends or purposes that nurse and client endeavor to reach; usually goals or aims are stated in client-centered terms to facilitate evaluation of the client's progress.

grief
Mourning as a response to loss, actual or imagined, of a meaningful person, object, or situation.

grief work
The process of reacting to loss in which anger, denial, and idealization of what was lost may play a part before detachment and restitution can occur.

group
Collection of two or more persons who are interdependent to some extent and who share meaningful interaction.

group therapy
A treatment modality that involves several persons in the same session and that utilizes interpersonal group behaviors to produce corrective or supportive interactions.

groupthink
Tendency of groups to replace rational thought processes with irrational, impulsive, ideas and decisions.

guilt
A sense of culpability and self-blame due to transgressions against one's internalized values and principles.

H

habeus corpus
The right of persons who are detained involuntarily, to a legal hearing to determine whether the detainment should continue.

hallucination
A false perception in the absence of any external sensory stimuli.

hallucinogen
A substance that produces a temporary psychotic state in which contact with and perceptions of reality are impaired.

helplessness
Belief on the part of individuals that they cannot help themselves.

hemiplegia
Paralysis of one lateral half of the body.

hemophilia
Impaired ability of the blood to coagulate; in its classic form the condition is hereditary, transmitted by females but limited to males.

hermaphrodite
An individual with genitals of both sexes.

holism
The study of the whole or total configuration of an organism; the view of human beings as unified biopsychosocial organisms interacting with their internal and external environments.

homeostasis
The tendency of organisms to maintain balance by preserving a constant internal environment.

homosexuality
Sexual attraction or preference for persons of the same sex.

hopelessness
Belief on the part of individuals that no one can help them.

hostility
Impulses or urges directed toward the destruction of a person or object.

Huntington's chorea
A hereditary disease characterized by rapid involuntary movements, speech disturbance, and mental deterioration due to degeneration of the cerebral cortex and basal ganglia. The condition appears in mature adulthood, with incapacitation and death occurring over a period of about 15 years.

hyperactivity
Behavior characterized by high energy expenditure and excessive activity.

Accelerated motor activity, emotional lability, and flight of ideas may be present.

hyperventilation
Rapid respiration due to high levels of anxiety.

hypochondriasis
A state of exaggerated concern for one's physical well-being in the absence of actual physiological problems.

hypokalemia
Abnormally low levels of blood potassium.

hysteric
An individual who deals with anxiety by means of self-dramatization, excitability, and attention-seeking behavior.

I

id
In psychoanalytic theory, the component of the personality that is present at birth and is the repository of drives and instincts.

ideas of reference
The belief that certain events or objects have a special meaning or significance for oneself.

identification
A process in which the attributes and traits of another are adopted and made part of oneself.

identity
The sense of selfhood that makes possible and sustains an integrated, consistent personality structure.

ideology
A belief system.

illusion
Misinterpretation of a sensory stimulus.

implosive therapy
A desensitization process in which a technique called *flooding* is used; the subject confronts an anxiety-producing object or situation at full intensity for prolonged periods of time. Anxiety is thought to diminish with repeated exposure to the flooding process.

incest
Sexual relationships between persons related biologically.

incorporation
A process in which persons introject or make part of themselves the qualities and attributes of another.

individuation
A developmental process in which the person separates from others and develops a unique, distinct identity.

indoleamines
A group of biogenic amines, including serotonin.

inferiority complex
Intense, generalized feelings of inadequacy that influence the way an individual behaves and relates to others.

inhibition
Control or restraint imposed on an unacceptable impulse, thought, or action; usually but not always self-imposed.

insanity
A synonym for mental disorder or psychosis; rarely applied by professionals except in legal matters.

insight
The ability to recognize and understand the connection between behavior and underlying motives and feelings.

integrity
Commitment to honesty, ethics, and values in various aspects of life.

intellectualization
Use of rationalization to avoid uncomfortable insights or awareness.

intelligence quotient (IQ)
Originally, the mental age of an individual multiplied by 100 and divided by chronological age; an arbitrary measure obtained by standardized intelligence tests.

interdisciplinary team
A team composed of members of different disciplines who engage in joint services and responsibilities.

interpersonal
Arising or generated between two or more persons.

intrapsychic
Arising, generated, or residing within the self.

introjection
A dysfunctional variant of identification in which the qualities of another person are totally incorporated by the individual.

introspection
Self-examination of one's mental processes and emotional reactions.

involutional melancholia
A form of affective disturbance that occurs in middle age; it may appear as agitated or retarded depression and is more common in women than men. Although self-limiting, the condition is severe; suicide potential is high and various delusions may be present.

isolation
Separation of thoughts, ideas, or actions from their emotional aspects.

isotope
Two or more forms of an element having the same or closely related physical properties.

J

judgment
The ability to predict the consequences of an action and modify one's behavior accordingly; the ability to make rational decisions based on cognition and reality.

K

kinesics
Body movements that may be seen as a component of nonverbal communication.

Klinefelter's syndrome
A condition in which the testes are abnormally small, Leydig's cells are dysfunctional, and urinary gonadotropins are increased; the condition is associated with abnormality of the sex chromosomes.

Korsakoff's syndrome
An organic brain syndrome attributed to polyneuritis and thiamine deficits occurring as a result of alcoholism; amnesia, confusion, and confabulation are among the manifestations.

L

la belle indifference
A total lack of concern for the disabling effects of a conversion reaction.

labeling
Consigning an individual to a category or classification based on behavior patterns, personality configuration, or psychiatric diagnosis.

lability
Changeable and poorly controlled emotional state.

learned helplessness
Attitudes and behaviors that indicate unreadiness or inability to participate or take responsibility for solving one's problems; causes vary from repeated failures, secondary gains, and depression to knowledge that someone else is available to help.

learning disability
An impairment in one or more cognitive processes such as attention, memory, visual perception, or written or spoken language. Examples are dyslexia and dysgraphia.

lesbian
Female homosexual.

liaison nursing
The linking of two or more nursing groups for the promotion of effective

collaboration between the groups, resulting in improved client care.

libido
A psychoanalytic term applied to instinctual energy; it usually denotes sexual drive or energy.

limit setting
Actions that encourage others to respect rules and norms; consequences attached to failure to adhere to rules and norms.

lithium carbonate
A drug effective for the treatment of acute mania and a prophylactic for the prevention of depressive and manic recurrences.

local adaptation syndrome (LAS)
A stress reaction limited to a particular part of the body.

longitudinal
Pertaining to length in relation to time or space.

loose associations
Unrelated ideas or events that activate connections with other ideas and events; a frequent manifestation during schizophrenic episodes.

M

magical thinking
The belief that thinking about a possible occurrence can make it happen; a primitive, immature form of thinking.

malingering
Conscious, deliberate feigning or exaggeration of disability or incapacity.

malpractice
Actions that have been performed incorrectly, have not been performed in the best interests of the client, have violated agency policy, or have failed to adhere to current standards of the ANA or to conform to state or national legislation.

mania
A state of accelerated activity, mental and physical; generally thought to be a defense against depression.

manipulation
Exertion of indirect control or influence over the actions of others in order to obtain one's own purpose.

marital schism
A dysfunctional form of family structure characterized by discordance and factionalism.

masochism
Gratification obtained by experiencing pain, abuse, or humiliation from others; usually applied to deviant sexual actions.

masturbation
Sexual gratification obtained by self-stimulation of the genitals.

maturation
Development resulting from heredity rather than learning.

maturational crisis
A developmental episode in which life transitions occur and the individual is vulnerable to disequilibrium.

mature elderly doctrine
Guideline which determines that the level of mental capacity rather than physical capacity be the deciding factor of competency with regard to treatment.

mental retardation
Significantly subaverage general intellectual functioning existing concurrently with deficits in adaptive behavior and manifested during the developmental period.

mental status exam
A formal, structured format for assessing a client's intelligence, mood and affect, appearance, thought processes, and capacity for insight.

metacommunication
Communications about the messages being transmitted; includes connotative as well as denotative components of communication.

migraine
A severe form of headache, usually limited to one side of the head, often accompanied by nausea and vomiting; it is believed to be associated with the constriction or dilation of cerebral arteries. The condition is believed to have emotional components.

milieu
The immediate environment, physical and social, in which individuals function.

milieu therapy
A treatment modality that uses all aspects of the environment, physical and social, in order to promote adaptive change.

Minnesota Multiphasic Personality Inventory (MMPI)
A widely used, empirically validated measure of personality.

monamine oxidase (MAO) inhibitors
A group of antidepressants that act by blocking the metabolism of certain neurotransmitters, thereby increasing the amounts available. Although useful, these drugs require extensive dietary restrictions.

monozygotic
Term usually applied to identical twins derived from one fertilized ovum (zygote).

moral management
An early, relatively humane psychiatric approach to care that included consideration of mind and spirit as well as body.

morbid
Unhealthy; pathological; unwholesome.

mourning
Psychological and physiological response of individuals to loss; a necessary process involving gradual renunciation of what was lost followed by the ability to form new attachments.

multidisciplinary team
A team composed of members of different disciplines who provide discipline-specific services.

multiple personality
A reaction in which two or more different personality configurations are present in the same body.

mutations
Changes in a gene that can cause new characteristics to appear in offspring.

N

narcissism
Self-love or egocentricity.

narcolepsy
Periods of sleep or trancelike episodes that occur suddenly without intent or control by the affected individual.

necrophilia
Sexual gratification related to sexual acts performed on a corpse; fantasies of such acts may be sufficient to produce sexual arousal and orgasm.

negative reinforcers
The removal of undesirable consequences in order to increase the behaviors they follow.

negativism
Refusal to cooperate or follow directions; exhibiting behaviors contrary to what is desired or expected.

negligence
Failure to perform any of a wide range of actions in accord with the best interests of the client, agency policy, ANA standards, or with state of national legislation.

neologism
Coining of new words or phrases; the attribution of new, private meanings to familiar words and phrases.

neurasthenia
A condition characterized by mental and physical fatigue and vague complaints without organic basis; a disorder related to anxiety.

neuroleptic
A pharmacological agent that produces antipsychotic effects.

neurology
Study of the brain and nervous system; the branch of medicine concerned with disorders and dysfunctions of the nervous system.

neuron
An individual nerve cell.

neurosis
An emotional disturbance accompanied by various avoidance behaviors and actions aimed at the reduction of anxiety; manifestations vary, but contact with reality is not lost.

neurotransmitters
Chemical substances that transmit impulses from one neuron to another.

norm
A standard of behavior upheld by a family, group, or community.

normal distribution
The tendency for most persons in a population to cluster round a central point with the remaining persons scattered near opposing extremes.

nosology
Study of the classification of diseases.

nuclear family
A two-generational family consisting of parents and their offspring, natural or adopted; the family of procreation established by the parental dyad.

nursing care plan
A comprehensive guide for the therapeutic utilization of the nursing process. It is based on the nursing process and delineates the means by which the nurse hopes to preserve, promote, or improve the adaptive behaviors of the client. It is also a means of facilitating communication between care providers, evaluating revising aspects of nursing process.

nursing diagnosis
The basic meaning of the term *diagnosis* is "thorough knowledge"; thus, a nursing diagnosis is a problem-oriented statement of a client's needs based on accumulated data and the nurse's identification of significant factors affecting the client in the past, present, and future.

nursing intervention
The initiation of action by the nurse on behalf of the client. Intervention is a specific aspect of the implementation phase of the nursing process; it is a consequence of assessment, diagnosis, and planning and a precipitant of evaluation.

nursing process
A cooperative process enabling the nurse to involve a client in a systematic process of problem solving designed to maintain, restore, or enhance the health of the client, whether individual, family, or community. Nursing process includes the ongoing activities of assessment, nursing diagnoses, planning, implementation, and evaluation.

nursing research
A process involving scientific principles of research studies and data analysis in laboratory and clinical settings to solve problems, test hypotheses, and contribute to the growing body of nursing theory, with the ultimate goal of improving health care.

O

obesity
Weight that exceeds accepted standards by more than 20 percent.

obsession
A recurring thought or idea that cannot be removed from conscious awareness.

obsessive-compulsive disorder
A behavioral style characterized by perfectionism, rigidity, and excessive need for control of the self and the environment.

occupational therapy
A therapeutic method involving planned, purposeful activity in which tangible products or discernible goals are accomplished.

oculogyric reaction
Uncontrollable upward movement of the eyes due to the side effects of antipsychotic medication.

Oedipus complex
In psychoanalytic theory, the child's attachment to the parent of the opposite sex and hostility toward the parent of the same sex.

operant conditioning
Behavior modification that changes behavior by manipulating stimuli and the consequences of reactions to stimuli.

organic brain syndrome
Any mental disorder caused by or associated with impairment of brain tissue structure; it may be acute or chronic, reversible or irreversible; etiology may be endogenous or exogenous.

orientation
Awareness of time, place, and person.

orthostatic hypotension
A decrease in blood pressure due to postural changes; a frequent side effect of psychotropic medication.

overload
Sensory input or performance demands that are beyond the tolerance or capacity of the individual.

overt
open; direct; unconcealed.

P

paleological thinking
Thought patterns in which connections are made not between topics or subjects of sentences but between

predicates. This leads to incoherent thinking and incomprehensible communication.

panic attack
Severe disorganization caused by intense anxiety; characterized by cognitive, emotional, and behavioral distortion.

paranoia
Extreme suspiciousness of others; usually related to use of the defense mechanism projection, whereby anxiety-producing thoughts and feelings are disowned by the individual and attributed to other people.

paraphilia
Sexual deviance in which unusual objects, rituals, or events are employed to obtain full sexual gratification.

paraphrase
Restating of what has been communicated in order to validate the accuracy of one's understanding and comprehension.

paraprofessional
An individual who has experience or training in a field but is not a professional.

parataxic
A mode of experience that is individualistic and idiosyncratic and in which consensual language and capacity for symbolism are limited.

parasympathetic nervous system
A division of the autonomic nervous system that controls most of the metabolic processes needed for the maintenance of life.

Parkinson's disease
A progressive disease of later life characterized by a masklike facial expression, tremor of muscles at rest, slow voluntary movements, ataxia, and muscle weakness. Mental capacity is not usually affected. When the symptoms occur in response to medication or are secondary to another disorder, the resultant syndrome is called Parkinsonism.

passive-aggressive
Behavior employed to express hostility and aggression indirectly.

patient classification system
Process of grouping clients according to some observable or inferred characteristic to determine nursing care requirements.

pedophilia
Sexual attraction of an adult toward children.

peer review
A system for evaluating professional practice within any health care discipline by a panel of peer reviewers concerned with admission criteria and continued stay review. In the review process, norms, criteria, and standards available in written form are used to screen large numbers of cases so as to identify appropriate and adequate care and to discover exceptions, if any.

perception
The individualistic process of viewing, comprehending, and interpreting the world and one's own experiences.

perseveration
Inappropriate repetition of a word or action once it is initiated.

personality
The accumulated configuration of traits, attributes, behaviors, qualities, and attitudes that characterize an individual.

personality disorders
A group of disorders, manifested in various behavioral patterns, in which the prevailing feature is relatively little anxiety and a tendency to project blame on others.

perspective
Sets of concepts, beliefs, or viewpoints used to direct and organize observations and/or data.

perversion
Deviation from what is considered normal and acceptable by the majority.

phallic
Pertaining to the penis.

phenylketonuria (PKU)
A congenital disease resulting from a defect in the metabolism of the amino acid phenylalanine; this hereditary condition is transmitted by recessive genes of parents apparently healthy but if tested shown to be carriers. If untreated, the disease causes mental retardation and other abnormalities.

phobia
An extreme, irrational fear of certain objects or circumstances.

pica
Ingestion or desire to ingest unnatural or unusual substances.

pleasure principle
A psychoanalytic concept describing the tendency of the id to find gratification and avoid discomfort; it is gradually modified by the reality principle, which imposes delayed gratification on the individual.

positive reinforcers
Desirable consequences given as the result of a desirable behavior.

posttraumatic stress syndrome
A delayed reaction to overwhelming stress, such as war or rape. Emotional instability, psychic numbing, and flashbacks are aspects of the clinical picture.

premorbid
That which existed prior to the onset of a disorder.

preoperational stage
The second Piagetian developmental stage, during which the thinking of the child is egocentric and inflexible.

The child at this stage achieves *object permanence*, or the realization that people and objects exist apart from the child. This stage also introduces symbolization into the child's thinking and language.

primal therapy
A form of therapy that reduces the defenses of the client, fostering regression so that the client may retrospectively experience painful events of the past, thus reducing residual tension, and putting the client in touch with the authentic, newly liberated self. The purpose of this therapy is to evoke pain and to elicit outcries known as "primal screaming." Some clients report reliving the traumatic experience of their own birth.

primary gain
A decrease in anxiety as a result of measures taken by individuals to deal with stress or conflict. The measures used include thoughts, actions, or reactions that may be conscious or unconscious but have the effect of lowering anxiety.

primary group
The social group, usually the family, that has the most profound influence on an individual.

primary nursing
A nursing model in which one nurse is responsible for the health care of a client 24 hours a day.

primary prevention
Measures used to promote health and reduce the incidence of disorder or dysfunction by opposing causative agents.

primary process thinking
Primitive, infantile thought processes that seek instant outlets; in psychoanalytic theory, those thought processes controlled by id forces.

process
An ongoing or continuing method or development involving a series of steps or changes.

progressive relaxation
A systematic technique to induce relaxation in various muscle groups of the body, progressing until total relaxation is achieved.

projection
Attribution of blame or responsibility for one's own acts and feelings to other people.

projective tests
Test forms in which ambiguous items are used to elicit information regarding psychological tendencies and personality traits of the subjects. The ambiguity of the items causes subjects to project aspects of themselves onto the answers, thus disclosing data that must be expertly interpreted and analyzed.

prospective payment
Payment rates for health care set in advance and considered fixed for a certain period of time.

prototaxic
A mode of experiences characteristic of the first months of life that is perceived by the infant as continuous, boundless, undifferentiated, and wordless.

proxemics
Spatial relationships in social interactions.

pseudodementia
Syndrome in which dementia is mimicked by a functional psychiatric illness, most often depression.

pseudohostility
Family dissension that avoids genuine sources of conflict.

pseudomutuality
Family harmony that is superficial and maintained at the expense of one or more family members.

psychic determinism
The psychoanalytic axiom that human behavior is neither random nor accidental, but is determined by preceding experiences and events.

psychoanalysis
A theoretical and therapeutic approach that explores anxiety-producing events of early life. Through the defense mechanism of repression, the memory of such events becomes unconscious; the purpose of psychoanalysis is to bring repressed material into conscious awareness so that it may be dealt with adaptively.

psychodrama
The use of dramatization under professional direction in order to help clients act out life experiences before an audience of peers who offer constructive alternative suggestions for coping.

psychodynamic
Pertaining to the causes and consequences of behavior and experience, with attention to underlying motivation, conscious and unconscious.

psychogenic
Psychological in origin.

psychometry
Measurement or testing of mental or psychological ability, potential, or functioning.

psychosocial theory
A theoretical framework proposed by Erikson and others pertaining to the interrelated psychological and social development of individuals. Implicit in Erikson's formulation is the physiological developmental influence.

psychosomatic
Physical symptoms of psychological origin; also any associated relationship between mind and body.

psychosurgery
Surgical intervention for psychiatric disorders, usually involving neural pathways or areas of the brain.

psychotherapy
Measures and interventions employed to offer support or to modify behavior. It may include identification of emotional problems troubling the client, goal setting, and negotiation of a therapeutic regimen.

psychotropic
Having an effect on the mind.

Q

quality assurance
A system of monitoring the level of health care by applying principles of internal accountability and self-regulation. Quality assurance uses peer review methods and utilization review to ensure that available services are being used properly and are of high quality as well as cost effective.

R

rape
Sexual intercourse with a minor (statutory rape); sexual intercourse without the consent of the partner (forcible rape).

rapport
Shared understanding and harmony between two people based on mutual trust.

rational emotive therapy
A treatment approach that emphasizes taking responsibility for one's own behavior, utilizing concepts based on existentialism.

rationalization
Fabrication of socially acceptable reasons to justify actions, thoughts, or feelings that might be unacceptable to the self or others.

reaction formation
Control or eradication of unacceptable ideas or impulses by engaging in opposite forms of behavior or attitudes.

reality
The world as it actually is; the external world as opposed to the internal world of daydreams and fantasy.

reality principle
A psychoanalytic concept applied to the gradual development of the ability to delay gratification and modify one's desires in accordance with the demands of society and external reality.

reality testing
An essential ego function that enables the individual to distinguish internal stimuli from external stimuli; differentiating subjective from objective experience.

reality therapy
A treatment approach that employs the existential concepts of responsibility, self-determination, and progress toward goals.

recidivism
Recurrence of deliquency or criminality despite punishment, incarceration, or treatment.

reciprocal inhibition
A behavior modification procedure in which an anxiety-producing stimulus is paired with an anxiety-reducing stimulus until anxiety is lowered to a comfortable level.

reference group
Any group with which one identifies and whose beliefs and values are influential.

reflection
A communication technique in which ideas or feelings expressed by one person are verbalized by the other in order to clarify meaning and encourage amplification.

regression
A retreat to less mature levels of thought and action in an attempt to deal with stressful or anxiety-producing situations.

reinforcement
The strengthening of behavior, particularly desirable behavior, by positive methods (rewards) or negative methods (removing punishments).

relationship therapy
A form of therapy often used by nurses to help clients establish trust and maintain contact with reality, thus fostering more adaptive patterns of thinking, feeling, and behaving.

relaxation therapy
Utilization of consciously induced states of relaxation in order to reduce tension and various dysfunctional responses to stress.

reliability
Data, results, or scores that are dependable and consistent.

REM sleep
Transitional stage of sleep during which dreaming often occurs.

remotivation therapy
A therapeutic approach designed to stimulate the interest and promote the socialization of chronic clients.

repression
Removal of unpleasant, anxiety-producing thoughts, desires, or memories from conscious awareness.

resistance
The tendency to maintain dysfunctional patterns of thinking and behaving despite therapeutic intervention.

Resource Utilization Groups (RUGS)
Method of categorization developed to determine resource consumption of long-term care clients.

reversal
Behavior in which instinctual feelings are expressed by opposing actions.

risk factors
Those factors—social, psychological, environmental, or physiological—that render certain individuals, families, or communities vulnerable to particular dysfunctions, disorders, or agents.

role
A set of behavioral expectations associated with an individual's status and functions in the family, group, or community.

role enactment
The performance of the functions, responsibilities, privileges, and obligations attached to the position or role one assumes in a family or group.

Rorschach Test
A projective psychological test designed to reveal basic attitudes and conflicts by having the individual interpret a series of inkblots.

S

sadism
Gratification obtained by inflicting pain, abuse, or humiliation on others; usually applied to sexually deviant acts.

scapegoat
An individual who is the target of aggression from others but who may not be the actual cause of hostility or frustration in others.

schism
A term applied to families characterized by severe conflict and dissension.

schizophrenia
A psychotic disorder of thought and perception characterized by withdrawal, impaired social relationships, loose associations, flat affect, autism, ambivalence, and regression. Manifestations may vary from person to person depending on the defense mechanisms and coping ability of the client.

school phobia
Aversion to school often generated by fears of separation from parents; also known as school avoidance behavior.

seclusion
Placing an individual in a room away from others so as to reduce stimuli and foster self-control; seclusion rooms may or may not be locked.

secondary gain
An additional gain or reward, such as attention, derived from any illness or disability.

secondary prevention
Measures designed to reduce the prevalence of dysfunction and disorders through early detection and adequate care.

secondary process thinking
Rational, mature thought processes considered to be under the control of the ego.

security operations
Any behavior employed to increase psychological comfort and reduce anxiety; may be conscious or unconscious.

self-actualization
The process of reaching one's full potential.

self-awareness
Recognition of what one is experiencing and how one is reacting.

self-concept
The sum of an individual's knowledge and beliefs about the self and its relation to the physical and social environment.

self-differentiation
The extent to which the individual preserves a sense of identity and separateness from the group.

self-esteem
Feelings held by individuals regarding their own worth and value.

self-fulfilling prophecy
A phenomenon in which expectations shape and maintain behavior, events, and interpersonal transactions.

self-system
Term coined by H. S. Sullivan to describe the integration of the "good me," "bad me," and "non-me" aspects of self.

sensate focus
A therapeutic sexual technique in which the partners evoke erotic responses, by fondling and touching without necessarily engaging in coitus.

sensorimotor stage
The initial stage in the cognitive development of the child as the child explores the environment through the senses and through motor activity, as described by Piaget.

sensory deprivation
Reduction of sensory input or stimuli below levels necessary to maintain self-awareness and support normal central nervous system function.

separation anxiety
Apprehension generated by loss or fear of loss of the mothering person; subsequent loss of significant persons or objects may reactivate separation anxiety.

serotonin
Neurotransmitter that is instrumental in regulating certain brain activities, including emotion.

sexual deviance
Sexual behavior that does not conform to standards of the population majority.

sexual dysfunction
Impaired ability to give or receive sexual gratification.

shaping
A form of behavior modification in which any behaviors resembling the desired goal are rewarded (reinforced); eventually only the closest approximate behaviors are rewarded; finally only the desired behavior is rewarded.

sibling rivalry
Competition between brothers and sisters for recognition and affection

sick role
Set of behaviors, privileges, and obligations expected from persons designated as being ill.

sickle cell anemia
A genetic defect commonly affecting blacks, characterized by abnormal hemoglobin, anemia, reticulocytosis, jaundice, recurrent fever, and pain. The name is derived from the crescent or sickle-shaped erythrocytes caused by varying proportions of hemoglobin.

significant others
Essential persons, often but not always related to the individual, who are sources of support for the individual.

situational crisis
Disturbed equilibrium that develops as a result of the impact of a specific event.

skew
Term applied to families in which relationships are distorted.

sleep apnea
Periodic halting or cessation of respirations during sleep.

social skills training
Teaching using forms of social behavior for rehearsal and performance of social tasks.

socialization
The process of acquiring the values, attitudes, and behaviors considered appropriate in a particular culture.

sociogram
A technique used in family counseling to observe and note the routes and lines of communication between family members.

sociology
Branch of social science dealing with relationships of individuals and groups to social institutions and society at large.

sodomy
Sexual intercourse involving the anus; anal penetration in sexual intercourse.

somnambulism
Sleepwalking.

spasm
Intense, involuntary contraction of muscles, usually accompanied by severe pain.

spasticity
Continued muscle contraction, causing hypertonicity, rigidity, and coordination problems.

specialist
A person whose expertise has a circumscribed focus accompanied by advanced preparation or skill in that particular area.

species
Any distinctive group or class distinguished by shared biological characteristics.

spina bifida
A defect of the spinal column resulting from imperfect union of paired vertebral arches, sometimes extensive enough to cause herniation of the meninges and spinal cord.

standardization
Utilization of methods designed to establish the expected range of scores on a test.

standards of practice
Authoritative statements or approved concepts that provide guidance to the nursing profession and its members in the actual delivery of care.

Stanford-Binet Test
A standardized intelligence test for children.

stereotype
A generalization of how members of a particular group or category are likely to look or act.

stigma
A condition or situation considered substandard or associated with disgrace.

stress
Any situation or condition requiring adjustment on the part of the individual, family, or group.

stressor
A stimulus, event, or experience that demands changed or new behavior. Stressors usually require expenditure of considerable energy, thus arousing alarm and mobilization responses.

structure
Arrangement of the parts of a whole by means of systematic organization or placement.

sublimation
Conscious transformation of unacceptable drives and impulses into socially acceptable behavior in order to satisfy the drive or impulse.

successive approximation
See shaping.

superego
In psychoanalytic theory, the aspect of the personality that monitors thoughts and actions; comparable to the conscience or internal censor.

suppression
Conscious inhibition or control of certain desires, thoughts, or emotions.

symbol
The representation of an idea or concept by means of an object, sign, or signal that conveys connotative and denotative meanings.

sympathetic nervous system
That part of the autonomic nervous system that is activated by stressful conditions, actual or perceived.

syndrome
A grouping or cluster of symptoms that represent the usual clinical manifestations of a disorder.

syntaxic
A mode of experience that is characterized by shared, consensually validated language and meanings and by the capacity for abstract thinking.

system
A set of interrelated components defined by boundaries, interdependent and interacting in such a manner that any stimulus affecting one component affects every other component, as well as acting on the system as a whole.

systematic desensitization
The reduction of anxiety-laden responses by gradually exposing the subject to approximations of feared objects or situations until the subject can tolerate the actual object or experience.

systems theory
The interdependent behavior of various entities or components functioning in reciprocal interactions, usually for a common purpose.

T

tardive dyskinesia
An irreversible side effect of major tranquilizers that causes involuntary grimacing and disfiguring movements of the tongue, mouth, and lower jaw.

Tay-Sachs disease
An inherited recessive condition prevalent among Jewish infants, which results in retardation and blindness.

team nursing
A hierarchical nursing model in which the most experienced nurse usually acts as team leader and other team members perform tasks according to their ability and the clients' needs.

theoretical framework
A systematic formulation of concepts and principles related to phenomena that have been observed and verified to some extent.

theory
A systematic statement of related concepts and principles.

therapeutic community
A form of environmental interpersonal therapy that is much like milieu therapy but usually less hierarchical. Administration and planning are delegated to an interdisciplinary team rather than to an acknowledged leader.

time out
A behavioral technique used when an impasse develops in which reinforcers are not being used effectively to modify disruptive behavior. Taking "time out" from the interaction introduces an element of rationality. It allows disruptive behavior and dysfunctional exchanges to be terminated for a time.

token economy
A behavioral modification system in which desired objects, in the form of tokens or various privileges, are bestowed in return for desirable behavior. The granting of tokens is a form of positive reinforcement.

tolerance
A condition in which increasingly large doses of a drug or other substance must be taken to obtain the same effect previously produced with smaller doses or amounts.

transactional analysis
Method of examining a verbal exchange between individuals to determine which part of a multiple nature—parent, adult, child—the person is relating from.

transcultural nursing
A subspecialty within nursing concerned with identifying and meeting the special needs of cultural groups within this pluralistic society and acting when necessary as advocates on behalf of such diverse groups.

transference
A psychological distortion in which the client acts or feels as if another individual is a significant person from early life; the distortion is usually unconscious.

transsexual
Sex identity confusion in which the individual has a strong wish to belong to the opposite sex; also, a person who has undergone surgical and hormonal intervention to achieve this purpose.

transvestite
An individual who derives sexual pleasure from dressing in garments usually worn by the opposite sex.

tricyclic antidepressants
Antidepressants that prevent reuptake of neurotransmitters into the presynaptic cleft, thus increasing the amounts available.

Turner's syndrome
A condition characterized by retarded growth and sexual development; it is associated with absence or abnormality of the second X chromosome in females.

type
A class, group, or subgroup sharing common characteristics.

type A
A personality type characterized by traits of competitiveness, time urgency, and high tension levels; type A's are believed by some investigators to be prone to stressrelated disorders.

U

undoing
Performance of activities designed to atone for errors or misdeeds, thus cancelling them.

unidisciplinary team
A team composed of members of the same discipline.

unipolar disorder
A disorder of mood and affect in which only episodes of depression occur.

V

vaginismus
Involuntary muscle spasms of the vaginal orifice and wall, preventing sexual penetration.

validity
Data, results, or scores that are sound, relevant, and convincing.

vicarious learning
The effect of observing the expressions and/or actions of a model upon the behavior and affect of the observer.

violence
Expression of aggressive impulses by acting destructively toward others.

visualization therapy
A form of self-hypnosis or conditioning used to promote relaxation or to mobilize the defenses of the individual against physical and psychological distress. The person using visualization therapy may depict in imagination a place of security and comfort or a state of active participation and assertiveness.

voluntary admission
Process in which individuals are admitted to a psychiatric hospital with their consent.

voyeurism
A sexual deviation in which gratification is obtained by witnessing sexual activities or by viewing sexually attractive persons, usually without their knowledge.

W

waxy flexibility
A condition seen in persons with catatonic schizophrenia; the individual retains a position or stance for long periods of time before gradually changing the position; also known as *cerea flexibilitas*.

Wechsler Intelligence Scale for Children
A standardized intelligence test for children.

Wernicke's syndrome
A complication of chronic alcoholism due to thiamine deficiency characterized by paralysis of the eye muscles and mental deterioration; it occasionally appears as a manifestation of other disorders.

withdrawal
Behaviors adopted to avoid interacting with others.

word salad
Incoherent use of words by disoriented or psychotic persons.

Z

zoophilia
See bestiality.

zygote
A fertilized cell formed by the union of male and female gametes.

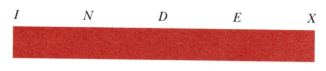

DATE DUE

APR 1 6 1997			

HIGHSMITH 45-220